The Law of Journalism and Mass Communication

Sixth Edition

For our families

Sara Miller McCune founded SAGE Publishing in 1965 to support the dissemination of usable knowledge and educate a global community. SAGE publishes more than 1000 journals and over 800 new books each year, spanning a wide range of subject areas. Our growing selection of library products includes archives, data, case studies and video. SAGE remains majority owned by our founder and after her lifetime will become owned by a charitable trust that secures the company's continued independence.

Los Angeles | London | New Delhi | Singapore | Washington DC | Melbourne

The Law of Journalism and Mass Communication

Sixth Edition

Robert Trager
University of Colorado, Boulder

Susan Dente Ross
Washington State University

Amy Reynolds
Kent State University

FOR INFORMATION:

CQ Press
An Imprint of SAGE Publications, Inc.
2455 Teller Road
Thousand Oaks, California 91320
E-mail: order@sagepub.com

SAGE Publications Ltd.
1 Oliver's Yard
55 City Road
London EC1Y 1SP
United Kingdom

SAGE Publications India Pvt. Ltd.
B 1/I 1 Mohan Cooperative Industrial Area
Mathura Road, New Delhi 110 044
India

SAGE Publications Asia-Pacific Pte. Ltd.
3 Church Street
#10-04 Samsung Hub
Singapore 049483

Acquisitions Editor: Terri Accomazzo
Content Development Editor: Anna Villarruel
Editorial Assistant: Erik Helton
Production Editor: Bennie Clark Allen
Copy Editor: Melinda Masson
Typesetter: C&M Digitals (P) Ltd.
Proofreader: Gretchen Treadwell
Indexer: Jean Casalegno
Cover Designer: Janet Kiesel
Marketing Manager: Jillian Oelson

Printed in the United States of America

Library of Congress Cataloging-in-Publication Data

Names: Trager, Robert, author. | Ross, Susan Dente, author. | Reynolds, Amy, 1967- author.

Title: The law of journalism and mass communication / Robert Trager, University of Colorado, Boulder; Susan Dente Ross, Washington State University; Amy Reynolds, Kent State University.

Description: Sixth edition. | Washington, D.C. : CQ Press, a division of Sage, [2018] | Includes bibliographical references and index.

Identifiers: LCCN 2017032750 | ISBN 9781506363226 (pbk. : alk. paper)

Subjects: LCSH: Mass media—Law and legislation—United States. | Press law—United States. | Freedom of the press—United States.

Classification: LCC KF2750 .T73 2018 | DDC 343.7309/9—dc23
LC record available at https://lccn.loc.gov/2017032750

SFI label applies to text stock

18 19 20 21 10 9 8 7 6 5 4 3 2

BRIEF CONTENTS

DETAILED CONTENTS

LIST OF FEATURES

PREFACE

This book is intended and designed primarily to serve those of you who plan to work in journalism, public relations, advertising or marketing in new or old media. We strive to produce a truly readable book centered on the most significant aspects of the law situated within the social and political contexts that give them meaning. We have trained our eyes sharply on the legal issues related to gathering and disseminating information in today's multimedia digital age that we believe are most relevant to you as a public communicator. Our goal is to improve your understanding of the protections and constraints imposed by the law upon the ways you communicate.

Our unique approach to *The Law of Journalism and Mass Communication* developed in response to the way we teach and the way we believe students learn best. We see the law as a product of specific decisions at a particular time and in a specific place. As such, the law is best understood when we see and feel its effects on real people, mundane conflicts and actions not only of our government but also of our friends, neighbors and families. Yet we recognize that time shifts rapidly, and decisions are both local and global.

Our goal is to make *The Law of Journalism and Mass Communication* as fresh and new as possible—to make it interesting and, yes, sometimes even fun or funny; not only to incorporate the latest court rulings and legislative enactments but also to present the trials and resolutions outside of court and beyond the judiciary that show how the law affects the ways mass communications work and how people perceive and receive that work. That means this edition deals with tweets and public protests, alcohol ads in university newspapers, global data privacy and cybersecurity, libel on the internet, free speech on college campuses and much more.

FEATURES

With this sixth edition, *The Law of Journalism and Mass Communication* enters those often-awkward teen years, ushering in the opportunity for some alterations beyond the customary biannual updates. All of the updated content you look for in each new edition—from the Supreme Court as well as both federal and state courts, Congress, executive agencies, federal and state policymakers and advisory groups, and media organizations and allies—is here, as always. As usual, these updates encompass at least one-third of a text that has been carefully edited to make it both interesting and readable. More than 150 photographs, color and graphics punctuate the text and respond to the need for a dynamic reading environment that encourages critical engagement. Each chapter embraces new case law and policy alongside new breakout boxes that highlight key rules of law, emerging legal issues and intersections with international law and policy. Boxes broaden the lens through which we view the law; emphasize that digital means local *is* global; draw out the intersections between the law and the people; and underscore key rules, tests and principles.

An initial quotation provides each chapter with a unique perspective or real-life example of the law at work. A ***Suppose . . .*** hypothetical engages readers with a central issue of the law raised in that chapter and resolved in one of the two **Cases for Study** that close the chapter. These cases allow students to read the actual decisions that construct *The Law of Journalism and Mass Communication*. **Landmark Cases in Context** point out when the web became our favorite public forum and when radio seemed like an alien intruder in our homes. Definitions in the margins and in a glossary at the back make it easier to comprehend and retain the often-unfamiliar terminology of the law.

ORGANIZATION AND COVERAGE

This sixth edition also brings some more notable changes the authors believe will help to clarify fast-moving areas of the law, better juxtapose related material to highlight emerging intersections and weed more carefully through the plethora of legal details to emphasize core concepts and precepts for new students of the law of journalism and mass communication. We hope these alterations more fully engage students and aid comprehension and retention of the material as they facilitate teaching innovation and provide greater opportunity for creative classroom activities.

To this end, the authors have reduced the number of chapters from 13 to 12 and reorganized several chapters in response to requests from adopters and reviewers. Specifically, readers will find a new approach to the opening chapters. The chapter on speech distinctions moves its focus more precisely onto how the Supreme Court's application of the First Amendment has evolved through time to differentially protect sometimes-fuzzy categories of speech. In this edition, you will find discussion of violence in video games in this chapter rather than in the later discussion of obscenity. The changes here are intended to make clear to readers how speech categories are not always precise and how court precedents constrain but do not absolutely bind subsequent decision making.

A sharpened chapter on libel and emotional distress is followed by a reorganized chapter on libel defenses to highlight those defenses most commonly used today. The privacy chapter now highlights the traditional privacy torts first, then offers a new section on privacy and data protection before ending with how the Supreme Court has approached emerging issues of electronic privacy. In this edition, two chapters on information gathering and overseeing the courts replace the three chapters that formerly dealt separately with newsgathering, reporter's privilege and access to the courts. The new structure places reporter's privilege within the uncertain protections afforded to the gathering of information and better integrates the protections for and limits to public access to judicial proceedings. The information gathering chapter is expanded from purely news situations to highlight issues of special relevance to public relations and marketing professionals.

A reorganized chapter on electronic media regulation makes the material more engaging and better explains both the regulatory history in this area and how changes in technology go hand in hand with regulation. Finally, the chapter on advertising has received a facelift to begin with a clarified discussion of how the definition of commercial speech has evolved before examining how the Supreme Court's protection of advertising has changed through time. Students of marketing are likely to find much in this chapter of interest.

WHAT'S NEW IN THE SIXTH EDITION

As with every edition, we have made every effort to keep the contents of this sixth edition abreast of the most recent law and policy actions of significance, the cutting-edge research in the field, and the social, technological and economic shifts affecting public communicators and their products. Just as Congress and the courts have altered the law in the two years since our last edition, updates and new information have reshaped every area of this edition of *The Law of Journalism and Mass Communication*. Some of the significant changes in this edition include:

- Clearer definitions in the margins and the glossary

- A new foundational discussion of the rule of law

- A focus on the shifts in the U.S. Supreme Court and the legacy of Justice Antonin Scalia

- A new discussion of and excerpt from *Reed v. Town of Gilbert* in light of its growing impact

- A new examination of the Communications Decency Act's Sec. 230 protections for online carriers of terrorist speech

- A discussion of the new Federal Aviation Administration regulations on commercial drone use

- Expanded coverage of the public right to record

- A new discussion of ag-gag and related limits on public access

- An updated review of driver's license privacy

- Expanded coverage of the use of anti-SLAPP laws, particularly with libel suits

- Updates on the opinion defense in the context of social media and fake news

- A new discussion of privacy concerns around personally identifiable data and the Federal Trade Commission's role in protecting consumer data

- A revised discussion of court-imposed gag orders

- New coverage of the right to a speedy trial

- A discussion of developments in the area of social media use in trials

- Updates on state reporter's privilege and shield law protections

- A discussion of protection from newsroom searches in light of federal seizure of Associated Press phone records

- An expanded exploration of the Federal Communications Commission's regulation of multichannel video programming distributors and online video providers

- An updated discussion of the Federal Communications Commission's must-carry and retransmission consent rules

- More extensive coverage of virtual child pornography

- A new exploration of disparaging trademarks and First Amendment protection

- A discussion of several recent Supreme Court cases involving intellectual property

- More extensive coverage of the transformative use test in copyright, especially as applied to new technologies

- A new and expanded discussion of the evolving meaning of commercial speech

- More extensive coverage of the Lanham Act

- A new exploration of Federal Trade Commission and Food and Drug Administration commercial speech actions

- Coverage of new Federal Trade Commission disclosure requirements related to commercial speech

Despite all the revisions, updates and new content, we believe this sixth edition of *The Law of Journalism and Mass Communication* will feel familiar to our former readers. We hope the breadth and diversity of media law you will discover in this volume provide the framework for a dynamic, engaged experience with the law. We also hope you find this text in good order, for, as Aristotle said, "Good law is good order."

DIGITAL RESOURCES

The wealth of online materials we provide through a companion website, located at **http://study.sagepub.com/medialaw6e**, encompasses both student learning aids and teaching tools. The following resources have been updated and revised to enhance student use of this new edition.

Password-protected **Instructor Resources** include the following:

- A **Microsoft® Word test bank** contains multiple-choice, true/false, short-answer and essay questions for each chapter. The test bank provides you with a diverse range of prewritten options as well as the opportunity for editing any question and/or inserting your own personalized questions to assess students' progress and understanding.

- Editable, chapter-specific Microsoft® **PowerPoint® slides** offer you complete flexibility in easily creating a multimedia presentation for your course, for you can highlight essential content and features.

- An **Instructor Manual** features chapter overviews, chapter outlines, classroom activities and links to professional resources.

- Lively and stimulating **class activities** can be used in class to reinforce active learning. The activities apply to individual or group projects.

- **Tables and figures** are available in an easily downloadable format for use in papers, handouts and presentations.

Our **Student Study Site** is completely open-access and offers a wide range of additional features:

- Mobile-friendly **eFlashcards** reinforce understanding of key terms and concepts that have been outlined in the chapters.

- Mobile-friendly **web quizzes** allow for independent assessment of progress made in learning course material.

- Insightful **chapter summaries** help students study and reinforce key concepts.

- **Links to professional resources** help students further explore chapter concepts and facilitate research.

- An archive of **case studies** provides the opportunity to engage directly and personally with the legal decisions that construct *The Law of Journalism and Mass Communication*.

ACKNOWLEDGMENTS

As with our previous editions, this book is a collaborative effort not only among its authors but also between us and the community we serve. The knowledge, insights, and comments of a large and expanding group of people have helped us update and improve this book. We offer our deep respect and gratitude to all those who have shaped our understanding of the field, gently pointed out our faults of commission or omission, and reinforced the strengths of this edition of *The Law of Journalism and Mass Communication*. You have been more generous than we deserve.

Beyond the friends, families, students, and colleagues who have encouraged and supported us in uncounted ways, we extend special thanks to all the anonymous reviewers who provided valuable feedback or, perhaps, favored our text among other books in the field. We also thank the talented editors, designers, and staff at CQ Press who helped bring this new edition to you.

Finally, and most important, we thank you, our readers.

The authors and SAGE also gratefully acknowledge the contributions of the following reviewers:

Roy S. Gutterman, *Syracuse University*

Maria Moore, *Illinois State University*

Elizabeth A. Skewes, *University of Colorado, Boulder*

Martin D. Sommerness, *Northern Arizona University*

John C. Watson, *American University*

ABOUT THE AUTHORS

Robert Trager is professor emeritus in journalism and mass communication at the University of Colorado. He taught courses in communication law, freedom of expression and media institutions. He is the founding editor of the law journal *Communication Law and Policy*. Before joining the University of Colorado faculty, he was an attorney with a major cable television company and practiced media law with a Washington, D.C., firm.

Susan Dente Ross is professor of English at Washington State University. A former newspaper owner and editor and head of the Association for Education in Journalism and Mass Communication Law Division, she is a Fulbright scholar whose international research, speaking, and training focus on free speech and press for the disempowered and as a tool for global equity, problem solving, and justice. She publishes on law, policy, and media's role in conflict transformation and reconciliation. She is a writer of creative nonfiction.

Amy Reynolds is dean of the College of Communication and Information at Kent State University. Her research focuses on dissent, First Amendment history, and media sociology. She has written or edited seven books. Prior to becoming a dean, she was a journalism professor at Louisiana State University and Indiana University. Before earning her PhD at the University of Texas, she worked as a reporter, producer, and editor at newspapers and television stations.

The obligation to follow precedent begins with necessity, and a contrary necessity marks its outer limit. . . . [W]e recognize that no judicial system could do society's work if it eyed each issue afresh in every case that raised it. . . . [Yet] it is common wisdom that the rule of *stare decisis* is not an "inexorable command."

—Planned Parenthood of Southeastern Pennsylvania v. Casey[1]

The Electoral College in 2017 affirmed the election of Donald Trump despite partisan claims that the rule of law required it to endorse Hillary Clinton, who won the popular vote.[2]

THE RULE OF LAW
Law in a Changing Communication Environment

SUPPOSE . . .

. . . it costs a lot to get elected, and people with money can affect election outcomes. In response, the federal government adopts laws that limit contributions to and spending by political candidates. The laws try to balance the right of individuals and groups to support candidates and the need to protect elections from corruption. Big money interests challenge the campaign finance laws in court. After decades of upholding similar laws, the U.S. Supreme Court in 2007 strikes down a federal[3] ban on certain political advertisements as unconstitutional. Writing in dissent, Justice David Souter argues, "The court (and, I think, the country) loses when important precedent is overruled without good reason."[4]

In the lead-up to the 2008 presidential election, a federal district court relied heavily on earlier Supreme Court decisions to uphold a law that prohibited a nonprofit organization called Citizens United from running advertisements and airing a film about then-presidential candidate Hillary Clinton.[5] On appeal, the Supreme Court ruling in *Citizens United v. Federal Election Commission*[6] struck down many campaign finance restrictions and raised questions about the stability and predictability of the law. This chapter and the case excerpts that follow explore the relative constancy or uncertainty of the rule of law.

The ancient Greek philosopher Aristotle said people are basically self-interested; they pursue their own interests to the exclusion of the greater good or the cause of justice. However, self-interest is ultimately shortsighted and self-destructive. A lumber company that seeks only to generate the greatest immediate profit ultimately deforests the timberlands it depends on and eliminates its own future.[7] Astute people therefore recognize that personal interests and short-term goals must sometimes give way to communal, universal or long-term objectives. Everyone benefits when people adopt a system of rules to promote a balance between gain and loss, between cost and benefit and between personal desires and universal concerns. Aristotle called this balance the "golden mean." Human interests are served and justice is achieved when a society adopts a system of law to balance conflicting human objectives and allow people to live together and achieve desired goals.[8]

rule of law The standards of a society that guide the proper and consistent creation and application of the law.

Belief in the power of law to promote this balance and restrain human injustice is the foundation of the U.S. Constitution and the **rule of law**. The U.S. Supreme Court said the notion that "our government is a government of laws, not of men" is central to our constitutional nature.[9] In essence, laws establish a contract that governs interactions among residents and between the people and their government. Legal rules establish the boundaries of acceptable behavior and empower government to punish violations. The rule of law limits the power of government because it prohibits government from infringing on the rights and liberties of the people. This system constrains the actions of both the people and the government to enhance liberty, freedom and justice for all.

In 1964, as the United States expanded what many then believed was an illegal military action in Vietnam, Harvard legal scholar Lon Fuller articulated what would become a foundational understanding of the rule of law. In Fuller's view, the rule of law was a set of standards intended to create norms and procedures that provide for consistent, neutral decision making equally for all. Fuller's formal, conceptual definition has been criticized because it does not provide specific guidance to those drafting, interpreting or applying the law.[10] As one legal scholar noted, this understanding of the rule of law is created through its application. It "cannot be answered in the abstract."[11]

LANDMARK CASES IN CONTEXT

Key ■ Event
◆ Cases

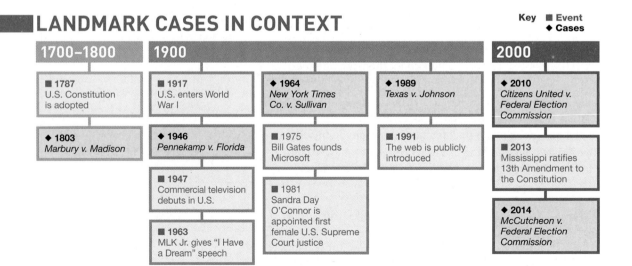

1700–1800	1900			2000
■ 1787 U.S. Constitution is adopted	■ 1917 U.S. enters World War I	◆ 1964 *New York Times Co. v. Sullivan*	◆ 1989 *Texas v. Johnson*	◆ 2010 *Citizens United v. Federal Election Commission*
◆ 1803 *Marbury v. Madison*	◆ 1946 *Pennekamp v. Florida*	■ 1975 Bill Gates founds Microsoft	■ 1991 The web is publicly introduced	■ 2013 Mississippi ratifies 13th Amendment to the Constitution
	■ 1947 Commercial television debuts in U.S.	■ 1981 Sandra Day O'Connor is appointed first female U.S. Supreme Court justice		◆ 2014 *McCutcheon v. Federal Election Commission*
	■ 1963 MLK Jr. gives "I Have a Dream" speech			

⬤ INTERNATIONAL LAW

Four Foundations of the Rule of Law

The World Justice Project has articulated four foundations of the rule of law based on internationally accepted universal standards. Accordingly, a system of the rule of law exists when:

1. All individuals and private entities are accountable under the law.

2. The laws are clear, public, stable and just; are applied evenly; and protect fundamental rights.

3. The process by which the laws are enacted, administered and enforced is accessible and fair.

4. Justice is delivered in a timely manner by competent, ethical, independent and neutral representatives who serve the public good.[1]

Even when endorsing these principles, many argue that any universal rule of law is a form of imperialism that tramples the unique priorities of individual nations and limits the freedom of different peoples to create distinct, culturally appropriate systems of law.[2]

---

1. World Justice Project, *Rule of Law Index 2014*, worldjusticeproject.org/sites/default/files/files/introduction_key_findings.pdf.
2. Rosa Ehrenreich Brooks, *The New Imperialism: Violence, Norms, and the "Rule of Law,"* 101 Mich. L. Rev. 2275 (2003); *but see* David Pimental, *Rule of Law Reform Without Cultural Imperialism?*, 2 Hague J. on Rule L. 1 (2010).

For Fuller, the rule of law established eight "desiderata," or desired outcomes, to guide how laws should be created and employed. The rule of law requires laws to be (1) general and not discriminatory; (2) widely known and disseminated; (3) forward-looking in their application rather than retroactive; (4) clear and specific; (5) self-consistent and complementary of each other; (6) capable of being obeyed; (7) relatively stable over time; and (8) applied and enforced in ways that reflect their underlying intent.

As a mechanism for ordering human behavior, the law functions best when it makes clear, comprehensible and consistent distinctions between legal and illegal behavior. People can only obey laws that they know about and understand. Good laws must be publicly disseminated and sufficiently clear and precise to properly inform citizens of when and how the laws apply (as well as when they do not).

Vague laws fail to define their terms or are unclear. They are unacceptable because people may avoid participating in legal activities because they are uncertain whether they will run afoul of the law. For example, ongoing legal battles seek to clarify the boundary between the First Amendment right to assemble and statutes governing unlawful assemblies.[12] In California, protesters were arrested under a state law that makes it a misdemeanor for two or more people to gather to commit an unlawful act or to perform a lawful action in a "violent, boisterous or tumultuous manner."[13] Without clarifying the boundaries of protected assemblies, a judge ruled in 2016 that the contested facts in the dispute did not support an NAACP request to ban police arrests of people gathering at the site of a fatal police shooting.[14]

vague laws Laws that either fail to define their terms or use such general language that neither citizens nor judges know with certainty what the laws permit or punish.

● REAL WORLD LAW

U.S. Legal System Not Equally Accessible for All

The World Justice Project's annual, global index of how citizens experience the rule of law in their home country ranked the United States 18 among 113 countries in 2016.[1] The report put the United States behind the Nordic countries, which topped the list, and below Estonia, the Czech Republic and Japan but well ahead of Cambodia, Afghanistan and Venezuela, which ranked last.

The study found two primary weaknesses in the U.S. justice system. Civil justice is far more expensive in the United States than in other countries, which distinctly disadvantages poor people. The U.S. justice system also fell behind in terms of equal treatment and absence of discrimination under the law.

1. World Justice Project, *Rule of Law Index 2016*, data.worldjusticeproject.org.

discretion The authority to determine the proper outcome.

overbroad law A principle that directs courts to find laws unconstitutional if they restrict more legal activity than necessary.

stare decisis The doctrine that courts follow precedent; the basis of common law, it literally means to stand by the previous decision.

precedent The outcome of a previous case that establishes a rule of law that courts within the same jurisdiction rely on to determine cases with similar issues.

Clear laws define their terms and detail their application in order to limit government officials' **discretion**. In this way, clear laws advance the rule of law by reducing the ability of officials to apply legal rules differently to their friends and foes. "True freedom requires the rule of law and justice, and a judicial system in which the rights of some are not secured by the denial of rights to others," one observer noted.[15]

Good laws accomplish their objectives with minimum infringement on the freedoms and liberties of the people. Well-tailored laws advance specific government interests or prevent particular harms without punishing activities that pose no risk to society. A law that sought to limit noisy disturbances of residential neighborhoods at night, for example, would be poorly tailored and **overbroad** if it prohibited all discussion out of doors, anywhere at any time.

The rule of law requires the law to be internally consistent, logical and relatively stable. To ensure slow evolution rather than rapid revolution of legal rules, judges in U.S. courts interpret and apply laws based upon the precedents established by other court rulings. Precedent, or **stare decisis**, is the legal principle that tells courts to stand by what courts have decided previously. As the U.S. Supreme Court has written, "[T]he very concept of the rule of law underlying our own Constitution requires such continuity over time that a respect for precedent is, by definition, indispensable."[16] The principle holds that subsequent court decisions should adhere to the example and reasoning of earlier decisions on the same point. Reliance on **precedent** is the heart of the common law (discussed later) and encourages predictable application of the law. But precedent is not absolutely binding; it is not always followed; and sometimes precedents seem to conflict. The rule of law can be ambiguous and unclear.[17] Especially where constitutional values are at issue, courts must "not allow principles of stare decisis to block correction of error," as the California Supreme Court said in 2015.[18]

Laws are not inflexible. Even the U.S. Constitution—the foundational contract between the U.S. government and the people—can be changed through amendment. Other laws—regulations, orders and rules—may be repealed or amended by the federal, state and local bodies that adopted them, and they may be interpreted or invalidated by the courts. In its landmark 1803 ruling in *Marbury v. Madison* (excerpted at the end of this chapter), the Supreme Court established the courts' power to interpret laws: "It is emphatically the province and duty of the judicial department to say what the law is. Those who apply the rule to particular cases must of necessity expound and interpret that rule."[19]

INTERNATIONAL LAW

Executive Orders Flow With the Stream of the Rule of Law

President Barack Obama addresses young African leaders at the White House in 2014.

In a 2014 address to African leaders, President Barack Obama stepped into the long-standing political controversy over the meaning and global application of the rule of law. He said:

> If you do not have a basic system of rule of law, of respect for civil rights and human rights, if you do not give people a credible, legitimate way to work though the political process . . . if there are not laws in place in which everyone is equal under the law . . . if you don't have those basic mechanisms, it is very rare for a country to succeed.[1]

The speech renewed attention to the tension between a commitment to universal standards of human rights and self-governance, and a need for laws to embody the unique social, cultural and historical conception of justice in a specific country at a particular time.

A United Nations paper on the global debate said, "The rule of law is a concept that resonates across borders and boundaries while reflecting a diverse set of perspectives. . . . It highlights the importance of context and specificity."[2]

---

1. Dave Boyer, *Obama to Give Africa $38M, but Tells Young African Leaders: Stop "Making Excuses" for Economy*, Wash. Times, July 28, 2014, www.washingtontimes.com/news/2014/jul/28/obama-give-africa-38m-tells-young-leaders-stop-mak.
2. Louis-Alexandre Berg and Deval Desai, *Draft United Nations Development Program Background Paper: Overview on the Rule of Law and Sustainable Development for the Global Dialogue on Rule of Law*, Aug. 2013, www.undp.org/content/dam/undp/library/Democratic%20Governance/Access%20to%20Justice%20and%20Rule%20of%20Law/Global%20Dialogue%20Background%20Paper%20-%20Rule%20of%20Law%20and%20Sustainable%20Developme....pdf.

BODY OF THE LAW

The body of law in the United States has grown in size and complexity as American society has become increasingly diverse and complicated. Many forms of communication and the laws that govern them today did not exist in the 1800s. Technology has been a driving force for change in the law of journalism and mass communication. U.S. law also has developed in response to social, political, philosophical and economic changes. Legislatures create new laws to reflect evolving understandings of individual rights, liberties and responsibilities. Employment and advertising laws, for example, emerged and multiplied as the nation's workforce shifted and the power of corporations grew. Even well-established legal concepts, such as defamation, have evolved to reflect new realities of the role of communication in society and the power of mass media to harm individuals.

constitutional law
The set of laws that establish the nature, functions and limits of government.

statutory law
Written law formally enacted by city, county, state and federal legislative bodies.

black-letter law
Formally enacted, written law that is available in legal reporters or other documents.

equity law Law created by judges to decide cases based on fairness and ethics and also to determine the proper remedy.

common law
Judge-made law comprised of the principles and traditions established through court rulings; precedent-based law.

doctrines
Principles or theories of law that shape judicial decision making (e.g., the doctrine of content neutrality).

administrative law
The orders, rules and regulations promulgated by executive branch administrative agencies to carry out their delegated duties.

The laws of journalism and mass communication generally originate from six sources.

1. **Constitutional law** establishes the nature, functions and limits of government. The U.S. Constitution, the fundamental law of the United States, was framed in 1787 and ratified in 1789. Each of the states also has a constitution.

2. City, county, state and federal legislative bodies enact **statutory law**. Like constitutions, statutes are written down; both types of law are called **black-letter law**.

3. and 4. Judges create law in the form of both **equity law** and **common law**. When judges apply general principles of ethics and fairness to determine the proper remedy for a legal harm, they create equity law. Thus, restraining orders that prevent reporters from intimidating child celebrities are a form of equity law. Judges craft the common law when they use legal custom, tradition and prior court decisions to guide their decisions in pending cases. Common law often arises in situations not covered expressly by statutes when judges base their decision on precedent and legal **doctrines** established in similar cases. For example, under common law, publishers and distributors of indecent communications have been treated differently from other publishers (see Chapter 10). Some believe judges will move away from this distinction as online publishing increasingly replaces print.[20]

5. Constitutions and legislatures grant authority to government executives and to specialized agencies to make decisions and create rules that form the body of **administrative law**. Administrative agencies, such as the Federal Communications Commission (FCC) or the Federal Trade Commission (FTC), create the rules, regulations, orders and decisions that execute, or apply, laws enacted by Congress.

6. Government executives, such as the president, can issue **executive orders**, another source of law. In his 2014 State of the Union address, for example, President Barack Obama controversially said he planned to use executive orders to improve opportunities for Americans "wherever and whenever I can take steps without legislation."[21] Early in his administration, President Donald Trump signed an executive order that banned immigrants from seven nations, heightened vetting protocols for immigrants and suspended the nation's acceptance of refugees from Syria.[22] Acting quickly, the Ninth Circuit Court of Appeals refused to overturn a court injunction that blocked implementation of the executive order. The court did not determine whether the law, described by the president as a "Muslim ban," was an establishment of religion that violated the First Amendment.[23]

The six sources of law are explored further below.

Constitutions

Constitutions at the federal and state levels establish the structure of government and delegate and limit government power. The U.S. Constitution establishes the basic character, concepts and principles of government; organizes the federal government; and provides a minimum level of individual rights and privileges throughout the country. It creates three separate and coequal branches of government—the executive, the legislative and the judicial—and designates the distinct functions and responsibilities of each. The executive

⦿ POINTS OF LAW

Six Sources of Law
• Constitutions
• Statutes
• Equity law
• Common law
• Administrative law
• Executive orders

executive orders
Orders from a government executive, such as the president, a governor or a mayor, that have the force of law.

branch oversees government and administers, or executes, laws. The legislative branch enacts laws, and the judicial branch interprets laws and resolves legal conflicts.

Separation of government into branches provides the checks and balances within government that help uphold the rule of law. For example, "restrictions derived from the separation of powers doctrine prevent the judicial branch from deciding **political questions** . . . that revolve around policy choices and value determinations" because the Constitution gives the legislative and executive branches express authority to make political decisions.[24]

political questions
Questions not subject to judicial review because they fall into areas properly handled by another branch of government.

In many ways, state constitutions are distinct and independent from the U.S. Constitution they mirror. Under the principle of **federalism**, states are related to, yet independent of, the federal government and each other. Federalism encourages experimentation and variety in government. Each state has the ability to structure its own government and to craft state constitutional protections that exceed the rights granted by the U.S. Constitution. For example, the U.S. Constitution says nothing about municipalities; states create and determine the authority of cities or towns. While the federal right to privacy exists only through the U.S. Supreme Court's interpretation of the protections afforded by the First Amendment to the Constitution, Washington State's constitution contains an explicit privacy clause that protects individuals from disturbances of their private affairs.[26] State constitutions can be amended only by a direct vote of the people.

federalism
A principle according to which the states are related to yet independent of each other and are related to yet independent of the federal government.

Congress has approved only 33 of the thousands of proposed amendments to the U.S. Constitution, and the states have ratified only 27 of these. The first 10 amendments to the Constitution, which form the Bill of Rights, were ratified in 1791 after several states called for increased constitutional protection of individual liberties. In fewer than 500 words, the Bill of Rights expressly guarantees fundamental rights and limits government power. For example, the First Amendment (see Chapter 2) prevents government from abridging the people's right to speak and worship freely.

supremacy
Article 4, Part 2 of the U.S. Constitution (commonly called the Supremacy Clause) establishes that federal law takes precedence over, or supersedes, state laws.

Statutes

The U.S. Constitution explicitly delegates the power to enact statutory laws to the popularly elected legislative branch of government: the U.S. Congress and the state, county and city legislatures. Legislatures make laws to respond to—or predict and attempt to prevent—social problems. Thus, statutory law can be very specific to define the legal limits of particular activities. All criminal laws are statutes, for example. Statutes also establish the

THE BILL OF RIGHTS TO THE U.S. CONSTITUTION

National Archive

The Bill of Rights embodies the first 10 amendments to the U.S. Constitution. The ordering of the amendments was not intentional and does not reflect any hierarchy of principles. That is to say, the First Amendment does not override the Second or the Fourth.

The U.S. Constitution is both the pinnacle and the foundation of the law of the United States. Its own text establishes the **supremacy** of the Constitution over other laws of the land.

The supremacy clause resolves conflicts among laws by establishing that all state laws must give way to federal law, and state or federal laws that conflict with the Constitution are invalid. In a similar way, some federal laws pre-empt state laws, which in turn may pre-empt city statutes.

As the bedrock of the law, the Constitution dictates the proper actions of all divisions of government and is relatively difficult to change. There are two ways to amend the Constitution. The first and only method actually used is for both chambers of Congress to pass a proposed constitutional amendment by a two-thirds vote in each. The second method is for two-thirds of the state legislatures to vote for a Constitutional Convention, which then proposes one or more amendments. All amendments to the Constitution also must be ratified by three-fourths of the state legislatures. In 2013, when Mississippi became the last state to ban slavery by ratifying the 13th Amendment to the Constitution, the vote was only symbolic. The needed three-fourths of states ratified the amendment in 1865.[25]

⊙ POINTS OF LAW

The Three Branches of Federal Government

The Executive

The president, the cabinet and the administrative agencies execute laws.

The Legislative

The Senate and the House of Representatives pass laws.

The Judicial

The three levels of courts review laws and adjudicate disputes.

rules of copyright, broadcasting, advertising and access to government meetings and information. Statutes are formally adopted through a public process and are meant to be clear and stable. They are written down in statute books and codified, which means they are compiled into topics by codes, and anyone can find and read them in public repository libraries.

When the language of a statute is unclear, imprecise or ambiguous, courts determine the law's proper meaning and application through a review process called **statutory construction**. Statutes may be difficult to interpret because they fail to define key terms. For example, if the word *meeting* is not defined in an open-meetings law, it is unclear whether the law applies to virtual meetings online.[28] When a statute suggests more than one meaning, courts generally look to the law's preamble, or statement of purpose, for guidance on how the legislature intended the law to apply. Courts may use legislative committee reports, debates and public statements to guide their statutory interpretation.

Courts tend to engage in **strict construction**, which narrowly defines laws to their literal meaning and clearly stated intent. The effort to interpret laws according to the "plain meaning" of the words—the **facial meaning** of the law—limits any tendency courts might have to rewrite laws through creative or expansive interpretation. This **deference** to legislative intent reflects courts' recognition that the power to write laws lies with the publicly elected legislature. The power of courts to engage in statutory construction is inherently nondemocratic because judges in many states are not elected.

Win McNamee/Getty Images

With the 2017 swearing in of the 115th Congress and inauguration of President Donald Trump, the Republican Party controlled both branches of government. This marked the 17th time since World War II that one party controlled both the Congress and the White House.[27]

statutory construction The process by which courts determine the proper meaning and application of statutes.

strict construction Courts' narrow interpretation and application of a law based on the literal meaning of its language. Especially applied in interpreting the Constitution.

facial meaning The plain and straightforward meaning.

deference The judicial practice of interpreting statues and rules by relying heavily on the judgments and intentions of the administrative experts and legislative agencies that enacted the laws.

Courts may invalidate state statutes that conflict with federal laws, or city statutes that conflict with either state or federal law. However, courts generally interpret the plain meaning of a statute in a way that avoids conflict with other laws, including the

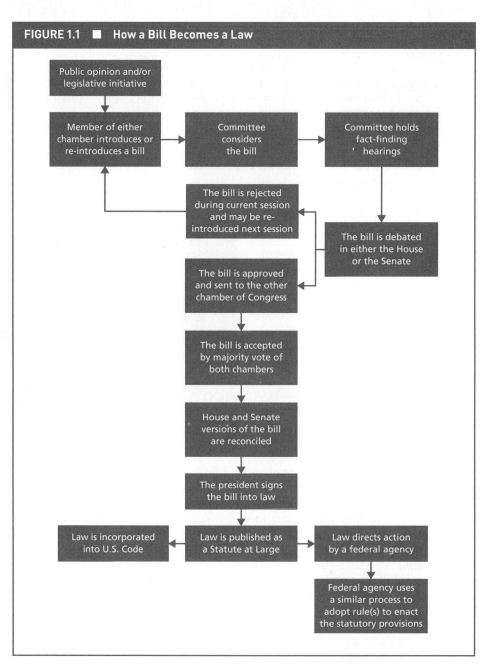

FIGURE 1.1 ■ How a Bill Becomes a Law

⦿ POINTS OF LAW

What's in a Face?

Some constitutional challenges to laws are raised before a law is applied. Such **facial challenges** argue that a law that may seem constitutional "on its face" is nonetheless unconstitutional in every instance. First Amendment challenges for vagueness and overbreadth often arise as facial challenges.

Laws are unconstitutionally vague if they are too unclear for a person to reasonably know whether the law applies to specific conduct. Vague laws often "chill" the exercise of constitutional rights and liberties because people fear their behavior might be punished under the law.

Laws intended to target illegal acts are overbroad if they harm constitutionally protected rights. For example, when the Supreme Court struck down a law prohibiting the depiction of animal cruelty, the Court said a law is unconstitutionally overbroad if "a substantial number of its applications are unconstitutional, judged in relation to the statute's plainly legitimate sweep."[1] The determination of overbreadth is based on a reasonable reading of the law's language.

---

1. United States v. Stevens, 559 U.S. 460 (2010) (mem.).

Constitution. Courts review the constitutionality of a statute only as a last resort. When engaging in constitutional review, courts generally attempt to preserve any portions of the law that can be upheld without violating the general intent of the statute. For example, the U.S. Supreme Court struck down the Communications Decency Act,[29] without undermining the balance of the comprehensive Telecommunications Act of 1996 (see Chapter 9).

More than two centuries ago, the U.S. Supreme Court essentially granted itself the power to strike down any laws it said conflicted with the U.S. Constitution. In 1803 in *Marbury v. Madison*,[30] the Court said the Constitution's system of checks and balances provided the judicial branch with inherent authority to limit the power of the legislative branch and bar it from enacting unconstitutional laws. The Court decided that although the Constitution gave the legislative branch the power to make laws, the judicial branch was empowered to interpret laws and discover what limits the Constitution placed on legislatures' lawmaking authority. In this controversial decision, the Court established its power of **judicial review**.

Judicial review allows all courts to examine government actions to determine whether they conform to the U.S. and state constitutions. However, courts other than the U.S. Supreme Court rarely use their power of judicial review. If a state supreme court determined that a statute was constitutional under its state constitution, the decision could be appealed to the U.S. Supreme Court, which could decide that the law did not meet the standards set by the U.S. Constitution. The Supreme Court tries to use its power of review sparingly and rarely strikes down laws as unconstitutional. As a general rule, the Court will defer to the lawmaking authority of the executive and legislative branches of government by interpreting laws in ways that do not conflict with the Constitution.

facial challenge A legal argument that the challenged law or policy is unconstitutional in every application; there are no situations in which the law can be interpreted to be constitutional.

judicial review The power of the courts to determine the meaning of the Constitution and decide whether laws violate the Constitution.

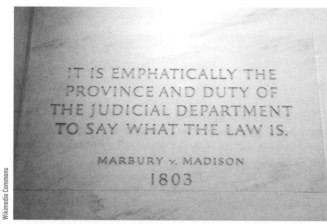

IT IS EMPHATICALLY THE
PROVINCE AND DUTY OF
THE JUDICIAL DEPARTMENT
TO SAY WHAT THE LAW IS.

MARBURY v. MADISON
1803

Wikimedia Commons

The U.S. Supreme Court building displays a plaque bearing a quotation from *Marbury v. Madison*, 5 U.S. 137, establishing its authority of judicial review.

Common Law

The common law is judge-made law. The common law consists of the rules and principles developed through custom and precedent. The common law is a vast and unwritten body of legal doctrines established through hundreds of years of dispute resolution that reaches past the founding of this country and across the Atlantic to England. For centuries prior to the settlement of the American colonies, English courts "discovered" the doctrines people traditionally used to resolve disagreements. Judges then applied these "common" laws to guide court decisions. The resulting decisions, and the reasoning that supported them, came to be known as English common law, which became the foundation of U.S. common law.

Eventually, common law grew to reflect more than the problem-solving principles of the common people. Today, U.S. common law rests on the presumption that prior court rulings, or precedent, should guide future decisions. The essence of precedent, stare decisis, is that courts should follow each other's guidance. Once a higher court has established a principle relevant to a certain set of facts, fairness requires lower courts to try to apply the same principle to similar facts. This establishes consistency and stability in the law.

Under the rule of stare decisis, the decision of a higher court, such as the U.S. Supreme Court, establishes a precedent that binds lower court rulings. A binding precedent of the U.S. Supreme Court constrains all lower federal courts throughout the country, and the decisions of each circuit court of appeals bind the district courts in that circuit. Similarly, lower state courts must follow the precedents of their own state appellate and supreme courts. However, courts from different and coequal jurisdictions do not establish binding precedent upon their peers. Courts in Rhode Island are not bound to follow precedents established in Wyoming, and federal district courts are not bound to apply precedents established by appellate courts in other federal circuits. In fact, different federal appellate courts sometimes hand down directly conflicting decisions. To avoid such conflicts, however, courts often look to each other's decisions for guidance.

Even when the power of stare decisis is at its greatest, lower courts may choose not to adhere to precedent. At the risk of the judges' credibility, courts may simply ignore precedent. After all, the common law must be discovered through research in the thousands of court decisions collected into centuries of volumes, called court reporters. Courts also may depart from precedent with good reason. Courts examining a new but similar question may decide to **modify precedent**—that is, to alter the precedent to respond to changed realities. Thus, the U.S. Supreme Court might find that contemporary attitudes and practices no longer support a 20-year-old precedent permitting government to maintain the secrecy of computer compilations of public records.[31]

modify precedent To change rather than follow or reject precedent.

● REAL WORLD LAW

Scalia Said Rules, History Should Guide Court Interpretations

Widely regarded as the most conservative justice on the Supreme Court,[1] Justice Antonin Scalia was also one of the longest-seated justices in the Court's history when he died in 2016 after almost 30 years on that bench.[2] His long tenure and strong views on constitutional and statutory interpretation shaped many areas of contemporary mass communication law as well as the rule of law. Regarding the rule of law, he argued that the Supreme Court should "curb—even reverse—the tendency of judges to imbue authoritative texts with their own policy preferences." Clearly delineated and consistently applied rules are necessary, he said, to "provide greater certainty in the law and hence greater predictability and greater respect for the rule of law."[3]

Justice Scalia relied on two complementary principles to keep the discretion of judges in check. First, he was a strong proponent of originalism, which holds that the Constitution's meaning should be based upon how the text was understood when it was adopted. Justice Scalia said the Supreme Court's constitutional rulings relied too often on broad, amorphous principles rather than "a historical criterion that is conceptually . . . separate from the preferences of the judge himself."[4] Second, he preferred concrete, discrete, bright-line rules to multipart tests or balancing.

"When . . . I adopt a general rule . . . I not only constrain lower courts, I constrain myself as well," he said.[5] Justice Scalia valued the predictability of rules to "enhance the legitimacy of decisions . . . [and] embolden the decision maker to resist the will of a hostile majority," one observer said.[6]

1. William M. Landes & Richard A. Posner, *Rational Judicial Behavior: A Statistical Study*, 1 J. OF LEGAL ANALYSIS 775 (2009).
2. John G. Roberts, Jr., *Statement by Chief Justice John G. Roberts, Jr.*, Feb. 13, 2016, www.supremecourt.gov/publicinfo/press/pressreleases/pr_02-13-16. (William O. Dougla, the longest-serving justice, served 36 and a half years. *See also* Supreme Court of the United States, *Frequently Asked Questions*, Mar. 14, 2016, www.supremecourt.gov/faq_justices.aspx.)
3. Antonin Scalia & Bryan A. Garner, READING LAW: THE INTERPRETATION OF LEGAL TEXTS, xxviii–xxix (2012).
4. Antonin Scalia, *Originalism: The Lesser Evil*, 57 U. CIN. L. REV. 849, 862–4 (1989).
5. Antonin Scalia, *The Rule of Law as a Law of Rules*, 56 U. CHI. L. REV. 1175 (1989).
6. Alex Kozinski, *My Pizza With Nino*, 12 CARDOZA L. REV. 1583, 1588–89 (1991).

Courts also may **distinguish from precedent** by asserting that factual differences between the current case and the precedent case outweigh similarities. For example, the Supreme Court 40-plus years ago distinguished between newspapers and broadcasters in terms of any right of public access.[32] The Court said the public has a right to demand that broadcasters provide diverse content on issues of public importance because broadcasters use the public airwaves. The Court did not apply that reasoning when it later considered virtually the same question as applied to newspapers. Newspapers, the Court said, are independent members of the press with a protected right to control their content.

distinguish from precedent To justify an outcome in a case by asserting that differences between that case and preceding cases outweigh any similarities.

Finally, courts very occasionally will **overturn precedent** outright and reject the fundamental premise of that decision. This is a radical step and generally occurs only to remedy past errors or to reflect a fundamental rethinking of the law. In one such instance, the Supreme Court in 1997 overruled a 12-year-old Court precedent that had prohibited public school teachers from providing remedial education in parochial schools.[33] The Court said the precedent had mistakenly confused government efforts to fulfill its mandate to educate all children with unconstitutional government establishment of religion.

overturn precedent To reject the fundamental premise of a precedent.

The Ninth Circuit Court of Appeals sitting en banc in 2014.

Equity Law

Judges, not legislatures, make equity law in order to provide fair remedies and relief for various harms. Equity law is based on the presumption that fairness is not always achieved through the rigid application of strict rules, and fines are not always the correct remedy for a legal harm. No specific, black-letter laws dictate equity. Rather, judges determine what is fair and issue decrees to ensure that justice is achieved. Thus, restraining orders that require paparazzi to stay a certain distance away from celebrities are a form of equity law. An injunction in 1971 that temporarily prevented The New York Times and The Washington Post from publishing stories based on the Pentagon Papers was another form of equity relief. While the law of equity is related to common law, the rules of equity law are more flexible and are not governed by precedent.

Administrative Rules

The legislative branch of government often delegates authority to expert administrative agencies in the executive branch to interpret and implement statutory laws. Administrative law may constitute the largest proportion of contemporary law in the United States. An alphabet soup of state and federal administrative agencies with specific areas of expertise—such as the FCC, which oversees interstate electronic communication—incorporates both legislative and judicial functions. These agencies adopt orders, rules and regulations to carry out the laws enacted by Congress and signed by the president. Regulatory rules have the force of law. Administrative agencies enforce the administrative laws they adopt; they conduct hearings in which they grant relief, resolve disputes and levy fines or penalties.

Courts generally have the power to hear challenges or appeals to the rules and decisions of administrative agencies after agency appeal procedures are exhausted. Courts engage in regulatory construction and judicial review of administrative agency rules and decisions in much the same way that they review statutory laws. However, the power of courts to void agency rules and actions is limited to situations in which the agency clearly has exceeded its authority, violated its rules and procedures or provided no evidence to support its ruling. In other situations, courts are expected to show deference to the agency's decision, giving weight to the expert judgment of the agency.

The authority, or even the existence, of administrative agencies can change. Legislatures may adopt or amend laws to revise the responsibilities of administrative agencies. Thus, when Congress adopted the Telecommunications Act of 1996, it substantially revised the responsibilities of the FCC, originally authorized by the Communications Act of 1934.

Executive Orders

Heads of the executive branch of government—the president, governors and mayors—have limited power to issue executive orders, which have the force of law. For example, each president of the United States issues orders that determine what types of records will be classified as secret, how long they will remain secret and who has access to them. Recent presidential executive orders have limited media access to military zones, excluded the public from meetings of groups advising the president on energy policy and redefined access to presidential records. Similarly, mayors and governors have issued orders— particularly under perceived emergency conditions—that limit public freedom of movement. For example, mayors across the country have imposed city curfews that prohibit teenagers from being on the streets after a certain hour and have established no-protest zones at controversial events.

STRUCTURE OF THE JUDICIAL SYSTEM

A basic understanding of the structure of the court system in the United States is fundamental to an appreciation of the functioning of the law. Trial courts, or federal district courts, do fact-finding, apply the law and settle disputes. Courts of appeal, including federal circuit courts and supreme courts in each system, review how lower courts applied the law. The courts create equity and common law and apply and interpret constitutions, statutes and orders. Through their judgments, courts can reshape laws or even throw them out as unconstitutional.

● REAL WORLD LAW

Senator Says Supreme Court Interpretation Violates the Rule of Law

In 2015, the Supreme Court interpreted the Affordable Care Act (ACA) to determine its constitutionality.[1] The politically charged challenge to the law argued that the law's plain language required only those states that operated their own health exchanges to provide tax credits to qualifying individuals.

But the Court upheld the law's application to all states by saying that the key phrase—"an exchange established by the state under" the law—was ambiguous. The Court also found the lower court's deference to an administrative agency interpretation inappropriate.

"[T]he fundamental canon of statutory construction [is] that the words of a statute must be read in their context and with a view to their place in the overall statutory scheme."[2] The proper interpretation of the key phrase is not determined in isolation, the Court said, but should be "compatible with the rest of the law."[3] The Court concluded that the only permissible interpretation was that the law's requirement applied to every state.

But Sen. Orrin Hatch (R-Utah), among others, said the Court's reasoning violated the rule of law by failing to follow the Court's clearly established precedent requiring that when a "statute is silent or ambiguous with respect to the specific question, the issue for the court is whether the agency's answer is based on a permissible construction of the statute."[4]

The Court's decision, Sen. Hatch said, "would have us believe that statutes are infinitely malleable. . . . [But] the text matters. Words matter. What the statute *says* is what matters because . . . fidelity to text is the foundation of the rule of law."[5]

1. 135 S. Ct. 2480 (2015).
2. *Id.* at 2489.
3. *Id.* at 2484.
4. Chevron U.S.A. Inc., v. Natural Resources Defense Council Inc., 467 U.S. 837 (1984).
5. Orrin G. Hatch, King v. Burwell *and the Rule of Law*, 63 UCLA L. Rev. Disc. 2 (2015).

▲ EMERGING LAW

A Shifting Balance of Power?

Early in 2017, the 115th Congress began proposing bills to scale back regulations adopted by executive agencies under the Obama administration. Shortly after his election, President Trump had promised to repeal two federal regulations for every one adopted under his administration.[1] Administrative agencies enact regulations that enable laws adopted by Congress to take effect.

Targets of the Republican-controlled Congress included federal land-use regulations, school accountability measures and Planned Parenthood funding.[2] One pending bill, the REINS Act, would make it more difficult for regulatory agencies to enact new rules.[3] The proposed law would require both houses of Congress to confirm any regulation within 70 days for it to take effect. If the REINS Act does not become law, agencies will continue to issue regulations without congressional review.[4]

Writing in formal opposition to the REINS Act, the League of Women Voters called the bill "an extraordinarily extreme measure" that "would effectively amend every existing regulatory statute . . . and neuter them. . . . Either house of Congress could kill any future [regulatory] safeguard simply by failing to act."[5]

In contrast, the Heritage Foundation said the REINS Act "would increase accountability for and transparency in the federal regulatory process."[6] The REINS Act mirrored a similar bill, supported by conservatives, that had stalled in the Wisconsin legislature in 2016.[7]

1. Clyde W. Crews Jr., *Donald Trump Promises to Eliminate Two Regulations for Every One Enacted*, Forbes, Nov. 22, 2016, https://www.forbes.com/sites/waynecrews/2016/11/22/donald-trump-promises-to-eliminate-two-regulations-for-every-one-enacted/#4bebadc04586.
2. Michelle Cottle, *How Republicans Plan to Roll Back Obama-Era Regulations*, Atlantic, Jan. 6, 2017, www.theatlantic.com/politics/archive/2017/01/how-republicans-plan-to-roll-back-obama-era-regulations/512348.
3. H.R. 26, 115th Cong. (2017) (Regulations From the Executive in Need of Scrutiny Act).
4. *How Laws Are Made and How to Research Them*, usa.gov.
5. *League Opposes H.R. 26, REINS Act of 2017*, lwv.org/content/league-opposes-hr-26-reins-act-2017.
6. *"Yes" on the REINS Act*, Heritage Found., Jan. 4, 2017, *at* heritageaction.com/key-votes/yes-reins-act-hr26.
7. *REINS Act Stalls in the Senate?*, MacIver News Serv., Mar. 11, 2016, www.maciverinstitute.com/2016/03/reins-act-stalls-in-the-senate.

Jurisdiction

An independent court system operates in each state, the District of Columbia and the federal government. The military and the U.S. territories, such as Puerto Rico, also have court systems.

Each of these systems of courts operates under the authority of the relevant constitution. For example, the U.S. Constitution requires the establishment of the Supreme Court of the United States and authorizes Congress to establish other courts it deems necessary to the proper functioning of the federal judiciary. **Jurisdiction** refers to a court's authority to hear a case. Every court has its own jurisdiction—that is, its own geographic or topical area of responsibility and authority. In libel, for example, the traditional standard has been that any court in any locale where the statement in question could be seen or heard would have jurisdiction.[34] A court may dismiss a lawsuit outside of its jurisdiction. New technologies present new challenges to the determination of jurisdiction. Consider online libel. Given that statements published online are potentially seen anywhere, any court could claim jurisdiction (see Chapter 10 for discussion of internet regulation).

The U.S. Constitution spells out the areas of authority of the federal courts. Within their geographic regions, federal courts exercise authority over cases that relate to interstate

jurisdiction The geographic or topical area of responsibility and authority of a court.

or international controversies or that interpret and apply federal laws, treaties or the U.S. Constitution. Thus, federal courts hear cases involving copyright laws. The federal courts also decide cases in which the federal government is a party, such as when the news media ask the courts to hold open public proceedings when considering the deportation of aliens from the United States. Cases involving controversies between states, between citizens of different states or between a state and a citizen of another state also are heard in federal courts. Thus, a libel suit brought by a resident of Oregon against a newspaper in Washington would be heard in federal court.

● REAL WORLD LAW

Executive Orders Ebb, Flow, May Be Unpublished

One of President Barack Obama's executive orders addressed national cybersecurity and allowed pre-emptive U.S. cyberattacks to ward off threats.

As a form of law, executive orders give presidents unilateral authority to create law. Some argue that such orders, which bypass Congress's constitutionally enumerated power to adopt laws, vest too much power in the executive, which is intended to implement laws. The Constitution neither defines nor requires the publication of executive orders. Even today an uncertain portion of such orders are issued informally and not recorded officially.[1]

The number of executive orders issued by presidents has risen and fallen, reaching its peak with Franklin D. Roosevelt's New Deal pronouncements. President Roosevelt issued an average of 307 executive orders each year, or more than one order on every weekday throughout his presidency.[2]

While the first 17 presidents issued fewer than four executive orders annually, President Ulysses S. Grant signed an average of 27 (or roughly one order every two weeks) during the Civil War. More recently, Bill Clinton averaged 46 executive orders a year; George W. Bush issued an average of 36; and Barack Obama issued 34. In response to partisan attacks that his executive orders were unconstitutional, President Obama said, "America does not stand still, and neither will I."[3] In his first 100 days in office, President Donald Trump issued the most executive orders of any president in recent history, perhaps in history.[4]

To be legal, the U.S. Supreme Court has said, executive orders must arise from the president's explicit power under Article 11, Sec. 2 of the Constitution, his role as commander and chief, or the president's responsibility to ensure that laws are faithfully executed.

1. Michael Elliot, *The Legality of Obama's Executive Orders*, Berkeley Pol. Rev., May 11, 2016, bpr.berkeley.edu/2016/05/11/the-legality-of-obamas-executive-orders-and-why-you-should-care.
2. Gerhard Peters & John T. Woolley, *Executive Orders*, The Amer. Presidency Proj., Dec. 20, 2016, www.presidency.ucsb.edu/data/orders.php.
3. *Obama: America Does Not Stand Still, and Neither Will I*, NBC News, Jan. 28, 2014, www.nbcnewyork.com/news/national-international/NATL-Obama-to-Face-Pessimistic-Public-With-State-of-the-Union-242482621.html.
4. Marshall Cohen & Wade Payson-Denney, *By the Numbers, How Donald Trump Stacks Up*, May 1, 2017, www.cnn.com/2017/04/29/politics/donald-trump-100-days-data/index.html.

◎ POINTS OF LAW

A Test for Court Jurisdiction of Internet Disputes

As online activity expands and routinely crosses national boundaries, and access to the internet becomes accepted as an essential public utility,[1] nations struggle individually and collectively to determine who has legal jurisdiction over online disputes.[2] The U.S. test to establish jurisdiction over online disputes requires courts to answer three questions in the affirmative[3]:

1. Did the defendant purposefully conduct activities in the jurisdiction of the court?

2. Did the plaintiff's claim arise out of the defendant's activities in this locale?

3. Is it constitutionally reasonable for the court to exercise jurisdiction?

---

1. Daniel Bennett, *Obama: The Internet Is a Utility*, ATLANTIC, Nov. 10, 2014, www.theatlantic.com/technology/archive/2014/11/obama-internet-utility-fcc-regulation-net-neutrality/382561.

2. Matthew Chivvis, *Reexamining the Yahoo! Litigations: Toward an Effects Test for Determining International Cyberspace Jurisdiction*, 41 U.S.F.L. REV. 699 (2007).

3. Calder v. Jones, 465 U.S. 783, 789 (1983).

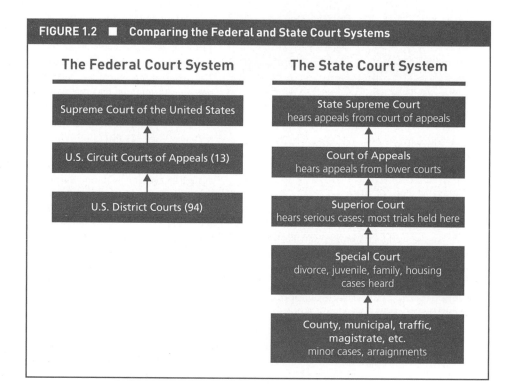

FIGURE 1.2 ■ Comparing the Federal and State Court Systems

The Federal Court System

Supreme Court of the United States

↑

U.S. Circuit Courts of Appeals (13)

↑

U.S. District Courts (94)

The State Court System

State Supreme Court
hears appeals from court of appeals

↑

Court of Appeals
hears appeals from lower courts

↑

Superior Court
hears serious cases; most trials held here

↑

Special Court
divorce, juvenile, family, housing cases heard

↑

County, municipal, traffic, magistrate, etc.
minor cases, arraignments

But what if a nationally circulated newspaper is the subject of the suit? Then the plaintiff might initiate the lawsuit in any court and would likely pursue the case in the court he or she thinks is most likely to render a favorable decision. In 2013, the U.S. Supreme Court issued a broad ruling that some said put an end to this practice, called **forum shopping**.[35] The dispute filed in federal court in California involved human rights abuses in Argentina that allegedly involved the German automobile manufacturer Mercedes-Benz, which has subsidiaries in the United States, including California. Following a detailed discussion of jurisdiction, a unanimous Supreme Court held that unless there is a link between the forum of the court and the source of injury, a company may only be sued "at home."[36] Accordingly, a national newspaper's "home" is only in two places: where it is incorporated or its main place of business.

Trial Courts

The separate court systems in the United States are organized similarly; most court systems have three tiers. At the lowest level, trial courts are the courts where nearly all cases begin. Each state contains at least one of the nation's 94 trial-level federal courts, which are called district courts. Trial courts reach decisions by finding facts and applying existing law to them. They are the only courts to use juries. They do not establish precedents. Some judges view the routine media coverage of legal actions taking place in trial courts as a threat to the fairness of trials (see Chapter 8). Some judges also fear that media coverage will cast their court in disrepute and reduce public trust in the judicial system.

Courts of Appeal

Anyone who loses a case at trial may appeal the decision. However, courts of appeal generally do not make findings of fact or receive new evidence in the case. Only in rare cases do courts of appeal review case facts **de novo**, a phrase meaning "new" or "over again." Instead, appellate courts review the legal process of the lower court. Courts of appeal examine the procedures and tests used by the lower court to determine whether **due process** was carried out—that is, whether the proper law was applied and whether the judicial process was fair and appropriate.

Decisions in appellate courts are based primarily on which are arguments, or briefs, and on short oral arguments from the attorneys representing each side of the case. Individuals and organizations that are not parties to the case may, with permission of the court, submit briefs for consideration. Those nonlitigants are called **amicus curiae** ("friends of the court"), and their filing is called an **amicus brief.**

Most court systems have two levels of appellate courts: the intermediate courts of appeal and the supreme court. In the federal court system, there are 13 intermediate-level appellate courts, called circuit courts. A panel of three judges hears all except the most important cases in the federal circuit courts of appeal. Only rarely do all the judges of the circuit court sit **en banc** to hear an appeal. *En banc* literally means "on the bench" but is used to mean "in full court." Twelve of the federal circuits represent geographic regions. For example, the U.S. Court of Appeals for the Ninth Circuit bears responsibility for the entire West Coast, Hawaii and Alaska, and the U.S. Court of Appeals for the D.C. Circuit covers the District of Columbia. The 13th circuit, the U.S. Court of Appeals for the Federal Circuit, handles

forum shopping A practice whereby the plaintiff chooses a court in which to sue because he or she believes the court will rule in the plaintiff's favor.

de novo Literally, "new" or "over again." On appeal, the court may review the facts de novo rather than simply reviewing the legal posture and process of the case.

due process Fair legal proceedings. Due process is guaranteed by the Fifth and 14th Amendments to the U.S. Constitution.

amicus brief A submission to the court from **amicus curiae**, or "friends of the court," which are interested individuals or organizations that are parties in the case.

en banc Literally, "on the bench" but now meaning "in full court." The judges of a circuit court of appeals will sit en banc to decide important or controversial cases.

TABLE 1.1 ■ Comparing Federal and State Courts

The federal government and each state government have their own court systems.

The Federal Court System

Structure

- Article III of the Constitution invests the judicial power of the United States in the federal court system. Article III, Section 1 specifically creates the U.S. Supreme Court and gives Congress the authority to create the lower federal courts.

- Congress has used this power to establish the 13 U.S. Courts of Appeals, the 94 U.S. District Courts, the U.S. Court of Claims, and the U.S. Court of International Trade. U.S. Bankruptcy Courts handle bankruptcy cases. Magistrate Judges handle some District Court matters.

- Parties dissatisfied with a decision of a U.S. District Court, the U.S. Court of Claims, and/or the U.S. Court of International Trade may appeal to a U.S. Court of Appeals.

- A party may ask the U.S. Supreme Court to review a decision of the U.S. Court of Appeals, but the Supreme Court usually is under no obligation to do so. The U.S. Supreme Court is the final arbiter of federal constitutional questions.

Selection of Judges

The Constitution states that federal judges are to be nominated by the President and confirmed by the Senate.

They hold office during good behavior, typically, for life. Through Congressional impeachment proceedings, federal judges may be removed from office for misbehavior.

Types of Cases Heard

- Cases that deal with the constitutionality of a law;
- Cases involving the laws and treaties of the U.S.;
- Legal issues related to ambassadors and public ministers;
- Disputes between two or more states;
- Admiralty law;
- Bankruptcy; and
- Habeas corpus issues.

Article I Courts

Congress created several Article I, or legislative courts, that do not have full judicial power. Judicial power is the authority to be the final decider in all questions of Constitutional law, all questions of federal law and to hear claims at the core of habeas corpus issues. Article I courts are:

- U.S. Court of Appeals for Veterans Claims
- U.S. Court of Appeals for the Armed Forces
- U.S. Tax Court

The State Court System

Structure

- The Constitution and laws of each state establish the state courts. A court of last resort, often known as a Supreme Court, is usually the highest court. Some states also have an intermediate Court of Appeals. Below these appeals courts are the state trial courts. Some are referred to as Circuit or District Courts.
- States also usually have courts that handle specific legal matters, e.g., probate court (wills and estates); juvenile court; family court; etc.
- Parties dissatisfied with the decision of the trial court may take their case to the intermediate Court of Appeals.
- Parties have the option to ask the highest state court to hear the case.
- Only certain cases are eligible for review by the U.S. Supreme Court.

Selection of Judges

State court judges are selected in a variety of ways, including

- election,
- appointment for a given number of years,
- appointment for life, and
- combinations of these methods, e.g., appointment followed by election.

Types of Cases Heard

- Most criminal cases, probate (involving wills and estates)
- Most contract cases, tort cases (personal injuries), family law (marriages, divorces, adoptions), etc.

State courts are the final arbiters of state laws and constitutions. Their interpretation of federal law or the U.S. Constitution may be appealed to the U.S. Supreme Court. The Supreme Court may choose to hear or not to hear such cases.

Article I Courts

N/A

Source: United States Courts, www.uscourts.gov/about-federal-courts/court-role-and-structure; www.uscourts.gov/aboutfederal-courts/court-role-and-structure/comparing-federal-state-courts.

specialized appeals. In addition, separate, specialized federal courts handle cases dealing with the armed forces, international trade or veterans' claims, among other things.

Courts of appeal may **affirm** the decision of the lower court with a majority opinion, which means they ratify or uphold the prior ruling and leave it intact. They may also **overrule** the lower court, reversing the previous decision. Any single judge or minority of the court may write a **concurring opinion** agreeing with the result reached by the court opinion but relying on different reasoning or legal principles or elaborating on significant issues. Judges who disagree with the opinion of the court may write a **dissenting opinion**, explaining the basis for the divergent conclusion.

affirm To ratify, uphold or approve a lower court ruling.

overrule To reverse the ruling of a lower court.

concurring opinion A separate opinion of a minority of the court or a single judge or justice agreeing with the majority opinion but applying different reasoning or legal principles.

dissenting opinion A separate opinion of a minority of the court or a single judge or justice disagreeing with the result reached by the majority and challenging the majority's reasoning or the legal basis of the decision.

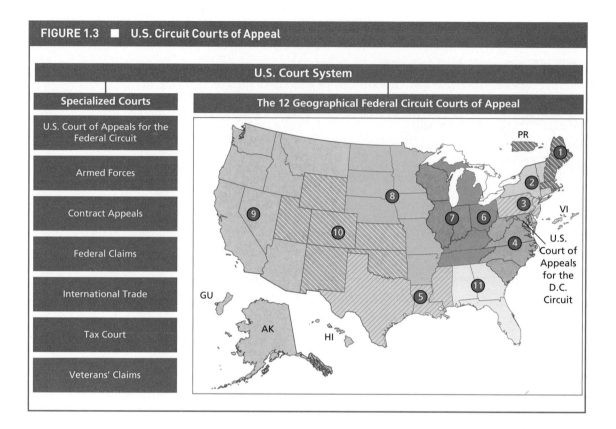

FIGURE 1.3 ■ U.S. Circuit Courts of Appeal

A dissenting opinion may challenge the majority's reasoning or the legal basis for its conclusion.

Majority decisions issued by courts of appeal establish precedent for lower courts within their jurisdiction. Their rulings also may be persuasive outside their jurisdiction. If only a plurality of the judges hearing a case supports the opinion of the lower court, the decision does not establish binding precedent. Similarly, dissenting and concurring opinions do not have the force of law, but they often are highly influential to subsequent court decisions.

remand To send back to the lower court for further action.

Courts of appeal also **remand**, or send back, decisions and require the lower court to reconsider the facts of the case. A decision to remand a case may not be appealed. Courts of appeal often remand cases when they believe that the lower court did not fully explore the facts or issues in the case and needs to develop a more complete record of evidence as the basis for its decision.

A circuit court of appeals decision must be signed by at least two of the three sitting judges and is final. The losing party may ask the court to reconsider the case or may request a rehearing en banc. Such requests are rarely granted. Losing parties also may appeal the verdict of any intermediate court of appeals to the highest court in the state or to the U.S. Supreme Court.

TABLE 1.2 ■ The U.S. Supreme Court at a Glance, 2017

	Justice	Born	Nominating President	Year Appointed
	Chief Justice John Roberts	1955	George W. Bush	2005
	Associate Justice Anthony Kennedy	1936	Ronald Reagan	1988
	Associate Justice Clarence Thomas	1948	George H. W. Bush	1991
	Associate Justice Ruth Bader Ginsburg	1933	Bill Clinton	1993
	Associate Justice Stephen Breyer	1938	Bill Clinton	1994

(Continued)

TABLE 1.2 ■ (Continued)

	Justice	Born	Nominating President	Year Appointed
	Associate Justice Samuel Alito	1950	George W. Bush	2006
	Associate Justice Sonia Sotomayor	1954	Barack Obama	2009
	Associate Justice Elena Kagan	1960	Barack Obama	2010
	Associate Justice Neil M. Gorsuch	1967	Donald Trump	2017

All photos: U.S. Supreme Court Collection, www.supremecourt.gov/about/biographies.aspx.

original jurisdiction The authority to consider a case at its inception, as contrasted with appellate jurisdiction.

The U.S. Supreme Court

Established in 1789, the Supreme Court of the United States functions primarily as an appellate court, although the Constitution establishes the Court's **original jurisdiction** in a few specific areas. In general, Congress has granted lower federal courts jurisdiction in these same areas, so almost no suits begin in the U.S. Supreme Court. Instead, the Court hears cases on appeal from all other federal courts, federal regulatory agencies and state supreme courts.

Cases come before the Court either on direct appeal from the lower court or through the Court's grant of a **writ of certiorari**. Certain federal laws, such as the Bipartisan Campaign Reform Act,[37] guarantee a direct right of appeal to the U.S. Supreme Court. More often, the Court grants a writ of certiorari for compelling reasons, such as when a case poses a novel or pressing legal question. The Court often grants certiorari to cases in which different U.S. circuit courts of appeal have issued conflicting opinions. The Court also may consider whether an issue is ripe for consideration, meaning that the case presents a real and present controversy rather than a hypothetical concern. In addition, the Court may reject some petitions as **moot** because the controversy is no longer "live." Mootness may be an issue, for example, when a student who has challenged school policy graduates before the case is resolved. The Court sometimes accepts cases that appear to be moot if it believes the problem is likely to arise again.

The Court's Makeup. The chief justice of the United States and eight associate justices make up the Supreme Court. The president nominates and the Senate confirms the chief justice as well as the other eight members of the Court, who sit "during good behavior"[38] for life or until retirement. This gives the president considerable influence over the Court's political ideology. After the Senate refused to hold hearings to consider President Obama's nominee to replace Justice Antonin Scalia, who died early in 2016, the power to nominate Supreme Court justices became a major issue in that year's presidential election.

Justice Sonia Sotomayor is the only true liberal among the sitting justices. Liberal justices tend to believe that government should play an active role in ensuring individual liberties. They also tend to support regulation of large businesses and corporations and to reduce emphasis on property rights. Justice Elena Kagan is perceived as "a center-left pragmatist" and swing vote,[39] and her first three terms demonstrated her willingness to inject a "critical voice that could make the case for liberals within the court and beyond."[40] Justice Ruth Bader Ginsburg is sometimes viewed as the Court's only liberal-leaning moderate, but her voting patterns place her in the political center of the Court, along with Justice Stephen Breyer.

Chief Justice John Roberts and Justices Anthony Kennedy, Clarence Thomas and Samuel Alito create a pro-business, conservative bloc in the Court.[41] Conservative justices, in general, want to reduce the role of the federal government, including the Supreme Court. They tend to favor a narrow, or close, reading of the Constitution that relies more heavily on original intent than on contemporary realities. However, one legal scholar said, "The unifying element of the Court's conservative leanings is not a commitment to any particular conservative judicial doctrine (e.g., originalism) but a commitment to the political and ideological positions espoused by conservative Republicans in the 1980s. Further, the Court . . . is quite willing to push a conservative agenda quite aggressively."[42] Justice Neil Gorsuch, appointed in 2017, is a reliable, thoughtful conservative who shares much of the philosophy of his predecessor.[43]

writ of certiorari A petition for review by the Supreme Court of the United States; *certiorari* means "to be informed of."

moot Term used to describe a case in which the issues presented are no longer "live" or in which the matter in dispute has already been resolved; a case is not moot if it is susceptible to repetition but evades review.

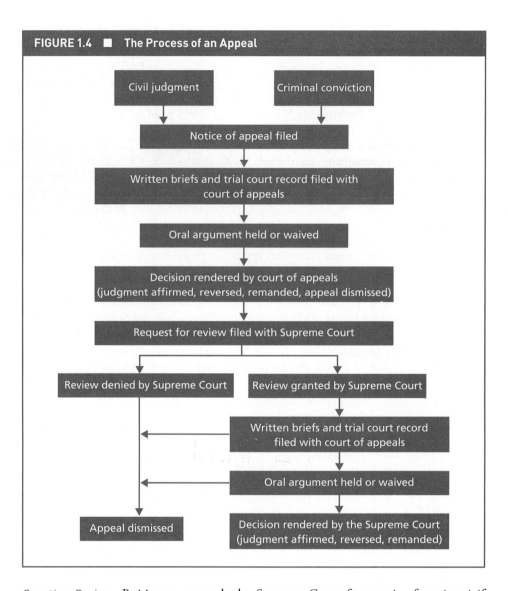

FIGURE 1.4 ■ The Process of an Appeal

Civil judgment

Criminal conviction

Notice of appeal filed

Written briefs and trial court record filed with court of appeals

Oral argument held or waived

Decision rendered by court of appeals (judgment affirmed, reversed, remanded, appeal dismissed)

Request for review filed with Supreme Court

Review denied by Supreme Court

Review granted by Supreme Court

Written briefs and trial court record filed with court of appeals

Oral argument held or waived

Appeal dismissed

Decision rendered by the Supreme Court (judgment affirmed, reversed, remanded)

Granting Review. Petitioners may ask the Supreme Court for a writ of certiorari if the court of appeals or the highest state court denies them a hearing or issues a verdict against them. Writs are granted at the discretion of the Court. All seated justices consider a writ, which is granted only if at least four justices vote to hear the case. This is called the rule of four. Neither the decision to grant nor the decision to deny a writ of certiorari indicates anything about the Court's opinion regarding the merits of the lower court's ruling. Denial of certiorari generally means that the justices do not think the issue is sufficiently important or timely to decide. In recent years, an average of 8,200 petitions have been filed with the Court, which grants less than 1 percent of them.[44] Approximately one-fourth of the petitions filed are accompanied by the required fee of $150. The vast majority of petitions are filed without the fee—often by prisoners who cannot pay the required filing fee.

Reaching Decisions. Once the Court agrees to hear a case, the parties file written briefs outlining the facts and legal issues in the case and summarizing their legal arguments. The justices review the briefs prior to oral argument in the case, which generally lasts one hour. The justices may sit silently during oral argument, or they may pepper the attorneys with questions.

Reproduced from an 1885 lithograph titled "Our Overworked Supreme Court."

Following oral argument, the justices meet in a private, closed conference to take an initial vote on the outcome. Discussion begins with the chief justice and proceeds around the table in order of descending seniority of the associate justices. Then voting proceeds from the most junior member of the Court and ends with the chief justice. The chief justice or the most senior justice in the majority determines who will draft the majority opinion.

A majority of the justices must agree on a point of law for the Court to establish binding precedent. Draft opinions are circulated among the justices, and negotiations may attempt to shift votes. It may take months for the Court to achieve a final decision, which is then announced on decision day.

Two other options exist for the Supreme Court. It may issue a **per curiam opinion**, which is an unsigned opinion by the Court as a whole. Although a single justice may draft the opinion, that authorship is not made public. Per curiam opinions often do not include the same thorough discussion of the issues found in signed opinions. The Supreme Court also can resolve a case by issuing a **memorandum order**. A memorandum order simply announces the vote of the Court without providing an opinion. This quick and easy method to dispense with a case has become more common with the Court's growing tendency to issue fewer and fewer signed opinions.

per curiam opinion An unsigned opinion by the court as a whole.

memorandum order An order announcing the vote of the Supreme Court without providing an opinion.

The ideological leanings of the individual justices, and of the Court as a whole, come into play in the choice of cases granted review and the ultimate decisions of the Court.[45] In 2010, for example, the Court was "bitterly divided" in its decision in *Citizens United v. Federal Election Commission* (the case mentioned at the beginning and excerpted at the end of this chapter) that declared some campaign finance regulations unconstitutional. Many agreed that the decision's "sweeping changes in federal election law"[46] "represented a sharp doctrinal shift" that split the Court "five-to-four along typical ideological lines."[47] Some observers said the Court had ignored binding precedent. Others argued that "the central principle which critics of this ruling find most offensive—that corporations possess 'personhood' and are thus entitled to Constitutional and First Amendment rights—has also been affirmed by decades of Supreme Court jurisprudence."[48] Thus, the conflict centered more on *which* precedents to follow than on whether to apply precedent at all.

originalists
Supreme Court justices who interpret the Constitution according to the perceived intent of its framers.

textualists
Judges—in particular, Supreme Court justices—who rely exclusively on a careful reading of legal texts to determine the meaning of the law.

The U.S. Supreme Court relies on a wide range of sources to guide its interpretation of the Constitution and its determination of the constitutionality of statutes. **Originalists** and **textualists** seek the meaning of the Constitution primarily in its explicit text, the historical context in which the document developed and the recorded history of its deliberation, ratification and originally intended meaning. Originalists are relatively unmoved by arguments that neither the meaning of nor the debates over the Constitution are clear. Some justices look beyond the text to discover how best to apply the Constitution today. Their interpretation relies more expressly on deep-seated personal and societal values, well-established ethical and legal concepts and the evolving interests of a shifting society. The Court's reasoning at times also builds on international standards, treaties or conventions, such as the Universal Declaration of Human Rights, or the decisions of courts outside the United States as well as state and other federal courts. On occasion, such as when the Court discovered a right to privacy embedded in the First Amendment, the justices refer to the views and insights of legal scholars.[49]

● **REAL WORLD LAW**

Court Opinions Are Like Sausages

Observers disagree about how the Supreme Court makes decisions. Law professors generally say decision making follows the internal logic of jurisprudence; justices adhere to legal rules, principles and precedents. Political scientists argue that external factors and the political ideologies of individual justices shape decisions. Favoring an internal logic for the law, Justice Antonin Scalia wrote in 1991,

The judicial power . . . must be . . . the power "to say what the law is," not the power to change it. . . . [Justices] make [the law] . . . as though they were "finding" it—discerning what the law is, rather than decreeing what it is today changed to, or what it will tomorrow be.[1]

In contrast, the external view sees the law as inherently ambiguous and subject to multiple interpretations. Interpretation necessarily reflects the unique situation of the interpreter. From this perspective,

there is a potentially never-ending debate about the best reading of a text. . . . As with other interpreters, the justices' expectations, interests and prejudices will shape their interpretive views. . . . Politics is always a part of the adjudicative process because legal interpretation is never mechanical.[2]

Research suggests the external view predicts Supreme Court decisions fairly effectively.[3] The largely secret process of Supreme Court deliberation obscures the specific components of judicial decision making. Like sausages, the court's decisions may be more acceptable if we don't know how they are made!

1. James B. Beam Distilling Co. v. Georgia, 501 U.S. 529, 549 (1991) (Scalia, J., concurring in judgment).
2. Stephen M. Feldman, *The Rule of Law or the Rule of Politics? Harmonizing the Internal and External Views of Supreme Court Decision Making*, 30 Law & Soc. Inquiry 89, 96, 101, 108 (2005).
3. *Id.* at 129; Greg Stohr, *Speech Rights Triumph as U.S. High Court Limits Government Power*, Bloomberg Business, June 27, 2011, www.bloomberg.com/news/articles/2011-06-28/speech-rights-triumph-as-u-s-high-court-limits-government-power.

PROCESSES OF THE LAW

Although each court and each case follows a somewhat idiosyncratic path, patterns can be traced through the judicial process. In a criminal matter, the case starts when a government agency investigates a possible crime. After gathering evidence, the government arrests someone for a crime, such as distributing obscene material through the internet. The standard of evidence needed for an arrest or to issue a search warrant is known as **probable cause**. Probable cause involves more than mere suspicion; it is a showing based on reliable information that a crime was committed and that the accused individual is likely the person who committed it.

The case then goes before a **grand jury** or a judge. Unlike trial juries (also called petit juries), grand juries do not determine guilt. Instead, grand juries are summoned on occasion to hear the state's evidence and determine whether that evidence establishes probable cause to believe that a crime has been committed. A grand jury may be convened on the county, state or federal level; with 12 to 23 members, grand juries are usually larger than trial juries. If the case proceeds without a grand jury, the judge makes a probable cause determination at a proceeding called a preliminary hearing. If the state fails to establish probable cause, the case may not proceed. If probable cause is found, the person is indicted.

Then the case moves to a court arraignment, where the defendant is formally charged and pleads guilty or not guilty. Often, a plea bargain may be arranged in which the defendant pleads guilty in exchange for a reduction in the charges or an agreed-upon sentence. Plea bargains account for almost 95 percent of all felony convictions in the United States.[50] If a not-guilty plea is entered, the case ordinarily proceeds to trial. The judge may set bail. Proof beyond a reasonable doubt is required to establish guilt in a criminal trial. Upon a verdict of guilty, the judge normally requests a presentencing report from the probation department outlining the defendant's background and holds a sentencing hearing. A criminal sentence may include time in a county jail, time in a state or federal prison and one or more fines.

Civil Suits

Civil cases generally involve two private individuals or organizations that cannot resolve a dispute. The courts provide a process to settle the conflict. The person who files a civil complaint or sues because she believes she has been harmed by an intrusion on her privacy or the inaccuracy of a news report, for example, is the **plaintiff**. The person responding to the suit is the **defendant**. The civil harm involved is called a **tort**. A tort is a private or civil injury one person or organization inflicts on another, and tort law provides a mechanism for the injured party to establish fault and receive compensation.

Many communication lawsuits are civil suits in which the plaintiff must prove his or her case by the preponderance of evidence. This standard of proof is lower than in criminal cases.

Civil suits begin when the plaintiff files a pleading with the clerk of court that outlines the complaint and the desired result and requires the defendant to appear in court. Most plaintiffs seek money damages. To receive a damage award, a plaintiff generally must show that the harm occurred, that the defendant caused the harm and that the defendant was

probable cause The standard of evidence needed for an arrest or to issue a search warrant. More than mere suspicion, it is a showing through reasonably trustworthy information that a crime has been or is being committed.

grand jury A group summoned to hear the state's evidence in criminal cases and decide whether a crime was committed and whether charges should be filed; grand juries do not determine guilt.

plaintiff The party who files a complaint; the one who sues.

defendant The party accused of violating a law, or the party being sued in a civil lawsuit.

tort A private or civil wrong for which a court can provide remedy in the form of damages.

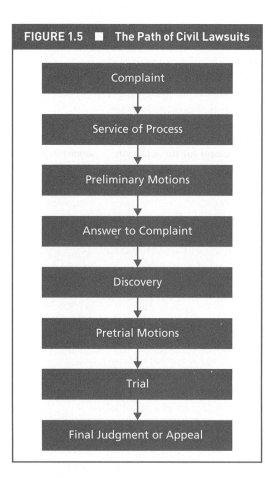

FIGURE 1.5 ■ The Path of Civil Lawsuits

Complaint

↓

Service of Process

↓

Preliminary Motions

↓

Answer to Complaint

↓

Discovery

↓

Pretrial Motions

↓

Trial

↓

Final Judgment or Appeal

---

strict liability
Liability without fault; liability for any and all harms, foreseeable or unforeseen, which result from a product or an action.

motion to dismiss
A request to a court to reject a complaint because it does not state a claim that can be remedied by law or is legally lacking in some other way.

---

at fault, meaning the defendant acted either negligently or with malicious intent. Under a **strict liability** standard, the plaintiff does not need to demonstrate fault on the part of the defendant in order to win the suit. Strict liability applies in the case of certain manufactured products as well as in cases involving inherently dangerous activities. Under strict liability, the individual who produced the product or took the action is liable for all resulting harms.

Following a complaint, the court schedules a hearing and issues a summons to the defendant, requiring him or her to appear in court. The defendant may answer the complaint by filing a countersuit, by denying the charge, by filing a **motion to dismiss** or by filing a motion for summary judgment. A motion to dismiss, or **demurrer**, asks a court to reject a complaint because it is legally insufficient in some way. For example, a media defendant may admit that it published a news story but argue that the story did not cause any legally actionable harm to the plaintiff. If the court grants the motion to dismiss, the plaintiff may appeal.

Before a case goes to trial, the disputing parties may agree to an out-of-court settlement. When this occurs, there is no public record of the outcome of the case. Out-of-court resolutions often prohibit the parties from discussing the terms of the settlement. Sometimes, as when Nike settled a recent lawsuit,[51] some terms of the settlement are publicized. After a lengthy legal battle over claims that Nike's statements about working conditions at its overseas factories amounted to false advertising, the parties settled. Without admitting liability, Nike reported on its website that it would pay a total of $1.5 million toward independent oversight of its factories and worker training.[52]

If the issues in a civil suit are narrow or the parties are close to resolution, the judge may attempt to settle the case through a court conference. More often, the two sides do not agree on the facts and begin to gather evidence through a process called **discovery**. The discovery process can last for months, during which either side may file motions asking the court to take action on various issues or amend earlier complaints. In trying to build a case, one or both parties may issue a **subpoena**, which is a legal command for someone, sometimes a journalist, to appear and testify in court or turn over evidence, such as outtakes and notes. With few exceptions, citizens are legally obligated to comply with subpoenas. The judge may issue a contempt of court citation, levy fines or put in jail individuals who refuse to comply with subpoenas.

Civil suits are settled by the parties before trial almost 97 percent of the time.[53]

If no settlement is reached, the case may then proceed to a jury trial, which is required if either party requests it. The court summons jurors to the courthouse from a local pool, usually from the voters' rolls. The locality of a lawsuit, where the original court hears the suit, is called the **venue**. The location from which a court draws its pool of jurors is the **venire**. The lawyers and judge select jurors through a process of questioning called **voir dire**, which literally means "to speak the truth." While the theoretical goal is to form an impartial jury to hear the evidence, attorneys on both sides hope to give themselves an advantage in the adversarial process. Today a large number of firms provide expert consulting on jury selection, witness preparation, post-trial media interviews and the like. Either side's attorney may challenge potential jurors "for cause," such as when a prospective juror knows a party in the suit. Attorneys also may eliminate a limited number of potential jurors through **peremptory challenges**, in which they need not show a reason for the rejection.

demurrer A request that a court dismiss a case on the grounds that although the claims are true they are insufficient to warrant a judgment against the defendant.

● REAL WORLD LAW

Arrests Inhibit Reporters

Mark Sagliocco/WireImage/Getty Images

In September 2016, police arrested award-winning *Democracy Now!* reporter Amy Goodman in Standing Rock, N.D., for covering what she called the "standoff" between protesters seeking to protect Native American water rights and security officers attempting to enable ongoing construction of the Dakota access oil pipeline.[1]

For her live reporting that went viral, Goodman was charged with riot, a misdemeanor punishable by jail and fine. Some said her reporting, which effectively ended media silence on the months-long confrontation, "may well have influenced the Obama administration's decision to halt work on the pipeline several days later."

The local prosecutor explained the charge against Goodman by saying she was not a reporter but "a protester, basically. Everything she reported on was from the position of justifying the protest actions." A spokesperson for the Committee to Protect Journalists said, "This arrest warrant is a transparent attempt to intimidate reporters from covering protests of significant public interest."

When Goodman appeared in court, the judge summarily dismissed the charge. In what some saw as a trend to suppress freedom of the press, journalists covering protests in Louisiana, Missouri and New York and across the nation were attacked, detained or arrested by police for criminal trespass, obstructing public roads or impeding an officer.[2] In several cases, police arrested reporters who were eventually released without charges.

1. Lizzy Ratner, *Amy Goodman Is Facing Jail Time for Reporting...*, NATION, Oct. 15, 2016, www.thenation.com/article/amy-goodman-is-facing-prison-for-reporting-on-the-dakota-access-pipeline-that-should-scare-us-all.
2. Reporters Without Borders, *Reporters Covering Black Lives Matter Arrested for Obstructing a Highway*, www.ifex.org/united_states/2016/07/14/blm_reporter_coverage.

After evidence is presented at trial, the judge issues instructions to the jury on how to apply the law to the facts of the case. Then the jury deliberates. If the jury cannot reach a verdict, the judge may order a new trial with a new jury. More typically, a jury deliberates until it reaches a verdict. The judge generally accepts the verdict and enters it as the judgment of the court. However, the judge has the authority to overturn the verdict if it is contrary to the law. If the plaintiff is successful, he or she will usually be awarded damages. Either the plaintiff or the defendant may appeal the judgment of the court. For example, if a party believes the jury was not properly instructed on the law, he or she may appeal on the basis of violation of due process. The person who appeals, called the petitioner or **appellant**, challenges the decision of the court. The respondent to the appeal, or the **appellee**, wants the verdict to be affirmed. It can take years and cost hundreds of thousands of dollars to appeal a case.

Summary Judgment

When parties ask a court to dismiss a case, they file a motion for **summary judgment**. A summary judgment is just what the name implies: A judge summarily decides the case and issues a judgment. Parties moving for summary judgment seek to avoid the cost and risk of losing at trial by providing evidence that neither party disputes the underlying facts. Thus, a summary judgment results in a legal determination by a court *without* a full trial.

A court's summary judgment may be issued based on the merits of the case as a whole or on specific issues critical to the case. In a libel case, this may occur when a plaintiff is clearly unable to meet one or more elements of the burden of proof, such as the falsity of the published material (see Chapter 4). If the judge determines evidence supports an uncontested conclusion that one party should win the case, the judge hands down a summary judgment in that party's favor.

A summary judgment can occur at any of several points in litigation, but usually prior to trial. The U.S. Supreme Court has said that courts considering motions for summary judgment "must view the facts and inferences to be drawn from them in the light most favorable to the opposing party."[54] In libel cases, this means that courts must take into account the burden the plaintiff is required to meet at trial. The Court created this obstacle to summary judgment because the nonmoving party loses the opportunity to present his or her case when a judge grants summary judgment to the opposing side.[55] Nonetheless, one study found increased use of summary judgments in the second half of the 20th century, with nearly 8 percent of civil cases in federal courts ending through summary judgment.[56]

Summary judgments can be important tools for protecting free expression, particularly in an environment in which plaintiffs may file frivolous lawsuits to harass the media.[57] Societal interest in free and open debate can be jeopardized by frivolous lawsuits because the high cost of defending against them may chill robust exercise of First Amendment rights.

FINDING THE LAW

This textbook provides an introduction and overview to key areas of the law of journalism and mass communication. Many students will wish, or their professors will require them, to supplement this text with research in primary legal sources. Primary sources are the actual documents that make up the law (e.g., statutes, case decisions, administrative rules and committee reports). Legal research often begins in secondary sources that analyze, interpret and discuss the primary documents. Perhaps the most useful secondary sources for beginning researchers in communication law are "American Jurisprudence 2d," "Corpus Juris Secundum" and "Media Law Reporter." The first two are legal encyclopedias that summarize legal subjects and reference relevant cases and legal articles. "Media Law Reporter" provides both topical summaries and excerpts of key media law cases organized by subject. However, "Media Law Reporter" is not comprehensive. It contains only the cases

U.S. Supreme Court Collection

selected by the editors to highlight prominent issues in media law. Law review articles provide invaluable scholarship and references to contemporary legal topics. However, primary source research in administrative, legislative and court documents is necessary to thoroughly research a legal topic.

The main reading room in the U.S. Supreme Court Library.

This text cannot provide a detailed explanation of how to navigate through these complex and diverse legal materials. However, access to primary legal materials is available online and in databases such as Westlaw and LexisNexis.

The notes at the end of this book contain citations to many of the important cases in the law of journalism and mass communication. These legal citations provide the names of the parties in the case, the number of the volume in which the case is reported, the abbreviated name of the official legal reporter (or book) in which the case appears, the page of the reporter on which the case begins and the year in which the case was decided. For example, one citation in note 4 of this chapter looks like this: "FEC v. Wisconsin Right to Life Inc., 551 U.S. 449 (2007)." This citation shows that the first party, the Federal Election Commission, filed an appeal from a decision in favor of the second party, Wisconsin Right to Life Inc. The decision in this case striking down a ban on issue advertising prior to elections or primaries can be found in the United States Reports (U.S.), which contains U.S. Supreme Court opinions. The case appears in volume 551 (the number *before* the name of the reporter), beginning on page 449 (the number *after* the name of the reporter). The case was decided in 2003 (the number in parentheses).

READING CASE LAW

This chapter shows that the law of journalism and mass communication contains many terms and concepts that may be unfamiliar to the general reader. Key definitions in the margins and the glossary at the back of the book should help you begin reading the law, which is a bit like reading a foreign language. Because judges write opinions for lawyers trained in legal terminology and doctrines, their use of unfamiliar terms may make it

peremptory challenge During jury selection, a challenge in which an attorney rejects a juror without showing a reason. Attorneys have the right to eliminate a limited number of jurors through peremptory challenges.

appellant The party making the appeal; also called the petitioner.

appellee The party against whom an appeal is made.

summary judgment The resolution of a legal dispute without a full trial when a judge determines that undisputed evidence is legally sufficient to render judgment.

difficult for newcomers to grasp the underlying meaning and importance of a case. With practice, however, people who are not judges or lawyers or even law students can learn the language and read case law with relative ease.

The following steps will help you read the law more quickly and with better comprehension. You will understand the law far better and more easily if you give yourself sufficient time to use these three steps:

1. ***Pre-read the case.*** Pre-reading is designed to identify the *structure* of the decision; the various *rules or doctrines* that underlie the court's reasoning; and the *outcome* of the case. These three elements provide a context to help you highlight the most important elements of the court's reasoning. To pre-read, quickly skim

   a. The topic sentence of each paragraph to get the gist of the opinion and identify its most important sections

   b. The first few paragraphs of the opinion, which should establish the parties, the issues and the history of the case

   c. The last few paragraphs of the opinion to understand the **holding** (which is the legal principle taken from the decision of the court) or to get a summary of the outcome of the case

2. ***Skim the entire case.*** Skimming involves scanning lightly over the entire case. Mark the start of key sections of the case for more careful reading but wait to highlight or underline.

3. ***Read carefully the sections you have identified as important.*** Underline or highlight as you go. You may want to identify different elements differently. In particular, take note of the following:

   a. ***The issue.*** In this text, the chapter titles generally signal the issue on which the case excerpt will focus. The case itself also often includes language that identifies the issue. Such language includes, "The question before the Court is whether . . ." and "The issue in this case is . . ." Knowing the issue in the case helps you know which elements of the history and facts are significant.

   b. ***The facts.*** Recognize that some facts are central to the issue whereas others are peripheral. To identify the important facts, ask yourself whether the dispute in the case is about a question of fact (e.g., what happened) or a question of law (e.g., which test, doctrine or category of speech is relevant). A libel decision that turns on the identity of the individual whose reputation was harmed would represent a question of fact.[58]

   c. ***The case history.*** The circumstances surrounding a decision often are pivotal to the issue before the Court. Sometimes the relevant history is one of shifting legal doctrine, as when the Court gradually affords commercial speech greater constitutional protection.[59] Sometimes the important context is factual, as when the Court protects defamatory comments situated within a generally accurate portrayal of the violent oppression of blacks during the civil rights movement.[60]

holding The decision or ruling of a court.

d. ***The common law rule of law.*** The rule is the heart of the decision; it is the common law developed in this case. To identify the rule, ask whether the Court has created a new test, engaged in balancing or applied an established doctrine in a new way. What are the elements of the rule, and what are its exceptions? Under what conditions or to what type of communication does the rule apply?

e. ***The analysis.*** Here the court applies the rule to the facts. In libel law, for example, public officials must prove actual malice to win their suit. How does the court apply this element of the test? What does that tell you about actual malice and about public officials?

Reading the law in this way is the first stage in conducting legal research. This careful reading also positions you well to write case briefs, which summarize the key elements of a court decision.

Briefing Cases

Case briefs simplify and clarify a court's sometimes lengthy opinions by selecting the five most important elements of the decision. Briefs focus on key elements and set aside content that does not directly inform the court's decision.

The five components of a case brief are often referred to as FIRAC. They are Facts, Issue, Rule of Law, Analysis and Conclusion.

1. ***The Facts.*** The facts summary should include all the information needed to understand the issue and the decision of the court. The facts statement consists of a brief but inclusive discussion of what happened in the legal dispute before it reached this court. It should include who the parties are, what happened in the trial court and the basis for appeal. What happened between the parties that gave rise to the case? Who initiated the lawsuit? What was the substance of the complaint, and what type of legal action was brought? What was the defense? What did other courts reviewing the case decide? What legal errors provide the basis for the appeal?

2. ***The Issue.*** Here, one sentence summarizes the specific question decided by the court in this case. The issue should be phrased as a single question that can be answered "yes" or "no."

3. ***The Rule of Law.*** The rule of law states, preferably in one sentence, the precedent established by this decision that will bind lower courts.

4. ***The Application.*** This section, also called the *rationale*, details why the court reached its decision. In this section, it is important to discuss the details of the court's reasoning. The analysis section needs to identify how and why the current decision creates new law. Consider whether it establishes a new test, clarifies existing legal distinctions, defines a new category or highlights changing realities that affect the law. A thorough analysis must describe the reasoning for all the opinions in the decision and highlight the specific points on which concurring and dissenting opinions diverge from the opinion of the court.

5. ***The Conclusion.*** This is a simple declarative statement of the holding reached by the present court. Did the court affirm, remand or reverse? Provide the vote of the court.

Analyzing *Marbury v. Madison*

The following case brief previews the first case excerpted at the end of this chapter.

FACTS: William Marbury was one of President John Adams' 42 "midnight appointments" on the eve of his departure from the White House. The necessary paperwork and procedures to secure his and several other appointments were completed, but Secretary of State John Marshall—himself a midnight appointee—failed to deliver Marbury's commission. Upon assuming the presidency, Thomas Jefferson ordered his secretary of state—James Madison—not to deliver the commission. Under authority of the Judiciary Act of 1789, Marbury sued to ask the Supreme Court to order Madison, through a writ of mandamus, to deliver the commission. A writ of mandamus is a court order requiring an individual or organization either to perform or to stop a particular action.

ISSUE: Does the Supreme Court have the power to review acts of Congress and declare them void if they violate the Constitution?

RULE of LAW: Under Article VI, Sec. 2 of the U.S. Constitution, the Supreme Court is implicitly given the power to review acts of Congress and to strike them down as void if they are "repugnant" to the Constitution.

APPLICATION: A commission signed by the president and sealed by the secretary of state is complete and legally binding. Denial of Marbury's commission violates the law, creating a governmental obligation to remedy the violation. A writ of mandamus is such a remedy. The Constitution is the "supreme law of the land" (Art. VI). As such, it is "superior" and "fundamental and paramount." It establishes "certain limits" on the power of the government it creates, including the power of Congress. Accordingly, "a legislative act contrary to the Constitution is not law." The Constitution also establishes that "[it] is emphatically the province and duty of the judicial department to say what the law is." The Supreme Court, therefore, must determine the law that applies in a specific case and decide the case according to the law. If the Court finds that "ordinary" statutory law conflicts with the dictates of the Constitution, the "fundamental" constitutional law must govern. If Congress enacted legislation the Constitution forbids, the Court must strike it down to give the Constitution its due weight.

Under Article III of the Constitution, Congress has the power to regulate the appellate jurisdiction, but not the original jurisdiction, of the Supreme Court. The Court's original jurisdiction is defined completely and exclusively by Article III and cannot be altered except by amendment of the Constitution. Through the Judiciary Act of 1789, Congress *added* matters of mandamus to the original jurisdiction of the Court. Being outside the power given to Congress by the Constitution, this act is illegitimate. Neither was the power of mandamus granted to the Court by the Constitution. Following these principles, the Court does not have the power to order mandamus on behalf of Marbury.

The Court held the provision of the Judiciary Act unconstitutional and declared the mandamus void.

CONCLUSION: Marshall, C.J. 6–0. Yes. Relying heavily on the inherent "logical reasoning" of the Constitution, rather than on any explicit text, the Court dismissed the case for lack of jurisdiction but found that Congress' grant of original power of mandamus to the Court violated the division of power established in Article III of the Constitution.

CHAPTER SUMMARY

THE RULE OF LAW provides a relatively clear, neutral and stable mechanism for resolving conflicts. Legal rules bind both government and citizens by defining the boundaries of acceptable behavior, establishing the power and range of punishment and dictating procedures for creating, applying, interpreting and changing the law. Well-crafted laws are clear and narrowly drawn. Court reliance on precedent discourages rapid law change but permits flexibility in response to change.

Laws in the United States come from six sources. Constitutions at the state and federal levels are the highest law of the land. Congress and the legislatures of every state, city and county enact statutes. Equity and common law are judge-made law and are not compiled into books. Thousands of executive branch administrative agencies establish legal rules that determine everything from the definition of false advertising to the number of different media a given corporation may control. At each level of government, executives issue orders that have the force of law.

The U.S. Supreme Court rarely exercises its power to review the constitutionality of laws and government actions. Through judicial review, courts have the power to interpret constitutions and to determine when government violates the Constitution.

Largely independent court systems exist at the federal level, in each of the states, the District of Columbia and the territories and the military. There are three levels of courts: trial courts, intermediate appellate courts and supreme courts. The U.S. Constitution establishes the U.S. Supreme Court and provides for other federal courts. The U.S. Supreme Court has power to review the constitutionality of final rulings of the highest state courts. It is the court of last resort and generally chooses which cases to review. Most cases reach the Court through a petition for certiorari. State courts have jurisdiction over issues arising within the state and relating to state law. New technologies that transcend traditional court boundaries make the determination of court jurisdiction increasingly difficult.

Trial courts review the facts and are the entry level for most legal disputes. Appeals courts, including the 13 federal circuit courts of appeal, review the legal reasoning and process of the lower courts. Three-judge panels decide most cases in the federal courts of appeals. Majority opinions of a court of appeals establish binding precedent within the court's jurisdiction.

Lawsuits are either criminal or civil. In criminal cases, the government brings an action against an individual for violating a criminal statute. In a civil lawsuit, a private individual (the plaintiff) initiates the process by filing a complaint. Both criminal and civil suits involve a variety of pretrial processes, and juries hear both types of cases. Jurors are called and questioned through voir dire, which provides an opportunity for attorneys to remove jurors for cause or through peremptory challenge. Court decisions may be appealed. Judges also may end a case through dismissal or summary judgment.

Online sources supplement and ease legal research once conducted exclusively in the numerous volumes held by legal, academic and government libraries. Law review articles are extremely valuable aids to legal research, as are legal encyclopedias. Legal researchers must be able to read and analyze case law. ■

CASES FOR STUDY

For study resources and a case archive go to **study.sagepub.com/medialaw6e.**

THINKING ABOUT IT

Critics of campaign finance regulations designed to prevent corruption in elections won several legal decisions in 2010 in the wake of the Supreme Court's ruling in *Citizens United v. Federal Election Commission*.[61] As one legal scholar noted, "The relevance of Citizens United has become an issue in every new campaign finance case" since the decision was handed down in January 2010.[62] This aspect of the Court's decision is developed in Chapter 2 when the First Amendment implications of campaign finance laws are discussed. Here we look instead at what *Citizens United* demonstrates about precedent and the rule of law. The debate raised in the Court's opinions has spawned vibrant public discussion about whether the doctrine of stare decisis serves "as an agent of stability" or "to destabilize the rule of law."[63] The second case excerpt below begins with Chief Justice John Roberts' concurring opinion in *Citizens United*, in which he "elaborated on when it *is* acceptable for the Court to overturn precedent."[64] Justice John Paul Stevens' rather acerbic dissent forms the second part of this contemporary Court debate on the role of precedent.

The first case excerpt is from *Marbury v. Madison*,[65] the decision in which the Supreme Court established its own power of judicial review. A central question resolved by the Supreme Court in *Marbury v. Madison* was whether, under the Constitution, the Court had authority to void duly enacted laws that it deemed to violate the U.S. Constitution.

As you read these case excerpts, keep the following questions in mind:

- How do the sitting justices differ in their interpretation of the binding nature of Supreme Court precedent?
- In the case of *Citizens United*, which justices are exercising "restraint" or "activism"? Why?
- What are the legal foundations for the different opinions?
- What do these decisions suggest about the stability or "transformation" of the rule of law under judicial review and stare decisis?

Marbury v. Madison
SUPREME COURT OF THE UNITED STATES
5 U.S. 137 (1803)

CHIEF JUSTICE JOHN MARSHALL
delivered the Court's opinion:
. . . The constitution vests the whole judicial power of the United States in one supreme court, and such inferior courts as congress shall, from time to time, ordain and establish. This power is expressly extended to all cases arising under the laws of the United States; and consequently, in some form, may be exercised over the present case; because the right claimed is given by a law of the United States.

In the distribution of this power it is declared that "the supreme court shall have original jurisdiction in all cases affecting ambassadors, other public ministers and consuls, and those in which a state shall be a party. In all other cases, the supreme court shall have appellate jurisdiction."

It has been insisted at the bar, that as the original grant of jurisdiction to the supreme and inferior courts is general, and the clause, assigning original jurisdiction to the supreme court, contains no negative or restrictive words; the power remains to the legislature, to assign original jurisdiction to that court in other cases than those specified in the article which has been recited; provided those cases belong to the judicial power of the United States.

If it had been intended to leave it to the discretion of the legislature to apportion the judicial power between the supreme and inferior courts according to the will of that body, it would certainly have been useless to have proceeded further than to have defined the judicial power, and the tribunals in which it should be vested. The subsequent part of the section is . . . entirely without meaning, if such is to be the construction. If congress remains at liberty to give this court appellate jurisdiction, where the constitution has declared their jurisdiction shall be original; and original jurisdiction where the constitution has declared it shall be appellate; the distribution of jurisdiction, made in the constitution, is form without substance. . . .

It cannot be presumed that any clause in the constitution is intended to be without effect; and therefore such a construction is inadmissible, unless the words require it. . . .

When an instrument organizing fundamentally a judicial system, divides it into one supreme, and so many inferior courts as the legislature may ordain and establish; then enumerates its powers, and proceeds so far to distribute them, as to define the jurisdiction of the supreme court by declaring the cases in which it shall take original jurisdiction, and that in others it shall take appellate jurisdiction, the plain import of the words seems to be, that in one class of cases its jurisdiction is original, and not appellate; in the other it is appellate, and not original. If any other construction would render the clause inoperative,

that is an additional reason for rejecting such other construction, and for adhering to their obvious meaning.

To enable this court then to issue a mandamus, it must be shown to be an exercise of appellate jurisdiction, or to be necessary to enable them to exercise appellate jurisdiction.

It has been stated at the bar that the appellate jurisdiction may be exercised in a variety of forms, and that if it be the will of the legislature that a mandamus should be used for that purpose, that will must be obeyed. This is true; yet the jurisdiction must be appellate, not original.

It is the essential criterion of appellate jurisdiction, that it revises and corrects the proceedings in a cause already instituted, and does not create that case. Although, therefore, a mandamus may be directed to courts, yet to issue such a writ to an officer for the delivery of a paper, is in effect the same as to sustain an original action for that paper, and therefore seems not to belong to appellate, but to original jurisdiction. Neither is it necessary in such a case as this, to enable the court to exercise its appellate jurisdiction.

The authority, therefore, given to the supreme court, by the act establishing the judicial courts of the United States, to issue writs of mandamus to public officers, appears not to be warranted by the constitution; and it becomes necessary to enquire whether a jurisdiction, so conferred, can be exercised.

The question, whether an act, repugnant to the constitution, can become the law of the land, is a question deeply interesting to the United States; but, happily, not of an intricacy proportioned to its interest. It seems only necessary to recognise certain principles, supposed to have been long and well established, to decide it.

That the people have an original right to establish, for their future government, such principles as, in their opinion, shall most conduce to their own happiness, is the basis, on which the whole American fabric has been erected. The exercise of this original right is a very great exertion; nor can it, nor ought it to be frequently repeated. The principles, therefore, so established, are deemed fundamental. And as the authority, from which they proceed, is supreme, and can seldom act, they are designed to be permanent.

This original and supreme will organizes the government, and assigns to different departments their respective powers. It may either stop here; or establish certain limits not to be transcended by those departments.

The government of the United States is of the latter description. The powers of the legislature are defined, and limited; and that those limits may not be mistaken, or forgotten, the constitution is written. To what purpose are powers limited, and to what purpose is that limitation committed to writing; if these limits may, at any time, be passed by those intended to be restrained? The distinction between a government with limited and unlimited powers is abolished, if those limits do not confine the persons on whom they are imposed, and if acts prohibited and acts allowed are of equal obligation. It is a proposition too plain to be contested, that the constitution controls any legislative act repugnant to it; or, that the legislature may alter the constitution by an ordinary act.

Between these alternatives there is no middle ground. The constitution is either a superior, paramount law, unchangeable by ordinary means, or it is on a level with ordinary legislative acts, and like other acts, is alterable when the legislature shall please to alter it.

If the former part of the alternative be true, then a legislative act contrary to the constitution is not law: if the latter part be true, then written constitutions are absurd attempts, on the part of the people, to limit a power in its own nature illimitable.

Certainly all those who have framed written constitutions contemplate them as forming the fundamental and paramount law of the nation, and consequently the theory of every such government must be, that an act of the legislature repugnant to the constitution is void.

This theory is essentially attached to a written constitution, and is consequently to be considered by this court as one of the fundamental principles of our society. It is not therefore to be lost sight of in the further consideration of this subject.

If an act of the legislature, repugnant to the constitution, is void, does it, notwithstanding its invalidity, bind the courts, and oblige them to give it effect? Or, in other words, though it be not law, does it constitute a rule as operative as if it was a law? This would be to overthrow in fact what was established in theory; and would seem, at first view, an absurdity too gross to be insisted on. It shall, however, receive a more attentive consideration.

It is emphatically the province and duty of the judicial department to say what the law is. Those who apply the rule to particular cases, must of necessity expound and interpret that rule. If two laws conflict with each other, the courts must decide on the operation of each. So if a law be in opposition to the constitution; if both the law and the constitution apply to a particular case, so that the court must either decide that case conformably to the law, disregarding the constitution; or conformably to the constitution, disregarding the law; the court must determine which of these conflicting rules governs the case. This is of the very essence of judicial duty.

If then the courts are to regard the constitution; and the constitution is superior to any ordinary act of the legislature; the constitution, and not such ordinary act, must govern the case to which they both apply.

Those then who controvert the principle that the constitution is to be considered, in court, as a paramount law, are reduced to the necessity of maintaining that courts must close their eyes on the constitution, and see only the law.

This doctrine would subvert the very foundation of all written constitutions. It would declare that an act, which, according to the principles and theory of our government, is entirely void, is yet, in practice, completely obligatory. It would declare, that if the legislature shall do what is expressly forbidden, such act, notwithstanding the express prohibition, is in reality effectual. It would be giving to the legislature a practical and real omnipotence with the same breath which professes to restrict their powers within narrow limits. It is prescribing limits, and declaring that those limits may be passed at pleasure.

That it thus reduces to nothing what we have deemed the greatest improvement on political institutions—a written constitution, would of itself be sufficient, in America where written constitutions have been viewed with so much reverence, for rejecting the construction. But the peculiar expressions of the constitution of the United States furnish additional arguments in favour of its rejection.

The judicial power of the United States is extended to all cases arising under the constitution. Could it be the intention of those who gave this power, to say that, in using it, the constitution should not be looked into? That a case arising under the constitution should be decided without examining the instrument under which it arises?

This is too extravagant to be maintained. . . .

[I]t is apparent, that the framers of the constitution contemplated that instrument, as a rule for the government of courts, as well as of the legislature.

Why otherwise does it direct the judges to take an oath to support it? This oath certainly applies, in an especial manner, to their conduct in their official character. How immoral to impose it on them, if they were to be used as the instruments, and the knowing instruments, for violating what they swear to support!

The oath of office, too, imposed by the legislature, is completely demonstrative of the legislative opinion on the subject. It is in these words, "I do solemnly swear that I will administer justice without respect to persons, and do equal right to the poor and to the rich; and that I will faithfully and impartially discharge all the duties incumbent on me as according to the best of my abilities and understanding, agreeably to the constitution, and laws of the United States."

Why does a judge swear to discharge his duties agreeably to the constitution of the United States, if that constitution forms no rule for his government? If it is closed upon him, and cannot be inspected by him?

If such be the real state of things, this is worse than solemn mockery. To prescribe, or to take this oath, becomes equally a crime.

It is also not entirely unworthy of observation, that in declaring what shall be the supreme law of the land, the constitution itself is first mentioned; and not the laws of the United States generally, but those only which shall be made in pursuance of the constitution, have that rank.

Thus, the particular phraseology of the constitution of the United States confirms and strengthens the principle, supposed to be essential to all written constitutions, that a law repugnant to the constitution is void; and that courts, as well as other departments, are bound by that instrument.

The rule must be discharged.

Citizens United v. Federal Election Commission
SUPREME COURT OF THE UNITED STATES
558 U.S. 310 (2010)

JUSTICE ANTHONY KENNEDY delivered the Court's opinion.

CHIEF JUSTICE ROBERTS, with whom JUSTICE SAMUEL ALITO joined, concurring: The Government urges us in this case to uphold a direct prohibition on political speech. It asks us to embrace a theory of the First Amendment that would allow censorship not only of television and radio broadcasts, but of pamphlets, posters, the internet, and virtually any other medium that corporations and unions might find useful in expressing their views on matters of public concern. Its theory, if accepted, would empower the Government to prohibit newspapers from running editorials or opinion pieces supporting or opposing candidates for office, so long as the newspapers were owned by corporations—as the major ones are. First Amendment rights could be confined to individuals, subverting the vibrant public discourse that is at the foundation of our democracy.

The Court properly rejects that theory, and I join its opinion in full. The First Amendment protects more than just the individual on a soapbox and the lonely pamphleteer. I write separately to address the important principles of judicial restraint and *stare decisis* implicated in this case.

Judging the constitutionality of an Act of Congress is "the gravest and most delicate duty that this Court is called upon to perform." Because the stakes are so high, our standard practice is to refrain from addressing constitutional questions except when necessary to rule on particular claims before us. This policy underlies both our willingness to construe ambiguous statutes to avoid constitutional problems and our practice "'never to formulate a rule of constitutional law broader than is required by the precise facts to which it is to be applied.'"

The majority and dissent are united in expressing allegiance to these principles. But I cannot agree with my dissenting colleagues on how these principles apply in this case.

The majority's step-by-step analysis accords with our standard practice of avoiding broad constitutional questions except when necessary to decide the case before us. The majority begins by addressing—and quite properly rejecting—Citizens United's statutory claim that [the Bipartisan Campaign Reform Act of 2002] does not actually cover its production and distribution of *Hillary: The Movie* (hereinafter *Hillary*). If there were a valid basis for deciding this statutory claim in Citizens United's favor (and thereby avoiding constitutional adjudication), it would be proper to do so. . . .

It is only because the majority rejects Citizens United's statutory claim that it proceeds to consider the group's various constitutional arguments, beginning with its narrowest claim (that *Hillary* is not the functional equivalent of express advocacy) and proceeding to its broadest claim (that *Austin v. Michigan Chamber of Commerce* (1990) should be overruled). . . .

The dissent advocates an approach to addressing Citizens United's claims that I find quite perplexing. It presumably agrees with the majority that Citizens United's narrower statutory and constitutional arguments lack merit—otherwise its conclusion that the group should lose this case would make no sense. Despite agreeing that these narrower arguments fail, however, the dissent

argues that the majority should nonetheless latch on to one of them in order to avoid reaching the broader constitutional question of whether *Austin* remains good law. It even suggests that the Court's failure to adopt one of these concededly meritless arguments is a sign that the majority is not "serious about judicial restraint."

This approach is based on a false premise: that our practice of avoiding unnecessary (and unnecessarily broad) constitutional holdings somehow trumps our obligation faithfully to interpret the law. It should go without saying, however, that we cannot embrace a narrow ground of decision simply because it is narrow; it must also be right. Thus while it is true that "[i]f it is not necessary to decide more, it is necessary not to decide more," sometimes it is necessary to decide more. There is a difference between judicial restraint and judicial abdication. When constitutional questions are "indispensably necessary" to resolving the case at hand, "the court must meet and decide them." . . .

This is the first case in which we have been asked to overrule *Austin*, and thus it is also the first in which we have had reason to consider how much weight to give *stare decisis* in assessing its continued validity. The dissent erroneously declares that the Court "reaffirmed" *Austin*'s holding in subsequent cases. Not so. Not a single party in any of those cases asked us to overrule *Austin*, and as the dissent points out, the Court generally does not consider constitutional arguments that have not properly been raised. *Austin*'s validity was therefore not directly at issue in the cases the dissent cites. The Court's unwillingness to overturn *Austin* in those cases cannot be understood as a *reaffirmation* of that decision.

Fidelity to precedent—the policy of *stare decisis*—is vital to the proper exercise of the judicial function. "*Stare decisis* is the preferred course because it promotes the even-handed, predictable, and consistent development of legal principles, fosters reliance on judicial decisions, and contributes to the actual and perceived integrity of the judicial process." For these reasons, we have long recognized that departures from precedent are inappropriate in the absence of a "special justification."

At the same time, *stare decisis* is neither an "inexorable command," nor "a mechanical formula of adherence to the latest decision," especially in constitutional cases. If it were, segregation would be legal, minimum wage laws would be unconstitutional, and the Government could wiretap ordinary criminal suspects without first obtaining warrants. As the dissent properly notes, none of us has viewed *stare decisis* in such absolute terms.

Stare decisis is instead a "principle of policy." When considering whether to reexamine a prior erroneous holding, we must balance the importance of having constitutional questions *decided* against the importance of having them *decided right*. As Justice Jackson explained, this requires a "sober appraisal of the disadvantages of the innovation as well as those of the questioned case, a weighing of practical effects of one against the other."

In conducting this balancing, we must keep in mind that *stare decisis* is not an end in itself. It is instead "the means by which we ensure that the law will not merely change erratically, but will develop in a principled and intelligible fashion." Its greatest purpose is to serve a constitutional ideal—the rule of law. It follows that in the unusual circumstance when fidelity to any particular precedent does more to damage this constitutional ideal than to advance it, we must be more willing to depart from that precedent.

Thus, for example, if the precedent under consideration itself departed from the Court's jurisprudence, returning to the "'intrinsically sounder' doctrine established in prior cases" may "better serv[e] the values of *stare decisis* than would following [the] more recently decided case inconsistent with the decisions that came before it." Abrogating the errant precedent, rather than reaffirming or extending it, might better preserve the law's coherence and curtail the precedent's disruptive effects.

Likewise, if adherence to a precedent actually impedes the stable and orderly adjudication of future cases, its *stare decisis* effect is also diminished. This can happen in a number of circumstances, such as when the precedent's validity is so hotly contested that it cannot reliably function as a basis for decision in future cases, when its rationale threatens to upend our settled jurisprudence in related areas of law, and when the precedent's underlying reasoning has become so discredited that the Court cannot keep the precedent alive without jury-rigging new and different justifications to shore up the original mistake.

These considerations weigh against retaining our decision in *Austin*. First, as the majority explains, that decision was an "aberration" insofar as it departed from the robust protections we had granted political speech in our earlier cases . . . [and] does not explain why corporations may be subject to prohibitions on speech in candidate elections when individuals may not.

Second, the validity of *Austin*'s rationale—itself adopted over two "spirited dissents"—has proved to be the consistent subject of dispute among Members of this Court ever since. The simple fact that one of our decisions remains controversial is, of course, insufficient to justify overruling it. But it does undermine the precedent's ability to contribute to the stable and orderly development of the law. In such circumstances, it is entirely appropriate for the Court—which in this case is squarely asked to reconsider *Austin*'s validity for the first time—to address the matter with a greater willingness to consider new approaches capable of restoring our doctrine to sounder footing.

Third, the *Austin* decision is uniquely destabilizing because it threatens to subvert our Court's decisions even outside the particular context of corporate express advocacy. The First Amendment theory underlying *Austin*'s holding is extraordinarily broad. *Austin*'s logic would authorize government prohibition of political speech by a category of speakers in the name of equality—a point that most scholars acknowledge (and many celebrate), but that the dissent denies.

It should not be surprising, then, that Members of the Court have relied on *Austin*'s expansive logic to justify greater incursions on the First Amendment, even outside the original context of corporate advocacy on behalf of candidates running for office. The dissent in this case succumbs to the same temptation, suggesting that *Austin* justifies prohibiting corporate speech because such speech might unduly influence "the market for legislation." The dissent reads *Austin* to permit restrictions on corporate speech based on nothing more than the fact that the corporate form may help individuals coordinate and present their views more effectively. A speaker's ability to persuade, however, provides no basis for government regulation of free and open public debate on what the laws should be.

If taken seriously, *Austin*'s logic would apply most directly to newspapers and other media corporations. They have a more profound impact on public discourse than most other speakers. These corporate entities are, for the time being, not subject to [the statute's] otherwise generally applicable prohibitions on corporate political speech. But this is simply a matter of legislative grace. The fact that the law currently grants a favored position to media corporations is no reason to overlook the danger inherent in accepting a theory that would allow government restrictions on their political speech.

These readings of *Austin* do no more than carry that decision's reasoning to its logical endpoint. In doing so, they highlight the threat *Austin* poses to First Amendment rights generally, even outside its specific factual context of corporate express advocacy. Because *Austin* is so difficult to confine to its facts—and because its logic threatens to undermine our First Amendment jurisprudence and the nature of public discourse more broadly—the costs of giving it *stare decisis* effect are unusually high.

Finally and most importantly, the Government's own effort to defend *Austin*—or, more accurately, to defend something that is not quite *Austin*—underscores its weakness as a precedent of the Court. The Government concedes that *Austin* "is not the most lucid opinion," yet asks us to reaffirm its holding. But while invoking *stare decisis* to support this position, the Government never once even mentions the compelling interest that *Austin* relied upon in the first place: the need to diminish "the corrosive and distorting effects of immense aggregations of wealth that are accumulated with the help of the corporate form and that have little or no correlation to the public's support for the corporation's political ideas." *Austin*'s specific holding on the basis of two new and potentially expansive interests—the need to prevent actual or apparent quid pro quo corruption, and the need to protect corporate shareholders. Those interests may or may not support the result in *Austin*, but they were plainly not part of the reasoning on which *Austin* relied. . . .

To its credit, the Government forthrightly concedes that *Austin* did not embrace either of the new rationales it now urges upon us. To be clear: The Court in *Austin* nowhere relied upon the only arguments the Government now raises to support that decision. . . .

To the extent that the Government's case for reaffirming *Austin* depends on radically reconceptualizing its reasoning, that argument is at odds with itself. *Stare decisis* is a doctrine of preservation, not transformation. It counsels deference to past mistakes, but provides no justification for making new ones. There is therefore no basis for the Court to give precedential sway to reasoning that it has never accepted, simply because that reasoning happens to support a conclusion reached on different grounds that have since been abandoned or discredited.

Doing so would undermine the rule-of-law values that justify *stare decisis* in the first place. It would effectively license the Court to invent and adopt new principles of constitutional law solely for the purpose of rationalizing its past errors, without a proper analysis of whether those principles have merit on their own. This approach would allow the Court's past missteps to spawn future mistakes, undercutting the very rule-of-law values that *stare decisis* is designed to protect.

None of this is to say that the Government is barred from making new arguments to support the outcome in *Austin*. On the contrary, it is free to do so. And of course the Court is free to accept them. But the Government's new arguments must stand or fall on their own; they are not entitled to receive the special deference we accord to precedent. They are, as grounds to support *Austin*, literally unprecedented.

Moreover, to the extent the Government relies on new arguments—and declines to defend *Austin* on its own terms—we may reasonably infer that it lacks confidence in that decision's original justification.

Because continued adherence to *Austin* threatens to subvert the "principled and intelligible" development of our First Amendment jurisprudence, I support the Court's determination to overrule that decision. . . .

JUSTICE JOHN PAUL STEVENS, with whom Justice Ruth Bader Ginsburg, Justice Stephen Breyer and Justice Sonia Sotomayor join, concurring in part and dissenting in part:
. . . The majority's approach to corporate electioneering marks a dramatic break from our past. Congress has placed special limitations on campaign spending by corporations ever since the passage of the Tillman Act in 1907. We have unanimously concluded that this "reflects a permissible assessment of the dangers posed by those entities to the electoral process," and have accepted the "legislative judgment that the special characteristics of the corporate structure require particularly careful regulation." The Court today rejects a century of history when it treats the distinction between corporate and individual campaign spending as an invidious novelty born of *Austin v. Michigan Chamber of Commerce.* Relying largely on individual dissenting opinions, the majority blazes through our precedents, overruling or disavowing a body of case law.

In his landmark concurrence in *Ashwander v. TVA* (1936), Justice Brandeis stressed the importance of adhering to rules the Court has "developed . . . for its own governance" when deciding constitutional questions. Because departures from those rules always enhance the risk of error, . . . I emphatically dissent from its principal holding.

The Court's ruling threatens to undermine the integrity of elected institutions across the Nation. The path it has taken to reach its outcome will, I fear, do damage to this institution. Before turning to the question whether to overrule *Austin* and part of *McConnell*, it is important to explain why the Court should not be deciding that question.

The first reason is that the question was not properly brought before us. . . . [T]he majority decides this case on a basis relinquished below, not included in the questions presented to us by the litigants, and argued here only in response to the Court's invitation. This procedure is unusual and inadvisable for a court. Our colleagues' suggestion that "we are asked to reconsider *Austin* and, in effect, *McConnell*," would be more accurate if rephrased to state that "we have asked ourselves" to reconsider those cases. . . .

It is all the more distressing that our colleagues have manufactured a facial challenge, because the parties have advanced numerous ways to resolve the case that would facilitate electioneering by nonprofit advocacy corporations such as Citizens United, without toppling statutes and precedents. Which is to say, the majority has transgressed yet another "cardinal" principle of the judicial process: "[I]f it is not necessary to decide more, it is necessary not to decide more." . . .

The final principle of judicial process that the majority violates is the most transparent: *stare decisis.* I am not an absolutist when it comes to *stare decisis*, in the campaign finance area or in any other. No one is. But if this principle is to do any meaningful work in supporting the rule of law, it must at least demand a significant justification, beyond the preferences of five Justices, for overturning settled doctrine. "[A] decision to overrule should rest on some special reason over and above the belief that a prior case was wrongly decided." No such justification exists in this case, and to the contrary there are powerful prudential reasons to keep faith with our precedents.

The Court's central argument for why *stare decisis* ought to be trumped is that it does not like *Austin.* The opinion "was not well reasoned," our colleagues assert, and it conflicts with First Amendment principles. This, of course, is the Court's merits argument, the many defects in which we will soon consider. I am perfectly willing to concede that if one of our precedents were dead wrong in its reasoning or irreconcilable with the rest of our doctrine, there would be a compelling basis for revisiting it. But neither is true of *Austin*, and restating a merits argument with additional vigor does not give it extra weight in the *stare decisis* calculus.

Perhaps in recognition of this point, the Court supplements its merits case with a smattering of assertions. The Court proclaims that "*Austin* is undermined by experience since its announcement." This is a curious claim to make in a case that lacks a developed record. The majority has no empirical evidence with which to substantiate the claim; we just have its *ipse dixit* that the real world has not been kind to *Austin*. Nor does the majority bother to specify in what sense *Austin* has been "undermined." Instead it treats the reader to a string of non sequiturs: "Our Nation's speech dynamic is changing"; "[s]peakers have become adept at presenting citizens with sound bites, talking points, and scripted messages"; "[c]orporations . . . do not have monolithic views." How any of these ruminations weakens the force of *stare decisis*, escapes my comprehension.

The majority also contends that the Government's hesitation to rely on *Austin*'s anti-distortion rationale "diminishe[s]" "the principle of adhering to that precedent." Why it diminishes the value of *stare decisis* is left unexplained. We have never thought fit to overrule a precedent because a litigant has taken any particular tack. Nor should we. Our decisions can often be defended on multiple grounds, and a litigant may have strategic or case-specific reasons for emphasizing only a subset of them. Members of the public, moreover, often rely on our bottom-line holdings far more than our precise legal arguments; surely this is true for the legislatures that have been regulating corporate electioneering since *Austin*. The task of evaluating the continued viability of precedents falls to this Court, not to the parties.

Although the majority opinion spends several pages making these surprising arguments, it says almost nothing about the standard considerations we have used to determine *stare decisis* value, such as the antiquity of the precedent, the workability of its legal rule, and the reliance interests at stake. It is also conspicuously silent about *McConnell*, even though the *McConnell* Court's decision to uphold [the Bipartisan Campaign Reform Act (BCRA)] relied not only on the anti-distortion logic of *Austin* but also

on the statute's historical pedigree, and the need to preserve the integrity of federal campaigns.

We have recognized that "[s]tare decisis has special force when legislators or citizens 'have acted in reliance on a previous decision, for in this instance overruling the decision would dislodge settled rights and expectations or require an extensive legislative response.'" *Stare decisis* protects not only personal rights involving property or contract but also the ability of the elected branches to shape their laws in an effective and coherent fashion. Today's decision takes away a power that we have long permitted these branches to exercise. State legislatures have relied on their authority to regulate corporate electioneering, confirmed in *Austin*, for more than a century. The Federal Congress has relied on this authority for a comparable stretch of time, and it specifically relied on *Austin* throughout the years it spent developing and debating BCRA. The total record it compiled was *100,000 pages* long. Pulling out the rug beneath Congress after affirming the constitutionality of [the statutory provision] six years ago shows great disrespect for a coequal branch.

By removing one of its central components, today's ruling makes a hash out of BCRA's "delicate and interconnected regulatory scheme." . . .

Beyond the reliance interests at stake, the other *stare decisis* factors also cut against the Court. Considerations of antiquity are significant for similar reasons. *McConnell* is only six years old, but *Austin* has been on the books for two decades, and many of the statutes called into question by today's opinion have been on the books for a half-century or more. The Court points to no intervening change in circumstances that warrants revisiting *Austin*. Certainly nothing relevant has changed since we decided WRTL [*Federal Election Commission v. Wisconsin Right to Life Inc.*] two Terms ago. And the Court gives no reason to think that *Austin* and *McConnell* are unworkable.

In fact, no one has argued to us that *Austin*'s rule has proved impracticable, and not a single for-profit corporation, union, or State has asked us to overrule it. Quite to the contrary, leading groups representing the business community, organized labor and the nonprofit sector, together with more than half of the States, urge that we preserve *Austin*. As for *McConnell*, the portions of BCRA it upheld may be prolix, but all three branches of Government have worked to make §203 as user-friendly as possible. For instance, Congress established a special mechanism for expedited review of constitutional challenges; the FEC has established a standardized process, with clearly defined safe harbors, for corporations to claim that a particular electioneering communication is permissible under WRTL; and, as noted above, The Chief Justice crafted his controlling opinion in WRTL with the express goal of maximizing clarity and administrability. The case for *stare decisis* may be bolstered, we have said, when subsequent rulings "have reduced the impact" of a precedent "while reaffirming the decision's core ruling."

In the end, the Court's rejection of *Austin* and *McConnell* comes down to nothing more than its disagreement with their results. Virtually every one of its arguments was made and rejected in those cases, and the majority opinion is essentially an amalgamation of resuscitated dissents. The only relevant thing that has changed since *Austin* and *McConnell* is the composition of this Court. Today's ruling thus strikes at the vitals of *stare decisis*, "the means by which we ensure that the law will not merely change erratically, but will develop in a principled and intelligible fashion" that "permits society to presume that bedrock principles are founded in the law rather than in the proclivities of individuals."

Freedom of expression is the matrix, the indispensable condition, of nearly every other form of freedom.

—U.S. Supreme Court Justice Benjamin N. Cardozo[1]

University of Wisconsin students turned out in 2016 to protest Ben Shapiro, editor-in-chief of the conservative DailyWire.com, who said university efforts to prevent "microaggressions" and create "safe spaces" violate the free speech rights of students and faculty.

2 THE FIRST AMENDMENT
Speech and Press Freedoms in Theory and Reality

SUPPOSE . . .

. . . an anonymous source gives two national newspapers copies of classified federal government documents that show the government has been lying publicly about the U.S. war abroad and the number of U.S. casualties. When the newspapers begin publishing stories based on the documents, the government obtains an injunction, or court order to stop further stories, on the grounds coverage will jeopardize the lives of U.S. soldiers, threaten military operations and undermine national security. The newspapers challenge the ban in court, arguing that they have a First Amendment right to publish the information and the public has a need to know the truth.

Does the government's power to classify government records as secret allow it to prevent public distribution of government information once disclosed? Does the First Amendment allow government to prevent media coverage of issues of national importance? Does it matter how the newspapers obtained the documents? Look for the answers to these questions in this chapter's discussion of *New York Times Co. v. United States* and its case excerpt at the end of the chapter.

The First Amendment to the U.S. Constitution includes only 45 words. "Congress shall make no law respecting an establishment of religion, or prohibiting the free exercise thereof; or abridging the freedom of speech, or of the press; or the right of the people peaceably to assemble, and to petition the government for a redress of grievances." Since the adoption of the Bill of Rights in 1791, thousands of articles, books and legal cases have tried to interpret the First Amendment and to define the boundaries of the six freedoms it protects. A literal interpretation of the First Amendment would completely ban Congress, and only Congress, from "abridging" the freedom of speech or of the press in any way. However, in 1925, the U.S. Supreme Court said the First Amendment applied to state legislatures as well as to Congress.[2] The Supreme Court since has struck down both federal and state laws, court rulings, administrative agency actions and executive orders because they violate the First Amendment.

Supreme Court decisions make clear that although the First Amendment says government "shall make no law," the First Amendment's ban is *not* absolute.[3] Instead, the justices interpret the meaning of the amendment in various ways.

WHAT THE FIRST AMENDMENT MEANS

Some justices are textualists who believe reading the First Amendment's own words provides a complete explanation of its meaning and protections. But the text offers little guidance on whether, for example, court orders requiring WikiLeaks to disclose its source of access to confidential government documents would unconstitutionally "abridge" the freedom of "the press" or whether Facebook "likes" are protected under the Constitution's "freedom of speech."[4] Although the Supreme Court rarely distinguishes between free speech and a free press and often combines them under the label "free expression," legal historians and Justice Potter Stewart have argued that the distinct free press clause was intended to provide special protections for journalists and the mass media to check the power of government.[5]

Justice Stewart was among those who look to history to help them decide what the First Amendment means. Such members of the Court seek the **original intent** of the framers of

original intent
The perceived intent of the framers of the First Amendment that guides some contemporary First Amendment application and interpretation.

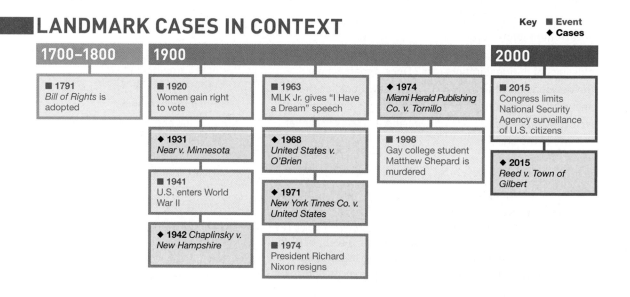

LANDMARK CASES IN CONTEXT

Key ■ Event
      ◆ Cases

1700–1800	1900			2000
■ 1791 *Bill of Rights* is adopted	■ 1920 Women gain right to vote	■ 1963 MLK Jr. gives "I Have a Dream" speech	◆ 1974 *Miami Herald Publishing Co. v. Tornillo*	■ 2015 Congress limits National Security Agency surveillance of U.S. citizens
	◆ 1931 *Near v. Minnesota*	◆ 1968 *United States v. O'Brien*	■ 1998 Gay college student Matthew Shepard is murdered	◆ 2015 *Reed v. Town of Gilbert*
	■ 1941 U.S. enters World War II	◆ 1971 *New York Times Co. v. United States*		
	◆ 1942 *Chaplinsky v. New Hampshire*	■ 1974 President Richard Nixon resigns		

● REAL WORLD LAW

Testing the Balance

Instagram/Justin Timberlake

Recent First Amendment controversies included battles over whether voters have the right to take "selfies" while voting.

When Justin Timberlake distributed a picture of himself voting in Memphis, he was among the most visible individuals potentially facing charges for violating state law.[1] The law in Tennessee and 17 other states prohibits voter selfies to protect the fundamental right to a secret ballot. Advocates argue that these laws reduce the risk of voter coercion and vote buying, but at least two courts said such laws violate the protection of freedom of speech.

"The prohibition on ballot selfies reaches and curtails the speech rights of all voters, not just those motivated to cast a particular vote for illegal reasons," the First Circuit Court of Appeals ruled. The court said that banning ballot selfies to achieve the highly speculative goal of deterring vote buying was like "burning down the house to roast the pig."[2]

In November 2016, laws in Alabama, Alaska, Colorado, Florida, Georgia, Illinois, Kansas, Massachusetts, Michigan, Mississippi, Nevada, New Jersey, New Mexico, New York, North Carolina, South Carolina, South Dakota and Wisconsin made voter selfies illegal.[3] In another 13 states including Tennessee, the legal boundaries to taking pictures of your ballot or yourself while voting are mixed or unclear.

Tennessee officials declined to prosecute Timberlake.

1. Abby Ohlheiser, *Yes, Your Ballot Selfie Might Be Illegal. Sorry,* Wash. Post, Nov. 8, 2016, www.washingtonpost.com/news/the-intersect/wp/2016/10/26/yes-your-ballot-selfie-still-might-be-illegal-sorry/?utm_term=.4e9c70bdc9ac.
2. Rideout v. Gardner, 838 F.3d 65 (1st Cir. 2016).
3. AP, *Ballot Selfies: A Look at Where They Are Legal and Not,* Oct. 23, 2016, www.apnews.com/04c313da0672422ba28bb57c4e4a7ca0.

the Constitution to help them determine whether occupying the streets of Ferguson, Mo., or burning a flag to protest government actions is a form of speech protected by the First Amendment.[6] Unfortunately, intent is slippery, and the authors of the First Amendment left few records to indicate what they meant by "the freedom of speech, or of the press."

Some justices view the Constitution as a living document that responds to societal changes. They argue that the flexibility of constitutional language is its greatest strength, not its failing. They believe that even a clear understanding of what the words of the First Amendment meant in 1791 would rarely be relevant today.

In contrast, other justices say malleability in the Constitution's meaning gives the Court unlimited power to change the protections of the First Amendment at whim. Through time, in fact, the Court has decreased both the percentage of First Amendment cases it reviews and its rulings in favor of First Amendment claims, according to a 2012 study.[7] In practice, the Supreme Court tends to avoid broad statements about the First Amendment and decides what the First Amendment means in the particular context of each specific case.

ad hoc balancing
Making decisions according to the specific facts of the case under review rather than more general principles.

To reach its decisions, the Court often weighs the constitutional interests on one side of a case against the competing interests on the other side. When courts make decisions according to the specific facts of the case under review rather than based on general principles, it is called **ad hoc balancing**. No clear rule dictates the Court's ad hoc balancing of interests. Instead, the justices carefully examine the competing rights and decide which side has greater constitutional merit. For example, in 2014, the Supreme Court balanced the interests of a government agency to control the speech of its employees against the right of the individual to testify truthfully in court. In *Lane v. Franks*, the Court ruled that

● REAL WORLD LAW

Speech Favoritism?

Danita Delimont/Alamy

Chief Justice of the United States John Roberts.

The Supreme Court's support for the First Amendment declined during the first five years of Chief Justice John Roberts' leadership, according to academic studies.[1] The Roberts Court not only found no free speech violation more frequently than had either the Rehnquist or Berger courts, which were known as defenders of the First Amendment; it also demonstrated a willingness to favor the free speech claims of corporations but not those of government whistle-blowers, grassroots organizations and unions, according to legal scholars.[2]

"What really animates [the Roberts Court's] decisions is a hostility to campaign finance laws much more than a commitment to expanding speech," argued Erwin Chemerinsky.[3] But others see a different agenda. "The Roberts court strongly protects speech that it likes, while allowing regulation of speech it disfavors," said Adam Winkler, according to a news report.[4]

1. Mark Tushnet, *Opinions: Five Myths About the Roberts Court*, WASH. POST, Oct. 11, 2013, www.washingtonpost.com/opinions/five-myths-about-the-roberts-court/2013/10/11/69924370-30f4-11e3-8627-c5d7de0a046b_story.html.
2. Monica Young, *The Roberts Court's Free Speech Double Standard*, ACSBLOG, Nov. 29, 2011, www.acslaw.org/acsblog/the-roberts-court's-free-speech-double-standard.
3. Erwin Chemerinsky, *Not a Free Speech Court*, 53 ARIZ. L. REV. 723 (2011), www.arizonalawreview.org/2011/53-3/chemerinsky.
4. Greg Stohr, *Speech Rights Triumph as U.S. High Court Limits Government Power*, BLOOMBERG BUSINESS, June 27, 2011, www.bloomberg.com/news/articles/2011-06-28/speech-rights-triumph-as-u-s-high-court-limits-government-power.

the First Amendment protects the right of public employees to testify in court on matters of public concern.[8] In 2010, the Supreme Court relied on its own "historical and traditional" interpretation of the First Amendment to strike down a law prohibiting depictions of animal cruelty.[9]

The Court also uses categories of speech to reach some First Amendment decisions. The Court has defined a range of broad categories, such as political speech or commercial speech, to help it determine the appropriate First Amendment protection. Simply put, the Court has created categories that give some types of speech a lot of protection; some, less; others, none at all. Decades ago in *Chaplinsky v. New Hampshire*,[10] the Court first noted that "certain well-defined and narrowly limited classes of speech . . . are no essential part of any exposition of ideas, and are of such slight social value as a step to truth" that government may prevent and punish this speech without violating the First Amendment.

Courts since have used categories that are sometimes unclear and quite broad or find the First Amendment does not protect certain types of speech. When speech falls into one of these categories, the courts do not balance the value of the speech against society's interests. Using the categorical approach, the courts' only question is whether a specific act of expression falls within a fully protected, less protected or unprotected class.

In *Chaplinsky*, the Court did not fully develop the different "narrow" categories of speech, but subsequent rulings make clear that political speech enjoys full constitutional protection, while fighting words and obscenity are unprotected categories. The First Amendment also does not prohibit laws that punish blackmail, extortion, perjury, false advertising and disruptive speech in the public school classroom, for example. Recent Court opinions suggest that child pornography, cross burning and true threats (particularly to national security) warrant little, if any, First Amendment protection.

When speech categories are less well defined, they provide limited guidance to courts seeking to resolve cases involving similar speech. Then courts generally use **categorical balancing** to determine the outcome. They look beyond the category of the speech alone to consider the particular circumstances and the harm caused by the speech to determine whether the expression is punishable. Judges do this on a case-by-case basis because it is difficult to judge the gravity of harm caused by speech in advance or in the abstract.

Thus, in its 2014 decision in *Lane v. Franks*, the Court clarified the boundary between public employee speech and citizen speech. "When public employees make statements pursuant to their official duties, the employees are not speaking as citizens for First Amendment purposes"[11] but are speaking as workers under control of the government, the Court wrote. In contrast, a public worker's speech "outside the scope of his ordinary job duties is speech as a citizen for First Amendment purposes,"[12] and it "holds special value precisely because those employees gain knowledge of matters of public concern through their employment."[13]

Whether a government employee's speech deserves First Amendment protection depends on the balance between the public value of the speech and the significance of the government interest in prohibiting the speech. In *Lane*, government could not punish an employee who provided truthful testimony about political corruption under oath in court. The balance weighed in the employee's favor.

The Supreme Court faced the question of how much First Amendment protection is given to false speech when it considered whether a federal law that made it a crime to lie

categorical balancing The practice of deciding cases by weighing different broad categories, such as political speech, against other categories of interests, such as privacy, to create general rules that may be applied in later cases with similar facts.

about being awarded U.S. military honors violated the Constitution.[14] In its decision in *United States v. Alvarez*, a majority of the Court struck down the Stolen Valor Act, but only four justices held that the First Amendment absolutely protects such false statements as pure speech. Reasoning for this plurality, Justice Anthony Kennedy said there is no "general exception to the First Amendment for false statements." He argued that speech may be excluded from First Amendment protection only in the rare and extreme circumstances of the "historic categories" that pose a grave and imminent threat. False claims about military awards pose no such threat.

Two justices concurred with the holding, forming the majority, but reasoned that laws may punish false statements of easily determined facts in specific contexts with proof of the harm they cause. In 2013, Congress amended the Stolen Valor Act to make it illegal to profit from such lies.[15] In 2014, the Ninth Circuit Court of Appeals upheld the power of government to punish the wearing of unearned military medals.[16] The court distinguished between the wearing of false medals and lying about military honors and found that the First Amendment protected only the false statements.

WHERE THE FIRST AMENDMENT CAME FROM

Historians of the First Amendment generally agree that it was never meant to pose a complete ban to all government action involving freedom of speech or of the press. Instead, the First Amendment was intended to prevent the U.S. government from adopting the types of suppressive laws that flourished in England following the introduction of the printing press in 1450. Beginning in the early 1500s, the British Crown controlled all presses in England through its licensing power. King Henry VIII and the Roman Catholic Church feared that broad public distribution of printed materials would erode their control of information and their authority. The church and the crown sought to suppress challenges to their power by outlawing critical views as heresy (criticism of the church) or sedition. They jointly imposed a strict system of licensing of printers and prior review of all texts.

Through prior review, the king's officers banned books and censored disfavored ideas. Printers suspected of publishing outlawed texts faced fines, prison, torture or even execution. The crown also gave lucrative monopoly printing contracts to favored printers in exchange for their unofficial help enforcing the licensing law. Licensed printers reported and attacked unlicensed printers and destroyed their presses. Despite the danger, unlicensed texts continued to appear in England.

Foundations of First Amendment Theory

In 1643, the power of prior review shifted from the king's officers to the British Parliament, with government censors reviewing all publications before printing. Authors and publishers protested against government control of content and developed theories to justify press freedom. In 1644, English poet John Milton's unlicensed "Areopagitica" argued that an open marketplace of ideas advanced the interests of society and humankind. Milton, who was angered by church and state attempts to destroy his earlier unlicensed pamphlet advocating divorce, said the free exchange of ideas was vital to the discovery of truth. He wrote, famously,

Though all the winds of doctrine were let loose to play upon the earth, so Truth be in the field, we do injuriously by licensing and prohibiting to misdoubt her strength. Let her and Falsehood grapple; who ever knew Truth put to the worse in a free and open encounter?[17]

By the late 1600s, English philosopher and political theorist John Locke argued that government censorship was an improper exercise of power.[18] Locke first said that all people have fundamental natural rights, including life, personal liberty and self-fulfillment. Freedom of expression is central to these natural rights. In contrast, government has no innate rights or natural authority and exists only through the grant of power from the people. Therefore, government actions are legitimate only within the sphere of granted power. Because the people do not grant government the power to limit their natural human rights, government censorship is always illegitimate.

Locke's vision of government was revolutionary. Nearly three-quarters of a century later, French political philosopher Jean-Jacques Rousseau advanced a similar view of a social contract between the people and their government.[19] Rousseau said all people are born free and equal but, without the constraints of morality and law, would become uncivilized and violent. Accordingly, people willingly form a social contract in which they exchange some freedom for a limited government that advances their collective interest. Because the people retain their sovereignty and their rights under this contract, government censorship can never be justified.

In 1694, the British Parliament failed to renew the Licensing Act, and official **prior restraint** of publications ended. But for the next 100 years, the British government enacted and enforced laws that punished immoral, illegal or dangerous speech after the fact. Political thinkers of the day generally did not view punishment after the fact as censorship because it allowed people to speak and publish and merely held them accountable for the harms their speech was believed to cause, such as sedition, **defamation** (criticism of individuals) and blasphemy (sacrilegious speech about God). In 1769, legal scholar Sir William Blackstone expressed this view of English common law.[20] He wrote,

> The liberty of the press is indeed essential to the nature of a free state, but this consists in laying no previous restraints upon publications, and not in freedom from censure for criminal matter when published. Every freeman has an undoubted right to lay what sentiments he pleases before the public, to forbid this is to destroy the freedom of the press, but if he publishes what is improper, mischievous, or illegal, he must take the consequences of his own temerity.[21]

Blackstone's view of freedom of the press and shadows of British licensing, taxation and common law restraints on speech and press moved across the ocean into the American colonies.[22] Presses in the colonies were licensed, and government censors previewed publications until the 1720s. The crime of **seditious libel** made it illegal to publish anything harmful to the reputation of a colonial governor. Truth was not a defense because truthful criticism still harmed the governor's reputation, and the governor had a legal right to be compensated for that harm.

prior restraint Action taken by the government to prohibit publication of a specific document or text before it is distributed to the public; a policy that requires government approval before publication.

defamation A false communication that harms another's reputation and subjects him or her to ridicule and scorn; incorporates both libel and slander.

seditious libel Communication meant to incite people to change the government; criticism of the government.

● REAL WORLD LAW

A U.S. War on the Press in 2017?

Media barely noticed a prior restraint imposed on a New Jersey newspaper amid frenzy over the Trump administration's guidelines to federal agencies to limit their communications with the public.

The largely unreported January 2017 court hearing involved a 3-month-old judge's order barring a Trentonian reporter from publishing information he had obtained from a confidential child abuse complaint.[1] The New Jersey Division of Child Protection and Permanency obtained the injunction to prevent reporter Isaac Avilucea from publishing details of the complaint against a 5-year-old boy's parents and grandmother.

The case began when school authorities reported that the unnamed child had, on two separate occasions, brought substantial quantities of heroin and crack cocaine to school. The state challenged Avilucea's assertion that he obtained the court order legally from the child's mother.

Within days of Donald Trump's inauguration, officials at the Environmental Protection Agency and the U.S. Department of Agriculture told staff that all external communications about their work would cease. The agencies told their scientists they could discuss neither agency research nor the speech restriction with anyone outside the agency.[2]

While many railed against this "unprecedented" censorship, others pointed out that presidential clampdowns were nothing new. Citing examples from Theodore Roosevelt and Dwight Eisenhower to Barack Obama, one reporter wrote: "There have been presidents in the past who lied with a smile, who silenced the press with a finger to the lips or a cup to the ear. . . . Presidents are going to wage war against the press."[3] From his earliest days in office, an assault on media appeared to be a mainstay of Trump's presidency.[4]

1. Salvador Rizzo, *N.J. Judge Holds Hearing in Press Censorship Case*, NorthJersey.com, Jan. 23, 2017, www.northjersey.com/story/news/new-jersey/2017/01/20/nj-judge-holds-hearing-press-censorship-case/96856868.
2. Dina Fine Maron, *Trump Administration Restricts News From Federal Scientists at USDA, EPA*, Scientific Am., Jan. 24, 2017, www.scientificamerican.com/article/trump-administration-restricts-news-from-federal-scientists-at-usda-epa.
3. D.C. McAllister, *Sorry, Journalists: Trump Isn't the First President to Threaten the Press*, Federalist, Jan. 24, 2017, www.thefederalist.com/2017/01/24/sorry-journalists-trump-isnt-first-president-threaten-press.
4. Steve Rosenfeld, *Donald Trump's Escalating War Against the Media*, Salon, Jan. 25, 2017, www.salon.com/2017/01/25/donald-trumps-escalating-war-against-the-media_partner.

With growing independence, the colonies attempted to dismantle some British common law traditions. In one case, the publisher of a newspaper in the colony of New York, John Peter Zenger, clearly had broken the sedition law by printing criticism of colonial Gov. William Cosby. Cosby jailed Zenger to stop the publications. Arguing for the defense, Andrew Hamilton said no one should be jailed for publishing truthful and fair criticism of government. The jury agreed and acquitted Zenger in 1734.

Very few trials for seditious libel occurred after that. However, the struggle to define the acceptable limits of free speech and a free press in the colonies continued. Colonial legislatures used their power to question, convict, jail and fine publishers for breach of parliamentary privilege if they published almost anything negative about the legislature.

This mixed history shaped First Amendment freedoms of speech and of the press. The Constitution's framers understood both the British tradition of punishment for sedition, blasphemy and libel, and the colonists' growing enthusiasm for increasingly wide-open debate. It seems clear the authors of the First Amendment intended to provide a ban on prior restraints. Less clear is whether they intended to eliminate the common law regarding sedition, blasphemy and libel.[23]

Seven years after the adoption of the First Amendment, the Sedition Act imposed heavy fines and jail time on individuals who stirred up public emotions or expressed malicious views against the government. As the 18th century ended, government leaders continued to support laws that punished criticism of government. More than a dozen prosecutions and convictions under the Alien and Sedition Acts targeted outspoken publishers and political opponents of President John Adams.[24] The Alien and Sedition Acts expired without the U.S. Supreme Court reviewing their constitutionality, but more than 150 years later, Justice William J. Brennan said that "the court of history" clearly decided the Sedition Act was unconstitutional.[25]

⬤ INTERNATIONAL LAW

The Great Firewall of China[1]

Chinese officers check IDs in a Zaozhuang, China, internet café to enforce required use of real names online.

Imaginechina via AP

Long viewed as a nation comfortable with suppressing the speech and assembly rights of its citizens, China is now regarded as imposing "the world's largest system of censorship."[2] Despite accounting for 40 percent of the world's online sales, China continues to close gaps and build new mechanisms for controlling the web, in what it calls its movement toward "internet sovereignty." Its internet censorship and surveillance program, which the United States has called an impediment to international trade, is estimated to affect 700 million users. China's "golden shield" blocks tens of thousands of websites, including Facebook, Twitter and Instagram. In 2016, for example, Apple said its iTunes Movies and iBooks were no longer available in China.

China also limited the ability of citizens to bypass its censorship through the use of virtual private networks (VPNs) by extending its limits on content to these providers.

Lu Wei, China's internet czar, said the country had achieved the perfect balance between control and freedom and should become a model for the West. "This path is the choice of history," he said.

1. Christopher Stevenson, Breaching the Great Firewall: China's Internet Censorship and the Quest for Freedom of Expression in a Connected World, 30 B.C. INT'L & COMP. L. REV. 532 (2007).
2. Simon Denyer, *China's Scary Lesson to the World: Censoring the Internet Works*, WASH. POST, May 23, 2016, washingtonpost.com/world/asia_pacific/chinas-scary-lesson-to-the-world-censoring-the-internet-works/2016/05/23/413afe78-fff3-11e5-8bb1-f124a43f84dc_story.html?utm_term=.72ae14910e46.

WHY WE VALUE THE FIRST AMENDMENT

The Supreme Court has interpreted the First Amendment as an instrument to achieve specific social functions or advance certain fundamental values. This approach protects freedom of speech and freedom of the press only when they advance particular societal interests.[26] Speech deserves protection because it aids the search for truth, advances self-governance, provides a check on government abuse of power and offers a safety valve for social discontent.[27] Some scholars argue that the most significant value of the First Amendment is to improve the ability of minority groups in society to be heard[28] or to encourage the development of a tolerant society.[29] Thus, Court decisions have upheld broadcast regulation to increase the diversity of ideas reaching U.S. voters. In *New York Times Co. v. Sullivan,* the Court ruled that robust criticism of government is so vital to democracy that the First Amendment protects news media from punishment for unintentional defamation of government officials (see Chapter 4).[30]

Those who value free speech in and of itself—as an end rather than a means—see free speech as a natural right. For them, the Constitution protects freedom of speech because speech is fundamental to individual natural liberty, essential to what it means to be human.[31]

These two perspectives on free speech are useful when they help courts determine what types of speech deserve to be protected or punished. Neither does a very good job of this, however. Neither provides strict guidelines or clear lines (what the law calls bright-line distinctions) to delineate protected speech. For instance, the functional approach fails to establish a clear boundary between speech that helps democratic self-governance and speech that does not. When is a march and rally in Washington, D.C., protected political expression? If speech is protected because it is the essence of being human, where is the logical limit to the right of self-expression? Does the Constitution protect our right to express ourselves by shooting guns in the middle of the city, by wearing unearned military medals or by making harassing telephone calls?

Two apparently contradictory landmark Supreme Court rulings on a public right of access to the media demonstrate the dilemmas presented by value-based decision making. In the first of these, *Red Lion Broadcasting Co. v. Federal Communications Commission,* the Court ruled years ago that regulations requiring broadcasters to seek out and broadcast competing views on controversial public issues were constitutional.[32] Broadcasters had said FCC rules requiring them to notify and provide free broadcast time for political candidates to reply to on-air attacks or to editorials endorsing their opponents violated their First Amendment right to choose the information they aired. The Court disagreed and said,

> The right of free speech of a broadcaster . . . or any other individual does not embrace a right to snuff out the free speech of others. . . . [The broadcaster] has no constitutional right to . . . monopolize a radio frequency to the exclusion of his fellow citizens.[33]

Here the Court held that *public* speech over the public airwaves was of paramount value. Five years later, with three new members, the Supreme Court ruled in *Miami Herald Publishing Co. v. Tornillo* that the First Amendment barred the government from requiring a newspaper to provide free reply space to political candidates attacked in the paper. The Court said "compelling editors or publishers to publish that which 'reason tells them should not be published'" is unconstitutional.[34] Although newspapers are a platform for public debate, "press responsibility is not mandated by the Constitution, and like many other virtues it cannot be legislated."[35] The Court lauded the autonomy of the printed press:

> A newspaper is more than a passive receptacle or conduit for news, comment and advertising. The choice of material to go into a newspaper, and the decisions made as to limitations on the size and content of the paper, and treatment of public issues and public officials—whether fair or unfair—constitute the exercise of editorial control and judgment. It has yet to be demonstrated how governmental regulation of this crucial process can be exercised consistent with First Amendment guarantees of a free press.[36]

⊙ POINTS OF LAW

Some Core Values of Free Speech

Most people believe the First Amendment serves a number of important interests: individual and social, instrumental and inherent.[1] Supreme Court decisions frequently identify core values of free speech:

- *Individual liberty.* The freedom of speech is deeply intertwined with fundamental natural rights.[2] In this sense, free speech is an inalienable right.

- *Self-government.*[3] The freedom to discuss political candidates and policies and to render judgments is an essential cornerstone of responsible self-governance. The freedom of speech enables "the people" to pursue "democratic self-determination."[4]

- *Limited government power.* Free speech is an "invaluable bulwark against tyranny."[5] The free speech of "the people" serves as a "check"[6] on authoritarian rule and a limit to the abuse of power by the few.

- *Attainment of truth.* Free speech advances the "marketplace of ideas" to increase knowledge and the discovery of truth. By challenging "certain truth" and "received wisdom," open public discussion allows a society to expand understanding.[7]

- *Safety valve.* Free speech allows people to express problems and grievances before they escalate into violence. Except during "the worst of times,"[8] free speech is a mechanism for "letting off steam" and helping to balance social stability and change, compromise and conflict, tolerance and hate.[9]

- *Its own end.* Free speech, like clean air, or beauty, or justice, is an end in and of itself, a valuable good and a cherished right.[10]

---

1. Thomas I. Emerson, *Toward a General Theory of the First Amendment*, 72 YALE L.J. 877 (1963).
2. *See* JOHN LOCKE, II TWO TREATISES OF GOVERNMENT 4 (Peter Laslett ed., Cambridge Univ. Press 1988) (1698).
3. For detailed discussion, *see* Alexander Meiklejohn, Free Speech and Its Relation to Self-Government (1948).
4. Robert Post, Managing Deliberation: The Quandary of Democratic Dialogue, 103 ETHICS 654, 672 (1993).
5. James Madison, *Report on the Virginia Resolutions* (Jan. 1800), reprinted in 5 THE FOUNDERS' CONSTITUTION (Philip B. Kurland & Ralph Lerner eds., 1987).
6. Vincent Blasi, *The Checking Value in First Amendment Theory*, 1977 AM. B. FOUND. RES. J. 521, 523 (1977).
7. Zechariah Chafee Jr., *Freedom of Speech in War Time*, 32 HARV. L. REV. 932 (1919); ZECHARIAH CHAFEE JR., FREEDOM OF SPEECH 37 (1920).
8. Vincent Blasi, *The Pathological Perspective and the First Amendment*, 85 COLUM. L. REV. 449, 464 (1985).
9. C. Edwin Baker, *Scope of the First Amendment Freedom of Speech*, 25 UCLA L. REV. 964 (1978).
10. Ronald Dworkin, A Moral Reading of the American Constitution (1996).

WHEN "THE PRESS" CHANGES

In 1791, when the First Amendment was adopted, speaking to crowds in town squares and printing flyers, pamphlets, leaflets, posters, books and newspapers were the primary ways to distribute your message. The printed word, the press, was *the* medium of mass communication, but the masses reached were small. The largest 18th-century newspapers had circulations of no more than 200 or so readers. Word of mouth, speech, remained a fundamental means of spreading timely information.

▲ EMERGING LAW

Whose Free Press?

iStock/hocus-focus

U.S. protections of open internet access for everyone in the name of freedom of speech[1] necessarily raise questions about whose freedom of a "press" is most important when social media, not traditional news providers, provide a lion's share of the news.[2]

"As news organizations . . . become not just digital first but digital only, journalism and free expression become part of a commercial sphere where the activities of news and journalism are marginal," one scholar said.[3] Such observers worry that profit-oriented tech firms, such as Facebook and Twitter, now control the distribution of news to a public to whom they bear no responsibility. They argue that the commercial priorities of internet service providers (ISPs) will distort the content of the news.

Others say government attempts to prevent ISPs from providing preferred access to profitable news will undermine the Supreme Court's unique protection of "the press." They fear net neutrality's equal-access-for-all requirements undermine the ability of content providers to make independent editorial decisions.[4]

Early in 2017, the new head of the Federal Communications Commission signaled his desire to provide internet access to un(der)served regions and promote competition among internet services. Some observers believed his pro-market approach would dismantle net neutrality regulations.[5]

1. T.C. Sottek, *Get Ready for the FCC to Say the Internet Is a Utility*, THE VERGE, Feb. 2, 2015, www.theverge.com/2015/2/2/7966363/net-neutrality-proposal.
2. Elise Hu, *Silicon Valley's Power Over the Free Press: Why It Matters*, ALL TECH CONSIDERED, Nov. 24, 2014, www.npr.org/sections/alltechconsidered/2014/11/24/366327398/silicon-valleys-power-over-the-free-press-why-it-matters.
3. *Id.*
4. Fred B. Campbell, Jr., *Freedom of the Press Is Bad News for Net Neutrality*, HILL, Dec. 1, 2015, thehill.com/blogs/congress-blog/technology/261519-freedom-of-the-press-is-bad-news-for-net-neutrality.
5. Nelson Granados, *The FCC Hints at the Future of Net Neutrality Under Trump*, FORBES, Feb. 1, 2017, www.forbes.com/sites/nelsongranados/2017/02/01/the-fcc-hints-at-the-future-of-net-neutrality-under-trump/#72764c5a46c0.

🖥 SOCIAL MEDIA LAW

What's Speech?

When an employee clicks "like" on a Facebook post, is that speech?

In 2012, a U.S. district court in Virginia ruled that Facebook "likes" are not speech.[1] Two sheriff's employees who clicked "like" on the campaign Facebook page of their boss's election opponent were fired. They sued, saying the termination violated their First Amendment rights. The district court granted summary judgment for the sheriff and found that the employees were not engaged in protected expression.

On appeal, the Fourth Circuit court disagreed and remanded the case.[2] It wrote:

On the most basic level, clicking on the "like" button literally published the statement that the User "likes" something, which is itself a substantive statement. . . . That a user may use a single mouse click to produce that message that he likes the page instead of typing the same message with several individual key strokes is of no constitutional significance.

Liking a political candidate's campaign page communicates the user's approval of the candidate and supports the campaign by associating the user with it. In this way, it is the internet equivalent of displaying a political sign in one's front yard, which the Supreme Court has held is substantive speech.

1. Bland v. Roberts, 857 F.Supp.2d 599 (E.D. Va. 2012).
2. Bland v. Roberts, 730 F.3d 368, 386 (4th Cir. 2013).

Today, the First Amendment faces a very different reality. Mass communication has changed dramatically. As each new medium—motion pictures, radio, television, telephones, cable and the internet—provided new communication options, citizens used media more and differently; their communications shifted from interpersonal to global, from paper to digital. Observers have decried each new medium as a threat to families, communities and democracy.[37] Established media viewed each newcomer as a competitor, even as the new arrivals proclaimed they increased quantity and diversity of the speech they enabled.

For its part, the Supreme Court has struggled to decide whether and how the First Amendment protects new media.[38] For a time, the Court generally treated each medium differently on the grounds that each presented unique First Amendment capabilities. In 1949, for example, one justice argued that "the moving picture screen, the radio, the newspaper, the handbill, the sound truck and the street corner orator have differing natures, values, abuses and dangers. Each, in my view, is a law unto itself."[39] The Court accepted regulatory differences "justified by some special characteristic of the press"[40] or by specific distinctions among the media. Government could regulate broadcasters differently from newspapers because broadcasters act as trustees of the scarce public airwaves.[41] Unique regulations on cable operators did not violate the First Amendment, the Court said, because cable threatened the survival of free over-the-air broadcasts.[42]

Even with newspapers in economic distress and media ownership patterns difficult to discern,[43] fewer owners control more and more diverse media, and the Court's carefully drawn distinctions no longer fit reality.[44] Newspapers and movies and TV shows are all viewed online and owned increasingly by nonmedia companies like Amazon or Warren Buffett's Berkshire Hathaway Inc. Journalists complain that increased emphasis on profits seriously undermines the quality of news,[45] but what is the news and what is "the press" when more and more people keep up through Saturday Night Live or memes? The Court must answer these difficult questions to apply the First Amendment's protections today, and it is said that hard questions make bad law.

HOW GOVERNMENT RESTRAINS FIRST AMENDMENT FREEDOMS

The Supreme Court has established one bedrock principle: Freedom of speech and of the press cannot coexist with prior restraint. Prior restraint stops speech before it is spoken and halts presses before they print. It is the essence of censorship. But in today's world of instant Snaps and posts, how and where should government step in to avoid the harms speech may cause?

The Court's modern understanding of prior restraint originates in 1931.[46] In *Near v. Minnesota*, the Court said that prior restraint, especially any outright ban on expression, is the least tolerable form of government intervention in the speech marketplace.[47] The case began after Jay Near, publisher of The Saturday Press in Minneapolis, printed charges that city officials were standing by as Jewish gangsters operated gambling, bootlegging and racketeering businesses across the city. When Near could not convince the judge that the attacks were true and published with good intent, a court order shut down the paper under a state public nuisance law that punished publication of "scandalous or defamatory material."

The Supreme Court reviewed the case and ruled that the permanent ban on future issues of The Saturday Press was unconstitutional. The Court said the First Amendment stands as a nearly absolute barrier to classic prior restraints like this Minnesota law banning "nuisance" publications. A classic prior restraint has three components: (1) It imposes government oversight over whole categories of speech, content or publication; (2) it allows the government to choose what content is acceptable; and (3) it empowers government to censor content before it reaches the public.

In 1971, the Supreme Court ruled in *New York Times Co. v. United States* (excerpted at the end of this chapter) that a court order preventing publication of news stories based on leaked Pentagon reports was an unconstitutional prior restraint.[48] The New York Times had begun a series of news stories based on the Pentagon Papers, as people called the top-secret Department of Defense study of the then-ongoing U.S. involvement in Vietnam. The Nixon administration asked for a court **injunction** to stop the publication of the

injunction A court order prohibiting a person or organization from doing some specified act.

⦿ POINTS OF LAW

Near v. Minnesota's First Amendment Safeguards

In 1931, the Supreme Court established that the First Amendment placed a heavy burden on government prior restraints on the press. The Court wrote:

> Liberty of speech, and of the press, is not an absolute right, and the State may punish its abuse. . . . [However, a] statute authorizing . . . restraint of publication is inconsistent with the conception of the liberty of the press as historically conceived and guaranteed. . . .

> The chief purpose of the guaranty is to prevent previous restraints upon publication. . . . The liberty of the press has been especially cherished in this country as respects publications censuring public officials and charging official misconduct. . . . The fact that the liberty of the press may be abused by miscreant purveyors of scandal does not make any the less necessary the immunity from previous restraint in dealing with official misconduct.[1]

The Court added that the First Amendment's

> protection even as to previous restraint is not absolutely unlimited. But the limitation has been recognized only in exceptional cases: When a nation is at war many things that might be said in time of peace are such a hindrance to its effort that their utterance will not be endured. . . . No one would question but that a government might prevent actual obstruction to its recruiting service or the publication of the sailing dates of transports or the number and location of troops. On similar grounds, the primary requirements of decency may be enforced against obscene publications. The security of the community life may be protected against incitements to acts of violence and the overthrow by force of orderly government, [and] the constitutional guaranty of free speech does not protect a man from an injunction against uttering words that may have all the effect of force.[2]

---

1. Near v. Minnesota, 283 U.S. 697, 708, 716, 720 (1931).
2. *Id.* at 716.

classified information on the status of the war. The government said publication threatened national security and the safety of U.S. troops. The district court agreed and enjoined publication.

Acting with unusual speed, the Supreme Court said the injunction violated the Constitution because the government had not shown that the ban was essential to prevent a real and immediate risk of harm to a compelling government interest. The Court said, "[A]ny system of prior restraints of expression comes to this Court bearing a heavy presumption against its constitutional validity."[49] The Court decision left open the possibility that prior restraints might be constitutional if the government could meet this very rigorous test.

The Court since has said prior restraints are generally unconstitutional because they pose too great a risk that government will censor ideas it disfavors and distort the marketplace of ideas. The Court once declared that if "a threat of criminal or civil sanctions after

AP Photo

Dr. Daniel Ellsberg (left), the RAND Corporation employee and U.S. Defense Department consultant who leaked the Pentagon Papers, speaks to reporters after his 1971 arraignment on charges of illegal possession of the classified documents.

publication 'chills' speech, prior restraint 'freezes' it."[50] The First Amendment poses its greatest obstacle to direct prior restraints on the news media because every moment of a ban on reporting causes direct harm to the First Amendment rights of both the media and the public.[51] Yet news organizations increasingly report that policies imposed on government agencies and the "management" of reporters through government public relations offices have the effect of prior restraint.[52] The government says it has the power to classify information and has good reasons to prohibit employees from speaking out (see below for discussion of government speakers).

Today, apparent prior restraints often arise in the form of court orders that stop speech or publication. For example, the Supreme Court long ago said a state court injunction preventing the scheduled broadcast of an investigative news report was unconstitutional; indefinite delay of news was unacceptable under the First Amendment.[53] As another court noted, "News delayed is news denied."[54] The Supreme Court decision involved CBS News' intended broadcast of undercover footage of a South Dakota meatpacking plant. Although the broadcast relied on "calculated misdeeds" and might cause significant harm to the meatpacking company, the Court ruled that the "most extraordinary remedy" of an injunction was unwarranted because it was not essential.

Nonetheless, the speed and breadth of online dissemination sometimes leads courts to impose injunctions. In 2010, for example, a district court in New Jersey imposed an injunction requiring TheFlyontheWall.com to delay distribution of stock tips it aggregated from more than five dozen investment firms.[55] The firms had sued the online publisher for "hot news" misappropriation, a form of unfair competition, for distributing their

● POINTS OF LAW

What Is a Prior Restraint?

A prior restraint is what we think of as good, old, garden-variety censorship. When government prohibits publication or suppresses particular material, this is prior restraint. Prior restraint exists when

1. Any government body or representative
2. Reviews speech or press *prior* to distribution and
3. Stops the dissemination of ideas *before* they reach the public

The Supreme Court has called prior restraint "the most serious and the least tolerable infringement on First Amendment rights."[1]

_____

1. Nebraska Press Ass'n v. Stuart, 427 U.S. 539, 559 (1976).

⬤ INTERNATIONAL LAW

English Publication Ban Doesn't Keep Threesomes Private[1]

Courtesy of News Syndication. Reprinted with permission.

An English celebrity, PJS, in 2016 received a court injunction in England to prevent a popular tabloid from publishing news of his extramarital affairs.[2]

When a U.S. publication released the story and named names online, the report was blocked for readers in England and Wales. Other foreign websites and social media quickly distributed the details. Many said the names were "an open secret."[3]

Upon appeal from The Sun on Sunday, the court removed the ban, saying the public interest in the information and the press's right to publish automatically outweighed the celebrity's limited right to privacy about his infidelities.

But England's high court quickly overturned the ruling and said neither side's interests automatically took precedent. Rather, the proper outcome required that the rights of both be carefully balanced in light of the specific facts. In this case, the court said, the private information was of no legitimate public interest, despite the fact that a prurient public wanted to know.

The high court also reasoned that a "qualitative difference" existed between the intrusiveness and distress caused by online publications abroad and unlimited English publication. The court said it would protect the individual's right to privacy in England and Wales regardless of the information's general availability elsewhere.

1. Claire Overman & Andrew Wheelhouse, *PJS v News Group Newspapers: Threesomes! Privacy! Social Media!*, Oxford Hum. Rights Hub, Sept. 8, 2016, ohrh.law.ox.ac.uk/pjs-v-news-group-newspapers-threesomes-privacy-social-media.
2. Berwin Leighton Paisner LLP, *Privacy Injunctions in the Internet Age: The Supreme Court Judgment in PJS*, May 31, 2016, www.lexology.com/library/detail.aspx?g=ac131e82-8fdd-4273-acd0-c89491a5e556.
3. Ray Wang, *Name the Scottish Celebrity Couple Who Have Injunction in England?*, Quora, Apr. 17, 2016, www.quora.com/Name-the-Scottish-celebrity-couple-who-have-injunction-in-England.

confidential stock recommendations before they were made public. On appeal, the Second Circuit Court quickly struck down the injunction and subsequently reversed the lower court, freeing TheFlyontheWall.com to continue rapid publication of the stock tips.[56] Courts also struggle with the use of injunctions as a means to reduce the potential harms of free speech online. Prior restraints on internet content may be ineffective because of the ability to publish outside the court's jurisdiction or to publish anonymously. In one case, the court-ordered shutdown of the WikiLeaks website, in response to a suit from a Cayman Islands bank, lasted only one week. The case was dismissed after the material appeared elsewhere.[57] Yet courts have blocked selected website information or entire websites for days or months.

A prior restraint on the media can be justified only in exceptional situations. Prior restraints may be permitted either when there is clear and convincing evidence that the speech will cause great and certain harm that cannot be addressed by less intrusive measures or when the speaker clearly engaged in criminal activity to obtain the information being banned.[58]

Despite the Supreme Court's opposition to prior restraints, many laws prevent or limit specific speakers from discussing particular topics, such as threats to national security. Judges' orders prohibiting trial participants from discussing the ongoing trial also generally are acceptable. Laws that limit use of copyrighted material are mandated by the Constitution, and laws that criminalize obscenity are accepted. Police also may legally prevent the speech involved when individuals conspire to commit a crime or to incite violence.

In addition, some government actions that appear to restrain freedom of speech are permitted because the Court does not view them as prior restraints. These laws generally impose content-neutral restrictions on the time, place or manner of expression, which means they do not target or restrict particular messages because of their content. Following this reasoning, courts prior to 2015 generally upheld town statutes that regulated signs to protect community safety and aesthetics.[59]

In *Reed v. Town of Gilbert*, the Supreme Court unanimously struck down a city sign ordinance as content based on its face.[60] The town had created 23 categories of signs (e.g., temporary directional, political) and applied different restrictions to each. A majority of the Court said a law is content based if it "applies to particular speech because of the topic discussed or the idea or message expressed."[61] Regulations that on their face "draw distinctions based on the message, . . . [or that] defin[e] regulated speech by particular subject matter . . . [or] by its function or purpose . . . are subject to **strict scrutiny**."[62] When the Court applies strict scrutiny, its most rigorous review, the Court finds most laws unconstitutional. Because the town's sign law could not pass strict scrutiny, it was unconstitutional.

Five justices used their concurrences to try to limit the breadth of the decision. One justice said the majority's "mechanical use of categories" was problematic and argued that all content distinctions should not automatically trigger the use of strict scrutiny.[63] Another argued that because the town's justification for the distinctions did not pass "even the laugh test," it was unnecessary to address whether the law was content based.[64]

A subsequent decision from the U.S. Appeals Court for the Seventh Circuit concluded that, under *Reed*, "Any law distinguishing one kind of speech from another by reference to [the] meaning [of the speech] now requires a compelling justification" rather than merely the important government interest required for content-neutral restrictions to be found constitutional.[65]

Some laws restricting anti-abortion protests and counseling outside family planning facilities[66] and bans on campaigning or distribution of election materials within a certain distance of the polls have been found content-neutral and constitutional.[67] More discussion of **content-neutral laws** follows.

HOW THE SUPREME COURT REVIEWS LAWS AFFECTING FIRST AMENDMENT RIGHTS

Some laws do not involve speech at all. Minimum-wage regulations and laws that prevent monopolies fall within the power of Congress to regulate commerce.[68] The Court generally presumes that these **laws of general application** are constitutional. The Supreme Court reviews challenges to such laws under minimum scrutiny, also called **rational review**. Rational review presumes the laws are constitutional; government only needs a

● REAL WORLD LAW

The Pentagon Papers of Our Time?

Many compared the 2010 WikiLeaks posting of more than 90,000 classified U.S. military documents on the war in Afghanistan to the publication of the Pentagon Papers during the Vietnam War.[1]

Both leaks hinged on media providing greater transparency to an ongoing and controversial war involving U.S. troops. Both highlighted mainstream media's importance in establishing the credibility of the documents. One observer who noted WikiLeaks' use of The New York Times to vet the documents prior to release said, "Transparency is moot without authority."[2]

Such comparisons obscure significant differences between the WikiLeaks and Pentagon Papers situations. The government imposed a prior restraint on the Pentagon Papers but not on WikiLeaks. The Pentagon Papers documents were at least three years old and were released as U.S. troops began to withdraw; some WikiLeaks material dated back only months, when the war in Afghanistan was ramping up.[3]

Although the Obama White House condemned the WikiLeaks release,[4] it did not seek an injunction to stop the documents' publication, perhaps because "[i]njunctions [do] not work once the cat is out of the bag or the genie out of the bottle"[5] or the information is already available worldwide on the web.

1. Janie Lorber, *Early Word: WikiLeaked*, N.Y. Times, July 30, 2010, thecaucus.blogs.nytimes.com.
2. Adam Kirsch, *Why WikiLeaks Still Needs The New York Times*, New Republic, July 26, 2010, www.tnr.com/blog/foreign-policy.
3. WikiLeaks, wikileaks.org.
4. Alexandra Topping, *WikiLeaks Condemned by White House Over War Documents*, Guardian, July 26, 2010, www.guardian.co.uk/world.
5. Lyrissa Lidsky, Pentagon Papers II? WikiLeaks and Information Control in the Internet Era, PrawfsBlawg, July 26, 2010, prawfsblawg.blogs.com.

rational purpose for such laws. Laws reviewed under minimum scrutiny must be reasonable and serve a legitimate government purpose to be constitutional.

Many laws do involve the freedom of speech and press protected by the First Amendment. When asked to decide whether such laws violate the Constitution, the Supreme Court first determines whether the law targets the ideas expressed or aims at some goal unrelated to the content of the message. The Court calls the first type of law "content based" and the second "content neutral." **Content-based laws** regulate what is being said; they single out certain messages or types of speech for particular treatment. Laws that prohibit the "desecration" of the U.S. flag are content based. **Content-neutral laws** restrict where, when and how ideas are expressed. Also called **time/place/manner laws**, content-neutral restrictions often advance public interests unrelated to speech. Laws that limit noise in hospital zones generally are content neutral. The Court applies intermediate scrutiny to such laws and generally finds them constitutional if they restrict speech as little as necessary to advance the related government interest.

Content-Based Laws

The Supreme Court generally presumes content-based laws are unconstitutional. Like prior restraints, laws that punish the expression of specific ideas after the fact pose a direct and serious threat of government censorship. To stop government censorship of disfavored ideas, the Supreme Court applies a very rigorous test to determine when content-based laws are constitutional. The toughest standard of review, strict scrutiny finds laws that discriminate on the basis of content unconstitutional unless they use (1) the least restrictive means (2) to advance a compelling government interest.

content-based laws Laws enacted because of the message, the subject matter or the ideas expressed in the regulated speech.

content-neutral laws Laws enacted to advance a government purpose unrelated to the content of speech.

time/place/manner laws A First Amendment concept that laws regulating the conditions of speech are more acceptable than those regulating content; also, the laws that regulate these conditions.

compelling
interest A
government
interest of the
highest order,
an interest the
government
is required to
protect.

Laws employ the least restrictive means only if they are extremely well tailored to their goals and restrict the smallest possible amount of protected speech. The Supreme Court generally finds that a law is least restrictive if the government has no other reasonable method to achieve its goals that would be less harmful to free speech rights. To pass strict scrutiny, laws also must directly advance a compelling or paramount government interest. The Court has said a **compelling interest** is an interest of the highest order that relates to core constitutional concerns or the most significant functions of government. Compelling government interests include national security, the electoral process and public health and safety.

In *Simon & Schuster v. Crime Victims Board*, for example, the Supreme Court struck down a New York law that required convicted criminals to turn over the profits of their publications that made even passing comments about their crimes.[69] The state enacted the

▲ EMERGING LAW

Reed's Deregulatory First Amendment Sword

In 2015, five Supreme Court justices expressed a new understanding of content-based regulations many said would require the Court to strike down a broad range of well-established laws.[1]

In *Reed v. Town of Gilbert*, a unanimous Court struck down the town's sign law, and a majority held that laws that distinguish among speech categories are content based on their face and must be reviewed under strict scrutiny. The majority said that even when a regulation does not obviously address speech content, it is content based if it cannot be "justified without *reference* to the content of the regulated speech."[2]

Some fear *Reed* eroded the distinction between content-based and content-neutral regulations and increased the likelihood that laws based on categories of speech would be found unconstitutional.[3] One legal expert said *Reed* posed a fundamental threat to the understanding of the First Amendment and "endangered all sorts of laws, including ones that regulate misleading advertising."[4]

Lower courts diverged on how to apply *Reed*. The Second and the Eleventh Circuit Courts reached opposite conclusions about laws restricting the way merchants communicate about higher prices charged for credit card purchases.[5] While the Second Circuit declined to apply *Reed* and said the law regulated commerce, the Eleventh Circuit used *Reed* to strike down the regulation as unconstitutionally content based.

On appeal of the Second Circuit's decision, the Supreme Court in 2017 did not apply *Reed* or clarify it. Instead, the Court vacated the decision and remanded the case for review as a regulation of speech about prices rather than control of prices themselves.[6]

1. *Free Speech Doctrine After* Reed v. Town of Gilbert, 129 Harv. L. Rev. 1981 (2016), harvardlawreview.org/2016/05/free-speech-after-reed-v-town-of-gilbert.
2. Reed v. Town of Gilbert, 135 S. Ct. 2218, 2227 (2015) (emphasis added).
3. *See, e.g.*, Adam Liptak, *Court's Free-Speech Expansion Has Far-Reaching Consequences*, N.Y. Times, Aug. 17, 2015, www.nytimes.com/2015/08/18/us/politics/courts-free-speech-expansion-has-far-reaching-consequences.html.
4. *Id.*
5. Expressions Hair Design v. Schneiderman, 808 F.3d 118 (2d Cir. 2015), *cert. granted*, 137 S. Ct. 30 (2016), *vacated*, 137 S. Ct. 1144 (2017); Dana's Railroad Supply v. Florida, 807 F.3d 1235 (11th Cir. 2015). *See also* Int'l Franchise Ass'n v. City of Seattle, 803 F.3d 389, 409 (9th Cir. 2015), *cert. denied*, 136 S. Ct. 1838 (2016) (upholding a lower court's refusal to grant a preliminary injunction); State v. Packingham, 777 S.E.2d 738, 741 (N.C. 2015), *cert. granted*, 137 S. Ct. 368 (2016) (upholding state ban on use of social media by registered sex offenders), *rev'd*, 137 S. Ct. 1730 (2017); Cahaly v. Larosa, 796 F.3d 399, 405–06 (4th Cir. 2015) (striking down a statute prohibiting political robocalls as content based under *Reed*); Norton v. City of Springfield, 806 F.3d 411, 412–13 (7th Cir. 2015), cert. denied, 136 S. Ct. 1173 (2016) (striking down a regulation prohibiting panhandling as content based).
6. Expressions Hair Design v. Schneiderman, 137 S. Ct. 1144 (2017).

◉ POINTS OF LAW

Strict Scrutiny

The Supreme Court has said content-based laws are constitutional only if they pass strict scrutiny. To be constitutional, a content-based law must

1. Be necessary and

2. Use the least restrictive means

3. To advance a compelling government interest

Strict scrutiny is the most rigorous test used by the Court to determine whether a law is constitutional. Few laws pass this test.

law following a well-publicized series of killings and said the money would compensate crime victims, increase victim compensation and decrease the "fruits" of crime.

Simon & Schuster, which had published a true-crime autobiography of mafia figure Henry Hill, challenged the law as facially unconstitutional on the grounds that it targeted specific content for punishment by the government. The Supreme Court said the content-based law did advance a compelling government interest but punished writings that deserved full First Amendment protection.[70] The law was not the least intrusive means to achieve this goal.

Content-Neutral Laws

The Supreme Court is more willing to uphold the constitutionality of laws that affect speech but do not discriminate on the basis of content. Content-neutral laws generally regulate the nonspeech elements of messages, such as the time, the place or the manner (size or volume) in which the speech occurs. If content-neutral laws advance a legitimate government goal and do not distinguish among ideas, the Court has tended to find them constitutional even if they reduce the method, location or quantity of speech.

The Court established its foundational First Amendment test for content-neutral laws in a case involving anti–Vietnam War protests. The Court reviewed the conviction of David O'Brien for burning his draft card on the steps of the South Boston Courthouse. O'Brien had violated a federal law that made it a crime to knowingly destroy a draft card. The government said the law aided the functioning of the draft and the U.S. military and protected the national security.[71] O'Brien argued that the law was unconstitutional on its face (see Chapter 1) and as applied in this case because it infringed on freedom of speech.

In *United States v. O'Brien*, the Supreme Court disagreed and upheld O'Brien's conviction.[72] Looking at the actual words of the law—a type of review called statutory construction (see Chapter 1)—the Supreme Court said Congress had enacted the statute to ensure the operation of the military draft. The Court found that any infringement the law caused to O'Brien's speech was minimal and incidental to the government's compelling interest in protecting this very important interest. The law did not target disfavored viewpoints

In Ankara in 2016, an estimated 800 Turkish journalists protested a wave of reporter arrests and detentions.

symbolic expression Action that warrants some First Amendment protection because its primary purpose is to express ideas.

and left O'Brien free to express his opposition to the draft in other ways. Moreover, when speech and action are intimately intertwined into **symbolic expression**, as in the burning of a draft card, the government's legitimate regulation of the actions may constitutionally place a small, content-neutral burden on protected speech.

Finding the law content neutral, the Court applied **intermediate scrutiny** and crafted a new test, known as the ***O'Brien test***. The *O'Brien* test's three substantive parts hold that a law is content neutral and will be constitutional if it (1) is not related to the suppression of speech, (2) advances an important government interest, and (3) is narrowly tailored to achieve that interest with only an incidental restriction of free expression. Most laws reviewed under intermediate scrutiny are upheld. If the Court finds a law content neutral, the law does not target ideas disfavored by government and also generally is unrelated to suppression of speech. Laws said to serve government goals unrelated to content tend to meet this standard. Under the *O'Brien* test, a law also must serve an **important government interest**. A government interest is important when it is more than merely convenient or reasonable. Important interests are weighty or significant; they are not compelling or of the highest order.

The third part of the *O'Brien* test, sometimes called the narrow-tailoring standard, requires a law to "fit" its purpose. A law "fits" when it advances the government interest without imposing an unnecessary burden on speech.[73] The calculation is not precise. Narrowly tailored laws must be clear and specific and may not give officials unlimited discretion.[74] The Supreme Court often defers to the expertise of administrative agencies and legislatures to decide the best means to achieve content-neutral objectives.

The Court applied the *O'Brien* test to uphold a regulation requiring New York City employees to control the volume and sound mix of performers in Central Park.[75] Performers said the rule unconstitutionally allowed the city to control their expression

⊙ POINTS OF LAW

Intermediate-Level Scrutiny

The Supreme Court generally applies some form of intermediate scrutiny to content-neutral laws that affect the freedom of speech. To be constitutional under intermediate scrutiny, a law must

1. Fall within the power of government and

2. Advance an important or substantial government interest that is unrelated to suppression of speech and

3. Be narrowly tailored to impose only an incidental restriction on First Amendment freedoms.

even when it served no important government interest. The Court, however, said the city's complete control of sound was a narrowly tailored means for the city to protect nearby (wealthy) residents from disturbance. *Ward v. Rock Against Racism* established that a content-neutral law is narrowly tailored if government interest would suffer in the absence of a law that advances the government's interest reasonably well.

Thus, when states passed laws restricting access and speech around family planning clinics, the Court generally finds the laws constitutional. In *Hill v. Colorado*, for example, the Court held that a state law creating moving, nonprotest zones around people entering abortion clinics was a valid, narrowly tailored, content-neutral restriction that directly advanced the government's significant interest in protecting the public from harassment.[76] But in 2014 in *McCullen v. Coakley*, the Court held that a fixed, 35-foot buffer zone around clinics was an unconstitutional prior restraint.[77] The Supreme Court said the Massachusetts law imposed a serious burden on those who sought to "counsel" women seeking abortions because it was not narrowly tailored to promote "public safety, patient access to healthcare, and unobstructed use of public sidewalks and roadways." The difference rested on the Court's conclusion that fixed buffer zones made it "substantially more difficult" to engage in one-on-one conversations.

Mario Tama/Getty Images

Police clash with anti-Trump protesters in Washington, D.C., in 2017.

intermediate scrutiny A standard applied by the courts to review laws that implicate core constitutional values; also called heightened review.

***O'Brien* test** A three-part test used to determine whether a content-neutral law is constitutional.

important government interest An interest of the government that is substantial or significant (i.e., more than merely convenient or reasonable) but not compelling.

SPEAKING POLITICS

Political speech lies at the "core of what the First Amendment is designed to protect."[78] The Supreme Court has said political speech involves any "communication concerning political change."[79] This encompasses ballots and voting, electioneering speeches and lobbying, campaign spending and yard signs, political advertisements, cartoons and blogs, petitions and buttons and maybe even protests. Believing that political speech is integral to democratic government, the Court generally has used strict scrutiny to review laws that seem to infringe on political speech.[80]

A key lawsuit began during the 2010 election, when an anti-abortion group planned a billboard campaign claiming that Steve Driehaus, candidate for the U.S. House of Representatives, backed taxpayer-funded abortion through his support of the Affordable Care Act. When Driehaus sought a ban to block the ads as false, the billboard owner refused to run the ad, and the anti-abortion group challenged the constitutionality of a state law making it illegal to lie in campaign ads. Although the Sixth Circuit said Driehaus could sue for defamation based on the false statements,[81] he could not prove that the defamatory statement was made with knowledge of its falsity, which is required for public officials (see Chapter 4).

On remand from the Supreme Court,[82] the Sixth Circuit Court of Appeals found the law unconstitutional because the law's content-based restriction on core political speech was not narrowly tailored to advance the state's compelling interest in preserving the integrity of its elections.[83] Some say the decision could affect similar laws in 15 states.[84]

Despite the Supreme Court's position that political speech deserves the highest level of constitutional protection, news organizations and government may be permitted to punish employees whose political expression violates their policies. For example, The (Colorado Springs) Gazette placed reporter Barrett Tryon on administrative leave after he refused to remove a link on his Facebook page to a Los Angeles Times article about the sale of The Gazette.[85] The case did not go to court. In an older ruling, the Washington State Supreme Court held that the First Amendment protection of editorial autonomy allows newspapers in Washington to prohibit reporters from engaging in political activity.[86]

SPEAKING FOR AND AS THE GOVERNMENT

Courts have attempted to distinguish the ability of government to control the speech of its employees from the freedom of individuals who work in government to engage in protected speech outside of their employment. Government employees do not lose their personal freedom of speech when they accept government work,[87] but the government has the authority to classify sensitive materials and control their distribution, especially in the name of national security. The government also may advance its interests by imposing codes of silence and controlling the content of employee speech and work products.[88]

In 2016, the Supreme Court ruled that the First Amendment prevented a city police department from demoting an employee in order to stop the employee's "overt involvement" in a political campaign.[89] After a police officer reported seeing Paterson, N.J., police detective Jeffrey Heffernan picking up a campaign sign for the opposing mayoral candidate, the chief of police demoted Heffernan to foot patrol. The Court said it was immaterial to its decision that Heffernan was, in fact, getting the sign for his mother. The police department's intention to punish Heffernan for engaging in protected political activity was sufficient to demonstrate that it had intentionally violated his First Amendment rights.

The Supreme Court in *Garcetti v. Ceballos* clarified the distinction between speech *as* a government employee and independent speech *of* a government employee.[90] The Court said the First Amendment did not prohibit government from limiting or punishing an employee's inappropriate work-related expression. The ruling came after Los Angeles County deputy district attorney Richard Ceballos wrote to his superiors about alleged inaccuracies in a sheriff's affidavit. Ceballos then was reassigned, transferred and denied a promotion. He sued, arguing that the actions unconstitutionally punished his protected speech. The government argued that the communication was punishable employee speech unrelated to matters of public concern. In a 5–4 ruling, the Supreme Court agreed with the government and said the government has authority "over what [expression] the employer itself has commissioned or created."[91]

In another case, a local police chief sued claiming the town council had retaliated against him for his successful challenge to their attempt to fire him.[92] In *Borough of Duryea v. Guarnieri*, the Supreme Court called the chief's claim "an ordinary workplace grievance."[93] The unanimous Court held that the right of the employee to petition for redress must be balanced "against the government's interest . . . in the effective and efficient management of its internal affairs."[94] The Court said the government's need to manage its affairs "requires proper restraints on the invocation of rights by employees."[95]

In a 2014 ruling, the Supreme Court suggested that this power over the speech of government workers extends only to "full-fledged" public employees.[96] The Court said the state of Illinois could not compel home health care workers funded through Medicaid to pay a "fair share" of union dues if the workers did not join the union. The caregivers, the Court said, are not truly public employees because they are hired by the Medicaid clients.

A year earlier, the Court said government control of employee speech extends only to speech related directly to the government employment.[97] The Supreme Court struck

● REAL WORLD LAW

Never-Ending Campaign Triggers Ban on Politicking[1]

A line of Supreme Court decisions based on the specific case facts distinguishes between the protected personal speech of government employees and their work-related speech and writing.[2]

The distinction became significant when President Donald Trump declared his candidacy for re-election the day after he took the oath of office in 2017 because the 1939 Hatch Act prohibits federal employees from conducting political activity in the workplace.[3] Most presidents wait years to announce their candidacy, so federal workers do not immediately start tiptoeing the boundary between protected personal comments and impermissible politicking.[4]

"Because the 2020 election is still more than three years away, at this time not all expressions of support or opposition to President Trump constitute political activity for purposes of the Hatch Act," new guidelines from the Office of Special Counsel said.

The Office of Special Counsel, a government agency independent of the White House, quickly informed federal employees they may not express views about whether the president should be re-elected or defeated in 2020 while on duty or at work. Otherwise, employees are free to express support or disapproval of the president and his policies.

The memo distinguished between protected views about current events and matters of public interest and illegal political activity. The ban does not apply to signs, pins, clothing, pictures or other communications related to the president's 2016 campaign except to the extent that such "displays or communications that expressly advocate for or against President Trump's reelection" violate the law's broad prohibition.

A separate guideline said the ban does not permit covered employees—even when off duty and away from work—to "'share' a post from a campaign Facebook page, 'retweet' a message from a political party, or 'like' a post that requests contributions for a candidate."[5]

---

1. Jonathan Weisman, Eric Lichtblau & Charlie Savage, *With the President Already Running for Re-election, Federal Workers Get Guidance on Office Politics*, N.Y. TIMES, Feb. 9, 2017, www.nytimes.com/2017/02/09/us/politics/donald-trump-administration.html?smprod=nytcore-iphone&smid=nytcore-iphone-share.
2. Pickering v. Bd. of Educ., 391 U.S. 563 (1968).
3. Hatch Act, 5 U.S.C.A. § 7324 (1939).
4. U.S. Office of Special Counsel, *Guidance on President Trump's Status as a Candidate and Its Effect on Activity in the Federal Workplace*, Feb. 7, 2017, www.documentcloud.org/documents/3457194-2017-Hatch-Act-Trump-Guidance.html.
5. U.S. Office of Special Counsel, *Hatch Act Social Media and Email Guidance*, osc.gov/Pages/Hatch-Act-Social-Media-and-Email-Guidance.aspx; U.S. Office of Special Counsel, *The Hatch Act Frequently Asked Questions on Federal Employees and the Use of Social Media and Email*, osc.gov/Pages/The-Hatch-Act-Frequently-Asked-Questions-on-Federal-Employees-and-the-Use-of-Social-Media-and-Email.aspx.

down part of a federal law that required nongovernmental organizations fighting HIV/AIDS to explicitly oppose prostitution and sex trafficking as a condition for receipt of federal funding.[98] The Court said the law unconstitutionally sought "to leverage funding to regulate speech outside the contours of the program itself."[99] Nonetheless, in 2016, with only eight members on the Supreme Court, the justices split evenly on whether government agencies could require employees to contribute to unions that used the funding to support political or ideological causes the employees disfavored.[100] The split vote left in place the Ninth Circuit Court's decision finding mandatory employee contributions constitutional.

Although the First Amendment limits government regulation of private speech, it does not deal expressly with the speech of the government itself. The 2015 decision in *Walker v. Texas Division, Sons of Confederate Veterans* illustrates the Supreme Court's emerging doctrine on the government's right to speak and, sometimes, to control or prevent the speech of others. In *Walker*, the Court said the First Amendment does not require states to approve specific specialty license plate slogans because license plates are government speech, not forums for private speakers.[101]

Years earlier, the Supreme Court ruled in *Pleasant Grove v. Summum* that government could select the monuments it displays in its parks.[102] A religious group raised a First Amendment challenge to a city's decision not to post the group's "Seven Aphorisms" on a permanent monument.[103] In reviewing the case, the Court first said that various limitations inherent to public displays make it impractical for government to accommodate all speakers. Instead, the Court said, the selection of speakers was a form of government speech subject to government control of content. The Court concluded "that the City's decision to accept certain privately donated monuments while rejecting respondent's is best viewed as a form of government speech . . . not subject to the Free Speech Clause."[104]

POLITICAL CAMPAIGNING AND FINANCING ELECTIONS

More than a decade ago, Congress passed the Bipartisan Campaign Reform Act (BCRA), banning "soft money" contributions to national political parties and imposing limits on the amount and source of funds candidates may accept and spend. The law limited individual spending and prohibited corporate (including nonprofit and union) funding of political messages during a certain period prior to an election. That was the law until the Supreme Court in *Citizens United v. Federal Election Commission* found the law's restrictions on corporate and union election spending facially unconstitutional.[105] The Court reasoned that the BCRA's requirements that political donors be disclosed adequately addressed the government's concern that unrestricted corporate election spending might lead to political corruption. Direct limits on how corporations and unions could fund "electioneering communications" violated the First Amendment. Courts since have applied *Citizens United* to strike down numerous restrictions on political spending.[106]

Then the Court struck down another piece of the law, removing the cap on aggregate individual political contributions.[107] In *McCutcheon v. FEC*, the Court majority said the aggregate limit reduced an individual's ability to participate in the political process without advancing the government's interest in preventing corruption. "Congress may target only a specific type of corruption—'quid pro quo' corruption,"[108] Chief Justice

● REAL WORLD LAW

Opening the Floodgates

The Supreme Court's *Citizens United*[1] decision, which struck down limits on election spending by corporations and unions that the Court had upheld only seven years earlier, prompted widespread criticism. "The consequences for our democracy of today's deeply misguided decision will be grave, opening the door for wealthy donors to give, in aggregate, millions of dollars in direct contributions in a single election cycle. . . . Despite today's damaging decision, Americans remain committed to restoring a political system of, by, and for the people."[2]

Then when the Court's *McCutcheon*[3] decision eliminated a cap on individual spending, thousands of people turned out nationwide to protest what one newspaper called "one of the worst Supreme Court decisions of all time."[4] Organizations inundated Congress with demands that they amend the Constitution to "effectively regulate election spending."[5]

Congress had not acted as of 2017.

1. Citizens United v. FEC, 558 U.S. 310 (2010).
2. *PFAW Statement on the McCutcheon v. FEC Decision*, Apr. 20, 2014, www.pfaw.org/press-releases/2014/04/pfaw-statement-mccutcheon-v-fec-decision.
3. McCutcheon v. FEC, 134 S. Ct. 1434 (2014).
4. Mansar Gidfar, *McCutcheon Is One of the Worst Supreme Court Decisions of All Time—Here's What You Need to Know*, HuffPost Politics, Apr. 20, 2014, www.huffingtonpost.com/mansur-gidfar/mccutcheon-supreme-court_b_5077459.html.
5. *Id.*

John Roberts wrote for the Court. Quid pro quo corruption is bribery, the payment for a specific action by a candidate.

In the wake of *McCutcheon*, Charles and David Koch allegedly spent almost $900 million in the 2016 federal election.[109] In 2017, the nomination of Education Secretary Betsy DeVos drew criticism from those who said she had bought her cabinet seat through her family's substantial political contributions. During her Senate confirmation hearing, DeVos said it was possible her family had contributed $200 million to political campaigns "through the years."[110]

The Supreme Court also has ruled that government may refuse to assist employee political contributions.[111] The Court employed rational review to uphold an Idaho state ban on the use of government payroll deductions for political contributions. The majority reasoned that the Constitution imposed no affirmative obligation on government to facilitate such political activities and the ban advanced the state's interest in avoiding the appearance of partisan political activity.

SPEAKING ANONYMOUSLY

The Supreme Court has said anonymous political speech has an "honorable tradition" that "is a shield from the tyranny of the majority."[112] Finding a state ban on anonymous campaign literature unconstitutional, the Court said the state's interest in preventing fraud and political influence was sufficiently important, but the law was not narrowly tailored. A long line of cases protects anonymous political speech.[113]

However, in 2010 the Court suggested that citizens engaged in the political process do not have an absolute right to keep their identities secret.[114] The case involved a citizen referendum to repeal a Washington state law granting new rights to same-sex domestic partners. The state open records law (see Chapter 7) required release of the names of all those who had endorsed the referendum, but the referendum supporters feared reprisal and argued that disclosure violated the First Amendment. The Supreme Court applied strict scrutiny to find the ban constitutional on the grounds that public disclosure of referendum petitions was substantially related to the important government interest in preserving the integrity of balloting and elections. On remand, the lower court ruled that the First Amendment did not protect anonymity even when disclosure might facilitate harassment.[115]

● INTERNATIONAL LAW

Uncertain Speech Rights Online

David Paul Morris/Bloomberg via Getty Images

Because speech online reaches around the globe, any country's laws may affect speakers elsewhere.[1] Sometimes.[2] And court decisions about online speech vary.

For example, in 2014, the Supreme Court of Canada ruled that personal privacy rights prevented telecommunications companies from releasing internet user information to police without a court order.[3] Users have a reasonable expectation of anonymity online, the Canadian court ruled. Similarly, the U.S. Supreme Court in 2014 protected a suspect's cell phone from a warrantless search (see Chapter 6).[4]

In contrast, the U.K. House of Lords gave tentative support in 2014 for removing protection for anonymous online speech in order to facilitate detection and prosecution of speech crimes online.[5] "There is little point in criminalizing certain behavior and at the same time legitimately making that same behavior impossible to detect," the report said.

1. Liat Clark, *European Ruling on Anonymous Comment Liability Shouldn't Be Universally Damaging*, WIRED, Oct. 14, 2013, www.wired.co.uk/news/archive/2013-10/14/european-courts-privacy-ruling.
2. Danny O'Brien, *UK's Lords and EU Take Aim at Online Anonymity*, Aug. 5, 2014, www.eff.org/deeplinks/2014/08/uks-lords-and-eu-take-aim-online-anonymity.
3. Jacob Gershman, *Canadians Have a Right to Online Anonymity, Nation's Top Court Rules*, WALL STREET J. LAW BLOG, June 13, 2014, blogs.wsj.com/law/2014/06/13/canadians-have-a-right-to-online-anonymity-nations-top-court-rules.
4. Riley v. California, 134 S. Ct. 2473 (2014).
5. O'Brien, *supra* note 2.

ASSEMBLING AND SPEAKING IN PUBLIC AND NONPUBLIC PLACES

Daily events across the United States assemble citizens on public property to exchange ideas and associate freely. Each of these gatherings occurs in what the Supreme Court calls a **public forum**. The concept of public forums recognizes the long and central role of public oratory in the United States. The idea is that a lot of government property is essentially held in trust for use by the public; it is the public's space. An early Supreme Court decision involving a challenge to a city ordinance prohibiting the distribution of pamphlets in city streets and parks explained the idea as follows:

> Wherever the title of streets and parks may rest, they have immemorially been held in trust for the use of the public and, time out of mind, have been used for purposes of assembly, communicating thoughts between citizens, and discussing public questions. Such use of the streets and public places has, from ancient times, been a part of the privileges, immunities, rights, and liberties of citizens.[116]

The people have a First Amendment right to use such public property to express themselves. Access to public spaces without fear of government censorship or punishment is critical to open public debate and dissent.[117] The Court has ruled that the Constitution allows Nazis, Vietnam War protesters, civil rights activists and the homeless to march and assemble in public places.[118]

In 2011 in *Snyder v. Phelps*, the Court ruled that even "outrageous" speech on a public sidewalk about a public issue cannot be punished.[119] The father of a Marine killed in the Iraq War had sought damages from Westboro Baptist Church members for harm caused by their picketing at his son's funeral with signs reading "Thank God for dead soldiers" and "Fag troops." But the Court held that the First Amendment protects public picketing even when the messages "fall short of refined social or political commentary."

The people's right to speak and assemble in public forums is not absolute; it is balanced against other considerations. Public use of public forums must be compatible with the normal activity in that place. The Supreme Court has established a hierarchy of three types of public forums according to the nature of the place, the pattern of its primary activities and the history of public access.[120]

Lands historically intended for public use—such as parks, streets and sidewalks adjacent to many public buildings—are **traditional public forums**.[121] The public has a general and presumed right to use these places for expression. Thus, in 2013 the Sixth Circuit Court of Appeals struck down Michigan's 94-year-old ban on "begging in a public place." The court said begging is a protected form of speech and the state could not ban "an entire category of activity that the First Amendment protects."

Government may set up rules, hours and policies to facilitate use of traditional public forums. Rules that close public parks after dark or require permits for gatherings are constitutional if they are fairly applied and content neutral, meaning they are tailored to their purpose and do not discriminate because of the content of the group's ideas or politics. Appeals courts recently found restrictions on rallies on a town lawn[122] and disorderly gatherings in public places[123] unconstitutional because they prohibited more protected speech

public forum Government property held for use by the public, usually for purposes of exercising rights of speech and assembly.

traditional public forum Lands designed for public use and historically used for public gathering, discussion and association (e.g., public streets, sidewalks and parks). Free speech is protected in these areas.

▲ EMERGING LAW

Are Government Online Sites Public Forums?

In what may be a case of first impression, the Honolulu Police Department (HPD) paid attorney's fees to a gun advocacy group that filed suit after HPD deleted the group's comments and blocked its future postings to the department's Facebook page.[1] The case was "dismissed with prejudice" when HPD agreed to pay the fees and to develop a policy to govern its treatment of public Facebook comments with the assistance of the American Civil Liberties Union.

HPD said its Facebook page was "a forum open to the public," but it had regularly deleted comments, removed links to articles and banned comments by disfavored users without explanation, notice or opportunity for the user to challenge the actions.[2]

The court did not reach the First Amendment issue in the case, but the outcome may have implications for the many other police departments and government agencies that maintain a Facebook page and control public comments to it without a clearly established policy.[3]

1. Haw. Def. Found. v. Honolulu, 2014 U.S. Dist. LEXIS 83871 (D. Haw., June 19, 2014).
2. Haw. Def. Found. v. Honolulu, 2014 U.S. Dist. LEXIS 84266 (D. Haw., Apr. 22, 2014).
3. Brian Lee, *Police Butt Heads With Social Media Users*, Telegram & Gazette, Apr. 7, 2013, www.telegram.com/article/20130407/NEWS/104079799&Template=printart.

than needed to serve the town objectives. Government must demonstrate a compelling interest to ban all expressive activities or assembly in a traditional public forum.

The Supreme Court also has held that government may ban public picketing and protests from traditional public forums to protect core privacy, safety or health interests. Thus, the Court upheld a ban on targeted picketing outside a doctor's residence and no-protest buffer zones outside abortion clinics.[124] In 2012, the Court did not decide whether the First Amendment protected a protester's right to comment directly in 2006 to then–Vice President Dick Cheney at a public gathering.[125] In *Reichle v. Howards*, the protester claimed his arrest for harassment after criticizing Cheney violated the First Amendment. The Supreme Court disagreed; the Secret Service agents protecting Cheney were immune from suit because they acted "reasonably" under the established law.

designated public forum Government spaces or buildings that are available for public use (within limits).

The primary purpose of some government spaces or buildings is not to serve public assembly or speech. Yet public schools and university classrooms, high school newspapers and fairgrounds may provide ideal settings for public expression. In these spaces, when government chooses to allow public use, it creates **designated public forums**,[126] and government may limit their public use.

The government may restrict the times, places or manners of public use of a designated public forum to ensure that it does not conflict with the primary function of the property. Government may impose well-tailored, reasonable, content-neutral licensing and usage regulations. In general, the Supreme Court reviews regulations of designated, or limited, public forums under intermediate scrutiny, balancing the citizen right of free expression against the primary role of the facility. When the government facility is operating as a public forum, government officials may not have unfettered discretion over that use and may not make content-based discriminations among users.[127] Public access cannot be denied entirely without a compelling reason.

Some government property simply is not available for public use. **Nonpublic forums** exist where public access, assembly and speech would conflict with the proper functioning of the government service and where there is no history of public access. Courts generally defer to the government to determine when government property is off limits. In nonpublic forums, government behaves more like a private property owner and controls the space to achieve government objectives. Military bases, prisons, post office walkways, utility poles, airport terminals and private mailboxes are all nonpublic forums.[128] Government may exclude the entire public or certain speakers or messages from nonpublic forums on the basis of a reasonable or rational, viewpoint-neutral interest.[129]

nonpublic forum
Government-held property that is not available for public speech and assembly purposes.

Private Property as a Public Forum

Public forums, sometimes, though rarely, exist on private property. When private property replaces or functions as a traditional public space, it may be treated as a public forum. The law in this area is unclear. However, when the open area of an enclosed shopping mall or a large private parking lot is used widely for public assembly and expression, the Supreme

● REAL WORLD LAW

But Where Can I Speak?

The Supreme Court long has held that "the freedom of speech and of the press guaranteed by the Constitution embraces at least the liberty to discuss *publicly* and truthfully all matters of public concern without prior restraint or fear of subsequent punishment."[1] To advance this goal, the Court's public forum doctrine has established three types of public forum with varying free speech rights.[2]

- *Traditional public forums.* In areas established for public gatherings or where expressive activity historically has occurred, the Court applies a heightened form of intermediate scrutiny to protect speech from undue regulation.

- *Limited/designated public forum.* When government permits public use of spaces with other primary purposes, such as school buildings, restrictions on permitted public usage receive the same heightened intermediate scrutiny review. Outside the permitted public usage, the Court applies rational review to regulations of these spaces.

- *Nonpublic forum.* On property where the government's primary purpose precludes public use (e.g., inside the Pentagon or a prison), the Court subjects speech regulations to rational review.

One district court ruling suggests that social media and other communication technologies may provide virtual public forums.[3] Justice Anthony Kennedy might support that idea. He has said, "Minds are not changed in the streets and parks as they once were. To an increasing degree, the more significant interchanges of ideas and shaping of public consciousness occur in mass and electronic media."[4]

1. Thornhill v. Alabama, 310 U.S. 88, 101–02 (1940) (emphasis added).
2. *See, e.g.,* Madsen v. Women's Health Ctr., 512 U.S. 753 (1994); United States v. Kokinda, 497 U.S. 720 (1990); Frisby v. Schultz, 487 U.S. 474 (1988); United States v. Grace, 461 U.S. 171 (1983); Cox v. Louisiana, 379 U.S. 536 (1965); Schneider v. New Jersey, 308 U.S. 147 (1939).
3. Haw. Def. Found. v. Honolulu, 2014 U.S. Dist. LEXIS 83871 (D. Haw., June 19, 2014).
4. Denver Area Educ. Telecom. Consortium Inc. v. FCC, 518 U.S. 727, 802–03 (1996) (Kennedy, J., dissenting).

Court has said the private property owner sometimes may be required to allow public gatherings and free expression.[130]

The U.S. Supreme Court also has held that citizens' free speech and petition rights may remain intact in a privately owned shopping center.[131] The owners of a California shopping center argued that they had a right to exclude teenagers circulating a petition. In a very narrow ruling based in part on the broad speech protections of the California constitution, the Court in *PruneYard Shopping Center v. Robins* reasoned that protecting the free speech rights of the teenagers did not unduly impose on the rights of the property owner. The large mall was a peculiarly public space, the Court said, and the slight intrusion created by those circulating the petition did not infringe on the owner's own freedom of speech.

Some U.S. Supreme Court justices have suggested that *PruneYard* allows government to "coerce [the] creation of a speaker's forum" only in California.[132] Some believe that the First Amendment freedom of press should provide a right for news media to enter private property to gather information,[133] but most people agree that *PruneYard* does not extend to newsgathering situations.

Virtual Forums and Government Speakers

Sometimes government funds that subsidize expression create a virtual public forum. When government funds support general speech and associational activities, the government may not discriminate on the basis of the ideas expressed.[134] Selection criteria must be content neutral. Government may not discriminate when it imposes taxes or benefits on expression. Government spending may not, for example, disfavor large newspapers, general interest magazines or commercial publications.[135] Government collection and distribution of money does not always create a public forum. In fact, the Court has acknowledged that some government funding procedures have the express purpose of discriminating among applicants according to the ideas they express.

The National Endowment for the Arts (NEA), for example, funds artists based on the value and quality of the artistic proposals it reviews. NEA grants are designed to advance the NEA's objectives, not to create a public forum for art. Accordingly, the NEA may choose not to fund art it disfavors or finds indecent or offensive.[136] The same is true of book purchases for public school libraries. School libraries are not public forums for all printed materials; they provide curriculum- and age-appropriate materials to school students. Therefore, library choices based on the school-age appropriateness of books do not violate the Constitution.[137]

REQUIRING SPEECH

The First Amendment protects the right to remain silent. More than 40 years ago, New Hampshire law required license plates to display the state slogan, "Live Free or Die." George Maynard, a Jehovah's Witness, covered up the slogan he found "morally, ethically, religiously and politically abhorrent." The Court ruled that Maynard had a constitutional right "not to be coerced by the state into advertising a slogan" that violated his beliefs; the First Amendment protects an individual's right "to refrain from speaking."[138]

The Court also has ruled in a group of cases that private organizations cannot be forced to include individuals or to support messages with which they disagree.[139] In one famous case, organizers of the huge annual St. Patrick's Day parade in Boston refused to allow an LGBTQ alliance to participate. The alliance sued, arguing that its exclusion from the parade violated its freedom of speech. The trial court agreed. Because the parade had no expressive purpose, the court said, forced inclusion of alliance members in the event would cause no harm to the parade organizer's First Amendment rights.

A unanimous Supreme Court reversed. The Court said it was unnecessary to the alliance's message that it participate in the organizer's event. The alliance could reach the desired audience in a number of ways that would not infringe on the organizer's freedom of association and speech. The Court said, "Whatever the reason [for excluding the group], it boils down to the choice of a speaker not to propound a particular point of view, and that choice is presumed to lie beyond the government's power of control."[140] An LGBTQ alliance participated in Boston's St. Patrick's Day parade for the first time in 2015.[141]

Based on a desire not to compel undesired speech but on the basis that all film producers should be treated equally, the Tenth Circuit Court of Appeals refused to apply campaign disclosure requirements to political films made by Citizens United.[142] The court said the group's films were not "electioneering communication" and could find no legitimate basis to distinguish between the advocacy group's movies on political subjects and "legitimate press functions."[143] The First Amendment, it said, required film producers to be exempt from disclosure requirements.

CHAPTER SUMMARY

THE U.S. SUPREME COURT CONSISTENTLY has said the First Amendment does not prevent government from all regulations of speech or press. The framers of the First Amendment did not define "the freedom of speech and of the press," but British arguments against government censorship as a form of thought control beyond the limited power granted to government by the people influenced American thinking. The framers did *not* embrace the British notion that punishment for truthful criticism of government was acceptable. In colonial times, the First Amendment clearly prohibited licensing and direct government censorship, called prior restraint, of speech or press.

The Court has not established a clear, fixed definition of the freedoms of speech and press. The Court tends to avoid broad declarations of the meaning of the First Amendment and to interpret in the context of a specific case. Various theories, values and tools aid the Court in understanding the First Amendment's meaning. Different justices and Court opinions view First Amendment freedoms as fundamental rights or as mechanisms to advance important interests, such as self-governance. Today, with new media reshaping both speech and press, the Court provides different degrees of protection to different speakers and to different types of speech.

A range of tests and strategies are available to help the Court apply the First Amendment. When a government action falls within the power delegated to government, the Court uses minimum scrutiny, or rational review, and assumes the law is constitutional. If a law affects constitutionally protected rights, such as speech and press, the Court uses a heightened form of review. Using its form of scrutiny, the Court has determined that the Constitution places a near absolute ban on prior restraint and strongly disfavors any regulations that target content. However, the Court reviews laws that are *not* applied on the basis of the content of speech, content-neutral rules, under intermediate scrutiny and finds many are constitutional.

It is unclear how the Court's 2015 decision in *Reed* may affect its use of categories and locations of speech to help it determine case outcomes. Many Supreme Court precedents establish that political speech and speech in traditional public forums receive the strictest scrutiny and the greatest constitutional protection from government abridgement. Other types of speech and speech in locations where unhindered free speech may be disruptive generally receive intermediate scrutiny and less constitutional protection.

The First Amendment does not infringe on the right of the government to speak, establish policies and control the work-related speech of its employees. However, government may not limit public employees' speech unrelated to work. The Supreme Court has said the First Amendment also protects an individual's right to speak anonymously and to refrain from speaking. ■

CASES FOR STUDY

For study resources and a case archive go to **study.sagepub.com/medialaw6e**.

The first of this chapter's two case excerpts examines the First Amendment protection from prior restraints on the press. In *New York Times Co. v. United States*, the Supreme Court provided expedited review of a federal injunction against war reporting by The Times and The Washington Post based on leaked classified documents. The Court's careful delineation of the government's limited ability to exercise prior restraint on speech underscored the importance of the separation of powers and reaffirmed that the government has very limited authority over the press. The second excerpt, *Reed v. Town of Gilbert*, presents the Supreme Court's 2015 decision articulating what some believe is a new understanding of which laws are reviewed under strict scrutiny because they are defined as content based. Although the justices reach a unanimous decision, they do not all endorse the majority's definition of content-based laws or its automatic application of strict scrutiny to such laws.

THINKING ABOUT IT

The two case excerpts explore two fundamental approaches to understanding the First Amendment. One Supreme Court decision establishes the extent and limits of the First Amendment's protection from government prior restraint on the press. Another redefines the basic distinction between laws that regulate on the basis of content and those that do not. As you read these case excerpts, keep the following questions in mind:

- What justification does the Court offer *in New York Times Co. v. United States* for the First Amendment's nearly absolute ban on prior restraints?

- In *Reed v. Town of Gilbert*, why do the justices disagree on the definition of content neutrality?

- What do the two decisions indicate about the power of the First Amendment to limit government regulations of "the press" and of the people's right to speak through signs?

- Does the Court use the same level of scrutiny in both cases? How do you know?

New York Times Co. v. United States
SUPREME COURT OF THE UNITED STATES
403 U.S. 713 (1971)

PER CURIAM OPINION:
We granted certiorari in these cases in which the United States seeks to enjoin the New York Times and the Washington Post from publishing the contents of a classified study entitled "History of U.S. Decision-Making Process on Viet Nam Policy."

"Any system of prior restraints of expression comes to this Court bearing a heavy presumption against its constitutional validity." The Government "thus carries a heavy burden of showing justification for the imposition of such a restraint." The [lower courts] held that the Government had not met that burden. We agree.

The judgment of the Court of Appeals for the District of Columbia Circuit is therefore affirmed. The order of the Court of Appeals or the Second Circuit is reversed, and the case is remanded with directions to enter a judgment affirming the judgment of the District Court for the Southern District of New York. The stays entered June 25, 1971, by the Court are vacated. The judgments shall issue forthwith.

So ordered.

JUSTICE HUGO BLACK, with whom JUSTICE WILLIAM DOUGLAS joined, concurring:

I adhere to the view that the Government's case against the Washington Post should have been dismissed, and that the injunction against the New York Times should have been vacated without oral argument when the cases were first presented to this Court. I believe that every moment's continuance of the injunctions against these newspapers amounts to a flagrant, indefensible, and continuing violation of the First Amendment. . . .

In the First Amendment, the Founding Fathers gave the free press the protection it must have to fulfill its essential role in our democracy. The press was to serve the governed, not the governors. The Government's power to censor the press was abolished so that the press would remain forever free to censure the Government. The press was protected so that it could bare the secrets of government and inform the people. Only a free and unrestrained press can effectively expose deception in government. And paramount among the responsibilities of a free press is the duty to prevent any part of the government from deceiving the people and sending them off to distant lands to die of foreign fevers and foreign shot and shell. In my view, far from deserving condemnation for their courageous reporting, the New York Times, the Washington Post, and other newspapers should be commended for serving the purpose that the Founding Fathers saw so clearly. In revealing the workings of government that led to the Vietnam war,

the newspapers nobly did precisely that which the Founders hoped and trusted they would do. . . .

The word "security" is a broad, vague generality whose contours should not be invoked to abrogate the fundamental law embodied in the First Amendment. The guarding of military and diplomatic secrets at the expense of informed representative government provides no real security for our Republic. The Framers of the First Amendment, fully aware of both the need to defend a new nation and the abuses of the English and Colonial governments, sought to give this new society strength and security by providing that freedom of speech, press, religion, and assembly should not be abridged. . . .

JUSTICE WILLIAM DOUGLAS, with whom JUSTICE HUGO BLACK joined, concurring:

. . . It should be noted at the outset that the First Amendment provides that "Congress shall make no law . . . abridging the freedom of speech, or of the press." That leaves, in my view, no room for governmental restraint on the press. . . .

The dominant purpose of the First Amendment was to prohibit the widespread practice of governmental suppression of embarrassing information. It is common knowledge that the First Amendment was adopted against the widespread use of the common law of seditious libel to punish the dissemination of material that is embarrassing to the powers-that-be. The present cases will, I think, go down in history as the most dramatic illustration of that principle. . . .

Secrecy in government is fundamentally antidemocratic, perpetuating bureaucratic errors. Open debate and discussion of public issues are vital to our national health. On public questions there should be "uninhibited, robust, and wide-open" debate. . . .

JUSTICE WILLIAM BRENNAN, concurring:

. . . The error that has pervaded these cases from the outset was the granting of any injunctive relief whatsoever, interim or otherwise. The entire thrust of the Government's claim throughout these cases has been that publication of the material sought to be enjoined "could," or "might," or "may" prejudice the national interest in various ways. But the First Amendment tolerates absolutely no prior judicial restraints of the press predicated upon surmise or conjecture that untoward consequences may result. Our cases, it is true, have indicated that there is a single, extremely narrow class of cases in which the First Amendment's ban on prior judicial restraint may be overridden. Our cases have thus far indicated that such cases may arise only when the Nation "is at war," during which times "[n]o one would question but that a government might prevent actual obstruction to its recruiting service or the publication of the dates of transports or the number and location of troops." Even if the present world situation were assumed to be tantamount to a time of war, or if the power of presently available armaments would justify even in peacetime the suppression of information that would set in motion a nuclear holocaust, in neither of these actions has the Government presented or even alleged that publication of items from or based upon the material at issue would cause the happening of an event of that nature. "[T]he chief purpose of [the First Amendment's] guaranty [is] to prevent previous restraints upon publication." Thus, only governmental allegation and proof that publication must inevitably, directly, and immediately cause the occurrence of an event kindred to imperiling the safety of a transport already at sea can support even the issuance of an interim restraining order. . . . Unless and until the Government has clearly made out its case, the First Amendment commands that no injunction may issue. . . .

JUSTICE POTTER STEWART, with whom
JUSTICE BYRON WHITE joined, concurring:
. . . If the Constitution gives the Executive a large degree of unshared power in the conduct of foreign affairs and the maintenance of our national defense, then, under the Constitution, the Executive must have the largely unshared duty to determine and preserve the degree of internal security necessary to exercise that power successfully. It is an awesome responsibility, requiring judgment and wisdom of a high order. I should suppose that moral, political, and practical considerations would dictate that a very first principle of that wisdom would be an insistence upon avoiding secrecy for its own sake.

For when everything is classified, then nothing is classified, and the system becomes one to be disregarded by the cynical or the careless, and to be manipulated by those intent on self-protection or self-promotion. I should suppose, in short, that the hallmark of a truly effective internal security system would be the maximum possible disclosure, recognizing that secrecy can best be preserved only when credibility is truly maintained. . . .

JUSTICE BYRON WHITE, with whom
JUSTICE POTTER STEWART joined,
concurring:
I concur in today's judgments, but only because of the concededly extraordinary protection against prior restraints enjoyed by the press under our constitutional system. I do not say that in no circumstances would the First Amendment permit an injunction against publishing information about government plans or operations. . . . But I nevertheless agree that the United States has not satisfied the very heavy burden that it must meet to warrant an injunction against publication in these cases, at least in the absence of express and appropriately limited congressional authorization for prior restraints in circumstances such as these. . . .

CHIEF JUSTICE WARREN BURGER,
dissenting:
. . . As I see it, we have been forced to deal with litigation concerning rights of great magnitude without an adequate record, and surely without time for adequate treatment either in the prior proceedings or in this Court. . . .

I agree generally with Mr. Justice Harlan and Mr. Justice Blackmun, but I am not prepared to reach the merits.

JUSTICE JOHN HARLAN, with whom
CHIEF JUSTICE WARREN BURGER
and JUSTICE HARRY BLACKMUN join,
dissenting:
. . . The power to evaluate the "pernicious influence" of premature disclosure is not, however, lodged in the Executive alone. I agree that, in performance of its duty to protect the values of the First Amendment

against political pressures, the judiciary must review the initial Executive determination to the point of satisfying itself that the subject matter of the dispute does lie within the proper compass of the President's foreign relations power. . . . Moreover, the judiciary may properly insist that the determination that disclosure of the subject matter would irreparably impair the national security be made by the head of the Executive Department concerned. . . .

But, in my judgment, the judiciary may not properly go beyond these two inquiries and re-determine for itself the probable impact of disclosure on the national security. . . .

JUSTICE HARRY BLACKMUN, dissenting:
. . . The First Amendment, after all, is only one part of an entire Constitution. . . . Each provision of the Constitution is important, and I cannot subscribe to a doctrine of unlimited absolutism for the First Amendment at the cost of downgrading other provisions. First Amendment absolutism has never commanded a majority of this Court. What is needed here is a weighing, upon properly developed standards, of the broad right of the press to print and of the very narrow right of the Government to prevent. Such standards are not yet developed.

Reed v. Town of Gilbert
SUPREME COURT OF THE UNITED STATES
135 S. Ct. 2218 (2015)

JUSTICE CLARENCE THOMAS delivered the Court's opinion:
The town of Gilbert, Arizona (or Town), has adopted a comprehensive code governing the manner in which people may display outdoor signs (Sign Code or Code). The Sign Code identifies various categories of signs based on the type of information they convey, then subjects each category to different restrictions. One of the categories is "Temporary Directional Signs Relating to a Qualifying Event," loosely defined as signs directing the public to a meeting of a nonprofit group. The Code imposes more stringent restrictions on these signs than it does on signs conveying other messages. We hold that these provisions are content-based regulations of speech that cannot survive strict scrutiny.

The Sign Code prohibits the display of outdoor signs anywhere within the Town without a permit, but it then exempts 23 categories of signs from that requirement. These exemptions include everything from bazaar signs to flying banners. Three categories of exempt signs are particularly relevant here.

The first is "Ideological Sign[s]." This category includes any "sign communicating a message or ideas for noncommercial purposes that is not a Construction Sign, Directional Sign, Temporary Directional Sign Relating to a Qualifying Event, Political Sign, Garage Sale Sign, or a sign owned or required by a governmental agency." Of the three categories discussed here, the Code treats ideological signs most favorably, allowing them to be up to 20 square feet in area and to be placed in all "zoning districts" without time limits.

The second category is "Political Sign[s]." This includes any "temporary sign designed to influence the outcome of an election called by a public body." The Code treats these signs less favorably than ideological signs. The Code allows the placement of political signs up to 16 square feet on residential property and up to 32 square feet on nonresidential property, undeveloped municipal property, and "rights-of-way." These signs may be displayed up to 60 days before a primary election and up to 15 days following a general election.

The third category is "Temporary Directional Signs Relating to a Qualifying Event." This includes any "Temporary Sign intended to direct pedestrians, motorists, and other passersby to a 'qualifying event.'" A "qualifying event" is defined as any "assembly, gathering, activity, or meeting sponsored, arranged, or promoted by a religious, charitable, community service, educational, or other similar non-profit organization." The Code treats temporary directional signs even less favorably than political signs. Temporary directional signs may be no larger than six square feet. They may be placed on private property or on a public right-of-way, but no more than four signs may be placed on a single property at any time. And, they may be displayed no more than 12 hours before the "qualifying event" and no more than 1 hour afterward.

Petitioners Good News Community Church (Church) and its pastor, Clyde Reed, wish to advertise the time and location of their Sunday church services. The Church is a small, cash-strapped entity that owns no building, so it holds its services at elementary schools or other locations in or near the Town. In order to inform the public about its services, which are held in a variety of different locations, the Church began placing 15 to 20 temporary signs around the Town, frequently in the public right-of-way abutting the street. The signs typically displayed the Church's name, along with the time and location of the upcoming service. Church members would post the signs early in the day on Saturday and then remove them around midday on Sunday. The display of these signs requires little money and manpower, and thus has proved to be an economical and effective way for the Church to let the community know where its services are being held each week.

This practice caught the attention of the Town's Sign Code compliance manager, who twice cited the Church for violating the Code. The first citation noted that the Church exceeded the time limits for displaying its temporary directional signs. The second citation referred to the same problem, along with the Church's failure to include the date of the event on the signs. Town officials even confiscated one of the Church's signs, which Reed had to retrieve from the municipal offices.

Reed contacted the Sign Code Compliance Department in an attempt to reach an accommodation. His efforts proved unsuccessful. The Town's Code compliance manager informed the Church that there would be "no leniency under the Code" and promised to punish any future violations.

Shortly thereafter, petitioners filed a complaint . . . arguing that the Sign Code abridged their freedom of speech in violation of the First and Fourteenth Amendments. The District Court denied the petitioners' motion for a preliminary injunction. The Court of Appeals for the Ninth Circuit affirmed, holding that the Sign Code's provision regulating temporary directional signs did not regulate speech on the basis of content. . . . It then remanded for the District Court to determine in the first instance whether the Sign Code's distinctions among temporary directional signs, political signs, and ideological signs nevertheless constituted a content-based regulation of speech.

On remand, the District Court granted summary judgment in favor of the Town. The Court of Appeals again affirmed, holding that the Code's sign categories were content neutral. The court concluded that "the distinctions between Temporary Directional Signs, Ideological Signs, and Political Signs . . . are based on objective factors relevant to Gilbert's creation of the specific exemption from the permit requirement and do not otherwise consider the substance of the sign." . . . [T]he Court of Appeals concluded that the Sign Code is content neutral. As the court explained, "Gilbert did not adopt its regulation of speech because it disagreed with the message conveyed" and its "interests in regulat[ing] temporary signs are unrelated to the content of the sign." Accordingly, the court believed that the Code was "content-neutral as that term [has been] defined by the Supreme Court." In light of that determination, it applied a lower level of scrutiny to the Sign Code and concluded that the law did not violate the First Amendment.

We granted certiorari, and now reverse.

The First Amendment, applicable to the States through the Fourteenth Amendment, prohibits the enactment of laws "abridging the freedom of speech." Under that Clause, a government, including a municipal government vested with state authority, "has no power to restrict expression because of its message, its ideas, its subject matter, or its content." Content-based laws—those that target speech based on its communicative content—are presumptively unconstitutional and may be justified only if the government proves that they are narrowly tailored to serve compelling state interests.

Government regulation of speech is content based if a law applies to particular speech because of the topic discussed or the idea or message expressed. This commonsense meaning of the phrase "content based" requires a court to consider whether a regulation of speech "on its face" draws distinctions based on the message a speaker conveys. Some facial distinctions based on a message are obvious, defining regulated speech by particular subject matter, and others are more subtle, defining regulated speech by its function or purpose. Both are distinctions drawn based on the message a speaker conveys, and, therefore, are subject to strict scrutiny.

Our precedents have also recognized a separate and additional category of laws that, though facially content neutral, will be considered content-based regulations of speech: laws that cannot be "justified without reference to the content of the regulated speech," or that were adopted by the government "because of disagreement with the message [the speech] conveys." Those laws, like those that are content based on their face, must also satisfy strict scrutiny.

The Town's Sign Code is content based on its face. It defines "Temporary Directional Signs" on the basis of whether a sign conveys the message of directing the public to church or some other "qualifying event." It defines "Political Signs" on the basis of whether a sign's message is "designed to influence the outcome of an election." And it defines "Ideological Signs" on the basis of whether a sign "communicat[es] a message or ideas" that do not fit within the Code's other categories. It then subjects each of these categories to different restrictions.

The restrictions in the Sign Code that apply to any given sign thus depend entirely on the communicative content of the sign. . . . [T]he Church's signs inviting people to attend its worship services are treated differently from signs conveying other types of ideas. On its face, the Sign Code is a content-based regulation of speech. We thus have no need to consider the government's justifications or purposes for enacting the Code to determine whether it is subject to strict scrutiny.

In reaching the contrary conclusion, the Court of Appeals offered several theories to explain why the Town's Sign Code should be deemed content neutral. None is persuasive.

The Court of Appeals first determined that the Sign Code was content neutral because the Town "did not adopt its regulation of speech [based on] disagree[ment] with the message conveyed," and its justifications for regulating temporary directional signs were "unrelated to the content of the sign." In its brief to this Court, the United States similarly contends that a sign regulation is content neutral—even if it expressly draws distinctions based on the sign's communicative content—if those distinctions can be "'justified without reference to the content of the regulated speech.'"

But this analysis skips the crucial first step in the content-neutrality analysis: determining whether the law is content neutral on its face. A law that is content based on its face is subject to strict scrutiny regardless of the government's benign motive, content-neutral justification, or lack of "animus toward the ideas contained" in the regulated speech. We have thus made clear that "[i]llicit legislative intent is not the sine qua non of a violation of the First Amendment," and a party opposing the government "need adduce no evidence of an improper censorial motive." Although "a content-based purpose may be sufficient in certain circumstances to show that a regulation is content based, it is not necessary." In other words, an innocuous justification cannot transform a facially content-based law into one that is content neutral.

That is why we have repeatedly considered whether a law is content neutral on its face before turning to the law's justification or purpose. Because strict scrutiny applies either when a law is content based on its face or when the purpose and justification for the law are content based, a court must evaluate each question before it concludes that the law is content neutral and thus subject to a lower level of scrutiny.

The Court of Appeals and the United States misunderstand our decision in Ward [v. Rock Against Racism]. [It] had nothing to say about facially content-based restrictions because it involved a facially content-neutral ban on the use, in a city-owned music venue, of sound amplification systems not provided by the city. In that context, we looked to governmental motive, including whether the government had regulated speech "because of disagreement" with its message, and whether the regulation was "'justified without reference to the content of the speech.'" But Ward's framework "applies only if a statute is content neutral." Its rules thus operate "to protect speech," not "to restrict it."

The First Amendment requires no less. Innocent motives do not eliminate the danger of censorship presented by a facially content-based statute. . . . That is why the First Amendment expressly targets the operation of the laws—i.e., the "abridg[ement] of speech"—rather than merely the motives of those who enacted them. "The vice of content-based legislation . . . is not that it is always used for invidious, thought-control purposes, but that it lends itself to use for those purposes."

For instance, . . . one could easily imagine a Sign Code compliance manager who disliked the Church's substantive teachings deploying the Sign Code to make it more difficult for the Church to inform the public of the location of its services. Accordingly, we have repeatedly "rejected the argument that 'discriminatory . . . treatment is suspect under the First Amendment only when the legislature intends to suppress certain ideas.'"

The Court of Appeals next reasoned that the Sign Code was content neutral because it "does not mention any idea or viewpoint, let alone single one out for differential treatment." It reasoned that, for the purpose of the Code provisions, "[i]t makes no difference which candidate is supported, who sponsors the event, or what ideological perspective is asserted."

The Town seizes on this reasoning, insisting that "content based" is a term of art that "should be applied flexibly" with the goal of protecting "viewpoints and ideas from government censorship or favoritism." In the Town's view, a sign regulation that "does not censor or favor particular viewpoints or ideas" cannot be content based. The Sign Code allegedly passes this test because its treatment of temporary directional signs does not raise any concerns that the government

is "endorsing or suppressing 'ideas or viewpoints,'" and the provisions for political signs and ideological signs "are neutral as to particular ideas or viewpoints" within those categories.

This analysis conflates two distinct but related limitations that the First Amendment places on government regulation of speech. Government discrimination among viewpoints—or the regulation of speech based on "the specific motivating ideology or the opinion or perspective of the speaker"—is a "more blatant" and "egregious form of content discrimination." But it is well established that "[t]he First Amendment's hostility to content-based regulation extends not only to restrictions on particular viewpoints, but also to prohibition of public discussion of an entire topic."

Thus, a speech regulation targeted at specific subject matter is content based even if it does not discriminate among viewpoints within that subject matter. For example, a law banning the use of sound trucks for political speech—and only political speech—would be a content-based regulation, even if it imposed no limits on the political viewpoints that could be expressed. The Town's Sign Code likewise singles out specific subject matter for differential treatment, even if it does not target viewpoints within that subject matter. Ideological messages are given more favorable treatment than messages concerning a political candidate, which are themselves given more favorable treatment than messages announcing an assembly of like-minded individuals. That is a paradigmatic example of content-based discrimination.

Finally, the Court of Appeals characterized the Sign Code's distinctions as turning on "the content-neutral elements of who is speaking through the sign and whether and when an event is occurring." That analysis is mistaken on both factual and legal grounds.

To start, the Sign Code's distinctions are not speaker based. The restrictions for political, ideological, and temporary event signs apply equally no matter who sponsors them. If a local business, for example, sought to put up signs advertising the Church's meetings, those signs would be subject to the same limitations as such signs placed by the Church. And if Reed had decided to display signs in support of a particular candidate, he could have made those signs far larger—and kept them up for far longer—than signs inviting people to attend his church services. If the Code's distinctions were truly speaker based, both types of signs would receive the same treatment.

In any case, the fact that a distinction is speaker based does not, as the Court of Appeals seemed to believe, automatically render the distinction content neutral. Because "[s]peech restrictions based on the identity of the speaker are all too often simply a means to control content," we have insisted that "laws favoring some speakers over others demand strict scrutiny when the legislature's speaker preference reflects a content preference." Thus, a law limiting the content of newspapers, but only newspapers, could not evade strict scrutiny simply because it could be characterized as speaker based. Likewise, a content-based law that restricted the political speech of all corporations would not become content neutral just because it singled out corporations as a class of speakers. . . .

Nor do the Sign Code's distinctions hinge on "whether and when an event is occurring." The Code does not permit citizens to post signs on any topic whatsoever within a set period leading up to an election, for example. . . .

And, just as with speaker-based laws, the fact that a distinction is event based does not render it content neutral. . . . A regulation that targets a sign because it conveys an idea about a specific event is no less content based than a regulation that targets a sign because it conveys some other idea. Here, the Code singles out signs bearing a particular message: the time and location of a specific event. This type of ordinance may seem like a perfectly rational way to regulate signs, but a clear and firm rule governing content neutrality is an essential means of protecting the freedom of speech, even if laws that might seem "entirely reasonable" will sometimes be "struck down because of their content-based nature."

Because the Town's Sign Code imposes content-based restrictions on speech, those provisions can stand only if they survive strict scrutiny, "which requires the Government to prove that the restriction furthers a compelling interest and is narrowly tailored to achieve that interest." Thus, it is the Town's

burden to demonstrate that the Code's differentiation between temporary directional signs and other types of signs, such as political signs and ideological signs, furthers a compelling governmental interest and is narrowly tailored to that end. The Town cannot do so. It has offered only two governmental interests in support of the distinctions the Sign Code draws: preserving the Town's aesthetic appeal and traffic safety. Assuming for the sake of argument that those are compelling governmental interests, the Code's distinctions fail as hopelessly underinclusive.

Starting with the preservation of aesthetics, temporary directional signs are "no greater an eyesore," than ideological or political ones. Yet the Code allows unlimited proliferation of larger ideological signs while strictly limiting the number, size, and duration of smaller directional ones. The Town cannot claim that placing strict limits on temporary directional signs is necessary to beautify the Town while at the same time allowing unlimited numbers of other types of signs that create the same problem.

The Town similarly has not shown that limiting temporary directional signs is necessary to eliminate threats to traffic safety, but that limiting other types of signs is not. The Town has offered no reason to believe that directional signs pose a greater threat to safety than do ideological or political signs. If anything, a sharply worded ideological sign seems more likely to distract a driver than a sign directing the public to a nearby church meeting.

In light of this underinclusiveness, the Town has not met its burden to prove that its Sign Code is narrowly tailored to further a compelling government interest. . . .

Our decision today will not prevent governments from enacting effective sign laws. The Town asserts that an "'absolutist'" content-neutrality rule would render "virtually all distinctions in sign laws . . . subject to strict scrutiny," but that is not the case. Not "all distinctions" are subject to strict scrutiny, only content-based ones are. Laws that are content neutral are instead subject to lesser scrutiny.

The Town has ample content-neutral options available to resolve problems with safety and aesthetics. For example, its current Code regulates many aspects of signs that have nothing to do with a sign's message:

size, building materials, lighting, moving parts, and portability. And on public property, the Town may go a long way toward entirely forbidding the posting of signs, so long as it does so in an evenhanded, content-neutral manner. Indeed, some lower courts have long held that similar content-based sign laws receive strict scrutiny, but there is no evidence that towns in those jurisdictions have suffered catastrophic effects.

We acknowledge that a city might reasonably view the general regulation of signs as necessary because signs "take up space and may obstruct views, distract motorists, displace alternative uses for land, and pose other problems that legitimately call for regulation." At the same time, the presence of certain signs may be essential, both for vehicles and pedestrians, to guide traffic or to identify hazards and ensure safety. A sign ordinance narrowly tailored to the challenges of protecting the safety of pedestrians, drivers, and passengers—such as warning signs marking hazards on private property, signs directing traffic, or street numbers associated with private houses—well might survive strict scrutiny. The signs at issue in this case, including political and ideological signs and signs for events, are far removed from those purposes. As discussed above, they are facially content based and are neither justified by traditional safety concerns nor narrowly tailored.

•••

We reverse the judgment of the Court of Appeals and remand the case for proceedings consistent with this opinion.

It is so ordered.

JUSTICE SAMUEL ALITO, with whom JUSTICE ANTHONY KENNEDY and JUSTICE SONIA SOTOMAYOR joined, concurring.

I join the opinion of the Court but add a few words of further explanation.

As the Court holds, what we have termed "content-based" laws must satisfy strict scrutiny. Content-based laws merit this protection because they present, albeit sometimes in a subtler form, the same dangers as laws that regulate speech based on viewpoint.

Limiting speech based on its "topic" or "subject" favors those who do not want to disturb the status quo. Such regulations may interfere with democratic self-government and the search for truth.

As the Court shows, the regulations at issue in this case are replete with content-based distinctions, and as a result they must satisfy strict scrutiny. This does not mean, however, that municipalities are powerless to enact and enforce reasonable sign regulations. . . .*

In addition to regulating signs put up by private actors, government entities may also erect their own signs consistent with the principles that allow governmental speech. They may put up all manner of signs to promote safety, as well as directional signs and signs pointing out historic sites and scenic spots.

Properly understood, today's decision will not prevent cities from regulating signs in a way that fully protects public safety and serves legitimate esthetic objectives.

———————

* Of course, content-neutral restrictions on speech are not necessarily consistent with the First Amendment. Time, place, and manner restrictions "must be narrowly tailored to serve the government's legitimate, content-neutral interests." But they need not meet the high standard imposed on viewpoint- and content-based restrictions.

JUSTICE STEPHEN BREYER, concurring.

I join JUSTICE KAGAN's separate opinion. Like JUSTICE KAGAN, I believe that categories alone cannot satisfactorily resolve the legal problem before us. The First Amendment requires greater judicial sensitivity both to the Amendment's expressive objectives and to the public's legitimate need for regulation than a simple recitation of categories, such as "content discrimination" and "strict scrutiny," would permit. In my view, the category "content discrimination" is better considered . . . as a rule of thumb, rather than as an automatic "strict scrutiny" trigger, leading to almost certain legal condemnation.

To use content discrimination to trigger strict scrutiny sometimes makes perfect sense. There are cases in which the Court has found content discrimination an unconstitutional method for suppressing a viewpoint. And there are cases where the Court has found content discrimination to reveal that rules governing a traditional public forum are, in fact, not a neutral way of fairly managing the forum in the interest of all speakers. In these types of cases, strict scrutiny is often appropriate, and content discrimination has thus served a useful purpose.

But content discrimination, while helping courts to identify unconstitutional suppression of expression, cannot and should not always trigger strict scrutiny. To say that it is not an automatic "strict scrutiny" trigger is not to argue against that concept's use. I readily concede, for example, that content discrimination, as a conceptual tool, can sometimes reveal weaknesses in the government's rationale for a rule that limits speech. . . . I also concede that, whenever government disfavors one kind of speech, it places that speech at a disadvantage, potentially interfering with the free marketplace of ideas and with an individual's ability to express thoughts and ideas that can help that individual determine the kind of society in which he wishes to live, help shape that society, and help define his place within it.

Nonetheless, in these latter instances to use the presence of content discrimination automatically to trigger strict scrutiny and thereby call into play a strong presumption against constitutionality goes too far. That is because virtually all government activities involve speech, many of which involve the regulation of speech. Regulatory programs almost always require content discrimination. And to hold that such content discrimination triggers strict scrutiny is to write a recipe for judicial management of ordinary government regulatory activity. . . .

I recognize that the Court could escape the problem by watering down the force of the presumption against constitutionality that "strict scrutiny" normally carries with it. But, in my view, doing so will weaken the First Amendment's protection in instances where "strict scrutiny" should apply in full force.

The better approach is to generally treat content discrimination as a strong reason weighing against the constitutionality of a rule where a traditional public forum, or where viewpoint discrimination, is threatened, but elsewhere treat it as a rule of thumb, finding it a helpful, but not determinative legal tool, in an appropriate case, to determine the strength of a justification. I would use content discrimination as a supplement to a more basic analysis, which, tracking most of our First Amendment cases, asks whether the regulation at issue works harm to First Amendment interests that is disproportionate in light of the relevant regulatory objectives. Answering this question requires examining the seriousness of the harm to speech, the importance of the countervailing objectives, the extent to which the law will achieve those objectives, and whether there are other, less restrictive ways of doing so. . . .

Here, regulation of signage along the roadside, for purposes of safety and beautification is at issue. There is no traditional public forum nor do I find any general effort to censor a particular viewpoint. Consequently, the specific regulation at issue does not warrant "strict scrutiny." Nonetheless, for the reasons that JUSTICE KAGAN sets forth, I believe that the Town of Gilbert's regulatory rules violate the First Amendment. I consequently concur in the Court's judgment only.

JUSTICE ELENA KAGAN, with whom JUSTICE RUTH BADER GINSBURG and JUSTICE STEPHEN BREYER joined, concurring.

Countless cities and towns across America have adopted ordinances regulating the posting of signs, while exempting certain categories of signs based on their subject matter. For example, some municipalities generally prohibit illuminated signs in residential neighborhoods, but lift that ban for signs that identify the address of a home or the name of its owner or occupant. In other municipalities, safety signs such as "Blind Pedestrian Crossing" and "Hidden Driveway" can be posted without a permit, even as other permanent signs require one. Elsewhere, historic site markers—for example, "George Washington Slept Here"—are also exempt from general regulations. And similarly, the federal Highway Beautification Act limits signs along interstate highways unless, for instance, they direct travelers to "scenic and historical attractions" or advertise free coffee.

Given the Court's analysis, many sign ordinances of that kind are now in jeopardy. Says the

Justice Steven Breyer

majority: When laws "single[] out specific subject matter," they are "facially content based"; and when they are facially content based, they are automatically subject to strict scrutiny. And although the majority holds out hope that some sign laws with subject-matter exemptions "might survive" that stringent review, the likelihood is that most will be struck down. After all, it is the "rare case[] in which a speech restriction withstands strict scrutiny." To clear that high bar, the government must show that a content-based distinction "is necessary to serve a compelling state interest and is narrowly drawn to achieve that end."

So on the majority's view, courts would have to determine that a town has a compelling interest in informing passersby where George Washington slept. . . . The consequence—unless courts water down strict scrutiny to something unrecognizable—is that our communities will find themselves in an unenviable bind: They will have to either repeal the exemptions that allow for helpful signs on streets and sidewalks, or else lift their sign restrictions altogether and resign themselves to the resulting clutter

Although the majority insists that applying strict scrutiny to all such ordinances is "essential" to protecting First Amendment freedoms, I find it challenging to understand why that is so. This Court's decisions articulate two important and related reasons for subjecting content-based speech regulations to the most exacting standard of review. The first is "to preserve an uninhibited marketplace of ideas in which truth will ultimately prevail." The second is to ensure that the government has not regulated speech "based on hostility—or favoritism—towards the underlying message expressed." Yet the subject-matter exemptions included in many sign ordinances do not implicate those concerns. . . .

We apply strict scrutiny to facially content-based regulations of speech, in keeping with the rationales just described, when there is any "realistic possibility that official suppression of ideas is afoot." That is always the case when the regulation facially differentiates on the basis of viewpoint. It is also the case (except in non-public or limited public forums) when a law restricts "discussion of an entire topic" in public debate.

Indeed, the precise reason the majority applies strict scrutiny here is that "the Code singles out signs bearing a particular message: the time and location of a specific event." We have stated that "[i]f the marketplace of ideas is to remain free and open, governments must not be allowed to choose 'which issues are worth discussing or debating.'" And we have recognized that such subject-matter restrictions, even though viewpoint-neutral on their face, may "suggest[] an attempt to give one side of a debatable public question an advantage in expressing its views to the people." Subject-matter regulation, in other words, may have the intent or effect of favoring some ideas over others. When that is realistically possible—when the restriction "raises the specter that the Government may effectively drive certain ideas or viewpoints from the marketplace"—we insist that the law pass the most demanding constitutional test.

But when that is not realistically possible, we may do well to relax our guard so that "entirely reasonable" laws imperiled by strict scrutiny can survive.

This point is by no means new. . . . Our cases have been far less rigid than the majority admits in applying strict scrutiny to facially content-based laws—including in cases just like this one [when] the law's enactment and enforcement revealed "not even a hint of bias or censorship. . . . The majority could easily have taken [that] tack here.

The Town of Gilbert's defense of its sign ordinance—most notably, the law's distinctions between directional signs and others—does not pass strict scrutiny, or intermediate scrutiny, or even the laugh test. . . . The absence of any sensible basis for [the law's] distinctions dooms the Town's ordinance under even the intermediate scrutiny that the Court typically applies to "time, place, or manner" speech regulations. Accordingly, there is no need to decide in this case whether strict scrutiny applies to every sign ordinance in every town across this country containing a subject-matter exemption.

I suspect this Court and others will regret the majority's insistence today on answering that question in the affirmative. . . . Because I see no reason why such an easy case calls for us to cast a constitutional pall on reasonable regulations quite unlike the law before us, I concur only in the judgment.

The character of every act depends upon the circumstance in which it is done. . . . The question in every case is whether the words used are used in such circumstances and are of such a nature as to create a clear and present danger that they will bring about the substantive evils that Congress has a right to prevent. It is a question of proximity and degree.

—U.S. Supreme Court Justice Oliver Wendell Holmes[1]

In 2016, the Third Circuit Court of Appeals reinstated Anthony Elonis' conviction for threatening his wife and others on Facebook. True threats, even when disguised as rap lyrics, are not protected speech, the court said.

3 SPEECH DISTINCTIONS
Different Categories Trigger Distinct Treatment

SUPPOSE . . .

. . . a man posts original rap lyrics filled with violent language about his wife and children, the police, a kindergarten class and an FBI agent on his Facebook page. He includes statements that the lyrics are "fictitious" artistic First Amendment expression not directed toward real individuals. The jury decides a reasonable reader would find the posts threatening, convicts him of the federal crime of conveying threats across state lines and sentences him to four years in jail. The appeals court affirms. But can song lyrics pose a criminal threat if you didn't intend to threaten? Does it matter that you communicated them online to your Facebook "friends"? Look for the U.S. Supreme Court's answers in the discussion and excerpt of *Elonis v. United States*[2] in this chapter.

Based on the foundation established in Chapter 2, this chapter examines how courts determine the boundaries of protected speech. It explores the various types of expression at the fringes of First Amendment protection and the special case of speech in and around public schools and universities.

A cornerstone of First Amendment analysis is that it does not prohibit all laws that infringe upon speech. To determine when laws violate the First Amendment, courts sometimes balance the benefits of the expression against any harm it poses to competing values. This ad hoc balancing is highly fact specific and does not provide clear rules that allow people to generalize the outcome to other, similar situations.

Cases for Study

- *Tinker v. Des Moines Independent Community School District*
- *Elonis v. United States*

Courts primarily use a categorical approach to resolve First Amendment conflicts. This process subjects broad categories of speech to predetermined types of court review. Once a court determines that the expression belongs to a specific category, it then applies the rules developed in earlier cases to decide the case outcome. Some categories of speech—blackmail, perjury, false advertising and obscenity, for example—are unprotected categories. If the speech category is protected, courts then look to the location of the speech and the nature of the law to determine the appropriate scrutiny to review the case.

Some categories of speech, such as hate speech and true threats, are not defined clearly. When conflicts involve these categories, courts look at the language of the statute, the circumstances and the level of harm to determine whether the speech is protected. If the harm is likely to be cataclysmic, society's interest generally outweighs concerns about protecting the speech. One difficulty, though, is that the seriousness of harm caused by the speech can only be guessed in advance.

NATIONAL SECURITY AND TRANQUILITY

It is difficult to determine when speech threatens national security or what speech must be curbed to provide for the public peace and tranquility. Decisions tend to reflect the national mood and the contemporary realities. During times of war or national unrest, courts often see radical speech and protest as more dangerous than they would during times of calm.[3] The Supreme Court has not created legal rules that consistently counterbalance the urge to stifle speech during times of instability.[4] Because the country moves from peace to war and back, the relative freedom to express unpopular ideas also shifts, undermining the promised stability of the law.[5]

LANDMARK CASES IN CONTEXT

Key   ■ Event
◆ Cases

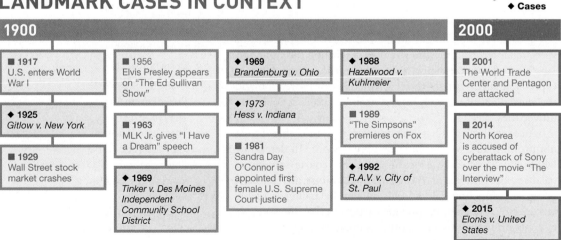

1900

- ■ 1917
  U.S. enters World War I
- ◆ 1925
  Gitlow v. New York
- ■ 1929
  Wall Street stock market crashes

- ■ 1956
  Elvis Presley appears on "The Ed Sullivan Show"
- ■ 1963
  MLK Jr. gives "I Have a Dream" speech
- ◆ 1969
  Tinker v. Des Moines Independent Community School District

- ◆ 1969
  Brandenburg v. Ohio
- ◆ 1973
  Hess v. Indiana
- ■ 1981
  Sandra Day O'Connor is appointed first female U.S. Supreme Court justice

- ◆ 1988
  Hazelwood v. Kuhlmeier
- ■ 1989
  "The Simpsons" premieres on Fox
- ◆ 1992
  R.A.V. v. City of St. Paul

2000

- ■ 2001
  The World Trade Center and Pentagon are attacked
- ■ 2014
  North Korea is accused of cyberattack of Sony over the movie "The Interview"
- ◆ 2015
  Elonis v. United States

● REAL WORLD LAW

Democracy's Unreasoned, Uncivil Promise

Vehement expression of opposing ideas is not the antithesis of free speech, but it does not necessarily produce informed democratic debate.[1] When raucous name-calling, hate-filled signs and near-threats in the streets replace the reasoned exchange of ideas, free speech may seem pathological.

Law professor Martin Redish suggests that concern about speech "pathology pervades the flow of American political history," and the Supreme Court rules accordingly. "Virtually all periods of strong political dissent throughout the nation's history have been met with a corresponding rise in repress[ion]."[2]

Uncivil discord may not advance democratic debate or inform citizens, but it may be a cost of democracy.

"The labels 'civility' and 'incivility' . . . effectively function as exclusion instruments," according to one legal scholar. "Although they create the appearance of inclusiveness and openness to contrarian views," they work to silence dissenting voices.[3]

---

1. David Estlund, *Democracy and the Real Speech Situation, in* Deliberative Democracy and Its Discontents 76 (Samantha Besson & Jose Luis Marti eds., 2006).
2. Martin Redish, The Logic of Persecution: Free Expression and the McCarthy Era 54, 62 (2006).
3. Barack Orbach, *On Hubris, Civility, and Incivility*, 54 Ariz. Law Rev. 443 (2012), ssrn.com/abstract=2046796.

Threats to National Security

Government efforts to punish speech that threatens its authority or undermines the security of the nation did not end in 1801 when the Sedition Act (discussed in Chapter 2) expired. Both federal and state legislatures have enacted laws to protect the public from speakers who would incite violence or the overthrow of government. Sometimes such laws infringe protected speech, but well-crafted laws that target the speech related to illegal conspiracies, advocacy of terrorism and treason generally are constitutional.

In *Holder v. Humanitarian Law Project (HLP)*, the U.S. Supreme Court ruled 6–3 that a federal ban on "material support" to terrorists did not violate the First Amendment, even when the law prevented support of legal expressive activities.[6] The **USA PATRIOT Act**'s[7] ban defined "material support" as *any* service, training, expert advice or assistance to a designated terrorist organization. The law placed a range of political organizing, activism and speech within the category of support for terrorism. The State Department said the ban played "a critical role in our fight against terrorism."[8]

Humanitarian Law Project involved a nonprofit organization that said the ban prevented it from offering training on how to negotiate peace to members of the Kurdistan Workers' Party, also known as the PKK, a federally designated terrorist organization. The group said the ban was overbroad and had a **chilling effect** on speech and associations protected by the First Amendment. Government actions that discourage the exercise of a constitutional right cause a chilling effect.

The Supreme Court said that, "given the sensitive interests in national security and foreign affairs at stake," it would defer to the government's judgment regarding the dangers of the group's activities.[9] The Court upheld the ban and said the law **as applied** to HLP was neither vague nor overbroad. Although "the scope of the material-support

USA PATRIOT Act The Uniting and Strengthening America by Providing Appropriate Tools Required to Intercept and Obstruct Terrorism Act of 2001. The act gave law enforcement agencies greater authority to combat terrorism.

chilling effect The discouragement of a constitutional right, especially free speech, by any government practice that creates uncertainty about the proper exercise of that right.

as applied A legal phrase referring to interpretation of a statute on the basis of actual effects on the parties in the present case.

statute may not be clear in every application, . . . the statutory terms are clear in their application to plaintiffs' proposed conduct," the Court wrote.[10] The law's ban on training of the PKK constitutionally advanced the government's compelling interest in "provid[ing] for the common defense," the Court concluded.[11]

In 2013, the First Circuit Court of Appeals relied on the Patriot Act's material support ban to uphold Tarek Mehanna's conviction for terrorism for his online postings of his accurate translations of al-Qaida materials.[12] Relying on the Supreme Court's ruling in *Humanitarian Law Project*,[13] the court concluded that Mehanna knowingly "coordinated" with and provided material support to a foreign terrorist organization through his posts.[14] Although the conviction clearly targeted Mehanna's online speech, the court said that congressional debate over the Patriot Act had ensured the law did not violate the First Amendment. The American Civil Liberties Union argued that such deference to Congress eliminated the role of the courts as independent reviewer of political judgments about when speech illegally advances terrorism.[15] The Patriot Act was signed within weeks of the terrorist attack on the United States on 9/11.

Critics argue that the Patriot Act as well as other laws that increase government surveillance to advance the war on terrorism threaten fundamental civil liberties.[16] However, as Chief Justice William H. Rehnquist once said, "It is neither desirable nor is it remotely likely that civil liberty will occupy as favored a position in wartime as it does in peacetime."[17]

Some Supreme Court decisions support Rehnquist's view. For example, during the post–World War II "Red Scare," the Court said the First Amendment did not stop government from requiring its employees to swear loyalty oaths and reject communism. The Court later said the Constitution permitted the U.S. attorney general to exclude a foreign economist from visiting and speaking at U.S. universities simply because he was a Marxist.[18]

When online content advances terrorism or other extreme harms, Section 230 of the Communications Decency Act protects digital service providers from liability for third-party content. In 2016, the First Circuit Court of Appeals dismissed a suit brought by three minors, who were victims of sexual trafficking, against an online advertising site.[19] In what some called a "big win" for freedom of speech,[20] the court said the difficult balance between protecting young women from "circumstances that evoke outrage" and protecting the freedom of speech advanced through online providers must be struck in favor of the speech. The court said the broad protections of the CDA clearly establish "the right to publish the speech of others in the information age." The Supreme Court declined to review the case of *Jane Doe v. Backpage.com*.[21]

A federal district court judge similarly held that Section 230 of the CDA protected Twitter from a claim that it had materially contributed to the spread of Islamic State group propaganda and terrorism that caused the murder of a contractor in Jordan.[22] The court dismissed Tamara Fields' argument that Twitter's "refusal to take any meaningful action" to deter IS incitement of violence through pro-terrorist posts made it liable for her husband's murder by IS.

EVOLVING COURT TESTS TO PROTECT DISRUPTIVE SPEECH

The Supreme Court has developed several tests to help it decide when unpopular or disturbing speech must be protected in order to encourage robust discussion and when it may be punished. The Court has said free expression is not protected if it causes imminent harm or plays "no essential part of any exposition of ideas, and [is] of such slight social value as a step to truth that any benefit that may be derived from [it] is clearly outweighed by the social interest in order and morality."[23] No bright lines define the boundaries of this category. The border between protected and unprotected speech is not fixed. The Court's tests afford leeway in response to changing circumstances.

From a Bad Tendency to a Clear and Present Danger

Almost a century ago, Justice Oliver Wendell Holmes wrote for a unanimous Supreme Court that government had a right and a duty to prevent speech that presented a "**clear and present danger**" to the nation.[24] The case of *Schenck v. United States* began when Charles Schenck, a Socialist Party member, mailed anti-draft pamphlets to men in Philadelphia. The pamphlets encouraged readers to reject the government's pro-war philosophy and oppose U.S. participation in World War I. Schenck was convicted of violating the Espionage Act of 1917, which was enacted to unify the nation behind the war effort.

In affirming Schenck's conviction, the Court said the mailing had a "bad tendency" that could endanger national security. Justice Holmes said ordinarily harmless words may become criminal during times of war because of the heightened danger they pose: "It is a question of proximity and degree."[25] Common sense indicates that "the most stringent protection of free speech would not protect a man in falsely shouting fire in a theatre and causing a panic."[26] Nor would it protect an individual in a military recruitment office falsely shouting, "I have a bomb."

A unanimous Court affirmed other convictions under the Espionage Act of anti-war protests, speeches and pamphlets the Court said might tend to endanger the nation. In one case, the Court upheld a 10-year prison term for publishing writings that questioned the constitutionality of the draft and the merits of the war.[27] The Court said the publications presented "a little breath [that] would be enough to kindle a flame" of unrest.[28] The Court also upheld the conviction of a speaker who told Socialist Party conventioneers, "You are fit for something better than slavery and cannon fodder."[29] The jury relied on the speaker's court testimony that he abhorred the war to demonstrate both his intent and the likelihood he would harm the war effort.

The Court also used this so-called bad-tendency standard to uphold a Sedition Act conviction of five friends whose pamphlets criticized U.S. interference in the Russian Revolution and encouraged strikes at U.S. munitions factories.[30] The leaflets told workers to oppose "the hypocrisy of the United States and her allies." This time writing in dissent, Justice Holmes said the "surreptitious publishing of a silly leaflet by an unknown man" did not pose a sufficiently grave and imminent danger to permit punishment.[31] The First Amendment requires government to protect diverse and loathsome opinions, he wrote, "unless they so imminently threaten immediate interference with the lawful and pressing purposes of the law that an immediate check is required to save the country."[32] This Holmes dissent in *Abrams v. United States* transformed his interpretation of the First Amendment and created the clear and present danger test.

The Court relied on the clear and present danger test for 50 years most often to affirm punishment of communists.[33] During the Red Scare of the 1920s, the Court affirmed the conviction of an immigrant for publication and distribution of Socialist Party literature

clear and present danger Doctrine establishing that restrictions on First Amendment rights will be upheld if they are necessary to prevent an extremely serious and imminent harm.

● REAL WORLD LAW

Just Clowning Around

Don Emmert/Getty

Chabad headquarters in Brooklyn, N.Y.

A New Jersey man was sentenced in federal court to more than two years in prison for online comments supporting terror attacks and hinting that his followers should target Jewish organizations.[1]

Yousef al-Khattab, founder of Revolution Muslim, posted a photo and map of the Brooklyn headquarters of the Chabad Jewish organization with comments that readers of his website should find Chabad's leaders and "deal with them directly at their homes."

Al-Khattab pleaded guilty to using the internet to advocate violence and put people in fear of injury, but he said he was a "clown" who never intended to call for violence and should be held responsible only "for what I say, not how other people understand it."

Prosecutors connected at least a dozen al-Khattab followers to terrorist plots or organizations, according to court records.

1. Matt Azpotosky, *New Jersey Man Sentenced to Prison for Extremist Islamic Web Posts*, WASH. POST, Apr. 25, 2014, www.washingtonpost.com/local/crime/new-jersey-man-to-be-sentenced-for-extremist-islamic-web-posts/2014/04/24/406e65a8-cbc4-11e3-93eb-6c0037dde2ad_story.html; *Jewish Man Who Became Radical Islamist Sentenced to Prison*, NPR, Apr. 25, 2014, www.npr.org/blogs/thetwo-way/2014/04/25/306905860/jewish-man-who-became-radical-islamist-sentenced-to-prison.

urging the rise of socialism in the United States.[34] Without evidence that the pamphlets caused any harm or disruption, the Supreme Court upheld the conviction for criminal anarchy and advocacy to overthrow the government. In *Gitlow v. New York*, the Court said the pamphlets lit a "revolutionary spark" that might ignite a "sweeping and destructive conflagration."[35] The majority said the writings "endanger[ed] the foundations of organized government and threaten[ed] its overthrow by unlawful means."[36]

In dissent, Justice Holmes declared, "Every idea is an incitement" and most ideas "should be given their chance and have their way" in the dialogue of a free and democratic society.[37] The mere dissemination of ideas does not endanger the nation.

The majority of the Court did not embrace Holmes' view, but it used *Gitlow* to expand free speech protection by establishing the doctrine of incorporation. The **incorporation doctrine** applies the 14th Amendment's due process clause to limit the power of state and local governments to abridge the guarantes of the Bill of Rights.[38] In other words, incorporation prevents the states, as well as the federal government, from abridging protected First Amendment rights.

In the years leading up to U.S. involvement in World War II, the Court used the clear and present danger test to uphold the conviction of a labor activist for participating in meetings of the Communist Labor Party.[39] The Court ruled that the First Amendment did not bar California from making it a crime to belong to a group that advocated

incorporation doctrine The 14th Amendment concept that most of the Bill of Rights applies equally to the states.

violence as a means to bring about political change. The Court accepted, without evidence, that the Communist Labor Party was violent. Mere party membership was sufficient to pose an imminent threat that was "relatively serious."[40] In his concurrence in *Whitney v. California*, Justice Louis Brandeis said a clear and present danger existed when previous conduct suggested a group *might contemplate* advocacy of immediate serious violence.[41]

During the anti-communist frenzy in the 1950s, the Court used the clear and present danger test to uphold a federal law that required labor union officers to swear they were not communists. In dissent, Justice Hugo Black said the test did not sufficiently protect unpopular political speech or association from overzealous regulation: "Too often it is fear which inspires such passions, and nothing is more reckless or contagious. In the resulting hysteria, popular indignation tars with the same brush all those who have ever been associated with any member of the group under attack."[42]

Members of the Court increasingly questioned the ability of the clear and present danger test to protect radical speech. They ruled that regulation of speech is unconstitutional if it is not narrowly tailored to avoid infringing on protected speech and does not address a problem more severe than abstract expressions about revolt.[43] They asserted that it is constitutional to regulate speech that advocates illegal action, but government may not punish speech that simply expresses a radical political idea. This doctrine is established in a case involving incitement.

From Clear and Present Danger to Incitement

By 1969, the Court had determined that the clear and present danger test was too easily swayed by political realities or social concerns to consistently protect innocuous speech.[44] To resolve the problem, the Court adopted a new test that drew a bright-line distinction between advocating violence as an abstract concept and inciting imminent violence. In *Brandenburg v. Ohio*, the Supreme Court ruled that the First Amendment protects the right to advocate but not to incite, or provoke, immediate violence.[45]

The case involved Clarence Brandenburg, a television repairman and Ku Klux Klan leader, who spoke to a dozen KKK members in the woods of rural Ohio. Brandenburg made vague threats to take "revengeance" against various government leaders, and his racist speech was later televised. Brandenburg was convicted under a state law that made it a crime to conspire to violently overthrow government. He said the conviction violated his right of free speech.

The Supreme Court struck down Brandenburg's conviction, ruling that the First Amendment protects people's right to advocate abhorrent ideas about social, political and economic change. Brandenburg's anti-Semitic and racist comments were highly offensive, the Court said, but "[m]ere advocacy of the use of force or violence does not remove speech from the protection of the First Amendment."[46] The expression of abstract ideas about the necessity of violence is protected speech. To protect it from government intrusion, the Court created a test that said government could punish the advocacy of force only when government could prove the advocacy (1) was directed to and (2) was likely to incite imminent lawless action.[47]

In a second case, *Hess v. Indiana*, Gregory Hess used profanity at an anti–Vietnam War rally after sheriff's officers moved demonstrators out of the street. When the U.S. Supreme Court heard Hess' appeal of his conviction for disorderly conduct, it overturned

◉ POINTS OF LAW

The Incitement Test

Almost five decades ago, the Supreme Court replaced its "clear and present danger" standard with the *Brandenburg/ Hess* incitement test.[1] The test establishes that speech loses First Amendment protection when it is likely to prompt imminent violence. The incitement test allows government constitutionally to prohibit speech that is

1. Directed toward inciting immediate violence or illegal action and

2. Likely to produce that action.

The *Brandenburg* decision established that government may punish criticism of government or advocacy of radical ideas only when speakers intend to incite illegal activity that is so imminent no other recourse would suffice to remove the threat.
  That remains the rule today.

1. Brandenburg v. Ohio, 395 U.S. 444 (1969); Hess v. Indiana, 414 U.S. 105 (1973) (per curiam).

the verdict. The First Amendment protected his speech that was not intended to, and not likely to, provoke an imminent violation of the law.[48] The Court in *Brandenburg* and *Hess* established that unless a speaker so inflamed a crowd that people responded to their emotions with immediate, illegal acts, the speech was protected.

When applied to the claims that media provoke violence, the incitement test requires a showing that exposure to the media content would cause immediate violent or unlawful activity. That is nearly impossible to prove. Media content does not ordinarily provoke such a rapid response. After seeing, reading or hearing media material, there is time to think before taking action, even time to prevent a person from committing violent acts. The incitement test also requires proof media content is likely to cause a reasonable person to act illegally. Rarely will a court find that a reasonable person would commit violence in response to media content.

DO MEDIA INCITE HARM?

If a court uses the incitement test when a member of the media is sued for causing physical harm, the plaintiff rarely wins. Plaintiffs generally fail to convince courts that media intentionally encouraged people to harm themselves or others. In one rare case, 17-year-old Devin Thompson, also known as Devin Moore, killed two police officers during his arrest for carjacking. A key argument in Thompson's complex defense was that his extensive play of two "Grand Theft Auto" games had caused post-traumatic stress and prompted the killings.[49] "60 Minutes" profiled the case. Thompson was convicted and sentenced to death.[50] After multiple proceedings, the Alabama Supreme Court upheld his conviction and separately allowed a wrongful death suit brought by the slain officers' families to proceed against the makers of the game.

The most relevant case heard by a federal court involved a Hustler magazine article titled "Orgasm of Death," describing autoerotic asphyxiation. The parents of a 14-year-old boy who hanged himself with a copy of Hustler open to the story nearby sued Hustler. The Fifth Circuit Court of Appeals said Hustler was not liable and did not incite the boy's actions.[51] The magazine not only did not urge readers to perform the act described; it repeatedly warned against it.

Courts have not found media incited violence even when media knew criminal activity might be related to their content. For example, Paramount Pictures continued distributing the movie "The Warriors" despite knowledge of two killings near California theaters that showed the film. Two days after the California murders, a teenager was stabbed and killed by another youth after leaving "The Warriors." The murdered boy's father sued Paramount, but the state supreme court held that the film's fictional portrayal of gang warfare did not constitute incitement because it did not advocate violent or unlawful acts.[52]

In the only decision of its kind, a court held a book publisher liable because it intended for criminals to buy and use the book "Hit Man: A Technical Manual for Independent Contractors" as a how-to for real murder.[53] A federal appellate court said the First Amendment did not protect Paladin Press because it encouraged, aided and abetted a crime. The killer mimicked the book's detailed, graphic instructions almost to the letter in brutally murdering a woman, her son and the son's nurse. The victims' relatives sued. The appellate court said, "[E]very court that has addressed the issue" agrees the First Amendment does not necessarily prevent finding a mass medium liable for assisting

● INTERNATIONAL LAW

Israel Moves to Stop Online Incitement

Top Facebook representatives met with Israeli officials in 2016 to try to work out mechanisms to prevent incitement through the online network.[1]

Government officials argued that online provocations, many through Facebook, set off a wave of violence with the Palestinians. They said they would work with Facebook to set up teams to monitor and remove inflammatory content. Under the established procedure, Israeli authorities complained to Facebook about content they deemed to be incitement. Then the company determined whether to remove the material based on its evaluation of community standards. One Israeli source said Facebook grants roughly 95 percent of Israel's requests to remove inciting content.[2]

A Facebook statement said, "There is no place for terrorists or content that promotes terrorism on Facebook. . . . Online extremism can only be tackled with a strong partnership between policymakers, civil society, academia and companies, and this is true in Israel and around the world."

Without further news on the Facebook negotiations, Israel's parliament in 2017 advanced legislation that would allow Israeli courts to force social networks to remove content that Israel considers to be incitement.[3]

1. *Israel and Facebook Join Hands to Decide What Is Censored*, Express Tribune, Sept. 14, 2016, tribune.com.pk/story/1181781/israel-facebook-joined-hands-determine-censored/.
2. *Facebook and Israel to Work to Monitor Posts That Incite Violence*, Assoc. Press, Sept. 12, 2016, www.theguardian.com/technology/2016/sep/12/facebook-israel-monitor-posts-incite-violence-social-media.
3. *Israel Advances Bill to Remove Online Incitement*, News24, Jan. 4, 2017, www.news24.com/World/News/israel-advances-bill-to-remove-online-incitement-20170103.

a crime, even if that aid "takes the form of the spoken or written word."[54] Paladin Press settled the case for $5 million.[55]

PHYSICAL HARMS

People tend to exaggerate the harms of media.[56] Some blame television for youth violence.[57] However, a Federal Trade Commission report on violent content in video games marketed to children said research generally establishes "that exposure to violence in entertainment media alone does not cause a child to commit a violent act."

Although there is little agreement on how exposure to television, video games, music and movie violence influences youth aggression,[58] some have tied obsessive exposure to these media to the mass murders at Sandy Hook Elementary School and

▲ EMERGING LAW

Pokémon Go Craze Does Not Spawn Predicted Lawsuits

Edward Berthelot/Getty Images

Within weeks of the 2016 free release of Pokémon Go, personal injury attorneys blanketed the internet with warnings of injuries related to use of the augmented virtual reality game and predicted a wave of liability lawsuits against the game maker, Take-Two.[1] Some attorneys said the game was an "attractive nuisance" that could lure players unsuspectingly into dangerous situations.

The surge of Pokémon Go play led to reports of players suffering serious injuries as they visited a series of "PokéStops" in their effort to capture, train and develop their Pokémon monster. Some of these stops were located on private property and at libraries, churches, restaurants or museums.

A pair of trespassing lawsuits arose, but court records show no lawsuits brought against Take-Two for personal injuries caused by the game. Few product liability claims against game makers for harm to players have been successful. For example, the Alabama Supreme Court granted summary judgment in a $600 million lawsuit brought against "Grand Theft Auto: Vice City" for copycat killings.[2]

The law in this area remains uncertain. Without court rulings, it remains an open question whether game makers may be held liable for injuries to players so engaged in gameplay that they fall off a cliff, get hit by a car or drive into a tree.

1. Bruce H. Raymond, *Expanded Video Game Liability Post-Pokémon Go?*, NAT'L L. REV., Jul. 26, 2016, www.natlawreview.com/article/expanded-video-game-liability-post-pok-mon-go; *see also* Hayley Tsukayama, *Pokémon Go's Unexpected Side Effect: Injuries*, www.washingtonpost.com/news/the-switch/wp/2016/07/08/pokemon-gos-unexpected-side-effect-injuries/?utm_term=.c02f1dfde866.
2. Rudie Obias, *11 Times Video Games Led to Lawsuits*, MENTAL FLOSS, Feb. 19, 2014, mentalfloss.com/article/55078/11-times-video-games-led-lawsuits.

the Aurora, Colo., movie theater.[59] Lawsuits claim that injury resulted from imitating the violence in movies like "Natural Born Killers" and video games like "Doom," and courts have been asked to determine the level of media responsibility.[60]

Similar lawsuits began decades ago when 13-year-old Ronny Zamora shot and killed his 83-year-old neighbor. Zamora's parents sued, claiming the television networks had failed to exercise "ordinary care to prevent their son from being 'impermissibly stimulated, incited and instigated' to duplicate the atrocities he viewed on television."[61] A federal district court said the networks did not have any duty to stop showing violent programs and could not be held responsible for the teen's actions. To dictate a limit on violent content would violate the First Amendment rights of the networks and the public, the court held.[62]

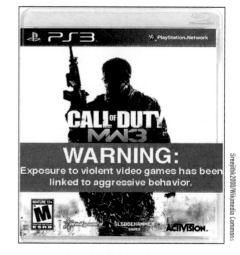

The violent images of video games, such as the flamethrower and guns seen here in "Doom," generate public and legislative concern.

Although lawsuits have proliferated, courts have not found the media liable for violent content.[63] Courts generally conclude that the media did not act negligently or did not intend to cause harm. The Supreme Court weighed in when it struck down a California law.[64] In *Brown v. Entertainment Merchants Association*, a video game merchants' group challenged the California law that prohibited the sale of violent video games to minors and required package labeling for violent content.[65] The law attempted to narrowly target only violent video games that, similar to unprotected obscenity, (1) appealed to deviant or morbid interests, (2) were patently offensive under contemporary community standards and (3) lacked serious artistic or other value (see related discussion in Chapter 10). The state said the law was intended to advance the important government interest in preventing psychological harm to minors.

But the Supreme Court struck down the law that singled out video games from other media and regulated them because of their interactivity and their unique attractiveness to children.[66] The Court refused to create a new category of disfavored speech for video game violence. California's attempt to create this new category of unprotected speech was both "unprecedented and mistaken," the Court said.[67]

In *Brown*, the Court said that violent video games deserve full First Amendment protection. "It is difficult to distinguish politics from entertainment," Justice Antonin Scalia wrote for the Court, "and dangerous to try. . . . Like the protected books, plays, and movies that preceded them, video games communicate ideas and even social messages. . . . That suffices to confer First Amendment protection."[68] Reviewing the law under strict scrutiny, the Court found it facially unconstitutional.

In his concurring opinion, Justice Samuel Alito urged care before broadly sweeping video games under the media umbrella. He wrote:

In considering the application of unchanging constitutional principles to new and rapidly evolving technology, this Court should proceed with caution. We should make every effort to understand the new technology. We should take into account the possibility that developing technology may have important societal implications that will become apparent only with time. We should not jump to the conclusion that new technology is fundamentally the same as some older thing with which we are familiar. And we should not hastily dismiss the judgment of legislators, who may be in a better position than we are to assess the implications of new technology.[69]

Negligence

negligence
Generally, the failure to exercise reasonable or ordinary care.

Plaintiffs suing the media for causing physical harm most often argue the media negligently distributed material that led to injury or death. When suits such as these are based on the tort of **negligence** (discussed in Chapter 4), the plaintiff must show the media defendant had a duty of due care, the defendant breached that duty and the breach caused the plaintiff's injury.

A court found NBC was not negligent when a girl was raped after the network aired the film "Born Innocent." Four days after the network aired the film that suggested four reform school inmates raped another with a toilet plunger, a 9-year-old suffered a similar attack at a San Francisco beach. The girl's parents sued NBC, claiming it was negligent in showing the movie when children could watch it. A state appellate court said the First Amendment barred any finding that NBC had a duty of care to the girl.[70] To do otherwise, the court said, would cause NBC to engage in self-censorship.

Foreseeability. To determine a defendant's duty of care, courts often ask whether the defendant should have foreseen the plaintiff's injury. Should the media have anticipated their action would cause harm? If a reasonable person would not foresee the harm, there was no duty.

Following the shooting deaths of 13 people at Columbine High School in Littleton, Colo., one family sued video game and movie producers on the grounds that the shooters copied their actions from the movie "The Basketball Diaries" and video games "Mortal Kombat," "MechWarrior," "Nightmare Creatures," "Doom," "Quake" and "Redneck Rampage." A federal district court rejected the suit, saying the media defendants did not have an obligation to protect the victim because they could not foresee the harm.[71]

In a similar case, a federal appellate court held there was insufficient proof that video game, movie and internet companies should have foreseen that their products could lead a 14-year-old boy to shoot several of his fellow high school students.[72] Even if media content prompted the shootings, the defendants could not have foreseen the violent response. It is "simply too far a leap from shooting characters on a video screen . . . to shooting people in a classroom," the court said.[73] The defendants did not owe the students a duty of care because the shooter's actions were unforeseeable.

Soldier of Fortune magazine publishes ads and stories about hunting, war and guns for "a male who owns camouflage clothing and more than one gun."[74] Ads promoting "GUN FOR HIRE . . . All jobs considered" led to two murder attempts, one of which was successful. A federal district court rejected the magazine's argument that the First Amendment protected its right to publish the ads.[75] The court said free speech is not absolute, and a jury could find the ads "had a substantial probability of ultimately causing harm to some individuals."[76] The magazine had a duty of due care because it was foreseeable that the ads could lead to physical injury. In a second case, a federal appellate court said Soldier of Fortune was obligated to determine whether the language of an ad, on its face, created an unreasonable risk of causing violent crime.[77]

However, Soldier of Fortune could not foresee harm from an ad that read: "EX-MARINES—67–69 'Nam Vets, Ex-DI, weapons specialist—jungle warfare, pilot, M.E., high risk assignments, U.S. or overseas."[78] In response to the ad, John Wayne Hearn received $10,000 from Robert Black to kill his wife. Hearn murdered Sandra Black, and her mother and son sued the magazine. The appellate court said the magazine had "no duty to refrain from publishing a facially innocuous classified advertisement when the ad's context—at most—made its message ambiguous."[79]

Proximate Cause If a defendant's actions led to the plaintiff's injury, the defendant caused the injury. But unless the defendant's action was the **proximate cause** of the harm, courts will not hold the defendant liable. To determine proximate cause, courts decide whether there is a direct relationship between the defendant's action and the plaintiff's injury.

proximate cause The legal determination of whether it is reasonable to conclude the defendant's actions led to the plaintiff's injury.

⭘ POINTS OF LAW

Media Liability for Negligence

To win a lawsuit for injury caused by media negligence, the plaintiff must prove breach of media's duty of care because the content posed a

1. Reasonable foreseeability of harm or
2. Proximate (directly related) cause of the harm.

For example, when a teenager committed suicide while listening to an Ozzy Osbourne album that includes the song "Suicide Solution," the teenager's parents sued. A California appellate court said the connection between the suicide and the song's lyrics was too tenuous to show proximate cause.[80]

Courts often refuse to find proximate cause if there is an unforeseeable event between the defendant's action and the plaintiff's later physical injury. In one case, a mother sued the manufacturer of "Dungeons & Dragons"[81] on the grounds that her son lost touch with reality because of his devotion to the game. A federal appellate court said the child's suicide was independent of the gameplay. The child's loss of reality and decision to commit suicide were intervening events.

SPEECH HARMS

Contrary to the childhood chant, words *can* hurt you. Speakers—sometimes intentionally, sometimes not—insult, denigrate and degrade. People call each other

More than 45 years after Paul Robert Cohen became famous as the voice of free speech and anti-war protest, he said his association with the anti-draft slogan was an accident. He only took the case up to the Supreme Court, he said, because he wanted to avoid serving 30 days in jail.

names; they hurl hateful insults and hurtful epithets at each other. They threaten; they harass; they offend. They fill the streets with dissent and discontent. The words and images they use alienate, cause fear and increase conflict.

Offensive Speech

Although many different flavors of speech offend or cause discomfort, mental anguish or suffering, the Supreme Court has said the First Amendment protects our right to express ourselves in our own words. In *Cohen v. California*,[82] Paul Robert Cohen was convicted of disturbing the peace for opposing the Vietnam War by wearing a jacket bearing the phrase "Fuck the Draft" into the Los Angeles courthouse. Cohen appealed and said the First Amendment protected his pure political speech. The Supreme Court agreed. Although court officials have broad authority to maintain decorum, they cannot punish speech that does not disrupt the court's functioning simply because they find the words offensive.

The Court went further and said the First Amendment protected both the content and the emotional value of a message. Meaningful protection for free speech goes beyond the "cognitive content" of the message to protect its "emotive function," the Court said. It is not simply *what* you say but *how* you say it that enjoys constitutional protection. As Justice John Harlan famously wrote, "One man's vulgarity is another's lyric."[83]

After Lester Packingham was convicted of taking indecent liberties with a minor, he became subject to a North Carolina law that prohibited convicted sex offenders from using social media.[84] After his release from prison, Packingham posted on Facebook about his happiness at having a parking ticket dismissed, and he was arrested. He challenged the law as an unconstitutional abridgement of his First Amendment right to free speech, but the state supreme court ruled that the law was a constitutional limit on conduct, not a restriction of speech.[85] On review in 2017, the U.S. Supreme Court ruled in *State v. Packingham* that the North Carolina law barring sex offenders from using social media websites like Facebook and Twitter was unconstitutional.[86] The Court relied on *Ashcroft v. Free Speech Coalition*[87] to find that the law was overly broad because it impermissibly suppressed lawful speech as well as unlawful speech and failed to demonstrate a compelling need to prevent illegal online speech to minors.

A 2015 federal district court ruling relied in part on *Cohen* to determine whether a state may punish speech by convicted criminals that causes mental anguish.[88] A Pennsylvania state law allowed prosecutors or crime victims to bring civil lawsuits to obtain an injunction to stop any "conduct" by a convicted criminal that perpetuates the harms of the crime and "causes a temporary or permanent state of mental anguish" to the victim.[89] The Revictimization Relief Act took effect within weeks of a small private Pennsylvania college announcing that its commencement speaker would be alumnus Mumia Abu-Jamal, who had been convicted of killing a police officer. One sponsor of the law said it was a means to prohibit "these rascals, these bad people from becoming entertainment values."[90]

Abu-Jamal challenged the act, and its application to him, as unconstitutionally vague, overbroad and content-based without the justification of a compelling government interest. The court agreed. The law's explicit and impermissible intent is to prevent "expression that causes mental anguish in crime victims," the court said. Yet the Supreme Court has made clear that when a law's action is triggered by "the impact an expression has on its listeners, [it] is the essence of content-based regulation."[91] The district court imposed a permanent injunction against application of the law, concluding, "The First Amendment's guarantee of free speech extends to convicted felons whose expressive conduct is *ipso facto* controversial or offensive."[92]

Fighting Words

The First Amendment protects people's right to vent anger in words. Accordingly, free speech serves as a societal safety valve; it allows people to blow off steam before they resort to physical violence.[93] Nonetheless, the Supreme Court recognizes that to vent anger also may "set fire to reason."[94]

The Supreme Court's 75-year-old ruling in *Chaplinsky v. New Hampshire*[95] first articulated the logic that violent listener reaction may provide the basis for limits on the freedom of speech. When residents complained that Walter Chaplinsky was distributing Jehovah's Witness pamphlets on the streets, a police officer warned him to stop because he was disturbing the peace. A group of people later became restless because of Chaplinsky's pamphlet distribution, and an officer detained Chaplinsky. The officer and Chaplinsky encountered the first officer, who warned Chaplinsky again, and Chaplinsky called the officer a "goddamned racketeer" and a "damned Fascist." He was convicted under a state law that defined disturbing the peace as publicly calling someone "any offensive, derisive or annoying word . . . or name . . . with intent to deride, offend or annoy."

In its landmark ruling, the U.S. Supreme Court upheld the conviction, holding that the First Amendment did not protect narrow categories of speech that make no contribution to the discussion of ideas or the search for truth. The Court said Chaplinsky's comments were unprotected **fighting words** that "by their very utterance inflict injury or tend to incite immediate breach of peace."[96]

fighting words Words not protected by the First Amendment because they cause immediate harm or illegal acts.

⦿ POINTS OF LAW

Fighting Words

Under the Supreme Court's fighting words doctrine, the First Amendment does not protect words that

1. Are directed at an individual and

2. Automatically inflict emotional harm or trigger violence.

▌ SOCIAL MEDIA LAW

Cyberbullying

A mom created a Myspace profile for a nonexistent 16-year-old boy to flirt with and then break up with her daughter's classmate. The day the mom, posing as the boy, told the classmate, "The world would be a better place without you in it," the girl committed suicide.

The mother was accused of violating Myspace's anti-harassment rules and the Computer Fraud and Abuse Act[1] that makes it illegal to use a computer to commit a crime or tort. The prosecutors said the mom violated the law by violating the Myspace terms of use. Although the jury found her guilty of misdemeanor violation of the Myspace terms of use agreement, a federal district judge set aside the verdict because the vague terms of the CFAA were never intended to apply to cyberbullying.[2] The law was intended to prevent unauthorized access, or hacking, of computer accounts.

The court said the CFAA was unconstitutionally vague because it provided neither the required fair warning of what constituted illegal activity nor objective criteria by which to determine when a crime had occurred.[3]

Today 23 states punish cyberbullying; 18 of those make it a crime.[4]

1. 18 U.S.C. § 1030.
2. United States v. Drew, 259 F.R.D. 449, 451 n.2 (C.D. Calif. 2009).
3. *Id.* at 463.
4. Sameer Hinduja & Justin W. Patchin, *State Cyberbullying Laws*, Jan. 2016, www.cyberbullying.us/Bullying-and-Cyberbullying-Laws.pdf.

In 1949, the Supreme Court heard the case of a priest who was arrested for disorderly conduct when his anti-Semitic and pro-Fascist comments to a sympathetic audience riled a group outside the assembly hall to violence. Illinois courts upheld his conviction, ruling that the law punished only unprotected fighting words that "stir[] the public to anger, invite[] dispute, bring[] about a condition of unrest . . . create[] a disturbance or . . . molest[] the inhabitants in the enjoyment of peace and quiet by arousing alarm."[97]

The Supreme Court reversed. It reasoned that "a function of free speech under our system of government is to *invite* dispute."[98] The Court in *Terminiello v. Chicago* said speech "may indeed best serve its high purpose when it induces a condition of unrest, creates dissatisfaction with conditions as they are, or even stirs people to anger."[99] The First Amendment protects such speech "unless shown likely to produce a clear and present danger of a serious substantive evil that rises far above public inconvenience, annoyance or unrest."[100] Subsequent Supreme Court rulings[101] have confirmed that the Constitution permits government to prohibit only those face-to-face comments that are inherently likely to trigger an immediate reaction of disorder or violence.

Hate Speech

hate speech
A category of speech that includes name-calling and pointed criticism that demeans others on the basis of race, color, gender, ethnicity, religion, national origin, disability, intellect or the like.

Contemporary concerns about the harms caused by intolerance, racism and bigotry have generated state and local speech codes to regulate so-called **hate speech**, but courts generally find these laws unconstitutional. *Hate speech* is not a legal term, but it is commonly understood to involve name-calling, slurs and epithets that demean others on the basis of race, color, gender, ethnicity, sexual preference, religion, national origin, disability or the like. Few cases dealing squarely with hate speech have reached the Supreme Court, but lower courts consistently have found anti-bias and anti-hate-speech laws unconstitutional.

The primary Supreme Court decision dealing with hate speech, *R.A.V. v. City of St. Paul*, involved several white teenage boys who, late one night, made a crude wooden cross from a broken chair and set it ablaze in the yard of a black family.[102] They were convicted of violating a local statute that punished the display of symbols—such as a burning cross—that arouse "anger, alarm or resentment in others on the basis of race, color, creed, religion or gender." The Minnesota Supreme Court upheld the conviction, reasoning that the bias-motivated crime statute punished only unprotected fighting words.

● INTERNATIONAL LAW

European Laws Punish Hate Speech

In response to a flood of refugees from the war in Syria, a vocal wave of xenophobia led to new barriers to immigration across the European Union.

Foundational documents of European law prohibit "any advocacy of national, racial, or religious hatred that constitutes incitement to discrimination, hostility, or violence" and provide the basis for national bans on speech that harms "the reputation and rights of others."[1]

The imprecision of these framing legal documents has led to differential laws that nonetheless allow for the punishment of speech that is protected under the U.S. Constitution's First Amendment. The U.S. Supreme Court has said that insulting speech is protected unless it incites immediate violence or disturbance of the peace.

In Denmark, it is a crime to spread "racial hatred," which includes publicly using threatening, vilifying or insulting language. French law makes it illegal to incite racial discrimination, hatred or violence based on ethic, national, racial or religious origins or affiliations. It violates the law in the Netherlands to publicly incite hatred or insult others based on race, religion, sexual orientation or personal convictions. In the United Kingdom, you can be punished for expression intended to stir up racial hatred.

Many European countries also outlaw denial of genocide, including the Holocaust, to protect descendants of the victims.[2] Some observers criticize the lone-wolf stance of the United States regarding hate speech. They argue that "Americans [need] to take more seriously the damage such speech does, and to overcome the 'knee-jerk, impulsive and thoughtless' arguments" against punishing speech that assaults.[3] Others say we need to protect hate speech "not because we doubt the speech inflicts harm, but because we fear the censorship more."[4]

1. *European Hate Speech Laws*, LEGAL PROJECT, 2017, www.legal-project.org/issues/european-hate-speech-laws.
2. Peter R. Teachout, *Making "Holocaust Denial" a Crime: Reflections on European Anti-Negationist Laws From the Perspective of U.S. Constitutional Experience*, 30 Vt. L. Rev. 655 (2006).
3. Michael W. McConnell, *You Can't Say That*, N.Y. TIMES BOOK REV., June 24, 2012, at BR14, www.nytimes.com (quoting JEREMY WALDRON, The Harm in Hate Speech (2012)).
4. McConnell, *supra* n. 3.

underinclusive A First Amendment doctrine that disfavors narrow laws that target a subset of a recognized category for discriminatory treatment.

viewpoint-based discrimination Government censorship or punishment of expression based on the ideas or attitudes expressed. Courts will apply a strict scrutiny test to determine whether the government acted constitutionally.

A unanimous U.S. Supreme Court reversed, but the justices did not agree on why. Five justices said the law was too narrow, or **underinclusive**, because it punished only a specific subset of fighting words that the government found particularly objectionable. Thus, the law imposed unconstitutional **viewpoint-based discrimination** because it punished certain forms of racist speech (cross burnings) but not others. The remaining four justices said the law was overbroad; it punished too much speech, not too little. They said the law unconstitutionally went beyond fighting words to punish speech that did not arise in face-to-face encounters and whose only harm was to prompt "generalized reactions" of hurt feelings, resentment or offense. Since *R.A.V.*, most efforts to tailor a constitutional hate speech ordinance have failed.

Current Standard

In the past 60 years, the Supreme Court has shied away from directly applying the fighting words category to determine the expanse of constitutional protection for free speech. Instead, the Court has tended to judge the constitutionality of laws that attempt to regulate highly volatile speech directed at specific individuals on the basis of the reach of the law. The Court has struck down a variety of laws that attempt to punish specific types of offensive speech on the grounds that the laws are not sufficiently narrowly tailored to prevent intrusion on protected speech. In one such ruling, the Court rearticulated the category of fighting words and said this type of speech sometimes does warrant protection by the First Amendment. In *R.A.V. v. City of St. Paul*, the Court wrote:

> Our cases [on fighting words] surely do not establish the proposition that the First Amendment imposes no obstacle whatsoever to regulation of particular instances of such proscribable expression, so that the government "may regulate [them] freely." . . . Such a simplistic, all-or-nothing-at-all approach to First Amendment protection is at odds with common sense and with our jurisprudence as well. It is not true that "fighting words" have at most a "de minimus" expressive content, or that their content is in all respects "worthless and undeserving of constitutional protection"; sometimes they are quite expressive indeed. We have not said that they constitute "no part of the expression of ideas," but only that they constitute "no essential part of any expression of ideas." . . . [T]he unprotected features of [fighting] words are, despite their verbal character, essentially a "nonspeech" element of communication.[103]

Supreme Court decisions make the precise level of protection the Constitution affords fighting words unclear. They suggest that speech loses its constitutional protection when the speaker intends to provoke violence or incite immediate unrest in a targeted individual or group.

Harmful Images

The Supreme Court reaffirmed its sole power to determine what categories of speech are, and are not, fully protected by the First Amendment. In reviewing one federal and one state statute, the Court reiterated its position that the Constitution fully protects even violent and deeply disturbing expression.

In *United States v. Stevens*, the Supreme Court denied Congress the power to exclude images of animal cruelty from First Amendment protection.[104] Robert J. Stevens had been convicted and given a 37-month sentence under the federal Animal Crush Video Prohibition Act for trafficking in "depictions of animal cruelty." He had compiled and sold videotapes of dogfights, though he had not arranged or participated in the fights. In a ruling written by Chief Justice John Roberts, with Justice Samuel Alito alone in dissent, the Court struck down the law as substantially overbroad because it penalized speech that did not fit within a historically recognized First Amendment exception. Neither Congress nor the Supreme Court has "freewheeling authority to declare new categories of speech outside the scope of the First Amendment," the Court concluded.[105]

Intimidation and Threats

When speech crosses certain lines, government may restrict messages that are sufficiently detrimental to important competing interests.

A decade ago, the Supreme Court began to shape a category of speech that moves beyond offensiveness. The case involved three cross burnings, one at a Ku Klux Klan rally and two in the yard of an African-American neighbor. In *Virginia v. Black*, the Court ruled that the First Amendment allows states to punish individuals who set crosses ablaze with the intent to intimidate.[106] The Court said laws may constitutionally target a specific subset of fighting words, such as cross burnings, that is so "inextricably intertwined" with a clear and pervasive history of violence that it constitutes a **true threat**. The Court said a burning cross is such a threatening instrument of racial terror and imminent violence that its power to intimidate overshadows free speech concerns. In dissent, Justice Clarence Thomas said the law punished only illegal acts and was unrelated to First Amendment concerns: "Those who hate cannot terrorize and intimidate to make their point."[107]

Writing for a 5–4 majority of the Court, Justice Sandra Day O'Connor reasoned that despite the inextricable connection between cross burnings and the KKK's "reign of terror in the South," history alone does not transform merely offensive speech into unprotected threats or intimidation. For speech to become punishable as a true threat, a speaker must (1) direct the threat toward one or more individuals (2) with the intent of causing the listener(s) (3) to fear bodily harm or death.[108] In this case, the majority reasoned that cross burning was constitutionally punishable because the intimidation is intended to create pervasive fear of violence in the targeted individual or group.

In *Elonis v. United States*, the Supreme Court sidestepped the First Amendment question of when internet posts constitute true threats punishable by law.[109] The Court returned the case to the Third Circuit Court of Appeals to determine under what conditions words convey a "true threat" that may be punished without violating the First Amendment.[110]

The case involved a Pennsylvania man convicted of making Facebook threats to his estranged wife and law enforcement officers. Anthony Elonis said he did not intend any threats and was composing "therapeutic" rap lyrics to express his depression and frustration after his wife took their two children and left him. One post read:

There's one way to love you

but a thousand ways to kill you.

I'm not going to rest

true threat
Speech directed toward one or more specific individuals with the intent of causing listeners to fear for their safety.

until your body is a mess,

soaked in blood and dying from all the little cuts.

Another read:

That's it, I've had about enough

I'm checking out and making a name for myself

Enough elementary schools in a ten mile radius to initia0te the most heinous school shooting ever imagined

And hell hath no fury like a crazy man in a Kindergarten class

The only question is . . . which one?

At trial, Elonis' wife testified that she was terrified by the posts, had filed a protective order against him and feared for her life and that of her children. The jury convicted Elonis, and the judge sentenced him to 50 months in jail.

In its 8–1 decision, the Supreme Court relied on statutory construction to conclude only that a conviction for threats online, like any criminal conviction, requires a showing that the defendant *intended* to violate the law and make a true threat.[111]

"Wrongdoing must be conscious to be criminal," Chief Justice John Roberts wrote for the majority. ". . . [T]his principle is as universal and persistent in mature systems of law as belief in freedom of the human will and a consequent ability and duty of the normal individual to choose between good and evil."[112] The Court reversed and remanded the case.

In his opinion concurring in part, Justice Samuel Alito criticized the Court's failure to establish whether recklessness was sufficient to trigger criminal liability. He wrote, "The Court's disposition of this case is certain to cause confusion and serious problems."[113]

On remand, the Third Circuit said that the subjective element of a threat involves the intent of the speaker, who must knowingly communicate an intention to cause harm.[114] The court said the objective standard requires that a reasonable person would view the

● POINTS OF LAW

Is That a True Threat?

Almost 75 years ago, the U.S. Supreme Court defined a threat as an "utterance in a context of violence [that] can lose its significance as an appeal to reason and become part of an instrument of force." As such, it is "not meant to be sheltered by the Constitution."[1] In *Virginia v. Black*,[2] the Court concluded that punishment of true threats is acceptable under the Constitution. The Court examined both speaker intent and a reasonable person's objective response in determining that cross burnings were true threats because of their historic power to terrorize.

1. Milk Wagon Drivers Union of Chicago v. Meadowmoor Dairies, 312 U.S. 287, 293 (1941).
2. 538 U.S. 343 (2003).

▌ SOCIAL MEDIA LAW

Rap Art or a Road Map to Threats?

In their appeal to the Supreme Court, the attorneys for Anthony Elonis argued that his criminal conviction based solely on readers' fearful reaction to his Facebook posts failed to recognize that "modern media allow personal reflections intended for a small audience (or no audience) to be viewed widely by people who are unfamiliar with the context."[1] This wide and unintended audience, largely unfamiliar with the speaker, may "interpret the statements much differently than the speakers intended."[2] They may not understand that his posts were artistic rap lyrics and protected expression, not threats, the attorneys claimed.

In response during oral argument, Justice Samuel Alito said that "sounds like a road map for threatening a spouse and getting away with it. . . . So you put it in a rhyme . . . and you say, 'I'm an aspiring rap artist,' and so then you are free from prosecution."[3]

The Court declined to rule on the issue.

1. Elonis v. United States, 135 S. Ct. 2001 (2015).
2. Elonis v. United States, *pet. for cert.*, at 35, law.virginia.edu/pdf/scotus/elonis_cert_petition.pdf.
3. Amy Howe, *Court Difficult to Read on Facebook Threats: In Plain English*, SCOTUSblog, Dec. 1, 2014, scotusblog.com/2014/12/court-difficult-to-read-on-facebook-threats-in-plain-english/.

communication as a threat. Applying these two elements, the subjective and the objective, the court affirmed Elonis' conviction. Elonis was released in 2016 after serving 44 months in jail.

Two court of appeals rulings before the Supreme Court's *Elonis* decision disagreed on what requirements must be met for government to constitutionally sanction speech it deems threatening. The Ninth Circuit Court of Appeals applied a two-part test like that in *Elonis* to reverse a conviction for blog comments the court said neither intentionally nor reasonably threatened the life of then-presidential candidate Barack Obama.[115] The Sixth Circuit used only the objective element to uphold an ex-husband's threat conviction for a YouTube musical rant against the child custody process.[116] Observers have encouraged the Supreme Court to act quickly to clarify whether a punishable threat exists whenever a reasonable person would fear for her own safety or whether it also requires the speaker to have intended to communicate a threat.[117]

SYMBOLIC SPEECH

Much expression that might anger or upset people does not cross the line into hate speech, fighting words, threats or incitement. Sometimes it does not even take the form of words. Nonverbal expression, in the form of burning flags, wearing armbands or marching through the public streets, is what the Supreme Court has called symbolic speech. The Court has said symbolic speech deserves First Amendment protection in some cases, but it has rejected "the view that an apparently limitless variety of conduct can be labeled speech whenever the person engaging in the conduct intends thereby to express his idea."[118] Only actions that are "closely akin to 'pure speech'" are viewed as symbolic speech.[119]

A hooded member of the Ku Klux Klan sets a cross on fire.

William Campbell/Sygma via Getty Images

Some of the most vehement and heated debate in the 1960s involved symbolic speech. Amid the civil rights movement and protests against the Vietnam War, the Court held that the Constitution protected the rights of protest groups to express the most radical and unpopular political ideas. However, there were limits, and the line between protected political protest and illegal activity, incitement or fighting words was not always obvious.

Burning Speech

In the first of these cases (which is discussed in Chapter 2), the Supreme Court affirmed the power of government to punish David O'Brien for burning his draft card in violation of a federal law intended to facilitate the military draft. The *O'Brien* ruling established intermediate scrutiny as the standard of judicial review of content-neutral laws that incidentally infringe on protected speech. In affirming O'Brien's conviction, the Court focused on why the government had enacted the law (intent) and how the law operated (effect) while acknowledging the expressive content of the public destruction of a draft card.[120]

Fast-forward 20 years, and the Court reviewed a case in which Gregory Lee Johnson had been convicted, sentenced to a year in prison and fined $2,000 for burning the American flag during a protest at the Republican National Convention in Dallas. In *Texas v. Johnson*, the Supreme Court used strict scrutiny to strike down a Texas law that made it a crime to desecrate the flag.[121] The state of Texas said its ban on flag desecration preserved an important symbol of national unity and prevented breach of the peace. Johnson argued that the law violated his right to free speech. The Supreme Court agreed. Finding flag burning to be a form of symbolic speech, the Court struck down the Texas law as unconstitutional.

A sharply divided Supreme Court held that the law failed to pass strict scrutiny because it served no compelling interest. The state's interest was insufficient to justify content-based suppression of speech. In fact, the government interest in preserving the sanctity of the flag represented an unconstitutional attempt to punish ideas the government disliked. The law's sole purpose was to prohibit expression the state found offensive.

"If there is a bedrock principle underlying the First Amendment," Justice William Brennan wrote for the Court, "it is that the government may not prohibit the expression of an idea simply because society finds the idea itself offensive or disagreeable."[122] The law was unconstitutional because it failed to serve a compelling interest and did not use the least intrusive means to advance its goals.

The Constitution also generally protects exaggeration, hyperbole and excess in speech by looking to the context to determine whether the words should be taken on their face. For example, the Court said an anti-war protester's comment to fellow marchers that "we'll take the fucking street later" did not present the clear and present danger of violence required under the incitement test because it was unlikely to prompt any immediate action.[123]

SPEECH IN THE SCHOOLS

There is nothing in the wording of the First Amendment itself to suggest that it protects the rights of minors, public school students or campus media differently from the rights of others. However, society has unique interests in protecting and educating its youth. Sometimes courts have accepted the idea that the nation's interest in developing its youth outweighs the free speech rights of public school students.

Courts have struggled to determine both how and where to draw the line between advancing the important concerns of parents and educators and protecting the sometimes-conflicting rights of students to freedom of speech and association.

Nearly 40 years ago, the Supreme Court said students' free speech rights prevented schools from removing books from the school library simply because someone might find them offensive.[124] Over the objections of a library review committee, a school board removed 10 books from the school libraries that some board members said were "objectionable," "anti-American, anti-Christian, anti-[Semitic], and just plain filthy."[125] Several students sued, and the Supreme Court said the book removal violated the First Amendment.

Although schools must ensure that curriculum is age appropriate and of good quality, schools may not constitutionally remove library books to placate a hypersensitive few. When the readings are optional, individual student freedom of choice prevails. The Court said that "access [to controversial materials] prepares students for active and effective participation in the pluralistic, often contentious society in which they will soon be adult members."[126] Decisions to remove books may not be made "in a narrowly partisan or political manner"[127] and are more likely to be constitutional if they advance a curricular purpose.

Flickr/Kascia Samel

In 2012, a U.S. district court judge required a public high school to stop using an internet filtering system that discriminated against websites that expressed pro-LGBTQ concepts and values.[128] The school's filter tagged anti-gay sites under "religion," which allowed access, but tagged pro-gay sites with "sex," which triggered blocking. "These filters are a new version of book-banning or pulling books off the shelf," a spokesperson for the American Library Association said.[129]

U.S. libraries mark Banned Books Week with public displays.

The U.S. Supreme Court has said, "The right to speak and the right to refrain from speaking are complementary components of the broader concept of individual freedom of mind."[130] Accordingly, government may not force citizens, even young school students, to express ideas with which they disagree.

More than 70 years ago, students who were Jehovah's Witnesses challenged the mandatory flag salute and Pledge of Allegiance in school as a violation of their religious beliefs. The Court agreed.[131] Despite the important role of public schools in teaching students civic values and responsibilities,[132] schools may not indoctrinate students into particular ideologies or silence teachers who wish to speak out on issues of public concern, the Court said.[133] "If there is any fixed star in our constitutional constellation," the Court wrote, "it is that no official, high or petty, can prescribe what shall be orthodox in politics, nationalism, religion or other matters of opinion or force citizens to confess by word or act their faith therein."[134]

Public Forum Analysis

The courts have used several different approaches to determine when student press and speech are protected. In many cases, the Supreme Court has viewed public schools and universities—including school-sponsored events, publications, funding and physical spaces—as limited public forums. Under public forum doctrine, and applying the *O'Brien* test (discussed in Chapter 2), schools may impose reasonable content-neutral time, place and manner regulations on student speech activities to advance educational objectives. What this means in practice is that schools and universities may adopt regulations to achieve their educational goals even if the rules incidentally limit the freedom of speech of students and teachers. School officials generally may not dictate the content of student speech except to prevent speech that would directly undermine the school's educational mission. Courts have upheld public school restrictions on, among other things, the clothing of students, the hours facilities may be used by outsiders, the school-related expression of teachers and the content of school-sponsored student speech and publications.

In several other approaches, the Court looked to the age, impressionability and maturity of the students; the location of the expression; the content of the speech; and the specific educational goals of the institution to determine the case outcome. Political turbulence and social unrest also play a part. As one Court observer noted, sometimes "the very concept of academic freedom is under fire."[135] Such case-specific decisions do not provide clear rules of law. The variety of tests yields different outcomes among primary, secondary and postsecondary schools as well as between a high school newspaper and a university student's speech during an open public debate.

The *Tinker* Test

Establishing the second line of cases, the *Tinker* test, as it is known, arose from the Court's 1969 review of a case involving symbolic anti-war protest.[136] In *Tinker v. Des Moines Independent Community School District*, the Court established the school classroom as a location that is "peculiarly the marketplace of ideas" where speech may be regulated only to prevent a "substantial disruption" to school activities.

The case began when a brother and sister, in junior and senior high, respectively, attended school wearing black armbands, which was a common means of protesting the Vietnam War. The students did not disrupt classes, but the school suspended them for violating a new policy prohibiting black armbands. The students sued, claiming the suspensions violated their right to free speech.

○ POINTS OF LAW

Non-University-Student Speech

Recent Supreme Court decisions on student expression generally approach non-university-student speech cases in one of three ways:

1. Is the speech disruptive? If the speech disrupts the functioning of the public school or violates the rights and interests of other students, it may be regulated.[1]

2. Is the speech of low value? If the speech is lewd or if it conflicts with the school's pedagogical goals or public values, it may be regulated.[2]

3. Is the speech sponsored by the school and therefore perceived to reflect the school's official position and attitude? If the speech occurs in a school-sponsored forum or event, if it is part of the school's official curriculum or if it appears to entangle the school with a particular religious viewpoint, it may be regulated.[3]

1. *See, e.g.,* Tinker v. Des Moines Indep. Cmty. Sch. Dist., 393 U.S. 503, 509 (1969).
2. *See, e.g.,* Bethel Sch. Dist. v. Fraser, 478 U.S. 675 (1986); Hazelwood v. Kuhlmeier, 484 U.S. 260 (1988).
3. *See, e.g.,* Hazelwood v. Kuhlmeier, 484 U.S. 260 (1988); Lemon v. Kurtzman, 403 U.S. 602 (1971); Bd. of Regents of Univ. of Wis. System v. Southworth, 529 U.S. 217 (2000).

In what has been called "the most important Supreme Court case in history protecting the constitutional rights of students,"[137] the Court in *Tinker* agreed with the students. The Court said the symbolic expression of the armbands was "akin to pure speech" and was protected under the First Amendment.[138] When novel or deviant issues are expressed, the First Amendment must weigh heavily in favor of the expression and against the bureaucratic urge to suppress, the Court said. Officials do not have the authority to suppress student expression simply to avoid unpleasantness or discomfort. The Constitution prohibits school officials from limiting free speech to "only that which the State chooses to communicate."[139] The Constitution makes it "unmistakable" that individuals do not "shed their constitutional rights to freedom of speech or expression at the schoolhouse gate."[140] Unless student expression materially or substantially disrupts the school's educational activities, school administrators lack authority to regulate the speech, the Court said.[141]

For nearly four decades, the rule was clear: Only when speech inside or adjacent to the school during school hours disrupts school activities may it be punished.[142] Then the Court's ruling in *Morse v. Frederick* seemed to muddy the test. In *Morse*, the Court held

Bettmann/Getty Images

The Tinkers (Lorena, Paul and Mary Beth, left to right) speak with the press in 1969 after learning the U.S. Supreme Court upheld the teens' right to wear anti-war armbands in school.

that the "substantial disruption" rule established in *Tinker* was not the only proper test for restricting student speech.[143]

The case began when high school senior Joseph Frederick and others displayed a banner reading "Bong Hits 4 Jesus" during a school field trip. Frederick said he did it for a laugh and to get himself on TV. The school's principal, Deborah Morse, apparently was not laughing when she told him to remove the banner. When he refused, she tore down the sign and suspended him for 10 days for violating a school policy that banned the advocacy of illegal drug use. Frederick sued, alleging that the principal had violated his right to free speech. The district court sided with the principal, but the U.S. Court of Appeals for the Ninth Circuit reversed, ruling that school officials may not "punish and censor non-disruptive" speech by students at school-sponsored events simply because they object to the message.

In a 5–4 ruling, the Supreme Court sided with the principal. The Court ruled that school officials may prohibit messages that advocate illegal drug use without running afoul of the First Amendment. For the majority, Chief Justice John Roberts wrote that the freedom of student speech does not extend to speech that directly contravenes an important school anti-drug policy. The majority flatly rejected the dissent's contention that the case implicated political speech. Instead, the Court reasoned that the "special environment" and the educational mandate of the schools permitted officials to prohibit student speech that raises a "palpable" danger to established school policy. "The First Amendment does not require schools to tolerate at school events student expression that contributes to [the] dangers" of illegal drug use, Justice Roberts wrote for the majority.[144] In dissent, Justice John Paul Stevens argued that "the Court's ham-handed, categorical approach is deaf to the constitutional imperative to permit unfettered debate, even among high-school students."[145] He said it condoned content-based discrimination.

George Wittenstein/akg

Student protest of social injustice has a long history. During World War II, Sophie Scholl (pictured center), her brother Hans and Christoph Probst were executed by the Nazis for their "White Rose Resistance" movement urging students to rise up against the Nazi regime.

The *Fraser* Approach

Decades ago, the Supreme Court was asked to determine the limits of students' right to offensive speech in public schools. The case of *Bethel School District v. Fraser* involved a speech by Matthew Fraser nominating a classmate for student government.[146] Employing a number of clever and humorous metaphors for male sexual prowess, Fraser addressed nearly 600 high school students, including some 14-year-olds, who were required to attend the school-sponsored assembly. The assistant principal said the speech violated a school policy forbidding profanity and obscenity that "materially and substantially interferes with the educational process." She suspended Fraser for three days and prohibited his selection as graduation speaker.

Fraser challenged the action as a violation of his First Amendment rights. On review, the Supreme Court upheld the school's decision. The Court said that when student speech occurs during a school-sponsored event, the student's liberty of speech may be curtailed to protect the school's educational purpose, especially when young students are in the audience. This is particularly true if the forum for the student speech suggests that the student is speaking for the school.

In *Fraser*, the Court said eliminating vulgarity and profanity from school events advanced the obligation of schools to "inculcate . . . habits and manners of civility."[147] Rather than view student First Amendment rights as paramount, the Court said it was "perfectly appropriate" for a school to impose student sanctions to disassociate the school from speech that threatened its core purpose.

The *Hazelwood* Test

Two years later, the Court reaffirmed school authority over school-sanctioned activities and speech. In this case, students in the journalism class at Hazelwood East High School in St. Louis, Mo., published a student newspaper, Spectrum, under the supervision of a faculty adviser who reviewed the content. The principal also reviewed each issue before publication, but school policy said students enjoyed freedom of "responsible" speech.

After the principal removed two pages of the newspaper that included one story about teen pregnancy at the school and a second about the impact of divorce on students at the school, student editors sued. The principal said the targeted stories invaded the privacy of students and parents interviewed and contained material inappropriate for younger students. Other unoffensive stories were also eliminated by removal of the pages to expedite printing before the school year ended. The trial court rejected the students' challenge, but the court of appeals reversed, saying the school could edit the newspaper's content only to avoid legal liability, not to advance grammatical, journalistic or social values.

In *Hazelwood v. Kuhlmeier*, the Supreme Court again reversed and said school administrators, not student reporters and editors, have authority to determine the appropriate content of a school-sponsored student newspaper.[148] When a school creates and supervises a forum for student speech, such as a student assembly or a teacher-supervised student newspaper, the school endorses that speech and is not only permitted but required to control the content to achieve educational goals, the Court said.[149] Schools not only are free from any obligation to "promote particular student speech"[150] but must exercise their supervisory function to promote a positive educational environment in all "school-sponsored publications, theatrical productions and other expressive activities that students, parents and members of the public might reasonably perceive to bear the imprimatur of the school."[151] In a footnote, however, the Court made clear that the decision did not apply to the university student press.[152]

Choosing the Proper Test

The *Morse* decision recognizing a school's authority to punish off-campus, school-related student speech led to conflicting rulings among U.S. circuit courts because it appeared to grant school officials new latitude to sanction nondisruptive speech. In recent years, courts of appeal demonstrate increased uncertainty about when *Tinker* applies and when *Fraser*, *Hazelwood* or *O'Brien* should dictate the outcome. In 2013, for example, the Second Circuit

Court of Appeals applied *Hazelwood* to rule that a middle school had authority to ban a class president from a scheduled speech unless she deleted a closing religious blessing because the speech constituted school-sponsored expression.[153] The court said *Tinker* applies only when "a student's personal expression . . . happens to occur on the school premises."

The Third Circuit Court of Appeals applied forum analysis to find unconstitutional an elementary school ban on student distribution of materials from nonschool organizations.[154] The school had prevented a fifth grader from the nondisruptive distribution of invitations to a Christmas party at her church. But the Tenth Circuit used *Tinker* as the basis for ruling that school officials did not violate the First Amendment when they prevented high school students from distributing rubber fetus dolls in school.[155] And, again applying *Tinker*, the Fourth Circuit upheld student punishment for wearing a Confederate flag T-shirt to school because "school officials could reasonably forecast" that the shirts "would materially and substantially disrupt the work and discipline of the school."[156]

In contrast, the Third Circuit Court of Appeals relied on *Fraser* when it allowed a middle school student lawsuit to proceed.[157] The court said the plaintiffs had a good likelihood of winning their challenge to the school's prohibition of breast-cancer-awareness bracelets reading "i ♥ boobies! (KEEP A BREAST)." The school had said the bracelets were "lewd, vulgar, profane, or plainly offensive." But the court said they were nondisruptive, discussed an important social issue and, thus, likely were protected free speech.

Seventh Circuit Court of Appeals Judge Richard Posner seemed a model of understatement. In a ruling summarily affirming the right of students to wear T-shirts critical of homosexuality, he said *Tinker*'s "substantial disruption test [has not] proved a model of clarity in its application," but it does distinguish between speech that simply hurts feelings, which a school may not bar, and speech that substantially disrupts school, which it may.[158]

The Eighth Circuit Court of Appeals ruled that a school could expel a Hannibal (Mo.) High School student for sending threatening text messages off-campus.[159] Then-10th grader Dylan J. Mardis sent off-campus instant messages to a friend saying "he wanted Hannibal to be known for something" and he wanted to kill at least five classmates. The court found his online messages sufficiently threatening and disruptive to warrant discipline because school officials have a paramount responsibility to protect students. However, "school officials cannot constitutionally reach out to discover, monitor, or punish [just] any type of out-of-school speech."[160]

A decision from the Fourth Circuit Court of Appeals held that a West Virginia high school could punish a student's off-campus, non-school-related speech via a Myspace group web page because it harassed another student and substantially interfered with school functions.[161] The disruption at issue was the harassed student's decision to miss one day of school. The court said the First Amendment permits schools to punish speech that it is "reasonably foreseeable" would reach school and impact school functioning. This standard had been used by the Second Circuit (which then included Judge Sonia Sotomayor).[162] In 2008, the Second Circuit upheld a Connecticut high school's punishment of a student for off-campus blog posts denigrating school officials and encouraging students to call an administrator and "piss her off." The court reasoned that such postings, which "foreseeably create[d] a risk of substantial disruption," were not entitled to First Amendment protection.

But in two decisions, the Third Circuit Court of Appeals held that neither middle nor high school students could be suspended for insulting online social media parodies of their principals even though the parodies likely were disruptive.[163] The court said that *Tinker* did not explicitly grant schools authority to punish vulgar speech that reached inside the schoolhouse gate.

Without deciding the "metaphysical question of where [the] speech occurred when [the student] used the internet as the medium," the Third Circuit said the school had failed to establish a sufficiently close connection between the after-hours, off-campus speech and school functions. Although online communications may have moved the schoolhouse gate beyond the brick-and-mortar buildings, the court said schools carry a heavier burden to justify regulating off-campus speech.

The U.S. Supreme Court has not reviewed any of these cases. As a consequence, the standard for deciding the free speech rights of students in public schools is less than clear. In general, rules affecting expression in public schools likely are constitutional if the policies neither (1) limit expressive content that is compatible with the school's educational priorities nor (2) target specific content without a strong educational justification.

The Supreme Court has refused to grant university administrators "the same degree of deference" it grants to high school administrators to regulate student expression[164] because college students are "less impressionable than younger students"[165] and because the free speech rights of public school students are "not automatically coextensive with the rights of adults in other settings."[166] The Court generally protects the free speech and free press rights of university students as an essential part of their educational experience. The university and, to a lesser degree, its faculty control the content of the curriculum. Otherwise, university policies and procedures generally must provide a neutral platform for broad student discussion of issues.[167]

Campus Speech

The Supreme Court has established that universities have a greater obligation to create and maintain forums for broad public discussion than do the public schools. As mentioned in Chapter 2, when a university's funding "program [is] designed to facilitate private speech," the funding creates a public forum that prohibits government control of the content of the speech.[168] Consequently, neither the students who contribute the fees nor the university administrators who oversee their allocation may discriminate among student groups because of the ideas they express.[169] Public universities must fund all student groups on the basis of the same content-neutral policies.

Thus, the Supreme Court upheld a University of Wisconsin policy to use mandatory student fees to fund an array of student organizations, including organizations with political or ideological objectives opposed by some students who paid the fees. The Court said the fees established a public forum, and the university was obliged to support all student expression without consideration of content. Writing in concurrence, Justice David Souter said the power of school authorities "to limit expressive freedom of students . . . is confined to high schools, whose students and their schools' relation to them are different and at least arguably distinguishable from their counterparts in college education."[170]

Many years earlier in its per curiam decision in *Papish v. Board of Curators of the University of Missouri*, the U.S. Supreme Court established that "the mere dissemination of ideas—no matter how offensive to good taste—on a state university campus may not be shut off in the name alone of 'conventions of decency.'"[171] The Court said the university violated the First Amendment rights of 32-year-old journalism graduate student Barbara Papish when it expelled her for distributing a campus newspaper containing what university officials labeled "indecent speech." Papish had distributed an issue of the Free Press Underground that contained a political cartoon depicting policemen raping the Statue of Liberty and the Goddess of Justice, and an article under the title, "M—f— Acquitted."

The Court distinguished colleges from public schools and held that a university's "mission is well served if students have the means to engage in dynamic discussions of philosophical, religious, scientific, social and political subjects in their extracurricular campus life outside the lecture hall."[172] As a consequence,[173] public universities not only may but must support all messages without regard to content to enhance wide-open extracurricular debate and free speech interests.[174]

Recently the Court reshaped this concept when it ruled in *Christian Legal Society v. Martinez* that a California law school could deny funding and other benefits to an explicitly

● **REAL WORLD LAW**

Are College Campuses Becoming Free Speech–Free Zones?

Violent protests at the University of California, Berkeley, led administrators to cancel a planned event by Breitbart senior editor and "right-wing provocateur" Milo Yiannopoulos early in 2017. The maelstrom at what was once the birthplace of the free speech movement prompted the most recent and visible cancelation by university administrators seeking to avoid potentially violent confrontations over the alt-right crusader's frequently vicious sexist, racist and inflammatory speech.[1]

Within days of the Berkeley cancellation, two Tennessee state representatives sponsored the "Milo bill . . . designed to implement oversight of administrators' handling of free speech issues." Republican Sen. Joey Hensley said, "We've heard stories from many students that are honestly on the conservative side that have those issues stifled in the classroom."[2] According to the state bill, universities "have abdicated their responsibility to uphold free speech principles, and these failures make it appropriate for all state institutions of higher education to restate and confirm their commitment in this regard."

As one observer concluded, it is a bedrock principle of the First Amendment that public universities, as representatives of government power, should adopt rules that are applied evenhandedly regardless of "the ideas those speakers espouse, even if their ideas are hateful. . . . The university has an obligation to ensure that [the student] right to protest does not prevent [other students] from hearing their invited guest."[3]

Beyond campus, Simon & Schuster canceled a ballyhooed deal for a Yiannopoulos memoir after a recording on YouTube showed him asserting that sexual relationships "between younger boys and older men . . . can be hugely positive experiences."[4]

1. Kasia Kovacs, *Inflammatory and Turned Away*, INSIDE HIGHER Ed, Oct. 21, 2016, www.insidehighered.com/news/2016/10/21/several-universities-cancel-appearances-conservative-writer-milo-yiannopoulos.
2. Adam Tamurin, *Breitbart's Milo Yiannopoulos Inspires Tennessee "Free Speech" Bill*, TENNESSEAN, Feb. 9, 2017, www.tennessean.com/story/news/politics/2017/02/09/breitbarts-milo-yiannopolous-inspires-tennessee-free-speech-bill/97690656.
3. Peter Beinart, *Everyone Has a Right to Free Speech, Even Milo*, ATLANTIC, Feb. 3, 2017, www.theatlantic.com/politics/archive/2017/02/everyone-has-a-right-to-free-speech-even-milo/515565.
4. Elle Hunt, *Milo Yiannopoulos Book Deal Cancelled After Outrage Over Child Abuse Comments*, GUARDIAN, Feb. 21, 2017, www.theguardian.com/books/2017/feb/21/milo-yiannopoulos-book-deal-cancelled-outrage-child-abuse-comments.

religious student group whose members were required to sign a statement of faith.[175] The Court said the law school's requirement that official student groups be open to "all comers" was a reasonable, viewpoint-neutral policy and advanced school interests in non-discriminatory access for students. Through failure to recognize Christian Legal Society's status as an official student group, the university denied CLS the ability to maintain tables at university recruitment fairs, to send bulk emails to all registered law students or to post messages on law school bulletin boards—benefits that clearly implicate First Amendment rights. Yet Justice Ruth Bader Ginsburg argued for the majority that alternative, non-university means of communication available to CLS "reduce[d] the importance of those [university] channels" as an essential means of reaching law school students and adequately protected the group's speech interests.[176] The decision blurred or erased the established distinction between adult and younger students by relying on *Tinker* and deferring to the judgment of law school administrators "in light of the special characteristics of the school environment."[177]

In dissent, Justice Samuel Alito wrote that the decision meant that there is "no freedom for expression that offends prevailing standards of political correctness in our country's institutions of higher learning."[178]

Despite the fact that student fees, or even university allocations, support student newspapers and yearbooks, the Supreme Court generally has viewed campus publications as forums for student expression in which universities may not control content. "Colleges and universities are supposed to be bastions of unbridled inquiry and expression," as one writer put it, "but they probably do as much to repress speech as any other institution in young people's lives."[179] The author referenced a recent study that found that only about one-third of students and fewer than one in five faculty members strongly agreed that it is "safe to hold unpopular positions on campus."

Nonetheless, courts have applied *Hazelwood* to review whether university administrators may censor school-subsidized and -approved publications.[180] One case began when a dean at Governors State University, a public college in Illinois, required her approval of the student newspaper's content before publication. Three student editors sued, claiming the action violated their First Amendment rights. The U.S. Court of Appeals for the Seventh Circuit applied *Hazelwood* to find that the student newspaper was a limited-purpose public forum beyond the control of the university's administration. However, the dean was not liable because the law on the issue was unsettled and the dean had no reason to know it, the court said.

Sitting en banc, the Sixth Circuit Court of Appeals earlier ruled similarly when Kansas State University officials confiscated a student yearbook because they found some of its content objectionable.[181] The court held that *Hazelwood* did not apply because a university "yearbook [must] be analyzed as a limited public forum—rather than a nonpublic forum," which was the case with the high school newspaper.[182] The determination of when a university-funded publication constitutes a public forum rests upon the intent and actions of the administrators, the court said. The court said the university had neither the need nor the authority to control the content of speech in this student yearbook.

The Ninth Circuit Court of Appeals found that editors of a conservative student newspaper at Oregon State University had a legitimate First Amendment claim to nondiscriminatory access to campus to distribute their publication.[183] The case involved an independent newspaper published by the OSU Student Alliance and distributed via campus newspaper boxes. Under a new unwritten policy to clean up campus, university employees removed all of the newspaper's distribution boxes but left the boxes for national papers, such as USA Today. The Ninth Circuit held that a written policy designated most of the OSU campus a public forum and, therefore, university constraints on free speech on campus were subject to the most stringent scrutiny. The court concluded that university officials purposefully engaged in content discrimination and used a "standardless policy" to arbitrarily deprive the newspaper of its ability to circulate.

Several court decisions establish greater latitude for colleges to punish speech by students. In *Tatro v. University of Minnesota*, the Minnesota Supreme Court upheld university sanctions on a student for "satirical commentary and violent fantasy" she posted on Facebook about a school cadaver.[184] As required by the anatomy lab in her mortuary science program, Amanda Tatro signed an agreement to make only "respectful and discreet" comments about cadavers or face "eviction" from the course. On Facebook, Tatro said she liked working with cadavers because it provided opportunity

● REAL WORLD LAW

Do the Speech Categories Make Sense?

Mark S. Scarberry.

Legal scholar Mark S. Scarberry asks whether there is a legally justifiable reason to distinguish between speech that incites a crowd to attack someone (incitement of violence) and speech that provokes a crowd to shout down or attack a speaker (heckler's veto).[1]

Thus far, the Supreme Court has treated the two types of speech as distinct and separate. Incitement that falls under the *Brandenburg* line of cases focused on prevention of imminent violence.[2] In contrast, the Court has reviewed instances of heckler's veto from the perspective of properly tailored time, place and manner regulations, with no mention of the *Brandenburg* standard (except in dissent).

Yet, Scarberry argues that there is "good reason" to treat both forms of speech in the same way. Both heckler's veto and incitement of violence present threats to free speech, personal safety and public order. As such, their punishment should be justifiable only "if the danger is sufficiently great and imminent, and the speaker continues" despite knowledge of this fact.

What do you think?

1. Email from Mark S. Scarberry, Professor, Pepperdine School of Law, Mar. 4, 2015 (on file with author).
2. Brandenburg v. Ohio, 395 U.S. 444 (1969).

Alex Wong/Getty

for "lots of aggression to be taken out" with an embalming knife that she wanted to use to "stab a certain someone in the throat."[185] In response, Tatro received an F in the lab, was placed on probation and was required to take ethics and have a psychiatric examination.

She sued, arguing that the sanctions violated her freedom of speech, which she said were "the same . . . as members of the general public."[186] The university argued that it had authority to regulate any student speech "reasonably related to legitimate pedagogical concerns."

Rather than rely on established tests to review the case, the court held that the university's action did not violate the First Amendment because the rules were "narrowly tailored and directly related to established professional conduct standards."[187] The court said the core mission of the university professional training program was to instill professional standards of ethics and behavior in its students.[188] Therefore, the university could "constitutionally regulate off-campus conduct that violate[s] specific professional obligations," although it could not "regulate a student's personal expression at any time, in any place, for any claimed curriculum-based reason."[189]

Although the Minnesota court in *Tatro* emphasized the narrowness of its ruling, a growing number of federal appeals courts has upheld the authority of colleges to punish or even expel college students, especially graduate students, for speech that violates the "professional standards" of their chosen field. Future teachers[190] and nurses[191] have been expelled for speech in and outside the class setting when their speech was deemed "unfitting" of professional students. While these courts recognize that greater latitude is provided to college student speech than to the free expression of less mature students,[192] circuit courts have split on whether to apply *Hazelwood* to these university speech cases.[193]

In one 2015 decision, the Ninth Circuit Court of Appeals crafted its own test for review of sanctions on university student speech related to professional standards. In *Oyama v. University of Hawaii*, the Ninth Circuit affirmed the constitutionality of the university's effective expulsion of a student based on his unprofessional and inappropriate speech.[194] Mark Oyama was denied a required student teacher placement after he made derogatory comments in classes about students with disabilities and said he favored consensual sexual relations with children. Oyama sued, saying the punishment violated his First Amendment rights.

The Ninth Circuit said *Hazelwood* did not apply because its "key rationales for restricting students' speech are to ensure that students are not exposed to material that may be inappropriate for their level of maturity and learn whatever lessons the activity is designed to teach. Neither of these rationales is relevant here."[195] Instead, the court leaned heavily on *Tatro* to find the university's punishment was constitutional because it "related directly to defined and established professional standards, was narrowly tailored to serve the University's foundational mission of evaluating Oyama's suitability for teaching,

AP Photo/Robert W. Klein

In the mid-1960s, massive student protests at the University of California, Berkeley, set off the free speech movement across the country. Here, Mario Savio, leader of the Berkeley Free Speech Movement, speaks to the assembled crowd in 1964.

Members of the alt-right supported claims that progressives armed with political correctness were silencing conservatives on U.S. campuses and shrinking the range of acceptable public debate.

and reflected reasonable professional judgment."[196] The university could deny Oyama's student teaching placement because his statements indicated that he had not absorbed, and likely would not comply with, defined and established standards for the teaching profession.[197]

In 2016, the Eighth Circuit Court of Appeals relied squarely on *Hazelwood* in deciding *Keefe v. Adams*.[198] Craig Keefe had posted angry comments about a classmate on Facebook that made the fellow nursing student "feel extremely uncomfortable and nervous."[199]

After meeting with Keefe, school administrators removed him from the nursing program for "behavior unbecoming of the profession and transgression of professional boundaries" in violation of the student handbook and the Code of Ethics for Nurses.[200] The court ruled that "college administrators and educators in a professional school have discretion to require compliance with recognized standards of the profession, both on and off campus, so long as their actions are reasonably related to legitimate pedagogical concerns."[201] Turning *Hazelwood* on its head, the court in *Keefe* said a "university may have an even stronger interest in the content of its curriculum and imposing academic discipline than did the high school at issue in Hazelwood."[202] Although several First Amendment organizations filed an amicus brief urging the Supreme Court to hear the case and provide "clarity . . . that off-campus speech is entitled to greater protection than speech inside of the classroom during school," the Supreme Court denied certiorari.[203]

The lower court rulings, according to the Student Press Law Center, "leave[] college students with diminished free-speech protection in all forums—including when speaking on off-campus social media on their personal time—if their speech can be deemed unprofessional."[204] They also allow "colleges to punish speech without having to demonstrate a substantial disruption to school activities."[205]

Some university administrators continue to try to influence the content of student media by pressuring faculty or staff advisers. In a recent example, the top editors of the University of Georgia's student newspaper resigned en masse, claiming nonstudent managers hired to oversee The Red and Black had interfered with their editorial autonomy.[206] One editor said the newly hired managers of the independent student paper had veto power on editorial content. A copy of a memo on content guidelines circulated among the paper's publishing board questioned the journalistic value of "content that catches people or organizations doing bad things." Within days of the walkout, the university reiterated its support of student control of content and reinstated the student editors.[207]

In a previous fight over content of a university student newspaper, a federal district court reversed itself to rule that the First Amendment did not prohibit Kansas State University from removing and reassigning the adviser of The Collegian.[208] The adviser was dismissed amid controversy over the newspaper's coverage of campus diversity issues and events.[209] Complaints surfaced and adviser Ron Johnson was reassigned after the newspaper failed to cover the university-hosted annual Big 12 Conference on Black Student Government.[210] The Collegian's editors joined Johnson's lawsuit, claiming that the removal amounted to censorship. The head of the journalism school said a content analysis of the newspaper supported the adviser's removal,[211] and university administrators said budget concerns drove the decision.[212]

Joe Kohen via Getty Images

The Department of Justice has reviewed several cases of burning a pride flag to determine whether to prosecute the act as a hate crime that is not protected by the First Amendment.

Speech Codes

In what some called a concession to political correctness[213] and others saw as an important step toward a more tolerant and inclusive society,[214] universities across the United States began adopting and strengthening campus speech codes in the 1980s.[215] The codes varied widely but generally prohibited verbal harassment of minorities, hate-filled invective, bigotry and offensive speech on campus. Courts consistently and resoundingly found these codes unconstitutional because they targeted disfavored speech and reduced the flow of information and ideas.[216] As one federal district court wrote, "The Supreme Court has consistently held that statutes punishing speech or conduct solely on the grounds that they are unseemly or offensive are unconstitutionally overbroad."[217]

Yet campus hate speech codes continue to be adopted.[218] One study found that although restrictions are declining, nearly 60 percent of the 400 universities examined maintained policies that "seriously infringe upon the free speech rights of students."[219] The universities argue that the codes are essential to the protection of informed discourse and serve the core educational mission of universities. Courts have not accepted the notion that limiting hateful speech enhances the diversity of ideas discussed in the university environment.

OTHER HARMS

Any person or company involved with preparing or publishing news, entertainment and advertising may be sued for any number of legal claims. Media are not exempt when laws, such as contract laws, apply generally to any competent adult. Thus, when media make contractual agreements, they may be sued for breaching a contract. A contract may be an oral or a written agreement.

For example, when documentary filmmakers interviewed art critic Donald Wildmon for their film about American art censorship, the filmmakers signed a contract stating that the interview would not be distributed beyond a single British channel without Wildmon's

● **REAL WORLD LAW**

Professor Punished for Violating Anti-Harassment Policy

In 2017, the University of Oregon found law professor Nancy Shurtz guilty of harassment under the campus anti-harassment policy for off-campus behavior that created a hostile learning environment for her students.[1]

The university publicly released an independent investigation of the incident during which Shurtz wore blackface, a white lab coat and a stethoscope to her Halloween party. She said she was dressed as Dr. Damon Tweedy, a black psychiatrist who wrote about racism in medical school in his memoir, "Black Man in a White Coat." Shurtz said she intended her costume to be an anti-racist statement.

She had used campus email and class announcements to invite her students to the party. Some students said they felt compelled to attend and to remain even though they were uncomfortable.[2]

Shurtz apologized but complained that the release of the report was a form of public shaming and "supremely public retaliation."[3]

The university found that although the party was in Shurtz's home, and she did not intend to offend anyone, her actions damaged race relations in the law school, caused anxiety to students, disrupted the business of the university and harmed the learning environment. The seriousness of the disruptions outweighed her right to freedom of speech and academic freedom, the university concluded.

The university temporarily suspended Shurtz and took other disciplinary action that it did not disclose, citing university policy and "faculty records law."[4]

---

1. U. Oregon News Release: Provost Issues Statement and Report Regarding Investigation, US Official News, Jan. 2, 2107, editorial@plusmedia solutions.com.
2. Scott Jaschik, *Oregon: Professor in Blackface Violated Anti-Harassment Policy*, Inside Higher Ed, Jan. 3, 2017, www.thefire.org/media-coverage/oregon-professor-in-blackface-violated-anti-harassment-policy.
3. Associated Press, *University of Oregon Professor Who Wore Blackface Blasts Report*, Seattle Times, Dec. 24, 2016, www.seattletimes.com/seattle-news/university-of-oregon-professor-who-wore-blackface-blasts-school-report.
4. Paul Caron, *University of Oregon Withholds From Public Discipline of Tax Prof Nancy Shurtz for Wearing Blackface*, TaxProf Blog, Feb. 27, 2017, taxprof.typepad.com/taxprof_blog/2017/02/university-of-oregon-withholds-from-public-disciplinary-records-of-tax-prof-nancy-shurtz-for-wearing.html.

permission. After the film won numerous awards and was selected to open a documentary festival in New York City, Wildmon sued. The filmmakers argued that the contract referred only to the complete interview, not the brief portions used in the film. Although neither the contract's wording nor the parties' intentions were clear, the court interpreted the contract to prevent reuse of the raw interview footage.[220] However, the original documentary, including the interview excerpts, could be exhibited wherever the producer wanted. The *Cohen v. Cowles Media Co.* decision, discussed in Chapter 8, in which newspapers revealed the name of a source to whom confidentiality was promised, also is a breach of contract case.

If someone who has an opportunity to gain financially believes another interfered with that opportunity, she may file a tort suit. The tort has different names in different states. In one example, a utility company executive pressured a newspaper that reported on energy matters not to use articles by a freelance writer whom the executive thought was biased. The writer sued the utility company for interfering with her economic relationship with the paper. A California appellate court ruled that the writer could pursue her economic interference claim because the utility executive might have improperly influenced the paper.[221] The First Amendment may be a defense against an economic interference claim.

CHAPTER SUMMARY

FOR YEARS, THE U.S. SUPREME COURT struggled to develop a test that would clearly delineate between dangerous incitement to violence and the legitimate right of people to express themselves vehemently and angrily. During periods of national instability, fear or war, the freedom of expression tends to become more susceptible to government restraint. Stopping imminent violence and protecting the national security are sufficiently important concerns to outweigh speech protection under certain conditions.

The Court's loose "clear and present danger" test frequently upheld the constitutionality of laws that punished unpopular political speech. The test evolved over the years and eventually became the current *Brandenburg/Hess* incitement test that limits government punishment to speech that is intended to and likely to produce imminent illegal action. In evaluating laws that limit speech, courts tend to balance the interests at stake, usually categorically.

Lawsuits against the media for promoting or causing physical harm rarely succeed. The Supreme Court requires plaintiffs to show that the media intended to encourage people to do themselves or others immediate harm. Media information and depictions rarely meet this standard. If plaintiffs claim the media acted negligently, leading to injury or death, they must prove the media had a duty of care that they breached and that the breach was the proximate cause of the injury. Courts rarely find media liable because a reasonable person is unlikely to have foreseen the harm.

The Supreme Court has established that offensive expression, and even what many view as hate speech, is protected by the Constitution because freedom of expression includes both the cognitive and the emotional elements of expression. Fighting words, a very narrowly defined category of face-to-face utterances that by their very expression inflict injury, are not protected. Laws that target highly offensive speech are constitutional only if they are extremely narrowly tailored to address real and demonstrable harms. Attempts to prohibit unpopular or racist speech as a subset of fighting words will rarely be constitutional. When speech becomes an overt act of threat or intimidation, it may be regulated and punished.

Some symbolic acts constitute speech and are protected by the First Amendment. Rulings on speech acts suggest that nondisruptive political protest that does not undermine core governmental interests is generally protected from government regulation.

The freedom of speech of students, and others, inside schools and universities is governed by a complex and shifting set of distinctions and tests that turn on specific facts. Case outcomes hinge on statutory language, the intensity of the threat or offense and the societal interest involved. Few bright lines or broad precedents exist in this evolving area of First Amendment law.

Contract law and laws against unfair competition, or interference with economic gain, do not run afoul of the First Amendment even though they affect the media, professional communicators and communications businesses. ∎

CASES FOR STUDY

For study resources and a case archive go to **study.sagepub.com/medialaw6e**.

THINKING ABOUT IT

The two case excerpts that follow highlight the Supreme Court's attempts to balance the First Amendment freedom of speech with concerns for educational goals and personal safety. Both cases help identify the parameters of First Amendment protection: The first clarifies the extent to which important competing values—in this case, education of the young—may limit the freedom of speakers. The second helps define when words that express ideas, even in artistic form, may lose constitutional protection because they threaten others and engender fear.

- Consider what each decision, as well as the two taken together, demonstrates about the different categories of speech in the Court's jurisprudence.

- In these two decisions defining the extent of First Amendment freedoms, does the Court focus on the nature of the speech, the intent of the law, the impact of the regulation or something else to reach its conclusion?

- To what extent does the Court's decision in *Tinker* turn on the category of speech, the type of speaker, the location of speech or other factors involved?

- Does *Elonis* provide a workable definition of true threats and a clear test to determine when such speech is unprotected?

Tinker v. Des Moines Independent Community School District
SUPREME COURT OF THE UNITED STATES
393 U.S. 503 (1969)

JUSTICE ABE FORTAS delivered the Court's opinion:

. . . The District Court recognized that the wearing of an armband for the purpose of expressing certain views is the type of symbolic act that is within the Free Speech Clause of the First Amendment. As we shall discuss, the wearing of armbands in the circumstances of this case was entirely divorced from actually or potentially disruptive conduct by those participating in it. It was closely akin to "pure speech" which, we have repeatedly held, is entitled to comprehensive protection under the First Amendment.

First Amendment rights, applied in light of the special characteristics of the school environment, are available to teachers and students. It can hardly be argued that either students or teachers shed their constitutional rights to freedom of speech or expression at the schoolhouse gate. This has been the unmistakable holding of this Court for almost 50 years. . . .

. . . On the other hand, the Court has repeatedly emphasized the need for affirming the comprehensive authority of the States and of school officials, consistent with fundamental constitutional safeguards, to prescribe and control conduct in the schools. . . . Our problem lies in the area where students in the exercise of First Amendment rights collide with the rules of the school authorities.

The problem posed by the present case . . . does not concern aggressive, disruptive action or even group demonstrations. Our problem involves direct, primary First Amendment rights akin to "pure speech."

The school officials banned and sought to punish petitioners for a silent, passive expression of opinion, unaccompanied by any disorder or disturbance on the part of petitioners. There is here no evidence whatever of petitioners' interference, actual or nascent, with the school's work or of collision with the rights of other students to be secure and to be let alone. Accordingly, this case does not concern speech or action that intrudes upon the work of the schools or the rights of other students. . . .

. . . Outside the classrooms, a few students made hostile remarks to the children wearing armbands, but there were no threats or acts of violence on school premises.

The District Court concluded that the action of the school authorities was reasonable because it was based upon their fear of a disturbance from the wearing of the armbands. But, in our system, undifferentiated fear or apprehension of disturbance is not enough to overcome the right to freedom of expression. Any departure from absolute regimentation may cause trouble. Any variation from the majority's opinion may inspire fear. Any word spoken, in class, in the lunchroom, or on the campus, that deviates from the views of another person may start an argument or cause a disturbance. But our Constitution says we must take this risk; and our history says that it is this sort of hazardous freedom—this kind of openness—that is the basis of our national strength and of the independence and vigor of Americans who grow up and live in this relatively permissive, often disputatious, society.

In order for the State in the person of school officials to justify prohibition of a particular expression of opinion, it must be able to show that its action was caused by something more than a mere desire to avoid the discomfort and unpleasantness that always accompany an unpopular viewpoint. Certainly where there is no finding and no showing that engaging in the forbidden conduct would "materially and substantially interfere with the requirements of appropriate discipline in the operation of the school," the prohibition cannot be sustained.

. . . [T]he record fails to yield evidence that the school authorities had reason to anticipate that the wearing of the armbands would substantially interfere with the work of the school or impinge upon the rights of other students. . . .

On the contrary, the action of the school authorities appears to have been based upon an urgent wish to avoid the controversy which might result from the expression, even by the silent symbol of armbands, of opposition to this Nation's part in the conflagration in Vietnam. It is revealing, in this respect, that the meeting at which the school principals decided to issue the contested regulation was called in response to a student's statement to the journalism teacher in one of the schools that he wanted to write an article on Vietnam and have it published in the school paper. (The student was dissuaded.)

It is also relevant that the school authorities did not purport to prohibit the wearing of all symbols of political or controversial significance. The record shows that students in some of the schools wore buttons relating to national political campaigns, and some even wore the Iron Cross, traditionally a symbol of Nazism. . . . Instead, a particular symbol—black armbands worn to exhibit opposition to this Nation's involvement in Vietnam—was singled out for prohibition. Clearly, the prohibition of expression of one particular opinion, at least without evidence that it is necessary to avoid material and substantial interference with schoolwork or discipline, is not constitutionally permissible.

In our system, state-operated schools may not be enclaves of totalitarianism. School officials do not possess absolute authority over their students. Students in school as well as out of school are "persons" under our Constitution. They are possessed of fundamental rights, which the State must respect, just as they themselves must respect their obligations to the State. In our system, students may not be regarded as closed-circuit recipients of only that which the State chooses to communicate. They may not be confined to the expression of those sentiments that are officially approved. In the absence of a specific showing of constitutionally valid reasons to regulate their speech, students are entitled to freedom of expression of their views. . . .

. . . A student's rights, therefore, do not embrace merely the classroom hours. When he is in the cafeteria, or on the playing field, or on the campus during the authorized hours, he may express his opinions, even on controversial subjects like the conflict in Vietnam, if he does so without "materially and substantially interfer[ing] with the requirements of appropriate discipline in the operation of the school" and without colliding with the rights of others. But conduct by the student, in class or out of it, which for any reason—whether it stems from time, place, or type of behavior—materially disrupts class work or involves substantial disorder or invasion of the rights of others is, of course, not immunized by the constitutional guarantee of freedom of speech.

Under our Constitution, free speech is not a right that is given only to be so circumscribed that it exists in principle but not in fact. Freedom of expression would not truly exist if the right could be exercised only in an area that a benevolent government has provided as a safe haven for crackpots. . . . [W]e do not confine the permissible exercise of First Amendment rights to a telephone booth or the four corners of a pamphlet, or to supervised and ordained discussion in a school classroom.

If a regulation were adopted by school officials forbidding discussion of the Vietnam conflict, or the expression by any student of opposition to it anywhere on school property except as part of a prescribed classroom exercise, it would be obvious that the regulation would violate the constitutional rights of students, at least if it could not be justified by a showing that the students' activities would materially and substantially disrupt the work and discipline of the school. In the circumstances of the present case, the prohibition of the silent, passive "witness of the armbands," as one of the children called it, is no less offensive to the Constitution's guarantees. . . .

JUSTICE POTTER STEWART, concurring:

Although I agree with much of what is said in the Court's opinion, and with its judgment in this case, I cannot share the Court's uncritical assumption that, school discipline aside, the First Amendment rights of children are coextensive with those of adults. . . . I continue to hold the view [that] . . . [a] State may permissibly determine that, at least in some precisely delineated areas, a child—like someone in a captive audience—is not possessed of that full capacity for individual choice which is the presupposition of First Amendment guarantees.

JUSTICE BYRON WHITE, concurring:

While I join the Court's opinion, I deem it appropriate to note, first, that the Court continues to recognize a distinction between communicating by words and communicating by acts or conduct which sufficiently impinges on some valid state interest. . . .

JUSTICE HUGO BLACK, dissenting:

The Court's holding in this case ushers in what I deem to be an entirely new era in which the power to control pupils by the elected "officials of state supported public schools . . ." in the United States is in ultimate effect transferred to the Supreme Court. The Court brought this particular case here on a petition for certiorari urging that the First and Fourteenth Amendments protect the right of school pupils to express their political views all the way "from kindergarten through high school." Here, the constitutional right to "political expression" asserted was a right to wear black armbands during school hours and at classes in order to demonstrate to the other students that the petitioners were mourning because of the death of United States soldiers in Vietnam and to protest that war which they were against. . . .

. . . [T]he crucial . . . questions are whether students and teachers may use the schools at their whim as a platform for the exercise of free speech— "symbolic" or "pure"—and whether the courts will allocate to themselves the function of deciding how the pupils' school day will be spent. While I have always believed that, under the First and Fourteenth

Amendments, neither the State nor the Federal Government has any authority to regulate or censor the content of speech, I have never believed that any person has a right to give speeches or engage in demonstrations where he pleases and when he pleases. . . .

I think the record overwhelmingly shows that the armbands did exactly what the elected school officials and principals foresaw they would, that is, took the students' minds off their class work and diverted them to thoughts about the highly emotional subject of the Vietnam War. And I repeat that, if the time has come when pupils of state-supported schools, kindergartens, grammar schools, or high schools, can defy and flout orders of school officials to keep their minds on their own schoolwork, it is the beginning of a new revolutionary era of permissiveness in this country fostered by the judiciary. . . .

It may be that the Nation has outworn the old-fashioned slogan that "children are to be seen, not heard," but one may, I hope, be permitted to harbor the thought that taxpayers send children to school on the premise that at their age they need to learn, not teach. . . . Iowa's public schools . . . are operated to give students an opportunity to learn, not to talk politics by actual speech, or by "symbolic" speech. And, as I have pointed out before, the record amply shows that public protest in the school classes against the Vietnam War "distracted from that singleness of purpose which the State [here Iowa] desired to exist in its public educational institutions." . . .

This case, therefore, wholly without constitutional reasons, in my judgment, subjects all the public schools in the country to the whims and caprices of their loudest-mouthed, but maybe not their brightest, students. I, for one, am not fully persuaded that school pupils are wise enough. . . . I wish, therefore, wholly to disclaim any purpose on my part to hold that the Federal Constitution compels the teachers, parents, and elected school officials to surrender control of the American public school system to public school students. I dissent.

JUSTICE JOHN HARLAN, dissenting:

I certainly agree that state public school authorities in the discharge of their responsibilities are not wholly exempt from the requirements of the Fourteenth Amendment respecting the freedoms of expression and association. At the same time I am reluctant to believe that there is any disagreement between the majority and myself on the proposition that school officials should be accorded the widest authority in maintaining discipline and good order in their institutions. To translate that proposition into a workable constitutional rule, I would, in cases like this, cast upon those complaining the burden of showing that a particular school measure was motivated by other than legitimate school concerns—for example, a desire to prohibit the expression of an unpopular point of view, while permitting expression of the dominant opinion.

Finding nothing in this record which impugns the good faith of respondents in promulgating the armband regulation, I would affirm the judgment below.

Elonis v. United States
SUPREME COURT OF THE UNITED STATES
135 S. Ct. 2001 (2015)

CHIEF JUSTICE JOHN ROBERTS delivered the opinion of the Court.

Federal law makes it a crime to transmit in interstate commerce "any communication containing any threat . . . to injure the person of another." 18 U. S. C. § 875(c). Petitioner was convicted of violating this provision under instructions that required the jury to find that he communicated what a reasonable person would regard as a threat. The question is whether the statute also requires that the defendant be aware of the threatening nature of the communication, and—if not—whether the First Amendment requires such a showing.

Anthony Douglas Elonis was an active user of the social networking web site Facebook. . . . In May 2010, Elonis's wife of nearly seven years left him, [and] . . . Elonis began "listening to more violent music" and posting self-styled "rap" lyrics . . . [that] included graphically violent language and imagery. This material was often interspersed with disclaimers that the lyrics were "fictitious," with no intentional "resemblance to real persons." Elonis posted an explanation to another Facebook user that "I'm doing this for me. My writing is therapeutic."

Elonis's co-workers and friends viewed the posts in a different light. Around Halloween of 2010, Elonis posted a photograph of himself and a co-worker at a "Halloween Haunt" event at the amusement park where they worked. In the photograph, Elonis was holding a toy knife against his co-worker's neck, and in the caption Elonis wrote, "I wish." . . . [The] chief of park security was a Facebook "friend" of Elonis, saw the photograph, and fired him.

In response, Elonis posted a new entry on his Facebook page:

"Moles! Didn't I tell y'all I had several? Y'all sayin' I had access to keys for all the f***in' gates. That I have sinister plans for all my friends and must have taken home a couple. Y'all think it's too dark and foggy to secure your facility from a man as mad as me? You see, even without a paycheck, I'm still the main attraction. Whoever thought the Halloween Haunt could be so f***in' scary?" . . .

Elonis's posts frequently included crude, degrading, and violent material about his soon-to-be ex-wife. Shortly after he was fired, Elonis posted an adaptation of a satirical sketch that he and his wife had watched together. In the actual sketch, called "It's Illegal to Say . . . ," a comedian explains that it is illegal for a person to say he wishes to kill the President, but not illegal to explain that it is illegal for him to say that. When Elonis posted the script of the sketch, however, he substituted his wife for the President. The posting was part of the basis for Count Two of the indictment, threatening his wife:

"Hi, I'm Tone Elonis.

Did you know that it's illegal for me to say I want to kill my wife? . . .

It's one of the only sentences that I'm not allowed to say. . . .

Now it was okay for me to say it right then because I was just telling you that it's illegal for me to say I want to kill my wife. . . .

Um, but what's interesting is that it's very illegal to say I really, really think someone out there should kill my wife. . . .

But not illegal to say with a mortar launcher.

Because that's it's own sentence. . . .

I also found out that it's incredibly illegal, extremely illegal to go on Facebook and say something like the best place to fire a mortar launcher at her house would be from the cornfield behind it because of easy access to a getaway road and you'd have a clear line of sight through the sun room. . . .

Yet even more illegal to show an illustrated diagram [of the house]. . . ."

The details about the home were accurate. At the bottom of the post, Elonis included a link to the video of the original skit, and wrote, "Art is about pushing limits. I'm willing to go to jail for my Constitutional rights. Are you?"

After viewing some of Elonis's posts, his wife felt "extremely afraid for [her] life." A state court granted her a three-year protection-from-abuse order against Elonis (essentially, a restraining order). Elonis referred to the order in another post on his "Tone Dougie" page, also included in Count Two of the indictment:

"Fold up your [protection-from-abuse order] and put it in your pocket

Is it thick enough to stop a bullet?

Try to enforce an Order

that was improperly granted in the first place

Me thinks the Judge needs an education

on true threat jurisprudence

And prison time'll add zeros to my settlement . . .

And if worse comes to worse

I've got enough explosives to take care of the State Police and the Sheriff 's Department."

At the bottom of this post was a link to the Wikipedia article on "Freedom of speech." . . . That same month, . . . Elonis posted [this] entry . . . :

"That's it, I've had about enough

I'm checking out and making a name for myself

Enough elementary schools in a ten mile radius to initiate the most heinous school shooting ever imagined

And hell hath no fury like a crazy man in a Kindergarten class

The only question is . . . which one?"

. . . A grand jury indicted Elonis for making threats to injure . . . in violation of 18 U. S. C. §875(c). In the District Court, Elonis moved to dismiss the indictment for failing to allege that he had intended to threaten anyone. The District Court denied the motion, holding that Third Circuit precedent required only that Elonis "intentionally made the communication, not that he intended to make a threat." At trial, Elonis testified that his posts emulated the rap lyrics of the well-known performer Eminem . . . In Elonis's view, he had posted "nothing . . . that hasn't been said already." The Government presented as witnesses Elonis's wife and co-workers, all of whom said they felt afraid and viewed Elonis's posts as serious threats.

Elonis requested a jury instruction that "the government must prove that he intended to communicate a true threat." The District Court denied that request. The jury instructions instead informed the jury that

"A statement is a true threat when a defendant intentionally makes a statement in a context or under such circumstances wherein a reasonable person would foresee that the statement would be interpreted by those to whom the maker communicates the statement as a serious expression of an intention to inflict bodily injury or take the life of an individual."

The Government's closing argument emphasized that it was irrelevant whether Elonis intended the postings to be threats—"it doesn't matter what he thinks." A jury convicted Elonis . . . [and] sentenced [him] to three years, eight months' imprisonment and three years' supervised release.

Elonis renewed his challenge to the jury instructions in the Court of Appeals, contending that the jury should have been required to find that he intended his posts to be threats. The Court of Appeals disagreed, holding that the intent required by Section 875(c) is only the intent to communicate words that the defendant understands, and that a reasonable person would view as a threat.

We granted certiorari.

. . . This statute requires that a communication be transmitted and that the communication contain a threat. It does not specify that the defendant must have any mental state with respect to these elements. In particular, it does not indicate whether the defendant must intend that his communication contain a threat.

Elonis argues that the word "threat" itself in Section 875(c) imposes such a requirement. According to Elonis, every definition of "threat" or "threaten" conveys the notion of an intent to inflict harm. . . . For its part, the Government argues that Section 875(c) should be read in light of its neighboring provisions . . . [that] expressly include a mental state requirement of an "intent to extort." According to the Government, the[se] express "intent to extort" requirements . . . should preclude courts from implying an unexpressed "intent to threaten" requirement in Section 875(c).

. . . The most we can conclude from the language of Section 875(c) and its neighboring provisions is that Congress meant to proscribe a broad class of threats in Section 875(c), but did not identify what mental state, if any, a defendant must have to be convicted. . . .

The fact that the statute does not specify any required mental state, however, does not mean that none exists. We have repeatedly held that "mere omission from a criminal enactment of any mention of criminal intent" should not be read "as dispensing with it." This rule of construction reflects the basic principle that "wrongdoing must be conscious to be criminal." . . . The "central thought" is that a defendant must be "blameworthy in mind" before he can be found guilty. . . . Although there are exceptions, the "general rule" is that a guilty mind is "a necessary element in the indictment and proof of every crime." We therefore generally "interpret[] criminal statutes to include broadly applicable scienter requirements, even where the statute by its terms does not contain them."

This is not to say that a defendant must know that his conduct is illegal before he may be found guilty. The familiar maxim "ignorance of the law is no excuse" typically holds true. Instead, our cases have explained that a defendant generally must "know the facts that make his conduct fit the definition of the offense," even if he does not know that those facts give rise to a crime. . . .

[I]n *United States v. X-Citement Video* (1994), we considered a statute criminalizing the distribution of visual depictions of minors engaged in sexually explicit conduct. We rejected a reading of the statute which would have required only that a defendant knowingly send the prohibited materials, regardless of whether he knew the age of the performers. We held instead that a defendant must also know that those depicted were minors, because that was "the crucial element separating legal innocence from wrongful conduct."

When interpreting federal criminal statutes that are silent on the required mental state, we read into the statute "only that *mens rea* which is necessary to separate wrongful conduct from 'otherwise innocent conduct.'" . . .

Section 875(c), as noted, requires proof that a communication was transmitted and that it contained a threat. . . . The parties agree that a defendant under Section 875(c) must know that he is transmitting a communication. But communicating *something* is not what makes the conduct "wrongful." Here "the crucial element separating legal innocence from wrongful conduct" is the threatening nature of the communication. The mental state requirement must therefore apply to the fact that the communication contains a threat.

Elonis's conviction, however, was premised solely on how his posts would be understood by a reasonable person. Such a "reasonable person" standard is a familiar feature of civil liability in tort law, but is inconsistent with "the conventional requirement for criminal conduct—*awareness* of some wrongdoing." Having liability turn on whether a "reasonable person" regards the communication as a threat—regardless of what the defendant thinks—"reduces culpability on the all-important element of the crime to negligence," and we "have long been reluctant to infer that a negligence standard was intended in criminal statutes." Under these principles, "what [Elonis] thinks" does matter.

The Government is at pains to characterize its position as something other than a negligence standard, emphasizing that its approach would require proof that a defendant "comprehended [the] contents and context" of the communication. . . . Elonis can be convicted, the Government contends, if he himself knew the contents and context of his posts, and a reasonable person would have recognized that the posts would be read as genuine threats. That is a negligence standard.

●●●

In light of the foregoing, Elonis's conviction cannot stand. The jury was instructed that the Government need prove only that a reasonable person would regard Elonis's communications as threats, and that was error. Federal criminal liability generally does not turn solely on the results of an act without considering the defendant's mental state. That understanding "took deep and early root in American soil" and Congress left it intact here: Under Section 875(c), "wrongdoing must be conscious to be criminal." . . .

Our holding makes clear that negligence is not sufficient to support a conviction under Section 875(c), contrary to the view of nine Courts of Appeals. . . . The judgment of the United States Court of Appeals for the Third Circuit is reversed, and the case is remanded for further proceedings consistent with this opinion.

It is so ordered.

JUSTICE ALITO, concurring in part and dissenting in part.

. . . The Court's disposition of this case is certain to cause confusion and serious problems. . . . The Court holds that the jury instructions in this case were defective because they required only negligence in conveying a threat. But the Court refuses to explain what type of intent was necessary. Did the jury need to find that Elonis had the *purpose* of conveying a true threat? Was it enough if he *knew* that his words conveyed such a threat? Would *recklessness* suffice? The Court declines to say. Attorneys and judges are left to guess. . . .

This Court has not defined the meaning of the term "threat" in §875(c), but in construing the same term in a related statute, the Court distinguished a "true 'threat'" from facetious or hyperbolic remarks. In my view, the term "threat" in §875(c) can fairly be defined as a statement that is reasonably interpreted as "an expression of an intention to inflict evil, injury, or damage on another." Conviction under §875(c) demands proof that the defendant's transmission was in fact a threat, *i.e.*, that it is reasonable to interpret the transmission as an expression of an intent to harm another. In addition, it must be shown that the defendant was at least reckless as to whether the transmission met that requirement. . . . I would hold that a defendant may be convicted under §875(c) if he or she consciously disregards the risk that the communication transmitted will be interpreted as a true threat. . . .

There remains the question whether interpreting §875(c) to require no more than recklessness with respect to the element at issue here would violate the First Amendment. . . .

Elonis argues that the First Amendment protects a threat if the person making the statement does not actually intend to cause harm. . . .

Elonis also claims his threats were constitutionally protected works of art. Words like his, he contends, are shielded by the First Amendment because they are similar to words uttered by rappers and singers in public performances and recordings. . . . But context matters. "Taken in context," lyrics in songs that are performed for an audience or sold in recorded form are unlikely to be interpreted as a real threat to a real person. Statements on social media that are pointedly directed at their victims, by contrast, are much more likely to be taken seriously. . . .

Threats of violence and intimidation are among the most favored weapons of domestic abusers, and the rise of social media has only made those tactics more commonplace. A fig leaf of artistic expression cannot convert such hurtful, valueless threats into protected speech. . . .

We have sometimes cautioned that it is necessary to "exten[d] a measure of strategic protection" to otherwise unprotected false statements of fact in order to ensure enough "'breathing space'" for protected speech. A similar argument might be made with respect to threats. But we have also held that the law provides adequate breathing space when it requires proof that false statements were made with reckless disregard of their falsity. Requiring proof of recklessness is similarly sufficient here.

Finally, because the jury instructions in this case did not require proof of recklessness, I would vacate the judgment below and remand for the Court of Appeals to decide in the first instance whether Elonis's conviction could be upheld under a recklessness standard.

JUSTICE THOMAS, dissenting.

We granted certiorari to resolve a conflict in the lower courts over the appropriate mental state for threat prosecutions under 18 U. S. C. §875(c). . . . Rather than resolve the conflict, the Court casts aside the approach used in nine Circuits and leaves nothing in its place. Lower courts are thus left to guess at the appropriate mental state for §875(c). All they know after today's decision is that a requirement of general intent will not do. But they can safely infer that a majority of this Court would not adopt an intent-to-threaten requirement, as the opinion carefully leaves open the possibility that recklessness may be enough.

This failure to decide throws everyone from appellate judges to everyday Facebook users into a state of uncertainty. . . . Because the Court of Appeals properly applied the general-intent standard, and because the communications transmitted by Elonis were "true threats" unprotected by the First Amendment, I would affirm the judgment below. . . .

Because §875(c) criminalizes speech, the First Amendment requires that the term "threat" be limited to a narrow class of historically unprotected communications called "true threats." To qualify as a true threat, a communication must be a serious expression of an intention to commit unlawful physical violence, not merely "political hyperbole"; "vehement, caustic, and sometimes unpleasantly sharp attacks"; or "vituperative, abusive, and inexact" statements. It also cannot be determined solely by the reaction of the recipient, but must instead be "determined by the interpretation of a *reasonable* recipient familiar with the context of the communication," lest historically protected speech be suppressed at the will of an eggshell observer. There is thus no dispute that, at a minimum, §875(c) requires an objective showing: The communication must be one that "a reasonable observer would construe as a true threat to another." And there is no dispute that the posts at issue here meet that objective standard. . . .

Our default rule in favor of general intent applies with full force to criminal statutes addressing speech. Well over 100 years ago, this Court considered a conviction under a federal obscenity statute that punished anyone "'who shall knowingly deposit, or cause to be deposited, for mailing or delivery,'" any "'obscene, lewd, or lascivious book, pamphlet, picture, paper, writing, print, or other publication of an indecent character.'" In that case, as here, the defendant argued that, even if "he may have had . . . actual knowledge or notice of [the paper's] contents" when he put it in the mail, he could not "be convicted of the offence . . . unless he knew or believed that such paper could be properly or justly characterized as obscene, lewd, and lascivious." The Court rejected that theory . . .

Applying ordinary rules of statutory construction, I would read §875(c) to require proof of general intent. To "know the facts that make his conduct illegal" under §875(c), a defendant must know that he transmitted a communication in interstate or foreign commerce that contained a threat. . . . A defendant like Elonis, however, who admits that he "knew that what [he] was saying was violent" but supposedly "just wanted to express [him]self," acted with the general intent required under §875(c), even if he did not know that a jury would conclude that his communication constituted a "threat" as a matter of law. . . .

Requiring general intent in this context is not the same as requiring mere negligence. . . . [T]he defendant must *know*—not merely be reckless or negligent with respect to the fact—that he is committing the acts that constitute the . . . offense.

But general intent requires *no* mental state (not even a negligent one) concerning the "fact" that certain words meet the *legal* definition of a threat. . . .

Elonis also insists that we read an intent-to-threaten element into §875(c) in light of the First Amendment. But our practice of construing statutes "to avoid constitutional questions . . . is not a license for the judiciary to rewrite language enacted by the legislature." . . .

Elonis does not contend that threats are constitutionally protected speech, nor could he: "From 1791 to the present, . . . our society . . . has permitted restrictions upon the content of speech in a few limited areas," true threats being one of them. Instead, Elonis claims that only *intentional* threats fall within this particular historical exception. . . .

Elonis also insists that our precedents require a mental state of intent when it comes to threat prosecutions under §875(c). . . .

We generally have not required a heightened mental state under the First Amendment for historically unprotected categories of speech. For instance, the Court has indicated that a legislature may constitutionally prohibit "'fighting words,' those personally abusive epithets which, when addressed to the ordinary citizen, are, as a matter of common knowledge, inherently likely to provoke violent reaction," without proof of an intent to provoke a violent reaction. Because the definition of "fighting words" turns on how the "ordinary citizen" would react to the language, this Court has observed that a defendant may be guilty of a breach of the peace if he "makes statements likely to provoke violence and disturbance of good order, even though no such eventuality be intended," and that the punishment of such statements "as a criminal act would raise no question under [the Constitution]." . . . I see no reason why we should give threats pride of place among unprotected speech.

[D]ebate on public issues should be uninhibited, robust, and wide-open, and . . . it may well include vehement, caustic, and sometimes unpleasantly sharp attacks on government and public officials. . . . [E]rroneous statement is inevitable in free debate, and . . . it must be protected if the freedoms of expression are to have the "breathing space" that they "need . . . to survive."

—U.S. Supreme Court Justice William Brennan[1]

Montgomery, Ala., police commissioner L.B. Sullivan (second from right) sued The New York Times for libel in the 1960s. The U.S. Supreme Court decision in *New York Times Co. v. Sullivan* is one of the most important legal cases in the history of U.S. constitutional law.

4 LIBEL AND EMOTIONAL DISTRESS
The Plaintiff's Case

SUPPOSE...

... that a civil rights group buys space in a major national newspaper. Its full-page editorial calls attention to the plight of people engaged in nonviolent demonstrations. Some recent events are described. The overall thrust of the text is accurate, but it also contains some minor factual errors. In addition, the editorial is critical of how some public officials—police officers, in particular—handled one demonstration. Several public officials, including the police commissioner, believe the editorial damaged their reputations and sue for defamation. Given the false statements in the text, should the plaintiffs win their lawsuit? Should it make any difference that they are public officials? Look for the answers to these questions when the case of *New York Times Co. v. Sullivan* is discussed later in this chapter and in an excerpt at the end of this chapter.

L ibel law is meant to protect an individual's reputation. It allows a person who believes his or her reputation has been injured to file a claim against the party responsible, asking for monetary damages to compensate for harm and to restore his or her reputation.

The idea that a person's reputation is valuable and worth protecting is a centuries-old concept. Throughout the course of Western civilization, people have closely associated reputation with one's ability to participate in a community's social and economic life.[2] "The right of a man to the protection of his own reputation from unjustified invasion and wrongful hurt reflects no more than our basic concept of the essential dignity and worth of every human being—a concept at the root of any decent system of ordered liberty," wrote former Chief Justice William Rehnquist.[3]

According to the U.S. Supreme Court, the common law of slander and libel is designed to achieve society's "pervasive and strong interest in preventing and redressing attacks upon reputation."[4] The challenge becomes "balanc[ing] the State's interest in compensating private individuals for injury to their reputation against the First Amendment interest in protecting this type of expression."[5]

One important consideration in libel claims is truth. Should one who makes a truthful statement that damages a person's reputation be subject to penalty under the law? Centuries ago, truthful statements that damaged reputation could be libelous. That is no longer the case.

The word "defamation" generally refers to false communication about another person that damages that person's reputation or brings him or her into disrepute. Both slander and libel are forms of defamation. The general purpose of libel laws is to allow people who are defamed to restore their reputations. Libel laws also serve as a deterrent. When a successful plaintiff—the party initiating the lawsuit—is awarded damages, three objectives are served: The plaintiff is compensated for his or her reputational and other losses, the defendant is punished, and the defendant and others are discouraged from committing the same kind of libelous conduct in the future. Thus, a societal benefit may result, particularly if as much attention is given to setting the record straight as was given to the reputation-damaging remarks.

LANDMARK CASES IN CONTEXT

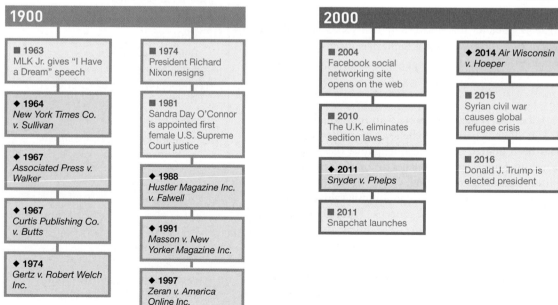

Key ■ Event
     ◆ Cases

1900

■ 1963
MLK Jr. gives "I Have a Dream" speech

◆ 1964
New York Times Co. v. Sullivan

◆ 1967
Associated Press v. Walker

◆ 1967
Curtis Publishing Co. v. Butts

◆ 1974
Gertz v. Robert Welch Inc.

■ 1974
President Richard Nixon resigns

■ 1981
Sandra Day O'Connor is appointed first female U.S. Supreme Court justice

◆ 1988
Hustler Magazine Inc. v. Falwell

◆ 1991
Masson v. New Yorker Magazine Inc.

◆ 1997
Zeran v. America Online Inc.

2000

■ 2004
Facebook social networking site opens on the web

■ 2010
The U.K. eliminates sedition laws

◆ 2011
Snyder v. Phelps

■ 2011
Snapchat launches

◆ 2014 Air Wisconsin v. Hoeper

■ 2015
Syrian civil war causes global refugee crisis

■ 2016
Donald J. Trump is elected president

● POINTS OF LAW

Slander vs. Libel

Historically, people associate "slander" with spoken words that damage reputation and "libel" with written defamation. The laws governing each are similar but distinct—damages awarded for libel are usually higher than for slander. Why? Because a written communication likely caused more harm because it lasted longer and its audience was larger. The evolution of mass communication technology has blurred that distinction. Defamatory content in broadcasting is deemed libel in most states, slander in some others. Some states hold that if broadcast defamation is from scripted (i.e., written) material, it is libel. Otherwise, it is slander.

The distinction between libel and slander is largely a historical artifact because slander lawsuits rarely emerge. When they do, the distinction between libel and slander matters because it changes what the plaintiff must prove to win.

A BRIEF HISTORY

Western civilization's earliest recorded prosecution for reputation-damaging remarks is arguably the trial and execution of Socrates in 399 B.C. In response to charges of slandering Greek gods and corrupting Athens youth, the philosopher was brought before a Heliastic court (a public court unique to ancient Athens). He admitted his "slanderous" teachings and, by a vote of 277 to 224, was found guilty. Socrates accepted his execution to dramatize the primacy of the life of the mind and the need for freedom of thought.[6]

Although ancient Greece contributed to the development of libel law in Western societies, the English common law—a descendant of Roman law—is where American libel law finds its most significant roots. Generally, English defamation law tells us slander is a false accusation that results in the humiliation of its victims. The law tries to suppress such language, "which is seen to pose various threats to the social order."[7]

Many people believe that laws against defamation help maintain the status quo, particularly when libel laws are enforced to punish criticism of those in positions of power.[8] Consequently, the development of libel law depends a great deal on the social and political forces at play in a given historical period.

In 15th-century England, two courts heard defamation complaints: the court of common law or the infamous court of the Star Chamber. The court of the Star Chamber evolved from the meetings of the king's royal council. Established in 1487, it was named after the star painted on the ceiling of the room in which it met. In the early 1600s, the court of the Star Chamber declared libel a criminal offense because it tended to cause breach of the peace. If the libel was "against a magistrate, or other public person, it [was] a greater offence."[9] The court of the Star Chamber generally viewed written defamation as more serious than spoken. Penalties for defamation included the possibility that the defamer "may be punished by fine and imprisonment, and if the case be exorbitant, by pillory and loss of his ears."[10] The Star Chamber was disbanded in 1641, and common law courts resumed their jurisdiction over defamation cases. It was not until about 1660 that the common law courts consistently began to distinguish between libel and slander.[11]

Libel

The word "libel" comes from the Latin *libellus*, or "little book." The legal term derives from the practice in ancient Rome of publishing little books or booklets that one Roman used to defame another. The history of valuing and protecting reputation is centuries old.

damages
Monetary compensation that may be recovered in court by any person who has suffered loss or injury. Damages may be compensatory for actual loss or punitive as punishment for outrageous conduct.

Sedition Act of 1798 Federal legislation under which anyone "opposing or resisting any law of the United States, or any act of the President of the United States," could be imprisoned for up to two years. The act also made it illegal to "write, print, utter, or publish" anything that criticized the president or Congress. The act expired in 1801 and ultimately was seen as a direct violation of the First Amendment.

Eighteenth-century English Judge Sir William Blackstone and his "Commentaries on the Law of England" played a major role in the development of law in the United States. Libel law is no exception. Punishment for defamation, Blackstone believed, was not inconsistent with the concept of freedom of the press. A free press, he wrote, "consists in laying no previous restraints upon publications, and not in freedom from censure for criminal matter when published."[12] Anyone can express his sentiments to the public, he added, "but if he publishes what is improper, mischievous, or illegal, he must take the consequences of his own temerity."[13]

Those consequences were to take the form of monetary **damages** sought by a plaintiff in compensation for a tarnished reputation. As a chief justice of the United States later described its evolution, "Defamation law developed not only as a means of allowing an individual to vindicate his good name, but also for the purpose of obtaining redress for harm caused by such statements. As the common law developed in this country, apart from the issue of damages, one usually needed only allege an unprivileged publication of false and defamatory matter to state a cause of action for defamation."[14]

That legal principle was brought to the American colonies and into the states after independence. But England also provided America with legal theories that were less desirable in a republic committed to individual freedoms. Among them was the concept of seditious libel. At various times throughout American history, authorities have been especially sensitive to criticism of the government. In response, laws have been passed criminalizing such expression. One of those eras was the post–Revolutionary War period. The **Sedition Act of 1798** made it a crime to write "any false, scandalous and malicious" statements against either the president or Congress.[15] While the act permitted a defendant to escape penalty by proving the truth of the writing, and juries were permitted to decide critical questions of law and fact, there was no doubt that it was intended to silence critics of the entrenched political powers.

Echoing Blackstone, John Marshall—a public official of the same era who would become Chief Justice of the United States—defended the Sedition Act as being consistent with the First Amendment because it did not impose a prior restraint.[16] "It is known to all," he wrote, that those who publish libels or who "libel the government of the state" may "be both sued and indicted."[17] Among the act's opponents was James Madison, the principal author of the First Amendment, who said, "It would seem a mockery to say that no laws should be passed preventing publications from being made, but that laws might be passed punishing them in case they should be made."[18] Madison and his supporters ultimately prevailed, with the act expiring in 1801.

THE ELEMENTS OF LIBEL: THE PLAINTIFF'S CASE

Just as defamation was recognized first as a harm committed by the spoken word and later as one that could also be committed through writing, the opportunities for libelous speech have increased exponentially with the development of communication technologies. In the global digital age—complete with blogs and social media—and because of the ease and speed of communicating, the possibilities for libel are on the rise.

Libel law serves to check the power of the media by opening its newsgathering and decision-making processes to public scrutiny and accountability. Although the best cure for bad speech may be more speech,[19] contemporary American society is often unwilling to rely only on corrective speech as a remedy for false and damaging statements to reputations. Libel law is one of the checks and balances in that process. The right of individuals to be secure in their reputations is weighed against the rights of others to be heard on issues of importance.

Unlike in the era of common law libel, when the defendant was required to prove that a defamatory statement was true, the entire initial **burden of proof** is now on the plaintiff in libel cases. To win, the plaintiff must prove that all of the required elements apply to the allegedly libelous material. Each of these elements requires definition and explanation.

burden of proof
The requirement for a party to a case to demonstrate one or more claims by the presentation of evidence. In libel law, for example, the plaintiff has the burden of proof.

⬤ **INTERNATIONAL LAW**

Criminal Defamation Laws in Turkey

The International Press Institute (IPI), a global network of news outlets and media professionals, is exposing what it calls "the negative effects that disproportionate defamation laws have on press freedom and freedom of expression in Europe," particularly in Turkey.[1] The European Federation of Journalists called Turkey the "world's biggest journalist-prison," following a failed coup attempt in July 2016.[2] The Committee to Protect Journalists is also drawing attention to Turkish authorities' use of "repressive laws" to silence critics.[3]

In November 2016, Turkish police arrested more than a dozen journalists at the independent Turkish newspaper Cumhuriyet, including the editor-in-chief. Those arrests spawned the hashtag #FreeTurkeyJournalists, which various free press organizations use to draw attention to the arrests and subsequent trials of journalists in the country. IPI notes that during the six-month period after the failed coup attempt, Turkish President Recep Tayyip Erdoğan has "overseen the filing of nearly 2,000 criminal cases of 'insult to the president.' . . . The result is an entire society afraid to speak its mind."[4]

1. International Press Institute, *The Abuse of Defamation Laws in Europe 2016–17: Exposing and Addressing the Threat to Media Freedom and Pluralism*, medialaws database, Jan. 5, 2017, legaldb.freemedia.at/defamation-laws-in-europe/.
2. European Federation of Journalists, *Turkey: 107 Journalists in Prison and 2,500 Others Left Unemployed*, europeanjournalists.org, Jan. 5, 2017, europeanjournalists.org/blog/2016/10/24/turkey-107-journalists-in-prison-and-2500-others-left-unemployed/.
3. Committee to Protect Journalists, *Turkish Journalist Sentenced to 21 Months in Prison for Insulting Erdoğan*, CPJ.org, Jan. 5, 2017, cpj.org/2016/03/turkish-journalist-sentenced-to-21-months-in-priso.php.
4. International Press Institute, *supra* note 1.

⊙ POINTS OF LAW

The Plaintiff's Libel Case

1. A statement of fact
2. That is published,
3. That is of and concerning the plaintiff,
4. That is defamatory,
5. That is false,
6. That causes damage (or harm) and
7. For which the defendant is at fault.

Statement of Fact

In order to be libelous, a statement must make an assertion of fact. During the 2016 presidential election, many politicians and their partisan supporters argued about facts and sometimes presented opinions as facts. The hashtag #alternativefacts went viral in 2016 after President Donald Trump's senior adviser used the phrase in response to allegations that the White House was providing false information to the public. The dictionary defines a fact as "a piece of information presented as having objective reality."[20] The dictionary defines opinion as "a view, judgment or appraisal formed in the mind about a particular matter; a belief stronger than impression and less strong than positive knowledge."[21] Understanding the difference between fact and opinion is important because an expression of opinion cannot be libelous.

How can you tell the difference between fact and opinion? If you write that in December 2016 the U.S. unemployment rate was 4.7 percent, you are offering an assertion of fact that can be proven true or false. If you write that you think the U.S. unemployment rate is too high, that is opinion. Opinion is not libelous because an opinion cannot be false—and falsity is another requirement of the plaintiff's libel case. (The opinion defense is explained in detail in Chapter 5.) For now, it is enough to understand that whether material can be considered an expression of opinion requires a rigorous analysis.

Publication

In order for a statement to be libelous, the plaintiff must show that the statement was made public. To satisfy this standard, only one person in addition to the source and subject of the allegedly defamatory statement must have seen or heard the information in question. When information is presented through the mass media, including social media, publication is presumed. Under the law of libel, material is considered published any time it is printed in a periodical, broadcast over the airwaves or posted on the internet.

Republication. Repeating libelous information is as potentially harmful to someone's reputation as publishing it in the first place. Thus, the person who republishes can be held just as responsible as the originator. Republishing libelous information is seen as a new publication in the eyes of the law. This is true even when careful attribution occurs. The law's rationale here is to prevent individuals or the media from freely committing defamation simply by attributing the libelous material to another source.

Particularly in an age of rapidly changing communication technologies, the republication rule would seem at odds with the wish to promote the free flow of ideas—clearly a tenet of the First Amendment. Even in a slightly less technological age, some courts began to allow for some degree of protection for republication of otherwise libelous information. Section 230 of the Communications Decency Act, the neutral reportage defense and the wire service defense, discussed in Chapter 5, confront this issue.

Republication on the internet illustrates how new technologies and platforms open the door to refinements in the law. For example, in New York a judge held that new comments made to older messages in order to return them to prominent positions on a website

Map 4.1 ■ Criminal Defamation Laws in the EU and EU Candidate Countries

Defamation is a Criminal Offence Punishable with Imprisonment
Defamation is a Criminal Offence (Not Punishable with Imprisonment)
Criminal Defamation Laws Repealed*

Source: International Press Institute (interactive map: legaldb.freemedia.at/defamation-laws-in-europe/)

▲ EMERGING LAW

Injunctions and Defamatory Speech Online

A significant challenge to defamation law in the age of the internet is how to deal with defamatory content online that is easily shared. Courts have seen a surge of defamation cases in which plaintiffs seek not only damages but also a court-ordered prohibition (called injunctive relief) to stop future publication of defamatory content on the internet.[1]

In 2015, the Seventh Circuit Court of Appeals struck down a broad injunction in a complicated case filed in 2008 that involved a Catholic nun who claimed to have experienced a series of apparitions of the Virgin Mary in 1956. Judge Richard Posner wrote, "An injunction against defamatory statements, if permissible at all, must not through careless drafting forbid statements not yet determined to be defamatory, for by doing so it could restrict lawful expression."[2]

Despite affirming that an injunction would harm not only the speaker but also listeners, the Court opened the door for the district judge in the case to decide whether to issue a new injunction and correct errors of vagueness, overbreadth and lack of specific findings. In her concurrence, Judge Diane Sykes wrote, "More fundamentally, the question whether an injunction is permissible *at all* in this context is a sensitive and difficult matter of First Amendment law."[3]

In 2014, the Supreme Court of Texas held that while injunctions against future publication of defamatory content are a form of prior restraint, post-trial orders to remove defamatory speech from websites are a permissible remedy.[4] A year later, in Washington, a state appellate court held that a permanent injunction against posting defamatory material is not a prior restraint.[5] In 2016, a California appeals court required Yelp to remove a defamatory post, a decision consistent with the Texas Supreme Court ruling.[6]

---

1. Ann C. Motto, *First Amendment: "Equity Will Not Enjoin a Libel"*: Well, Actually, Yes, It Will, 11 Seventh Cir. Rev. 271 (Spring, 2016).
2. McCarthy v. Fuller, 810 F.3d 456, 462 (7th Cir. 2015), *cert. denied*, 136 S. Ct. 1726 (2016).
3. McCarthy, 810 F.3d at 464 (Sykes, J., concurring).
4. Kinney v. Barnes, 443 S.W.3d 87 (Tex. 2014), *cert. denied*, 135 S. Ct. 1164 (2015).
5. *In re* Janzen, 43 Med. L. Rep. 3211 (Wash. Ct. App. Oct. 22, 2015).
6. Hassell v. Bird, 203 Cal. Rptr. 3d 203 (Cal. Ct. App. 2016).

Several women have sued Bill Cosby for defamation after Cosby's attorney said they lied when they accused the comedian of sexual assault.

to keep a conversation alive—"bump messages"—do not count as republication in the context of libel.[22] However, a recent court decision in Utah held that a defendant did meet the requirement of republication when she updated text on a website on which she had posted numerous defamatory statements about a residential youth treatment facility.[23]

In another case, a New York trial court held that adding a "share button" to online archived articles is not republication, even though the buttons facilitate content sharing. The court based its decision on the idea that the target audience, newspaper readers, did not change with the addition of the button. Moreover, readers always had the option to share even without the button; they could print, email or distribute articles in other ways. The court said the use of a share button was "akin to a delayed circulation of the original rather than republication."[24]

Is retweeting a form of republication? Many legal experts say that Section 230 of the Communications Decency Act (see Chapter 5) protects retweets as long as new defamatory remarks are not added, although this is still an open legal question and no cases have yet determined this. Courts now generally apply the same logic to hyperlinking. The New York Court of Appeals, the state's highest court, has held that continuous access to an article posted via hyperlinks is not a republication. This changes, however, if new content is added. For example, in a 2016 case, a New York district court held that a software company could proceed with a defamation claim after a computer support website added potentially defamatory statements to a post that contained an old hyperlink.[25]

Vendors and Distributors. Publisher liability in libel is determined by whether publishers are or should be aware of the material they disseminate, possibly including a presumption that they have read and edited the content. To prove publication, a libel plaintiff must show not just that libelous material was published; the plaintiff must also identify a specific person, group or business responsible for the publication. Among those who are granted a republication exception are vendors and distributors. For example, bookstores, libraries and newsstands are not publishers of the works they stock. They cannot be sued for libel based on the works they make available because they do not control the content of those products.

Given this "vendor exception," how should the law treat internet service providers (ISPs)? Protection for ISPs did not exist until one section of the **Communications Decency Act** was put to the test about 20 years ago. Before Congress passed the CDA

Communications Decency Act The part of the 1996 Telecommunications Act that largely attempted to regulate internet content. The Communications Decency Act was successfully challenged in *Reno v. American Civil Liberties Union* (1997).

▌ SOCIAL MEDIA LAW

Twitter, Politics and Insults

If the president-elect of the United States calls you a "major loser" or a "real dummy" on Twitter, is that defamatory content? In 2017, a New York judge dismissed a defamation suit filed against then President-elect Donald Trump by a veteran political strategist and TV pundit, writing that Trump's Twitter insults are generally viewed as opinion. "His tweets about his critics, necessarily restricted to 140 characters or less, are rife with vague and simplistic insults such as 'loser' or 'total loser' or 'totally biased loser,' 'dummy' or 'dope' or 'dumb,' 'zero/no credibility,' 'crazy' or 'wacko' and 'disaster,' all deflecting serious consideration," the judge wrote.[1]

Trump launched a Twitter tirade toward Cheryl Jacobus after she made critical comments about him and his campaign on CNN. Trump's insults included a claim that Jacobus had "begged" his campaign for a job and was only critical of him because his campaign didn't hire her. Jacobus said that was false. The judge determined that while "the intemperate tweets are clearly intended to belittle and demean the plaintiff," it was impossible to show that they had damaged her reputation even if the claim about her wanting a job was false.[2]

1. Mark Mooney, *Trump Defamation by Twitter Case Tossed Out*, cnnmoney, Feb. 4, 2017, money.cnn.com/2017/01/10/media/trump-cheryl-jacobus-twitter-defame/.
2. *Id.*

The Alfred P. Murrah Federal Building after the Oklahoma City bombing in 1995.

in 1996 as part of the Telecommunications Act, court rulings in this area had been mixed. Some judges ruled that ISPs should be regarded as publishers,[26] while others said that they were only distributors of information that others had published.[27] The discrepancy was resolved when Section 230 of the CDA was tested by a libel claim against AOL (then America Online Inc.).[28]

Kenneth Zeran claimed AOL injured his reputation by not quickly removing false information about him. His claim arose after an anonymous AOL user posted an advertisement for T-shirts with images and a slogan glorifying the 1995 Oklahoma City bombing. The ad included Zeran's telephone number, although he claimed no role in or knowledge of the ad. Ultimately, a federal appeals court ruled, "By its plain language, Section 230 creates a federal immunity to any cause of action that would make service providers liable for information originating with a third-party user of that service."[29] The court said Section 230 prevents courts from even considering claims that place an ISP in the role of publisher[30] because Congress recognized that a law requiring ISPs to restrict or eliminate speech to avoid liability would create an "obvious chilling effect" on speech.[31]

In 2007, the First Circuit Court of Appeals ruled that the definition of "provider of an interactive computer service" includes service providers who do not directly connect their users to the internet.[32] Unlike AOL in the *Zeran* case, the defendant here did not provide users with access to the internet but managed a series of websites. The court reasoned that narrowing protection only to services that provide internet access would undermine congressional intent in passing the CDA and that Section 230 immunity should be broadly construed.[33]

Blogs provide an example of a "publisher." A blogger is responsible for the material he or she posts. But is the blogger legally responsible for items others may post on his or her site? What if the postings are anonymous? In a ruling that also relied on Section 230, a federal judge dismissed a libel claim against a website operator whose site included anonymous postings that the plaintiff claimed damaged his reputation.[34]

Unknown Publisher/Anonymous Speech. Sometimes material is published, but the speaker is unknown. A hallmark of the internet and interaction through some mobile applications and social media is anonymous communication. The ability to speak anonymously can allow ideas and viewpoints that otherwise might remain unexpressed to enter the marketplace of ideas by reducing the fear of reprisal. "Under our constitution, anonymous pamphleteering is not a pernicious, fraudulent practice, but an honorable tradition of advocacy and of dissent," U.S. Supreme Court Justice Antonin Scalia once wrote. "Anonymity is a shield from the tyranny of the majority."[35] As Chapter 2 notes, the Supreme Court has recognized a First Amendment right to anonymous speech. But what happens when the wish to protect anonymous speech collides with the imperative of holding people accountable for libelous expression?

Generally speaking, state courts have taken three approaches to "unmasking" anonymous posters on the internet in libel cases. In Virginia, plaintiffs must show they have a legitimate, good faith basis to claim an actionable offense within the court's jurisdiction, and that the identity of the anonymous speaker is central to advancing their case.[36] Most other state courts have rejected this standard because it does not offer the speaker sufficient First Amendment protection.

In *Dendrite v. John Doe #3*, a New Jersey court held that the plaintiff must present the court with prima facie ("on its face") evidence that is sufficient to prove the plaintiff has a case that can withstand a motion to dismiss. A motion to dismiss is a formal request to the court to dismiss a case. It is often filed immediately by a defendant after a plaintiff files suit, although it may be filed at any time during legal proceedings by either party. Grounds for dismissing a lawsuit are determined by each jurisdiction's laws. If the plaintiff's case can withstand a motion to dismiss, then the court should balance the First Amendment rights of the anonymous speaker against the strength of the prima facie case and the need to disclose the anonymous speaker.[37] The Delaware Supreme Court has held that a defamation plaintiff must "satisfy a 'summary judgment' standard before obtaining the identity of an anonymous defender." Under a summary judgment standard, a judge must view certain points in the light most favorable to the defendant and make a judgment from that perspective. This approach is the most protective of anonymous speech. The Delaware Supreme Court wrote, "Indeed, there is reason to believe that many defamation plaintiffs bring suit merely to unmask the identities of anonymous critics. . . . The goals of this new breed of libel action are largely symbolic, the primary goal being to silence John Doe and others like him."[38]

Identification

A libel plaintiff is required to show that he or she was the specific person whose reputation was harmed or, possibly, that he or she was a member of a small group that was defamed. Early common law asked whether the statement was "of and concerning" the plaintiff—a standard still employed. This test asks whether the statement reasonably refers to the plaintiff. There are several ways a person can be identified. The most obvious is by name, but people can be identified in other ways—by title, through photographic images or within a context in which their identity can be inferred. As long as someone other than the plaintiff and the defendant recognize that the content is about the plaintiff, identification has taken place. In addition, the intention of the publisher is not critical to this determination; a publisher may not have intended to implicate the plaintiff, but identification might have occurred nonetheless.

Group Identification. In some circumstances, libel law allows any member of a group to sue when the entire group has been libeled. The key is whether in libeling the group, the information is also "of and concerning" the specific individual bringing the lawsuit. In general, the smaller the group, the more likely it is that its individual members have been identified. According to one authority, "It is not possible to set definite limits as to the size of the group or class, but the cases in which recovery [of damages] has been allowed usually have involved numbers of 25 or fewer."[39]

A court will evaluate each situation on its specific facts. Some rulings in this category indicate that if a group has fewer than 100 members, any one of them could file a successful libel claim, depending on the libelous material in question. As a group grows in size, the inclusiveness of the language that allegedly libeled its members becomes a factor.[40]

Defamation

Another element in the plaintiff's case involves the allegedly libelous content itself. In order for the plaintiff to win, the material at issue must be defamatory. The challenge is defining and establishing a standard of defamation. The standard begins with the premise that when reputation is damaged, defamation occurs.

Some words by themselves may qualify as defamatory. Some kinds of statements convey such defamatory meaning that they are considered to be defamatory as a matter of law; on its face and without further proof, the content is defamatory. This is **libel per se**. Libel per se typically involves accusations of criminal activity, unethical activity or practice, unprofessional behavior and/or immoral actions (sometimes called moral turpitude, which is conduct contrary to community standards). For example, in 2014 the Eighth Circuit reversed a lower court ruling in favor of rock musician Sammy Hagar. Hagar had written in his 2011 autobiography that a woman who claimed she was pregnant with his baby was lying about the baby's paternity in an attempt to extort money from him. The appeals court held that calling someone a liar was libel per se in Iowa (the jurisdiction), and although she wasn't named in the book, her friends and family members recognized her immediately based on Hagar's allegations.[41]

Distinguishing defamatory from nondefamatory statements is more art than science. Within various contexts, the following definitions of "defamatory" have been offered:

- Words or images that are false and injurious to another

- Words or images that expose another person to hatred, contempt or ridicule

- Words or images that tend to harm the reputation of another so as to lower him or her in the estimation of the community or deter third persons from associating or dealing with him or her[42]

- Words or images that subject a person to the loss of goodwill or confidence from others[43]

- Words or images that subject a person to scorn or ridicule

- Words or images that tend to expose a person to hatred, contempt or aversion, or tend to induce an evil or unsavory opinion of him or her in the minds of a substantial number in the community

- Words or images that tend to prejudice someone in the eyes of a substantial and respectable minority of the community[44]

Whatever the standard, courts traditionally have said that the matter must be viewed from the perspective of "right-thinking" people.[45] Some examples of recent cases that

libel per se A statement whose injurious nature is apparent and requires no further proof.

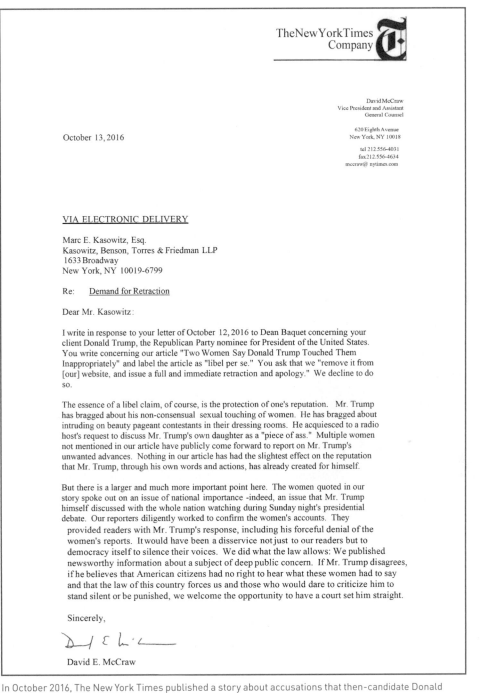

TheNewYorkTimes
Company

David McCraw
Vice President and Assistant
General Counsel

620 Eighth Avenue
New York, NY 10018

tel 212.556-4031
fax 212.556-4634
mccraw@nytimes.com

October 13, 2016

VIA ELECTRONIC DELIVERY

Marc E. Kasowitz, Esq.
Kasowitz, Benson, Torres & Friedman LLP
1633 Broadway
New York, NY 10019-6799

Re: Demand for Retraction

Dear Mr. Kasowitz:

I write in response to your letter of October 12, 2016 to Dean Baquet concerning your
client Donald Trump, the Republican Party nominee for President of the United States.
You write concerning our article "Two Women Say Donald Trump Touched Them
Inappropriately" and label the article as "libel per se." You ask that we "remove it from
[our] website, and issue a full and immediate retraction and apology." We decline to do
so.

The essence of a libel claim, of course, is the protection of one's reputation. Mr. Trump
has bragged about his non-consensual sexual touching of women. He has bragged about
intruding on beauty pageant contestants in their dressing rooms. He acquiesced to a radio
host's request to discuss Mr. Trump's own daughter as a "piece of ass." Multiple women
not mentioned in our article have publicly come forward to report on Mr. Trump's
unwanted advances. Nothing in our article has had the slightest effect on the reputation
that Mr. Trump, through his own words and actions, has already created for himself.

But there is a larger and much more important point here. The women quoted in our
story spoke out on an issue of national importance -indeed, an issue that Mr. Trump
himself discussed with the whole nation watching during Sunday night's presidential
debate. Our reporters diligently worked to confirm the women's accounts. They
provided readers with Mr. Trump's response, including his forceful denial of the
women's reports. It would have been a disservice not just to our readers but to
democracy itself to silence their voices. We did what the law allows: We published
newsworthy information about a subject of deep public concern. If Mr. Trump disagrees,
if he believes that American citizens had no right to hear what these women had to say
and that the law of this country forces us and those who would dare to criticize him to
stand silent or be punished, we welcome the opportunity to have a court set him straight.

Sincerely,

David E. McCraw

In October 2016, The New York Times published a story about accusations that then-candidate Donald
Trump had inappropriately touched women. Trump's lawyer demanded a retraction and threatened to sue
the Times, calling the article "libel per se." The New York Times' attorney's powerful response went viral.

explored the meaning of defamation include a New York appellate court's decision that a false allegation of homosexuality is no longer defamatory per se. The court cited New York's Marriage Equality Act as evidence of changing attitudes toward homosexuality.[46] Rhode Island's Supreme Court held that deliberately and falsely stating that a political event is "off the record" is not defamatory. A plaintiff argued that a newspaper portrayed him falsely as "someone to be disliked because he is a political insider who attacks the First Amendment."[47] Similarly, in Massachusetts, an appellate court held that when a newspaper wrote that it could not reach a person for comment, such a statement isn't defamatory even if it is false. In Florida, a state court said that reporting that a plaintiff refused to cooperate or comment in a televised news story is not defamatory.[48]

libel per quod A statement whose injurious nature requires proof.

In contrast with libel per se is **libel per quod**. It arises when the matter by itself does not appear to be defamatory, but knowledge of additional information would damage the plaintiff's reputation. An example of libel per quod would be a news report that the plaintiff was seen visiting 123 Main Street. By itself, that report would not seem defamatory. But if many readers are aware there is a drug-manufacturing lab at that address, then the report would have accused the plaintiff of involvement in illegal activity.

 # REAL WORLD LAW

Terrorism and Defamation

In the immediate aftermath of the Boston Marathon bombing, speculative media coverage led to a defamation lawsuit.

As noted, one definition of defamation is words that tend to expose a person to hatred, contempt or aversion, or tend to induce an evil or unsavory opinion of him or her in the minds of a substantial number in the community. An example of this is wrongly identifying someone as a terrorist.

In the manhunt that ensued after the 2013 Boston Marathon bombing, a picture of two young men who attended the Boston Marathon appeared on the front page of the New York Post under the headline "BAG MEN." Although a small text box on the front page noted that no evidence linked them to the bombing, the article that accompanied the image said that police investigators had been circulating photos of two men whom witnesses saw chatting near the finish line.[1]

The First Circuit held that a reasonable reader could interpret the article to suggest the two men were suspects. "When taken in context of the widespread reporting on the bombing, the 'BAG MEN' headline could be construed to imply that the plaintiffs' bags had been used to carry the bombs."[2] The New York Post settled the case out of court.

1. Kevin T. Baine, Grey C. Callaham & Nicholas Gamse, *Defamation Law Case Summaries for PLI*, 2 Comm. L. in the Digital Age 15 (2014); Barhoum v. NYP Holdings Inc., 2014 Mass. Super. LEXIS 52 (Mass. Super. Ct. Mar. 10, 2014).
2. Baine, Callaham & Gamse, *supra* note 1.

Article headlines can occasionally be the source of successful libel claims. As with captions and teasers, their abbreviated nature and shortened message may still be interpreted in a defamatory way. Whether the headline is "of and concerning" the plaintiff becomes material—as, of course, do the other elements of the plaintiff's case. In a lawsuit spawned by the murder trial of O.J. Simpson, the National Examiner was found liable for the headline "Cops Think Kato Did It." The implication regarding Brian "Kato" Kaelin was clear: The "it" being referred to was the murder of Nicole Brown Simpson and Ronald Goldman. The article itself clarified that the "it" mentioned in the front-page headline was actually perjury related to his trial testimony. Kaelin sued, claiming his reputation was damaged.[49] A defense witness who admitted that "the front page of the tabloid paper is what we sell the paper on, not what's inside it,"[50] only served to strengthen the plaintiff's case.

Article illustrations and photographs can also result in libel if they are juxtaposed in a way that creates a defamatory impression. Recently, a New York court held that an archived crime scene photo used as a visual with an article about gang violence was capable of defamatory meaning. The photo of a 10-year-old African-American boy looking over yellow police tape at a crime scene was placed underneath the headline "Call to Get Tougher on Gang Activities." The appeals court said that the juxtaposition of the photo and the text could create a defamatory impression and that connecting a person to a serious crime like gang activity constitutes libel per se.[51]

Among the challenges for a court is deciding what the words or images at issue in a libel case mean and whether they can be considered defamatory. Whether they are actionable cannot simply be determined according to whether they harmed the plaintiff's reputation. The allegedly libelous matter may conceivably harm reputation without rising to the level of defamation. Thus, another element of defamation that plaintiffs must show is that the material "is reasonably capable of sustaining defamatory meaning."[52] A judge decides whether the words constituting the statement at issue are capable of conveying defamatory meaning. If so, the case may move to trial to determine whether, in fact, the words did convey a defamatory meaning.

Business Reputation. While businesses and corporations do not have reputations in the same sense that individuals do, they can suffer a kind of reputational harm that can impair their ability to conduct business. In addition, individuals within businesses and corporations may have a legitimate libel claim when criticism of the business falsely implies wrongdoing on their part.

Trade Libel. Trade libel pertains to criticism of products rather than criticism of people or businesses. When it applies to food products, it is sometimes colloquially called "veggie libel." These are state laws that became popular in the 1990s. In one of the most famous cases, a group of Texas cattlemen sued Oprah Winfrey for remarks she made about mad cow disease. During that time, international media had reported on the disease after several people in the U.K. died from eating infected beef. An episode of "The Oprah Winfrey Show" titled "Dangerous Food" explored the topic of diseased

Oprah Winfrey.

beef. Although neither Texas nor any of the plaintiffs was mentioned, the Texas Beef Group and several other Texas-based cattle companies filed suit. They claimed the show's producers "intentionally edited . . . much of the factual and scientific information that would have calmed the hysteria it knew one guest's false exaggerations would create."[53] The plaintiffs added that this "malicious" treatment "caused markets to immediately" crash and they suffered damages as a result.[54] When Winfrey commented during the show that the information about tainted beef had "just stopped me cold from eating another burger,"[55] the flames were fanned. The plaintiffs sought $100 million in damages. Winfrey won at trial and on appeal.[56]

Falsity

For a statement to be libelous, it must be false. The plaintiff is responsible for demonstrating that the statement at issue is false rather than the defendant proving the statement is true.

Historically this was reversed: The burden of proof to show a statement is true was placed on the defendant. This was the case in English common law. Moreover, when the English government used libel law in an effort to silence critics, truth was rejected as a defense. True but defamatory statements about the government, it was believed, were even more harmful than false criticism. Later, the common law recognized truth as a defense in civil libel cases.

Libel law in the United States now clearly places the burden of proof regarding falsity on the plaintiff. The U.S. Supreme Court has emphatically reinforced this aspect of libel law. Justice Sandra Day O'Connor, writing for the Court in a case involving a Philadelphia newspaper, emphasized the importance of protecting and encouraging the free flow of information and ideas:

> We believe that the Constitution requires us to tip [the scales] in favor of protecting free speech. . . . The burden of proving truth upon media defendants who publish speech of public concern deters such speech because of the fear that liability will unjustifiably result. . . . Because such a "chilling" effect would be antithetical to the First Amendment's protection of true speech on matters of public concern . . . a plaintiff must bear the burden of showing that the speech at issue is false before recovering damages for defamation from a media defendant. To do otherwise could only result in a deterrence of the speech which the Constitution makes free.[57]

Substantial Truth. Libel law provides some latitude with regard to falsity. Minor error or discrepancy does not necessarily make a statement false. As long as the statement is substantially true, it cannot meet the standard for falsity and therefore cannot be libelous. The Supreme Court said that substantial truth "would absolve a defendant even if she cannot justify every word of the alleged defamatory matter; it is sufficient if the substance of the charge is proved true, irrespective of the slight inaccuracy in the details. . . . Minor inaccuracies do not amount to falsity so long as the substance, the gist, the sting of the libelous charge can be justified."[58]

● REAL WORLD LAW

"Pink Slime" and the Decline of Beef Products Inc.

A worker inspects raw chunks of meat for processing.

A series of reports by ABC News in 2012 that called a processed meat product "pink slime" were the focus of a trade libel suit brought by Beef Products Inc. (BPI). The company sought $1.2 billion in damages under South Dakota's "veggie libel" law. BPI says it was defamatory to call its "lean finely textured beef," made from raw chunks of meat and fat beef trimmings, "pink slime," a term that originated from a United States Department of Agriculture (USDA) microbiologist.[1]

BPI's product was used by many fast-food chains and sold by large grocery store chains. ABC News reports said the product was made with "low grade" meat, including scraps and waste, and was supposedly made partially from connective animal tissue. The producers maintain that the product was made from muscle, or meat. The public pressured fast-food chains to eliminate the textured beef product, and BPI's revenues plummeted, resulting in the closure of three of its processing plants and the loss of 700 jobs.[2]

ABC maintained the use of the term "pink slime" was protected expression of opinion and sought to have the complaint dismissed. A South Dakota court held that "the use of the term 'pink slime' with a food product can be reasonably interpreted as implying that the food product is not meat and is not fit to eat, which are objective facts which can be proven," and allowed the lawsuit to move forward.[3] In addition to ABC News, BPI sued several others. In 2016, the judge hearing the case approved the dismissal of five defendants, but the case moved forward against ABC, news anchor Diane Sawyer and one ABC news correspondent.[4] In 2017, ABC and BPI settled out of court. ABC News did not retract or apologize for its report, noting that the company reached "an amicable resolution" with BPI.[5]

1. Kelly/Warner Law Firm, *Current High Profile Trade Libel Suit: The Case of the Pink Slime,* kellywarnerlaw.com, July 17, 2013, kellywarnerlaw.com/trade-libel-basics/.
2. Amanda Radke, *Update on BPI Lawsuit Against ABC,* beefmagazine.com, Oct. 12, 2016, www.beefmagazine.com/blog/update-bpi-lawsuit-against-abc.
3. Beef Prods. Inc. v. ABC, No. CIV12292, 2014 WL 1245307 (S.D. Cir. Mar. 27, 2014).
4. Radke, *supra* note 2.
5. Daniel Victor, *ABC Settles With Mean Producer in "Pink Slime" Defamation Case,* N.Y. Times, June 28, 2017, www.nytimes.com/2017/06/28/business/media/pink-slime-abc-lawsuit-settlement.html?_r=0.

⊙ POINTS OF LAW

The Burden of Proof as Deterrent

The burden of proof of falsity occasionally serves as a deterrent to potential plaintiffs. The requirement to delve deeply into the allegedly libelous statement and refute its veracity is sometimes so distasteful that would-be plaintiffs choose not to file libel claims in the first place. The information revealed in the process may be more embarrassing and damaging to reputation than the allegedly libelous statement. In addition, this proof of falsity requirement leads targets of some news media investigations to conclude that a libel claim is not their best course of action. That is, under some circumstances, plaintiffs may not want the truth or falsity of a news report's claims analyzed. The possibility that the allegations could be proved true or substantially true can be discouraging to a potential plaintiff. (See, e.g., the examination of the *Food Lion* case in Chapter 7.)

One appellate court has used a test to determine whether a published statement is substantially true by considering both the gist of the statement and "whether the alleged defamatory statement was more damaging to the plaintiff's reputation, in the mind of the average listener, than a truthful statement would have been."[59] The nonlibelous nature of substantially true statements would mean, for example, that if a news website reports that an individual was in police custody when, in fact, the individual had been released on bail, the story is likely substantially true because the individual had been in custody and it was only an error in timing that had caused the mistake. If, however, a news website publishes a story saying that a person has been charged with a crime when in fact he or she has only been investigated by the police, it is unlikely the story will be judged to be substantially true. If something is not at least substantially true, then it is false.

Libel by Implication. While individual statements within an article or report may be factually accurate, taken together they may paint a different picture. Through implication or innuendo, one can create libelous messages. In a case dismissed by a Washington state appeals court, for example, a crane operator sued a newspaper for what he said was implied in headlines. After an accident, Seattle Post-Intelligencer headlines read "Operator in crane wreck has history of drug abuse" and "Man completed mandated rehab program after his last arrest in 2000." The crane operator's tests for drugs after the accident were negative. He filed several claims including libel, though he admitted that there were no false statements in the newspaper. Still, he claimed "defamation by implication" due to the juxtaposing of true statements in a way that created a false impression.[60] This case followed an Iowa Supreme Court ruling that public plaintiffs there can sue for "defamation by implication." The court said that if a true fact is not properly and thoroughly explained, it can become defamatory if, when read in a particular way, it carries false implications.[61]

Libel by implication can also happen through the juxtaposition of images. In 2016, the Third Circuit Court of Appeals concluded that the juxtaposition of a photo did create a defamatory impression in a case that involved a Philadelphia firefighter who appeared in a picture next to a story about a sex scandal within the city's fire department. The court decided that a reasonable person could conclude that the inclusion of the firefighter's picture and name juxtaposed to the story would incorrectly implicate him in the sex scandal.[62] In the Ninth Circuit Court of Appeals, the court unanimously decided in favor of an unidentified performer in the pornography industry after a stock photo of her appeared within a story about a female performer testing positive for HIV, which temporarily shut down the porn industry in California. The unidentified performer was one of the most popular soft porn actresses on the internet. While the story text noted that the unidentified performer who tested positive was new to the industry, the court held that the photo juxtaposition resulted in a reasonable implication that the statements in the story referred to the model/actress used in the stock photo, even though she was not named.[63]

Fault

To support a libel claim, a plaintiff must show that the defendant was at fault in making public the allegedly false and defamatory statement of fact. Prior to *New York Times Co. v. Sullivan*, fault was not an element of common law libel. The landmark case did away with the concept of libel as a no-fault tort, and subsequent Supreme Court cases explained what level of fault is used in libel suits. As a general rule, public officials and public figures must prove actual malice as a standard of fault, and private individuals must prove negligence.

New York Times Co. v. Sullivan. One of the most important legal cases in the history of American constitutional law is a libel case, *New York Times Co. v. Sullivan.*[64] The U.S. Supreme Court's ruling in that case has had a monumental impact not just on journalism but on society as a whole.

The circumstances of *New York Times Co. v. Sullivan* arose within the context of the civil rights movement of the 1960s. African-American groups seeking racial equality under the law frequently engaged in nonviolent marches in southern states. These events were minimized or ignored by the local southern press but were covered elsewhere, including frequently in The New York Times. Many southern leaders resented the Times and other northern newspapers that covered the marches.

Against that backdrop, a coalition of civil rights leaders purchased space in The New York Times for a full-page statement. Carrying the headline "Heed Their Rising Voices," the "advertorial" made charges against officials in southern states who, the statement claimed, had used violent and illegal methods to suppress the marches. Although the gist of the statement was factually accurate, there were some errors of fact. Asserting he had been defamed, L.B. Sullivan, the police commissioner of Montgomery, Ala., filed a libel claim against the Times and some of the civil rights leaders who had purchased the newspaper space. He sought $500,000 in damages from the Times, which was at the time financially vulnerable.

Although Sullivan was not identified by name in the statement, he maintained that it was nevertheless "of and concerning" him. The ad criticized public officials who, it said, used illegal tactics and violence to counter peaceful demonstrations. Sullivan maintained that the statements implicated him. He and his attorneys were able to file a libel claim in Alabama because several copies of the paper had been circulated in Montgomery County. A trial court there quickly ruled in Sullivan's favor, awarding him $500,000 in damages. The Alabama Supreme Court upheld both the verdict and the award.

The New York Times appealed the case to the U.S. Supreme Court, arguing that because Sullivan was a public official, a higher standard should be applied to his claim. The case came at a critical time both in the history of the civil rights movement and for The New York Times, which could have suffered crippling financial damage if the judgment against it was affirmed. In a landmark ruling that rewrote U.S. libel law, the Court ruled 9–0 in favor of the Times, reversing the judgment of the Alabama Supreme Court.

The Court's decision in *Sullivan* was based on the premise that to readily punish a media organization for publishing criticism of government officials was contrary to "the central meaning of the First Amendment," an argument that for the first time applied the protections of the First Amendment to the law of libel. The Court's decision rested on the principle that media defendants did not have sufficient protection from libel suits. Awarding victories to libel plaintiffs too easily, the Court reasoned, threatened to choke off the free flow of information that is essential to the maintenance of a democratic society. Fear of making even minor errors would result in a chilling effect on the media, unduly restricting press freedom. Moreover, this freedom was especially important when it came to criticism of the government and government officials. This kind of political speech is a core First Amendment value.[65] To allow libel plaintiffs who are government officials to be successful without a showing of fault would be tantamount to reinstituting seditious libel—prohibiting criticism of the government.

actual malice
In libel law, a statement made knowing it is false or with reckless disregard for its truth.

For Sullivan to win his case, Justice William Brennan wrote, the police commissioner would have to prove that The New York Times published the editorial-advertisement knowing it contained false information or with reckless disregard for its truth. This new standard of fault, Brennan wrote, was called "**actual malice**." Media defendants must have some room for error—"breathing space."[66] After this ruling, plaintiffs who are public officials had to prove that the content was published with actual malice—a new level of fault.

Justice Brennan explained: "We consider this case against the background of a profound national commitment to the principle that debate on public issues should be uninhibited, robust, and wide-open."[67] This debate should be open not just to members of the press but also to members of the public, who otherwise may not have access to the press.[68] If libel plaintiffs were not required to show actual malice before they could win libel suits, he wrote, such debate would be unduly limited because of self-censorship by both the public and the press.[69] His opinion emphasized that when people enter government service, they assume roles in which their job performance is rightly scrutinized and often criticized. Thus, the open debate the Court sought to protect "may well include vehement, caustic, and sometimes unpleasantly sharp attacks on government and public officials."[70]

Furthermore, because public officials have easy access to the news media, they have an avenue by which to correct any reputational harm they may have suffered. Thus, they must meet a more difficult standard than the one applied to cases involving private plaintiffs.

THE NEW YORK TIMES, TUESDAY, MARCH 29, 1960

> **"** *The growing movement of peaceful mass demonstrations by Negroes is something new in the South, something understandable. . . . Let Congress heed their rising voices, for they will be heard.* **"**
>
> —*New York Times editorial*
> *Saturday, March 19, 1960*

Heed Their Rising Voices

AS the whole world knows by now, thousands of Southern Negro students are engaged in widespread non-violent demonstrations in positive affirmation of the right to live in human dignity as guaranteed by the U. S. Constitution and the Bill of Rights. In their efforts to uphold these guarantees, they are being met by an unprecedented wave of terror by those who would deny and negate that document which the whole world looks upon as setting the pattern for modern freedom. . .

In Orangeburg, South Carolina, when 400 students peacefully sought to buy doughnuts and coffee at lunch counters in the business district, they were forcibly ejected, tear-gassed, soaked to the skin in freezing weather with fire hoses, arrested en masse and herded into an open barbed-wire stockade to stand for hours in the bitter cold.

In Montgomery, Alabama, after students sang "My Country, 'Tis of Thee" on the State Capitol steps, their leaders were expelled from school, and truckloads of police armed with shotguns and tear-gas ringed the Alabama State College Campus. When the entire student body protested to state authorities by refusing to re-register, their dining hall was padlocked in an attempt to starve them into submission.

In Tallahassee, Atlanta, Nashville, Savannah, Greensboro, Memphis, Richmond, Charlotte, and a host of other cities in the South, young American teenagers, in face of the entire weight of official state apparatus and police power, have boldly stepped forth as protagonists of democracy. Their courage and amazing restraint have inspired millions and given a new dignity to the cause of freedom.

Small wonder that the Southern violators of the Constitution fear this new, non-violent brand of freedom fighter. . . even as they fear the upswelling right-to-vote movement. Small wonder that they are determined to destroy the one man who, more than any other, symbolizes the new spirit now sweeping the South—the Rev. Dr. Martin Luther King, Jr., world-famous leader of the Montgomery Bus Protest. For it is his doctrine of non-violence which has inspired and guided the students in their widening wave of sit-ins; and it is this same Dr. King who founded and is president of the Southern Christian Leadership Conference—the organization which is spearheading the surging right-to-vote movement. Under Dr. King's direction the Leadership Conference conducts Student Workshops and Seminars in the philosophy and techniques of non-violent resistance.

Again and again the Southern violators have answered Dr. King's peaceful protests with intimidation and violence. They have bombed his home almost killing his wife and child. They have assaulted his person. They have arrested him seven times—for "speeding," "loitering" and similar "offenses." And now they have charged him with "perjury"—a *felony* under which they could imprison him for *ten years.* Obviously, their real purpose is to remove him physically as the leader to whom the students and millions

of others—look for guidance and support, and thereby to intimidate *all* leaders who may rise in the South. Their strategy is to behead this affirmative movement, and thus to demoralize Negro Americans and weaken their will to struggle. The defense of Martin Luther King, spiritual leader of the student sit-in movement, clearly, therefore, is an integral part of the total struggle for freedom in the South.

Decent-minded Americans cannot help but applaud the creative daring of the students and the quiet heroism of Dr. King. But this is one of those moments in the stormy history of Freedom when men and women of good will must do more than applaud the rising-to-glory of others. The America whose good name hangs in the balance before a watchful world, the America whose heritage of Liberty these Southern Upholders of the Constitution are defending, is *our* America as well as theirs. . .

We must heed their rising voices—yes—but we must add our own.

We must extend ourselves above and beyond moral support and render the material help so urgently needed by those who are taking the risks, facing jail, and *even death* in a glorious re-affirmation of our Constitution and its Bill of Rights.

We urge you to join hands with our fellow Americans in the South by supporting, with your dollars, this combined appeal for all three needs—the defense of Martin Luther King—the support of the embattled students—and the struggle for the right-to-vote.

Your Help Is Urgently Needed . . . NOW!!

Stella Adler	Dr. Alan Knight Chalmers	Anthony Franciosa	John Killens	L. Joseph Overton	Maureen Stapleton
Raymond Pace Alexander	Richard Coe	Lorraine Hansbury	Eartha Kitt	Clarence Pickett	Frank Silvera
Harry Van Arsdale	Nat King Cole	Rev. Donald Harrington	Rabbi Edward Klein	Shad Polier	Hope Stevens
Harry Belafonte	Cheryl Crawford	Nat Hentoff	Hope Lange	Sidney Poitier	George Tabor
Julie Belafonte	Dorothy Dandridge	James Hicks	John Lewis	A. Philip Randolph	Rev. Gardner C.
Dr. Algernon Black	Ossie Davis	Mary Hinkson	Viveca Lindfors	John Raitt	Taylor
Marc Blitzstein	Sammy Davis, Jr.	Van Heflin	Carl Murphy	Elmer Rice	Norman Thomas
William Branch	Ruby Dee	Langston Hughes	Don Murray	Jackie Robinson	Kenneth Tynan
Marlon Brando	Dr. Philip Elliott	Morris Iushewitz	John Murray	Mrs. Eleanor Roosevelt	Charles White
Mrs. Ralph Bunche	Dr. Harry Emerson	Mahalia Jackson	A. J. Muste	Bayard Rustin	Shelley Winters
Diahann Carroll	Fosdick	Mordecai Johnson	Frederick O'Neal	Robert Ryan	Max Youngstein

We in the south who are struggling daily for dignity and freedom warmly endorse this appeal

Rev. Ralph D. Abernathy *(Montgomery, Ala.)*	Rev. Matthew D. McCollom *(Orangeburg, S.C.)*	Rev. Walter L. Hamilton *(Norfolk, Va.)*	Rev. A. L. Davis *(New Orleans, La.)*
Rev. Fred L. Shuttlesworth *(Birmingham, Ala.)*	Rev. William Holmes Borders *(Atlanta, Ga.)*	I. S. Levy *(Columbia, S.C.)* Rev. Martin Luther King, Sr. *(Atlanta, Ga.)*	Mrs. Katie E. Whickham *(New Orleans, La.)*
Rev. Kelley Miller Smith *(Nashville, Tenn.)*	Rev. Douglas Moore *(Durham, N.C.)*	Rev. Henry C. Bunton *(Memphis, Tenn.)*	Rev. W. H. Hall *(Hattiesburg, Miss.)*
Rev. W. A. Dennis *(Chattanooga, Tenn.)*	Rev. Wyatt Tee Walker *(Petersburg, Va.)*	Rev. S.S. Seay, Sr. *(Montgomery, Ala.)*	Rev. J. E. Lowery *(Mobile, Ala.)*
Rev. C. K. Steele *(Tallahassee, Fla.)*		Rev. Samuel W. Williams *(Atlanta, Ga.)*	Rev. T. J. Jemison *(Baton Rouge, La.)*

COMMITTEE TO DEFEND MARTIN LUTHER KING AND THE STRUGGLE FOR FREEDOM IN THE SOUTH

312 West 125th Street, New York 27, N.Y. UNiversity 6-1700

Chairmen: A. Philip Randolph, Dr. Gardner C. Taylor; *Chairmen of Cultural Division:* Harry Belafonte, Sidney Poitier; *Treasurer:* Nat King Cole; *Executive Director:* Bayard Rustin; *Chairmen of Church Division:* Father George B. Ford, Rev. Harry Emerson Fosdick, Rev. Thomas Kilgore, Jr., Rabbi Edward E. Klein; *Chairman of Labor Division:* Morris Iushewitz

Please mail this coupon TODAY!

> **Committee To Defend Martin Luther King and The Struggle For Freedom in The South**
>
> 312 West 125th Street, New York 27, N.Y.
> UNiversity 6-1700
>
> I am enclosing my contribution of 5 for the work of the Committee.
>
> Name _____
>
> Address _____
>
> City ____ Zone ____ State ____
>
> ☐ I want to help   ☐ Please send further information
>
> **Please make checks payable to:**
> **Committee to Defend Martin Luther King**

The New York Times "advertorial" that prompted L.B. Sullivan's libel lawsuit against the newspaper.
Source: Originally published in the *New York Times* March 29, 1960. From the National Archives.

● **REAL WORLD LAW**

Can President Trump Change U.S. Libel Laws?

At a campaign rally in 2016, Republican presidential candidate Donald Trump said he would "open up our libel laws so when [the media] write purposely negative and horrible and false articles, we can sue them and win lots of money."[1]

As president, can Trump change libel laws? As already noted, libel law is a matter of state law. Presidents cannot directly change state laws. Because of *New York Times Co. v. Sullivan* and subsequent cases, the First Amendment limits public officials and public figures from recovering for libel without a showing of actual malice. *New York Times Co. v. Sullivan* constitutionalized libel law. First Amendment scholar Harry Kalven Jr. wrote that the *Sullivan* decision embraced free press principles that decry chilling effects and include a speech-protective approach. "Political freedom ends when government can use its powers and its courts to silence its critics."[2]

Legal experts say that if President Trump wants to change the libel laws, he has to get the Supreme Court to overturn the *Sullivan* decision and its progeny. This is unlikely to happen for several reasons. For decades, the Supreme Court has shown little interest in libel law. Libel is not a conservative vs. liberal issue—historically, both camps have shown support for protecting core First Amendment principles of free speech. Finally, one media law expert notes, "Changing the laws to make it easier to sue would essentially be used to harm him. He's more likely to be a libel defendant than a libel plaintiff."[3]

---

1. Jenna Johnson, *"I Will Give You Everything." Here Are 282 of Donald Trump's Campaign Promises*, Wash. Post, Nov. 28, 2016, www.washington-post.com/politics/i-will-give-you-everything-here-are-282-of-donald-trumps-campaign-promises/2016/11/24/01160678-b0f9-11e6-8616-52b15787add0_story.html?tid=a_inl&utm_term=.28ef219eddd1.
2. Harry Kalven Jr., *The* New York Times *Case: A Note on "The Central Meaning of the First Amendment,"* 1964 Sup. Ct. Rev. 191, 205.
3. Sydney Ember, *Can Libel Laws Be Changed Under Trump?* N.Y. Times, Nov. 13, 2016, www.nytimes.com/2016/11/14/business/media/can-libel-laws-be-changed-under-trump.html.

The opinion emphasized that the First Amendment permitted—even encouraged—an aggressive press. This was especially true with regard to the media's role as a "watchdog" in democratic society, keeping an eye on those in government. Allowing libel suits to proceed too easily against this vital organ of democratic society would damage democracy. Referring to the consequences of large damage awards against newspapers, Brennan wrote, "Whether or not a newspaper can survive a succession of such judgments, the pall of fear and timidity imposed upon those who would give voice to public criticism is an atmosphere in which the First Amendment freedoms cannot survive."[71]

Enjoying added protection from lawsuits in public official libel cases, the news media were more aggressive in the wake of the *Sullivan* case. In the years immediately following the ruling, aggressive coverage of events such as the civil rights movement, the Vietnam War and the Watergate scandal followed.[72]

Thus, with *New York Times Co. v. Sullivan*, libel law was "constitutionalized." The phrase "freedom of the press" was given new meaning. Restricting the flow of information, as the Court observed was possible under prior libel standards, is antithetical to the philosophy and spirit of the First Amendment.

Actual Malice

"Actual malice" is defined as knowledge of falsity or reckless disregard for the truth. Although the examination of this concept began within the discussion of *New York Times Co. v. Sullivan*, additional scrutiny is required given the developments that followed the landmark ruling.

● POINTS OF LAW

Actual Malice

- Knowledge of falsity or
- Reckless disregard for the truth

Knowledge of Falsity. Knowledge of falsity is nothing more than lying—publishing information knowing it is false. Knowledge of falsity is uncommon in the news media, where truth and accuracy are universal standards. Nonetheless, a news report in which the publisher "stacks the deck" to produce an intentionally distorted representation may rise to the level of knowledge of falsity. During the 1964 presidential campaign, for example, some people questioned the fitness for office of the Republican Party nominee, Sen. Barry Goldwater. The publisher of Fact magazine, Ralph Ginzburg, sent a questionnaire to hundreds of psychiatrists that asked them to analyze Goldwater's mental condition. Ginzburg received a variety of responses but published in a "psychobiographical" article only those that reflected poorly on the senator. When Goldwater sued for libel, the court concluded Ginzburg's conduct qualified as knowledge of falsity.[73]

Does knowingly changing the statements of an interview subject also qualify as knowledge of falsity, especially when those words are enclosed in quotation marks in print? Not necessarily. Reporter Janet Malcolm did just that in articles published in The New Yorker in 1983. The articles were based on more than 40 hours of taped interviews with psychoanalyst Jeffrey Masson. When Masson sued for libel, a decade-long journey through the courts began. At one stop along the way, the U.S. Supreme Court noted that in those hours of recorded interviews, no statements identical to the challenged passages appeared. In its decision, the Court ruled that while readers presume that words within quotation marks are verbatim reproductions of what the interviewee said, it would be unrealistic for the law to require the press to meet such a standard. Justice Anthony Kennedy wrote, "A deliberate alteration of the words uttered by a plaintiff does not equate with knowledge of falsity . . . unless the alteration results in a material change in the meaning conveyed by the statement."[74] Absent an alteration that changes the meaning, the words remain substantially true. Courts today often refer to the outcome in the *Masson* case as the material change of meaning doctrine.

In 2014, the U.S. Supreme Court further clarified the material change of meaning doctrine in a case involving a former pilot who sued an airline for defamation after the airline reported his "suspicious" behavior to the Transportation Security Administration (TSA).[75] In a 6–3 vote, the Supreme Court held the Aviation and Transportation Security Act (ATSA), which has an immunity provision for reporting suspicious behavior, provided immunity to the airline unless the disclosure to the TSA was made with actual malice. The court applied the *New York Times Co. v. Sullivan* actual malice standard and wrote that immunity applied unless the statements to the TSA were materially false.[76] Writing for the majority, Justice Sonia Sotomayor said that to accept the plaintiff's demand for precise wording in reporting suspicious behavior to the TSA "would vitiate the purpose of ATSA immunity," and that "baggage handlers, flight attendants, gate agents and other airline employees who report suspicious behavior to the TSA should not face financial ruin if, in the heat of a potential threat, they fail to choose their words with exacting care."[77]

Reckless Disregard for the Truth. Reckless disregard for the truth may be thought of as very sloppy journalism. The sloppiness must be both careless and irresponsible. In its *New York Times Co. v. Sullivan* ruling, the U.S. Supreme Court made it clear that the failure by the newspaper in that case to check the advertisement against its own records did not rise to the level of reckless disregard. A few years later, the Court considered two cases simultaneously that added to the understanding of reckless disregard. In the first, a weekly magazine, The Saturday Evening Post, published an article in 1963 about an attempt to fix a 1962 college football game. The magazine's source claimed he had been "patched" into a telephone conversation between the athletic director at the University of Georgia, Wally Butts, and the head football coach at the University of Alabama, Paul "Bear" Bryant. Moreover, the source claimed that in the call he heard the two men arranging the fix. The source, George Burnett, said he took careful notes of the conversation.

The Saturday Evening Post based its article on Burnett's recollection but never asked to see his notes. No effort was made by the magazine to corroborate the information with other sources, nor were other potential sources of information consulted, such as football experts, game films or witnesses. Burnett's credibility also went unchecked. It turned out he had a criminal record. The magazine's editors—and Burnett—failed to do their jobs adequately. As Justice John Harlan wrote in his opinion for the Court, "In short, the evidence is ample to support a finding of highly unreasonable conduct constituting an extreme departure from the standards of investigation and reporting ordinarily adhered to by responsible publishers."[78] The Court indicated that the omissions of responsibility by The Saturday Evening Post clearly qualified as the kind of conduct that rises to the level of reckless disregard for the truth.

In the second case, a retired major general, Edwin Walker, sued The Associated Press (AP) for its reports on his role in incidents surrounding efforts to keep the peace at the University of Mississippi when it was

Donald J. Trump ✔
@realDonaldTrump
 ఽ- Follow   ⌄

The FAKE NEWS media (failing @nytimes, @NBCNews, @ABC, @CBS, @CNN) is not my enemy, it is the enemy of the American People!

RETWEETS 51,167   LIKES 162,613

1:48 PM - 17 Feb 2017

↩ 79K   ⇄ 51K   ♥ 183K

U.S. President Donald Trump frequently attacks the media, suggesting they report lies and "fake news."

Source: Twitter post. Donald Trump, @realDonaldTrump. "THE FAKE NEWS Media." 02/17/2017 1:48 p.m.

● **REAL WORLD LAW**

Lessons Learned From the Rolling Stone Defamation Lawsuit

In 2016, a Virginia jury awarded a University of Virginia administrator $3 million in damages for a discredited Rolling Stone article. The 2014 article, "A Rape on Campus," relied on a single source when it told the story of a gang rape at a fraternity party. The rape never happened. The jury found that several statements in the article, as well as from the reporter in postpublication interviews, were made with actual malice and ordered both the magazine and the writer of the story to pay damages.[1]

In 2015, a report by the Columbia University Graduate School of Journalism called the article a "failure of journalism." This resulted in Rolling Stone retracting the story and removing it from its website.[2]

Libel defense attorneys suggested several lessons came from the Rolling Stone case[3]:

- Reporters should be aware that what they say in postpublication interviews and on their social media feeds can bring the possibility of individual liability. Media defense attorneys discourage reporters from talking with the press about their work.

- After concerns about the original article came to light, Rolling Stone published two editor notes to clarify/apologize. These notes generated additional publicity and brought the article to the attention of a new audience. This was considered republication and calls into question whether wholesale retraction is needed in cases like this one.

- The Rolling Stone verdict is unusual because of the focus on the individual reporter, who was found to be an independent publisher for her postpublication remark. This is an area of libel law to watch.

Another lawsuit, brought by the fraternity named in the article, settled out of court in 2017 for $1.65 million.[4]

1. Hawes Spencer and Ben Sisario, *In Rolling Stone Defamation Case, Magazine and Reporter Ordered to Pay $3 Million*, NYTimes.com, Nov. 7, 2016, www.nytimes.com/2016/11/08/business/media/in-rolling-stone-defamation-case-magazine-and-reporter-ordered-to-pay-3-million.html.
2. Sheila Coronel, Steve Coll & Derek Kravitz, *Rolling Stone and UVA: The Columbia University Graduate School of Journalism Report: An Anatomy of a Journalistic Failure*, April 5, 2015, RollingStone.com, www.rollingstone.com/culture/features/a-rape-on-campus-what-went-wrong-20150405.
3. Defamation and Related Claims, Comm. L. in the Digital Age 2016 (November 10, 2016).
4. T. Rees Shapiro, *Fraternity Chapter at U-Va. to Settle Suit Against Rolling Stone for $1.65 Million*, Wash. Post, June 13, 2017, www.washington-post.com/local/education/fraternity-chapter-at-u-va-to-settle-suit-against-rolling-stone-for-165-million/2017/06/13/35012b46-503d-11e7-91eb-9611861a988f_story.html?utm_term=.03e28824adcb.

enrolling its first African-American student in 1962. AP reported that Walker had taken command of a violent crowd of protesters and had personally led a charge against federal marshals sent there to enforce a court decree and to assist in preserving order. The report also described Walker as encouraging rioters to use violence and giving them technical advice on combating the effects of tear gas.[79] These false statements were distributed to several other media outlets.

In distinguishing the two cases, the Court cited one significant factor: "The evidence showed that the Butts story was in no sense 'hot news,' and the editors of the magazine recognized the need for a thorough investigation of the serious charges. . . . In contrast to the Butts article, the dispatch which concerns us in *Walker* was news which required immediate dissemination. . . . Considering the necessity for rapid dissemination, nothing in this series of events gives the slightest hint of a severe departure from accepted publishing standards."[80]

Thus, the urgency of a story has a significant bearing on whether the methods used by the news media defendant exhibit reckless disregard for the truth. The Court is willing to

⦿ POINTS OF LAW

"Reckless Disregard" Criteria

- *Urgency of the story.* Is there time to check the information?
- *Source reliability.* Is the source trustworthy?
- *Number of sources.* More than one source?
- *Story believability.* Is further examination necessary?

allow the news media some "wiggle room" when there is deadline pressure. In addition, the reliability of a story's source and the believability of the information are factors in the judgment.

The following year, the Supreme Court further developed its reckless disregard standard. First, the Court admitted that "reckless disregard" cannot be summarized in a single infallible definition. But it went on to say that reckless conduct is not measured merely by whether a reasonably prudent person would have published or would have investigated before publishing. "There must be sufficient evidence to permit the conclusion that the defendant in fact entertained serious doubts as to the truth of his publication. Publishing with such doubts shows reckless disregard for the truth or falsity and demonstrates actual malice."[81]

Thus, the Supreme Court had now infused the reckless disregard standard with an element of subjectivity. It was no longer enough to merely examine the evidence related to the publisher's actions; now it was also necessary to determine the publisher's state of mind. But does this standard place a premium on ignorance? Does it reward a publisher who has doubts about the information but does nothing prior to publication to investigate? Evidence of investigation could be used against the publisher in court. The Supreme Court admitted that this possibility existed but said the purpose of the actual malice standard was to emphasize free expression. If it were going to err in its definition of reckless disregard, the Court said it would do so on the side that enhanced rather than chilled expression.

deposition
Testimony by a witness conducted outside a courtroom and intended to be used in preparation for trial.

More than a decade later, the Supreme Court considered whether evidence could be used to help make judgments about a libel defendant's state of mind. During a **deposition**, a "60 Minutes" segment producer had refused to answer certain questions related to his editorial decisions concerning a 1973 broadcast about a government cover-up of atrocities during the Vietnam War, claiming the First Amendment protected them from being disclosed. The Supreme Court disagreed and ruled that the plaintiff could look into the defendant's mental processes.[82]

A decade later, the Court further indicated that a judgment concerning reckless disregard does not necessarily need to focus on any single lapse by the defendant but may rest on an evaluation of the record as a whole. In other words, the more mistakes that are made, the more readily a court may conclude that a defendant acted with reckless disregard.

The Court ruled that an Ohio newspaper acted with actual malice when it failed to interview the one witness who could have verified its story about alleged corruption in a local election for a judgeship; the newspaper did not listen to a tape it had been told would exonerate the plaintiff, a tape that the plaintiff delivered to the newspaper at the newspaper's request; an editorial the newspaper published prior to the libelous report indicated the editor had already decided to publish the allegations at issue regardless of evidence to the contrary; and discrepancies in the testimony of the defendant's own witnesses supported the idea that the defendant had failed to conduct a complete investigation with the deliberate intent of avoiding the truth.[83]

Public Officials. **New York Times Co. v. Sullivan** also established that not only is the content of the allegedly libelous material important, so is the nature of the plaintiff. The ruling said public official plaintiffs must show that fault on the part of the defendant is at the level of actual malice. Private figures, on the other hand, are usually required to show some lesser, easier-to-prove level of fault, typically negligence.

But who qualifies as a public official? The U.S. Supreme Court, through Justice Brennan, has said, "It is clear that the 'public official' designation applies at the very

● INTERNATIONAL LAW

Fake News and Defamation

In 2016, a fake news conspiracy theory about a popular pizza restaurant in Washington, D.C., led police to arrest a man who fired shots inside the restaurant. The false election-related story held that a Hillary Clinton-linked pizzeria ran a pedophile ring. The theory spread mostly on Reddit but was also shared on social media.[1]

After the restaurant was falsely accused, some wondered if Congress could craft a legal remedy for fake news victims without stepping on the First Amendment. A Harvard University constitutional and international law professor suggested that the European Union's "right to be forgotten" law might provide some remedy. The law, discussed in Chapter 6, allows search engines to block or remove some internet posts.[2]

"Regulating search engines by legal order, the way the European right-to-forget system does, is probably the trickiest part, legally speaking," writes Noah Feldman. "It's also the most practically important. U.S. takedown orders won't reach all who publish fake news. But they might well cover the major search engines that people use to spread the articles, as well as social networking sites that spread fake news."[3]

Facebook began to take steps to combat the spread of fake news in 2016. In 2017, it started a trial of new filtering tools in Germany ahead of elections there. The filter allows users to report stories as fake, which would send them to a third-party fact-checker. "If a story is deemed false, Facebook will flag it, decline to prioritize it and warn users who want to share it."[4]

---

1. Faiz Siddiqui & Susan Svrluga, *N.C. Man Told Police He Went to D.C. Pizzeria With Gun to Investigate Conspiracy Theory*, WASH. POST, Dec. 5, 2016, www .washingtonpost.com/news/local/wp/2016/12/04/d-c-police-respond-to-report-of-a-man-with-a-gun-at-comet-ping-pong-restaurant/? utm_term=.dc4c70415d58.
2. Noah Feldman, *Closing the Safe Harbor for Libelous Fake News*, BLOOMBERG, Dec. 16, 2016, www.bloomberg.com/view/articles/2016-12-16/ free-speech-libel-and-the-truth-after-pizzagate.
3. *Id.*
4. Jon Fingas, *Facebook Tests Fake News Filtering Outside of the US*, ENGADGET, Jan. 15, 2017, www.engadget.com/2017/01/15/facebook-tests- fake-news-filtering-in-germany/.

least to those among the hierarchy of government employees who have or appear to have to the public substantial responsibility for or control over the conduct of governmental affairs."[84] The idea is that people who meet that definition are people whom the public is justified in wanting to know about because they serve the public. Information about them may relate to the officials' qualifications, conduct and character. But not all those paid by government for their work meet the criteria.

Conversely, one can meet the public official standard without being a government employee. For example, a libel plaintiff in New Hampshire who was hired by three elected county commissioners to supervise a public recreation facility owned by the county was deemed to be a public official by the Supreme Court in 1966. "Where a position in government has such apparent importance that the public has an independent interest in the qualifications and performance of the person who holds it, beyond the general public interest in the qualifications, conduct and performance of all government employees, both elements we identified in New York Times are present, and the New York Times malice standards apply," the Court wrote.[85]

A person usually remains a public official even after leaving a position that includes substantial responsibility for or control over the conduct of governmental affairs, as long as the allegedly libelous material pertains to the person's conduct while in that post. However, the U.S. Supreme Court has said that it is possible, though rare, for the passage of time to erode the public's interest in the official's conduct in office so much that the actual malice standard would no longer apply.[86]

Public Figures. Do other public people need to prove actual malice when they sue for libel? After *New York Times Co. v. Sullivan*, the U.S. Supreme Court answered this question in the affirmative in *Curtis Publishing Co. v. Butts* and *Associated Press v. Walker*, the two cases described previously and considered simultaneously by the Court. Chief Justice Earl Warren wrote, "To me, differentiation between 'public figures' and 'public officials' and the adoption of separate standards of proof for each has no basis in law, logic, or First Amendment policy. Increasingly in this country, the distinctions between governmental and private sectors are blurred."[87] One reason a higher level of fault is required of public officials is that they typically have access to the media to correct damage to their reputation. **Public figures**, Warren claimed, are no different:

public figure
In libel law, a plaintiff who is in the public spotlight, usually voluntarily, and must prove the defendant acted with actual malice in order to win damages.

> "Public figures," like "public officials," often play an influential role in ordering society. And surely as a class these "public figures" have as ready access as "public officials" to the mass media of communication, both to influence policy and to counter criticism of their views and activities. Our citizenry has a legitimate and substantial interest in the conduct of such persons, and freedom of the press to engage in uninhibited debate about their involvement in public issues and events is as crucial as it is in the case of "public officials." The fact that they are not amenable to the restraints of the political process only underscores the legitimate and substantial nature of the interest, since it means that public opinion may be the only instrument by which society can attempt to influence their conduct.[88]

One question remained, however: Who qualifies as a public figure?

All-Purpose Public Figures. The U.S. Supreme Court has defined two categories of public figures. Both must prove that a defendant acted with actual malice. In *Gertz v. Robert Welch Inc.*, the Court said that some people "occupy positions of such persuasive power and influence that they are deemed public figures for all purposes."[89] An **all-purpose public figure** is anyone whom a court labels to be "public" under all circumstances. That is, no matter the context, the individual's name is widely recognizable to at least some segments of the public. However, some courts demand that an additional requirement be met for all-purpose public figure status: The person must also have written or spoken about a broad range of issues. These are people who have acquired some degree of fame outside the public official sphere—"celebrities," for example. This could include not only those in the entertainment field but also some athletes, activists, religious leaders and business leaders.

Limited-Purpose Public Figures. More common than all-purpose public figures are those people who have attained public status only within a narrow set of circumstances. These people, in the words of the Court, "have thrust themselves to the forefront of particular public controversies in order to influence the resolution of the issues involved."[90] Like an all-purpose public figure, a **limited-purpose public figure** invites attention and comment. An individual may be a limited-purpose public figure within a particular community or a particular field. In the *Gertz* ruling, Justice Lewis Powell echoed Justice Brennan's *New York Times Co. v. Sullivan* rationale, noting that an individual who seeks government office must accept "certain necessary consequences of that involvement in public affairs. He runs the risk of closer public scrutiny than might otherwise be the case."[91] He then added the key declaration: "Those classed as public figures stand in a similar position."[92]

Although the groundwork had already been established,[93] another series of rulings by the Court more precisely articulated who qualifies as a public figure. In one case, a man had been in the news 16 years prior to a false characterization in a book, but he had not voluntarily thrust himself into the public eye. The Supreme Court ruled he was not a public figure.[94] In another case, when a wealthy and well-known socialite sued for libel over a report about her behavior that led to divorce, the Court said she was private because her involvement in the divorce was not voluntary.[95] In yet another case, the Court held that a scientist who had received federal grants and who had published papers in scientific journals was nevertheless a private figure. The defendant tried to claim the scientist had become a public figure through the notoriety of his libel suit. The Court ruled that libel

all-purpose public figure In libel law, a person who occupies a position of such persuasive power and influence as to be deemed a public figure for all purposes. Public figure libel plaintiffs are required to prove actual malice.

Lee Balterman/The LIFE Picture Collection/Getty Images

Lawyer Elmer Gertz was known well beyond *Gertz v. Robert Welch Inc.*—he represented famous author Henry Miller and accused murderer Jack Ruby.

◉ POINTS OF LAW

Limited-Purpose Public Figure

- A public controversy must exist before the publication of the allegedly libelous statement.
- The plaintiff must have in some way participated voluntarily in trying to resolve this controversy.
- The plaintiff's participation actively sought to influence public opinion regarding the controversy.

limited-purpose public figure In libel law, those plaintiffs who have attained public figure status within a narrow set of circumstances by thrusting themselves to the forefront of particular public controversies in order to influence the resolution of the issues involved; this kind of public figure is more common than the all-purpose public figure.

bootstrapping In libel law, the forbidden practice of a defendant claiming that the plaintiff is a public figure solely on the basis of the statement that is the reason for the lawsuit.

defendants cannot, in effect, create a public figure through the defamation claim itself or media coverage of it.[96]

This and similar cases illustrate what is described as **bootstrapping**. Bootstrapping occurs when media defendants "attach" themselves to the protection of the actual malice standard by citing media coverage—including the very media coverage they generate—of the plaintiff as evidence that the plaintiff is a public figure. Courts have noted that the public controversy at issue must have existed prior to the publication upon which the defamation claim is based in order for the plaintiff to be categorized as a public figure. As the Supreme Court said, "Clearly, those charged with defamation cannot, by their own conduct, create their own defense by making the claimant a public figure."[97] However, a possible side effect can occur when a court rigidly applies the pre-existing controversy requirement. Such an approach may punish legitimate reporting that uncovers specific acts of wrongdoing. Courts therefore attempt to carefully decide which came first: the controversy or the allegedly libelous story about the controversy.

Just as media are not permitted to bootstrap themselves onto their own material to strengthen their defense, a plaintiff may not avoid the actual malice standard by claiming that the attention was unwanted. The proper question for a court is not whether the plaintiff volunteered for the publicity but whether the plaintiff volunteered for an activity from which publicity would foreseeably arise.

Even if an individual is not active in a particular field of endeavor, mere presence within that field may satisfy a court's public figure requirements. One court explains that where a person has "chosen to engage in a profession which draws him regularly into regional and national view and leads to fame and notoriety in the community . . . he invites general public discussion. . . . If society chooses to direct massive public attention to a particular sphere of activity, those who enter that sphere inviting such attention overcome the *Times* standard."[98] Thus, voluntary entry into a sphere of activity is sufficient to satisfy this element of the public figure inquiry.

Because the Supreme Court has said that a public figure is someone with widespread fame or notoriety, the individual's prominence is important in determining public figure status. Moreover, that prominence may apply to a narrowly drawn context. Merely being an executive within a prominent and influential company does not by itself make one a public figure. Professionals are typically not public figures, but under certain circumstances they can be. For example, voluntary use of controversial or unorthodox techniques may be enough to confer public figure status. Publicly defending such methods or adopting other controversial stands also tends to bring about public figure status: A doctor who had written extensively on health issues as a newspaper columnist, who had authored several journal articles on the subject and who had appeared on at least one nationally broadcast television program discussing health and nutrition issues was held to be a public figure for a limited range of issues—those pertaining to health and nutrition.[99]

An individual may assume public figure status within small publics but may revert to being a private figure in larger spheres. For example, a university professor may be a public figure on campus and in the adjacent academic community but a private person beyond those boundaries. The professor therefore may be a public figure for purposes of an article in the university newspaper but not if featured in a regional newspaper or a national magazine. Thus, the professor's public figure status is limited. Similarly, an individual may attain the status of an all-purpose public figure within a particular geographical area.[100]

● REAL WORLD LAW

The Governor vs. The Sniper

AP/Star Tribune/Elizabeth Flores

Former Minnesota Gov. Jesse Ventura leaves a federal courthouse after day one at his 2014 defamation trial against "American Sniper" Chris Kyle's estate.

In 2014, a federal jury in Minnesota awarded former professional wrestler and former Minnesota Gov. Jesse Ventura $1.8 million from the estate of Chris Kyle. Kyle was a Navy SEAL sniper whose life was featured in the 2014 film "American Sniper," an adaptation of his best-selling memoir by the same name.[1]

In 2016, the Eighth Circuit Court of Appeals reversed the Minnesota jury's verdict on "unjust enrichment" and suggested that Kyle was prevented from having a fair trial. Unjust enrichment means that someone unfairly made money at the expense of someone else.[2]

In 2014, Ventura had successfully argued that Kyle's description in his book of an alleged bar fight between the two men was false and defamatory. The appeals court noted that at least seven witnesses testifying on behalf of Kyle's estate offered generally similar accounts of the bar fight. The Eighth Circuit panel also vacated part of the jury verdict by noting that Ventura's lawyers offered improper and prejudicial statements that suggested that the insurance policy covering Kyle's book, rather than Kyle's estate, would pay damages awarded to Ventura.[3]

Ventura's appeal to the U.S. Supreme Court was denied, and the Eight Circuit has remanded the defamation judgment for a new trial.[4]

---

1. Joseph Lindberg, *Jesse Ventura Goes After "American Sniper" Publisher Now*, Minn. Pioneer Press, Dec. 16, 2014, www.twincities.com/localnews/ci_27147200/jesse-ventura-sues-american-sniper-publisher-now?source=pkg.
2. Ventura v. Kyle, 825 F.3d 876 (8th Cir. 2016).
3. *Id.*
4. *Id.*

Involuntary Public Figures. In the same ruling that categorized public figures as all-purpose and limited-purpose, the U.S. Supreme Court also suggested that there may be a third category: **involuntary public figures**. These are people who do not necessarily thrust themselves into public controversies voluntarily but who are drawn into specific issues.[101] An individual could be drawn into a matter of public controversy through unforeseen or unintended circumstances, becoming a public figure through no purposeful action. The Court added, however, that the occurrence of such public figures is "exceedingly rare."[102]

involuntary public figure In libel law, a person who does not necessarily thrust himself or herself into public controversies voluntarily but is drawn into a given issue.

Nevertheless, cases surface occasionally where plaintiffs are declared involuntary public figures. For example, a Connecticut court ruled that a plaintiff who had served time in prison for a crime he did not commit was just such an involuntary public figure. "There are . . . individuals who have not sought publicity or consented to it, but through their own conduct or otherwise have become a legitimate subject of public interest. They have, in other words, become 'news,'" the court decided.[103]

Losing Public Figure Status. It is theoretically possible for one-time public figures to revert to private status with the passage of time. However, the courts have been inconsistent in their application of this concept. How much time must pass before a person loses his or her public status is difficult to pin down. One consideration is whether the person's role in a particular matter remains in the public consciousness or is of public concern. To return to private status, it is likely that a plaintiff would need to demonstrate not only that he or she is no longer a subject of public concern but also that his or her libel claim is not connected to events or controversies of which the public remains aware.

Private Figures. A libel plaintiff who does not qualify as a public official or public figure is considered a **private figure**. Private figures usually do not have to prove actual malice as the level of fault in their cases. Typically, they need to show only that the libel defendant acted with negligence, although this is not universally true.

While the definition of negligence varies from state to state, it is in all cases easier to prove than actual malice. Negligence is the failure to exercise reasonable or ordinary care. What constitutes negligence can vary from one professional setting to another. When establishing what constitutes negligence in the field of journalism, it can be difficult to arrive at a single definition because news media operate according to a variety of professional standards, especially as new forms of media have emerged on the internet. What is "acceptable" in television news reporting may not be so in a daily newspaper or on social media. In other words, unlike professions such as medicine and law, journalism has no single authoritative code of conduct.

private figure In libel law, a plaintiff who cannot be categorized as either a public figure or a public official. Generally, in order to recover damages, a private figure is required to prove not actual malice but merely negligence on the part of the defendant.

That said, some common examples of negligent behavior in the news media have emerged. These include, but are not limited to, the following:

- Relying on a single or anonymous source

- Relying on other media reports without independent investigation

- Careless misstatements of the contents of documents

- Possessing ill will toward the plaintiff

- Conclusions or inferences unreasonably deduced

- Failure to follow established internal practices and policies

- Errors in taking notes and quoting sources

In sum, journalistic negligence may be viewed as the failure to take reasonable care to ensure that a report is accurate and that its subjects are treated fairly.

The Nature of the Statement. Whether a plaintiff is considered a public figure for purposes of a libel suit can depend on the nature of the material being published—specifically whether it relates to a matter of public concern. In one case that reached the U.S. Supreme Court, a credit reporting agency issued a credit report that erroneously reported the bankruptcy filing of a Vermont construction contractor. The credit report had been sent to five subscribers who, by agreement, could not repeat the information. The contractor sued for libel. The U.S. Supreme Court upheld a lower court ruling that the contractor was a private figure, making it easier for the company to make a case that it had been libeled. The reason: The statement about its supposed bankruptcy was not a matter of public concern.[104] The Court's opinion stated that the purpose of the speaker and the nature and size of the audience are relevant in determining when speech involves matters of public concern.[105] In determining whether a statement is libelous, therefore, the Court identified the importance of both the status of the plaintiff and the nature of the statement in question.

There was some concern in the media that this ruling might dilute libel protections and allow strict liability if plaintiffs were no longer required to prove fault on the part of media outlets reporting on matters that were not of public concern. Strict liability (introduced in Chapter 1) means that a defendant is automatically held responsible for damages when an inherently dangerous or wrongful act occurs. Fault is not required to recover damages. When a court applies strict liability, the person injured doesn't have to prove negligence to receive monetary damages.

In *Dun & Bradstreet Inc. v. Greenmoss Builders Inc.*, the question surfaced as to whether plaintiffs could be required to prove actual malice even when suing a nonmedia defendant. The Court stated that since its inception, the standard had been applied to nonmedia defendants.[106] That application, however, is facilitated when the statement is a matter of public concern.

Generally speaking, a majority of lower court decisions involving libel in the private person–private information context have concluded that states can impose liability without fault. But, in a U.S. District Court in Oregon in 2011, the application of strict liability to a libel case raised new concerns about bloggers and their status as journalists. It also raises concerns about how courts determine whether matters are of public concern.[107]

Kevin Padrick, a senior executive with Obsidian Finance Group, sued blogger Crystal Cox for criticisms she posted about him and Obsidian on her personal, issue-specific website www.obsidianfinancesucks.com, as well as on some third-party websites. Cox suggested, among other things, that Padrick and Obsidian committed fraud, were corrupt and paid off the media and politicians, as well as that Padrick had hired a hitman to kill her.[108] Only one of Cox's posts proceeded to trial. The court rejected Cox's claim that it should treat her as a media defendant. The judge instructed the jury to treat the case as a strict liability tort—meaning the plaintiff did not have to show fault. The court made its determination of Cox's status as a private figure because she provided no evidence of education in journalism, no connections with established news organizations and no adherence to basic journalistic standards. The court also held that her post about Obsidian Finance did not involve matters of public concern.[109]

In November 2011, a jury awarded damages of $1 million to Obsidian Finance and $1.5 million to Padrick. In 2012, Cox filed a motion for a new trial, arguing that the jury instructions misstated the law and that the verdict was excessive. That motion was denied. Subsequently, both Cox and Obsidian appealed to the Ninth Circuit. In 2014, the Ninth Circuit agreed with First Amendment scholar Eugene Volokh, who argued on Cox's behalf that she is entitled to the same protection afforded media defendants in the *Gertz* case. He said the court must apply at least a negligence standard of fault and that the speech at issue was a matter of public concern.[110]

The Ninth Circuit panel decision held that bloggers are entitled to the protection provided by *Gertz* when a blog post involves a matter of public concern. Rejecting the notion that First Amendment protection applies only to trained and credentialed journalists, the panel quoted the Supreme Court's ruling in *Citizens United*: "We have consistently rejected the proposition that the institutional press has any constitutional privilege beyond that of other speakers." The Ninth Circuit panel added, "As the Supreme Court has accurately warned, a First Amendment distinction between the institutional press and other speakers is unworkable. . . . In defamation cases, the public-figure status of a plaintiff and the public importance of the statement at issue—not the identity of the speaker—provide the First Amendment touchstones."[111]

EMOTIONAL DISTRESS

Sometimes people who bring a libel lawsuit will also claim a harm that does not simply involve reputation. A news story could cause **emotional distress** even though it is not defamatory. Or a libelous story injuring a plaintiff's reputation might also upset him or her emotionally. There are two categories of emotional distress suits: **intentional infliction of emotional distress** and **negligent infliction of emotional distress**.

Just as a libel defendant may act with actual malice—that is, intentionally or recklessly publishing false material—so may an intentional or **reckless** act or statement cause emotional distress. Acting recklessly is not caring what the result of an action will be. Also, being negligent—an act or statement made by mistake or without anticipating the possible harm the act or statement could cause—may inflict emotional distress, just as a negligently published article may defame someone. Emotional distress cases sometimes are called "emotional injury" or "mental distress" suits.

The law defines "emotional distress" as being frightened or extremely anxious. A plaintiff must show the emotional injury is very serious or severe, that she or he experienced considerable mental pain or anguish.[112] Merely being upset, angry, embarrassed or resentful is

emotional distress Serious mental anguish.

intentional infliction of emotional distress Extreme and outrageous intentional or reckless conduct causing plaintiffs severe emotional harm; public official and public figure plaintiff must show actual malice on defendant's part.

negligent infliction of emotional distress Careless breach of a duty that causes the plaintiff severe emotional harm.

reckless Word used to describe actions taken with no consideration of the legal harms that might result.

not enough to win a lawsuit based on infliction of emotional distress.[113] However, emotions such as severe disappointment or an intense feeling of shame or humiliation may cause the extreme mental pain that the emotional distress tort requires.[114]

INTENTIONAL INFLICTION OF EMOTIONAL DISTRESS

Intentional or reckless conduct that is extreme and outrageous and causes severe emotional harm can be grounds for a successful lawsuit.[115] The key to intentional infliction of emotional distress (IIED) is that the defendant's actions must have been outrageous—that is, actions a civilized society considers intolerable and beyond all bounds of decency.[116]

Usually insults do not amount to outrageous conduct, nor do words that annoy, or even statements that are mild threats. Courts understand the verbal jousting people experience in 21st-century America can cause hurt feelings. People are not always polite and considerate. The law expects people to ignore unpleasant comments. The high standard plaintiffs must meet—the defendant's conduct must be beyond all possible bounds of decency—is meant to prevent lawsuits being filed over mere insults, annoying comments and other remarks that are aggravating but not outrageous.[117] That some harms suffered in life do not rise to the level of legally actionable claims is captured in the Latin phrase *de minimis non curat lex*, "the law does not concern itself with trifles."

In addition to outrageousness, an IIED plaintiff must prove severe emotional distress caused by the defendant's action or expression. This requires more than mild annoyance or embarrassment.

Outrageousness

Media defendants win most intentional infliction of emotional distress cases primarily because courts do not find the media acted in an outrageous manner. For example, there was nothing extreme or outrageous when a photographer on assignment for Harper's Magazine took a picture of a soldier's body lying in an open casket at the soldier's funeral.

⦿ POINTS OF LAW

Intentional Infliction of Emotional Distress

Plaintiff's Case
   Defendant's intentional or reckless conduct

- Was extreme and outrageous—beyond the bounds of decency tolerated in civilized society;

- Involved actual malice, if plaintiff is a public official or public figure; and

- Caused plaintiff's severe emotional distress.

Defense
   There is no defense if plaintiff proves his or her case.

The soldier, who died while serving in Iraq, was the first member of the Oklahoma National Guard to be killed in action in more than 50 years. Harper's published the photograph along with others showing Americans and Iraqis mourning those killed in the war. A federal appellate court rejected a lawsuit for intentional infliction of emotional distress brought by the soldier's family, ruling that the photograph was not "so extreme and outrageous as to go beyond all possible bounds of decency."[118]

Broadcasting the identity of undercover narcotics police officers has not been found outrageous. A federal appellate court said publishing "upsetting but true news reports" is not "so extreme and outrageous as to permit recovery" in an intentional infliction of emotional distress lawsuit.[119]

Not even incorrectly suggesting a scientist sent anthrax-laced letters was deemed outrageous. In a series of newspaper columns, New York Times columnist Nicholas Kristof wrote that the FBI should focus on a Mr. Z in the investigation into the mailing of letters containing anthrax that caused five deaths. The columnist later identified Mr. Z as Dr. Steven J. Hatfill, a research scientist employed by the U.S. Department of Defense. Hatfill sued the Times for intentional infliction of emotional distress and other torts. A federal appellate court found Hatfill could not show that publishing the columns constituted extreme and outrageous conduct.[120] The U.S. government exonerated Hatfill in 2008 and awarded him $4.6 million to settle a lawsuit he brought against the government.[121]

However, plaintiffs have proved outrageousness in several intentional infliction of emotional distress cases brought against the media. Eran Best sued for intentional infliction of emotional distress based on an episode of the A&E network reality program "Female Forces." The program follows female police officers through their workday. An episode focused on the Naperville, Ill., police department. A male Naperville officer stopped Best and called for a female officer, who arrived with a "Female Forces" camera crew. The officers gave Best a field sobriety test and arrested her for driving on a suspended driver's license. They handcuffed Best, searched her car and took her to the police station, all recorded by the camera crew.

In the police car, the male officer told Best her arrest would not be on "Female Forces" if she did not sign a consent form. At the police station, a "Female Forces" producer urged Best to sign. Best repeatedly refused and did not sign a consent form. Despite that, footage of her arrest appeared on "Female Forces," including the sobriety test and her being handcuffed. Best's face is visible and her voice heard. The program also included a scene in which the two officers kidded about Best's "expensive taste" while searching her car. One officer said Best "likes Coach purses, bags, and shoes." The other commented on Best's driving a Jaguar. The court held Best could show outrageousness based on the program's airing footage that included the mocking comments, knowing Best objected, and ignoring the assurances given her that the footage would not be televised.[122]

Courts have ruled that some newsgathering techniques by themselves are outrageous. For instance, a television news reporter and cameraman approached a house next door to one where, earlier in the day, a woman had murdered her two small children and then committed suicide. The reporter talked with a 5-year-old child, her 7-year-old sister and their 11-year-old babysitter, who were home without an adult present. The reporter asked the children what had happened next door. After the children said they knew nothing about it, the reporter said, "Well, the mom has killed the two little kids and herself." With the camera continuing to film, the reporter asked about the family next door.

Although the station did not show the videotape, the children's parents sued for intentional infliction of emotional distress. Ruling in favor of the plaintiff, a California appellate court noted that the reporter approached the children suddenly and with no warning; a cameraman pointed bright lights at the children; the reporter pushed the door open; the reporter blurted out "information with emotionally devastating potential"; the children were not allowed to object to being interviewed on videotape and were too young to understand they could refuse.[123] The court said these actions could be seen as extreme and outrageous, especially because they involved children under 12 years old.

Entertainment programs as well as news reports may be the basis of intentional infliction of emotional distress cases. A court may find remarks are extreme and outrageous if the person who made the statements knew or should have known that the plaintiff was particularly susceptible to emotional distress. For instance, after Melinda Duckett's 2-year-old son disappeared, CNN's Nancy Grace recorded a telephone conversation with Duckett. The recording was for Grace's show the following day. Just before the program aired, Duckett committed suicide. CNN ran the recording as scheduled and several times after that. Duckett's estate, her parents and her sister sued CNN and Grace for intentional infliction of emotional distress. The court said if the defendants knew Duckett already suffered emotional and psychological stress because her son had disappeared, as the plaintiffs alleged, "'the potential for severe emotional distress is enormously increased.'"[124]

In addition to proving that the defendant's actions or statements were outrageous, a plaintiff suing for intentional infliction of emotional distress must prove the defendant acted intentionally or recklessly.[125]

Actual Malice

Public officials and public figures have an additional hurdle to overcome to win an intentional infliction of emotional distress case. The U.S. Supreme Court requires public people to prove actual malice in addition to the tort's other elements. As discussed earlier in this chapter, in *New York Times Co. v. Sullivan* the Court defined "actual malice" as publishing with knowledge of falsity or a reckless disregard for the truth.[126] When the Rev. Jerry Falwell sued Larry Flynt and Hustler magazine for intentional infliction of emotional distress, the Court extended its actual malice ruling to IIED cases in *Hustler Magazine Inc. v. Falwell*.[127] Flynt published what he claimed was a parody of a Campari advertising campaign. At the time, Campari, a liquor manufacturer, published ads in which celebrities discussed their "first time," an obvious double entendre about tasting Campari and having sex.

In Flynt's satire, Falwell, the leader of a national organization named the Moral Majority, described his "first time" as being with his mother in an outhouse. The magazine portrayed Falwell, who was known for speaking out against immorality, as a hypocrite for engaging in immoral activities. Hustler included a disclaimer saying "ad parody—not to be taken seriously," and the magazine's table of contents cited the page as "Fiction—Ad and Personality Parody."

Falwell sued Flynt for libel, appropriation and intentional infliction of emotional distress. A federal district court jury rejected the libel claim because the satire was so outlandish no one would believe it was a statement of fact. At trial on that issue, a jury said Flynt intentionally inflicted emotional distress, and it awarded Falwell $100,000 in compensatory damages and $100,000 in punitive damages.[128] A federal appellate court affirmed, saying the satire was outrageous and intentionally published.[129]

But the Supreme Court reversed that decision, holding that as a public figure Falwell had to present proof of actual malice.[130] The Court found that, as satire, the First Amendment protected the magazine's Campari ad. Biting, even hurtful, humor is the stock-in-trade of satirical works, the Court found, and it was simply not possible to create a constitutionally valid distinction between political cartoons and satires and the arguably tasteless Campari ad spoof. If juries were permitted to award damages for such satires, the Court warned, jurors could decide what was outrageous based on their political leanings, which would violate the First Amendment.

Not all parodies and satires were protected, the *Falwell* Court said. A public figure or public official who could prove that a satire included a false statement of fact published with actual malice could win a lawsuit for intentional infliction of emotional distress. Because the jury in this case had found there were no factual statements in the piece—it was just a parody—Falwell could not successfully sue for intentional infliction of emotional distress.

The Court also suggested Falwell might have used intentional infliction of emotional distress as a replacement for his rejected libel claim. If public figures had to prove actual malice to win libel cases, they should carry that burden for intentional infliction as well, the Court implied. In both torts, actual malice served to protect the press's First Amendment right to make caustic comments about public people.

In 2011, the U.S. Supreme Court again ruled that an IIED claim infringed the First Amendment. The Court said in *Snyder v. Phelps* that speech about matters of public concern, even "particularly hurtful" expression, is protected against an IIED lawsuit.[131] In *Snyder v. Phelps*, protesters from Westboro Baptist Church of Topeka, Kan., picketed the funeral of a Marine killed in action in Iraq. Westboro's 75

⭕ POINTS OF LAW

Parody or Satire?

The Supreme Court has explained that there is a difference between "parody" (in which the copyrighted work is the target) and "satire" (in which the copyrighted work is merely used to poke fun at another target): "Parody needs to mimic an original to make its point, and so has some claim to use the creation of its victim's (or collective victims') imagination, whereas satire can stand on its own two feet and so requires justification for the very act of borrowing."[1]

1. Campbell v. Acuff-Rose Music, 510 U.S. 569, 580–81 (1994).

congregants, most of whom were church founder Fred Phelps' family members, believed "God hates and punishes the United States for its tolerance of homosexuality, particularly in America's military," according to the Court.[132] The group expressed its views by picketing, frequently near military funerals.

Phelps and six of his family picketed 1,000 feet from the Marine's hometown Catholic church for 30 minutes before the funeral. They displayed signs saying, for example, "God Hates the USA/Thank God for 9/11," "Thank God for Dead Soldiers," "Pope in Hell" and "Priests Rape Boys." Another sign said "God Hates Fags," although the Marine was not gay. Only the tops of the signs were visible to those in the funeral procession as it passed close to the protesters. Later that evening, while watching a televised news report about the demonstration, the Marine's father, Albert Snyder, saw what the signs said.

Snyder sued for IIED and other torts. He said several of the signs, such as those saying "You're Going to Hell" and "God Hates You," were directed at him. The jury granted a multimillion-dollar award for the IIED and other claims.

The satire that prompted Jerry Falwell to sue Larry Flynt and Hustler magazine.

Hustler/LFP

Westboro appealed. The U.S. Court of Appeals for the Fourth Circuit reversed, holding that the First Amendment protected Westboro's statements because they dealt with matters of public concern, could not be proven false and were hyperbole.[133]

The U.S. Supreme Court agreed with the appellate court. Westboro's signs related to matters of public concern, and as *New York Times Co. v. Sullivan* emphasized, the First Amendment stands for "a profound national commitment to the principle that debate on public issues should be uninhibited, robust, and wide-open," the Court ruled.[134] Citing *Hustler Magazine Inc. v. Falwell*, the Court said the First Amendment may be a defense against an intentional infliction of emotional distress claim.

In response to the *Snyder* decision, Congress adopted a law forbidding protests two hours before or after a military funeral and demonstrations closer than 300 feet from such funerals with a possible award of $50,000 in statutory damages.[135]

Chip Somodevilla/Getty Images

Westboro Baptist Church members in front of the U.S. Supreme Court building as the Court hands down its *Snyder v. Phelps* decision.

The Court did not decide whether expression directed to a private individual or disorderly demonstrations would be protected against an IIED claim even if the content addressed matters of public concern. The *Snyder* Court said it did not consider whether the Marine's father was a public or private figure. Had he been found a public figure he would have had to prove actual malice, as the Court said in *Falwell*. But in *Snyder* the Court said the Westboro picketers were aiming their expression at the general public, not at Albert Snyder or his family. Because the expression was about matters of public concern and was directed toward a broad audience, the speech was protected regardless of what elements Snyder had to prove to win an IIED lawsuit.

NEGLIGENT INFLICTION OF EMOTIONAL DISTRESS

If one person carelessly causes another emotional harm, the injured person may sue using a tort called negligent infliction of emotional distress (NIED). The law asks whether the defendant should have anticipated that her or his careless action would injure the plaintiff. More formally, a plaintiff suing for NIED must prove (1) the defendant had a duty to use due care, (2) the defendant negligently breached that duty, (3) the breach caused the plaintiff's injury and (4) the breach was the proximate cause of the plaintiff's severe emotional distress.[136]

A "duty of due care" means the defendant should have foreseen that negligence could cause harm to the person or people to whom he or she owed a duty. Breaching the duty means the defendant did not act as a reasonable person would. Causing the plaintiff's emotional distress means the defendant's actions were the direct reason the plaintiff was emotionally harmed. This may be called "cause-in-fact." Proximate cause is the law's way of asking if it is reasonable to conclude the defendant caused the plaintiff's injury. NIED suits against the media often turn on the proximate cause question. Courts usually find that actions taken by a media organization are only tangentially related to the plaintiff's injury. If the connection between what the organization did and how the plaintiff was injured is too indirect to find the mass medium responsible, the plaintiff cannot prove proximate cause.

Courts in some states also require plaintiffs to show a degree of physical harm.[137] The harm may be that the defendant physically injured (or even just touched) the plaintiff, causing emotional harm, or that the defendant caused emotional harm resulting in physical symptoms.[138] The plaintiff's problem is convincing courts that an emotional distress claim is real. Courts see the NIED tort as caught between two important concerns. First, the law wants to compensate people whose emotional injuries are caused by others' negligence. But second, judges want to avoid suits for trivial, de minimus, harms or fraudulent emotional harm claims.[139] These competing interests have "caused inconsistency and incoherence in the law," one court said.[140]

NIED suits against the media usually fail, although plaintiffs have successfully sued for NIED when the media have put them in harm's way. For example, after a woman had been physically attacked, but before the assailant was apprehended by police, a newspaper published the woman's name and address. After the newspaper published the article, the assailant terrorized his victim several more times. A Missouri appellate court upheld the victim's NIED suit.[141]

CHAPTER SUMMARY

THE VALUE OF INDIVIDUAL REPUTATION, the importance of protecting it and the ability to restore it once it is damaged are centuries-old concepts. As with much of law in the United States, libel stems in large part from the English common law. The threat of a libel suit can create a chilling effect in the media—a reluctance to publish freely and pursue stories aggressively. For those who either file or defend libel claims, it is an expensive process, taking a toll both financially and emotionally. Many claims are settled out of court.

The libel plaintiff's case has several elements, all of which must be proved in court to win. The material in question must be (1) a statement of fact (2) that is published, (3) that is of and concerning the plaintiff, (4) that is defamatory, (5) that is false, (6) that causes damage (or harm) and (7) that is the result of fault by the defendant. The first five elements are examined in the preceding sections. No matter where libel occurs or in what communicative medium, the plaintiff must prove the same elements.

Libel plaintiffs must show that the defendant is at fault for publishing the defamatory material. The level of fault that must be proved varies according to the plaintiff's status. Public officials and public figures must show the defendant acted with actual malice, meaning with knowledge of falsity or reckless disregard for the truth. Private figures usually must prove negligence on the part of the defendant, a much less difficult standard to meet. Sometimes questions about fault include an evaluation of whether the statement(s) in question involve a matter of public concern. The distinction in fault standards began with the landmark 1964 U.S. Supreme Court ruling in *New York Times Co. v. Sullivan.* Justice Brennan's opinion for the Court transformed the law and journalism. By affording the media more "breathing space" for error, the ruling reduces the possible chilling effect of libel suits and encourages the journalistic tradition of close oversight and criticism of government.

Either intentional or reckless extreme or outrageous conduct that results in severe emotional harm may amount to intentional infliction of emotional distress. The most important element is the defendant's actions. Outrageous actions, defined as being beyond all bounds of decency, may lead to successful intentional infliction of emotional distress suits. In addition to proving outrageous intentional or reckless conduct and severe emotional harm, public officials and public figures must show the defendant acted with actual malice to win an intentional infliction of emotional distress case. The First Amendment protects speech on matters of public concern from a successful IIED suit. Also, the First Amendment likely will not allow successful IIED suits based on satires and parodies.

A plaintiff suing for negligent infliction of emotional distress must prove the defendant had a duty of due care and breached that duty, causing the plaintiff's severe emotional distress, and that there is proximate cause to find the defendant liable for the harm. Some states require that physical harm accompany emotional trauma. ■

CASES FOR STUDY

For study resources and a case archive go to **study.sagepub.com/medialaw6e**.

THINKING ABOUT IT

The two case excerpts that follow are considered landmark cases about both libel and intentional infliction of emotional distress. As you read these case excerpts, keep the following questions in mind:

- How do the two decisions help define the meaning of actual malice as it applies to public officials and public figures?

- What are the important concepts that each of these decisions adds to laws about libel and intentional infliction of emotional distress?

- How, according to the Supreme Court in *New York Times Co. v. Sullivan* and in *Hustler Magazine Inc. v. Falwell*, does libel law implicate the First Amendment?

- What approach does the Supreme Court take in trying to balance First Amendment rights against the right not to be emotionally harmed and to protect your reputation?

New York Times Co. v. Sullivan
SUPREME COURT OF THE UNITED STATES
376 U.S. 254 (1964)

JUSTICE WILLIAM BRENNAN delivered the Court's opinion:

We are required in this case to determine for the first time the extent to which the constitutional protections for speech and press limit a State's power to award damages in a libel action brought by a public official against critics of his official conduct.

Respondent L.B. Sullivan is one of the three elected Commissioners of the City of Montgomery, Alabama. He testified that he was "Commissioner of Public Affairs and the duties are supervision of the Police Department, Fire Department, Department of Cemetery and Department of Scales." He brought this civil libel action against the four individual petitioners, who are Negroes and Alabama clergymen, and against petitioner the New York Times Company, a New York corporation which publishes the New York Times, a daily newspaper. A jury in the Circuit Court of Montgomery County awarded him damages of $500,000, the full amount claimed, against all the petitioners, and the Supreme Court of Alabama affirmed. . . .

Of the 10 paragraphs of text in the advertisement, the third and a portion of the sixth were the basis of respondent's claim of libel. . . .

It is uncontroverted that some of the statements contained in the two paragraphs were not accurate descriptions of events which occurred in

Montgomery. Although Negro students staged a demonstration on the State Capitol steps, they sang the National Anthem and not "My Country, 'Tis of Thee." Although nine students were expelled by the State Board of Education, this was not for leading the demonstration at the Capitol, but for demanding service at a lunch counter in the Montgomery County Courthouse on another day. Not the entire student body, but most of it, had protested the expulsion, not by refusing to register, but by boycotting classes on a single day; virtually all the students did register for the ensuing semester. . . .

Because of the importance of the constitutional issues involved, we granted the separate petitions for certiorari of the individual petitioners and of the Times. We reverse the judgment. We hold that the rule of law applied by the Alabama courts is constitutionally deficient for failure to provide the safeguards for freedom of speech and of the press that are required by the First and Fourteenth Amendments in a libel action brought by a public official against critics of his official conduct. We further hold that under the proper safeguards the evidence presented in this case is constitutionally insufficient to support the judgment for respondent. . . .

The publication here was not a "commercial" advertisement . . . [that] communicated information, expressed opinion, recited grievances, protested claimed abuses, and sought financial support on behalf of a movement whose existence and objectives are matters of the highest public interest and concern. That the Times was paid for publishing the advertisement is as immaterial in this connection as is the fact that newspapers and books are sold. . . . Any other conclusion would discourage newspapers from carrying "editorial advertisements" of this type, and so might shut off an important outlet for the promulgation of information and ideas by persons who do not themselves have access to publishing facilities—who wish to exercise their freedom of speech even though they are not members of the press. . . . To avoid placing such a handicap upon the freedoms of expression, we hold that, if the allegedly libelous statements would otherwise be constitutionally protected from the present judgment, they do not forfeit that protection because they were published in the form of a paid advertisement. . . .

The general proposition that freedom of expression upon public questions is secured by the First Amendment has long been settled by our decisions. The constitutional safeguard, we have said, "was fashioned to assure unfettered interchange of ideas for the bringing about of political and social changes desired by the people. . . ."

. . . The First Amendment, said Judge Learned Hand, "presupposes that right conclusions are more likely to be gathered out of a multitude of tongues, than through any kind of authoritative selection. To many this is, and always will be, folly; but we have staked upon it our all." . . .

Thus we consider this case against the background of a profound national commitment to the principle that debate on public issues should be uninhibited, robust, and wide-open, and that it may well include vehement, caustic, and sometimes unpleasantly sharp attacks on government and public officials. The present advertisement, as an expression of grievance and protest on one of the major public issues of our time, would seem clearly to qualify for the constitutional protection. The question is whether it forfeits that protection by the falsity of some of its factual statements and by its alleged defamation of respondent. . . .

That erroneous statement is inevitable in free debate, and . . . it must be protected if the freedoms of expression are to have the "breathing space" that they "need . . . to survive. . . ."

Injury to official reputation affords no more warrant for repressing speech that would otherwise be free than does factual error. . . .

If neither factual error nor defamatory content suffices to remove the constitutional shield from criticism of official conduct, the combination of the two elements is no less inadequate. . . .

. . . A rule compelling the critic of official conduct to guarantee the truth of all his factual assertions—and to do so on pain of libel judgments virtually unlimited in amount—leads to a comparable "self-censorship." Allowance of the defense of truth, with the burden of proving it on the defendant, does not mean that only false speech will be deterred. . . . The constitutional guarantees require, we think, a federal rule that prohibits a public official from recovering damages for a defamatory falsehood relating to his official conduct unless he proves that the statement was made with "actual malice"—that is, with knowledge that it was false or with reckless disregard of whether it was false or not. . . .

. . . As Madison said, "the censorial power is in the people over the Government, and not in the Government over the people." It would give public servants an unjustified preference over the public they serve, if critics of official conduct did not have a fair equivalent of the immunity granted to the officials themselves. . . .

We hold today that the Constitution delimits a State's power to award damages for libel in actions brought by public officials against critics of their official conduct. Since this is such an action, the rule requiring proof of actual malice is applicable. . . .

Applying these standards, we consider that the proof presented to show actual malice lacks the convincing clarity which the constitutional standard demands, and hence that it would not constitutionally sustain the judgment for respondent under the proper rule of law. . . .

Finally, there is evidence that the Times published the advertisement without checking its accuracy against the news stories in the Times' own files. The mere presence of the stories in the files does not, of course, establish that the Times "knew" the advertisement was false, since the state of mind required for actual malice would have to be brought home to the persons in the Times' organization having responsibility for the publication of the advertisement. . . .

The judgment of the Supreme Court of Alabama is reversed and the case is remanded to that court for further proceedings not inconsistent with this opinion.

Reversed and remanded.

Hustler Magazine Inc. v. Falwell
SUPREME COURT OF THE UNITED STATES
485 U.S. 46 (1988)

CHIEF JUSTICE WILLIAM REHNQUIST delivered the Court's opinion:
Petitioner Hustler Magazine Inc. is a magazine of nationwide circulation. Respondent Jerry Falwell, a nationally known minister who has been active as a commentator on politics and public affairs, sued petitioner and its publisher, petitioner Larry Flynt, to recover damages for invasion of privacy, libel, and intentional infliction of emotional distress. . . .

The inside front cover of the November 1983 issue of Hustler Magazine featured a "parody" of an advertisement for Campari Liqueur that contained the name and picture of respondent and was entitled "Jerry Falwell talks about his first time." This parody was modeled after actual Campari ads that included interviews with various celebrities about their "first times." Although it was apparent by the end of each interview that this meant the first time they sampled

Campari, the ads clearly played on the sexual double entendre of the general subject of "first times." Copying the form and layout of these Campari ads, Hustler's editors chose respondent as the featured celebrity and drafted an alleged "interview" with him in which he states that his "first time" was during a drunken incestuous rendezvous with his mother in an outhouse. The Hustler parody portrays respondent and his mother as drunk and immoral, and suggests that respondent is a hypocrite who preaches only when he is drunk. In small print at the bottom of the page, the ad contains the disclaimer, "ad parody—not to be taken seriously." The magazine's table of contents also lists the ad as "Fiction; Ad and Personality Parody."

[Falwell sued. He failed on the libel and privacy claims.] The jury ruled for respondent on the intentional infliction of emotional distress claim, however, and stated that he should be awarded $100,000 in compensatory damages, as well as $50,000 each in punitive damages. . . .

On appeal, the United States Court of Appeals for the Fourth Circuit affirmed the judgment against petitioners. . . .

At the heart of the First Amendment is the recognition of the fundamental importance of the free flow of ideas and opinions on matters of public interest and concern. . . . We have therefore been particularly vigilant to ensure that individual expressions of ideas remain free from governmentally imposed sanctions. . . .

The sort of robust political debate encouraged by the First Amendment is bound to produce speech that is critical of those who hold public office or those public figures who are "intimately involved in the resolution of important public questions or, by reason of their fame, shape events in areas of concern to society at large." . . . Such criticism, inevitably, will not always be reasoned or moderate; public figures as well as public officials will be subject to "vehement, caustic, and sometimes unpleasantly sharp attacks." . . .

Of course, this does not mean that any speech about a public figure is immune from sanction in the form of damages. Since *New York Times Co. v. Sullivan*, we have consistently ruled that a public figure may hold a speaker liable for the damage to reputation caused by publication of a defamatory falsehood, but only if the statement was made "with knowledge that it was false or with reckless disregard of whether it was false or not." False statements of fact are particularly valueless; they interfere with the truth-seeking function of the marketplace of ideas, and they cause damage to an individual's reputation that cannot easily be repaired by counterspeech, however persuasive or effective. But even though falsehoods have little value in and of themselves, they are "nevertheless inevitable in free debate," and a rule that would impose strict liability on a publisher for false factual assertions would have an undoubted "chilling" effect on speech relating to public figures that does have constitutional value. "Freedoms of expression require 'breathing space.'" This breathing space is provided by a constitutional rule that allows public

figures to recover for libel or defamation only when they can prove both that the statement was false and that the statement was made with the requisite level of culpability. . . .

Generally speaking, the law does not regard the intent to inflict emotional distress as one which should receive much solicitude, and it is quite understandable that most if not all jurisdictions have chosen to make it civilly culpable where the conduct in question is sufficiently "outrageous." But in the world of debate about public affairs, many things done with motives that are less than admirable are protected by the First Amendment. . . .

[Although] a bad motive may be deemed controlling for purposes of tort liability in other areas of the law, we think the First Amendment prohibits such a result in the area of public debate about public figures.

Were we to hold otherwise, there can be little doubt that political cartoonists and satirists would be subjected to damages awards without any showing that their work falsely defamed its subject. . . .

. . . Several famous examples of this type of intentionally injurious speech were drawn by Thomas Nast, probably the greatest American cartoonist to date, who was associated for many years during the post–Civil War era with Harper's Weekly. In the pages of that publication Nast conducted a graphic vendetta against William M. "Boss" Tweed and his corrupt associates in New York City's "Tweed Ring." It has been described by one historian of the subject as "a sustained attack which in its passion and effectiveness stands alone in the history of American graphic art." . . .

Despite their sometimes caustic nature, from the early cartoon portraying George Washington as an ass down to the present day, graphic depictions and satirical cartoons have played a prominent role in public and political debate. . . .

Respondent contends, however, that the caricature in question here was so "outrageous" as to distinguish it from more traditional political cartoons. There is no doubt that the caricature of respondent and his mother published in Hustler is at best a distant cousin of the political cartoons described above, and a rather poor relation at that. If it were possible by laying down a principled standard to separate the one from the other, public discourse would probably suffer little or no harm. But we doubt that there is any such standard, and we are quite sure that the pejorative description "outrageous" does not supply one. "Outrageousness" in the area of political and social discourse has an inherent subjectiveness about it which would allow a jury to impose liability on the basis of the jurors' tastes or views, or perhaps on the basis of their dislike of a particular expression. An "outrageousness" standard thus runs afoul of our longstanding refusal to allow damages to be awarded because the speech in question may have an adverse emotional impact on the audience. . . .

We conclude that public figures and public officials may not recover for the tort of intentional infliction of emotional distress by reason of publications such as the one here at issue without showing in addition that the publication contains a false statement of fact which was made with "actual malice," *i.e.,* with knowledge that the statement was false or with reckless disregard as to whether or not it was true. This is not merely a "blind application" of the *New York Times* standard, it reflects our considered judgment that such a standard is necessary to give adequate "breathing space" to the freedoms protected by the First Amendment.

Here it is clear that respondent Falwell is a "public figure" for purposes of First Amendment law. The jury found against respondent on his libel claim when it decided that the Hustler ad parody could not "reasonably be understood as describing actual facts about [respondent] or actual events in which [he] participated." The Court of Appeals interpreted the jury's finding to be that the ad parody "was not reasonably believable," and in accordance with our custom we accept this finding. Respondent is thus relegated to his claim for damages awarded by the jury for the intentional infliction of emotional distress by "outrageous" conduct. But, for reasons heretofore stated, this claim cannot, consistently with the First Amendment, form a basis for the award of damages when the conduct in question is the publication of a caricature such as the ad parody involved here. The judgment of the Court of Appeals is accordingly

Reversed.

Under the First Amendment there is no such thing as a false idea. However pernicious an opinion may seem, we depend for its correction not on the conscience of judges and juries but on the competition of other ideas. But there is no constitutional value in false statements of fact.

—U.S. Supreme Court Justice Lewis Powell[1]

Section 230 of the Communications Decency Act offers immunity to websites in libel claims, although the protection is not absolute. A recent California case involving Yelp.com has sparked broader discussion about the limits of Section 230.

5 LIBEL
Defenses and Privileges

SUPPOSE . . .

. . . that a newspaper columnist writes about a school board hearing that is investigating possible neglect or wrongdoing on the part of school employees. The column contains accusations that some people lied at the hearing. One of the accused, believing that the statement was false and damaged his reputation, sues the columnist and his newspaper for libel. The defendants claim the column is an expression of opinion and the First Amendment protects their opinion. These were the circumstances in *Milkovich v. Lorain Journal Co.*, discussed in this chapter and excerpted at the end.

Parties sued for libel can use many defenses, any of which has the potential to be successful, depending on the circumstances of the case. There is one important difference between the plaintiff's case and the defendant's challenges: Although the plaintiff must prove every element of her case, a successful defendant needs only one suitable defense. The libel defense attorney is like a carpenter who must choose the right tool for a given job. A carpenter has many tools to choose from, yet it is crucial to choose the proper one to get the job done. The libel defense attorney is no different.

TRUTH

Defending a libel suit may consist of merely taking the elements of the plaintiff's case, explained in Chapter 4, and proving their opposite. A libel defendant may be able to demonstrate that there is no liability for publishing the statement at issue if it is not defamatory, it was not published or the plaintiff was not identified or does not meet the elements of a libel case. Truth or substantial truth is the appropriate counterargument to the plaintiff's claim that the material at issue is false. Truth is sometimes viewed as the most basic and ironclad of all libel defenses. The plaintiff is responsible for demonstrating that the statement at issue is false rather than the defendant proving the statement is true.

As noted in Chapter 4, historically this was reversed: The burden of proof to show a statement is true was placed on the defendant. This was the case in English common law. Today, libel law in the United States clearly places the burden of proof regarding falsity on the plaintiff. Additionally, minor error or discrepancy does not necessarily make a statement false. As long as the statement is substantially true, it cannot meet the standard for falsity and therefore cannot be libelous.

As part of a defense strategy, a libel defendant may attempt to demonstrate to a court that it conducted itself in a responsible way in gathering and reporting the news. The defendant is then more likely to garner support for its argument that it should not be found legally responsible for committing libel. The media defendant, for example, may need to disprove the plaintiff's claim that its employees acted with reckless disregard for the truth or that they were negligent.

In attempting to prove that a libel defendant acted with reckless disregard, a plaintiff is likely to attempt to build a case bit by bit, demonstrating a series of irresponsible or careless acts in the newsgathering and publishing process. Courts have said that no single element is sufficient to prove clearly and convincingly that a defendant acted with reckless disregard, but each can be used as evidence to build a case.

LANDMARK CASES IN CONTEXT

Key ■ Event
◆ Cases

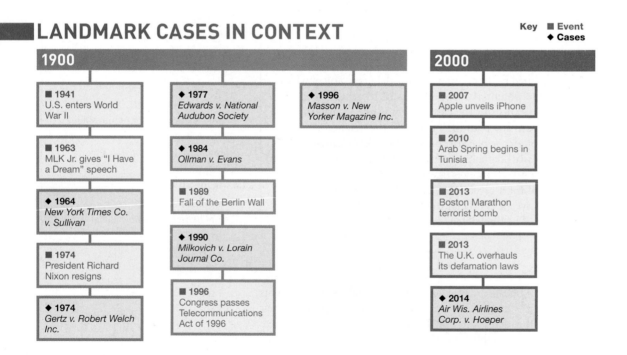

1900

■ 1941
U.S. enters World War II

■ 1963
MLK Jr. gives "I Have a Dream" speech

◆ 1964
New York Times Co. v. Sullivan

■ 1974
President Richard Nixon resigns

◆ 1974
Gertz v. Robert Welch Inc.

◆ 1977
Edwards v. National Audubon Society

◆ 1984
Ollman v. Evans

■ 1989
Fall of the Berlin Wall

◆ 1990
Milkovich v. Lorain Journal Co.

■ 1996
Congress passes Telecommunications Act of 1996

◆ 1996
Masson v. New Yorker Magazine Inc.

2000

■ 2007
Apple unveils iPhone

■ 2010
Arab Spring begins in Tunisia

■ 2013
Boston Marathon terrorist bomb

■ 2013
The U.K. overhauls its defamation laws

◆ 2014
Air Wis. Airlines Corp. v. Hoeper

A libel defendant wants to strengthen his or her position by showing as many of the following as possible:

- The story was investigated thoroughly.

- Interviews were conducted with people who had knowledge of facts related to the story, including the subject of the report.

- Previously published material was not relied on.

- Biased stories were not relied on.

- The reporting was careful, systematic and painstaking.

- Multiple viewpoints were sought and, when possible, included in the report.

- There was a willingness to retract or correct if facts warranted such action.

- If applicable, there was a demonstrable deadline.

- There was no ill will or hatred toward the plaintiff.

Attorney Gloria Allred represents several women separately suing President Donald Trump and comedian Bill Cosby for defamation after both men called them liars. In both cases, women alleged sexual misconduct or assault. Central to their claims is the notion of truth.

In addition to defending a libel case on the elements, those accused of libel have several defenses at their disposal that may not directly correspond with any element of the plaintiff's case.

ANTI-SLAPP PROTECTION

Chilling speech is the goal of some defamation lawsuits. In those cases, libel law is used not as a shield against threatened harms or as a means of correcting them, but as a weapon to prevent speech from occurring in the first place. These are called **SLAPPs** (strategic lawsuits against public participation).[2] They are meant to silence critics.

Plaintiffs rarely win these cases. Noting that SLAPPs are often used to suppress a party's First Amendment rights, some states have enacted anti-SLAPP legislation.[3] Courts have upheld the constitutionality of these laws. Thirty-one states, the District of Columbia and one U.S. territory (Guam) have either enacted an anti-SLAPP statute or have state courts that recognize anti-SLAPP protections as a matter of case law. State courts consider new anti-SLAPP statutes as they emerge.

In the past few years, some plaintiffs have brought anti-SLAPP claims in federal court, and the outcome is mixed. The First, Fifth and Ninth U.S. Circuit Courts have applied anti-SLAPP acts in part or in whole. The Eleventh U.S. Circuit Court in 2014 rejected the application of Georgia's anti-SLAPP law, noting that a part of the Georgia law conflicted with the Federal Rules of Civil Procedure and therefore could not apply in federal court.[4]

SLAPP (strategic lawsuit against public participation) A lawsuit whose purpose is to harass critics into silence, often to suppress those critics' First Amendment rights.

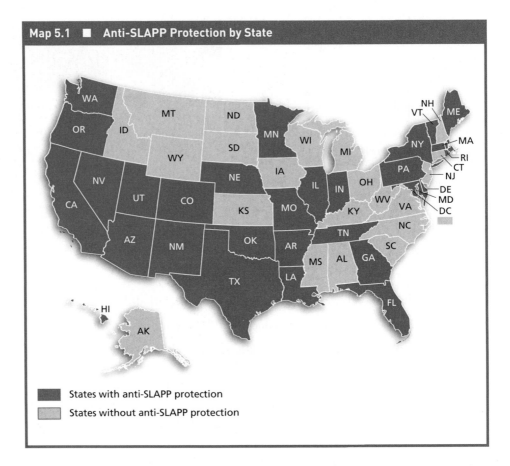

Map 5.1 ■ Anti-SLAPP Protection by State

■ States with anti-SLAPP protection
■ States without anti-SLAPP protection

The D.C. Circuit Court ruled similarly in 2015 that a federal court could not apply a state or locality's anti-SLAPP provisions because federal courts are required to follow the Federal Rules and applying the anti-SLAPP statute was too burdensome on courts.[5] Even though the circuit court would not apply the D.C. anti-SLAPP statute, it still found that the defamation claim brought by the son of current Palestinian leader Mahmoud Abbas should be dismissed because his case was not based on factual representations.[6]

In a more recent D.C. Circuit court case, a different panel of judges held that the *Abbas* ruling got it wrong, noting instead that the burden is the same, whether applying the Federal Rules or the D.C. anti-SLAPP statute.[7] Additionally, the court held that the denial of an anti-SLAPP motion is immediately appealable. The case originated when noted climate scientist Michael Mann filed a libel suit against the National Review and Competitive Enterprise Institute. Dr. Mann claimed that their articles criticizing his conclusions about global warming and accusing him of deception and academic and scientific misconduct defamed him.[8] The D.C. Circuit Court applied the D.C. anti-SLAPP statue and concluded that Dr. Mann "hurdled the Anti-SLAPP statute's threshold, showing likelihood of success on the merits" because he presented legally sufficient evidence to support the fact that the articles were defamatory and published with actual malice.[9]

⬤ POINTS OF LAW

Success on the Merits

The phrase "success on the merits" is a term that courts use to describe one factor when evaluating whether to grant a preliminary injunction, which is central to an anti-SLAPP motion. The party that wants the injunction "has to be able to convince the court, on a preliminary basis—meaning before the record is fully developed—that one of the reasons it is entitled to temporary relief is that it will probably win the case anyway," according to the American Bar Association.[1]

1. *Likelihood of Success*, ABA JOURNAL, Feb. 19, 2017, www.abajournal.com/blawg/likelihood-of-success.

In 2016, the Ninth Circuit upheld an anti-SLAPP motion in a case involving a variety of state law claims.[10] In another decision, the court upheld the application of the anti-SLAPP motion, but one of the judges noted in his concurrence that anti-SLAPP motions do not belong in federal court because they directly conflict with the Federal Rules.[11] Given the different applications of anti-SLAPP statutes and motions in various federal courts, legal experts suggest this issue is ripe for hearing by the U.S. Supreme Court.[12]

FAIR REPORT PRIVILEGE

The **fair report privilege** is based on the idea that keeping citizens informed about matters of public concern is sometimes more important than avoiding occasional damage to individual reputations. It gives reporters some breathing room to report on official governmental conduct without having to first prove the truth of what the government says. How does the privilege work? When a journalist relies on official government records or proceedings, the privilege may apply. Even if a contributor to an official proceeding makes a statement that is false and defamatory—or if an official government record does the same—a news organization whose report is based exclusively on the statement will not be liable for defamation as long as the story accurately and fairly reflects the content of the report or proceeding.

fair report privilege A privilege claimed by journalists who report events on the basis of official records. The report must fairly and accurately reflect the content of the records; this is the condition that sometimes leads to this privilege being called "conditional privilege."

⬤ POINTS OF LAW

Fair Report Privilege

1. The information must be obtained from a record or proceeding recognized as "official."

2. The news report must fairly and accurately reflect what is in the public record or what was said during the official proceeding.

3. The source of the statement should be clearly noted in the news report.

4. Not all states recognize the fair report privilege.

A few courts have considered whether a reporter's intent to harm a person's reputation may terminate the fair report privilege. This question surfaced in a Minnesota case in which a citizen mentioned the name of a police officer during a city council meeting. The citizen accused the officer of dealing drugs. The reporter who covered the meeting did not report the accusation immediately but instead investigated the situation. When the reporter published several articles, the officer sued, claiming that the articles were inaccurate and were written with ill will. (This is not the same as actual malice, discussed in Chapter 4.) Lower courts said the fair report privilege could be lost if the defendants were motivated by ill will, but ultimately the Minnesota court ruled that the reporter in this case had no intent to injure the plaintiff.[13] Nevertheless, the question of whether ill will could possibly eliminate the privilege in some jurisdictions remains.

The fair report privilege covers officials and proceedings in the executive, judicial and legislative branches of state, local and federal governments and, often, private individuals communicating with the government. Law enforcement agencies are also covered, including reports of police activity. For example, a former Belleville, Ill., police chief sued the local newspaper for libel after the newspaper reported that he was the subject of a rape investigation. A three-judge panel of the state appellate court unanimously dismissed the case, ruling that the newspaper was protected by the fair report privilege because its article was a fair and accurate report based on a local prosecutor's comments.[14]

Not every statement by a police officer is privileged, however. This generally is determined on a case-by-case fact basis with different outcomes in different states. One state supreme court, for example, refused to apply the fair report privilege to statements made by a police officer to a reporter during an interview.[15] The court ruled that the officer's participation in the interview and his remarks were not considered to be part of his official duties—a key determinant in deciding whether the privilege applies.

More recent decisions have taken a different approach. In South Carolina, a court held that the fair report privilege applied to an email the sheriff's department sent to a newspaper and was not limited to official records and press releases. In Michigan, a U.S. district court applied the privilege to unofficial statements made to the press by police officers.[16] The Sixth Circuit, applying Tennessee law, upheld a summary judgment in favor of a local TV news station that videotaped a story based on a ride-along with the U.S. Marshals Service during which the marshals erroneously arrested an individual with the same name as the fugitive. A day after the ride-along, the station aired its report of the arrest. Although the arrest itself was in error, the court held that the television report was a fair and accurate account of an official government action. Because the station didn't know the marshals had arrested the wrong person, the court found no evidence of actual malice to overcome the privilege.[17]

More recently, a Massachusetts court did not recognize the fair report privilege in the "BAG MEN" case (noted in Chapter 4). In the manhunt that ensued after the 2013 Boston Marathon bombing, the New York Post published a picture of two young men who attended the Boston Marathon on the front page under the headline "BAG MEN."[18] The New York Post argued that the fair report privilege applied because the photograph it used came from an FBI email. The court said the article had not fairly and accurately reported the information, so the fair report privilege did not apply. The case was ultimately settled out of court.[19] Journalists should note that different outcomes, including failure to recognize privilege, occur in different states and court systems. This happened recently when a federal court in Maine noted that the state does not recognize the fair report privilege.[20]

The justification for the fair report privilege stems from another kind of privileged situation. Within various government processes, for example, it is so vitally important that people be allowed to speak and communicate information without fear of being sued for libel that they are granted immunity from liability. The rationale is that citizens in a participatory democracy are entitled to

The courtrrom from the O.J. Simpson murder trial in 1994. Documents related to the judicial branch are typically privledged.

such information.[21] As a Massachusetts judge, Oliver Wendell Holmes Jr. was among those who reasoned that the public should be provided with information about judicial proceedings because "those who administer justice should act under a sense of public responsibility."[22] Nearly a century later, another Massachusetts court echoed Holmes and held that the value of granting privilege to media reports about the courts is "the security which publicity gives for the proper administration of justice."[23]

This privilege—called **absolute privilege**—typically occurs within the context of carrying out the business of government. An open society demands that members of the public have access to information relating to government proceedings. It logically follows that people reporting on these proceedings or information related to these proceedings also have some protection. That protection, though, is only available when the news report is fair and accurate. Thus, in addition to this protection sometimes being referred to as the fair report privilege, it is called **conditional (or qualified) privilege**.

Reports about judicial activities—the courts—are conditionally privileged. Therefore, media accounts of testimony, depositions, attorney arguments, trials, verdicts, opinions and orders—those aspects that are typically open or available to the public—are among the proceedings covered. Also, documents that relate to the judicial branch are typically privileged. For example, the New Jersey Supreme Court ruled that journalists who report accurately from court filings, including pretrial documents, are protected from libel claims.[24] In Maryland, a state court in 2012 applied the fair report privilege to a newspaper's coverage of a murder trial that included reporting based on a discovery memo in the case file that was not offered as evidence at trial.[25]

In 2013, a Pennsylvania state court applied the fair report privilege to an article about a convicted drug dealer, even though there was a minor discrepancy between the news account and the court record. The newspaper said the plaintiff owned the car in which he was arrested, but the court report stated that the plaintiff was actually a passenger. The court said the fact difference was minor and immaterial.[26] A New York court came to a similar decision when it held that minor inaccuracies, including when those errors are about the precise legal significance of court orders and filings, are protected by the state's fair report privilege.[27]

absolute privilege
A complete exemption from liability for the speaking or publishing of defamatory words of and concerning another because the statement was made within the performance of duty such as in judicial or political contexts.

conditional (or qualified) privilege An exemption from liability for repeating defamatory words of and concerning another because the original statement was made within the performance of duty such as in judicial or political contexts; usually claimed by journalists who report statements made in absolutely privileged situations; this privilege is conditional (or qualified) on the premise that the reporting is fair and accurate.

The fair report privilege is important to the news media given that much of what they do is report on the activities, people, records and documents of the various levels of government. The privilege can be forfeited if the allegedly defamatory material is published with significant inaccuracies or if reported unfairly. This unfair reporting can include ill will toward the plaintiff, if the gist of the article is not substantially true, or if the author draws conclusions or adds comments to the official report. For example, in 2015 a Connecticut court did not uphold the application of the state's fair report privilege when a newspaper implied that a plaintiff's lawsuits were frivolous. The court said the publication was not immune simply because it republished comments from a waiver-of-court-fees amendment that described the plaintiff as someone who frequently files frivolous lawsuits. Instead, the court said the claim of frivolousness amounted to opinion and was not defamatory. On the flip side, the same court held that other republished statements about the plaintiff's litigation history were protected by the fair report privilege because they accurately reported official proceedings about a matter of public concern.[28]

The fair report privilege protects media reports of official government actions, regardless of possible defamatory elements within those reports and proceedings. The Detroit News, for example, successfully used the fair report privilege when it was sued for libel for printing the names of convicted felons working in Detroit public schools. The newspaper had obtained the names from state records. One of the people named sued for libel, claiming the felony charges against her would soon be dismissed. "The privilege precludes damages in a libel suit," the Michigan Court of Appeals ruled, "where a defendant engages in the publication of the contents of a public record, provided the defendant presents a 'fair and true' report of the public record."[29]

● REAL WORLD LAW

Fair Report Privilege and Press Conferences

In 2014, various media outlets, including the celebrity gossip website TMZ, accurately reported information from a press conference held by the attorney general of New York. In that press conference and in a subsequent press release the attorney general discussed the arrest of a woman for her alleged involvement in a drug and prostitution ring. TMZ's headline for its story read, "Super Bowl Prostitution Bust Was Asian Invasion."

The problem: The attorney general indicted and arrested the wrong person, and the woman identified by TMZ and others sued for defamation and negligent, reckless and intentional infliction of emotional distress. In 2015, a federal court in New Jersey dismissed the libel and other claims because it applied that state's fair report privilege. The court held that the media defendants accurately reported the information from the attorney general's press conference and press release, even though the attorney general presented inaccurate information at the press conference.[1]

The court also highlighted that the media organizations did not imply that the woman had been convicted of the allegations. The woman has appealed the decision to the Third Circuit.[2]

---

1. Lee v. TMZ Prods. Inc, 43 Med. L. Rep. 3243 (D.N.J. Aug. 10, 2015).
2. Shayna Posses, *NY Daily News Must Face Libel Suit at 3rd Circ.*, LAW360.COM, Oct. 21, 2016, www.law360.com/articles/854069/ny-daily-news-must-face-libel-suit-at-3rd-circ.

FAIR COMMENT AND CRITICISM

Fair comment and criticism is a common law privilege that protects critics from lawsuits brought by individuals in the public eye. As noted in the chapter opening, the Supreme Court has held that, "under the First Amendment there is no such thing as a false idea. . . . But there is no constitutional value in false statements of fact."[30] The key to this common law defense and the stronger constitutional opinion defense (explained in detail below) is the separation of fact and opinion. A critic can be anyone who comments on these individuals and their work. Being in the public eye is not the same as being a public figure for purposes of actual malice. A person in the public eye is anyone who enters a public sphere: artists, entertainers, dramatists, writers, members of the clergy, teachers—anyone who moves in and out of the public eye, either professionally or as an amateur. By placing their work products or services into the public sphere, these individuals invite criticism.

The privilege also protects commentary on institutions whose activities are of interest to the public or where matters of public interest are concerned. Thus, not only are written works subject to fair comment and criticism, but so are works of art and other products of businesses such as restaurants that implicitly invite reviews of their offerings.

A libel suit involving a book review is instructive: An author sued The New York Times for a reviewer's criticisms of his book. Among other things, the reviewer wrote that the book contained "too much sloppy journalism to trust the bulk of [its] 512 pages including its whopping 64 pages of footnotes."[31] A federal appeals court held that the review was not defamatory, ruling that the genre of the writing and the context within which it appeared must be considered. "The statements at issue in the instant case are assessments of a book, rather than direct assaults on [the author's] character, reputation, or competence as a journalist," the court wrote. " . . . While a critic's latitude is not unlimited, he or she must be given the constitutional 'breathing space' appropriate to the genre."[32]

Historically, the fair comment and criticism privilege was incorporated into the common law to afford legal immunity for the honest expression of opinion on matters of legitimate public interest based on a true or privileged statement of fact.[33] Comment was generally privileged when it addressed a matter of public concern, was based on true or privileged facts, represented the actual opinion of the speaker and was not made solely for the purpose of causing harm.[34] The privilege of fair comment applied only to an expression of opinion and not to a false statement of fact, whether it was expressly stated or implied from an expression of opinion.[35] As the U.S. Supreme Court has stated, "The privilege of 'fair comment' was the device employed to strike the appropriate balance between the need for vigorous public discourse and the need to redress injury to citizens wrought by invidious or irresponsible speech."[36]

State Historical Society of Iowa

In 1898, a well-known stage act, the Cherry Sisters, sued for libel after a bad review from an Iowa newspaper.

With the rise in popularity of user-created reviews on websites like Yelp and Angie's List, opportunities for lawsuits about criticism are increasing. Especially notable is a steady stream of defamation lawsuits brought by businesses that argue they are sustaining damages in the form of lost future customers. One example is a case involving Jane Perez, who wrote a Yelp and an Angie's List review criticizing a contractor who she said failed to deliver promised services. Perez also implied he might be responsible for jewelry missing from her home.

The contractor filed a defamation lawsuit seeking $750,000. In 2012, a county circuit court in Virginia ordered a preliminary injunction, instructing Perez to remove portions of her negative review, including references she had made to an earlier lawsuit in which she won a judgment against the contractor for unpaid bills. The court also barred her from repeating her accusations in future posts.[37] The Virginia Supreme Court quickly overturned the injunction, saying it amounted to an unreasonable prior restraint of Perez's right to free speech. The court noted that the contractor also had adequate remedy by suing Perez for damages.

In 2014, a Virginia state court resolved the defamation lawsuit. A jury found that Perez had defamed the contractor—but the jury also determined that comments the contractor posted on Yelp and Angie's List in direct response to Perez's accusations were also defamatory. As a result, neither party received damages in the case. Legal experts say lawsuits tied to user-generated reviews on websites such as Yelp remain unpredictable with variable outcomes from jurisdiction to jurisdiction.[38]

OPINION

Although similar to fair comment and criticism, the libel defense of opinion is distinct. The primary difference is that fair comment and criticism is rooted in the common law. Opinion stems from the First Amendment and is therefore a constitutional defense and thus stronger and more effective. It is considered to be an unqualified defense in that, once proved, it cannot be lost. The question, however, becomes whether specific case circumstances permit the application of the opinion defense.

Holding and expressing opinions is a right guaranteed by the First Amendment. "Under the First Amendment there is no such thing as a false idea. However pernicious an opinion may seem, we depend for its correction not on the conscience of judges and juries but on the competition of other ideas," wrote U.S. Supreme Court Justice Lewis Powell.[39] The First Amendment "rests on the assumption that the widest possible dissemination of information from diverse and antagonistic sources is essential to the welfare of the public."[40] Moreover, as Justice Louis Brandeis wrote early in the 20th century, "[F]reedom to think as you will and speak as you think are means indispensable to the discovery and spread of political truth."[41] Thus, a libel defendant may put forth an argument that, in part, echoes Justice William Brennan's opinion in *New York Times Co. v. Sullivan*.[42] The question becomes, "Does the speech contribute to the 'profound national commitment to the principle that debate on public issues should be uninhibited, robust, and wide-open'?"[43] At a fundamental level, a libel defense may be constructed on constitutional grounds—a claim that limiting ability to convey information is an abridgment of the First Amendment guarantees of free speech and press. Denying an individual the opportunity to express an opinion would be such an abridgment.

The challenge comes in attempting to distinguish statements of fact from statements of opinion. To attempt to separate fact from opinion is to venture onto one of the law's slipperiest of slopes. Yet to do so is vital in establishing the boundaries of the opinion defense's protection. Stating an opinion involves far more than attaching "In my opinion," "I believe" or similar qualifiers to a statement. The distinguishing attributes of opinion were developed and ultimately solidified by a federal appeals court. That court articulated a four-part test to determine whether a statement was one of fact or an expression of opinion.[44] Not all of the test's elements need to be satisfied; rather, the answers to its questions are to be evaluated in total.

The *Ollman* test (named for the case from which it stems, *Ollman v. Evans*,[45] excerpted at the end of this chapter) appeared to provide a sound and relatively straightforward instrument, in four parts, to assess opinion:

1. Is the statement verifiable—objectively capable of proof or disproof? In other words, can the statement be proved either true or false? Opinion is indirectly linked to the falsity/truth element of libel. That is, if a statement cannot be proved true or false, then it may satisfy the legal definition of an expression of opinion.

2. What is the common usage or meaning of the words?

3. What is the journalistic context in which the statement occurs? This element is especially important for the media. It provides added weight for an opinion defense when the material in question appears in a part of a publication (or, e.g., a broadcast or website) traditionally reserved for opinions—for example, the op-ed pages, personal columns, social media or a blog. The material must be considered as a whole. The language of an entire opinion column, for example, may signal that a specific statement, standing alone, which would appear to be factual, is in fact an expression of opinion.

4. What is the broader social context into which the statement fits? For example, was the statement at issue made within a context or in a place where the expression of opinions is common or expected? Or was it made within a context in which opinion is not commonplace and, instead, statements are presumed to be statements of fact?

Over time, opinion was granted a wide berth of protection. Newsweek magazine, for example, was vindicated in publishing a reference to a false accusation that a former South Dakota governor had sexually assaulted a teenage girl. The words appeared to some people to constitute a statement of fact, but the court found them to be "imprecise, unverifiable" and "presented in a forum where spirited writing is expected and involves criticism of the motives and intentions of a public official."[46] Other plaintiffs who sued because they were called unscrupulous charlatans, neo-Nazis, sleazebags and ignorant and spineless politicians lost their cases because these charges were determined to be expressions of opinion rather than statements of fact.[47]

The latitude afforded to opinion was extensive, but then came a case that put the "no such thing as a false idea"[48] doctrine to the test. Six years after the *Ollman* test was created, the U.S. Supreme Court reframed what had appeared to be a nearly absolute opinion defense. The case involved a high school wrestling team that brawled with a competing team during a match. Several people were injured. After a hearing, the coach of one team was censured, and his team was placed on probation. A lawsuit was filed in an attempt to prevent the team probation.

At a hearing, the coach, Michael Milkovich, denied that he had incited the brawl. In the next day's newspaper, a local sports columnist wrote that Milkovich, along with a

● REAL WORLD LAW

Has "Truthiness" Changed Our View of the Law?

Aurora/Alamy

Stephen Colbert

On the debut episode of "The Colbert Report" in 2005, Stephen Colbert's satirical character introduced the concept of "truthiness": A truth that a person making an argument claims to know intuitively or because it "feels right"—even if the claim is without evidence. Colbert suggested truthiness comes from "the gut," and said, "I don't trust books. They're all fact and no heart. And that's exactly what's pulling the country apart today. Face it folks, we are a divided nation . . . divided between those who think with their head and those who know with their heart."[1]

In a 2006 interview, Colbert said, "It doesn't seem to matter what facts are. It used to be everyone was entitled to their own opinion, but not their own facts. But that's not the case anymore. Facts matter not at all. Perception is everything."[2]

Since 2005, the word "truthiness" has made it into the dictionary, been featured in a lengthy entry on Wikipedia and become a part of U.S. political discourse. In a recent analysis of a case involving a challenge to an Ohio statute that "criminalizes making false statements about a political candidate" with actual malice, Slate .com's legal analyst asked, "What's scarier than truthiness in politics? A law banning it."[3]

At issue was an effort by the Susan B. Anthony List (SBA List) to put up a billboard that would have read "Shame on Steve Driehaus! Driehaus voted FOR taxpayer-funded abortion." The SBA List distributed this message through other channels, but the billboard company refused to post the ad, fearing it was in violation of the Ohio law. The SBA List made its claim about Driehaus based on the pro-life Democrat running for re-election to the U.S. House of Representatives voting for the Affordable Care Act (also called Obamacare).[4]

A federal court found that the SBA List wasn't harmed by the billboard company's actions and dismissed the suit for lack of standing because Driehaus withdrew his complaint about the ad to the Ohio Elections Commission. The Ohio statute and the subsequent SBA List lawsuit shows that although "truthiness" is a made-up word, it may well remain a staple of our discussions about the increasing fuzziness between fact and opinion and how that fuzziness plays out in the political arena.

1. Stephen Colbert, *The Word—Truthiness*, THE COLBERT REPORT, Oct. 17, 2005, thecolbertreport.cc.com/videos/63ite2/the-word—truthiness.
2. Nathan Rabin, *Stephen Colbert*, A.V. CLUB, Jan. 25, 2006, www.avclub.com/article/stephen-colbert-13970.
3. Dahlia Lithwick, *What's Scarier Than Truthiness in Politics? A Law Banning It*, SLATE.COM, Apr. 14, 2014, www.slate.com/articles/news_and_politics/supreme_court_dispatches/2014/04/susan_b_anthony_list_v_driehaus_the_supreme_court_gets_an_earful_on_truthiness.html.
4. *Id.*

⬤ POINTS OF LAW

The *Ollman* Test for Opinion

1. Verifiability
2. Common meaning
3. Journalistic context
4. Social context

school superintendent, misrepresented the truth in an effort to keep the team from being placed on probation. "Anyone who attended the meet . . . knows in his heart that [they] lied at the hearing after each having given his solemn oath to tell the truth," the column read. "But they got away with it." The columnist added that the entire episode provided a lesson for the student body: "If you get in a jam, lie your way out."[49]

The coach sued for libel. After 15 years and several appeals, the Ohio Court of Appeals held that the column was constitutionally protected opinion, but the U.S. Supreme Court reversed.[50] The Court rejected the broad application of the concept that there is "no such thing as a false idea." "[T]his passage has become the opening salvo in all arguments for protection from defamation actions on the ground of opinion," wrote Chief Justice William Rehnquist, "even though [the original] case did not remotely concern the question."[51] The passage was not intended to create a wholesale defamation exemption for anything that might be labeled "opinion," he continued. "Not only would such an interpretation be contrary to the tenor and context of the passage, but it would also ignore the fact that expressions of 'opinion' may often imply an assertion of objective fact."[52]

Chief Justice Rehnquist wrote that facts can disguise themselves as opinions, and, when they do, they imply knowledge of hidden facts that led to the opinion. Merely embedding statements of fact in a column does not transform those statements into expressions of opinion. They remain statements of fact and, if false, may be the basis of a libel suit. Whether the material is verifiable—whether it can be proved true or false—is paramount. The Supreme Court said the key question in this case was whether a reasonable reader could conclude that the statements in the column implied that Milkovich had lied in the judicial proceeding. The Court believed that such an implication had been made and ruled for Milkovich. Even though the material was in a column and thus satisfied the "journalistic context" part of the *Ollman* test, the Court said it was not opinion.[53]

Letters to the Editor and Online Comments

The approach that courts take to applying protection to online comments is based substantially on earlier cases that focused on letters to the editor of a newspaper. Letters to the editor are typically viewed as expressions of opinion rather than statements of fact. For that reason, historically, newspapers and magazines have won most cases based on the publication of such letters. Courts have sought to provide protection for the publication

● REAL WORLD LAW

Modern Application of *Milkovich*

More than two decades since the *Milkovich* ruling, court decisions involving the opinion defense continue to distinguish fact from opinion. In 2012, a New York trial court dismissed a libel case on the grounds that criticism published on an online review website amounted to pure opinion and did not include provable defamatory facts. In that case, a medical doctor sued over comments that claimed she was "a terrible doctor" and was "mentally unstable and has poor skills."[1] The court held that the comments were opinion in the context of the internet and said that anonymous comments on the Web "can be understood as a platform for 'unsupported and often baseless assertions of opinion' rather than fact."[2]

That same year, an appellate court in California affirmed the dismissal of a libel case against the Gizmodo tech blog. In that case, the plaintiff challenged an article that criticized him for overhyping his startups and new tech products. Gizmodo's use of the word "scam" was central to the plaintiff's argument, but the court looked at the article as a whole and said it was opinion that had "the tone and style of a sarcastic product or movie review."[3] The court also noted that Gizmodo allowed readers to draw their own conclusions about the plaintiff's products through links to product source materials.[4]

---

1. *New Developments 2012*, MLRC BULLETIN, Dec. 2012, at 52.
2. *Id.*
3. *Id.; see also* Redmond v. Gawker Media LLC, 2012 Cal. App. Unpub. LEXIS 5879 (Cal. App. Aug. 10, 2012) (unpublished).
4. *Id.*

of letters, often viewing them as part of an open forum for the general public. Today, based on the same rationale, courts generally offer the same protection for opinions published as opinion blogs or as comments on review or comment-based websites as well as comments that appear below news articles on newspaper or related websites.

Where a letter appears within a publication is likely to have a significant bearing in determining whether it qualifies as opinion. This stems directly from the "journalistic context" element of the *Ollman* test. That is, by appearing within a section of a publication that is clearly set aside for the expression of opinions—including opinions from readers—a letter (versus an article) or an online comment (that appears below an article) is much more likely to be viewed by a court as an expression of opinion. The same is true in the context of publication on specific websites. For example, a court in New York recently held that two women who called an ex-boyfriend a liar and a cheater were expressing opinion because their words appeared in the context of a website whose sole purpose is to air complaints about dishonest romantic partners.[54]

An example of the idea that authors of letters to the editor enjoy the same constitutional protection for their opinions as newspaper reporters was provided by an early 21st-century case. In the ruling, a state court said, "The robust exchange of ideas that occurs each day on the editorial pages of our state's newspapers could indeed suffer if the nonmedia authors of letters to the editor published in these forums were denied the same constitutional protections enjoyed by the editors themselves."[55] Thus, the authors of letters or online comments that the news media publish are as shielded as the media themselves.

In cases in which letters were not protected as opinion, courts have held that those letters combined opinion and facts. Often cases based on such expressions are resolved in favor of libel plaintiffs. For example, a Florida appellate court ruled that a letter questioning a child psychologist's qualifications was defamatory because it was just such a mixed expression and therefore not privileged.[56]

Rhetorical Hyperbole, Parody and Satire

The history of successful libel defense includes this premise: If the material on which a libel claim is based is so outrageous that no reasonable person could believe it, damage to the plaintiff's reputation could not have happened. The most infamous example lies within the circumstances of *Hustler Magazine Inc. v. Falwell,*[57] discussed in Chapter 4.

As with other libel defenses, context can be a critical element when it comes to the defense of rhetorical hyperbole, parody and satire. The context of the material in question can play a big role in determining whether a reasonable person would believe it to be a statement of fact.

The U.S. Supreme Court first recognized rhetorical hyperbole as protected speech—and therefore a libel defense—when a developer sued the publisher of a newspaper after the newspaper printed articles reporting that some people characterized the developer's

⊙ POINTS OF LAW

Innocent Construction Rule

Libel cases can hinge on what words mean, and determining meaning in a specific circumstance may depend on context. In most states, if a statement has two possible meanings—and one is defamatory and one is not—a jury decides how the words are understood. But this situation is treated differently in Illinois. Under the innocent construction rule, as long as the words at issue have one nondefamatory (or innocent) meaning, the defendant wins. In establishing the rule, the Illinois Supreme Court said that allegedly libelous words capable of being read innocently "must be so read and declared nonactionable as a matter of law."[1]

A federal appeals court affirmed the ruling of a lower federal court in Illinois that deferred to the innocent construction rule. The case centered on a nonfiction book written by a former police officer. The book contained "fantasy sequences" in which the author created fictional scenes to symbolically describe her experiences. This included a story that she had been beaten. Though her former adviser was mentioned in the book, it was never by name within these sequences. Still, he believed he had been identified and sued for libel. The Seventh Circuit Court of Appeals ruled that these sequences could be read in a way that did not call into question the plaintiff's integrity or reputation. The court added, "Statements that cannot reasonably be interpreted as stating actual facts are protected under the First Amendment."[2]

There is some evidence that the innocent construction rule exists in Ohio, Missouri and New Mexico. In addition, a few states hold that statements susceptible to the application of the rule are actionable only when special damages can be proved. They are Alabama, Mississippi, Iowa, Montana and Oklahoma.[3]

---

1. John v. Tribune Co., 24 Ill. 2d 437, 442 (1962).
2. Madison v. Frazier, 539 F.3d 646, 654 (7th Cir. 2008).
3. *See* ROBERT D. SACK, SACK ON DEFAMATION: LIBEL, SLANDER, AND RELATED PROBLEMS 2–68–2–69 (1999, rev. 2008) (citations omitted).

negotiating tactics as blackmail.[58] The developer argued that the word "blackmail" implied that the developer had committed the crime of blackmail. The Supreme Court rejected the developer's argument, holding that the word "blackmail" was not slander when spoken and not libel when reported because "even the most careless reader must have perceived that the word was no more than rhetorical hyperbole, a vigorous epithet used by those who considered [the developer's] negotiating position extremely unreasonable."[59]

Rhetorical hyperbole is rampant on the internet. For example, would you stay at a hotel labeled the No. 1 Dirtiest Hotel of the year by online reviewers? When the Grand Resort Hotel and Convention Center in Pigeon Forge, Tenn., nabbed this top spot on a 2011 list, major television news outlets and websites reported the distinction. The list on TripAdvisor.com included a link to the hotel with a photograph of a ripped bedspread and a user quote that read, "There was dirt at least ½ inch thick in the bathtub which was filled with lots of dark hair."[60]

The Grand Resort took issue with a system of online reviews that resulted in this ranking. It argued that such a distinction "maliciously" caused customers to lose confidence in the resort and the TripAdvisor rating caused "great injury and irreparable damage to . . . destroy [its] business and reputation by false and misleading means."[61] The hotel sued TripAdvisor for libel and said the numerical ranking system the site used to determine each year's top 10 dirtiest hotels was based solely on customer reviews.

AP Photo/Bebeto Matthews

NBC's Saturday Night Live is famous for its political parody and satire. In February 2017, actress Melissa McCarthy made a surprise appearance as then-White House Press Secretary Sean Spicer.

A federal district court in Tennessee dismissed the hotel's libel suit, holding that the online ranking was clearly rhetorical hyperbole, even though it offered a numerical ranking system based on user reviews. The appeals court agreed: "TripAdvisor's placement of Grand Resort on the '2011 Dirtiest Hotels' list is not capable of being defamatory." The court added that the list is protected opinion because "the list employs loose, hyperbolic language and its general tenor undermines any assertion . . . that the list communicates anything more than the opinions of TripAdvisor's users."[62]

Similar to rhetorical hyperbole, satire or parody meant to be humorous or offer social commentary is often not libelous. For example, an artist was sued for libel because one of his paintings portrayed the plaintiffs holding knives and attacking a young woman. The artist knew the plaintiffs, also artists, but had become embroiled in a spat with them over their views on art. The painting was meant to satirize the views of those depicted. An appellate court considered the context and identified it as symbolic expression with no accusation of criminal conduct.[63]

Compare that to a situation in which a newspaper published a fictional article describing a Texas juvenile court judge who ordered the detention of a first grader for making a threat in a book report. The fictional student was described as appearing before the judge in handcuffs and ankle shackles.[64] The problem arose because the judge named in this otherwise made-up story was real. The satirical article came out after a real court case in which that same judge had ordered the detention of a 13-year-old student who wrote a Halloween horror story depicting the shooting death of a teacher and two students.

The newspaper did not dispute that its article on the first grader was completely made-up. It was meant to be a commentary on the judge and his heavy-handed justice. But the judge and a district attorney sued for libel, claiming that the article could be understood by a reasonable reader as making false statements of fact about them and that they were made with actual malice. The newspaper defended itself by claiming the article was satire and parody and therefore protected by the First Amendment. Ultimately, the Texas Supreme Court ruled for the newspaper.[65] The court cited clues in the article that would alert a reasonable reader that the article was not a statement of fact but instead a criticism or opinion. Though the article did have a superficial degree of plausibility, the court said, that is the hallmark of satire.

SECTION 230 IMMUNITY

Media and technology attorneys and experts suggest that Section 230 of the federal Communications Decency Act (CDA) of 1996[66] is critical to the functioning of the internet.[67] As mentioned in Chapter 4, Section 230 offers immunity to websites in libel claims, although the protection is not absolute. Section 230 generally provides legal protection to website operators and internet service providers when issues arise from the content created by others. For 20 years, courts have rejected attempts to limit the application of Section 230 to only "traditional" ISPs like Verizon or AOL. Instead, they have extended protection to the many diverse entities commonly called "interactive computer service providers."[68] Under this broader definition, blog sites and other interactive services like YouTube, Facebook or Twitter that rely on user-generated content, information provided from third-party RSS feeds or reader comments also may receive immunity from libel claims under Section 230.

The key to determining whether Section 230 protects against a libel claim is to identify the source of the content and the extent to which the ISP interacted directly with the content. For example, courts have ruled that when bloggers allow third parties to add readers' comments or other materials to their blogs, then Section 230 protects them. What is less clear is whether those who edit comments or selectively publish reader comments also would fall under Section 230 immunity.[69]

In 2011, a California state court considered whether Facebook qualified for immunity under Section 230 for its "Sponsored Story" advertising system. Five plaintiffs sued Facebook for placing their usernames and profile pictures in Sponsored Stories on friends' Facebook pages. For example, plaintiff Angel Fraley "liked" Rosetta Stone's Facebook profile in order to receive a free software demonstration. Subsequently, Fraley's friends' Facebook pages showed a Sponsored Story advertisement with the Rosetta Stone logo and her "like" for Rosetta Stone.[70]

Facebook argued that it is protected under Section 230 because it is an "interactive computer service" with content provided by third parties. But, the court disagreed in the

○ POINTS OF LAW

Does Section 230 Immunity Apply?

Yes, it does apply to internet service providers and websites if:

- The ISP/website is a content distributor and not a content creator
- The ISP/website did not interact directly with the content

Section 230 immunity also applies when:

- ISPs/websites correct, edit, add or remove content—so long as they do not substantially alter the meaning of the content
- ISPs/websites solicit or encourage users to submit content
- ISPs/websites pay a third party to create or submit content—so long as they do not substantially alter the meaning of the content
- ISPs/websites provide forms or drop-downs to facilitate content submission by users—so long as the forms and drop-downs are neutral

context of the Sponsored Story feature, saying that because Facebook creates and develops the commercial content without user consent, Facebook is not immune. "Although Facebook meets the definition of an interactive computer service under the CDA . . . it also meets the statutory definition of an information content provider. . . . Furthermore, '[the fact that members] are information content providers does not preclude [Facebook] from also being an information content provider by helping "develop" at least "in part" the information' posted in the form of Sponsored Stories."[71] In this case, the court is making a clear distinction between content creation and distribution.

A 2014 ruling by the Sixth Circuit Court of Appeals further extends Section 230 protection if the operator of a website creates or adds content to a post that is potentially libelous. In a case that involved TheDirty.com, a U.S. district court in Kentucky held that the website should not receive immunity for potentially defamatory comments third-party posters made on the website. TheDirty.com is a popular website that allows users to "anonymously upload comments, photographs, and video, which [the website owner] then selects and publishes along with his own distinct, editorial comments. In short, the website is a user-generated tabloid primarily targeting non-public figures."[72]

The Sixth Circuit panel reversed the lower court decision, holding that the website owner's additional comments did not materially contribute to the defamatory content of the third-party statements. This means that Section 230 immunity remains for an ISP even if it encourages defamatory posts, selects the defamatory post for publication and/or "adopts or ratifies" the defamatory posts through its own comments.[73] This is called the "material contribution test," which means that a website operator does not forgo Section 230 immunity unless the operator "materially contributes" to the defamatory content produced by the users.[74]

🔲 SOCIAL MEDIA LAW

Social Media and Defamation

Scott Dudelson/WireImage/Getty Images

Courtney Love

According to legal experts, defamation cases tied to social media are on the rise, "reflect[ing] the growing impact and importance of new media compared with traditional news providers."[1] Lawsuits against individuals are becoming more common because Section 230 makes it difficult for a plaintiff who has suffered online defamation to recover damages from an internet service provider or website, like Facebook or Twitter. Many years ago, plaintiffs were inclined to sue an ISP or a website because these companies are wealthy and could afford to pay damages. But, as court decisions increasingly apply Section 230 immunity to a variety of website functions, lawsuits against individuals offer a more likely avenue for remedy.[2]

An example from 2014 is the first Twitter libel case to ever go before a jury. In that California case, rock musician Courtney Love's former attorney sued her for a tweet suggesting he had been "bought off." But the attorney did not prevail because he could not meet the actual malice standard.[3]

Today, many businesses and professional organizations offer "best practices" guides for using social media. These guides often highlight the challenges that social media bring to the area of defamation, including real-time interaction or the ability to post a comment quickly "on the fly," which can lead to less careful or precise use of language.[4]

If you frequently use social media or produce user-generated content online, experts say you should always ensure that the information you post or retweet either is truthful or would not injure a person's reputation. Additionally, recognize that modified photos and videos can defame a person or a business and the "less obvious and absurd the modification, the more likely it is that a court will find it defamatory."[5]

1. Roy Greenslade, *23% Increase in Defamation Actions as Social Media Claims Rise*, The Guardian (London), Oct. 20, 2014, www.theguardian.com/media/greenslade/2014/oct/20/medialaw-social-media.
2. *Defamation and Social Media: What You Need to Know*, Findlaw.com, Feb. 24, 2015, injury.findlaw.com/torts-and-personal-injuries/defamation-and-social-media—what-you-need-to-know.html.
3. Gordon & Holmes v. Courtney Michelle Love, No. BC462438 (Cal. Super. Ct. 2014).
4. *Top 10 Legal Issues in Social Media*, Nealmcdevitt.com, Feb. 24, 2015, www.nealmcdevitt.com/assets/news/Top_10_Social_Media_Legal_Issues_FINAL.PDF.
5. *Id.*

Although Section 230 is a robust defense for ISPs and information content providers, it is far from ironclad. In 2016, the Ninth Circuit Court of Appeals refused to grant immunity under Section 230 to Internet Brands Inc. in a case that involved the Model Mayhem networking website it operated for people in the modeling industry. The plaintiff in the case, identified only as Jane Doe, posted her information to the site and was then contacted by two men posing as talent scouts who lured her to a fake audition where they drugged her, raped her and recorded the rape for sale and distribution as pornography. Doe sued Internet Brands under a California law that requires a warning of harm when a person has a "special relationship to either the person whose conduct needs to be controlled or . . . to the foreseeable victim of that conduct."[75] Doe asserted that Internet Brands knew its website was being used by sexual predators and failed to warn users. "The duty to warn allegedly imposed by California law would not require Internet Brands to remove any user content or otherwise affect how it publishes or monitors such content," according to the Ninth Circuit. "Any alleged obligation to warn could have been satisfied without changes to the content posted by the website's users and without conducting a detailed investigation. Internet Brands could have given a warning to Model Mayhem users, perhaps by posting a notice on the website or by informing users by email what it knew."[76] For now, this ruling applies only under state law in California.

OTHER DEFENSES

Neutral Reportage

As explained in Chapter 4, someone who repeats libelous information is as potentially responsible as the originator of that same information. Republication is not a valid libel defense. But that longtime rule of libel law was loosened somewhat by the doctrine of neutral reportage.

neutral reportage
In libel law, a defense accepted in some jurisdictions that says that when an accusation is made by a responsible and prominent organization, reporting that accusation is protected by the First Amendment even when it turns out the accusation was false and libelous.

Neutral reportage recognizes that the First Amendment principle of the free flow of information and ideas is important. The doctrine suggests that among the kinds of information that should be free to reach people are accusations made by one individual about another. In some circumstances, the news value lies not in whether the accusation is true but simply in the fact that the accusation was made or who made it. According to neutral reportage, the news media should not be restrained from merely reporting an accusation as long as the reporting is done in a fair, objective and balanced (i.e., neutral) manner. Even if the publisher of the reported accusations has serious doubts about their veracity, the neutral reportage doctrine could provide a successful defense.

The neutral reportage defense was established in 1977 and only applied to cases involving public figures.[77] Since then, the scope of that application has sometimes expanded beyond public figures, but the nation's courts have not uniformly embraced neutral reportage. Its recognition, in fact, has been spotty. One obstacle to more widespread acceptance is that the U.S. Supreme Court has had virtually nothing to say about neutral reportage. Because it has been left to individual state and federal districts to determine how to handle neutral reportage, the legal landscape is uncertain.[78] Thus, while neutral reportage remains an option in the libel defendant's arsenal, the inconsistent manner in which courts have

▲ EMERGING LAW

Gaps in Section 230 Immunity?

While Section 230 immunity has expanded over the past two decades, in 2016 the outcome in several cases suggested gaps exist. One case to watch is *Hassell v. Bird*, which at the time of publication of this text was on appeal at the California Supreme Court. The case involves an attorney (Hassell) who sued a former client (Bird) for defamation for a negative review she posted on Yelp. When Bird failed to show up in court twice for the defamation claim, the court awarded Hassell more than a half-million dollars in damages and ordered Bird to remove the negative reviews. As noted in Chapter 4, courts have seen a surge of defamation cases in which plaintiffs seek not only damages but also a court-ordered prohibition (called injunctive relief) to stop future publication of defamatory content on the internet and/or the removal of defamatory content.[1]

When Hassell approached Yelp to remove the reviews, Yelp attempted to intervene in the case arguing that it was protected under Section 230. The case is procedurally complicated because Yelp was never a party in the original lawsuit. The court rejected Yelp's First Amendment argument that it was a content curator. Instead, the court said it was unprotected as a passive technology conduit required to comply with an injunction against speech already deemed to be defamatory, and therefore unprotected.[2]

Eric Goldman, a legal expert on Section 230, wrote that the decision "rips a [big] hole" in Section 230 immunity and effectively becomes an easy way for people to "scrub" unflattering content from the internet.[3]

More than 40 organizations, companies and law professors decried the decision. "The decision has already been used to try to expand the law in dangerous ways," Google wrote. Glassdoor, a jobs and recruiting site, noted, "Since *Hassell* was published, we have begun receiving demand letters citing the opinion as grounds for demanding that Glassdoor remove content and reviews deemed objectionable."[4]

---

1. RonNell Andersen Jones, *Developments in the Law of Social Media*, Comm. L. in the Digital Age (2016).
2. Hassell v. Bird, 203 Cal. Rptr. 3d 203 (Ct. App. 2016).
3. Eric Goldman, *Yelp Forced to Remove Defamatory Reviews—Hassell v. Bird*, Tech. & Marketing L. Blog, June 8, 2016, blog.ericgoldman.org/archives/2016/06/yelp-forced-to-remove-defamatory-reviews-hassell-v-bird.htm.
4. Eric Goldman, *The Internet Rallies Against a Terrible Section 230 Ruling—Hassell v. Bird*, Tech. & Marketing L. Blog, Aug. 22, 2016, blog.ericgoldman.org/archives/2016/08/hassell-v-bird.htm.

● POINTS OF LAW

Neutral Reportage

The First Amendment is a defense in a libel case if the following apply:

- The story is newsworthy and related to a public controversy.
- The accusation is made by a responsible person or group.
- The charge is about a public official, public figure or public organization.
- The story is accurate, containing denials or other views.
- The reporting is neutral.

accepted it makes its application in a specific case questionable. Much depends on how a court in a given jurisdiction may have ruled on neutral reportage previously.

Wire Service Defense

The wire service defense is related to the neutral reportage doctrine. It is similar to neutral reportage in that it provides a defense for republication on the condition that the reporting meets certain standards. The wire service defense reflects and acknowledges the extent to which news media are dependent on news services, particularly for nonlocal news. To expect verification of every report is unreasonable. This defense holds that the accurate republication of a story provided by a reputable news agency does not constitute fault as a matter of law. The wire defense is available to libel defendants if four factors are met: (1) The defendant received material containing the defamatory statements from a reputable newsgathering agency, (2) the defendant did not know the story was false, (3) nothing on the face of the story reasonably could have alerted the defendant that it may have been incorrect, and (4) the original wire service story was republished without substantial change.

The wire service defense has succeeded even when a newspaper published a story that relied on past wire service articles[79] and when a network affiliate broadcast news reports of its parent network.[80] Also, like the neutral reportage privilege, the wire service defense has been accepted in a limited number of jurisdictions.

Single-Publication Rule

single-publication rule A rule that limits libel victims to only one cause of action even with multiple publications of the libel, common in the mass media and on websites.

Another issue related to republication is the availability of an article subsequent to its initial publication. Does the republication of a work weeks, months or years after its original publication constitute a publication, therefore subjecting it to additional, separate libel claims? According to the **single-publication rule**, no. The rule states that the entire edition of a newspaper or magazine is a single publication. Subsequent sales or reissues are not new publications. Courts across the United States also apply the single-publication rule to internet publications and to emerging online publishing platforms as well as with digital archiving.[81] Thus, a new libel suit with merit is not possible in any of these circumstances. However, if in the republication process, content changes in a way that creates a new libel, the single-publication rule is unlikely to apply.

● POINTS OF LAW

The Wire Service Defense

The wire service defense may be applied as long as the following are present:

1. The defendant received material containing the defamatory statements from a reputable newsgathering agency.

2. The defendant did not know the story was false.

3. Nothing on the face of the story reasonably could have alerted the defendant that it may have been incorrect.

4. The original wire service story was republished without substantial change.

The Libel-Proof Plaintiff

When an individual's reputation is already so bad that additional false accusations could not harm it further, the individual may be without the ability to win a defamation suit. Under these circumstances, a libel defendant may be able to invoke the concept of the **libel-proof plaintiff**. Since the concept was first articulated as a libel defense,[82] two different ways to implement it have emerged.

One way stipulates that any reputational harm to the plaintiff caused by a false accusation only incrementally injures the reputation beyond its already damaged condition. Suppose, for example, that an individual is identified in an article as a thief, child molester and tax evader. If all of those charges are true, does it make any difference if the article also falsely identifies the individual as a kidnapper? No—in such a case, the publisher could probably win, arguing that the single false statement causes harm that is negligible (or incremental) beyond what already exists and therefore is not grounds for a libel suit. The plaintiff is libel-proof. Under these kinds of circumstances, the false statement causes very little harm to the plaintiff's reputation beyond where it stood prior to the most recent publication.

Like other common law libel privileges, the acceptance of this part of the doctrine has not been universal. For example, a federal appeals court rejected the libel-proof plaintiff doctrine in 1984.[83] A journalist described the founder of an organization as a racist, fascist, anti-Semitic neo-Nazi and wrote that he had founded the organization to pursue his

libel-proof plaintiff A plaintiff whose reputation is deemed to be so damaged already that additional false statements of and concerning him or her cannot cause further harm.

● REAL WORLD LAW

Managing Your Reputation Online

The internet allows for a permanent record of our past, and search engines and social media facilitate the easy spread of blog posts, images, commentary, status updates and other information. Other than going to court to seek an injunction to remove negative content or to try to prevent the sharing of defamatory content (an emerging area of law), what can you do to help protect your reputation online?

"Set up a Google alert for yourself. Contribute things that are of professional interest, and do it occasionally," according to the founder of Reputation.com. "You don't have to tweet every day—doing it a few times a month is a good idea, especially if it is relevant to what you do. And don't use Facebook a lot; if you do, maximize your privacy settings. Also, don't post a lot of photos to social media, in general, about your families. Basically, don't over-share."[1]

The founder of another reputation management company, Metal Rabbit Media, equates a person's online reputation to his or her credit score: "Americans have had to learn to manage their credit cards and bills to maintain a good credit score. The Web . . . contains the modern day version of inaccurate credit reports."[2]

1. Carolyn O'Hara, *10 Things You Need to Know About Online Reputation Management*, FORBES.COM, Nov. 20, 2013, www.forbes.com/sites/learnvest/2013/11/20/10-things-you-need-to-know-about-online-reputation-management/#7fdd7b585a36.
2. Nick Bilton, *The Growing Business of Online Reputation Management*, NYTIMES.COM, April 4, 2011, bits.blogs.nytimes.com/2011/04/04/the-growing-business-of-online-reputation-management/?_r=0.

goals. The defense argued that previous publications had already so irreparably tarnished the plaintiff's reputation that the libel-proof doctrine should apply. In an opinion written by then-Judge Antonin Scalia, an appellate court rejected the claim, ruling that "we cannot envision how a court would go about determining that someone's reputation had already been 'irreparably' damaged—i.e., that no new reader could be reached by the freshest libel."[84] In writing that no matter how bad one's reputation is, it can always be worsened, Scalia offered an analogy: "It is shameful that Benedict Arnold was a traitor; but he was not a shoplifter to boot, and one should not have been able to make that charge while knowing its falsity with impunity."[85]

Courts may also recognize the second aspect of the libel-proof doctrine, which says that libel plaintiffs with tarnished reputations with regard to a particular issue are libel-proof only with respect to that issue. Libel claims pursued in this context present the question of whether previous publicity and the issue before the court are within the same framework.

INTERNATIONAL LAW

International Jurisdiction in Libel Actions

Because U.S. libel law is more protective of defendants than are laws in other countries, U.S. citizens have historically been more susceptible to libel verdicts against them in foreign courts. International plaintiffs have been known to engage in "libel tourism," shopping for a country other than the United States in which to file a libel claim.

The U.S. Congress passed a libel tourism bill in 2010. The law prevents federal courts from enforcing a foreign libel judgment against an American journalist, author or publisher if it is inconsistent with the protections afforded by the First Amendment. It also allows individuals who have a foreign judgment levied against them to demonstrate that it is not enforceable in the United States.[1]

For many years, London was considered the "libel capital of the world," but the enactment of the U.K. Defamation Bill, which became law in 2013, largely put an end to libel tourism in the U.K. The law now includes a requirement that plaintiffs prove serious harm; it removes presumption in favor of a jury trial; it introduces the defenses of "responsible publication on matters of public interest," truth and opinion; and it provides more protection for websites that host user-generated content. It also adopts the single-publication rule.[2]

What about libel actions that cross the U.S. borders? In 2016 the Texas Supreme Court held that a Mexican recording artist who lived in Texas could exercise specific personal jurisdiction in Texas, even though broadcasts at the center of her complaint originated in Mexico. Specific personal jurisdiction refers to jurisdiction based on a person's minimum contact with a state when a legal claim is related to that contact. The Court said that the defendant, TV Azteca, intentionally targeted the Texas market and that it was not unreasonable or burdensome for foreign nationals to have to comply with the laws of the jurisdiction in which they do business and in which the Mexican recording artist lived.[3]

1. *U.S. Passes Historic SPEECH Act*, EUROPENEWS, July 28, 2010, europenews.dken/node/34081.
2. Defamation Bill 2012–13, services.parliament.uk/bills/2012-13/defamation.html.
3. TV Azteca v. Ruiz, 490 S.W. 3d 29 (Tex. 2016), *cert. denied*, 2017 WL 2722433 (June 26, 2017).

For example, a plaintiff challenged a newspaper report that he had tested positive for drug use. The court found that although the report was incorrect, the plaintiff was libel-proof regarding this specific issue because he had previously admitted using drugs.[86] Had the new report falsely damaged his reputation regarding a topic unrelated to drug use, the libel-proof plaintiff doctrine could not have been invoked. The plaintiff still had a positive reputation to protect in those other areas.

Thus, the doctrine of the libel-proof plaintiff may serve a defendant who has published otherwise defamatory statements about an individual whose reputation is already so sullied as to render additional accusations moot, regardless of their falsity. Depending on the circumstances, the doctrine may apply to accusations of any nature or to those that relate only to a specific issue.

The libel-proof plaintiff doctrine remains a valuable defense weapon, particularly against frivolous libel suits and especially given the U.S. Supreme Court's opinion that states are free to adopt the doctrine as they see fit.[87]

ADDITIONAL DEFENSE CONSIDERATIONS

Summary Judgment

A libel defendant can ask a court to dismiss a lawsuit by filing a motion for summary judgment. As noted in Chapter 1, a summary judgment is just what the name implies: A judge promptly decides certain points of a case and grants the motion to dismiss the case. It can occur at any of several points in litigation but usually occurs prior to trial.

A judge may issue a summary judgment on grounds that there is no genuine dispute about any material fact. With libel, this generally means a plaintiff is clearly unable to meet at least one element in his or her burden of proof. On numerous occasions, the U.S. Supreme Court said that when considering motions for summary judgment, courts "must view the facts and inferences to be drawn from them in the light most favorable to the opposing party."[88] Particularly in libel cases, this means that courts must take into account the burden the plaintiff must meet at trial. The rationale behind this view is that if the summary judgment is granted, the plaintiff's opportunity to prove a case ends, but if a defendant's motion for summary judgment is denied, the defendant still has an opportunity to prove his or her case at trial.[89]

Summary judgments can be important tools for protecting free expression, particularly in an environment in which plaintiffs have harassed the media by filing frivolous lawsuits (e.g., see the description of SLAPPs earlier in this chapter). One federal judge wrote that in the First Amendment area, summary procedures are even more essential. Free debate is at stake if the harassment succeeds. One purpose of the *New York Times Co. v. Sullivan* actual malice principle, the judge wrote, is to prevent people from being discouraged in the full and free exercise of First Amendment rights with respect to the conduct of their government.[90]

Motion to Dismiss for Actual Malice

Until 1979, summary judgment was a preferred method of dealing with libel cases involving actual malice. When the defense submitted a motion for summary judgment—based on the contention that the plaintiff could not prove actual malice—the judge would either grant or deny it. If granted, the case was over. In 1979, the U.S. Supreme Court cast doubt on the appropriateness of summary judgment in libel cases because any examination of actual malice "calls a defendant's state of mind into question." Such a circumstance "does not readily lend itself to summary disposition."[91] Although some lower courts took the admonition to heart—using it as a basis for denying summary judgment—motions for summary judgment are still granted more often than not. In 1986, the Court ruled that in deciding whether to grant motions for summary judgment, trial judges should decide whether public plaintiffs who file lawsuits claiming they have been libeled can meet the actual malice standard by "clear and convincing evidence." If not, summary judgment for the party they have sued should be granted.[92]

This issue was revisited by the Supreme Court about a decade ago. In 2007, the U.S. Supreme Court significantly changed the standard for the motion to dismiss in *Bell Atlantic Corp. v. Twombly.*[93] Two years later, it affirmed its decision in *Ashcroft v. Iqbal.*[94] Since then, a new standard has emerged—called the *Iqbal/Twombly* Rule—that has, in essence, made a motion to dismiss equivalent to a motion for summary judgment. Under the *Iqbal/Twombly* Rule, judges should use "judicial common sense" to determine the plausibility of a claim and the sufficiency of the evidence. The Supreme Court justified the change by noting the increasing legal costs to defendants. One study suggests that, since the decision, more motions to dismiss have succeeded in courts across the country in many different areas of the law.[95]

In 2012, two federal appeals courts applied the *Iqbal/Twombly* Rule to actual malice proceedings. The First Circuit became the first to apply the standard to actual malice and granted a motion to dismiss in a case involving a political candidate's complaint that a political attack ad defamed him. The court said that the use of "actual malice buzzwords" was not sufficient to make a claim and that the candidate must "lay out enough facts from which [actual] malice might reasonably be inferred."[96] In the Fourth Circuit, the court granted a motion to dismiss a case involving NASCAR driver Jeremy Mayfield, who sued NASCAR for reporting that he tested positive for recreational or performance-enhancing drugs. Mayfield said NASCAR knew the test result was a false positive because he was taking prescription medication at the time. The court said Mayfield's evidence was insufficient.[97]

Legal experts now consider the *Iqbal/Twombly* Rule another form of defense for defamation claims. In 2016, the Eleventh Circuit Court of Appeals joined six other circuits in holding that the standard from *Iqbal/Twombly* applies to the actual malice element in defamation cases.[98]

NASCAR driver Jeremy Mayfield.

Todd Warshaw/Getty Images for NASCAR

Jurisdiction

A court may dismiss a lawsuit on the grounds that the court lacks jurisdiction. Traditionally in libel, the standard has been that wherever the material in question could be seen or heard, a court in any of those locales would have jurisdiction.[99]

Thus, a plaintiff could go "forum shopping" in an attempt to find a jurisdiction most favorable to his or her case.

Given that statements published on the internet can potentially be seen anywhere, any court could claim jurisdiction. A plaintiff could initiate the lawsuit in any court, including those that might be most favorable. But early in the 21st century, significant restrictions were placed on this practice. The U.S. Court of Appeals for the Fourth Circuit applied a three-pronged test for determining the exercise of jurisdiction: (1) whether the defendant purposefully conducted activities in the state, (2) whether the plaintiff's claim arises out of the defendant's activities there and (3) whether the exercise of jurisdiction would be constitutionally reasonable.[100]

To understand the test, it is helpful to examine the circumstances surrounding the case in which it was first applied. Two Connecticut newspapers were investigating conditions of confinement at a Virginia prison. The story was relevant in Connecticut because some of the overflow prison population in Connecticut was being transferred to a Virginia facility. Articles that included content critical of the Virginia prison and its management appeared in the newspaper in both its print and online editions. The Virginia prison warden sued in federal court in Virginia, claiming that the online content was seen in Virginia and had defamed him there. The appeals court ruled that because the newspapers did not direct their website content to a Virginia audience, courts there had no jurisdiction. The court

▲ EMERGING LAW

Internal Communication and Social Media as Evidence

"Dance like nobody is watching, but email like it may one day be subpoenaed and read aloud in a deposition." This good, general advice returned front-of-mind for journalists after a North Carolina jury handed down a $9 million libel verdict ($7.5 million punitive) against The (Raleigh) News & Observer. The damages were later reduced to $6 million by a state law cap that limits punitive damages.[1]

The case involved a state firearms agent who sued the newspaper, claiming that a 2010 front-page investigative series about questionable practices at the State Bureau of Investigation defamed her. Email correspondence between the reporter and an editor played a role in the outcome. While the story in question relied on multiple sources, all of the sources testified that they were misquoted.

While plaintiffs have had the opportunity to subpoena journalists' emails and notes in the past (see Chapter 7), legal experts note that litigants are increasingly turning to work-related emails as well as publicly available social media feeds to scrutinize journalists' comments outside of their stories to potentially support a defamation claim. The connection to defamation claims is a newer trend.[2]

In light of the allegations surrounding Russian hacking of political campaign emails in 2016, many are encouraging journalists and other communication professionals to remember that comments and posts on social media are public and that they should never assume that work-related emails might not be read by outsiders, including the courts.[3]

---

1. Corey Hutchins, *A Daily's Loss in Court May Cause Journalists to Rethink How They Communicate*, CJR.ORG, Oct. 25, 2016, www.cjr.org/united_states_project/libel_lawsuit_journalists_email_slack.php?Newsletter.
2. Tom Hentoff, *Defamation and Related Claims*, COMM. L. IN THE DIGITAL AGE (2016).
3. *Id.*

carefully reviewed the articles and determined they were aimed at a local (Connecticut) audience.[101] Placing content online, the court ruled, is not sufficient by itself to subject a person to the jurisdiction in another state just because the information could be accessed there.[102] Otherwise, a person who places information on the internet could be sued anywhere the information could be accessed. The bottom line, according to this ruling, is that jurisdiction rests where the publication's intended audience is located.

Statutes of Limitations

Statutes of limitations apply for virtually all crimes and civil actions. Charges of most criminal activity and civil actions can be filed only during a limited time after the alleged violation of the law. Courts do not like old claims. While not a defense per se, delay in filing a libel lawsuit can work to the benefit of a defendant, sometimes requiring dismissal where the lawsuit is barred by the statute of limitations.

In libel, the length of statutes of limitations is one, two or three years, depending on the state. The clock begins ticking on the date the material was made available to the public. With some printed publications, this can be prior to the date of publication on the cover. Many monthly magazines, for example, are mailed to subscribers and appear on newsstands or online well before the official publication date.

On a related note, the single-publication rule also applies to statutes of limitations. The reissue of a printed publication or a post online does not restart the statute of limitations calendar as a truly new publication would. A modification to a website—when the modification is unrelated to the allegedly defamatory statement—does not amount to a new publication. For purposes of libel claims and statutes of limitations, the date of publication remains the date on which the material was originally posted.

Retractions

While not a libel defense per se, retractions and corrections published to correct content can play a role in helping libel defendants by mitigating the damage to the plaintiff that resulted from the libelous publication. The degree to which a retraction is offered promptly, is displayed prominently and is plainly stated will likely help the defendant's cause. The rationale for this is that a retraction can help reduce the damage to the plaintiff's reputation; the defendant therefore should be required to pay less in damages.

While issuing a retraction is certainly the responsible action to undertake, doing so may work against the defendant if the offended party files a lawsuit. Depending on their wording,

● POINTS OF LAW

A Test for Jurisdiction

1. Whether the defendant purposefully conducted activities in the state,

2. Whether the plaintiff's claim arises out of the defendant's activities there and

3. Whether the exercise of jurisdiction would be constitutionally reasonable

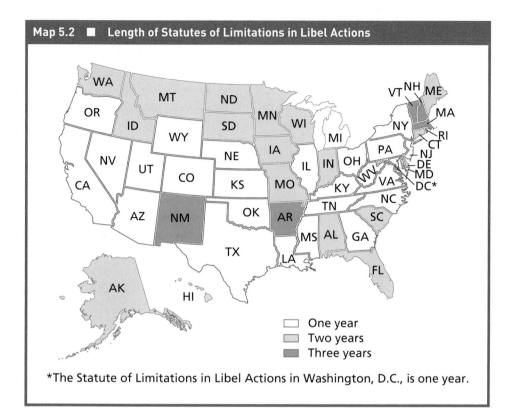

Map 5.2 ■ Length of Statutes of Limitations in Libel Actions

One year
Two years
Three years

*The Statute of Limitations in Libel Actions in Washington, D.C., is one year.

retractions may be viewed as an admission of guilt. Consequently, libel defense attorneys may advise against issuing them in the first place. In part as a response to this paradox, a majority of states have adopted **retraction statutes**. Increasingly, these laws prevent plaintiffs from recovering some damages after publication of a retraction.[103] Retraction statutes vary in their strength and coverage.[104] The protection they offer differs in many ways, from prohibitions on punitive damages to restricting damages to out-of-pocket losses.[105] Most of these statutes look favorably on media defendants who issue retractions. Rather than penalizing media organizations that indirectly acknowledge some degree of negligence, these statutes offer a kind of compensation by reducing their obligation to pay damages.

Retraction statutes do not always fare well under judicial review in their respective states. Some have been ruled unconstitutional. The Arizona Supreme Court, for example, ruled that the retraction statute in that state violated the state constitution.[106] The law limited plaintiffs to recovering only special damages when retractions were published.[107] But the Arizona Constitution holds that "[t]he right of action to recover damages for injuries shall never be abrogated, and the amount recovered shall not be subject to any statutory limitation."[108] Because the law conflicted with the Arizona Constitution, it did not survive judicial scrutiny. However, although a retraction or correction of a news report in Arizona may no longer immunize a libel defendant from all punitive damage claims, it may serve to reduce those damages.

retraction statutes
In libel law, state laws that limit the damages a plaintiff may receive if the defendant had issued a retraction of the material at issue. Retraction statutes are meant to discourage the punishment of any good-faith effort of admitting a mistake.

CHAPTER SUMMARY

THOSE SUED FOR LIBEL HAVE SEVERAL DEFENSE OPTIONS from which to choose, any one of which can lead to success. Truth is one of the most straightforward defenses, given that material must be false to be libelous. Even material that is less than completely accurate may be regarded as substantially true. Chilling speech is the goal of some defamation lawsuits. In those cases, libel law is used not as a shield against threatened harms or as a means of correcting them, but as a weapon to prevent speech from occurring in the first place. These are called SLAPPs (strategic lawsuits against public participation). Noting that SLAPPs are often used to suppress a party's First Amendment rights, some states have enacted anti-SLAPP legislation. The constitutionality of these laws has been upheld.

Journalists are able to report on certain events without fear of libel as long as their reporting is fair and accurate. The fair report privilege generally applies to reporting on official government proceedings (e.g., hearings, trials) or records, but not all states recognize this privilege. Another defense, fair comment and criticism, pertains to honest evaluation of works of legitimate public interest.

Expressing an opinion is regarded as a basic First Amendment right. Opinion is protected speech not susceptible to a libel claim. However, for material to qualify as protected opinion, it must satisfy the four-part *Ollman* test. Published letters to the editor, online comments and websites or blogs purely used to express opinions are typically viewed as protected opinion because of context. If a statement is unbelievable, then it cannot be libelous. Thus, parody, satire and rhetorical hyperbole can be used as libel defenses when it is clear to a reasonable person that their use is not to be taken seriously.

Section 230 of the Communications Decency Act offers immunity to websites and internet service providers in libel claims, although the protection is not absolute. The key to determining whether Section 230 protects against a libel claim is to identify the source of the content and the extent to which the service provider or website interacted directly with the content. Correcting, editing, adding or removing content does not strip a website or an ISP of Section 230 immunity so long as it doesn't substantially alter the meaning of the content.

Some libel defenses allow for a kind of republication. These include neutral reportage and the wire service defense. Under the single-publication rule, multiple issues of the same publication do not make the defendant vulnerable to multiple libel claims. Courts across the United States also apply the single-publication rule to internet publications and to emerging online publishing platforms.

Sometimes false, defamatory material is published about someone whose reputation cannot be lowered beyond its current level. Under those circumstances, a defendant may argue the plaintiff is libel-proof. Additional defense considerations include summary judgment, motion to dismiss for actual malice, jurisdiction, statutes of limitations and retractions. ■

CASES FOR STUDY

For study resources and a case archive go to **study.sagepub.com/medialaw6e**.

THINKING ABOUT IT

The two case excerpts that follow are very important libel cases. Note that only one of them is from the U.S. Supreme Court. The other is from the D.C. Circuit Court of Appeals. At the center of each is the libel defense of opinion. As you read these case excerpts, keep the following questions in mind:

- How do the two decisions help define the meaning of opinion?

- Does either ruling outline any kind of test or standard to help judge opinion? If so, what is that?

- Do these rulings expand or narrow the definition of opinion?

Ollman v. Evans
U.S. COURT OF APPEALS FOR THE DISTRICT OF COLUMBIA CIRCUIT
750 F.2d 970 (1984)

JUDGE KENNETH STARR delivered the court's opinion:

This defamation action arises out of the publication of a syndicated column by Rowland Evans and Robert Novak in May 1978. The question before us is whether the allegedly defamatory statements set forth in the column are constitutionally protected expressions of opinion or, as appellant contends, actionable assertions of fact. We conclude, as did the District Court, that the challenged statements are entitled to absolute First Amendment protection as expressions of opinion. . . .

The plaintiff, Bertell Ollman, is a professor of political science at New York University. . . . In March 1978, Mr. Ollman was nominated by a departmental search committee to head the Department of Government and Politics at the University of Maryland. The committee's recommendation was "duly approved by the Provost of the University and the Chancellor of the College Park campus."

With this professional move from Washington Square to College Park, Maryland thus in the offing, the Evans and Novak article appeared. . . .

This case presents us with the delicate and sensitive task of accommodating the First Amendment's protection of free expression of ideas with the common law's protection of an individual's interest in reputation. It is a truism that the free flow of ideas and opinions is integral to our democratic system of government. Thomas Jefferson well expressed this principle in his First Inaugural Address, when the Nation's memory was fresh with the passage of the notorious Alien and Sedition Acts:

If there be any among us who would wish to dissolve this Union or to change its republican form, let them stand undisturbed as monuments of the safety with which error of opinion may be tolerated where reason is left free to combat it.

At the same time, an individual's interest in his or her reputation is of the highest order. Its protection is an eloquent expression of the respect historically afforded the dignity of the individual in Anglo-American legal culture. A defamatory statement may destroy an individual's livelihood, wreck his standing in the community, and seriously impair his sense of dignity and self-esteem. . . .

. . . In *Gertz*, the Supreme Court in *dicta* seemed to provide absolute immunity from defamation actions for all opinions and to discern the basis for this immunity in the First Amendment. The Court began its analysis of the case by stating:

Under the First Amendment there is no such thing as a false idea. However pernicious an opinion may seem, we depend for its correction not on the conscience of judges and juries but on the competition of other ideas. But there is no constitutional value in false statements of fact. Neither the intentional lie nor the careless error materially advances society's interest in "uninhibited, robust, and wide-open debate on the public issues." . . .

. . . *Gertz*'s implicit command thus imposes upon both state and federal courts the duty as a matter of constitutional adjudication to distinguish facts from opinions in order to provide opinions with the requisite, absolute First Amendment protection. At the same time, however, the Supreme Court provided little guidance in *Gertz* itself as to the manner in which the distinction between fact and opinion is to be discerned. . . .

. . . With largely uncharted seas having been left in *Gertz*'s wake, the lower federal courts and state courts have, not surprisingly, fashioned various approaches in attempting to articulate the *Gertz*-mandated distinction between fact and opinion. . . .

In formulating a test to distinguish between fact and opinion, courts are admittedly faced with a dilemma. Because of the richness and diversity of language, as evidenced by the capacity of the same words to convey different meanings in different contexts, it is quite impossible to lay down a bright-line or mechanical distinction. . . . While this dilemma admits of no easy resolution, we think it obliges us to state plainly the factors that guide us in distinguishing fact from opinion and to demonstrate how these factors lead to a proper accommodation between the competing interests in free expression of opinion and in an individual's reputation. . . .

While courts are divided in their methods of distinguishing between assertions of fact and expressions of opinion, they are universally agreed that the task is a difficult one. . . .

The degree to which such kinds of statements have real factual content can, of course, vary greatly. We believe, in consequence, that courts should analyze the totality of the circumstances in which the statements are made to decide whether they merit the absolute First Amendment protection enjoyed by opinion. To evaluate the totality of the circumstances of an allegedly defamatory statement, we will consider four factors in assessing whether the average reader would view the statement as fact or, conversely, opinion. . . .

First, we will analyze the common usage or meaning of the specific language of the challenged statement itself. Our analysis of the specific language under scrutiny will be aimed at determining whether the statement has a precise core of meaning for which a consensus of understanding exists or, conversely, whether the statement is indefinite and ambiguous. . . .

Second, we will consider the statement's verifiability—is the statement capable of being objectively characterized as true or false? . . . Third, moving from the challenged language itself, we will consider the full context of the statement—the entire article or column, for example—inasmuch as other, unchallenged language surrounding the allegedly defamatory statement will influence the average reader's readiness to infer that a particular statement has factual content. . . . Finally, we will consider the broader context or setting in which the statement appears. Different types of writing have, as we shall more fully see, widely varying social conventions which signal to the reader the likelihood of a statement's being either fact or opinion. . . .

. . . [O]nce our inquiry into whether the statement is an assertion of fact or expression of opinion has concluded, the factors militating either in favor of or against the drawing of factual implications from any statement have already been identified. A separate inquiry into whether a statement, already classified in this painstaking way as opinion, implies allegedly defamatory facts would, in our view, be superfluous.

In short, we believe that the application of the four-factor analysis set forth above, and drawn from the considerable judicial teaching on the subject, will identify those statements so "factually laden" that they should not receive the benefit of the opinion privilege. . . .

Now we turn to the case at hand to apply the foregoing analysis. As we have seen, Mr. Ollman alleges various instances of defamation in the Evans and Novak column. Before analyzing each such instance, we will first examine the context (the third and fourth factors in our approach) in which the alleged defamations arise. We will then assess the manner in which this context would influence the average reader in interpreting the alleged defamations as an assertion of fact or an expression of opinion.

From the earliest days of the Republic, individuals have published and circulated short, frequently sharp and biting writings on issues of social and political interest. From the pamphleteers urging revolution to abolitionists condemning the evils of slavery, American authors have sought through pamphlets and tracts both to stimulate debate and to persuade. Today among the inheritors of this lively tradition are the columnists and opinion writers whose works appear on the editorial and Op-Ed pages of the Nation's newspapers. The column at issue here is plainly part and parcel of this tradition of social and political criticism.

The reasonable reader who peruses an Evans and Novak column on the editorial or Op-Ed page is fully aware that the statements found there are not "hard" news like those printed on the front page or elsewhere in the news sections of the newspaper. Readers expect that columnists will make strong statements, sometimes phrased in a polemical manner that would hardly be considered balanced or fair elsewhere in the newspaper. That proposition is inherent in the very notion of an "Op-Ed page." Because of obvious space limitations, it is also manifest that columnists or commentators will express themselves in condensed fashion without providing what might be considered the full picture. Columnists are, after all, writing a column, not a full-length scholarly article or a book. This broad understanding of the traditional function of a column like Evans and Novak will therefore predispose the average reader to regard what is found there to be opinion. . . .

. . . Evans and Novak made it clear that they were not purporting to set forth definitive conclusions, but instead meant to ventilate what in their view constituted the central questions raised by Mr. Ollman's prospective appointment. . . . Prominently displayed in the Evans and Novak column, therefore, is interrogatory or cautionary language that militates in favor of treating statements as opinion. . . .

Nor is the statement that "[Mr. Ollman] is widely viewed in his profession as a political activist" a representation or assertion of fact. . . . While Mr. Ollman argues that this assertion is defamatory since it *implies* that he has no reputation as a scholar, we are rather skeptical of the strength of that implication, particularly in the context of this column. . . .

Next we turn to Mr. Ollman's complaints about the column's quotations from and remarks about his writings. . . . When a critic is commenting about a book, the reader is on notice that the critic is engaging in interpretation, an inherently subjective enterprise, and therefore realizes that others, including the author, may utterly disagree with the critic's interpretation. . . . The reader is thus predisposed to view what the critic writes as opinion. . . .

Evans' and Novak's statements about Mr. Ollman's article clearly do not fall into the category of misquotation or misrepresentation. . . .

Professor Ollman also objects to the column's posing the question, prompted in Evans' and Novak's view by Mr. Ollman's article, of whether he intended to use the classroom for indoctrination. As we noted previously, the column in no wise affirmatively stated that Mr. Ollman was indoctrinating his students. Moreover, indoctrination is not, at least as used here in the setting of academia, a word with a well-defined meaning. . . .

Finally, we turn to the most troublesome statement in the column. In the third-to-last paragraph, an anonymous political science professor is quoted as saying: "Ollman has no status within the profession but is a pure and simple activist." . . .

Certainly a scholar's academic reputation among his peers is crucial to his or her career. . . .

We are of the view, however, that under the constitutionally based opinion privilege announced in *Gertz*, this quotation, under the circumstances before us, is protected. . . . [H]ere we deal with statements by well-known, nationally syndicated columnists on the Op-Ed page of a newspaper, the well-recognized home of opinion and comment. In addition, the thrust of the column, taken as a whole, is to raise questions about Mr. Ollman's scholarship and intentions, not to state conclusively from Evans' and Novak's first-hand knowledge that Professor Ollman is not a scholar or that his colleagues do not regard him as such. . . .

. . . [W]e are reminded that in the accommodation of the conflicting concerns reflected in the First Amendment and the law of defamation, the deep-seated constitutional values embodied in the Bill of Rights require that we not engage, without bearing clearly in mind the context before us, in a Talmudic parsing of a single sentence or two, as if we were occupied with a philosophical enterprise or linguistic analysis. Ours is a practical task, with elemental constitutional values of freedom looming large as we go about our work. And in that undertaking, we are reminded by *Gertz* itself of our duty "to assure to the freedoms of speech and press that 'breathing space' essential to their fruitful exercise." For the contraction of liberty's "breathing space" can only mean inhibition of the scope of public discussion on matters of general interest and concern. The provision of breathing space counsels strongly against straining to squeeze factual content from a single sentence in a column that is otherwise clearly opinion. . . .

The judgment of the District Court is therefore *Affirmed.*

Judge Robert Bork, concurring:

. . . [T]he statement challenged in this lawsuit, in terms of the policies of the first amendment, is functionally more like an "opinion" than a "fact" and should not be actionable. It thus falls within the category the Supreme Court calls "rhetorical hyperbole." . . .

. . . Ollman, by his own actions, entered a political arena in which heated discourse was to be expected and must be protected; the "fact" proposed to be tried is in truth wholly unsuitable for trial, which further imperils free discussion; the statement is not of the kind that would usually be accepted as one of hard fact and appeared in a context that further indicated it was rhetorical hyperbole.

Plaintiff Ollman, as will be shown, placed himself in the political arena and became the subject of heated political debate. . . .

. . . [I]n order to protect a vigorous marketplace in political ideas and contentions, we ought to accept the proposition that those who place themselves in a political arena must accept a degree of derogation that others need not. . . .

. . . [T]he core function of the first amendment is the preservation of that freedom to think and speak as one please which is the "means indispensable to the discovery and spread of political truth." Necessary to the preservation of that freedom, of course, is the willingness of those who would speak to be spoken to and, as in this case, to be spoken about. . . .

. . . Ollman has, as is his undoubted right, gone well beyond the role of the cloistered scholar, and he did so before Evans and Novak wrote about him. . . . Professor Ollman was an active proponent not just of Marxist scholarship but of Marxist politics. . . . It was plain that Ollman was a political activist and that he saw his academic post as, among other things, a means of advancing his political goals. . . .

. . . Ollman was not simply a scholar who was suddenly singled out by the press or by Evans and Novak. . . . He had entered the political arena before he put himself forward for the department chairmanship. . . . [H]e must accept the banging and jostling of political debate, in ways that a private person need not, in order to keep the political arena free and vital. . . .

. . . Ollman entered a first amendment arena and had to accept the rough treatment that arena affords. . . .

. . . [I]t is indisputable that this swirling public debate provided a strong context in which charges and countercharges should be assessed. In my view, that context made it much less likely that what Evans and Novak said would be regarded as an assertion of plain fact rather than as part of the judgments expressed by each side on the merits of the proposed appointment. . . .

When we come to the context in which this statement occurred, it becomes even more apparent that few people were likely to perceive it as a direct assertion of fact, to be taken at face value. That context was one of controversy and opinion, and it is known to be such by readers. It is significant, in the first place, that the column appeared on the Op-Ed pages of newspapers. These are pages reserved for the expression of opinion, much of it highly controversial opinion. That does not convert every assertion of fact on the Op-Ed pages into an expression of opinion merely by its placement there. It does alert the reader that he is in the context of controversy and politics, and that what he reads does not even purport to be as balanced, objective, and fair-minded as he has a right to hope to be the case with what is contained in the news columns of the paper. . . .

. . . I am persuaded that Ollman may not rest a libel action on the statement contained in the Evans and Novak column.

Judge Antonin Scalia, dissenting:

More plaintiffs should bear in mind that it is a normal human reaction, after painstakingly examining and rejecting thirty invalid and almost absurd contentions, to reject the thirty-first contention as well, and make a clean sweep of the matter. I have no other explanation for the majority's affirmance of summary judgment dismissing what seems to me a classic and coolly crafted libel, Evans and Novak's disparagement of Ollman's professional reputation. . . .

. . . [T]o say, as the concurrence does, that hyperbole excuses not merely the exaggeration but *the fact sought to be vividly conveyed by the exaggeration* is to mistake a freedom to enliven discourse for a freedom to destroy reputation. The libel that "Smith is an incompetent carpenter" is not converted into harmless and nonactionable word-play by merely embellishing it into the statement that "Smith is the worst carpenter this side of the Mississippi." . . .

Appendix

"The Marxist Professor's Intentions"

by Rowland Evans and Robert Novak

The Washington Post

May 4, 1978

What is in danger of becoming a frivolous public debate over the appointment of a Marxist to head the University of Maryland's department of politics and government has so far ignored this unspoken concern within the academic community: the avowed desire of many political activists to use higher education for indoctrination.

The proposal to name Bertell Ollman, professor at New York University, as department head has generated wrong-headed debate. Politicians who jumped in to oppose Ollman simply for his Marxist philosophy have received a justifiable going-over from defenders of academic freedom in the press and the university. Academic Prince Valiants seem arrayed against McCarythite [*sic*] know-nothings.

But neither side approaches the central question: not Ollman's beliefs, but his intentions. His candid writings avow his desire to use the classroom as an instrument for preparing what he calls "the revolution." Whether this is a form of indoctrination that could transform the real function of a university and transcend limits of academic freedom is a concern to academicians who are neither McCarthyite nor know-nothing.

To protect academic freedom, that question should be posed not by politicians but by professors. But professors throughout the country troubled by the nomination, clearly a minority, dare not say a word in today's campus climate.

While Ollman is described in news accounts as a "respected Marxist scholar," he is widely viewed in his profession as a political activist. Amid the increasingly popular Marxist movement in university life, he is distinct from philosophical Marxists. Rather, he is an outspoken proponent of "political Marxism."

He twice sought election to the council of the American Political Science Association as a candidate of the "Caucus for a New Political Science" and finished last out of 16 candidates each time. Whether or not that represents a professional judgment by his colleagues, as some critics contend, the verdict clearly rejected his campaign pledge: "If elected . . . I shall use every means at my disposal to promote the study of Marxism and Marxist approaches to politics throughout the profession."

Ollman's intentions become explicit in "On Teaching Marxism and Building the Movement," his article in the Winter 1978 issue of New Political Science. Most students, he claims, conclude his course with a "Marxist outlook." Ollman concedes that will be seen "as an admission that the purpose of my course is to convert students to socialism."

That bothers him not at all because "a correct understanding of Marxism (as indeed of any body of scientific truths) leads automatically to its acceptance." Non-Marxist students are defined as those "who do not yet understand Marxism." The "classroom" is a place where the students' "bourgeois ideology is being dismantled." "Our prior task" before the revolution, he writes, "is to make more revolutionaries. The revolution will only occur when there are enough of us to make it."

He concludes by stressing the importance to "the movement" of "radical professors." If approved for his new post, Ollman will have a major voice in filling a new professorship promised him. A leading prospect is fellow Marxist Alan Wolfe; he is notorious for his book "The Seamy Side of Democracy," whose celebration of communist China extols the beneficial nature of "brainwashing."

Ollman's principal scholarly work, "Alienation: Marx's Conception of Man in Capitalist Society," is a ponderous tome in adoration of the master (Marxism "is like a magnificently rich tapestry"). Published in 1971, it does not abandon hope for the revolution forecast by Karl Marx in 1848. "The present youth rebellion," he writes, by "helping to change the workers of tomorrow" will, along with other factors, make possible "a socialist revolution."

Such pamphleteering is hooted at by one political scientist in a major eastern university, whose scholarship and reputation as a liberal are well known. "Ollman has no status within the profession, but is a pure and simple activist," he said. Would he say that publicly? "No chance of it. Our academic culture does not permit the raising of such questions."

"Such questions" would include these: What is the true measurement of Ollman's scholarship? Does he intend to use the classroom for indoctrination? Will he indeed be followed by other Marxist professors? Could the department in time be closed to non-Marxists, following the tendency at several English universities?

Even if "such questions" cannot be raised by the faculty, they certainly should not be raised by politicians. While dissatisfaction with pragmatism by many liberal professors has renewed interest in the comprehensive dogma of the Marxists, there is little tolerance for confronting the value of that dogma. Here are the makings of a crisis that, to protect its integrity and true academic freedom, academia itself must resolve.

Milkovich v. Lorain Journal Co.
SUPREME COURT OF THE UNITED STATES
497 U.S. 1 (1990)

CHIEF JUSTICE William REHNQUIST delivered the Court's opinion:

Respondent J. Theodore Diadiun authored an article in an Ohio newspaper implying that petitioner Michael Milkovich, a local high school wrestling coach, lied under oath in a judicial proceeding about an incident involving petitioner and his team which occurred at a wrestling match. Petitioner sued Diadiun and the newspaper for libel, and the Ohio Court of Appeals affirmed a lower court entry of summary judgment against petitioner.

This judgment was based in part on the grounds that the article constituted an "opinion" protected from the reach of state defamation law by the First Amendment to the United States Constitution. We hold that the First Amendment does not prohibit the application of Ohio's libel laws to the alleged defamations contained in the article.

This case is before us for the third time in an odyssey of litigation spanning nearly 15 years. Petitioner Milkovich, now retired, was the wrestling coach at Maple Heights High School in Maple Heights, Ohio.

In 1974, his team was involved in an altercation at a home wrestling match with a team from Mentor High School. Several people were injured. In response to the incident, the Ohio High School Athletic Association (OHSAA) held a hearing at which Milkovich and H. Don Scott, the Superintendent of Maple Heights Public Schools, testified. Following the hearing, OHSAA placed the Maple Heights team on probation for a year and declared the team ineligible for the 1975 state tournament. OHSAA also censured Milkovich for his actions during the altercation. Thereafter, several parents and wrestlers sued OHSAA in the Court of Common Pleas of Franklin County, Ohio, seeking a restraining order against OHSAA's ruling on the grounds that they had been denied due process in the OHSAA proceeding. Both Milkovich and Scott testified in that proceeding. The court overturned OHSAA's probation and ineligibility orders on due process grounds.

The day after the court rendered its decision, respondent Diadiun's column appeared in the News-Herald, a newspaper which circulates in Lake County, Ohio, and is owned by respondent Lorain Journal Co. The column bore the heading "Maple beat the law with the 'big lie,'" beneath which appeared Diadiun's photograph and the words "TD Says." The carryover page headline announced ". . . Diadiun says Maple told a lie." The column contained the following passages:

> . . . [A] lesson was learned (or relearned) yesterday by the student body of Maple Heights High School, and by anyone who attended the Maple-Mentor wrestling meet of last Feb. 8.
>
> A lesson which, sadly, in view of the events of the past year, is well they learned early.
>
> It is simply this: If you get in a jam, lie your way out.
>
> If you're successful enough, and powerful enough, and can sound sincere enough, you stand an excellent chance of making the lie stand up, regardless of what really happened.
>
> The teachers responsible were mainly head Maple wrestling coach, Mike Milkovich,

and former superintendent of schools H. Donald Scott.

. . .

> Anyone who attended the meet, whether he be from Maple Heights, Mentor, or impartial observer, knows in his heart that Milkovich and Scott lied at the hearing after each having given his solemn oath to tell the truth.
>
> But they got away with it.
>
> Is that the kind of lesson we want our young people learning from their high school administrators and coaches?
>
> I think not.[109]

Petitioner commenced a defamation action against respondents in the Court of Common Pleas of Lake County, Ohio, alleging that the headline of Diadiun's article and the nine passages quoted above "accused plaintiff of committing the crime of perjury, an indictable offense in the State of Ohio, and damaged plaintiff directly in his life-time occupation of coach and teacher, and constituted libel *per se.*" The action proceeded to trial, and the court granted a directed verdict to respondents on the ground that the evidence failed to establish the article was published with "actual malice" as required by *New York Times Co. v. Sullivan.* The Ohio Court of Appeals for the Eleventh Appellate District reversed and remanded, holding that there was sufficient evidence of actual malice to go to the jury. The Ohio Supreme Court dismissed the ensuing appeal for want of a substantial constitutional question, and this Court denied certiorari.

On remand, relying in part on our decision in *Gertz v. Robert Welch Inc.* (1974), the trial court granted summary judgment to respondents on the grounds that the article was an opinion protected from a libel action by "constitutional law," and alternatively, as a public figure, petitioner had failed to make out a *prima facie* case of actual malice. The Ohio Court of Appeals affirmed both determinations. On appeal, the Supreme Court of Ohio reversed and remanded. The court first decided that petitioner was neither a public figure nor a public official under the relevant decisions of this Court. The court then found that "the statements in issue are factual assertions as a matter of law, and are not constitutionally protected as the opinions of the writer. . . . The plain import of the author's assertions is that Milkovich, *inter alia*, committed the crime of perjury in a court of law." This Court again denied certiorari.

Meanwhile, Superintendent Scott had been pursuing a separate defamation action through the Ohio courts. Two years after its Milkovich decision, in considering Scott's appeal, the Ohio Supreme Court reversed its position on Diadiun's article, concluding that the column was "constitutionally protected opinion." Consequently, the court upheld a lower court's grant of summary judgment against Scott.

The *Scott* court decided that the proper analysis for determining whether utterances are fact or opinion was set forth in the decision of the United States Court of Appeals for the District of Columbia Circuit in *Ollman v. Evans* (1984). Under that analysis, four factors are considered to ascertain whether, under the "totality of circumstances," a statement is fact or opinion. These factors are: (1) "the specific language used"; (2) "whether the statement is verifiable"; (3) "the general context of the statement"; and (4) "the broader context in which the statement appeared." The court found that application of the first two factors to the column militated in favor of deeming the challenged passages actionable assertions of fact. That potential outcome was trumped, however, by the court's consideration of the third and fourth factors. With respect to the third factor, the general context, the court explained that "the large caption 'TD Says' . . . would indicate to even the most gullible reader that the article was, in fact, opinion." As for the fourth factor, the "broader context," the court reasoned that because the article appeared on a sports page—"a traditional haven for cajoling, invective, and hyperbole"—the article would probably be construed as opinion.

Subsequently, considering itself bound by the Ohio Supreme Court's decision in *Scott*, the Ohio Court of Appeals in the instant proceedings affirmed a trial court's grant of summary judgment in favor of respondents, concluding that "it has been decided, as a matter of law, that the article in question was constitutionally protected opinion." The Supreme Court of Ohio dismissed petitioner's ensuing appeal for want of a substantial constitutional question. We granted certiorari, to consider the important questions raised by the Ohio courts' recognition of a constitutionally required "opinion" exception to the application of its defamation laws. We now reverse. . . .

Respondents would have us recognize, in addition to the established safeguards discussed above, still another First-Amendment-based protection for defamatory statements which are categorized as "opinion" as opposed to "fact." For this proposition they rely principally on the following dictum from our opinion in *Gertz:*

"Under the First Amendment there is no such thing as a false idea. However pernicious an opinion may seem, we depend for its correction not on the conscience of judges and juries but on the competition of other ideas. But there is no constitutional value in false statements of fact."

Judge Friendly appropriately observed that this passage "has become the opening salvo in all arguments for protection from defamation actions on the ground of opinion, even though the case did not remotely concern the question." Read in context, though, the fair meaning of the passage is to equate the word "opinion" in the second sentence with the word "idea" in the first sentence. Under this view, the language was merely a reiteration of Justice Holmes' classic "marketplace of ideas" concept. . . . ("[T]he ultimate good desired is better reached by free trade in ideas . . . the best test of truth is the power of the thought to get itself accepted in the competition of the market").

Thus, we do not think this passage from *Gertz* was intended to create a wholesale defamation exemption for anything that might be labeled "opinion." . . . (The "marketplace of ideas" origin of this passage "points strongly to the view that the 'opinions' held to be constitutionally protected were the sort of thing that could be corrected by discussion"). Not only would such an interpretation be contrary to the tenor and context of the passage, but it would also ignore the fact that expressions of "opinion" may often imply an assertion of objective fact.

If a speaker says, "In my opinion John Jones is a liar," he implies a knowledge of facts which lead to the conclusion that Jones told an untruth. Even if the speaker states the facts upon which he bases his opinion, if those facts are either incorrect or incomplete, or if his assessment of them is erroneous, the statement may still imply a false assertion of fact. Simply couching such statements in terms of opinion does not dispel these implications; and the statement, "In my opinion Jones is a liar," can cause as much damage to reputation as the statement, "Jones is a liar." As Judge Friendly aptly stated: "[It] would be destructive of the law of libel if a writer could escape liability for accusations of [defamatory conduct] simply by using, explicitly or implicitly, the words 'I think.'" It is worthy of note that, at common law, even the privilege of fair comment did not extend to "a false statement of fact, whether it was expressly stated or implied from an expression of opinion."

. . . [R]espondents do not really contend that a statement such as, "In my opinion John Jones is a liar," should be protected by a separate privilege for "opinion" under the First Amendment. But they do contend that in every defamation case the First Amendment mandates an inquiry into whether a statement is "opinion" or "fact," and that only the latter statements may be actionable. They propose that a number of factors developed by the lower courts (in what we hold was a mistaken reliance on the *Gertz* dictum) be considered in deciding which is which. But we think the "'breathing space'" which "'freedoms of expression require in order to survive'" is adequately secured by existing constitutional doctrine without the creation of an artificial dichotomy between "opinion" and fact.

Foremost, we think [precedent] stands for the proposition that a statement on matters of public concern must be provable as false before there can be liability under state defamation law, at least in situations, like the present, where a media defendant is involved. Thus, unlike the statement, "In my opinion Mayor Jones is a liar," the statement, "In my opinion Mayor Jones shows his abysmal ignorance by accepting the teachings of Marx and Lenin," would not be actionable. [Precedent] ensures that a statement of opinion relating to matters of public concern which does not contain a provably false factual connotation will receive full constitutional protection. . . .

We are not persuaded that, in addition to these protections, an additional separate constitutional privilege for "opinion" is required to ensure the freedom of expression guaranteed by the First Amendment. The dispositive question in the present case then becomes whether a reasonable factfinder could conclude that the statements in the Diadiun column imply an assertion that petitioner Milkovich perjured himself in a judicial proceeding. We think this question must be answered in the affirmative. As the Ohio Supreme Court itself observed, "The clear impact in some nine sentences and a caption is that [Milkovich] 'lied at the hearing after . . . having given his solemn oath to tell the truth.'" This is not the sort of loose, figurative, or hyperbolic language which would negate the impression that the writer was seriously maintaining that petitioner committed the crime of perjury. Nor does the general tenor of the article negate this impression.

We also think the connotation that petitioner committed perjury is sufficiently factual to be susceptible of being proved true or false. A determination whether petitioner lied in this instance can be made on a core of objective evidence by comparing, *inter alia*, petitioner's testimony before the OHSAA board with his subsequent testimony before the trial court. As the *Scott* court noted regarding the plaintiff in that case, "Whether or not H. Don Scott did indeed perjure himself is certainly verifiable by a perjury action with evidence adduced from the transcripts and witnesses present at the hearing. Unlike a subjective assertion, the averred defamatory language is an articulation of an objectively verifiable event." So too with petitioner Milkovich.

[Previous] decisions . . . establishing First Amendment protection for defendants in defamation actions surely demonstrate the Court's recognition of the Amendment's vital guarantee of free and uninhibited discussion of public issues. But there is also another side to the equation; we have regularly acknowledged the "important social values which underlie the law of defamation," and recognized that "[s]ociety has a pervasive and strong interest in preventing and redressing attacks upon reputation." . . .

We believe our decision in the present case holds the balance true. The judgment of the Ohio Court of Appeals is reversed, and the case is remanded for further proceedings not inconsistent with this opinion.

Reversed.

Modern cellphones are not just another technological convenience. With all they contain and all they may reveal, they hold for many Americans "the privacies of life." The fact that technology now allows an individual to carry such information in his hand does not make the information any less worthy of the protection for which the Founders fought.

—**Supreme Court Chief Justice John Roberts**[1]

In a recent U.S. Supreme Court ruling about cellphone privacy, Chief Justice John Roberts remarked, "The proverbial visitor from Mars might conclude [cellphones] were an important feature of human anatomy."[2]

6

PROTECTING PRIVACY
Conflicts Between the Press, the Government, and the Right to Privacy

SUPPOSE...

... police, in two unrelated incidents, stop two men and, without a warrant, search their cellphones. In the first case involving a routine traffic stop, the information taken from the phone ties the man to a gang and to a gang-related shooting. In the second case, the cellphone contents connect the man, arrested for trying to sell drugs, to a specific apartment. When the police search the apartment, they find illegal drugs, a weapon and cash. Based on this evidence gained through the information collected through the warrantless search of his flip phone, the man is sentenced to more than 20 years in prison.

In court, both men argued that the police search of their phones without a warrant violated their Fourth Amendment right against "unreasonable searches and seizures." Does the Fourth Amendment protect the contents of cellphones from warrantless searches? Does the Fourth Amendment protect the privacy of cellphones, or is police review of the digital photo gallery on a smartphone found in a suspect's pockets the legal equivalent of a routine search through a suspect's pockets? More broadly, how has technology changed society's understanding of a "reasonable expectation of privacy"? Look for the answers to these questions when you read the discussion of *Riley v. California* in this chapter and an excerpt of the case decision at the end of the chapter.

Americans have been concerned about their privacy since the United States' inception. The U.S. Constitution reflects this. For example, the framers adopted the Fourth Amendment, protecting "the right of the people to be secure in their persons, houses, papers, and effects, against unreasonable searches and seizures."[3] The U.S. Constitution, state and federal laws and court decisions offer some limited privacy protection. Although the word "privacy" is not in the federal Constitution, the U.S. Supreme Court has said the Constitution protects certain privacy rights.[4] The Court said the word "liberty" in the 14th Amendment—"[N]or shall any State deprive any person of life, liberty, or property, without due process of law"—includes personal privacy.[5] Additionally, the Constitution includes the Third, Fourth and Fifth Amendments protecting different aspects of personal privacy.[6]

State and federal governments have adopted statutes protecting privacy. Most of these laws stop government agencies from providing confidential information without an individual's permission. In recent decades, federal agencies have also started to play a greater role in protecting privacy. The Federal Trade Commission protects consumers and promotes competition. Today, the FTC has the power to police companies' data security practices, and it enforces various laws that address data security and personal privacy.

PRIVACY LAW'S DEVELOPMENT

The use of tort law—in civil law, a tort is an injury one person or entity inflicts on another—to sue the media for invading privacy is a relatively new idea. Although libel has been recognized for four centuries, the notion that courts or legislatures should protect privacy rights is only about 130 years old. Concerns about the press delving into

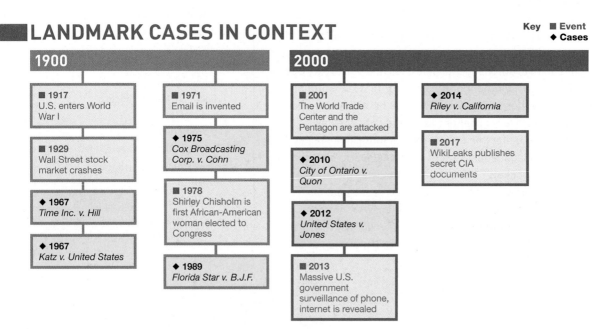

LANDMARK CASES IN CONTEXT

Key ■ Event
◆ Cases

1900

■ **1917**
U.S. enters World War I

■ **1929**
Wall Street stock market crashes

◆ **1967**
Time Inc. v. Hill

◆ **1967**
Katz v. United States

■ **1971**
Email is invented

◆ **1975**
Cox Broadcasting Corp. v. Cohn

■ **1978**
Shirley Chisholm is first African-American woman elected to Congress

◆ **1989**
Florida Star v. B.J.F.

2000

■ **2001**
The World Trade Center and the Pentagon are attacked

◆ **2010**
City of Ontario v. Quon

◆ **2012**
United States v. Jones

■ **2013**
Massive U.S. government surveillance of phone, internet is revealed

◆ **2014**
Riley v. California

■ **2017**
WikiLeaks publishes secret CIA documents

individuals' private lives date back at least to the 19th century in the United States, but it took two Boston lawyers to put privacy on the legal map.[7] Samuel Warren and his law partner, then– future Supreme Court Justice Louis Brandeis, wrote an article for the Harvard Law Review—perhaps the country's most prestigious academic law journal—titled "The Right to Privacy."[8] Published in 1890, the article argued that human dignity required protecting individual privacy. Warren and Brandeis knew that no statutes shielded people's private lives from prying journalists, but the lawyers contended that the common law should recognize privacy rights.[9] The article elaborated for the first time a legal theory as to why the courts should recognize a right to privacy, and it proved influential when the Supreme Court eventually recognized a right to privacy based in the U.S. Constitution and its underlying principles.

U.S. Supreme Court Justice Louis Brandeis.

During the seven decades after Warren and Brandeis' article, courts in a few states accepted a common law right of privacy, and several other states adopted laws protecting privacy.[10] Sixty years ago, William Prosser, a torts expert and law school dean, published an article trying to clarify the conflicting state statutes that had emerged over the years.[11] Prosser suggested that states divide privacy law into four categories: false light, appropriation, intrusion and private facts. Courts and state legislatures adopted and continue to use Prosser's categories, but not all states allow plaintiffs to sue for each of the four privacy torts. Additionally, the appropriation tort currently includes two different torts: commercialization and right to publicity.

In 2017, 34 states recognize the false light tort, and 10 have rejected it; 46 states recognize private facts, and four have rejected that doctrine; 42 states recognize the intrusion tort, while two have rejected it; and 46 states recognize appropriation torts, while four states have not had the opportunity to rule on the issue. The District of Columbia and the U.S. Virgin Islands both recognize all four privacy torts, while Puerto Rico only recognizes appropriation.[12]

Only living individuals may sue for three of the privacy torts: intrusion, private facts and false light.[13] Like a person's reputation in a libel case, privacy is considered a personal right. The dead do not have personal rights. Also, businesses, associations, unions and other groups do not have personal rights and most often cannot sue for a privacy tort.[14] Only individuals may sue for appropriation in many states. But a few states allow businesses, nonprofit organizations and associations to bring appropriation lawsuits. Additionally, in many states, the right of publicity is extended to heirs.

FALSE LIGHT

False light is a first cousin to libel. It exists in some states because not all false statements are defamatory. The false light tort includes statements both disparaging and flattering.

Libel protects reputation—a person's good name. In contrast, false light compensates for the emotional distress a false report causes. An article making a person appear to be

false light A privacy tort that involves making a person seem in the public eye to be someone he or she is not. Several states do not allow false light suits.

⦿ POINTS OF LAW

The Four Privacy Torts

1. *False light:* Intentionally or recklessly publicizing false information a reasonable person would find highly offensive
2. *Appropriation:* Using another's name or likeness for advertising or other commercial purposes without permission (Appropriation includes two different torts, commercialization and right of publicity.)
3. *Intrusion:* Intentionally intruding on another's solitude or seclusion
4. *Private facts:* Publicizing private, embarrassing information

someone he or she is not, even if it does not injure the person's reputation, may be grounds for a false light suit.[15] For example, an unauthorized biography said that a former baseball player was a war hero, but he was not. The book said the player won a medal for outstanding heroism, but he did not. If the player sued the author and the publisher, would he sue for libel? No, instead the player might sue for false light. Warren Spahn, a Hall of Fame pitcher, did just that and won the case.[16]

Some state courts say the false light tort is too similar to defamation and refuse to recognize it. They also say false light is so vague it encroaches on First Amendment rights. Some courts do not want to consider lawsuits based on content that makes people appear better than they really are. California sees false light and libel as such close relatives that a false light plaintiff must prove reputational injury.[17] A number of courts allow a plaintiff to sue for both defamation and false light based on the same facts.

Plaintiff's Case

Most states recognizing false light require a plaintiff to prove (1) the material was published, (2) the plaintiff was identified, (3) the published material was false or created a false impression, (4) the statements or pictures put the plaintiff in a false light that would be highly offensive to a reasonable person and (5) the defendant knew the material was false or recklessly disregarded its falsity.[18] Only individuals can bring a false light suit.[19]

Publication. The false light tort requires material to have been widely distributed to the public generally or to a large segment of the community.[20] An oral comment to a few people does not amount to publicity for the false light tort. Courts in a few states allow publication to be proved by dissemination to just one person or a few people.[21] For these courts, that smaller group must have a special relationship with the plaintiff so the plaintiff would be highly offended if the group saw or heard the publication.[22]

Identification. The plaintiff must prove the material in question was about her or him. The courts of some states, such as California, define identification for false light just as they do for libel. It is sufficient if one or more persons say the article identified the plaintiff.[23] Most courts hold that because the publication requirement means many people must be exposed to the story, a large segment of the public must reasonably believe the false material refers to the plaintiff.

Falsity. Published material supporting a false light suit must be false or imply false information. If the publication is true, it cannot be grounds for a false light suit even if the material emotionally upsets the plaintiff. Minor errors ordinarily do not make a story sufficiently incorrect to meet the falsity standard.

Some courts hold that true facts can lead to false implications if the defendant intended that result. For example, The New York Times published a story implying that a businessman named Robert Howard might be using an alias and really was another person, Howard Finkelstein, a convicted felon. The story included only true statements: Records showed that Finkelstein used the name Robert Howard; Howard denied he was Finkelstein, yet rumors circulated saying he might be. A jury found that the reporter did not libel Howard because the story did not absolutely say he was Finkelstein. A federal appellate court said the story's implication that the businessman might be the felon could sustain a false light suit.[24] However, there must be a clear connection between the statements leading to a false light suit and the implied falsehood the plaintiff claims.

Highly Offensive. At a false light trial, the **fact finder**—the jury, if there is one, or the judge—must determine whether the published material would be highly offensive to a reasonable person. There are no definite standards. Defining "highly offensive" is a very subjective task. It is made even more difficult because a publication may be highly offensive even though it is positive. Some legal scholars try to clarify the term "highly offensive" by putting false light cases into three categories: **embellishment, distortion** and **fictionalization**. Categorizing may highlight the false statements' offensive nature.

fact finder In a trial, a judge or the jury determining which facts presented in evidence are accurate.

embellishment Occurs when false material is added to otherwise true facts.

distortion Occurs when facts are omitted or the context in which material is published makes an otherwise accurate story appear false.

fictionalization Occurs when some truth, such as a person's name or identifying characteristics, is part of a largely fictional piece.

⊙ POINTS OF LAW

False Light

Plaintiff's Case

- Publicizing
- False facts
- About an identified individual
- That would be highly offensive to a reasonable person
- With intent or recklessness (according to the Supreme Court) or negligence if the plaintiff is a private person (according to some courts)

Defense

- Libel defenses

● REAL WORLD LAW

Fake News and False Light

Laura Hunter
@LauraHunterCDR

Conservative News Journalist

📍 Las Vegas, NV

🔗 conservativedailypost.com

📅 Joined August 2016

Can the misleading use of a photograph to endorse a conservative website constitute false light? In 2017, the reigning Miss World winner sued Gravitas Advertising and others for using her photo without permission and creating a fake Facebook profile that suggested she was a spokesperson for the Conservative Daily Review website.[1]

According to Laura Hunter's complaint, the top Google search result for her name was the fake Facebook page, which had nearly 900,000 followers and likes in early 2017. The fake Facebook page posted multiple articles each day that redirected readers to conservativedailypost.com. "They have stolen her identity and used her as a spokeswoman for and purported author of content and viewpoints antithetical to her own beliefs," according to her legal complaint. Hunter also said the website is "dedicated to spreading false information about American politics; it is part of the epidemic of 'fake news' sites that plagued the 2016 presidential election."[2]

One First Amendment attorney noted that the case is based on the fact that Hunter is not conservative and is in no way affiliated with the website. He predicted the false light claim could survive in court.[3]

1. Jack Greiner, *Fighting Fake News in Court*, Cincinnati.com, March 16, 2017, www.cincinnati.com/story/money/2017/03/16/fighting-fake-news-court/98982054/.
2. Mike Heuer, *Ms. World Says Right-Wing Facebook Page Is Fake*, CourthouseNewsService.com, Feb. 24, 2017, www.courthousenews.com/ms-world-says-right-wing-facebook-page-is-fake/.
3. Greiner, *supra* note 1.

A story is embellished when false material is added to otherwise true facts. For example, a series of newspaper columns told a true story of a mother giving up a baby for adoption, the baby being adopted, a court giving the natural father custody four years later and the father hiring a psychologist to help the child adjust to a new home. One column falsely said the psychologist "has readily admitted that she sees her job as doing whatever the natural parents instruct her to do." A jury could find it highly offensive to a reasonable person to suggest a psychologist would ignore her professional commitments, a court ruled.[25]

Distortion occurs when facts are omitted or the context in which material is published makes an otherwise accurate story appear false. For example, a young woman consented to having a photographer take her picture for his portfolio. A magazine later used the picture to illustrate a story headlined "In Cold Blood—An Exposé of the Baltimore Teen Murders." The accompanying article said the high murder rate among the city's African-American teenagers was due to drug abuse and poor economic conditions. Used in other circumstances, the photo might not have led to a lawsuit. This context, however, implied that the young woman was poor, abused drugs or perhaps even was connected to a murder.[26]

Fictionalization in false light occurs when some truth, such as a person's name or identifying characteristics, is part of a largely fictional piece. In one case, a supermarket tabloid newspaper published a picture of 97-year-old Arkansas resident Nellie Mitchell to illustrate a story with the headline, "Pregnancy Forced Granny to Quit Work at Age 101." The story was a fictional account of an Australian woman who left her paper route at the age of 101 because she became pregnant during an extramarital affair with a rich client. Mitchell, in fact, delivered newspapers in her hometown for nearly 50 years. Mitchell won her false light suit and, after the newspaper's appeals, was awarded $1 million in damages.[27]

Fault. Decades ago, the U.S. Supreme Court decided its only two false light cases: *Time Inc. v. Hill* and *Cantrell v. Forest City Publishing Co.* Despite private individual plaintiffs in both cases, not public officials or public figures, the Court held that they had to prove actual malice to win.

The seven Hill family members sued Time Inc., publisher of Life magazine, for a story based on the family's experience of being held hostage by escaped convicts. News stories across the country reported that three prison escapees held the Hills hostage for 19 hours. The convicts did not harm the Hills, and the family later said they were treated with respect. The family moved from the Philadelphia suburbs to Connecticut, trying to return to a private life. Within a year of the incident, a novel about the fictional Hilliard family of four, held hostage by escaped convicts, was published. In the novel, the convicts beat the fictional father and son and subjected the daughter to verbal sexual insults. The novel was turned into a play, portraying the same fictional family and violent convicts. Life published an article about the play, including pictures of actors staging scenes in the Hills' Philadelphia house. The Hills claimed that the text and accompanying photographs suggested the convicts had treated the real Hill family as ruthlessly as the convicts treated the fictional hostages. The Hills said the convicts had treated them well. Implying they had been treated badly put the family in a false light. The Hills sued and won in the New York state courts. Richard Nixon, who was elected U.S. president in 1968, represented Time Inc., in its appeal to the U.S. Supreme Court.

The Supreme Court reversed, saying the jury should have been told that the Hills could win only if they proved actual malice.[28] The First Amendment protects the press from being sued for negligent misstatements when reporting stories of public interest, the Court reasoned. After pursuing their case for more than 10 years, the Hills decided not to return to trial court. At trial, they would have to show that Life either knew the article and photographs were false or recklessly disregarded whether they were false.

In the *Cantrell* case, decided seven years after *Hill*, the Court again said a private plaintiff had to prove actual malice. A bridge in West Virginia collapsed, killing 43 people, including Margaret Cantrell's husband. Five months later, Cleveland Plain Dealer reporter Joe Eszterhas went with a photographer to the Cantrell home. Eszterhas talked with the Cantrell children, and the photographer took dozens of pictures. Margaret Cantrell was not at home while Eszterhas was at her residence. According to the Supreme Court, Eszterhas' article about the bridge disaster in The Plain Dealer stressed the family's abject poverty. The children's old, ill-fitting clothes and the deteriorating condition of their home were detailed in both the text and the accompanying photographs. Eszterhas used the Cantrell family to illustrate the impact of the bridge collapse on the lives of the people in the Point Pleasant area.

The Supreme Court upheld a jury verdict in the Cantrell family's favor because the trial judge had told the jury actual malice was part of the plaintiff's false light case. The Court said there was sufficient evidence to show that portions of the article were false and were published with knowing falsity or reckless disregard for the truth. Cantrell and the Hills were not public officials, limited-purpose public figures or universal public figures. They were private people who, the Court said, had to prove in their false light suits that the media defendants had acted with actual malice.

Lower courts are supposed to follow U.S. Supreme Court rulings. But state courts are divided about requiring private persons to prove actual malice in false light cases. Courts in at least five states and the District of Columbia have applied *Gertz v. Robert Welch Inc.* (discussed in Chapter 4) to false light cases, as they suggest the Supreme Court would if it heard another false light appeal.[29] These courts would require only that a private individual prove negligence in a false light suit, not malice. Courts in at least 11 other states follow the Supreme Court dictates in *Hill* and *Cantrell*, requiring all false light plaintiffs to show actual malice.[30]

Defenses

Because not all state courts recognize the false light tort, parts of it remain in flux. However, many courts say that if a false light plaintiff proves all elements of his case, a media defendant may use the libel defenses to defeat the claim.[31]

People with absolute privilege if sued for libel—those involved in judicial proceedings or government meetings, certain public officials and others discussed in Chapter 5—also are absolutely privileged in false light suits. The press has a conditional privilege to report what people with absolute privilege and in absolutely privileged documents say. It also is likely in false light cases that the media may use a defense of fair and accurate reporting about government meetings and activities.[32]

Truth is a defense to a false light suit. A defendant can prove truth by showing that the story is substantially true. If a person agrees to an interview in which she reveals highly offensive false facts or agrees to an article containing those false facts being published, consent will be an effective defense. The few courts deciding the issue disagree about whether opinion is a defense for a false light suit.[33]

States disagree about the appropriate statute of limitations for false light suits. A state may apply the general statute of limitations for torts, the same one used for battery or trespass, for example. Or the statute of limitations for privacy suits may be based on the time period for filing a libel suit. The statute of limitations period for libel suits usually is shorter than the general torts limitation period.[34]

More recently, some appellate courts have also applied anti-SLAPP statutes to false light claims. As noted in Chapter 5, anti-SLAPP statutes are used to challenge lawsuits meant to chill free speech. In 2016, the Ninth Circuit Court of Appeals said California's anti-SLAPP statute applied to a lawsuit filed against the producers and distributers of the film "The Hurt Locker." Army sergeant Jeffrey Sarver alleged that the main character in the film was based on him, and he sued for misappropriation, invasion of privacy, defamation, false light, intentional infliction of emotional distress and other torts.

With respect to defamation and false light, Sarver alleged that the film's depiction of his work with improvised explosive devices during the Iraq War was false. The Ninth Circuit applied the anti-SLAPP statute to the lawsuit noting that the focus on the Iraq War was an issue of public concern.[35] California's anti-SLAPP statute is broadly applicable, so the Ninth Circuit applied it to all of Sarver's claims. "'The Hurt Locker' film and the narrative of its central character Will James spoke directly to issues of a public nature," the court wrote. Additionally, the film is "speech that was fully protected by the First Amendment, which safeguards the storytellers and artists who take the raw materials of life and transform them into art, such as movies."[36] California's anti-SLAPP statute is one of the strongest in the country, so the appellate courts' application of the statute to a range of privacy claims in this circumstance might not be replicated in other jurisdictions.[37]

Summit Entertainment/Photofest

In 2015, an appeals court held that "The Hurt Locker" was transformative. An army sergeant said Jeremy Renner's character was based on him.

APPROPRIATION

Appropriation, generally using a person's name, picture or voice without permission for commercial or trade purposes, is an area of privacy tort law that is currently a "hot mess," according to one privacy law expert.[38] Why? Because the Supreme Court has decided only one appropriation case (*Zacchini v. Scripps-Howard Broadcasting Co.*, which is discussed later in this section), and that case predates many of the modern technologies and media platforms to which the Supreme Court has since given First Amendment protection. State courts take a range of approaches to resolve appropriation cases, often based on whether the alleged appropriation arises in a commercial context (see Chapter 12 for more on commercial speech) or another First Amendment context. As Chapter 3 noted, the courts often apply strict scrutiny, rather than a balancing of interests, when reviewing cases involving the media. However, many courts apply a balancing approach to resolve some right of publicity claims.[39] Before addressing these issues, the next section will define the commercialization and right of publicity torts as well as what plaintiffs are required to prove.

Commercialization and Right of Publicity

Appropriation includes two different torts: **commercialization** and the **right of publicity**. Most people do not want their names or pictures to be in advertisements because they want to remain private. The appropriation tort used to protect people who want privacy is called "commercialization" or "misappropriation." Commercialization, the word this chapter uses, prohibits using another person's name or likeness for commercial purposes without permission. No state has refused to allow appropriation suits, though courts in some have not yet ruled on the issue.[40]

Some people, however, want their names and pictures to be publicized and they want to control when, how and where their names and pictures will be used for advertising and other commercial purposes. They also want to be paid for giving their permission. Courts often refer to this part of the appropriation tort as the "right of publicity."[41]

appropriation
Using a person's name, picture, likeness, voice or identity for commercial or trade purposes without permission.

commercialization
The appropriation tort used to protect people who want privacy; prohibits using another person's name or likeness for commercial purposes without permission.

right of publicity
The appropriation tort protecting a celebrity's right to have his or her name, picture, likeness, voice and identity used for commercial or trade purposes only with permission.

New York state adopted the country's first appropriation law in 1903.[42] Two years later, Georgia became the first state to recognize appropriation as a common law privacy tort. A federal appeals court judge, Jerome Frank, first used the phrase "right of publicity" nearly 60 years ago.[43] The court ruled that professional baseball players had a right to earn money when their names were used on baseball cards. The players' goal was to control when their names were used publicly—and to be paid when that happened. Courts generally find that everyone has both a right to protect his or her privacy and a right to decide when his or her name or picture may or may not be used commercially by others.[44] The commercial value of a celebrity's name or picture, though, will be much greater than that of a relatively unknown individual. The court also said a right of publicity could be transferred, as a car can be sold. But the right of privacy cannot be transferred.

Although both commercialization and the right of publicity prevent the use of someone's name, picture, likeness, voice or identity for advertising or other commercial purposes without permission, they differ in two important ways. One difference is that commercialization protects an individual's dignity connected with personal privacy, while the right of publicity protects the monetary value of using well-known individuals' names and pictures.

A second difference is that courts generally consider commercialization to be a personal right, one that does not survive a person's death. However, the right of publicity may be considered a property right, not a personal right. Just as a person may say who gets his or her car after he or she dies—through a will or by state law—a person may choose who will control her right of publicity after death.[45] In many states, the right of publicity survives after a person's death.[46] The right may last for a specific number of years (from 20 to 100 years, depending on the state), as long as the right is used, or, in at least one state, forever.[47]

Recently, a handful of state legislatures have explored efforts to extend or alter the right of publicity after death. Maryland, Massachusetts and New Hampshire failed to extend the application of their statutes to 70 years beyond death, but Indiana lawmakers

● POINTS OF LAW

Appropriation

The appropriation tort may be divided into two torts:

1. *Commercialization:* Applying to someone who wants to remain private and unknown except to family and friends. Using this person's name, picture, likeness or voice for advertising or other commercial purposes without permission is commercialization. It is invading this person's privacy, causing emotional distress.

2. *Right of publicity:* Applying to someone who wants to be known far and wide, to be a celebrity—a musician, athlete, movie star or television personality. Using this person's name, picture, likeness, voice or identity— or a look-alike or sound-alike—for advertising or other commercial purposes without permission invades this person's right of publicity. It diminishes the person's economic value.

passed an amendment to the state's existing statute and applied post-mortem publicity rights retroactively.[48] The law exempts people who became famous as a result of a criminal charge or conviction. Some federal courts have recently resolved issues of jurisdiction in postmortem right of publicity cases. For example, a few years ago the Ninth Circuit Court of Appeals ruled that Marilyn Monroe's publicity rights died with her more than 50 years ago because she lived in New York at the time of her death and New York does not recognize a right of publicity after death. Her estate argued that because she died in California that state's postmortem right of publicity statute should apply.[49] The trend in similar cases is to apply the law of the state of primary residence of the celebrity at the time of death.[50]

At the state level, in 2014, an Arizona appeals court held that the right of publicity is a property right that can be transferred to a descendant.[51] After the death of Prince in 2016, the Minnesota legislature tried to push through a right of publicity bill that extended postmortem rights because of concerns about a lack of protection for Prince's estate. The bill was pulled weeks later after the bill's sponsor decided it was more prudent to leave the matter for state courts to decide.[52] In California, a state appeals court ruled that the state's right to publicity began when the state enacted a "deceased personality" publicity statute 20 years ago and allowed the second family of Bing Crosby to assert a publicity right dating back to 1996.[53]

In recent years, rapper 50 Cent has filed multiple lawsuits in multiple jurisdictions to protect his right of publicity.

Plaintiff's Case

To win a commercialization or right of publicity case, a plaintiff must prove her or his name or likeness was used for advertising or other commercial purposes without permission. The plaintiff also must show the commercial use was of and concerning her or him and was widely distributed.

Name or Likeness. Appropriation occurs most obviously when a person's name, picture or likeness—clearly identifying the person—is used commercially without permission. Having the same name that is used in an advertisement is usually not enough to show identification. Something in the ad must show the ad was of and concerning that plaintiff.[54] A name can sometimes be the primary basis of a claim. For example, in 2016, Hasbro and Fox News anchor Harris Faulkner settled a case in New Jersey after Faulkner accused the toy maker of violating her right of publicity. A New Jersey court refused to dismiss Faulkner's claim, based largely on the use of her name. Hasbro had named a toy hamster from its "Littlest Pet Shop" line Harris Faulkner. Legal experts predicted that arguments claiming the hamster looked like Faulkner would probably fail, but suggested that Faulkner had a strong claim on a name-based right of publicity.[55]

It is not sufficient that the commercial use only hints at the plaintiff's identity or may remind some people of the plaintiff.[56] Rather, there must be reasonable grounds for identifying the plaintiff. What if the name used is not a person's real name? In one

Fox News anchor Harris Faulkner; Hasbro's Harris Faulkner hamster.

Mike Coppola/Getty Images, Hasbro

case, an Oldsmobile commercial used the name Lew Alcindor. Kareem Abdul-Jabbar sued because he had not given permission. Oldsmobile said Alcindor no longer was Abdul-Jabbar's name, so he had no right to protect it. A federal appellate court disagreed. Abdul-Jabbar was named Ferdinand Lewis ("Lew") Alcindor at birth. He played college and several years of professional basketball under that name. When he converted to Islam, he took the name Kareem Abdul-Jabbar, later legally adopting that as his name. The court said the name Lew Alcindor still identified Abdul-Jabbar.[57]

In 2016, a court in Illinois dismissed a right of publicity case brought by a Guinness World Records record holder against Wendy's. The fast-food chain ran a kid's meal promotion with Guinness in 2013. All kid's meals included one of six Guinness-themed toys, one of which was a footbag. An accompanying card listed Guinness facts about the footbag, including this: "How many times in a row can you kick this footbag without it hitting the ground? Back in 1997, Ted Martin made his world record of 63,326 kicks in a little less than nine hours!"[58] The court said that the use of Martin's name on the instruction card did not amount to an endorsement and did not violate Martin's right of publicity. Rather, the instruction card was part of a product, not an advertisement, and it never suggested that Martin endorsed anything.

In a recent case involving the rapper 50 Cent, a court held that his likeness was invoked for commercial purpose when a website posted reproduced and screened photos of the rapper in its masthead. The court said that even though the images were of poor visual quality, visitors to the website could still see that the pictures were of 50 Cent.[59] When an advertisement uses a person who looks like a celebrity, can the celebrity prove identification? An actor looking very much like New Orleans chef Paul Prudhomme urged television viewers to buy Folgers coffee. A federal district court said people could be confused, justifiably believing the real Prudhomme endorsed Folgers.[60]

sound-alike
Someone whose voice sounds like another person's voice. Sound-alikes may not be used for commercial or trade purposes without permission or a disclaimer.

Voice. Individuals' voices are protected against use for commercial or trade purposes. Further, advertisers may not use **sound-alikes**, just as they may not use look-alikes, without permission or a disclaimer. Singer and actress Bette Midler refused to allow Ford Motor Co. to use her hit recording "Do You Want to Dance?" in a commercial. Ford's advertising agency then hired a member of Midler's backup singing group. The singer was told to imitate Midler's rendition of the song. After the radio commercial aired, a number of people told Midler they thought she had performed in the ad. The commercial failed to say Midler was not the singer. Midler sued Ford and its advertising agency. The defendants had appropriated part of Midler's identity, a federal appellate court said.[61] The court said a "voice is as distinctive and personal as a face" and "is one of the most palpable ways identity is manifested."

⬤ POINTS OF LAW

Appropriation

Plaintiff's Case

- Using a person's name, picture, likeness (such as a drawing or avatar), voice or identity
- For advertising or other commercial uses
- Without permission

Defenses

- News
- Public domain
- First Amendment
- Incidental use
- Advertising for a mass medium
- Consent

Identity. Do people have characteristics beyond their face or voice that the appropriation tort should protect? Game show hostess Vanna White sued Samsung Electronics for appropriation after the company ran a series of magazine ads showing its products in futuristic settings. One ad pictured a Samsung VCR on a game show set. A robot standing by a letter board wore an evening gown, jewelry and a long blond wig. The advertising agency wanted the scene to look like the set from "Wheel of Fortune." A federal appellate court agreed that it did, and said the ad appropriated White's identity.[62] Although the ad did not use White's name, picture, likeness or voice, it nonetheless used White, the court said.

Two actors from the television show "Cheers" brought a lawsuit that extended the rule from the Vanna White court decision. A company wanted to install in airport bars a set that looked like the scene from the television program "Cheers." Two animatronic figures named Hank and Bob were to sit at the bar, and customers could have a drink sitting next to the figures. Paramount, which owned the "Cheers" copyright, granted permission. However, George Wendt, who played Norm on "Cheers," and John Ratzenberger, who played Cliff, refused to give consent. Wendt and Ratzenberger sued, claiming the company would appropriate their identities without permission.

The animatronic figures resembled Wendt's and Ratzenberger's characters in their size, clothing and sitting positions at the bar. But the figures' faces were different from the actors'. A federal appellate court said the figures sufficiently resembled the actors and that Wendt and Ratzenberger could bring a suit claiming appropriation of their identities.[63] The parties settled the case out of court.[64]

Actors impersonating celebrities in noncommercial or non-advertising situations, such as in a satire or parody, are not appropriating the celebrities' likenesses or voices. The First Amendment protects such expression.[65] But the Vanna White case shows that protection does not extend to impersonations in advertisements or other commercial situations. The appellate court specifically rejected Samsung's contention that the robot ad was meant as a satire.

Defenses

Even if a plaintiff can prove that his or her name or likeness was used for commercial purposes without permission, there are several defenses for appropriation.

Newsworthiness. Newsworthiness is the most common defense. Media publish newsworthy material despite having a commercial purpose. As one federal court said, "Speech is protected even though it is carried in a form that is sold for profit."[66] Courts have defined the word "newsworthy" broadly. Courts see a bright line between commercial use and trade use on one side, and nearly everything else on the other side. The newsworthiness defense sometimes shows up in unlikely cases. For example, in 2014, rapper 50 Cent argued that his creation of an explicit sex video directed at rival rapper Ricky Ross was newsworthy. A New York state court disagreed, specifically noting that the posting of explicit sex tapes is not newsworthy.[67]

Judges do not carefully analyze content to determine whether it is newsworthy. Rather, if the content is not on the commercial/trade-use side of the bright line, it will be found

● REAL WORLD LAW

Facebook's Sponsored Stories

AP Photo/Jeff Chiu

Recently, Facebook settled a class action lawsuit tied to its "Sponsored Story" advertising system. Five plaintiffs sued Facebook for misappropriation in a California state court. They argued that placing their usernames and profile pictures into Sponsored Stories on friends' Facebook pages violated their right of publicity because Facebook did not obtain their consent. For example, plaintiff Angel Fraley "liked" Rosetta Stone's Facebook profile in order to receive a free software demonstration. Subsequently, Fraley's friends' Facebook pages showed a Sponsored Story advertisement with the Rosetta Stone logo and her "like" for Rosetta Stone.[1]

The terms of the settlement included no acknowledgement of wrongdoing on the part of Facebook, which denied liability. Facebook agreed to pay $20 million into a fund that will pay out up to $10 per person for claims from people who appeared in a Sponsored Story.[2]

1. Kashmir Hill, *Facebook Sends Most of America an Offer to Settle a Class Action Lawsuit for $10*, ABOVE THE LAW, Jan. 22, 2013, abovethelaw.com/tag/fraley-v-facebook/.
2. GCG, *Fraley v. Facebook Inc.: Overview of the Proposed Settlement*, Mar. 28, 2013, www.fraleyfacebook settlement.com.

● REAL WORLD LAW

The Proliferation of Mugshot Websites

Michael Ochs/Getty

Frank Sinatra's mugshot from an arrest in 1938 for having an affair with a married woman.

When a news media outlet publishes a mugshot (the police photo of a person's face), it is considered newsworthy and not a violation of privacy. Additionally, mugshots are usually considered public records, not private. In the past few years, dozens of for-profit mugshot websites have emerged, posting publicly available mugshots for widespread viewing. Some of the websites charge people money to have their mugshots removed. Others try to attract advertising to their websites for commercial gain and develop a following on social media.[1]

Recently, some private (noncelebrity) plaintiffs have argued that those websites violate their right of publicity. A federal court in Pennsylvania dismissed one such case for lack of evidence but left open the question of whether mugshot websites constitute a form of a news report.[2]

By 2017, many states had passed laws prohibiting companies that publish mugshots from charging fees to remove or correct information. Currently, a federal class action lawsuit is pending against Mugshots.com and a related company. The lawsuit alleges that Mugshots.com intentionally posts incomplete information so that a sister website can solicit fees from people seeking to make corrections.[3]

---

1. David Kravets, *Shamed by Mugshot Sites Arrestees Try Novel Lawsuit*, WIRED, Dec. 12, 2012, www.wired.com/2012/12/mugshot-industry-legal-attack/.
2. Taha v. Bucks County, 9 F. Supp. 3d 490 (E.D. Pa. 2014).
3. Becky Yerak, *Lawsuit: Mug Shot Website Posts Incomplete Records So Sister Site Can Solicit "Takedown" Fees*, CHICAGOTRIBUNE.COM, Mar. 13, 2017, www.chicagotribune.com/business/ct-mug-shot-websites-0312-biz-20170310-story.html.

newsworthy. The U.S. Supreme Court has heard only one appropriation case. The Court's decision, applied to a unique set of facts, rejected a television station's claim that it had a newsworthiness defense to a right of publicity suit. Hugo Zacchini was a human cannonball. A television station recorded 15 seconds of Zacchini's act, including the most critical part—his flight from the cannon to the net—and showed the recording on its news program. People who saw the entire act on television were less likely to attend the performance in person, according to the Court. The Court focused on the economic value of his act. The television station's First Amendment rights were not more important than protecting Zacchini's financial interest in his performance, the Court said.[68]

Public Domain. Courts have held that names and associated information may be widely available to the public and therefore cannot be protected by right of publicity. For example, an online fantasy baseball league operator could use Major League Baseball players' names and statistics without MLB's permission, the U.S. Court of Appeals for the Eighth Circuit ruled.[69] The court said that information is widely available in the public domain. That is,

Bettmann/ Getty Images

The U.S. Supreme Court said human cannonball Hugo Zacchini could win an appropriation lawsuit against a television station that aired only 15 seconds of his performance. The station claimed the newsworthiness defense, but the Court rejected it. The station showed Zacchini's entire act, the Court said, threatening the performance's economic value.

many print, electronic and digital sources provide players' names and statistics, making that information factual rather than personal to the players.

First Amendment. Does the First Amendment protect using a celebrity's name or picture if the use is not commercial? Courts have considered whether merchandise—such as posters, dolls, T-shirts and games—has First Amendment protection.[70] The first case in which a court used the term "right of publicity" involved baseball cards included in bubble gum packages. Players could give a company an exclusive right to use their pictures because a baseball player has a right to exploit the value of his name or likeness, a federal appellate court said.[71]

The First Amendment may protect the satirical use of personal information. The Major League Baseball Players Association sued a company selling baseball cards with recognizable caricatures of baseball players accompanied by satiric comments. For example, the player on one card is named Treasury Bonds, a spoof of Barry Bonds' name.[72] A federal appellate court said the First Amendment fully protects the baseball cards. The cards are "an important form of entertainment and social commentary that deserve First Amendment protection," the court concluded.[73]

Posters are not like satirical baseball cards. Courts most often have decided posters do not have First Amendment protection. Courts found appropriation when posters of singer Elvis Presley, model Christie Brinkley and professional wrestlers were distributed without permission.[74] But courts have also said the First Amendment protects selling posters with pictures of newsworthy individuals or events, such as a poster with a picture of comedian Pat Paulsen when he ran for president and one showing former San Francisco 49ers quarterback Joe Montana celebrating the team's 1990 Super Bowl victory.[75] Courts drew a distinction between merchandise exploiting celebrities' names or likenesses and posters conveying newsworthy information of public interest.

The question of First Amendment protection versus right of publicity is arising more frequently when a well-known person is used in an artistic work. For example, recently a federal judge in New York ruled that hip-hop star Pitbull did not violate actress Lindsay Lohan's right of publicity by including the line "I'm toptoein', to keep flowin', I got it locked up, like Lindsay Lohan" in his hit song "Give Me Everything." Rather, the song is a work of art protected by the First Amendment.[76]

One approach used to resolve this kind of conflict is the artistic relevance test. This test asks whether using a celebrity's name or picture is relevant to a work's artistic purpose. If it is, the First Amendment, which applies to artistic as well as journalistic works, may allow using the celebrity's name without permission. However, consent is needed if the name or celebrity's likeness is used primarily to give the work commercial appeal. For example, Italian movie director Federico Fellini made a film titled "Ginger and Fred." To movie fans, the obvious reference is to the Ginger Rogers and Fred Astaire films. The Fellini movie was about two cabaret dancers who were given the nicknames Ginger and Fred because they imitated Rogers and Astaire. Rogers sued, claiming the movie title infringed on her right to use her name for commercial purposes. In *Rogers v. Grimaldi*, a federal appellate court applied the **artistic relevance test**.[77] The court said Rogers could not win unless the movie title had no artistic relevance to the film itself or misled consumers about the film's contents. The movie's title and contents were artistically related, the court held.

Not all song titles clearly relate to the song's lyrics. For example, the rap duo OutKast recorded a song titled "Rosa Parks." Parks was a major figure during the civil rights struggles of the 1950s and 1960s. In 1955, riding in the middle of a racially segregated Montgomery, Ala., bus, Parks refused to give her seat to a white person and move to the back of the bus, as city law required. Her defiant act spurred a 381-day bus boycott by Montgomery blacks and touched off other boycotts, sit-ins and demonstrations throughout the South.[78]

Applying the *Rogers* test, a federal appellate court concluded that a jury could find the title "Rosa Parks" had no artistic relevance to the lyrics, despite the phrase "move to the back of the bus" being used repeatedly in the chorus. The lyrics, containing profanity and explicit sexual references, only meant that OutKast had recorded a new album, the court concluded. Using Rosa Parks' name in the title also was misleading, the court held. It could make potential consumers believe the song in fact was about Parks, although the lyrics in no way referred to her.

Instead of the *Rogers* artistic relevance test, some courts have used a **transformative use test** to decide whether a challenged work has First Amendment protection against a right of publicity suit.[79] These courts ask whether the new work only copies the original—an artist makes an exact drawing of a celebrity and sells copies of that picture—or instead transforms the original by adding new creative elements. If an artist drawing a caricature exaggerates a person's facial or body features, perhaps for comic effect, the caricature transforms the original—that is, changes the person's actual physical features. The First Amendment protects caricatures that have enough originality.

The California Supreme Court developed the transformative use test in a case involving the Three Stooges.[80] An artist created a charcoal sketch of the Three Stooges, transferred the sketch to T-shirts and lithographs and sold thousands of the items. A company owning the Three Stooges' publicity rights sued.[81] The California court acknowledged the conflict between the artist's First Amendment right to express himself, particularly about public personalities, and the right of celebrities to protect their property and financial interests in their images. The sketch was an expressive work, the court said. Commentary about celebrities is part of a public discussion about public matters.

The court proposed the transformative use test to distinguish protected artistic expression about celebrities from expression that encroaches on the right of publicity. The First Amendment protects a work that adds enough new elements to the original to transform it. Changing the original by giving it a new meaning or a different message justifies First Amendment protection.

artistic relevance test A test to determine whether the use of a celebrity's name, picture, likeness, voice or identity is relevant to a disputed work's artistic purpose. It is used in cases regarding the infringement of a celebrity's right of publicity.

transformative use test A test to determine whether a creator has transformed a person's name, picture, likeness, voice or identity for artistic purposes. If so, the person cannot win a right of publicity suit against the creator.

Transformative works may be satires, news reports or works of fiction or social criticism, the court said. However, the court concluded, "When artistic expression takes the form of a literal depiction or imitation of a celebrity for commercial gain, directly trespassing on the right of publicity without adding significant expression beyond that trespass," the celebrity's rights outweigh First Amendment protections.[82] The court found that the Three Stooges drawing was a "literal, conventional" depiction of the three men, with no discernible transformative elements. Because the drawing did not transform the Three Stooges' pictures, it had no First Amendment protection.

Recently, courts have heard several cases that test the application of the transformative use test to athletes and video games. The most prominent cases, which settled for $60 million after a lengthy appeals process in the Ninth Circuit Court of Appeals, involve three college athletes who filed class action lawsuits against the video game company Electronic Arts as well as the National Collegiate Athletic Association and the Collegiate Licensing Company (now known as IMG College Licensing).[83] Class action lawsuits are filed by individuals acting on behalf of a group with a common legal interest. In 2009, Ed O'Bannon, the star of UCLA's 1995 championship basketball team, and Sam Keller, former quarterback from Arizona State University and the University of Nebraska, argued in a U.S. district court in California that EA's NCAA-themed video games violated their right of publicity because their likenesses were used without compensation.[84] The players noted that the video games depicted every distinctive characteristic of them except their names. At the same time, former Rutgers quarterback Ryan Hart made the same claim in a U.S. district court in New Jersey.[85]

In both cases, EA argued that its First Amendment rights trumped the players' right of publicity. Although the facts in both cases are nearly identical, the lower courts came to different decisions. In California, the court applied the transformative use test and held that EA's use of Keller was not transformative and did not deserve First Amendment protection. In New Jersey, the court also applied the transformative use test but came to the opposite conclusion and ruled in favor of EA. The New Jersey decision critically referenced the California decision, noting that "it is logically inconsistent to consider the setting in which the character sits . . . yet ignore the remainder of the game."[86] The Third Circuit Court of Appeals eventually reversed the district court's summary judgment decision.[87] Both cases settled out of court with agreements to pay millions of dollars to the student athletes named in the class action suits.[88]

On the heels of the settlements, 10 former college football and basketball players filed a similar right of publicity lawsuit in federal court against major broadcast companies, athletic conferences and licensers. Former Vanderbilt University football player Javon Marshall was the lead plaintiff in the lawsuit, which sought damages for the misappropriation of the names, images and likenesses of college athletes in broadcasts and advertisements without their consent.[89] In 2016, the Sixth Circuit affirmed a Tennessee district court ruling, which dismissed the case and noted that a common law right of publicity does not exist in that state.[90]

In 2016, the NCAA appealed the Ninth Circuit's decision in the O'Bannon case to the U.S. Supreme Court, arguing the case was wrongly decided. The Supreme Court declined to hear the case. The NCAA's interest in the ruling stemmed from additional claims that the organization's rules violate antitrust laws by not allowing student athletes compensation for the use of their names and likenesses.[91] Nonetheless, courts still generally are applying the transformative use test to affirm First Amendment rights in lawsuits that involve movies, television and video games. For example, a few years ago the Weinstein Co. prevailed in a lawsuit brought by legendary soul singer Sam Moore who said the film "Soul Men" violated his right of publicity because it told his life story. An appeals court applied the transformative use test and said the film added "significant expressive elements," so it was protected on First Amendment grounds.[92]

The transformative use test can result in First Amendment protection for artists. The California Supreme Court used the test to rule that a comic book artist transformed images of two musicians, Johnny and Edgar Winter.[93] The California Supreme Court said, "An artist depicting a celebrity must contribute something more than a 'merely trivial' variation" of the celebrity's image. The artist "must create something recognizably 'his own'" for a court to find "significant transformative elements" in the artist's work.[94]

Another way to balance the First Amendment and the right of publicity is the **predominant use test**. The question is whether a person's name or image is used more for commercial purposes or substantive expression. The Missouri Supreme Court applied this test in ruling that a comic book creator named a character "Antonio 'Tony Twist' Twistelli" more to sell the comics than for free speech purposes. In the comic, Twistelli was portrayed as an organized crime leader. A real Tony Twist, a former professional hockey player, sued for misuse of his name. A jury awarded $15 million in damages, and the state's high court affirmed the ruling.[95]

Courts have long held that the First Amendment protects using celebrities' names in biographies and fiction, including movies and television programs. Although this was part of appropriation law long before the California Supreme Court used the transformative use test, the reasons are similar. Books, news stories, movies and television programs add transformative elements by putting the names in a context. For example, a movie called "Panther," combining fact and fiction, portrayed several members of the Black Panther Party, a political group active in the 1960s and 1970s that promoted black power and social activism. Bobby Seale, a prominent member of the Black Panthers, sued. A federal district court rejected Seale's appropriation claim, saying the First Amendment protected using his name in the film.[96]

Some celebrities, such as the now-deceased wealthy recluse Howard Hughes, have tried to limit who may write their biographies.[97] But no person, or deceased person's relative, has the right to prevent anyone from writing about another's life.[98] Even fiction including the names of real people is protected by the First Amendment. However, if an author claims that a work is a biography, but the work is much more fiction than fact, the First Amendment may not protect it.

Ads for the Media. Another First Amendment–based appropriation defense holds that mass media may run advertisements for themselves without consent when using the names and likenesses of public figures if those figures were part of their original content. Courts recognized this defense when a magazine, Holiday, ran ads for itself in two other publications. One ad urged people to subscribe, and the other ad suggested advertising agencies place their clients' ads in Holiday. Both ads included pictures of actress Shirley Booth that Holiday had published in one of its issues. Booth sued under New York's

predominant use test In a right of publicity lawsuit, a test to determine whether the defendant used the plaintiff's name or picture more for commercial purposes or protected expression.

appropriation law. The state's highest court said that in order to stay in business and to use its First Amendment rights, the magazine had to attract subscribers and advertisers. Illustrating the magazine's contents and quality by showing what it publishes does not violate Booth's rights, the court concluded.[99]

Holiday magazine won the suit in part because it did not suggest Booth endorsed the magazine. However, a men's magazine's advertisement for itself used a picture of the actress and singer Cher that had accompanied a published interview with her. A cartoon balloon over Cher's head included the words, "So join Cher and FORUM's hundreds of thousands of other adventurous readers today." Cher sued, saying the magazine had implied her endorsement of the magazine without permission. A federal appellate court agreed with her.[100]

More recently, former Chicago Bulls star Michael Jordan sued a grocery store chain based on a magazine ad in which Jewel Food Stores congratulated him for being inducted into the Basketball Hall of Fame. The Seventh Circuit Court of Appeals found that because the grocery store's logo was prominently featured along with its marketing slogan and then linked in the ad text to Jordan, it constituted image advertising. The case was remanded to the lower court, but the Seventh Circuit said a First Amendment defense would not apply in the case.[101]

Consent. The best appropriation defense is consent. That is why professional photographers use releases—contracts prepared by lawyers and signed by all parties involved—when taking pictures for advertisements or other commercial use. Oral consent can be a defense, but proving it can be difficult if the plaintiff claims she or he did not give permission. Also, the law does not allow certain people to give consent, such as minors and those who are not mentally or emotionally capable of agreeing. And consent is limited to the agreement's terms. Consent to use a picture in an ad during 2018, for example, does not allow its use in 2020. Similarly, if a person gives consent to use a picture in a shampoo ad, the picture cannot be used to advertise bedsheets. If a person gives sweeping consent—to use a picture at any time in the future in any advertisement—a court likely will hold that the agreement is more limited than indicated.

Consent most often is explicit. A person agrees to allow his or her name to be used. But consent may be implied. In one case, two people sat on a bench at a dog-racing track. Track personnel announced that a picture would be taken of the area where the people sat, and the camera was within their view. The two people did not move from the bench. When the track used the picture in an advertising brochure, both sued for appropriation. A court ruled that the plaintiffs gave implied consent by not moving when they knew their picture would be taken.[102]

Incidental Use. The use of a person's name or likeness may be incidental to a work's primary purpose. A court could rule that a person's name or likeness was used so briefly that the purpose was not to make a profit or gain commercial benefit. For example, a name applied to a fictional terrorist in a comic book appeared in 1 of 116 panels spanning 24 pages. A person who said the comic book applied his name to the terrorist sued under New York's appropriation law. A federal district court said the name's use was incidental to the comic book's primary purpose and could not sustain a privacy suit.[103] Similarly, if

---

FIGURE 6.1   ■   Model Release Form

Model Release

I, _____ , hereby give consent to _____ and all agents or employees of
_____ . This gives them the right to make any recordings of me in the form of
photographs, video or audio recordings. The session begins on _____ and ends on
_____ . The recordings can be used presently and in the future with no purpose or time
limitation. I further give consent for my identity to be released in association with the recordings made
of me. I release the right to exhibit the recordings to _____ and all agents and employees
of _____ for private or public use. I understand there will be no future compensation made
to me for subsequent use of the material.

I have read and understood the content of this form.

Signature	Date

---

a photograph of a large crowd of people is used in an advertisement, it is unlikely one person in the group could claim successfully that her picture is being used for commercial purposes.

INTRUSION

Critics say the press is obsessed with publishing the sensational, and some argue this obsession prompts journalists to intrude into personal privacy through whatever means necessary—planting microphones, using telescopic camera lenses and infrared heat-sensing film, trespassing on private property, even lying. But journalists say unconventional newsgathering techniques may be necessary in order to provide information about the targets of investigative reporting.

Invasive newsgathering techniques may amount to intrusion or, as courts say, **intrusion upon seclusion**.[104] A journalist may be sued for intrusion if he intentionally interferes with another person's solitude or meddles in the person's private concerns, and if the intrusion would highly offend a **reasonable person** (the law's version of an average person). The intrusion may be physical, such as entering someone's house without permission, or technological, such as using a miniature camera. The intrusion tort is intended to ensure people retain their dignity by preventing unwanted encroachment into their physical space and their private affairs. Only New York state and Virginia have refused to recognize the intrusion tort.[105] (Information-gathering techniques that may be classified as intrusion are discussed further in Chapter 7.)

intrusion upon seclusion Physically or technologically disturbing another's reasonable expectation of privacy.

reasonable person The law's version of an average person.

Methods of Intruding

The more technology develops, the more ways intrusion can occur. For example, as of 2016, 35 states enacted laws addressing a variety of concerns, including privacy protection,

mailforristock.com

In 2016, new Federal Aviation Administration rules made it easier for businesses to fly lightweight drones.

with unmanned aircraft systems, often called drones.[106] But even older technology, such as a camera's telephoto lens, can be a means of intruding.

In one case, a woman mysteriously disappeared from her home. The woman's sister-in-law, husband and children visited the woman's home. They were in bathing suits at the home's swimming pool, surrounded by a seven-foot-high fence, when a CBS television network cameraman stood on a neighbor's porch and, using a telephoto lens, videotaped the family. A federal district court permitted the family to sue CBS for intrusion, saying, "We find that the plaintiffs' allegations that they were swimming in the backyard pool of a private home surrounded by a seven-foot privacy fence are sufficient to allege both that they believed they were in a secluded place and that the activity was private."[107]

Intrusion suits have been brought based on news reporters finding information in public records. Courts hold that there is no reasonable expectation of privacy in public records.[108]

Intrusion on Private Property

Journalists might obtain information by intentionally entering private property without permission. Anyone who does so has committed intrusion, an act similar to trespass (discussed in Chapter 7). Trespass is both a crime and a tort. A trespasser may be sued for intrusion.

Intrusion may occur only if a person has a reasonable expectation of privacy. For instance, there is a reasonable expectation others will not enter into private property, such as a house or apartment, without consent. Without consent, a journalist entering a private residence is intruding. Simply entering private land, however, may not be intruding. In a lawsuit involving Google's Street View feature, which provides panoramic views of streets in metropolitan areas, a couple sued Google for intrusion. Street View showed the couple's house and swimming pool. The couple claimed the pictures could be obtained only by driving up the private street on which their home is located, a street marked as "Private Road, No Trespassing." However, no reasonable person would be highly offended by Google's entry onto the road, the Third Circuit Court of Appeals said, because guests and delivery trucks entered the road and saw what Street View's pictures showed.[109] Ordinarily, there is not a reasonable expectation of privacy on public streets and sidewalks and in public parks where people can be seen or overheard. However, there may be circumstances when people do have a reasonable expectation of privacy in public places.

For example, the U.S. Supreme Court upheld a Colorado law that created an eight-foot bubble around individuals entering a health care facility.[110] The statute made it illegal to approach within eight feet of a person going into an abortion clinic—the law's primary focus—to hand her a leaflet, show her a sign or talk with her without her consent. The law applied within a 100-foot radius around a health care facility's entrance.

In *Hill v. Colorado*, the Court said the law was neither content based nor viewpoint based. Therefore, the Court did not apply a strict scrutiny standard. The state needed to show only a substantial interest. The Court said Colorado's interests in public health and in protecting the rights of individuals to avoid unwanted communication met the intermediate scrutiny test. Colorado's law implies that people entering health clinics have a reasonable expectation of privacy.

Courts may not permit journalists to exceed acceptable means of obtaining information. Following Princess Diana's death, California passed an anti-paparazzi law.[111] The California law says that offensively trespassing to photograph or record a person's personal or family activities is an invasion of privacy. A plaintiff may receive three times the damages a jury awards and may receive punitive damages under the California statute. Another California statute makes it a misdemeanor to attempt to photograph or videotape the children of celebrities in a harassing manner.[112]

Journalists should not assume people involved in a news event occurring on public property do not have a reasonable expectation of privacy. For example, an automobile accident victim reasonably expected discussions with emergency personnel to be private even if medical treatment took place on the side of a public road, a court held.[113]

It is not always easy to determine whether property is private or public. Taxpayers own government land, but they may not always be permitted on the property. Reporters entering a naval base without permission to cover protests could be arrested, a federal district court ruled.[114] Businesses invite the public to enter to buy their products or services. However, reporters entering for other reasons may be intruding. A television news crew burst into a New York City restaurant with cameras on and bright lights blazing to report on a health code violation. The court said the journalists had trespassed because the restaurant allowed the public to enter only for the purpose of dining, not to take pictures and generate news reports.[115]

Defenses

Consent is the only defense for an intrusion suit based on trespass in nearly all cases. Newsworthiness is not a defense because publishing is not an element of the tort. The

⊙ POINTS OF LAW

Intrusion by Trespass

Plaintiff's Case

- A reasonable expectation of privacy
- Intentional intrusion on the privacy
- The intrusion would be highly offensive to a reasonable person

Defense

- Consent

intrusion happens in the newsgathering process. However, the U.S. Court of Appeals for the Ninth Circuit said a story's newsworthiness may reduce the intrusion's offensiveness.[116] This is important because a plaintiff must prove the intrusion was highly offensive.

Consent. A person cannot claim a reasonable expectation of privacy if he or she gave consent for someone to be on his or her private property. For example, a restaurant owner allowed a television news crew to videotape a health inspector evaluating the restaurant. After the station ran an unflattering story, the restaurant sued for intrusion. Because a trial jury found that the restaurant owner had given the television crew consent to enter the premises, an appeals court rejected the restaurant's claim.[117] Consent can also be implied. For example, if a journalist enters private property and the property owner responds to the reporter's questions, there is implied consent to remain and continue the interview.[118]

False Pretenses. Using false pretenses to enter private property is a long-standing reporting technique. Courts are not in agreement, but generally they say reporters may use deceit to gain entry. At least two federal courts have reached that conclusion. In one case, a producer for the ABC television network program "Primetime Live" sent seven people, posing as patients and equipped with hidden cameras, to eye clinics owned by Dr. J.H. Desnick. "Primetime Live" used portions of the hidden video recordings in a story it aired suggesting that Desnick's clinics performed unnecessary cataract surgery. Desnick sued ABC for intrusion and other torts. The clinics were open to anyone who wanted an eye examination, a federal appellate court said. The people posing as patients were allowed into the clinics, just as anyone else would have been. That the "patients" meant to deceive did not invalidate the consent to enter, the court held.[119]

The U.S. Court of Appeals for the Seventh Circuit observed that many people use deception to enter private or semiprivate premises. For example, a restaurant owner might refuse entry to a food critic known to write harsh reviews. But restaurant critics usually do not identify themselves to the owner. They enter and eat anonymously as ordinary patrons. The court said this deception does not negate the restaurant owner's consent. The court indicated, however, that this analysis might not apply to someone using false pretenses to enter with no substantive reason to be there, citing as an example someone who pretends to be a utilities meter reader to enter a private home. In contrast, the hypothetical restaurant critic—and the eye clinic "patients"—did have valid reasons to be on private property, the court said.

What if the context involves medical treatment? In one case, a photographer recorded video of emergency room personnel treating a man who had a bad reaction to a drug. The photographer, dressed in hospital apparel, asked the man to sign a release form and said the video would be used to help train hospital personnel. The patient signed the form, thinking the photographer was a doctor. After a portion of the video ran on a cable program, "Trauma: Life in the ER," the patient sued for intrusion and other claims. A court agreed with the patient's argument that he was in a "zone of physical and sensory privacy and he had a reasonable expectation of seclusion" in a hospital emergency room. The court said the photographer's deception invalidated the patient's consent.[120]

Entering a home using false pretenses may provide grounds for an intrusion suit in most circumstances. At least one court said that combining false pretenses with surreptitious image and audio recording after entering a home was intrusive. To investigate a person practicing medicine without a license, a Life magazine reporter and a photographer claimed to be patients and were admitted to the man's home. The reporter had a microphone in her purse, and the photographer used a small, concealed camera to take pictures. A federal appellate court ignored the false pretenses question and focused on the surreptitious reporting. The court said people have a reasonable expectation of privacy in their homes. Even though a person might expect a visitor to repeat what is said in the house and describe the scene, it is not expected that "what is heard and seen will be transmitted by photograph or recording, or in our modern world, in full living color and [high fidelity] to the public at large or to any segment of it that the visitor may select."[121] The court added, "The First Amendment is not a license to trespass, to steal, or to intrude by electronic means into the precincts of another's home or office."[122]

Most states have laws making it illegal to pretend to be a law enforcement officer. In some states, it is unlawful to pretend to be any public official.

Newsworthiness. Newsworthiness rarely is a defense to an intrusion suit based on trespass or surreptitious surveillance because publication is not part of the plaintiff's burden of proof.[123] Intrusion is determined on the basis of the techniques used to gather information. Publishing that information may lead to other torts, such as libel. But publication alone does not prove that the journalist committed intrusion. Therefore, the story's newsworthiness is not an intrusion defense.

Newsworthiness may be a defense in rare circumstances, however. One court held that reporters using false pretenses to enter a medical laboratory and then secretly recording activities in that lab was not highly offensive because the journalists were investigating laboratory errors in testing for certain cancers. The public's interest in important health issues prevailed over privacy interests, the court said.[124] Another court said that "the legitimate motive of gathering the news" could "negate the offensiveness element of the intrusion tort."[125]

PRIVATE FACTS

A court first recognized the private facts tort in 1927, holding that placing a large sign in the window of a car repair business correctly stating that a local veterinarian owed $49.67 could violate the veterinarian's right of privacy.[126] Journalists and others can be sued for the **private facts** tort if they publicize truthful private information that is not of legitimate public concern and if publicizing the facts would be highly offensive to a reasonable person.[127] The private facts tort is intended to protect a person's dignity and peace of mind by discouraging the publication of intimate facts. If intimate private facts are publicized, a jury may award monetary damages to compensate for the resulting emotional injury.[128] Courts recognize a First Amendment defense to a private facts lawsuit.[129]

private facts
The tort under which individuals or media are sued for publishing highly embarrassing private information that is not newsworthy or lawfully obtained from a public record.

Intimate Facts

Intimate facts are those that a person would not want the community to know. This information must be more than just embarrassing. There are many facts a person might want

○ POINTS OF LAW

Private Facts

Plaintiff's Case

- Publicizing
- Private, intimate facts
- That would be highly embarrassing to a reasonable person
- And are not of legitimate concern to the public

Defenses

- First Amendment: Truthful information lawfully obtained from public records

---

to keep private simply because they are not for public knowledge. Private facts suits can relate to a person's financial condition,[130] medical information,[131] domestic difficulties[132] and similar intimate facts. Often, private facts suits concern sexual activities.[133]

It is not always clear why a court does or does not find publishing a fact offensive. Private facts cases focus on the community's reaction to disseminating the intimate information.[134] The question before a court hearing a private facts case is: Would it outrage the community's notions of decency if the intimate information were published?[135]

Not all facts about a person are private; not even all intimate facts about a person are private. Information in a public record, such as a court filing or an arrest record, by definition is public information, not private. Nor are facts private if a person made them public. Courts hold that information told to a few close relatives or friends remains private. A person may define her or his own circle of intimacy.[136] But if a person reveals intimate facts publicly, the private facts tort does not limit the media from also publishing the information.

One illustrative case involves a friendship between two high school girls that deteriorated into a bitter feud. The first girl accused the second of being pregnant, and that girl teased the first about her Jewish heritage, seeking psychological counseling and having plastic surgery. The second girl's family self-published a book about the feud. The book included school, police and legal documents connected with the situation. The first girl sued for private facts, among other torts. She claimed the book included "1) excerpts and summaries from her Myspace.com webpage; 2) three statements related to her Jewish ancestry; 3) her enrolment (sic) at [a university]; 4) two statements regarding Plaintiff's decision to seek professional psychological care or counseling; 5) Plaintiff's transfer from one high school to another under a superintendent's agreement; and 6) two statements regarding plastic surgery on Plaintiff's nose."[137] The court held categories 1, 2, 3 and 5 were not private, noting the plaintiff agreed she could not conceal what she posted on her Myspace page. She also wrote on her Myspace page that she sought psychological help. As to plastic surgery, the court said it "questions whether this matter is truly private: cosmetic surgery on one's face is by its nature exposed to the public eye."[138]

Legitimate Public Concern

Even if intimate facts were private before being published, a plaintiff cannot win a private facts lawsuit if the information is newsworthy or of legitimate public concern. The media help determine what is newsworthy by reporting on some stories and not others. Stories about crimes, suicides, divorces, catastrophes, diseases and other topics may include intimate information the people involved do not want published. If newsworthy, these private facts cannot be the basis of a successful private facts suit.[139] Courts give the media considerable freedom to determine what is newsworthy. Judges do not want to infringe on journalists' First Amendment rights to report the news. But courts do draw lines, finding that very intimate facts are not newsworthy if publishing the information would outrage the community.

Many courts have adopted a test to determine newsworthiness, first used by a federal appeals court in a case in which a Southern California surfer sued Sports Illustrated magazine.[140]

● REAL WORLD LAW

"Revenge Porn" Websites: Invasion of Privacy or Simply Unethical?

Websites featuring nonconsensual pornography, commonly known as revenge porn, allow people to post sexually explicit videos or nude pictures of others without their consent. The owner of the pioneering revenge porn site IsAnybodyUp.com said at the site's peak he was earning $10,000 a month in advertising revenue based on 30 million reported page views. That site is no longer active, but the owner of a different site modeled after it says he makes $3,000 a month, with some of that money coming from the $250 he charges people to remove pictures or videos from the site.[1]

Legal experts say a private facts lawsuit is hard to win in revenge porn cases because often the victim initially shared the explicit image with someone, usually a friend or sexual partner. Many courts have found that the act of voluntarily sharing the image makes it no longer private.[2]

What's the solution? Some have suggested that courts should accept an argument of implied confidentiality—"explicit images and videos are unlikely to be created or shared with an intimate without some expectation or implication of confidence." No court has yet accepted confidentiality as a legally viable argument in these cases.[3]

Many organizations, like the Cyber Civil Rights Initiative, are fighting revenge porn by appealing to state legislatures. That seems to be working. In 2017, 35 states and the District of Columbia had laws that criminalized revenge porn.[4] At the federal level, a California congresswoman introduced the Intimate Privacy Protection Act of 2016 in the House of Representatives, but the bill did not move forward.[5]

---

1. Joe Mullin, *Revenge Porn Is "Just Entertainment," Says Owner of IsAnybodyDown*, ARSTECHNICA.COM, Feb. 4, 2013, arstechnica.com/tech-policy/2013/02/revenge-porn-is-just-entertainment-says-owner-of-isanybodydown.
2. Woodrow Hartzog, *How to Fight Revenge Porn*, THE ATLANTIC, May 10, 2013, www.theatlantic.com/technology/archive/2013/05/how-to-fight-revenge-porn/275759/.
3. *Id.*
4. The 35 states are Alaska, Arizona, Arkansas, California, Colorado, Connecticut, Delaware, Florida, Georgia, Hawaii, Idaho, Illinois, Kansas, Louisiana, Maine, Maryland, Michigan, Minnesota, Nevada, New Hampshire, New Jersey, New Mexico, North Carolina, North Dakota, Oklahoma, Oregon, Pennsylvania, South Dakota, Tennessee, Texas, Utah, Vermont, Virginia, Washington and Wisconsin, as well as the District of Columbia. Cyber Civil Rights Initiative, *35 States + DC Have Revenge Porn Laws*, CYBERCIVILRIGHTS.ORG, Mar. 31, 2017, www.cybercivilrights.org/revenge-porn-laws/.
5. Intimate Privacy Protection Act, H.R. 5896, 114th Cong., 2nd Sess. (2016), www.congress.gov/bill/114th-congress/house-bill/5896/text.

A Sports Illustrated story included information about Mike Virgil, who bodysurfed at the Wedge, a public beach near Newport Beach, Calif. The Wedge is reputed to be the world's most dangerous place to bodysurf. To illustrate the surfers' daredevil attitudes, the story said Virgil put out a cigarette on his tongue, burned holes through a dollar bill that rested on the back of his hand, dove headfirst down a flight of stairs to impress women, ate spiders and jumped off billboards. Virgil spoke with the Sports Illustrated reporter but withdrew his consent to the story before publication. The surfer sued the magazine for publishing private facts.

The court said the First Amendment did not protect publicity of highly intimate facts unless they were of public concern. Defining newsworthiness, the court distinguished between information the public is entitled to know and facts published for a morbid or sensational reason. Surfing at the Wedge could be of public concern, the court grudgingly admitted. But did that justify revealing intimate details of Virgil's life? The court sent the case back to the trial court,[141] which held that the information in the article about eating spiders, diving down stairs and other private facts in the article was embarrassing but not morbid and sensational. The facts helped describe people who bodysurfed at the Wedge, the court said in ruling for Sports Illustrated.[142]

Several courts have taken a slightly different approach to defining what is newsworthy when stories concern people involuntarily put in the public eye. These courts determine whether there is a logical connection between the news event and the private facts revealed. Well-known persons such as actors, athletes, politicians and musicians are inherently more newsworthy than others. The public wants to know about them, and they have chosen to be in the public eye. Even celebrities, though, have a right to keep private those facts that would be highly embarrassing if publicized.

For example, in part based on a private facts claim, actress Pamela Anderson Lee and rock musician Bret Michaels successfully prevented distribution of their sex tape.[143] More recently, former professional wrestler Hulk Hogan, whose real name is Terry Bollea, sued Gawker Media for reporting on and showing excerpts of a sex tape that showed him having sex with the wife of a friend, Todd Clem, who is a radio shock jock named Bubba the Love Sponge. Clem made the recording and gave Gawker the tape; the media outlet did not pay for it. Bollea sued Clem and his wife for invasion of privacy and settled out of court after Clem acknowledged that Bollea did not know his sexual encounter was being recorded. Bollea also sued Gawker for invasion of privacy, seeking $100 million in damages.[144]

Initially, the case focused largely on whether issuing an injunction to prevent the publication of the tape was appropriate under the First Amendment. In ruling on the injunction, the judge wrote that Hogan's public discussions—with TMZ, on the Howard Stern show and in his autobiography—about his many affairs showed that the subject was not truly private and that reporting on the sex tape was a matter of public concern.[145]

When Bollea's privacy lawsuit finally ended up in front of a jury, he argued that his celebrity status as Hulk Hogan should not deprive him of privacy protections; that he did not know the sexual encounter was being recorded; that Gawker did not seek his permission to publish the video; and that Gawker was not a journalist but rather was acting solely for its own commercial gain. The jury found in favor of Bollea, determining that the publication of the sex tape was offensive and not a matter of legitimate public concern.

It recommended awarding $140 million in both actual and punitive damages, an award later upheld by a judge.

Nick Denton, Gawker's CEO, began an appeal and later declared personal bankruptcy, as did Gawker Media. Univision bought Gawker Media's assets, not including the flagship Gawker website, and in late 2016, Gawker and Bollea settled the invasion of privacy lawsuit for $31 million, ending the appeals process. Ultimately, Gawker.com was shut down, and Univision took down all of the other articles involved in the litigation.[146] Many legal experts suggest that Gawker and Denton might have prevailed on appeal based on First Amendment grounds but that the legal fight would be too costly after the revelation that billionaire Peter Thiel, the founder of PayPal, was financing Bollea's lawsuit.[147]

Newsworthiness can be a defense to a private facts suit. In the past, media defendants had the burden of showing that the facts were of legitimate public interest, and some courts continue to put the newsworthiness burden on the defendant. Many courts instead now require the plaintiff in a private facts suit to prove the intimate facts were not newsworthy. This change came when a newspaper reported that a student body president was a transsexual.[148] Toni Diaz, born Antonio Diaz, underwent sex reassignment

▲ EMERGING LAW

The Monetary Value of Privacy

Privacy law experts say they have noticed an emerging trend toward juries, rather than judges, determining newsworthiness as well as larger jury verdicts in privacy cases.[1]

In 2016, sports broadcaster Erin Andrews won $55 million in damages from a stalker and from a hotel owner and management group after she was the victim of unlawful videotaping. Andrews' serial stalker secretly recorded her in adjacent hotel rooms and leaked nude videos of Andrews, which went viral. The stalker went to prison, and a jury awarded Andrews damages for invasion of privacy and other torts.[2] Media law experts assert that the size of the damage award shows that privacy is becoming a more important value.

Gawker Media declared bankruptcy after a jury awarded professional wrestler Hulk Hogan $140 million in damages for the unauthorized publication of a sex tape. A billionaire's private financing of the Hogan case meant it would be financially challenging for Gawker to proceed with its appeal on First Amendment grounds.[3] In 2017, New York Giants defensive end Jason Pierre-Paul settled an invasion of privacy suit with ESPN after reporter Adam Schefter tweeted photos of Pierre-Paul's hospital records from a 2015 hand injury. ESPN argued that its reporting was newsworthy, and while a federal judge dismissed Pierre-Paul's claim that the tweet violated Florida's medical privacy statute, she allowed the privacy claim to move forward.[4]

Whether one agrees with the outcomes in these cases, media law experts argue that these trends could have a chilling effect on media coverage of issues of legitimate public concern.

1. Thomas Leatherbury, *2015–16 Developments in Newsgathering and Privacy Liability*, COMM. LAW IN DIGITAL AGE, Nov. 10, 2016.
2. Cindy Boren, *The Erin Andrews Verdict: It's Not About the $55 Million in Peephole Lawsuit*, WASH. POST, Mar. 8, 2016, www.washingtonpost.com/news/early-lead/wp/2016/03/08/the-erin-andrews-verdict-its-not-about-the-55-million-in-peephole-lawsuit/?utm_term=.46a6f3f942d7.
3. Sydney Ember, *Gawker and Hulk Hogan Reach $31 Million Settlement*, N.Y. TIMES, Nov. 2, 2016, www.nytimes.com/2016/11/03/business/media/gawker-hulk-hogan-settlement.html?_r=1.
4. Kevin Draper, *Jason Pierre-Paul and ESPN Settle Invasion of Privacy Suit*, DEADSPIN.COM, Feb. 3, 2017, deadspin.com/jason-pierre-paul-and-espn-settle-invasion-of-privacy-s-1791981170.

surgery before entering a community college. Elected student body president, she charged school administrators with mishandling student funds. A local newspaper columnist wrote of Diaz, "Now I realize, that in these times, such a matter is no big deal, but I suspect his female classmates in P.E. 97 may wish to make other showering arrangements." Diaz, who had told only close relatives and friends of her operation, sued the paper and columnist.

A court ruled that Diaz, as plaintiff, had to prove the private facts were not newsworthy because putting the burden on the media could lead to self-censorship. The court ruled that Diaz could show it was not newsworthy to publish remarks about her gender and that her gender had no connection with her ability to be student body president.

Some private facts plaintiffs have argued that the passage of time may mean that information is no longer of legitimate concern to the public. Either the plaintiff was newsworthy many years before the media published the intimate information, or the private facts relate to events that happened long ago. Courts have rejected this contention, saying that newsworthiness does not disappear over time.[149]

Publicity

A private facts plaintiff must prove that the defendant publicized the intimate information. Publicity in the private facts tort is not the same as publication in a libel suit. In libel, publication to a third party, someone other than the plaintiff and defendant, is sufficient. For the private facts tort, most courts require widespread publicity.[150] Revealing intimate information in the media will meet the definition of publicity.[151] Some courts hold that revealing private facts to small groups of people who have a special relationship with the plaintiff is sufficient. This could include the plaintiff's fellow workers, church members, colleagues in a social organization or neighbors.[152]

Publishing private facts is permissible if the information is newsworthy or of legitimate public concern. Judges or juries determine newsworthiness in private facts cases. The criteria many courts use is that private facts are newsworthy if the publication was not intended to be sensational and morbid. Courts also consider whether there is a logical connection between the news event and the published private facts. Most courts require a private facts plaintiff to prove the article was not newsworthy. Some courts regard newsworthiness as a defense to a private facts lawsuit. Most courts require the plaintiff to prove the information was widely published.

First Amendment Defense

When the media face a private facts lawsuit, they often argue that the First Amendment protects publishing truthful information. One way to balance privacy interests against free speech interests is to focus on the source of the information. Should the press lose a private facts suit if the intimate information came from a **public record**?

public record
A government record, particularly one that is publicly available.

The U.S. Supreme Court has said the First Amendment protects publishing truthful information of public significance lawfully obtained from public records, unless punishing the media would serve a compelling state interest. Court decisions have not held that the First Amendment always will protect publishing truthful information taken from public records,[153] but the Supreme Court has not yet found a compelling state interest that overrides the press's First Amendment rights.

Public Significance. In determining whether a publication is about a matter of public significance, the Supreme Court focuses on the story's subject, not individuals named in the article.[154] In *Florida Star v. B.J.F.*, for example, the Supreme Court held that the First Amendment protected a newspaper that published the name of a rape victim, reasoning that violent crime is a publicly significant topic.[155]

Three-and-a-half decades ago, a woman identified as B.J.F. reported to a Florida sheriff's department that she had been robbed and sexually assaulted. The sheriff's department prepared an incident report that identified B.J.F. by her full name and placed the report in its pressroom, which was open to the public. An inexperienced reporter for the Florida Star saw the report, and the paper published a brief story on the case, including B.J.F.'s full name. This was contrary to the paper's policy of not naming rape victims. B.J.F. sued

● INTERNATIONAL LAW

EU's Right to Be Forgotten

A few years ago, the European Court of Justice (in essence, a "supreme court" for the European Union) issued a landmark privacy decision with global consequences. The case involved a concept called the "right to be forgotten" as it applied to the EU's 1995 Data Protection Directive. In 2010, a Spanish man asked a government agency to force newspaper La Vanguardia to remove items from its website that announced that his property would be auctioned to pay his debts. Although the man had resolved his financial situation, the announcement popped up whenever someone searched his name on the La Vanguardia site. The man also asked the agency to force Google to remove the links from searches for his name.[1]

The European Court of Justice upheld a decision to allow the newspaper to retain the information but to require Google to unlink the articles from a search of the man's name. Google said it would apply the EU decision only to the European versions of its websites (such as google.be or google.fr), not to its global site: google.com. Google reported that since the ruling, it had received 704,541 "right to be forgotten" requests, leading it to review nearly two million links. It granted 56.8 percent of the requests.[3]

The European Court's decision applies only to search engines. Throughout 2016, Google negotiated with EU data protection regulators over the reach of the "right to be forgotten" after a 2015 order in France required Google to delist search results across all of its domains. Google faced sanctions from France's Commission Nationale de l'Informatique et des Libertés in 2016 for refusing to comply with the order, arguing that the French regulator was overreaching.[4]

In 2016, the EU formally adopted new privacy rules, the General Data Protection Regulation, to replace the 1995 directive. The GDPR expands the right to be forgotten by providing for a "right to erasure," which gives EU citizens "the right to obtain from [a data] controller the erasure of personal data concerning him or her without undue delay" in specific contexts. Full compliance with the new regulation comes in mid-2018, and it's still unclear how the new "right to erasure" will work in practice.[5]

1. Case C-131/12, Google Spain SL v. Agencia Española de Protección de Datos (Court of Justice of European Union, 2014), curia.europa.eu/juris/document/document.jsf?docid=152065&doclang=en.
2. Jeffrey Toobin, *The Solace of Oblivion*, THE NEW YORKER, Sept. 29, 2014, www.newyorker.com/magazine/2014/09/29/solace-oblivion.
3. Google, *European Privacy Requests for Search Removals*, GOOGLE.COM, Mar. 31, 2017, www.google.com/transparency report/removals/europeprivacy/.
4. Jane Kirtley, *EU Adopts General Data Protection Regulation: Global Privacy and Data Protection*, COMM. LAW IN THE DIGITAL AGE 2016 (2016).
5. *Id.*, at 193.

the sheriff's department and the Florida Star under a state law making it illegal for media to publish the name of a sexual assault victim. The sheriff's department settled before trial, and B.J.F. won her case against the newspaper, a result that was upheld by a Florida appellate court.

The newspaper appealed the case to the U.S. Supreme Court, which reversed, holding that the First Amendment protects a newspaper that publishes truthful information lawfully obtained from public records, provided no compelling state interest requires otherwise. Although protecting the identity of a sexual assault victim could in principle be a compelling state interest, the Court said, three factors worked against that conclusion in this case. First, the government itself supplied the information. Second, the state law forbidding names from being published had no exceptions, not even if the community already knew the victim's name. Third, the state law applied only to the media, allowing others to disseminate a victim's name. Under these circumstances, the Court said, the right to a free press outweighed the state's interest in preventing publication of B.J.F.'s name.

Lawfully Obtained. In three other decisions, the Supreme Court ruled that where the press had legally obtained truthful information from public records it was not liable for publishing private facts. Nearly 50 years ago in *Cox Broadcasting Corp. v. Cohn*, excerpted at the end of this chapter, the Court said for the first time that truthful information lawfully obtained from a public record could not be the basis of a private facts lawsuit.[156] The case involved the rape and murder of a 17-year-old girl in Georgia. At a court proceeding some months after the crime, a reporter covering the incident learned the name of the victim from indictments filed against six defendants and reported it. The victim's father sued the television station for broadcasting the name of his daughter. He won at trial and again on the television station's appeal to the Georgia Supreme Court. But the U.S. Supreme Court reversed, noting that the First Amendment protects the press against a private facts tort if the information is obtained from generally available public records.

In a separate case originating in Oklahoma in 1976, news media violated a juvenile court judge's order by publishing the name and picture of an 11-year-old boy charged with second-degree murder for shooting a railroad employee. Reporters were in the courtroom when the juvenile appeared, and the court put his name on the public record. Photographers took pictures as the minor left the courthouse. The Supreme Court said the press had lawfully obtained information available to the public and held that the First Amendment prohibits punishing the press for revealing information taken from public records.[157]

In a third case, newspaper reporters who had been monitoring a police scanner in West Virginia responded to a crime scene and learned from witnesses and investigators the name of a 14-year-old boy charged with killing a classmate. State prosecutors obtained an indictment against the press for publishing the boy's name in violation of a state law. The Supreme Court, however, ruled in favor of the newspaper, reasoning that the First Amendment protects news reports where journalists have lawfully obtained truthful information from publicly available sources. The Court said protecting the minor's privacy was not a compelling reason to restrict the freedom of the press.[158]

The Supreme Court has also held that the First Amendment sometimes protects publication of private information even where it was not lawfully obtained—so long as the media were not involved in illegally acquiring the information. In *Bartnicki v. Vopper* (discussed further in Chapter 7), the Court said the media were not liable for publishing an intercepted cellphone conversation between two labor negotiators. Punishing the media for publishing information they obtained without acting illegally would not further a compelling government interest, the Court said.[159]

Public Record. Publicly available facts are not private. Names, addresses and telephone numbers are widely available, so they are not confidential.[160] Information in government records available to the public cannot be considered private. Facts presented in public meetings also are not secret. Unless a judge seals a record, making it unavailable, court records are public. A private facts suit cannot be based on intimate information contained in publicly accessible records.

Some government records are not publicly accessible and may not be considered public records in a private facts lawsuit. For example, grand jury proceedings are closed and not available to the public or press.[161] Also, information about individuals' medical conditions, tax filings and other personal data may not be considered a public record.[162] In 2017, after candidate and then-President Donald Trump refused to release his tax returns, the ranking member of the Senate Finance Committee introduced the Presidential Tax Transparency Act, which would amend the Ethics in Government Act of 1978 if passed. The newly proposed bill would require all sitting presidents to release their three most recent years of tax returns to the Office of Government Ethics and would require that presidential candidates, within 15 days of becoming a party's nominee, release their most recent three years of returns.[163] The disclosure of President Trump's tax returns was a heated, partisan issue during the 2016 campaign.

Similarly, not all publicly accessible places are "public." Publishing a picture and a conversation obtained by entering a private hospital room may not be protected even if the hospital generally is open to the public.[164]

PRIVACY AND DATA PROTECTION

Today, people's concerns about privacy persist alongside an additional threat from marketers, data brokers and other businesses that amass personally identifiable data. For example, Google, Microsoft and many popular websites install tracking devices on users' computers, some able to record and transmit keystrokes for data gathering and analysis. Courts have allowed websites and advertisers to put cookies—technology that tracks what websites people visit—on computers.[165] Many smartphone applications send users' sensitive information to advertisers and third-party data collectors.[166]

In 2016, the popular ride-hailing app Uber added new features, including access to a user's ride history, personal contacts, calendar and other information, that raised privacy concerns.[167] The announcement of the additional data collection by Uber came on the heels of the company settling a case with New York state authorities for two data breaches that occurred in 2014 and 2015. As part of the settlement, Uber was required to encrypt rider geolocation information and offer other security features that protect riders' personal information from potential abuse by Uber staff.[168]

About five years ago, the Federal Trade Commission issued a substantive report about consumer privacy protection and called on companies to adopt its recommended best practices. The FTC is the chief federal agency that protects consumer privacy and enforces federal privacy laws. The one exception to this is the FCC's regulation of privacy practices as they apply to broadband internet service providers, discussed in Chapter 9.

The FTC report suggested that companies build in consumer privacy protections at all stages of product development. Those protections should include consumer data security, limited data collection and retention, and procedures to promote data accuracy. The report also recommended giving consumers the option to control how they share their information and the ability to choose a "Do Not Track" mechanism, and the FTC encouraged companies to strive toward transparency in how they collect and use consumer information.[169]

Current federal and state privacy laws do not sufficiently protect American consumers, according to the FTC. The burden of understanding websites' privacy policies is with online users who must affirmatively try to ensure their own privacy.[170] For example, Facebook's privacy policy is thousands of words long and, like most other social media websites, requires users to opt out if they want privacy. That is, users' posted information is publicly available and becomes private only if a user clicks on the appropriate settings. Facebook continually updates its privacy and information security policies, even relocating where a user can find the privacy and security icons as it changes its basic design. In 2017, Facebook had 2 billion monthly users worldwide.[171] It's unclear how many have read the policy and opted for privacy.

data broker
An entity that collects and stores personal information about consumers, then sells that information to other organizations.

Data brokers collect and store billions of pieces of personal data that cover nearly every U.S. consumer and sell that information to other organizations. In 2014, the FTC issued a report on data brokers to educate the public about how these companies use, maintain and disseminate the personal data they collect. The report noted that none of the nine major data brokers obtained their data directly from consumers. Instead, the data originated from both public and private sources, online and offline. Information collected included Social Security numbers, interest in heath issues, voter records, viewed news reports, social media posts, information from travel websites and transaction data from retailers.[172]

Data brokers analyze and repackage the information they collect for sale for marketing or risk mitigation purposes and/or for people searches. The FTC said consumers could benefit from the data these brokers collect and analyze but found little transparency in the industry. Additionally, the report said these brokers unnecessarily store consumer data indefinitely, which can increase security risks for consumers (for example, increased risk of identity theft).[173]

The FTC has urged Congress to regulate data brokers and increase consumer control over their personal information. Specific FTC legislative suggestions include requiring the brokers to disclose their sources of information, giving consumers the opportunity to correct inaccurate information and allowing consumers to opt out of data collection.[174]

In a 2015 FTC report, "Internet of Things: Privacy and Security in a Connected World," the federal agency reiterated many of its earlier recommendations and suggested

● REAL WORLD LAW

Protection From Doxxing

Doxxing is the practice of finding personally identifiable information about someone from publicly available data, and using that information to threaten or harass her. The word is derived from the phrase "document tracing." Recently, a doxxing website exposed the Social Security numbers, credit reports, mortgage information, addresses, phone numbers and other sensitive information of celebrities and prominent government officials. The doxxing website posted the FBI director's credit report and the Social Security numbers of Jay Z, Beyoncé, Kim Kardashian and Ashton Kutcher, among other celebrities.[1]

Harvard's Nieman Lab recently offered suggestions for journalists to protect themselves since they are increasingly the targets of doxxing attacks.

- Request digital security training from your employer, including how to keep personal information private, which sites target reporters and how to send and receive encrypted files;

- Use only an official email address and phone number for work, and don't use your personal information. Never give your home address, and have packages delivered only to the office. Freelancers should consider getting a P.O. box and using Skype or Google Voice phone numbers in place of personal cell or landline numbers;

- If you are doxxed, report the harassment to the police and have a lawyer with you who understands the issues. Share any identifying information you know about the harassers.[2]

Usually a doxxing episode is followed by a call to action. In real incidents, this has ranged from threatening phone calls to unwanted food delivery to more dangerous activities such as swatting (making a prank call to 911 in hopes of deploying the SWAT team) or "posting a claim on Craigslist that (the victim) has rape fantasies and encouraging men to visit."[3]

1. Associated Press, *Financial Info. on Celebs, Officials Leaked Online*, Politico.com, March 12, 2013, www.politico.com/story/2013/03/financial-info-on-celebs-officials-leaked-online-88740.html.
2. Rose Eveleth, *How to Deter Doxxing*, Niemanreports.org, July 17, 2015, niemanreports.org/articles/how-to-deter-doxxing/.
3. *Id.*

that it is imperative for companies to earn consumers' trust by protecting their personal data. The FTC defined the "internet of things" as consumer devices or sensors—other than computers, smartphones and tablets—that connect, store or transmit information via the internet. These include, for example, home thermostats and appliances. The report notes that the number of connected devices worldwide (then more than 25 billion) would continue to grow significantly and that security should be a priority for companies developing new devices. The report suggests building security into devices from the start, training employees about the importance of consumer privacy, adopting measures that prevent unauthorized users from accessing consumer data stored on a network, monitoring devices and updating security patches. The report also said that companies should inform consumers what data are collected, give them choices about how their information is used and consider limiting the collection and storage duration of consumer data.[175]

In recent years, state and federal courts have connected legal issues to privacy and data collection. In 2013, 38 states reached a privacy settlement with Google for $7 million after a privacy breach with the Google Street View car fleet. For two years, the cars collected passwords, messages and other private data from unsecured Wi-Fi networks as they drove past homes and businesses. Following the settlement, Google said it had secured the information and would destroy it without using it. Google also agreed to initiate a new consumer privacy employee-training program and a national advertising campaign to educate users on how to protect their privacy.[176]

In 2015, a federal judge in California dismissed a class action lawsuit that claimed Samsung and other smartphone manufacturers violated users' privacy by collecting consumers' data from their phones using Carrier IQ software. The primary allegation was that Carrier IQ's software, which is automatically installed on various Android phones, collected and transferred sensitive data from the smartphones. The judge said that while the companies did intercept communications such as text messages, the plaintiffs had not established sufficient evidence that the companies actually received the intercepted texts as required by law.[177]

In 2016, the U.S. Supreme Court decided *Spokeo Inc. v. Robins*, a case involving a people search engine. Spokeo operates an online search engine that contains personal information about people for its users, which includes employers who want to evaluate prospective employees.[178] Thomas Robins filed a class action suit against Spokeo after he determined that the search engine contained incorrect information that misrepresented his marital status and employment status and inflated both his income and his level of education. Robins argued that the inaccuracies violated the Fair Credit Reporting Act.

In a 6–2 decision, the Supreme Court held that Robins did not have standing to sue for damages because he could not show that he suffered "concrete" harm as a result of Spokeo's alleged FCRA violation.[179] Legal experts noted that the ruling could extend to numerous other statutes used in class action lawsuits when those lawsuits are based on alleged technical violations of law that do not cause harm. They added that the decision did not give much guidance for other cases involving the increased risk to individuals when personal data are misused or incorrect.[180]

One statute that could be subjected to the outcome in *Spokeo* is the Video Privacy Protection Act, which courts have revived in the context of online streaming video websites and mobile applications. Congress enacted the VPPA after Supreme Court nominee Robert Bork's video rental records were disclosed to the media during his confirmation hearing in 1987. The law prevents video service providers from knowingly disclosing a consumer's personally identifiable information to a third party (with a few exceptions).[181]

While at the time of its enactment the VPPA was meant to apply only to physical video rentals, a federal court in California applied the law to streaming websites and mobile applications because they were sharing personally identifiable information with third-party advertisers and data brokers.[182] What the decision did not clarify was how to determine whether a person is a subscriber under the VPPA. The distinction between a subscriber and a consumer of free content, whether from an online video streaming website or from a free mobile application, is at the core of whether courts believe the data privacy protections from the VPPA should be extended. The First and Eleventh Circuit Courts of Appeals have come to different determinations, highlighting the difficulty in applying the decades-old law in a digital context.[183]

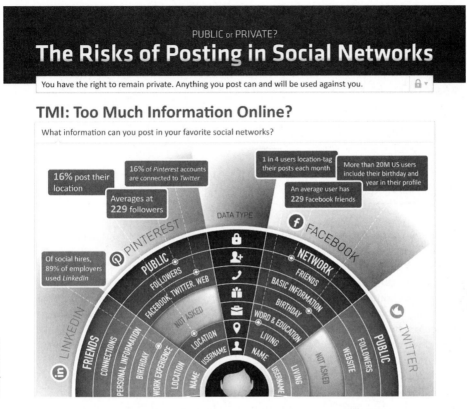

PUBLIC or PRIVATE?

The Risks of Posting in Social Networks

You have the right to remain private. Anything you post can and will be used against you.

TMI: Too Much Information Online?

What information can you post in your favorite social networks?

16% post their location

16% of *Pinterest* accounts are connected to *Twitter*

Averages at **229** followers

Of social hires, **89%** of employers used *LinkedIn*

1 in 4 users location-tag their posts each month

More than 20M US users include their birthday and year in their profile

An average user has **229** Facebook friends

Courtesy of Trend Micro

Social networks prompt users to share personal information, like their hometowns or their birthdays, online. No matter what service you use, it's important that you find out where the privacy settings live before sharing information on social media.

ELECTRONIC PRIVACY AND THE SUPREME COURT

In the past decade, the U.S. Supreme Court has decided a series of landmark privacy cases that involve electronic communication. These cases tackle questions about how courts should apply decades-old precedents to technology that did not exist at the time the Court issued those decisions. In 2010, the Court held that government employers may see public employees' text messages sent and received on government-issued equipment if the searches have a legitimate work-related purpose and the public employees have been told not to expect privacy.[184]

The case, *City of Ontario v. Quon,* involved an Ontario, Calif., police officer who used a department-issued pager to communicate with fellow officers. The city gave permission to use the pagers for a limited number of personal messages. When the city audited officers' pagers, it found one officer had sent sexually explicit text messages to and received them from both his wife and his mistress. The officer claimed the city violated his reasonable expectation of privacy. The Court said even if the officer did have a reasonable expectation of privacy, the city's search of his pager did not violate it. Although the Court stressed its ruling was narrowly applied to the case facts, it could relate to government-issued cellphones, computers and other communication technologies.

● POINTS OF LAW

Constitutional Right to Privacy

- Protection comes from the Third, Fourth, Fifth and 14th Amendments.
- The Constitution protects from governmental invasion of privacy.
- Harlan's "reasonable expectation of privacy" test from *Katz* establishes a Fourth Amendment right to privacy when:
  1. A person exhibits an actual expectation of privacy and
  2. Society is prepared to recognize this expectation as reasonable.

The *Quon* decision is not the first time the Supreme Court ruled that employees have limited privacy rights. Thirty years ago, the Court said a search of a public employee's desk and filing cabinet did not violate his Fourth Amendment rights, which protect against unreasonable searches and seizures.[185] May a private employer look at an email message on an employee's computer? Courts have said the First Amendment does not bar companies from doing so because the company's interest in preventing illegal activity or unprofessional comments outweighs an employee's privacy interest.[186]

Privacy protection diminished after Sept. 11, 2001. At airports, employees of the Transportation Security Administration, a federal government agency, may open and look through travelers' luggage. The USA PATRIOT Act allows the government to obtain information about anyone from public libraries, businesses, hospitals and internet service providers. The government has to say only that the information is being sought for a terrorism investigation. The person revealing the information is not allowed to tell anyone else that the government asked for it.[187]

Although the *Quon* decision and the Patriot Act diminish privacy expectations, three recent Supreme Court cases expand privacy protection as it relates to "unreasonable searches and seizures" under the Fourth Amendment. In *United States v. Jones*, the Supreme Court unanimously held that physically mounting a GPS transmitter on a car amounts to a search and violates the Fourth Amendment.[188] In *Jones*, the Court relied partially on its 1967 decision in *Katz v. United States*. Katz had been convicted of illegal betting over a telephone line in a public phone booth. The government recorded his phone conversations without a warrant, and those recordings led to his conviction. The Supreme Court threw out that evidence, calling it a Fourth Amendment violation. In his concurrence, Justice John Marshall Harlan II wrote, "[A] person has a constitutionally protected reasonable expectation of privacy," and "electronic as well as physical intrusion into a place that is in this sense private may constitute a violation of the Fourth Amendment."[189]

Subsequent courts have recognized Justice Harlan's concurrence in *Katz* as the Harlan "reasonable expectation of privacy test." The test requires that an individual exhibit an actual expectation of privacy and that this expectation is one that society is prepared to recognize as reasonable.[190] Referencing *Katz*, the *Jones* Court said that "a violation occurs when government officers violated a person's 'reasonable expectation of privacy.'"[191]

In *Florida v. Jardines*, the Supreme Court held that the use of drug-sniffing dogs to search an area around a house after a tip that the homeowner was growing marijuana amounts to a Fourth Amendment violation. Police obtained a search warrant after the dog found the drugs, but the Supreme Court said the warrant was not valid because it was based on the illegal search by the K-9 officer and his dog. The majority reasoned that "while law enforcement officers need not 'shield their eyes' when passing by the home 'on public thoroughfares,' an officer's leave to gather information is sharply circumscribed when he steps off those thoroughfares and enters the Fourth Amendment's protect[ed] areas."[192]

The U.S. Supreme Court held that searching a cellphone without a warrant violates the Fourth Amendment.

Does a police officer's "leave to gather information" extend to a search of a suspect's smartphone? In 2014 in *Riley v. California*, which is excerpted at the end of this chapter, a unanimous Supreme Court said "no." The decision involved two cases in which suspects arrested for criminal activity were convicted based on evidence found on their cellphones—one a smartphone, the other a flip phone. The government argued that searching a cellphone found on a person at the time of arrest fell under the "incident to arrest" exception, which allows for a search of a person without a warrant at the time of an arrest.

Writing for the Court, Chief Justice John Roberts said the "incident to arrest" exception does not apply to a cellphone. "Modern cellphones, as a category, implicate privacy concerns far beyond those implicated by the search of a cigarette pack, a wallet, or a purse," he wrote. "A conclusion that inspecting the contents of an arrestee's pockets works no substantial additional intrusion on privacy beyond the arrest itself may make sense as applied to physical items, but any extension of that reasoning to digital data has to rest on its own bottom. Cellphones differ in both a quantitative and a qualitative sense from other objects that might be kept on an arrestee's person."[193]

Legal scholars note that since the *Katz* case offered the reasonable expectation of privacy test in 1967, the Supreme Court has decided very few Fourth Amendment cases dealing with advanced technology. But the decisions in *Jones*, *Jardines* and *Riley* show that the Court has decided in the 21st century both to reaffirm the traditional privacy expectation near the home (*Jardines*) and to extend protection to newer technologies that have given rise to public concern (*Jones* and *Riley*). One legal scholar wrote that the *Riley* decision "left no doubt that the Court's intention was to extend the Fourth Amendment's protection to digitally stored information without regard to the particular storage device. . . . [It] reaffirmed the nation's commitment to protecting privacy in the face of advancing technology."[194]

Congress is also attempting to produce legislation that clarifies how law enforcement and the government may use advanced technologies, such as geolocation information services. In 2013, a bipartisan group in the House of Representatives introduced the

Geolocation Privacy and Surveillance Act that would require police to obtain a warrant to collect location data from a cellphone, tablet or other portable electronic device.[195] Although the House's version of the GPSA died in committee, the Senate introduced its own version in 2015 and again in 2017 to strengthen privacy provisions tied to geolocation software and information systems.[196]

Additional pending legislation in Congress that deals with privacy and the security of an individual's information includes an update to the 1986 Electronic Communications Privacy Act,[197] which privacy advocates say is woefully inadequate to handle today's issues.[198] In 2017, the House passed the Email Privacy Act, which narrowly amends the ECPA to extend a search warrant requirement to communications that are stored for more than 180 days. An earlier version of the bill also required a warrant notification of an email search to most users. The non-profit Electronic Privacy Information Center has encouraged Congress to update the ECPA in several other ways, including improving protection for location data and better encryption for commercial email services, but these concerns are not addressed in the current bill.[199]

CHAPTER SUMMARY

THE U.S. CONSTITUTION, STATE AND federal laws and court decisions offer some limited privacy protection. Although the word "privacy" is not in the federal Constitution, the U.S. Supreme Court has said the Constitution protects certain privacy rights. For the media, privacy questions usually arise in tort suits. In 1960, Prosser divided privacy law into four torts: false light, appropriation, intrusion and private facts.

Not all states allow false light suits. Most that do require a plaintiff to prove (1) publicity, (2) identification, (3) the published material was false or created a false impression, (4) the statements or pictures put the plaintiff in a false light that would be highly offensive to a reasonable person and (5) the defendant knew the material was false or recklessly disregarded its falsity. In the only two false light cases the U.S. Supreme Court has decided, it said all plaintiffs must prove actual malice. Some lower courts require all false light plaintiffs to prove actual malice. Others require only public officials and public figures to prove actual malice.

Courts recognize most libel defenses as defenses in false light cases, including conditional privilege, fair reporting and truth. States may use the shorter statute of limitations applied to libel cases, or the longer limitations period used for other torts, in false light cases. Appropriation is divided into commercialization and right of publicity. Commercialization protects individuals from having their names, pictures, likenesses, voices and identities used for commercial or trade purposes without their permission. Commercialization applies to famous and ordinary people alike. Courts recently have recognized a right of publicity that protects celebrities from being exploited.

A successful appropriation plaintiff must prove his or her name, picture, likeness, voice or identity was used for commercial or trade purposes without his or her permission. Even a pseudonym or stage name is protected. An advertisement may use a model who looks like another person only if a disclaimer explains the person not pictured in the ad is not endorsing the product or service. Similarly, a person who sounds like another when talking or singing may be used in an advertisement if accompanied by a disclaimer. Some courts also allow a plaintiff to sue for appropriation if his or her identity is used for commercial or trade purposes without permission.

Courts recognize several defenses to an appropriation suit. The press most often uses the newsworthiness defense. Courts consider media content to be newsworthy if it is not used in an advertisement or other commercial context. The Supreme Court has held that the media lose the newsworthiness defense if they show a performer's entire act in a news program.

Courts recognize a First Amendment defense in right of publicity cases. Courts use several tests in balancing celebrities' rights to earn money from their names and likenesses against the media's free speech rights. One is to determine whether a celebrity's name or likeness is used in conveying information of public concern. Another is to assess whether using a celebrity's name or likeness is artistically relevant to the work. A third is to decide whether the disputed work transformed the celebrity's likeness, making it into something new.

Courts allow the media to use someone's name or likeness in an advertisement for the mass medium itself if the ad does not suggest the person is endorsing the mass medium. Also, if a person consents to a commercial use of his or her name or likeness, the person cannot sue successfully for appropriation unless the use goes beyond the consent given. Finally, an incidental use of a person's name or likeness is not appropriation.

Intrusion occurs if a person intentionally interferes with another's solitude or private concerns through physical or technological means. Physical intrusion is also trespass. Trespass is both a crime and a tort. To win an intrusion suit, a plaintiff must prove the defendant acted intentionally to intrude into private matters in a way a reasonable person would find highly offensive. If highly offensive intrusion occurs, a plaintiff is able to show he had a reasonable expectation of privacy that the defendant violated. Intrusion concerns how information is gathered. Publication is not part of the intrusion tort.

Generally, people on public property have no reasonable expectation of privacy, but particularly aggressive newsgathering even on public property can be considered intrusion. Consent is the defense for intrusion by trespass. The person who owns or is using the property must give consent. Courts have ruled that law enforcement officials may not give journalists consent to enter private property. Courts generally, but not unanimously, hold that consent is valid even if obtained by using false pretenses.

Journalists may use visible equipment to photograph or record on public property. However, secret recording is intrusion if the circumstances suggest a person should have a reasonable expectation of privacy in public, such as during a medical emergency. Secretly videotaping on private property is usually intrusion. Consent is a defense in an intrusion suit. Newsworthiness rarely is an effective defense against an intrusion suit.

A private facts plaintiff must show the widely disseminated facts were private, dealt with intimate or highly personal matters and were not of legitimate public concern. A plaintiff also must prove that publication would be highly offensive to a reasonable person. Facts are not private if they are from public records or are generally known. The First Amendment protects publishing truthful information of public significance lawfully obtained from public records. However, this would not be a defense to a private facts lawsuit if a court determined that punishing the media would serve a compelling state interest. The U.S. Supreme Court, though, has never found a state interest compelling enough to allow such punishment, even where the media has revealed the name of a rape victim.

The topic of a news story, rather than the individual people discussed in the story, determines whether the story is of public significance. Information is lawfully obtained as long as a journalist does nothing illegal to obtain it. Information is public if it is in government records or otherwise available to the public. Newsworthiness does not diminish over time. Once newsworthy, facts and people remain newsworthy.

Today, people's concerns about privacy persist alongside an additional threat from marketers, data brokers and other businesses that amass personally identifiable data. The Federal Trade Commission is the chief federal agency that protects consumer privacy and enforces federal privacy laws. This area of the law continues to evolve.

Some privacy protection diminished after Sept. 11, 2001. The Patriot Act allows the government to obtain information about anyone from public libraries, businesses, hospitals and internet service providers. The U.S. Supreme Court in 2010 held that government employers may see public employees' text messages sent and received on government-issued equipment if the searches have a legitimate work-related purpose and the public employees have been told not to expect privacy. Three recent Supreme Court decisions that explored privacy and the Fourth Amendment reaffirmed the traditional privacy expectation near the home and unanimously held that physically mounting a GPS transmitter on a car amounts to a search and violates the Fourth Amendment as does the warrantless search of a cellphone at the time of an arrest. Congress is increasingly interested in updating federal privacy-related laws that deal with new technology. ∎

CASES FOR STUDY

For study resources and a case archive go to **study.sagepub.com/medialaw6e**.

THINKING ABOUT IT

The two case excerpts that follow are landmark privacy cases. As you read these case excerpts, keep the following questions in mind:

- Think back to Chapter 1 and the discussion of originalism (interpretation of the Constitution according to the perceived intent of its framers). Can you spot originalist ideas in a modern-day decision about how advances in technology impact the right to privacy as protected by the Fourth Amendment in the *Riley* case?

- How do the two decisions try to balance right of privacy against other important rights?

- How has technology changed our societal understanding of a "reasonable expectation of privacy"?

Cox Broadcasting Corp. v. Cohn
SUPREME COURT OF THE UNITED STATES
420 U.S. 469 (1975)

JUSTICE BYRON WHITE delivered the Court's opinion:

The issue before us in this case is whether, consistently with the First and Fourteenth Amendments, a State may extend a cause of action for damages for invasion of privacy caused by the publication of the name of a deceased rape victim which was publicly revealed in connection with the prosecution of the crime.

In August 1971, appellee's 17-year-old daughter was the victim of a rape and did not survive the incident. Six youths were soon indicted for murder and rape. Although there was substantial press coverage of the crime and of subsequent developments, the identity of the victim was not disclosed pending trial, perhaps because of Ga. Code Ann. § 26-9901 (1972), which makes it a misdemeanor to publish or broadcast the name or identity of a rape victim. In April 1972, some eight months later, the six defendants appeared in court. Five pleaded guilty to rape

or attempted rape, the charge of murder having been dropped. The guilty pleas were accepted by the court, and the trial of the defendant pleading not guilty was set for a later date.

In the course of the proceedings that day, appellant Wassell, a reporter covering the incident for his employer, learned the name of the victim from an examination of the indictments which were made available for his inspection in the courtroom. That the name of the victim appears in the indictments and that the indictments were public records available for inspection are not disputed. Later that day, Wassell broadcast over the facilities of station WSB-TV, a television station owned by appellant Cox Broadcasting Corp., a news report concerning the court proceedings. The report named the victim of the crime and was repeated the following day.

In May 1972, appellee brought an action for money damages against appellants, relying on § 26-9901 and claiming that his right to privacy had been invaded by the television broadcasts giving the name of his deceased daughter. Appellants admitted the broadcasts but claimed that they were privileged under both state law and the First and Fourteenth Amendments. The trial court, rejecting appellants' constitutional claims and holding that the Georgia statute gave a civil remedy to those injured by its violation, granted summary judgment to appellee as to liability, with the determination of damages to await trial by jury.

On appeal, the Georgia Supreme Court, in its initial opinion, held that the trial court had erred in construing § 26-9901 to extend a civil cause of action for invasion of privacy and thus found it unnecessary to consider the constitutionality of the statute. . . . Upon motion for rehearing the Georgia court countered the argument that the victim's name was a matter of public interest and could be published with impunity by relying on § 26-9901 as an authoritative declaration of state policy that the name of a rape victim was not a matter of public concern. This time the court felt compelled to determine the constitutionality of the statute and sustained it as a "legitimate limitation on the right of freedom of expression contained in the First Amendment." The court could discern "no public interest or general concern about the identity of the victim of such a crime as will make the right to disclose the identity of the victim rise to the level of First Amendment protection."

. . . [W]e conclude that we have jurisdiction to review the judgment of the Georgia Supreme Court rejecting the challenge under the First and Fourteenth Amendments to the state law authorizing damage suits against the press for publishing the name of a rape victim whose identity is revealed in the course of a public prosecution. . . .

Georgia stoutly defends both § 26-9901 and the State's common-law privacy action challenged here. Its claims are not without force, for powerful arguments can be made, and have been made, that however it may be ultimately defined, there *is* a zone of privacy surrounding every individual, a zone within which the State may protect him from intrusion by the press, with all its attendant publicity. Indeed, the central thesis of the root article by Warren and Brandeis, The Right to Privacy, was that the press was overstepping its prerogatives by publishing essentially private information and that there should be a remedy for the alleged abuses.

More compellingly, the century has experienced a strong tide running in favor of the so-called right of privacy. In 1967, we noted that "[it] has been said that a 'right of privacy' has been recognized at common law in 30 States plus the District of Columbia and by statute in four States." We there cited the 1964 edition of Prosser's Law of Torts. The 1971 edition of that same source states that "[in] one form or another, the right of privacy is by this time recognized and accepted in all but a very few jurisdictions." Nor is it irrelevant here that the right of privacy is no recent arrival in the jurisprudence of Georgia, which has embraced the right in some form since 1905 when the Georgia Supreme Court decided the leading case of *Pavesich v. New England Life Ins. Co.*

These are impressive credentials for a right of privacy, but we should recognize that we do not have at issue here an action for the invasion of privacy involving the appropriation of one's name or photograph, a physical or other tangible intrusion into a private area, or a publication of otherwise private information that is also false although perhaps not defamatory. The version of the privacy tort now before us—termed in Georgia "the tort of public disclosure"—is that in which the plaintiff claims the right to be free from unwanted publicity about his private affairs, which, although wholly true, would be offensive to a person of ordinary sensibilities. Because the gravamen of the claimed injury is the publication of information, whether true or not, the dissemination of which is embarrassing or otherwise painful to an individual, it is here that claims of privacy most directly confront the constitutional freedoms of speech and press. The face-off is apparent, and the appellants urge upon us the broad holding that the press may not be made criminally or civilly liable for publishing information that is neither false nor misleading but absolutely accurate, however damaging it may be to reputation or individual sensibilities. In this sphere of collision between claims of privacy and those of the free press, the interests on both sides are plainly rooted in the traditions and significant concerns of our society. Rather than address the broader question whether truthful publications may ever be subjected to civil or criminal liability consistently with the First and Fourteenth Amendments, or to put it another way, whether the State may ever define and protect an area of privacy free from unwanted publicity in the press, it is appropriate to focus on the narrower interface between press and privacy that this case presents, namely, whether the State may impose sanctions on the accurate publication of the name of a rape victim obtained from public records—more specifically, from judicial records which are maintained in connection with a public prosecution and which themselves are open to public inspection. We are convinced that the State may not do so.

In the first place, in a society in which each individual has but limited time and resources with which to observe at first hand the operations of his government, he relies necessarily upon the press to bring to him in convenient form the facts of those operations. Great responsibility is accordingly placed upon the news media to report fully and accurately the proceedings of government, and official records and documents open to the public are the basic data of governmental operations. Without the information provided by the press most of us and many of our representatives would be unable to vote intelligently or to register opinions on the administration of government generally. With respect to judicial proceedings in particular, the function of the press serves to guarantee the fairness of trials and to bring to bear the beneficial effects of public scrutiny upon the administration of justice.

Appellee has claimed in this litigation that the efforts of the press have infringed his right to privacy by broadcasting to the world the fact that his daughter was a rape victim. The commission of crime, prosecutions resulting from it, and judicial proceedings arising from the prosecutions, however, are without question events of legitimate concern to the public and consequently fall within the responsibility of the press to report the operations of government.

The special protected nature of accurate reports of judicial proceedings has repeatedly been recognized. This Court, in an opinion written by MR. JUSTICE DOUGLAS, has said:

"A trial is a public event. What transpires in the court room is public property. If a transcript of the court proceedings had been published, we suppose none would claim that the judge could punish the publisher for contempt. And we can see no difference though the conduct of the attorneys, of the jury, or even of the judge himself, may have reflected on the court. *Those who see and hear what transpired can report it with impunity.* There is no special perquisite of the judiciary which enables it, as distinguished from other institutions of democratic government, to suppress, edit, or censor events which transpire in proceedings before it."

The developing law surrounding the tort of invasion of privacy recognizes a privilege in the press to report the events of judicial proceedings. The Warren and Brandeis article noted that the proposed new right would be limited in the same manner as actions for libel and slander where such a publication was a privileged communication: "the right to privacy is not invaded by any publication made in a court of justice. . . . and (at least in many jurisdictions) reports of any such proceedings would in some measure be accorded a like privilege."

The Restatement of Torts, § 867, embraced an action for privacy. . . . According to this draft, ascertaining and publishing the contents of public records are simply not within the reach of these kinds of privacy actions.

Thus even the prevailing law of invasion of privacy generally recognizes that the interests in privacy fade when the information involved already appears on the public record. The conclusion is compelling when viewed in terms of the First and Fourteenth Amendments and in light of the public interest in a vigorous press. The Georgia cause of action for invasion of privacy through public disclosure of the name of a rape victim imposes sanctions on pure expression—the content of a publication—and not conduct or a combination of speech and nonspeech elements that might otherwise be open to regulation or prohibition.

The publication of truthful information available on the public record contains none of the indicia of those limited categories of expression, such as "fighting" words, which "are no essential part of any exposition of ideas, and are of such slight social value as a step to truth that any benefit that may be derived from them is clearly outweighed by the social interest in order and morality."

By placing the information in the public domain on official court records, the State must be presumed to have concluded that the public interest was thereby being served. Public records by their very nature are of interest to those concerned with the administration of government, and a public benefit is performed by the reporting of the true contents of the records by the media. The freedom of the press to publish that information appears to us to be of critical importance to our type of government in which the citizenry is the final judge of the proper conduct of public business. In preserving that form of government the First and Fourteenth Amendments command nothing less than that the States may not impose sanctions on the publication of truthful information contained in official court records open to public inspection.

We are reluctant to embark on a course that would make public records generally available to the media but forbid their publication if offensive to the sensibilities of the supposed reasonable man. Such a rule would make it very difficult for the media to inform citizens about the public business and yet stay within the law. The rule would invite timidity and self-censorship and very likely lead to the suppression of many items that would otherwise be published and that should be made available to the public. At the very least, the First and Fourteenth Amendments will not allow exposing the press to liability for truthfully publishing information released to the public in official court records. If there are privacy interests to be protected in judicial proceedings, the States must respond by means which avoid public documentation or other exposure of private information. Their political institutions must weigh the interests in privacy with the interests of the public to know and of the press to publish. Once true information is disclosed in public court documents open to public inspection, the press cannot be sanctioned for publishing it. In this instance as in others reliance must rest upon the judgment of those who decide what to publish or broadcast.

Appellant Wassell based his televised report upon notes taken during the court proceedings and obtained the name of the victim from the indictments handed to him at his request during a recess in the hearing. Appellee has not contended that the name was obtained in an improper fashion or that it was not on an official court document open to public inspection. Under these circumstances, the protection of freedom of the press provided by the First and Fourteenth Amendments bars the State of Georgia from making appellants' broadcast the basis of civil liability.

Reversed.

CHIEF JUSTICE WARREN BURGER concurs in the judgment.

JUSTICE LEWIS POWELL, Jr., concurring, with whom **JUSTICE WILLIAM DOUGLAS** joins. . . .

JUSTICE WILLIAM DOUGLAS, concurring in the judgment.

I agree that the state judgment is "final," and I also agree in the reversal of the Georgia court. On the merits, the case for me is on all fours with *New Jersey State Lottery Comm'n v. United States*. For the reasons I stated in my dissent from our disposition of that case, there is no power on the part of government to suppress or penalize the publication of "news of the day."

JUSTICE WILLIAM REHNQUIST, dissenting.

Because I am of the opinion that the decision which is the subject of this appeal is not a "final" judgment or decree, as that term is used in 28 U. S. C. § 1257, I would dismiss this appeal for want of jurisdiction. . . .

Riley v. California
SUPREME COURT OF THE UNITED STATES
134 S. Ct. 2473 (2014)

CHIEF JUSTICE JOHN ROBERTS delivered the Court's opinion:

These two cases raise a common question: whether the police may, without a warrant, search digital information on a cellphone seized from an individual who has been arrested.

In the first case, petitioner David Riley was stopped by a police officer for driving with expired registration tags. In the course of the stop, the officer also learned that Riley's license had been suspended. The officer impounded Riley's car, pursuant to department policy, and another officer conducted an inventory search of the car. Riley was arrested for possession of concealed and loaded firearms when that search turned up two handguns under the car's hood.

An officer searched Riley incident to the arrest and found items associated with the "Bloods" street gang. He also seized a cellphone from Riley's pants pocket. . . .

At the police station about two hours after the arrest, a detective specializing in gangs further examined the contents of the phone. The detective testified that he "went through" Riley's phone "looking for evidence, because . . . gang members will often video themselves with guns or take pictures of themselves with the guns." . . . The police also found photographs of Riley standing in front of a car they suspected had been involved in a shooting a few weeks earlier.

Riley was ultimately charged, in connection with that earlier shooting, with firing at an occupied vehicle, assault with a semiautomatic firearm, and attempted murder. . . . Prior to trial, Riley moved to suppress all evidence that the police had obtained from his cellphone. He contended that the searches of his phone violated the Fourth Amendment, because they had been performed without a warrant and were not otherwise justified by exigent circumstances. The trial court rejected that argument. At Riley's trial, police officers testified about the photographs and videos found on the phone, and some of the photographs were admitted into evidence. Riley was convicted on all three counts and received an enhanced sentence of 15 years to life in prison. . . .

In the second case, a police officer performing routine surveillance observed respondent Brima Wurie make an apparent drug sale from a car. Officers subsequently arrested Wurie and took him to the police station. At the station, the officers seized two cellphones from Wurie's person. The one at issue here was a "flip phone." . . . Five to ten minutes after arriving at the station, the officers noticed that the phone was repeatedly receiving calls from a source identified as "my house" on the phone's external screen. A few minutes later, they . . . pressed one button on the phone to access its call log, then another button to determine the phone number associated with the "my house" label. They next used an online phone directory to trace that phone number to an apartment building.

When the officers went to the building, they saw Wurie's name on a mailbox and observed through a window a woman who resembled the woman in the photograph on Wurie's phone. They secured the apartment while obtaining a search warrant and, upon later executing the warrant, found and seized 215 grams of crack cocaine, marijuana, drug paraphernalia, a firearm and ammunition, and cash.

Wurie was charged with distributing crack cocaine, possessing crack cocaine with intent to distribute, and being a felon in possession of a firearm and ammunition. He moved to suppress the evidence obtained from the search of the apartment, arguing that it was the fruit of an unconstitutional search of his cellphone. The District Court denied the motion. Wurie was convicted on all three counts and sentenced to 262 months in prison.

A divided panel of the First Circuit reversed the denial of Wurie's motion to suppress and vacated Wurie's convictions for possession with intent to distribute and possession of a firearm as a felon. The court held that cellphones are distinct from other physical possessions that may be searched incident to arrest without a warrant, because of the amount of personal data cellphones contain and the negligible threat they pose to law enforcement interests.

We granted certiorari.

The Fourth Amendment provides: "The right of the people to be secure in their persons, houses, papers, and effects, against unreasonable searches and seizures, shall not be violated, and no Warrants shall issue, but upon probable cause, supported by Oath or affirmation, and particularly describing the place to be searched, and the persons or things to be seized."

As the text makes clear, "the ultimate touchstone of the Fourth Amendment is 'reasonableness.'" Our cases have determined that "[w]here a search is undertaken by law enforcement officials to discover evidence of criminal wrongdoing, . . . reasonableness generally requires the obtaining of a judicial warrant." Such a warrant ensures that the inferences to support a search are "drawn by a neutral and detached magistrate instead of being judged by the officer engaged in the often competitive enterprise of ferreting out crime." In the absence of a warrant, a search is reasonable only if it falls within a specific exception to the warrant requirement.

The two cases before us concern the reasonableness of a warrantless search incident to a lawful arrest.

. . . These cases require us to decide how the search incident to arrest doctrine applies to modern cellphones, which are now such a pervasive and insistent part of daily life that the proverbial visitor from Mars might conclude they were an important feature of human anatomy. A smart phone of the sort taken from Riley was unheard of ten years ago; a significant majority of American adults now own such phones. Even less sophisticated phones like Wurie's, which have already faded in popularity since Wurie was arrested in 2007, have been around for less than 15 years.

. . . Digital data stored on a cellphone cannot itself be used as a weapon to harm an arresting officer or to effectuate the arrestee's escape. Law enforcement officers remain free to examine the physical aspects of a phone to ensure that it will not be used as a weapon—say, to determine whether there is a razor blade hidden between the phone and its case. Once an officer has secured a phone and eliminated any potential physical threats, however, data on the phone can endanger no one.

. . . The United States and California both suggest that a search of cellphone data might help ensure officer safety in more indirect ways, for example by alerting officers that confederates of the arrestee are headed to the scene. There is undoubtedly a strong government interest in warning officers about such possibilities, but neither the United States nor California offers evidence to suggest that their concerns are based on actual experience. . . . Accordingly, the interest in protecting officer safety does not justify dispensing with the warrant requirement across the board.

. . . Both Riley and Wurie concede that officers could have seized and secured their cellphones to prevent destruction of evidence while seeking a warrant. That is a sensible concession. And once law enforcement officers have secured a cellphone, there is no longer any risk that the arrestee himself will be able to delete incriminating data from the phone.

The United States and California argue that information on a cellphone may nevertheless be vulnerable to two types of evidence destruction unique to digital data—remote wiping and data encryption. . . .

As an initial matter, these broader concerns about the loss of evidence are distinct from . . . focus on a defendant who responds to arrest by trying to conceal or destroy evidence within his reach. With respect to remote wiping, the Government's primary concern turns on the actions of third parties who are not present at the scene of arrest. And data encryption is even further afield. There, the Government focuses on the ordinary operation of a phone's security features, apart from *any* active attempt by a defendant or his associates to conceal or destroy evidence upon arrest.

We have also been given little reason to believe that either problem is prevalent. . . .

. . . Moreover, in situations in which an arrest might trigger a remote-wipe attempt or an officer discovers an unlocked phone, it is not clear that the ability to conduct a warrantless search would make much of a difference. The need to effect the arrest, secure the scene, and tend to other pressing matters means that law enforcement officers may well not be able to turn their attention to a cellphone right away. Cellphone data would be vulnerable to remote wiping from the time an individual anticipates arrest to the time any eventual search of the phone is completed, which might be at the station house hours later. Likewise, an officer who seizes a phone in an unlocked state might not be able to begin his search in the short time remaining before the phone locks and data becomes encrypted.

In any event, as to remote wiping, law enforcement is not without specific means to address the threat. Remote wiping can be fully prevented by disconnecting a phone from the network. . . . The search incident to arrest exception rests not only on the heightened government interests at stake in a volatile arrest situation, but also on an arrestee's reduced privacy interests upon being taken into police custody. . . .

The fact that an arrestee has diminished privacy interests does not mean that the Fourth Amendment falls out of the picture entirely. Not every search "is acceptable solely because a person is in custody." To the contrary, when "privacy-related concerns are weighty enough" a "search may require a warrant, notwithstanding the diminished expectations of privacy of the arrestee." . . .

The United States asserts that a search of all data stored on a cellphone is "materially indistinguishable" from searches of . . . physical items. That is like saying a ride on horseback is materially indistinguishable from a flight to the moon. Both are ways of getting from point A to point B, but little else justifies lumping them together. Modern cellphones, as a category, implicate privacy concerns far beyond those implicated by the search of a cigarette pack, a wallet, or a purse. A conclusion that inspecting the contents of an arrestee's pockets works no substantial additional intrusion on privacy beyond the arrest itself may make sense as applied to physical items, but any extension of that reasoning to digital data has to rest on its own bottom.

Cellphones differ in both a quantitative and a qualitative sense from other objects that might be kept on an arrestee's person. The term "cellphone" is itself misleading shorthand; many of these devices are in fact minicomputers that also happen to have the capacity to be used as a telephone. They could just as easily be called cameras, video players, rolodexes, calendars, tape recorders, libraries, diaries, albums, televisions, maps, or newspapers.

One of the most notable distinguishing features of modern cellphones is their immense storage capacity. Before cellphones, a search of a person was limited by physical realities and tended as a general matter to constitute only a narrow intrusion on privacy. Most people cannot lug around every piece of mail they have received for the past several months, every picture they have taken, or every book or article they have read—nor would they have any reason to attempt to do so. . . .

But the possible intrusion on privacy is not physically limited in the same way when it comes to cellphones. The current top-selling smart phone has a standard capacity of 16 gigabytes (and is available with up to 64 gigabytes). Sixteen gigabytes translates to millions of pages of text, thousands of pictures, or hundreds of videos. Cellphones couple that capacity with the ability to store many different types of information: Even the most basic phones that sell for less than $20 might hold photographs, picture messages, text messages, Internet browsing history, a calendar, a thousand-entry phone book, and so on. We expect that the gulf between physical practicability and digital capacity will only continue to widen in the future.

The storage capacity of cellphones has several interrelated consequences for privacy. First, a cellphone collects in one place many distinct types of information—an address, a note, a prescription, a bank statement, a video—that reveal much more in combination than any isolated record. Second, a cellphone's capacity allows even just one type of information to convey far more than previously possible. The sum of an individual's private life can be reconstructed through a thousand photographs labeled with dates, locations, and descriptions; the same cannot be said of a photograph or two of loved ones tucked into a wallet. Third, the data on a phone can date back to the purchase of the phone, or even earlier. A person might carry in his pocket a slip of paper reminding him to call Mr. Jones; he would not carry a record of all his communications with Mr. Jones for the past several months, as would routinely be kept on a phone.

Finally, there is an element of pervasiveness that characterizes cellphones but not physical records. Prior to the digital age, people did not typically carry a cache of sensitive personal information with them as they went about their day. Now it is the person who is not carrying a cellphone, with all that it contains, who is the exception. According to one poll, nearly three-quarters of smart phone users report being within five feet of their phones most of the time, with 12% admitting that they even use their phones in the shower. A decade ago police officers searching an arrestee might have occasionally stumbled across a highly personal item such as a diary. But those discoveries were likely to be few and far between. Today, by contrast, it is no exaggeration to say that many of the more than 90% of American adults who own a cellphone keep on their person a digital record of nearly every aspect of their lives—from the mundane to the intimate. Allowing the police to scrutinize such records on a routine basis is quite different from allowing them to search a personal item or two in the occasional case.

Although the data stored on a cellphone is distinguished from physical records by quantity alone, certain types of data are also qualitatively different. An Internet search and browsing history, for example, can be found on an Internet-enabled phone and could reveal an individual's private interests or concerns—perhaps a search for certain symptoms of disease, coupled with frequent visits to WebMD. Data on a cellphone can also reveal where a person has been. Historic location information is a standard feature on many smart phones and can reconstruct someone's specific movements down to the minute, not only around town but also within a particular building.

Mobile application software on a cellphone, or "apps," offer a range of tools for managing detailed information about all aspects of a person's life. . . . There are over a million apps available in each of the two major app stores; the phrase "there's an app for that" is now part of the popular lexicon. The average smart phone user has installed 33 apps, which together can form a revealing montage of the user's life.

In 1926, Learned Hand observed . . . that it is "a totally different thing to search a man's pockets and use against him what they contain, from ransacking his house for everything which may incriminate him." If his pockets contain a cellphone, however, that is no longer true. Indeed, a cellphone search would typically expose to the government far *more* than the most exhaustive search of a house: A phone not only contains in digital form many sensitive records previously found in the home; it also contains a broad array of private information never found in a home in any form—unless the phone is.

To further complicate the scope of the privacy interests at stake, the data a user views on many modern cellphones may not in fact be stored on the device itself. Treating a cellphone as a container whose contents may be searched incident to an arrest is a bit strained as an initial matter. But the analogy crumbles entirely when a cellphone is used to access data located elsewhere, at the tap of a screen. That is what cellphones, with increasing frequency, are designed to do by taking advantage of "cloud computing." Cloud computing is the capacity of Internet-connected devices to display data stored on remote servers rather than on the device itself. Cellphone users often may not know whether particular information is stored on the device or in the cloud, and it generally makes little difference. Moreover, the same type of data may be stored locally on the device for one user and in the cloud for another. . . .

[A]t oral argument California suggested a different limiting principle, under which officers could search cellphone data if they could have obtained the same information from a pre-digital counterpart. But the fact that a search in the pre-digital era could have turned up a photograph or two in a wallet does not justify a search of thousands of photos in a digital gallery. The fact that someone could have tucked a paper bank statement in a pocket does not justify a search of every bank statement from the last five years. And to make matters worse, such an analogue test would allow law enforcement to search a range of items contained on a phone, even though people would be unlikely to carry such a variety of information in physical form. In Riley's case, for example, it is implausible that he would have strolled around with video tapes, photo albums, and an address book all crammed into his pockets. But because each of those items has a pre-digital analogue, police under California's proposal would be able to search a phone for all of those items—a significant diminution of privacy.

In addition, an analogue test would launch courts on a difficult line-drawing expedition to determine which digital files are comparable to physical records. Is an e-mail equivalent to a letter? Is a voicemail equivalent to a phone message slip? It is not clear how officers could make these kinds of decisions before conducting a search, or how courts would apply the proposed rule after the fact. An analogue test would "keep defendants and judges guessing for years to come."

We cannot deny that our decision today will have an impact on the ability of law enforcement to combat crime. Cellphones have become important tools in facilitating coordination and communication among members of criminal enterprises, and can provide valuable incriminating information about dangerous criminals. Privacy comes at a cost.

Our holding, of course, is not that the information on a cellphone is immune from search; it is instead that a warrant is generally required before such a search, even when a cellphone is seized incident to arrest. Our cases have historically recognized that the warrant requirement is "an important working part of our machinery of government," not merely "an inconvenience to be somehow 'weighed' against the claims of police efficiency." Recent technological advances similar to those discussed here have, in addition, made the process of obtaining a warrant itself more efficient.

Moreover, even though the search incident to arrest exception does not apply to cellphones, other case-specific exceptions may still justify a warrantless search of a particular phone. "One well-recognized exception applies when 'the exigencies of the situation' make the needs of law enforcement so compelling that [a] warrantless search is objectively reasonable under the Fourth Amendment." Such exigencies could include the need to prevent the imminent destruction of evidence in individual cases, to pursue a fleeing suspect, and to assist persons who are seriously injured or are threatened with imminent injury. . . .

In light of the availability of the exigent circumstances exception, there is no reason to believe that law enforcement officers will not be able to address some of the more extreme hypotheticals that have been suggested: a suspect texting an accomplice who, it is feared, is preparing to detonate a bomb, or a child abductor who may have information about the child's location on his cellphone. The defendants here recognize—indeed, they stress—that such fact-specific threats may justify a warrantless search of cellphone data. The critical point is that, unlike the search incident to arrest exception, the exigent circumstances exception requires a court to examine whether an emergency justified a warrantless search in each particular case.

Our cases have recognized that the Fourth Amendment was the founding generation's response to the reviled "general warrants" and "writs of assistance" of the colonial era, which allowed British officers to rummage through homes in an unrestrained search for evidence of criminal activity. Opposition to such searches was in fact one of the driving forces behind the Revolution itself. . . .

Modern cellphones are not just another technological convenience. With all they contain and all they may reveal, they hold for many Americans "the privacies of life." The fact that technology now allows an individual to carry such information in his hand does not make the information any less worthy of the protection for which the Founders fought. Our answer to the question of what police must do before searching a cellphone seized incident to an arrest is accordingly simple—get a warrant.

We reverse the judgment of the California Court of Appeal in No. 13-132 and remand the case for further proceedings not inconsistent with this opinion. We affirm the judgment of the First Circuit in No. 13-212.

It is so ordered.

JUSTICE SAMUEL ALITO, concurring in part and concurring in the judgment.

I agree with the Court that law enforcement officers, in conducting a lawful search incident to arrest, must generally obtain a warrant before searching information stored or accessible on a cellphone. I write separately to address two points.

First, I am not convinced at this time that the ancient rule on searches incident to arrest is based exclusively (or even primarily) on the need to protect the safety of arresting officers and the need to prevent the destruction of evidence. This rule antedates the adoption of the Fourth Amendment by at least a century. . . .

I agree that we should not mechanically apply the rule used in the pre-digital era to the search of a cellphone. Many cellphones now in use are capable of storing and accessing a quantity of information, some highly personal, that no person would ever have had on his person in hard-copy form. This calls for a new balancing of law enforcement and privacy interests.

The Court strikes this balance in favor of privacy interests with respect to all cellphones and all information found in them, and this approach leads to anomalies. . . .

While the Court's approach leads to anomalies, I do not see a workable alternative. Law enforcement officers need clear rules regarding searches incident to arrest, and it would take many cases and many years for the courts to develop more nuanced rules. And during that time, the nature of the electronic devices that ordinary Americans carry on their persons would continue to change.

This brings me to my second point. While I agree with the holding of the Court, I would reconsider the question presented here if either Congress or state legislatures, after assessing the legitimate needs of law enforcement and the privacy interests of cellphone owners, enact legislation that draws reasonable distinctions based on categories of information or perhaps other variables.

The regulation of electronic surveillance provides an instructive example. After this Court held that electronic surveillance constitutes a search even when no property interest is invaded, Congress responded by enacting Title III of the Omnibus Crime Control and Safe Streets Act of 1968. Since that time, electronic surveillance has been governed primarily, not by decisions of this Court, but by the statute, which authorizes but imposes detailed restrictions on electronic surveillance.

Modern cellphones are of great value for both lawful and unlawful purposes. They can be used in committing many serious crimes, and they present new and difficult law enforcement problems. At the same time, because of the role that these devices have come to play in contemporary life, searching their contents implicates very sensitive privacy interests that this Court is poorly positioned to understand and evaluate. Many forms of modern technology are making it easier and easier for both government and private entities to amass a wealth of information about the lives of ordinary Americans, and at the same time, many ordinary Americans are choosing to make public much information that was seldom revealed to outsiders just a few decades ago.

In light of these developments, it would be very unfortunate if privacy protection in the 21st century were left primarily to the federal courts using the blunt instrument of the Fourth Amendment. Legislatures, elected by the people, are in a better position than we are to assess and respond to the changes that have already occurred and those that almost certainly will take place in the future.

News must not be unnecessarily cut off at its source, for without freedom to acquire information the right to publish would be impermissibly compromised. Accordingly, a right to gather news, of some dimensions, must exist.

—U.S. Supreme Court Justice Lewis Powell[1]

White House Press Secretary Sean Spicer began President Trump's first term battling regularly with the media over "fake news" reports and leaks of information from the White House and other executive branch offices.

7 GATHERING INFORMATION
Opportunities and Obstacles

SUPPOSE...

...that a team of law enforcement officers executes a search warrant on what they believe is the home of a suspect. A newspaper reporter and photographer accompany the officers, who forcibly enter the home in the early morning, awakening two residents, who are the suspect's parents. The couple assures the officers their son is not there. The photographer takes several pictures, though none are published. After a search of the home, the officers and journalists leave. Was the journalists' presence illegal? If so, who is responsible—the journalists or the law enforcement agency? Look for the answers to these questions when the case of *Wilson v. Layne* is discussed later in this chapter and excerpted at the end of the chapter.

ACCESS TO PLACES

While legal scholars and media advocates argue that the First Amendment should be understood to protect the right to gather information and report the news,[2] the U.S. Supreme Court has said merely that newsgathering plays an important role in advancing First Amendment interests.[3] Courts consistently rule that no explicit newsgathering right exists under the First Amendment. Journalists and other professional communicators enjoy no constitutional privilege to enter locations where news occurs.

Although professional communicators and social media junkies rely increasingly on online and other electronic sources, many remain committed to more traditional techniques. Some information is best obtained at the scene of the

Student Records

Medical Records

Driver's Information

Cases for Study

- ◆ *U.S. Department of Justice v. Reporters Committee for Freedom of the Press*
- ◆ *Wilson v. Layne*

news. Protections for access to public spaces and government meetings and records and the ability to gather information on- or offline are established by a complex array of statutes and court precedents.

Access to Public Property

Sidewalks, parks and a lot of public property are public forums reserved for use by the public with some limitations (see Chapter 2). Government may restrict access to ensure the proper functioning of public services and to protect public safety. Accordingly, police and other public safety officials may order individuals, including the press, to stay away from a crime scene or other event on public land or in public buildings. Anyone who disobeys a lawful order may be arrested for interfering with police functions.

Public officials do not have unlimited power over individuals at a scene, however. In one case, the city of New York agreed to pay an $18 million settlement for the arrest and detention—from a couple of hours to more than a day—of nearly 1,800 protesters, journalists and onlookers at the 2004 Republican National Convention.[4] In another case, the Seventh Circuit Court of Appeals found unconstitutional a Chicago ordinance that made it a crime for an individual to knowingly disregard police orders to disperse near a site of disorderly conduct. The case involved an individual's arrest for refusal to stay on the sidewalk near where the officer judged protesters to be causing "serious inconvenience, annoyance or alarm."[5] The court said the law was too broad, vague and subjective to pass constitutional review.

Some land and buildings, such as military bases and polling sites, are government owned or controlled but not open to general admission by the public or journalists.

LANDMARK CASES IN CONTEXT

Key   ■ Event
       ◆ Cases

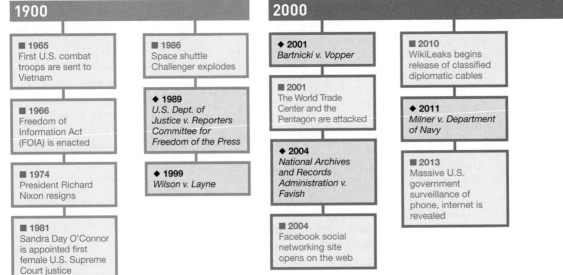

1900

■ 1965
First U.S. combat troops are sent to Vietnam

■ 1966
Freedom of Information Act (FOIA) is enacted

■ 1974
President Richard Nixon resigns

■ 1981
Sandra Day O'Connor is appointed first female U.S. Supreme Court justice

■ 1986
Space shuttle Challenger explodes

◆ 1989
U.S. Dept. of Justice v. Reporters Committee for Freedom of the Press

◆ 1999
Wilson v. Layne

2000

◆ 2001
Bartnicki v. Vopper

■ 2001
The World Trade Center and the Pentagon are attacked

◆ 2004
National Archives and Records Administration v. Favish

■ 2004
Facebook social networking site opens on the web

■ 2010
WikiLeaks begins release of classified diplomatic cables

◆ 2011
Milner v. Department of Navy

■ 2013
Massive U.S. government surveillance of phone, internet is revealed

Nonetheless, polling places should be open to the press, the U.S. Court of Appeals for the Sixth Circuit ruled.[6] An Ohio law required all nonvoters to stay well away from the polls. Applying strict scrutiny to what it viewed as a content-based restriction on nonvoter speech, the court found the law violated the press's First Amendment rights. The state had a compelling interest in ensuring orderly elections, but the law was not narrowly drawn to achieve that end, the court said.

The Third Circuit Court of Appeals disagreed.[7] A newspaper challenged Pennsylvania's law requiring people to remain 10 feet away from the polls. The court viewed the law as a limit not on speech but on newsgathering, which the First Amendment does not protect. The Third Circuit applied the two-pronged *Press-Enterprise* test that determines the public right of access to courtrooms (discussed in Chapter 8).[8] The *Press-Enterprise* test presumes access to sites and processes that traditionally have been open and whose purpose is logically advanced by public access. The government must meet a "weighty" burden to overcome this presumed access.

In reviewing the law restricting access to the polls, the Third Circuit said: First, although voting might once have been open, it was now more secret. Second, openness might benefit the process by reducing voter fraud or intimidation, but it also might deter some voters from exercising their right. The court concluded that both prongs of the test required affirming the limit on public access.

The Ninth Circuit Court of Appeals also used the *Press-Enterprise* test to decide whether the Bureau of Land Management violated the rights of reporters seeking access to government land.[9] A photojournalist sued to remove limits to her access to the holding facilities for wild horses rounded up by the BLM. The court remanded the case, noting that the two-pronged test should be used "to evaluate attempts to access a wide range of civil and administrative government activities." Despite finding that the horse roundups had been open traditionally and public access advanced the process,[10] the court upheld the restrictions. The court said the limits appropriately advanced the BLM's overriding interest in the safety of observers and did not unduly infringe First Amendment rights.

Christopher Ketcham, a widely published freelance journalist and former Knight Science Journalism fellow at the Massachusetts Institute of Technology, brought a suit against the U.S. National Park Service for its policy banning observers at the annual "cull" of buffalo from Yellowstone.[11] In denying Ketcham's request for an injunction to stop the policy, the federal district court in 2015 refused to apply the *Press-Enterprise* test "outside the context of trial proceedings." However, in dicta, the court said the culls had been closed historically and closures were narrowly tailored to protect the safety of workers and the public. Additionally, the court said, "viewing the culling of bison is not protected First Amendment speech or activity." It added that even were it to

Some of the estimated 900 bison culled from Yellowstone in 2015 awaiting slaughter in the Stephens Creek Capture Facility in Montana.

apply the First Amendment, it would find the park was a nonpublic forum and the ban was content-neutral.

A recent Department of Defense policy increased access to social media by military personnel, which opens new avenues for contact with enlisted military.[12] The policy requires all military units to allow access to social networking sites that do not contain restricted content, such as pornography. As a consequence, both the Marine Corps and the Army lifted permanent bans.

Long-standing military restrictions, such as bans on the reporting of troop locations and movements, still apply. Some arose after what many called the first televised war, the Vietnam conflict. Some blamed the nightly television coverage for the decline of U.S. public support for the war, and government officials resolved to better control media coverage of future military operations. More than a decade later, after government banned media access to the U.S. invasion of the Caribbean nation of Grenada, a congressional study recommended the use of "pool reporting"—reporting by a small, government-selected group of journalists who share their information and video with other media. Pool reporting since has restricted media movements and reporting on numerous military engagements and some high-profile trials.

● REAL WORLD LAW

Ejection of Embedded Journalist Raises Coverage Concerns

Wayne Anderson was an embedded journalist in Afghanistan when, despite the objections of those overseeing his embedded status, he reported on shootings of U.S. troops by Afghan National Army members. Based on its finding that Anderson had violated his embed agreement, the Army dismissed him, withdrew his credentials and sent him home.[1]

Anderson sued saying he had not violated his embed agreement. He sought to reverse his dismissal and reinstate his reporting credentials on the grounds that the military's actions violated the rights of a free press and harmed his reputation and his future employment.

The D.C. Circuit Court of Appeals declined to do so. Emphasizing the privilege of reporting in a war zone and minimizing any harm the dismissal caused, the court held that sovereign immunity and the military's authority to control the field of war barred Anderson's lawsuit. The Supreme Court declined to hear his appeal.[2]

Former Army intelligence analyst Chelsea Manning says dismissals like this, and the subsequent military blacklisting of the journalists involved, are central to the power of officials to control press coverage of military actions. "This creates reporting that flatters senior decision makers. A result is that the American public's access to the facts is gutted, which leaves them with no way to evaluate the conduct of American officials."[3]

---

1. Jacob Fischler, *Embedded Reporter Takes Army Ejection to Supreme Court*, LAW360, May 13, 2016, www.law360.com/articles/796298/embedded-reporter-takes-army-ejection-to-supreme-court.
2. Anderson v. Carter, 802 F.3d 4 (D.C. Cir. 2015), *cert. denied*, 137 S. Ct. 65 (2016).
3. Chelsea Manning, *The Fog Machine of War*, N.Y. TIMES, Jun. 14, 2014, www.nytimes.com/2014/06/15/opinion/sunday/chelsea-manning.

● REAL WORLD LAW

How to Sue for Police Harassment

The First Amendment clearly protects the right to speak on matters of public concern. The Fourth Amendment protects against unreasonable searches and seizures.[1]

If you believe you have been harassed by police and want to sue, you may use 42 U.S.C. § 1983, which Congress enacted to protect the civil rights of African-Americans in the post–Civil War era.[2] Section 1983, as it routinely is called, is an efficient mechanism for bringing private action in federal court to protect your constitutional rights. Section 1983 lawsuits may be used only against "state actors" "acting under the color of law," which includes law enforcement officials conducting their official duties.

One benefit of a Section 1983 lawsuit is that, if you win, your attorney's fees become the responsibility of the defendant. Because case law is well established in this area, police generally cannot rely on a qualified immunity defense. Qualified immunity protects state actors from liability only when their alleged violations involve rights that courts have not clearly established.

1. Fordyce v. City of Seattle, 55 F.3d 436 (9th Cir. 1995); Glik v. Cunniffe, 655 F.3d 78 (1st Cir. 2011); ACLU v. Alvarez, 679 F.3d 583 (7th Cir.), *cert. denied*, 133 S. Ct. 651 (2012); Bell v. Keating, 697 F.3d 445 (7th Cir. 2012); Allen Etzler, *U.S. Justice Department Issues Letters Supporting Citizens Recording Police Officers*, CAP. NEWS SERV., Apr. 26, 2013, cnsmaryland.org/2013/04/26/u-s-justice-department-issues-letters-supporting-citizens-recording-police-officers/.
2. Jon Loevy, *Section 1983 Litigation in a Nutshell: Make a Case of It!*, 17 J. DUPAGE CITY B. ASSOC., 2004–05, www.dcabrief.org/vol171004art2.html.

The DOD has collaborated with media to embed journalists in military units since the U.S. invasion of Iraq. Embedding provides reporters greater access and in-person war coverage but raises questions about loss of objectivity by reporters who identify too closely with the military units on whom they rely and report.[13]

Access to Quasi-Public Property

Some seemingly public property is closed to the public. If access to a specific area of public property is restricted, individuals must comply. Obtaining access through trespass, harassment or misrepresentation is illegal. For example, when an airplane crashed at a publicly owned airport, officers kept unauthorized people away. A television photojournalist followed an emergency vehicle through a roadblock and was ordered to leave. He then jumped a fence and began taking pictures of the site. He again was ordered to leave and was arrested when he refused to stop taking pictures unless he was arrested.

The Wisconsin Supreme Court upheld the photojournalist's conviction for disorderly conduct. It rejected the argument that the First Amendment requires news media access to emergency sites and pointed out that access was restricted, not denied, in this situation. Journalists who followed the airport's media guidelines were taken to the crash site.[14]

ACCESS TO GOVERNMENT MEETINGS AND RECORDS

"Knowledge will forever govern ignorance; and a people who mean to be their own governors must arm themselves with the power which knowledge gives."[15] The words are James Madison's. They epitomize both the spirit of, and the need for, openness in a democratic government. Liberal democratic theory maintains that government authorities have an obligation to shed light on their decision making and provide access to the information necessary to self-governance.

The creation of hundreds of specialized federal agencies through the mid-20th century increased the size and complexity of government and prompted citizen concerns about growing difficulty to understand or oversee government workings. Government business was being conducted on multiple levels outside the U.S. Capitol. Increasingly closed and complicated federal operations led to a public call for greater government transparency and laws to ensure greater access to government.[16] Today two types of laws enhance citizen access to government meetings and government records. (Access to courts and their records is addressed in Chapter 8.)

Open Federal Meetings

Journalists and members of the public gain valuable information from government meetings and records. The public's business is conducted through a myriad of meetings held by governing and policymaking bodies at all levels of government. Because the processes of meetings as well as their results are of legitimate public interest, the **Government in the Sunshine Act**—also known as the "Federal Open Meetings Law"—was passed 40 years ago.[17] The act requires the 50 or so federal agencies, commissions and boards with some independent authority and with members appointed by the president to conduct their business in public. They must give public notice of their meetings and record decisions.

Ten exemptions allow boards to close meetings or hold executive sessions to debate specific topics. Exemptions 1 through 9 are similar to those of the federal Freedom of Information Act detailed below.[18] Exemption 10 applies to agency litigation or arbitration. A frequent reason for closure is that the board will discuss matters related to personnel, and closure protects the privacy of those involved.

Approximately 1,000 advisory boards provide expert guidance to the federal government. They play a major role in the development of government policy but are not covered by the Government in the Sunshine Act because they have no independent authority. The Federal Advisory Committee Act opens their meetings and records to the public unless the committee is "composed wholly of full-time officers or employees of the federal government."[19]

Open State Meetings

All states and the District of Columbia have laws or constitutional provisions ensuring some degree of public access to government meetings.[20] The laws vary widely, as do the penalties for violating them. In general, open-meetings laws trigger public access whenever a quorum of a decision-making body deliberates public business.

Government in the Sunshine Act Sometimes referred to as the Federal Open Meetings Law, an act passed in 1976 that mandates that meetings of federal government agencies be open to the public unless all or some part of a meeting is exempted according to exceptions outlined in the law.

● POINTS OF LAW

State Open-Meetings Laws: The New York Example

The following is excerpted from the New York State Open Meetings Law's section on opening meetings and executive sessions:

(a) Every meeting of a public body shall be open to the general public, except that an executive session of such body may be called and business transacted thereat in accordance with section one hundred five of this article. (b) Public bodies shall make or cause to be made all reasonable efforts to ensure that meetings are held in facilities that permit barrier-free physical access to the physically handicapped, as defined in subdivision five of section fifty of the public buildings law. (c) A public body that uses videoconferencing to conduct its meetings shall provide an opportunity to attend, listen and observe at any site at which a member participates. (d) Public bodies shall make or cause to be made all reasonable efforts to ensure that meetings are held in an appropriate facility which can adequately accommodate members of the public who wish to attend such meetings.[1]

---

1. New York Open Meetings Law, N.Y. Pub. Off. Law § 103 (1976).

Most state laws define a meeting as either a physical gathering or videoconference that allows members to interact in real time.[21] Applying this logic, some observers believe open-meetings laws should apply to online chats. Boards may meet the need for public access either through space in their meeting room or through electronic access. Most state laws require agencies to provide public notice in advance of meetings and to record minutes of their business. A few states also require boards to keep minutes of their executive sessions, which become available to the public if closure is improper or once the need for closure has passed.

Several states outline provisions for the enforcement of open-meetings laws. In Michigan, for example, any citizen may challenge in court a decision made by a public body to deny access. If the court determines that the closure violated the law, the court can invalidate that decision and any actions taken during the closure. In addition, a public official who intentionally breaks the law is subject to a fine up to $1,000. A second deliberate violation can result in a fine up to $2,000, a jail term of up to one year or both.[22]

In a ruling related to open meetings, the Ninth Circuit Court of Appeals recently struck down a California city ordinance that permitted the city council to evict members of the public from its meetings for "disorderly, insolent or disruptive behavior."[23] The court said the law was unconstitutionally overbroad because it permitted the counsel to expel citizens who were merely "impertinent, insolent or essentially offensive" but caused no disruption.

Library of Congress (LC-USZ62-95680)

Lyndon Johnson usually signed bills into laws with a crowd, but the Freedom of Information Act was signed at the last minute at his ranch in Texas.

Freedom of Information Act
The federal law that requires records held by federal government agencies to be made available to the public, provided that the information sought does not fall within one of nine exempted categories.

legislative history
Congressional reports and records containing reports of discussions about proposed legislation.

Open Federal Records

Congress passed the **Freedom of Information Act** more than 50 years ago. It was intended to permit any person access to records held by federal executive branch agencies. The act has been amended, most recently with the Open Government Act of 2007.[24]

The U.S. Supreme Court has said the law's presumption is that "disclosure, not secrecy, is the dominant objective."[25] Exemptions that allow government to withhold information must be interpreted narrowly to afford the greatest possible access.

The language of FOIA provides access to records held by federal agencies. This raises two questions:

1. *What is an agency?* "Agency" is defined as "any executive department, military department, Government corporation, Government controlled corporation, or other establishment in the executive branch of the Government, including the Executive Office of the President, or any independent regulatory agency."[26] This includes all federal executive offices, such as the Office of Management and Budget and the Office of Policy Development but excludes the White House itself, including the president's closest advisers and their staffs.[27] It also excludes Congress and the federal courts as well as quasi-executive organizations that receive federal funding but are not under the direct control of the federal government—for example, the Corporation for Public Broadcasting.

   Covered federal agencies, departments, commissions and government-controlled corporations include cabinet-level departments such as Defense, Homeland Security and Justice; regulatory agencies such as the Federal Communications Commission and the Securities and Exchange Commission; and NASA and the U.S. Postal Service.

2. *What is a record?* Neither the text of FOIA nor its **legislative history** defines "record,"[28] but courts interpret the act to apply to all tangible or fixed items that (a) document government actions and (b) may be reproduced. Thus, computer files, paper reports, films, videotapes, photographs and audio recordings are records under the law. A record already exists; it is not something government could compile from the diverse information it holds.

While the definitions of agency and record are relatively clear, the criteria necessary to link an agency and a record in order for something to qualify as an "agency record" remain in dispute. The "statutory silence"[29] on the precise definition of covered agency records leaves courts to construe the key legal phrase.[30] The U.S. Supreme Court has reasoned that "[t]he use of the word 'agency' as a modifier demonstrates that Congress contemplated

▐ SOCIAL MEDIA LAW

Report Urges Transparency Renaissance

Nine out of 10 open government experts "fear the new administration will worsen freedom of information and government transparency," a 2017 report concludes.[1]

Calling for a "renaissance" in freedom of information to reverse the "steady decline in transparency and . . . in public records access" during the second half of the Obama administration, the report urges a new focus on this fundamental aspect of democratic self-governance.

The report urges a rebirth of a national commitment to government transparency through:

1. The banding together of citizens, journalists, civil society organizations and government officials to advance open government;

2. The networking of state action centers, or hubs, to provide quick response to access problems, advocate legislative change as needed and propel access litigation;

3. A publicity campaign to promote awareness, education and advocacy for freedom of information; and

4. Development and distribution of state-of-the-art digital technologies to facilitate the distribution of government information to the public.

---

1. David Cuillier, *Forecasting Freedom of Information*, KNIGHT FOUNDATION, Mar. 11, 2017, www.knightfoundation.org/reports/forecasting-freedom-of-information.

---

some relationship between an 'agency' and the 'record' requested."[31] In Senate hearings, the term "agency record" was assumed to include "all papers which an agency preserves in the performance of its functions."[32]

Shortly after adoption of FOIA, a federal appellate court provided a construction of agency record.[33] A party sought a congressional transcript held by the CIA. The CIA argued that the transcript was a congressional document exempt from FOIA coverage. The court agreed and ruled that the agency's mere possession of a document did not transform it into an agency record.[34]

Reporters have relied on FOIA to obtain information including data related to NASA mishaps,[35] design deficiencies in the Ford Pinto and the Hubble Space Telescope, dangers to local communities from nuclear weapons plants and hazardous lead levels in imported wines. Requesting a record from a federal government agency is relatively easy. (Obtaining the record may be another matter.) Familiarity with FOIA and the preferred procedures enhances the likelihood that the request will be granted.

Requests for records may be done by telephone, email or mail. Agencies enjoy some discretion on whether to release records, so understanding human nature may ease the process.[36] It may help to begin with a friendly telephone call to identify the record holder and perhaps obtain the records without further effort. A written request keeps better track of the date of the request, the records requested and the agency's responses, all of which are essential if you later sue the agency to obtain the records. Sometimes agencies ignore friendly requests, so pointed reminders of the law also may be useful in getting their attention.[37]

⦿ POINT OF LAW

Records Under FOIA

In light of the Freedom of Information Act's unclear definition of agency record, courts have developed the following criteria:

- A record is anything in documentary form to be provided in the preferred format of the requester.
- An agency record must be part of the legitimate conduct of the agency's official duties.
- An agency record likely includes any document created and possessed by the agency.
- A record possessed but not created by an agency may not qualify as an agency record.
- An agency is not required to create a record that does not exist or to obtain a requested record not under agency control.

Federal agency websites offer instructions on how to file FOIA requests. The Reporters Committee for Freedom of the Press also provides a useful online guide,[38] with an online FOIA letter generator[39] and step-by-step help with letter preparation.

Requests should be as detailed and specific as possible as you may be charged for time-consuming records searches. Agencies may charge search and/or duplicating fees at cost, or they may waive fees. FOIA provides for fee waivers for news media and fee reductions for nonprofit organizations. Other users find that requests for fee waivers may trigger lengthy delays.

Agencies have 20 working days to respond to FOIA requests. "Respond" does not mean comply, but the U.S. Court of Appeals for the District of Columbia Circuit recently held that the agency "must at least indicate within the relevant time period the scope of the documents it will produce and the exemptions it will claim with respect to any withheld documents."[40] Appeals may be filed to unreasonable delays, and denials may be challenged in a federal court.

The presumption of access places the burden of proof on government to show why any delay or nondisclosure is valid. The agency must cite the specific exemption that justifies nondisclosure and must limit nondisclosure to only those portions of the requested records that qualify. For example, a federal judge ruled that the National Nuclear Security Administration unreasonably delayed response to numerous requests for records on nuclear waste sites in New Mexico. The vague justification that the records were complex and sensitive did not meet the agency's obligations under FOIA.[41]

The federal FOIA Improvement Act of 2016 mandates a "presumption of openness" that permits agencies to withhold records only if it is "reasonably foreseeable" that disclosure would harm one of the interests protected by FOIA's exemptions.[42]

Courts have allowed federal agencies essentially to say, "We don't have to tell you if we have the documents." This nonreply reply is called a "Glomar response," taken from the CIA's refusal to disclose whether it had information related to rumored involvement of Howard Hughes' Glomar Explorer in U.S. attempts to recover a lost Soviet submarine. More recently, though, the D.C. Circuit Court of Appeals refused to allow the CIA to use the Glomar response when the American Civil Liberties Union requested documents about drones used for targeted killings. The court said national security would not be harmed by the CIA's revealing whether it had such documents given that public officials had revealed the CIA's involvement in the drone program.[43]

● REAL WORLD LAW

Sample FOIA Request Letter[1]

Agency Head [or Freedom of Information Act Officer]

Name of Agency

Address of Agency

City, State, Zip Code

Re: Freedom of Information Act Request

Dear _____:

    This is a request under the Freedom of Information Act.

    I request that a copy of the following documents [or documents containing the following information] be provided to me: [identify the documents or information as specifically as possible].

    In order to help to determine my status to assess fees, you should know that I am (insert a suitable description of the requester and the purpose of the request).

    [Sample requester descriptions:

    a representative of the news media affiliated with the _____ newspaper (magazine, television station, etc.), and this request is made as part of news gathering and not for a commercial use.

    affiliated with an educational or noncommercial scientific institution, and this request is made for a scholarly or scientific purpose and not for a commercial use.

    an individual seeking information for personal use and not for a commercial use.

    affiliated with a private corporation and am seeking information for use in the company's business.]

    [Optional] I am willing to pay fees for this request up to a maximum of $___. If you estimate that the fees will exceed this limit, please inform me first.

    [Optional] I request a waiver of all fees for this request. Disclosure of the requested information to me is in the public interest because it is likely to contribute significantly to public understanding of the operations or activities of the government and is not primarily in my commercial interest. [Include a specific explanation.]

    Thank you for your consideration of this request.

Sincerely,

Name

Address

City, State, Zip Code

Telephone number [Optional]

---

1. *Sample FOIA Request Letters*, National Freedom of Information Coalition, www.nfoic.org/sample-foia-request-letters.

Electronic
Freedom of
Information Act A
1996 amendment
to the Freedom
of Information
Act that applies
the act to
electronically
stored
information.

Some 20 years ago, Congress passed an amendment to FOIA known as the **Electronic Freedom of Information Act** to extend FOIA to computer records.[44] The law established that computer searches to retrieve records do not constitute creation of a new record, a justification some agencies had used to deny access to electronic records.

EFOIA requires agencies to deliver documents in "any form or format requested" that is "readily reproducible by the agency." A federal appeals court said this required the DOD to provide files in zipped format because the agency used such files as part of its "business as usual."[45] When agencies subcontract with private companies to computerize their hard-copy records, the records are not in the agency's possession, and request for access may be denied.

EFOIA requires federal agencies to create a FOIA section on their websites and to provide "electronic reading rooms" filled with online copies of records, policy statements, administrative opinions and indexes of frequently sought documents. EFOIA encourages agencies to provide expedited access to records when the requester can demonstrate a compelling safety or public interest need for rapid access. While EFOIA applies only to federal records, many states adopted specific provisions to ensure and improve electronic access to state records.[46]

Open State Records

Given that most communication professionals work at the local level, they are likely to rely often on state, rather than federal, open-records laws.[47] Every state and the District of Columbia has an access-to-information statute. Some follow the model of FOIA; others look very different. Some require more or less disclosure than FOIA. In Texas, for example, a state agency has only 10 days to comply with a request.[48]

The tradition of state open-records laws runs deeper than the federal version. As early as 1849, Wisconsin provided for inspection of public records. The explicit purpose of state open-records laws tends to be government accountability. Illinois links the right of access to enabling "people to fulfill their duties of discussing public issues fully and freely" and making "informed political judgments."[49]

Because there is so much state-to-state variation in open-records laws, characterizing them broadly is virtually impossible. Even those that appear similar may, in reality, differ in their details. Generally speaking, however, some observations are helpful:

- Like federal agencies, state agencies are not required to create or acquire records in response to a request.

- Few states require agencies to produce record indexes.

- Some states require that requesters be state residents.

- Many states have exemptions similar to those of FOIA.

- Most states' open-records laws cover electronic and computer-stored records, but some states do not require that these records be transformed into a user-friendly format.

- Some states' open-records laws cover the legislature, executive branch and courts.

▲ EMERGING LAW

If You Work for Government, Your Work Emails Are Public

Public employees increasingly use their own devices to conduct the government's business. Sometimes employee devices are vital to agencies with extremely tight budgets. Sometimes, the motivation is convenience or, more rarely, an attempt to avoid creating records the employees might have to make public under federal or state open-records laws.

Whether on personal or government devices, public employees often commingle personal communications with government work. Agencies faced with records requests must determine how best to segregate the personal messages deserving privacy protection from disclosable public records. In Illinois, employees must turn over all records, and "public bodies conduct a reasonable search for these responsive records, which includes searching public employees' private emails."[1] In California, Washington and Wisconsin, the employees themselves search their devices and disclose what is public.[2]

In 2016, the District of Columbia Circuit Court of Appeals ruled that emails of federal employees held in personal email accounts also may be public records under FOIA. The case sought access to the emails of a science adviser to Hillary Clinton. In remanding the case to be heard on its merits, the judge said, "If a department head can deprive the citizens of their right to know what his department is up to by the simple expedient of maintaining his departmental emails on another domain, [FOIA's] purpose is hardly served."[3]

---

1. Josh Herman, *Public Employee Emails Subject to FOIA*, MILLER, HALL & TRIGGS LLC, Aug. 16, 2016, mhtlaw.com/2016/08/16/public-employee-emails-subject-foia.
2. City of San Jose v. Superior Court (Smith), 389 P.3d 848 (Cal. 2017); Nissen v. Pierce County, 357 P.3d 45 (Wash. 2015); Schill v. Wisconsin Rapids School Dist., 786 N.W.2d 177 (Wis. 2010).
3. Competitive Enterprise Inst. v. Office of Science & Technology Policy, 827 F.3d 145 (D.C. Cir. 2016).

- Some states' open-records laws do not specify response time limits. Delays can be lengthy.

- Some states do not specify penalties for agencies violating the law.

State open-records laws apply not only to state government agencies and departments but also to cities, school districts and other state governing authorities. Like FOIA, state laws apply to the digital age. The law in Tennessee covers "all documents, papers, letters, maps, books, photographs, microfilms, electronic data processing files and output, sound recordings, or other materials regardless of physical form made or received pursuant to law or ordinance or in connection with the transaction of official business by a governmental agency."[50]

A question raised in one case was whether unreadable **metadata** were part of a public record.[51] Metadata are hidden data that may include the creation date, authorship and edit history of a file. The case began when a Phoenix police officer sought the metadata because he suspected information had been altered in the records provided in response to his request. The city argued that the metadata were not part of the record and therefore not subject to the state open-records law. The Arizona Supreme Court disagreed, ruling that metadata are "part of the underlying document; [this type of data] does not stand on its own."[52]

metadata A set of data that describes and gives information about other data.

In a decision establishing that the public records act applied to public information stored on a personal computer, the Washington Supreme Court also ruled that metadata are subject to disclosure because they may contain information that relates to the conduct of government.[53]

A growing number of courts have ruled that government employees cannot avoid disclosure under state open records laws by using personal devices to conduct the public's business.[54] In 2016, the Washington State Supreme Court found that a prosecutor's call logs and work-related voice and text messages on his private cell phone were subject to disclosure when they relate to the employee's official duties.[55] However, while "an individual has no constitutional privacy interest in a *public* record," the court said the employee had a legitimate privacy interest in his personal information.[56] To accommodate the personal privacy interest, the court said "an employee's good-faith search for public records on his personal device can satisfy an agency's obligation" for disclosure under the public records law.[57]

In 2017, the California Supreme Court relied expressly on the Washington Supreme Court decision to hold that the employee could search his own accounts and devices for the public records that required disclosure. The court unanimously ruled that when a government "employee uses a personal account to communicate about the conduct of public business the writings may be subject to disclosure under the California Public Records Act."[58]

▣ SOCIAL MEDIA LAW

Access to State Records in the Digital Age

Social media websites such as Facebook allow government officials to exchange information in ways not considered when most open-records and open-meetings laws were adopted. States grapple with how to apply open-records laws to computerized records, including information that appears in social media. Simply because people may be able to view some of the information online does not relieve a government entity from the obligation to provide the information to other citizens on request.[1]

In addition, "internet exchanges that create virtual records can also create virtual meetings," according to two lawyers who analyzed how to apply open-records and open-meeting laws in Texas.[2] As technology provides for online meetings, it is also expanding the definition of "meeting" and the application of laws permitting access.

---

1. *See* Alan J. Bojorquez & Damien Shores, *Open Government and the Net: Bringing Social Media Into the Light*, 11 Tex. Tech. Admin. L. J. 45, 59 (2009).
2. *Id.*

Timely response and effective enforcement of open-records laws are often important to people seeking records. Like justice delayed, access delayed may, in effect, be access denied. Thirty-four states and the District of Columbia provide civil and/or criminal sanctions for failure to comply with records requests.[59]

PROMISES OF CONFIDENTIALITY

Journalists contact a lot of people and gather a lot of information in the course of their work. To obtain information that may be sensitive or of interest to law enforcement, reporters may agree to limit how the information is used or provide confidentiality for the source. A promise of anonymity may be the only way a reporter can gain access to key information.

Anonymous Sources and Confidential Leaks

The use of confidential sources is a long-standing journalistic practice.[60] The promise of confidentiality is "one form of currency that journalists use to get something they want and need, which is information."[61] One estimate indicates that at least one-third of newspaper accounts and the vast majority of newsmagazine stories contain veiled attribution.[62]

Reporters and their news organizations typically keep promises of confidentiality, even when courts ask them to break them (see Chapter 8). Keeping such promises is both ethical and practical. Individuals and organizations that break promises develop a reputation for being untrustworthy. Sources vanish.

Breaking Promises

When an organization breaks a promise and reveals the identity of a source promised anonymity, the source may sue and win.[63] Promises, even unwritten promises, can be legally binding under the principle of **promissory estoppel**. Promissory estoppel requires courts to enforce a promise if the individual who received the promise relied on it and its breach created a harm that should be remedied by law. Promissory estoppel is a **generally applicable law** that applies with equal force to news organizations as to anyone else.

The U.S. Supreme Court ruled 25 years ago that the First Amendment did not protect journalists from the consequences of broken promises.[64] The case of *Cohen v. Cowles Media Co.* involved Dan Cohen, a political campaign worker, who offered four reporters prejudicial information about a political opponent just days before the election. On the condition that his identity be kept secret, Cohen told the reporters the opponent had been arrested for unlawful assembly and petty theft more than 10 years earlier. Two newspaper reporters accepted the offer, and, after heated newsroom debate, both editors ran the stories clearly identifying Cohen. Editors said the public deserved to know about Cohen's political "dirty tricks."

As a result, Cohen was fired from his job. He sued the newspapers, claiming breach of a contractual agreement. At trial, the jury agreed and awarded Cohen $200,000 in compensatory damages and $500,000 in punitive damages. An appeals court threw out the punitive damages, and the Minnesota Supreme Court reversed the ruling and rejected the application of promissory estoppel to the newspapers. To do otherwise, the court said, would violate the First Amendment.

promissory estoppel A legal doctrine requiring liability when a clear promise is made and relied on and injury results from the broken promise.

generally applicable law A law that is enforced evenly, across the board. Within First Amendment contexts, it is the idea that the freedom of the press clause does not exempt news organizations or personnel from obeying general laws.

On appeal, the U.S. Supreme Court ruled in Cohen's favor and said the First Amendment imposed no ban on the application of promissory estoppel to the press. "Generally applicable laws do not offend the First Amendment simply because their enforcement against the press has incidental effects on its ability to gather and report the news," Justice Byron White wrote in *Cohen*.[65]

RECORDING

In recent years, conflicts between both citizens and journalists and police over the right to record police have increased. Police have confiscated or destroyed the footage of journalists and citizen observers recording encounters ranging from large public protests to traffic stops and detained or arrested press and private photographers.

Right to Record

In a recent case, Antonio Buehler was arrested on multiple occasions by police in Austin, Texas. The officers said he refused their lawful orders to stop recording, which interfered with their performance of their duties. Buehler sued, and the district court held that Buehler's arrest violated his clearly established First Amendment right to record the police. However, the court dismissed the case. It said the officers were immune from liability because a grand jury had found probable cause to charge Buehler with disobeying a legal order. The Fifth Circuit Court of Appeals agreed. Buehler's appeal to the U.S. Supreme Court was denied.[66]

One recent case involved the seizure of the cellphone and arrest of a woman who sat in her car and told an officer she was using her phone to film his nearby traffic stop of her friend. In its ruling, the First Circuit Court of Appeals said the First Amendment protects an individual's right to peacefully and nondisruptively record public police activity.[67] Three years earlier, the First Circuit had said that because police could not prove the cellphone filming of their arrest in a public park hindered performance of their duties, the arrest violated the First Amendment.[68]

More than half a dozen lower courts reaching from Maryland to Missouri also recently heard right-to-photograph-or-record cases and broadly rejected police motions to dismiss and claims of immunity.[69] The Department of Justice intervened in two of these cases to assert the public's "right to record police officers while performing their duties in a public place, as well as the right to be protected from warrantless seizure and destruction of those recordings."[70] A Texas court of appeals also struck down a state law prohibiting "improper photography" without the person's consent and "with intent to . . . arouse or gratify the sexual desire of any person."[71] The court said the law unconstitutionally restricted an individual's thoughts and the right to take photographs.

The Seventh Circuit Court of Appeals also held that the First Amendment protects audio recording of police officers, even when state law requires the consent of all parties.[72] The Seventh Circuit ruled that a law prohibiting public recording of police activities in a traditional public forum violates the First Amendment because the burden on speech outweighs any substantial state interest in prohibiting recording of what other witnesses might readily overhear.

Certain properties also may be protected by a variety of laws limiting recording. State "ag-gag" laws initially prohibited recording, photographing or entering agricultural facilities to document animal abuse or other illegal activity without the owners' informed permission. Idaho's law, one of three original ag-gag laws challenged as unconstitutional, was struck down in 2015 for violating both the First Amendment and the equal protection clause by penalizing lawful employees who wanted to expose "matters of utmost public concern."[73] An appeal is pending.

Not to be deterred, Idaho passed a second law in 2016.[74] It joined seven other states that either punish recording or hamper investigations of livestock facilities by requiring that evidence of each single incident of animal abuse be turned over to police almost immediately.[75] These newer "disclosure" laws require individuals to disclose their identities before they have gathered sufficient evidence to demonstrate the pattern of abuse necessary for successful prosecution.

In one high-profile arrest, internationally renowned photojournalist George Steinmetz was charged with trespassing after he took photographs while paragliding over a cattle feedlot in Kansas.[76] He was on assignment for National Geographic magazine. "It was quite a surprise to me," Steinmetz said. "I've been detained in Iran and Yemen, and questioned about spying, but never arrested. And then I get thrown in jail in America."[77]

A federal law, the Animal Enterprise Terrorism Act of 2014, defines activities intended to "harm or interfere with" animal facilities as a form of terrorism subject to prison terms and hefty fines. Such activities include "nonviolent obstruction of an animal enterprise," although the law includes guidance that it should not be "construed to prohibit any expressive activity . . . protected by the First Amendment."[78]

Face-to-Face and Participant Recording

People often record interviews. Recording audio or video in an interview with plainly visible equipment does not violate any state or federal law. There is nothing secret about recording this way.

If a reporter records an interview without the interviewee's knowledge, over the phone or with a hidden recorder, laws may be triggered. Thirty-eight states and the District of Columbia allow the use of a hidden recorder for a face-to-face interview.[79] These are called "one-party" states. The person doing the recording has the necessary knowledge of the recording.

Twelve states are not so lenient.[80] These all-party states require all participants in an interview or conversation to give consent, or recording is not permitted. Vermont is the only state without a law specifically addressing audio or video recording of interviews, but the state's highest court has held that hidden recordings of communications in a home violate personal privacy.[81] Another thirteen states specifically outlaw the use of hidden cameras in private places.[82]

George Steinmetz

George Steinmetz's paragliding photograph of Brookover Ranch Feed Yard and adjacent crop circles in Garden City, Kansas.

INTERNATIONAL LAW

You Can't Watch Everyone

Late in 2016, the European Union's top court struck down the United Kingdom's new mass surveillance program as unconstitutional.

The court said, "The Charter of Fundamental Rights of the European Union must be interpreted as precluding national legislation which, for the purpose of fighting crime, provides for general and indiscriminate retention of all traffic and location data of all subscribers and registered users relating to all means of electronic communication."[1]

The ruling struck down what many had called the most extreme surveillance law of any democratic nation. Cameras in public places as well as a fleet of drones recorded the public's activities across the country.[2] Under the law, the UK retained data of virtually every online and telephone communication of the nation's entire population.

The so-called "Snooper's Charter" of 2016 exempted the Parliament and the House of Lords from this surveillance.

---

1. Cory Doctorow, *Europe's Top Court Says UK Surveillance Rules Are Unconstitutional*, BOING BOING, Dec. 21, 2016, boingboing.net/2016/12/21/europes-top-court-says-uk-su.html.
2. *Surrey Now Has the UK's "Largest" Police Drone Project*, WIRED, Apr. 12, 2016, www.wired.co.uk/article/surrey-police-uk-largest-drone-trial.

POINTS OF LAW

States That Forbid Hidden Cameras in Private Places[1]

- Alabama*
- Arkansas
- California
- Delaware*
- Georgia*
- Hawaii*
- Kansas*
- Maine*
- Michigan*
- Minnesota*
- New Hampshire
- South Dakota*
- Utah*

---

1. Reporters Committee for Freedom of the Press, *The First Amendment Handbook*, www.rcfp.org/handbook/c03p02.html (last visited July 26, 2017).

*States that also prohibit trespassing on private property to conduct surveillance of people.

California is an all-party state[83] that makes it illegal to record a "confidential communication" unless all parties give consent.[84] One California case involved two reporters who entered an office of the Association of Community Organizations for Reform Now claiming they wanted help obtaining a home mortgage. One was wearing a hidden camera and also used his cellphone to record the audio, according to a federal district court.[85] The two told the ACORN worker "they intended to fill the house with underage girls working as prostitutes . . . [and] needed help filling out tax forms so the income from this illegal operation would appear legitimate," the court said. They asked whether the conversation was confidential and were told it was.

The individuals posted an edited videotape on the internet showing the ACORN employee "conspiring to promote an underage prostitution business," according to the court. The ACORN employee sued, claiming the recording violated California law.

The key question, the court said, was whether the ACORN employee had a reasonable expectation that the conversation would be confidential. The discussion inside the employee's office dealt with personal client matters. Under those circumstances, according to the court, the ACORN employee could reasonably believe the conversation was sensitive and would remain confidential. Therefore, the employee did not give implicit consent to the recording. The case settled out of court with a payment of $100,000 to the ACORN employee for "any pain" caused by distribution of the edited recording.[86]

Noncovert Recording

Access to public property is generally permitted to any member of the public, and whatever can be viewed from public property generally can be recorded. However, recording of certain events

● REAL WORLD LAW

Recording in Public Places

A New Jersey man was arrested for recording video in a plaza outside a federal courthouse in New York City. Antonio Musumeci shot video of a man handing out pamphlets, then interviewed that man. The interviewee was arrested by the Federal Protective Service. Afterward, the memory card from Musumeci's camera was confiscated, and he was arrested and charged with violating a federal regulation restricting photography on federal property.[1]

The regulation requires advance permission to photograph certain agency-occupied areas, with some exceptions for news photography. Musumeci argued that the law violated his First and 14th Amendment rights.[2]

The federal government settled and agreed that no federal regulations bar photography of federal courthouses from publicly accessible property. The government also agreed to inform federal employees of the rights of photographers.[3]

---

1. 41 C.F.R. § 102–74.420.
2. Musumeci v. U.S. Dep't of Homeland Security, S.D.N.Y., Index No. 10 CIV 3370 (2010); *see also* Heicklen v. U.S. Dep't of Homeland Security, 2011 WL 3841543 (S.D.N.Y., Aug. 30, 2011).
3. Musumeci v. U.S. Dep't of Homeland Security, N.Y. Civil Liberties Union, www.nyclu.org/en/cases/musumeci-v-us-department-homeland-security-challenging-government-regulation-restricting (last visited July 26, 2017).

may be restricted. The Maryland Legislature, for example, prohibits reporters with recording devices from attending its sessions. When reporters challenged the restriction, a Maryland appeals court said that while newsgathering is entitled to some First Amendment protection, banning recorders does not infringe on that right.[87] It called the ban "a mere inconvenience."[88] Similar reasoning guides the U.S. Supreme Court, the federal court system and the few state judiciaries that continue to limit cameras in courtrooms, as explained in Chapter 8.[89]

OBSTACLES TO GATHERING INFORMATION

tortious newsgathering The use of reporting techniques that are wrongful and unlawful and for which the victim may obtain damages in court.

Small digital devices and cellphones make surveillance and recording easier and more covert. And the ubiquity of cellphones eases repeated contact that may be annoying or worse. Individuals wishing to avoid contact or public coverage may seek protection under criminal harassment and stalking laws designed to protect crime victims.[90] While prosecutors and judges tend to strike down the application of these laws to journalists who persist in asking questions, anti-harassment statutes in nine states leave the door open for prosecution for repeated, aggressive contacts to gather information.[91]

Harassment and Stalking

When newsgathering is too aggressive, it can become harassment. Notable examples involve photographers known as "paparazzi" pursuing celebrities. Decades ago a court ordered a photographer to stay a fixed distance away from former first lady Jacqueline Kennedy Onassis, her children and their homes and schools.[92] Both Onassis and the Secret Service sued the photographer for continually interfering with the agents performing their protective duties. The court flatly rejected the photographer's claim that the First Amendment was a complete defense to his behavior.[93]

David Parker /Alamy Stock Photo

A group of bronze paparazzi dogs roves the globe to suggest that the pack mentality of photojournalists exceeds the limits of reasonable behavior, according to the artists, Gillie and Marc.

The concept of **tortious newsgathering** developed in response to the "ambush-and-surveillance" journalism practiced by photojournalists and some television programs. Tortious newsgathering broadly encompasses the range of problematic behaviors explored in this chapter. One case symbolizes the evolution of the law—and the media—in this area. Employees of the television program "Inside Edition" were working on a story on an insurance company. When requests for interviews were denied, producers targeted two executives in the company by staking out their home, following them and their 3-year-old and using hidden cameras, powerful microphones and extreme telephoto lenses. To escape, the family vacationed in Florida. The "Inside Edition" crew followed the family when they tried to escape by vacationing in Florida. The crew anchored a boat 50 yards offshore of the family house.

● REAL WORLD LAW

"Celebrities v. Paparazzi"

Spread Pictures, LLC

Justin Bieber.

California recently increased the criminal penalties for intentionally harassing a child because of a parent's job.[1] The revision greatly increased jail terms and fines for those who photograph children in a harassing fashion and without parental permission or who trespass or invade a celebrity's privacy to obtain a photograph.[2] The original law allowed separate charges for driving recklessly in pursuit of celebrity photos or blocking sidewalks to create a sort of "false imprisonment."[4] It also applied steeper penalties if children were endangered as a result. A separate law prohibits paparazzi use of drones to record audio or video of people without their permission.[3]

News organizations and the California Newspaper Publishers Association said the laws are overly broad and threaten legitimate newsgathering. They argue that existing laws address public concerns without implicating the First Amendment.

The California Supreme Court declined to review the appeal brought by photographer Paul Raef to what may be the only conviction under the law. Raef brought a facial First Amendment challenge to the increased penalties imposed for his high-speed pursuit of Justin Bieber to obtain photographs. The lower court found the law constitutional because it targeted neither the intent nor the communicative aspects of the newsgathering activity involved and any infringement on speech was incidental.[4]

1. Laura Olson, *Paparazzi Bill Passes in California, Protecting Children of Public Figures*, Huffington Post, Sept. 25, 2013, www.huffingtonpost.com/2013/09/25/paparazzi-bill-passes_n_3991404.html.
2. Dennis Romero, *Stiff Penalties for Aggressive Paparazzi in California Likely*, L.A. Weekly, Sept. 1, 2010, blogs.laweekly.com informer/hollywood/paparazzi-bill-passes/.
3. *California Governor Outlaws Paparazzi Drones, Days After Approving Police UAVs*, RT, Oct. 1, 2014, rt.com/usa/192120-california-bans-paparazzi-drones/.
4. Raef v. Superior Court, 193 Cal. Rptr. 3d 159 (Ct. App. 2015).

A judge in Philadelphia granted the family an injunction.[94] The "*legal* newsgathering activities" of the "Inside Edition" crew would not be "irreparably harmed by an injunction narrowly tailored to preclude them from continuing their harassing conduct." The injunction targeted illegal newsgathering tactics.

Fraud and Misrepresentation

Journalists are subject to prosecution when they use illegal means to gather news. Years ago, ABC News magazine reporters used false names and fake work histories to go undercover in Food Lion grocery stores to investigate alleged unsanitary practices.[95] They wore hidden miniature cameras and microphones to work.[96] Their jobs gave them access to nonpublic areas of the stores, where they filmed allegedly unsanitary meat-handling practices. Food Lion sharply criticized their story, denied the accusations and sued.

Food Lion did not sue for libel, where it would have to prove ABC's claims were false. It sued ABC for fraud, trespass, unfair trade practices and breach of a duty of loyalty.[97] The

● REAL WORLD LAW

Undercover at Work

The practice of journalists working for the company or industry the reporter wants to expose has a long history. From Upton Sinclair writing about the terrible conditions in the meatpacking business in "The Jungle" to ABC reporters working in Food Lion grocery stores, undercover work is a journalistic tradition. When ABC journalists lied on their job applications to Food Lion, the U.S. Court of Appeals for the Fourth Circuit ruled that the journalists were not liable for lying to get jobs but were liable for trespass. Although Food Lion gave them access to the nonpublic parts of the stores, the court said it was trespass because Food Lion did not know the reporters were filming a story. The decision suggests that "a reporter or producer can be liable for trespass if, while working undercover, he works for the company he is reporting on."[1]

1. Shelly Rosenfeld, Note: *Lights, Camera, Sanction? Whether a Proposed Anti-Paparazzi Ordinance Would Limit Investigative Journalism in the News Business*, 6 Hastings Bus. L.J. 483, 493 (2010).

court said, "Food Lion attacked the methods used by defendants to gather the information ultimately aired on 'PrimeTime Live.'" The choice of suit supported a presumption that the content of the story was true.[98] The jury found for Food Lion, awarding the grocery chain more than $5.5 million in punitive damages. A chill went through the media.

Although the judge reduced the award to $315,000, ABC appealed. The Court of Appeals for the Fourth Circuit reversed the verdict for Food Lion on all but the trespass and breach of loyalty claims, but the case remains a cautionary tale for the press.[99] Not only had the lower court called some newsgathering techniques illegal; the dissenting judge on the federal appeals court would have sustained the fraud claim and the punitive damages against ABC.[100]

ABC ultimately paid only $2 in damages, but a few factors should not be overlooked:

- First, the attorney fees were costly.[101]

- Second, those costs and the verdict had a sobering effect on newsgathering techniques that involve deception.

- Third, the jury evidenced extreme animosity toward the news media, particularly toward big, powerful and seemingly smug and well-to-do news organizations.[102]

- ABC's successful appeal relied on specific state laws in the states where the reporting occurred. A different result might arise in a different state.

In Minnesota, a court later ruled against a Minneapolis television station when an employee hid her media job to work as a volunteer in a facility for the mentally disabled. She wore a hidden camera and used the video in broadcasts critical of the facility. The facility sued for fraud and trespass, and the Minnesota appeals court ruled that the station misrepresented itself and trespassed on private property.[103] The parties reached a confidential settlement.

Misrepresentation also can occur when journalists honestly disclose who they are but disguise the nature of the story they are developing. When truckers declined to participate in an NBC "Dateline" story about the trucking industry, NBC promised one truck driver and his boss that their report would be positive and would not include comments from anyone from Parents Against Tired Truckers. The "Dateline" segment was not positive. It included statements like "American highways are a trucker's killing field."[104] It also contained interviews with PATT members.

The driver and his boss sued NBC for fraud and misrepresentation. The First Circuit Court of Appeals favored NBC on nearly every point and ruled that the network's vague promise to produce a "positive portrayal" was insufficient basis for a claim.[105] But the court said damages could be awarded based on NBC's specific and unequivocal promise not to include anyone from PATT. The parties settled for an undisclosed amount.[106]

Intrusion, Trespass and Voyeurism

Trespass is entering another's property without permission.[107] The law against trespassing is generally applicable; no one, journalists included, may trespass. Permission to enter the property may be given or denied only by the owner or the resident, who may not be the owner. When law enforcement officials obtain a search warrant or have emergency control of property, they have the legal authority to enter without permission. But that permission does not extend to others.

The well-established tradition of the **ride-along**—in which journalists accompany public officers to various scenes—provided media with material for stories and increased officers' visibility. However, when the scenes were on private property, the residents' Fourth Amendment protection against unreasonable searches of their dwellings and

ride-along A term given to the practice of journalists or other private citizens accompanying government officials—usually those in law enforcement or other emergency response personnel—as they carry out their duties.

● REAL WORLD LAW

Chilling Hospital PR: Patient Approval Required

In 2016, New York–Presbyterian Hospital agreed to pay $2.2 million in fines to federal regulators for recording patients without patient consent. The decision involved ABC's reality show "NY Med" airing the dying moments of an 83-year-old man who had been struck by a car.[1]

The U.S. Department of Health and Human Services used the fine to clarify that medical facilities violate the rights of patients if they allow media into treatment areas without patient approval. Many said the ruling would end popular television and cable shows recorded in hospitals.

"I think this will have a chilling effect on hospitals going forward," said the chairman of the ethics committee of the American College of Emergency Physicians. "Any hospital legal counsel worth his salt or any P.R. director would be committing malpractice in order to allow it to occur. It's now embodied in a federal directive."[2]

1. Charles Ornstein, *NY Hospital to Pay $2.2 Million Over Unauthorized Filming of 2 Patients*, N.Y. TIMES, Apr. 21, 2016, www.nytimes.com/2016/04/22/nyregion/new-york-hospital-to-pay-fine.
2. *Id.*

unreasonable intrusion or trespass came into play. A series of rulings balancing the residents' privacy against the media's First Amendment rights has significantly limited news media access.

In one, a television crew accompanied Los Angeles Fire Department paramedics into the home of a heart attack victim. The unsuccessful resuscitation efforts were videotaped and broadcast on a local newscast that night and later as part of a documentary. The victim's family sued. Trespassing was among their claims. In ruling for the plaintiffs, a California appeals court said, "Personal security in a society saturated daily with publicity about its members requires protection not only from governmental intrusion, but some basic bulwark of defense against private commercial enterprises which derive profits from gathering and disseminating information."[108]

Noting the importance of newsgathering, the court said the "First Amendment has never been construed to accord newsmen immunity from torts or crimes committed

● REAL WORLD LAW

You Have No First Amendment Right to Trespass

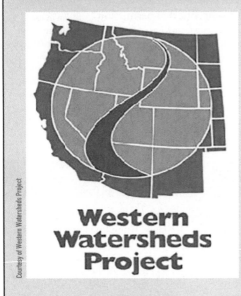

Courtesy of Western Watersheds Project

Two recent Wyoming laws impose criminal and civil penalties on people who enter private lands without permission to provide "resource data" on land use to government agencies.[1] Wyoming recently revised its trespass laws to make it a crime to enter on "open land," including public property, to "unlawfully collect resource data" such as water samples to test E. coli contamination from cattle waste runoff.[2]

Several groups, including one that monitors the impact of intensive cattle ranching on the health of neighboring public waterways, challenged the constitutionality of the laws.[3] They said the laws intentionally stifled legitimate criticism of matters of great public importance protected by the First Amendment.

The district court dismissed the suit as "erroneously premised upon their perceived First Amendment right to trespass upon private property."[4] Hearing Western Watersheds Project's appeal in 2016, the Tenth Circuit Court of Appeals seemed skeptical that conservation groups had a First Amendment right to gather data from public lands that included the right to cross private property to do so.[5] The court's decision was pending as of press date.

1. Wyo. Stat. §§ 6-3-414 (2015); 40-27-101 (2015).
2. *Update on Wyoming Trespass Law and Lawsuit*, Western Watersheds Project, www.westernwatersheds.org/2015/05/om-311 (last visited July 26, 2017). The state argued that the laws permissibly prevent trespass on private property to gain access to public lands.
3. Western Watersheds Project v. Michael, 196 F. Supp. 3d 1231 (D. Wyo. 2016).
4. Adam Lidgett, *Wyo. Urges 10th Cir. to Uphold "Open Land" Suit*, LAW 360, Dec. 21, 2016, www.law360.com/articles/875396/wyo-urges-10th-circ-to-uphold-open-land-suit-ruling.
5. Emma Gannon, *Conservationists Argue at 10th Circuit for Right to Cross Private Lands in Wyoming*, COURTHOUSE NEWS SERVICE, May 8, 2017, www.courthousenews.com/conservationists-argue-10th-circuit-right-cross-private-lands-wyoming.

⭕ POINTS OF LAW

Wilson v. Layne: The State of Ride-Alongs

- A search warrant entitles officers, but not reporters, to enter a home.
- The presence of reporters is unrelated to the authorized intrusion.
- The presence of reporters serves no legitimate law enforcement purposes.
- Inviting reporters for the execution of a search warrant violates the Fourth Amendment.

during the course of newsgathering. The First Amendment is not a license to trespass, to steal, or to intrude by electronic means into the precincts of another's home or office."[109]

The U.S. Supreme Court reinforced that doctrine. When U.S. Fish and Wildlife Service agents searched a 75,000-acre Montana ranch, the lead agent was wearing a CNN microphone and the officers were using CNN video cameras without the residents' knowledge. Officials suspected the family had shot or poisoned eagles, violating federal wildlife laws.[110] The family sued, claiming the FWS officers violated their Fourth Amendment right to be free from unreasonable searches and seizures. In *Hanlon v. Berger*, the Supreme Court said a jury should review the merits of the Fourth Amendment claim because CNN's actions were intended to serve an "entertainment" purpose, not law enforcement.[111] The case settled out of court.[112]

In *Wilson v. Layne*, excerpted at the end of this chapter, the Supreme Court dealt another blow to ride-alongs. Armed with a search warrant, federal and local law enforcement officers allowed a Washington Post photographer to accompany their early morning raid of a private home to arrest a fugitive. The photographer took pictures as officers wrestled a man to the floor and a woman emerged from the bedroom. None of the photos was published. The pair were the parents of the fugitive, who was not at home. The couple sued on the grounds that the presence of journalists violated their Fourth Amendment protection.[113]

The U.S. Supreme Court in *Wilson v. Layne* ruled in favor of the couple. While the warrant entitled the officers to enter the home, it did not authorize officers to invite journalists along.[114] The presence of reporters was unrelated to the warrant's purpose and the limited intrusion it allowed.[115] Any benefits ride-alongs provide to help minimize police abuses, protect suspects, advance government anti-crime and law enforcement activities or improve news reporting of law enforcement were too far removed from the warrant's objective to override the residents' Fourth Amendment rights.[116]

The rule that emerged is that it generally is a violation of the Fourth Amendment for police to bring third parties into a home during the execution of a warrant unless that third party is there to help execute the warrant.[117] The law is now clearly on the side of residents. Media ride-alongs on public property are safer for journalists, but reporters are not immune from liability even in those circumstances.[118]

● REAL WORLD LAW

It Is Not Just Illegal; It Is Embarrassing

First Amendment scholar Rodney Smolla tells journalists to be cautious about ride-alongs because they place the media and government officials "dangerously close" to working together. That proximity endangers press autonomy and the adversarial relationship necessary to hold those in government accountable.

It is vital to avoid even the appearance of any quid pro quo relationship. At the very least, Smolla says, journalists should make the distinction between public and private spaces. Cruising neighborhoods is one thing; being part of executing a warrant, especially on private property, is another.

While ride-alongs may provide journalists unique and valuable access, journalists should find it an embarrassment when law enforcement officials defend themselves by claiming journalists were working with them, as happened in *Wilson v. Layne*, Smolla says.[1]

---

1. Rodney A. Smolla, *Privacy and the Law: The Media's Intrusion on Privacy: Privacy and the First Amendment Right to Gather News*, 67 Geo. Wash. L. Rev. 1097 (1999).

Problems With Covert Recording

Journalists and others often record conversations and behavior, sometimes without the knowledge of those being recorded. This may be the only way to gather evidence of possible wrongdoing, and recordings can establish the facts of what happened or what was said. But there is always some deception involved in covert recording; hidden recording devices are, by definition, unknown to some parties. The proliferation of miniature cameras and cellphones increased concerns about covert recording and prompted laws meant to protect against video voyeurism.

Described in various ways, video voyeurism includes photography in private areas and covert photos of people's intimate anatomy, such as photos up a woman's skirt, without the knowledge of the subjects. The federal Video Voyeurism Prevention Act[119] prohibits unauthorized photography of an individual's private areas. A total of 24 states also have laws that specifically address this issue. The remaining 26 states have general "anti-voyeurism" or "peeping" laws.[120]

After a Texas appellate court struck down as overbroad that state's sweeping "improper photography" law in 2014,[121] the state revised the law. The state's more targeted "invasive photography" law now makes it illegal to take or distribute images without the person's consent (1) of the person's intimate areas, (2) when a person is in a changing room or bathroom or (3) with the intention of invading the person's privacy.[122]

Some media organizations enforce policies about the use of hidden recordings or recordings without consent. In addition, various state and federal laws come into play. While the use of hidden cameras by the news media does not itself constitute an illegal intrusion, 13 states specifically prohibit the unauthorized use or installation of cameras in private places.[123] Recording may be acceptable in one state but not another.[124] Covert recording also may violate federal laws.

Not necessarily covert, aerial photography often occurs without the permission of the subjects. In 2016, the Federal Aviation Administration adopted new rules governing the use of drones to minimize the risks posed by their increasing popularity.[125] In addition to other requirements, the rules prohibited drones from flying over "any persons" not directly involved in their operation. Drones may not fly above national parks, military bases, stadiums, sporting events or sites of emergencies. There is also a no-fly zone within five miles of airports (except with prior authorization) and in Washington, D.C.

Subject to these restrictions, noncommercial drone photographers and news operations generally may photograph from drones. Commercial operators must apply for FAA exemptions to photograph and obtain authorization from air-traffic controllers to fly in controlled airspace. Many state and municipal laws impose additional limits on drone photography.[126]

A 2017 national legislative roundup identified 27 states with regulations addressing the use of drones.[127] These laws vary dramatically in their breadth and focus. California was among the first to ban drone recording.[128] In the most stringent of these laws, Texas generally bans drone recording for any use except education, research, limited development and commercial purposes and for police, military and state reasons.[129]

In 2015, the FAA sought a $1.9 million fine from SkyPan, a company providing aerial photography for real estate purposes.[130] In seeking the extraordinary fine, the FAA said the company had flown scores of unapproved flights over highly congested airspace above New York and Chicago. SkyPan settled the dispute in 2017 by paying $200,000 without acknowledging any violation of the FAA rules,[131] which continue to evolve. The FAA has considered but not implemented specific privacy protections.

● INTERNATIONAL LAW

Hacking Into Arrest

One illegal way to gather information is by hacking into another's computer or phone. An international scandal erupted when news broke that England's News of the World newspaper hacked into 600 people's cellphones as part of its newsgathering activities.[1]

The hacking "led to civil suits, criminal investigations [and] a parliamentary inquiry." British police identified "more than 100 reporters, editors, investigators, executives and public officials . . . implicated in wrongdoing."[2] Arrests and convictions of corporate executives, editors and other employees prompted the closure of the News of the World, once a very profitable Sunday tabloid.[3]

The British Parliament responded by adopting a press code that established an independent regulator to oversee Britain's press. Any paper refusing to abide by the standards of the "voluntary" oversight process would face punitive damages of up to $1.5 million.

British editors protested the new press code and said it violated the country's centuries-long history of press freedom.[4]

---

1. *See* Alan Cowell & John F. Burns, *Britain: 7 Appear in Court in Phone Hacking Case*, N.Y. TIMES, Aug. 17, 2012, at A6.
2. Stephen Castle & Alan Cowell, *Britain: Newspapers Protest New Press Rules*, N.Y. TIMES, Mar. 20, 2013, at A6.
3. Thomas S. Leatherbury & Travis R. Wimberly, *2012 Update: Developments in the Law of Newsgathering Liability*, in 3 COMM. L. IN THE DIGITAL AGE 2012, at 595–96; John F. Burns, *Six More Journalists Held in British Hacking Case*, N.Y. TIMES, Feb. 14, 2013, at A6.
4. Stephen Castle & Alan Cowell, *British Newspapers Challenge New Press Rules*, N.Y. TIMES, Mar. 19, 2013, www.nytimes.com/2013/03/20/world/europe/british-newspapers-new-press-rules.html.

Wiretap Act
A federal law to protect the privacy of phone calls and other oral communications that makes it illegal to intercept, record, disseminate or use a private communication without a participant's permission. The law allows the government to bring criminal charges and those whose privacy was violated to sue for civil damages.

Recording or Intercepting "Wire" Conversations

Federal laws protect the privacy of "wire communication," which includes technologies that may not be wired but transfer voice communications from a point of origin to a point of reception.[132] Landline telephones, cellphones and computer-based voice services such as Skype, Google Hangouts and FaceTime[133] all fall under that regulatory umbrella. The federal **Wiretap Act**[134] prohibits the interception (and recording) of a call or voice communication in transit via these methods. It does not protect messages that are stored after transmission. The data packets stored following internet calls are subject to the Stored Communications Act,[135] which offers "considerably less protection" than the Wiretap Act.[136] Investigative agencies can access live or stored calls with warrants and subpoenas.

The federal Electronic Communications Privacy Act prohibits the unauthorized interception of an electronic communication while it is in transit or storage.[138] Although computer or phone hacking does not involve covert recording, it does involve the breach of users' expectations of privacy and generally is both unethical and illegal. The ECPA and the Computer Fraud and Abuse Act together prohibit both phone and computer hacking.[139] All 50 states also make it illegal to hack into someone's computer or phone to obtain previously recorded conversations or messages or to gain another person's phone records by misrepresenting your identity.[140]

Late in 2016, Yahoo CEO Marissa Mayer announced that two separate hacks involved the names and birth dates, telephone numbers, passwords and security questions of 1.5 billion Yahoo users.[137]

In 2015, however, the Department of Justice declined to prosecute News Corp. and its sister company, Twentieth Century Fox, for the phone-hacking scandal that broke in Great Britain a decade earlier.[141] The DOJ spent years investigating thousands of emails after the high-profile investigation in the U.K. uncovered News Corp.'s routine reliance on hacking into cellphones to gather personal and sometimes sensational tidbits about the subjects of news stories.

Alleged violation of the ECPA has been among the claims in suits against internet service providers who reveal the identity of anonymous contributors. Courts generally have favored ISPs that disclose identities according to the standards outlined in the act. In one case, the plaintiff posted a message on AOL (then America Online) that harassed the soon-to-be ex-wife of the plaintiff's lover. When AOL investigated, it terminated the poster's contract for violating AOL's "Rules of the Road." Under subpoena and in compliance with an exception provided by the ECPA, AOL provided the identity of the poster to the subject of the post. A federal court ruled that such disclosure did not violate the poster's privacy.[142]

The Foreign Intelligence Surveillance Act allows government foreign intelligence investigators to use wiretaps, surveillance and tracking of personal communications without a court order.[143] Journalists are subject to FISA, as are news organizations, and

Peter Kramer/NBC/NBC NewsWire via Getty Images

"the extent to which the government currently uses FISA to obtain journalists' sources . . . is unknown," according to the Reporters Committee for Freedom of the Press.[144]

Recording In-State Calls. State laws regulating telephone calls that originate and end within that state may present problems for reporters who want to record an interview (or other conversation) conducted over telephone or the internet. Some state courts insist on applying that state's laws even if the case involves an interstate phone call.[145] As with face-to-face recording, 12 states' laws (the same all-party states related to face-to-face interviews) make it illegal to record a telephone conversation without all parties consenting.[146] Some of these all-party laws apply only to confidential conversations. Thirty-seven states, the District of Columbia and federal law allow recording a phone call if only one party to the conversation agrees.

Several organizations urge journalists to err on the side of caution when recording calls. The safest strategy is to assume that the stricter law will apply and assume it is necessary to request permission to record from all parties.[147]

Recording Interstate Calls. Both federal law and the Federal Communications Commission have authority over calls that cross state lines. Federal law allows recording if only one party consents.[148] However, an FCC rule requires obtaining all parties' consent and notifying all parties at the beginning of a call that it will be recorded, or using a regularly repeating beep tone so all parties know the call is being recorded.[149] The FCC says the federal law is meant to help law enforcement officers listen to calls as part of their duties, but the commission rule is meant to dissuade the public from recording calls without permission.[150]

Broadcasting Recorded Calls. The Federal Communications Commission requires radio and television stations to notify callers if the station intends to broadcast the call live or record the call for later broadcast. Consent is not necessary, only notification. There is an exception for programs that customarily air calls live or broadcast recorded calls, such as radio call-in shows. These callers have a reasonable expectation that their conversations will be aired or recorded.[151]

The U.S. Supreme Court has ruled that the First Amendment allows media to use an illegal recording so long as they were not involved in its creation. In *Bartnicki v. Vopper*, an unidentified person intercepted and recorded a cellphone conversation between two teachers' union negotiators and sent it to local media. The discussion involved heated negotiations over a collective bargaining agreement. One negotiator is recorded to say, "[W]e're gonna have to go to their, their homes . . . [t]o blow off their front porches, we'll have to do some work on some of those guys."[152] Local radio stations played the tape, and newspapers printed its contents.

The negotiator who made the remarks sued, arguing that the media intentionally "disclosed" the private exchange they should have known was obtained illegally. That violates the federal wiretap law, the negotiator said.[153] The media claimed the First Amendment allowed the use of the taped discussion of matters of significant concern because journalists were not involved in the wiretapping.

MAP 7.1 ■ Recording Laws by State

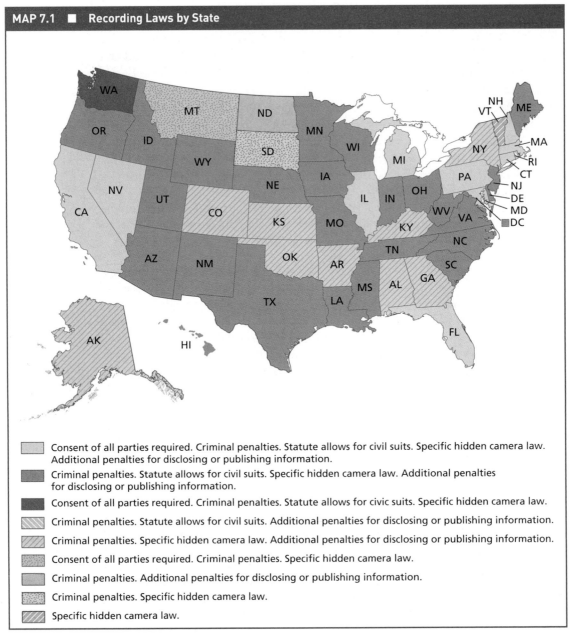

Consent of all parties required. Criminal penalties. Statute allows for civil suits. Specific hidden camera law. Additional penalties for disclosing or publishing information.

Criminal penalties. Statute allows for civil suits. Specific hidden camera law. Additional penalties for disclosing or publishing information.

Consent of all parties required. Criminal penalties. Statute allows for civic suits. Specific hidden camera law.

Criminal penalties. Statute allows for civil suits. Additional penalties for disclosing or publishing information.

Criminal penalties. Specific hidden camera law. Additional penalties for disclosing or publishing information.

Consent of all parties required. Criminal penalties. Specific hidden camera law.

Criminal penalties. Additional penalties for disclosing or publishing information.

Criminal penalties. Specific hidden camera law.

Specific hidden camera law.

Source: Reporters Committee for Freedom of the Press, *Reporter's Recording Guide*, Aug. 1, 2012, www.rcfp.org/reporters-recording-guide.

The U.S. Supreme Court agreed with the media. The First Amendment protects a journalist who shares or reports on illegally intercepted private conversations when the conversation is newsworthy and the journalist was not involved in the interception. The Court said the media were protected because they (1) played no part in the illegal interception, (2) had lawful access to the information on the tapes and (3) correctly judged the conversation to be of public concern.[154]

Finding the ban on disclosing illegally intercepted communications to be a prohibition on speech content, the Court applied strict scrutiny and held that the law failed to serve the government's alleged compelling interest of dissuading people from intercepting private communications. More importantly, the Court said, the media in *Bartnicki* did not intercept the conversation. The Court acknowledged the government's important interest in minimizing harm to private callers by discouraging distribution of illegally intercepted calls, but it said informing people about matters of public interest can be more important. "[A] stranger's illegal conduct does not suffice to remove the First Amendment shield from speech about a matter of public concern,"[155] the Court concluded.

Under federal and many state laws, a recording made to commit a crime or a tort is illegal regardless of who consents. For example, rap artists Andre Young, Snoop Dogg, Ice Cube and Eminem were scheduled to perform in Detroit as part of a nationwide tour. In each of 10 cities before Detroit, a short video introduced Andre Young and Snoop Dogg. But Detroit police told tour producers the video violated obscenity laws and could not be shown. Tour representatives secretly recorded the meeting and included parts of the recording in a music video sold internationally.

City officials sued under the federal wiretap law that makes it illegal to record a private conversation without the consent of at least one party.[156] Tour representatives said they gave themselves permission, but the court said one-party consent is not sufficient if recording is for an illegal purpose or to commit a tort.[157] Here the tour representatives made the video intending to use it to commit the tort of appropriation—taking the material without consent for commercial purposes (see Chapter 6).

● POINTS OF LAW

Media Distribution of Illegally Intercepted Calls

Under the U.S. Supreme Court's ruling in *Bartnicki v. Vopper*,[1] the First Amendment protects media from liability for distributing illegally intercepted communications when:

- The media had no involvement in the interception.
- The media gained access to the intercepted calls legally.
- The content of the intercepted calls relates to matters of public concern.
- 532 U.S. 514, 518–19 (2001).

Social Media Sources

Using material from social media may be perilous because many of the circulated claims are both anonymous and without supporting evidence. The Washington Post among other prominent media has been caught publishing material based on tweets only to find the purported tweeter did not exist. One media critic discovered that his intentionally planted misinformation with no named source took 10 minutes to go viral. In 2017, Twitter remained in the headlines for weeks at the center of debate over President Donald Trump's unsubstantiated tweets claiming that the media were purveyors of "fake news."

Many news organizations warn reporters to be cautious about using social media accounts as sources. The Associated Press, for example, says, "Fake accounts are rampant in the social media world and can appear online within minutes of a new name appearing in the news. . . . [N]ever lift quotes, photos or video from social networking sites and attribute them to the name on the profile or feed where you found the material."[158]

OBSTACLES TO GATHERING GOVERNMENT INFORMATION

The laws that provide a right of access to government information have limitations on that access. A number of other laws also limit the range of government information available to the public.

Exceptions to Government Openness

FOIA Exemptions. Federal agencies are not compelled to hand over every record requested. Nine FOIA exemptions allow agencies to withhold requested records. However, the wording of FOIA exemptions *permits* but does not require agencies to refuse to disclose information covered by an exemption. The exemptions to disclosure are permissive, and the law requires agencies to interpret the exemptions narrowly. Guidelines encouraging federal employees to read the exemptions narrowly result in agencies releasing more information more often; broader interpretations reduce disclosure. Agencies often exercise their discretion in favor of nondisclosure.

When an agency denies all or part of a FOIA request, the law requires the agency to show that the record falls under one or more specific exemptions. Thus, record keepers are required to strike out, or redact, only the particular portions of records covered by the law's exemptions. The physical process of redacting records word by word is painstaking and can result in lengthy backlogs. However, if a portion of a record may be exempted from disclosure, the agency may elect to release it, though this is unlikely.

Agency interpretations of FOIA's nine exemptions have generated court challenges. After the Sept. 11, 2001, terrorist attacks, for example, U.S. Attorney General John Ashcroft issued a memorandum to the heads of all federal agencies urging restraint with any discretionary grant of access to records that might fall under one or more exemptions.[159] The memo instructed federal agencies to withhold information sought through FOIA requests whenever a "sound legal basis" might justify secrecy and to disclose information "only after full and deliberate consideration of the institutional, commercial and personal privacy interests that could be implicated."[160]

● POINTS OF LAW

Freedom of Information Act: The Nine Exemptions

1. National security
2. Internal agency rules and procedures
3. Disclosures forbidden by other statutes
4. Trade secrets
5. Agency memoranda
6. Personal privacy
7. Law enforcement records
8. Financial records
9. Geological information

This represented an about-face to established policy to grant more liberal public access to federal government records in response to FOIA requests. An audit of federal agencies that receive the vast majority of FOIA requests found that, after the Ashcroft memo, the system was in "extreme disarray," with slow response times, lackadaisical document searches, lost requests and no accountability.[161] Another post–Sept. 11 development was the passage of the Homeland Security Act of 2002, which provided broad exemptions from FOIA disclosure for information related to the security of critical infrastructure or protected systems, including computer systems and information.[162]

On his first day in office in 2009, President Barack Obama issued a memo affirming FOIA as "the most prominent expression of a profound national commitment to ensuring an open Government."[163] However, a 2010 study by the National Security Archive concluded that the Obama administration "clearly stated a new policy direction for open government but has not [been effectively] communicating and enforcing that message throughout the executive branch."[164] In 2015, news sources reported that for the second consecutive year the federal government had set records in nondisclosure and censorship of public records.[165] Many criticized President Obama whose pre-election rhetoric proclaimed a commitment to a new transparency in government.

Exemption 1: National Security. Records fall under the exemption of national security if they are classified as confidential, secret or top secret. Members of the executive branch use each classification to reflect rising sensitivity of the information and the potential for harm if released.[166] Records requests denied on the basis of this exemption have been the most difficult to overturn.

An amendment to FOIA empowers judges to determine whether information was properly classified as a potential threat to national security or foreign policy if released. Typically, judges rule in favor of classification. The U.S. Supreme Court, for example,

TOP SECRET

confinement box. The other inquiry involved claims that the SERE training caused two individuals to engage in criminal behavior, namely, felony shoplifting and downloading child pornography onto a military computer. According to this official, these claims were found to be baseless. Moreover, he has indicated that during the three and a half years he spent as ████████ ████████ of the SERE program, he trained 10,000 students. Of those students, only two dropped out of the training following the use of these techniques. Although on rare occasions some students temporarily postponed the remainder of their training and received psychological counseling, those students were able to finish the program without any indication of subsequent mental health effects.

You have informed us that you have consulted with ████████████ who has ten years of experience with SERE training ████████████████████████████████████ ██ He stated that, during those ten years, insofar as he is aware, none of the individuals who completed the program suffered any adverse mental health effects. He informed you that there was one person who did not complete the training. That person experienced an adverse mental health reaction that lasted only two hours. After those two hours, the individual's symptoms spontaneously dissipated without requiring treatment or counseling and no other symptoms were ever reported by this individual. According to the information you have provided to us, this assessment of the use of these procedures includes the use of the waterboard.

Additionally, you received a memorandum from the ████████████████████ ████████████████████████████████████ which you supplied to us. ██████ has experience with the use of all of these procedures in a course of conduct, with the exception of the insect in the confinement box and the waterboard. This memorandum confirms that the use of these procedures has not resulted in any reported instances of prolonged mental harm, and very few instances of immediate and temporary adverse psychological responses to the training. ████████████ reported that a small minority of students have had temporary adverse psychological reactions during training. Of the 26,829 students trained from 1992 through 2001 in the Air Force SERE training, 4.3 percent of those students had contact with psychology services. Of those 4.3 percent, only 3.2 percent were pulled from the program for psychological reasons. Thus, out of the students trained overall, only 0.14 percent were pulled from the program for psychological reasons. Furthermore, although ████████████ indicated that surveys of students having completed this training are not done, he expressed confidence that the training did not cause any long-term psychological impact. He based his conclusion on the debriefing of students that is done after the training. More importantly, he based this assessment on the fact that although training is required to be extremely stressful in order to be effective, very few complaints have been made regarding the training. During his tenure, in which 10,000 students were trained, no congressional complaints have been made. While there was one Inspector General complaint, it was not due to psychological concerns. Moreover, he was aware of only one letter inquiring about the long-term impact of these techniques from an individual trained

TOP SECRET

5

An example of a redacted document that was released under FOIA. This is one page from a memo to the CIA's general counsel written by the assistant attorney general in 2002.

referred to the exemption as the "keystone of a congressional scheme that balances deference to the Executive's interest in maintaining secrecy with continued judicial and congressional oversight."[167] Even when information is widely known, such as the CIA's use of waterboarding and other "enhanced interrogation techniques, an agency may refuse a FOIA request on the basis of national security," the Second Circuit Court of Appeals ruled in 2012.[168]

Exemption 2: Internal Agency Rules and Procedures. The exemption related to internal agency rules is a "housekeeping" exemption. It covers records related exclusively to the practices of the agency itself: vacation policies, lunch break rules, parking space assignments and so on. Its purpose is not so much to prevent any harm from disclosure but to eliminate the time and expense of retrieving these mundane records. The exemption also covers any internal policy that might be used inappropriately. For example, break or shift change procedures used by federal prison guards could conceivably be used to breach facility security.

This exemption cannot be used to conceal all agency practices. If an agency policy or procedure is of public concern and its disclosure would not undermine agency regulations, a court could rule that related records do not qualify for Exemption 2 and order their release.

The U.S. Supreme Court addressed this issue in a case seeking records related to Air Force Academy honor and ethics hearings. The Court said, "[T]he general thrust of the exemption is simply to relieve agencies of the burden of assembling and maintaining for public inspection matter in which the public could not reasonably be expected to have an interest."[169] In another decision, the Court ruled that Exemption 2 applies only to human resource and "employee relations" records, not to other records an agency might possess.[170] Therefore, the Court said, the U.S. Navy could not use Exemption 2 to reject a FOIA request for information about explosives at a naval base in Puget Sound, Wash. The location of the munitions is unrelated to employee records.

Exemption 3: Statutory Exemptions. This exemption stipulates that FOIA cannot override other laws that forbid the disclosure of certain information. When litigation surfaces related to this exemption, courts usually require the government to show that (1) the information being sought falls within the scope of the statute being cited and (2) the statute grants no discretionary authority to the government agency holding the information (i.e., the nondisclosure is mandatory). If those standards are met, the decision of nondisclosure is generally upheld.

Exemption 4: Trade Secrets. The private business information provided to various government agencies, which includes profit-and-loss statements, market-share information and secret formulas and the like, is generally exempt from disclosure under FOIA. No government agency or personnel created the information; agencies merely collect and keep it to assist other government objectives, such as enforcement of copyright law or regulation of broadcasters. Trade secret information is confidential, and its release would cause considerable competitive harm or loss to a business or make it more difficult to collect similar information in the future. Other businesses might use the information to the competitive disadvantage of the businesses required to make the disclosures, which is why FOIA exempts such information from disclosure. When faced with challenges to disclosure, the courts ask agencies to show that the information sought is, in fact, a trade secret.

In one Exemption 4 case, Chrysler Corp. had turned over documents related to its affirmative action program and workforce composition to a government agency. When the agency received and signaled its intent to grant a FOIA request for those records, Chrysler objected and challenged the records' release. In ruling in the *Chrysler* case, the U.S. Supreme Court found the automaker had no claim to a trade secret exemption. FOIA, it said, "is an attempt to meet the demand for open government while preserving workable confidentiality in governmental decisionmaking."[171]

Exemption 5: Agency Memos. Sometimes referred to as the "working papers" or "discovery" exemption, Exemption 5 protects from disclosure agency memoranda, studies or drafts that are prepared and used internally to create final reports or policies. One court ruled that this exemption helps both to protect the integrity of the decision-making process and to avoid confusing the public by disclosing preliminary policy decisions.[172] Opponents argue that this exemption obscures the decision-making process. In 2016, Congress limited the exemption for records of "deliberative process," or debate, to 25 years.[173]

In one situation, an association faced an Exemption 5 denial when it sought documents related to water allocation that various Native American tribes had transmitted to the Department of the Interior and the Bureau of Indian Affairs. Ultimately, the Supreme Court ruled in favor of full disclosure. The Court emphasized that Exemption 5 is not intended to protect government secrets.[174] The key here was whether the documents qualified as "inter-agency or intra-agency memoranda or letters." The Court said they did not.

This exemption also protects information exchanged between an agency and its attorney(s). Exemption 5 recognizes that the traditional attorney–client privilege is not waived merely because the client is a federal agency. Anything that is considered discovery material—the evidence gathered in a civil trial and made available to both sides as part of the trial process—is covered by this exemption.

Exemption 6: Personal Privacy. Privacy is at the heart of Exemptions 6 and 7. Under Exemption 6, "personnel and medical files and similar files, the disclosure of which would constitute a clearly unwarranted invasion of personal privacy," may be withheld. The phrase "similar files" has been the source of much dispute. It has generally been interpreted broadly to include lists, files, records and letters.

Courts attempt to balance privacy concerns against the purpose of FOIA. Sometimes courts consider the purpose of the request and any public interest in disclosure. "Exemption Six overwhelmingly favors the disclosure of information relating to a violation of the public trust by a government official," a federal appeals court once ruled.[175]

However, the U.S. Supreme Court favored privacy when it recognized that FOIA's purpose is allowing the activity of government—not private citizens—to be open to

● **REAL WORLD LAW**

NASA and FOIA

An illustration of FOIA Exemption 6 at work occurred when The New York Times sued NASA. Several months after the 1986 explosion of the space shuttle Challenger killed all seven astronauts aboard, The New York Times filed a FOIA request with NASA for cockpit voice recordings and accompanying transcripts. NASA provided the transcripts but refused to release any recordings, citing Exemption 6. The Times sued.

The newspaper claimed there was a public interest in the cockpit recording because there was substantial interest in the disaster and in NASA's conduct before, during and after the tragedy. NASA maintained that the privacy protection of Exemption 6 extends to the families of the astronauts. Moreover, NASA claimed that voice recordings could shed no additional light on the event beyond that revealed by the transcripts.

After an appeal and remand, the U.S. District Court for the District of Columbia determined that the privacy interests clearly outweighed the public interest and ruled against The New York Times.[1]

1. New York Times Co. v. NASA, 782 F. Supp. 628 (D.D.C. 1991).

public scrutiny.[176] The Court said Exemption 6 applies to individuals, not corporations, because the ordinary meaning of the word "personal" refers to human beings.[177] Federal agencies, then, cannot use this exemption to reject FOIA requests for information about corporations and other businesses.

Exemption 7: Law Enforcement Records. Records compiled within the context of law enforcement investigations may be exempt from FOIA disclosure. There are limits, however, to the exemption. For the government to deny disclosure, release of a record must reasonably be expected to do one of the following:

a. Interfere with enforcement proceedings, or

b. Deprive a person of the right to a fair trial with an impartial jury, or

c. Constitute an unwarranted invasion of privacy, or

d. Disclose the identity of a confidential source, or

e. Disclose law enforcement techniques and procedures, or

f. Endanger the life or physical safety of any individual.

At one time, items such as rap sheets, arrest records, convictions records and department manuals were not exempt. In *U.S. Department of Justice v. Reporters Committee for Freedom of the Press*,[178] excerpted at the end of this chapter, a journalist filed a FOIA request with the FBI for its criminal records on four members of a family suspected of criminal activity. The FBI complied with the requests pertaining to three deceased family members but not to the remaining living member of the family. That decision was challenged on the grounds that there was a public interest in learning about his past arrests or convictions. The survivor allegedly had improper dealings with a corrupt congressman and was an officer of a corporation with defense contracts. But the Supreme Court upheld the nondisclosure on the basis of Exemption 7. "Disclosure of records regarding private citizens, identifiable by name, is not what the framers of FOIA had in mind,"[179] Justice John Paul Stevens wrote for the Court.

In 2004, the U.S. Supreme Court affirmed the authority of several federal agencies and organizations to withhold death scene photographs of Vincent Foster Jr.[180] Foster had been legal counsel to President Bill Clinton. The U.S. Park Police conducted an investigation into Foster's death and took color photographs of the death scene, including 10 pictures of Foster's body. That investigation and subsequent investigations by the FBI, Congress and independent counsels all concluded that Foster committed suicide by shooting himself with a revolver.

People including attorney Allan Favish believed disclosure of the pictures was vital to public understanding of whether Foster was the victim of a murder disguised as a suicide. Favish filed FOIA requests with two different federal agencies. Both were denied. Lawsuits followed.

In affirming rulings against Favish, the U.S. Supreme Court held that the right of privacy under FOIA extends to surviving family members. The Supreme Court rejected Favish's conspiracy theory as sufficient basis to overcome the family's right to privacy because people seeking information that implicates personal privacy interests must demonstrate a clear connection between the information sought and a significant public interest. More important, the Court said when

> the public interest being asserted is to show that responsible officials acted negligently or otherwise improperly in the performance of their duties, the requester must establish more than a bare suspicion in order to obtain disclosure. Rather, the requester must produce evidence that would warrant a belief by a reasonable person that the alleged Government impropriety might have occurred.[181]

Thus, rather than requiring broad disclosure of records that might shed some light on possible government malfeasance, the Court said Favish could overcome the family's privacy interest only if he provided substantial evidence to demonstrate the public interest in the records. The Court relied on an earlier decision in which it had said FOIA is intended to provide access to "official information that sheds light on an agency's performance of its statutory duties, . . . [which] is not fostered by disclosure of information about private citizens that is accumulated in various governmental files but that reveals little or nothing about an agency's own conduct."[182]

In 2011, the U.S. Supreme Court narrowed and clarified this privacy exemption. A group had submitted a FOIA request to the Federal Communications Commission for AT&T's records that revealed it overbilled the federal government for telephone and other services. The company said Exemption 7 should keep those records secret. The FCC argued that AT&T did not qualify for the personal privacy exemption. The Supreme Court agreed that the privacy exemption is for individuals, not corporations. Chief Justice John Roberts concluded the Court's opinion: "We trust that AT&T will not take it personally."[183]

Exemption 8: Financial Records. This exemption allows for nondisclosure of sensitive financial reports or audits. The burden on the government agency is to show that the disclosure of certain reports would undermine public confidence in banks and other financial institutions. Although seldom used, this exemption assumes greater significance during periods when financial scandals take place. This sweeping exemption left many questions unanswered during the massive financial crisis of savings and loan organizations during the 1980s. When Congress repealed portions of the Dodd-Frank Act that had exempted the Securities and Exchange Commission from FOIA in 2010, it allowed Exemption 8 to apply to the SEC.[184]

Skepticism about the 1993 alleged suicide of Vincent Foster Jr. (left), seen here in 1988 with his wife, Lisa, and Hillary and Bill Clinton, led to a FOIA request for photos.

Exemption 9: Geological Data. Exemption 9 rarely comes into play within a news media context although it is broad. It is designed to prevent oil and gas exploration companies from obtaining information from federal agencies that can provide them a competitive advantage. Much like the trade secrets exemption, this exemption protects potentially profitable confidential geological information from being obtained through FOIA.

The Privacy Act

The federal Privacy Act requires government agencies to use the information in their files that contain individual, personal information only for the reason it was collected.[185] They also may share the information with the subject of the file, but federal government agencies may not disclose the information to anyone else without the written consent of the person involved. That is true unless FOIA mandates disclosure. Whenever the two statutes are in opposition, FOIA prevails.

Student Records

The **Family Educational Rights and Privacy Act**, sometimes referred to as the Buckley Amendment,[186] forbids federally funded educational institutions from releasing students' academic records unless they, as adults, or their parents provide consent. The adult students and the parents of minor children are permitted access to the records. The law shields records that contain personally identifiable information, which the Department of Education defines to include a family member's name, the student's Social Security or student ID number and personal characteristics or other information that would make it easy to determine the student's identity.[187] Government-supported schools also are forbidden from releasing grades or information related to a student's health, although they can disclose "directory" information such as a student's name, address, telephone number,

Family Educational Rights and Privacy Act A federal law that protects the privacy of student education records. Also known as the Buckley Amendment.

date and place of birth, major field of study, dates of attendance and degrees and awards received. Violating the law puts an institution's government funding at risk.

University officials have said FERPA prevents them from releasing information such as campus police records or student disciplinary records to journalists. While nondisclosure may protect individuals, the news media argue that the public has a right to know information related to possible crimes and justice systems on the campuses of public institutions.

The federal Campus Security Policy and Campus Crime Statistics Act, or the Clery Act as it is now known, requires universities to compile and publish statistics on campus

● REAL WORLD LAW

The Fight Over Photos

AP Photo

The Associated Press permits publication of its Abu Ghraib photographs for "editorial use only," such as in this book.

A battle over whether the Department of Defense should release photos of U.S. detainees in Afghanistan and Iraq, including the Abu Ghraib prison, focused on Freedom of Information Act Exemptions 6 and 7. The DOD initially claimed FOIA's privacy exemptions applied. Later, the Pentagon said the photos were exempted under another part of Exemption 7 because they could reasonably endanger the life or physical safety of any individual. It was referring to U.S. troops abroad.

The Second Circuit Court of Appeals ruled in favor of the photographs' release and said: "FOIA's purpose is to encourage public disclosure of information in the possession of federal agencies so that the people may know what their government is up to. The release of information of this sort represents FOIA's basic purpose: to ensure an informed citizenry, vital to the functioning of a democratic society, needed to check against corruption and to hold the governors accountable to the governed."[1] The court concluded that the exemption required a specific anticipated danger to a particular individual rather than diffuse risks to "any" members of the U.S. forces.

Soon after, Congress enacted a law allowing the secretary of defense to block the pictures' release. At the urging of his national security advisers, President Barack Obama asked the Justice Department to argue in court that releasing the photos would inflame anti-American sentiment abroad and endanger U.S. troops. Without comment, the U.S. Supreme Court vacated the lower court ruling in light of the new law.[2]

1. ACLU v. U.S. Dep't of Defense, 543 F.3d 59, 66 (2nd Cir. 2008) (internal quotations omitted).
2. U.S. Dep't of Defense v. ACLU, 558 U.S. 1042 (2009).

▲ EMERGING LAW

GMO Foods Grow in the DARK

In 2014, Republican Rep. Mike Pompeo of Kansas, the state that ranks first in wheat production and seventh in total agriculture production in the nation, introduced a bill that would prohibit any state or federal body from requiring the labeling of genetically modified organisms.[1]

Pompeo proposed the ban, which critics dubbed the Deny Americans the Right to Know or DARK Act, after two states passed laws mandating GMO labeling and more than two dozen others considered similar legislation.[2] If enacted, the law would prohibit mandatory GMO labeling and allow genetically engineered foods to be labeled "natural." Pompeo's bill was identical to model legislation drafted by the Grocery Manufacturers Association. In 2015, the House of Representatives passed the federal DARK Act, but the Senate was expected to reject the law's nationwide ban on enforced labeling of GMOs.[3]

In 2013, the attorney general of Washington State filed suit against the GMA, claiming the association "illegally collected and spent a sum of $7.2 million to defeat Washington's [GMO] labeling initiative, while hiding the identity of its contributors" in violation of the state's campaign disclosure laws.[4] In response, the GMA agreed to disclose its contributors.[5] Calling the GMA's contributions the "largest amount of money ever concealed," the attorney general said he would seek penalties,[6] and within months, the GMA filed suit seeking a ruling that Washington's campaign finance laws were unconstitutional.[7]

1. Sara Sciammacco, *Big Food's "Dark Act" Introduced in Congress*, EWG, Apr. 9, 2014, www.ewg.org/release/big-food-s-dark-act-introduced-congress.
2. Scott Faber, *Pompeo's DARK Act Will Keep Consumers in the Dark*, AGMAGBLOG, Apr. 19, 2014, www.ewg.org/agmag/2014/04/pompeo-s-dark-act-will-keep-consumers-dark.
3. Stefanie Spear, *House Passes DARK Act, Banning States From Requiring GMO Labels on Food*, ECOWATCH, July 24, 2015, ecowatch.com/2015/07/24/house-passes-dark-act.
4. *Washington State Attorney General Files Lawsuit Against Grocery Manufacturers Association*, JUST LABEL IT, Oct. 16, 2013, www.justlabelit.org/press-room/washington-state-attorney-general-files-lawsuit-against-grocery-manufacturers-association/.
5. Nick Rees, *Washington AG: Grocery Manufacturers Association Agrees to Disclose Financing*, LEGAL NEWSLINE, Oct. 21, 2013, LexisNexis.
6. *Washington Mandatory Labeling of Genetically Engineered Food Measure, Initiative 522 (2013)*, BALLOTPEDIA, Washington_Mandatory_Labeling_of_Genetically_Engineered_Food_Measure,_Initiative_522_(2013).
7. Zach C. Miller, *Grocery Manufacturers Association Sues the State of Washington Over GMO Labeling Fight: GMA More Evil Than Monsanto*, NATURAL NEWS, Feb. 17, 2014, www.naturalnews.com/043937_Grocery_Manufacturers_Association_GMO_labeling_Washington_State.html.

crime each year.[188] Reporting using these statistics has unveiled significant problems on campuses, such as the excesses in fraternity hazing and gay bashing at the University of Georgia uncovered when student journalists obtained records of university disciplinary hearings.[189] The Georgia Supreme Court held that disciplinary records were not student records under FERPA because they were not concerned with student academic performance, financial aid or academic probation.[190]

Such campus information is more difficult to obtain in the wake of a Sixth Circuit Court of Appeals ruling in response to a DOE argument that student disciplinary records are shielded by FERPA.[191] The weekly Chronicle of Higher Education and the Miami University of Ohio student newspaper sought the records of the university's internal discipline committees to examine crime trends on campus. The Sixth Circuit supported the DOE position and said the law's language made clear that disciplinary proceedings were part of student records and could not be released without consent.

Medical Records

Health Insurance
Portability and
Accountability
Act A federal
law protecting
against health
professionals
and institutions
revealing
individuals'
private medical
records.

The **Health Insurance Portability and Accountability Act** prevents health professionals and institutions from revealing individuals' personal medical records.[192] After Congress passed HIPAA in 1996, the Department of Health and Human Services crafted the first federal medical privacy regulations, called the Standards for Privacy of Individually Identifiable Health Information. These rules were designed to give patients more control over their health information and to limit the use and release of health records to third parties. Generally, the privacy standards established a federal requirement that most health care providers obtain a patient's written consent before disclosing the patient's personal health information. The rules restrict the use of such records for marketing and research purposes.

Driver's Information

Driver's Privacy
Protection
Act Federal
legislation that
prohibits states
from disclosing
personal
information that
drivers submit in
order to obtain a
driver's license.

The federal **Driver's Privacy Protection Act** of 1994 prohibits states from releasing information obtained from driver's license and vehicle registration records without permission except under specific circumstances.[193] At one time, many states sold this information for millions of dollars annually. Congress stopped this practice in part to prevent stalkers from obtaining information about potential targets. However, the law also prevents journalists from using these records to find information for stories. The U.S. Supreme Court upheld the law against a constitutional challenge, finding that Congress' power over interstate commerce allowed it to adopt the statute.[194]

In 2015, the Seventh Circuit Court of Appeals refused to dismiss the district court's ruling that the Sun-Times newspaper of Chicago was punishable for disclosing "private information" from the driver's licenses of several police officers.[195] The Sun-Times received photographs and physical descriptions of the officers after the state attorney general required their release under the state's freedom of law. In its published criticism of the officers' participation in a homicide lineup, the Sun-Times included each officer's birth date, height, weight, hair color and eye color, details it said were essential to demonstrate the problematic composition of the police lineup. The newspaper argued that it had published accurate, legally obtained information that was not defined as private under the law.

The Seventh Circuit held that the DPPA's ban on disclosure of private information applied and the newspaper enjoyed no First Amendment protection from penalty. The court reasoned that the ban was both content-neutral and rationally related to the government's legitimate interest in protecting the information from unauthorized disclosure. The Supreme Court declined to review the decision.

CHAPTER SUMMARY

THE U.S. CONSTITUTION provides no special right of access to journalists or others seeking information to distribute to the public. While journalists share the general right of access to public spaces, everyone must obey legal orders from emergency officers that may include moving away from crime scenes. Legal police orders respond to the need for officers to conduct their official functions. Unless recording interferes with officials' duties, courts generally uphold the public right to record in public. This is not true in nonpublic areas.

Access to U.S. military operations can be challenging. The history in this area is one of give-and-take, with the government attempting to exert more control in recent decades. Courts disagree on what public access is provided, or allowed, to polling sites, where orderly elections are paramount. Two appeals courts used the *Press-Enterprise* logic and experience test to deny access to public polls and to Bureau of Land Management horse roundups, but a federal district court in 2015 said the test should not apply outside of court procedures.

The Government in the Sunshine Act and the Federal Advisory Committee Act provide public access to meetings of federal governing and advisory boards. Separate laws in each state and the District of Columbia cover access to government meetings at the state and local levels. The laws vary widely, and some lack definitions of key terms, such as "meeting." A meeting generally occurs when a quorum of a body gathers either physically or virtually.

The Freedom of Information Act and the Electronic Freedom of Information Act provide a public right of access to the records of federal executive branch agencies and departments, regardless of the record's format. A record is any tangible item that may be reproduced and that records government actions. The laws presume access to most records but do not require covered agencies to create records in response to requests. EFOIA requires records be provided in the requester's preferred format. Exemptions to the law are permissive and should be interpreted narrowly. Similar laws exist on the state level.

Promises of confidentiality for disclosure of information are a journalistic tradition. If sources rely on promises that are breached, resulting in harm to the source, the promise may be upheld in court. Misrepresentations and fraud, which may arise in undercover reporting, may violate the law.

Both federal and state laws protect specific locations from photography. Other laws prevent electronic intrusion and regulate photography by drones. Overt face-to-face video or audio recording does not violate federal or state laws. However, laws at the federal and state levels restrict recording under some conditions when all parties are not fully informed. People have a right to be free from trespass, intrusion and "peeping" into their homes and in their private electronic communications.

Laws that provide a right of public access to government records and meetings provide exemptions. Other laws protect personal privacy and the privacy of student, medical and driver's records. ◼

CASES FOR STUDY

For study resources and a case archive go to **study.sagepub.com/medialaw6e**.

THINKING ABOUT IT

The two case excerpts that follow cover different subsets in the broad area of information gathering. The first case relates to the Freedom of Information Act. The second addresses the concept of the ride-along. As you read these case excerpts, keep the following questions in mind:

- Just how much information does the Freedom of Information Act provide? Are the limits that have been established fair?

- In the *Reporters Committee* case, what factor does the Supreme Court identify as critical in deciding whether to disclose a private document?

- The *Reporters Committee* case was decided in 1989. Has the nature of privacy changed in such a way that the ruling might be different today?

- Note that in the *Wilson* ride-along case, a media organization is not a party to the case. Nevertheless, it is a ruling that affects the media significantly. How and why?

- In *Wilson*, why were members of the news media on the scene? Did their presence help in the execution of the warrant?

U.S. Department of Justice v. Reporters Committee for Freedom of the Press
SUPREME COURT OF THE UNITED STATES
489 U.S. 749 (1989)

JUSTICE JOHN PAUL STEVENS delivered the Court's opinion:

The Federal Bureau of Investigation (FBI) has accumulated and maintains criminal identification records, sometimes referred to as "rap sheets," on over 24 million persons. The question presented by this case is whether the disclosure of the contents of such a file to a third party "could reasonably be expected to constitute an unwarranted invasion of personal privacy" within the meaning of the Freedom of Information Act (FOIA).

In 1924 Congress appropriated funds to enable the Department of Justice (Department) to establish a program to collect and preserve fingerprints and other criminal identification records. That statute authorized the Department to exchange such information with "officials of States, cities and other institutions." . . . Congress created the FBI's identification division, and gave it responsibility for "acquiring, collecting, classifying, and preserving criminal identification and other crime records and the exchanging of said criminal identification records with the duly authorized officials of governmental agencies, of States, cities, and penal institutions." Rap sheets compiled pursuant to such authority contain certain descriptive information, such as date of birth and physical characteristics, as well as a history of arrests, charges, convictions, and incarcerations of the subject. Normally a rap sheet is preserved until its subject attains age 80. Because of the volume of rap sheets, they are sometimes incorrect or incomplete and sometimes contain information about other persons with similar names.

The local, state, and federal law enforcement agencies throughout the Nation that exchange rap-sheet data with the FBI do so on a voluntary basis. The principal use of the information is to assist in the detection and prosecution of offenders; it is also used by courts and corrections officials in connection with sentencing and parole decisions. As a matter of executive policy, the Department has generally treated rap sheets as confidential and, with certain exceptions, has restricted their use to governmental purposes. Consistent with the Department's basic policy of treating these records as confidential, Congress in 1957 amended the basic statute to provide that the FBI's exchange of rap-sheet information with any other agency is subject to cancellation "if dissemination is made outside the receiving departments or related agencies."

As a matter of Department policy, the FBI has made two exceptions to its general practice of prohibiting unofficial access to rap sheets. First, it allows the subject of a rap sheet to obtain a copy, and second, it occasionally allows rap sheets to be used in the preparation of press releases and publicity designed to assist in the apprehension of wanted persons or fugitives. . . .

Although much rap-sheet information is a matter of public record, the availability and dissemination of the actual rap sheet to the public is limited. Arrests, indictments, convictions, and sentences are public events that are usually documented in court records. In addition, if a person's entire criminal history transpired in a single jurisdiction, all of the contents of his or her rap sheet may be available upon request in that jurisdiction. That possibility,

however, is present in only three States. All of the other 47 States place substantial restrictions on the availability of criminal-history summaries even though individual events in those summaries are matters of public record. Moreover, even in Florida, Wisconsin, and Oklahoma, the publicly available summaries may not include information about out-of-state arrests or convictions.

The statute known as FOIA is actually a part of the Administrative Procedure Act (APA). Section 3 of the APA as enacted in 1946 gave agencies broad discretion concerning the publication of governmental records. In 1966 Congress amended that section to implement "'a general philosophy of full agency disclosure.'" The amendment required agencies to publish their rules of procedure in the Federal Register, and to make available for public inspection and copying their opinions, statements of policy, interpretations, and staff manuals and instructions that are not published in the Federal Register . . . In addition, [it] requires every agency "upon any request for records which . . . reasonably describes such records" to make such records "promptly available to any person." If an agency improperly withholds any documents, the district court has jurisdiction to order their production. Unlike the review of other agency action that must be upheld if supported by substantial evidence and not arbitrary or capricious, FOIA expressly places the burden "on the agency to sustain its action" and directs the district courts to "determine the matter de novo."

Congress exempted nine categories of documents from FOIA's broad disclosure requirements. Three of those exemptions are arguably relevant to this case. Exemption 3 applies to documents that are specifically exempted from disclosure by another statute. Exemption 6 protects "personnel and medical files and similar files the disclosure of which would constitute a clearly unwarranted invasion of personal privacy." Exemption 7(C) excludes records or information compiled for law enforcement purposes, "but only to the extent that the production of such [materials] . . . could reasonably be expected to constitute an unwarranted invasion of personal privacy."

Exemption 7(C)'s privacy language is broader than the comparable language in Exemption 6 in two respects. First, whereas Exemption 6 requires that the invasion of privacy be "clearly unwarranted," the adverb "clearly" is omitted from Exemption 7(C). This omission is the product of a 1974 amendment adopted in response to concerns expressed by the President. Second, whereas Exemption 6 refers to disclosures that "would constitute" an invasion of privacy, Exemption 7(C) encompasses any disclosure that "could reasonably be expected to constitute" such an invasion. This difference is also the product of a specific amendment. Thus, the standard for evaluating a threatened invasion of privacy interests resulting from the disclosure of records compiled for law enforcement purposes is somewhat broader than the standard applicable to personnel, medical, and similar files.

This case arises out of requests made by a CBS news correspondent and the Reporters Committee for Freedom of the Press (respondents) for information concerning the criminal records of four members of the Medico family. The Pennsylvania Crime Commission had identified the family's company, Medico Industries, as a legitimate business dominated by organized crime figures. Moreover, the company allegedly had obtained a number of defense contracts as a result of an improper arrangement with a corrupt Congressman.

FOIA requests sought disclosure of any arrests, indictments, acquittals, convictions, and sentences of any of the four Medicos. Although the FBI originally denied the requests, it provided the requested data concerning three of the Medicos after their deaths. In their complaint in the district court, respondents sought the rap sheet for the fourth, Charles Medico (Medico), insofar as it contained "matters of public record." . . .

Exemption 7(C) requires us to balance the privacy interest in maintaining, as the government puts it, the "practical obscurity" of the rap sheets against the public interest in their release.

The preliminary question is whether Medico's interest in the nondisclosure of any rap sheet the FBI might have on him is the sort of "personal privacy" interest that Congress intended Exemption 7(C) to protect. As we have pointed out before, "[t]he cases sometimes characterized as protecting 'privacy' have in fact involved at least two different kinds of interests. One is the individual interest in avoiding disclosure of personal matters, and another is the interest in independence in making certain kinds of important decisions." Here, the former interest, "in avoiding disclosure of personal matters," is implicated. Because events summarized in a rap sheet have been previously disclosed to the public, respondents contend that Medico's privacy interest in avoiding disclosure of a federal compilation of these events approaches zero. We reject respondents' cramped notion of personal privacy.

To begin with, both the common law and the literal understandings of privacy encompass the individual's control of information concerning his or her person. In an organized society, there are few facts that are not at one time or another divulged to another. Thus the extent of the protection accorded a privacy right at common law rested in part on the degree of dissemination of the allegedly private fact and the extent to which the passage of time rendered it private. According to Webster's initial definition, information may be classified as "private" if it is "intended for or restricted to the use of a particular person or group or class of persons: not freely available to the public." Recognition of this attribute of a privacy interest supports the distinction, in terms of personal privacy, between scattered disclosure of the bits of information contained in a rap sheet and revelation of the rap sheet as a whole. The very fact that federal funds have been spent to prepare, index, and maintain these criminal-history files demonstrates that the individual items of information in the summaries would not otherwise be "freely available" either to the officials who have access to the underlying files or to the general public. Indeed, if the summaries were "freely available," there would be no reason to invoke FOIA to obtain access to the information they contain. Granted, in many contexts the fact that information is not freely available is no reason to exempt that information from a statute generally requiring its dissemination. But the issue here is whether the compilation of otherwise hard-to-obtain information alters the privacy interest implicated by disclosure of that information. Plainly there is a vast difference between the public records that might be found after a diligent search of courthouse files, county archives, and local police stations throughout the country and a computerized summary located in a single clearinghouse of information.

This conclusion is supported by the web of federal statutory and regulatory provisions that limits the disclosure of rap-sheet information. That is, Congress has authorized rap-sheet dissemination to banks, local licensing officials, the securities industry, the nuclear-power industry, and other law enforcement agencies. Further, the FBI has permitted such disclosure to the subject of the rap sheet and, more generally, to assist in the apprehension of wanted persons or fugitives. Finally, the FBI's exchange of rap-sheet information "is subject to cancellation if dissemination is made outside the receiving departments or related agencies." This careful and limited pattern of authorized rap-sheet disclosure fits the dictionary definition of privacy as involving a restriction of information "to the use of a particular person or group or class of persons." Moreover, although perhaps not specific enough to constitute a statutory exemption under FOIA Exemption 3, these statutes and regulations, taken as a whole, evidence a congressional intent to protect the privacy of rap-sheet subjects, and a concomitant recognition of the power of compilations to affect personal privacy that outstrips the combined power of the bits of information contained within.

Other portions of FOIA itself bolster the conclusion that disclosure of records regarding private citizens, identifiable by name, is not what the framers of FOIA had in mind. Specifically, FOIA provides that "[t]o the extent required to prevent a clearly unwarranted invasion of personal privacy, an agency may delete identifying details when it makes available or publishes an opinion, statement of policy, interpretation, or staff manual or instruction." Additionally, FOIA assures that "[a]ny reasonably segregable portion of a record shall be provided to any person requesting such record after deletion of the portions which are exempt under Section (b)." These provisions, for deletion of identifying references and disclosure of segregable portions of records with exempt information deleted, reflect a congressional understanding that disclosure of records containing personal details about private citizens can infringe significant privacy interests.

Also supporting our conclusion that a strong privacy interest inheres in the nondisclosure of compiled computerized information is the Privacy Act of 1974. The Privacy Act was passed largely out of concern over "the impact of computer data banks on individual privacy." The Privacy Act provides generally that "[n]o agency shall disclose any record which is contained in a system of records . . . except pursuant to a written request by, or with the prior written consent of, the individual to whom the record pertains." Although the Privacy Act contains a variety of exceptions to this rule, including an exemption for information required to be disclosed under FOIA, Congress' basic policy concern regarding the implications of computerized data banks for personal privacy is certainly relevant in our consideration of the privacy interest affected by dissemination of rap sheets from the FBI computer.

Given this level of federal concern over centralized data bases, the fact that most States deny the general public access to their criminal-history summaries should not be surprising. As we have pointed out, in 47 States nonconviction data from criminal-history summaries are not available at all, and even conviction data are "generally unavailable to the public." State policies, of course, do not determine the meaning of a federal statute, but they provide evidence that the law enforcement profession generally assumes— as has the Department of Justice—that individual subjects have a significant privacy interest in their criminal histories. It is reasonable to presume that Congress legislated with an understanding of this professional point of view.

In addition to the common-law and dictionary understandings, the basic difference between scattered bits of criminal history and a federal compilation, federal statutory provisions, and state policies, our cases have also recognized the privacy interest inherent in the nondisclosure of certain information even where the information may have been at one time public. . . .

In sum, the fact that "an event is not wholly 'private' does not mean that an individual has no interest in limiting disclosure or dissemination of the information." The privacy interest in a rap sheet is substantial. The substantial character of that interest is affected by the fact that in today's society the computer can accumulate and store information that would otherwise have surely been forgotten long before a person attains age 80, when the FBI's rap sheets are discarded.

Exemption 7(C), by its terms, permits an agency to withhold a document only when revelation "could reasonably be expected to constitute an unwarranted invasion of personal privacy." We must next address what factors might warrant an invasion of the interest described in Part IV.

Our previous decisions establish that whether an invasion of privacy is warranted cannot turn on the purposes for which the request for information is made. Except for cases in which the objection to disclosure is based on a claim of privilege and the person requesting disclosure is the party protected by the privilege, the identity of the requesting party has no bearing on the merits of his or her FOIA request. Thus, although the subject of a presentence report can waive a privilege that might defeat a third party's access to that report, and although the FBI's policy of granting the subject of a rap sheet access to his own criminal history is consistent with its policy of denying access to all other members of the general public, the rights of the two press respondents in this case are no different from those that might be asserted by any other third party, such as a neighbor or prospective employer. As we have repeatedly stated, Congress "clearly intended" FOIA "to give any member of the public as much right to disclosure as one with a special interest [in a particular document]." . . . "The Act's sole concern is with what must be made public or not made public."

Thus whether disclosure of a private document under Exemption 7(C) is warranted must turn on the nature of the requested document and its relationship to "the basic purpose of the Freedom of Information Act 'to open agency action to the light of public scrutiny'" . . . rather than on the particular purpose for which the document is being requested. In our leading case on FOIA, we declared that the Act was designed to create a broad right of access to "official information." . . .

This basic policy of "'full agency disclosure unless information is exempted under clearly delineated statutory language'" indeed focuses on the citizens' right to be informed about "what their government is up to." Official information that sheds light on an agency's performance of its statutory duties falls squarely within that statutory purpose. That purpose, however, is not fostered by disclosure of information about private citizens that is accumulated in various governmental files but that reveals little or nothing about an agency's own conduct. In this case—and presumably in the typical case in which one private citizen is seeking information about another—the requester does not intend to discover anything about the conduct of the agency that has possession of the requested records. Indeed, response to this request would not shed any light on the conduct of any Government agency or official. . . .

Respondents argue that there is a twofold public interest in learning about Medico's past arrests or convictions: He allegedly had improper dealings with a corrupt Congressman, and he is an officer of a corporation with defense contracts. But if Medico has, in fact, been arrested or convicted of certain crimes, that information would neither aggravate nor mitigate his allegedly improper relationship with the Congressman; more specifically, it would tell us nothing directly about the character of the Congressman's behavior. Nor would it tell us anything about the conduct of the Department of Defense (DOD) in awarding one or more contracts to the Medico Company. Arguably a FOIA request to the DOD for records relating to those contracts, or for documents describing the agency's procedures, if any, for determining whether officers of a prospective contractor have criminal records, would constitute an appropriate request for "official information." Conceivably Medico's rap sheet would provide details to include in a news story, but, in itself, this is not the kind of public interest for which Congress enacted FOIA. In other words, although there is undoubtedly some public interest in anyone's criminal history, especially if the history is in some way related to the subject's dealing with a public official or agency, FOIA's central purpose is to ensure that the Government's activities be opened to the sharp eye of public scrutiny, not that information about private citizens that happens to be in the warehouse of the Government be so disclosed. Thus, it should come as no surprise that in none of our cases construing FOIA have we found it appropriate to order a Government agency to honor a FOIA request for information about a particular private citizen.

What we have said should make clear that the public interest in the release of any rap sheet on Medico that may exist is not the type of interest protected by FOIA. Medico may or may not be one of the 24 million persons for whom the FBI has a rap sheet. If respondents are entitled to have the FBI tell them what it knows about Medico's criminal history, any other member of the public is entitled to the same disclosure—whether for writing a news story, for deciding whether to employ Medico, to rent a house to him, to extend credit to him, or simply to confirm or deny a suspicion. There is, unquestionably, some public interest in providing interested citizens with answers to their questions about Medico. But that interest falls outside the ambit of the public interest that FOIA was enacted to serve.

Finally, we note that Congress has provided that the standard fees for production of documents under FOIA shall be waived or reduced "if disclosure of the information is in the public interest because it is likely to contribute significantly to public understanding of the operations or activities of the government and is not primarily in the commercial interest of the requester." Although such a provision obviously implies that there will be requests that do not meet

such a "public interest" standard, we think it relevant to today's inquiry regarding the public interest in release of rap sheets on private citizens that Congress once again expressed the core purpose of FOIA as "contribut[ing] significantly to public understanding of the operations or activities of the government."

Both the general requirement that a court "shall determine the matter de novo" and the specific reference to an "unwarranted" invasion of privacy in Exemption 7(C) indicate that a court must balance the public interest in disclosure against the interest Congress intended the Exemption to protect. Although both sides agree that such a balance must be undertaken, how such a balance should be done is in dispute. The Court of Appeals majority expressed concern about assigning federal judges the task of striking a proper case-by-case, or ad hoc, balance between individual privacy interests and the public interest in the disclosure of criminal-history information without providing those judges standards to assist in performing that task. Our cases provide support for the proposition that categorical decisions may be appropriate and individual circumstances disregarded when a case fits into a genus in which the balance characteristically tips in one direction. . . .

. . . [W]e hold as a categorical matter that a third party's request for law enforcement records or information about a private citizen can reasonably be expected to invade that citizen's privacy, and that when the request seeks no "official information" about a Government agency, but merely records that the Government happens to be storing, the invasion of privacy is "unwarranted." The judgment of the Court of Appeals is reversed.

It is so ordered.

Wilson v. Layne
SUPREME COURT OF THE UNITED STATES
526 U.S. 603 (1999)

CHIEF JUSTICE WILLIAM REHNQUIST delivered the Court's opinion:
While executing an arrest warrant in a private home, police officers invited representatives of the media

to accompany them. We hold that such a "media ride-along" does violate the Fourth Amendment, but that because the state of the law was not clearly established at the time the search in this case took place, the officers are entitled to the defense of qualified immunity.

In early 1992, the Attorney General of the United States approved "Operation Gunsmoke," a special national fugitive apprehension program in which United States Marshals worked with state and local police to apprehend dangerous criminals. The "Operation Gunsmoke" policy statement explained that the operation was to concentrate on "armed individuals wanted on federal and/or state and local warrants for serious drug and other violent felonies." This effective program ultimately resulted in over 3,000 arrests in 40 metropolitan areas.

One of the dangerous fugitives identified as a target of "Operation Gunsmoke" was Dominic Wilson, the son of petitioners Charles and Geraldine Wilson. Dominic Wilson had violated his probation on previous felony charges of robbery, theft, and assault with intent to rob, and the police computer listed "caution indicators" that he was likely to be armed, to resist arrest, and to "assault police." The computer also listed his address as 909 North Stone Street Avenue in Rockville, Maryland. Unknown to the police, this was actually the home of petitioners, Dominic Wilson's parents. Thus, in April 1992, the Circuit Court for Montgomery County issued three arrest warrants for Dominic Wilson, one for each of his probation violations. The warrants were each addressed to "any duly authorized peace officer," and commanded such officers to arrest him and bring him "immediately" before the Circuit Court to answer an indictment as to his probation violation. The warrants made no mention of media presence or assistance.

In the early morning hours of April 16, 1992, a Gunsmoke team of Deputy United States Marshals and Montgomery County Police officers assembled to execute the Dominic Wilson warrants. The team was accompanied by a reporter and a photographer from the Washington Post, who had been invited by the Marshals to accompany them on their mission as part of a Marshal's Service ride-along policy.

At around 6:45 a.m., the officers, with media representatives in tow, entered the dwelling at 909 North Stone Street Avenue in the Lincoln Park neighborhood of Rockville. Petitioners Charles and Geraldine Wilson were still in bed when they heard the officers enter the home. Petitioner Charles Wilson, dressed only in a pair of briefs, ran into the living room to investigate. Discovering at least five men in street clothes with guns in his living room, he angrily demanded that they state their business, and repeatedly cursed the officers. Believing him to be an angry Dominic Wilson, the officers quickly subdued him on the floor. Geraldine Wilson next entered the living room to investigate, wearing only a nightgown. She observed her husband being restrained by the armed officers.

When their protective sweep was completed, the officers learned that Dominic Wilson was not in the house, and they departed. During the time that the officers were in the home, the Washington Post photographer took numerous pictures. The print reporter was also apparently in the living room observing the confrontation between the police and Charles Wilson. At no time, however, were the reporters involved in the execution of the arrest warrant. The Washington Post never published its photographs of the incident.

Petitioners sued the law enforcement officials in their personal capacities for money damages. . . . They contended that the officers' actions in bringing members of the media to observe and record the attempted execution of the arrest warrant violated their Fourth Amendment rights. . . .

. . . [G]overnment officials performing discretionary functions generally are granted a qualified immunity and are "shielded from liability for civil damages insofar as their conduct does not violate clearly established statutory or constitutional rights of which a reasonable person would have known."

. . . A court evaluating a claim of qualified immunity "must first determine whether the plaintiff has alleged the deprivation of an actual constitutional right at all, and if so, proceed to determine whether that right was clearly established at the time of the alleged violation." This order of procedure is designed to "spare a defendant not only unwarranted liability, but unwarranted demands customarily imposed upon those defending a long drawn-out lawsuit."

Deciding the constitutional question before addressing the qualified immunity question also promotes clarity in the legal standards for official conduct, to the benefit of both the officers and the general public. We now turn to the Fourth Amendment question.

In 1604, an English court made the now-famous observation that "the house of every one is to him as his castle and fortress, as well for his defence against injury and violence, as for his repose." In his Commentaries on the Laws of England, William Blackstone noted that

> the law of England has so particular and tender a regard to the immunity of a man's house, that it stiles it his castle, and will never suffer it to be violated with impunity: agreeing herein with the sentiments of ancient Rome. . . . For this reason no doors can in general be broken open to execute any civil process; though, in criminal causes, the public safety supersedes the private.

The Fourth Amendment embodies this centuries-old principle of respect for the privacy of the home: "The right of the people to be secure in their persons, houses, papers, and effects, against unreasonable searches and seizures, shall not be violated, and no Warrants shall issue, but upon probable cause, supported by Oath or affirmation, and particularly describing the place to be searched, and the persons or things to be seized."

Our decisions have applied these basic principles of the Fourth Amendment to situations, like those in this case, in which police enter a home under the authority of an arrest warrant in order to take into custody the suspect named in the warrant. In *Payton v. New York* (1980), we noted that although clear in its protection of the home, the common-law tradition at the time of the drafting of the Fourth Amendment was ambivalent on the question of whether police could enter a home without a warrant. We were ultimately persuaded that the "overriding respect for the sanctity of the home that has been embedded in our traditions since the origins of the Republic" meant that absent a warrant or exigent circumstances, police could not enter a home to make an arrest. We decided that "an arrest warrant founded on probable cause implicitly carries with it the limited authority to enter a dwelling in which the suspect lives when there is reason to believe the suspect is within."

Here, of course, the officers had such a warrant, and they were undoubtedly entitled to enter the Wilson home in order to execute the arrest warrant for Dominic Wilson. But it does not necessarily follow that they were entitled to bring a newspaper reporter and a photographer with them. . . .

Certainly the presence of reporters inside the home was not related to the objectives of the authorized intrusion. Respondents concede that the reporters did not engage in the execution of the warrant, and did not assist the police in their task. The reporters therefore were not present for any reason related to the justification for police entry into the home—the apprehension of Dominic Wilson.

This is not a case in which the presence of the third parties directly aided in the execution of the warrant. Where the police enter a home under the authority of a warrant to search for stolen property, the presence of third parties for the purpose of identifying the stolen property has long been approved by this Court and our common-law tradition.

Respondents argue that the presence of the Washington Post reporters in the Wilsons' home nonetheless served a number of legitimate law enforcement purposes. They first assert that officers should be able to exercise reasonable discretion about when it would "further their law enforcement mission to permit members of the news media to accompany them in executing a warrant." But this claim ignores the importance of the right of residential privacy at the core of the Fourth Amendment. It may well be that media ride-alongs further the law enforcement objectives of the police in a general sense, but that is not the same as furthering the purposes of the search. Were such generalized "law enforcement objectives" themselves sufficient to trump the Fourth Amendment, the protections guaranteed by that Amendment's text would be significantly watered down.

Respondents next argue that the presence of third parties could serve the law enforcement purpose of publicizing the government's efforts to combat crime, and facilitate accurate reporting on law enforcement activities. There is certainly language in our opinions interpreting the First Amendment which points to the importance of "the press" in informing the general public about the administration of criminal justice. . . . But the Fourth Amendment also protects a very important right, and in the present case it is in terms of that right that the media ride-alongs must be judged.

Surely the possibility of good public relations for the police is simply not enough, standing alone, to justify the ride-along intrusion into a private home. And even the need for accurate reporting on police issues in general bears no direct relation to the constitutional justification for the police intrusion into a home in order to execute a felony arrest warrant.

Finally, respondents argue that the presence of third parties could serve in some situations to minimize police abuses and protect suspects, and also to protect the safety of the officers. While it might be reasonable for police officers to themselves videotape home entries as part of a "quality control" effort to ensure that the rights of homeowners are being respected, or even to preserve evidence, such a situation is significantly different from the media presence in this case. The Washington Post reporters in the Wilsons' home were working on a story for their own purposes. They were not present for the purpose of protecting the officers, much less the Wilsons. A private photographer was acting for private purposes, as evidenced in part by the fact that the newspaper and not the police retained the photographs. Thus, although the presence of third parties during the execution of a warrant may in some circumstances be constitutionally permissible, the presence of these third parties was not.

The reasons advanced by respondents, taken in their entirety, fall short of justifying the presence of media inside a home. We hold that it is a violation of the Fourth Amendment for police to bring members of the media or other third parties into a home during the execution of a warrant when the presence of the third parties in the home was not in aid of the execution of the warrant.

Since the police action in this case violated the petitioners' Fourth Amendment right, we now must decide whether this right was clearly established at the time of the search. As noted above, government officials performing discretionary functions generally are granted a qualified immunity and are "shielded from liability for civil damages insofar as their conduct does not violate clearly established statutory or constitutional rights of which a reasonable person would have known." What this means in practice is that "whether an official protected by qualified immunity may be held personally liable for an allegedly unlawful official action generally turns on the 'objective legal reasonableness' of the action, assessed in light of the legal rules that were 'clearly established' at the time it was taken." . . .

We hold that it was not unreasonable for a police officer in April 1992 to have believed that bringing media observers along during the execution of an arrest warrant (even in a home) was lawful. First, the constitutional question presented by this case is by no means open and shut. The Fourth Amendment protects the rights of homeowners from entry without a warrant, but there was a warrant here. The question is whether the invitation to the media exceeded the scope of the search authorized by the warrant. Accurate media coverage of police activities serves an important public purpose, and it is not obvious from the general principles of the Fourth Amendment that the conduct of the officers in this case violated the Amendment.

Second, although media ride-alongs of one sort or another had apparently become a common police practice, in 1992 there were no judicial opinions holding that this practice became unlawful when it entered a home. . . .

Finally, important to our conclusion was the reliance by the United States marshals in this case on a Marshal's Service ride-along policy which explicitly contemplated that media who engaged in ride-alongs might enter private homes with their cameras as part of fugitive apprehension arrests. The Montgomery County Sheriff's Department also at this time had a ride-along program that did not expressly prohibit media entry into private homes.

Such a policy, of course, could not make reasonable a belief that was contrary to a decided body of case law. But here the state of the law as to third parties accompanying police on home entries was at best undeveloped, and it was not unreasonable for law enforcement officers to look and rely on their formal ride-along policies.

Given such an undeveloped state of the law, the officers in this case cannot have been "expected to predict the future course of constitutional law." Between the time of the events of this case and today's decision, a split among the Federal Circuits in fact developed on the question whether media ride-alongs that enter homes subject the police to money damages. If judges thus disagree on a constitutional question, it is unfair to subject police to money damages for picking the losing side of the controversy.

For the foregoing reasons, the judgment of the Court of Appeals is affirmed.

It is so ordered.

[W]e note that unfair and prejudicial news comment on pending trials has become increasingly prevalent. Due process requires that the accused receive a trial by an impartial jury free from outside influences. Given the pervasiveness of modern communications and the difficulty of effacing prejudicial publicity from the minds of the jurors, the trial courts must take strong measures to ensure that the balance is never weighed against the accused. . . . The cure lies in those remedial measures that will prevent the prejudice at its inception.

—U.S. Supreme Court Justice Tom Clark[1]

Judge Debra Nelson reads instructions to the jury during the 2013 murder trial of George Zimmerman.

Gary W. Green/Orlando Sentinel/MCT via Getty Images

8 OVERSEEING THE COURTS
Protecting Procedures and Watchdogs

SUPPOSE...

... that a reporter promises a source anonymity in exchange for sensitive information that relates to criminal activity. When the article is published, law enforcement officials learn the reporter has additional information that could help their investigation. The reporter receives a subpoena to appear before a grand jury. When asked to reveal his source's identity, he refuses. He says to do so would infringe his and his newspaper's First Amendment rights.

Does the First Amendment provide a right for journalists to refuse to disclose the identity of a source, even when a grand jury investigates whether to charge a crime? Should a journalist who refuses to disclose confidential information go to jail? Look for the answers to these questions when the case of *Branzburg v. Hayes* is discussed later and excerpted at the end of the chapter.

The Sixth Amendment to the U.S. Constitution gives criminal defendants the right to a speedy public trial by an impartial jury of their peers in the locale of the crime. In the 50 years since U.S. Supreme Court Justice Tom Clark suggested that courts must remedy the inherent conflict between fair trials and a free and robust press, we have moved to real-time social media clips of unfolding crimes that circulate the globe. News media tweet information instantly. Reporters describe crime scenes and evidence. They interview neighbors, family, police and victims throughout investigations. Media disseminate gory photographs, and public relations experts carefully craft an image of the victim.[2] They

Cases for Study

- *Branzburg v. Hayes*
- *Richmond Newspapers Inc. v. Virginia*

inform; they persuade; sometimes they convince.[3] The stories they tell affect suspects' livelihoods and even the charges filed.

Studies show that people who rely on media coverage to understand crime—most people—misunderstand the nature and frequency of crime in their neighborhood and around the world. They increasingly view crimes and trials as entertainment.[4]

ACCESS TO COURTS AND COURT RECORDS

The Sixth Amendment guarantees the right to a fair and open public trial. Some four decades ago, the U.S. Supreme Court said the public's long-standing common law right to view public trials must be balanced to protect a fair trial.[5] The Court's landmark ruling in *Gannett v. DePasquale* arose after Judge Daniel DePasquale granted pretrial motions to suppress evidence and confessions and to exclude the public and the press from the trial for the murder of an off-duty police officer. No one at the pretrial hearing, including a Gannett reporter, objected to the court's rulings.

After Gannett later objected to the court closure, the judge upheld the motions and said the defendant's right to a fair trial outweighed the right of the press to cover the hearing. On review, the Supreme Court considered whether a criminal defendant may waive his right to a public trial regardless of whether the public, including the media, wants to attend. The Court found that publicity could prejudice the defendant's right to a fair trial and affirmed the power of judges to use means that "are not strictly and inescapably necessary" to protect a fair trial.[6] Justice Potter Stewart wrote:

LANDMARK CASES IN CONTEXT

Key ■ Event
     ◆ Cases

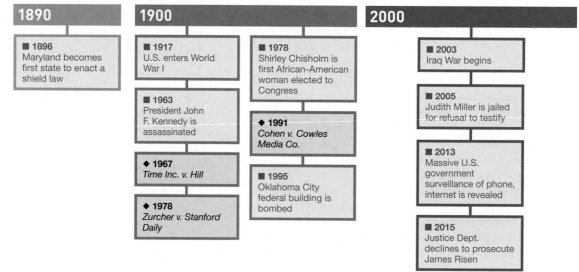

1890

- **■ 1896**
  Maryland becomes first state to enact a shield law

1900

- **■ 1917**
  U.S. enters World War I

- **■ 1963**
  President John F. Kennedy is assassinated

- **◆ 1967**
  Time Inc. v. Hill

- **◆ 1978**
  Zurcher v. Stanford Daily

- **■ 1978**
  Shirley Chisholm is first African-American woman elected to Congress

- **◆ 1991**
  Cohen v. Cowles Media Co.

- **■ 1995**
  Oklahoma City federal building is bombed

2000

- **■ 2003**
  Iraq War begins

- **■ 2005**
  Judith Miller is jailed for refusal to testify

- **■ 2013**
  Massive U.S. government surveillance of phone, internet is revealed

- **■ 2015**
  Justice Dept. declines to prosecute James Risen

● REAL WORLD LAW

Courts Can't Be Just for English Speakers

State courts in Hawaii recently expanded their language program to help individuals with "limited English proficiency" to participate fully in court proceedings and processes.[1] The state provided interpreters in thousands of court procedures to improve access to the courts for people whose first language is not English. Approximately 13 percent of Hawaiians have limited proficiency in English.[2]

The Department of Justice paid Hawaii to train court interpreters and publicize its language services following complaints that the state failed to provide equal access to its judiciary for limited-proficiency English speakers. The courts' website now allows individuals to print out "language ID" cards to inform public officials of the need for a translator in a specific language.

1. *Department of Justice Applauds Hawaii State Judiciary for Continued Commitment in Expanding Language Assistance Services*, LEGAL MONITOR WORLDWIDE, Mar. 25, 2015.
2. Chad Blair, *Hawaii State Courts Resolve Language Access Issues*, HONOLULU CIVIL BEAT, Mar. 25, 2015, www.civilbeat.com/2015/03/hawaii-state-courts-resolve-language-access-issues/.

There can be no blinking the fact that there is a strong societal interest in public trials. Openness in court proceedings may improve the quality of testimony, induce unknown witnesses to come forward with relevant testimony, cause all trial participants to perform their duties more conscientiously, and generally give the public an opportunity to observe the judicial system. But there is a strong societal interest in other constitutional guarantees extended to the accused as well.[7]

In a concurring opinion joined by three other justices, Justice Harry Blackmun argued that court closure "may implicate interests beyond those of the accused . . . [including] important social interests relating to the integrity of the trial process."[8] He said judges must weigh those competing interests fully even if no one objects to closure. Judges should presume that court processes should be open and require the party seeking closure to demonstrate (1) the probability that publicity would infringe on the right to a fair trial, (2) the inadequacy of alternatives to closure and (3) the effectiveness of closure.

Presuming the Openness of Trials

Then, in 1980, the Supreme Court generally adopted Justice Blackmun's position. In *Richmond Newspapers Inc. v. Virginia*,[9] the Court found that the Sixth Amendment right to a public trial does not belong to the defendant alone. The Court said criminal trials are presumptively open and the First Amendment prohibits closing them without a full exploration of alternatives.[10]

Chief Justice Warren Burger wrote that "absent an overriding interest articulated in findings, the trial of a criminal case must be open to the public."[11] Open criminal trials serve the public interest and advance the core First Amendment goal of protecting "freedom of communications on matters relating to the functioning of government."[12] Access to the criminal process enables citizens to evaluate government performance, to maintain faith in the judicial system and to seek catharsis for the trauma of crimes.[13]

⊙ POINTS OF LAW

Open Courts

According to the U.S. Supreme Court's rulings in the two cases involving the Press-Enterprise newspaper, court proceedings are presumptively open if logic and experience dictate openness. Accordingly, court processes are presumed to be open if:

1. The proceeding in question has a largely uninterrupted history of openness, and

2. Openness contributes to the proper functioning of the proceeding itself.

The Supreme Court of South Dakota applied this reasoning recently to recognize a qualified First Amendment right of access to civil trials in that state.[14] The state high court found that the presumption of openness outweighed the agreement of all trial parties and the judge to close the trial about a popular tourist attraction. In addition, the desire to reduce prejudicial publicity does not justify gag orders in civil cases decided by a judge, the court said.

On the heels of *Richmond Newspapers Inc.*, the Supreme Court ruled that states may not require closure of specific portions of criminal trials.[15] In *Globe Newspaper Co. v. Superior Court for Norfolk County*, the Supreme Court struck down a Virginia law that closed courtrooms during all testimony of any minor who was a sexual assault victim. The Court said the Constitution requires judges to demonstrate the need for closures; "the institutional value of the open criminal trial is recognized in both logic and experience."[16]

A pair of cases involving the Press-Enterprise newspaper in California created the **experience and logic test** to determine when the constitutional presumption of openness applies. The Supreme Court said that court procedures are presumptively open when (1) "the place and process have historically been open to the press and general public," and (2) "public access plays a significant positive role in the functioning of the particular process in question." The Court found a presumptive public right of access to both jury selection and preliminary hearings.[17] Preliminary hearings generally determine whether there is sufficient evidence to proceed to trial.

> **experience and logic test** A doctrine that evaluates both the history of openness and the role it plays in ensuring the credibility of a process to determine whether it is presumptively open.

The Court said access to the hearings themselves, not simply to transcripts released later, is vital to ensure public confidence. It recognized that some particularly sensitive questions to potential jurors during jury selection, or voir dire, might raise privacy concerns sufficient to warrant closure. Such closures must be narrowly tailored to protect only those matters that raise serious concerns. Some courts justify closed voir dire and juror anonymity, saying that access to jury selection and juror identity erodes the candor of potential jurors and harms an integral judicial process.

In 2010, the Supreme Court reaffirmed that the Sixth Amendment right to a public trial applies to voir dire.[18] In *Presley v. Georgia*, the Court's 8–2 decision reiterated that "the public has a right to be present whether or not any party has asserted the right."[19] "Courts are obligated to take every reasonable measure to accommodate public attendance at criminal trials."[20]

Broadcasting and Recording Court Proceedings

Although the Constitution provides a right of access to courts, openness is not absolute. Judges may limit attendance, including the number of media present, and they may exclude recording devices to ensure decorum in their courts.

In *Chandler v. Florida*, the U.S. Supreme Court said the right of access to public trials does not include presumptive access for cameras.[21] Although cameras are no longer presumed to be inherently prejudicial, the Court said individual states should determine whether to permit cameras in courtrooms. It said print coverage sufficiently protects the

▲ EMERGING LAW

Tea Leaves, Cameras and Inevitability

The Supreme Court bans cameras from the high court, meaning only 50 members of the public can view Court sessions in person.[1]

In 2017, the Court's newest appointee, Justice Neil M. Gorsuch, said he had an "open mind" about cameras in the Supreme Court.[2]

Supreme Court Justice Sonia Sotomayor recently reversed her position supporting cameras in the courtroom. "I think the process could be more misleading than helpful," she said. "It's like reading tea leaves."[3]

In contrast, Justice Stephen G. Breyer said increased media coverage could be "helpful." In helping the public better understand the courts, he said, it offers "tremendous potential."[4]

Congress has failed many times to pass laws that would presume broadcast access to the Court unless a majority of the justices voted for closure to protect specific, enumerated interests.[5] Justice Anthony Kennedy said a congressional mandate would violate established "etiquette" if not the letter of the law.[6]

Some say, "It is inevitable that television will be in the Supreme Court, and I would not provoke the constitutional controversy by requiring them to do it."[7]

Chip Somodevilla/Getty Images

U.S. Supreme Court Justice Sonia Sotomayor.

1. La Monica Everett-Haynes, *Experts Evaluate the "New Media" and Courts*, Univ. Ariz. News, Sept. 9, 2008, uanews.org/node/21471.
2. Ashley Killough, *Neil Gorsuch Says He Has an "Open Mind" on Cameras in the Supreme Court*, CNN Politics, Mar. 21, 2017, www.cnn.com/2017/03/21/politics/gorsuch-cameras-supreme-court.
3. *Battles to Gain Camera/Audio Access to State and Federal Courtrooms Continue*, Silha Bull., Fall 2011.
4. Sam Baker, *Justice Sotomayor No Longer Backs Television Cameras in Supreme Court*, Feb. 7, 2013, thehill.com/homenews/news/281765-sotomayor-no-longer-backs-cameras-in-supreme-court.
5. *Connolly Sponsors Bill to Allow Cameras in U.S. Supreme Court Proceedings*, Jan. 4, 2013, connolly.house.gov/news/connolly-sponsors-bill-to-allow-cameras-in-us-supreme-court-proceedings/.
6. *See, e.g.*, Anthony E. Mauro, *Let the Cameras Roll: Cameras in the Court and the Myth of Supreme Court Exceptionalism*, 1 Reynolds Cts. & Media L.J. 259 (2011).
7. *Id.*

public interest in open trials. The Court also noted that electronic coverage effects the trial process and participants in unpredictable ways.

In 2016, the U.S. Judicial Conference ended its four-year national trial project[22] allowing cameras in civil proceedings in 14 federal district courts.[23] Despite support for cameras from a large majority of participating judges and attorneys, the national policy body maintained the ban on recording in federal trial courts.[24] Federal Rule of Criminal Procedure 53 generally prohibits cameras in federal criminal trial courts, and federal policy bans televised civil proceedings. Video coverage of some district court proceedings is allowed in the Second and Ninth Circuits.[25]

In a narrow ruling, the Supreme Court recently prevented the broadcast of a federal district court trial on California's ballot measure banning same-sex marriage. The defense opposed the coverage. The Court said the trial court's decision to permit live streaming of the proceeding failed to "follow the appropriate procedures set forth in federal law,"[26] and public viewing might cause harassment of trial participants. The trial court struck down the voter-approved same-sex marriage ban.[27]

The U.S. Supreme Court does not permit still or video cameras during oral arguments. The 13 federal circuit courts of appeal each decide whether to allow televised or other news media coverage. Judges in federal appellate courts generally permit cameras in the courtroom at least some of the time. Court rules determine the specific conditions that apply when cameras are allowed.

Cameras are allowed in some courtrooms some of the time in all 50 states.[28] Many states limit the number and location of cameras. Roughly 20 states are extremely permissive about cameras in the courtroom. In Florida, a judicially created presumption permits camera coverage of virtually all cases.[29] Massachusetts rules generally permit journalists to record or provide real-time transmission of court proceedings unless there is evidence of a "substantial likelihood of harm" to parties or a fair trial.[30] South Dakota rules allow broadcast coverage of trials with the consent of the judge and all parties, except for filming of jurors or proceedings when the jury is excluded.[31] The Illinois code of judicial conduct limits broadcasting of court proceedings to "the extent authorized by order of the Supreme Court"[32] and prohibits broadcasting or recording of any compelled witness testimony.[33]

States from Alabama to Utah limit camera coverage of trials based on the type of case or the ages of the witnesses. In nine states, judges may limit the number and location of cameras, prohibit recording of jurors or vulnerable witnesses or require pooled cameras. In another six states, including Delaware and Illinois, courts are virtually closed to cameras.

TABLE 8.1 ■ Cameras in Federal Courts	
U.S. Supreme Court	No cameras
U.S. Circuit Courts	Civil trials at judges' discretion; barred from criminal proceedings by Federal Rule of Criminal Procedure 53
U.S. District Courts	Cameras in some proceedings in Second and Ninth Circuit trial courts

Source: Adapted from *Cameras and Electronic Devices in the Federal Courtroom*, Fed. Evidence Rev. (2014), federalevidence.com/node/1345.

⬤ INTERNATIONAL LAW

India's Supreme Court Allows Cameras in Courts

The Supreme Court of India in 2017 ordered an immediate trial installation of closed-circuit TV cameras, without audio, in 24 courts across the country.[1] The order said the cameras would monitor the courts, the judges' chambers and "such important locations of the court complexes." However, the recordings are expressly exempt from disclosure under India's Right to Information Act without permission of the court involved. Participating courts were required to report results of the one-month trial recording.

The order followed a petition from a man seeking to record the trial of his "matrimonial dispute to ensure a fair trial" and years of government pressure to record the courts to increase transparency. India's Department of Justice said cameras would keep an eye on trial participants' conduct and provide electronic records of proceedings. The high court had resisted audio-video recordings and said "wider consultation" was needed to ensure that cameras did not imperil fair trials.

1. Utkarsh Anand, *Shedding Reluctance, Supreme Court Agrees to Open Courtrooms to Cameras*, INDIAN EXPRESS, Mar. 29, 2017, indianexpress.com/article/india/no-audio-initially-no-rti-either-shedding-reluctance-sc-agrees-to-open-courtrooms-to-cameras-supreme-court-4590136.

To ensure they do not violate court rules, those wishing to record court proceedings must be familiar with the details of the laws in the states where they report.

Using Newer Technologies in the Courts

Studies of the effects on courts of accelerating news cycles, 24-hour news coverage, blogs, webcasts and other "new media" mechanisms suggest these media sensationalize rather than educate or inform the public.[34] A 2017 study said that the ubiquity of social media threatens the impartiality of the jury,[35] and courts concerned about their uncertain impact are not racing to embrace new media.[36] In one recent case, the Tennessee Supreme Court sent a first-degree murder conviction back for review by the trial court because the judge had failed to question a juror who had exchanged Facebook messages with one of the state's witnesses during jury deliberation.[37] Jury deliberations are absolutely sealed.

Led by California and Massachusetts, courts are integrating social media into their administrative offices, their courtrooms and their public outreach. Courts use closed-circuit coverage of sensitive witnesses, and some stream or have blogs that offer instant public access. Some state and federal courts allow reporters to webcast and use social media posts to provide play-by-play coverage of unfolding trials.[38] One judge—overseeing a $1 million recording industry lawsuit against a Boston University student for copyright infringement through Kazaa—echoed the *Press-Enterprise* standard and said nothing in "life or logic" prevents livestreaming of court proceedings, especially in a case involving digital technology.[39] However, the First Circuit Court of Appeals refused to allow webcasting of the appeal.[40]

The Michigan Supreme Court became the first to ban all electronic communication by jurors during trials, and a number of courts declared mistrials because of juror use of new media during trial.[41] Similar bans were spreading across the country,[42] and courts struggle to determine whether to use new media evidence in trials.

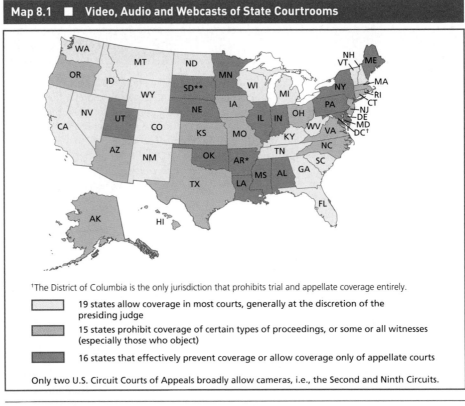

Map 8.1 ■ Video, Audio and Webcasts of State Courtrooms

†The District of Columbia is the only jurisdiction that prohibits trial and appellate coverage entirely.

19 states allow coverage in most courts, generally at the discretion of the presiding judge

15 states prohibit coverage of certain types of proceedings, or some or all witnesses (especially those who object)

16 states that effectively prevent coverage or allow coverage only of appellate courts

Only two U.S. Circuit Courts of Appeals broadly allow cameras, i.e., the Second and Ninth Circuits.

Source: Cameras in the Court: A State-by-State Guide, Nov. 15-26, 2012, rtdna.org/article/cameras_in_the_court_a_state_by_state_guide_updated#.Uielybx1Ets.

▌ SOCIAL MEDIA LAW

Managing New Media in Courts

A Media Law Resource Center model policy for electronic media in the court system recommends that:

1. People in courtrooms may use electronic devices to silently take notes and/or transmit texts without prior authorization from the presiding judge.

2. A judge may prohibit or restrict use of electronic devices if they pose any threat to safety or security or compromise the integrity of the proceeding.

3. Reporters', bloggers' and other court observers' use of electronic devices to post online commentary during the proceedings is presumptively permitted so long as it meets the conditions set out in [2].[1]

1. Media Law Resource Center, Newsgathering Committee Defense Counsel Section (2010), www.medialaw.org/Content/NavigationMenu/ Member_Resources/Litigation_Resources/Litigation_Resources.htm.

Accessing Court Records

The public right to access court records is grounded in common law and the U.S. and state constitutions. Decisions to close, or seal, court records generally are subject to the same constitutional limits as court closure. They are strongly disfavored and must pass the stringent *Press-Enterprise* experience and logic test.

Four decades ago, the Supreme Court limited the common law right of access to court records. The criminal trial of some Watergate conspirators relied on tape recordings of former President Richard Nixon as evidence. Federal law provides delayed public access to presidential records, including the Nixon tapes, but the district court denied media access to the tapes during the trial. It said broadcast of the tapes might prejudice defense appeals. The court of appeals reversed.

In *Nixon v. Warner Communications*, the U.S. Supreme Court held that courts are not required to provide access to all records in their custody, particularly when the records are

■ SOCIAL MEDIA LAW

Twitter on Trial

The defense in the high-profile Trayvon Martin murder case embraced social media to counter an "avalanche of misinformation" about defendant George Zimmerman.[1] The judge, in the trial that focused media attention on white shootings of unarmed African-American males, provided Zimmerman's attorney with some of Martin's private records and allowed the defense to use a website,[2] a Twitter page and a Facebook account to rebuff negative coverage of Zimmerman.[3]

Martin's family first used Twitter to bring attention to the 17-year-old's death, and social media galvanized the public after it learned Martin was unarmed when he was killed in Florida. But later both the prosecution and the defense "agree[d] that social media [were] playing a highly invasive role in the court proceedings and [might] even affect the outcome."[4]

"Has the jury tweeted a verdict?"

The defense suggested that, without social media, Zimmerman "may never have been charged" with second-degree murder. The prosecution said social media focused the world attention on the case as a test of justice in the United States.[5]

1. Lizette Alvarez, *Social Media, Growing in Legal Circles, Find a Role in Florida Murder Case*, N.Y. Times, Nov. 7, 2012, www.nytimes.com/2012/11/07/us/social-media-finds-a-role-in-case-against-zimmerman.html?pagewanted=all&_r=0.
2. Yamiche Alcindor, *Trayvon Martin's Postings, Records Spark Court Debate*, USA Today, Oct. 19, 2012, www.usatoday.com/story/news/nation/2012/10/19/trayvon-zimmerman-sanford-racial/1644403/.
3. Lizette Alvarez, *Judge in Trayvon Martin Case Denies Request for Silence*, N.Y. Times, Oct. 30, 2012, A-16, www.nytimes.com/2012/10/30/us/judge-in-trayvon-martin-case-denies-request-for-silence.html.
4. Heather Manes, *Lawyers of Trayvon Martin Case Lament Social Media Engagement*, Opposing Views, Apr. 28, 2013, www.opposingviews.com/i/money/jobs-and-careers/lawyers-trayvon-martin-case-lament-social-media-engagement.
5. *See, e.g.,* Tom Foreman, Analysis: *The Race Factor in George Zimmerman's Trial*, CNN, July 15, 2013, www.cnn.com/2013/07/14/justice/zimmerman-race-factor.

available through alternative means.[43] The Court said the press had no First Amendment right to inspect or copy the tapes because the media have no rights of access superior to those of the general public.[44] More recently, the Supreme Court did not review a sweeping ban on public release of information from the secret Foreign Intelligence Surveillance Court trials of alleged terrorists.[45] Forty years ago, the Foreign Intelligence Surveillance Act established broad government power to conduct covert physical and electronic surveillance of foreign nationals and countries suspected of espionage.[46] Cases involving the act are heard in special FISA courts where both sessions and records are secret.

A U.S. district court also found that the common law right of access to trials does not provide access to trial exhibits not held by the court.[47] However, court records that do not unduly harm due process or privacy rights should be open.

State court rules and policies generally determine the openness of court records. To limit harms to trial fairness and invasion of privacy, rules seal court records of information disclosed mandatorily or under discovery unless the material is presented in open court. States generally impose penalties on employees who violate these rules. The U.S. Supreme Court ruled in *Florida Star v. B.J.F.* that states may not punish media for publishing truthful information obtained legally from court files unless the penalty is "narrowly tailored to a state interest of the highest order."[48] (See Chapter 6 for a discussion of this case.)

Unclear judicial standards lead to wide disparities in the sealing of court records.[49] Although access restrictions must be narrowly tailored to meet a compelling interest, few courts offer evidence to justify records closures. Some courts also exclude sealed cases from their dockets and electronic case management systems, effectively preventing challenges to closure or even knowledge that the cases exist. Where state open-records laws do apply, these rules also vary. In Indiana, the open-records law covers all court records not closed by a specific exemption.[50] Washington's broad Public Disclosure Act excludes the courts.[51] An Ohio Supreme Court ruling said neither the constitution nor the state's open-records law prevented a judge from sealing an entire court record weeks after the defendant was acquitted of criminal charges.[52] The court said that "limit[ing] the life of a particular record" did not harm the public's right to know.

In New York, a trial court in 2016 unsealed records of a state legislator's extramarital affairs while he was awaiting sentencing for fraud, extortion and money laundering.[53] The court said disclosure threatened neither the defendant's privacy right nor his right to a fair trial in any potential retrial. Public access to the evidence submitted under seal advanced the public interest because the evidence itself is often "as important as the trial" in assuring public confidence in judicial procedures, the court said. The court order required the redaction of the identity of two Jane Does to preserve their legitimate privacy interest.

Electronic Access to Court Records

Numerous national court and judicial organizations have worked to facilitate online public access to court records while protecting important interests in privacy.[54] Both the National Center for State Courts and the Justice Management Institute advocated that court records be posted online and be presumptively open.

The Public Access to Court Electronic Records site (www.pacer.gov) provides online access to federal court records, but electronic access to state court records is "remarkably disparate."[55] State rules vary broadly on which records are online and for what purposes and to whom they are open. Most states provide some access to civil and family law case records online.[56] For example, about half of Florida circuit and county courts have their court records online.[57] Minnesota maintains a searchable online database of all public information on its courts that includes some court records.[58] Some states' online access systems are free and comprehensive; many others charge fees. Information gatherers wanting detailed information on state laws on access to court records on- and offline may find it through the National Center for State Courts.[59]

Electronic access to public records has increased fears about how easily searchable data compilations alter the nature and extent of access to courts. Such concerns are not new. In 1890, noted jurists Louis Brandeis and Samuel Warren argued that the people have a "right to be let alone."[60] Many states limit access to records containing sensitive information, such as the financial records or addresses of individuals, especially when it is aggregated online.[61]

In a foundational decision long before online access to court records was common, the Supreme Court ruled in *U.S. Department of Justice v. Reporters Committee for Freedom of the Press* that federal law did not allow journalists access to an FBI electronic compilation of rap (arrest) sheets.[62] The reporter wanted to compile the background of a suspected mobster, but the Court said access to the aggregated information posed an impermissible threat to individual privacy.

The *Reporters Committee* case involved the federal Freedom of Information Act, not court rules, but courts have applied similar reasoning to electronic access. For example, a Washington state court rule requires people who request criminal conviction data to agree to use the information responsibly.[63] The Minnesota court records committee suggests that large fees be charged for court databases in order to make money. The checkered and fast-shifting pattern of electronic access to court records requires those seeking records to know their state rules and procedures.

ADVANCING FAIRNESS IN TRIALS

Potential jurors do not live in a vacuum. Like everyone, they swim daily in a sea of crime coverage. The U.S. Supreme Court recognized the potential harms media publicity might cause to fair trials in the early days of television. More than 50 years ago in *Estes v. Texas*, the Court ruled that televised coverage of the criminal trial of a Texas financier charged with a multimillion-dollar con was inherently prejudicial.[64]

A huge, highly publicized national investigation preceded the case, with the financier appearing on the cover of Time magazine in 1962. A Texas newspaper editor won the 1963 Pulitzer Prize for bringing the fraud "to national attention with resultant investigation, prosecution and conviction of Estes."[65]

Despite defense requests to ban cameras from the court, cameras and reporters swarmed the trial where Estes was convicted of conspiracy and fraud. On appeal, the U.S. Supreme Court found that intensive broadcast coverage prior to the state trial *automatically* alters juror perceptions of the case and creates prejudice and a form of harassment of the defendant. The Court said judges must take steps to reduce the significant potential harms of publicity on trials. The Court later rejected the assumption that all broadcast coverage of trials is inevitably prejudicial,[66] but it said judges must ensure that media publicity does not undermine trial fairness.

In a second case, *Sheppard v. Maxwell*, the Supreme Court overturned a murder conviction when a judge allowed extensive pretrial and trial publicity to turn the proceedings into a "Roman holiday."[67] Prominent Cleveland physician Sam Sheppard was charged with the beating death of his wife. Dr. Sheppard said a stranger had broken in to their home, knocked him unconscious and committed the crime. The media frenzy began the day of the crime and pervaded every aspect of what was called "the trial of the century."[68] Media broadcast live coverage and printed verbatim transcripts of the second-degree murder trial. Sheppard was convicted and sentenced to life imprisonment.

The Supreme Court overturned his conviction because intense and prejudicial press coverage prevented a fair trial. It said judges must protect the fair trial rights of a defendant by controlling the trial process and participants, including the media. The Court acknowledged the important role of free press in a democracy and in the administration of justice. However, the Court said the press has no right to inflame the minds of jurors, jeopardize the fairness of trials or make a mockery of the solemn judicial process.

While limited press coverage may coexist with a fair trial, the Court said "massive and pervasive" coverage that reaches the jurors and permeates the trial may be *presumed* to be prejudicial. After 10 years in jail, Sheppard was retried and found not guilty.

The *Sheppard* Court encouraged judges to use narrowly tailored measures to protect trial fairness. These measures include:

continuance
Postponement of a trial to a later time.

1. **Continuance**, or delay, of the trial until publicity has subsided

2. Change of the venue, or location, of the trial to avoid areas permeated by media coverage

▲ EMERGING LAW

Judges' Instructions Reduce Potential Bias From Social Media

A recent study of federal and state jurors concluded that "there is no perfect solution to the growing risk of juror misconduct associated with social media."[1]

Legal experts worry about the potential for social media to impact the impartiality of the jurors who are required to reach a verdict based solely on evidence presented in court.

Criminal defense attorney Michael Kenny said, "The ubiquitous nature of social media today . . . [presents] the potential for instances when the attorneys or the court would be unaware of some contact or independent evidence gathering by a jury."[2]

However, the study found that jurors take very seriously their oath to reach a verdict based on in-court evidence, and they strive to follow judges' instructions. The best strategy to mitigate social media–introduced bias is for courts to "employ specialized social-media instructions early and often during trial," the study concluded.[3]

---

1. Amy J. St. Eve et al., *More From the #Jury Box: The Latest on Juries and Social Media*, 12 Duke L. & Tech. Rev. 64, 90 (2014).
2. Comment: *Social Media's Attack on the Impartial Jury*, Kemp, Ruge & Green LG, 2017, kemprugegreen.com/social-medias-attack-on-the-impartial-jury/.
3. St. Eve. et al., *supra* note 1, at 90.

3. **Sequestration**, or isolation, of the jury from the public

4. Extensive voir dire, or questioning, of potential jurors to identify prejudice

5. **Gag orders** on participants to limit discussion of the case outside the courtroom

6. Protection of potential witnesses from outside influences

7. Instructions, or **admonitions**, to the jury to avoid prejudicial influences and to set aside any preconceptions they may have

8. Retrial if the jury or the judicial process has been contaminated by media coverage

9. Limitations on press attendance, through measures such as pool reporting, to reduce the impact of their presence on jurors and witnesses

Following Sheppard

The *Sheppard* ruling was applauded for its protection of defendants' rights and criticized for prompting judges to limit the openness of judicial proceedings.[69] Judges apply the measures suggested by the Supreme Court in *Sheppard v. Maxwell* to prevent or correct prejudice in the jury. Judges determine from where and how the jury is chosen, where and when the trial takes place and the amount of speech freedom jury members and other trial participants will have during the trial.

In one case, media were barred from a 2011 pretrial hearing in Miami involving four men accused of the murder of Washington Redskins star Sean Taylor.[70] The judge agreed with defense attorneys that media coverage of the hearing on the admissibility of alleged confessions might prejudice prospective jurors. Attorneys for the Miami Herald and Post-Newsweek unsuccessfully argued that Miami's juror pool was large enough to find unbiased jurors.

Selecting Jurors. When a court wants to select a jury for a trial, the clerk of court chooses names at random from a list, such as adult licensed drivers or registered voters, in the county where the trial will be held. The location from which the pool of jurors is drawn is called the "venire." Each potential juror receives a **summons** to appear in court.

The judge and/or attorneys for both sides question members of the jury pool to select individuals able to weigh objectively the evidence presented during trial. Public relations litigation specials may help either side find favorable jurors. Jury questioning is called "voir dire," which means "to speak the truth." The voir dire process is designed to ensure that overtly biased individuals do not sit on a jury.

Either side may pose a **for-cause challenge** to a potential juror if the individual's responses suggest a prejudice relevant to the case. Each attorney also may use a limited number of peremptory challenges to remove potential jurors without any explanation. Once both sides accept the jury, jurors are **impaneled** (selected and seated) and sworn in.

A trial by an impartial jury does not require jurors to have no information about the defendant or the crime. Impartial jurors assure the court they will give the facts full and unbiased consideration and render a verdict solely on the basis of evidence presented in court. Impartial jurors must have no fixed opinion of the guilt or innocence of the defendant.[71]

---

sequestration The isolation of jurors to avoid prejudice from publicity in a sensational trial.

gag orders A nonlegal term used to describe court orders that prohibit publication or discussion of specific materials.

admonitions Judges' instructions to jurors warning them to avoid potentially prejudicial communications.

summons A notice asking an individual to appear at a court. Potential jurors receive such a summons.

for-cause challenge In the context of jury selection, the ability of attorneys to remove a potential juror for a reason the law finds sufficient, as opposed to a peremptory challenge.

impanel To select and seat a jury.

The twelve members of a seated petit jury.

A potential juror is not disqualified for cause simply because he or she has seen or read news about the crime or the defendant. Similarly, prejudice may not be assumed simply because of a juror's race or gender.[72]

In a recent case that received extensive media coverage and social media debate, the Kentucky Supreme Court remanded a man's conviction for killing a young girl while driving impaired. The appeal involved a seated juror who lied during voir dire about being a Facebook "friend" with the victim's mother.[73] Reviewing only the issue of whether the dishonest voir dire response created "reversible error" in due process, the high court said "'friendships' on Facebook and other similar social networking websites do not *necessarily* carry the same weight as true friendships or relationships in the community" and do not automatically create impermissible bias.[74]

Rehearing the case, the lower court found the juror's lie inadvertent and allowed the conviction to stand. On review of the entire trial record, the state supreme court found that for-cause release of 50 potential jurors had exhausted the entire jury pool. One seated juror knew the defendant had a history of substance abuse and reckless behavior.[75] In reversing the conviction, the state supreme court strongly reminded lower courts that "trial judges are possessed of great authority to enlarge jury panels or change venues. They don't have to imperil their cases with such miserly voir dire practices."[76]

Instructing the Jury. Judges routinely issue admonitions, or instructions and warnings, to jurors, to tell them to avoid potential prejudice. Typical admonitions tell jurors not to view news coverage and not to discuss the case among themselves or with others prior to jury deliberations. The judge in a 2015 murder and child-abuse case refused to find prejudice despite a juror's almost daily tweets about the case throughout the trial.[77] During the second week of the trial, one tweet read: "In my book, everybody's guilty until proven innocent."[78] Although the judge acknowledged the juror's use of Twitter violated his instructions, he refused to grant a retrial. Attorneys for the defense said they would appeal.

Judges also give instructions on the law to the jury prior to deliberation. These instructions generally advise jurors about the applicable law and remind them of their duty to reach a verdict in the case on the basis only of the evidence presented in court.

Sequestering the Jury. Sometimes, though rarely, a judge will sequester, or isolate, a jury during a trial. Sequestration generally houses jurors in a hotel near the courthouse and prohibits them from having unsupervised contact with anyone outside of court. Sequestration may protect trial fairness and the safety of jurors who face threats, but jurors dislike it, and it may alter juror attitudes and the outcome of the trial.

Relocating the Trial. Although the Sixth Amendment protects a criminal defendant's right to a trial in the location where the crime occurred, either the prosecution or the defense may request a change of venue, or location. If conditions in the initial location, including media coverage, are substantially likely to endanger a fair trial, a change of venue may relocate the trial. Changing venue is expensive, and media coverage often follows the trial.

Recently, when selection of unbiased jurors in the Boston Marathon bombing trial of Dzhokhar Tsarnaev proved difficult, the judge three times denied the defense request to relocate the trial outside of Boston.[79] The defense said almost 70 percent of nearly 1,400 prospective jurors identified a personal connection to the case and belief in the defendant's guilt. The First Circuit Court of Appeals supported the judge's decision that the defense failed to demonstrate that irreparable harm would occur if the trial were not moved. Intense media attention "does not equate to disqualifying prejudice."[80]

Delaying the Trial. In 2016, the Supreme Court ruled that the right to a speedy trial does not require speedy sentencing.[81] The case involved a man who waited in jail for more than 14 months for sentencing after he pleaded guilty to bail-jumping and failure to appear in court. After he was sentenced to seven years in prison, he appealed arguing that the sentencing delay violated his Sixth Amendment right. The Supreme Court disagreed. Its short, unanimous ruling said the "heart" of the Sixth Amendment is the desire to protect the "presumption of innocence and therefore loses force upon conviction."[82] While a defendant's due process right to liberty continues after conviction, the Court said that issue was not raised in this appeal.

In 2015, a Delaware trial court found that court-requested delays of nearly three years between an arrest for drunk driving and the trial unfairly prejudiced the defendant.[83] The court dismissed the charges after the defendant's attorney argued that delays caused his client severe anxiety and violated his right to a speedy trial. The judge said, "When a

● REAL WORLD LAW

Does Publicity Bias Jurors?

Experts say pretrial publicity alters the outcome of a trial only when[1]:

- Jurors are exposed to pretrial publicity.

- The evidence in court does not point convincingly to a clear verdict.

- The information provided by the media seems better—more convincing, more likely or more reliable—than the evidence presented in court.

- The media consistently lean toward one verdict.

- All the remedies available to the court fail at the same time.

1. Jon Bruschke & William E. Loges, Free Press vs. Fair Trials: Examining Publicity's Role in Trial Outcomes 134–37 (2004).

trial is delayed, a defendant is presumed to be prejudiced to some degree. . . . [Although] 'time's erosion of exculpatory evidence and testimony can rarely be shown,' it is nonetheless the most serious type of prejudice."[84]

Criminal defendants may waive their Sixth Amendment right to a speedy trial. Defendants and their attorneys may seek a delay, or continuance, to try to reduce the prejudicial impact of publicity. The prosecution or other parties to the trial may oppose a continuance because postponements often reduce the availability and recall of witnesses.[85]

Making Jurors Anonymous. Some courts refuse to release the names and identities of jurors in high-profile cases or in cases where jurors may legitimately be concerned for their personal safety.[86] Some courts refuse to release information about jurors by claiming that the release would violate the jurors' personal privacy interests. The Texas criminal code requires anonymous juries unless there is a showing that openness serves the public good.[87] Criminal defense attorneys often argue that shielding jurors' identities increases juror anxiety and perception that the crime is severe and the defendant guilty. Many courts do not find anonymous juries inherently prejudicial.

The question of public access to juror information remains unsettled. Although two federal appellate courts held that the public has a constitutional right to timely access to juror names in a criminal proceeding,[88] one member of the Seventh Circuit Court of Appeals panel requested a full review of the decision.[89] Court bans on press photographs of jurors outside the courtroom generally must pass strict scrutiny because they constitute a form of prior restraint on a free press.

Limiting Speech Outside of Court. Members of the legal community tend to believe that when government and court officials—police and attorneys, for example—publicly discuss ongoing trials, their speech influences jurors' perceptions of witnesses' guilt or innocence. In *Sheppard*, the Supreme Court encouraged judges to prevent trial participants from discussing potentially prejudicial information outside the courtroom. Judges use **restraining orders**, or gag orders, to control the flow of information from its source.

restraining order A court order forbidding an individual or group of individuals from doing a specified act until a hearing can be conducted.

Some 25 years ago, the Supreme Court ruled in *Mu'Min v. Virginia* that restraining attorneys' speech outside the courtroom during a trial did not violate the First Amendment.[90] The Court reasoned that insiders to a vital government process have special access to sensitive information and unique power to derail justice. Consequently, courts may control their trial-related speech when it poses a "substantial likelihood" of jeopardizing a fair trial.[91]

Gag orders on trial participants generally are upheld if (1) narrowly drawn and (2) supported by evidence that unfettered speech poses a substantial likelihood of jeopardizing a fair trial and (3) by careful consideration of alternatives. Narrowly drawn restraining orders end as soon as the threat to the trial process passes.[92] A different test applies to gag orders on the media (see Advancing the Flow of News below).

In high-profile cases, judges concerned about prejudicial pretrial publicity may issue sweeping gag orders on all trial participants. Thus, the judge in the murder trial of Aurora, Colo., theater shooter James Eagan Holmes imposed a ban on all parties from

■ SOCIAL MEDIA LAW

Tweets and "Friends" of the Court

An appeals court in Florida decided that the judge in a criminal case should have disqualified himself because he was a Facebook "friend" of the prosecutor.[1]

In presenting the question to the state's high court, one appeals court judge said,

Judges do not have the unfettered social freedom of teenagers. . . . Maintenance of the appearance of impartiality requires the avoidance of entanglements and relationships that compromise that appearance.[2]

A federal district court in Pennsylvania earlier refused to place any value on Facebook relationships:

[T]he court assigns no significance to the Facebook "friends" reference. . . . "Friendships" on Facebook may be as fleeting as the flick of a delete button.[3]

---

1. Eric Goldman, *Social Media Law Roundup*, Tech. & Marketing L. Blog, Jan. 18, 2013, blog.ericgoldman.org/archives/2013/01/social_media_ev_2.htm.
2. Domville v. State, 103 So. 3d 184 (Fla. Ct. App. 2012).
3. Quigley Corp. v. Karkus, 2009 U.S. Dist. LEXIS 41296 at *16 (E.D. Pa., May 19, 2009).

disseminating any information about the case.[93] Despite prominent opposition to the ban,[94] the judge let it stand throughout the trial.[95]

In 2016, the Michigan Supreme Court lifted a judge's sweeping gag order in the criminal corruption trial of two government officials.[96] The order prevented "all potential trial participants from making any extra judicial statements regarding this case to members of the media."[97] The appeals court upheld the order and said it "placed no direct restraint of any kind on the Free Press" because the newspaper could not produce any individual who wished to speak that the order restrained.[98] The state supreme court vacated the order as an impermissible prior restraint.

In 2015, the U.S. Court of Appeals for the Fourth Circuit vacated[99] a West Virginia judge's "extensive" ban on comments to the media about a criminal trial related to the 2010 Upper Big Branch Mine disaster that killed 29 miners.[100] The trial judge said the ban "restricting the parties and potential trial participants' statements to the press at the outset helps preserve the defendant's right to a fair and just tribunal."[101] But the Fourth Circuit applied a test from the *Press-Enterprise* cases requiring that public access to trial processes cannot be denied without "specific findings . . . demonstrating that, first, there is a substantial probability that the defendant's right to a fair trial will be prejudiced by publicity that closure would prevent and, second, reasonable alternatives to closure cannot adequately protect the defendant's fair trial rights."[102]

Impartial Judges

Sometimes the fairness of the judge is cast into doubt. In *Sheppard*, the Court said the fact that both the judge and the prosecutor were running for election during the trial posed the potential for prejudice.[103] The Supreme Court also has ruled that the Constitution requires judges to disqualify themselves from hearing a case when a risk of prejudice exists because "a person with a personal stake [in the case outcome] . . . had a significant and disproportionate influence" in the judge's election or appointment to the bench.[104] But the Supreme Court struck down a Minnesota state law that banned judges from campaigning on issues that might come before their court.[105] The Court said the law violated the First Amendment by directly limiting speech vital to elections.[106]

BALANCING INTERESTS

Decades ago the U.S. Supreme Court said it for centuries has been a "fundamental maxim that the public has a right to every man's evidence."[107] While law enforcement is responsible for identifying relevant evidence, judges must determine which evidence may be admitted into court. Because justice is best served when everyone reveals information relevant to the case, judges may require parties to testify or to produce relevant evidence. It is unequivocally "the obligation of all citizens to give relevant testimony with respect to criminal conduct," the Court said.[108]

Requiring Evidence

reporter's privilege
The concept that reporters may keep information such as source identity confidential. The rationale is that the reporter–source relationship is similar to doctor–patient and lawyer–client relationships.

Many argue that the First Amendment's recognition of the value of newsgathering should protect journalists from forced disclosure of information in court. This rationale holds that the First Amendment guarantee of freedom of the press includes a **reporter's privilege** not to divulge confidential information. In this view, a requirement to testify constitutes an unconstitutional government infringement on the free flow of ideas. The Supreme Court has recognized only a limited constitutional protection for reporters (discussed later in this chapter). Court rulings tend to rely on fundamental principles of law and laws of general application to find that justice often depends on evidence that sometimes is held by journalists.

search warrant
A written order issued by a judge, directed to a law enforcement officer, authorizing the search and seizure of any property for which there is reason to believe it will serve as evidence in a criminal investigation.

Courts provide **search warrants** and subpoenas to collect evidence and ensure that it is presented in court. A search warrant permits law enforcement officers to search a specified place for particular items or people. The Fourth Amendment to the U.S. Constitution requires that searches be conducted reasonably. To receive a search warrant, investigators must show probable cause that the items or people are vital to the investigation in the specified location. Some national security mechanisms allow searches and seizures without a warrant or with a secret warrant.[109]

quash To nullify or annul, as in quashing a subpoena.

Both search warrants and subpoenas are court orders that require cooperation, but a search warrant implies greater urgency. Search warrants demand immediate compliance. There is no legal way to delay, resist or prevent a legally warranted search. Subpoenas do not require on-the-spot compliance. They order the named person to appear at some future judicial proceeding. In the interim, the recipient can file a motion to **quash** the subpoena. A motion to quash is a request to a court to vacate the order. Concern that evidence might be destroyed by the lapse between service of a subpoena and the date of the required court appearance is one justification for search warrants.

▲ EMERGING LAW

When Is Evidence Prejudicial?

Illustration by Corinna Marin. https://www.corinnamarin.com

Amid controversy over court restrictions on the use of violent hip-hop lyrics as evidence in criminal trials, one court ruled that rap lyrics may be used only if they demonstrate "a strong nexus" to the crime.

The New Jersey Supreme Court recently upheld a state appeals court's ruling overturning the attempted murder conviction of Vonte Skinner, a rapper.[1] The court said the prosecution's heavy reliance on Skinner's "violent, profane, and disturbing rap lyrics," written years before the crime, was "highly prejudicial" and provided little or no evidence of "any motive or intent" behind the charges.[2]

The court's decision echoed the position of legal observers who argue that the use of a rapper's artistic self-expression as evidence of the author's bad character or criminal motive violates the First Amendment and misconstrues the use of hyperbole in hip-hop.[3]

1. State v. Skinner, 95 A.3d 236 (N.J. Sup. Ct. 2014).
2. Id.
3. See, e.g., Clay Calvert, Amicus Curiae Brief of the Marion T. Brechner First Amendment Project in Support of Petitioner, in re Elonis v. United States, Aug. 18, 2014, www.americanbar.org/content/dam/aba/publications/ supreme_court_preview/BriefsV4/13-983_pet_amcu_mbbfap .authcheckdam.pdf.

Forty years ago, the Supreme Court ruled directly on the amount of protection the First Amendment provides from searches of newsrooms. After a campus demonstration during which some police officers were assaulted, investigators with a search warrant sought unpublished photographs taken by staff of the Stanford University student newspaper to identify demonstration participants. The Stanford Daily sued the police claiming the search violated the newspaper's First and Fourth Amendment rights. The Fourth Amendment protects against unreasonable searches and seizures.

Because no one at the newspaper was suspected of a crime, the trial judge ruled the search warrant was unreasonable without a showing that a subpoena was impractical. The appellate court agreed. The court's decision was based on five points:

1. Searches will be physically disruptive to such an extent that timely publication will be impeded.

2. Confidential sources of information will dry up, and the press will also lose opportunities to cover issues and events of public importance if news participants fear that press files will be readily available to authorities.

3. Reporters will be deterred from recording and preserving their recollections for future use if such information is subject to seizure.

● REAL WORLD LAW

Encrypted Data Not Safe From Government Eyes

In 2016, months of public legal wrangling between the U.S. Department of Justice and Apple over access to the iPhone used by one of the shooters in the San Bernardino terrorist attack ended when the DOJ paid hackers to break into Apple's encrypted system. A senior administration official said the break-in was appropriate "on both national security and on law enforcement grounds because of the potential use [of encryption] by terrorists and other national security concerns" to thwart government law enforcement.[1]

In another case, journalists and activists paid close attention when the FBI subpoenaed and gagged Open Whisper Systems to obtain access to information in iPhones protected by their popular encryption system, Signal.[2]

Amid growing concern over government use of subpoenas in tandem with gag orders to prevent discussion of government demands for protected digital information, National Public Radio, Fox News, The Washington Post, the American Civil Liberties Union and many of the major players in the U.S. tech industry supported a lawsuit by Microsoft that said bans on discussion of governmental snooping into customers' information violated the First Amendment.[3]

Microsoft said the government had subpoenaed its customer data 5,600 times between September 2014 and March 2016, with almost half of the requests accompanied by gag orders. Most of the gags never expire.

1. Ellen Nakashima, *FBI Paid Professional Hackers One-Time Fee to Crack San Bernardino iPhone*, Wash. Post., April 12, 2016, www.washingtonpost .com/world/national-security/fbi-paid-professional-hackers-one-time-fee-to-crack-san-bernardino-iphone/2016/04/12/5397814a-00de-11 e6-9d36-33d198ea26c5_story.html?utm_term=.33d992d3b0c7.
2. Nicole Perlroth & Katie Benner, *Subpoenas and Gag Orders Show Government Overreach, Tech Companies Argue*, N.Y. Times, Oct. 4, 2016, www .nytimes.com/2016/10/05/technology/subpoenas-and-gag-orders-show-government-overreach-tech-companies-argue.html?_r=0.
3. Nick Wingfield, *Microsoft's Challenge to Government Secrecy Wins Dozens of Supporters*, N.Y. Times, Sept. 2, 2016, www.nytimes.com/2016/09/03/ technology/microsofts-challenge-to-government-secrecy-wins-dozens-of-supporters.html.

4. The processing and dissemination of news will be chilled by the prospect of searches that would disclose internal editorial deliberations.

5. The press will resort to self-censorship to conceal its possession of information of potential interest to the police.

In *Zurcher v. Stanford Daily*, the Supreme Court rejected this reasoning and ruled that newsrooms are entitled to no special treatment beyond that afforded any citizen.[110] The Court said that nothing in the Fourth Amendment restricted searches of newsrooms. Implicitly, the ruling suggested that nothing in the First Amendment did either.

Penalizing Failure to Disclose

As professional collectors of news and information, journalists may be more likely than most to have information of importance to the court.[111] Subpoenas may order them to appear in court to testify or produce evidence. The need to uncover "every man's evidence" generally requires journalists to comply with subpoenas (see below on strategies used to oppose subpoenas).

If reporters refuse to testify and disclose information sought under subpoena, judges may use their power of contempt to punish them.[112] A finding of criminal contempt results in a fixed jail term and/or fine. Under civil contempt, journalists are jailed until they comply with the order to disclose or until the matter is resolved in another method. Contempt citations must be obeyed.

When former New York Times reporter Judith Miller refused to comply with a subpoena to testify before a grand jury about her knowledge of a White House leak that outed an undercover CIA agent, she was cited with contempt and spent 85 days in jail.[113] The prosecutor argued that Miller's testimony was necessary and that "journalists are not entitled to promise complete confidentiality—no one in America is."[114] The U.S. Supreme Court rejected her appeal.[115] Miller was released from jail and testified after her source relieved her of her confidentiality agreement.[116]

Times Chairman Arthur Sulzberger Jr. said:

> There are times when the greater good of democracy demands an act of conscience. Judy has chosen such an act in honoring her promise of confidentiality to her sources. She believes as do we, that the free flow of information is critical to an informed citizenry.[117]

Two freelancers served lengthy jail terms for refusing to name sources. Freelance photographer Josh Wolf was jailed for 226 days for refusal to give a grand jury videotape

● POINTS OF LAW

Contempt of Court

Through contempt of court orders, judges have broad, discretionary power to punish deliberate disobedience of a court order or any misconduct in or interference with the court. Some state laws and the First Amendment limit judges' power of contempt.[1]

Civil Contempt

Civil contempt citations may compel an individual to do something, such as name a source or turn over notes. They also arise when someone intentionally disobeys a court order. Civil contempt sometimes is called "indirect contempt" because the instigating event generally occurs outside the direct supervision of the judge.

Criminal Contempt

Criminal contempt is conduct in or near the court that willfully disobeys a court order or obstructs court proceedings. Because it generally interferes directly with the proceedings of the court, it sometimes is called "direct contempt."

Under the First Amendment, judges may issue contempt citations against harsh news criticism only if the comments intimidate jurors or undermine the fairness of the trial. Individuals given lengthy jail terms for contempt have a right to a jury trial.[2]

1. Pennekamp v. Florida, 328 U.S. 331 (1946).
2. See, e.g., Bloom v. Illinois, 391 U.S. 194, 203 n.6 (1968).

Jailed for more than five months for refusal to disclose her sources to a grand jury, aspiring crime writer Vanessa Leggett later received the PEN First Amendment Award for her protection of freedom of the press.

he made of a San Francisco demonstration.[118] He was released when he agreed to upload all of his demonstration footage.[119] In another case, English teacher Vanessa Leggett refused to provide her notes from interviews about a murder to the grand jury.[120] She served 168 days in jail and was released after the grand jury ended.

Protecting Juveniles

Courts generally provide different levels of access to legal proceedings involving juveniles. The government's substantial interest in reducing trauma that might impede rehabilitation and healing of juvenile victims, defendants and witnesses limits public access to juvenile proceedings. The Supreme Court has said that historically confidential juvenile processes reduce the stigmatization of minors.[121] Fifty years ago, the Supreme Court said juvenile court procedures must ensure that minors receive the full "reach of constitutional guarantees applicable to adults."[122] The Court next ruled that juvenile defendants have the right to counsel and notice.[123]

Federal law permits, but does not require, closure of juvenile proceedings and records on a case-by-case basis. Most federal courts do not consider juvenile proceedings to be presumptively open, and about a third of the states presume that juvenile proceedings are closed while another third provide a broad right of public access to juvenile courts.[124] Washington state, for example, presumes that juvenile proceedings will be open. Georgia and Los Angeles County have open juvenile courts, and in 2014 Kentucky initiated a pilot project to explore whether juvenile courts should be presumptively open.[125]

All states allow certain juveniles to be treated as adults within the justice system, but Maryland, New Jersey and Wisconsin may prohibit the media from revealing the identity of a juvenile.[126] Communicators who legally obtain sealed information about juveniles may publish the information without fear of punishment. A recent Massachusetts Supreme Court decision confirmed that state courts cannot ban media from releasing the legally obtained name of a minor.[127] Most states bar cameras from juvenile courts.[128]

To determine their right of access to juvenile proceedings, individuals should consult their state laws and reports on juvenile justice from the Reporters Committee for Freedom of the Press and the National Center for Juvenile Justice.[129]

In Massachusetts (where the law makes juvenile murder trials presumptively open, while other juvenile proceedings are presumptively closed) a trial judge denied a 14-year-old murder suspect's motion to seal the highly prejudicial video recording and transcript of his police interview.[130] The court said the records were presumptively open once entered into evidence. Police had interviewed the teen alone. He received life in prison for the rape and murder of a math teacher.[131]

Connecticut, Illinois, Massachusetts and Vermont in 2017 considered raising the juvenile court age to 21.[132]

Protecting Sexual Assault Victims

In cases of sexual assault, every state and the District of Columbia has a rape shield law to protect the alleged victim from questions that might prejudice jurors against the victim.[133] Except for Mississippi, every state has a statute excluding evidence of the complaining witness's past sexual activity.[134] Some states also shield the victim's identity and other personal information.[135]

In 2014, the Sixth Circuit Court of Appeals rejected a challenge to Michigan's rape shield law.[136] The court ruled that the Sixth Amendment permitted limits on the extent and nature of the defendant's cross-examination of his minor nephew, the molestation victim who experienced a nervous breakdown.

Protecting State Secrets and National Security

Sixty-five years ago, the Supreme Court granted the executive branch power to keep secret—with little judicial review—information that it said would present a "reasonable danger" to national security.[137] One study found administrations since the 9/11 terrorist

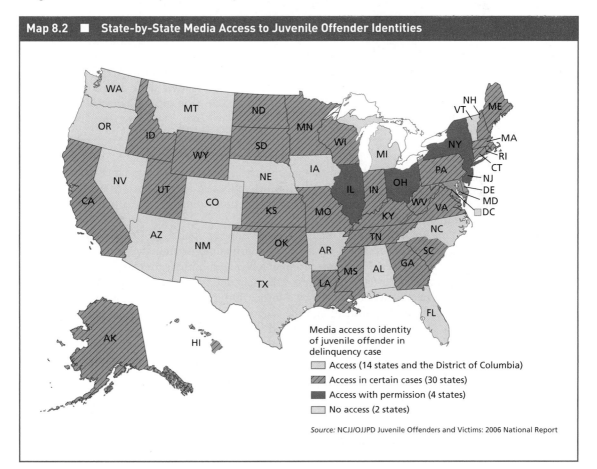

Map 8.2 ■ **State-by-State Media Access to Juvenile Offender Identities**

Media access to identity of juvenile offender in delinquency case

- Access (14 states and the District of Columbia)
- Access in certain cases (30 states)
- Access with permission (4 states)
- No access (2 states)

Source: NCJJ/OJJPD Juvenile Offenders and Victims: 2006 National Report

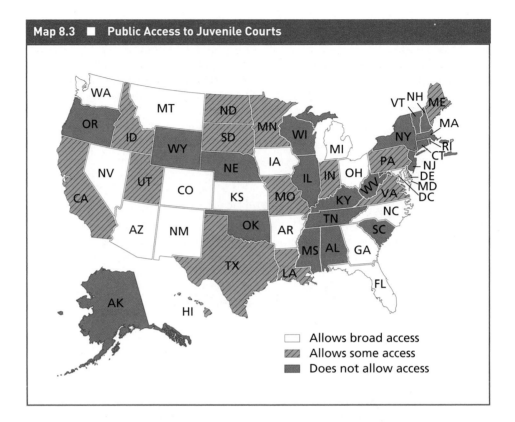

Map 8.3 ■ Public Access to Juvenile Courts

Allows broad access

Allows some access

Does not allow access

attack have "aggressively used the 'state secrets' privilege, insisting that entire cases could be exempt from judicial review."[138] Another study said administrations use the power to declare "state secrets" to thwart open judicial proceedings and even prevent cases from going to trial.[139]

In one case, the Ninth Circuit Court of Appeals upheld the Obama administration's use of state secrets to shield details of the Bush administration's extraordinary rendition program during a criminal prosecution of a Boeing subsidiary for removing alleged terrorists from the United States.[140] In the D.C. Circuit, a judge refused state secrets privilege and reinstated a lawsuit brought by a former Drug Enforcement Administration official against the State Department and the CIA for illegally wiretapping his communications overseas.[141] Unprivileged evidence existed for the case to proceed.

National security concerns justify the secrecy of virtually all Foreign Intelligence Surveillance Act court actions. The courts are presumptively closed, and the court docket is "super-sealed" to hide evidence of even the existence of the case.[142]

Closing Courts

In *Press-Enterprise I* and *II*, the Supreme Court said, "The presumption of openness may be overcome only by an overriding interest based on findings that closure is essential to preserve higher values and is narrowly tailored to serve that interest."[143] *Press-Enterprise II* established that general privacy concerns alone do not justify closing a courtroom or voir dire. Anyone seeking to close a presumptively open hearing must show that (1) the openness has a "substantial probability" of significantly threatening the fair trial process and (2) closure is a last resort "essential" to preserving fair trial rights. Courts must apply this test to withhold information, including the names and addresses of jurors, from the public.[144]

Before closing a courtroom, judges must determine that facts demonstrate *all* of the following:

- Openness poses a substantial threat to a fair proceeding.

- No alternative exists that would effectively eliminate the threat to fairness.

- Closure will effectively eliminate the threat.

- Closure will be narrowly tailored to eliminate the threat and protect maximum public access to the judicial process.

Before closing any or all of a trial, judges must permit interested parties and the public to raise objections.

Despite this high standard, courts continue to close their doors and seal their records. Courts generally accept the commonsense notion that media coverage has an effect on the fairness of a trial.[145] Judges sometimes close trials of their own accord without hearings or findings of prejudice.[146] Studies, however, show that the effects of media coverage appear to be highly specific and inconsistent.[147]

When the trial judge banned media from voir dire in the fraud trial of home décor guru Martha Stewart, the Second Circuit Court of Appeals ruled the judge's actions unconstitutional. "The mere fact of intense media coverage of a celebrity defendant, without further compelling justification, is simply not enough to justify closure."[148]

Courts sometimes close trials and records in business cases that involve trade secrets and proprietary information. When the parties settled the "landmark monopolization case of the 21st Century"[149] between computer industry giant Intel and its chief competitor, Advanced Micro Devices, media argued that the court's seal improperly shielded Intel business practices from public scrutiny.[150] The settlement ended the media request to unseal "hundreds of millions of pages of documentation" held in the court's records.[151] In a related case heard in the European Union, the U.S. Supreme Court ordered disclosure to AMD of some 600,000 pages of Intel records.[152]

In another business case, a federal judge closed the courtroom and sealed documents to protect the secrets of Facebook and ConnectU. Another federal judge sealed the courtroom and records in a lawsuit brought by the Motion Picture Association of America to prevent RealDVD from selling decryption software.[153]

The Supreme Court has not ruled directly on whether hearings to consider the suppression of evidence or plea bargains must be open. At least one federal appeals court has upheld the authority of judges to hold conferences in closed chambers or to conduct whispered bench conferences in the courtroom with the lawyers during the trial. Courts also protect the secrecy of jury deliberations. In 2016, however, the Supreme Court held that a conviction should be reviewed when it is discovered that a juror reached the

⦿ POINTS OF LAW

The *Press-Enterprise* Test for Court Closure

In *Press-Enterprise (II) v. Superior Court of California*, the U.S. Supreme Court established that an individual seeking to close open court records or proceedings, including pretrial hearings, must provide:

1. Specific, on-the-record findings that there is a "substantial probability" that openness will jeopardize the defendant's right to a fair trial

2. Convincing evidence that closure is "essential" to preserve the trial's fairness[1]

---

1. *Press-Enterprise (II) v. Superior Court of California*, 478 U.S. 1 (1986).

verdict based on racial animus toward the defendant.[154] The right of public access does not extend to all criminal trial proceedings. Grand jury hearings and their documents generally are sealed.

ADVANCING THE FLOW OF NEWS

In the years following *Sheppard v. Maxwell*, state media, bar associations and members of the judiciary developed agreements to guide reporting on the courts. The so-called bench/bar/press guidelines aimed to limit prejudicial media coverage by restricting both the content and the tone of trial coverage. They balanced the media and public interest in information against the courts' concerns about privacy and fairness. State rules vary, but some agreements create boards able to punish media violations.

Days after the murder of six family members in Nebraska, a neighbor confessed to the crime. National news media converged on the murder trial, and the judge issued an order barring publication of specific evidence and ordering the media to follow Nebraska's bench/bar/press guidelines. The voluntary guidelines encouraged media not to disclose information about confessions, guilt or innocence, lab tests, witness credibility or statements that reasonably would be expected to influence the outcome of the trial.

The state press association appealed. The Nebraska Supreme Court upheld the order, and in *Nebraska Press Association v. Stuart* the U.S. Supreme Court reversed.[155] The Court said decisions about appropriate news content are the domain of editors, not judges. That remains the law. The Court has never said courts may bind media to bench/bar/press guidelines.

Some courts continue to enforce the voluntary bench/bar/press guidelines on media. One state court in Washington excluded the press from a pretrial hearing after it ruled that its prior pretrial coverage violated the guidelines.[156] Another trial judge made press adherence to the guidelines a condition for media to attend a pretrial hearing open to the public. The Washington Supreme Court upheld this procedure.[157]

Guiding Media Coverage of Courts

The Supreme Court's landmark decision in *Nebraska Press Association v. Stuart* called press gags an extraordinary remedy that is presumptively unconstitutional.[158] The Supreme Court classified gag orders on the media as the most serious and least tolerable prior restraint on First Amendment rights. Court orders that bar the media from publicizing legally obtained information about ongoing trials must meet the highest standard of review. For example, states may not punish witnesses to secret grand juries who discuss their own testimony after the conclusion of the grand jury investigation.[159]

After *Nebraska Press Association*, courts must consider three things before imposing a media gag: (1) the quantity and content of media coverage, (2) the potential effectiveness of alternatives to a gag and (3) the likelihood that a gag would remedy the harmful publicity. Judges must determine that the gag is a last resort that narrowly targets information that poses a clear threat to the fair trial and limits as little press freedom as possible. Constitutionally valid media gag orders are rare.

But the U.S. Supreme Court declined to review a press appeal challenging two Florida court orders directing that "no party shall further disclose the contents of the transcript of testimony before the grand jury" that had been leaked to the press.[160] In his opinion, Justice Anthony Kennedy denied certiorari "despite indications that a prior restraint may have been imposed."[161] The Supreme Court also upheld a restraining order that prevented two newspapers from publicizing the confidential membership and donor list of a religious group obtained from the discovery process in a libel lawsuit.[162] The Court unanimously found the restraining order constitutional because it did not prevent the newspapers from publishing the same information if they obtained it outside of trial discovery.

Courts continue to place gags on the media. An Alabama trial judge briefly banned The Montgomery Advertiser and USA Today from publishing information in the public record about the age and condition of gas pipes across Alabama.[163] The judge entered

○ POINTS OF LAW

What Is Fair Coverage of Criminal Trials?

Media standards of professional and ethical performance as well as bench/bar/press guidelines establish fair reporting standards on criminal proceedings. Most guidelines say that only an overwhelming justification should permit media to report:

1. The existence or content of a confession

2. Statements or opinions of guilt or innocence

3. The results of lab tests

4. Statements or opinions on the credibility of witnesses, the evidence or the investigative process or personnel

5. Other information reasonably likely to affect the trial verdict

⊙ POINTS OF LAW

Closing Media Mouths: The *Nebraska Press* Standard

Nebraska Press Association v. Stuart established that a judge must justify gags imposed on the media with convincing evidence that:

1. Disclosure of the information would present a substantial threat to a fair trial.
2. There is no effective alternative to a gag on the press.
3. The gag will effectively eliminate the danger to the fair trial, and
4. The gag is narrowly tailored to restrict only the information that must be kept secret.

U.S. Army via Getty Images

Mark Boal's interviews with U.S. Army Sgt. Bowe Bergdahl became the basis of the second season of the investigative podcast *Serial*.

the gag in response to Alabama Gas Corp.'s claim that publication of the information raised a risk to national security of sabotage and terrorism.

Protecting Confidential Information

Although individuals who receive subpoenas are expected to comply, recipients may move to quash the subpoena. When journalists are subpoenaed to testify about confidential information, they may use either a state reporter's privilege or state shield laws in efforts to quash the subpoena.

Late in 2016, screenwriter and producer of National Public Radio's podcast "Serial" Mark Boal settled his six-month lawsuit against the government to stop a subpoena for 25 hours of unedited tapes of his interviews with accused U.S. Army deserter Bowe Bergdahl.[164] Bergdahl was a prisoner of the Taliban in Afghanistan and Pakistan for five years. The military court trying Bergdahl had threatened Boal with a contempt citation. Military courts do not recognize reporter's privilege, but Boal argued that federal court precedents should apply. The settlement details were not released, but the government agreed to drop the subpoena and to allow Boal to protect all confidential material from his interviews with Bergdahl.

Providing a Limited Privilege

The concept of reporter's privilege, sometimes called "journalist's privilege," is an extension of other forms of privilege. Courts long have granted certain privileges not to testify to parties in a special relationship—lawyer–client, doctor–patient, husband–wife or clergy–parishioner, for example. Journalists argue that the reporter–source relationship is precisely one of these privileged relationships[165] that the First Amendment protects. Compelling a journalist to violate a promise of confidentiality, they say, impinges on freedom of the press and harms the flow of information.

One distinction between lawyer–client and reporter–source relationships is that attorney–client privilege "belongs" to the client, and reporter's privilege belongs to both the source and the reporter. A client may release an attorney from the agreement while a journalist may argue for privilege even after released from the promise.[166]

Reporter's privilege as we know it originated in the landmark U.S. Supreme Court case *Branzburg v. Hayes*.[167] *Branzburg* consolidated four cases. Two involved Paul Branzburg's sources on illegal drug use reported in The (Louisville) Courier-Journal. Two were related to sources within the Black Panthers contacted in separate reporting by TV reporter Paul Pappas and New York Times reporter Earl Caldwell. All three refused to testify before grand juries and were cited with contempt.

All three reporters claimed the First Amendment provided a privilege that protected them from revealing confidential information. They argued that their ability to report news would be irreparably harmed. Sources would dry up. Mere appearance before a closed grand jury could chill their access to sources who would never know what the reporter revealed. Forced grand jury appearance alone would reduce the information available to the public in violation of the First Amendment.

By a 5–4 majority, the Supreme Court disagreed. The Court balanced the benefits of a reporter's privilege not to testify before a grand jury against the public interest in justice and favored the latter. Obtaining evidence is critical to justice, the Court said. The fact that the necessary evidence is held by a reporter is immaterial. Grand juries are entitled to "every man's evidence," journalists included.[168] Writing in concurrence, Justice Lewis Powell emphasized "the limited nature" of the Court's holding.[169] Reporter's privilege to withhold information should be determined case by case. Refusal to provide information may be permissible if the information fails to serve "a legitimate need of law enforcement."[170]

Writing in dissent, only Justice William Douglas argued that journalists have an absolute privilege to withhold information, including sources' names.[171] Three justices criticized the "Court's crabbed view of the First Amendment"[172] and said reporters have a limited First Amendment privilege to refuse to reveal sources.[173] The First Amendment guarantee is "not for the benefit of the press so much as for the benefit of all of us."[174]

Writing for the three, Justice Potter Stewart said a First Amendment privilege to withhold information should exist unless officials could meet "a heavy burden of justification" to overcome the privilege.[175] He said that burden could be met only when (1) there is probable cause to believe the reporter has information clearly relevant to a specific

New York Times General Counsel James C. Goodale arrives at court June 17, 1971, to oppose the court's restraining order on continued publication of the Pentagon Papers (the Supreme Court ruling discussed in Chapter 2).

AP Photo/Davis

⬤ INTERNATIONAL LAW

Canada Says Stop Trampling on Reporters' Rights

Without providing a broad statement on reporter's privilege, the Canadian Supreme Court urged judges to use caution when forcing journalists to reveal sources.[1]

In the ruling in a libel lawsuit brought against a Globe and Mail reporter, the court said:

If relevant information is available by other means and, therefore, could be obtained without requiring a journalist to break the undertaking of confidentiality, then those avenues ought to be exhausted. The necessity requirement . . . acts as a further buffer against fishing expeditions and any unnecessary interference with the work of the media.[2]

1. Julia Zebley, *Canada Supreme Court Broadens Journalists' Rights to Protect Sources*, Paper Chase, Oct. 22, 2010, jurist.org/paperchase/2010/10/canada-supreme-court-broadens-journalists-rights-to-protect-sources.php.
2. *Id.*

---

violation of law, (2) the information being sought cannot be obtained by other means that are less intrusive of First Amendment values and (3) there is a compelling and overriding interest in the information.[176]

Many courts adopted this approach, which is called the "reporter's privilege test." Among federal appellate courts, only the Sixth Circuit Court of Appeals has not recognized a journalist's privilege to protect confidential sources.[177]

The *Branzburg* decision is narrow, speaking only to a journalist being called before a grand jury. The various *Branzburg* opinions did not make clear how to decide cases not pertaining to grand juries, but they suggest a willingness to consider a reporter's privilege under certain conditions. Thus, a sort of "unofficial majority" of the Court said that a qualified reporter's privilege may be contemplated outside of grand jury circumstances.

In 2016, a federal district court in Massachusetts ordered radio and television commentator Glenn Beck to provide the identities of at least two of the confidential sources he relied on to link the plaintiff, Abdulrahman Alharbi, to the 2013 Boston Marathon bombing.[178] Alharbi sued Beck for libel for repeatedly reporting that Alharbi helped finance the bombing. Beck claimed qualified privilege from disclosure and sought summary judgment on the libel charge, asserting that the stories were accurate reports of information from confidential government sources. The court said disclosure of two of Beck's six sources was necessary due to Beck's vague and often contradictory testimony about their identities and the information they provided. Accurate reports of what they said were essential to Alharbi's case.

In a highly visible recent case the Justice Department investigated, questioned and subpoenaed Pulitzer Prize–winning New York Times reporter James Risen for more than six years, to discover the source of classified information used in his book, "State of War: The Secret History of the CIA and the Bush Administration."[179] The government finally dropped charges against Risen only after convicting former CIA agent Jeffrey Sterling for the leak. But in *United States v. Sterling*, the Fourth Circuit Court of Appeals said no

First Amendment or common law privilege exists for journalists.[180] The Fourth Circuit said Risen did not have protection against testifying because he could provide a "direct, firsthand account of the [alleged] criminal conduct . . . [that] cannot be obtained by alternative means, as [Risen] is without dispute the only witness who can offer this critical testimony."[181]

In 2016, a New York appeals court held that reporter's privilege protected a New York Times reporter from forced disclosure of information from her jailhouse interview of a man charged with a decades-old high-profile murder. The court said Frances Robles' notes of interviews with the "Baby Hope" murder suspect were neither "critical [n]or necessary" to the prosecution.[182] An Arizona appellate court also recognized a qualified First Amendment privilege for newsgathering materials and held that the trial court should have quashed a subpoena for the interview notes of a Phoenix reporter.[183]

Relying on Delaware's Reporters' Privilege Act, a state trial court used a balancing test to let stand a subpoena against the New Journal for the unedited video of one reporter's entire interview with murder suspect Christopher Rivers.[184] The court said the newspaper failed to show how release of the information in the interview would chill its reporting. Moreover, the information was material to the prosecution, unavailable elsewhere and intended for public display.

Some lower courts have balanced *Branzburg's* three factors (possession, alternatives and relevance) against the asserted damage to newsgathering and the First Amendment. If one factor clearly favors the journalist, the journalist may have reporter's privilege protection. For example, one federal district court ruled reporter's privilege shielded a journalist from being questioned because there were alternative ways to obtain the information.[185] Another federal district court upheld reporter's privilege on the grounds that the information sought was not materially relevant to the charges involved in the case.[186]

When faced with subpoenas to identify those who posted anonymously on their websites, news organizations discover reporter's privilege may not protect them. In Idaho, for example, a county Republican Committee official sought the source of allegedly defamatory comments about her that appeared on a blog administered by a reporter of The Spokesman-Review. The newspaper claimed reporter's privilege protection under the First

● POINTS OF LAW

The Reporter's Privilege Test

A reporter's privilege to withhold information likely does not exist if the government can demonstrate:

1. Possession: Probable cause to believe that the reporter has information clearly connected to a specific violation of law

2. No Alternatives: That the information sought cannot be obtained by alternative means less destructive of First Amendment values

3. Relevance: That there is a compelling and overriding interest in the information

Amendment and the state constitution. The court denied protection, reasoning that the privilege did not apply to the journalist who was "not acting as a reporter" but serving as "a facilitator of commentary."[187]

Reporter's privilege may not protect freelance journalists or filmmakers. The U.S. Court of Appeals for the Second Circuit ruled that a documentary filmmaker could not use reporter's privilege because attorneys representing the film's subjects helped with the movie's production. That meant the filmmaker was not a journalist because he did not function with journalistic independence, the court said.[188] However, a federal district court refused to rule that documentary filmmaker Ken Burns had become an advocate and thereby lost his reporter's privilege protection when he produced "The Central Park Five," a film about the five men convicted for raping a jogger in New York's Central Park.[189] The court quashed a subpoena for outtakes from the Burns film. "If the film-maker is independent, . . . the fact that the filmmaker develops an opinion or additional motivations will not remove the protections of the privilege," the court said.[190]

Applying Shield Laws

The U.S. Supreme Court's opinion in *Branzburg* essentially invited legislatures to determine whether "a statutory newsman's privilege is necessary and desirable."[191] Although 17 states had enacted **shield laws** prior to *Branzburg*, most others passed laws to protect journalists in some situations from contempt citations for refusing to reveal a source.[192] Wyoming is the only holdout, but Hawaii's shield law expired in 2013.[193] Late in 2016, efforts to enact a new Hawaiian shield law failed.[194]

Shield laws vary widely from state to state. They all grant some degree of reporter's privilege and reduce the discretion of the court about whether privilege exists and for whom. The wording of the shield law may limit who and what it protects. When Montana recently closed a loophole in its shield law, it "became the first state in the nation to specifically protect reporters' privileged electronic communications from government intrusion," according to the governor.[195] The revised law no longer permits state or local governments to request reporters' confidential information from third parties such as email providers and social networking sites. Recent attempts to strengthen shield laws in Colorado and Maryland failed.[196]

There is no federal shield law. Journalists involved in federal court cases may rely on the uncertain common law privilege. A decade ago, the Pennsylvania Supreme Court broke ground when it rejected the assumption that shield laws do *not* protect against grand jury subpoenas. After a newspaper reporter used a confidential source to report on a grand jury proceeding, the state high court ruled that the Pennsylvania shield law grants an absolute privilege to journalists and protects their sources in all cases.[197]

In a dozen ongoing legal battles in Minnesota, a county attorney demanded that the reality crime television show, "The First 48," turn over all of its footage of several criminal defendants. The show's producers refused the request and argued that the footage was protected by the state's shield law. But the county said the footage was critical to both sides of the case and the shield should not apply because the show "is an entertainment device; it's not a device seeking truth or justice. It gets in the way of us doing our job."[198] One district court judge agreed, requiring disclosure of the footage relevant to the double-murder case of Antonio Fransion Jenkins Jr.[199]

shield laws State laws that protect journalists from being found in contempt of court for refusing to reveal sources.

⊙ POINTS OF LAW

Whom Shield Laws Protect

Foundational definitions in state shield laws determine the breadth and application of the law. For example, West Virginia's law includes the following:

"Reporter" means a person who regularly gathers, prepares, collects, photographs, records, writes, edits, reports, or publishes news or information that concerns matters of public interest for dissemination to the public for a substantial portion of the person's livelihood, or a supervisor, or employer of that person in that capacity: Provided that a student reporter at an accredited educational institution who meets all of the requirements of this definition, except that his or her reporting may not provide a portion of his or her livelihood, meets the definition of reporter for purposes of this section.[1]

On its face, this law applies only to individuals who disseminate news for a living (including freelancers whose major income comes from news) and those working in and with campus media.

1. W. Va. Code § 57-3-10.

Some shield laws recognize the difficulty of defining "journalist" by applying protection to several categories of people. The Minnesota shield law protects anyone "directly engaged in the gathering, procuring, compiling, editing, or publishing of information . . . to the public."[200] Some states shield those who report or write "motion picture news." Freelance writers, book authors, internet writers and many others are left out of many shield laws. Some states also exclude magazine writers.

In 2017, a Pennsylvania court found that the state's shield law made no distinction based on the form of publication. Two people brought suit against a blog to obtain the identity of individuals who made allegedly libelous comments to his posts.[201] The court said the state shield protected the blog operator because he was an author who gathered, compiled and published news through a general-circulation publication comparable to a newspaper. The shield protected sources whom the blogger had promised confidentiality but did not automatically protect commenters who were not confidential sources.[202]

In Arizona, an ex-mobster demanded the notes of an author writing a book about political corruption in the state. An Arizona appellate court let the subpoena stand because its shield law does not protect authors who do not report news or regularly disseminate information.[203]

Several state courts have excluded bloggers from shield protection. A New Jersey court found that state's shield law did not protect an online bulletin-board poster who did not employ customary journalistic practices such as checking facts, including different views or promising sources confidentiality.[204] The New Jersey Supreme Court agreed and said the law shields those connected with or employed by "news media."[205] Electronic bulletin boards that are "little more than forums for discussion" do not meet this definition, the court said.

One judge initially said the Illinois shield law did not protect bloggers on a website containing technology news and commentary. The decision was reversed when the website disclosed that it also included reviews and undertook fact checking. When a blog contributes to information flow by reporting recent events, it can be considered a news medium, according to the court.[206] Courts in Indiana and Kentucky have ruled that their states' shield laws do not apply to anonymous posters.[207] Shield laws in Colorado, Florida, Montana, Oregon and North Carolina protect the identities of anonymous posters by broadly defining what they protect.[208]

In 2016, courts in at least three states applied state shield laws and upheld subpoenas for newsgathering records or confidential sources.[209] But in Washington, an appellate court applied the state's shield law to protect the identity of hackers who posted Kazakh government emails online that an opposition newspaper used to write articles critical of the government.[210] The court said the hackers were protected sources despite the fact that they did not provide the information directly to the newspaper.

Courts are most likely to protect source confidentiality in civil cases in which journalists are not parties to the litigation. In such cases, courts tend to assume the existence of alternative sources for the information that do not implicate the First Amendment.

Applying shield law, an Illinois appellate court vacated a contempt order against a journalist whose testimony was sought in a multiple murder case.[211] But in a complex defamation and right-to-record suit involving NBC Universal's "Dateline" show, the Tenth Circuit Court of Appeals said Colorado's shield law protects confidential sources but does not prevent legitimate discovery of nonconfidential information even from journalists.[212]

Like other privileges, reporter's privilege can be waived. Particularly when a journalist is on the verge of going to court, confidential sources may grant permission to the reporter to disclose their identities. Courts tend to diminish the weight of privilege once a source releases a reporter from the promise of secrecy.

Clarifying What Shield Laws Cover

The information protected by shield laws also varies by state. Tennessee's shield law applies to any information or source of information used for publication or broadcast. Most statutes do not protect journalists called to testify about events they witnessed, especially crimes. Also, the shield often crumbles when journalists are defendants—for example, in a libel case. Access to the reporter's knowledge, notes and sources may be vital to the plaintiff's effort to prove the journalist acted with negligence or actual malice.

A federal district court in Oregon said the state's shield law did not protect a self-identified investigative blogger who was a defendant in a libel suit.[213] The blog was not a "medium of communication," the court said, because it was not "affiliated with any newspaper, magazine, periodical, book, pamphlet, news service, wire service, news or feature syndicate, broadcast station or network, or cable, television system." The court also said the blogger was not a journalist because she presented no evidence of journalistic training, affiliation or practices.[214] In a related decision, the same judge defended his narrow reading of the Oregon shield law. He said he did not mean "that a person who 'blogs' could never be considered 'media.'"[215] Rather, the absence of *any* journalistic practice prevented her categorization as a journalist.

A Texas court said the state's shield law did not apply to someone who blogged about oil and gas drilling's impact on the environment. The blogger was an activist, not a journalist, because she had no journalism background, was not objective and did not adhere to journalistic ethics, the court said.[216] In refusing to apply the New Jersey shield law to a blogger seeking to use it in defense of a libel suit, the state supreme court said the law applies to individuals who communicate to the public on- or offline and have a relationship to their publication similar to that of reporters with traditional media.[217]

Finding Other Protections

Other defenses may exist if a state's reporter's privilege or shield law does not protect journalists from revealing information. Any subpoena in a federal criminal case must comply with Rule 17(c) of the Federal Rules of Criminal Procedure. The rule says a subpoena may be issued only for materials "admissible as evidence." The U.S. Supreme Court said to justify a subpoena, the materials must be relevant, otherwise unavailable and necessary for the trial. The subpoena may not be a "fishing expedition."[218] Rule 26 of the Federal Rules of Civil Procedure prohibits a judge from granting a subpoena for materials in a civil trial if the materials can be obtained elsewhere or if the burden to get the materials outweighs any benefit.

The Privacy Protection Act. After the *Stanford Daily* newsroom search case, Congress passed the Privacy Protection Act of 1980 that significantly limits both state and federal agencies' use of search warrants against public communicators. The law prohibits government agents from searching or seizing a journalist's "work product" or "documentary materials" in the journalist's possession as part of a criminal investigation. Work product includes notes and drafts of news stories. Documentary materials include videotapes, audiotapes and computer files.[219] The law also protects outtakes not included in the final product.

Limited exceptions under the Privacy Protection Act exist if the news organization has refused an order to disclose and all other remedies have been exhausted. Agents may seize certain information related to national security, child pornography or evidence that a journalist committed a crime. Investigators also may seize documentary materials to prevent their destruction or the death or other serious injury of individuals. Journalists may sue government employees for violating the law and seek damages, attorney's fees and court costs.

In at least one case, the U.S. Department of Justice accused a reporter of a crime in an effort to circumvent the Privacy Protection Act. To justify a targeted search of a Fox News reporter's emails, the DOJ claimed the reporter conspired with a State Department analyst to obtain classified documents.[220] Subsequent rules prevented the FBI and others from using an accusation of conspiracy to obtain a search warrant for a reporter's materials.[221]

Yet searches continue. In 2016, New Jersey police armed with a warrant seized a water meter and other materials from a newspaper after it reported on alleged corruption in a city water department.[222] The online story included images of a stolen water meter the paper said a water department employee claimed was "proof that a crime has been committed." The police chief said the interest of "a criminal investigation kind of outweighs" any investigation by the newspaper.

Facing National Security Claims. As discussed elsewhere, national security claims often trump other legal protections. However, the U.S. Court of Appeals for the Ninth Circuit recently ruled that Homeland Security's border agents do not have unlimited power to search people's electronic devices.[223] The case involved finding child pornography on a laptop, but the court signaled that the DHS must have "reasonable suspicion" before searching individuals' electronic devices. However, the Ninth Circuit said "a quick look" or "unintrusive search of a laptop," such as asking that the computer be turned on, is acceptable.

For undisclosed reasons, the Justice Department in 2013 confirmed that it had obtained two months of records from 20 Associated Press phone lines, including general switchboard numbers and an office-wide shared fax line.[224] The department only notified AP of the search after the fact. It never justified the seizure or explained how it obtained the records. Justice Department regulations require notice and notification, and they require subpoenas of journalists' records to be narrowly tailored and a last resort.

A Washington Times reporter settled her lawsuit against the DHS for seizure of newsgathering materials—including information about a whistleblower. The materials were taken from her home under a warrant seeking evidence in a case unrelated to the reporter or her reporting.[225] Under a secret settlement, DHS agreed to improve its protection of newsgathering materials in future searches.

● REAL WORLD LAW

Open Your Mouth and Open Courts

The Federal Judicial Center provides advice on how to object to improper attempts at closure.[1] The Society of Professional Journalists provides this script:

I respectfully protest closure of [this record or this proceeding]. The U.S. Supreme Court has ruled that the First Amendment forbids exclusion of the public from pretrial and trial proceedings without findings of fact identifying the overriding interest to be protected and the necessity of closure to protect that interest.

The Court also has ruled that openness is a constitutional presumption. More than speculation or conclusory assertion of harm is required to justify closure. I ask the court to follow the rulings of the U.S. Supreme Court.

Or, if you plan to involve an attorney, then you might say,

I request that the court delay further proceedings to allow time for counsel to appear and file a motion in opposition to closure.

Finally, if you actually are barred from entering the courtroom, you may give a note containing one of the above statements to the court bailiff or clerk to transmit to the judge. As a reporter, you likely will want to file a story on the closure as well!

---

1. Sealing Court Records and Proceedings: A Pocket Guide (2010), www.fjc.gov/sites/default/files/2012/Sealing_Guide.pdf.

Challenging Closures

The public has a right to challenge court closures, sealed public records and seizures of personal materials. Anyone may challenge a judge's order closing records or criminal proceedings. Such requests should be made in writing and/or in open court. When challenging court closures, individuals should stand and request recognition by the judge and then state an objection to the closure. Anyone also may ask the court to delay proceedings to seek the advice of an attorney in order to object to the closure.

CHAPTER SUMMARY

THE SIXTH AMENDMENT RIGHT to an open public trial belongs to the public as well as the defendant. The Supreme Court established that both the First Amendment and common law provide a public right to attend criminal trials. The presumption of openness extends to pretrial hearings, voir dire and other historically open proceedings. The *Press-Enterprise* cases created tests that often determine whether proceedings are presumptively open and when they may be closed.

Although cameras are not inherently prejudicial to fair trials, broadcast and new media access to courts is not guaranteed. The Supreme Court disfavors cameras. Some courts in every state allow cameras. Judicial discretion, rules of criminal procedure and precedent generally determine access for cameras, broadcasting and new media. Court administrative offices increasingly use these technologies.

Common law access to court records is balanced against competing interests. Most records presented in court are presumptively open. Courts generally must exhaust all reasonable alternatives before sealing presumptively open records. Precedent establishes that access restrictions must be narrowly tailored. Few courts justify their sealing of records. Wide disparities exist among states on electronic access to court records. Some states charge for electronic access. Media cannot be punished for accurately disseminating information legally obtained from court records.

The Sixth Amendment guarantee of a speedy trial does not extend to speedy sentencing. The right to a fair trial by an impartial jury in the district where the crime was committed does not mean jurors must be ignorant of the crime. It means they have no fixed idea about guilt or innocence and will determine their verdict based only on the evidence presented in court. Careful voir dire, judges' admonitions, instructions, sequestrations and even contempt citations help protect the fairness of jurors. Judges disfavor jury sequestration and rarely postpone or relocate a trial or order a retrial.

Closures of presumptively open trial proceedings must be justified on the grounds that they are essential to preserve the fair trial process. Such closures should meet the *Press-Enterprise* test that requires them to be narrowly tailored and the only effective alternative to prevent a substantial threat to a fair trial. Special rules and conditions limit access to trials involving juveniles, sexual assaults or state secrets and national security issues.

Laws that automatically close presumptively open trials are unconstitutional. Court restraining orders that limit trial participants' extrajudicial discussion of trials generally are constitutional if a substantial likelihood exists that publicity would harm the fair trial. Direct gags on the media rarely are constitutional. Bench/bar/press guidelines suggest limits to the content of media coverage of ongoing law enforcement investigations and trials.

Subpoenas that order reporters to appear in court and testify (even to the identities of confidential sources) are legal. An uncertain and qualified reporter's privilege to refuse to disclose confidential information may offer protection. Some state constitutions and state shield laws also may protect news personnel from disclosing confidential information. The scope and application of shield laws vary broadly.

Reporters may challenge subpoenas in court on First Amendment grounds or under federal criminal and civil rules. The three-part *Branzburg* test often determines whether the privilege stands. If the subpoena is not quashed, reporters must comply. Failure to comply may result in contempt rulings, jail and fines.

Properly issued search warrants of reporters and newsrooms are legal under the First Amendment, the Supreme Court held. The Privacy Protection Act limits law enforcement's authority to search newsrooms. National security concerns may override legal protections.

Trial observers may challenge the closure of court sessions but should get an objection on the court's record at the time of the closure order. ■

CASES FOR STUDY

For study resources and a case archive go to **study.sagepub.com/medialaw6e**.

THINKING ABOUT IT

The two case excerpts that follow address very different aspects of fair trials. The first is the U.S. Supreme Court ruling that established a test for a qualified reporter's privilege, which offers limited protection to reporters from an obligation to disclose confidential sources. The second Supreme Court ruling dealt with the right of the public, independent from the parties at trial, to attend criminal trials. As you read these case excerpts, keep the following questions in mind:

- What is the extent (and the limit) of privilege given to reporters by the *Branzburg v. Hayes* decision?
- Among the plurality, concurrences and dissents, whose opinion established the *Branzburg* test? What is the significance of this origin of the test?
- What are the foundations the Court draws upon in *Richmond Newspapers Inc. v. Virginia* to conclude that the public has a right of access to criminal trials?
- What does the Court's decision in *Richmond Newspapers* suggest about any broader public right of access to judicial proceedings?
- Consider how these two decisions have affected a defendant's right to a fair trial. Do they privilege the public's right to know or the media's right to gather news over a fair trial?

Branzburg v. Hayes
SUPREME COURT OF THE UNITED STATES
408 U.S. 665 (1972)

JUSTICE BYRON WHITE
delivered the Court's opinion:

The issue in these cases is whether requiring newsmen to appear and testify before state or federal grand juries abridges the freedom of speech and press guaranteed by the First Amendment. We hold that it does not. . . .

On November 15, 1969, the Courier-Journal carried a story under petitioner's by-line describing in detail his observations of two young residents of Jefferson County synthesizing hashish from marihuana. . . . The article stated that petitioner

had promised not to reveal the identity of the two hashish makers.

Petitioner was shortly subpoenaed by the Jefferson County grand jury; he appeared but refused to identify the individuals he had seen possessing marihuana or the persons he had seen making hashish from marihuana. A state trial court judge ordered petitioner to answer these questions and rejected his contention that the Kentucky reporters' privilege statute, Ky. Rev. Stat. § 421.100 (1962), the First Amendment of the United States Constitution, or §§ 1, 2, and 8 of the Kentucky Constitution authorized his refusal to answer. . . . [T]he Court of Appeals . . . held that petitioner had abandoned his First Amendment argument . . . and tacitly rejected his argument based on the Kentucky Constitution. It also construed Ky. Rev. Stat. § 421.100 as affording a newsman the privilege of refusing to divulge the identity of an informant who supplied him with information, but held that the statute did not permit a reporter to refuse to testify about events he had observed personally, including the identities of those persons he had observed.

The second case involving petitioner Branzburg arose out of his later story . . . , which described in detail the use of drugs in Frankfort, Kentucky. The article reported that . . . petitioner had "spent two weeks interviewing several dozen drug users in the capital city" and had seen some of them smoking marihuana. A number of conversations with and observations of several unnamed drug users were recounted. Subpoenaed to appear before a Franklin County grand jury "to testify in the matter of violation of statutes concerning use and sale of drugs," petitioner Branzburg moved to quash the summons; the motion was denied, although an order was issued protecting Branzburg from revealing "confidential associations, sources or information" but requiring that he "answer any questions which concern or pertain to any criminal act, the commission of which was actually observed by [him]." . . .

[P]etitioner sought mandamus and prohibition from the Kentucky Court of Appeals, arguing that if he were forced to go before the grand jury or to answer questions regarding the identity of informants or disclose information given to him in confidence, his effectiveness as a reporter would be greatly damaged. The Court of Appeals once again denied the requested writs, reaffirming its construction of Ky. Rev. Stat. § 421.100, and rejecting petitioner's claim of a First Amendment privilege. It . . . [announced] "the generally recognized rule that the sources of information of a newspaper reporter are not privileged under the First Amendment." It characterized petitioner's fear that his ability to obtain news would be destroyed as "so tenuous that it does not, in the opinion of this court, present an issue of abridgement of the freedom of the press within the meaning of

that term as used in the Constitution of the United States." . . .

[Paul] Pappas, a television newsman-photographer working out of . . . Providence, Rhode Island, . . . intended to cover a Black Panther news conference at that group's headquarters in a boarded-up store. Petitioner found the streets around the store barricaded, but he ultimately gained entrance to the area and recorded and photographed a prepared statement read by one of the Black Panther leaders. . . . [On a later visit,] Pappas agreed not to disclose anything he saw or heard inside the store except an anticipated police raid. . . . [T]here was no police raid, and petitioner wrote no story and did not otherwise reveal what had occurred in the store. . . .

[Summoned before the grand jury, Pappas] refused to answer any questions about what had taken place inside headquarters while he was there, claiming that the First Amendment afforded him a privilege to protect confidential informants and their information. His motion to quash on First Amendment and other grounds was denied. The [appeals] court then reaffirmed prior Massachusetts holdings that testimonial privileges were "exceptional" and "limited," stating that "the principle that the public 'has a right to every man's evidence'" had usually been preferred, in the Commonwealth, to countervailing interests." . . .

Petitioners . . . press First Amendment claims that may be simply put: that to gather news it is often necessary to agree either not to identify the source of information published or to publish only part of the facts revealed, or both; that if the reporter is nevertheless forced to reveal these confidences to a grand jury, the source so identified and other confidential sources of other reporters will be measurably deterred from furnishing publishable information, all to the detriment of the free flow of information protected by the First Amendment. Although the newsmen in these cases do not claim an absolute privilege against official interrogation in all circumstances, they assert that the reporter should not be forced either to appear or to testify before a grand jury or at trial until and unless sufficient grounds are shown for believing that the reporter possesses information relevant to a crime the grand jury is investigating, that the information the reporter has is unavailable from other sources, and that the need for the information is sufficiently compelling to override the claimed invasion of First Amendment interests occasioned by the disclosure.

Principally relied upon are prior cases emphasizing the importance of the First Amendment guarantees to individual development and to our system of representative government, decisions requiring that official action with adverse impact on First Amendment rights be justified by a public interest that is "compelling" or "paramount," and those precedents establishing the principle that justifiable governmental goals may not be achieved by unduly broad means having an unnecessary impact on protected rights of speech, press, or association. The heart of the claim is that the burden on news gathering resulting from compelling reporters to disclose confidential information outweighs any public interest in obtaining the information.

We do not . . . [suggest] that news gathering does not qualify for First Amendment protection; without some protection for seeking out the news, freedom of the press could be eviscerated. But these cases involve no intrusions upon speech or assembly, no prior restraint or restriction on what the press may publish, and no express or implied command that the press publish what it prefers to withhold. No exaction or tax for the privilege of publishing, and no penalty, civil or criminal, related to the content of published material is at issue here. The use of confidential sources by the press is not forbidden or restricted; reporters remain free to seek news from any source by means within the law. No attempt is made to require the press to publish its sources of information or indiscriminately to disclose them on request.

The sole issue before us is the obligation of reporters to respond to grand jury subpoenas as other citizens do and to answer questions relevant to an investigation into the commission of crime. Citizens generally are not constitutionally immune from grand jury subpoenas; and neither the First Amendment nor any other constitutional provision protects the average citizen from disclosing to a grand jury information that he has received in confidence. The claim is, however, that reporters are exempt from these

obligations because if forced to respond to subpoenas and identify their sources or disclose other confidences, their informants will refuse or be reluctant to furnish newsworthy information in the future. This asserted burden on news gathering is said to make compelled testimony from newsmen constitutionally suspect and to require a privileged position for them.

. . . The Court [elsewhere] has emphasized that "the publisher of a newspaper has no special immunity from the application of general laws. He has no special privilege to invade the rights and liberties of others." . . . The prevailing view is that the press is not free to publish with impunity everything and anything it desires to publish. Although it may deter or regulate what is said or published, the press may not circulate knowing or reckless falsehoods damaging to private reputation without subjecting itself to liability for damages, including punitive damages, or even criminal prosecution.

It has generally been held that the First Amendment does not guarantee the press a constitutional right of special access to information not available to the public generally. . . .

Despite the fact that news gathering may be hampered, the press is regularly excluded from grand jury proceedings, our own conferences, the meetings of other official bodies gathered in executive session, and the meetings of private organizations. Newsmen have no constitutional right of access to the scenes of crime or disaster when the general public is excluded, and they may be prohibited from attending or publishing information about trials if such restrictions are necessary to assure a defendant a fair trial before an impartial tribunal. . . .

It is thus not surprising that the great weight of authority is that newsmen are not exempt from the normal duty of appearing before a grand jury and answering questions relevant to a criminal investigation. At common law, courts consistently refused to recognize the existence of any privilege authorizing a newsman to refuse to reveal confidential information to a grand jury. . . .

The prevailing constitutional view of the newsman's privilege is very much rooted in the ancient role of the grand jury that has the dual function of determining if there is probable cause to believe that a crime has been committed and of protecting citizens against unfounded criminal prosecutions. . . . [T]he grand jury's authority to subpoena witnesses is not only historic, but essential to its task. Although the powers of the grand jury are not unlimited and are subject to the supervision of a judge, the longstanding principle [is] that "the public . . . has a right to every man's evidence," except for those persons protected by a constitutional, common-law, or statutory privilege. . . .

A number of States have provided newsmen a statutory privilege of varying breadth, but the majority have not done so, and none has been provided by federal statute. Until now the only testimonial privilege for unofficial witnesses that is rooted in the Federal Constitution is the Fifth Amendment privilege against compelled self-incrimination. We are asked to create another by interpreting the First Amendment to grant newsmen a testimonial privilege that other citizens do not enjoy. This we decline to do. . . .

This conclusion itself involves no restraint on what newspapers may publish or on the type or quality of information reporters may seek to acquire, nor does it threaten the vast bulk of confidential relationships between reporters and their sources. Grand juries address themselves to the issues of whether crimes have been committed and who committed them. Only where news sources themselves are implicated in crime or possess information relevant to the grand jury's task need they or the reporter be concerned about grand jury subpoenas. Nothing before us indicates that a large number or percentage of all confidential news sources falls into either category and would in any way be deterred by our holding that the Constitution does not, as it never has, exempt the newsman from performing the citizen's normal duty of appearing and furnishing information relevant to the grand jury's task.

The preference for anonymity of those confidential informants involved in actual criminal conduct is presumably a product of their desire to escape criminal prosecution, and this preference, while understandable, is hardly deserving of constitutional protection. . . . The Amendment does not reach so far as to override the interest of the public in ensuring that neither reporter nor source is invading the rights of other citizens through reprehensible conduct forbidden to all other persons. To assert the contrary proposition "is to answer it, since it involves in its very statement the contention that the freedom of the press is the freedom to do wrong with impunity and implies the right to frustrate and defeat the discharge of those governmental duties upon the performance of which the freedom of all, including that of the press, depends. . . . It suffices to say that, however complete is the right of the press to state public things and discuss them, that right, as every other right enjoyed in human society, is subject to the restraints which separate right from wrong-doing."

Thus, we cannot seriously entertain the notion that the First Amendment protects a newsman's agreement to conceal the criminal conduct of his source, or evidence thereof, on the theory that it is better to write about crime than to do something about it. Insofar as any reporter in these cases undertook not to reveal or testify about the crime he witnessed, his claim of privilege under the First Amendment presents no substantial question. The crimes of news sources are no less reprehensible and threatening to the public interest when witnessed by a reporter than when they are not.

There remain those situations where a source is not engaged in criminal conduct but has information suggesting illegal conduct by others. Newsmen frequently receive information from such sources pursuant to a tacit or express agreement to withhold the source's name and suppress any information that the source wishes not published. Such informants presumably desire anonymity in order to avoid being entangled as a witness in a criminal trial or grand jury investigation. They may fear that disclosure will threaten their job security or personal safety or that it will simply result in dishonor or embarrassment.

The argument that the flow of news will be diminished by compelling reporters to aid the grand jury in a criminal investigation is not irrational, nor are the records before us silent on the matter. But we remain unclear how often and to what extent informers are actually deterred from furnishing information when newsmen are forced to testify before a grand jury. The available data indicate that some newsmen rely a great deal on confidential sources and that some informants are particularly sensitive to the threat of exposure and may be silenced if it is held by this Court that, ordinarily, newsmen must testify pursuant to subpoenas, but the evidence fails to demonstrate that there would be a significant constriction of the flow of news to the public if this Court reaffirms the prior common-law and constitutional rule regarding the testimonial obligations of newsmen. Estimates of the inhibiting effect of such subpoenas on the willingness of informants to make disclosures to newsmen are widely divergent and to a great extent speculative. . . .

Reliance by the press on confidential informants does not mean that all such sources will in fact dry up because of the later possible appearance of the newsman before a grand jury. The reporter may never be called and if he objects to testifying, the prosecution may not insist. Also, the relationship of many informants to the press is a symbiotic one which is unlikely to be greatly inhibited by the threat of subpoena: quite often, such informants are members of a minority political or cultural group that relies heavily on the media to propagate its views, publicize its aims, and magnify its exposure to the public. Moreover, grand juries characteristically conduct secret proceedings, and law enforcement officers are themselves experienced in dealing with informers, and have their own methods for protecting them without interference with the effective administration of justice. There is little before us indicating that informants whose interest in avoiding exposure is that it may threaten job security, personal safety, or peace of mind, would in fact be in a worse position, or would think they would be, if they risked placing their trust in public officials as well as reporters. We doubt if the informer who prefers anonymity but is sincerely interested in furnishing evidence of crime will always or very often be deterred by the prospect of dealing with those public authorities characteristically charged with the duty to protect the public interest as well as his. . . .

We note first that the privilege claimed is that of the reporter, not the informant, and that if the authorities independently identify the informant, neither his own reluctance to testify nor the objection of the newsman would shield him from grand jury inquiry, whatever the impact on the flow of news or on his future usefulness as a secret source of information. More important, it is obvious that agreements to conceal information relevant to commission of crime have very little to recommend them from the standpoint of public policy. . . .

Of course, the press has the right to abide by its agreement not to publish all the information it has, but the right to withhold news is not equivalent to a First Amendment exemption from the ordinary duty of all other citizens to furnish relevant information to a grand jury performing an important public function. Private restraints on the flow of information are not so favored by the First Amendment that they override all other public interests. . . .

Neither are we now convinced that a virtually impenetrable constitutional shield, beyond legislative or judicial control, should be forged to protect a private system of informers operated by the press to report on criminal conduct, a system that would be unaccountable to the public, would pose a threat to the citizen's justifiable expectations of privacy, and would equally protect well-intentioned informants and those who for pay or otherwise betray their trust to their employer or associates. . . .

We are admonished that refusal to provide a First Amendment reporter's privilege will undermine the freedom of the press to collect and disseminate news. But this is not the lesson history teaches us. As noted previously, the common law recognized no such privilege, and the constitutional argument was not even asserted until 1958. From the beginning of our country the press has operated without constitutional protection for press informants, and the press has flourished. The existing constitutional rules have not been a serious obstacle to either the development or retention of confidential news sources by the press.

It is said that currently press subpoenas have multiplied, that mutual distrust and tension between press and officialdom have increased, that reporting styles have changed, and that there is now more need for confidential sources, particularly where the press seeks news about minority cultural and political groups or dissident organizations suspicious of the law and public officials. These developments, even if true, are treacherous grounds for a far-reaching interpretation of the First Amendment fastening a nationwide rule on courts, grand juries, and prosecuting officials everywhere. The obligation to testify in response to grand jury subpoenas will not threaten these sources not involved with criminal conduct and without information relevant to grand jury investigations, and we cannot hold that the Constitution places the sources in these two categories either above the law or beyond its reach.

The argument for such a constitutional privilege rests heavily on those cases holding that the infringement of protected First Amendment rights must be no broader than necessary to achieve a permissible governmental purpose. We do not deal, however, with a governmental institution that has abused its proper function, as a legislative committee does when it "expose[s] for the sake of exposure." . . . The investigative power of the grand jury is necessarily broad if its public responsibility is to be adequately discharged. . . .

The privilege claimed here is conditional, not absolute; given the suggested preliminary showings and compelling need, the reporter would be required to testify. Presumably, such a rule would reduce the instances in which reporters could be required to appear, but predicting in advance when and in what circumstances they could be compelled to do so would be difficult. Such a rule would also have implications for the issuance of compulsory process to reporters at civil and criminal trials and at legislative hearings. If newsmen's confidential sources are as sensitive as they are claimed to be, the prospect of being unmasked whenever a judge determines the situation justifies it is hardly a satisfactory solution to the problem. For them, it would appear that only an absolute privilege would suffice.

We are unwilling to embark the judiciary on a long and difficult journey to such an uncertain destination. The administration of a constitutional newsman's privilege would present practical and conceptual difficulties of a high order. Sooner or later, it would be necessary to define those categories of newsmen who qualified for the privilege, a questionable procedure in light of the traditional doctrine that liberty of the press is the right of the lonely pamphleteer who uses carbon paper or a mimeograph just as much as of the large metropolitan publisher who utilizes the latest photocomposition methods. Freedom of the press is a "fundamental personal right" which "is not confined to newspapers and periodicals. It necessarily embraces pamphlets and leaflets. . . . The press in its historic connotation comprehends every sort of publication which affords a vehicle of information and opinion." The informative function asserted by representatives of the organized press in the present cases is also performed by lecturers, political pollsters, novelists, academic researchers, and dramatists. Almost any author may quite accurately assert that he is contributing to the flow of information to the public, that he relies on confidential sources of information, and that these sources will be silenced if he is forced to make disclosures before a grand jury.

In each instance where a reporter is subpoenaed to testify, the courts would also be embroiled in preliminary factual and legal determinations with respect to whether the proper predicate had been laid for the reporter's appearance . . . Thus, in the end, by considering whether enforcement of a particular law served a "compelling" governmental interest, the courts would be inextricably involved in distinguishing between the value of enforcing different criminal laws. By requiring testimony from a reporter in investigations involving some crimes but not in others, they would be making a value judgment that a legislature had declined to make, since in each case the criminal law involved would represent a considered legislative judgment, not constitutionally suspect, of what conduct is liable to criminal prosecution. The task of judges, like other officials outside the legislative branch, is not to make the law but to uphold it in accordance with their oaths.

At the federal level, Congress has freedom to determine whether a statutory newsman's privilege is necessary and desirable and to fashion standards and rules as narrow or broad as deemed necessary to deal with the evil discerned and, equally important, to refashion those rules as experience from time to time may dictate. There is also merit in leaving state legislatures free, within First Amendment limits, to fashion their own standards in light of the conditions and problems with respect to the relations between law enforcement officials and press in their own areas. It goes without saying, of course, that we are powerless to bar state courts from responding in their own way and construing their own constitutions so as to recognize a newsman's privilege, either qualified or absolute.

In addition, there is much force in the pragmatic view that the press has at its disposal powerful mechanisms of communication, and is far from helpless to protect itself from harassment or substantial harm. Furthermore, if what the newsmen urged in these cases is true—that law enforcement cannot hope to gain and may suffer from subpoenaing newsmen before grand juries—prosecutors will be loath to risk so much for so little. Thus, at the federal level the Attorney General has already fashioned a set of rules for federal officials in connection with subpoenaing members of the press to testify before grand juries or at criminal trials. These rules are a major step in the direction the reporters herein desire to move. They may prove wholly sufficient to resolve the bulk of disagreements and controversies between press and federal officials.

Finally, as we have earlier indicated, news gathering is not without its First Amendment protections, and grand jury investigations if instituted or conducted other than in good faith, would pose wholly different issues for resolution under the First Amendment. Official harassment of the press undertaken not for purposes of law enforcement but to disrupt a reporter's relationship with his news sources would have no justification. Grand juries are subject to judicial control and subpoenas to motions to quash. We do not expect courts will forget that grand juries must operate within the limits of the First Amendment as well as the Fifth. . . .

Justice Lewis Powell, concurring:
I add this brief statement to emphasize what seems to me to be the limited nature of the Court's

holding. The Court does not hold that newsmen, subpoenaed to testify before a grand jury, are without constitutional rights with respect to the gathering of news or in safeguarding their sources. . . .

As indicated in the concluding portion of the opinion, the Court states that no harassment of newsmen will be tolerated. If a newsman believes that the grand jury investigation is not being conducted in good faith, he is not without remedy. Indeed, if the newsman is called upon to give information bearing only a remote and tenuous relationship to the subject of the investigation, or if he has some other reason to believe that his testimony implicates confidential source relationships without a legitimate need of law enforcement, he will have access to the court on a motion to quash, and an appropriate protective order may be entered. The asserted claim to privilege should be judged on its facts by the striking of a proper balance between freedom of the press and the obligation of all citizens to give relevant testimony with respect to criminal conduct. The balance of these vital constitutional and societal interests on a case-by-case basis accords with the tried and traditional way of adjudicating such questions.

In short, the courts will be available to newsmen under circumstances where legitimate First Amendment interests require protection.

Justice Potter Stewart, with whom Justice William Brennan and Justice Thurgood Marshall join, dissenting:
The Court's crabbed view of the First Amendment reflects a disturbing insensitivity to the critical role of an independent press in our society. The question whether a reporter has a constitutional right to a confidential relationship with his source is of first impression here, but the principles that should guide our decision are as basic as any to be found in the Constitution. . . . [T]he Court in these cases holds that a newsman has no First Amendment right to protect his sources when called before a grand jury. The Court thus invites state and federal authorities to undermine the historic independence of the press by attempting to annex the journalistic profession as an investigative arm of government.

Not only will this decision impair performance of the press' constitutionally protected functions, but it will, I am convinced, in the long run harm rather than help the administration of justice.

I respectfully dissent.

The reporter's constitutional right to a confidential relationship with his source stems from the broad societal interest in a full and free flow of information to the public. It is this basic concern that underlies the Constitution's protection of a free press, because the guarantee is "not for the benefit of the press so much as for the benefit of all of us." Enlightened choice by an informed citizenry is the basic ideal upon which an open society is premised, and a free press is thus indispensable to a free society. Not only does the press enhance personal self-fulfillment by providing the people with the widest possible range of fact and opinion, but it also is an incontestable precondition of self-government. The press "has been a mighty catalyst in awakening public interest in governmental affairs, exposing corruption among public officers and employees and generally informing the citizenry of public events and occurrences. . . ."

As private and public aggregations of power burgeon in size and the pressures for conformity necessarily mount, there is obviously a continuing need for an independent press to disseminate a robust variety of information and opinion through reportage, investigation, and criticism, if we are to preserve our constitutional tradition of maximizing freedom of choice by encouraging diversity of expression. In keeping with this tradition, we have held that the right to publish is central to the First Amendment and basic to the existence of constitutional democracy.

A corollary of the right to publish must be the right to gather news. The full flow of information to the public protected by the free-press guarantee would be severely curtailed if no protection whatever were afforded to the process by which news is assembled and disseminated. We have, therefore, recognized that there is a right to publish without prior governmental approval, a right to distribute information, and a right to receive printed matter.

No less important to the news dissemination process is the gathering of information. News must not be unnecessarily cut off at its source, for without freedom to acquire information the right to publish would be impermissibly compromised. Accordingly, a right to gather news, of some dimensions, must exist. As Madison wrote: "A popular Government, without popular information, or the means of acquiring it, is but a Prologue to a Farce or a Tragedy, or perhaps both."

The right to gather news implies, in turn, a right to a confidential relationship between a reporter and his source. This proposition follows as a matter of simple logic once three factual predicates are recognized: (1) newsmen require informants to gather news; (2) confidentiality—the promise or understanding that names or certain aspects of communications will be kept off the record—is essential to the creation and maintenance of a news gathering relationship with informants; and (3) an unbridled subpoena power— the absence of a constitutional right protecting, in any way, a confidential relationship from compulsory process—will either deter sources from divulging information or deter reporters from gathering and publishing information.

It is obvious that informants are necessary to the news-gathering process as we know it today. If it is to perform its constitutional mission, the press must do far more than merely print public statements or publish prepared handouts. Familiarity with the people and circumstances involved in the myriad background activities that result in the final product called "news" is vital to complete and responsible journalism, unless the press is to be a captive mouthpiece of "newsmakers."

It is equally obvious that the promise of confidentiality may be a necessary prerequisite to a productive relationship between a newsman and his informants. An officeholder may fear his superior; a member of the bureaucracy, his associates; a dissident, the scorn of majority opinion. All may have information valuable to the public discourse, yet each may be willing to relate that information only in confidence to a reporter whom he trusts, either because of excessive caution or because of a reasonable fear of reprisals or censure for unorthodox views. The First Amendment concern must not be with the motives of any particular news source, but rather with the conditions in which informants of all shades of the spectrum may make information available through the press to the public. . . .

Finally, and most important, when governmental officials possess an unchecked power to compel newsmen to disclose information received in confidence, sources will clearly be deterred from giving information, and reporters will clearly be deterred from publishing it, because uncertainty about exercise of the power will lead to "self-censorship." The uncertainty arises, of course, because the judiciary has traditionally imposed virtually no limitations on the grand jury's broad investigatory powers.

After today's decision, the potential informant can never be sure that his identity or off-the-record communications will not subsequently be revealed through the compelled testimony of a newsman. . . . The potential source must, therefore, choose between risking exposure by giving information or avoiding the risk by remaining silent. The reporter must speculate about whether contact with a controversial source or publication of controversial material will lead to a subpoena. In the event of a subpoena, under today's decision, the newsman will know that he must choose between being punished for contempt if he refuses to testify, or violating his profession's ethics and impairing his resourcefulness as a reporter if he discloses confidential information. . . .

The impairment of the flow of news cannot, of course, be proved with scientific precision, as the Court seems to demand. Obviously, not every newsgathering relationship requires confidentiality. And it is difficult to pinpoint precisely how many relationships do require a promise or understanding of nondisclosure. But we have never before demanded that First Amendment rights rest on elaborate empirical studies demonstrating beyond any conceivable doubt that deterrent effects exist; we have never before required proof of the exact number of people potentially affected by governmental action, who would actually be dissuaded from engaging in First Amendment activity.

Rather, on the basis of common sense and available information, we have asked, often implicitly, (1) whether there was a rational connection between the cause (the governmental action) and the effect (the deterrence or impairment of First Amendment activity), and (2) whether the effect would occur with some regularity, i.e., would not be de minimis. And, in making this determination, we have shown a special solicitude towards the "indispensable liberties" protected by the First Amendment, for "[f]reedoms such as these are protected not only against heavy-handed frontal attack, but also from being stifled by more subtle governmental interference." Once this threshold inquiry has been satisfied, we have then examined the competing interests in determining whether there is an unconstitutional infringement of First Amendment freedoms. . . .

. . . We can and must accept the evidence developed in the record, and elsewhere, that overwhelmingly supports the premise that deterrence will occur with regularity in important types of news-gathering relationships. Thus, we cannot escape the conclusion that when neither the reporter nor his source can rely on the shield of confidentiality against unrestrained use of the grand jury's subpoena power, valuable information will not be published and the public dialogue will inevitably be impoverished.

Posed against the First Amendment's protection of the newsman's confidential relationships in these cases is society's interest in the use of the grand jury to administer justice fairly and effectively. The grand jury serves two important functions: "to examine into the commission of crimes" and "to stand between the prosecutor and the accused, and to determine whether the charge was founded upon credible testimony or was dictated by malice or personal ill will." And to perform these functions, the grand jury must have available to it every man's relevant evidence.

Yet the longstanding rule making every person's evidence available to the grand jury is not absolute. The rule has been limited by the Fifth Amendment, the Fourth Amendment, and the evidentiary privileges of the common law. . . . [T]he Court noted that "some confidential matters are shielded from considerations of policy, and perhaps in other cases for special reasons a witness may be excused from telling all that he knows." . . . "[A]ny exemption from the duty to testify before the grand jury "presupposes a very real interest to be protected."

Such an interest must surely be the First Amendment protection of a confidential relationship. . . .

[T]his protection does not exist for the purely private interests of the newsman or his informant, nor even, at bottom, for the First Amendment interests of either partner in the newsgathering relationship. Rather, it functions to insure nothing less than democratic decisionmaking through the free flow of information to the public, and it serves, thereby, to honor the "profound national commitment to the principle that debate on public issues should be uninhibited, robust, and wide-open."

In striking the proper balance between the public interest in the efficient administration of justice and the First Amendment guarantee of the fullest flow of information, we must begin with the basic proposition that because of their "delicate and vulnerable" nature, and their transcendent importance for the just functioning of our society, First Amendment rights require special safeguards. . . .

In no previous case have we considered the extent to which the First Amendment limits the grand jury subpoena power. But the Court has said that "the Bill of Rights is applicable to investigations as to all forms of governmental action. Witnesses cannot be compelled to give evidence against themselves. They cannot be subjected to unreasonable search and seizure. Nor can the First Amendment freedoms of speech, press . . . or political belief and association be abridged." [Elsewhere], it was stated: "It is particularly important that the exercise of the power of compulsory process be carefully circumscribed when the investigative process tends to impinge upon such highly sensitive areas as freedom of speech or press, freedom of political association, and freedom of communication of ideas."

The established method of "carefully" circumscribing investigative powers is to place a heavy burden of justification on government officials when First Amendment rights are impaired. The decisions of this Court have "consistently held that only a compelling state interest in the regulation of a subject within the State's constitutional power to regulate can justify limiting First Amendment freedoms." And "it is an essential prerequisite to the validity of an investigation which intrudes into the area of constitutionally protected rights of speech, press, association and petition that the State convincingly show a substantial relation between the information sought and a subject of overriding and compelling state interest." Thus, when an investigation impinges on First Amendment rights, the government must not only show that the inquiry is of "compelling and overriding importance," but it must also "convincingly" demonstrate that the investigation is "substantially related" to the information sought.

Governmental officials must, therefore, demonstrate that the information sought is clearly relevant to a precisely defined subject of governmental inquiry. They must demonstrate that it is reasonable to think the witness in question has that information. And they must show that there is not any means of obtaining the information less destructive of First Amendment liberties.

These requirements, which we have recognized in decisions involving legislative and executive investigations, serve established policies reflected in numerous First Amendment decisions arising in other contexts. The requirements militate against vague investigations that, like vague laws, create uncertainty and needlessly discourage First Amendment activity. They also insure that a legitimate governmental purpose will not be pursued by means that "broadly stifle fundamental personal liberties when the end can be more narrowly achieved." . . .

I believe the safeguards developed in our decisions involving governmental investigations must apply to the grand jury inquiries in these cases. Surely the function of the grand jury to aid in the enforcement of the law is no more important than the function of the legislature, and its committees, to make the law. . . .

Accordingly, when a reporter is asked to appear before a grand jury and reveal confidences, I would hold that the government must (1) show that there is probable cause to believe that the newsman has information that is clearly relevant to a specific probable violation of law; (2) demonstrate that the information sought cannot be obtained by alternative means less destructive of First Amendment rights; and (3) demonstrate a compelling and overriding interest in the information.

This is not to say that a grand jury could not issue a subpoena until such a showing were made, and it is not to say that a newsman would be in any way privileged to ignore any subpoena that was issued. Obviously, before the government's burden to make such a showing were triggered, the reporter would have to move to quash the subpoena, asserting the basis on which he considered the particular relationship a confidential one.

The crux of the Court's rejection of any newsman's privilege is its observation that only "where news sources themselves are implicated in crime or possess information relevant to the grand jury's task need they or the reporter be concerned about grand jury subpoenas." But this is a most misleading construct. For it is obviously not true that the only persons about whom reporters will be forced to testify will be those "confidential informants involved in actual criminal conduct" and those having "information suggesting illegal conduct by others." As noted above, given the grand jury's extraordinarily broad investigative powers and the weak standards of relevance and materiality that apply during such inquiries, reporters, if they have no testimonial privilege, will be called to give information about informants who have neither committed crimes nor have information about crime. It is to avoid deterrence of such sources and thus to prevent needless injury to First Amendment values that I think the government must be required to show probable cause that the newsman has information that is clearly relevant to a specific probable violation of criminal law.

Similarly, a reporter may have information from a confidential source that is "related" to the commission of crime, but the government may be able to obtain an indictment or otherwise achieve its purposes by subpoenaing persons other than the reporter. It is an obvious but important truism that when government aims have been fully served, there can be no legitimate reason to disrupt a confidential relationship between a reporter and his source. To do so would not aid the administration of justice and would only impair the flow of information to the public. Thus, it is to avoid deterrence of such sources that I think the government must show that there are no alternative means for the grand jury to obtain the information sought. . . .

The error in the Court's absolute rejection of First Amendment interests in these cases seems to me to be most profound. For in the name of advancing the administration of justice, the Court's decision, I think, will only impair the achievement of that goal. People entrusted with law enforcement responsibility, no less than private citizens, need general information relating to controversial social problems. Obviously, press reports have great value to government, even when the newsman cannot be compelled to testify before a grand jury. The sad paradox of the Court's position is that when a grand jury may exercise an unbridled subpoena power, and sources involved in sensitive matters become fearful of disclosing information, the newsman will not only cease to be a useful grand jury witness; he will cease to investigate and publish information about issues of public import. I cannot subscribe to such an anomalous result, for, in my view, the interests protected by the First Amendment are not antagonistic to the administration of justice. Rather, they can, in the long run, only be complementary, and for that reason must be given great "breathing space." . . .

Richmond Newspapers Inc. v. Virginia
SUPREME COURT OF THE UNITED STATES
448 U.S. 555 (1980)

Chief JUSTICE WARREN BURGER delivered the Court's opinion:
The narrow question presented in this case is whether the right of the public and press to attend criminal trials is guaranteed under the United States Constitution. . . .

Stevenson was indicted for the murder of a hotel manager who had been found stabbed to death on

December 2, 1975. Tried promptly in July, 1976, Stevenson was convicted of second-degree murder in the Circuit Court of Hanover County, Va. The Virginia Supreme Court reversed the conviction in October, 1977, holding that a bloodstained shirt purportedly belonging to Stevenson had been improperly admitted into evidence. Stevenson was retried in the same court. This second trial ended in a mistrial on May 30, 1978, when a juror asked to be excused after trial had begun and no alternate was available. A third trial, which began in the same court on June 6, 1978, also ended in a mistrial . . . because a prospective juror had read about Stevenson's previous trials in a newspaper and had told other prospective jurors about the case before the retrial began.

Stevenson was tried in the same court for a fourth time beginning on September 11, 1978. Present in the courtroom when the case was called were . . . reporters for appellant Richmond Newspapers, Inc. Before the trial began, counsel for the defendant moved that it be closed to the public:

"[T]here was this woman that was with the family of the deceased when we were here before. She had sat in the Courtroom. I would like to ask that everybody be excluded from the Courtroom because I don't want any information being shuffled back and forth when we have a recess as to what—who testified to what."

The trial judge, who had presided over two of the three previous trials, asked if the prosecution had any objection to clearing the courtroom. The prosecutor stated he had no objection and . . . the trial judge . . . ordered "that the Courtroom be kept clear of all parties except the witnesses when they testify." The record does not show that any objections to the closure order were made by anyone present at the time. . . .

Later that same day, however, appellants sought a hearing on a motion to vacate the closure order. The trial judge granted the request and scheduled a hearing to follow the close of the day's proceedings. When the hearing began, the court ruled that the hearing was to be treated as part of the trial; accordingly, he again ordered the reporters to leave the courtroom, and they complied.

At the closed hearing, counsel for appellants observed that no evidentiary findings had been made by the court prior to the entry of its closure order, and pointed out that the court had failed to consider any other, less drastic measures within its power to ensure a fair trial. Counsel for appellants argued that constitutional considerations mandated that before ordering closure, the court should first decide that the rights of the defendant could be protected in no other way.

Counsel for defendant Stevenson pointed out that this was the fourth time he was standing trial. He also referred to "difficulty with information between the jurors," and stated that he "didn't want information to leak out," be published by the media, perhaps inaccurately, and then be seen by the jurors. Defense counsel argued that these things, plus the fact that "this is a small community," made this a proper case for closure.

The trial judge noted that counsel for the defendant had made similar statements at the morning hearing. The court also stated: "One of the other points that we take into consideration in this particular Courtroom is layout of the Courtroom. I think that having people in the Courtroom is distracting to the jury. Now, we have to have certain people in here and maybe that's not a very good reason. When we get into our new Court Building, people can sit in the audience so the jury can't see them. The rule of the Court may be different under those circumstances. . . ."

The prosecutor again declined comment, and the court summed up by saying: "I'm inclined to agree with [defense counsel] that, if I feel that the rights of the defendant are infringed in any way, [when] he makes the motion to do something and it doesn't completely override all rights of everyone else, then I'm inclined to go along with the defendant's motion." The court denied the motion to vacate and ordered the trial to continue the following morning "with the press and public excluded."

What transpired when the closed trial resumed the next day was disclosed in the following manner by an order of the court entered September 12, 1978: "[In] the absence of the jury, the defendant, by counsel, made a Motion that a mistrial be declared, which motion was taken under advisement. "At the conclusion of the Commonwealth's evidence, the attorney for the defendant moved the Court to strike the Commonwealth's evidence on grounds stated to the record, which Motion was sustained by the Court." "And the jury having been excused, the Court doth find the accused NOT GUILTY of Murder, as charged in the Indictment, and he was allowed to depart." . . . The Virginia Supreme Court . . . finding no reversible error, denied the petition for appeal. . . .

The criminal trial which appellants sought to attend has long since ended, and there is thus some suggestion that the case is moot. This Court has frequently recognized, however, that its jurisdiction is not necessarily defeated by the practical termination of a contest which is short-lived by nature. If the underlying dispute is "capable of repetition, yet evading review," it is not moot. . . .

In prior cases the Court has treated questions involving conflicts between publicity and a defendant's right to a fair trial. . . . But here for the first time the Court is asked to decide whether a criminal trial itself may be closed to the public upon the unopposed request of a defendant, without any demonstration that closure is required to protect the defendant's superior right to a fair trial, or that some other overriding consideration requires closure.

The origins of the proceeding which has become the modern criminal trial in Anglo-American justice can be traced back beyond reliable historical records. . . . What is significant for present purposes is that, throughout its evolution, the trial has been open to all who cared to observe. . . . From these early times, although great changes in courts and procedure took place, one thing remained constant: the public character of the trial at which guilt or innocence was decided. . . .

We have found nothing to suggest that the presumptive openness of the trial, which English courts were later to call "one of the essential qualities of a court of justice," was not also an attribute of the judicial systems of colonial America. . . . In some instances, the openness of trials was explicitly recognized as part of the fundamental law of the Colony. . . . Other contemporary writings confirm the recognition that part of the very nature of a criminal trial was its openness to those who wished to attend. . . .

As we have shown, . . . the historical evidence demonstrates conclusively that, at the time when our organic laws were adopted, criminal trials both here and in England had long been presumptively open. This is no quirk of history; rather, it has long been recognized as an indispensable attribute of an Anglo-American trial. . . . Jeremy Bentham not only recognized the therapeutic value of open justice but regarded it as the keystone:

"Without publicity, all other checks are insufficient: in comparison of publicity, all other checks are of small account. Recordation, appeal, whatever other institutions might present themselves in the character of checks, would be found to operate rather as cloaks than checks; as cloaks in reality, as checks only in appearance." . . .

. . . The early history of open trials in part reflects the widespread acknowledgment . . . that public trials had significant community therapeutic value. . . . [P]eople sensed from experience and observation that, especially in the administration of criminal justice, the means used to achieve justice must have the support derived from public acceptance of both the process and its results.

When a shocking crime occurs, a community reaction of outrage and public protest often follows. Thereafter the open processes of justice serve an important prophylactic purpose, providing an outlet for community concern, hostility, and emotion. Without an awareness that society's responses to criminal conduct are underway, natural human reactions of outrage and protest are frustrated and may manifest themselves in some form of vengeful "self-help," as indeed they did regularly in the activities of vigilante "committees" on our frontiers. . . .

Civilized societies withdraw both from the victim and the vigilante the enforcement of criminal laws, but they cannot erase from people's consciousness the fundamental, natural yearning to see justice done—or even the urge for retribution. The crucial prophylactic aspects of the administration of justice cannot function in the dark; no community catharsis can occur if justice is "done in a corner [or] in any covert manner." It is not enough to say that results alone will satiate the natural community desire for "satisfaction." A result considered untoward may undermine public confidence, and where the trial has been concealed from public view, an unexpected outcome can cause a reaction that the system at best has failed and at worst has been corrupted. To work effectively, it is important that society's criminal process "satisfy the appearance of justice," and the appearance of justice can best be provided by allowing people to observe it. . . .

People in an open society do not demand infallibility from their institutions, but it is difficult for them to accept what they are prohibited from observing. When a criminal trial is conducted in the open, there is at least an opportunity both for understanding the system in general and its workings in a particular case: "The educative effect of public attendance is a material advantage. Not only is respect for the law increased and intelligent acquaintance acquired with the methods of government, but a strong confidence in judicial remedies is secured which could never be inspired by a system of secrecy." . . .

. . . Instead of acquiring information about trials by firsthand observation or by word of mouth from those who attended, people now acquire it chiefly through the print and electronic media. In a sense, this validates the media claim of functioning as surrogates for the public. While media representatives enjoy the same right of access as the public, they often are provided special seating and priority of entry so that they may report what people in attendance have seen and heard. This "[contributes] to public understanding of the rule of law and to comprehension of the functioning of the entire criminal justice system. . . ."

From this unbroken, uncontradicted history, supported by reasons as valid today as in centuries past, we are bound to conclude that a presumption of openness inheres in the very nature of a criminal trial under our system of justice. . . .

Despite the history of criminal trials being presumptively open since long before the Constitution, the State presses its contention that neither the Constitution nor the Bill of Rights contains any provision which, by its terms, guarantees to the public the right to attend criminal trials. Standing alone, this is correct, but there remains the question whether, absent an explicit provision, the Constitution affords protection against exclusion of the public from criminal trials. . . .

The Bill of Rights was enacted against the backdrop of the long history of trials being presumptively open. Public access to trials was then regarded as an important aspect of the process itself; . . . In guaranteeing freedoms such as those of speech and press, the First Amendment can be read as protecting the right of everyone to attend trials so as to give meaning to those explicit guarantees. "The First Amendment goes beyond protection of the press and the self-expression of individuals to prohibit government from limiting the stock of information from which members of the public may draw." Free speech carries with it some freedom to listen. . . . What this means in the context of trials is that the First Amendment guarantees of speech and press, standing alone, prohibit government from summarily closing courtroom doors which had long been open to the public at the time that Amendment was adopted. . . .

. . . It is not crucial whether we describe this right to attend criminal trials to hear, see, and communicate observations concerning them as a "right of access," or a "right to gather information," for we have recognized that "without some protection for seeking out the news, freedom of the press could be eviscerated." The explicit, guaranteed rights to speak and to publish concerning what takes place at a trial would lose much meaning if access to observe the trial could, as it was here, be foreclosed arbitrarily.

The right of access to places traditionally open to the public, as criminal trials have long been, may be seen as assured by the amalgam of the First Amendment guarantees of speech and press; and their affinity to the right of assembly is not without relevance. . . . [A] trial courtroom also is a public place where the people generally—and representatives of the media—have a right to be present, and where their presence historically has been thought to enhance the integrity and quality of what takes place.

The State argues that the Constitution nowhere spells out a guarantee for the right of the public to attend trials, and that, accordingly, no such right is protected. . . . But arguments such as the State makes have not precluded recognition of important rights not enumerated. . . . We hold that the right to attend criminal trials is implicit in the guarantees of the First Amendment; without the freedom to attend such trials, which people have exercised for centuries, important aspects of freedom of speech and "of the press could be eviscerated."

Having concluded there was a guaranteed right of the public under the First and Fourteenth Amendments to attend the trial of Stevenson's case, we return to the closure order challenged by appellants. . . . Despite the fact that this was the fourth trial of the accused, the trial judge made no findings to support closure; no inquiry was made as to whether alternative solutions would have met the need to ensure fairness; there was no recognition of any right under the Constitution for the public or press to attend the trial.

There exist in the context of the trial itself various tested alternatives to satisfy the constitutional demands of fairness. . . . There was no suggestion that any problems with witnesses could not have been dealt with by their exclusion from the courtroom or their sequestration during the trial. Nor is there anything to indicate that sequestration of the jurors would not have guarded against their being subjected to any improper information. All of the alternatives admittedly present difficulties for trial courts, but none of the factors relied on here was beyond the realm of the manageable. Absent an overriding interest articulated in findings, the trial of a criminal case must be open to the public. Accordingly, the judgment under review is

Reversed. . . .

JUSTICE JOHN PAUL STEVENS concurring:
This is a watershed case. Until today, the Court has accorded virtually absolute protection to the dissemination of information or ideas, but never before has it squarely held that the acquisition of newsworthy matter is entitled to any constitutional protection whatsoever. . . .

Today, however, for the first time, the Court unequivocally holds that an arbitrary interference with access to important information is an abridgment of the freedoms of speech and of the press protected by the First Amendment. . . .

. . . I agree that the First Amendment protects the public and the press from abridgment of their rights of access to information about the operation of their government, including the Judicial Branch; given the total absence of any record justification for the closure order entered in this case, that order violated the First Amendment.

JUSTICE WILLIAM BRENNAN, with whom JUSTICE THURGOOD MARSHALL joined, concurring:
. . . I agree with those of my Brethren who hold that, without more, agreement of the trial judge and the parties cannot constitutionally close a trial to the public.

While freedom of expression is made inviolate by the First Amendment, and, with only rare and stringent exceptions, may not be suppressed, the First Amendment has not been viewed by the Court in all settings as providing an equally categorical assurance of the correlative freedom of access to information. Yet the Court has not ruled out a public access component to the First Amendment in every circumstance. Read with care and in context, our decisions must therefore be understood as holding only that any privilege of access to governmental information is subject to a degree of restraint dictated by the nature of the information and countervailing interests in security or confidentiality. These cases neither comprehensively nor absolutely deny that public access to information may at times be implied by the First Amendment and the principles which animate it.

The Court's approach in right-of-access cases simply reflects the special nature of a claim of First Amendment right to gather information. . . . [T]he First Amendment . . . has a structural role to play in securing and fostering our republican system of self-government. Implicit in this structural role is not only "the principle that debate on public issues should be uninhibited, robust, and wide-open," but also the antecedent assumption that valuable public debate—as well as other civic behavior—must be informed. The structural model links the First Amendment to that process of communication necessary for a democracy to survive, and thus entails solicitude not only for communication itself, but also for the indispensable conditions of meaningful communication. . . .

First, the case for a right of access has special force when drawn from an enduring and vital tradition of public entree to particular proceedings or information. Such a tradition commands respect, in part, because the Constitution carries the gloss of history. More importantly, a tradition of accessibility implies the favorable judgment of experience. Second, the value of access must be measured in specifics. Analysis is not advanced by rhetorical statements that all information bears upon public issues; what is crucial in individual cases is whether access to a particular government process is important in terms of that very process.

To resolve the case before us, therefore, we must consult historical and current practice with respect to open trials, and weigh the importance of public access to the trial process itself. . . . [S]ignificantly for our present purpose, [the Court has] recognized that open trials are bulwarks of our free and democratic government: public access to court proceedings is one of the numerous "checks and balances" of our system, because "contemporaneous review in the forum of public opinion is an effective restraint on possible abuse of judicial power." Indeed, the Court focused with particularity upon the public trial guarantee "as a safeguard against any attempt to employ our courts as instruments of persecution," or "for the suppression of political and religious heresies." Thus, . . . open trials are indispensable to First Amendment political and religious freedoms. . . .

Publicity serves to advance several of the particular purposes of the trial (and, indeed, the judicial) process. . . . But, as a feature of our governing system

of justice, the trial process serves other, broadly political, interests, and public access advances these objectives as well. To that extent, trial access possesses specific structural significance. . . . Secrecy is profoundly inimical to this demonstrative purpose of the trial process. . . .

But the trial is more than a demonstrably just method of adjudicating disputes and protecting rights. . . . It follows that the conduct of the trial is preeminently a matter of public interest. . . .

. . . [R]esolution of First Amendment public access claims in individual cases must be strongly influenced by the weight of historical practice and by an assessment of the specific structural value of public access in the circumstances. With regard to the case at hand, our ingrained tradition of public trials and the importance of public access to the broader purposes of the trial process, tip the balance strongly toward the rule that trials be open. What countervailing interests might be sufficiently compelling to reverse this presumption of openness need not concern us now, for the statute at stake here authorizes trial closures at the unfettered discretion of the judge and parties. Accordingly, [the law] violates the First and Fourteenth Amendments, and the decision of the Virginia Supreme Court to the contrary should be reversed.

JUSTICE POTTER STEWART concurring:
. . . [The presumption of open criminal proceedings] does not mean that the First Amendment fight of members of the public and representatives of the press to attend civil and criminal trials is absolute. Just as a legislature may impose reasonable time, place, and manner restrictions upon the exercise of First Amendment freedoms, so may a trial judge impose reasonable limitations upon the unrestricted occupation of a courtroom by representatives of the press and members of the public. Much more than a city street, a trial courtroom must be a quiet and orderly place. Moreover, every courtroom has a finite physical capacity, and there may be occasions when not all who wish to attend a trial may do so. And while there exist many alternative ways to satisfy the constitutional demands of a

fair trial, those demands may also sometimes justify limitations upon the unrestricted presence of spectators in the courtroom.

Since, in the present case, the trial judge appears to have given no recognition to the right of representatives of the press and members of the public to be present at the Virginia murder trial over which he was presiding, the judgment under review must be reversed.

JUSTICE HARRY BLACKMUN concurring:

. . . I remain convinced that the right to a public trial is to be found where the Constitution explicitly placed it—in the Sixth Amendment.

The Court, however, has eschewed the Sixth Amendment route. The plurality turns to other possible constitutional sources and invokes a veritable potpourri of them—the Speech Clause of the First Amendment, the Press Clause, the Assembly Clause, the Ninth Amendment, and a cluster of penumbral guarantees recognized in past decisions. This course is troublesome, but it is the route that has been selected and, at least for now, we must live with it. . . .

. . . [W]ith the Sixth Amendment set to one side in this case, I am driven to conclude, as a secondary position, that the First Amendment must provide some measure of protection for public access to the trial. . . . It is clear and obvious to me, on the approach the Court has chosen to take, that, by closing this criminal trial, the trial judge abridged these First Amendment interests of the public.

I also would reverse, and I join the judgment of the Court.

JUSTICE WILLIAM REHNQUIST dissenting:

. . . I do not believe that either the First or Sixth Amendment, as made applicable to the States by the Fourteenth, requires that a State's reasons for denying public access to a trial, where both the prosecuting attorney and the defendant have consented to an order of closure approved by the judge, are subject to any additional constitutional review at our hands. . . .

The issue here is not whether the "right" to freedom of the press conferred by the First Amendment to the Constitution overrides the defendant's "right" to a fair trial conferred by other Amendments to the Constitution; it is, instead, whether any provision in the Constitution may fairly be read to prohibit what the trial judge in the Virginia state-court system did in this case. Being unable to find any such prohibition in the First, Sixth, Ninth, or any other Amendment to the United States Constitution, or in the Constitution itself, I dissent.

Broadband networks are the most powerful and pervasive connectivity in history. Broadband is reshaping our economy and recasting the patterns of our lives. . . . There are three simple keys to our broadband future. Broadband networks must be fast. Broadband networks must be fair. Broadband networks must be open.

—Former FCC Chair Tom Wheeler[1]

When comedian John Oliver aired a segment about net neutrality on his weekly show, his viewers generated 45,000 comments to the Federal Communications Commission and crashed the comment system.

9 ELECTRONIC MEDIA REGULATION
From Radio to the Internet

SUPPOSE . . .

. . . an author publishes a book that criticizes a politically conservative presidential candidate. In reviewing the book, a newspaper columnist says the author must be sympathetic to terrorist groups. Could the newspaper be forced to give the author space to reply to the columnist? No, the First Amendment protects the paper from being required to grant a reply (see Chapter 2). But if a radio or television station airs similar criticism of the author, could the author force the station to allow a reply? If so, what would the rationale be for the courts to uphold that requirement despite the First Amendment? What differentiates broadcast stations from other forms of media? Look for answers to these questions in the discussion of *Red Lion Broadcasting Co. Inc. v. Federal Communications Commission* and in the case excerpt at the end of the chapter.

Legal issues discussed in this book apply to the electronic and digital media just as they apply to the print media. In a 21st-century media environment, we think less about the distinction between electronic and print media because content is so readily available across a variety of platforms, including the internet. Yet, the distinction between electronic and print media is still important within mass communication law. The **electronic media**, particularly radio and television, must comply with regulations that are not applicable to print.

DEVELOPMENT OF BROADCAST REGULATION

electronic media
Broadcast and newer forms of media that utilize electronic technology or the digital encoding of information to distribute news and entertainment. Does not include media, like newspapers, historically distributed in printed form.

electromagnetic spectrum
The range of wavelengths or frequencies over which electromagnetic radiation extends.

Electronic media developed long after the United States adopted the First Amendment. In the late 19th century, European physicists began to understand how to use the electromagnetic spectrum to transmit signals. In 1888, a German physicist created the first electromagnetic radio waves in his lab. A few years later, British physicist Sir Oliver Lodge sent the first message using radio waves in Oxford, England. In 1897, Nikola Tesla, after whom Elon Musk named his global electric car company Tesla Motors, filed U.S. patents that explained how electrical energy could be transmitted without wires. He later realized that his patents could be used for wireless communication.[2]

At the turn of the 20th century, Italian inventor Guglielmo Marconi was sending radio signals across the Atlantic Ocean without using wires. He transmitted his signals using radio frequencies, which are part of the electromagnetic spectrum. At a basic level, the **electromagnetic spectrum** is made up of light waves and other types of energy that radiate from where they are produced—called electromagnetic radiation. Together, they form the electromagnetic spectrum, which includes the visible light that we see as well as electromagnetic waves we can't see, for example microwaves and radio waves.

In 1902, an American physicist and inventor applied his knowledge of telegraphs to advance radio tuning to try to overcome the problem of interference. A few years later, a Canadian engineer became the first person to transmit the human voice using radio waves. Subsequently, the invention of an electronic component by an American engineer named Lee de Forest allowed for the manufacture of smaller radios to spur radio's development. In what is hailed as the birth of public radio in the United States, de Forest transmitted the

LANDMARK CASES IN CONTEXT

Key ■ Event
◆ Cases

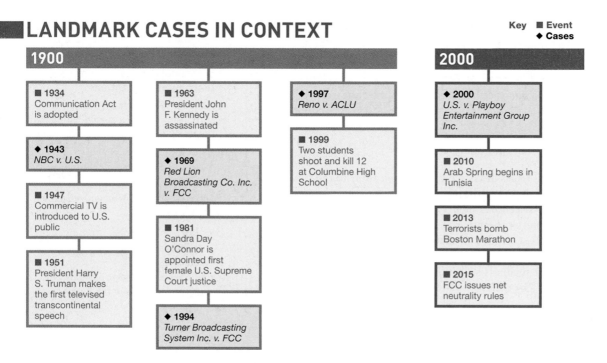

1900

■ 1934
Communication Act is adopted

◆ 1943
NBC v. U.S.

■ 1947
Commercial TV is introduced to U.S. public

■ 1951
President Harry S. Truman makes the first televised transcontinental speech

■ 1963
President John F. Kennedy is assassinated

◆ 1969
Red Lion Broadcasting Co. Inc. v. FCC

■ 1981
Sandra Day O'Connor is appointed first female U.S. Supreme Court justice

◆ 1994
Turner Broadcasting System Inc. v. FCC

◆ 1997
Reno v. ACLU

■ 1999
Two students shoot and kill 12 at Columbine High School

2000

◆ 2000
U.S. v. Playboy Entertainment Group Inc.

■ 2010
Arab Spring begins in Tunisia

■ 2013
Terrorists bomb Boston Marathon

■ 2015
FCC issues net neutrality rules

first public broadcast in New York City in 1910. The broadcast featured the voices of the Metropolitan Opera. Members of the public and the press used earphones to listen at locations across the city.[3]

As with most new technological innovations, these patent holders and creators soon worked to commercialize and profit from their inventions. At the time, a legal structure did not exist to regulate or manage radio transmissions. Often messages interfered with each other during this early period of experimentation, and it became clear to lawmakers that regulation was needed.

The Titanic.

Radio Regulation

Congress passed the first federal regulation of broadcast in 1910. The Wireless Ship Act required oceangoing vessels to carry radio equipment and operators, but Congress had not considered the law's impact on the spectrum, especially since the mandate had global implications for ships traveling across the ocean.[4] Other nations pressured Congress to establish standards that every country could adopt, allowing messages to reach their destinations without interference. Then tragedy struck. In 1912, the Titanic hit an iceberg, plunging thousands to their deaths. Many passengers could have been saved if a rescue ship had arrived. The Titanic sent a distress signal, but it did not reach authorities because of interference with the Titanic's signal and because the radio operator on the nearest ship was off-duty and did not hear the message.[5]

The Titanic disaster prompted Congress to pass the Radio Act of 1912, which required oceangoing ships to have radio operators on duty around the clock. It also gave the U.S. secretary of commerce power to grant radio station licenses, stipulating what frequency each licensee would use. A **radio frequency** is any one of the electromagnetic wave frequencies that lies within a specified range that is used for communication. The intent was to prevent message interference.[6]

However, the law did not give the secretary power to refuse a license or substantially regulate radio. Anyone applying for a license would get one, as long as no two applications were for the same frequency. The commerce secretary also had no authority to limit the power used to broadcast, which allowed the most powerful stations to drown out others. Amateur radio operators began ignoring the law, changing the frequencies they used and even relocating to other cities without the secretary's approval.[7]

During the 1920s, a number of commercial radio stations began broadcasting. Because radio was playing an increasingly important role in American commerce, Congress adopted the Radio Act of 1927 to solve these growing issues.[8] The law established the **Federal Radio Commission**, a federal agency charged with issuing or denying radio licenses and assigning frequencies to prevent stations from interfering with each other. The law gave the FRC the power to regulate stations as necessary to allow radio's development.

radio frequency Any one of the electromagnetic wave frequencies that lie in the range extending from around 3 kHz to 300 GHz, which includes those frequencies used for communications or radio signals.

Federal Radio Commission A federal agency established by the Radio Act of 1927 to oversee radio broadcasting. The Federal Communications Commission succeeded the Federal Radio Commission in 1934.

The 1927 law included several provisions that remain in effect today. First, the act said the FRC could not censor radio content. Second, it said the public, not station licensees, owned the spectrum. That is, the spectrum is considered a public resource. Because of this, the law required the FRC to make decisions based on the "public interest, convenience and necessity." A federal court interpreted the 1927 act to say the federal government, not the states, had exclusive control over radio broadcasting.[9]

Shortly after passing the 1927 act, Congress realized that radio needed continued oversight. In addition to the FRC, a number of different federal agencies had authority over various aspects of the radio industry. To resolve these problems, Congress rescinded the 1927 act and adopted the Communications Act of 1934.[10] Although often amended, the 1934 law is still in place. It gave the newly established **Federal Communications Commission** authority to regulate over-the-air radio and television, which was also an emerging broadcast

● REAL WORLD LAW

Radio Killed the Video Star?

Andrew Harrer/Bloomberg via Getty Images

The first video that MTV aired when it launched nearly 40 years ago was "Video Killed the Radio Star." Yet today, 93 percent of Americans—about 245 million people, over the age of 12—still listen to the radio. On average, they listen 12 hours per week.[1]

"[T]he future of digital media is being defined by the convergence of three forces: social, local and mobile," Federal Communications Commission Chairman Ajit Pai said recently. "[W]hoever can harness these three forces" is poised to "succeed in the digital future. Now, when you think about social, local, mobile, that's radio!" Pai added that radio is also vital to communities after a disaster when "over-the-air radio is a lifeline."[2]

Pai said that the FCC should continue to work on its AM Radio Revitalization Initiative that could help solve AM radio band technical problems and open up new markets for AM radio to better compete with FM and digital radio. In 2015, the FCC unanimously adopted a set of AM radio reforms designed to give AM stations more flexibility, for example the ability to purchase an FM translator in a secondary market.[3]

Not only are many forms of broadcast radio still popular today, but digital radio, especially music-streaming services on the internet, is well-positioned for substantial growth over the next decade. Currently, more than one-third of Americans use their mobile phones to stream music, and Pandora is one of the top five most popular apps in the United States. As Forbes magazine recently noted, "There has never been a more opportune time to maximize internet radio experiences."[4]

1. Ajit Pai, *Remarks of FCC Chairman Ajit Pai at the North American Broadcasters Association's Future of Radio and Audio Symposium*, FCC, Feb. 16, 2017, www.fcc.gov/document/chairman-pai-remarks-future-radio-and-audio-symposium.
2. *Id.*
3. *Id.*
4. David Porter, *Why Internet Radio Is the Biggest Advertising Opportunity of the Future*, FORBES, Mar. 18, 2015, www.forbes.com/sites/davidporter/2015/03/18/why-internet-radio-is-the-biggest-advertising-opportunity-of-the-future/#45bfcfc471af.

medium during this period. States still did not have the authority to regulate broadcasting. The 1934 act also allowed the commission to oversee long-distance telephone companies and other industries providing interstate communication services by wire.

Federal Communications Commission

The 1934 act established the FCC as an independent federal agency. The U.S. president selects the five commissioners, who are appointed to five-year terms. The president also designates one of the commissioners to be FCC chair—the commission's chief executive officer. The U.S. Senate must approve commissioner nominations, including the chair. No more than three sitting commissioners may be from the same political party. Commissioners may not have financial interests in any company or industry the FCC oversees and must be U.S. citizens. The FCC operates under the Administrative Procedure Act, a law telling federal agencies how they may propose and adopt regulations and giving federal courts power to rule on challenges to those decisions. Congress gives the FCC its funding, increasing or decreasing the budget each year as Congress chooses.

Today the commission's responsibilities include regulating all "interstate and international communications by radio, television, wire, satellite and cable." The FCC is the "primary authority for communications law, regulation and technological innovation . . . associated with rapidly evolving advances in global communications." The FCC not only enforces the Communications Act of 1934 and FCC rules, but it also notes that it encourages "the highest and best use of spectrum domestically and internationally," promotes "competition, innovation and investment in broadband services and facilities," and provides "leadership in strengthening the defense of the nation's communication infrastructure."[11] FCC rules cover a wide range of issues such as the sale of stolen cellphones and GPS devices, deceptive practices by telemarketers and even the loudness of television commercials.[12]

At the most basic level, the commissioners adopt rules and regulations. The process starts when commissioners identify an issue. FCC staff members prepare a **notice of proposed rulemaking** explaining what the commissioners plan to do and why. Members of the public, interested companies and industry organizations may submit comments to the commission. The FCC also provides an opportunity to submit replies that respond to the original submissions. FCC staff members consider all the submissions and draft a report and order. The commissioners discuss the draft, suggest changes and vote on a final version in a public meeting. Companies, organizations and individuals who object to the commission's final decision may ask the commissioners to reconsider. The FCC rarely will reconsider its decisions. The final regulations then become part of the FCC's rules.

Federal Communications Commission An independent U.S. government agency, directly responsible to Congress, charged with regulating interstate and international communications by radio, television, wire, satellite, cable and broadband. The Communications Act of 1934 established the Federal Communications Commission; its jurisdiction covers the 50 states, the District of Columbia and U.S. possessions.

AP/George R. Skadding

President Franklin D. Roosevelt signed the Communications Act of 1934.

● **REAL WORLD LAW**

The Current FCC

In 2017, President Donald Trump nominated sitting FCC Commissioner Ajit Pai to become the Federal Communications Commission chair. Before becoming a commissioner in 2012, Pai worked as a lawyer for the U.S. Department of Justice, the U.S. Senate, the FCC's Office of General Counsel and Verizon Communications.[1] Pai has said that as chair he will prioritize the following issues:

- Making broadband service available to all Americans. He proposes to do this in many ways and emphasizes that the wireless infrastructure in the United States needs to be streamlined and moved from big towers to small cells.

- Pushing for Next Generation 911, an internet-based system that Pai said will ensure that people can always reach emergency services.

- Implementing ways to make the FCC more efficient, including faster response to public petitions and reviewing various FCC rules he considers obsolete.[2]

In addition to Pai (a Republican), the other commissioners who remained in their positions after the election of President Trump are Mignon Clyburn (a Democrat in her second term) and Michael O'Reilly (a Republican in his second term). In August 2017, Congress confirmed the nominations of Brendan Carr, a Republican who most recently served as the FCC's general counsel under Pai, and former Democratic commissioner Jessica Rosenworcel.[3]

1. FCC, AJIT PAI BIO, www.fcc.gov/about/leadership/ajit-pai (last visited April 4, 2017).
2. *Id.*
3. David Oxenford, *A Full House at the FCC as Two "New" Commissioners Confirmed*, BROADCASTLAWBLOG.COM, Aug. 7, 2017, www.broadcastlawblog .com/2017/08/articles/a-full-house-at-the-fcc-as-two-new-commissioners-confirmed/?utm_source=David+Oxenford%2C+Esq+-+ Broadcast+Law+Blog&utm_medium=email&utm_campaign=87e37a82c6-RSS_EMAIL_CAMPAIGN&utm_term=0_550fd6c4c6- 87e37a82c6-70193957.

A company, an industry association or an individual affected by a commission decision may challenge the FCC policy in a federal appellate court. Usually the appeal is to the U.S. Court of Appeals for the District of Columbia Circuit, although other circuits also may hear an appeal of a commission decision. A federal court ruling overrides an FCC decision.

notice of proposed rulemaking A notice issued by the Federal Communications Commission announcing that the commission is considering changing certain of its regulations or adopting new rules.

The commission's rules have the effect of law. Companies, industries and individuals must comply with the FCC's rules or face sanctions. The commission has a range of possible punishments, from a letter of reprimand in a licensee's file, to a fine, to revoking or not renewing a license. Commonly, the FCC punishes by issuing a fine, called a "forfeiture."

One important responsibility of the FCC is to grant a license to broadcast. **Broadcasting** is formally defined by the Communications Act of 1934 as use of the electromagnetic spectrum to send signals to many listeners and viewers simultaneously.[13] It is not a broadcast when the CBS television network sends a signal to the CBS station in Des Moines, Iowa. That is a private transmission from the network to the station.[14] It is a broadcast when the Des Moines station sends the signal through its transmitter to thousands of television sets and to the local cable system. CBS, then, does not broadcast;

rather, the stations owned by or affiliated with CBS broadcast. The FCC's broadcast regulations apply to radio and television stations.

It is unlawful to operate any broadcast station in the United States without an FCC license, which is granted for an eight-year period and may be renewed for subsequent eight-year periods. Renewal is ensured unless the licensee has not operated in the public interest, has repeatedly violated FCC rules or has shown a pattern of abusing the law. There is no limit on the number of renewals a station owner may receive; a corporate owner may retain a station license as long as the corporation exists. An FCC license is not transferable: A licensee wanting to sell a broadcast station may sell the building, equipment, transmitter and trucks—but not the license. The FCC acts on behalf of the public in allowing a licensee to use the spectrum for the license period.

FCC Chair Ajit Pai.

If a frequency is not already used for broadcasting and two or more competing applicants want a license for the frequency, the FCC holds an auction.[15] The bidder offering to pay the government the most money is awarded the station license.

To obtain a license, an individual must be an American citizen.[16] A foreign corporation may not hold a license, nor may a corporation with more than 20 percent foreign ownership. A foreign government may not be a licensee, nor may a corporation controlled by another corporation with more than 25 percent foreign ownership.[17] These foreign ownership restrictions, first adopted in the 1927 law and continued in the 1934 act, were justified by national security concerns. Congress did not want U.S. media used for foreign propaganda.

For decades, the FCC also limited the number of stations a single licensee could own, both in one metropolitan area and nationally. Over time, the commission removed some and changed other ownership restrictions. For example, there now is no limit on how many radio stations one licensee may own nationally. A single company may own from five to eight radio stations in one metropolitan area, depending on the number of radio stations in that area.[18] One company may own television stations reaching a maximum of 39 percent of the country's television households[19] and may own two television stations in the same community if (1) no more than one of the stations is among the four highest-rated stations in the city and (2) at least eight independently owned commercial or noncommercial television stations remain in the community.[20] Also, one owner may have licenses for up to two television stations and, at the same time, from one to six radio stations in the same community, depending on how many independent media voices (primarily local broadcast stations and local newspapers) remain in the community.[21] FCC rules forbid a company from owning more than one of the top four broadcast television networks—that is: ABC, CBS, Fox and NBC.[22]

A commission rule applying only to the country's 20 largest metropolitan areas would allow a radio station licensee also to own a newspaper in the same city.[23] The FCC revised

broadcasting
Defined by the Communications Act of 1934 as use of the electromagnetic spectrum to send signals to many listeners and viewers simultaneously.

● **INTERNATIONAL LAW**

Expand Foreign Ownership?

FCC Commissioner Michael O'Reilly recently suggested that the commission consider reducing barriers to foreign investment in the U.S. communications marketplace. He noted that the FCC has the authority to permit a higher foreign ownership limit (above the current 25 percent cap) or to waive the limit altogether. O'Reilly argues that greater foreign investment in U.S. communications companies would provide new sources of funding for growth and job creation, add new diverse voices to the marketplace and help remove other international trade barriers.[1]

The FCC has chosen to consider broadcast licensee requests to exceed the cap on foreign investment on a case-by-case basis.

---

1. Michael O'Reilly, *Affirmatively Expand Permissible Foreign Ownership*, FCC Bʟᴏɢ, Mar. 3, 2015, www.fcc.gov/blog/affirmatively-expand-permissible-foreign-ownership.

its newspaper/broadcast cross-ownership rules in 2006, but a 2011 court decision and ongoing FCC reviews have maintained the ban on ownership of both a daily newspaper and a full-power broadcast station (radio or TV) in the same market.[24]

In 2014, the FCC voted 3–2 to adopt a rule to cut down on joint ad sales agreements among television stations. A joint ad sales agreement is an agreement between stations to jointly sell advertising. The FCC sees these agreements as unfair to small companies, especially new entrants, and as a way to circumvent the FCC's limit on owning more than one full-power television station in the same market.[25]

The FCC's 2014 rule barred companies from using one advertising sales staff for two or more stations in the same local market. It effectively meant that any television station that handled more than 15 percent of ad sales for another station would be considered to own both stations under FCC rules. The FCC allowed stations two years to seek a waiver to the rules or to unwind cooperative ad sales agreements. The FCC encouraged waivers to joint sales agreements that would enhance diversity in media ownership.

In 2016, the Third Circuit Court of Appeals struck down the 2014 rule, noting that the FCC expanded the reach of the ownership rules without first justifying the change in policy. Congress requires a quadrennial review process (occurring every four years). The 2010 and 2014 quadrennial reviews of the media ownership rules had not happened when the FCC issued the new joint sales rule in 2014.[26]

In 2016, the FCC also largely retained its media ownership rules, noting the continuing importance of newspapers and broadcast television stations as the predominant sources of local news and information. The FCC concluded that the existing newspaper/broadcast and the newspaper/radio cross-ownership limits remained necessary to protect the public interest in viewpoint diversity.[27]

The 2016 FCC order included a new rule encouraged to limit the number of new television acquisitions by some companies, but it did not require any companies to sell existing stations. Rather, the new rule could bar new acquisitions of television stations. In early 2017, new FCC Chair Ajit Pai said he expected the FCC to lose a legal challenge by

Twenty-First Century Fox to the 2016 rule that was pending in the U.S. Court of Appeals. The FCC said it would repeal the rule and would then "launch a comprehensive review of the national ownership cap" at the end of 2017.[28] The FCC's next quadrennial review proceeding, in which it will determine whether the broadcast ownership rules remain necessary to serving the public interest, is in 2018.

The broadcast and newspaper industries long have maintained that the FCC's ownership rules are overly burdensome in the fast-evolving and highly competitive media marketplace. Consumer interest groups have argued that the ownership rules are necessary to preserve the public interest in viewpoint diversity.

● REAL WORLD LAW

The Redskins Objection

Redskins owner Dan Snyder.

For many years, American Indians and others have protested the team name of the NFL's Washington Redskins. They argue that the word "redskins" is a highly offensive ethnic slur and the team's name should be changed. The team's owner, Dan Snyder, has refused and said the word is a tribute to American Indians' strength and courage.[1]

A George Washington University law professor filed a formal objection with the Federal Communications Commission, opposing the license renewal application of local Washington, D.C.–area radio station WWXX, also owned by Snyder. The law professor's petition said that WWXX's repeated broadcasting of the word "redskins" is profanity and a form of hate speech.[2]

One former FCC chair supported the petition, noting, "It is inappropriate for broadcasters to use racial epithets as part of normal, everyday reporting." But First Amendment scholar Eugene Volokh cited FCC and court decisions that hold that the First Amendment protects the broadcast of racial epithets despite their offensiveness.[3]

Ultimately, the FCC rejected the petition and concluded that "licensees have broad discretion—based on their right to free speech—to choose, in good faith, the programming they believe serves the needs and interests of their communities. This holds true even if the material broadcast is insulting to a particular minority or ethnic group in a station's community."[4]

1. Steve Lovelady, *Petitioner Wants FCC to Ref "Redskins" Debate*, CommLawBlog, Sept. 29, 2014, www.commlawblog.com/2014/09/articles/broadcast/petitioner-wants-fcc-to-ref-redskins-debate/.
2. *Id.*
3. Eugene Volokh, *No, the FCC May Not Ban the Use of "Redskins" on Radio and TV Broadcasting*, Wash. Post, Oct. 1, 2014, www.washingtonpost.com/news/volokh-conspiracy/wp/2014/10/01/no-the-fcc-may-not-ban-the-use-of-redskins-on-radio-and-tv-broadcasting/.
4. Mike Florio, *FCC Dismisses Petition Attacking Washington Name*, ProFootballTalk, Dec. 19, 2014, profootballtalk.nbcsports.com/2014/12/19/fcc-dismisses-petition-attacking-washington-name/.

Reasons to Regulate Broadcasting

Radio and television station licensees often tell courts there is no valid reason to regulate broadcasting because the First Amendment should apply equally to all mass media. The U.S. Supreme Court has rejected this argument in two ways. First, the Court's decisions have allowed for the different treatment of mass media under the First Amendment. The Court has held that movies, for example, do not have the same First Amendment rights as print media.[29] Each mass medium has its own peculiarities, although each has basic free speech protection, the Court has said (as discussed in Chapter 3).

Second, broadcasting uses the spectrum—a limited, publicly owned resource. Unlike print media or the internet—anyone with enough money can print a newspaper or publish a website—only a select few companies in a geographical area may use the spectrum.

Seventy-five years ago, the Supreme Court first established spectrum scarcity as the principal reason the government can regulate broadcasters.[30] In that case, the Court upheld the FCC's jurisdiction of broadcast networks. After the Communications Act of 1934 created the commission, radio station owners expected the FCC to prevent interference by carefully choosing licensees and controlling the power that stations used to broadcast. The commission took more control over the radio industry than expected. Among other decisions, the FCC adopted rules regulating the relationship between the emerging radio networks and local stations. The commission was concerned that networks exerted too much control over stations, requiring the stations to carry all network programs, for example. The networks sued the FCC, claiming that it overstepped its statutory responsibilities.

The U.S. Supreme Court supported the FCC. The Court said "the radio spectrum simply is not large enough to accommodate everybody." The few companies using the spectrum have a special privilege, making it reasonable to regulate them, the Court decided.[31]

The Court reinforced the spectrum scarcity rationale in *Red Lion Broadcasting Co. Inc. v. FCC* (excerpted at the end of this chapter). The Court upheld the FCC's rule requiring that a station offer free time to an individual personally attacked by comments made on air.[32] The audience's right to hear both sides of an issue was more important than the licensee's First Amendment freedom, according to the Court. The Court reiterated that the spectrum prevents everyone who wants to broadcast from doing so and that the spectrum is a public resource. As noted in Chapter 2, the Court ruled five years later that print media do not have the same right-of-reply requirement as broadcasters.[33]

spectrum scarcity
The limitation to the number of segments of the broadcast spectrum that may be used for radio or television in a specific geographical area without causing interference. Spectrum scarcity is the primary reason courts permit greater regulation of broadcasters than print media.

Spectrum scarcity remains the reason courts most often give for allowing broadcast regulation. Not everyone who wants a license to operate a television or radio station may have one because the spectrum has only enough room to accommodate a limited number of stations.

In continuing to use this reasoning, courts seem to ignore the development of direct broadcast satellite service, satellite radio, low-power radio and television stations (broadcasting signals available within a few miles of the transmitter), the internet and other emerging technologies. Although the Supreme Court has recognized the advent of newer technologies, it said the Court would not alter its spectrum scarcity rationale "without some signal from Congress or the FCC that technological developments have advanced so far that some revision of the system of broadcast regulation may be required."[34]

In addition to spectrum scarcity, courts use two other rationales to justify regulating radio and television. One is that the broadcast media are pervasive. Without regulation, children in particular could be exposed to inappropriate content.[35] A second reason is the perception that broadcast media have a greater influence on audiences—a "special impact"—than do print media.[36] Again, this rationale is especially concerned with children.

Although broadcasting remains the most regulated mass medium, the courts have permitted the FCC to roll back many regulations during the past three decades. However, the Supreme Court has yet to clearly state that spectrum scarcity is no longer a valid rationale for regulating over-the-air radio and television.

The Public Interest Standard

In the 1927 Radio Act and the 1934 Communications Act, Congress said the public interest comes before a station's interests. Both laws say federal regulation is to be guided by the "public interest, convenience and necessity."[37] But the law does not define the term "public interest." Through its first 50 years overseeing broadcasters, the FCC justified adopting regulations by citing public interest. Then in the 1980s, the commission said the public interest required deregulating the broadcast industry. The FCC's focus turned to the market rather than the commission to regulate broadcasting in the public interest. Then-FCC Chair Mark Fowler led the charge against regulation. Under Fowler and subsequent commission chairs, the FCC eliminated many program requirements, including rules obliging stations to survey their communities to determine programming preferences and limiting how many minutes per hour could be used for commercials.[38]

Even in the market-driven model, public interest considerations persist. One example is the rapid increase in use of smartphone and other technologies that requires substantial spectrum space. The FCC has spent the past few years exploring ways to reallocate the spectrum to accommodate consumers' pervasive use of **broadband** and other wireless technologies.[39] Broadband is a high-capacity transmission technique that uses a wide range of frequencies, which enables a large number of messages to be communicated simultaneously.

Five years ago Congress passed a law to create the First Responder Network Authority, commonly called FirstNet. FirstNet is a broadband network dedicated exclusively to the public safety community. Congress allocated spectrum and provided $7 billion to construct the secure FirstNet system of radio access networks in all U.S. localities. The 9/11 Commission recommended FirstNet in response to reports from police, firefighters, emergency medical personnel and others of many communication failures because they could not access broadband networks during the Sept. 11 terrorist attacks. Public safety officials' access to broadband was also a problem after Hurricane Katrina in New Orleans in 2005.[40]

broadband A high-capacity transmission technique that uses a wide range of frequencies, which enables a large number of messages to be communicated simultaneously.

U.S. Coast Guard

The U.S. Coast Guard surveys the damage to New Orleans from Hurricane Katrina in 2005.

▲ EMERGING LAW

Why Care About Spectrum Scarcity and the FCC?

In addition to radio and television broadcasts, your GPS, your exercise tracker, your smartphone and all other wireless communication devices use the spectrum. In the 21st century, the spectrum is crowded. It needs the Federal Communications Commission to help free up and reorganize space so you can continue to utilize all of the power and functionality of your wireless communication devices.

For almost 25 years, the FCC has conducted different kinds of auctions that allow companies to buy spectrum allocation. Recently, the FCC auctioned off a substantial amount of advanced wireless service (AWS-3) spectrum, freed up by transferring U.S. Defense Department and other government agencies to different bands. AWS-3 is the "high-frequency band" of the spectrum that carries lots of data but loses quality performance when it travels through building walls. A spectrum auction works like other auctions—spectrum goes to the highest bidder.[1]

Experts say the auction raised billions of dollars for the government and allows wireless providers to deliver faster networks to consumers.[2]

In 2017, the FCC is expected to conclude its incentive auction, which under the Spectrum Act of 2012 allowed the FCC to provide broadcasters with the ability to voluntarily relinquish their spectrum usage rights (in a reverse auction), then auction those rights to companies that need flexible-use wireless licenses in a forward auction. The FCC has used this process to "repack" the spectrum, reorganizing and reassigning broadcast television stations to channels in the TV band while allocating the blocks of cleared spectrum in the flexible wireless use band to wireless providers.[3]

The Spectrum Pipeline Act of 2015 also requires the FCC to hold more auctions to make additional spectrum available for mobile services by 2024.[4]

---

1. Roger Cheng, *The US Government's Wireless-Spectrum Auction: Why It Matters*, CNET, Oct. 19, 2014, www.cnet.com/news/the-us-government-is-auctioning-off-wireless-spectrum-why-you-should-care-faq/.
2. *Id.*
3. *How It Works: The Incentive Auction Explained*, FCC, April 4, 2017, www.fcc.gov/about-fcc/fcc-initiatives/incentive-auctions/how-it-works.
4. Bipartisan Budget Act of 2015, Pub. L. No. 114-74 §§ 1001-1008 (2015).

FirstNet has independent authority within the U.S. Department of Commerce.[41] As of 2014, FirstNet's Nationwide Public Safety Broadband Network was not complete, but emergency communications during the Boston Marathon bombing in 2013 showed the network's progress. Immediately after the bombings, the Boston Police Department was able to use social media to issue warnings and alerts to the public, and the FBI was able to receive information through video streams and tools like Google's Person Finder.[42] In 2016, the FCC put forth two notices of proposed rulemaking to seek comment on the process it will use for states that choose to deploy their own radio access network as part of FirstNet and on its order to relocate public safety stakeholders to a different band on the spectrum.[43]

fairness doctrine
The Federal Communications Commission rule requiring broadcast stations to air programs discussing public issues and include a variety of views about controversial issues of public importance.

Fairness Doctrine. In 1929, the FRC said radio stations should broadcast various views about public issues.[44] The FCC adopted regulations in 1949 stating how that policy, called the **fairness doctrine**, should be put into effect. Forty years later, in 1989, a federal appellate court allowed the doctrine to expire.

The FCC's 1949 rule said that television and radio stations must (1) air programs discussing public issues and (2) include a variety of views about controversial issues of public importance.[45] Different views did not have to be presented in one program, but the station's overall programming had to reflect important opinions about controversial topics. The commission justified the fairness doctrine by pointing to licensees' responsibilities to the public.[46] The U.S. Supreme Court upheld the doctrine in the 1969 *Red Lion* decision, saying that spectrum scarcity allowed the FCC to require broadcasters to present a variety of opinions.[47]

The FCC changed its rules in 1987, finding that the fairness doctrine violated broadcasters' First Amendment rights.[48] The commission said that broadcasters censored themselves under the fairness doctrine, choosing not to present discussions about important public issues rather than be forced to air a variety of opinions about those issues. In 1989, the D.C. Circuit Court of Appeals agreed with the broadcasters, and the fairness doctrine ended.[49]

Two features of the fairness doctrine formally remained on the books until recently. First, the commission's personal attack rule, the *Red Lion* decision's focus, required broadcast stations to provide free reply time to any person or group whose integrity, honesty or character was attacked on the air. The rule did not apply to public officials. Second, the political editorial rule required broadcasters to give free time for a legally qualified candidate to respond to an editorial opposing the candidate or promoting any of the candidate's rivals. In 2000, the D.C. Circuit said the FCC had not justified the rules and ordered their elimination.[50] Public stations still may not endorse or oppose a political candidate, although they may air editorials about public issues.[51] In 2011, then-FCC Chair Julius Genachowski formally eliminated the fairness doctrine, noting that the rule had not been enforced since the late 1980s.[52]

BROADCAST PROGRAM REGULATION

The FCC is not allowed to censor broadcast content.[53] But the FCC may set general programming rules, such as prohibiting hoaxes, requiring children's programming and regulating politicians' radio and television appearances.

Political Broadcasting

In both the 1927 and 1934 laws, Congress ensured that broadcasters could not favor one candidate for an elective office over another. Section 315 of the 1934 act guarantees equal opportunity rather than equal time to legally qualified candidates. Section 315 does not apply to ballot issues, such as referendums, state constitutional amendments, initiatives and recalls of elected officials.

"Equal opportunity" means all candidates are given the opportunity to reach approximately the same audience as an opponent. Being allowed to purchase a minute of time at midnight is not equal opportunity if the candidate's opponent purchased a minute at 9 p.m. Nor is being given one minute an equal opportunity if the candidate's opponent has used 30 minutes. Equal opportunity also means getting free time if a candidate's opponent appeared on a station or cable system without paying (with some exceptions, noted in "Exceptions to the Use Rule" later in this chapter).

Legally Qualified Candidate. FCC regulations explain that a legally qualified candidate is someone who has publicly announced a bid for office, has her or his name on the ballot or is a serious write-in candidate. The candidate also must be legally qualified to hold the office.[54]

In a closed primary election, Democrats oppose other Democrats for their party's nomination, and Republicans oppose other Republicans. But neither party's candidates oppose the other's, nor do they oppose independents or third-party candidates. Therefore, if a Democrat buys 60 seconds of advertising time on a radio station during a primary election period, a Republican running in the primary cannot invoke Section 315 to require the station to sell him or her a minute. During the general election, every legally qualified candidate may use the equal opportunity rule if another candidate for the office uses a broadcast station or cable system.

The Use Rule. Section 315's equal opportunity requirement applies when a legally qualified candidate uses a broadcast station or cable system. "Use" is defined as the candidate or the candidate's picture being seen or the candidate's voice being heard on a broadcast station or cable system. The broadcasting of a candidate's name without the candidate's picture or voice is not a use.

This applies to more than a candidate's commercials. If a candidate appears on a television station's outdoor recreation program to give a fly-fishing demonstration, the candidate has used the station. This is true even if the candidate does not mention that she is a candidate, discuss her platform or refer to politics in any way. Potential voters might have a more favorable impression of the candidate when she proves herself a fly-fishing expert instead of discussing her political platform in a commercial. Her legally qualified opponents, then, may request equal opportunity, or an equal amount of airtime for an equivalent price.

If one candidate uses the station or system without paying—for example, baking cookies as a guest on the station's cooking program—his opponents do not have to pay for their uses. Making one candidate pay while another gets free time is not equal opportunity. But if the first candidate pays for time, opponents also have to pay. Section 315 requires a station or system to charge politicians the **lowest unit rate**, equivalent to the rate the very best commercial advertiser pays.

lowest unit rate Generally a station's minimum advertising rate and the maximum rate a broadcaster or cable system may charge a politician for advertising time during the 45 days before primary elections and the 60 days before general elections.

Exceptions to the Use Rule. In 1959, Congress adopted four exceptions to the use rule. First, regularly scheduled news programs are exempt. This exemption was meant for local news programs. But when the commission defined this category as including "programs reporting about some area of current events, in a manner similar to more traditional newscasts,"[55] it also included such programs as "Entertainment Tonight"[56] and "Celebrity Justice."[57] If an anchor or reporter on a regularly scheduled news program is a legally qualified candidate for an elective office, equal opportunity will apply. If the reporter stays on the air in that role while running for office, all his or her opponents will be entitled to equivalent free airtime.

Second, regularly scheduled news interview programs are exempt. These must have been regularly scheduled for some time before the election. For example, scheduling four interview shows, one each week for a month before an election, does not qualify a program as "regularly scheduled." Although this exemption initially was for programs such as "Meet the Press" and "Face the Nation," the FCC has included "Jerry Springer"[58] and "The Howard Stern Show."[59]

● REAL WORLD LAW

Political Advertising and the 2016 Elections

Even though traditional advertising on television is declining, partially because of a continuing shift in viewing habits (for example, more people streaming shows via Netflix),[1] experts underscore the importance of advertising on local television to political campaigns.

According to one report, the content of Hillary Clinton's television ads and her failure to advertise on television early in key states may have been important factors in her loss to President Donald Trump—despite the fact that Clinton spent more money overall on television advertising than Trump.[2]

Nearly 60 percent of voters in swing states in 2016 said that TV was the top influencer in their voting decisions, more than all other platforms; 71 percent of voters said television caused them to be more aware of a candidate or an issue. A study by the Video Advertising Bureau said that 79 percent of undecided voters acknowledged that campaign advertising on television attracted their attention.[3] In total, experts believe that candidates for federal offices and their affiliated political action committees spent more than $4.4 billion in political advertising on television in 2016.[4]

1. Emily Steel & Sydney Ember, *Networks Fret as Ad Dollars Flow to Digital Media*, N.Y. TIMES, May 10, 2015, www.nytimes.com/2015/05/11/business/media/networks-fret-as-ad-dollars-flow-to-digital-media.html?ref=business&_r=0.
2. Steve Lanzano, *Local Broadcast TV Advertising Will Be Critical in 2018 Elections*, CAMPAIGNS & ELECTIONS, Apr. 3, 2017, www.campaignsandelections.com/campaign-insider/local-broadcast-tv-advertising-will-be-critical-in-2018-elections.
3. *Id.*
4. Danielle Kurtzleben, *2016 Campaigns Will Spend $4.4 Billion on TV Ads, but Why?* NPR, Aug. 19, 2015, www.npr.org/sections/itsallpolitics/2015/08/19/432759311/2016-campaign-tv-ad-spending.

Third, live coverage of bona fide news events is exempt. If a candidate's campaign speech is covered live, the candidate's on-air appearance will not be considered a use. Nor is it a use if candidates participate in a televised debate, no matter who sponsors the debate. Because debates are exempt from the use rule, the debate organizers may include and exclude any candidates they want.[60]

Fourth, candidates' appearances in documentaries do not trigger Section 315 if the appearance is incidental to the program's topic. For example, if a mayoral candidate is an expert on the state's tourist industry and appears in a documentary about that topic, it will not be considered a use. Of course, if the documentary is about the candidate's childhood in a housing project, his appearance would not be incidental to the program's topic and would be a use.

Invoking Section 315. A candidate wanting equal opportunity must request time from the station or cable system within seven days of his opponent's appearance. If the candidate fails to make a request within the seven-day period, the station or system need not honor a request for equal opportunity. The station or cable system is under no obligation to notify opponents of a political candidate's use of the station.

To reduce negative political advertising, a 2002 federal law requires candidates to promise stations they will refer to their opponents in a commercial only under specific conditions. To refer to an opponent, a candidate's (1) radio commercial must include

the candidate's voice approving the commercial's contents or (2) television commercial must show the candidate or the candidate's picture with a printed statement approving the commercial. If a candidate mentions an opponent and these requirements are not met, the lowest unit rate will not apply.[61]

The lowest unit rate is in effect during the 45 days before any primary election and the 60 days before any general election. Outside those periods, political candidates are charged a rate comparable to other advertisers.

This ad from the 2016 U.S. presidential election prominently displays the sponsorship identification required by the Federal Communications Commission.

FCC regulations also require any commercial on a broadcast station to identify who paid for the ad.[62] This rule applies to political advertisements as well. A candidate's ad, then, must say on radio or show in print for a televised ad something like "This advertisement paid for by the Pat Smith for Congress Committee."

Reasonable Time for Federal Candidates. Broadcast stations and cable systems cannot edit or censor political appearances. Because stations are not permitted to edit or censor, they also are not responsible for what candidates say. For example, if a candidate libels his opponent, the opponent may sue the candidate but not the station.[63] It is possible for a station to avoid all the complications of political broadcasting by never putting candidates on the air. If the first legally qualified candidate running for an office does not appear on a station, Section 315 would not be triggered for other candidates. Although this is legal under Section 315, the FCC has suggested stations should allow candidates airtime because it is in the public interest.

Congress recognized this Section 315 loophole and decided to close it—at least for itself. Section 312(a)(7) of the Communications Act requires radio and television stations to provide federal candidates with reasonable access.[64] This means even the first candidate for a federal office asking to buy commercial time must be sold the advertising spot.[65] The federal elective offices are senator, representative and president. Although the law does not specifically state that it applies to cable systems, the FCC assumes it does. Section 312(a)(7) exempts noncommercial stations from complying with the section's requirements.

Section 312(a)(7)'s requirement that commercial stations provide candidates for federal office with "reasonable access" is not clear. The U.S. Supreme Court, rejecting CBS Television Network's decision not to sell President Jimmy Carter 30 minutes of prime time, gave only limited direction in interpreting the statute.[66] Broadcasters must consider each federal candidate's request "on an individualized basis, and broadcasters are required to tailor their responses to accommodate, as much as reasonably possible, a candidate's stated purposes in seeking air time." However, broadcasters also may "give weight to such factors as the amount of time previously sold to the candidate, the disruptive impact on regular programming and the likelihood of requests for time by rival candidates."[67] Broadcasters may not use these criteria as an excuse to deny federal candidates the time requested. Rather, "broadcasters must cite a realistic danger of substantial program disruption" or the likelihood of too many requests.[68]

Aside from being assured they can get on the air, federal candidates are treated under Section 315 just as candidates for state and local offices are.

Candidates' Supporters. The FCC has determined that an opposing candidate's supporters may ask for equal opportunity under the same standards that Section 315 requires when the candidate's supporters use airtime. This means the candidate himor herself cannot ask for equal opportunity if his or her opponent's supporters use a station, but the candidate's supporters can ask for time. This is called the **Zapple rule**, named after a congressional staff attorney who first asked the FCC about these circumstances.

Zapple rule
A political broadcasting rule that allows a candidate's supporters equal opportunity to use broadcast stations if the candidate's opponents' supporters use the stations.

527 Groups. A 527 group is established by a section of the federal tax code exempting the organizations from paying taxes on contributions they receive.[69] Unlike a political action committee, a 527 group focuses on issues and not directly endorsing or opposing candidates. There are no limits on the amount of contributions an individual or business may give to a 527 group, unlike PACs, which are subject to limits. For example, in 2012, Fred Eshelman, founder of Pharmaceutical Product Development Inc., contributed more than $4 million to the conservative 572 group RightChange.com.[70]

527 groups may purchase advertisements focusing on political issues but may not support or oppose individual candidates for elective office. A 527 group could urge people to vote, for example. Neither the Federal Election Commission nor state election commissions oversee 527 groups unless a group supports or opposes a candidate. In 2006 and 2007, the FEC fined several 527 groups for violating the tax code rules during the 2004 presidential election. For example, Swift Boat Veterans for Truth spent $22.6 million on television ads opposing John Kerry, the Democratic presidential candidate, and MoveOn .org, a politically liberal group, opposed Republican George W. Bush's re-election. The FEC said that, as 527 groups, neither should have attempted to influence the presidential election.[71]

Children's Programming

In 1990, Congress passed the Children's Television Act.[72] The law sets general requirements for children's programming on broadcast television stations. The law also limits commercial time before, during and after children's programs on broadcast and cable television.

The statute requires broadcast television stations to provide programming intended for children up to 17 years old that meets their "educational and informational needs."[73] Before, during and after programming specifically meant for children 12 years old and younger, advertising is limited to 12 minutes per hour during the week and 10 1/2 minutes per hour on the weekends. These limits are prorated—a half-hour program may have six minutes of commercials on a weekday afternoon, for example. The FCC also has

The long-running and popular children's show "Sesame Street" has aired on PBS since its inception in 1969. In 2016, the show moved its first-run episodes to HBO. After a nine-month exclusivity window for first-run episodes, the show will then air on PBS member stations at no charge.

ruled that characters in children's programs cannot appear in commercials before, during or after those programs.[74] Cartoon characters in children's programs or children's program hosts also may not sell products in commercials during or adjacent to shows in which the character or host appears.[75] In the context of digital television, the commission's rules prevent displaying a website address during a children's show if the website uses the show's characters to sell products or the site offers products featuring the show's characters.

The FCC allowed individual stations to decide how much children's programming stations must carry[76] until 1996 when it adopted standards for complying with the 1990 law.[77] The commission ruled that broadcast television stations must carry three hours per week, averaged over a six-month period, of programming specifically intended to meet children's intellectual/cognitive and social/emotional needs. The programs must be at least 30 minutes long, regularly scheduled weekly and broadcast between 7 a.m. and 10 p.m. local time. The commission identifies this as "core programming."

A station not meeting the core programming standard may substitute shorter programs, public service announcements for children and programs not scheduled weekly. The FCC may choose not to renew a station's license if it does not meet the requirements. The FCC has said its children's programming rules are "reasonable, viewpoint-neutral" requirements for licensees who must operate in the public interest. Because the commission does not "tell licensees what topics they must address," the FCC is not acting as a censor, the commission said.[78]

With the enactment of the Child Safe Viewing Act of 2007, the FCC began to explore blocking technologies that could apply to devices other than television. CTIA, a wireless association, has also developed voluntary guidelines for classifying content as generally accessible (available to all ages) or restricted (for people 18 or older). Parents may use the guidelines to block the purchase of restricted content via some wireless service providers, but they do not yet have a way to restrict access to content generally available on the internet. The FCC said it supports industry efforts to help consumers manage the content their children can access on a mobile device or through social media, but it does not endorse or develop these specific guidelines.[79]

Hoaxes

FCC rules forbid stations to broadcast a hoax, which means knowingly broadcasting false reports of crimes or catastrophes that "directly cause" foreseeable, "immediate, substantial and actual public harm."[80] The Radio Act of 1912 made it illegal to transmit a false distress signal or fraudulent signal of any kind.[81] The Radio Act of 1927[82] and the Communications Act of 1934[83] were more limited, prohibiting false distress signals. Although that regulation remains in place today, the FCC adopted the current ban on broadcast hoaxes in 1992.

The most famous broadcast hoax was actually a radio drama. Orson Welles directed and starred in a radio broadcast based on H.G. Wells' novel "The War of the Worlds," which aired nationwide the night before Halloween in 1938. The radio drama described Martian monsters emerging from a meteor that landed in New Jersey. Despite Welles breaking in four times to say the broadcast was fictional, the program sounded real to many listeners. People ran from their homes, cars jammed streets, hospitals treated hysterical listeners and police station telephones were clogged with calls.[84] Some writers argue that newspaper stories exaggerated the public panic,[85] yet the FCC was sufficiently concerned to promise an inquiry. However, because the drama was not a false signal, the commissioners had no grounds to take any action.[86]

Almost 45 years later, the commission adopted a rule prohibiting the broadcast of false information concerning a crime or catastrophe if the station knows the story is false, it is foreseeable the broadcast will cause substantial public harm and harm does result. Public harm includes police and other public safety officials being diverted from their duties in reaction to a false broadcast.[87] The FCC has heard of very few incidents since 1992 that could be considered hoaxes and has not punished a single station under the new rule.

● REAL WORLD LAW

Emergency Alert: Zombie Attack?

"Civil authorities in your area have reported that the bodies of the dead are rising from the grave and attacking the living."[1] This is what viewers of some television stations in Michigan and Montana heard over the emergency alert system in 2013 after hackers broke into vulnerable EAS equipment with unsecured passwords. Following the attack on a handful of stations, the Federal Communications Commission ordered all broadcasters to inspect their systems, change their EAS passwords and properly secure equipment behind firewalls.

A hardware security analyst told the Chicago Tribune that he found at least 30 systems vulnerable to a similar attack. Another cybersecurity expert said that undermining the EAS would compromise the government's ability to communicate with the public in times of crisis. "While EAS may not control nuclear power or hydroelectric dams or air traffic control, it can be used to cause widespread panic," he said.[2]

1. *Zombie Hack Blamed on Easy Passwords*, Chi. Trib., Feb. 14, 2013, articles.chicagotribune.com/2013-02-14/business/chi-zombie-hack-blamed-on-easy-passwords-20130214_1_karole-white-ioactive-labs-passwords.
2. *Id.*

Public Broadcasting

The FCC oversees public broadcasting stations, which must comply with most of the same rules commercial broadcasters follow. Public stations do not carry advertising.[88] However, corporations and individuals make financial contributions to noncommercial stations and may receive on-air acknowledgments of those contributions.[89] A federal district court decision in California upheld this advertising ban. The FCC fined a public television station in San Francisco for what the commission said amounted to paid ads. The license holder of the station, Minority Television Project, appealed the fine and also challenged the law that prohibits all advertising—both political and commercial—on public television. The Ninth Circuit Court of Appeals upheld the lower court decision that supported the ban on all ads on noncommercial stations.[90]

Public stations receive funding from the Corporation for Public Broadcasting, established by The Public Broadcasting Act. Congress allocates money to the CPB, which also receives funds from other sources. The act says public stations must strictly adhere to "objectivity and balance in all programs or series of programs of a controversial nature."[91] Despite the Public Broadcasting Act's "objectivity" language, the Supreme Court has allowed public stations to air editorials favoring or opposing public and political issues.[92] Public stations have "important journalistic freedoms which the First Amendment jealously protects," the Court said.[93] The CPB helps support NPR and PBS, which provide programming to public television stations. In 2017, President Trump proposed the elimination of federal funding of the CPB.[94]

DEVELOPMENT OF CABLE AND SATELLITE REGULATION

Cable systems send signals through a wire—coaxial cable or fiber-optic lines—and do not use the spectrum. Cable television emerged because some people could not get a broadcast television signal, particularly in rural areas. In the 1940s, a power company employee built a large antenna in the Appalachian Mountains of Pennsylvania that received signals from Philadelphia television stations. A wire ran from the antenna to a building and from there to homes, giving birth to cable television.[95] For decades, it was called "community antenna television" or CATV.

Initially, the FCC decided it had no jurisdiction over CATV.[96] But broadcast television station owners feared CATV could take away their viewers and advertisers and urged the FCC to reconsider. In 1962, noting that some CATV operators used microwaves—hence spectrum—to transmit signals from stations to cable system antennas, the FCC decided it had jurisdiction over at least part of the CATV business.[97] When the commission adopted several CATV rules, cable operators challenged the commission's authority to control CATV, but the U.S. Supreme Court upheld the FCC's jurisdiction.[98] The Court said that because the commission was responsible for protecting the public's interest in broadcasting, it had the right to oversee CATV as ancillary to its responsibility toward broadcasting.

FCC rule changes in the mid-1970s allowed cable systems to move beyond delivery of local television signals to carry the signals of stations outside the local community. For example, HBO began a pay cable service in 1975. With distant station signals and HBO, cable television could offer programming not available on local television stations.

By the 1980s, controversy surrounded cable television. Communities wanted to regulate cable, arguing that system wires ran over public streets and sidewalks, and telephone companies wanted to offer cable services throughout the country. Cable operators did not want regulation. Trying to strike a compromise, Congress adopted the Cable Communications Policy Act of 1984.[99] The law gave local and state governments and the federal government shared authority over cable.

A few years later, critics said the 1984 law gave the cable industry monopoly power in communities and allowed cable companies to raise rates without limit, provide poor customer service and prevent competition. Congress responded by re-regulating cable in the Cable Television Consumer Protection and Competition Act of 1992.[100] The 1992 law regulated rates cable systems charged subscribers. It also required cable systems to carry local broadcast television stations and to deliver other programming, such as ESPN and MTV, to direct broadcast satellite companies and other cable competitors. The law also barred local governments from allowing one cable system to monopolize service if others wanted to compete.

Then Congress adopted the Telecommunications Act of 1996, loosening many of the cable regulations imposed in 1992.[101] Designed primarily to foster competition in the telephone industry, the 1996 law also deregulated cable subscriber rates, again allowing cable companies to raise most prices without government permission. The basic, lowest-level programming package remains rate regulated for most cable systems. The law also allows cable companies to offer local telephone service.

The 1984, 1992 and 1996 laws did not define cable's First Amendment status. The Supreme Court once decided the cable industry had protection similar to the print media,[102] then suggested it was not certain what First Amendment analysis applied to cable television[103] and finally applied strict scrutiny to cable content regulations.[104]

In ruling on cable's challenge to must-carry rules—regulations that require cable systems to transmit local broadcast television stations—the Supreme Court said cable sends signals by wire, not through the air. Therefore, the spectrum scarcity rationale behind broadcast regulation does not apply to cable. Nearly 25 years ago, in *Turner Broadcasting System Inc. v. FCC* (excerpted at the end of this chapter), the Court applied the First Amendment test it uses for print media to cable: If the regulation affects speech because of its content, apply strict scrutiny; if the regulation is content neutral, apply an intermediate standard.[105] (Strict scrutiny and intermediate scrutiny are discussed in Chapter 2.)

Two years after the *Turner Broadcasting* decision, in *Denver Area Educational Telecommunications Consortium Inc. v. FCC*, the Supreme Court could not agree on what First Amendment test to use for cable.[106] The Court did not clearly establish the First Amendment status of cable when it overturned a law allowing cable companies to reject sexually offensive material on certain channels.[107] Then in 2000, the Court justified regulation of adult programming on cable to protect children who might be exposed when cable's signal "bled" onto an adjacent channel. In *United States v. Playboy Entertainment Group Inc.*, the Court unanimously agreed that although shielding children from adult programming is a compelling governmental interest, the law was unconstitutional because an alternative exists: Subscribers can tell their cable company to block the adult channel's signal before it reaches their home.[108]

In the 1996 law under challenge, Congress had offered cable systems two options: First, they could fully scramble adult channels' signals so programming could not be seen even if the signals bled. Second, they could carry adult programming only late at night when most children were not watching.[109] But all nine Supreme Court justices said the restriction was content based because it applied only to sexually explicit programming. The Court struck down the law under strict scrutiny review, the Court's most rigorous test to protect a speaker's First Amendment rights.

In 2016, the FCC voted to propose new set-top box rules that would provide more equipment options to consumers. The cable industry strongly opposed the new rules and then-FCC Chair Tom Wheeler's pledge to "Unlock the Box." With the change in control of the FCC from Democrats to Republicans, legal experts predict the initiative may go away.[110]

Just as the emergence of cable required the FCC to consider its role in regulation, so did the emergence of direct broadcast satellite services to consumers. More than 34 million American households receive their television programming by subscribing to a DBS service.[111] DBS uses a small dish attached to a roof or the side of a house to receive signals from a high-powered satellite.

Years ago, the FCC encouraged DBS service to develop as a cable competitor by declining to classify satellite service as broadcasting. The commission's decision relieved DBS of the regulatory burdens that broadcasters, and to some extent cable, face. The commission instead categorized DBS as a point-to-multipoint nonbroadcast service, a ruling upheld in court.[112] Dissatisfied with the FCC's decision not to impose regulations on DBS, Congress passed the Cable Television Consumer Protection and Competition Act of 1992. The law required DBS providers to abide by the political broadcasting rules in Sections 315 and 312(a)(7).

DBS emerged as a challenger to cable's dominance when Congress allowed satellite services to offer subscribers their local television stations as well as satellite programming.[113] As DBS grew, the FCC imposed additional regulations. For example, the FCC required satellite operators to set aside 4 percent of their channel capacity for educational or informational programming.[114] The commission said carrying noncommercial or public broadcast stations would not satisfy this requirement. The FCC also required DBS systems to comply with the same advertising limits during children's programming the commission applied to broadcast television stations.[115]

In 2016, the FCC voted to propose new set-top box rules that would provide more equipment options to consumers. The cable industry strongly opposed the new rules and then-FCC Chair Tom Wheeler's pledged to "Unlock the Box." With the change in control of the FCC from Democrats to Republicans, legal experts predict the initiative may go away.

multichannel video programming distributors An entity, including cable or direct broadcast satellite services, that makes multiple channels of video programming available for purchase.

MULTICHANNEL VIDEO PROGRAMMING DISTRIBUTORS REGULATION

Today, the FCC defines both cable and DBS services as **multichannel video programming distributors**, or MVPDs. An MVPD is an entity that makes available for purchase multiple channels of video programming. In its most recent annual assessment to Congress, the FCC noted that its data show that cable accounts for 52.8 percent, DBS accounts for 33.8 percent and telephone accounts for 13 percent of all MVPD subscribers. Cable subscribers are declining, while DBS subscribers are holding steady and phone MVPD subscribers are increasing, with AT&T and Verizon emerging as the largest players.[116]

According to the FCC, the major MVPDs today offer hundreds of linear television channels and thousands of nonlinear video-on-demand and pay-per-view programs. In addition to delivering video programming to television sets, MVPDs deliver video programming to computer screens, tablets and mobile devices. The FCC notes that MVPDs also offer internet and phone services as core elements of their business models.[117]

Must-Carry and Retransmission Consent

The Cable Television Consumer Protection and Competition Act of 1992 contained two provisions that required the carriage of broadcast stations on cable, DBS and all MVPD systems—the **must-carry rule** and **retransmission consent**. The 1992 law prohibits these providers from retransmitting a broadcast station without the broadcaster's explicit permission. The law instead gives the broadcaster the ability to negotiate with the MVPD for carriage. When the 1992 law passed, broadcast programming was the most popular content available on cable and DBS systems. One of the key concepts behind retransmission consent was the idea that broadcasters like ABC or CBS were producing popular content carried on large cable systems such as Comcast and Time Warner, but very few consumers received their broadcast programs over the air using an antenna. This meant that the broadcasters did not receive advertising revenue for their programming. The 1992 law allowed broadcasters to negotiate with cable systems to permit retransmission of their content generally for a fee and did not give the FCC authority to force broadcasters to consent to carriage.[118]

Because not all broadcast channels were popular enough to be sought after by an MVPD, the law also granted broadcasters the option to require MVPDs to carry their programming rather than negotiating for retransmission. Must-carry, also called the cable carriage requirement, means that if a broadcast station chooses must-carry status it may not be dropped from an MVPD's channel lineup. By asserting its must-carry rights, the broadcaster cannot demand payment for its content from the system operator.

Every three years, commercial broadcast stations choose between must-carry and retransmission consent. Noncommercial stations may not choose retransmission consent; they are carried under the must-carry provision.

In the 1990s, the cable industry fought the must-carry rule in court. Cable companies argued that a system can carry only a limited number of networks. Finding room to carry a local station's signal could force a cable system to eliminate other programming it already was carrying—Food Network, for example. Cable companies also said the must-carry rules were content-specific regulations, forcing cable to choose a local station over some other programming. Congress would have to show it had a compelling interest to justify imposing a content-specific rule, cable companies argued, and no such compelling interest existed.

must-carry rule Regulations enacted under the federal cable law that require multichannel video programming distributors to transmit local broadcast television stations.

retransmission consent Part of the federal cable law allowing broadcast stations to negotiate.

In the second *Turner Broadcasting System Inc. v. FCC* decision, in 1997, the Supreme Court refused to accept the cable industry's argument that the must-carry rules were content specific.[119] The must-carry rules are content neutral because they do not dictate specific programming, the Court said. To determine the rules' constitutionality, the Court applied the test it established in *United States v. O'Brien*, discussed in Chapter 2.[120] The *O'Brien* test applies to regulations incidentally affecting speech when that is not the regulation's primary purpose. The rules protect broadcast stations, which is an important objective, the Court said. In enacting them, Congress did not intend to directly affect cable systems' speech. Rather, Congress needed to adopt the rules to achieve its purpose of ensuring consumers' access to local broadcast stations.

When the cable industry again challenged the must-carry rules, the U.S. Court of Appeals for the Second Circuit rejected the argument that must-carry rules violate cable operators' First Amendment rights.[121] The U.S. Supreme Court refused to hear the case.

In 2015, the FCC implemented the requirements of the Satellite Television Extension and Localism Act Reauthorization Act of 2014, which aimed to modernize the must-carry and retransmission consent rules but maintain the basic framework of the 1992 Cable Act.[122]

▲ EMERGING LAW

Next-Generation TV?

In 2017, the Federal Communications Commission gave the go-ahead for the voluntary adoption of ATSC 3.0, a new broadcast transmission standard. The FCC's Advanced Television Systems Committee developed the new standard, which gives broadcasters the ability to support interactivity, a superior picture (4K), targeted advertising and content, transmission to mobile devices and the integration of broadcast programming with other internet protocol services.[1]

FCC Chair Ajit Pai said the new standard, supported by broadcasters, would also allow for ultra-high definition and immersive audio, better access to content for the disabled and the development of a substantially more advanced emergency alert system. Commissioner Michael O'Reilly said the new transmission standard opens "the door to innovation."[2]

FCC Commissioner Mignon Clyburn said that if the new standard is required, she will worry about the maintenance of the older ATSC 1.0 standard for stations that cannot afford to make the switch to ATSC 3.0. She also said the new standard might disadvantage multichannel video programming distributors that do not want to carry the new standard.[3]

The FCC is expected to issue the final order on ATSC 3.0, also called "next-generation television," in late 2017. In the meantime, broadcasters may simulcast in both the current and new standard during the rollout, and MVPDs must continue to carry the existing, but not new, ATSC transmission standard.[4]

1. Kathleen Kirby, *Developments in Electronic Media Regulation*, Comm. Law. Digital Age 2016 (2016).
2. John Eggerton, *FCC's Pai Proposes ATSC 3.0 Rollout*, Broadcasting & Cable, Feb. 2, 2017, www.broadcastingcable.com/news/washington/fccs-pai-proposes-atsc-30-rollout/163020.
3. John Eggerton, *FCC Unanimously Approves ATSC 3.0 Rollout Proposal*, Multichannel News, Feb. 23, 2017, www.multichannel.com/news/policy/fcc-unanimously-approves-atsc-30-rollout-proposal/411086.
4. *Media Bureau Seeks Comment on Joint Petition for Rulemaking of America's Public Television Stations, The AWARN Alliance, The Consumer Technology Association, and The National Association of Broadcasters Seeking to Authorize Permissive Use of the "Next Generation TV" Broadcast Television Standard*, Public Notice, GN Docket No. 16-142, DA 16-451 (rel. Apr. 26, 2016).

Specifically, the law added a new **satellite market modification rule**, which allows a television station, satellite operator or county government to request the addition or deletion of communities from a broadcast station's local television market to better reflect current market realities. For example, in many communities existing satellite delivery of a local broadcast television station doesn't exist because it is not technically or economically feasible. When the FCC receives a market modification request, it considers five factors that would allow a petitioner to demonstrate they provide local service to the community, including the consideration of access to television stations located in the same state.[123]

The Federal Communications Commission has regulatory power over emerging internet-based video services like Sling TV because these services use a high-speed internet connection to deliver video content to consumers.

Additionally, the FCC initiated a review of the current process for evaluating whether broadcasters and MVPDs are negotiating for retransmission consent in good faith. The goal of the review of the retransmission consent rule is to ensure that negotiations are conducted fairly and "in a way that benefits consumers of video programming services."[124]

Public Access Channels

By the time Congress adopted the Cable Communications Policy Act of 1984, most cable franchises already included provisions for public, educational or governmental access channels. The 1984 statute made that reality the law. Congress saw **PEG access channels** as a way to allow the public, various educational institutions and local governments to have cable system access in ways Congress does not provide for newspapers, magazines, radio and television stations and other mass media. The 1984 law permits a cable company to set aside channels for public, educational or governmental use.[125] Although the law does not require cable system operators to agree, they usually do.

Public access channels generally allow local citizens, on a first-come basis, to put on programming they choose. Many municipalities have a government official or nonprofit organization oversee public channel programming.[126] Local school boards and colleges use educational channels. Government channels often carry city council and county board meetings. The 1984 cable act prohibits cable system operators from exercising any editorial control over PEG or leased access programming.[127]

The Cable Television Consumer Protection and Competition Act of 1992 also required DBS operators to offer leased access channels for noncommercial educational purposes,[128] but a federal appellate court rejected the PEG and leased access requirements as infringing on DBS providers' First Amendment rights.[129]

INTERNET REGULATION

The FCC has considered its role in internet regulation since 2005. Acknowledging Congress had not given the commission explicit authority over the internet, the FCC said

satellite market modification rule Part of the Satellite Television Extension and Localism Act Reauthorization Act of 2014 that allows a television station, satellite operator or county government to request the addition or deletion of communities from a broadcast station's local television market.

● REAL WORLD LAW

FCC Overturns Sports Blackout Rules

Recently, the Federal Communications Commission ended its 40-year enforcement of sports blackout rules, meaning it would allow multichannel video program distributors to transmit sports programming even if a sports event was blacked out on a local broadcast station. According to the FCC, "This action removes Commission protection of the private blackout policies of sports leagues, which require local broadcast stations to black out a game if a team does not sell a certain percentage of tickets by a certain time prior to the game."[1]

The FCC said the decision offers transparency to sports fans and allows sports leagues to choose to continue the blackout policies through private agreements with programming distributors. In the absence of FCC rules, MVPDs must still obtain the necessary rights to distribute a sporting event from an alternative source.[2]

---

1. FCC, GUIDE TO SPORTS BLACKOUTS, www.fcc.gov/guides/sports-blackouts (last visited Aug. 2, 2017).
2. Kathleen Kirby, *Communication Law 2016*, COMM. LAW IN DIGITAL AGE 2016 (2016).

PEG access channels
Channels that cable systems set aside for public, educational and government use.

it had ancillary jurisdiction under the Communications Act of 1934.[130] As noted earlier in the chapter, years before Congress adopted the first cable television law in 1984, the U.S. Supreme Court held that the 1934 act's language gave the FCC jurisdiction over cable as "ancillary" to its statutory right to regulate broadcasting.[131]

Although initially the FCC took a "hands off the internet" approach, more recently it claimed ancillary jurisdiction over broadband. The FCC's claim of jurisdiction over broadband has been both upheld and rejected by courts.

For example, in 2005, the Supreme Court held that cable television systems do not have to give their customers a choice of internet service providers.[132] The case before the Supreme Court turned on determining the legal category for cable internet services. The Telecommunications Act of 1996 says providers of telecommunications service are utilities that can be more strictly regulated than broadcasters. This includes requiring them to sell access to their networks.[133] However, the FCC decided in 2002 that cable internet access is not a telecommunications service but an information service.[134] Information services, according to the FCC, provide enhanced services, like web hosting, and are more than a basic utility that provides nothing more than transmission.

One way to gain high-speed internet access is through a cable modem offered by a cable television system. An ISP provides the internet connection. Many cable systems wanted their customers to use only an ISP the system owned or with which the system had an agreement. But other ISPs might want to use a cable system to provide high-speed internet access through cable modems. Must cable systems allow these other ISPs to offer access?

The Supreme Court said the 1996 law was ambiguous and the FCC had a right to interpret how the law applied to ISPs. The Court's ruling affirmed the authority of the FCC to categorize cable modem service as an information service, permitting cable system operators to choose which ISPs may offer high-speed internet access through cable modems. The ruling also prevented local cable television franchising authorities from regulating high-speed internet access through cable modems.

Three years ago, as part of its 2015 Open Internet Order, the FCC changed this classification. Today, internet services are treated as a basic telecommunications service. The implications of this are discussed in more detail below.

Online Video Distributor Regulation

Online video distributors are entities that provide video programming using the internet or internet protocol-based transmission paths provided by an outside entity. Currently, the FCC groups video content distribution into three categories: broadcast television stations, MVPDs and OVDs. The FCC is seeking comment on whether to expand its MVPD definition to include OVDs, but for now, OVDs are treated as a separate category.[135]

Consumers need a broadband connection to receive video content from OVDs. Under the FCC's current definition, an OVD is different from an MVPD.[136] OVDs are diverse and include a variety of types of distributors, such as movie companies that release their films online using the internet instead of distributing them for viewing in a movie theater. Examples of OVDs are Sling TV, Apple TV and Sony's PlayStation Vue.

Another way to think about an OVD is in the context of vertical integration, the idea that one company has developed two or more stages of a process, such as content creation and content distribution. The FCC notes that OVDs may "be involved in providing video storage and delivery services, content creation or aggregation (i.e., networks, studios, and sports leagues), or device manufacturing. Several technology companies, notably Amazon, Apple, Google, and Microsoft, also serve as OVDs. Each company takes a slightly different approach to integrating its online video services with storage services, apps, and devices to attract and retain customers."[137]

A recent FCC report noted that "the OVD industry is evolving, and no single business strategy has emerged as the dominant model. Unlike with MVPDs, which generally compete to be the sole provider for a consumer, a single consumer often uses or subscribes to multiple OVDs, [which] offer content to consumers via electronic sell-through, rental, subscription (with or without advertising), or for free (usually with advertising)."[138]

The 2015 Open Internet Order created a standard under which the FCC can prohibit, on a case-by-case basis, practices that unreasonably interfere with consumers' ability to access content, applications and services using the internet.[139] The FCC notes that an OVD attempting to enter the marketplace faces several challenges, including access to sufficient internet capacity to allow for a high-quality viewing experience. In 2016, the FCC announced an inquiry to determine if the FCC should address issues that independent video programmers face in gaining carriage in the current marketplace.[140]

Net Neutrality

As noted earlier, the FCC's 2015 Open Internet Order changed the classification of ISPs from an information service to a telecommunications service. This change in classification allows the FCC to regulate broadband providers as common carriers. This means they are treated like landline telephone providers, and they must make their services available to everyone on the same terms.

What is net neutrality? At its core, **net neutrality** simply means that ISPs cannot charge content providers to speed up the delivery of their content. Supporters of net neutrality say that the concept is important for the internet to maintain its democratic status.

online video distributor
An entity that provides video programming using the internet or internet protocol–based transmission paths.

net neutrality
The principle that holds that internet service providers cannot charge content providers to speed up the delivery of their goods—all internet traffic is treated equally.

They argue that ISPs should not favor some content providers over others simply because they can charge them more money to deliver their content, even if that content takes up a lot of broadband space (for example, video). Notable corporate supporters of net neutrality principles include Google, Microsoft, Netflix and Twitter.[141]

Opponents of net neutrality say that if ISPs cannot charge more money for different kinds of transmissions such as those required by OVDs, then it stifles innovation and runs against the ISPs' financial interests. Opponents to net neutrality principles include Verizon, AT&T and Comcast. The net neutrality issue also tends to fall along political party lines with Democrats supporting net neutrality principles and Republicans opposing them.[142]

The FCC issued its first net neutrality order in 2008.[143] In the first court challenge to that order, the D.C. Circuit Court held that the FCC did not have jurisdiction to regulate

● REAL WORLD LAW

FCC and ISP Privacy Rules

In 2017, Congress rolled back the Federal Communications Commission's 2016 privacy rules that required broadband internet service providers to protect consumer privacy. The 2016 privacy requirements applied to broadband ISPs but not to websites, apps or other "edge services" that provide a gateway to other internet services.[1] The rules were intended to implement the 2015 Open Internet Order that reclassified broadband as a telecommunications service subject to more expansive regulation.

The rules would have expanded protection for consumer information. The rule governed how an ISP handled a variety of consumer data beyond billing and service agreements to include app usage, internet browsing history, shopping records, medical and health information, biometric information, employment information and more.[2]

Privacy advocates argued that the FCC's rules were necessary to protect consumers because ISPs are able to collect substantially more information than other services, such as search engines or OVDs. They also argued that although consumers are free to switch from ISPs lacking privacy protections to those with enhanced privacy policies, many Americans have little choice when it comes to broadband service providers because of lack of competition in their area.[3]

FCC Chair Ajit Pai supported the congressional rollback, saying that the rules were unnecessary because the broadband market is highly competitive. He added that the regulations put a greater regulatory burden on ISPs than on websites and others who sell content to third parties, such as data brokers.[4]

As noted in Chapter 6, the Federal Trade Commission generally regulates consumer data privacy on the internet. The 2015 Open Internet Order's reclassification of broadband as a telecommunications service moved the regulatory oversight of ISPs from the FTC to the FCC. The FTC continues to have oversight of consumer data privacy protections on the internet, with broadband ISPs as the sole exception.

---

1. *In the Matter of Protecting the Privacy of Customers of Broadband and Other Telecommunications Services*, Notice of Proposed Rulemaking, FCC 16-39 (rel. Apr. 1, 2016).
2. Kathleen Kirby, *Developments in Electronic Media Regulation*, COMM. LAW IN DIGITAL AGE 2016 (2016).
3. Brian Fung, *The House Just Voted to Wipe Away the FCC's Landmark Internet Privacy Protections*, WASH. POST, March 28, 2017, www.washingtonpost .com/news/the-switch/wp/2017/03/28/the-house-just-voted-to-wipe-out-the-fccs-landmark-internet-privacy-protections/?utm_ term=.0dca240ec9f9.
4. Jon Brodkin, *Ajit Pai Says Broadband Market Too Competitive for Strict Privacy Rules*, ARS TECHNICA, April 5, 2017, arstechnica.com/ tech-policy/2017/04/ajit-pai-says-broadband-market-too-competitive-for-strict-privacy-rules/.

ISP broadband services.[144] After that court decision, the FCC tried again, issuing new net neutrality rules in its 2010 Open Internet Report and Order.[145] Verizon challenged the 2010 order. In 2014, the D.C. Circuit Court struck down the FCC's new net neutrality rules.[146] The court said the FCC's Open Internet Orders did not justify its shift away from the commission's previous decision to categorize ISPs as information services. The court's decision left open the door for the FCC to pursue new net neutrality rules if it reclassified ISPs as a telecommunications service.[147]

The FCC's 2015 Open Internet Order reclassified high-speed internet service as a telecommunications service under Title II of the Telecommunications Act of 1996 and effectively began treating broadband service providers like a public utility.[148] The 2015 FCC order bans throttling, blocking and paid prioritization of content. This means providers may not "impair or degrade" or block lawful internet traffic on the basis of content. The ban on paid prioritization cuts to the heart of net neutrality and prohibits broadband providers from creating paid "fast lanes" to favor some kinds of traffic over others.[149]

The FCC's 3–2 vote on the 2015 order divided along party lines. Then-Chair Tom Wheeler's comment on the order represented the sentiments of the three Democrats in the majority at the time: "Our challenge is to achieve two equally important goals: ensure incentives for private investment in broadband infrastructure so the U.S. has world-leading networks and ensure that those networks are fast, fair and open for all Americans. [We have] achieved those goals, giving consumers, innovators and entrepreneurs the protections they deserve, while providing certainty for broadband providers and the online marketplace."[150]

The two Republicans on the commission voted against the order. "Americans love the free and open internet. We relish our freedom to speak, to post, to rally, to learn, to listen, to watch and to connect online," wrote then-Commissioner Pai in dissent. "The internet has become a powerful force for freedom, both at home and abroad. So it is sad to witness the FCC's unprecedented attempt to replace that freedom with government control."[151]

Nearly 50 organizations sued to block the new rules that took effect in 2015; the D.C. Circuit Court consolidated all of the lawsuits[152] and in 2016 denied the petitions for review of the 2015 order.[153] When President Donald Trump nominated Pai to lead the FCC in 2017, many speculated that net neutrality would end. In mid-2017, Pai announced that the FCC would begin the process of loosening net neutrality enforcement regulations.[154]

The Internet's First Amendment Status

In overturning a congressional attempt to limit online sexual expression, the Supreme Court held in *Reno v. American Civil Liberties Union* that the internet has complete First Amendment protection.[155] *Reno v. ACLU* decided a challenge to the Communications Decency Act, a provision of the Telecommunications Act of 1996.[156] The CDA prohibited using the internet to transmit indecent, patently offensive or obscene material to minors.

To determine the CDA's constitutionality, the Court had to decide what First Amendment protections apply to the internet. The starting assumption is that the First Amendment protects expression communicated by any means. But the Court has said each mass medium has its own peculiarities, so there may need to be adjustments to a medium's First Amendment rights. Broadcasting, as discussed throughout this chapter,

◉ POINTS OF LAW

The FCC's 2015 Open Internet Order

In addition to reclassifying fixed and mobile broadband internet service providers as telecommunications services, the Federal Communications Commission's 2015 Open Internet Order bans three practices:

- Throttling: Broadband providers cannot impair or degrade internet traffic on the basis of content, applications or services.

- Paid Prioritization: No "fast lanes." Put another way, broadband providers may not favor some traffic over other traffic, and they may not prioritize delivery of content and services by their affiliates.

- Blocking: Broadband providers may not block access to legal content, applications or services.[1]

---

1. Protecting and Promoting the Open Internet, 80 Fed. Reg. 19737 (Apr. 13, 2015).

uses a scarce spectrum, justifying its limited First Amendment protection. In *Reno*, the Court said that the internet did not use the spectrum and was not as invasive as broadcasting. Families not wanting their children to have internet access do not need to subscribe to an internet service. Historically, the internet has not been "subject to the type of government supervision and regulation that has attended the broadcast industry."[157] Unlike broadcasting, the internet does not have any special characteristics that require decreasing its First Amendment rights, the *Reno* Court held.

Justice John Paul Stevens, writing for the Court majority, characterized the internet as "a unique medium" that is "a vast platform from which to address and hear from a worldwide audience of millions of readers, viewers, researchers and buyers. Any person or organization with a computer connected to the Internet can 'publish' information."[158]

Having held that internet content has full First Amendment protection, the Court overturned the CDA's restrictions on transmitting indecent and patently offensive material using the internet. The Court upheld the ban on obscene content sent over the internet. The First Amendment does not protect obscene material on the internet or in any medium (see Chapter 10).[159]

As noted at the start of this section on internet regulation, the Supreme Court has upheld the FCC's authority to regulate broadband internet services under the Communications Act of 1934. As with all electronic media regulation discussed in this chapter, the Supreme Court has never granted the FCC the authority to censor content; rather, the FCC is permitted only to institute program or other content-neutral regulations that serve the public interest.

CHAPTER SUMMARY

FEDERAL LAW FIRST REGULATED ELECTRONIC MEDIA—radio—in 1912. When cooperation among radio broadcasters was unsuccessful, Congress established the Federal Radio Commission in 1927 and gave it extensive power over radio broadcasting. The Federal

Communications Commission replaced the FRC in 1934. Today, the FCC uses its powers to adopt regulations affecting large segments of the electronic media, as well as licensing spectrum users and enforcing the commission's regulations.

The First Amendment rights of broadcasters are not equal to those enjoyed by the print media. Spectrum scarcity limits broadcasting to a select few who obtain FCC licenses. Courts say this justifies some limits on broadcasters' free speech rights. Courts also point to broadcasting's pervasiveness and impact on audiences, particularly children. The FCC regulates broadcasting to ensure it operates in the public interest, but the FCC is not allowed to censor broadcasting content.

Every broadcast station must have an FCC license. If there is an available frequency, or if a station is being sold, the commission grants licenses to applicants who meet certain criteria. An applicant must be an American citizen or a corporation not controlled by foreign interests. The commission has a complex, ever-changing set of rules limiting broadcast ownership.

Section 315 of the Communications Act of 1934 requires broadcasters and cable systems to give equal opportunity to use the airwaves to legally qualified candidates running for the same office. Federal candidates may obtain time even if their opponents have not appeared in a broadcast. A political "candidate" is someone who has announced he or she is running for office and has his or her name on the ballot or is a write-in candidate. "Use" of a station or cable system occurs whenever a candidate's image or voice appears on radio or television.

Federal law and FCC rules require broadcast television stations to show at least three hours per week of programming that meets children's intellectual/cognitive and social/emotional needs and to limit adjacent advertising. FCC rules prohibit broadcasting hoaxes. FCC rules require that sponsorship identification accompany all material a station did not create itself.

The FCC initially declined to regulate cable television. In 1984, a federal law spread cable television jurisdiction between local governments and the FCC. After some vacillating, the Supreme Court said the strict scrutiny test should be applied to regulations affecting cable content, and the intermediate scrutiny test should be applied to content-neutral regulations imposed on cable. The primary laws that regulate cable today are the Cable Television Consumer Protection and Competition Act of 1992 and the Telecommunications Act of 1996. Just as the emergence of cable required the FCC to consider its role in regulation, so did the emergence of direct broadcast satellite services. As DBS grew, the FCC began to impose DBS regulations similar to cable.

Today, the FCC defines both cable and DBS services as multichannel video programming distributors. The 1992 law contained two provisions that required the carriage of broadcast stations on cable and DBS systems—the must-carry rule and retransmission consent. The 1992 law prohibits MVPDs from retransmitting a broadcast station without the broadcaster's explicit permission. Must-carry holds that if a broadcast station chooses must-carry status, it will not be dropped from an MVPD's channel lineup. By asserting its must-carry rights, the broadcaster cannot demand compensation from the system operator. The Supreme Court has upheld the rules.

In 2015, the FCC implemented the Satellite Television Extension and Localism Act Reauthorization Act of 2014, which aimed to modernize the must-carry and retransmission consent rules but maintain the basic framework of the 1992 Cable Act. Specifically, the law added a new satellite market modification rule that allows a television station, satellite operator or county government to request the addition or deletion of communities from a broadcast station's local television market to better reflect current market realities.

Although initially the FCC took a "hands off the internet" approach, more recently it claimed ancillary jurisdiction over broadband. Broadband uses a wide range of frequencies to enable a large number of messages to be communicated simultaneously. Three years ago, as part of its 2015 Open Internet Order, the FCC changed broadband's classification from an information service to a basic telecommunications service. This change allows the FCC to regulate broadband providers as common carriers. This means they are treated like landline telephone providers, and they must make their services available to everyone on the same terms.

Net neutrality means that ISPs cannot charge content providers to speed up the delivery of their content. Unlike broadcasting, the internet does not have any special characteristics that require decreasing its First Amendment rights, according to the Supreme Court. The Court has upheld the FCC's authority to regulate broadband internet services under the Communications Act of 1934. As with all electronic media regulation discussed in this chapter, the Supreme Court has never granted the FCC the authority to censor content; rather, the FCC is permitted only to institute program or other content-neutral regulations that serve the public interest. ■

CASES FOR STUDY

For study resources and a case archive go to **study.sagepub.com/medialaw6e**.

THINKING ABOUT IT

The two case excerpts that follow deal with broadcasting and cable television. As you read these case excerpts, keep the following questions in mind:

- What reasons does the Court give for the way it applies the First Amendment to broadcasting and cable?

- Do these two decisions logically lead to the Court's ruling in *Reno v. ACLU* that the internet should have full First Amendment protection? Why or why not?

- In what ways are these two cases still relevant today, as technology has fundamentally changed the electronic media landscape?

Red Lion Broadcasting Co. Inc. v. Federal Communications Commission
SUPREME COURT OF THE UNITED STATES
395 U.S. 367 (1969)

JUSTICE BYRON WHITE delivered the Court's opinion:

The Federal Communications Commission has for many years imposed on radio and television broadcasters the requirement that discussion of public issues be presented on broadcast stations, and that each side of those issues must be given fair coverage. This is known as the fairness doctrine, which originated very early in the history of broadcasting and has maintained its present outlines for some time. It is an obligation whose content has been defined in a long series of FCC rulings in particular cases, and which is distinct from the statutory requirement of Section 315 of the Communications Act that equal time be allotted all qualified candidates for public office. Two aspects of the fairness doctrine, relating to personal attacks in the context of controversial public issues and to political editorializing, were codified more precisely in the form of FCC regulations in 1967. The two cases before us now, which

were decided separately below, challenge the constitutional and statutory bases of the doctrine and component rules. *Red Lion* involves the application of the fairness doctrine to a particular broadcast, and *RTNDA* [*Radio and Television News Directors Association*] arises as an action to review the FCC's 1967 promulgation of the personal attack and political editorializing regulations, which were laid down after the *Red Lion* litigation had begun.

The Red Lion Broadcasting Company is licensed to operate a Pennsylvania radio station, WGCB. On November 27, 1964, WGCB carried a 15-minute broadcast by the Reverend Billy James Hargis as part of a "Christian Crusade" series. A book by Fred J. Cook entitled "Goldwater—Extremist on the Right" was discussed by Hargis, who said that Cook had been fired by a newspaper for making false charges against city officials; that Cook had then worked for a Communist-affiliated publication; that he had defended Alger Hiss and attacked J. Edgar Hoover and the Central Intelligence Agency; and that he had now written a "book to smear and destroy Barry Goldwater." When Cook heard of the broadcast he concluded that he had been personally attacked and demanded free reply time, which the station refused. After an exchange of letters among Cook, Red Lion, and the FCC, the FCC declared that the Hargis broadcast constituted a personal attack on Cook; that Red Lion had failed to meet its obligation under the fairness doctrine . . . to send a tape, transcript, or summary of the broadcast to Cook and offer him reply time; and that the station must provide reply time whether or not Cook would pay for it. On review in the Court of Appeals for the District of Columbia Circuit, the FCC's position was upheld as constitutional and otherwise proper. . . .

Believing that the specific application of the fairness doctrine in *Red Lion*, and the promulgation of the regulations in *RTNDA*, are both authorized by Congress and enhance rather than abridge the freedoms of speech and press protected by the First Amendment, we hold them valid and constitutional, reversing the judgment below in *RTNDA* and affirming the judgment below in *Red Lion*.

The history of the emergence of the fairness doctrine and of the related legislation shows that the Commission's action in the *Red Lion* case did not exceed its authority, and that in adopting the new regulations the Commission was implementing congressional policy rather than embarking on a frolic of its own.

Before 1927, the allocation of frequencies was left entirely to the private sector, and the result was chaos. It quickly became apparent that broadcast frequencies constituted a scarce resource whose use could be regulated and rationalized only by the Government. Without government control, the medium would be of little use because of the cacophony of competing voices, none of which could be clearly and predictably heard. Consequently, the Federal Radio Commission was established to allocate frequencies among competing applicants in a manner responsive to the public "convenience, interest, or necessity."

Very shortly thereafter the Commission expressed its view that the "public interest requires ample play for the free and fair competition of opposing views, and the commission believes that the principle applies . . . to all discussions of issues of importance to the public." This doctrine was applied through denial of license renewals or construction permits, both by the FRC, and its successor FCC. After an extended period during which the licensee was obliged not only to cover and to cover fairly the views of others, but also to refrain from expressing his own personal views, the latter limitation on the licensee was abandoned and the doctrine developed into its present form.

There is a twofold duty laid down by the FCC's decisions and described by the 1949 Report on Editorializing by Broadcast Licensees. The broadcaster must give adequate coverage to public issues, and coverage must be fair in that it accurately reflects the opposing views. This must be done at the broadcaster's own expense if sponsorship is unavailable. Moreover, the duty must be met by programming obtained at the licensee's own initiative if available from no other source. . . .

When a personal attack has been made on a figure involved in a public issue, . . . [it is required] that the individual attacked himself be offered an opportunity to respond. Likewise, where one candidate is endorsed in a political editorial, the other candidates must themselves be offered reply time to use personally or through a spokesman. These obligations differ from the general fairness requirement that issues be presented, and presented with coverage of competing views, in that the broadcaster does not have the option of presenting the attacked party's side himself or choosing a third party to represent that side. But insofar as there is an obligation of the broadcaster to see that both sides are presented, and insofar as that is an affirmative obligation, the personal attack doctrine and regulations do not differ from the preceding fairness doctrine. The simple fact that the attacked men or unendorsed candidates may respond themselves or through agents is not a critical distinction, and indeed, it is not unreasonable for the FCC to conclude that the objective of adequate presentation of all sides may best be served by allowing those most closely affected to make the response, rather than leaving the response in the hands of the station which has attacked their candidacies, endorsed their opponents, or carried a personal attack upon them. . . .

The broadcasters challenge the fairness doctrine and its specific manifestations in the personal attack and political editorial rules on conventional First Amendment grounds, alleging that the rules abridge their freedom of speech and press. Their contention is that the First Amendment protects their desire to use their allotted frequencies continuously to broadcast whatever they choose, and to exclude whomever they choose from ever using that frequency. No man may be prevented from saying or publishing what he thinks, or from refusing in his speech or other utterances to give equal weight to the views of his opponents. This right, they say, applies equally to broadcasters.

Although broadcasting is clearly a medium affected by a First Amendment interest, differences in the characteristics of new media justify differences in the standards applied to them. For example, the ability of new technology to produce sounds more raucous than those of the human voice justifies restrictions on the sound level, and on the hours and places of use, of sound trucks so long as the restrictions are reasonable and applied without discrimination.

Just as the Government may limit the use of sound-amplifying equipment potentially so noisy that it drowns out civilized private speech, so may the Government limit the use of broadcast equipment. The right of free speech of a broadcaster, the user of a sound truck, or any other individual does not embrace a right to snuff out the free speech of others. . . .

It was . . . the chaos which ensued from permitting anyone to use any frequency at whatever power level he wished, which made necessary the enactment of the Radio Act of 1927 and the Communications Act of 1934. It was this reality which at the very least necessitated first the division of the radio spectrum into portions reserved respectively for public broadcasting and for other important radio uses such as amateur operation, aircraft, police, defense, and navigation; and then the subdivision of each portion, and assignment of specific frequencies to individual users or groups of users. Beyond this, however, because the frequencies reserved for public broadcasting were limited in number, it was essential for the Government to tell some applicants that they could not broadcast at all because there was room for only a few.

Where there are substantially more individuals who want to broadcast than there are frequencies to allocate, it is idle to posit an unabridgeable First Amendment right to broadcast comparable to the right of every individual to speak, write, or publish. If 100 persons want broadcast licenses but there are only 10 frequencies to allocate, all of them may have the same "right" to a license; but if there is to be any effective communication by radio, only a few can be licensed and the rest must be barred from the airwaves. It would be strange if the First Amendment, aimed at protecting and furthering communications, prevented the Government from making radio communication possible by requiring licenses to broadcast and by limiting the number of licenses so as not to overcrowd the spectrum.

This has been the consistent view of the Court. Congress unquestionably has the power to grant and deny licenses and to eliminate existing stations. No one has a First Amendment right to a license or to monopolize a radio frequency; to deny a station license because "the public interest" requires it "is not a denial of free speech."

By the same token, as far as the First Amendment is concerned those who are licensed stand no better than those to whom licenses are refused. A license permits broadcasting, but the licensee has no constitutional right to be the one who holds the license or to monopolize a radio frequency to the exclusion of his fellow citizens. There is nothing in the First Amendment which prevents the Government from requiring a licensee to share his frequency with others and to conduct himself as a proxy or fiduciary with obligations to present those views and voices which are representative of his community and which would otherwise, by necessity, be barred from the airwaves.

This is not to say that the First Amendment is irrelevant to public broadcasting. On the contrary, it has a major role to play as the Congress itself recognized in forbidding FCC interference with "the right of free speech by means of radio communication." Because of the scarcity of radio frequencies, the Government is permitted to put restraints on licensees in favor of others whose views should be expressed on this unique medium. But the people as a whole retain their interest in free speech by radio and their collective right to have the medium function consistently with the ends and purposes of the First Amendment. It is the right of the viewers and listeners, not the right of the broadcasters, which is paramount. It is the purpose of the First Amendment to preserve an uninhibited marketplace of ideas in which truth will ultimately prevail, rather than to countenance monopolization of that market, whether it be by the Government itself or a private licensee. "Speech concerning public affairs is more than self-expression; it is the essence of self-government." It is the right of the public to receive suitable access to social, political, esthetic, moral, and other ideas and experiences which is crucial here. That right may not constitutionally be abridged either by Congress or by the FCC.

Rather than confer frequency monopolies on a relatively small number of licensees, in a Nation of 200,000,000, the Government could surely have decreed that each frequency should be shared among all or some of those who wish to use it, each being assigned a portion of the broadcast day or the broadcast week. The ruling and regulations at issue here do not go quite so far. They assert that under specified circumstances, a licensee must offer to make available a reasonable amount of broadcast time to those who have a view different from that which has already been expressed on his station. The expression of a political endorsement, or of a personal attack while dealing with a controversial public issue, simply triggers this time sharing. As we have said, the *First Amendment* confers no right on licensees to prevent others from broadcasting on "their" frequencies and no right to an unconditional monopoly of a scarce resource which the Government has denied others the right to use.

In terms of constitutional principle, and as enforced sharing of a scarce resource, the personal attack and political editorial rules are indistinguishable from the equal-time provision of Section 315, a specific enactment of Congress requiring stations to set aside reply time under specified circumstances and to which the fairness doctrine and these constituent regulations are important complements. That provision, which has been part of the law since 1927, has been held valid by this Court as an obligation of the licensee relieving him of any power in any way to prevent or censor the broadcast, and thus insulating him from liability for defamation. The constitutionality of the statute under the First Amendment was unquestioned.

Nor can we say that it is inconsistent with the First Amendment goal of producing an informed public capable of conducting its own affairs to require a broadcaster to permit answers to personal attacks occurring in the course of discussing controversial issues, or to require that the political opponents of those endorsed by the station be given a chance to communicate with the public. Otherwise, station owners and a few networks would have unfettered power to make time available only to the highest bidders, to communicate only their own views on public issues, people and candidates, and to permit on the air only those with whom they agreed. There is no sanctuary in the First Amendment for unlimited private censorship operating in a medium not open to all. "Freedom of the press from governmental interference under the First Amendment does not sanction repression of that freedom by private interests."

It is strenuously argued, however, that if political editorials or personal attacks will trigger an obligation in broadcasters to afford the opportunity for expression to speakers who need not pay for time and whose views are unpalatable to the licensees, then broadcasters will be irresistibly forced to self-censorship and their coverage of controversial public issues will be eliminated or at least rendered wholly ineffective. Such a result would indeed be a serious matter, for should licensees actually eliminate their coverage of controversial issues, the purposes of the doctrine would be stifled.

At this point, however, as the Federal Communications Commission has indicated, that possibility is at best speculative. The communications industry, and in particular the networks, have taken pains to present controversial issues in the past, and even now they do not assert that they intend to abandon their efforts in this regard. It would be better if the FCC's encouragement were never necessary to induce the broadcasters to meet their responsibility. And if experience with the administration of these doctrines indicates that they have the net effect of reducing rather than enhancing the volume and quality of coverage, there will be time enough to reconsider the constitutional implications. The fairness doctrine in the past has had no such overall effect.

That this will occur now seems unlikely, however, since if present licensees should suddenly prove timorous, the Commission is not powerless to insist that they give adequate and fair attention to public issues. It does not violate the First Amendment to treat licensees given the privilege of using scarce radio frequencies as proxies for the entire community, obligated to give suitable time and attention to matters of great public concern. To condition the granting or renewal of licenses on a willingness to present representative community views on controversial issues is consistent with the ends and purposes of those constitutional provisions forbidding the abridgment of freedom of speech and freedom of the press. Congress need not stand idly by and permit those with licenses to ignore the problems which beset the people or to exclude from the airways anything but their own views of fundamental questions. The statute, long administrative practice, and cases are to this effect.

Licenses to broadcast do not confer ownership of designated frequencies, but only the temporary privilege of using them. . . . The statute mandates the issuance of licenses if the "public convenience, interest, or necessity will be served thereby." . . . [In 1943] the Court considered the validity of the Commission's chain broadcasting regulations, which among other things forbade stations from devoting too much time to network programs in order that there be suitable opportunity for local programs serving local needs. The Court upheld the regulations, unequivocally recognizing that the Commission was more than a traffic policeman concerned with the technical aspects of broadcasting and that it neither exceeded its powers under the statute nor transgressed the First Amendment in interesting itself in general program format and the kinds of programs broadcast by licensees. . . .

It is argued that even if at one time the lack of available frequencies for all who wished to use them justified the Government's choice of those who would best serve the public interest by acting as proxy for those who would present differing views, or by giving the latter access directly to broadcast facilities, this condition no longer prevails so that continuing control is not justified. To this there are several answers.

Scarcity is not entirely a thing of the past. Advances in technology . . . have led to more efficient utilization of the frequency spectrum, but uses for that spectrum have also grown apace. Portions of the spectrum must be reserved for vital uses unconnected with human communication, such as radio-navigational aids used by aircraft and vessels. Conflicts have even emerged between such vital functions as defense preparedness and experimentation in methods of averting midair collisions through radio warning devices. . . .

The rapidity with which technological advances succeed one another to create more efficient use of spectrum space on the one hand, and to create new uses for that space by ever growing numbers of people on the other, makes it unwise to speculate on the future allocation of that space. It is enough to say that the resource is one of considerable and growing importance whose scarcity impelled its regulation by an agency authorized by Congress. . . .

Even where there are gaps in spectrum utilization, the fact remains that existing broadcasters have often attained their present position because of their initial government selection in competition with others before new technological advances opened new opportunities for further uses. Long experience in broadcasting, confirmed habits of listeners and viewers, network affiliation, and other advantages in program procurement give existing broadcasters a substantial advantage over new entrants, even where new entry is technologically possible. These advantages are the fruit of a preferred position conferred by the Government. Some present possibility for new entry by competing stations is not enough, in itself, to render unconstitutional the Government's effort to assure that a broadcaster's programming ranges widely enough to serve the public interest.

In view of the scarcity of broadcast frequencies, the Government's role in allocating those frequencies, and the legitimate claims of those unable without governmental assistance to gain access to those frequencies for expression of their views, we hold the regulations and ruling at issue here are both authorized by statute and constitutional. . . .

Turner Broadcasting System Inc. v. Federal Communications Commission
SUPREME COURT OF THE UNITED STATES
512 U.S. 622 (1994)

JUSTICE ANTHONY KENNEDY delivered the opinion of the Court:

. . . [T]he Cable Television Consumer Protection and Competition Act of 1992 requires cable television systems to devote a portion of their channels to the transmission of local broadcast television stations. This case presents the question whether these provisions abridge the freedom of speech or of the press, in violation of the First Amendment. . . .

The role of cable television in the Nation's communications system has undergone dramatic change over the past 45 years. Given the pace of technological advancement and the increasing convergence between cable and other electronic media, the cable industry today stands at the center of an ongoing telecommunications revolution with still undefined potential to affect the way we communicate and develop our intellectual resources.

The earliest cable systems were built in the late 1940's to bring clear broadcast television signals to remote or mountainous communities. The purpose was not to replace broadcast television but to enhance it. Modern cable systems do much more than enhance the reception of nearby broadcast television stations. With the capacity to carry dozens of channels and import distant programming signals via satellite or microwave relay, today's cable systems are in direct competition with over-the-air broadcasters as an independent source of television programming.

Broadcast and cable television are distinguished by the different technologies through which they reach viewers. Broadcast stations radiate electromagnetic signals from a central transmitting antenna. These signals can be captured, in turn, by any television set within the antenna's range. Cable systems, by contrast, rely upon a physical, point-to-point connection between a transmission facility and the television sets of individual subscribers. Cable systems make this connection much like telephone companies, using cable or optical fibers strung above ground or buried in ducts to reach the homes or businesses of subscribers. The construction of this physical infrastructure entails the use of public rights-of-way and easements and often results in the disruption of traffic on streets and other public property. As a result, the cable medium may depend for its very existence upon express permission from local governing authorities.

Cable technology affords two principal benefits over broadcast. First, it eliminates the signal interference sometimes encountered in over-the-air broadcasting and thus gives viewers undistorted reception of broadcast stations. Second, it is capable of transmitting many more channels than are available through broadcasting, giving subscribers access to far greater programming variety. . . .

The cable television industry includes both cable operators (those who own the physical cable network and transmit the cable signal to the viewer) and cable programmers (those who produce television programs and sell or license them to cable operators). In some cases, cable operators have acquired ownership of cable programmers, and vice versa. Although cable operators may create some of their own programming, most of their programming is drawn from outside sources. These outside sources include not only local or distant broadcast stations, but also the many national and regional cable programming networks that have emerged in recent years, such as CNN, MTV, ESPN, TNT, C-Span, The Family Channel, Nickelodeon, Arts and Entertainment, Black Entertainment Television, CourtTV, The Discovery Channel, American Movie Classics, Comedy Central, The Learning Channel, and The Weather Channel. Once the cable operator has selected the programming sources, the cable system functions, in essence, as a conduit for the speech of others, transmitting it on a continuous and unedited basis to subscribers.

In contrast to commercial broadcast stations, which transmit signals at no charge to viewers and generate revenues by selling time to advertisers, cable systems charge subscribers a monthly fee for the right to receive cable programming and rely to a lesser extent on advertising. In most instances, cable subscribers choose the stations they will receive by selecting among various plans, or "tiers," of cable service. In a typical offering, the basic tier consists of local broadcast stations plus a number of cable programming networks selected by the cable operator. For an additional cost, subscribers can obtain channels devoted to particular subjects or interests, such as recent-release feature movies, sports, children's programming, sexually explicit programming, and the like. Many cable systems also offer pay-per-view service, which allows an individual subscriber to order and pay a one-time fee to see a single movie or program at a set time of the day.

On October 5, 1992, Congress overrode a Presidential veto to enact the Cable Television Consumer Protection and Competition Act of 1992. Among other things, the Act subjects the cable industry to rate regulation by the Federal Communications Commission (FCC) and by municipal franchising authorities; prohibits municipalities from awarding exclusive franchises to cable operators; imposes various restrictions on cable programmers that are affiliated with cable operators; and directs the FCC to develop and promulgate regulations imposing minimum technical standards for cable operators. At issue in this case is the constitutionality of the so-called must-carry provisions, which require cable operators to carry the signals of a specified number of local broadcast television stations. . . .

Congress enacted the 1992 Cable Act after conducting three years of hearings on the structure and operation of the cable television industry. . . . Congress found that the physical characteristics of cable transmission, compounded by the increasing concentration of economic power in the cable industry, are endangering the ability of over-the-air broadcast television stations to compete for a viewing audience and thus for necessary operating revenues. Congress determined that regulation of the market for video programming was necessary to correct this competitive imbalance.

In particular, Congress found that over 60 percent of the households with television sets subscribe to cable, and for these households cable has replaced over-the-air broadcast television as the primary provider of video programming. This is so, Congress found, because "most subscribers to cable television systems do not or cannot maintain antennas to receive broadcast television services, do not have input selector switches to convert from a cable to antenna reception system, or cannot otherwise receive broadcast television services." In addition, Congress concluded that due to "local franchising requirements and the extraordinary expense of constructing more than one cable television system to serve a particular geographic area," the overwhelming majority of cable operators exercise a monopoly over cable service. "The result," Congress determined, "is undue market power for the cable operator as compared to that of consumers and video programmers."

According to Congress, this market position gives cable operators the power and the incentive to harm broadcast competitors. The power derives from the cable operator's ability, as owner of the transmission facility, to "terminate the retransmission of the broadcast signal, refuse to carry new signals, or reposition a broadcast signal to a disadvantageous channel position." The incentive derives from the economic reality that "cable television systems and broadcast television stations increasingly compete for television advertising revenues." By refusing carriage of broadcasters' signals, cable operators, as a practical matter, can reduce the number of households that have access to the broadcasters' programming, and thereby capture advertising dollars that would otherwise go to broadcast stations. . . .

In light of these technological and economic conditions, Congress concluded that unless cable operators are required to carry local broadcast stations, "[t]here is a substantial likelihood that . . . additional local broadcast signals will be deleted, repositioned, or not carried"; the "marked shift in market share" from broadcast to cable will continue to erode the advertising revenue base which sustains free local broadcast television; and that, as a consequence, "the economic viability of free local broadcast television and its ability to originate quality local programming will be seriously jeopardized." . . .

There can be no disagreement on an initial premise: Cable programmers and cable operators engage in and transmit speech, and they are entitled to the protection of the speech and press provisions of the First Amendment. Through "original programming or by exercising editorial discretion over which stations or programs to include in [their] repertoire," cable programmers and operators "seek to communicate messages on a wide variety of topics and in a wide variety of formats." By requiring cable systems to set aside a portion of their channels for local broadcasters, the must-carry rules regulate cable speech in two respects: The rules reduce the number of channels over which cable operators exercise unfettered control, and they render it more difficult for cable programmers to compete for carriage on the limited channels remaining. Nevertheless, because not every interference with speech triggers the same degree of scrutiny under the First Amendment, we must decide at the outset the level of scrutiny applicable to the must-carry provisions.

We address first the Government's contention that regulation of cable television should be analyzed under the same First Amendment standard that applies to regulation of broadcast television. It is true that our cases have permitted more intrusive regulation of broadcast speakers than of speakers in other media. . . . But the rationale for applying a less rigorous standard of First Amendment scrutiny to broadcast regulation, whatever its validity in the cases elaborating it, does not apply in the context of cable regulation.

The justification for our distinct approach to broadcast regulation rests upon the unique physical limitations of the broadcast medium. As a general matter, there are more would-be broadcasters than frequencies available in the electromagnetic spectrum. And if two broadcasters were to attempt to transmit over the same frequency in the same locale, they would interfere with one another's signals, so that neither could be heard at all. The scarcity of broadcast frequencies thus required the establishment of some regulatory mechanism to divide the electromagnetic spectrum and assign specific frequencies to particular broadcasters. In addition, the inherent physical limitation on the number of speakers who may use the broadcast medium has been thought to require some adjustment in traditional First Amendment analysis to permit the Government to place limited content restraints, and impose certain affirmative obligations, on broadcast licensees. As we said in *Red Lion*, "where there are substantially more individuals who want to broadcast than there are frequencies to allocate, it is idle to posit an unabridgeable First Amendment right to broadcast comparable to the right of every individual to speak, write, or publish." . . .

. . . The broadcast cases are inapposite in the present context because cable television does not suffer from the inherent limitations that characterize the broadcast medium. Indeed, given the rapid advances in fiber optics and digital compression technology, soon there may be no practical limitation on the number of speakers who may use the cable medium. Nor is there any danger of physical interference between two cable speakers attempting to share the same channel. . . .

This is not to say that the unique physical characteristics of cable transmission should be ignored when determining the constitutionality of regulations affecting cable speech. They should not. But whatever relevance these physical characteristics may have in the evaluation of particular cable regulations, they do not require the alteration of settled principles of our First Amendment jurisprudence. . . .

... Our precedents thus apply the most exacting scrutiny to regulations that suppress, disadvantage, or impose differential burdens upon speech because of its content. Laws that compel speakers to utter or distribute speech bearing a particular message are subject to the same rigorous scrutiny. In contrast, regulations that are unrelated to the content of speech are subject to an intermediate level of scrutiny, because in most cases they pose a less substantial risk of excising certain ideas or viewpoints from the public dialogue. . . .

As a general rule, laws that by their terms distinguish favored speech from disfavored speech on the basis of the ideas or views expressed are content-based. By contrast, laws that confer benefits or impose burdens on speech without reference to the ideas or views expressed are in most instances content-neutral.

Insofar as they pertain to the carriage of full-power broadcasters, the must-carry rules, on their face, impose burdens and confer benefits without reference to the content of speech. Although the provisions interfere with cable operators' editorial discretion by compelling them to offer carriage to a certain minimum number of broadcast stations, the extent of the interference does not depend upon the content of the cable operators' programming. The rules impose obligations upon all operators, save those with fewer than 300 subscribers, regardless of the programs or stations they now offer or have offered in the past. Nothing in the Act imposes a restriction, penalty, or burden by reason of the views, programs, or stations the cable operator has selected or will select. The number of channels a cable operator must set aside depends only on the operator's channel capacity; hence, an operator cannot avoid or mitigate its obligations under the Act by altering the programming it offers to subscribers.

The must-carry provisions also burden cable programmers by reducing the number of channels for which they can compete. But, again, this burden is unrelated to content, for it extends to all cable programmers irrespective of the programming they choose to offer viewers. And finally, the privileges conferred by the must-carry provisions are also unrelated to content. The rules benefit all full power broadcasters who request carriage—be they commercial or noncommercial, independent or network-affiliated, English or Spanish language, religious or secular. The aggregate effect of the rules is thus to make every full power commercial and noncommercial broadcaster eligible for must-carry, provided only that the broadcaster operates within the same television market as a cable system. . . .

That the must-carry provisions, on their face, do not burden or benefit speech of a particular content does not end the inquiry. Our cases have recognized that even a regulation neutral on its face may be content-based if its manifest purpose is to regulate speech because of the message it conveys.

Appellants contend, in this regard, that the must-carry regulations are content-based because Congress' purpose in enacting them was to promote speech of a favored content. We do not agree. Our review of the Act and its various findings persuades us that Congress' overriding objective in enacting must-carry was not to favor programming of a particular subject matter, viewpoint, or format, but rather to preserve access to free television programming for the 40 percent of Americans without cable. . . .

In short, Congress' acknowledgment that broadcast television stations make a valuable contribution to the Nation's communications system does not render the must-carry scheme content-based. The scope and operation of the challenged provisions make clear, in our view, that Congress designed the must-carry provisions not to promote speech of a particular content, but to prevent cable operators from exploiting their economic power to the detriment of broadcasters, and thereby to ensure that all Americans, especially those unable to subscribe to cable, have access to free television programming—whatever its content. . . .

JUSTICE SANDRA DAY O'CONNOR, with whom JUSTICE ANTONIN SCALIA AND JUSTICE RUTH BADER GINSBURG joined, and with whom JUSTICE CLARENCE THOMAS joined in part, concurring in part and dissenting in part:

There are only so many channels that any cable system can carry. If there are fewer channels than programmers who want to use the system, some programmers will have to be dropped. In the must-carry provisions of the Cable Television Consumer Protection and Competition Act of 1992, Congress made a choice: By reserving a little over one-third of the channels on a cable system for broadcasters, it ensured that in most cases it will be a cable programmer who is dropped and a broadcaster who is retained. The question presented in this case is whether this choice comports with the commands of the First Amendment.

The 1992 Cable Act implicates the First Amendment rights of two classes of speakers. First, it tells cable operators which programmers they must carry, and keeps cable operators from carrying others that they might prefer. Though cable operators do not actually originate most of the programming they show, the Court correctly holds that they are, for First Amendment purposes, speakers. Selecting which speech to retransmit is, as we know from the example of publishing houses, movie theaters, bookstores, and Reader's Digest, no less communication than is creating the speech in the first place.

Second, the Act deprives a certain class of video programmers—those who operate cable channels rather than broadcast stations—of access to over one-third of an entire medium. Cable programmers may compete only for those channels that are not set aside by the must-carry provisions. A cable programmer that might otherwise have been carried may well be denied access in favor of a broadcaster that is less appealing to the viewers but is favored by the must-carry rules. It is as if the Government ordered all movie theaters to reserve at least one-third of their screening for films made by American production companies, or required all bookstores to devote one-third of their shelf space to nonprofit publishers. As the Court explains, cable programmers and operators stand in the same position under the First Amendment as do the more traditional media. . . .

I agree with the Court that some speaker-based restrictions—those genuinely justified without reference to content—need not be subject to strict scrutiny. But looking at the statute at issue, I cannot avoid the conclusion that its preference for broadcasters over cable programmers is justified with reference to content. . . .

Preferences for diversity of viewpoints, for localism, for educational programming, and for news and public affairs all make reference to content. They may not reflect hostility to particular points of view, or a desire to suppress certain subjects because they are controversial or offensive. They may be quite benignly motivated. But benign motivation, we have consistently held, is not enough to avoid the need for strict scrutiny of content-based justifications. The First Amendment does more than just bar government from intentionally suppressing speech of which it disapproves. It also generally prohibits the government from excepting certain kinds of speech from regulation because it thinks the speech is especially valuable.

This is why the Court is mistaken in concluding that the interest in diversity—in "access to a multiplicity" of "diverse and antagonistic sources"—is content neutral. Indeed, the interest is not "related to the *suppression* of free expression," but that is not enough for content neutrality. The interest in giving a tax break to religious, sports, or professional magazines, is not related to the suppression of speech; the interest in giving labor picketers an exemption from a general picketing ban, is not related to the suppression of speech. But they are both related to the *content* of speech—to its communicative impact. The interest in ensuring access to a multiplicity of diverse and antagonistic sources of information, no matter how praiseworthy, is directly tied to the content of what the speakers will likely say. . . .

Having said all this, it is important to acknowledge one basic fact: The question is not whether there will be control over who gets to speak over cable—the question is who will have this control. Under the FCC's view, the answer is Congress, acting within relatively broad limits. Under my view, the answer is the cable operator. Most of the time, the cable operator's decision will be largely dictated by the preferences of the viewers; but because many cable operators are indeed monopolists, the viewers' preferences will not always prevail. Our recognition that cable operators are speakers is bottomed in large part on the very fact that the cable operator has editorial discretion. . . .

But the First Amendment as we understand it today rests on the premise that it is government power, rather than private power, that is the main threat to free expression; and as a consequence, the Amendment imposes substantial limitations on the Government even when it is trying to serve concededly praiseworthy goals. Perhaps Congress can to some extent restrict, even in a content-based manner, the speech of cable operators and cable programmers. But it must do so in compliance with the constitutional requirements, requirements that were not complied with here. Accordingly, I would reverse the judgment below.

I have reached the conclusion . . . that under the First and Fourteenth Amendments criminal laws in this area are constitutionally limited to hard-core pornography. I shall not today attempt further to define the kinds of material I understand to be embraced within that shorthand description; and perhaps I could never succeed in intelligibly doing so. But I know it when I see it.

—U.S. Supreme Court Justice Potter Stewart[1]

Ninety million people witnessed Janet Jackson's Super Bowl halftime show "wardrobe malfunction." For a fraction of a second, her breast was exposed, leading to more than 500,000 viewer complaints to the Federal Communications Commission.[2]

10 OBSCENITY AND INDECENCY
Social Norms and Legal Standards

SUPPOSE...

... that a singer-actress and a television personality say four-letter expletives on live television broadcasts and a TV cop program briefly shows female nudity. These are words most people have heard from the time they were small children on the playground and images most teenagers and adults have seen. But, federal law has banned broadcasting such words and pictures for decades. Should the Federal Communications Commission find the broadcasts indecent? Should the FCC punish stations for airing them? Look for the answers to these questions when *Federal Communications Commission v. Fox Television Stations Inc.* is discussed later in this chapter and excerpted at the end of the chapter.

Sexual expression is ubiquitous in contemporary societies—as it has been for centuries. It can be found in art, in beer commercials, on websites and social media, in television programs and in movies. There is little agreement—aside from the Supreme Court's definition of "obscenity"—about what sexual expression should be protected and what should be illegal. The argument has two sides, each based on a different set of values. Some believe sexually explicit material does not deserve First Amendment protection. Others argue sexual expression is just that—expression.

The law as it is applied to sexual expression comes from Supreme Court First Amendment decisions as well as administrative law (see Chapter 1 for an overview of sources of law). First Amendment decisions mostly focus on obscenity. Administrative

pornography
A vague—not legally precise—term for sexually oriented material.

indecency A narrow legal term referring to sexual expression and expletives inappropriate for children on broadcast radio and television.

obscenity The dictionary defines it as relating to sex in an indecent, very offensive or shocking way. The legal definition of obscenity comes from *Miller v. California*—material is determined to be obscene if it passes the *Miller* test.

laws that apply to sexual expression come from the FCC (see Chapter 9 for an overview of the FCC) and focus on indecency. The FCC determines the rules and regulations for indecency as applied to different media—specifically, broadcast, cable and the internet.

Current federal and state laws have stripped material that meets the U.S. Supreme Court's definition of obscenity of all First Amendment protection. The dictionary defines obscenity simply as "relating to sex in an indecent or offensive way," or "very offensive in usually a shocking way."[3]

Generally speaking, there is not agreement on what word to use in describing all offensive sexual expression. What's the difference between obscenity, pornography and indecency? The word **pornography** is vague—not legally precise—because it encompasses both protected and unprotected sexual material. The term **indecency** has only a narrow legal meaning, referring to sexual expression and expletives inappropriate for children on broadcast radio and television. Until the mid-20th century, American courts used a broad definition of **obscenity**, allowing government officials to ban a wide range of materials.

OBSCENITY

Two centuries ago, American society considered religious blasphemy and heresy to be more troublesome than sexual expression. With few exceptions, governments—state and federal—did not adopt laws or bring criminal charges concerning sexual material.

Comstock and *Hicklin*

After the Civil War, some people claimed that U.S. citizens, particularly indigent men, lacked morality. Anthony Comstock, a store clerk, became the champion of young

LANDMARK CASES IN CONTEXT

Key ■ Event
◆ Cases

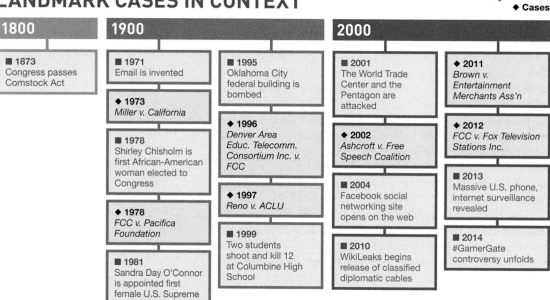

1800

■ **1873**
Congress passes Comstock Act

1900

■ **1971**
Email is invented

◆ **1973**
Miller v. California

■ **1978**
Shirley Chisholm is first African-American woman elected to Congress

◆ **1978**
FCC v. Pacifica Foundation

■ **1981**
Sandra Day O'Connor is appointed first female U.S. Supreme Court justice

■ **1995**
Oklahoma City federal building is bombed

◆ **1996**
Denver Area Educ. Telecomm. Consortium Inc. v. FCC

◆ **1997**
Reno v. ACLU

■ **1999**
Two students shoot and kill 12 at Columbine High School

2000

■ **2001**
The World Trade Center and the Pentagon are attacked

◆ **2002**
Ashcroft v. Free Speech Coalition

■ **2004**
Facebook social networking site opens on the web

■ **2010**
WikiLeaks begins release of classified diplomatic cables

◆ **2011**
Brown v. Entertainment Merchants Ass'n

◆ **2012**
FCC v. Fox Television Stations Inc.

■ **2013**
Massive U.S. phone, internet surveillance revealed

■ **2014**
#GamerGate controversy unfolds

men's decency and launched an anti-obscenity movement.[4] He believed that "anything remotely touching upon sex was . . . obscene."[5] In 1872, Comstock convinced the Young Men's Christian Association to support his campaign against sexual content in art, newspapers, books, magazines and other media. Comstock became secretary of the Society for the Suppression of Vice, funded in part by prominent and wealthy businessmen. The campaign lasted for more than 60 years. During that time, the society convinced schools and libraries to ban works by prominent authors.[6]

Although federal laws already banned importing and mailing obscene material, Comstock vigorously lobbied Congress to further tighten mailing restrictions. His campaign culminated in the Comstock Act, a federal law adopted in 1873 prohibiting the mailing of "obscene, lewd, or lascivious" material.[7] Initially used only to stop mailings concerning contraception and abortion, the law was amended in 1876 to ensure that it banned the mailing of pornographic materials.[8] After the law's adoption, Congress appointed Comstock as a special postal inspector to help enforce the statute. He held the post for 42 years. As a U.S. Postal Service special agent, Comstock prosecuted many people for selling and mailing material that he said was lewd. Comstock would order items through the mail and then, with the illicit item as evidence, take the seller to court.[9] The law remains in effect today, although now it applies only to obscene content.

When courts in the post–Civil War United States began hearing cases involving sexually explicit material, it became clear that any publication found obscene would not have First Amendment protection. The question was how to define obscenity. Beginning in the late 19th century and continuing for more than 60 years, federal courts applied the **_Hicklin_ rule** in deciding obscenity cases. The rule came from an 1868 British case, _Regina v. Hicklin_, stating that "the test of obscenity is this, whether the tendency of the matter charged as obscenity is to deprave and corrupt those whose minds are open to such immoral influences and into whose hands a publication of this sort may fall."[10] In essence, the _Hicklin_ rule meant adults could be exposed only to material acceptable for the most susceptible minds—the young. The newly established U.S. courts commonly held that if even a portion of a publication met the _Hicklin_ test, the entire publication was obscene. The _Hicklin_ rule remained dominant in the United States into the 1930s.

Deciding whether U.S. customs officials could prevent James Joyce's novel "Ulysses" from being imported, a federal district court in 1933 rejected the _Hicklin_ test. The court said the test for obscenity should be the entire work's impact on an "average person." The court said "Ulysses" was literary art and was not obscene.[11] Some federal and state courts continued to apply _Hicklin_ into the 1950s. However, the "Ulysses" decision effectively suggested that courts could determine what is obscene by reviewing the material in its

In addition to successfully lobbying Congress to pass what became the Comstock Act, Anthony Comstock effectively pushed all states to pass obscenity laws.

Hicklin **rule** Taken from a mid-19th-century English case and used in the United States until the mid-20th century, a rule that defines material as obscene if it tends to corrupt children.

● REAL WORLD LAW

The Second Circuit on James Joyce's "Ulysses"

Culture Club/Getty Images

In a 1934 decision in which the Second Circuit Court of Appeals upheld a district court ruling that James Joyce's "Ulysses" was not obscene, the court laid some of the groundwork for future obscenity tests. The court wrote, "It is settled, at least so far as this court is concerned, that works of physiology, medicine, science and sex instruction are not within the statute, though to some extent and among some persons they may tend to promote lustful thoughts. We think the same immunity should apply to literature as to science, where the presentation, when viewed objectively, is sincere, and the erotic matter is not introduced to promote lust and does not furnish the dominant note of the publication. The question in each case is whether a publication taken as a whole has a libidinous effect. The book before us has such portentous length, is written with such evident truthfulness in its depiction of certain types of humanity, and is so little erotic in its result, that it does not fall within the forbidden class."[1]

1. United States v. One Book Entitled Ulysses, 72 F.2d 705, 705–706 (2d Cir. 1934).

entirety instead of assessing isolated passages or pictures. The decision also suggested the test should ascertain a work's effect on an average person instead of on children.

Today, federal laws continue to prohibit mailing or importing obscene material and producing, transporting and selling obscene material across state lines.[12] Additionally, the U.S. Congress has adopted criminal laws prohibiting internet obscenity, particularly when addressed to minors.[13] States also have adopted obscenity laws.

Current Obscenity Definition

The U.S. Supreme Court handed down its first major obscenity decision in 1957. In *Roth v. United States*, the Court said the First Amendment does not protect obscene material. At the same time, it definitively rejected *Hicklin* and narrowed the obscenity definition to give sexual expression more freedom. The Court said material was obscene if, first, an "average person, applying contemporary community standards," found the work taken as a whole appealed to **prurient interest**, meaning that it "excites lustful thoughts." Second, obscene material must be "utterly without redeeming social importance."[14]

prurient interest
Lustful thoughts or sexual desires.

The Court refined the *Roth* test several times between 1957 and 1973. The test remained difficult for government prosecutors to meet, however, and there were relatively few obscenity convictions after *Roth*.

In 1973, the Court reconsidered obscenity law in *Miller v. California* and set down the definition of obscenity that remains to this day.[15] Defendant Marvin Miller sent brochures in a mass mailing to advertise four "adult" books and a film in California. The brochures included pictures, drawings and text "very explicitly depicting men and women in groups of two or more engaging in a variety of sexual activities, with genitals often prominently displayed."[16] Many of the brochures were mailed to people who had not requested the information. The manager of a Newport Beach, Calif., restaurant opened the mail one morning with his mother standing at his side. Five brochures slipped out of an unmarked envelope for all to see. The manager called the police. A jury convicted Miller of violating a California statute that forbid the intentional distribution of obscene materials. Miller appealed to the U.S. Supreme Court.

Before the Court could decide if Miller's brochures were obscene, it had to define obscenity. The justices established a complex, three-part definition of obscenity. Under the *Miller* test, to find material obscene a court must consider whether (1) "the average person, applying contemporary community standards," would find that the work, taken as a whole, appeals to prurient interests; (2) the work depicts or describes, in a patently offensive way, sexual conduct specifically defined by the applicable state law; and (3) the work, taken as a whole, lacks serious literary, artistic, political or scientific value.[17]

A work must meet every part of the test to be obscene. That is, the government must show a work, considered in its entirety, (1) arouses sexual lust, (2) is hard-core pornography and (3) has no serious social value. If the government cannot prove any part of this test, the work is not obscene, and the First Amendment protects it.

Prurient Interest and Local Standards. The first part of the *Miller* test requires showing that an average person would find the work, taken in its entirety, appeals to prurient interests, or "lustful thoughts." The Court said "prurient" refers to "morbid or lascivious longings."[18] Material arousing morbid or shameful sexual thoughts meets this part of the *Miller* test.

The *Miller* case confirmed what the U.S. Supreme Court held in earlier cases: To determine whether material appeals to prurient interests, the content must be considered

● INTERNATIONAL LAW

United Kingdom Revises Pornography Regulations

In 2014, the United Kingdom amended its 2003 Communication Act and banned some specific sex acts from content produced and sold in Britain. The legislation does not impact pornography produced outside the country. The regulations target video-on-demand online porn services and ban a range of activities, some of which are singled out because they were deemed life-threatening, including strangulation. Depictions of nonconsensual sex are included in the banned acts, as are full bondage and restraint. U.K. regulators say the purpose of the ban is to safeguard children and bring restrictions on video-on-demand content in line with other forms of pornography in the country. Opponents of the regulation say it may affect internet freedom and will create an unnecessary trade barrier for independent U.K. producers of pornography.[1]

1. Heather Saul, *UK Porn Legislation: What Is Now Banned Under New Government Laws*, INDEPENDENT (LONDON), Dec. 2, 2014, www.independent .co.uk/news/uk/home-news/uk-porn-legislation-what-is-now-banned-under-new-government-laws-9898541.html.

Justices Anthony Kennedy (left), Ruth Bader Ginsburg (center) and Stephen Breyer (right) acknowledge the challenge in applying community standards to the internet.

as a whole, not as discrete pictures or words. A photograph that might be found obscene on its own may be protected in a magazine by surrounding it with fiction and nonfiction articles by leading authors.

An assessment of whether the material appeals to prurient interests must be based on conclusions drawn by an average person, not a child or a particularly sensitive person. Jurors are not to use their own personal standards but instead to use those of an average person in the community.[19] The Court has not explained how a juror can know the standards of an average person. Some courts allow survey results to help jurors understand community attitudes, but not all courts permit social science data as evidence.

The standards are to be community-wide. Legislatures and courts decide what geographic area will be the community for setting obscenity standards. The Supreme Court has said the community may be the city or county where the jurors live. In the *Miller* decision, the Court allowed California to use statewide standards. Other states, such as Illinois, also have permitted statewide obscenity standards.[20] Even a "deviant sexual group, rather than the public at large," may be a community for determining appropriate standards, the Court has said.[21]

It is easy to apply local, not national, standards when a movie theater shows a film. Local authorities charge the theater owner with showing an obscene film, and a local jury decides whether the film meets the *Miller* obscenity definition. It is far more difficult to apply local standards when an internet site in San Jose, Calif., sends sexually explicit photographs to Memphis, Tenn. Which is the local community—San Jose or Memphis?

In one case, a U.S. postal inspector in Memphis using an assumed name gained access to a bulletin board operating on a website physically located in Milpitas, Calif., a city north of San Jose. The postal inspector downloaded sexually explicit images and ordered videotapes delivered to him in Memphis by a freight service. Robert and Carleen Thomas, the bulletin board operators, were charged with sending obscene material across state lines and other obscenity-related crimes. The charges were filed in Memphis, and a Memphis jury convicted the defendants. Appealing their conviction, the bulletin board operators said a local community standard cannot apply to the internet, a geographically limitless medium. The U.S. Court of Appeals for the Sixth Circuit disagreed, declining to use a national standard for determining obscenity.[22] The court also rejected the defendants' suggestion to use an "internet community." The court said it was appropriate to use the local Memphis standards. Sellers of sexually explicit material should make certain they do not have customers in communities with inhospitable standards, the court said.

The Thomases proposed the internet community would be the entire country. Websites may be viewed and their material downloaded in any U.S. city. Even an email message sent to one person can be read wherever the recipient is, not necessarily in the person's home community. Under the *Miller* standard, then, which community's standard determines whether the material appeals to prurient interests—where the message was sent, where it was received, where it might be accessed or a national standard? How can an online publisher avoid sending content to communities that would find the material appeals to prurient interests while also sending it to communities that would not? U.S. Supreme Court Justice Anthony Kennedy, joined by Justices Ruth Bader Ginsburg and David Souter, recognized that the "national variation in community standards constitutes a particular burden on Internet speech."[23] Similarly, Justice Stephen Breyer said applying "the community standards of every locality in the United States would provide the most puritan of communities with a heckler's Internet veto affecting the rest of the Nation."[24] Former Justice Sandra Day O'Connor also favored a national community for judging internet communications.[25]

Nonetheless, the Court has not yet chosen to adopt a national community standard in cases of internet obscenity. That leaves lower courts to decide, and courts disagree about whether an internet community is local or national. For example, the U.S. Court of Appeals for the Ninth Circuit ruled that a jury must use a national community standard when deciding if material transmitted on the internet is obscene.[26] However, the U.S. Court of Appeals for the Eleventh Circuit disagreed. Paul Little, also known as Max Hardcore, was convicted of using the internet to market obscene videos. Hearing Little's appeal, the Eleventh Circuit held that the *Miller* contemporary community requirement means a local or statewide standard "on the Internet or elsewhere."[27]

Patently Offensive. The second part of the *Miller* test requires the government to show the material is **patently offensive** according to state law. In *Miller*, the U.S. Supreme Court provided examples of patent offensiveness: (1) "representations or descriptions of ultimate sexual acts, normal or perverted, actual or simulated" or (2) "representations or descriptions of masturbation, excretory functions and lewd exhibition of the genitals."[28] As in

patently offensive
Term describing material with hard-core sexual conduct.

● REAL WORLD LAW

Feminist Views on Pornography

In the early 1980s, feminists became more vocal about their views on pornography, and three schools of thought emerged that remain part of feminist discussions about pornography today. Anti-pornography feminists typically argue that all pornography harms women in its making, and it harms society because women are viewed only through a sexual lens. Anti-censorship feminists are critical of misogynistic pornography (specifically, pornography that results in the mistreatment of women or promotes hatred toward women), but they don't share the anti-pornography feminists' view that all pornography is bad. Pro-pornography feminists believe that pornography liberates women's sexuality and helps challenge existing gender norms. Pro-pornography feminists also oppose censorship.[1]

1. Gail Dines & Robert Jensen, *Feminist Debates on Pornography*, Gail Dines, Sept. 10, 2009, gaildines.com/2009/09/pornography-feminist-debates-on/.

the first part of the *Miller* test, patent offensiveness is to be determined by contemporary community standards, the Court said.

The Supreme Court's examples of patent offensiveness mean that state definitions must meet a certain standard. Patently offensive material at least has to include hard-core sexual conduct. The Court made this clear when it rejected a jury's finding that the movie "Carnal Knowledge" was obscene.[29] The 1971 movie, directed by a leading Broadway and Hollywood director, Mike Nichols, contained some partial nudity but had no sex scenes. Starring Candice Bergen, Jack Nicholson and Ann-Margret, who received an Oscar nomination for her role, it had made several critics' Top 10 lists. An Albany, Ga., jury convicted a theater operator for showing the film, finding the movie to be obscene. The Supreme Court said the jury had the right to use local community standards in deciding whether the film appealed to prurient interests. However, the jury could not find the movie was patently offensive unless at a minimum it met the Court's understanding of that term, as illustrated by the Court's examples.

The Court has said the *Miller* examples of patently offensive material were just that—examples—not an exhaustive list. Sexually explicit material not included in the Court's list of sexual acts could be patently offensive.[30] Deciding whether material appeals to prurient interests, then, largely is in a jury's hands. But the Court said, "it would be a serious misreading of *Miller* to conclude that juries have unbridled discretion in determining what is 'patently offensive.'"[31] A jury could decide that local community standards set a higher level for patent offensiveness than the Court required. Jurors in San Francisco or New York, for example, might determine that in those communities patently offensive material must depict scenes even more offensive than the Court's examples. However, jurors in Albany, Ga., cannot decide that scenes of partly nude actors make a film patently offensive. Partial nudity is not the equivalent of the Court's criteria for finding patent offensiveness.

The second part of the *Miller* obscenity test requires states to define the specific sexual acts forbidden by state law. Courts require criminal laws to be clear and specific, allowing people to know what they must do or not do in order to obey the laws. The Supreme Court's language in *Miller* says that is how states must write obscenity laws—clearly and definitively.

Serious Social Value. The third part of the *Miller* obscenity test says material cannot be found obscene if it has serious literary, artistic, political or social value. Under *Miller*, the work has to lack serious social value to be considered obscene. There is a wide gap between any social value and serious social value. Material falling in the space between "any social value" and "serious social value" could be found obscene if it also meets the first two parts of the *Miller* test.

In *Pope v. Illinois*, decided after *Miller*, the Supreme Court said serious social value should be decided using national standards, not local criteria.[32] The *Pope* decision also said a determination of **serious social value** should be based on what a reasonable person would decide. Because this suggests an objective, rather than a subjective, analysis of a work's social value, juries may consider testimony of expert witnesses who express their opinions about a work's social value.

serious social value Material cannot be found obscene if it has serious literary, artistic, political or scientific value determined using national, not local/community, standards.

At the request of a county sheriff in Florida, a federal district court found a 2 Live Crew album, "As Nasty as They Wanna Be," to be obscene. On review, the Eleventh Circuit Court of Appeals observed that 2 Live Crew presented several expert witnesses at trial who testified the album had serious social value. The sheriff played the album at trial but offered no expert witnesses to support his contention that the recording was obscene. The appellate court said simply listening to a recording was not enough to determine whether the recording possessed serious social value. Expert witnesses' testimony was required.[33]

Jeff Kravitz/FilmMagic, Inc./Getty Images

In 1992, a Florida county sheriff asked a court to find 2 Live Crew's "As Nasty as They Wanna Be" album obscene but did not provide any evidence.

Enforcing Obscenity Laws

The *Miller v. California* decision did not answer all questions about obscenity. For example, is *Miller* the correct test to determine whether sexual material should be made available to minors? Even if it is illegal to produce, distribute, sell and exhibit obscene material, is it illegal to possess it? What is child pornography? The Supreme Court has worked its way through these and other matters concerning obscene material.

Variable Obscenity. Long ago, the Supreme Court held that government officials may not limit adults to seeing only material acceptable for children. In 1957, the Court struck

⬤ POINTS OF LAW

The *Miller* Test

Under the *Miller* test, to find material obscene, a court must consider whether

1. "the average person, applying contemporary community standards," would find that the work, taken as a whole, appeals to prurient interests;

2. the work depicts or describes, in a patently offensive way, sexual conduct specifically defined by the applicable state law; and

3. the work, taken as a whole, lacks serious literary, artistic, political or scientific value (often called the SLAPS test).[1]

1. Miller v. California, 413 U.S. 15, 22 (1973).

down a Michigan law making it illegal to distribute sexual material "tending to incite minors to violent or depraved or immoral acts."[34] The Court said the law violated the First Amendment because its effect "is to reduce the adult population of Michigan to reading only what is fit for children."[35]

However, the opposite is not true. In *Ginsberg v. New York*, the Court said minors do not have a First Amendment right to sexual material acceptable for adults. Under its power to protect the well-being of minors, the Court said, a state may "adjust the definition of obscenity to social realities."[36] Restricting minors' access to sexual material has been called **variable obscenity**: Material not obscene for adults may be obscene if the same material is given to minors.

variable obscenity
The concept that sexually oriented material not obscene for adults may be obscene if distributed to minors.

child pornography
Any image showing children in sexual or sexually explicit situations.

Child Pornography. Making, selling, distributing or possessing child pornography is illegal. Federal law defines **child pornography** as "any visual depiction . . . involving the use of a minor engaging in sexually explicit conduct . . . or such visual depiction [that] has been created . . . to appear that an identifiable minor is engaging in sexually explicit conduct."[37] The question is not whether children are appearing in videos, films or photographs that would be obscene under the *Miller v. California* test. Rather, the question is whether minors are being sexually exploited. In addition to the federal law, all states and the District of Columbia have child pornography laws.

Courts, Congress and child welfare organizations have recognized the harm child pornography causes. There is harm not only from the initial sexual act or depiction but also from the presence of the images on the internet. Thirty-five years ago in *New York v. Ferber*, the Supreme Court upheld New York's child pornography law, one of the nation's strictest.[38] Ferber sold pornographic films of young boys to an undercover officer. Hearing

▋ SOCIAL MEDIA LAW

Twitter, Reddit Ban Revenge Porn and Threats

As noted in Chapter 6, many state legislatures are passing laws to criminalize revenge porn, also called nonconsensual pornography. Revenge porn consists of sexually explicit videos or nude pictures of people that are posted online without the individuals' consent. Social media are one way that revenge porn is quickly distributed. In 2015, Twitter approved new community rules that prohibit posting "intimate photos or videos that were taken or distributed without the subject's consent."[1] Reddit enacted a similar policy.[2]

Under the new Twitter rules, the subject of a revenge porn image can report it to the company and request that Twitter review and remove the material. The user who posted the image can appeal a takedown decision, but if Twitter determines that an image violates the revenge porn prohibition, the company will not only block access to the image but also lock the account of the poster.[3]

---

1. Hayley Tsukayama, *Twitter Updates Its Rules to Specifically Ban "Revenge Porn,"* WASH. POST, Mar. 11, 2015, www.washingtonpost.com/blogs/the-switch/wp/2015/03/11/twitter-updates-its-rules-to-specifically-ban-revenge-porn/.
2. Andrea Peterson, *Reddit Is Finally Cracking Down on Revenge Porn,* WASH. POST, Feb. 24, 2015, www.washingtonpost.com/blogs/the-switch/wp/2015/02/24/reddit-is-finally-cracking-down-on-revenge-porn/.
3. Tsukayama, *supra* note 1.

Ferber's appeal of his conviction, the Court said child pornography laws are essential to protecting minors. Using children in sexual material harms minors' "physiological, emotional and mental health," the Court said.[39] First, the child endures psychological harm, knowing there is a permanent record of his participation in sexual activity. Second, making, selling and obtaining pornography showing children in sexual situations helps to perpetuate the sexual exploitation of children and encourages pedophilia.

Federal law is applied to visual depictions and defines child pornography as any image showing minors in "sexually explicit conduct."[40] The conduct may be actual or simulated "sexual intercourse," "masturbation" or lewd "exhibition of the genitals or pubic area."[41]

Courts strictly interpret child pornography laws. "Unlike the Court's obscenity standards, child pornography laws involve no fuzzy facts like 'community standards' or 'artistic value,' and prosecutors can make a case with little more than proof that the defendant possessed or made a visual depiction of sexual conduct by a minor," wrote a First Amendment scholar.[42] For example, a film showed preteen and teenaged girls younger than 17 years old wearing bikinis, leotards or underwear (but not nude) and gyrating to music. The "photographer would zoom in on the children's pubic and genital area and display a close-up view for an extended period of time," a federal appellate court said.[43] The film was child pornography and the federal child pornography law does not require nudity, the court said, holding that this broad interpretation of federal law does not make the law unconstitutionally overbroad.[44]

At least one court has taken to the extreme concern about child pornography's role in entangling minors in the sex trade. A Florida circuit court judge sentenced a 26-year-old man to life in prison without possibility of parole when he was found guilty of having hundreds of pornographic images of children on his computer.[45]

More than 20 years ago, Congress adopted the Child Pornography Prevention Act, criminalizing the sending or possessing of digital images of children in sexual poses or activities, even if the images were of young-looking adults and not of real children. The Supreme Court found the law unconstitutional, noting that two provisions in the law that dealt with virtual images of children were too broad and criminalized child pornography that did not involve actual minors.[46]

Fifteen years ago, Congress passed the Prosecutorial Remedies and Other Tools to End the Exploitation of Children Today (PROTECT) Act in response to the Court's decision. Under review, the Supreme Court held that the PROTECT Act was constitutional and did not violate the First Amendment. The Court was concerned that "the emergence of new technology and the repeated retransmission of picture files over the Internet . . . could make it nearly impossible to prove that a particular image was produced using real children [even though] there is no substantial evidence that any of the child pornography images being trafficked today were made other than by the abuse of real children," because virtual imaging is prohibitively expensive."[47]

Writing for the majority, Justice Antonin Scalia said, "Child pornography harms and debases the most defenseless of our citizens. Both the state and federal governments have sought to suppress it for many years, only to find it proliferating through the new medium of the Internet. This Court held unconstitutional Congress's previous attempt to meet this new threat, and Congress responded with a carefully crafted attempt to eliminate the

First Amendment problems we identified. As far as the provision at issue in this case is concerned, that effort was successful."[48]

Even though the Supreme Court determined that virtual child pornography that does not involve actual minors does not receive First Amendment protection, the courts continue to hear cases about child pornography and technology. In 2014, a defendant in the Eighth Circuit Court of Appeals challenged the federal definition of child pornography that includes "visual depictions . . . modified to appear" like a minor engaged in sexual conduct.[49] The defendant argued that the definition was overly broad because morphed images are not real, so sexual abuse cannot occur. The Eighth Circuit disagreed, noting that the government did not have a less restrictive means "to protect this child from the exploitation and psychological harm resulting from the distribution of the morphed image than to prevent [the defendant] from disseminating it."[50]

U.S. law allows child pornography victims to seek restitution not only from the person who created the images but also from those who possess the pictures.[51] The victim may recover for physical and psychological medical services, temporary housing, childcare, lost income, attorney's fees and other expenses. The person who created the images will be liable for these damages.[52] However, restitution from a person who did not make but only possessed the child pornography must be based on proof of harm. Ten U.S. courts of appeals have ruled that the victim must show that a person who only has, or perhaps also transmitted, the illegal images caused specific harms.[53] The Fifth Circuit Court of Appeals is the only federal appellate court to disagree.[54] It decided in 2012 that the victim need show only that he or she was harmed by the image being in circulation and anyone found guilty of possessing that image may be liable for damages.

◉ POINTS OF LAW

Virtual Child Pornography

Federal law applies to visual depictions and defines child pornography as any image showing minors in "sexually explicit conduct."[1] Fifteen years ago, in *Ashcroft v. Free Speech Coalition*, the Supreme Court struck down two provisions of the Child Pornography Prevention Act because it also prohibited material that was not obscene or traditional child pornography. The Court's decision prohibited the criminalization of pure virtual child pornography that did not involve actual minors.[2]

The year after *Ashcroft*, Congress responded by passing the Prosecutorial Remedies and Other Tools to end the Exploitation of Children Today Act, which replaced the problematic provisions in the CPPA. Subsequently, in *United States v. Williams*, the Supreme Court upheld the PROTECT Act provisions and noted that all child pornography, virtual or otherwise, is obscene and without First Amendment protection. In his dissent, Justice David Souter summarized the impact of the decision, which brings clarity to the question of virtual images: "If the (PROTECT) Act can be enforced, it will function just as it was meant to do, by merging the whole subject of child pornography . . . dispensing with the real-child element in the underlying subject."[3]

1. 18 U.S.C. §§ 2251(a), 2252(b)(4), 2256(8).
2. Ashcroft v. Free Speech Coalition, 535 U.S. 234 (2002).
3. United States v. Williams, 553 U.S. 285, 319 (2008) (Souter, J., dissenting).

In 2014, the U.S. Supreme Court took a closer look at the specific statutory language in the law and concluded in *Paroline v. United States* that Congress intended to limit restitution to only those losses proximately caused by the defendant.[55] A proximate cause is a cause that directly produces the effect. The possession of child pornography containing a plaintiff's image, unlike the creation of that image, may not qualify as a proximate cause that entitles the victim to compensation. Or, if it does, it might not justify awarding the full amount of damages the plaintiff claims.

Hearing the appeal in *Paroline*, the Supreme Court remanded the case for reconsideration with the guidance that a victim should receive restitution only in an amount that represents the extent of loss the defendant caused the victim. As of 2017, a district court in Texas had not yet ruled in its reconsideration of the case.[56]

The impact of the *Paroline* decision is still unclear. The court was split 5–4, with two dissenting opinions. In one, Chief Justice John G. Roberts, joined by Justices Scalia and Clarence Thomas, argued that the Court's ruling simply asks lower courts to pick "arbitrary" amounts for restitution. They said that is not "good enough for the criminal law" and would ultimately result in no restitution for victims who are repeatedly victimized in cases when many offenders (sometimes thousands) possess images of the child pornography victim.[57]

In her dissent, Justice Sonia Sotomayor argued that the Court's opinion could not be reconciled with the law Congress passed, which she said requires full restitution for a victim's losses. "Congress did not intend . . . to create a safe harbor for those who inflict upon their victims the proverbial death by a thousand cuts," she wrote. "Given the very nature of the child pornography market—in which a large class of offenders contribute jointly to their victims' harm by trading their images—[the Court's approach leaves] victims with little hope of recovery."[58]

One legal scholar has suggested that when Congress enacted the law it did not fully consider the nature of the harm of child pornography to the victims. She argued that restitution for victims of child pornography is not as straightforward as restitution for victims of other criminal acts. She suggested, as did the dissenting justices, that Congress should revisit the law. The appellate courts that have heard these cases have also urged Congress to clarify the language in the law to allow for consistent application.[59]

Sexting. Sexting is defined as "sending someone sexually explicit photographs or messages via a mobile phone."[60] Sometimes prosecutors classify sexting involving minors as child pornography.[61] If the act of sexting is child pornography, those who receive and retain sexually explicit images can be charged with possessing child pornography, a felony under state and federal laws.

Currently, 20 states have laws that specifically target sexting. Some of the laws are connected to laws that prohibit the distribution of revenge porn, also called nonconsensual pornography.[62] Some state legislatures—including those in Arizona, Connecticut, Louisiana and Illinois—have adopted laws imposing lighter sentences on teenage sexters than on adults convicted of making or possessing child pornography. In Louisiana, for example, a first offense for teen sexting warrants 10 days in jail, and a second offense could lead to 30 days in jail. The Arizona law categorizes sexting by those 8 to 18 years old as a petty offense if pictures are sent only to one other person.[63] Some states, for example Texas and Florida, take a rehabilitative approach to teen sexting and require education and community service as part of their accountability efforts.[64]

According to one legal scholar, teen sexting has declined slightly since 2009 when sexting laws became more common. A 2014 report suggests that about 40 percent of teenagers have posted or texted sexually suggestive messages.[65]

Possessing Obscene Material. Although courts have upheld laws against making, distributing, selling and exhibiting obscene material, the Supreme Court said the First Amendment protects possession of obscene material, except child pornography, in the privacy of one's home.

Overturning a conviction for possessing obscene films, the Supreme Court in *Stanley v. Georgia* said that merely categorizing films as obscene did not justify "a drastic invasion of personal liberties guaranteed by the First Amendment."[66] Police had found the obscene films during a search of a suspected bookmaker's home. The Court said there are reasons to have obscenity statutes, but the reasons do not allow authorities to "reach into the privacy of one's own home."[67] Government may not tell people what books they may read or films they may watch, the Court said.

The government may limit possession of child pornography.[68] The U.S. Supreme Court has said the underlying interests prohibiting the possession of child pornography are so vital that they support a ban on possession.[69] The justifications for punishing possession of child

▲ EMERGING LAW

Snapchat Sued for Sexually Explicit Content

In 2016, a 14-year-old user and his mother filed a class action lawsuit against the Snapchat messaging app that lets users send videos and pictures that automatically delete within a few seconds of viewing. The teenager had viewed several sexually explicit posts on the app's Discover section. One of the posts mentioned in the complaint and produced by BuzzFeed was titled "23 Pictures That Are Too Real If You've Ever Had Sex With a Penis," and featured Disney movie stills with explicit captions. The post allegedly "perverted" Disney characters into "obscene" images.[1]

The Discover section debuted in 2015 and features a range of content brands (for example, CNN, ESPN, BuzzFeed and Disney, among many others) that produce "daily refreshed" channels with stories and ads.[2] The complaint alleges that Snapchat curates the Discover articles. Snapchat is rated on iTunes as an app for people 12+, but its terms of use note that it might offer additional services that require "you to be even older to use."[3]

According to the complaint, Snapchat is engaged in "an insidious pattern and practice of intentionally exposing minors to harmful, offensive, prurient and sexually offensive content, without warning minors or their parents that they would be exposed to such explicit content."[4]

1. Eriq Gardner, *Snapchat Sued for Exposing Kids to Media Partners' Sexually Offensive Content*, Hollywood Reporter, July 7, 2016, www.hollywoodreporter.com/thr-esq/snapchat-sued-exposing-kids-media-909096.
2. Jordan Crook, *Snapchat Launches Discover*, Tech Crunch, Jan. 27, 2015, techcrunch.com/2015/01/27/snapchat-launches-discover/.
3. Mariella Moon, *Snapchat Faces Class-Action Suit for Sexually Explicit Content*, Engadget, July 8, 2016, www.engadget.com/2016/07/08/snapchat-class-action-sexually-explicit-discover/.
4. Gardner, *supra* note 1.

pornography—protecting children's physical and psychological well-being and ending the sexual exploitation of children—are sufficiently important to overcome First Amendment rights, the Court said.

Procedural Protections. The First Amendment protects filmmakers, according to the Supreme Court.[70] Nonetheless, the Court once allowed government censorship boards to license films for exhibition. That is, in some states and communities, a theater had to obtain board approval before it could show a film.[71] When they were active, some censorship boards assumed a given film was obscene and required

the movie producer to prove it was not. This violated the movie producer's rights, the Supreme Court said.[72]

There are no more government movie censors. The last movie censorship board, the Maryland State Board of Censors, stopped functioning in 1981. But the procedural safeguards the Supreme Court required of those committees set the standard for all obscenity prosecutions. For example, government officials must prove in court that a work is obscene. Officials cannot merely claim material is obscene and then ban it. Additionally, any prior restraint on allegedly obscene material must be for as short a time as possible until a court decides whether the work meets the obscenity definition.

Authorities also have tried to control obscenity using laws that target organized crime. Almost 50 years ago, Congress adopted the Racketeer Influenced and Corrupt Organizations Act.[73] Thirty-two states also have RICO acts. The RICO laws forbid using money earned from illegal activities—racketeering—to finance legal or illegal businesses or nonprofit enterprises engaged in interstate commerce.[74]

RICO prosecutions implicate the First Amendment because the laws allow the government to seize all assets acquired through racketeering activity. In one case, the owner of a dozen adult theaters and bookstores was convicted of violating obscenity laws. Under the state's RICO law, authorities seized the contents of the defendant's theaters and bookstores. The defendant claimed the seizure violated his First Amendment rights. In part, he said the seizure amounted to a prior restraint because not all his stores' books and his theaters' films were obscene. The seizure was for past criminal acts—selling obscene material, the Supreme Court said.[75] If the defendant wanted to open a new adult bookstore that sold sexually explicit but not obscene material, he could do so in the future. Therefore, there was no prior restraint.

INDECENCY

Consider obscene sexual expression on one side of an imaginary line and nonobscene sexual expression on the other side. Take the nonobscene sexual expression, add excretory

▲ EMERGING LAW

Online Adult Advertisements and Sex Trafficking

In 2017, the website Backpage.com said it would close its "adult section" in which advertisers solicited sexual services while it continues to fight several lawsuits in federal courts.[1] Law enforcement specialists who investigate child sexual exploitation and child prostitution argue that online advertising websites are the primary means for promoting the availability of children for sex. Some state sex trafficking laws target online advertising as one means to stop potential child sexual abuse.

Recently, more than 80 percent of state attorneys general have pressured Craigslist, the leading operator of online adult-oriented advertising, and Backpage.com to shut down their adult services sections that include ads for prostitutes, escort services and other adult-oriented services. Backpage.com refused to do so until a Senate investigative committee concluded that the website was knowingly assisting human traffickers.[2] Backpage.com called the subcommittee's findings "unconstitutional government censorship."[3]

State legislation has also targeted and shut down website advertisers that might facilitate commercial sex abuse of a minor. In Washington and Massachusetts, Backpage.com successfully argued that the First Amendment protected it from enforcement of state laws that created criminal liability for anyone who knowingly advertises "the commercial sexual abuse of a minor."[4] Backpage.com argued that the law would chill permissible ads and that Section 230 of the Communications Decency Act (see Chapter 5) protected it from liability. Federal courts have agreed.[5]

A 2012 study reported that while 70 percent of adult classified ads appeared on Backpage.com, sex ads persisted on Craigslist and could be found on Facebook, Twitter, Tumblr and About.com. Voice Media Group, the owner of Backpage.com, makes about $22 million per year on user-generated adult advertising, the report said.[6]

---

1. Steven Koff, *Backpage.com Still Appears to Be Running Ads for Prostitutes, Sexual Services*, Cleveland.com, Jan. 12, 2017, www.cleveland.com/metro/index.ssf/2017/01/backpagecom_might_not_have_act.html.
2. *Id.*
3. Derek Hawkins, *Backpage.com Shuts Down Adult Services Ads After Relentless Pressure From Authorities*, Wash. Post, Jan. 10, 2017, www.washingtonpost.com/news/morning-mix/wp/2017/01/10/backpage-com-shuts-down-adult-services-ads-after-relentless-pressure-from-authorities/?utm_term=.227390c60d61.
4. Doe v. Backpage.com LLC, 817 F.3d 12 (1st Cir. 2016), *cert. denied*, 137 S. Ct. 622 (2017); Backpage.com LLC v. McKenna, 881 F. Supp. 2d 1262 (W.D. Wash. 2012).
5. *Id.*
6. Tracy Clark-Flory, *Sex Ads: It Isn't Just Backpage.com*, Salon, May 24, 2012, www.salon.com/2012/05/24/sex_ads_it_isnt_just_backpage_com/.

functions and filthy words, and it becomes indecent speech. The Supreme Court has made clear that the First Amendment does not protect obscenity. Does the First Amendment protect indecency? Indecent speech is protected in print media, in movies, in recordings and on the internet. It is protected on most cable television programming. Indecent speech is not protected if broadcast by radio or television between 6 a.m. and 10 p.m. or if directed to children over the telephone.[76] As with obscenity, the problem is defining "indecency."

The Communications Act of 1934 makes it illegal to broadcast indecent material.[77] Many individuals and members of federal administrative agencies and Congress want to limit children's exposure to indecency. However, the courts and the FCC allow broadcast radio and television stations to air indecent material when it is likely that few children will be in the audience.

What is indecent speech? According to the U.S. Supreme Court, "The normal definition of 'indecent' merely refers to nonconformance with accepted standards of morality."[78] "Indecency" is not a synonym for "obscenity," the Court said.[79] Obscenity meets the *Miller v. California* definition.[80] Indecency does not; rather, indecency is content some people find offensive. Material that is patently offensive but does not have prurient appeal is not obscene but may be indecent.[81] Also, material may be indecent even if it has serious social value. The FCC once defined indecency as "language or material that, in context, depicts or describes in terms patently offensive as measured by contemporary community standards for the broadcast medium, sexual or excretory activities or organs."[82] However, this definition is flexible.

Broadcast Indecency

Indecent images and language are not the same as obscene material. What is indecency? Is it the repetition of certain four-letter and other unacceptable words? Is it patently offensive material that describes or shows sexual or excretory organs or activities? Is it the single utterance of an expletive? At various times, the FCC has said each of these definitions describes indecency.

In both the 1927 Radio Act and the Communications Act of 1934, Congress prohibited broadcasting "any obscene, indecent, or profane language."[83] Congress later eliminated this provision but inserted the ban on indecent broadcasts into the federal criminal code.[84] In 1960, Congress gave the FCC power to impose civil fines on broadcasters who violate the commission's indecency regulations.[85]

The law seems clear: no indecent material on broadcast radio or television. But the First Amendment protects indecent speech unless the government has a compelling interest in regulating it and chooses the least restrictive regulatory method.[86] Also, the law forbids the FCC from censoring radio or television broadcasts.[87] And among all media, only broadcasting is forbidden from carrying indecent material. How, then, can banning broadcast indecency be justified?

The FCC and the courts, with Congress' acquiescence, said the reason for limiting indecent programs is to protect children.[88] For example, in fining a radio station for discussing oral sex during an afternoon program, the commission emphasized "the presence of children in the broadcast audience."[89] Also, the First Amendment protects indecent material in nonbroadcast media because these media can separate children from adults in their audiences. Minors can be prevented from having access to indecent books, magazines and movies, for example. But broadcast radio and television are too pervasive; they are available everywhere and children continually are exposed to them. Those concerned about indecency, then, had to balance potential harms to children against broadcasters' First Amendment rights.

George Carlin.

Defining Broadcast Indecency. The FCC's statutory duty to limit indecent broadcasts lay dormant for many years. The FCC did not act against indecency until 1975. The commission responded to a father's complaint that in 1973 he and his young son heard a New York City radio station playing comedian George Carlin's "Filthy Words" monologue at 2 p.m. Carlin's 12-minute live performance contained the seven "words you couldn't say on television."[90] He then said them repeatedly.[91] Defining indecency as "language that describes, in terms patently offensive as measured by contemporary community standards for the broadcast medium, sexual or excretory activities and organs, at times of the day when there is a reasonable risk that children may be in the audience," the FCC fined the station's operator, Pacifica Foundation.[92]

When *FCC v. Pacifica Foundation* (excerpted below) reached the U.S. Supreme Court, the Court said indecent broadcast speech is material in "nonconformance with accepted standards of morality." Broadcasters have First Amendment protection, the Court noted, but the protection is limited because of spectrum scarcity (see Chapter 9). This allows courts to restrict indecency in broadcasting but not in other media, the Court said.

In determining whether the Carlin recording was indecent, the Court said the context of the challenged material is "all-important" and that an "occasional expletive" need not lead to sanctioning a broadcaster.[93] The Court focused on the "repetitive, deliberate use" of words that refer to "excretory or sexual activities or organs" in a "patently offensive" but nonobscene manner.[94] This suggested that indecency applied only to a Carlin-like monologue—defining indecency as "filthy words." Double entendre and sly suggestions about sex seemed not to be included in the Court's definition of indecent speech. The Court stressed radio and television's "uniquely pervasive presence in the lives of all Americans" but focused on children. The nature of broadcasting made it "uniquely accessible to children, even those too young to read." That concern and the unique facts of the case—Carlin's repeatedly saying the seven words—justified the FCC's fining the radio station, the Court said.[95]

For a decade after *Pacifica*, the FCC defined indecency as it did in that case—repeated dirty words—and took no action against broadcasters for violating the commission's indecency standard. Words not describing sexual activities or organs, and therefore not patently offensive, were not indecent unless they were Carlin-type words constantly repeated. When the words were only expletives, the commission said, "[D]eliberate and repetitive use in a patently offensive manner is a requisite to a finding of indecency."[96] At that time, a single expletive was not indecent.

In 1987, the FCC expressed concern that the "filthy words" indecency definition did not sufficiently protect children. Instead, the commission adopted a broader generic standard to define indecency.[97] The commission said it would consider a broadcast's context and tone as well as its language. This allowed the FCC to expand its indecency definition.[98] In the *Pacifica* decision, the Court said that community standards for broadcast determined when language or material was "patently offensive" and therefore indecent.[99] The *Pacifica* Court did not say what it meant by "patently offensive" as measured by "community standards for the broadcast medium," leaving broadcasters with little guidance beyond knowing what seven words George Carlin used in his monologue.

The FCC tried to clarify its standards in 2001 by adopting broadcast industry indecency guidelines. The commission again said material is indecent if it meets the generic *Pacifica* test, adding that it would consider several factors in determining whether broadcast material was patently offensive: (1) how explicitly or graphically the material describes

● **REAL WORLD LAW**

Accidental Porn on the Local News

In 2015, when WDBJ in Roanoke, Va., broadcast a news story about a porn star who volunteered with a local rescue organization, it accidentally aired an image of a naked man with "a hand moving up and down the length of the shaft of the erect penis."[1]

What happened? The station told the Federal Communications Commission that it did not realize that its use of an acceptable still image from a porn website would also include boxes simultaneously showing video clips from pornographic films. The sexually explicit video clip aired for three seconds. The FCC noted that "although the material did not extensively dwell on or contain repetitions of sexual material, . . . the duration of the material was sufficient to attract and hold viewers' attention; several complainants note that they viewed the material perfectly well."[2]

The FCC concluded that WDBJ was culpable and fined the station the maximum $325,000.[3]

---

1. Eugene Volokh, *FCC Proposes $325,000 Fine for Accidental Inclusion of Porn on Video Capture in News Story*, WASH. POST, March 24, 2015, www .washingtonpost.com/news/volokh-conspiracy/wp/2015/03/24/fcc-proposes-325000-fine-for-accidental-inclusion-of-porn-on-video-capture-in-news-story/.
2. In the Matter of WDBJ Television, 2015 F.C.C. LEXIS 858 (F.C.C. Mar. 23, 2015).
3. *Id.*

sexual activities, (2) whether the material dwells on sexual activities and (3) whether the material is meant to shock or sexually excite the audience. The FCC said it would consider the full context in which the material appeared.[100]

But the commission's clarified definition of indecency did not last long. When U2 band member Bono said, "This is really, really, fucking brilliant," while receiving a Golden Globe award during the 2003 ceremony telecast, complaints poured in to the FCC. The commission asserted, for the first time, that a "fleeting expletive"—a single, nonliteral use of a curse word—could be indecent.[101] The "'F-Word' is one of the most vulgar, graphic and explicit descriptions of sexual activity in the English language," and therefore "inherently has a sexual connotation," the commission said. This conclusion overruled previous FCC decisions that found a fleeting expletive not indecent. The commission also found Bono's comment "profane," discarding its earlier definitions limiting that word to meaning blasphemy.

Similarly, the FCC found singer and actress Cher's unscripted exclamation on the 2002 prime-time Billboard Music Awards program—"People have been telling me I'm on the way out every year, right? So fuck 'em"—and television personality Nicole Richie's

U2 lead singer Bono.

Axelle/Bauer-Griffin/FilmMagic/Getty Images

remark on the 2003 Billboard Music Awards program—"Have you ever tried to get cow shit out of a Prada purse? It's not so fucking simple"—to be indecent and profane.[102] The FCC also said the two programs were patently offensive because the material was explicit, shocking and gratuitous.

The Second Circuit Court of Appeals rejected the FCC's decision, saying the commission "failed to adequately explain why it had changed its nearly-30-year policy on fleeting expletives." The court noted that the FCC ruling "bore 'no rational connection to the Commission's actual policy,' because the FCC had not instituted a blanket ban on expletives."[103]

But the U.S. Supreme Court overturned the Second Circuit's decision. The Court in 2009 said the FCC did not act arbitrarily or capriciously when it ruled that a single use of an expletive is indecent. The FCC supplied sufficient reasons for its new policy, the Court said. The FCC admitted it overturned a long-standing regulation that a single use was not indecent. But the commission said the "F-Word" has a sexual meaning no matter how it is used, a meaning that insults and offends. That was enough justification for the Court, in a 5–4 decision, to uphold the FCC's new rule.[104]

The Supreme Court did not discuss the constitutional issue beyond instructing the Second Circuit to consider whether the FCC's "fleeting obscenity" rule abridged broadcasters' First Amendment rights. The Second Circuit said the rule did infringe broadcasters' free speech. The appellate court held that the commission's fleeting-expletive policy violated the First Amendment because it was vague, not allowing broadcasters to know what content would be found indecent and thus creating a chilling effect. The court said the chilling effect went beyond the fleeting-expletive regulation, forcing broadcasters not to take risks but rather to self-censor content that might or might not be found indecent under the FCC's definition. Also, some words might be indecent in entertainment shows but not necessarily in a news program or if used for educational or artistic purposes. For example, the commission rejected complaints that swear words in the movie "Saving Private Ryan" were indecent when a broadcast television network showed the film.[105]

The FCC appealed the Second Circuit's decision to the Supreme Court. In 2012, the Court told the FCC it could not fine broadcasters for carrying the Bono, Cher and Richie utterances because the FCC adopted the fleeting-expletive rule after those programs were aired.[106] Broadcasters could not be held liable for violating a rule they did not know would change, the Court said. The Supreme Court did not define, or give the FCC guidance in defining, indecency. Nor did the Court determine whether indecency regulations infringe broadcasters' First Amendment rights. Aside from telling the FCC it could not apply new rules retroactively, the Court did no more than say the commission may modify its indecency regulations, considering the public interest and legal requirements, and courts may review the current or modified indecency rules when appropriate cases arise.

While the Bono, Cher and Richie questions were bouncing back and forth in the courts, Justin Timberlake ever-so-briefly exposed (for 9/16 of one second) Janet Jackson's breast during the 2004 Super Bowl halftime show, and a frenzy ensued. Congress increased the maximum fine the FCC could impose for broadcasting indecent material "by a factor of 10."[107] Reacting to public and congressional outrage, the FCC said Jackson's partial nudity violated its indecency standard and imposed $550,000 in fines against Viacom-owned television stations that aired the Super Bowl.[108] Viacom Inc. owns CBS, the network that carried the Super Bowl in 2004.

The U.S. Court of Appeals for the Third Circuit overturned the commission's decision, saying that for three decades the FCC punished broadcasters for indecent programming only when the material was "so pervasive as to amount to 'shock treatment' for the audience. . . . [T]he Commission consistently explained that isolated or fleeting material did not fall within the scope of actionable indecency."[109]

The U.S. Supreme Court told the Third Circuit to reconsider its decision.[110] The Court said its 2009 ruling concerning Bono and Cher could mean the FCC did not act arbitrarily and capriciously in finding that CBS aired indecent material. In 2011, the Third Circuit issued a new ruling that said the 2009 *Fox* decision supported its conclusion in the Super Bowl case.[111] However, both the FCC and the Supreme Court acknowledged the commission changed the definition of indecency in its fleeting-expletive ruling, applying to both words and images. Additionally, as with the Bono and Cher broadcasts, the Janet Jackson incident occurred before the commission announced its new approach, so the CBS network and stations could not have anticipated the change. On this basis, the Third Circuit affirmed its previous ruling that the FCC could not impose fines for airing a fleeting image of Jackson's breast. The Supreme Court refused to hear an appeal of the Third Circuit's 2011 decision.

The Supreme Court's 2012 *Fox Television* decision (excerpted at the end of this chapter) and the Court's refusal to review the Third Circuit's Super Bowl ruling left broadcasters with little guidance. The Court gave the FCC a suggestion, though, when it said in *Fox Television*, "[T]his opinion leaves the Commission free to modify its current indecency policy in light of its determination of the public interest and applicable legal requirements."[112] In 2013, the FCC began reconsidering its indecency regulations. The commission sought public comment on whether the FCC should change its broadcast indecency policies but failed to take any action.[113]

Channeling Broadcast Indecency. Balancing the U.S. Supreme Court's expressed concern for children against broadcasters' free speech rights, and complying with a congressional mandate, the FCC adopted a **safe harbor policy** in 1993. The commission would not punish any station that broadcasts indecent programming in a certain time period, a scheduling practice called "channeling." An FCC rule says stations may air indecent—but not obscene—material from 10 p.m. to 6 a.m. local time.[114] Strictly speaking, broadcasting indecent material at any time violates federal law. But the commission, with court approval, agreed not to take action against indecent broadcasts aired at times when few children are expected to be in the audience.[115] The 10 p.m. to 6 a.m. period is a safe harbor, a time when stations safely may broadcast material that does not fully comply with the law's indecency ban.

Television Program Ratings and the V-Chip. Roughly 25 years ago, some members of Congress expressed a concern about the impact of violent content on children. Realizing that the First Amendment prevented government censorship of television

safe harbor policy A Federal Communications Commission policy designating 10 p.m. to 6 a.m. as a time when broadcast radio and television stations may air indecent material without violating federal law or FCC regulations.

programs, Congress considered other alternatives. After an acrimonious fight, Congress required television set manufacturers to include an electronic chip, the V-chip, to enable parents to block reception of certain programs. Congress also encouraged the FCC or the television industry to establish a program ratings system.

Preferring to adopt its own program ratings system rather than have the FCC recommend or require one, the National Association of Broadcasters, representing broadcast stations and networks; the National Cable Television Association (now the Internet & Television Association), representing cable system owners; and the Motion Picture Association of America, representing television program producers, created the TV Parental Guidelines. The guidelines create a voluntary ratings system. For more than a decade, all broadcast and basic cable networks have chosen to rate their programs, as have premium cable networks such as HBO and the major distributors of syndicated television programs such as "Oprah" and "Wheel of Fortune."[116]

The broadcast television, cable and program production industries also established an Oversight Monitoring Board to review ratings applied to television programs.[117] The board has no legal authority. It can only encourage the television, cable and production industries to apply the ratings accurately and consistently. Neither the V-chip requirement nor the ratings system has been challenged in court.

The television ratings system is similar to that adopted by the Motion Picture Association of America for movies. The MPAA system, also supported by the National Association of Theatre Owners, is voluntary for film producers and movie theaters, but the film industry generally follows it.[118]

Cable Indecency

Cable and broadcast television are very different media in the courts' and the FCC's eyes. Cable comes into a home only if the residents pay a monthly fee. Cable customers generally may select the cable networks they want to receive and not subscribe to others. However, radio and broadcast television programs are ubiquitous. They are everywhere—cars, stores, homes, restaurants. Broadcast indecency is channeled into the safe harbor period because children otherwise inadvertently could be exposed to it. The same rationale does not apply to cable television, according to the courts and the FCC.

HBO's development in 1975 spurred cable's popularity. Certain movies that HBO showed, and various other cable network content, so offended some state legislators and local officials that by the early 1980s they adopted laws forbidding cable indecency. Courts uniformly rejected these restrictions. For example, a Miami, Fla., ordinance prohibited cable systems from distributing "obscene or indecent" material.[119] A federal appellate court said the *Pacifica* restrictions on broadcasting indecent material did not apply to cable television. Parents may prevent their children from watching cable television by not subscribing. The court also said the Miami law was overbroad because it did not allow any period when a cable system could transmit indecent material. Courts struck down several similar laws that the Utah Legislature and many Utah cities adopted to ban indecent material on cable television.[120] Congress adopted the first federal law regulating cable in 1984 but did not use the statute to limit indecent content on cable television. Rather, the law said only the obvious: Cable systems could not transmit obscene material.[121] The 1984 Cable Communications Policy Act's one concession to those concerned about indecent

TELEVISION PROGRAM RATINGS

Following is a list of television parental guidelines. The first two ratings are for programs designed solely for children. The rest are for programs designed for general audiences.

- TV-Y (All children—This program is designed to be appropriate for all children.) Whether animated or live-action, the themes and elements in this program are specifically designed for a very young audience, including children from ages 2 to 6. This program is not expected to frighten younger children.

- TV-Y7 (Directed to older children—This program is designed for children age 7 and older.) It may be more appropriate for children who have acquired the developmental skills needed to distinguish between make-believe and reality. Themes and elements in this program may include mild fantasy or comedic violence or may frighten children under the age of 7. Therefore, parents may wish to consider the suitability of this program for their very young children. *Note:* For those programs where fantasy violence may be more intense or more combative than other programs in this category, such programs will be designated TV-Y7-FV.

- TV-G (General audience—Most parents would find this program suitable for all ages.) Although this rating does not signify a program designed specifically for children, most parents may let younger children watch this program unattended. It contains little or no violence, no strong language and little or no sexual dialogue or situations.

- TV-PG (Parental guidance suggested—This program contains material that parents may find unsuitable for younger children.) Many parents may want to watch it with their younger children. The theme itself may call for parental guidance, and/or the program contains one or more of the following: moderate violence (V), some sexual situations (S), infrequent coarse language (L) or some suggestive dialogue (D).

- TV-14 (Parents strongly cautioned—This program contains some material that many parents would find unsuitable for children under 14 years of age.) Parents are strongly urged to exercise greater care in monitoring this program and are cautioned against letting children under the age of 14 watch unattended. This program contains one or more of the following: intense violence (V), intense sexual situations (S), strong coarse language (L), or intensely suggestive dialogue (D).

- TV-MA (Mature audience only—This program is specifically designed to be viewed by adults and therefore may be unsuitable for children under 17.) This program contains one or more of the following: graphic violence (V), explicit sexual activity (S) or crude indecent language (L).[1]

---

1. FCC, V-Chip: Viewing Television Responsibly, www.fcc.gov/vchip (last visited Mar. 4, 2017).

In 2017, some viewers complained to the Federal Communications Commission about the use of the word "goddamn" in promos for "RuPaul's Drag Race," which airs on cable channel Logo TV.

material on cable networks was to require cable system operators to provide lockboxes to customers who requested them. Lockboxes allowed subscribers to block receipt of individual cable channels.[122]

The FCC has not attempted to extend its broadcast indecency regulations to cable television. Responding to complaints about the cable network FX show "Nip/Tuck," the commission stated clearly: "The Commission does not regulate cable indecency."[123] However, in 1992, Congress decided that indecent cable content required its attention. Legislation adopted that year included three provisions limiting indecent content on cable television. The law dealt only with two kinds of cable channels. First, community members, local schools and government agencies may use a cable system's public, educational and governmental access channels. Congress allowed cable operators—though not the government—to ban indecent programming on PEG access channels. Second, cable systems' leased-access channels can be rented by individuals and companies to show programming they want cable subscribers to see. (Both types of access channels are discussed in Chapter 9.) The law also said cable systems—again, not the government—could ban any leased-access programming a cable operator believes "describes or depicts sexual or excretory activities or organs in a patently offensive manner."

In *Denver Area Educational Telecommunications Consortium Inc. v. FCC*, the Supreme Court found two of the provisions unconstitutional.[124] The Supreme Court upheld the leased-access provision. But the Court said cable systems could not prohibit indecent programming on PEG access channels. Nor would the Court allow a requirement that cable systems put all indecent leased-access programming on one channel and deliver that channel only to subscribers who request it.[125]

The Court's *Denver Area* decision was fractious. Even when a group of justices agreed on a result, they could not agree on a reason for the outcome. Subsequently, Congress continued its efforts to limit indecency on PEG access channels. In the Telecommunications Act of 1996, Congress said cable operators could not exercise editorial control over PEG content, but they "may refuse to transmit any public access program or portion of a public access program which contains obscenity, indecency, or nudity."[126] This provision has yet to be challenged in court.

However, the Supreme Court overturned other sections of the 1996 act dealing with sexually explicit cable programming. Congress required cable operators to scramble the signal of any indecent programming on adult-oriented channels.[127] In part, Congress said, this was to prevent adult programming signals from bleeding into channels that children could see even in homes that did not subscribe to adult channels. Alternatively, Congress said, cable programmers could offer adult programming only during hours when children are unlikely to be watching. The FCC said the period would be 10 p.m. to 6 a.m.[128]

A unanimous Supreme Court said those provisions of the 1996 act were content-based regulations requiring a strict scrutiny analysis.[129] Protecting children from exposure to sexually explicit programming is a compelling state interest, but Congress had not adopted the least restrictive approach. Instead, the Court said, cable subscribers may ask cable companies to block channels and may request lockboxes. The availability of these alternatives makes the 1996 act's provisions unconstitutional, the Court ruled.

Internet Indecency

Many websites contain sexually explicit images. Although it is difficult to track, researchers who study the consumption of pornography on the internet estimate that between 4 and 15 percent of internet use involves pornographic content.[130] Congress has used two approaches in trying to separate children from indecent internet content.[131] First, it has limited content, making it illegal to provide children indecent material through the internet. Courts have found these attempts unconstitutional because some prohibitions on content for children also restrict adult access to protected material. Second, Congress and some local governments have limited children's access to content by, for example, requiring public and school libraries to block indecent material. The Supreme Court approved this method of preventing children's exposure to sexually explicit internet content.

The primary way that Congress attempted to regulate internet indecency was the Communications Decency Act, Title V of the Telecommunications Act of 1996.[132] The CDA made it illegal to knowingly transmit "obscene or indecent messages to any recipient under 18 years of age" or to make available "patently offensive messages" to anyone under 18 years old. People could not be convicted of violating the CDA if they either took "good faith" actions to prevent minors from seeing those materials or used procedures the law specified (such as a verified credit card) to confirm a recipient's age.

The Supreme Court rejected the CDA, finding it unconstitutionally overbroad in *Reno v. American Civil Liberties Union*.[133] The Court first said that, unlike broadcasting, the internet had full First Amendment protection. The internet is not limited by spectrum scarcity, as is broadcasting. Also, the internet is not as intrusive as broadcasting. Families

● REAL WORLD LAW

Popular Restaurants Add Porn-Blocking Filters

In 2016, Starbucks joined McDonald's, Chick-fil-A, Panera Bread and Subway in blocking Wi-Fi-enabled pornography websites from its public, in-store Wi-Fi. The coffee chain noted that it would work to ensure that its porn-blocking filters did not block unintended, nonpornographic content.[1]

The decision to install the porn-blocking filters came after a campaign by the National Center on Sexual Exploitation and Enough Is Enough. The groups distributed an online petition that garnered thousands of signatures as part of a larger #PornFreeWiFi campaign.[2]

1. David Kravets, *Sorry, There's No More Porn With Your Starbucks Latte*, Ars Technica, July 15, 2016, arstechnica.com/tech-policy/2016/07/sorry-theres-no-more-porn-with-your-starbucks-latte/.
2. *Id.*

not wanting children to access the internet at home need not subscribe to an internet service provider, the Court said. For these reasons, the Court refused to find the internet bound by the *Pacifica* case and rejected the CDA's complete ban on indecent internet content.

Because the CDA directly restricted speech, the Court used a strict scrutiny analysis. The Court acknowledged that Congress has a compelling interest in protecting children from sexually explicit content. But the Court decided the law was too sweeping. The CDA denied adults access to protected speech as a way to prevent minors from being exposed to potentially harmful content, the Court said. The Court noted that (at that time) there was no technology allowing adults to see internet material while preventing children from doing so. The Court also said the CDA was overbroad because Congress had not carefully defined the words "indecent" and "offensive."[134]

The Court's decision did not include the CDA's restriction on sending obscene material over the internet. This limitation remains part of the federal law. Congress enacted the Child Online Protection Act in 1998, intending to correct the CDA's constitutional problems.[135] Courts consistently have found the COPA unconstitutional. The COPA differed from the CDA in two important ways. First, the COPA banned internet distribution to children of material "harmful to minors," defined in part as being designed to pander to prurient interest, determined by applying contemporary community standards. The CDA more broadly limited obscene, indecent or offensive content. Second, the COPA's restriction on transmitting harmful content applied only to people intending to profit from using the internet. The law also defined minors as 16 years old and younger, not 17 years old and younger.

The COPA definition of harmful to minors resembled the *Miller* obscenity definition. This meant the COPA affected a narrower range of materials than did the CDA. But the definition focused on all materials inappropriate for minors, so the COPA reduced adult access to only materials appropriate for children—just as the CDA did.

Challenges to the COPA stayed in the courts for a decade. First, a federal district court preliminarily stopped the government from enforcing the law.[136] The U.S. Court of Appeals for the Third Circuit affirmed that decision, concluding that the community standards language was overbroad.[137] The U.S. Supreme Court disagreed with the Third Circuit and vacated the decision.[138] Reviewing the case again, the Third Circuit issued an injunction blocking the COPA's enforcement. The court said there were technological methods of limiting children's access to websites containing inappropriate material and that therefore a sweeping ban on "material harmful to children" was not the least restrictive way to achieve Congress' purpose.[139]

On review, the Supreme Court left the preliminary injunction in place, saying that blocking and filtering software could effectively limit children's access to harmful material. However, the Court sent the case back to the trial court to update information about internet technology. Courts must have current information to decide if the COPA limits more speech than necessary to protect children, the Court said. When a content-based speech regulation, such as the COPA, is challenged, the government must show there are no alternatives less restrictive of First Amendment rights. For example, filters could prevent children from seeing harmful material while allowing adults access to internet content, the Court said. Also, filters would not chill speech. Websites could include content unacceptable for children but constitutionally protected for adults. Additionally, filters are able to prevent children's access to pornography sent via email and available on websites located in other countries. The COPA applies only to websites located in the United States. A congressionally appointed commission found filtering software to be the most effective means of preventing children from seeing harmful material. For these reasons, it would be difficult for the government to show that the COPA would be more effective and less restrictive than filters, the Supreme Court concluded.[140]

A federal district court in 2007 found that the COPA was not narrowly tailored and not the least restrictive or most effective way to achieve Congress' compelling interest in protecting children.[141] The government once again appealed the decision.

Hearing the case one more time, the Third Circuit affirmed the district court's decision.[142] Applying strict scrutiny, the appellate court agreed that the government had a compelling interest in protecting children from exposure to harmful material on the internet. But the court said the COPA was not narrowly tailored to achieve that goal. The government failed to show the COPA was a better, less restrictive method of protecting children than using filters that could prevent a computer from receiving certain internet sites. The court also held that several words and phrases in the law, such as "minor," were vague and not clearly defined.[143]

● REAL WORLD LAW

Taylor Swift Purchases Porn Domains

Steve Granitz/WireImag/Getty Images

Taylor Swift.

In June 2015, the Internet Corporation for Assigned Names and Numbers expanded its top-level domains (for example, .com, .net and .org), adding .porn, .adult and .sucks to the mix. Prior to the June release of the new domains, ICANN invited some companies and high-profile individuals to register new domains before the general public.[1]

Pop superstar Taylor Swift was one of the celebrities who purchased .porn and .adult domains with her name (TaylorSwift.porn and TaylorSwift.adult). Commentators praised Swift for her business savvy, noting that she purchased the domains not for pornographic purposes but to prevent others from buying them.[2]

1. Patrick Ryan, *Taylor Swift Buys Porn-Site Domain Names*, USA TODAY, Mar. 23, 2015, www.usatoday.com/story/news/nation-now/2015/03/22/taylor-swift-buys-porn-site-domain-names/25193325/.
2. *Id.*

Almost a decade ago, the Supreme Court refused to hear the government's appeal of the Third Circuit's decision.[144] Eleven years after the COPA's adoption, courts definitively ruled it unconstitutional. Even before Congress adopted the COPA, it took another, indirect route to keeping sexual material off the internet. The Child Pornography Prevention Act, adopted in 1996, made it illegal to send or possess digital images of child pornography.[145] The law made it illegal to send or possess an image that "is, or appears to be, of a minor engaging in sexually explicit conduct," or if the image is advertised or distributed in a way "that conveys the impression" that a minor is "engaging in sexually explicit conduct."[146]

The Supreme Court said the CPPA abridged First Amendment rights and found it unconstitutional.[147] In *Ashcroft v. Free Speech Coalition*, the Court said the language making it illegal to send or possess images that were not obscene was overbroad. The law would prevent adults from seeing protected content in order to block children's exposure. Because the CPPA was a content-based regulation, the Court applied strict scrutiny. It said Congress had a compelling interest in protecting children from being involved in the sex trade. However, the Court said, since computer-generated pictures of minors are outlawed, the CPPA would prohibit child pornography that does not harm an actual child. That also would be true when adults who appear to be children are pictured.

As noted earlier in the chapter, Congress adopted the PROTECT Act of 2003 in response to the Court's decision.[148] The PROTECT Act makes it illegal to provide someone with or request from someone an image that "is indistinguishable from that of a minor" in a sexual situation. This wording differs from the "appears to be" and "conveys the impression" language in the CPPA. In 2008, the Supreme Court found the PROTECT Act constitutional. The Court said the act focused not on the material but on the speech—offering or requesting child pornography—that could put the material into distribution. The First Amendment does not protect offers to engage in illegal transactions, the Court said, because offering to give or receive unlawful material has no social value.[149]

In addition to the PROTECT Act, the Supreme Court found constitutional one other congressional attempt to deal with online content. Congress enacted the Children's Internet Protection Act in 2000. This law focused on schools and libraries that receive federal money. The CIPA would stop money from going to schools and libraries that do not install "technology protection measures" on their computers accessing the internet. Those schools and libraries wanting to continue receiving federal funds would have to install filtering software that blocks obscenity, child pornography or material "harmful to minors."[150] The Supreme Court held in *United States v. American Library Association* that Congress has the right to set conditions for receipt of federal money.[151] The Court said public libraries already choose to purchase or not purchase certain books and other materials. For example, most libraries exclude pornographic material from their print collections, the Court said. Limiting what internet sites are available on the computers that libraries provide to the public is an equivalent decision. The Court also said requiring adults to ask a librarian to unblock a computer does not infringe on adults' First Amendment rights.

CHAPTER SUMMARY

Sᴇxᴜᴀʟ ᴇxᴘʀᴇssɪᴏɴ ɪs ғᴏᴜɴᴅ ᴛʜʀᴏᴜɢʜᴏᴜᴛ history. Sexual expression did not concern most Americans until the late 19th century when Anthony Comstock made it a public issue. Congress adopted the Comstock Act making it illegal to mail obscene or lewd material. Generally speaking, there is not agreement on what word to use in describing all offensive sexual expression. The word "pornography" is vague—not legally precise—because it encompasses both protected and unprotected sexual material. The term "indecency" has only a narrow legal meaning, referring to sexual expression and expletives inappropriate for children on broadcast radio and television. Until the mid-20th century, American courts used a broad definition of obscenity, allowing government officials to ban a wide range of materials.

The U.S. Supreme Court in 1973 adopted the definition of obscenity courts still use today. For the government to prove material is obscene and therefore without First Amendment protection, it must show the work considered in its entirety (1) arouses sexual lust, (2) is hard-core pornography and (3) has no serious social value. If the government is unable to prove any one of these elements, called the *Miller* test, the material cannot be found obscene. Prurient interest, or arousing sexual lust, is determined using contemporary community standards. These may be citywide or statewide standards. The Supreme Court has provided examples of the kind of content that would be patently offensive or hard-core pornography. Jurors may not find material patently offensive if it does not at least meet the Court's standards. Whether material has serious literary, artistic, political or scientific value is determined using national criteria based on expert testimony. The standard applied (community or national) to internet obscenity is still unsettled.

It is illegal to provide minors with sexually explicit material that would not be obscene if given to an adult. Courts call this variable obscenity. The federal government and all states have laws making it illegal to make, distribute or possess material showing children in sexual situations. This is child pornography. However, the First Amendment protects possessing obscene material if it is not child pornography.

The First Amendment protects indecent material—except on broadcast television and radio. The Federal Communications Commission and the Supreme Court define broadcast indecency as patently offensive material describing or depicting sexual or excretory activities and organs. The FCC's rules consider whether the material explicitly or graphically describes and dwells on sexual activities and whether the material is meant to shock or sexually excite the audience. The FCC has adopted rules categorizing fleeting expletives as indecent. The Supreme Court did not determine whether these rules violated broadcasters' First Amendment rights. The Court said the FCC could modify its indecency regulations if it chooses to do so and courts could rule whether the current or modified regulations are constitutional. The Second Circuit has said the current indecency regulations are unconstitutionally vague. If indecency regulations are constitutionally acceptable, courts allow broadcasters to air indecent material between 10 p.m. and 6 a.m. local time. Because parents may choose not to subscribe to cable television, courts have not allowed the government to ban indecent material from cable. The one exception is that cable system operators may reject public access programs that are obscene or indecent or contain nudity.

The Supreme Court has rejected several congressional attempts to prevent children from seeing sexually oriented material on the internet. The Court did allow Congress to withhold government funds for computers and internet connections from public libraries and schools that do not install blocking software on computers available to the public. It also upheld the constitutionality of the Prosecutorial Remedies and Other Tools to End the Exploitation of Children Today (PROTECT) Act, which makes it illegal to provide someone with or request from someone an image that "is indistinguishable from that of a minor" in a sexual situation. ■

CASES FOR STUDY

For study resources and a case archive go to **study.sagepub.com/medialaw6e**.

THINKING ABOUT IT

The two case excerpts that follow offer the U.S. Supreme Court's definition of indecency and demonstrate how the FCC has applied the concept of indecency to specific contexts over time. As you read these case excerpts, keep the following questions in mind:

- Is the rationale of protecting children and the intrusiveness of broadcasting in the home, put forth by the Court in *FCC v. Pacifica Foundation*, still relevant today? Could new technologies and different ways to deliver content such as George Carlin's monologue change the outcome in this case if it were heard by the Court today?

- Considering the different views from the justices in *FCC v. Pacifica Foundation*, what are the various ways that each sees indecency as distinct from obscenity with respect to the First Amendment?

- In *Fox*, does the Supreme Court clearly justify why the law forbids indecency?

- If you were in charge of a broadcast channel, would you have enough specific guidance from the *Fox* decision to help you determine how to avoid getting fined for airing indecent content?

Federal Communications Commission v. Pacifica Foundation
SUPREME COURT OF THE UNITED STATES
438 U.S. 726 (1978)

JUSTICE JOHN PAUL STEVENS delivered the Court's opinion:

This case requires that we decide whether the Federal Communications Commission has any power to regulate a radio broadcast that is indecent but not obscene.

A satiric humorist named George Carlin recorded a 12-minute monologue entitled "Filthy Words" before a live audience in a California theater. He began by referring to his thoughts about "the words you couldn't say on the public, ah, airwaves, um, the ones you definitely wouldn't say, ever." He proceeded to list those words and repeat them over and over again in a variety of colloquialisms. The transcript of the recording . . . indicates frequent laughter from the audience.

At about 2 o'clock in the afternoon on Tuesday, October 30, 1973, a New York radio station, owned by respondent Pacifica Foundation, broadcast the "Filthy Words" monologue. A few weeks later a man, who stated that he had heard the broadcast while driving with his young son, wrote a letter complaining to the Commission. . . .

The complaint was forwarded to the station for comment. In its response, Pacifica explained that the monologue had been played during a program about contemporary society's attitude toward language and that, immediately before its broadcast, listeners had been advised that it included "sensitive language which might be regarded as offensive to some." Pacifica characterized George Carlin as "a significant social satirist" who . . . examines the language of ordinary people. . . . Carlin is not mouthing obscenities, he is merely using words to satirize as harmless and essentially silly our attitudes towards those words." . . .

On February 21, 1975, the Commission issued a declaratory order granting the complaint and holding that Pacifica "could have been the subject of administrative sanctions." The Commission did not impose formal sanctions . . .

In its memorandum opinion the Commission stated that it intended to "clarify the standards which will be utilized in considering" the growing number of complaints about indecent speech on the airwaves. Advancing several reasons for treating broadcast speech differently from other forms of expression, the Commission found a power to regulate indecent broadcasting in two statutes, [one] which forbids the use of "any obscene, indecent, or profane language by means of radio communications," and [another] which requires the Commission to "encourage the larger and more effective use of radio in the public interest."

The Commission characterized the language used in the Carlin monologue as "patently offensive," though not necessarily obscene, and expressed the opinion that it should be regulated by principles analogous to those found in the law of nuisance . . .

Applying these considerations to the language used in the monologue as broadcast by respondent, the Commission concluded that certain words depicted sexual and excretory activities in a patently offensive manner, noted that they "were broadcast at a time when children were undoubtedly in the audience (i.e., in the early afternoon)," and that the prerecorded language, with these offensive words "repeated over and over," was "deliberately broadcast." In summary, the Commission stated: "We therefore hold that the language as broadcast was indecent and prohibited."

After the order issued, the Commission was asked to clarify its opinion by ruling that the broadcast of indecent words as part of a live newscast would not be prohibited. The Commission issued another opinion in which it pointed out that it "never intended to place an absolute prohibition on the broadcast of this type of language, but rather sought to channel it to times of day when children most likely would not be exposed to it." The Commission noted that its "declaratory order was issued in a specific factual context," and declined to comment on various hypothetical situations presented by the petition. It relied on its "long standing policy of refusing to issue interpretive rulings or advisory opinions when the critical facts are not explicitly stated or there is a possibility that subsequent events will alter them."

The United States Court of Appeals for the District of Columbia Circuit reversed, with each of the three judges on the panel writing separately. . . .

Having granted the Commission's petition for certiorari, we must decide: (1) whether the scope of judicial review encompasses more than the Commission's determination that the monologue was indecent "as broadcast"; (2) whether the Commission's order was a form of censorship . . . ; (3) whether the broadcast was indecent . . . ; and (4) whether the order violates the First Amendment of the United States Constitution.

. . . [A] statutory question presented by this case is whether the afternoon broadcast of the "Filthy Words" monologue was indecent. . . . Even that question is narrowly confined by the arguments of the parties.

The Commission identified several words that referred to excretory or sexual activities or organs, stated that the repetitive, deliberate use of those words in an afternoon broadcast when children are in the audience was patently offensive, and held that the broadcast was indecent. Pacifica takes issue with the Commission's definition of indecency, but does not dispute the Commission's preliminary determination that each of the components of its definition was present. Specifically, Pacifica does not quarrel with the conclusion that this afternoon broadcast was patently offensive. Pacifica's claim that the broadcast was not indecent within the meaning of the statute rests entirely on the absence of prurient appeal.

The plain language of the statute does not support Pacifica's argument. The words "obscene, indecent, or profane" are written in the disjunctive, implying that each has a separate meaning. Prurient appeal is an element of the obscene, but the normal definition of "indecent" merely refers to nonconformance with accepted standards of morality.

Pacifica argues, however, that this Court has construed the term "indecent" in related statutes to mean "obscene," as that term was defined in *Miller v. California*. . . . In holding that the statute's coverage is limited to obscenity, the Court followed the lead of Mr. Justice Harlan [who] . . . thought that the phrase "obscene, lewd, lascivious, indecent, filthy or vile," taken as a whole, was clearly limited to the obscene, a reading well grounded in prior judicial constructions. . . .

. . . the Commission has long interpreted [the statute] as encompassing more than the obscene. The former statute deals primarily with printed matter enclosed in sealed envelopes mailed from one individual to another; the latter deals with the content of public broadcasts. It is unrealistic to assume that Congress intended to impose precisely the same limitations on the dissemination of patently offensive matter by such different means.

Because neither our prior decisions nor the language or history of [the statute] supports the conclusion that prurient appeal is an essential component of indecent language, we reject Pacifica's construction of the statute. When that construction is put to one side, there is no basis for disagreeing with the Commission's conclusion that indecent language was used in this broadcast.

Pacifica makes two constitutional attacks on the Commission's order. First, it argues that the Commission's construction of the statutory language broadly encompasses so much constitutionally protected speech that reversal is required even if Pacifica's broadcast of the "Filthy Words" monologue is not itself protected by the First Amendment. Second, Pacifica argues that inasmuch as the recording is not obscene, the Constitution forbids any abridgment of the right to broadcast it on the radio.

The first argument fails because our review is limited to the question whether the Commission has the authority to proscribe this particular broadcast. . . .

It is true that the Commission's order may lead some broadcasters to censor themselves. At most, however, the Commission's definition of indecency will deter only the broadcasting of patently offensive references to excretory and sexual organs and activities. While some of these references may be protected, they surely lie at the periphery of First Amendment concern. . . . Invalidating any rule on the basis of its hypothetical application to situations not before the Court is "strong medicine" to be applied "sparingly and only as a last resort." We decline to administer that medicine to preserve the vigor of patently offensive sexual and excretory speech.

When the issue is narrowed to the facts of this case, the question is whether the First Amendment denies government any power to restrict the public broadcast of indecent language in any circumstances. . . .

The words of the Carlin monologue are unquestionably "speech" within the meaning of the First Amendment. It is equally clear that the Commission's objections to the broadcast were based in part on its content. The order must therefore fall if, as Pacifica argues, the First Amendment prohibits all governmental regulation that depends on the content of speech. Our past cases demonstrate, however, that no such absolute rule is mandated by the Constitution.

. . . The government may forbid speech calculated to provoke a fight. It may pay heed to the "'commonsense differences' between commercial speech and other varieties." It may treat libels against private citizens more severely than libels against public officials. Obscenity may be wholly prohibited. . . .

The question in this case is whether a broadcast of patently offensive words dealing with sex and excretion may be regulated because of its content. Obscene materials have been denied the protection of the First Amendment because their content is so offensive to contemporary moral standards.

But the fact that society may find speech offensive is not a sufficient reason for suppressing it. Indeed, if it is the speaker's opinion that gives offense, that consequence is a reason for according it constitutional protection. For it is a central tenet of the First Amendment that the government must remain neutral in the marketplace of ideas. If there were any reason to believe that the Commission's characterization of the Carlin monologue as offensive could be traced to its political content—or even to the fact that it satirized contemporary attitudes about four-letter words—First Amendment protection might be required. But that is simply not this case. These words offend for the same reasons that obscenity offends. . . .

Although these words ordinarily lack literary, political, or scientific value, they are not entirely outside the protection of the First Amendment. Some uses of even the most offensive words are unquestionably protected. Indeed, we may assume, *arguendo*, that this monologue would be protected in other contexts. Nonetheless, the constitutional protection accorded to a communication containing such patently offensive sexual and excretory language need not be the same in every context. . . . Words that are commonplace in one setting are shocking in another. To paraphrase Mr. Justice Harlan, one occasion's lyric is another's vulgarity.

In this case it is undisputed that the content of Pacifica's broadcast was "vulgar," "offensive," and "shocking." Because content of that character is not entitled to absolute constitutional protection under all circumstances, we must consider its context in order to determine whether the Commission's action was constitutionally permissible.

We have long recognized that each medium of expression presents special First Amendment problems. And of all forms of communication, it is broadcasting that has received the most limited First Amendment protection. . . . [A]lthough the First Amendment protects newspaper publishers from being required to print the replies of those whom they criticize, it affords no such protection to broadcasters; on the contrary, they must give free time to the victims of their criticism.

The reasons for these distinctions are complex, but two have relevance to the present case. First, the broadcast media have established a uniquely pervasive presence in the lives of all Americans. Patently offensive, indecent material presented over the airwaves confronts the citizen, not only in public, but also in the privacy of the home, where the individual's right to be left alone plainly outweighs the First Amendment rights of an intruder.

Because the broadcast audience is constantly tuning in and out, prior warnings cannot completely protect the listener or viewer from unexpected program content. To say that one may avoid further offense by turning off the radio when he hears indecent language is like saying that the remedy for an assault is to run away after the first blow. One may hang up on an indecent phone call, but that option does not give the caller a constitutional immunity or avoid a harm that has already taken place.

Second, broadcasting is uniquely accessible to children, even those too young to read. Although Cohen's written message might have been incomprehensible to a first grader, Pacifica's broadcast could have enlarged a child's vocabulary in an instant. Other forms of offensive expression may be withheld from the young without restricting the expression at its source. Bookstores and motion picture theaters, for example, may be prohibited from making indecent material available to children. . . . The ease with which children may obtain access to broadcast material . . . amply justif[ies] special treatment of indecent broadcasting.

It is appropriate, in conclusion, to emphasize the narrowness of our holding. This case does not involve a two-way radio conversation between a cab driver and a dispatcher, or a telecast of an Elizabethan comedy. We have not decided that an occasional expletive in either setting would justify any sanction or, indeed, that this broadcast would justify a criminal prosecution. The Commission's decision rested entirely on a nuisance rationale under which context is all-important. The concept requires consideration of a host of variables. The time of day was emphasized by the Commission. The content of the program in which the language is used will also affect the composition of the audience, and differences between radio, television, and perhaps closed-circuit transmissions, may also be relevant. . . . We . . . hold that when the Commission finds that a pig has entered the parlor, the exercise of its regulatory power does not depend on proof that the pig is obscene.

The judgment of the Court of Appeals is reversed. *It is so ordered.*

JUSTICE LEWIS POWELL, with whom JUSTICE HARRY BLACKMUN joined, concurring in part and concurring in the judgment.

. . . The Court today reviews only the Commission's holding that Carlin's monologue was indecent "as broadcast" at two o'clock in the afternoon, and not the broad sweep of the Commission's opinion. . . .

I also agree with much that is said in Part IV of MR. JUSTICE STEVENS' opinion, and with its conclusion that the Commission's holding in this case does not violate the First Amendment. Because I do not subscribe to all that is said in Part IV, however, I state my views separately.

It is conceded that the monologue at issue here is not obscene in the constitutional sense. . . . Some of the words used have been held protected by the First Amendment in other cases and contexts. I do not think Carlin, consistently with the First Amendment, could be punished for delivering the same monologue to a live audience composed of adults who, knowing what to expect, chose to attend his performance. And I would assume that an adult could not constitutionally be prohibited from purchasing a recording or transcript of the monologue and playing or reading it in the privacy of his own home.

But it also is true that the language employed is, to most people, vulgar and offensive. . . . The Commission did not err in characterizing the narrow category of language used here as "patently offensive" to most people regardless of age.

The issue, however, is whether the Commission may impose civil sanctions on a licensee radio station for broadcasting the monologue at two o'clock in the afternoon. The Commission's primary concern was to prevent the broadcast from reaching the ears of unsupervised children who were likely to be in the audience at that hour. . . .

In most instances, the dissemination of this kind of speech to children may be limited without also limiting willing adults' access to it. Sellers of printed and recorded matter and exhibitors of motion pictures and live performances may be required to shut their doors to children, but such a requirement has no effect on adults' access.

The difficulty is that such a physical separation of the audience cannot be accomplished in the broadcast media. During most of the broadcast hours, both adults and unsupervised children are likely to be in the broadcast audience, and the broadcaster cannot reach willing adults without also reaching children. This, as the Court emphasizes, is one of the distinctions between the broadcast and other media to which we often have adverted as justifying a different treatment of the broadcast media for First Amendment purposes.

In my view, the Commission was entitled to give substantial weight to this difference in reaching its decision in this case.

A second difference, not without relevance, is that broadcasting—unlike most other forms of communication—comes directly into the home, the one place where people ordinarily have the right not to be assaulted by uninvited and offensive sights and sounds. Although the First Amendment may require unwilling adults to absorb the first blow of offensive but protected speech when they are in public before they turn away, but a different order of values obtains in the home. . . .

. . . In short, I agree that on the facts of this case, the Commission's order did not violate respondent's First Amendment rights.

. . . In my view, the result in this case does not turn on whether Carlin's monologue, viewed as a whole, or the words that constitute it, have more or less "value" than a candidate's campaign speech. This is a judgment for each person to make, not one for the judges to impose upon him.

The result turns instead on the unique characteristics of the broadcast media, combined with society's right to protect its children from speech generally agreed to be inappropriate for their years, and with the interest of unwilling adults in not being assaulted by such offensive speech in their homes. Moreover, I doubt whether today's decision will prevent any adult who wishes to receive Carlin's message in Carlin's own words from doing so, and from making for himself a value judgment as to the merit of the message and words. These are the grounds upon which I join the judgment of the Court as to Part IV.

JUSTICE WILLIAM BRENNAN AND JUSTICE POTTER STEWART, with whom Justice THURGOOD MARSHALL joined, dissenting.

I agree with MR. JUSTICE STEWART that . . . the word "indecent" must be construed to prohibit only obscene speech. I would, therefore, normally refrain from expressing my views on any constitutional issues implicated in this case. However, I find the Court's misapplication of fundamental First Amendment principles so patent, and its attempt to impose *its* notions of propriety on the whole of the American people so misguided, that I am unable to remain silent.

For the second time in two years, the Court refuses to embrace the notion, completely antithetical to basic First Amendment values, that the degree of protection the First Amendment affords protected speech varies with the social value ascribed to that speech by five Members of this Court. Moreover, as do all parties, all Members of the Court agree that the Carlin monologue aired by Station WBAI does not fall within one of the categories of speech, such as "fighting words," or obscenity, that is totally without First Amendment protection. This conclusion, of course, is compelled by our cases expressly holding that communications containing some of the words found condemnable here are fully protected by the First Amendment in other contexts. Yet despite the Court's refusal to create a sliding scale of First Amendment protection calibrated to this Court's perception of the worth of a communication's content, and despite our unanimous agreement that the Carlin monologue is protected speech, a majority of the Court nevertheless finds that, on the facts of this case, the FCC is not constitutionally barred from imposing sanctions on Pacifica for its airing of the Carlin monologue. This majority apparently believes that the FCC's disapproval of Pacifica's afternoon broadcast of Carlin's "Dirty Words" recording is a permissible time, place, and manner regulation. Both the opinion of my Brother STEVENS and the opinion of my Brother POWELL rely principally on two factors in reaching this conclusion: (1) the capacity of a radio broadcast to intrude into the unwilling listener's home, and (2) the presence of children in the listening audience. Dispassionate analysis, removed from individual notions as to what is proper and what is not, starkly reveals that these justifications, whether individually or together, simply do not support even the professedly moderate degree of governmental homogenization of radio communications—if, indeed, such homogenization can ever be moderate given the preeminent status of the right of free speech in our constitutional scheme—that the Court today permits.

Without question, the privacy interests of an individual in his home are substantial and deserving of significant protection. In finding these interests sufficient to justify the content regulation of protected speech, however, the Court commits two errors. First, it misconceives the nature of the privacy interests involved where an individual voluntarily chooses to admit radio communications into his home. Second, it ignores the constitutionally protected interests of both those who wish to transmit and those who desire to receive broadcasts that many—including the FCC and this Court—might find offensive.

. . . Even if an individual who voluntarily opens his home to radio communications retains privacy interests of sufficient moment to justify a ban on protected speech if those interests are "invaded in an essentially intolerable manner," the very fact that those interests are threatened only by a radio broadcast precludes any intolerable invasion of privacy; for unlike other intrusive modes of communication, such as sound trucks, "[the] radio can be turned off,"—and with a minimum of effort.

. . . The Court's balance, of necessity, fails to accord proper weight to the interests of listeners who wish to hear broadcasts the FCC deems offensive. It permits majoritarian tastes completely to preclude a protected message from entering the homes of a receptive, unoffended minority. No decision of this Court supports such a result. . . .

. . . Because the Carlin monologue is obviously not an erotic appeal to the prurient interests of children, the Court, for the first time, allows the government to prevent minors from gaining access to materials that are not obscene, and are therefore protected, as to them. . . .

The opinion of my Brother POWELL acknowledges that there lurks in today's decision a potential for "'[reducing] the adult population . . . to [hearing] only what is fit for children,'" but expresses faith that the FCC will vigilantly prevent this potential from ever becoming a reality. I am far less certain than my Brother POWELL that such faith in the Commission is warranted; and even if I shared it, I could not so easily shirk the responsibility assumed by each Member of this Court jealously to guard against encroachments on First Amendment freedoms.

In concluding that the presence of children in the listening audience provides an adequate basis for the FCC to impose sanctions for Pacifica's broadcast of the Carlin monologue, the opinions of my Brother POWELL, and my Brother STEVENS, both stress the time-honored right of a parent to raise his child as he sees fit—a right this Court has consistently been vigilant to protect. Yet this principle supports a result directly contrary to that reached by the Court. [Prior decisions] hold that parents, *not* the government, have the right to make certain decisions regarding the upbringing of their children. As surprising as it may be to individual Members of this Court, some parents may actually find Mr. Carlin's unabashed attitude towards the seven "dirty words" healthy, and deem it desirable to expose their children to the manner in which Mr. Carlin defuses the taboo surrounding the words. Such parents may constitute a minority of the American public, but the absence of great numbers willing to exercise the right to raise their children in this fashion does not alter the right's nature or its existence. Only the Court's regrettable decision does that.

As demonstrated above, neither of the factors relied on by both the opinion of my Brother POWELL and the opinion of my Brother STEVENS—the intrusive nature of radio and the presence of children in the listening audience—can, when taken on its own terms, support the FCC's disapproval of the Carlin monologue. . . . Taken to their logical extreme, these rationales would support the cleansing of public radio of any "four-letter words" whatsoever, regardless of their context. The rationales could justify the banning from radio of a myriad of literary works, novels, poems, and plays by the likes of Shakespeare, Joyce, Hemingway, Ben Jonson, Henry Fielding, Robert Burns, and Chaucer; they could support the suppression of a good deal of political speech, such as the Nixon tapes; and they could even provide the basis for imposing sanctions for the broadcast of certain portions of the Bible.

In order to dispel the specter of the possibility of so unpalatable a degree of censorship, and to defuse Pacifica's overbreadth challenge, the FCC insists that it desires only the authority to reprimand a broadcaster on facts analogous to those present in this case . . . For my own part, even accepting that this case is limited to its facts, I would place the responsibility and the right to weed worthless and offensive communications from the public airways where it belongs and where, until today, it resided: in a public free to choose those communications worthy of its attention from a marketplace unsullied by the censor's hand.

The absence of any hesitancy in the opinions of my Brothers POWELL and STEVENS to approve the FCC's censorship of the Carlin monologue on the basis of two demonstrably inadequate grounds is a function of their perception that the decision will result in little, if any, curtailment of communicative exchanges protected by the First Amendment. . . .

. . . [E]ven if an alternative phrasing may communicate a speaker's abstract ideas as effectively as those words he is forbidden to use, it is doubtful that the sterilized message will convey the emotion that is an essential part of so many communications.

. . . The airways are capable not only of carrying a message, but also of transforming it. A satirist's monologue may be most potent when delivered to a live audience; yet the choice whether this will in fact be the manner in which the message is delivered and received is one the First Amendment prohibits the government from making.

It is quite evident that I find the Court's attempt to unstitch the warp and woof of First Amendment law in an effort to reshape its fabric to cover the patently wrong result the Court reaches in this case dangerous as well as lamentable. Yet there runs throughout the opinions of my Brothers POWELL and STEVENS another vein I find equally disturbing: a depressing inability to appreciate that in our land of cultural pluralism, there are many who think, act, and talk differently from the Members of this Court, and who do not share their fragile sensibilities. It is only an acute ethnocentric myopia that enables the Court to approve the censorship of communications solely because of the words they contain.

... The words that the Court and the Commission find so unpalatable may be the stuff of everyday conversations in some, if not many, of the innumerable subcultures that compose this Nation. Academic research indicates that this is indeed the case. As one researcher concluded, "[words] generally considered obscene like 'bullshit' and 'fuck' are considered neither obscene nor derogatory in the [black] vernacular except in particular contextual situations and when used with certain intonations."

... In this context, the Court's decision may be seen for what, in the broader perspective, it really is: another of the dominant culture's inevitable efforts to force those groups who do not share its mores to conform to its way of thinking, acting, and speaking.

Pacifica, in response to an FCC inquiry about its broadcast of Carlin's satire on "'the words you couldn't say on the public . . . airways,'" explained that "Carlin is not mouthing obscenities, he is merely using words to satirize as harmless and essentially silly our attitudes towards those words." In confirming Carlin's prescience as a social commentator by the result it reaches today, the Court evidences an attitude toward the "seven dirty words" that many others besides Mr. Carlin and Pacifica might describe as "silly." Whether today's decision will similarly prove "harmless" remains to be seen. One can only hope that it will.

JUSTICE POTTER STEWART, with whom JUSTICE WILLIAM BRENNAN, JUSTICE BYRON WHITE, and JUSTICE

THURGOOD MARSHALL join, dissenting.

... The statute pursuant to which the Commission acted, makes it a federal offense to utter "any obscene, indecent, or profane language by means of radio communication." The Commission held, and the Court today agrees, that "indecent" is a broader concept than "obscene" as the latter term was defined in *Miller v. California*, because language can be "indecent" although it has social, political, or artistic value and lacks prurient appeal. But this construction of [the statute], while perhaps plausible, is by no means compelled. To the contrary, I think that "indecent" should properly be read as meaning no more than "obscene." Since the Carlin monologue concededly was not "obscene," I believe that the Commission lacked statutory authority to ban it. Under this construction of the statute, it is unnecessary to address the difficult and important issue of the Commission's constitutional power to prohibit speech that would be constitutionally protected outside the context of electronic broadcasting.

This Court has recently decided the meaning of the term "indecent" in a closely related statutory context [and held] that "indecent" . . . has the same meaning as "obscene" as that term was defined in the *Miller* case. . . .

I would hold, therefore, that Congress intended, by using the word "indecent" in §1464 to prohibit nothing more than obscene speech. Under that reading of the statute, the Commission's order in this case was not authorized, and on that basis I would affirm the judgment of the Court of Appeals.

Federal Communications Commission v. Fox Television Stations Inc.
SUPREME COURT OF THE UNITED STATES
567 U.S. 239 (2012)

JUSTICE ANTHONY KENNEDY delivered the Court's opinion:
In FCC v. Fox Television Stations, Inc. (2009) (Fox I), the Court held that the Federal Communication[s] Commission's decision to modify its indecency

enforcement regime to regulate so-called fleeting expletives was neither arbitrary nor capricious. The Court then declined to address the constitutionality of the policy, however, because the United States Court of Appeals for the Second Circuit had yet to do so. On remand, the Court of Appeals [in 2010] found the policy was vague and, as a result, unconstitutional. The case now returns to this Court for decision upon the constitutional question.

[The U.S. Criminal Code] provides that "[w]hoever utters any obscene, indecent, or profane language by means of radio communication shall be fined . . . or imprisoned not more than two years, or both." The Federal Communications Commission (Commission) has been instructed by Congress to enforce [that provision] between the hours of 6 a.m. and 10 p.m. And the Commission has applied its regulations to radio and television broadcasters alike. . . .

This Court first reviewed the Commission's indecency policy in FCC v. Pacifica Foundation (1978). In *Pacifica*, the Commission determined that George Carlin's "Filthy Words" monologue was indecent. It contained "language that describes, in terms patently offensive as measured by contemporary community standards for the broadcast medium, sexual or excretory activities and organs, at times of the day when there is a reasonable risk that children may be in the audience." This Court upheld the Commission's ruling. . . .

In 1987, the Commission determined it was applying the *Pacifica* standard in too narrow a way. It stated that in later cases its definition of indecent language would "appropriately includ[e] a broader range of material than the seven specific words at issue in [the Carlin monologue]." Thus, the Commission indicated it would use the "generic definition of indecency" articulated in its 1975 *Pacifica* order and assess the full context of allegedly indecent broadcasts rather than limiting its regulation to a "comprehensive index . . . of indecent words or pictorial depictions."

Even under this context based approach, the Commission continued to note the important difference between isolated and repeated broadcasts of indecent material. In the context of expletives, the Commission determined "deliberate and repetitive use in a patently offensive manner is a requisite to a finding of indecency." For speech "involving the description or depiction of sexual or excretory functions . . . [t]he mere fact that specific words or phrases are not repeated does not mandate a finding that material that is otherwise patently offensive . . . is not indecent."

In 2001, the Commission issued a policy statement intended "to provide guidance to the broadcast industry regarding [its] caselaw interpreting [the indecency law] and [its] enforcement policies with respect to broadcast indecency." In that document the Commission restated that for material to be indecent it must depict sexual or excretory organs or activities and be patently offensive as measured by contemporary community standards for the broadcast medium. Describing the framework of what it considered patently offensive, the Commission explained that three factors had proved significant:

"(1) [T]he explicitness or graphic nature of the description or depiction of sexual or excretory organs or activities; (2) whether the material dwells on or repeats at length descriptions of sexual or excretory organs or activities; (3) whether the material appears to pander or is used to titillate, or whether the material appears to have been presented for its shock value."

As regards the second of these factors, the Commission explained that "[r]epetition of and persistent focus on sexual or excretory material have been cited consistently as factors that exacerbate the potential offensiveness of broadcasts. In contrast, where sexual or excretory references have been made once or have been passing or fleeting in nature, this characteristic has tended to weigh against a finding of indecency." The Commission then gave examples of material that was not found indecent because it was fleeting and isolated, and contrasted it with fleeting references that were found patently offensive in light of other factors.

It was against this regulatory background that the three incidents of alleged indecency at issue here took place. First, in the 2002 Billboard Music Awards, broadcast by respondent Fox Television Stations, Inc., the singer Cher exclaimed during an unscripted acceptance speech: "I've also had my critics for the last 40 years saying that I was on my way out every year. Right. So f*** 'em." Second, Fox broadcast the Billboard Music Awards again in 2003. There, a person named Nicole Richie made the following unscripted remark while presenting an award: "Have you ever tried to get cow s*** out of a Prada purse? It's not so f***ing simple." The third incident involved an episode of NYPD Blue, a regular television show broadcast by respondent ABC Television Network. The episode broadcast on February 25, 2003, showed the nude buttocks of an adult female character for approximately seven seconds and for a moment the side of her breast. During the scene, in which the character was preparing to take a shower, a child portraying her boyfriend's son entered the bathroom. A moment of awkwardness followed. The Commission received indecency complaints about all three broadcasts.

After these incidents, but before the Commission issued Notices of Apparent Liability to Fox and ABC, the Commission issued a decision sanctioning NBC for a comment made by the singer Bono during the 2003 Golden Globe Awards. Upon winning the award for Best Original Song, Bono exclaimed: "'This is really, really, f***ing brilliant. Really, really great.'" Reversing a decision by its enforcement bureau, the Commission found the use of the F-word actionably indecent. The Commission held that the word was "one of the most vulgar, graphic and explicit descriptions of sexual activity in the English language," and thus found "any use of that word or a variation, in any context, inherently has a sexual connotation." Turning to the isolated nature of the expletive, the Commission reversed prior rulings that had found fleeting expletives not indecent. The Commission held "the mere fact that specific words or phrases are not sustained or repeated does not mandate a finding that material that is otherwise patently offensive to the broadcast medium is not indecent."

Even though the incidents at issue in these cases took place before the Golden Globes Order, the Commission applied its new policy regarding fleeting expletives and fleeting nudity. It found the broadcasts by respondents Fox and ABC to be in violation of this standard.

As to Fox, [in 2006] the Commission found the two Billboard Awards broadcasts indecent. Numerous parties petitioned for a review of the order in the United States Court of Appeals for the

Second Circuit. The Court of Appeals granted the Commission's request for a voluntary remand so that it could respond to the parties' objections. In its remand order, the Commission applied its tripartite definition of patently offensive material from its 2001 Order and found that both broadcasts fell well within its scope. As pertains to the constitutional issue in these cases, the Commission noted that under the policy clarified in the Golden Globes Order, "categorically requiring repeated use of expletives in order to find material indecent is inconsistent with our general approach to indecency enforcement." Though the Commission deemed Fox should have known Nicole Richie's comments were actionably indecent even prior to the Golden Globes Order, it declined to propose a forfeiture in light of the limited nature of the Second Circuit's remand. The Commission acknowledged that "it was not apparent that Fox could be penalized for Cher's comment at the time it was broadcast." And so, as in the Golden Globes case it imposed no penalty for that broadcast.

Fox and various intervenors returned to the United States Court of Appeals for the Second Circuit, raising administrative, statutory, and constitutional challenges to the Commission's indecency regulations. In a 2-to-1 decision, with Judge Leval dissenting, the Court of Appeals found the Remand Order arbitrary and capricious because "the FCC has made a 180-degree turn regarding its treatment of 'fleeting expletives' without providing a reasoned explanation justifying the about-face." While noting its skepticism as to whether the Commission's fleeting expletive regime "would pass constitutional muster," the Court of Appeals found it unnecessary to address the issue.

The case came here on certiorari. Citing the Administrative Procedure Act, this Court noted that the Judiciary may set aside agency action that is arbitrary or capricious. In the context of a change in policy (such as the Commission's determination that fleeting expletives could be indecent), the decision held an agency, in the ordinary course, should acknowledge that it is in fact changing its position and "show that there are good reasons for the new policy." There is no need, however, for an agency to provide detailed justifications for every change or to show that the reasons for the new policy are better than the reasons for the old one.

Judged under this standard, the Court in *Fox I* found the Commission's new indecency enforcement policy neither arbitrary nor capricious. The Court noted the Commission had acknowledged breaking new ground in ruling that fleeting and nonliteral expletives could be indecent under the controlling standards; the Court concluded the agency's reasons for expanding the scope of its enforcement activity were rational. Not only was it "certainly reasonable to determine that it made no sense to distinguish between literal and nonliteral uses of offensive words," but the Court agreed that the Commission's decision to "look at the patent offensiveness of even isolated uses of sexual and excretory words fits with the context-based approach [approved] . . . in *Pacifica*." Given that "[e]ven isolated utterances can . . . constitute harmful 'first blow[s]' to children," the Court held that the Commission could "decide it needed to step away from its old regime where nonrepetitive use of an expletive was *per se* nonactionable." Having found the agency's action to be neither arbitrary nor capricious, the Court remanded for the Court of Appeals to address respondents' First Amendment challenges.

On remand from *Fox I*, the Court of Appeals held the Commission's indecency policy unconstitutionally vague and invalidated it in its entirety. The Court of Appeals found the policy, as expressed in the 2001 Guidance and subsequent Commission decisions, failed to give broadcasters sufficient notice of what would be considered indecent. Surveying a number of Commission adjudications, the court found the Commission was inconsistent as to which words it deemed patently offensive. It also determined that the Commission's presumptive prohibition on the F-word and the S-word was plagued by vagueness because the Commission had on occasion found the fleeting use of those words not indecent provided they occurred during a bona fide news interview or were "demonstrably essential to the nature of an artistic or educational work." The Commission's application of these exceptions, according to the Court of Appeals, left

broadcasters guessing whether an expletive would be deemed artistically integral to a program or whether a particular broadcast would be considered a bona fide news interview. The Court of Appeals found the vagueness inherent in the policy had forced broadcasters to "choose between not airing . . . controversial programs [or] risking massive fines or possibly even loss of their licenses." And the court found that there was "ample evidence in the record" that this harsh choice had led to a chill of protected speech.

The procedural history regarding ABC is more brief. On February 19, 2008, the Commission issued a forfeiture order finding the display of the woman's nude buttocks in NYPD Blue was actionably indecent. The Commission determined that, regardless of medical definitions, displays of buttocks fell within the category of displays of sexual or excretory organs because the depiction was "widely associated with sexual arousal and closely associated by most people with excretory activities." The scene was deemed patently offensive as measured by contemporary community standards, and the Commission determined that "[t]he female actor's nudity is presented in a manner that clearly panders to and titillates the audience." Unlike in the Fox case, the Commission imposed a forfeiture of $27,500 on each of the 45 ABC-affiliated stations that aired the indecent episode. In a summary order the United States Court of Appeals for the Second Circuit vacated the forfeiture order, determining that it was bound by its *Fox* decision striking down the entirety of the Commission's indecency policy.

. . . These are the cases before us.

A fundamental principle in our legal system is that laws which regulate persons or entities must give fair notice of conduct that is forbidden or required. This requirement of clarity in regulation is essential to the protections provided by the Due Process Clause of the Fifth Amendment. It requires the invalidation of laws that are impermissibly vague. A conviction or punishment fails to comply with due process if the statute or regulation under which it is obtained "fails to provide a person of ordinary intelligence fair notice of what is prohibited, or is so standardless that it authorizes or encourages seriously discriminatory enforcement." As this Court has explained, a regulation is not vague because it may at times be difficult to prove an incriminating fact but rather because it is unclear as to what fact must be proved.

Even when speech is not at issue, the void for vagueness doctrine addresses at least two connected but discrete due process concerns: first, that regulated parties should know what is required of them so they may act accordingly; second, precision and guidance are necessary so that those enforcing the law do not act in an arbitrary or discriminatory way. When speech is involved, rigorous adherence to those requirements is necessary to ensure that ambiguity does not chill protected speech.

These concerns are implicated here because, at the outset, the broadcasters claim they did not have, and do not have, sufficient notice of what is proscribed. And leaving aside any concerns about facial invalidity, they contend that the lengthy procedural history set forth above shows that the broadcasters did not have fair notice of what was forbidden. Under the 2001 Guidelines in force when the broadcasts occurred, a key consideration was "'whether the material dwell[ed] on or repeat[ed] at length'" the offending description or depiction. In the 2004 *Golden Globes* Order, issued after the broadcasts, the Commission changed course and held that fleeting expletives could be a statutory violation. In the challenged orders now under review the Commission applied the new principle promulgated in the *Golden Globes* Order and determined fleeting expletives and a brief moment of indecency were actionably indecent. This regulatory history, however, makes it apparent that the Commission policy in place at the time of the broadcasts gave no notice to Fox or ABC that a fleeting expletive or a brief shot of nudity could be actionably indecent; yet Fox and ABC were found to be in violation. The Commission's lack of notice to Fox and ABC that its interpretation had changed so the fleeting moments of indecency contained in their broadcasts were a violation of [the indecency law] as interpreted and enforced by the agency "fail[ed] to provide a person of ordinary intelligence fair notice of what is prohibited." This would be true with respect to a regulatory change this abrupt on any subject, but it is surely the case when applied to the regulations in

question, regulations that touch upon "sensitive areas of basic First Amendment freedoms."

The Government raises two arguments in response, but neither is persuasive. As for the two fleeting expletives, the Government concedes that "Fox did not have reasonable notice at the time of the broadcasts that the Commission would consider non-repeated expletives indecent." The Government argues, nonetheless, that Fox "cannot establish unconstitutional vagueness on that basis . . . because the Commission did not impose a sanction where Fox lacked such notice." As the Court observed when the case was here three Terms ago, it is true that the Commission declined to impose any forfeiture on Fox, and in its order the Commission claimed that it would not consider the indecent broadcasts either when considering whether to renew stations' licenses or "in any other context." This "policy of forbearance," as the Government calls it, does not suffice to make the issue moot. Though the Commission claims it will not consider the prior indecent broadcasts "in any context," it has the statutory power to take into account "any history of prior offenses" when setting the level of a forfeiture penalty. Just as in the First Amendment context, the due process protection against vague regulations "does not leave [regulated parties] . . . at the mercy of *noblesse oblige*." Given that the Commission found it was "not inequitable to hold Fox responsible for [the 2003 broadcast]," and that it has the statutory authority to use its finding to increase any future penalties, the Government's assurance it will elect not to do so is insufficient to remedy the constitutional violation.

In addition, when combined with the legal consequence described above, reputational injury provides further reason for granting relief to Fox. As respondent CBS points out, findings of wrongdoing can result in harm to a broadcaster's "reputation with viewers and advertisers." This observation is hardly surprising given that the challenged orders, which are contained in the permanent Commission record, describe in strongly disapproving terms the indecent material broadcast by Fox, and Fox's efforts to protect children from being exposed to it. Commission sanctions on broadcasters for indecent material are widely publicized. The challenged orders could have an adverse impact on Fox's reputation that audiences and advertisers alike are entitled to take into account.

With respect to ABC, the Government with good reason does not argue no sanction was imposed. The fine against ABC and its network affiliates for the seven seconds of nudity was nearly $1.24 million. The Government argues instead that ABC had notice that the scene in NYPD Blue would be considered indecent in light of a 1960 decision where the Commission declared that the "televising of nudes might well raise a serious question of programming contrary to [the indecency law]." This argument does not prevail. An isolated and ambiguous statement from a 1960 Commission decision does not suffice for the fair notice required when the Government intends to impose over a $1 million fine for allegedly impermissible speech. . . .

The Commission failed to give Fox or ABC fair notice prior to the broadcasts in question that fleeting expletives and momentary nudity could be found actionably indecent.

Therefore, the Commission's standards as applied to these broadcasts were vague, and the Commission's orders must be set aside.

It is necessary to make three observations about the scope of this decision. First, because the Court resolves these cases on fair notice grounds under the Due Process Clause, it need not address the First Amendment implications of the Commission's indecency policy. It is argued that this Court's ruling in *Pacifica* (and the less rigorous standard of scrutiny it provided for the regulation of broadcasters) should be overruled because the rationale of that case has been overtaken by technological change and the wide availability of multiple other choices for listeners and viewers. The Government for its part maintains that when it licenses a conventional broadcast spectrum, the public may assume that the Government has its own interest in setting certain standards. These arguments need not be addressed here. In light of the Court's holding that the Commission's policy failed to provide fair notice it is unnecessary to reconsider *Pacifica* at this time.

This leads to a second observation. Here, the Court rules that Fox and ABC lacked notice at the time of their broadcasts that the material they were broadcasting could be found actionably indecent under then-existing policies. Given this disposition, it is unnecessary for the Court to address the constitutionality of the current indecency policy as expressed in the *Golden Globes* Order and subsequent adjudications. The Court adheres to its normal practice of declining to decide cases not before it.

Third, this opinion leaves the Commission free to modify its current indecency policy in light of its determination of the public interest and applicable legal requirements. And it leaves the courts free to review the current policy or any modified policy in light of its content and application.

•••

The judgments of the United States Court of Appeals for the Second Circuit are vacated, and the cases are remanded for further proceedings consistent with the principles set forth in this opinion.

It is so ordered.

Justice Sotomayor took no part in the consideration or decision of these cases.

We're going to aggressively protect our intellectual property. Our single greatest asset is the innovation and the ingenuity and creativity of the American people. It is essential to our prosperity, and it will only become more so in this century.

—**Barack Obama, former president of the United States**[1]

If a monkey takes a selfie, like this one, does it own the copyright to the image? After this monkey selfie emerged, the question was raised by People for the Ethical Treatment of Animals. A federal judge said animals do not have copyright privileges under the current law.

11 INTELLECTUAL PROPERTY
Protecting and Using Intangible Creations

SUPPOSE...

... that a startup tech company has developed an individualized antenna system that allows customers to watch over-the-air television broadcasts via the internet on any device. Broadcaster television networks claim this new system violates copyright law, specifically their public performance rights under the 1976 Copyright Act. If the individualized antenna system persists, broadcasters could lose millions of dollars in licensing fees they receive from cable companies, who have to pay for the right to carry the broadcasters' copyrighted programming. Does this new system violate the public performance rights of broadcasters? Or does this innovative new technology simply provide customers a more individualized, less expensive and convenient way to watch broadcast programs? Look for the answer to these questions in the case of *American Broadcasting Companies Inc. v. Aereo Inc.* discussed later in this chapter and excerpted at the end of the chapter.

P atent, trademark and copyright statutes all are categorized as **intellectual property law**. Generally, intellectual property laws—particularly patent and copyright statutes—are intended to encourage creativity. Ensuring that people will benefit financially from their creations encourages them to continue being creative. If people could use others' intellectual creations without permission, there would be no financial incentive to write, design or invent. Trademarks help businesses protect their brands and identity. Intellectual property law is increasingly

intellectual property law The legal category including copyright, trademark and patent law.

complex because of technological advances, but as with other areas of the law, core principles apply and the legal system continues to adapt to rapid changes.

COPYRIGHT

copyright An exclusive legal right used to protect intellectual creations from unauthorized use.

A **copyright** is an exclusive legal right protecting intellectual creations from unauthorized use. Copyright law balances the creator's right to restrict the use of his or her work and society's belief that some uses should be allowed without the creator's permission. Achieving the balance has been a difficult task since the United States adopted its first copyright law in 1790.

U.S. copyright law protects the rights of creators of "original works of authorship" to use their creations.[2] The work's creator—the copyright holder—determines who can use the work, for what purpose and for how long. The U.S. Constitution grants creators control over their works for only a "limited time."[3] Once the limit was 28 years. Today copyright for many works lasts for the creator's life plus 70 more years.

The concept of protecting creators' works emerged in the 15th century, when the invention of the printing press enabled cheaper copying. In England, the monarchy held that printers would control publication and the Crown would control printers. Authors might be paid for a manuscript, but then they dropped out of the picture.[4] Copyright's initial purpose was to prevent sedition—criticizing the king or queen. The Crown gave a group of printers, called the Stationers' Company, control over printing. Licensed printers received the right to publish a work in perpetuity.

LANDMARK CASES IN CONTEXT

Key ■ Event
◆ Cases

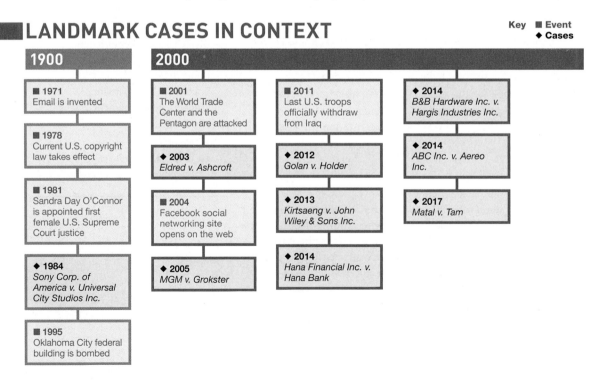

1900

■ **1971**
Email is invented

■ **1978**
Current U.S. copyright law takes effect

■ **1981**
Sandra Day O'Connor is appointed first female U.S. Supreme Court justice

◆ **1984**
Sony Corp. of America v. Universal City Studios Inc.

■ **1995**
Oklahoma City federal building is bombed

2000

■ **2001**
The World Trade Center and the Pentagon are attacked

◆ **2003**
Eldred v. Ashcroft

■ **2004**
Facebook social networking site opens on the web

◆ **2005**
MGM v. Grokster

■ **2011**
Last U.S. troops officially withdraw from Iraq

◆ **2012**
Golan v. Holder

◆ **2013**
Kirtsaeng v. John Wiley & Sons Inc.

◆ **2014**
Hana Financial Inc. v. Hana Bank

◆ **2014**
B&B Hardware Inc. v. Hargis Industries Inc.

◆ **2014**
ABC Inc. v. Aereo Inc.

◆ **2017**
Matal v. Tam

○ POINT OF LAW

The U.S. Constitution: Copyrights and Patents

The Congress shall have Power . . . [t]o promote the Progress of Science and useful Arts, by securing for limited Times to Authors and Inventors the exclusive Right to their respective Writings and Discoveries.[1]

1. U.S. CONST., art. 1, § 8, cls. 1, 8.

The license requirement ended in 1694, but the Stationers' Company did not disappear. Rather, it shifted its focus from printers to authors. The first copyright law in England, the **Statute of Anne** of 1710, protected authors' works[5] and granted authors copyright protection if they registered their works with the government. When the copyright period ended—after 14 years, or 28 years if the author renewed the copyright—the work entered the public domain, and anyone could use it without permission. Under the Statute of Anne, authors controlled their creations but often sold their rights to printers as a way of turning their works into ready cash.

Statute of Anne The first copyright law, adopted in England in 1710, protected authors' works if they registered them with the government.

The Development of U.S. Copyright Law

The U.S. Constitution followed England's lead, allowing Congress to adopt copyright and patent laws to encourage authors to create new works.[6] Before the Constitution was ratified, 12 of the 13 states passed their own copyright laws. The first Congress in 1790 adopted a law giving books, maps and charts a 14-year copyright.[7] The U.S. Supreme Court later ruled that the federal law took the place of state statutes and any common law copyright claims.[8] Today, the federal law is the country's only copyright statute.

During the 19th century, Congress amended the copyright law to protect musical compositions, photographs and paintings.[9] The 1870 act established the Library of Congress, giving it the power to register copyrights and requiring creators to deposit with the library two copies of a copyrighted published work.

In 1866, the Berne Convention for the Protection of Literary and Artistic Works was signed by several countries in a step toward protecting works globally. However, the United States did not join. The country was not concerned with protecting its citizens' works overseas and did not want to protect foreign creators' works in the United States. The **Berne Convention**, though, spurred a major revision of U.S. copyright law in 1909.[10] Among other changes, the law extended copyright protection to 28 years, with a renewal period of another 28 years.

As the 20th century progressed, entertainment, news, technology and other industries pressured Congress to update copyright law. In response, Congress adopted the Copyright Act of 1976, which took effect Jan. 1, 1978. In 1988, Congress amended the 1976 act in ways that permitted the United States to join the Berne Convention—more than a century after the treaty's initial adoption.[11]

Berne Convention The primary international copyright treaty adopted by many countries in 1886 and by the United States in 1988.

The copyright law passed in 1870 established the Library of Congress.

Sean Pavone/Alamy

The 1976 Copyright Act

The 1976 Copyright Act, amended several times since, specifies what may be protected by copyright, what rights that protection includes, any restrictions on those rights and the formalities necessary to exercise the rights.

The act remains the backbone of U.S. copyright law today. Although computers and a rudimentary internet existed in 1976, they were not part of Congress' thinking when it passed the current copyright law. In 1998, Congress adopted the Digital Millennium Copyright Act in an attempt to integrate the internet and other digital media more squarely into copyright law.[12] The DMCA bans software and hardware that facilitate circumventing copyright protection technology, with certain exceptions.[13] For example, the act forbids software that would disable anti-copying features in software that enables the copying of digital video.[14] The DMCA also prohibits removing or changing copyright information, such as the copyright owner's name.[15]

● REAL WORLD LAW

Samsung Electronics Co. v. Apple

In its first design patent decision in more than a century, the Supreme Court recently tried to clarify how Apple, under the Patent Act, could recover damages from Samsung for patent infringement.[1]

In 2012, a jury held that Samsung infringed on Apple's design patents. Design patents focus on how an article, or product, looks. Samsung faced nearly $1 billion in penalties because it was ordered to pay damages based on total profits from all of its phones that infringed.[2]

In a narrow ruling in 2016, a unanimous Supreme Court held that Samsung only needed to pay damages on the infringing components rather than on the entire phone. It sent the case back to the U.S. Court of Appeals for the Federal Circuit, which in 2017 began the process of trying to determine how much Samsung owed Apple for infringement.[3]

Samsung and Apple have sued each other over various intellectual property claims for nearly a decade. The lawsuits span the globe. One tech commentator said these cases are less about money than about control of the mobile device market. Experts suggest it will be years before all of the cases are resolved.[4]

1. Samsung Electronics Co. v. Apple, 137 S. Ct. 429 (2016).
2. *Id.*
3. Julian Chokkattu, *U.S. Court of Appeals Officially Reopens the Apple v. Samsung Patent Case*, DIGITAL TRENDS, Jan. 13, 2017, www.digitaltrends.com/mobile/apple-vs-samsung-supreme-court/.
4. Geoff Duncan, *Why Are Apple and Samsung Throwing Down? A Timeline of the Biggest Fight in Tech*, DIGITAL TRENDS, Apr. 4, 2014, www.digitaltrends.com/mobile/apple-vs-samsung-patent-war-timeline.

The Works Copyright Protects. U.S. copyright law protects a wide variety of works. Realizing that it could not list all possible works eligible for copyright, however, Congress provided two broad criteria, offered some examples and left it to the courts to provide more clarity. The 1976 law says that copyright protection applies to "original works of authorship" that are "fixed in any tangible medium of expression."[16] Congress used the word "authorship" to include artists, composers, journalists, sculptors and many other creators.

A work must be substantially original to be protected.[17] Copyright law does not define "original." As one court said, "[O]riginality" simply means "a work independently created by its author, one not copied from pre-existing works, and a work that comes from the exercise of the creative powers of the author's mind."[18]

A collection of previously created works can be protected if there is substantial originality in the choice or arrangement of the works.[19] The copyright law refers to this as a "compilation," such as a book consisting of selected magazine articles.[20] The statute grants a copyright to the creation of the compilation, but each work included in the collection retains its own copyright protection.

● POINTS OF LAW

The 1976 Copyright Act

Copyright protection applies to "original works of authorship" that are "fixed in any tangible medium of expression."[1] Works that are protected by copyright include:

- Literary works
- Musical works, including any accompanying words
- Dramatic works, including any accompanying music
- Pantomimes and choreographic works
- Pictorial, graphic and sculptural works
- Motion pictures and other audiovisual works
- Sound recordings
- Architectural works

The U.S. Copyright Office suggests viewing these categories broadly. For example, computer software is considered a literary work and protected by copyright law.[2] In a 2017 decision, the Supreme Court said clothing design elements could receive copyright protection as pictorial, graphic and sculptural works.[3]

1. 18 U.S.C. § 102(a).
2. U.S. Copyright Office, Copyright Basics, www.copyright.gov/circs/circ01.pdf (last visited Aug. 4, 2017).
3. Star Athletica LLC v. Varsity Brands Inc., 137 S. Ct. 1002 (2017).

Design 299B
Registration No. VA 1-319-226

Design 299A
Registration No. VA 1-319-228

Two cheerleading uniforms were at the center of the Supreme Court's recent decision to allow copyright of clothing design elements when they are perceived as a work of art.

In addition to being original, a work must be "fixed in a tangible medium." This means a work must be capable of being seen, "reproduced, or otherwise communicated, either directly or with the aid of a machine or device"—words or pictures on paper, images on videotape, a quilt made of cloth, a statue made of marble, music fixed in a digital file.[21]

What works are original and fixed in a tangible medium so they may be copyrighted? The 1976 Copyright Act lists eight categories of eligible works: (1) literary works; (2) musical works, including any accompanying words; (3) dramatic works, including any accompanying music; (4) pantomimes and choreographic works; (5) pictorial, graphic and sculptural works; (6) motion pictures and other audiovisual works; (7) sound recordings and (8) architectural works.[22] These categories are more illustrative than definitive. For example, software can be copyrighted (typically it is considered a literary work because it is written code), even though it is not listed separately among the eight categories. Designs, patterns and shapes also can have copyright protection.

In 2017, the Supreme Court added elements of clothing design to the list of copyrightable works. In a 6–2 decision, the Court held that design features in clothing could be eligible for copyright protection if those features are perceived as a work of art separate from the "useful article."[23] According to the U.S. Copyright Office, a useful article is an object that has a utilitarian function "that is not merely to portray the appearance of the article or to convey information."[24] Clothing and furniture are examples of useful articles.

At issue in the case was whether stripes, zigzags and chevrons on a cheerleading uniform could receive copyright protection. Before the case reached the Supreme Court, various circuit courts of appeal had reached different conclusions on the broader issue of clothing design, resulting in nine different variability tests to determine if copyright protection was appropriate.[25]

The Supreme Court said it accepted the case to resolve the widespread disagreement. Writing for the majority, Justice Clarence Thomas said, "a feature incorporated into the design of a useful article is eligible for copyright protection only if the feature (1) can be perceived as a two- or three-dimensional work of art separate from the useful article and (2) would qualify as protectable pictorial, graphic, or sculptural work—either on its own or fixed in some other tangible medium of expression—if it were imagined separately from the useful article into which it is incorporated."[26] Legal experts said the Court's decision is significant for the fashion industry, which has asserted for years that clothing not only is a useful article in that it protects the body, but it also is a form of creative expression.[27]

The 1976 statute protects all works eligible for copyright, both published and unpublished.[28] Before the 1976 statute was adopted, unpublished works were protected by state common law, not the federal statute. Common law protection for unpublished works and protection lasted forever.[29] The new law changed this, giving unpublished creations the same protection as published works.

A work that is not original or is not fixed in a tangible medium cannot be copyrighted. For example, a telephone directory's contents of names, addresses and phone numbers lacked originality, the U.S. Supreme Court ruled. There was insufficient creativity in an alphabetical list.[30] Ideas, history and facts cannot be copyrighted.[31] To qualify for copyright protection, there must be originality or novelty in the compiling or organizing of facts.[32]

As technology advances, new questions arise in this area—for example, is an individual point of interest within a GPS database copyrightable? A federal district court said "yes" because of the originality in selecting, categorizing and arranging the database.[33] In another case, a federal district court held that the HTML code and cascading style sheets (commonly called CSS) underlying an online advertiser's website were sufficiently original and creative to allow them to be copyrighted.[34]

Software is copyrightable as a literary work because it is written code.

A news story reporting an automobile accident can receive copyright protection. But the underlying facts—the accident itself—cannot be copyrighted. A reporter's description of the accident is original and is fixed in a tangible medium when typed into a computer or smartphone. However, the reporter may not successfully claim he or she was first on the scene and therefore no other journalist can write about the accident. Nor may a scholar write a book about a historical incident—even one that has not been described previously—and prevent anyone else from writing about the incident.

The law does not give copyright protection to words and phrases, including advertising slogans and titles of books, movies and television programs because they lack sufficient originality to qualify for copyright protection. However, a trademark can protect these creations. Also, works created by the U.S. government are not eligible for copyright protection.[35]

Using someone's work without identifying the source may be plagiarism rather than a copyright violation. **Plagiarism** commonly means using others' ideas without attribution.

plagiarism Using another's work or ideas without attribution.

Although plagiarism may not rise to the level of a copyright violation, it can have serious consequences. For example, Kendra Marr resigned from Politico, a prominent political website, after some of her articles were found to be rewrites of other reporters' work.[36] CNN and Time magazine suspended writer and television host Fareed Zakaria after one of his Time columns copied material from someone else's article.[37] And New York Times reporter Jayson Blair resigned after being charged with plagiarism.[38] Blair fabricated sources and material from other publications and pretended to have been places he never went.[39]

● **REAL WORLD LAW**

The Hot News Doctrine

Although copyright law does not protect news facts, one mass medium cannot persistently take information from another and present the news as its own. This concept, known as misappropriation of news and sometimes called the "hot news" doctrine, emerged in 1918 when the Supreme Court decided *International News Service v. Associated Press*.[1]

Courts find misappropriation of news when (1) a news organization spends money to gather news, (2) the information is time sensitive, (3) a competing person or company uses that information without permission or payment and (4) the news organization's ability to gather news is threatened by others' use of the information.[2]

A recent example of a "hot news" claim arose when The Associated Press sued Meltwater, a subscription service that uses software to "scrape" the web for its subscribers to monitor news articles that contain certain words and phrases. Most of Meltwater's clients are public relations firms that want to monitor news reports about their companies. A federal district judge held that Meltwater violated copyright law in its use of AP content, but the court did not address the AP's claim that the service also committed "hot news misappropriation."[3]

Although many media law attorneys have noted that the emergence of social media and other new distribution platforms make the "hot news" doctrine an evolving area of law, the AP settled the case out of court. It announced it would partner with Meltwater to jointly develop new products.[4]

1. International News Service v. Associated Press, 248 U.S. 215 (1918).
2. Nat'l Basketball Ass'n v. Motorola Inc., 105 F.3d 841, 845 (2d Cir. 1997).
3. AP v. Meltwater U.S. Holdings Inc., 931 F. Supp. 2d 537 (S.D.N.Y. 2013).
4. Brian Farkas, *Hot News to Meltwater*, GS2Law, Feb. 21, 2012, www.gs2law.com/hot_news_to_meltwater/.

○ **POINTS OF LAW**

When Copyright Takes Effect

Copyright automatically begins for an original work the moment it is created and fixed in a tangible medium, which could be digitally fixed to a hard drive, stored in the cloud or written on paper. Registration with the U.S. Copyright Office is not required.[1] However, if a copyright is infringed upon, the copyright holder cannot sue under the law unless the copyright has been registered.[2] The Copyright Office does not confirm that each submitted item is original. If a registered copyright is challenged, a court may find that the work does not comply with the requirements necessary to receive copyright protection. Also, the Copyright Office may refuse to register a copyright if it finds the work—such as a book title or advertising slogan—is not eligible for copyright protection.[3]

1. 17 U.S.C. § 408(a).
2. 17 U.S.C. § 411(a).
3. 37 C.F.R. § 202.1.

Copyright Ownership. A work's creator owns the work's copyright—with some exceptions.[40] For example, if two or more people create a work, the copyright is jointly owned, and all creators have all the protection a copyright gives. However, when a person creates a work as part of her or his employment, the law gives the copyright to the employer.[41] The copyright law calls such a creation a "**work made for hire**."[42]

work made for hire Work created when working for another person or company. The copyright in a work made for hire belongs to the employer, not the creator.

A work made for hire occurs in only two circumstances. First, an employee preparing a work as part of his or her regular employment will not own the copyright.[43] Instead, the employer will own the copyright. Second, and less common, a work may be for hire if the creator and employer agree to that in writing and if the work is specially ordered or commissioned for use in, for example, a compilation, a motion picture, a textbook or any of several other categories the law specifies.[44]

The U.S. Supreme Court has listed a number of factors for courts to consider in determining whether a person acted as an employee so that the works were made for hire.[45] These include (1) the organization's right to control how the work is accomplished, (2) who owns the equipment used to create the work, (3) where the work took place, (4) who determined the days and hours worked, (5) whether there was a long-term relationship between the two parties, (6) who hired any assistants that may have been used and several other factors. The more the company or organization controls the factors, the more the balance tips toward the work being made for hire. When the criteria more generally favor the creator, the more likely he or she will be an independent contractor and own the work's copyright.

Generally, freelancers own the copyrights to their work. The copyright law allows copyright ownership to be changed by contract. However, contracts transferring copyrights in freelancer material to a newspaper or magazine do not automatically transfer control to media organizations' online publications. The copyright law calls newspapers and magazines "collective works."[46]

More than 15 years ago, in *New York Times Co. Inc. v. Tasini*, the Supreme Court said online publication reproduced and distributed individual articles rather than the newspaper as a whole. The Court said when the Times placed articles published in its paper onto the internet, it took articles out of context because the website presented individual articles rather than articles in the context of the original newspaper page. The freelance writers retained their copyrights in the individual articles, the Court said. If a contract between a freelancer and a newspaper did not specifically include online publications, the agreement covered only the initial publication.[47]

Copyright Protection. The law specifies six exclusive rights copyright holders have in their works. This includes (1) the right to reproduce the work, (2) the right to make derivative works, (3) the right to distribute the work publicly, (4) the right to perform a work publicly, (5) the right to display a work publicly and (6) the right to transmit a sound recording through digital audio means.[48] No one may copy a work without the copyright holder's permission. There are exceptions to this copyright protection. The U.S. Supreme Court allowed home recording for personal use.[49] Also, Congress amended the Copyright Act to permit making a single copy of an analog or digital recording for personal use.[50]

A derivative work is a work that is obtained from or created in relation to an original work. For example, without the copyright holder's permission, no one may use a novel as the basis of a play or make a movie from a television program because it would be a derivative of a work protected by copyright. Recently, a federal court held that an e-book is not a derivative work because it does not recast, transform or adapt a pre-existing work and it is not an original work of authorship.[51]

In addition to controlling derivative works, the copyright owner also determines when a work will be publicly distributed. This includes public distribution of a work on social media. For example, a federal district court said merely posting photos on Twitter does not allow others to use them without permission.[52] Daniel Morel photographed scenes after the Haiti earthquake in 2010. He posted these photos to his Twitter account. Without Morel's permission, an employee of Agence France-Presse, an international news agency, sent eight of Morel's photos to the AFP photo desk. Morel sued AFP and several other media organizations for copyright infringement. AFP argued that when Morel posted his photos on Twitter, he accepted Twitter's terms of service, and those terms automatically granted permission to use the photos. A federal district court disagreed, holding that Twitter's terms of service do not state or mean that content posted to a Twitter account essentially falls into the public domain.[53] AFP infringed Morel's copyrights, the court ruled. Morel settled out of court with The Washington Post, CBS, ABC and CNN, all of which also had used Morel's photos without permission. A federal jury awarded Morel the maximum statutory penalty of $1.2 million from AFP and Getty Images for copyright infringement.[54]

The right to publicly perform a work applies to "literary, musical, dramatic and choreographic works, pantomimes, and motion pictures and other audiovisual works."[55] This restricts anyone from transmitting a movie to the public, for example, without the copyright holder's permission. One important consideration in this area of copyright law as a result of new technology is how to apply the Transmit Clause. When Congress passed the 1976 Copyright Act, it added the **Transmit Clause** to clarify how broadcasters and cable television systems "perform" within this area of copyright law. Congress said that, under the Transmit Clause, a broadcast network is performing when it transmits content; a local broadcaster is performing when it transmits the network broadcast; and a cable television system performs when it retransmits a broadcast to its subscribers.[56]

In cable television's infancy, the Supreme Court held that cable did not infringe anyone's copyright when it retransmitted broadcast station signals to subscribers.[57] The Court said retransmitting broadcast signals was not a performance under the 1909 copyright law and did not require copyright holder permission. Congress agreed to override the Court's decisions in the 1976 law and adopted a compromise that cable system owners had reached with the producers and broadcasters.[58] That law allows cable operators to retransmit radio and television broadcast signals without obtaining permission in exchange for a compulsory fee based on a percentage of a cable system's annual revenues. The U.S. Copyright Office collects and distributes the fees to copyright holders of the programs and other material cable broadcasts and retransmits. Multichannel video program distributors have a similar compulsory license to retransmit broadcast signals.[59] For example, direct broadcast satellite services pay royalties according to the number of their subscribers.

The application of the Transmit Clause to new technology is at the heart of the Supreme Court's 2014 decision in *American Broadcasting Companies Inc. v. Aereo Inc.* (excerpted at the end of this chapter).[60] At issue was whether Aereo's innovative system

Transmit Clause Part of the 1976 Copyright Act that says a broadcast network is performing when it transmits content; a local broadcaster is performing when it transmits the network broadcast; and a cable television system performs when it retransmits a broadcast to its subscribers.

of utilizing thousands of dime-sized antennas to offer its subscribers broadcast television content over the internet violated the Transmit Clause and constituted a public performance of copyrighted works. The Court held that it did, comparing Aereo's service to a cable system.[61] Immediately following the decision, Aereo suspended its video streaming service[62] and asked the Federal Communications Commission to grant it a license to retransmit broadcast material as a multichannel video programming distributor (see Chapter 9). If granted MVPD status, this would still require Aereo to apply for compulsory licensing (like a cable system) under the Copyright Act.[63]

Despite the Supreme Court's *Aereo* decision, unauthorized live streaming of broadcast programs continues on the internet. FilmOn X, a service nearly identical to Aereo, has continued to argue in multiple federal courts that it functions like a cable system and should receive a compulsory license to rebroadcast. District courts in Illinois and New York and in the Second Circuit have rejected FilmOn X's claim, noting that the service does not transmit signals directly to users. A conflicting decision in a California

◨ SOCIAL MEDIA LAW

Avoiding Copyright Issues on Social Media and Blogs

Most issues that arise with copyrights in blogs and social media involve images. Paragon Digital Marketing offers several useful tips for avoiding infringement on social media or a blog whether you are posting or tweeting from your personal account or working in some form of marketing/promotions[1]:

- Do not rely on a Google image search—most images found through a Google image search are protected by copyright.

- Always assume that an image you see on the internet is protected by copyright, even those included in a tweet.

- Do not crop out watermarks or other identifying information. The copyright information typically also is embedded in the digital image file.

- Always acknowledge authorship—include the person's name with a copyright symbol and link back to the source.

- Consider using Creative Commons, a nonprofit website that enables sharing without violating copyrights (creativecommons.org). Other websites also offer free images (either because they are in the public domain or because they have license agreements). These include stockfreeimages.com, Flickr photos or videos with a Creative Commons attribution license and the searchable photopin.com.

- When uncertain about use, seek permission from the copyright holder. One easy way to find the copyright holder is to perform a reverse image search in Google. Simply save a copy of an image on your desktop. Then copy that image into the search box at images.google.com. The search generates a list of websites where the image has appeared, which often leads to the copyright holder.

1. Paragon Digital Marketing, *Proper Image Use: How to Avoid Copyright Infringement on the Web*, paragondigital.com/blog/how-to-avoid-copyright-infringement/ (last visited May 10, 2017).

⦿ POINTS OF LAW

Exclusive Rights in Copyrighted Works

The copyright holder with exclusive rights may do the following:

1. Reproduce the copyrighted work

2. Prepare derivative works based upon the copyrighted work

3. Distribute copies of the copyrighted work to the public by sale or other transfer of ownership, or by rental, lease or lending (except CDs and computer software)

4. Perform the copyrighted work publicly in the case of literary, musical, dramatic and choreographic works; pantomimes; and motion pictures and other audiovisual works

5. Display the copyrighted work publicly in the case of literary, musical, dramatic and choreographic works; pantomimes; and pictorial, graphic or sculptural works, including the individual images of a motion picture or other audiovisual work

6. Perform the copyrighted work publicly by means of a digital audio transmission in the case of sound recordings[1]

---

1. 17 U.S.C. § 106.

district court that accepted FilmOn X's argument is on appeal to the Ninth Circuit Court of Appeals.[64]

In addition to public performance rights, copyright holders have the right to publicly display a work. This applies to "literary, musical, dramatic and choreographic works, [and] pantomimes," as does the right to perform a work publicly. The right to display adds protection for "pictorial, graphic, or sculptural works, including the individual images of a motion picture or other audiovisual work."[65] Under this provision, no one may display a painting, sculpture, photograph or similar work without the copyright owner's permission.

The final exclusive right maintained by a copyright holder is the right to transmit a sound recording through digital audio means.[66] This provision requires obtaining permission from a recording company to play one of its recordings via the internet, satellite radio or other digital media, including interactive services. Permission is not required to play a recording over a broadcasting station or in a live performance, but permission is required to play the composition embedded within the recording (unless its copyright protection has expired).

Copyright Law Limitations. Some protections are not absolute under U.S. copyright law. For example, libraries open to the public have a limited right to make photocopies for certain purposes.[67] Libraries may make a copy to respond to an interlibrary loan request or to replace a deteriorating copy of a work. Though not part of the law, Congress provided guidelines for teachers in not-for-profit educational institutions. A teacher may, no more than twice per term, copy one chapter from a book for the teacher's own use or copy an excerpt of no more than 1,000 words or 10 percent of a book to distribute to a class. The guidelines do not allow students to copy materials.

Copyright owners do not have the right to control individual copies of their works after distribution—with a few exceptions. A person who buys a copy of a novel may give away that book, sell it, rent it or throw it away.[68] The author has no right to stop the purchaser from taking any of those actions. This is called the "**first-sale doctrine**."[69] The copyright law says that once creators have distributed copies of a work, they no longer can regulate what happens to those copies. However, when copyright holders agree to transfer the physical object containing the copyrighted work—the book containing a novel, a DVD containing a movie, a magazine containing articles—they do not transfer any rights in the copyrighted work. The law still restricts copying the novel, making derivative works from a movie and so on. The first-sale doctrine distinguishes between the physical object and the intellectual creation itself. The doctrine does not change the copyright holder's control of the creation, only control of the object containing the creation.

The first-sale doctrine allows the buyer of a book manufactured and purchased in the United States or overseas to resell that book. The U.S. Supreme Court said the first-sale doctrine also allowed the purchase of foreign-manufactured books and the sale of them in the United States.[70]

The first-sale doctrine, like some other parts of the copyright law, was meant for a pre-digital world. The problem is when a digital copy is sent from one computer to another, the receiving computer makes an additional copy of the document, something the law does not allow.

Concerns about people making cheap copies of rented computer software or movies prompted Congress to limit the first-sale doctrine. Congress restricted rentals of recordings without the copyright holder's permission.[71] Five years ago, the U.S. Court of Appeals for the Second Circuit ruled that a company called ReDigi infringed Capitol Records' copyrights in its sound recordings. ReDigi allowed people to "sell their legally acquired digital music files and buy used digital music from others at a fraction of the price currently available on iTunes." Essentially, ReDigi acted as a used digital music store. The Second Circuit held that when a digital music file moves from one person's computer to another computer, the file is reproduced. Because reproduction is one of the rights guaranteed to a copyright owner, ReDigi infringed Capitol's rights under the copyright law, the court said.[72]

Transferring Copyrights. A copyright is a property right. Just like a car, a copyright can be given away, sold or leased.

Rights protected by copyright can be thought of as a bundle that includes a number of rights. For example, an author writes a novel and has the right, among others, to prevent unauthorized copying. If the author sells the right to reproduce the novel as a hardback book, the author still holds all the other copying rights. The author may sell the paperback copying rights to another publisher. The author may sell to a film studio one of the rights to a derivative work—the right to make a movie from the novel. That still leaves the author with many other rights. Or the author may choose to sell all of his or her rights to one person or company. Each time the author sells a right, he or she receives a lump sum payment or, often, a percentage of revenue from sales.

first-sale doctrine
Once a copyright owner sells a copy of a work, the new owner may possess, transfer or otherwise dispose of that copy without the copyright owner's permission.

Whoever buys a right from the author then owns that right unless a contract between the author and the buyer says otherwise. If the buyer wants to sell the right to a third person, the author cannot refuse to allow the sale unless the author has a contractual right to do so. A copyright does not disappear when the copyright holder dies. The copyright holder may transfer the right to someone else through a will.

Not only may copyright holders completely transfer their rights; they may license or lease rights. A license is a contract giving limited permission for use. For example, a photographer may license a picture to a company for use in an advertising campaign during the year 2018. The photographer has not given up any rights but, rather, retains the copyright on the picture and all the rights protected by the copyright. The agreement may give the company exclusive use of the photograph for advertising during 2018, or the photographer may retain the right to allow others also to use it.

The 1976 copyright law recognizes that creators often do not have equal bargaining rights with the large corporations purchasing creators' copyrights. To strike a more equal balance, the law gives creators a termination right.[73] This allows creators, or their heirs, to require the transferred rights be returned 35 to 40 years after the original transfer. This does not apply to works made for hire.

public domain
The sphere that includes material not protected by copyright law and therefore available for use without the creator's permission.

Copyright Duration. The Constitution gives Congress the right to adopt copyright and patent laws "for limited times."[74] Lobbying by corporate copyright holders—movie and television program producers, book publishers and others—convinced Congress to stretch the definition of limited times almost to the breaking point.

The 1976 copyright law gave copyright protection for the creator's lifetime plus 50 years after the creator's death with no renewal. The Sonny Bono Copyright Term Extension Act of 1998 extended all copyright periods by 20 years. After the Bono Act took effect, the copyright period for works created on or after Jan. 1, 1978, became the author's lifetime plus 70 years.[75] Works made for hire are protected for 95 years from publication or 120 years from creation, whichever is shorter.[76]

Copyright protection's duration depends on several factors. First, the current law did not affect works created in the United States that were in the **public domain** on Jan. 1, 1978. When the current copyright statute took effect, the public domain included many works because their copyrights had expired—such as Herman Melville's "Moby-Dick." Also, some works copyrighted under the 1909 law lost protection because their creators failed to renew copyrights.

The 1976 law also covers unpublished works, formerly given perpetual protection under state common law. The statute replaced common law protection and protected unpublished works for the author's life plus 70 years.

The Supreme Court upheld the Bono Act against claims that it violates the constitutional copyright clause and the First Amendment.[77] In *Eldred v. Ashcroft*, the Supreme Court said extending the copyright period is constitutional. Congress has

Sony Bono.

Harry Langdon/Getty Images

the right to determine what "limited" means as long as the copyright period is not forever, the Court said. Congress could justify extending the copyright period because people live longer now. Also, technological changes make copyrighted works last longer.

The creator's life plus 70 years is a limited time within the meaning of the Constitution's copyright clause, the Court said.[78] The phrase "limited time" does not mean a fixed time. The copyright period may be flexible. However, the Court did not define "limited time," nor did it offer a test for determining what period might go beyond "limited."

The Court also rejected First Amendment arguments against the Bono Act. The Constitution's adopters found no tension between the First Amendment and the copyright clause, according to the Court. The current law balances free speech and copyright protection concerns. And the fair use defense, discussed later in this chapter, allows the public to use portions of copyrighted works under certain circumstances, the Court said.

When the United States joined the Berne Convention, many works created in other countries had fallen into the public domain here but not in their creators' countries.[79] That allowed orchestras on limited budgets and school programs, for example, to perform compositions by 20th-century composers such as Dmitri Shostakovich and Igor

● REAL WORLD LAW

The Sonny Bono Law

Mickey Mouse as Steamboat Willie in the first Mickey cartoon.

AF archive/Alamy Stock Photo

Sonny Bono, formerly an entertainer and singer-actress Cher's first husband, was a member of the U.S. House of Representatives when he died. Congress named the copyright extension act in Bono's honor because Bono believed copyrights should last forever.[1]

Mickey Mouse's copyright protection, originally granted in 1928 when Mickey's first cartoon, "Steamboat Willie," was shown, would have expired in 2003. But the Walt Disney Co., which owns Mickey's copyright, lobbied Congress to lengthen the copyright period. By one estimate, Disney spent more than $6.3 million persuading members of Congress to change the law. The Copyright Term Extension Act—the Sonny Bono law—protects Mickey's copyright until 2023.[2] Considering that Mickey may be worth more than $3 billion, will Disney be talking with Congress then?[3]

1. *See* 3 MELVILLE B. NIMMER & DAVID NIMMER, NIMMER ON COPYRIGHT § 9.01 (2013).
2. Laurie Richter, *Reproductive Freedom: Striking a Fair Balance Between Copyright and Other Intellectual Property Protections in Cartoon Characters*, 21 ST. THOMAS L. REV. 441, 451–52 (2009).
3. Joseph Menn, *Disney's Rights to Young Mickey Mouse May Be Wrong*, L.A. TIMES, Aug. 22, 2008, at A1.

● POINTS OF LAW

The Public Domain

Material that no longer is under copyright protection is in the public domain. Material that never was copyrighted, such as federal government publications, also is in the public domain. Such public domain material, including text, photographs, drawings and other materials, some of which may be found on the internet, may be used without obtaining permission.[1] Be sure material is not protected before using it without permission. Some public domain material may include works that remain under copyright. And material that no longer is under copyright protection still may be protected by trademark.

Material also may be in the public domain if the creator says it is. The creator may disavow copyright protection and allow anyone to use the material without permission. This happened recently when a music publisher settled the copyright lawsuit over the English language's most popular song, "Happy Birthday to You," and asked a judge to declare the song in the public domain.[2]

---

1. Lloyd J. Jassin, *New Rules for Using Public Domain Materials*, www.copylaw.com/new_articles/PublicDomain.html (last visited May 11, 2017).
2. Eriq Gardner, *Warner Music Pays $14 Million to End "Happy Birthday" Copyright Lawsuit*, HOLLYWOOD REPORTER, Feb. 9, 2016, www.hollywoodreporter.com/thr-esq/warner-music-pays-14-million-863120.

Stravinsky without paying a royalty fee. Films Alfred Hitchcock directed in England and Pablo Picasso's paintings also were freely available. In 1994, Congress gave these foreign works copyright protection.[80] Works affected generally were those produced between 1923 and 1989 that still were under copyright in the country where created.[81]

Groups directly affected by losing free access to these works sued, arguing Congress's action was unconstitutional. In *Golan v. Holder*, the U.S. Supreme Court disagreed.[82] The Court said the Constitution's language allows Congress to give copyright protection to works that once were in the public domain. Congress's action did no more than put the United States in the same position as other countries that are parties to the Berne Convention.

The Court also said Congress might reasonably assert that the comportment of U.S. copyright law with the laws of other Berne members would help create a well-functioning international system and thus inspire new works. The Court rejected the plaintiffs' argument that their First Amendment rights were abridged because they no longer could perform the newly protected works. The Court said any work Congress brought under copyright protection remained available, just for a fee. The Court also emphasized Congress's freedom to broadly interpret the Constitution's copyright clause.[83]

Proving Copyright Infringement

Using any part of a copyrighted work is **infringement** unless there is an applicable defense. The copyright statute allows a court to award **statutory damages** even if the infringer does not make a profit from the creator's work.[84]

To sue for copyright infringement, the plaintiff first must show proof of a valid, registered copyright prior to bringing a lawsuit. Nearly 70 years ago, a landmark decision in the Second Circuit Court of Appeals defined the basic structure of most copyright infringement claims.[85] Called the *Arnstein* test, it first requires a determination of

infringement The unauthorized manufacture, sale or distribution of an item protected by copyright, patent or trademark law.

statutory damages Damages specified in certain laws. Under these laws, copyright being an example, a judge may award statutory damages even if a plaintiff is unable to prove actual damages.

whether a plaintiff's work was actually copied. Without proof of copying, there is no infringement. To prove that something was copied, juries and judges consider whether a defendant had access to the work and whether the works are substantially similar. Today, in some instances, expert witness testimony is allowed as part of the process to help better understand differences in various contexts—for example, a copyright infringement claim about music sampling could be different than a claim about software. It is common for courts to recognize the need for expert testimony in cases that are highly technical.[86]

● REAL WORLD LAW

"Blurred Lines" Infringes on Marvin Gaye Classic

Marvin Gaye.

Recently, a Los Angeles jury awarded the estate of Motown legend Marvin Gaye $7.3 million for copyright infringement. At issue was substantial similarity between the 2013 smash hit "Blurred Lines," written and performed by Robin Thicke, Pharrell Williams and Clifford Harris (better known as rapper T.I.), and Gaye's 1977 classic "Got to Give It Up."[1]

Thicke, Williams and Harris ended months of arguing with Gaye's family by filing a lawsuit asking the federal court to declare that their song did not infringe on "Got to Give It Up." The three argued that what they were trying to capture with "Blurred Lines" was a specific "feel," paying tribute to an era and a genre.

Gaye's estate filed a counterclaim, arguing that the two songs contained eight similarities that infringed, including a signature phrase in the main vocal melodies, hooks with similar notes and backup vocals and similarity of the core themes of the songs, among other similarities.[2] The case wound up before a jury.

Because Gaye's estate owned only the composition (the sheet music), not the sound recording, the court allowed the jury only to hear a stripped-down version of Gaye's recording of "Got to Give It Up." The jury sided with Gaye's estate, deciding that Thicke and Williams had infringed but Harris had not, nor had the distributors of the song (Universal Music, Interscope Records and Williams' Star Trak Entertainment).[3] One week after the verdict, Gaye's children asked for an injunction from the court to stop sales of "Blurred Lines" and to hold Harris and the record companies responsible for copyright infringement as well. A federal judge denied the request to stop sales, but noted that Thicke's record label and Harris are also liable for copyright infringement.[4]

1. Kory Grow, *Robin Thicke, Pharrell Lose Multi-Million Dollar "Blurred Lines" Lawsuit*, ROLLING STONE, Mar. 10, 2015, www.rollingstone.com/music/news/robin-thicke-and-pharrell-lose-blurred-lines-lawsuit-20150310.
2. Josh H. Escovedo, *The Blurred Lines of an Infringement Action*, IP LAW BLOG, Mar. 6, 2015, www.theiplawblog.com/2015/03/articles/copyright-law/the-blurred-lines-of-an-infringement-action/.
3. Grow, *supra* note 1.
4. Dee Lockett, *"Blurred Lines" Is Here to Stay—Though Now Even More People Are in Trouble for It*, VULTURE, July 15, 2015, www.vulture.com/2015/07/blurred-lines-is-here-to-stay.html.

○ POINTS OF LAW

Infringing Copyright

A copyright plaintiff must prove the following:

1. The work used is protected by a valid copyright—meaning it is an original work fixed in a tangible medium.
2. The plaintiff owns the copyright.
3. The valid copyright is registered with the Copyright Office.
4. And either:
   a. There is evidence the defendant directly copied the copyrighted work, or
   b. The infringer had access to the copyrighted work, and the two works are substantially similar.

About 40 years ago, the extrinsic/intrinsic test emerged in the Ninth Circuit Court of Appeals.[87] Sometimes called the *Krofft* test, it is a two-step test that explores the substantial similarity of the challenged work both (1) to the general idea and context and (2) to the specific expression of that idea in the copyrighted work. The first step is to conduct an extrinsic analysis that eliminates unprotected elements such as ideas, facts and generally contextual scenes within an established genre. The intrinsic examination determines whether a reasonable person would find the elements protected by copyright, when standing alone, are substantially similar. It asks how an ordinary person would respond to the "total concept and feel" of a work.[88]

The *Krofft* test is often applied in the context of music. The conceptual idea behind the test was further refined in a Second Circuit Court of Appeals decision in the early 1990s that involved computer programming. In *Computer Associates v. Altai*, the court crafted the "abstraction-filtration-comparison" or AFC test that "requires the court to identify which aspects . . . constitute . . . expression versus ideas ('abstraction'), remove from consideration unprotectable ideas ('filtration'), and only then compare whether the defendant copied the protectable elements ('comparison')."[89] The AFC test is now widely used when trying to determine substantial similarity in computer programs, and many legal experts argue that it should be more widely applied because it is consistent with the Supreme Court's definition of infringement, which focuses on copying the elements of an original work.[90]

No matter which test a court uses, the question of access to a copyrighted work always comes before consideration of substantial similarity. Legal experts note that the *Arnstein* decision deliberately empowered juries to play a central role in determining the answer to both questions. Today, experts argue that copyright law has become so complex that jury decisions create apparently ad hoc and arbitrary results. The Supreme Court has never weighed in on copyright infringement analyses, which is why courts differ in their approach to determining infringement. Regardless of the test applied, the keys to determining infringement are access and substantial similarity.

A plaintiff does not have to prove that a copyright infringement was deliberate. Accidental infringement violates the law. A court may reduce statutory damages imposed on a person who unintentionally infringed on another person's copyright and waive statutory damages completely if the innocent infringer works for a nonprofit library or public broadcaster.[91]

Contributory Infringement. A plaintiff does not have to prove that the defendant directly infringed on copyright. Showing that the defendant knowingly aided or contributed to copyright infringement is sufficient. Although **contributory infringement** is not specifically banned in the copyright law, the statute implies that contributory infringement violates the law, and courts long have held it actionable.[92]

Contributory infringement may be difficult to prove. Several television program producers sued Sony for making videocassette recorders that allowed viewers to tape copyrighted programs without permission. The producers claimed the VCRs enabled unauthorized copying. In *Sony Corp. of America v. Universal City Studios Inc.*, the U.S. Supreme Court said Sony might have known that viewers used VCRs to record television programs, but it could be fair use (discussed below) to record programs to watch later—time shifting.[93] Sony was not liable because the VCRs could be used for noninfringing purposes, the Court ruled.[94]

A quarter-century later, Cablevision Systems faced a similar challenge to its digital video recorder system. A group of movie studios and broadcast and cable networks argued that Cablevision's DVRs directly infringed on program copyrights by making unauthorized copies on computers and publicly performing the programs when customers later watched them. The U.S. Court of Appeals for the Second Circuit ruled that the cable customer, rather than Cablevision, copied the program. Cablevision's computers acted as a modern VCR. Because only one customer at one time viewed the program, the program was not publicly performed, "public" being a larger group than just one customer.[95]

Those who benefit financially from others' copyright infringement also may be liable under copyright law. This might include a store selling pirated DVDs copied without permission of the movies' copyright holders. These are called "vicarious copyright infringers."

Finally, the U.S. Supreme Court established a third type of indirect copyright infringer. These are individuals or companies who induce or encourage others to engage in copyright infringement. In the *Metro-Goldwyn-Mayer Studios Inc. v. Grokster Ltd.* decision, the Court held that Grokster infringed on MGM's copyright because it knew people used its software to download music files. The Court said it did not matter that the software could be used for legal purposes because Grokster induced, or encouraged, users to infringe on copyrights.[96]

contributory infringement The participation in, or contribution to, the infringing acts of another person.

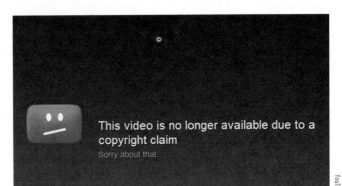

This video is no longer available due to a copyright claim

Sorry about that.

YouTube

YouTube has created a copyright center (www .youtube.com/ yt/copyright/) to teach users about copyright infringement and avoid video removals.

Websites allowing users to illegally download movies violate *Grokster*'s inducement rule, the Ninth Circuit Court of Appeals held in 2013.[97] Seven major movie studios showed that the defendant's peer-to-peer file-sharing sites directly helped site users locate specific movies and television programs to upload copyrighted works and burn copyrighted material onto DVDs to play on television sets. The court said this and other evidence showed the defendant induced site users to infringe the movie studio's copyrights.

However, embedding a video image on a website is not contributory infringement, the Seventh Circuit Court of Appeals ruled.[98] A gay pornography site sued MyVidster, a "social bookmarking" service. MyVidster subscribers can "bookmark" videos uploaded with or without permission to a server. The MyVidster site finds the embed code and stores it with an image from the video. Then MyVidster patrons can select the video, transmitted for viewing from the server, without going through any computer controlled by MyVidster. The pornography site claimed MyVidster contributed to copyright infringement by linking to websites containing illegal copies of the videos. The court disagreed. Just as a newspaper lists theaters where a movie is playing, MyVidster is not helping customers either copy or perform the videos, the court said.

Copyright Infringement Defense: Fair Use

A person sued for copyright infringement might claim that the plaintiff did not file within the law's three-year statute of limitations (or five years for criminal charges).[99] Or a defendant may argue that the copyright holder knowingly has abandoned the copyright, placing the work in the public domain.[100] The most common defense, however, is **fair use**.

Courts recognized the fair use defense long before Congress wrote it into the 1976 copyright law.[101] Courts understood that the copyright statutes—from 1790 to the present—give copyright holders the right to forbid any use of their works without permission. But what if an English teacher copies a few paragraphs from a novel for a class discussion? Or a movie reviewer shows 15 seconds of a film on television to illustrate a point about the movie? Or a comedian sings a portion of a song's lyrics in a parody? Courts have decided that these and similar uses could be fair to the copyright holder and to society. The 1976 Copyright Act included fair use as a defense.[102]

Fair use is difficult to define. One judge has said that to be fair "the use must be of a character that serves the copyright objective of stimulating productive thought and public instruction without excessively diminishing the incentives for creativity."[103] The 1976 law set out four criteria courts use in balancing the plaintiff's rights to forbid any use of a work without permission and the defendant's right to use a portion of the work under certain circumstances: (1) the purpose and character of the use, (2) the nature of the copyrighted work, (3) the amount and substantiality of the portion used and (4) the effect on the plaintiff's potential market.

1. The purpose and character of the use. In determining the purpose and character of the defendant's use of the copyrighted material, courts consider several factors, including whether the use is for commercial or nonprofit purposes. The law gives examples of uses that would tilt the balance toward a fair use: criticism, comment, news reporting, teaching (including multiple copies for classroom use), scholarship, parody, searchable databases and research.[104]

fair use A test courts use to determine whether using another's copyrighted material without permission is legal or an infringement. Also used in trademark infringement cases.

⬤ POINTS OF LAW

Fair Use Defense

1. For what purpose was the copyrighted work used without permission?
2. What was the nature of the copyrighted work that was used without permission?
3. How much and what portion of the copyrighted work was used without permission?
4. What effect did the unauthorized use have on the copyrighted work's market value?

News reporting may be considered a fair use, but this is not clear. For example, more than 30 years ago, The Nation magazine used 300 to 400 words from President Gerald R. Ford's memoirs without the book publisher's permission. The publisher had sold Time magazine the exclusive right to run excerpts. The U.S. Supreme Court acknowledged that Ford's thoughts were news, but that alone was not sufficient to qualify The Nation's copying as fair use.[105] The Court said it was not.

In a case involving a cover version of a popular song, the Supreme Court considered whether a parody changes the work it mocks or merely repeats without permission the copyrighted material.[106] The Court made transformative use a key part of fair use's first element. The more the parody transforms the work it mimics, the more likely it is that the nature of the use is fair.

The Court said fair use is more likely to be found if the new work "adds something new, with a further purpose or different character, altering the [copyrighted work] with new expression, meaning, or message."[107] A 2 Live Crew parody of Roy Orbison's song

⬤ POINTS OF LAW

Transformative Use

Transformative use is one of the primary defenses used today when arguing fair use. Transformative use is generally fair use if the answer to two questions is "yes":

1. "Has the material you have taken from the original work been transformed by adding new expression or meaning?"
2. "Was value added to the original by creating new information, new aesthetics, new insights and understandings?"[1]

Courts must also apply the other fair use factors (discussed in this section) to transformative use, but often it is the transformative use determination that carries the most weight.

---

1. *Fair Use: What Is Transformative?*, www.nolo.com/legal-encyclopedia/fair-use-what-transformative.html (last visited May 12, 2017).

"Oh, Pretty Woman" might be fair use because it did transform the original, the Court said.[108] The Court emphasized the importance of 2 Live Crew's transformation of the original but said the district court must reconsider whether the other fair use elements established fair use. The parties settled the case.[109]

Five years ago, the Seventh Circuit Court of Appeals ruled that a parody by the animated television program "South Park" of a viral video, "What What (In the Butt)," was fair use because South Park's intent was "to comment on and critique the social phenomenon that is the 'viral video.'"[110] In 2015, the Second Circuit held that an unauthorized derivative work of the film "Point Break" was also fair use and could itself be copyrighted because the parody added sufficient originality.[111] This case was unusual because the plaintiff did not use fair use as a defense but rather claimed that the derivative work was protected by copyright.

Transformative use can exist beyond parodies. A federal district court in New York held that a service that monitors and records television and radio broadcasts to turn them into a searchable database for its users amounts to fair use because the database is transformative.[112] Similarly, a federal judge held that the legal databases Lexis and Westlaw did not violate copyright law when they copied legal briefs in their entirety to create an interactive legal research tool. Although the use of the legal briefs was commercial (or for profit), the judge said the transformative nature of the database carried greater weight.[113]

In 2015, the Second Circuit Court of Appeals held that Google's mass digitization of millions of books, in connection with providing brief excerpts of books used in Google's search function, was a transformative fair use.[114] Several book publishers and the Authors Guild, which represents authors whose works were made into digital books without their permission, sued Google claiming copyright infringement. A federal district judge ruled that scanning the books amounted to fair use for purposes of preserving the works, making the books available to those with sight impairment and enabling the works to be searched.[115] The Second Circuit agreed and noted that Google's "snippet" view of the books added value and context to the basic transformative search function.[116]

AF archive /Alamy Stock Photo

A federal court of appeals found a "South Park" parody to be fair use.

In another case, the creator of the "Flying B" logo for the Baltimore Ravens, a professional football team, sued the team and the National Football League for using the logo in historical exhibits and in documentary videos. The team stopped using the logo in 1998. The Fourth Circuit considered use of the logo transformative. The court noted that the original purpose of the logo was to create a team brand but that the use in the NFL's video was incidental and that the main purpose for its inclusion in the NFL's "Top 10" series was to present a narrative about the Ravens' historical record.[117]

In 2016, the Second Circuit Court of Appeals reversed a decision by a federal district court that found the incorporation of Abbott and Costello's "Who's on First?" routine in a Broadway production was fair use. The Second Circuit held that the use of the routine in the production "Hand to God" was not transformative because it did not alter the original with new expression or meaning and the routine was performed for the exact same purpose as the original—for laughs. The court noted that the live performance even mimicked the original timing, tone and delivery of the Abbott and Costello routine.[118]

2. The nature of the copyrighted work. This factor examines whether the copyrighted work is largely creative, such as a feature film, or more informational or functional, like a compilation of court decisions.[119] Courts often find more copyright protection for creative works. Copying portions of factually based materials may tilt the balance toward a fair use.

The question of whether unpublished materials should have special protection against a fair use defense arose when a court allowed J.D. Salinger, the author of "The Catcher in the Rye," to stop distribution of an unauthorized biography including excerpts from his letters.[120] A federal appellate court held that unpublished materials are entitled to more protection than published works. Congress later amended the Copyright Act to clarify that unpublished materials are not necessarily protected if all four fair use factors show copying without permission should be permitted.[121]

3. The amount and substantiality of the portion used. Courts ask two questions with regard to the amount and substantiality factor. First, how much of the copyrighted work was used without permission? Courts may count how many words from a story or seconds from a movie were used or may consider what percentage of the original was used. Second, what particular portion of the copyrighted work was used, and how important was it to the copyrighted work? Quoting from the last page of a mystery novel—the words telling who committed the murder, how and why—would tip the balance toward copyright infringement, not fair use. The balance would tip toward infringement even if only a comparatively few words—but the most important words—were quoted from the mystery novel.

Copying the entirety of a copyrighted work does not necessarily mean the use was not fair. A group of students sued the company that owns Turnitin, a plagiarism detection service, because Turnitin archived their work in the company's computers. The students claimed the archiving effectively copied their work, thus infringing their copyrights. The U.S. Court of Appeals for the Fourth Circuit disagreed.[122] Although the company copied all of each student paper, the court found Turnitin's archiving to be fair use. In general, the court said, "as the amount of the copyrighted material that is used increases, the likelihood that the use will constitute a 'fair use' decreases."[123] However, the court balanced the amount used against other fair use factors, particularly the purpose. Here Turnitin uses each student paper for a limited purpose, that is, to enable students and teachers to expose plagiarism. In the database-related transformative use cases noted earlier, courts reinforced the idea that fair use can apply even if works are copied in their entirety.[124]

Similarly, a federal appellate court said reprinting full pictures of Grateful Dead posters and concert tickets did not preclude finding fair use when the images were scattered throughout a book in collages of images, text and graphic art. The court said the use was transformative because images were shown in reduced size and only a few unauthorized copyrighted works were published among 2,000 images.[125]

Professors, film and media studies students and documentary filmmakers generally may use short clips from movies for criticism, for commentary or even to make new, noncommercial videos, the Librarian of Congress ruled.[126]

4. The effect on the plaintiff's potential market. Many courts consider the extent to which the unauthorized copying diminished the copyright holder's likely profits from his or her creation the most important of the four fair use factors. Giving away the end of a mystery novel might mean potential readers would not purchase the book, which would have a financial impact on a copyright holder and the incentive to create. When a Kinko's store responded to professors' requests to make course packets by copying chapters from numerous books without permission, several publishers sued for copyright infringement. A court rejected Kinko's fair use defense, finding the fourth factor the "single most important" part of the fair use test in that case.[127] If students purchased the professor's course packet, they were not purchasing the textbook from which the chapters came.

The U.S. Supreme Court has said copying a substantial portion of a copyrighted work without permission may prove a "greater likelihood of market harm under the fourth" element of the fair use test.[128] That is, typically, the more of a work that someone copies, the less likely it is someone else will purchase the original. This would cause market harm to the copyright holder. With the increase in the application of transformative use in the first part of the fair use test (purpose and character of the use), some courts have acknowledged that under the fourth part of the test the transformative use of the work actually expands the market for the original work.[129] That is, copying the entire work for a searchable database, as Google has done, can make the full work more widely available in the marketplace, and that enhances the value of the copyrighted work.

The DMCA and Safe Harbor Protections

Copyright infringement can occur on the internet just as it can in print. Copying pictures from a magazine's website onto another website or into a class paper without permission violates the copyright law.[130] Downloading copyrighted music or movies infringes on copyright holders' rights. As noted earlier in this chapter, the Digital Millennium Copyright Act was an attempt to bring the internet and other digital media into the copyright law.[131] One of the concerns the DMCA addresses is whether internet service providers can lose copyright suits based on content their users post.

The DMCA shields ISPs and video-sharing sites from copyright infringement claims if they remove material that a copyright holder tells them is posted without permission.[132] This is called a "takedown notice." This protection is available if a website names an agent to receive takedown requests, lets site users know of the site's copyright infringement policy and complies with takedown requests it receives. ISPs must comply with takedown

▲ EMERGING LAW

APIs and Copyright

API stands for "application programming interface." Basically, APIs are computer operating system tools that enable developers to create software applications. One well-known API is Oracle's Java. Google's Android, a popular mobile phone platform, is software written in Java but containing its own APIs.[1]

In 2010, Oracle sued Google for copyright infringement arguing that the Android API copied the Java code along with the "structure, sequence and organization" of 37 Java API packages. A jury heard portions of the case and decided that Google did infringe, but at the same time a district court judge ruled that APIs like Java are a method of operation and are not copyrightable.[2]

These conflicting results generated several appeals. In 2014, a federal court of appeals reversed the district court judge's decision and said the Java API and its SSO did qualify for copyright protection because they included creative expression separate from their function. The appeals court reinstated the jury's verdict. Google had argued its use of the API constituted a fair use, and that claim resulted in a hung jury. So, the appeals court remanded that specific question to the district court.[3]

Google appealed to the U.S. Supreme Court, but after inviting the solicitor general to file a brief in the case,[4] the Court denied the petition. In 2016, a jury found Google's use of Oracle's API was fair use. The jury instructions in that case defined transformative use and noted that "when purely functional elements are embedded in copyrighted work and it is necessary to copy associated creative elements to utilize functional elements, [this] favors fair use."[5]

---

1. Colin Lecher, *The Oracle v. Google Case May Go to the Supreme Court*, THE VERGE, Oct. 9, 2014, www.theverge.com/2014/10/9/6953215/oracle-v-google-case-supreme-court-hearing.
2. Oracle America Inc. v. Google Inc., 872 F. Supp. 2d 974 (N.D. Cal. 2012).
3. Oracle Am. Inc. v. Google Inc., 750 F.3d 1339 (Fed. Cir. 2014), *cert. denied*, 135 S. Ct. 2887 (2015).
4. *Id.*
5. Bruce Keller, *Communications Law in the Digital Age: Intellectual Property*, COMM. L. IN THE DIGITAL AGE (2016).

requests that clearly identify the work claimed to infringe copyright and provide the URL of the infringing work.[133] A customer cannot sue the ISP for removing material even if the customer later shows the material did not violate a copyright holder's rights. ISPs that knowingly transmit material that violates copyright are not protected.

The DMCA offers other protection to video-sharing websites. It protects video-sharing websites from monetary damages when a user, rather than the site, posts copyrighted material without permission. The copyright holder cannot successfully sue the site operator if the operator (1) did not know the content infringed someone's copyright, (2) did not earn money directly from the posted material and (3) promptly complied with a takedown notice. These takedown protections, also known as **safe harbors**, limit video-sharing sites' liability.

The DMCA's safe harbors saved Veoh Networks, an internet-based video-sharing service, from losing a copyright infringement suit in 2013. Universal Music Group, one of the world's largest recording companies, sued Veoh over user-uploaded videos that included UMG-copyrighted songs. Veoh had implemented a copyright infringement policy and taken down videos when notified of violations but was not able to prevent all

safe harbor The takedown notification provision of the Digital Millennium Copyright Act that protects internet service providers and video-sharing websites from claims of infringement when they do not know about the infringement, do not earn money from the infringement and promptly comply with a takedown notice.

infringements. Despite failure to notify Veoh of all infringing videos, UMG said Veoh should have known some of its videos infringed copyright. The U.S. Court of Appeals for the Ninth Circuit said the DMCA requires specific notification to Veoh of videos that need to be removed.[134] Absent such notification, Veoh had neither the right nor the ability to prevent users from posting videos that infringed copyright, the court said. Simple labeling of "music video" postings was insufficient to show Veoh knew a video infringed UMG's copyright.

The DMCA's safe harbor provision also kept Google-owned YouTube from losing a $1 billion suit filed by Viacom. Viacom owns Paramount Pictures, the CBS television network and several cable networks such as MTV, VH1 and Comedy Central. On remand from a federal appellate court, a district judge in 2013 held that YouTube's removal of 100,000 videos that Viacom said infringed its copyrights did not show YouTube knew it carried Viacom's copyrighted material.[135] Without that knowledge, the safe harbor protected YouTube.

In 2014, a federal district court ruled that the DMCA safe harbor provision also protected Vimeo, another popular video-sharing website, with respect to user-uploaded

▲ EMERGING LAW

Copyright and the Music Marketplace

Recently, the U.S. Copyright Office released a yearlong study of how to reform the music licensing system that the office says is significantly "outmoded."[1] The concept of music licensing dates back to the early 20th century. Performing rights organizations (for example, the American Society of Composers, Authors and Publishers) grant licenses for the performance of copyrighted songs for specific purposes. In return for licenses, the organizations collect song fees from the song users and distribute royalties to the composers.

The 245-page report identifies shortcomings in the current music licensing system and notes that music is "culturally essential and economically important" and both music creators and innovators are "doing business in legal quicksand."[2] The report offers a new legal framework, ideas and principles to guide future reform.

The report attracted little media attention, but some tech bloggers noted that the report's proposed framework would increase songwriter royalties and could result in consumers paying more for popular streaming music services (like Pandora or Spotify).[3] Under current licensing practices, record labels bring in the majority of music industry revenues, and some believe that is unfair given their diminished role in the digital music marketplace. Many artists have objected vocally to the current system, which they say punishes songwriters. After Jay Z bought music streaming service Tidal for $54 million, he invited fellow songwriters to share in company profits. In 2017, he sold a stake in Tidal to Sprint.[4]

Some argue that a new legal structure must emerge to reform the music licensing system to better match today's digital music environment.[5]

---

1. U.S. COPYRIGHT OFFICE, COPYRIGHT AND THE MUSIC MARKETPLACE: A REPORT OF THE REGISTER OF COPYRIGHTS, Feb. 2015, copyright.gov/policy/musiclicensingstudy/copyright-and-the-music-marketplace.pdf.
2. *Id.*
3. Pulkit Chandna, *Proposed Changes in Copyright Law Could Render Online Music Streaming More Expensive*, TECHHIVE, Feb. 11, 2015, www.techhive.com/article/2882758/proposed-changes-in-copyright-law-could-render-online-music-streaming-more-expensive.html.
4. BBC, *Jay Z Sells Stake in his Tidal Music Streaming Service*, BBC, Jan. 23, 2017, www.bbc.com/news/business-38725806.
5. Aloe Blacc, Irina D. Manta & David S. Olson, *Sharelines (Commentary): Music Streaming Demands New Wav of Licensing Rules*, CHICAGO TRIB., Apr. 3, 2015, www.chicagotribune.com/news/opinion/commentary/ct-jay-z-pandora-songwriters-compensation-copyright-justice-perspec-0402-20150403-story.html.

videos that Vimeo's employees did not review. But the court did not give safe harbor to a handful of infringing videos that Vimeo employees did view.[136] This is sometimes called "**red flag knowledge**." The phrase from the *YouTube* decision refers to an ISP or website being "subjectively aware of facts that would have made the specific infringement 'objectively' obvious to a reasonable person."[137] If the website has red flag knowledge of infringing material and does not remove it, then a court could find it responsible for infringement. Vimeo argued that the videos reviewed by the employees did not contain "objectively obvious" infringement and should be protected by the safe harbor provision, but the court disagreed.[138]

When one Photobucket user sued the photo-sharing website for sharing her photos with Kodak's website and for not removing all infringing images, the Second Circuit Court of Appeals applied the *YouTube* decision and held that Photobucket did not have an affirmative requirement to police its site.[139] Kodak placed the shared photos onto various items and sold them without the plaintiff's permission. Photobucket complied with several DMCA takedown notices from the plaintiff, but some of her copyrighted work remained on the website. The Second Circuit held that Photobucket was entitled to safe harbor protection. The plaintiff also unsuccessfully sued Kodak.

In the context of a news website, the Tenth Circuit Court of Appeals held in 2016 that Examiner.com was protected under the DMCA safe harbor provision after individuals contributing to the website posted photographs without permission. The court's decision was based on the fact that the site's contributors are considered users under the DMCA and that the infringing photos were posted at their discretion. The website did not have red flag knowledge.[140]

A website or blog containing an embedded copyrighted video does not lose DMCA protection. As long as the video is a link to another site and no copy is maintained, the DMCA applies.[141]

Gareth Cattermole/Getty Images

Artists like Adele have barred their work from streaming services like Spotify because song royalties from streaming are low. In 2016, artists earned 17 cents for every 100 plays on free, ad-supported music streaming services.

red flag knowledge When an internet service provider or website is aware of facts that would make infringement obvious to a reasonable person.

Music, the Internet and File Sharing

Early in this century, shortly after an appeals court confirmed that technical innovations that facilitate copyright infringement violate the law, digital music file sharing via the internet was becoming popular. Some 35 million U.S. adults downloaded music online, and 67 percent of them said they did not care whether the music was protected by copyright.[142] Napster, one of the first music file-sharing services, allowed users to reach into each other's computers to retrieve files containing copyrighted music. Before the Ninth Circuit Court of Appeals ruled that Napster's operation violated the copyright law, millions of people used this peer-to-peer network to make unauthorized copies of sound recordings.[143] Napster's sole purpose was to aid copyright infringement by allowing users to share copyrighted music, according to the court.

Subsequent P2P systems generally avoided Napster's central server design, but the recording industry pursued individual downloaders. One federal appellate court affirmed a $222,000 award to the recording industry from a woman who distributed 24 songs using the Kazaa P2P network. That litigation ended in 2013 when the U.S. Supreme Court refused to hear her appeal.[144] Another federal appellate court upheld a jury's decision ordering a Boston University graduate student to pay $675,000 in damages for illegally downloading and sharing 30 songs.[145]

The recording and movie industries filed a copyright infringement lawsuit against two P2P networks, Grokster and Morpheus, claiming they contributed to copyright infringement by allowing network users to illegally download copyrighted songs and movies. The U.S. Supreme Court agreed and said Grokster and Morpheus promoted and encouraged their users to violate the copyright law.[146] In its unanimous decision, the Court said the P2P systems aided in copyright "infringement on a gigantic scale" and that "the probable scope of copyright infringement is staggering."[147]

Grokster and Morpheus argued they were no more responsible for copyright infringement than was Sony for making VCRs. But the Court said the difference between Sony's VCRs and the file-sharing services is "inducement."[148] Sony may have known VCRs could be used to infringe on copyright, but it did not encourage illegal copying. Grokster and Morpheus, however, aimed their services at former Napster users, did not develop filtering tools to prevent copyright infringement and sold advertising directed to people who were illegally downloading copyrighted digital content, the Court said. All this showed Grokster and Morpheus encouraged or induced their users to illegally download protected content, according to the Court.

Five years ago, in another attempt to limit online theft, the recording and movie industry activated the Copyright Alert System. Copyright holders will notify five major ISPs—Verizon, Comcast, AT&T, Cablevision and Time Warner—when any of the ISPs' customers engage in illegal downloading using P2P software. The customer then will receive up to six warning notices from the ISP before his or her bandwidth may be reduced, or a customer may automatically be sent to a website with information about copyright law. The Copyright Alert System may limit the hundreds of thousands of cases, most dismissed or settled, content providers have brought against illegal downloaders. The Center for Copyright Information reported that the system sent out 1.3 million alerts in its first year and received only 265 challenges. CCI also reported that its survey found that 62 percent of U.S. consumers said copyright infringement is never acceptable and they would stop infringement if they received an alert.[149]

TRADEMARKS

trademark A word, name, symbol or design used to identify a company's goods and distinguish them from similar products other companies make.

A **trademark** is a word, name, symbol or design used to identify a company's goods and distinguish them from similar products other companies make.[150] A service mark accomplishes the same purpose for services a firm provides. A trade name identifies a particular company rather than the company's product or service. Federal law also protects trade dress, which describes a product's total look, including size, shape, color, texture and graphics. The word "trademark" may be used generally to include all four of these categories. However, the law does not protect trade names or trade dress as completely as it protects trademarks and service marks.

Trademarks are valuable. Consider the importance of McDonald's, Google, Nike, Amazon, Kleenex and Coke as trademarks. Companies use trademarks to advertise their products and services. Customers use trademarks to ensure they are getting the goods or services from a particular company. Reaching for a soft drink, a customer does not want to have to read the small print on a label to confirm that a company named Coca-Cola in Atlanta, Ga., licenses the product. A customer simply wants to see the word "Coke" and know it is the product he or she wants. Coca-Cola's trademark is worth millions of dollars.

Trademarks may be brand names or logos designed to identify a company's product. The Nike "swoosh" is a well-known logo. But the list of what can be trademarked is lengthy: letters (CBS), numbers (VO5), domain names (Amazon.com), slogans ("Just do it"), shapes (Coke bottle), colors (Corning fiberglass pink insulation),[151] sounds (quacking noise made by guides and participants in duck boat tours)[152] and smells ("fresh cut grass" for tennis balls).[153]

The federal Lanham Act protects trademarks that are eligible for registration with the U.S. Patent and Trademark Office.[154] The law ensures that if a company complies with certain requirements, no other company may use a word, symbol, slogan or other such item that will confuse consumers about who supplies a particular product or service. The Lanham Act also prevents using a mark to falsely suggest a product's source even if the mark is not registered.[155]

Distinctiveness Requirement

Distinctive words, designs or other indicators of a product or service's origin are eligible for trademark registration.[156] A trademark will be protected only if it is distinctive. A trademark is distinctive if it distinguishes one company's goods from another's.

There is a spectrum of distinctiveness in trademark law. The less unique—that is, the more broadly descriptive—a mark is, the less likely it is to be eligible for trademark registration. The most distinctive category is "fanciful marks." These are invented marks, including made-up words. Lexus, Xerox and Exxon are examples of fanciful marks. A court found that Peterbilt and Kenworth are fanciful marks applied to trucks.[157] The trucks' manufacturer sued a website operator who used the words "Peterbilt" and "Kenworth" in the site's address without permission. Because fanciful marks are the strongest and most distinctive trademarks possible, the most trademark protection should be applied to fanciful marks, the court said. When a strong mark is infringed, it is more likely consumers will be confused, the court concluded.

"Arbitrary marks," the next most distinctive category, are words that have ordinary meanings unrelated to the product or service. For example, an apple is a fruit, but Apple is a trademark for computers and other products manufactured by Apple Inc. A dictionary will define the word "apple" as a fruit, but not as a computer. Numbers and letters arranged in a distinctive order may be arbitrary marks, such as bebe for clothes[158] or V8 for vegetable juice.[159]

"Suggestive marks" suggest a product's qualities or manufacturer's business but do not describe either. A suggestive mark requires consumers to use their imaginations to discern the company's exact business.[160] One court said Coppertone, Orange Crush and Playboy are good examples of suggestive marks "because they conjure images of the associated products without directly describing those products."[161] A court held that the word "CarMax" is a suggestive mark for a used car dealership.[162] The word suggests that CarMax is involved in the automobile business but does not say the company sells used cars.

A "descriptive mark" leaves little to a consumer's imagination. The mark describes the product or service and may or may not suggest what company provided it. Generally, commonly used descriptive terms cannot be trademarked. For example, many soft drink companies may use the word "refreshing" to describe their products. However, a descriptive mark may be a trademark if it has acquired a distinctive connection to the product for which it is used. Courts call this a "secondary meaning" beyond the word's common meaning. Distinctive, arbitrary and suggestive marks do not require a secondary meaning.

To obtain a secondary meaning, the public must associate a word with a product's source or producer, not the product. Courts do not agree on a test for finding a secondary meaning, but the Court of Appeals for the Ninth Circuit's approach is illustrative. It

● REAL WORLD LAW

Sports Trademarks

AP/Gene J. Puskar; Buma ISD

Penn State said a high school's logo (right) looked too much like the university's panther (left) and therefore could be a trademark infringement.

Professional and university sports leagues and teams protect their trademarks because they are worth millions of dollars. The leagues' and teams' logos are used on clothing and other merchandise, in advertising for game tickets and as part of televised sports events. When a T-shirt maker puts the phrase "Who Dat" on shirts, it has used a phrase the National Football League says it has trademarked and is used by New Orleans Saints fans.[1] The words "Super Bowl" and "Olympics" also are trademarks. So are "March Madness" and even "Elite Eight."

Colleges also protect their trademarked logos. In 2015, Texas A&M sued the NFL's Indianapolis Colts for allegedly infringing on their "12th Man" trademark. The Seattle Seahawks also use the "12th Man" trademark but pay Texas A&M to do so.[2]

The University of Florida ordered a private K–12 school to stop using an alligator as its mascot because it nearly matched Florida's Gator. The school said it could cost $60,000 to change its logo on everything from uniforms to the gym floor. Penn State told a Texas high school—1,400 miles from the university—its Cougar logo looked too much like Penn State's Nittany Lion. The University of Pittsburgh instructed a Toledo, Ohio, high school to stop using Pitt's trademarked Panther for sports teams and, more generally, to identify the schools. Using a trademark without permission for purposes similar to the trademark owner's use violates federal law.[3]

1. Ken Sugiura & Michael Carvell, *In Brief*, ATL. J-.CONST., Jan. 30, 2010, at 1C.
2. Tom Fornelli, *Texas A&M Suing the Indianapolis Colts for Trademark Infringement*, CBS SPORTS, Nov. 12, 2015, www.cbssports.com/college-football/news/texas-am-suing-the-indianapolis-colts-for-trademark-infringement/.
3. Adam Himmelsbach, *Colleges Fight to Keep Logos Off High School Playing Fields*, N.Y. TIMES, Nov. 27, 2010, at A1, A3.

⊙ POINTS OF LAW

Types of Marks

A trademark is only protected if it is distinctive. There is a spectrum of distinctiveness in trademark law. The more distinct or unique a mark, the more likely it will be eligible for trademark registration.

- **Fanciful marks**—invented marks, including made-up words (for example, Lexus) most likely to receive trademark protection.
- **Arbitrary marks**—words that have ordinary meanings unrelated to the product or service (for example, Apple).
- **Suggestive marks**—marks that suggest a product's source or manufacturer's business but do not describe what the product is (for example, Playboy).
- **Descriptive marks**—marks that describe the product or service and leave little to a consumer's imagination and that must attach a distinctive meaning to the product or service (called secondary meaning) to be trademarked.

considers "(1) whether actual purchasers of the product bearing the claimed trademark associate the trademark with the producer; (2) the degree and manner of advertising under the claimed trademark; (3) the length and manner of use of the claimed trademark; and (4) whether use of the claimed trademark has been exclusive."[163]

Certain groups of descriptive words, such as geographic terms, have difficulty acquiring a secondary meaning and cannot be a registered trademark if they only describe where the goods or services are made or offered. For example, a court refused to find that the word "Boston" had a secondary meaning in the phrase "Boston Beer."[164] Although the beer is manufactured in Boston, "Boston" means the Massachusetts city and is not connected in the public's mind with that brand of beer, the court said. The court did not allow Boston Beer to be a trademark. But a century ago, the Supreme Court held "The American Girl" to be an arbitrary trademark for a brand of shoes because it did not suggest the shoes were made in America or even that the product was shoes.[165] A geographic term also cannot be a registered trademark if it is deceptive. For example, a ham processor located in Nebraska cannot use the term "Danish ham" as a trademark for its product.

Similarly, people's names must acquire a secondary meaning to be protected. In one case, Fabrikant & Sons, a jewelry company, trademarked the word "Fabrikant." Several years later, Fabrikant Fine Diamonds began business as a buyer and seller of jewelry. Both companies are located in New York City, and both are owned by individuals named Fabrikant. A court ruled that Fabrikant Fine Diamonds had to either stop using the name Fabrikant or use a first name in front of the word to distinguish it from Fabrikant & Sons.[166] Otherwise the public would be confused, the court said. Courts often consider three factors to rule in competing name cases. As one court put it, the factors are "(a) the interest of the plaintiff in protecting the good will which has attached to his personal name trademark, (b) the interest of the defendant in using his own name in his business activities and (c) the interest of the public in being free from confusion and deception."[167]

The World's 10 Most Powerful Brands.
These are the world's most powerful brands, all awarded the top AAA+ brand rating based on Brand Finance's Brand Strength Index (BSI).

Brand Finance plc.

Every year, Brand Finance releases a report on the world's most valuable and powerful brands and their trademarks. Google was the most *valuable* global brand in 2017, worth about $109 billion. Lego was the most *powerful* global brand because of its high scores on familiarity, loyalty, promotion, marketing investment, staff satisfaction and corporate reputation.

Finally, generic words will not be given trademark protection. A graham cracker manufacturer cannot use the word "cracker" as a trademark, for example. A manufacturer is not allowed to take a word commonly used to describe a product category and use it exclusively for the company's own purpose. For instance, Harley-Davidson could not use the word "hog" as a mark for its motorcycles,[168] nor could a concert promoter obtain a trademark for the term "summer jam" to advertise its summer concerts.[169]

Some marks that once were protected became generic when the public used the mark to mean a category of goods rather than a particular manufacturer's product. Thermos, cellophane, brassiere, aspirin, shredded wheat and monopoly (the board game) all once were protected copyrights that became generic words.[170] Courts ask what a word's primary significance is to the public. If the public thinks of a word as describing a class of goods—a vacuum bottle is a thermos—the word is generic and cannot be a protected mark. If the word primarily means a particular manufacturer—Xerox makes Xerox copying machines—the word will remain a trademark.[171]

Companies can take several steps to prevent a trademark from becoming generic. Among other actions, a company should select a distinctive mark, advertise the goods using both the trademark and the product's generic word (Kleenex facial tissue), use advertisements to educate the public that the product's trademark is not a generic word and use the trademark on several different products.[172]

Registering a Trademark

A history of using a distinctive mark to identify a product can give the mark protection even if it is not registered. The first person or company to use the mark owns it. State courts recognize common law rights in marks within the geographic area where the mark is used. It is not necessary to register a mark to give it common law protection. An owner of a mark protected by common law may use the symbols ™ (trademark) or ℠ (service mark), but these are not recognized by statute.

A mark must be registered with the PTO to have statutory protection under the Lanham Act.[173] Registering a mark requires submitting an application form, a drawing of the mark and a filing fee to the PTO. Trademark law's complexity means a trademark attorney needs to be involved in registering a mark.

Section 2(a) of the Lanham Act prevents the PTO from registering a mark that is considered immoral, disparaging or deceptive.[174] These kinds of trademarks are often referred to as **disparaging marks**. Trademark registration also excludes marks with a flag or other insignia of any country or U.S. state or city, marks with a name or other identification of a living person without the individual's consent or marks that are only descriptive without secondary meaning.[175]

Nor will the PTO register a mark identical to or similar to an existing mark. Descriptive marks go on the Supplemental Register, with their owners hoping to move them to the Principal Register once secondary meaning has been established.[176]

In 2017, the U.S. Supreme Court considered whether the Lanham Act's ban on disparaging trademarks violates the First Amendment.[177] Simon Tam and his Asian-American band the Slants applied for a trademark in 2011 to protect the band name. The band says it uses the name to re-appropriate the slur sometimes applied to Asians. The PTO refused to register the trademark because it was disparaging. Sitting en banc, the D.C. Circuit Court of Appeals reversed and held that the PTO's ban on disparaging marks was an unconstitutional viewpoint-based restriction on speech.[178] "Courts have been slow to appreciate the expressive power of trademarks," the D.C. Circuit Court wrote. "The government cannot refuse to register disparaging marks because it disapproves of the expressive messages conveyed by the marks."[179] The Supreme Court agreed.

The government argued that trademarks, like license plates, are a form of government speech. Government's power to operate the trademark program includes the power to reject the disparaging mark. In *Matal v. Tam*, excerpted at the end of the chapter, the Supreme Court held that the disparagement clause violates the First Amendment. "Contrary to the Government's contention, trademarks are private, not government speech," Justice Samuel Alito wrote for the Court. "Because the "Free Speech Clause . . . does not regulate government speech," the government is not required to maintain viewpoint neutrality on its own speech. This Court exercises great caution in extending its government-speech precedents, for if private speech could be passed off as government speech by simply affixing a government seal of approval, government could silence or muffle the expression of disfavored viewpoints."[180]

Anthony Pidgeon/Redferns/Getty Images

A few years ago, the PTO canceled the NFL Washington Redskins' name and logo as disparaging. The Redskins' appeal of the decision is pending in the Fourth Circuit Court of Appeals. In 2016, the team asked to join the Slants trademark case before the Supreme Court, but that request was denied.[181] The Redskins instead filed an amicus brief in support of the Slants.[182]

Federal registration provides a mark more protection than common law does for a mark. Registration establishes the date of the mark's first use, protects nationwide use and lets competitors know that a company owns the mark.[183] A company may use the statutory symbol for registered marks. The symbol ® or the phrase "Registered U.S. Patent and Trademark Office" is acceptable. If a registered mark is infringed, its owner may sue in federal court. After five years of use, the mark gains nearly complete protection.[184] During the sixth year after registration, a mark owner must file an affidavit confirming the mark has been in continued use.[185] Marks registered after Nov. 16, 1989, have a 10-year term. Registrations may be renewed indefinitely.[186]

In addition to First Amendment concerns, the Oregon-based band the Slants said it needs its name trademarked in order to land a record label deal.

Domain Names

Congress adapted trademark law to the internet, but website addresses, or domain names, have been a particular problem for trademark law. Domain names may be trademarked and protected against infringement, although the domain name suffixes, such as .com or .org, are not considered part of a trademarked domain name.

Cybersquatters claim domain names that include trademarks or famous people's names. Before Congress passed the Anticybersquatting Consumer Protection Act, trademark owners often sued cybersquatters, frequently successfully, to try to stop the practice.[187] The ACPA provides civil and criminal remedies for registering a domain name with the intention of selling it to the trademark owner. The law applies to a domain name identical or confusingly similar to a trademark or that disparages or injures a well-known trademark. A defendant must have acted in bad faith to be liable under the statute.

In one ACPA case, a company named Spider Webs registered hundreds of domain names, including ErnestandJulioGallo.com. The Gallo winery sued. A federal appellate court held the ACPA constitutional and said the unauthorized domain name could injure Gallo's trademark.[188] Spider Webs admitted it registered the domain name hoping the ACPA would be found unconstitutional. That showed bad faith, the appellate court said, and it upheld a $25,000 damage award and a court order preventing Spider Webs from registering any domain name that used "Gallo" or "Ernest and Julio."

If two companies have identical or similar trademarks for two different products, the companies' domain names might be the same—chip.com for a computer chip company or for a potato chip company. In such a case, one court said trademark law takes precedence over domain registration. The court gave a disputed domain name—moviebuff—to the company that first used the mark.[189] However, if two domain names are similar and both describe the companies' products, courts may allow the firms to continue using the names. For example, the manufacturer of Beanie Babies sued a company using bargain-beanies.com as a domain name. The bargain beanies company sold used beanbag animals. A federal appellate court said preventing a firm from using a domain name describing its business would be like "forbidding a used car dealer who specializes in selling Chevrolets to mention" the car's name in the dealer's advertising.[190] The court allowed both companies to use their domain names.

Trademark Infringement

Anyone may use a protected trademark in a way that is not confusing. The Lanham Act says trademark infringement occurs when a mark "is likely to cause confusion, or to cause a mistake, or to deceive as to the affiliation, connection, or association of such person with another person, or as to the origin, sponsorship, or approval of his or her goods, services, or commercial activities by another person."[191] Including the words "Pontiac," "Tommy Hilfiger" and "Burger King" in this paragraph is not a trademark infringement. Using marks for informational purposes is a fair use.

The First Amendment protects using a competitor's trademark in comparative advertising, courts have ruled.[192] However, a competitor may not alter a mark in a comparative ad. In one case, a competitor to John Deere's lawn tractor business aired a comparative ad that distorted and animated Deere's trademarked deer logo, showing the deer jumping through a hoop that breaks apart, for instance. The ad diminished Deere's logo in consumers' minds, a court ruled.[193]

Recently, a federal court in California held that use of a competitor's trademark as an advertising keyword in a search is not likely to cause consumer confusion and is not a trademark infringement.[194] Facebook claimed likelihood of confusion and won a trademark infringement lawsuit against a social networking site named Teachbook. Teachbook marketed to teachers, stating that many schools forbid teachers from using Facebook because students might learn teachers' personal information. A federal district court found a likelihood of confusion between the two marks because the "Teachbook mark is highly similar to the registered Facebook mark in appearance, sound, meaning, and commercial impression."[195]

Similar—even identical—marks may not cause confusion if the goods for which the marks are used are not the same. Wendy's automobile parts may coexist with Wendy's restaurants if a court says consumers would not think the restaurant company also owns the auto parts store.

Companies may redesign or refresh logos but want to retain the original trademark. Trademark **tacking** allows a trademark owner to slightly alter a trademark without abandoning ownership of the original mark. In order to "tack" a trademark, the owner must show that "the two trademarks create the same, continuing commercial impression, and the later mark should not materially differ from or alter the character of the mark attempted to be tacked."[196] Courts review tacking claims with a higher likelihood of confusion standard. That is, rather than establishing the likelihood of confusion in the marketplace, when a trademark owner is arguing for tacking, that owner must show that consumers believe both trademarks represent the same company or product and that there is no marketplace confusion. In other words, a business owner can show tacking by demonstrating that the new trademark is basically the same as the original in the eyes of consumers—that is, to consumers it represents the same thing.

tacking Allows a trademark owner to slightly alter a trademark without abandoning ownership of the original mark.

For example, Pepsi-Cola was trademarked in 1903. Since then, its logo has evolved from the soda's name appearing in cursive font to a circle-shaped logo with "Pepsi" in the center. Since the 1940s, the logos incorporated red, white and blue as part of the circle.[197] Pepsi would likely be able to "tack" its logos since changes always incorporate previous, recognizable logo elements. The logo the company uses today combines the colors it started using in the 1940s with a font that contains a modern look but incorporates elements of the original logo.[198]

In 2015, the Supreme Court unanimously decided that a jury should decide questions of tacking because it involves a question of fact—whether the two marks create the same commercial impression to consumers.[199] As one trademark expert observed, "This makes sense: A jury is comprised of 12 ordinary people, and questions about trademarks usually revolve around whether ordinary consumers would be confused."[200]

Courts use a variety of criteria to determine whether consumers likely will be confused by similar marks used by different products or services. These include the marks' similarities, the similarities of products or services for which the marks are used, how consumers purchase the goods (impulse buying or careful consideration), how well known the first-used mark is, actual confusion that can be proved and how long both marks have been used without confusion.[201]

The evolution of the Pepsi logo would likely qualify as tacking.

Using a famous trademark in a way that disparages or diminishes the mark's effectiveness is known as "dilution." Dilution may happen in two ways.[202] First, a product name similar to a well-known trademark could make the famous mark less distinctive. What the law calls "blurring" whittles away a trademark's selling power. Second, a poorly made or unsavory product using a name similar to a famous trademark could cause consumers to think less of the well-known mark. This is "tarnishment."[203]

Congress revised federal anti-dilution law in response to a U.S. Supreme Court decision involving an "adult novelties" store in Elizabethtown, Ky., called Victor's Secret. After franchise Victoria's Secret asked the store's owners not to use the name Victor's Secret, the owners called it Victor's Little Secret. Victoria's Secret sued for trademark dilution. The Supreme Court said Victoria's Secret had to show actual dilution of its trademark, which might be difficult for the large corporation to do.[204] The Court said there is "a complete absence of evidence of any lessening of the capacity of the Victoria's Secret mark to identify . . . goods . . . sold in Victoria's Secret stores or advertised in its catalogs."[205]

Congress rejected that approach. It revised anti-dilution law to require companies with famous trademarks to show only a likelihood of dilution, not actual dilution of trademark effectiveness. But the core of the anti-dilution law remains the same: A company does not have to prove it is likely consumers will be confused between a famous trademark and a similar product or service name. Rather, the company only has to show another firm's similar mark has diminished the well-known mark's distinctiveness or injured its reputation.

Nearly half the states have anti-dilution statutes. These laws protect dilution of all marks used in the state, not just the famous marks the federal anti-dilution law protects.

Several remedies are available for trademark infringement. First, anyone notified of an alleged infringement may stop using the disputed mark voluntarily. Second, a court may issue an order requiring the infringing company to stop using the mark. If a mark owner is able to prove actual consumer confusion, a court may award monetary damages against the infringer.

Trademark Infringement Defenses

The Lanham Act lists nine defenses to a trademark infringement action.[206] Most turn on disputed facts. For example, a defendant might argue that the registered trademark was obtained fraudulently, that the trademark has been abandoned and no longer is in use or that the mark misrepresents a product's origin. A defendant also might claim to have used and registered the mark first.

The Lanham Act also provides a fair use defense.[207] This allows one company's trademark to describe another company's product. Courts will accept the fair use defense if the defendant used the mark to describe its goods and not as a trademark. Also, the use

🔲 SOCIAL MEDIA LAW

Trademarks and Social Media Services

In 2016, the Trademark Trial and Appeal Board upheld the Patent and Trademark Office's decision to refuse to register a company's Twitter page online community as a separate mark.

Florists' Transworld Delivery wanted to trademark "Say It Your Way," which is its online community for registered users. The problem? FTD's Twitter page did not offer the social networking service as a "separable service to others"; rather, the Twitter page was incidental to FTD's sales of its goods.[1]

The board noted that simply using Twitter for a company's purposes is not the same as establishing an online community in connection with a company's mark.[2]

Legal experts say the takeaway from the decision is that trademark applicants need to consider how they explain their services; they must clearly distinguish between a company's own services and the services provided by a social media platform.[3]

---

1. John L. Welch, *Precedential No. 14: FTD's Twitter Account Not a Separate, Registrable Service, Says TTAB*, THETTABLOG, May 16, 2016, thettablog .blogspot.com/2016/05/precedential-no-14-ftds-twitter-account.html.
2. *In re* Florists Inc. 119 U.S.P.Q.2d 1056 (T.T.A.B. 2016).
3. Sterne Kessler Goldstein & Fox, *Saying It YOUR Way, on THEIR Website: Not a Registrable Service*, LEXOLOGY, June 30, 2016, www.lexology.com/ library/detail.aspx?g=c0915e36-d789-4cd2-bf01-07dc332172a2.

cannot cause customer confusion. For example, a federal court in Utah recently held that NoMoreRack.com's use of the word "overstock" in its advertisements was a fair use and did not infringe on Overstock.com's trademark. The court said that use of such a general term, even though the websites directly compete with each other, did not create a likelihood of confusion.[208]

In another recent case, the Ninth Circuit Court of Appeals held that use of the phrase "web celeb" as part of an entertainment website and as a television award show category was fair use even though WEBCELEB is a trademark attached to a website that provides a marketplace for independent musicians and fans to buy music. The court held that the phrase "web celeb" was merely a common descriptive phrase for internet celebrities.[209]

Referring to the defendant's own product or service by using the plaintiff's mark without permission also may be a fair use. This may be done in comparative advertising, or in other contexts. In one case, two newspapers used the trademarked name of a band, New Kids on the Block, to promote the newspapers' telephone polls about the band. The papers used the band's name to describe the papers' own product: the telephone poll. A court found this a fair use because the band could not be identified without using its trademarked name and the papers did not suggest that the band endorsed the poll.[210]

The anti-dilution law also provides a fair use exception. Using a famous trademark for comparative advertising, parody or all forms of news reporting and commentary is not an infringement.[211]

CHAPTER SUMMARY

INTELLECTUAL PROPERTY LAW INCLUDES COPYRIGHTS, trademarks and patents. U.S. copyright law protects the rights of creators of "original works of authorship" in fixed form to use their creations. The U.S. Constitution gives Congress the right to adopt copyright laws. The United States adopted the major international copyright agreement, the Berne Convention, in 1988.

The 1976 Copyright Act is the backbone of U.S. copyright law. The law defines copyright as an original work fixed in a tangible medium. Works protected include literary, musical, dramatic, motion picture and many other works. Ideas, history and facts may not be copyrighted. Short phrases, titles and advertising slogans may not be copyrighted, though they may qualify for trademark protection. In 1998, Congress adopted the Digital Millennium Copyright Act in an attempt to bring the internet and other digital media into copyright law.

An original work is copyrighted from the moment it is fixed in a tangible medium. A work's creator owns the copyright to the work. However, if an employee creates a work, it is usually a work made for hire, and the copyright is held by the employer. Freelance journalists usually are considered independent contractors and thus own the copyrights to their work. According to the Supreme Court, if a contract between a freelancer and a newspaper does not specifically cover online publications, the agreement covers only the initial publication.

Copyright protects the creator's right to reproduce the work, make derivative works and distribute, perform or display a work. It also protects the right to transmit a sound recording through digital audio means. Individuals may record audio and video copies for their own personal use. The first-sale doctrine allows purchasers to dispose as they choose of objects containing copyrighted works, such as books and DVDs.

Copyrights on works created on or after Jan. 1, 1978, last for the creator's life plus 70 years. A work made for hire lasts for 95 years from publication or 120 years from creation, whichever is shorter. Works protected under the 1909 law and still in copyright when the current law took effect are protected for 95 years from the date they first were copyrighted.

To prove copyright infringement, the copyright holder must show (1) he or she has a valid copyright, (2) the work is registered and (3) the defendant either directly copied the work or had access to the copyrighted work and the two works are substantially similar.

Fair use, the most common copyright infringement defense, is a four-part balancing test. Courts consider (1) the purpose and character of the use, (2) the nature of the copyrighted work, (3) the amount and substantiality of the portion used and (4) the effect on the plaintiff's potential market. Criticism, news, scholarship, the creation of searchable databases and parody tend toward fair use. In evaluating the purpose and character of use, the transformative use test is becoming more prevalent. Using an important part of a work may suggest infringement. Harm to the plaintiff's potential profits may be the most important fair use criterion.

The Digital Millennium Copyright Act bans technologies that circumvent copyright protections. The law also protects internet service providers against copyright suits if the ISP takes down material a copyright holder says is posted without permission. This is commonly called safe harbor protection. Safe harbor protection does not apply if an ISP or website has red flag knowledge of user-posted infringing material.

The recording industry has sued services providing software that allows file sharing when the networks have been used for unauthorized copying of sound recordings. The recording and movie industries have instituted the Copyright Alert System to notify copyright infringers they are violating the law.

The federal Lanham Act protects trademarks from infringement. Marks may be words, designs, colors and other devices identifying the source of products or services. A trademark will be protected only if it is distinctive. Distinctiveness ranges from strongly distinctive to merely descriptive and generic. Merely descriptive and generic marks cannot be protected. The common law protects unregistered marks within the geographic area where they are used. Under the Lanham Act, trademark confusion occurs when the mark is likely to cause consumer confusion in the commercial marketplace. A mark must be registered with the U.S. Patent and Trademark Office to have protection under the Lanham Act. Registering is a complex process, and marks may be rejected for a variety of reasons. The Supreme Court decided in 2017 that trademarks are private, nongovernment speech, so disparaging trademarks can be registered.

Domain names may be registered as trademarks. The federal Anticybersquatting Consumer Protection Act is intended to prevent people from claiming domain names only to sell them to companies or individuals.

One form of trademark infringement is dilution, which is defined as using a famous trademark in a way that disparages the mark or diminishes its effectiveness. Trademark defenses can include tacking and fair use. Trademark tacking allows a trademark owner to slightly alter a trademark without abandoning ownership of the original mark. The Supreme Court said juries should decide questions of tacking. Courts accept the fair use defense if the defendant used the mark to describe its goods rather than as a trademark and the use did not confuse consumers. ■

CASES FOR STUDY

For study resources and a case archive go to **study.sagepub.com/medialaw6e**.

THINKING ABOUT IT

The U.S. Supreme Court decides few cases concerning intellectual property, but as technology rapidly advances, the Court appears to be paying more attention to this area of law. Both of these case excerpts are recent decisions. As you read them, keep the following questions in mind:

- Do you agree with the Court's reasoning in *Aereo*? Does it make sense to consider Aereo's service a public performance? Why or why not?

- Do you think the *Aereo* decision could affect or stifle the development of new technology?

- How does the Supreme Court's ruling about disparaging trademarks in *Matal v. Tam* address the issue of viewpoint discrimination?

Matal v. Tam
SUPREME COURT OF THE UNITED STATES
137 S. Ct. 1744 (2017)

JUSTICE SAMUEL ALITO (joined by CHIEF JUSTICE JOHN ROBERTS, JUSTICE CLARENCE THOMAS and JUSTICE STEPHEN BREYER) delivered the Court's opinion:

This case concerns a dance-rock band's application for federal trademark registration of the band's name, "The Slants." "Slants" is a derogatory term for persons of Asian descent, and members of the band are Asian-Americans. But the band members believe that by taking that slur as the name of their group, they will help to "reclaim" the term and drain its denigrating force.

The Patent and Trademark Office (PTO) denied the application based on a provision of federal law prohibiting the registration of trademarks that may "disparage . . . or bring . . . into contemp[t] or disrepute" any "persons, living or dead." We now hold that this provision violates the Free Speech Clause of the First Amendment. It offends a bedrock First

Amendment principle: Speech may not be banned on the ground that it expresses ideas that offend.

"The principle underlying trademark protection is that distinctive marks—words, names, symbols, and the like—can help distinguish a particular artisan's goods from those of others."

"[F]ederal law does not create trademarks." Trademarks and their precursors have ancient origins, and trademarks were protected at common law and in equity at the time of the founding of our country. . . . The foundation of current federal trademark law is the Lanham Act, enacted in 1946. By that time, trademark had expanded far beyond phrases that do no more than identify a good or service. Then, as now, trademarks often consisted of catchy phrases that convey a message.

Under the Lanham Act, trademarks that are "used in commerce" may be placed on the "principal register," that is, they may be federally registered. . . . "[N]ational protection of trademarks is desirable," we have explained, "because trademarks foster competition and the maintenance of quality by securing to the producer the benefits of good reputation." . . .

The Lanham Act contains provisions that bar certain trademarks from the principal register. . . .

At issue in this case is one such provision, which we will call "the disparagement clause." This provision prohibits the registration of a trademark "which may disparage . . . persons, living or dead, institutions, beliefs, or national symbols, or bring them into contempt, or disrepute." This clause appeared in the original Lanham Act and has remained the same to this day.

When deciding whether a trademark is disparaging, an examiner at the PTO generally applies a "two-part test." The examiner first considers "the likely meaning of the matter in question, taking into account not only dictionary definitions, but also the relationship of the matter to the other elements in the mark, the nature of the goods or services, and the manner in which the mark is used in the marketplace in connection with the goods or services." "If that meaning is found to refer to identifiable persons, institutions, beliefs or national symbols," the examiner moves to the second step, asking "whether that meaning may be disparaging to a substantial composite of the referenced group." If the examiner finds that a "substantial composite, although not necessarily a majority, of the referenced group would find the proposed mark . . . to be disparaging in the context of contemporary attitudes," a prima facie case of disparagement is made out, and the burden shifts to the applicant to prove that the trademark is not disparaging. What is more, the PTO has specified that "[t]he fact that an applicant may be a member of that group or has good intentions underlying its use of a term does not obviate the fact that a substantial composite of the referenced group would find the term objectionable."

Simon Tam is the lead singer of "The Slants." He chose this moniker in order to "reclaim" and "take ownership" of stereotypes about people of Asian ethnicity. The group "draws inspiration for its lyrics from childhood slurs and mocking nursery rhymes" and has given its albums names such as "The Yellow Album" and "Slanted Eyes, Slanted Hearts."

Tam sought federal registration of "THE SLANTS," on the principal register, but an examining attorney at the PTO rejected the request, applying the PTO's two-part framework and finding that "there is . . . a substantial composite of persons who find the term in the applied-for mark offensive." The examining attorney relied in part on the fact that "numerous dictionaries define 'slants' or 'slant-eyes' as a derogatory or offensive term." The examining attorney also relied on a finding that "the band's name has been found offensive numerous times"—citing a performance that was canceled because of the band's moniker and the fact that "several bloggers and commenters to articles on the band have indicated that they find the term and the applied-for mark offensive."

Tam contested the denial of registration before the examining attorney and before the PTO's Trademark Trial and Appeal Board (TTAB) but to no avail. Eventually, he took the case to federal court, where the en banc Federal Circuit ultimately found the disparagement clause facially unconstitutional under the First Amendment's Free Speech Clause. The majority found that the clause engages in viewpoint-based discrimination, that the clause regulates the expressive component of trademarks and consequently cannot be treated as commercial speech, and that the clause is subject to and cannot satisfy strict scrutiny. The majority also rejected the Government's argument that registered trademarks constitute government speech, as well as the Government's contention that federal registration is a form of government subsidy. And the majority opined that even if the disparagement clause were analyzed under this Court's commercial speech cases, the clause would fail the "intermediate scrutiny" that those cases prescribe. . . .

The Government filed a petition for certiorari, which we granted in order to decide whether the disparagement clause "is facially invalid under the Free Speech Clause of the First Amendment." . . .

Because the disparagement clause applies to marks that disparage the members of a racial or ethnic group, we must decide whether the clause violates the Free Speech Clause of the First Amendment. And at the outset, we must consider three arguments that would either eliminate any First Amendment protection or result in highly permissive rational-basis review. Specifically, the Government contends (1) that trademarks are government speech, not private speech, (2) that trademarks are a form of government subsidy, and (3) that the constitutionality of the disparagement clause should be tested under a new "government-program" doctrine. We address each of these arguments below.

The First Amendment prohibits Congress and other government entities and actors from "abridging the freedom of speech"; the First Amendment does not say that Congress and other government entities must abridge their own ability to speak freely. . . .

As we have said, "it is not easy to imagine how government could function" if it were subject to the restrictions that the First Amendment imposes on private speech. "'[T]he First Amendment forbids the government to regulate speech in ways that favor some viewpoints or ideas at the expense of others,'" but imposing a requirement of viewpoint-neutrality on government speech would be paralyzing. When a government entity embarks on a course of action, it necessarily takes a particular viewpoint and rejects others. . . .

But while the government-speech doctrine is important—indeed, essential—it is a doctrine that is susceptible to dangerous misuse. If private speech could be passed off as government speech by simply affixing a government seal of approval, government could silence or muffle the expression of disfavored viewpoints. For this reason, we must exercise great caution before extending our government-speech precedents.

At issue here is the content of trademarks that are registered by the PTO, an arm of the Federal Government. The Federal Government does not dream up these marks, and it does not edit marks submitted for registration. Except as required by the statute involved here, an examiner may not reject a mark based on the viewpoint that it appears to express. Thus, unless that section is thought to apply, an examiner does not inquire whether any viewpoint conveyed by a mark is consistent with Government policy or whether any such viewpoint is consistent with that expressed by other marks already on the principal register. Instead, if the mark meets the Lanham Act's viewpoint-neutral requirements, registration is mandatory. And if an examiner finds that a mark is eligible for placement on the principal register, that decision is not reviewed by any higher official unless the registration is challenged. Moreover, once a mark is registered, the PTO is not authorized to remove it from the register unless a party moves for cancellation, the registration expires, or the Federal Trade Commission initiates proceedings based on certain grounds.

In light of all this, it is far-fetched to suggest that the content of a registered mark is government speech. If the federal registration of a trademark makes the mark government speech, the Federal Government is babbling prodigiously and incoherently. It is saying many unseemly things. It is expressing contradictory views. It is unashamedly endorsing a vast array of commercial products and services. And it is providing Delphic advice to the consuming public.

For example, if trademarks represent government speech, what does the Government have in mind when it advises Americans to "make.believe" (Sony), "Think different" (Apple), "Just do it" (Nike), or "Have it your way" (Burger King)? Was the Government warning about a coming disaster when it registered the mark "EndTime Ministries"?

The PTO has made it clear that registration does not constitute approval of a mark. And it is unlikely that more than a tiny fraction of the public has any idea what federal registration of a trademark means. None of our government speech cases even remotely supports the idea that registered trademarks are government speech. . . .

Trademarks have not traditionally been used to convey a Government message. With the exception of the enforcement of 15 U.S.C. §1052(a), the viewpoint expressed by a mark has not played a role in the decision whether to place it on the principal register. And there is no evidence that the public associates the contents of trademarks with the Federal Government.

This brings us to the case on which the Government relies most heavily, *Walker*, which likely marks the outer bounds of the government-speech doctrine. Holding that the messages on Texas specialty license plates are government speech, the *Walker* Court cited three factors . . . First, license plates have long been used by the States to convey state messages. Second, license plates "are often closely identified in the public mind" with the State, since they are manufactured and owned by the State, generally designed by the State, and serve as a form of "government ID." Third, Texas "maintain[ed] direct control over the messages conveyed on its specialty plates." . . . [N]one of these factors are present in this case. . . .

Perhaps the most worrisome implication of the Government's argument concerns the system of copyright registration. If federal registration makes a trademark government speech and thus eliminates all First Amendment protection, would the registration of the copyright for a book produce a similar transformation?

The Government attempts to distinguish copyright on the ground that it is "'the engine of free expression,'" but as this case illustrates, trademarks often have an expressive content. Companies spend huge amounts to create and publicize trademarks that convey a message. It is true that the necessary brevity of trademarks limits what they can say. But powerful messages can sometimes be conveyed in just a few words.

Trademarks are private, not government, speech.

We next address the Government's argument that this case is governed by cases in which this Court has upheld the constitutionality of government programs that subsidized speech expressing a particular viewpoint. These cases implicate a notoriously tricky question of constitutional law. "[W]e have held that the Government 'may not deny a benefit to a person on a basis that infringes his constitutionally protected . . . freedom of speech even if he has no entitlement to that benefit.'" But at the same time, government is not required to subsidize activities that it does not wish to promote. Determining which of these principles applies in a particular case "is not always self-evident," but no difficult question is presented here.

Unlike the present case, the decisions on which the Government relies all involved cash subsidies or their equivalent. . . . In other cases, we have regarded tax benefits as comparable to cash subsidies.

The federal registration of a trademark is nothing like the programs at issue in these cases. The PTO does not pay money to parties seeking registration of a mark. Quite the contrary is true: An applicant for registration must pay the PTO a filing fee of $225–$600. And to maintain federal registration, the holder of a mark must pay a fee of $300–$500 every 10 years. The Federal Circuit concluded that these fees have fully supported the registration system for the past 27 years. . . .

Finally, the Government urges us to sustain the disparagement clause under a new doctrine that would apply to "government-program" cases. For the most part, this argument simply merges our government-speech cases and the . . . subsidy cases in an attempt to construct a broader doctrine that can be applied to the registration of trademarks. The only new element in this construct consists of two cases involving a public employer's collection of union dues from its employees. But those cases occupy a special area of First Amendment case law, and they are far removed from the registration of trademarks. . . .

Potentially more analogous are cases in which a unit of government creates a limited public forum for private speech. When government creates such a forum, in either a literal or "metaphysical" sense, some content- and speaker-based restrictions may be allowed. However, even in such cases, what we have termed "viewpoint discrimination" is forbidden.

Our cases use the term "viewpoint" discrimination in a broad sense, and in that sense, the disparagement clause discriminates on the bases of "viewpoint." To be sure, the clause evenhandedly prohibits disparagement of all groups. It applies equally to marks that damn Democrats and Republicans, capitalists and socialists, and those arrayed on both sides of every possible issue. It denies registration to any mark that is offensive to a substantial percentage of the members of any group. But in the sense relevant here, that is viewpoint discrimination: Giving offense is a viewpoint.

We have said time and again that "the public expression of ideas may not be prohibited merely because the ideas are themselves offensive to some of their hearers." For this reason, the disparagement clause cannot be saved by analyzing it as a type of government program in which some content- and speaker-based restrictions are permitted.

Having concluded that the disparagement clause cannot be sustained under our government-speech or subsidy cases or under the Government's proposed "government-program" doctrine, we must confront a dispute between the parties on the question whether trademarks are commercial speech . . . The Government and *amici* supporting its position argue that all trademarks are commercial speech. They note that the central purposes of trademarks are commercial and that federal law regulates trademarks to promote fair and orderly interstate commerce. Tam and his *amici*, on the other hand, contend that many, if not all, trademarks have an expressive component. In other words, these trademarks do not simply identify the source of a product or service but go on to say something more, either about the product or service or some broader issue. The trademark in this case illustrates this point. The name "The Slants" not only identifies the band but expresses a view about social issues.

We need not resolve this debate between the parties because the disparagement clause cannot withstand even *Central Hudson* review. Under *Central Hudson*, a restriction of speech must serve "a substantial interest," and it must be "narrowly drawn." The disparagement clause fails this requirement.

It is claimed that the disparagement clause serves two interests. The first is phrased in a variety of ways in the briefs. Echoing language in one of the opinions below, the Government asserts an interest in preventing "'underrepresented groups'" from being "'bombarded with demeaning messages in commercial advertising.'" An *amicus* supporting the Government refers to "encouraging racial tolerance and protecting the privacy and welfare of individuals." But no matter how the point is phrased, its unmistakable thrust is this: The Government has an interest in preventing speech expressing ideas that offend. And, as we have explained, that idea strikes at the heart of the First Amendment. Speech that demeans on the basis of race, ethnicity, gender, religion, age, disability, or any

other similar ground is hateful; but the proudest boast of our free speech jurisprudence is that we protect the freedom to express "the thought that we hate."

The second interest asserted is protecting the orderly flow of commerce. Commerce, we are told, is disrupted by trademarks that "involv[e] disparagement of race, gender, ethnicity, national origin, religion, sexual orientation, and similar demographic classification." Such trademarks are analogized to discriminatory conduct, which has been recognized to have an adverse effect on commerce.

A simple answer to this argument is that the disparagement clause is not "narrowly drawn" to drive out trademarks that support invidious discrimination. The clause reaches any trademark that disparages *any person, group, or institution*. It applies to trademarks like the following: "Down with racists," "Down with sexists," "Down with homophobes." It is not an anti-discrimination clause; it is a happy-talk clause. In this way, it goes much further than is necessary to serve the interest asserted.

The clause is far too broad in other ways as well. The clause protects every person living or dead as well as every institution. Is it conceivable that commerce would be disrupted by a trademark saying: "James Buchanan was a disastrous president" or "Slavery is an evil institution"?

There is also a deeper problem with the argument that commercial speech may be cleansed of any expression likely to cause offense. The commercial market is well stocked with merchandise that disparages prominent figures and groups, and the line between commercial and non-commercial speech is not always clear, as this case illustrates. If affixing the commercial label permits the suppression of any speech that may lead to political or social "volatility," free speech would be endangered.

●●●

For these reasons, we hold that the disparagement clause violates the Free Speech Clause of the First Amendment. The judgment of the Federal Circuit is affirmed.

It is so ordered.

JUSTICE ANTHONY KENNEDY and CLARENCE THOMAS, with whom Justice Ruth Bader Ginsburg, Justice Sonia Sotomayor and Justice Kagan join, concurring in part and concurring in the judgment.

The Patent and Trademark Office (PTO) has denied the substantial benefits of federal trademark registration to the mark THE SLANTS. The PTO did so under the mandate of the disparagement clause. . . .

As the Court is correct to hold, §1052(a) constitutes viewpoint discrimination—a form of speech suppression so potent that it must be subject to rigorous constitutional scrutiny. The Government's action and the statute on which it is based cannot survive this scrutiny.

The Court is correct in its judgment, and I join Parts I, II, and III-A of its opinion. This separate writing explains in greater detail why the First Amendment's protections against viewpoint discrimination apply to the trademark here. . . .

Those few categories of speech that the government can regulate or punish—for instance, fraud, defamation, or incitement—are well established within our constitutional tradition. Aside from these and a few other narrow exceptions, it is a fundamental principle of the First Amendment that the government may not punish or suppress speech based on disapproval of the ideas or perspectives the speech conveys.

The First Amendment guards against laws "targeted at specific subject matter," a form of speech suppression known as content based discrimination. This category includes a subtype of laws that go further, aimed at the suppression of "particular views . . . on a subject." A law found to discriminate based on viewpoint is an "egregious form of content discrimination," which is "presumptively unconstitutional."

At its most basic, the test for viewpoint discrimination is whether—within the relevant subject category—the government has singled out a subset of messages for disfavor based on the views expressed. In the instant case, the disparagement clause the Government now seeks to implement and enforce identifies the relevant subject as "persons, living or dead, institutions, beliefs, or national symbols." Within that category, an applicant may register a positive or benign mark but not a derogatory one. The law thus reflects the Government's disapproval of a subset of messages it finds offensive. This is the essence of viewpoint discrimination.

The Government disputes this conclusion. It argues, to begin with, that the law is viewpoint neutral because it applies in equal measure to any trademark that demeans or offends. This misses the point. A subject that is first defined by content and then regulated or censored by mandating only one sort of comment is not viewpoint neutral. To prohibit all sides from criticizing their opponents makes a law more viewpoint based, not less so. The logic of the Government's rule is that a law would be viewpoint neutral even if it provided that public officials could be praised but not condemned. The First Amendment's viewpoint neutrality principle protects more than the right to identify with a particular side. It protects the right to create and present arguments for particular positions in particular ways, as the speaker chooses. By mandating positivity, the law here might silence dissent and distort the marketplace of ideas.

The Government next suggests that the statute is viewpoint neutral because the disparagement clause applies to trademarks regardless of the applicant's personal views or reasons for using the mark. Instead, registration is denied based on the expected reaction of the applicant's audience. In this way, the argument goes, it cannot be said that Government is acting with hostility toward a particular point of view. For example, the Government does not dispute that respondent seeks to use his mark in a positive way. Indeed, respondent endeavors to use The Slants to supplant a racial epithet, using new insights, musical talents, and wry humor to make it a badge of pride. Respondent's application was denied not because the Government thought his object was to demean or offend but because the Government thought his trademark would have that effect on at least some Asian-Americans.

The Government may not insulate a law from charges of viewpoint discrimination by tying censorship to the reaction of the speaker's audience. The Court has suggested that viewpoint discrimination occurs when the government intends to suppress a speaker's beliefs, but viewpoint discrimination need not take that form in every instance. The danger of viewpoint discrimination is that the government is attempting to remove certain ideas or perspectives from a broader debate. That danger is all the greater if the ideas or perspectives are ones a particular audience might think offensive, at least at first hearing. An initial reaction may prompt further reflection, leading to a more reasoned, more tolerant position.

Indeed, a speech burden based on audience reactions is simply government hostility and intervention in a different guise. The speech is targeted, after all, based on the government's disapproval of the speaker's choice of message. And it is the government itself that is attempting in this case to decide whether the relevant audience would find the speech offensive. For reasons like these, the Court's cases have long prohibited the government from justifying a First Amendment burden by pointing to the offensiveness of the speech to be suppressed.

The Government's argument in defense of the statute assumes that respondent's mark is a negative comment. In addressing that argument on its own terms, this opinion is not intended to imply that the Government's interpretation is accurate. From respondent's submissions, it is evident he would disagree that his mark means what the Government says it does. The trademark will have the effect, respondent urges, of reclaiming an offensive term for the positive purpose of celebrating all that Asian-Americans can and do contribute to our diverse Nation. While thoughtful persons can agree or disagree with this approach, the dissonance between the trademark's potential to teach and the Government's insistence on its own, opposite, and negative interpretation confirms the constitutional vice of the statute.

. . . To the extent trademarks qualify as commercial speech, they are an example of why that term or category does not serve as a blanket exemption from the First Amendment's requirement of viewpoint neutrality. Justice Holmes' reference to the "free trade in ideas" and the "power of . . . thought

to get itself accepted in the competition of the market," was a metaphor. In the realm of trademarks, the metaphorical marketplace of ideas becomes a tangible, powerful reality. Here that real marketplace exists as a matter of state law and our common-law tradition, quite without regard to the Federal Government. These marks make up part of the expression of everyday life, as with the names of entertainment groups, broadcast networks, designer clothing, newspapers, automobiles, candy bars, toys, and so on. Nonprofit organizations—ranging from medical-research charities and other humanitarian causes to political advocacy groups—also have trademarks, which they use to compete in a real economic sense for funding and other resources as they seek to persuade others to join their cause. To permit viewpoint discrimination in this context is to permit Government censorship.

. . . It is telling that the Court's precedents have recognized just one narrow situation in which viewpoint discrimination is permissible: where the government itself is speaking or recruiting others to communicate a message on its behalf. The exception is necessary to allow the government to stake out positions and pursue policies. But it is also narrow, to prevent the government from claiming that every government program is exempt from the First Amendment. These cases have identified a number of factors that, if present, suggest the government is speaking on its own behalf; but none are present here.

There may be situations where private speakers are selected for a government program to assist the government in advancing a particular message. That is not this case either. The central purpose of trademark registration is to facilitate source identification. To serve that broad purpose, the Government has provided the benefits of federal registration to millions of marks identifying every type of product and cause. Registered trademarks do so by means of a wide diversity of words, symbols, and messages. Whether a mark is disparaging bears no plausible relation to that goal. While defining the purpose and scope of a federal program for these purposes can be complex, our cases are clear that viewpoint discrimination is not permitted where, as here, the Government "expends funds to encourage a diversity of views from private speakers."

•••

A law that can be directed against speech found offensive to some portion of the public can be turned against minority and dissenting views to the detriment of all. The First Amendment does not entrust that power to the government's benevolence. Instead, our reliance must be on the substantial safeguards of free and open discussion in a democratic society.

For these reasons, I join the Court's opinion in part and concur in the judgment.

American Broadcasting Companies Inc. v. Aereo Inc.
SUPREME COURT OF THE UNITED STATES
134 S. Ct. 2498 (2014)

JUSTICE STEPHEN BREYER delivered the Court's opinion:

The Copyright Act of 1976 gives a copyright owner the "exclusive righ[t]" to "perform the copyrighted work publicly." . . .

We must decide whether respondent Aereo, Inc., infringes this exclusive right by selling its subscribers a technologically complex service that allows them to watch television programs over the Internet at about the same time as the programs are broadcast over the air. We conclude that it does.

For a monthly fee, Aereo offers subscribers broadcast television programming over the Internet, virtually as the programming is being broadcast. Much of this programming is made up of copyrighted works. Aereo neither owns the copyright in those works nor holds a license from the copyright owners to perform those works publicly.

Aereo's system is made up of servers, transcoders, and thousands of dime-sized antennas housed in a central warehouse. It works roughly as follows: First, when a subscriber wants to watch a show that is currently being broadcast, he visits Aereo's website and selects, from a list of the local programming, the show he wishes to see.

Second, one of Aereo's servers selects an antenna, which it dedicates to the use of that subscriber (and that subscriber alone) for the duration of the selected show. A server then tunes the antenna to the over-the-air broadcast carrying the show. The antenna begins to receive the broadcast, and an Aereo transcoder translates the signals received into data that can be transmitted over the Internet.

Third, rather than directly send the data to the subscriber, a server saves the data in a subscriber-specific folder on Aereo's hard drive. In other words, Aereo's system creates a subscriber-specific copy—that is, a "personal" copy—of the subscriber's program of choice.

Fourth, once several seconds of programming have been saved, Aereo's server begins to stream the saved copy of the show to the subscriber over the Internet. . . . The subscriber can watch the streamed program on the screen of his personal computer, tablet, smart phone, Internet-connected television, or other Internet-connected device. The streaming continues, a mere few seconds behind the over-the-air broadcast, until the subscriber has received the entire show. . . .

Aereo emphasizes that the data that its system streams to each subscriber are the data from his own personal copy, made from the broadcast signals received by the particular antenna allotted to him. . . .

Petitioners are television producers, marketers, distributors, and broadcasters who own the copyrights in many of the programs that Aereo's system streams to its subscribers. They brought suit against Aereo for copyright infringement in Federal District

Court. They sought a preliminary injunction, arguing that Aereo was infringing their right to "perform" their works "publicly," as the Transmit Clause defines those terms.

The District Court denied the preliminary injunction. Relying on prior Circuit precedent, a divided panel of the Second Circuit affirmed. In the Second Circuit's view, Aereo does not perform publicly within the meaning of the Transmit Clause because it does not transmit "to the public." Rather, each time Aereo streams a program to a subscriber, it sends a *private* transmission that is available only to that subscriber. The Second Circuit denied rehearing en banc, over the dissent of two judges. We granted certiorari.

This case requires us to answer two questions: First, in operating in the manner described above, does Aereo "perform" at all? And second, if so, does Aereo do so "publicly"? We address these distinct questions in turn.

Does Aereo "perform"? . . . Phrased another way, does Aereo "transmit . . . a performance" when a subscriber watches a show using Aereo's system, or is it only the subscriber who transmits? In Aereo's view, it does not perform. . . . Like a home antenna and DVR, Aereo's equipment simply responds to its subscribers' directives. So it is only the subscribers who "perform" when they use Aereo's equipment to stream television programs to themselves.

Considered alone, the language of the Act does not clearly indicate when an entity "perform[s]" (or "transmit[s]") and when it merely supplies equipment that allows others to do so. But when read in light of its purpose, the Act is unmistakable: An entity that engages in activities like Aereo's performs.

History makes plain that one of Congress' primary purposes in amending the Copyright Act in 1976 was to overturn this Court's determination that community antenna television (CATV) systems (the precursors of modern cable systems) fell outside the Act's scope. In *Fortnightly Corp. v. United Artists Television, Inc.* (1968), the Court considered a CATV system that carried local television broadcasting, much of which was copyrighted, to its subscribers in two cities. . . .

Asked to decide whether the CATV provider infringed copyright holders' exclusive right to perform their works publicly, the Court held that the provider did not "perform" at all. . . . The Court reasoned that CATV providers were unlike broadcasters:

"Broadcasters select the programs to be viewed; CATV systems simply carry, without editing, whatever programs they receive. Broadcasters procure programs and propagate them to the public; CATV systems receive programs that have been released to the public and carry them by private channels to additional viewers."

Instead, CATV providers were more like viewers . . . Viewers do not become performers by using "amplifying equipment," and a CATV provider should not be treated differently for providing viewers the same equipment.

In *Teleprompter Corp. v. Columbia Broadcasting System, Inc.* (1974), the Court considered the copyright liability of a CATV provider that carried broadcast television programming into subscribers' homes from hundreds of miles away. Although the Court recognized that a viewer might not be able to afford amplifying equipment that would provide access to those distant signals, it nonetheless found that the CATV provider was more like a viewer than a broadcaster. . . .

The Court also recognized that the CATV system exercised some measure of choice over what to transmit. But that fact did not transform the CATV system into a broadcaster. A broadcaster exercises significant creativity in choosing what to air, the Court reasoned. . . .

In 1976 Congress amended the Copyright Act in large part to reject the Court's holdings in *Fortnightly* and *Teleprompter*. . . . Congress enacted new language that erased the Court's line between broadcaster and viewer, in respect to "perform[ing]" a work. The amended statute clarifies that to "perform" an audiovisual work means "to show its images in any sequence or to make the sounds accompanying it audible." . . . Under this new language, *both* the broadcaster *and* the viewer of a television program "perform," because they both show the program's images and make audible the program's sounds. . . .

Congress also enacted the Transmit Clause, which specifies that an entity performs publicly when it "transmit[s] . . . a performance . . . to the public." Cable system activities, like those of the CATV systems in *Fortnightly* and *Teleprompter,* lie at the heart of the activities that Congress intended this language to cover. . . . The Clause thus makes clear that an entity that acts like a CATV system itself performs, even if when doing so, it simply enhances viewers' ability to receive broadcast television signals.

Congress further created a new section of the Act to regulate cable companies' public performances of copyrighted works. Section 111 creates a complex, highly detailed compulsory licensing scheme that sets out the conditions, including the payment of compulsory fees, under which cable systems may retransmit broadcasts. . . . Congress made these three changes to achieve a similar end: to bring the activities of cable systems within the scope of the Copyright Act.

This history makes clear that Aereo is not simply an equipment provider. . . . Aereo's activities are substantially similar to those of the CATV companies that Congress amended the Act to reach. . . .

We recognize, and Aereo and the dissent emphasize, one particular difference between Aereo's system and the cable systems at issue in *Fortnightly* and *Teleprompter.* The systems in those cases transmitted constantly; they sent continuous programming to each subscriber's television set. In contrast, Aereo's system remains inert until a subscriber indicates that she wants to watch a program. . . .

This is a critical difference, says the dissent. . . . In our view, however, the dissent's . . . argument, in whatever form, makes too much out of too little. . . .

Next, we must consider whether Aereo performs petitioners' works "publicly," within the meaning of the Transmit Clause. Under the Clause, an entity performs a work publicly when it "transmit[s] . . . a performance . . . of the work . . . to the public." Aereo denies that it satisfies this definition. . . .

As we have said, an Aereo subscriber receives broadcast television signals with an antenna dedicated

to him alone. . . . The fact that each transmission is to only one subscriber, in Aereo's view, means that it does not transmit a performance "to the public."

. . . The text of the Clause effectuates Congress' intent. Aereo's argument to the contrary relies on the premise that "to transmit . . . a performance" means to make a single transmission. But the Clause suggests that an entity may transmit a performance through multiple, discrete transmissions. That is because one can "transmit" or "communicate" something through a *set* of actions. . . .

The fact that a singular noun ("a performance") follows the words "to transmit" does not suggest the contrary. . . .

The Transmit Clause must permit this interpretation, for it provides that one may transmit a performance to the public "whether the members of the public capable of receiving the performance . . . receive it . . . at the same time or at different times." . . .

Finally, we note that Aereo's subscribers may receive the same programs at different times and locations. This fact does not help Aereo, however, for the Transmit Clause expressly provides that an entity may perform publicly "whether the members of the public capable of receiving the performance . . . receive it in the same place or in separate places and at the same time or at different times." In other words, "the public" need not be situated together, spatially or temporally. For these reasons, we conclude that Aereo transmits a performance of petitioners' copyrighted works to the public, within the meaning of the Transmit Clause.

. . . In sum, having considered the details of Aereo's practices, we find them highly similar to those of the CATV systems in *Fortnightly* and *Teleprompter.* And those are activities that the 1976 amendments sought to bring within the scope of the Copyright Act. Insofar as there are differences, those differences concern not the nature of the service that Aereo provides so much as the technological manner in which it provides the service. We conclude that those differences are not adequate to place Aereo's activities outside the scope of the Act.

For these reasons, we conclude that Aereo "perform[s]" petitioners' copyrighted works "publicly," as those terms are defined by the Transmit Clause. We therefore reverse the contrary judgment of the Court of Appeals, and we remand the case for further proceedings consistent with this opinion.

It is so ordered.

JUSTICE ANTONIN SCALIA, with whom Justice Clarence Thomas and Justice Samuel Alito join, dissenting.

This case is the latest skirmish in the long-running copyright battle over the delivery of television programming. . . .

There are two types of liability for copyright infringement: direct and secondary. As its name suggests, the former applies when an actor personally engages in infringing conduct. Secondary liability, by contrast, is a means of holding defendants responsible for infringement by third parties, even when the defendants "have not themselves engaged in the infringing activity." It applies when a defendant "intentionally induc[es] or encourag[es]" infringing acts by others or profits from such acts "while declining to exercise a right to stop or limit [them]."

Most suits against equipment manufacturers and service providers involve secondary-liability claims. . . .

This suit, or rather the portion of it before us here, is fundamentally different. The Networks claim that Aereo *directly* infringes their public-performance right. Accordingly, the Networks must prove that Aereo "perform[s]" copyrighted works when its subscribers log in, select a channel, and push the "watch" button. That process undoubtedly results in a performance; the question is *who* does the performing. If Aereo's subscribers perform but Aereo does not, the claim necessarily fails.

. . . A comparison between copy shops and video-on-demand services illustrates the point. A copy shop rents out photocopiers on a per-use basis. One customer might copy his 10-year-old's drawings—a perfectly lawful thing to do—while another might duplicate a famous artist's copyrighted photographs—a use clearly prohibited. Either way, *the customer* chooses the content and activates the copying function; the photocopier does nothing except in response to the customer's commands. Because the shop plays no role in selecting the content, it cannot be held directly liable when a customer makes an infringing copy.

Video-on-demand services, like photocopiers, respond automatically to user input, but they differ in one crucial respect: *They choose the content.* When a user signs in to Netflix, for example, "thousands of . . . movies [and] TV episodes" carefully curated by Netflix are "available to watch instantly." That selection and arrangement by the service provider constitutes a volitional act directed to specific copyrighted works and thus serves as a basis for direct liability.

The distinction between direct and secondary liability would collapse if there were not a clear rule for determining whether *the defendant* committed the infringing act. . . .

So which is Aereo: the copy shop or the video-on-demand service? In truth, it is neither. Rather, it is akin to a copy shop that provides its patrons with a library card. Aereo offers access to an automated system consisting of routers, servers, transcoders, and dime-sized antennae. Like a photocopier or VCR, that system lies dormant until a subscriber activates it. . . .

Unlike video-on-demand services, Aereo does not provide a prearranged assortment of movies and television shows. Rather, it assigns each subscriber an antenna that—like a library card—can be used to obtain whatever broadcasts are freely available. Some of those broadcasts are copyrighted; others are in the public domain. The key point is that subscribers call all the shots: Aereo's automated system does not relay any program, copyrighted or not, until a subscriber selects the program and tells Aereo to relay it. Aereo's operation of that system is a volitional act and a but-for cause of the resulting performances, but, as in the case of the copy shop, that degree of involvement is not enough for direct liability.

In sum, Aereo does not "perform" for the sole and simple reason that it does not make the choice of content. And because Aereo does not perform, it cannot be held directly liable for infringing the Networks' public-performance right. That conclusion does not necessarily mean that Aereo's service complies with the Copyright Act. Quite the contrary. The Networks' complaint alleges that Aereo is directly *and* secondarily liable for infringing their public-performance rights *and also* their reproduction rights. Their request for a preliminary injunction—the only issue before this Court—is based exclusively on the direct-liability portion of the public-performance claim. . . .

The Court's conclusion that Aereo performs boils down to the following syllogism: (1) Congress amended the Act to overrule our decisions holding that cable systems do not perform when they retransmit over-the-air broadcasts; (2) Aereo looks a lot like a cable system; therefore (3) Aereo performs. . . .

I share the Court's evident feeling that what Aereo is doing (or enabling to be done) to the Networks' copyrighted programming ought not to be allowed. But perhaps we need not distort the Copyright Act to forbid it.

. . . [T]he proper course is not to bend and twist the Act's terms in an effort to produce a just outcome, but to apply the law as it stands and leave to Congress the task of deciding whether the Copyright Act needs an upgrade. . . .

I respectfully dissent.

Our question is whether speech which does "no more than propose a commercial transaction" is so removed from any "exposition of ideas" and from "truth, science, morality and arts in general, in its diffusion of liberal sentiments on the administration of Government," that it lacks all protection. Our answer is that it is not.

—U.S. Supreme Court Justice Harry Blackmun[1]

With states increasingly decriminalizing or legalizing medical and recreational marijuana use, marijuana merchants faced a confusing mix of federal and state law controlling its advertising, and the federal Drug Enforcement Administration considered reclassifying marijuana from a Schedule I drug treated like heroin under federal law.

12 ADVERTISING
When Speech and Commerce Converge

SUPPOSE...

... a state law prohibits drug marketers and data-mining companies from buying doctors' prescription records from pharmacies to help protect the privacy of doctors and prevent aggressive drug marketing to doctors. The law allows anyone other than a drug company marketer or companies that compile data for drug companies to access the prescription records. Legislative records show that the law is intended to encourage sales of generic over costlier brand-name drugs.

Does the law regulate commercial activity or commercial speech? If it regulates speech, is it a constitutional use of government authority, or does it unconstitutionally target speech because of government disfavor with its content? Look for answers to these questions when the case of *Sorrell v. IMS Health Inc.*[2] is discussed later in this chapter and excerpted at the chapter's end.

WHAT IS COMMERCIAL SPEECH?

Speech categories (as discussed in Chapter 3) are intended to help courts determine the proper application of First Amendment protections in specific cases. Speech categories work best to create clarity and stability in the law when they, themselves, are clear and unambiguously defined. That is not the case with commercial speech, which has evolved across decades through a series of fact-specific and sometimes confusing Supreme Court decisions.

The Supreme Court long denied advertising, or commercial speech, constitutional protection because advertising was tied directly to commerce and did not advance core free speech values.[3] Seventy-five years ago, a U.S. Supreme Court case about a submarine initiated modern commercial speech doctrine. F.J. Chrestensen docked a decommissioned U.S. Navy sub at a New York City pier and distributed handbills to attract people for paid tours. After Chrestensen learned that city law prohibited commercial handbill distribution, he printed a protest to that law on the flip side of the advertisement. When told that inclusion of this "political speech" did not immunize him from prosecution, he received an injunction to stop interference with his leafleting. The injunction was affirmed on appeal. The U.S. Supreme Court reversed.

The Supreme Court saw Chrestensen's handbill as little more than advertising, which it said had no First Amendment protection and was subject to reasonable regulation. The Court said, "The streets are proper places for the exercise of the freedom of communicating information and disseminating opinion," which government may not unduly limit.[4] However, "the Constitution imposes no such restraint on government as respects purely commercial speech."[5] Many, including judges, interpreted *Valentine v. Chrestensen* to mean that advertising fell outside the First Amendment.

The Court struggled to differentiate commercial speech from noncommercial paid content—such as paid political, informational or issue ads. As discussed in Chapter 4, the Supreme Court in *New York Times Co. v. Sullivan* provided First Amendment protection to the paid self-promotion of the civil rights movement at the center of this landmark libel ruling.[6] *Sullivan* limited the scope of *Chrestensen*. The Court distinguished the *Sullivan* ad,

LANDMARK CASES IN CONTEXT

Key ■ Event
◆ Cases

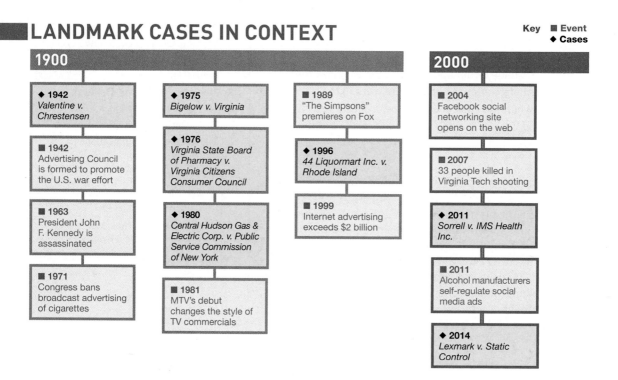

1900			2000

◆ **1942**
Valentine v. Chrestensen

◆ **1975**
Bigelow v. Virginia

■ **1989**
"The Simpsons" premieres on Fox

■ **2004**
Facebook social networking site opens on the web

■ **1942**
Advertising Council is formed to promote the U.S. war effort

◆ **1976**
Virginia State Board of Pharmacy v. Virginia Citizens Consumer Council

◆ **1996**
44 Liquormart Inc. v. Rhode Island

■ **2007**
33 people killed in Virginia Tech shooting

■ **1963**
President John F. Kennedy is assassinated

◆ **1980**
Central Hudson Gas & Electric Corp. v. Public Service Commission of New York

■ **1999**
Internet advertising exceeds $2 billion

◆ **2011**
Sorrell v. IMS Health Inc.

■ **1971**
Congress bans broadcast advertising of cigarettes

■ **1981**
MTV's debut changes the style of TV commercials

■ **2011**
Alcohol manufacturers self-regulate social media ads

◆ **2014**
Lexmark v. Static Control

● REAL WORLD LAW

A Bombardment of False and Deceptive Political Ads?

Politifact.com

The Political TV Ad Archive rounded up the top most-aired presidential ads from the largest markets in key swing states.

In the 2016 presidential election, seven out of the 10 most-aired political ads in the largest markets in key swing states were attack ads, according to PolitiFact.[1]

Some argued that the ad campaigns for the two nominees, especially the messages from super PACs, inundated voters with false and deceptive political claims. PolitiFact largely disagreed.

After fact-checking the claims of the top 10 campaign spots, PolitiFact found that 60 percent were true or mostly true. The truth of another two ads was unclear because the underlying information was largely true, but the absence of context may have misled the public.

Only 20 percent of the 10 most-aired political ads were largely false, and one of those involved contested statements about whether Hillary Clinton had used a private email server to share confidential information.

Research shows that attack ads do not sway voters; they alienate them.[2] Perhaps that fuels the public perception that they are drowning in political lies. It may be that disaffected voters perceive greater intentional distortion and deception in the ads they dislike.

1. Linda Qiu, *10 Most-Aired Political Ads, Fact Checked*, PolitiFact, Nov. 3, 2016, www.politifact.com/truth-o-meter/article/2016/nov/03/10-most-aired-political-ads-fact-checked.
2. Conor M. Dowling & Amber Wichowsky, *Attacks Without Consequence? Candidates, Parties, Groups and the Changing Face of Negative Advertising*, 59 Amer. J. of Polit. Sci. (2015), onlinelibrary.wiley.com/doi/10.1111/ajps.12094/abstract; Liam C. Malloy & Shanna Pearson-Merkowitz, *Going Positive: The Effects of Negative and Positive Advertising on Candidate Success and Voter Turnout*, Res. & Politics (2016), web.archive.org/web/20160506133711/rap.sagepub.com:80/content/3/1/2053168015625078.abstract.

which communicated information, expressed opinions and sought support "on behalf of a movement whose existence and objectives are matters of the highest public interest and concern,"[7] from the mere proposal of a commercial transaction. "That the Times was paid for publishing the advertisement is as immaterial in this connection as is the fact that newspapers and books are sold," the Court wrote.[8]

Lower courts struggle to define what is, and is not, commercial speech. In the midst of a trademark battle, the trial court ordered that one company retract its posted claims that the chief employee of the other was involved in a paternity suit and was a "deadbeat dad." On a First Amendment appeal to the retraction order, the Fifth Circuit Court of Appeals ruled that the order involved commercial speech because the individual "must have made [the post] with the economic interest of harming" the other's business.[9] The court upheld the retraction as a constitutional form of required disclosure to prevent consumer deception.[10]

When Army Sgt. Jeffrey Sarver sued the producers of the Oscar-winning film "The Hurt Locker" for appropriation, among other things, he characterized the film as commercial speech deserving lessened First Amendment protection. The Ninth Circuit Court of Appeals rejected that argument as well as his claim that his identity had a commercial market value.[11]

The Enigma software company brought a false advertising suit against Bleeping, which hosts an online forum and promotes affiliated software firms. Bleeping moved for dismissal, arguing that the user's comments were not commercial speech. But the trial court said that because the comments "lambasted" Enigma and recommended "a trustworthy alternative," the false advertising claim could proceed to trial.[12]

EVOLVING COMMERCIAL SPEECH PROTECTION

The Supreme Court has established that when truthful commercial speech is of core public interest, the First Amendment protection for the speech outweighs the government's interest in regulating advertising.[13] But the Court did not make clear exactly what level of First Amendment protection advertising enjoys.

In an early case involving a New York–based abortion service's paid newspaper ads, the Supreme Court ruled that Virginia could not prohibit the advertisements because abortions were legal.[14] By the time the Supreme Court heard *Bigelow v. Virginia*, its ruling in *Roe v. Wade*[15] had made most abortions legal, and the Court found it difficult to justify criminalizing advertisements for a legal service. Moreover, the Court again held that the ad was more than simply commercial speech; it "did more than simply propose a commercial transaction. It contained factual material of clear 'public interest.'"[16] In *Bigelow*, the Court "clearly establish[ed] that speech is not stripped of First Amendment protection merely because it appears in [the] form" of paid commercial advertisements.[17] The Court said *Chrestensen* had never been intended to permit any and all government regulation of commercial advertising.[18]

When the Court considered a Virginia state regulation prohibiting pharmacists from advertising prescription drug prices, it held that the ban violated the public's First Amendment right to receive factual information and the pharmacists' wish to communicate. In *Virginia State Board of Pharmacy v. Virginia Citizens Consumer Council*, the Court said the constitutional protection of commercial speech encourages the free flow of information to aid intelligent commercial decisions.[19] However, government may regulate false or misleading paid messages that do "*no more* than propose a commercial transaction" without offending the First Amendment.[20]

Soon thereafter, in *Central Hudson Gas & Electric Corp. v. Public Service Commission of New York*, the Court established when regulation of commercial speech is constitutional.[21] The Court defined commercial speech this time as "an expression related *solely* to the economic interests of the speaker and its audience," generally in the form of a commercial advertisement for the sale of goods and services, or speech proposing a commercial transaction.[22] The case arose during a national energy crisis and involved a New York state ban on utility company advertising that encouraged the use of energy. To decide the case, the Court developed a test.

In *Central Hudson*, the Court established that regulation of (1) nondeceptive advertising for legal products and services is constitutional *only* if (2) government demonstrates a substantial state interest in the regulation, (3) the regulation directly advances that interest and (4) the regulation uses the "least restrictive means," restricting as little speech as possible, to achieve the government's interest. Applying its new test, which bears striking resemblance

● POINTS OF LAW

The Free Flow of (Commercial) Information

In *Virginia State Board of Pharmacy v. Virginia Citizens Consumer Council*,[1] the U.S. Supreme Court established that:

- "Freedom of speech" applies to both the speaker and the receiver of information.

- "[S]peech does not lose its First Amendment protection because money is spent to project it, as in a paid advertisement."[2]

- Speech that only proposes a commercial transaction is not so removed from "any exposition of ideas" that it lacks all protection.

- The need to make intelligent, informed economic decisions in a free-enterprise economy drives the public interest in entirely commercial information.

- Some forms of commercial speech, including deceptive or misleading ads, may be regulated.

1. 425 U.S. 748 (1976).
2. *Id.* at 761.

to the *O'Brien* test for content-neutral regulations of speech, the Court found the total ban on energy-use advertising was unconstitutional. Under *Central Hudson*, the government may freely regulate commercial speech that is deceptive or that concerns unlawful activity.

In *Board of Trustees of the State University of New York v. Fox*, the Court modified its *Central Hudson* test.[23] The Court said advertising regulation did not need to employ the "least restrictive means" available to the state. Instead, regulation must demonstrate a "reasonable fit" to the state interest. "What our decisions require is a 'fit' between the legislature's ends and the means chosen to accomplish those ends—a fit that is not necessarily perfect, but reasonable," Justice Antonin Scalia wrote for the Court.[24] This revision made it easier for advertising regulations to be found constitutional.

● POINTS OF LAW

The Commercial Speech Doctrine

- The government may regulate advertising that is false, misleading or deceptive.
- The government may regulate advertising for unlawful goods and services.

Even accurate advertising for legal goods and services may be regulated if the government demonstrates:

- There is a substantial state interest behind the regulation.
- The regulation directly advances the state's interest.
- There is a reasonable fit between the state's interest and the regulation.

In two more recent decisions, the Court shifted its review toward greater First Amendment protection for truthful commercial speech about legal products, even dangerous or disfavored "vice" products. The first case, *44 Liquormart Inc. v. Rhode Island*, dealt with a state ban on price advertising by liquor stores intended to reduce alcohol consumption.[25] The Court said, "The First Amendment directs us to be especially skeptical of regulations that seek to keep people in the dark for what the government perceives to be their own good."[26]

The Court viewed the law's absolute ban as particularly egregious. Four justices voting with the majority said that *Central Hudson* itself called for "special care" in review of government attempts to impose blanket bans to achieve goals unrelated to the speech

● POINTS OF LAW

The *Central Hudson* Test After *Sorrell*

Although lower courts have been slow to follow the directive the Supreme Court issued in its decision in *Sorrell v. IMS Health Inc.*,[1] the Court clearly established a new layer to the review a court should conduct when it applies the *Central Hudson* test.[2]

After *Sorrell*, courts asked to rule on the constitutionality of a regulation on commercial speech must determine:

(1) Is the commercial speech false or related to an illegal activity?

    a. If yes, the speech may be banned or strictly regulated.

    b. If no, proceed with the test.

(2) Is the regulation of commercial speech based on its content?

    a. If yes, the court must apply heightened, or strict, scrutiny and presume that the rule is unconstitutional.

    b. If no, proceed with the test.

(3) Is the regulation of commercial speech content neutral?

    a. If yes, the court must apply the *Central Hudson* test and strike down the regulation unless the answer to all of the following is yes.

        i. Does the rule relate to a significant government interest?

        ii. Does the rule directly advance that government interest?

        iii. Is the regulation unrelated to the suppression of speech?

        iv. Does the regulation "fit" the government interest without unduly infringing on speech?

This new standard makes it very difficult for regulations of truthful commercial speech to survive First Amendment review unless the speech promotes an illegal activity.

1. 564 U.S. 552 (2011).

2. Central Hudson Gas & Electric Corp. v. Public Service Commission of New York, 447 U.S. 557, 561 (1980).

⊙ POINTS OF LAW

False and Misleading?

A Federal Trade Commission policy statement establishes the three-part federal definition of false and misleading advertising:

- First, the ad must involve a "material" representation, omission or practice.

- Second, the material representation must be likely to affect the consumer's conduct or decision with regard to a product or service.

- Third, the representation must be likely to mislead a reasonable consumer acting reasonably in the circumstances.[1]

---

1. FTC Policy Statement by Chairman James C. Miller III (Oct. 14, 1983), www.ftc.gov/public-statements/1983/10/ftc-policy-statement-deception.

---

involved.[27] Justice Clarence Thomas went further; in his concurrence, he said all regulations that prohibit truthful advertising for legal products are per se unconstitutional.[28]

Then in *Sorrell v. IMS Health Inc.* (excerpted at the end of the chapter), the Supreme Court said a heightened test applies to government attempts to prohibit dissemination of truthful, nonmisleading information about a lawful product.[29] The Vermont law at issue placed a ban on certain speakers and the content of their speech related to the prescribing patterns of physicians.

In 2016, the Ninth Circuit Court of Appeals remanded a case and established that review of a California restriction on alcohol advertising should be conducted under *Sorrell's* heightened *Central Hudson* test.[30] Only a year earlier, the Ninth Circuit had applied a more lenient *Central Hudson* test to remand the question of whether a city ordinance restricting in-window alcohol advertising by stores along a pedestrian mall "fit" the city's stated goals.[31]

Ruling after *Sorrell*, an en banc D.C. Circuit Court of Appeals also applied the *Central Hudson* test, ignoring its "directly advances" element, to affirm the constitutionality of U.S. Department of Agriculture meat-labeling requirements.[32] The court said the merchants' minimal First Amendment interest in refusing to disclose factual information was easily overcome by the consumer benefits of the information.[33]

CREATING DISTINCTIONS WITHIN COMMERCIAL SPEECH

Congress established the **Federal Trade Commission** in 1914 and expanded its powers in 1938. The FTC act prohibits "unfair or deceptive acts or practices in or affecting commerce."[34] The FTC has said the law's prohibitions of unfair and deceptive practices apply equally to all communication media.[35] Under the law, the FTC has imposed broad disclosure requirements designed to prevent consumer deception. Other state and federal agencies also impose disclosure requirements.

The **Lanham Act** of 1938 also prohibits any false or misleading description of goods, services or commercial activities in any forum, including commercial advertising or promotion.[36]

Federal Trade Commission A federal agency created in 1914. Its purpose is to promote free and fair competition in interstate commerce; this includes preventing false and misleading advertising.

Lanham Act A federal law that regulates the trademark registration process but also contains a section permitting business competitors to sue one another for false advertising.

Though the law initially was rarely applied to commercial advertising, it is now one foundation for lawsuits about ads using price or product comparisons.

False and Deceptive Advertising

A primary function of the FTC is to protect consumers by regulating advertising and ensuring that advertisers substantiate the accuracy of their claims.[37] Thirty-five years ago, the FTC defined false and misleading advertising as advertising that (1) makes a "material" claim or omission that (2) affects consumers' conduct or decisions and that (3) is likely to mislead a reasonable consumer.[38] Beyond deceptive, fraudulent or misleading advertising claims, FTC enforcement efforts target internet advertising, advertising to children, marketing of violent media and alcohol and tobacco marketing.

Some recent cases illustrate what constitutes deceptive advertising. In one, several employees changed firms and sent emails to their former clients falsely claiming that their new employer would be working with their previous firm. The original company sued for false advertising. On appeal, the Sixth Circuit Court of Appeals allowed the false advertising claim under the Lanham Act to proceed. The court rejected its earlier position that the "touchstone" of a false advertising claim is whether the contested content is "part of an organized campaign to penetrate the relevant market."[39] Instead, the appeals court said, "the types of sophisticated, tailored advertising in use today" no longer necessarily involve a broad advertising campaign. Today, the court said, false advertising claims may involve commercial speech "disseminated either widely enough to the relevant purchasing public to constitute advertising or promotion within that industry or to a substantial portion of the plaintiff's or defendant's existing customer or client base."[40]

When the National Association for the Advancement of Colored People sued anti-abortion advocates for false advertising to stop an online article titled "NAACP: National

● REAL WORLD LAW

Going to the Dogs

A Eukanuba dog food ad campaign claimed that a 10-year study of the company's food found that the life span of dogs eating its brand increased by 30 percent. One TV ad claimed, "With Eukanuba and proper care, dogs in the study were able to live beyond their typical life span." The Federal Trade Commission said the company lacked evidence to support the claim.[1]

The FTC ordered the company to stop making false health claims about its products and to have substantial, scientific evidence to support all such claims.

1. Fed. Trade Comm'n, *FTC Approves Final Order Settling Charges That Mars Petcare Made False Health Claims for Its Eukanuba Brand Dog Food* (Dec. 13, 2016), www.ftc.gov/news-events/press-releases/2016/12/ftc-approves-final-order-settling-charges-mars-petcare-made-false.

Association for the Abortion of Colored People," the Fourth Circuit Court of Appeals held that the speech did not violate the Lanham Act because it was not published "in connection with" the promotion or sale of goods or services.[41] It therefore was not advertising. In another case, a federal trial court in California allowed a suit to proceed against Uber to examine whether the "safe rides" statement it puts on its receipts is punishable as false advertising.[42]

Required Disclosures. The FTC generally requires notifications, called disclosures, to ensure that paid advertising on any platform does not mislead consumers about the nature or the source of the content they are viewing. More than 30 years ago, the Supreme Court upheld government authority to force disclosures that are reasonably related to a substantial government interest.[43]

FTC rules require companies to disclose any payment for endorsements of their products, and publishers must identify any content they produce or display in exchange for compensation. FTC guidelines require that disclosures for ads on websites, social media and mobile devices be sufficiently clear and conspicuous that a reasonable consumer will see them and understand that they apply to the appropriate content, even if the disclosure cannot be immediately adjacent to the ad. Space limitations, for example on Twitter, do not justify failure to provide appropriate disclosures.[44]

In 2015, the FTC said its disclosure requirements apply to **native advertising** in which ads are designed to resemble the editorial content of the medium where they appear. The FTC said native ads are deceptive when their overall impression so closely mimics nonpaid content as to be likely to confuse consumers.[45]

In its first enforcement against native ads, the FTC in 2016 issued a complaint against clothing retailer Lord & Taylor.[46] Lord & Taylor's marketing of a new women's clothing line included blog posts, digital photos, video uploads, native ads in online fashion magazines and a team of online "fashion influencers recruited for their fashion style and extensive base of followers on social media platforms."[47] The FTC said the "influencers" received undisclosed payment and free clothing to send preapproved Lord & Taylor posts and hashtags that reached an estimated 11.4 million Instagram users. Lord & Taylor also preapproved at least one online article and an Instagram photo without disclosing that the content was paid.

In settling the case, the FTC prohibited Lord & Taylor from making future misrepresentations that suggest paid content is independent or objective. The FTC required Lord & Taylor to ensure that all endorsers disclose their paid relationship with the retailer.[48] The settlement sanctioned only Lord & Taylor (the advertiser), not the influencers or the publishers, although FTC policy allows liability for all of these parties.[49]

In another case involving paid "influencers," an FTC order required Machinima, a multichannel YouTube network about video games and gaming culture, to ensure its ad campaigns carried proper disclosure. Microsoft and its advertising agency paid influencers to promote Microsoft's Xbox One through a Machinima video campaign. The FTC said that many influencers "gave the impression that their videos were independently produced and that their comments reflected the influencer's personal views."[50] The FTC's settlement sanctioned the publisher, Machinima, not Microsoft, the ad agency or the influencers.[51]

native advertising Ads designed to resemble the editorial content of the medium where they appear. The Federal Trade Commission has said this may be deceptive if it makes it difficult for consumers to distinguish advertising from editorial content.

In 2017, the FTC sent out more than 90 warning letters in one week to remind broadcasters, advertisers, marketers and "influencers" of their obligation to disclose all sponsored promotions and endorsements they distribute through social media. The letters are the first to target the influencers themselves and emphasize the shared responsibility for disclosure.[52]

A handful of FTC investigations suggest that the FTC also applies disclosure requirements to word-of-mouth campaigns by bloggers and noncelebrities.[53] In "word-of-mouth" marketing, a company encourages (and generally compensates) users of its products to "talk them up" on social media to their friends on the theory that recommendations from friends and real product users are more persuasive than other sources.[54]

▲ EMERGING LAW

Court Allows State to Force Disclosure of "Cancer Agent"

Richard Levine/Alamy Stock Photo

A California court in 2017 dismissed a case brought by chemical maker Monsanto to stop the state from requiring the company to label its popular weed killer, Roundup, with a cancer warning.[1] Monsanto introduced Roundup almost 45 years ago. It is a household and agricultural leader worldwide in eliminating weeds while limiting harm to crops or plants.[2]

In 2016, the nation's largest agricultural state took the first step toward requiring warning labels when it added Roundup's main colorless, odorless ingredient—glyphosate—to its list of known cancer-causing agents. Monsanto brought suit on First Amendment grounds, claiming that the forced labeling would violate its free speech and require it to make false and misleading claims.[3]

The U.S. Environmental Protection Agency does restrict the use of glyphosate, which it says has low toxicity. But California said the U.N. World Health Organization's International Agency for Research on Cancer was the "gold standard," and the state relied upon its classification of glyphosate as a "probable human carcinogen."[4]

Monsanto also argued unsuccessfully that California had delegated fact-finding unconstitutionally to an unelected foreign body. The company said it would challenge the state superior court ruling.[5]

---

1. *In re: Monsanto Co. v. Office of Environmental Health Hazard Assessment*, Case No. 16 CE CG 00183, Tentative Ruling for Dept. 403, Fresno Super. Ct. Cal., Jan. 26, 2017, www.fresno.courts.ca.gov/tentative_rulings/documents/01-27-17.pdf.
2. Scott Smith, *California Clears Hurdle for Cancer Warning Label on Roundup*, U.S. NEWS & WORLD REP., Jan. 27, 2016, www.usnews.com/news/news/articles/2017-01-27/california-fights-monsanto-on-labels-for-popular-weed-killer.
3. *Id.*
4. Scott Smith, *Warning Label on Roundup Could Be Coming Soon in California*, U.S. NEWS & WORLD REPORT, Jan. 27, 2017, www.usnews.com/news/news/articles/2017-01-27/california-fights-monsanto-on-labels-for-popular-weed-killer.
5. *Id.*

The FTC's reach encompasses unsolicited commercial messages, or spam. Unclearly labeled public relations and advertising messages emailed directly to users may violate the Controlling the Assault of Non-Solicited Pornography and Marketing Act.[55] The CAN-SPAM law prohibits "the transmission, to a protected computer, of a commercial electronic mail message, or a transaction or relationship message, that contains, or is accompanied by, header information that is materially false or materially misleading."[56] In addition, the FTC requires employees who send out personal messages about company products to disclose their conflict of interest and make clear that they are not speaking on behalf of the employer.[57]

Due process standards apply to disclosure requirements. When the U.S. Court of Appeals for the D.C. Circuit reviewed Federal Election Commission rules requiring disclosure of corporate but not other types of funding of broadcast "electioneering communications," it struck them down. The court said Congress had not "spoke[n] plainly" about its intentions, and the rules were "capricious" and unsupported by fact finding.[58]

Puffing Up Claims

The FTC distinguishes "**puffery**," which involves advertising that exaggerates the merits of products or services in such a way that no reasonable person would take the claim seriously, from deception. As one former FTC commissioner said,

> The FTC does not pursue subjective claims or puffery—claims like "this is the best hairspray in the world." But if there is an objective component to the claim—such as "more consumers prefer our hairspray to any other" or "our hairspray lasts longer than the most popular brands"—then you need to be sure that the claim is not deceptive and that you have adequate substantiation *before* you make the claim. These requirements apply both to explicit or express claims and to implied claims.[59]

Promoting Vice and Dangerous Products

Controversial commercial speech—such as advertising for **vice products** or advertising to susceptible audiences—is a prime arena for testing the limits of constitutional protection for commercial speech. The Supreme Court must often determine the limits of permissible regulation of advertising for alcohol, tobacco, drugs, gambling, guns and, more recently, marijuana.

Alcohol. When Coors Brewing Co. wanted to advertise and label its beer with the percentage of alcohol content, a federal law stood in the way. Coors challenged the law on First Amendment grounds, and the federal government said the law was a reasonable means to prevent "strength wars" that might increase beer potency and harm society. In *Rubin v. Coors Brewing Co.*, the Supreme Court concluded that while combating "strength wars" may be a substantial interest, a ban on alcohol content did not achieve that goal as well as would alternatives "less intrusive to the First Amendment's protections for commercial speech."[60]

The Fourth Circuit Court of Appeals similarly held that Virginia's ban on alcohol ads in college newspapers violated the First Amendment because it was not narrowly tailored

puffery
Advertising that exaggerates the merits of products or services in such a way that no reasonable person would take the ad seriously. Usually, puffery is not illegal given that a reasonable person understands the claim is not to be taken literally.

vice products
Products related to activities generally considered unhealthy or immoral or whose use is restricted by age or other condition. The category includes alcohol, tobacco, firearms, sexually explicit materials and drugs.

INTERNATIONAL LAW

Misleading Advertising in Europe

European Commission rules address the most frequent misleading advertising practices and scams in the European Union.[1]

Prior EU regulation did not adequately address concerns with deceptive contracts and internet offers, use of competitors' trademarks, false product and price comparisons, fake internet domain name sales and trademark protection as well as other internet-based frauds.

New EU regulations[2] largely parallel the U.S. Federal Trade Commission Act[3] and bar misleading, aggressive or "unfair commercial practices" in advertising and marketing that are likely to materially distort the economic decisions of a reasonable consumer. Misleading advertising "contains false information and is therefore untruthful or . . . deceives or is likely to deceive the average consumer."[4]

The commission said the rules protect consumers and small businesses that are particularly vulnerable to unfair business-to-business advertising practices.

---

1. European Commission, *Consumer Rights and Law: The Directive on Consumer Rights*, ec.europa.eu/justice/consumer-marketing/rights-contracts/directive/index_en.htm (last visited Aug. 6, 2017).
2. Council directive 2005/29.
3. 15 U.S.C §§ 41–58, *as amended*.
4. Council directive 2005/29, art. 6(1).

---

to the state's interest in reducing alcohol abuse on college campuses.[61] The same court earlier held that the ban was facially constitutional.[62] But the later decision found the regulation was not constitutional as applied because the majority of readers of the Virginia Tech newspaper were 21 or older. Both the newspaper and its readers "have a protected interest" in nonmisleading alcohol advertising, the court ruled.

Rhode Island fined one liquor store owner who tried to circumvent a state law forbidding liquor stores from advertising prices by placing the exclamation "Wow" next to certain bargain products in newspaper ads. The owner sued under the First Amendment, and the state argued that the law advanced the government's substantial interest in promoting temperance by preventing promotion of bargain alcohol prices that would increase consumption.

Viviane Moos/Getty Images

Camel cigarette advertising featuring Joe Camel.

The U.S. Supreme Court disagreed.[63] The Court found the law unconstitutional because the state showed no causal relationship between the ban on truthful advertising and the promotion of temperance.

Tobacco. The Lorillard brothers began advertising their tobacco products in a New York daily newspaper in 1789. Nearly two centuries later, the District of Columbia Circuit Court of Appeals ruled that the federal Public Health Cigarette Smoking Act's ban on broadcast TV and radio ads for cigarettes did not violate the free speech rights of tobacco companies because other outlets existed for their advertising.[64] The court said the government had the power to regulate tobacco advertising to protect minors and others from the

▲ EMERGING LAW

Weed Control?

Legalization of marijuana in some states has prompted many to regulate marijuana ads much as they control the promotion of alcohol products.

Marijuana is legal for medicinal or other purposes in nearly two dozen states,[1] but the federal government and several states are trying to limit or stop marijuana advertising.

In 2016, when California voters legalized the possession, growth, purchase and use of marijuana for recreational purposes,[2] the initiative also mandated packaging and labeling requirements and prohibited advertising to children.[3]

In Colorado, where adults may legally possess a limited amount of marijuana,[4] laws regulate both the method and the content of marijuana advertising. The laws effectively ban advertising via any medium with an audience that includes 30 percent minors. Although a federal court said two Colorado publications did not have standing to challenge the state's near total ban on marijuana advertising,[5] law professors debated whether the First Amendment prevented such laws.[6]

As part of the Trump administration's 2017 renewal of the national war on drugs, the Department of Justice was widely expected to increase enforcement of federal laws banning recreational use of marijuana and implicating, if not eliminating, its advertising.[7]

1. Marijuana Policy Project, *23 Legal Medical Marijuana States and DC*, medicalmarijuana.procon.org/view.resource.php?resourceID=000881 (last visited Aug. 6, 2017).
2. Katy Steinmetz, *What to Know About Marijuana Legalization in California*, TIME, Nov. 9, 2016, time.com/4565438/california-marijuana-faq-rules-prop-64.
3. *Submission of Amendment to Statewide Initiative Measure—Control, Regulate and Tax Adult Use of Marijuana Act, No. 15-0103*, OLSON, HAGEL & FISHBURN, Dec. 7, 2015, www.oag.ca.gov/system/files/initiatives/pdfs/15-0103%20(Marijuana)_1.pdf.
4. *Marijuana Laws in Colorado*, POTGUIDE.COM, COLORADO, www.coloradopotguide.com/marijuana-laws-in-colorado (last visited Aug. 6, 2017).
5. John Ingold, *Lawsuit Over Colorado's Marijuana Advertising Rules Suffers Setback*, DENVER POST, Feb. 17, 2014, www.denverpost.com/2014/02/17/lawsuit-over-colorado-marijuana-advertising-rules-suffers-setback.
6. Robert Mikos, *Commercial Marijuana Advertising and the First Amendment*, PRAWFSBLAWG, Feb. 27, 2017, prawfsblawg.blogs.com/prawfsblawg/2017/02/commercial-marijuana-advertising-and-the-first-amendment.html.
7. Tom Huddleston Jr., *The White House Expects "Greater Enforcement" of Federal Marijuana Laws*, FORTUNE, Feb. 23, 2017, fortune.com/2017/02/23/marijuana-enforcement-white-house; Sari Horwitz, *How Jeff Sessions Wants to Bring Back the War on Drugs*, WASH. POST, Apr. 8, 2017, www.washingtonpost.com/world/national-security/how-jeff-sessions-wants-to-bring-back-the-war-on-drugs/2017/04/08/414ce6be-132b-11e7-ada0-1489b735b3a3_story.html?utm_term=.f4e35fe82e93.

lure of tobacco. In response, tobacco producers increasingly advertised via print media, billboards and other means.

When Lorillard Tobacco Co. challenged a Massachusetts law that limited point-of-sale tobacco ads and banned outdoor tobacco ads within 1,000 feet of a school or playground, the Supreme Court applied the *Central Hudson* test to hold that the point-of-sale regulations advanced a legitimate state interest in preventing minors from accessing tobacco products that were illegal for them to consume. The Court in *Lorillard Tobacco Co. v. Reilly* said those restrictions addressed a state interest "unrelated to the communication of ideas."[65] However, the ban on outdoor advertising was unconstitutional because it did not reasonably fit the state's interest.

Almost 40 years ago, government attempts to protect susceptible people, especially children, from tobacco promotions targeted Camel's use of the cartoon character Joe Camel. Critics said Joe Camel prompted smoking by minors, for whom smoking was illegal. In fact, Camel cigarettes' share of the youth market rose from 4 percent to 13 percent after the introduction of Joe Camel.[66] When the Food and Drug Administration initiated rules "designed to stop sales and marketing of cigarettes and smokeless tobacco to children," a federal district court in North Carolina said the rules fell within the reasonable authority of the FDA.[67] The tobacco industry settled, agreeing to end all use of cartoon characters and all billboard and transit ads promoting tobacco products in all 50 states. In 2016, the FDA expanded its rules to apply to all tobacco products, including hookahs and e-cigarettes.[68]

As regulators struggled to balance consumer protection and tobacco company free speech rights, Congress enacted the Family Smoking Prevention and Tobacco Control Act,[69] and the FDA adopted new graphic labeling requirements for cigarettes.[70] The U.S. Courts of Appeals for the D.C. and Sixth Circuits disagreed on the constitutionally of the FDA rules requiring tobacco companies to "emblazon cigarette packaging with images of people dying from smoking-related disease, mouth and gum damage linked to smoking and other graphic portrayals of the harms of smoking."[71] Applying *Central Hudson*, the Sixth Circuit upheld most of the new labeling requirements because they regulated only commercial speech about risky tobacco products. The D.C. Circuit used strict scrutiny to find the labeling requirement largely unconstitutional,[72] and both courts said the rules required speech that was neither purely factual nor uncontroversial.[73] The Supreme Court declined review of both cases.[74]

The rationale that government interest in promoting certain messages generally does not outweigh a company's First Amendment right to refuse to carry government messages[75] has provided an obstacle to government efforts to impose advertising and labeling requirements on "foodstuffs" marketed to children.[76]

Gambling. When a federal law banned all broadcast lottery ads in states that prohibited gambling, a radio station in North Carolina challenged the law. Lotteries were illegal in North Carolina, but the station was located three miles from Virginia, where most of its listeners lived and where lotteries were legal. The U.S. Supreme Court upheld the ban, finding that the state power to ban gambling provided a legitimate government interest in discouraging gambling promotion.[77] The Court said that

Congress surely knew that stations in one state could often be heard in another but expressly prevented each and every North Carolina station, including Edge, from carrying lottery ads . . . [because] each North Carolina station would have an audience in that state, even if its signal reached elsewhere. . . . The statutory restriction . . . advance[d] the governmental purpose of supporting North Carolina's laws against gambling.[78]

Similar logic justified Federal Communications Commission rules that banned broadcasters in Louisiana from airing ads for private casino gambling because the ads reached states where such gambling was illegal. In a case brought by an association of broadcasters, a unanimous Supreme Court held that although the state had a substantial interest in reducing the social costs of gambling, the rules failed the *Central Hudson* test because they did not advance that interest.[79] The rules were underinclusive because they prohibited only advertising for private casinos (not for casinos operated by Native American tribes and not advertising of other forms of gambling). The rules simply directed gamblers to favored outlets, the Court said. Moreover, the rules were not as narrowly tailored as they could be.[80]

WARNING:
Smoking can kill you.

One of the proposed cigarette-package images abandoned by the Food and Drug Administration.

Prescription Medicines. Advertisements for prescription drugs promote highly controlled substances. But in its review of a Vermont law that prohibited drug marketing and data-mining companies from buying doctors' prescription records from pharmacies for marketing purposes, the Supreme Court applied strict scrutiny rather than the commercial speech doctrine.[81] The state law limited the sale or disclosure of pharmacy prescription records to brand-name drug marketers in order to protect doctors' privacy and prevent drug marketing that might alter doctors' prescribing practices and quash demand for cheaper generic drugs.[82]

In *Sorrell v. IMS Health Inc.* (excerpted at the end of this chapter), the Court said the law unconstitutionally limited pharmacies' sale and distribution of information and targeted only drug marketers. "The state has burdened a form of protected expression that it found too persuasive. At the same time, the state has left unburdened those speakers whose messages are in accord with its own views," the Supreme Court said. "This the state cannot do."[83] The Court said the restriction on pharmacies' speech was both content-based and viewpoint-discriminatory on its face. The law "does not simply have an effect on speech," Justice Anthony Kennedy wrote for the majority. "[It] is directed at certain content and is aimed at particular speakers."

Three justices sharply dissented and concluded that "[a]t best, the Court opens a Pandora's box of First Amendment challenges to many ordinary regulatory practices that may only incidentally affect a commercial message. . . . At worst, it reawakens [the] threat of substituting judicial for democratic decision-making where ordinary economic regulation is at issue."[84] Many said the decision eviscerated well-developed precedent that speech intended solely to generate profits and sales should not receive the full constitutional protection afforded to political, artistic or scientific speech.[85] A year later, some said the *Sorrell* decision already had distorted rulings on tobacco advertising in school zones and on cigarette package labels.[86] Under *Sorrell*, courts heighten the scrutiny applied to laws that regulate truthful, nondeceptive advertising.

Guns. A federal trial court in California allowed a preliminary injunction to prevent the state from applying its law limiting gun sale advertising.[87] The court reasoned that the First Amendment challenge to the law would likely succeed under *Central Hudson* because the state's goals of dampening demand and reducing violence were tenuous and only indirectly advanced by limiting the merchants' speech.

● REAL WORLD LAW

Smoke-Filled Rooms and Hazy Standards?

In *Lorillard*, the U.S. Supreme Court ruled that state bans on outdoor advertising of tobacco products near schools and playgrounds must clearly balance the "costs and benefits" of such restrictions on free speech.

The ruling in *Lorillard Tobacco Co. v. Reilly*[1] clarifies the U.S. Supreme Court's application of the *Central Hudson* test to commercial speech that reaches children. At issue were Massachusetts regulations that prohibited both outdoor and point-of-sale tobacco product advertising within 1,000 feet of a school or playground. Lorillard said the regulations would prohibit its advertising in about 90 percent of Massachusetts' biggest cities.

The Court found that the outdoor rules passed the first three prongs of the *Central Hudson* test. However, they did not present a reasonable "fit" to the state interest in reducing tobacco consumption by minors because they effectively banned tobacco ads in any urban areas with densely clustered schools and playgrounds.[2]

"Efforts to protect children from exposure to harmful material will undoubtedly have some spillover effect on the free speech rights of adults," and "finding the appropriate balance is no easy matter," the Court said.[3] However, the Court offered no "coherent limits" to the application of "the *Central Hudson* test to defeat objectionable legislation" or to determine when a law's "fit" was acceptable.[4]

1. 533 U.S. 525 (2001).
2. *Id.*
3. *Id.*
4. Charles Fischette, *A New Architecture of Commercial Speech Law*, 31 Harv. J.L. & Pub. Pol'y 663, 666–67 (2008).

Advertising That Offends

The FCC regulates offensive broadcast advertising, but no federal agency or law controls offensive ads or advertising of disfavored activities, such as racism or pornography, in other media. The protection of commercial speech that attacks others is uncertain and varied.

A divided Ninth Circuit Court of Appeals upheld the authority of Seattle Metro Transit to prohibit ads on its buses that criticized Israeli policies toward Palestinians.[88] In rejecting ads that read "ISRAELI WAR CRIMES . . . YOUR TAX DOLLARS AT WORK," the court said the county applied viewpoint-neutral, content-based review of speech in a limited public forum. The SMT ruling responded to "real and substantial" fears that the ads' display "presented a reasonably foreseeable threat of disruption" to transit passengers.

The First Circuit Court of Appeals also affirmed a Massachusetts ban on ads that "demean or disparage" individuals or groups from its transit vehicles.[89] One banned ad read "IN ANY WAR BETWEEN THE CIVILIZED MAN AND THE SAVAGE, SUPPORT THE CIVILIZED MAN. ☆ SUPPORT ISRAEL ☆ DEFEAT JIHAD." The court said the ad space was a nonpublic forum, and the ban a constitutional application of "reasonable, viewpoint-neutral limits."

In contrast, a federal district court ruled that the Philadelphia public transit authority's refusal to display ads that read "Islamic Jew-Hatred: It's in the Quran. Two Thirds of All US Aid Goes to Islamic Countries" violated the First Amendment.[90] The court reasoned that the ad was "exactly the sort of political expression that lies at the heart of the First Amendment . . . regardless of its alleged falsity." The court then enjoined the city's ban on the ads.[91]

Promoting Corporations and Professional Activities

The Supreme Court has distinguished the First Amendment right of a business to communicate political messages from its commercial speech. For example, when a bank wanted to pay to support a voter referendum, including public advertising for it, the Court affirmed the bank's constitutional right.[92] Relying on the public's right to free-flowing information and the nearly impossible differentiation of media companies from others, the Court provided businesses' noncommercial speech with greater protection than afforded under the commercial speech doctrine.[93] The Supreme Court's decision in *Citizens United v. Federal Election Commission* (see Chapters 1 and 2) also increased the First Amendment protection for corporate funding of political speech.[94]

Earlier, when Nike had sought to place itself in a positive light by communicating about an issue of public controversy, the case of *Nike Inc. v. Kasky* raised a new question for the Supreme Court.[95] Nike issued press releases and letters to newspapers and university athletic directors in response to accusations that

Workers in a Nike factory near Ho Chi Minh City, Vietnam.

AP/Richard Vogel

its overseas plants operated illegally and unsafely and abused workers. A California activist sued, claiming Nike's statements were knowingly false advertising.

The trial court dismissed the case, but the California Supreme Court ruled that the speech was commercial and might be punishable under state false advertising and unfair competition laws. The court said that Nike's speech to an audience consisting largely of its potential customers included representations of fact intended to maintain or increase Nike's sales.[96] The dissent argued that the speech was protected political speech and part of an important public discussion.[97]

Nike appealed to the U.S. Supreme Court and argued that, even if false, its political speech was absolutely protected by the First Amendment. Nike said commercial speech doctrine applied only to speech involving things such as product pricing or characteristics. The Supreme Court dismissed the case on the grounds that the activist did not have **standing**, leaving the core question unanswered. Nike settled and reportedly paid $1.5 million to the Fair Labor Association.

Corporate, business and professional ads designed to enhance sales and revenue generally involve commercial speech. When state bar associations of lawyers and judges prohibited advertising by lawyers, the Supreme Court struck down the ban.[98] The Court said the absolute prohibition on truthful advertising was unconstitutional, although "[r]easonable" restrictions—such as those pertaining to false advertising—might survive First Amendment scrutiny.[99] The Court did not indicate how it would review professional association's limits on advertising by professionals in other fields, such as public relations or marketing.

When a dentist with a specialty in endodontics was denied permission to list both "dentist" and "endodontist" on his signs, he challenged the Ohio law that prohibits dentists from advertising both general and specialized practices as an unconstitutional restraint of his speech. The trial court dismissed the claim, but the Sixth Circuit Court of Appeals reversed. It instructed the trial court to apply the *Central Hudson* test, which it said must place the burden on the government to justify the law's restraint of speech.[100]

standing The position of a plaintiff who has been injured or has been threatened with injury. No person is entitled to challenge the constitutionality of an ordinance or statute unless he or she has the required standing—that is, unless he or she has been affected by the ordinance or statute.

Advertising Online

The cost-effectiveness of internet advertising is attractive to companies. Not only do internet ads often reach hundreds of thousands of consumers or more, online ads enable collection of highly valuable user activity data that enable advertisers to target ads to consumer interests. In 2015, the FTC settled a complaint that app developers violated the Children's Online Privacy Protection Act[101] by enabling advertisers to use "persistent identifiers," or trackers, to target ads toward children.[102] The FTC's rules under COPPA classify persistent identifiers as personal information and prohibit their collection from children under 13 without parental notice and consent.[103]

The instantaneous nature of internet advertising and purchasing also provides fertile ground for fraud and unwanted ads. The FTC monitors illegal advertising on the internet and enforces laws against online fraud. The commission issued its first consent decree for deceptive online advertising after a service placed advertisements on the internet advising consumers to take illegal steps to repair their credit records.[104] The action required the advertiser to provide consumer compensation, to cease misrepresentations and to cooperate in FTC investigations of the sellers of the credit program materials.

INTERNATIONAL LAW

Advertisers Swarm to Facebook, Google

Peter Foley/Bloomberg via Getty Images

A total of $17.6 billion was spent on digital ads in the third quarter of 2016, an increase of 20 percent over the same period a year earlier.[1] But Google swallowed up more than a quarter of that market, and Facebook had a 16 percent share.

Together the two behemoths account for 90 percent of the growth in online advertising precisely because of the enormous amount of personal data they collect that allows advertisers to marry audiences to the ads that interest them. Meanwhile, other platforms—like Twitter and Snapchat—fail to gain market share and struggle for advertising revenue.

Some argue that stronger privacy laws in the United States, akin to those in the European Union, would better distribute advertising revenue across digital media and support more diverse digital content.[2] New EU regulations effective in 2018 will require companies to obtain permission from users to collect their data for use in targeting advertising content.[3]

1. Matthew Ingram, *How Google and Facebook Have Taken Over the Digital Ad Industry*, FORTUNE, Jan. 4, 2017, fortune.com/2017/01/04/google-facebook-ad-industry.
2. Klint Finley, *Stronger Privacy Laws Could Save Advertising From Itself*, WIRED, Apr. 12, 2017, www.wired.com/2017/04/stronger-privacy-laws-save-advertising.
3. *Id.*

For several years, the FTC has asked advertisers voluntarily to give consumers "effective and meaningful privacy protection" via an easy, internet-wide "Do Not Track" option.[105] The FTC has said that because mechanisms targeting advertising to consumers are invisible, consumers should have an easy way to opt out.[106] Some internet browsers, such as Internet Explorer 9,[107] enable users to block cookies, but the FTC has sought a simpler, more global solution for consumers.

Some believe the FTC should take action to resolve consumer complaints about unsolicited, unwanted email, or spam advertising. The federal CAN-SPAM Act[108] empowers internet service providers and the government to pursue spammers in federal courts. The law prohibits the use of false header information in commercial email and requires unsolicited messages to include opt-out instructions. It also punishes spam containing unmarked pornographic material. Penalties for violations include up to five years' imprisonment and fines of up to $6 million.[109]

Most states have their own anti-spam laws.[110] In Virginia, where laws target unsolicited commercial bulk emails,[111] Jeremy Jaynes, a man once considered one of the world's most

● REAL WORLD LAW

In the Amazon Jungle: Third-Party Liability

A New York court signaled that "third-party liability" may not exist in the world of internet advertising. The case involved Amazon, Google and several online companies.

Sellify, the parent company of an online marketer, complained when an Amazon-affiliated advertiser used Google keywords to pop up warnings like "Beware of the SCAM Artist" when users searched for Sellify ads. Sellify demanded that Amazon remove the pop-ups, but Amazon did not have that ability. Instead, it warned the company. The company failed to stop the pop-ups, so Amazon terminated its partnership.

Meanwhile, Sellify sued Amazon, claiming the retail giant was responsible for the problem ads. The New York court dismissed the case and held that Amazon could not be held liable for the actions of the third party it did not control. Merely allowing third parties to link to its website did not make Amazon responsible for third-party actions.[1]

---

1. Sellify Inc. v. Amazon.com Inc., 2010 U.S. Dist. LEXIS 118173 (S.D.N.Y. Nov. 4, 2010).

prolific spammers,[112] was charged with violating the law after he sent more than 55,000 unsolicited emails to subscribers of AOL (then America Online). The Virginia Supreme Court overturned Jaynes' conviction, finding the law's prohibition on false routing information overbroad and facially unconstitutional because it infringed the First Amendment right to engage in anonymous speech and targeted not only unsolicited commercial bulk emails but "the anonymous transmission of all unsolicited bulk e-mails including those containing political, religious or other speech protected by the First Amendment to the United States Constitution."[113]

The U.S. Court of Appeals for the Eighth Circuit addressed a similar problem related to fax advertisements. The Telephone Consumer Protection Act requires all unsolicited faxed ads to include instructions on how to opt out.[114] The appeals court said the opt-out provision applied even when the recipient consented to the faxes because the rule was intended to prevent recipients' limited consent from becoming global or permanent.[115] On remand, the sender faced a multimillion-dollar class action suit for failure to include opt-out language in faxes for which the recipient had given prior explicit consent.

REMEDYING PROBLEMS THROUGH EXECUTIVE AGENCIES

The federal government largely assumed responsibility for regulating advertising because commercial speech often crosses state lines and, therefore, falls under the U.S. Constitution's commerce clause.

Congress passed the Lanham Act in 1938 to prohibit any false or misleading description of goods, services or commercial activities in any forum, including commercial advertising or promotion.[116] Though initially the law was seldom used to curtail advertising practices, it became the foundation for suits, especially over ads using price or product comparisons.

The Supreme Court appeared to include product labeling under the act's mandate for truthful commercial speech. The Court ruled 8–0 that juice company POM Wonderful could sue Coca-Cola for false advertising in its labeling of Minute Maid pomegranate blueberry juice.[117] FDA rules allow the product, which contains only 0.3 percent pomegranate and 0.2 percent blueberry juice, to be labeled "a flavored blend of five juices."[118] But the Court held that the FDA rule did not prevent POM Wonderful from pursuing a claim that the label violated the FTC's ban on deceptive and misleading advertising. The Court found no support for Coca-Cola's claim "that because food and beverage labeling is involved, it has no Lanham Act liability here for practices that allegedly mislead and trick customers, all to the injury of the competitor."[119]

In another case, the Supreme Court also created a rule for when a plaintiff may bring a Lanham Act suit for false and misleading advertising.[120] The Court said the law protected interests beyond those of direct corporate competitors and consumers. When the plaintiff's challenge lies in the law's "zone of interest," the Court said, the individual has standing to sue. The Court did not define "zone of interest" but suggested it is roughly equivalent to congressional intent.

In addition, the Court said the Lanham Act does not require the false advertising to directly cause the injury at the heart of the suit. Rather, the injury must be "proximately caused" by the false advertising.[121] Consumer responses to a defendant's false advertising that harmed a company's sales and reputation established the "injury in fact" necessary to bring suit.

◦ SOCIAL MEDIA LAW

Piling on Unwanted Texts

Isabella Piccinini

Sometimes, simply sending a text or email is unfair and deceptive, according to the Federal Trade Commission.

Responding to a complaint against a "mind-boggling" number of commercial texts and emails marketing a mortgage refinancing service, the Federal Trade Commission ruled that the texts amounted to an unfair and deceptive practice because they (1) were sent without prior permission and (2) were annoying, frustrating and paid for by the recipients.[1] The marketing also misleadingly suggested government affiliation, the FTC said, because it provided a URL that contained ".gov," called itself "official" and featured an American flag.[2]

The FTC order, which permanently prohibited all unauthorized and unsolicited commercial texts to cellphones subject to fines and forfeitures of up to $18,000, added on to Federal Communications Commission rules that prohibited spam to cellphones and mandated an opt-out mechanism.[3]

1. Ronald G. London, *FTC Settlement Ups Ante on Need for Prior Express Consent to Lawfully Text-Message*, Privacy & Sec. L. Blog, Sept. 30, 2011, www.privsecblog.com/2011/09/articles/marketing-and-consumer-privacy/ftc-settlement-ups-ante-on-need-for-prior-express-consent-to-lawfully-text-message.
2. *Id.*
3. *Id.*

The Federal Trade Commission

The Federal Trade Commission learns of potentially problematic advertisements through complaints, congressional inquiries, news articles or public debate. Some issues arise directly from advertisers seeking advice to avoid problems. The FTC generally conducts nonpublic inquiries and fact-findings to protect its investigation and the privacy of those

● REAL WORLD LAW

The Jury's Out: Does Advertising Increase Product Demand?

Come to where the flavor is. Come to Marlboro Country.

Regulators and lawmakers sometimes target tobacco advertising, with disputes often settled in court.

A foundational basis for government regulation of advertising is that it alters consumer choices and increases product demand. In fact, the scientific jury may be out. One advertising study suggested that advertising increases demand for cigarettes. Another found that alcohol advertising does not increase demand but shifts consumption among brands.[1]

But the U.S. Supreme Court's rulings accept the following:

- A utility company would not have contested an advertising ban "unless it believed that promotion would increase sales."[2]

- Legislatures believe advertising "would serve to increase the demand for the product advertised. We think the legislature's belief is a reasonable one."[3]

- The "acknowledged [] theory [is] that product advertising stimulates demand for products, while suppressed advertising may have the opposite effect. . . . [N]umerous studies . . . support this theory in the case of tobacco products."[4]

Nevertheless, policy and empirical studies have produced mixed results. The Food and Drug Administration found a correlation between advertising and increased product demand,[5] but other federal agencies were "not convinced that advertising leads to increased consumption."[6]

---

1. Barry J. Seldon & Khosrow Doroodian, *A Simultaneous Model of Cigarette Advertising: Effects on Demand and Industry Response to Public Policy*, 71 Rev. Econ. & Stat. 673 (1989); Jon P. Nelson & John R. Moran, *Advertising and U.S. Alcoholic Beverage Demand: System-Wide Estimates*, 27 Applied Econ. 1225 (1995).
2. Cent. Hudson Gas & Electric Corp. v. Pub. Serv. Comm'n, 447 U.S. 557, 569 (1980).
3. Posadas de Puerto Rico Associates v. Tourism Co. of Puerto Rico, 478 U.S. 328, 342 (1986).
4. Lorillard Tobacco Co. v. Reilly, 533 U.S. 525, 557 (2001).
5. *See, e.g.,* Rosalind M. Kendellen, *The Food and Drug Administration Retreats From Patient Package Inserts for Prescription Drugs*, 40 Food Drug Cosm. L.J. 172 (1985) (showing the FDA's motivation for establishing a package insert plan for consumers).
6. 1 Antitrust & Trade Reg. Rep. (BNA) No. 1277, at 199 (Aug. 7, 1986).

● POINTS OF LAW

Lanham Act Standing

The U.S. Supreme Court established that a plaintiff has standing to bring suit under the Lanham Act when:

1. The defendant's actions occurred inside "the zone of interest" of the Lanham Act, and

2. The injury to the plaintiff is "proximately caused" by the defendant's actions.

investigated. FTC powers are designed to prevent problematic advertising or remedy deceptive ads to protect the public. FTC actions range from quite informal letters to serious, official legal actions.

Preventive Measures. The least formal FTC action is an **opinion letter** sent to an advertiser seeking advice. Opinion letters are not legally binding, but they provide an efficient means for businesses to avoid problems.

An FTC **advisory opinion** is part of the official public record, provides more information and provides transparency to FTC actions. These opinions may be both formal and harsh; they often oblige the advertiser to adhere to the opinion provided.

The FTC's broad **industry guides** outline policies about a particular product or service. For example, the FTC industry guide on advertising testimonials and endorsements establishes that endorsers, especially celebrity endorsers, may be personally liable for false claims.[122] "Material connections," such as payment for the endorsement, must be disclosed. "New media," specifically bloggers, social media and viral campaigners, also are subject to FTC enforcement action, as are "nontraditional" advertising endorsers, such as "on-air DJ's."[123]

FTC **trade regulation rules** target an entire trade. They differ from guides because they mandate rather than suggest a particular practice. FTC trade regulation rules deal with an entire group rather than each individual advertiser. Individual advertisers may challenge the rules to the commission and appeal FTC decisions in court.

The U.S. Court of Appeals for the D.C. Circuit in 2015 upheld an FTC rule requiring POM pomegranate juice manufacturers to stop advertising the products' health benefits unless valid clinical trials supported the claims.[124] However, the court said the First Amendment limited the conditions the FTC could impose on advertisers. POM had appealed the FTC finding that the ads deceptively claimed POM's extensive health benefits based on flawed studies. The court suggested advertiser free speech rights protected product claims of both specific and general health benefits without the rigorous clinical trials the FTC mandated.

opinion letter
An informal Federal Trade Commission communication providing general advice about advertising techniques.

advisory opinion
A Federal Trade Commission measure that offers formal guidance on whether a specific advertisement may be false or misleading and how to correct it.

Coca-Cola

industry guides
In advertising,
a Federal Trade
Commission
measure that
outlines the
FTC's policies
concerning
a particular
category of
product or
service.

**trade regulation
rule** A broadly
worded
statement by the
Federal Trade
Commission
that outlines
advertising
requirements for
a particular trade.

**voluntary
compliance**
The general
Federal Trade
Commission
practice to allow
advertisers to
follow FTC rules
and correct
violations before
the commission
takes action.

substantiation
The authority of
the Federal Trade
Commission to
demand that an
advertiser prove
its advertised
claims.

**corrective
advertising** The
Federal Trade
Commission
power to require
an advertiser
to advertise
or otherwise
distribute
information to
correct false
or misleading
advertisement
claims.

The FTC also oversees **voluntary compliance** with rules and regulations and response to consumer complaints. The commission generally asks for evidence of advertisers' own corrective actions before initiating investigations or corrective measures.

Corrective Measures. If an advertiser fails to comply voluntarily with regulatory directives, the FTC may begin corrective measures through a **consent order** or consent agreement. A consent order must be signed by the FTC and the advertiser and may contain a **cease and desist order** requiring an advertiser to stop particular practices. For example, the FTC ordered American Nationwide Mortgage Co. to cease and desist its direct mail ad campaign that stated, "30-Year Fixed. 1.95%." In a virtually illegible footnote, the ad stated, "4.981% Annual Percentage Rate." Small print on the ad's reverse side qualified and limited the duration of even the higher interest rate.[125] Under the FTC order, the mortgage company agreed to discontinue the advertisement.

A consent order is for settlement purposes only. It does not constitute an admission of guilt by the advertiser. There are practical reasons for advertisers to sign such an agreement. Failure to sign may trigger negative publicity and severe FTC penalties. When the FTC concluded that Rite Aid pharmacies failed to provide their advertised protection for the privacy of individuals' prescription drug information, the resulting consent order mandated specific corrective measures by Rite Aid and fined the company $1 million.[126]

If advertisers refuse to sign a consent order, the FTC may issue a **litigated order**. The FTC files litigated orders in an administrative court. If the court affirms the order, the advertiser may appeal to a federal court. Failure to follow a litigated order upheld by the courts may result in fines of up to $10,000 per day. In one litigated action, the promoters of two dietary supplements advertised for weight loss and disease prevention agreed to pay the FTC $4.5 million for their false or unsubstantiated product claims and deceptively formatted infomercials.[127]

Substantiation is an FTC tool that empowers the commission to require an advertiser to prove its claims with "competent and reliable evidence."[128] The FTC's demand to "prove it" was central to its case against Tropicana's Healthy Heart orange juice. In both television and print, Tropicana advertised that drinking its product increases "good" cholesterol and lowers blood pressure. The FTC said the clinical study Tropicana used to substantiate its claims was inadequate.[129] The FTC said the ads were false or misleading and ordered Tropicana to stop making the claims.

If an advertiser fails to substantiate its advertised claims, the FTC may order **corrective advertising** that requires the advertiser to correct the misleading claims through new ads or other means.

The FTC used a corrective advertising order 40 years ago against Listerine mouthwash. The FTC found that Listerine misled the public for more than half a century with ad claims that it helped prevent colds and sore throats. A federal appeals court ruled that the FTC's ordered corrective advertising did not violate the First Amendment because "Listerine's advertisements play[ed] a substantial role in creating or reinforcing in the public's mind a false belief about the product . . . [that would] linger on after the false advertising ceases."[130] Nearly a year of required corrective advertising was not "an unreasonably long time in which to correct a hundred years of cold claims," the court ruled.[131] The company spent $10 million on those ads.

⬤ POINTS OF LAW

FTC Mechanisms

Preventive Measures	Corrective Measures
• Opinion letters	• Cease and desist orders
• Advisory opinions	• Consent orders
• Industry guides	• Substantiation
• Trade rules	• Litigated orders
• Voluntary compliance	• Corrective advertising
	• Injunctions

The FTC issued a litigated corrective advertising order for unsubstantiated superiority claims in Doan's analgesic products' advertisements and packaging.[132] The commission said substantial evidence supported its finding that the ads' deceptive claims were material, affected consumer beliefs and created lingering effects that required remedy.[133] The order required Doan's to spend its average annual advertising budget on corrective ads for a minimum of one year.

The FTC also may seek court injunctions or restraining orders to stop advertising that is false or misleading and may cause immediate harm. These orders generally stop the advertising until a full hearing takes place. The FTC, however, sought permanent injunctions to stop companies from making unsubstantiated claims that required consumers to pay thousands of dollars in up-front fees to receive promised reductions in credit card debt.[134]

The Federal Communications Commission

Agencies beyond the FTC and the FDA also issue rules that impact commercial speech. The FCC's oversight of broadcast television includes regulation of certain types of content—including advertising—to serve the public good (see Chapter 9).

FCC rules prohibit paid for-profit business and campaign advertising on public television stations.[135] The Supreme Court denied certiorari to review the Ninth Circuit Court of Appeals' summary judgment in favor of the FCC against a public television station's First Amendment challenge to the FCC ban on paid political advertisements. The Ninth Circuit found that substantial evidence supported the FCC's conclusion that commercial and political advertising posed a legitimate threat to the noncommercial, educational "essence" of public television.[136] The court accepted the decades-old rationale that the scarcity of broadcast airwaves supports government's increased regulation of television.

consent order An agreement between the Federal Trade Commission and an advertiser stipulating the terms that must be followed to address problematic advertising; also called a consent agreement.

cease and desist order An administrative agency order prohibiting a person or business from continuing a particular course of conduct.

litigated order A Federal Trade Commission order filed in administrative court and enforceable by the courts whose violation can result in penalties, including fines of up to $10,000 per day.

CHAPTER SUMMARY

THE CATEGORY OF COMMERCIAL SPEECH has evolved through decades of Supreme Court decisions. The Court long denied First Amendment protection for commercial speech, which it viewed as solely an extension of commerce, not expression. In its libel judgment in *New York Times v. Sullivan*, the Court said the First Amendment protected the paid speech because it contributed to an important public dialogue. When truthful advertising involves more than matters of commerce, the First Amendment may outweigh the government's right to regulate commerce. Constitutional protection for commercial speech advances the free flow of information.

The Court's ruling in *Central Hudson* established that government may constitutionally regulate nondeceptive advertising only with regulations that use the least speech-restrictive means to directly advance a substantial government interest. Courts continue to rely on this test, but it has been modified by Supreme Court decisions that require heightened scrutiny of laws that infringe upon truthful advertising for legal products. Certain types of commercial speech may be regulated without constitutional problems.

False or deceptive ads and ads for illegal products may be banned under the Federal Trade Commission Act and the Lanham Act. The FTC assumes primary responsibility for overseeing false and misleading advertising that makes deceptive material claims likely to mislead a reasonable consumer. FTC rules require publishers in all media to disclose paid content and advertisers to disclose paid endorsements. Native advertisements designed to resemble the unpaid content of the forum in which they appear may be deceptive and require disclosures. The FTC has also required disclosures involving "word-of-mouth" campaigns and employee endorsements. Puffery that would not affect the purchase decision of a reasonable consumer is not regulated as false advertising.

In rulings involving alcohol and tobacco, the Supreme Court has struck down absolute bans on advertising for legal products and services to legal consumers but allowed strict regulations when the ads reach minors. The Court has also disfavored government attempts to redirect or reduce consumption in cases involving advertising foodstuffs to children, gambling and prescription drugs. The FTC prohibits companies from tracking children's online behavior that allows them to target ads to interested children.

A variety of decisions by the Supreme Court distinguish the political speech of corporations from commercial speech. Corporations' political speech may enjoy full First Amendment protection.

The FTC punishes spam and requires truthful labeling of unsolicited commercial bulk texts and emails. To enforce its rules, the FTC uses both preventive and corrective measures, ranging from informal advisories and letters to litigated orders that require advertisers to cease and desist illegal practices or to provide corrective advertising and information. Through substantiation, the FTC requires companies to provide a factual basis for substantive product claims. The Federal Communications Commission regulates offensive broadcast advertising, and the Food and Drug Administration oversees some aspects of the labeling and promoting of foodstuffs. ■

CASES FOR STUDY

For study resources and a case archive go to **study.sagepub.com/medialaw6e**.

THINKING ABOUT IT

The two case excerpts that follow address the regulation of commercial speech and whether specific regulations are consistent with the First Amendment. The first is the U.S. Supreme Court case that established the test for answering that question. In the second case, the U.S. Supreme Court declines to apply that test and shifts toward the scrutiny it employs in "pure" speech cases. As you read these case excerpts, keep the following questions in mind:

- What are the circumstances surrounding each case?

- Specifically, what type of speech is involved, and in what ways is it intermingled with commerce?

- What is the nature of the regulations being challenged?

- What is the state interest in each case? Are those interests legitimate?

- How does the Court's review in *Sorrell* differ from the test established by *Central Hudson*? What implications does this difference have for First Amendment protection of commercial speech?

Central Hudson Gas & Electric Corp. v. Public Service Commission of New York
SUPREME COURT OF THE UNITED STATES
447 U.S. 557 (1980)

JUSTICE LEWIS POWELL delivered the Court's opinion:

This case presents the question whether a regulation of the Public Service Commission of the State of New York violates the First and Fourteenth Amendments because it completely bans promotional advertising by an electrical utility.

In December, 1973, the Commission, appellee here, ordered electric utilities in New York State to cease all advertising that "promot[es] the use of electricity." The order was based on the Commission's finding that "the interconnected utility system in New York State does not have sufficient fuel stocks or sources of supply to continue furnishing all customer demands for the 1973–1974 winter."

Three years later, when the fuel shortage had eased, the Commission requested comments from the public on its proposal to continue the ban on promotional advertising. Central Hudson Gas & Electric Corp., the appellant in this case, opposed the ban on First Amendment grounds. After reviewing the public comments, the Commission extended the prohibition in a Policy Statement issued on February 25, 1977.

The Policy Statement divided advertising expenses "into two broad categories: promotional—advertising intended to stimulate the purchase of utility services . . . and institutional and informational, a broad category inclusive of all advertising not clearly intended to promote sales." The Commission declared all promotional advertising contrary to the national policy of conserving energy. It acknowledged that the ban is not a perfect vehicle for conserving energy. For example, the Commission's order prohibits promotional advertising to develop consumption during periods when demand for electricity is low. By limiting growth in "off-peak" consumption, the ban limits the "beneficial side effects" of such growth in terms of more efficient use of existing powerplants. And since oil dealers are not under the Commission's jurisdiction and thus remain free to advertise, it was recognized that the ban can achieve only "piecemeal conservationism." Still, the Commission adopted the restriction because it was deemed likely to "result in some dampening of unnecessary growth" in energy consumption.

The Commission's order explicitly permitted "informational" advertising designed to encourage "shifts of consumption" from peak demand times to periods of low electricity demand. Informational advertising would not seek to increase aggregate consumption, but would invite a leveling of demand throughout any given 24-hour period. The agency offered to review "specific proposals by the companies for specifically described [advertising] programs that meet these criteria."

When it rejected requests for rehearing on the Policy Statement, the Commission supplemented its rationale for the advertising ban. The agency observed that additional electricity probably would be more expensive to produce than existing output. Because electricity rates in New York were not then based on marginal cost, the Commission feared that additional power would be priced below the actual cost of generation. The additional electricity would be subsidized by all consumers through generally higher rates. The state agency also thought that promotional advertising would give "misleading signals" to the public by appearing to encourage energy consumption at a time when conservation is needed. . . .

The Commission's order restricts only commercial speech, that is, expression related solely to the economic interests of the speaker and its audience. The First Amendment, as applied to the States through the Fourteenth Amendment, protects commercial speech from unwarranted governmental regulation. Commercial expression not only serves the economic interest of the speaker, but also assists consumers and furthers the societal interest in the fullest possible dissemination of information. In applying the First Amendment to this area, we have rejected the "highly paternalistic" view that government has complete power to suppress or regulate commercial speech. . . .

Nevertheless, our decisions have recognized "the 'commonsense' distinction between speech proposing a commercial transaction, which occurs in an area traditionally subject to government regulation, and other varieties of speech." . . . The Constitution therefore accords a lesser protection to commercial speech than to other constitutionally guaranteed expression. The protection available for particular commercial expression turns on the nature both of the expression and of the governmental interests served by its regulation.

The First Amendment's concern for commercial speech is based on the informational function of advertising. Consequently, there can be no constitutional objection to the suppression of commercial messages that do not accurately inform the public about lawful activity. The government may ban forms of communication more likely to deceive the public than to inform it, or commercial speech related to illegal activity.

If the communication is neither misleading nor related to unlawful activity, the government's power is more circumscribed. The State must assert a substantial interest to be achieved by restrictions on commercial speech. Moreover, the regulatory technique must be in proportion to that interest. The limitation on expression must be designed carefully to achieve the State's goal. Compliance with this requirement may be measured by two criteria. First, the restriction must directly advance the state interest involved; the regulation may not be sustained if it provides only ineffective or remote support for the government's purpose. Second, if the governmental interest could be served as well by a more limited restriction on commercial speech, the excessive restrictions cannot survive. . . .

The second criterion recognizes that the First Amendment mandates that speech restrictions be "narrowly drawn." The regulatory technique may extend only as far as the interest it serves. The State cannot regulate speech that poses no danger to the asserted state interest, nor can it completely suppress information when narrower restrictions on expression would serve its interest as well. . . .

In this case, the Commission's prohibition acts directly against the promotional activities of Central Hudson, and, to the extent the limitations are unnecessary to serve the State's interest, they are invalid. . . .

In commercial speech cases, then, a four-part analysis has developed. At the outset, we must determine whether the expression is protected by the First Amendment. For commercial speech to come within that provision, it at least must concern lawful activity and not be misleading. Next, we ask whether the asserted governmental interest is substantial. If both inquiries yield positive answers, we must determine whether the regulation directly advances the governmental interest asserted, and whether it is not more extensive than is necessary to serve that interest.

We now apply this four-step analysis for commercial speech to the Commission's arguments in support of its ban on promotional advertising.

The Commission does not claim that the expression at issue either is inaccurate or relates to unlawful activity. Yet the New York Court of Appeals questioned whether Central Hudson's advertising is protected commercial speech. Because appellant holds a monopoly over the sale of electricity in its service area, the state court suggested that the Commission's order restricts no commercial speech of any worth. The court stated that advertising in a "noncompetitive market" could not improve the decisionmaking of consumers. The court saw no constitutional problem with barring commercial speech that it viewed as conveying little useful information.

This reasoning falls short of establishing that appellant's advertising is not commercial speech protected by the First Amendment. Monopoly over the supply of a product provides no protection from competition with substitutes for that product. . . .

Even in monopoly markets, the suppression of advertising reduces the information available for consumer decisions and thereby defeats the purpose of the First Amendment. The New York court's argument appears to assume that the providers of a monopoly service or product are willing to pay for wholly ineffective advertising. Most businesses—even regulated monopolies—are unlikely to underwrite promotional advertising that is of no interest or use to consumers. Indeed, a monopoly enterprise legitimately may wish to inform the public that it has developed new services or terms of doing business. A consumer may need information to aid his decision whether or not to use the monopoly service at all, or how much of the service he should purchase. In the absence of factors that would distort the decision to advertise, we may assume that the willingness of a business to promote its products reflects a belief that consumers are interested in the advertising. Since no such extraordinary conditions have been identified in this case, appellant's monopoly position does not alter the First Amendment's protection for its commercial speech.

The Commission offers two state interests as justifications for the ban on promotional advertising. The first concerns energy conservation. Any increase in demand for electricity—during peak or off-peak periods—means greater consumption of energy. The Commission argues, and the New York court agreed, that the State's interest in conserving energy is sufficient to support suppression of advertising designed to increase consumption of electricity. In view of our country's dependence on energy resources beyond our control, no one can doubt the importance of energy conservation. Plainly, therefore, the state interest asserted is substantial.

The Commission also argues that promotional advertising will aggravate inequities caused by the failure to base the utilities' rates on marginal cost. The utilities argued to the Commission that if they could promote the use of electricity in periods of low demand, they would improve their utilization of generating capacity. The Commission responded that promotion of off-peak consumption also would increase consumption during peak periods. If peak demand were to rise, the absence of marginal cost rates would mean that the rates charged for the additional power would not reflect the true costs of expanding production. Instead, the extra costs would be borne by all consumers through higher overall rates. Without promotional advertising, the Commission stated, this inequitable turn of events would be less likely to occur. The choice among rate structures involves difficult and important questions of economic supply and distributional fairness. The State's concern that rates be fair and efficient represents a clear and substantial governmental interest.

Next, we focus on the relationship between the State's interests and the advertising ban. Under this criterion, the Commission's laudable concern over the equity and efficiency of appellant's rates does not provide a constitutionally adequate reason for restricting protected speech. The link between the advertising prohibition and appellant's rate structure is, at most, tenuous. The impact of promotional advertising on the equity of appellant's rates is highly speculative. Advertising to increase off-peak usage would have to increase peak usage, while other factors that directly affect the fairness and efficiency of appellant's rates remained constant. Such conditional and remote eventualities simply cannot justify silencing appellant's promotional advertising.

In contrast, the State's interest in energy conservation is directly advanced by the Commission order at issue here. There is an immediate connection between advertising and demand for electricity. Central Hudson would not contest the advertising ban unless it believed that promotion would increase its sales. Thus, we find a direct link between the state interest in conservation and the Commission's order.

We come finally to the critical inquiry in this case: whether the Commission's complete suppression of speech ordinarily protected by the First Amendment is no more extensive than necessary to further the State's interest in energy conservation. The Commission's order reaches all promotional advertising, regardless of the impact of the touted service on overall energy use. But the energy conservation rationale, as important as it is, cannot justify suppressing information about electric devices or services that

would cause no net increase in total energy use. In addition, no showing has been made that a more limited restriction on the content of promotional advertising would not serve adequately the State's interests.

Appellant insists that, but for the ban, it would advertise products and services that use energy efficiently. These include the "heat pump," which both parties acknowledge to be a major improvement in electric heating, and the use of electric heat as a "backup" to solar and other heat sources. Although the Commission has questioned the efficiency of electric heating before this Court, neither the Commission's Policy Statement nor its order denying rehearing made findings on this issue. In the absence of authoritative findings to the contrary, we must credit as within the realm of possibility the claim that electric heat can be an efficient alternative in some circumstances.

The Commission's order prevents appellant from promoting electric services that would reduce energy use by diverting demand from less efficient sources, or that would consume roughly the same amount of energy as do alternative sources. In neither situation would the utility's advertising endanger conservation or mislead the public. To the extent that the Commission's order suppresses speech that in no way impairs the State's interest in energy conservation, the Commission's order violates the First and Fourteenth Amendments, and must be invalidated.

The Commission also has not demonstrated that its interest in conservation cannot be protected adequately by more limited regulation of appellant's commercial expression. To further its policy of conservation, the Commission could attempt to restrict the format and content of Central Hudson's advertising. It might, for example, require that the advertisements include information about the relative efficiency and expense of the offered service, both under current conditions and for the foreseeable future. In the absence of a showing that more limited speech regulation would be ineffective, we cannot approve the complete suppression of Central Hudson's advertising.

Our decision today in no way disparages the national interest in energy conservation. We accept without reservation the argument that conservation, as well as the development of alternative energy sources, is an imperative national goal. Administrative bodies empowered to regulate electric utilities have the authority—and indeed the duty—to take appropriate action to further this goal. When, however, such action involves the suppression of speech, the First and Fourteenth Amendments require that the restriction be no more extensive than is necessary to serve the state interest. In this case, the record before us fails to show that the total ban on promotional advertising meets this requirement.

Accordingly, the judgment of the New York Court of Appeals is

Reversed. . . .

JUSTICE WILLIAM REHNQUIST, dissenting:

The Court today invalidates an order issued by the New York Public Service Commission designed to promote a policy that has been declared to be of critical national concern. The order was issued by the Commission in 1973 in response to the Mideastern oil embargo crisis. It prohibits electric corporations "from promoting the use of electricity through the use of advertising, subsidy payments . . . or employee incentives." Although the immediate crisis created by the oil embargo has subsided, the ban on promotional advertising remains in effect. The regulation was re-examined by the New York Public Service Commission in 1977. Its constitutionality was subsequently upheld by the New York Court of Appeals, which concluded that the paramount national interest in energy conservation justified its retention.

The Court's asserted justification for invalidating the New York law is the public interest discerned by the Court to underlie the First Amendment in the free flow of commercial information. Prior to this Court's recent decision in *Virginia Pharmacy Board v. Virginia Citizens Consumer Council,* however, commercial speech was afforded no protection under the First Amendment whatsoever. Given what seems to me full recognition of the holding of *Virginia Pharmacy Board* that commercial speech is entitled to

some degree of First Amendment protection, I think the Court is nonetheless incorrect in invalidating the carefully considered state ban on promotional advertising in light of pressing national and state energy needs. . . .

This Court has previously recognized that, although commercial speech may be entitled to First Amendment protection, that protection is not as extensive as that accorded to the advocacy of ideas. . . . "We have not discarded the 'common-sense' distinction between speech proposing a commercial transaction, which occurs in an area traditionally subject to government regulation, and other varieties of speech. To require a parity of constitutional protection for commercial and noncommercial speech alike could invite dilution, simply by a leveling process, of the force of the Amendment's guarantee with respect to the latter kind of speech. Rather than subject the First Amendment to such a devitalization, we instead have afforded commercial speech a limited measure of protection, commensurate with its subordinate position in the scale of First Amendment values, while allowing modes of regulation that might be impermissible in the realm of noncommercial expression."

The Court's decision today fails to give due deference to this subordinate position of commercial speech. The Court in so doing returns to the bygone era . . . in which it was common practice for this Court to strike down economic regulations adopted by a State based on the Court's own notions of the most appropriate means for the State to implement its considered policies.

I had thought by now it had become well established that a State has broad discretion in imposing economic regulations. . . . The State of New York has determined here that economic realities require the grant of monopoly status to public utilities in order to distribute efficiently the services they provide, and in granting utilities such status it has made them subject to an extensive regulatory scheme. When the State adopted this scheme and when its Public Service Commission issued its initial ban on promotional advertising in 1973, commercial speech had not been held to fall within the scope of the First Amendment at all. . . .

The Court today holds not only that commercial speech is entitled to First Amendment protection, but also that when it is protected a State may not regulate it unless its reason for doing so amounts to a "substantial" governmental interest, its regulation "directly advances" that interest, and its manner of regulation is "not more extensive than necessary" to serve the interest. The test adopted by the Court thus elevates the protection accorded commercial speech that falls within the scope of the First Amendment to a level that is virtually indistinguishable from that of non-commercial speech. . . .

An ostensible justification for striking down New York's ban on promotional advertising is that this Court has previously "rejected the 'highly paternalistic' view that government has complete power to suppress or regulate commercial speech. '[P]eople will perceive their own best interests if only they are well enough informed and . . . the best means to that end is to open the channels of communication, rather than to close them. . . .'" Whatever the merits of this view, I think the Court has carried its logic too far here. . . .

While it is true that an important objective of the First Amendment is to foster the free flow of information, identification of speech that falls within its protection is not aided by the metaphorical reference to a "marketplace of ideas." There is no reason for believing that the marketplace of ideas is free from market imperfections any more than there is to believe that the invisible hand will always lead to optimum economic decisions in the commercial market. . . . Indeed, many types of speech have been held to fall outside the scope of the First Amendment, thereby subject to governmental regulation, despite this Court's references to a marketplace of ideas. . . .

I remain of the view that the Court unlocked a Pandora's Box when it "elevated" commercial speech to the level of traditional political speech by according it First Amendment protection in *Virginia Pharmacy Board v. Virginia Citizens Consumer Council.* The line between "commercial speech," and the kind of speech that those who drafted the First Amendment had in mind, may not be a technically or intellectually easy

one to draw, but it surely produced far fewer problems than has the development of judicial doctrine in this area since *Virginia Pharmacy Board.* . . .

The notion that more speech is the remedy to expose falsehood and fallacies is wholly out of place in the commercial bazaar, where if applied logically the remedy of one who was defrauded would be merely a statement, available upon request, reciting the Latin maxim *"caveat emptor."* But since "fraudulent speech" in this area is to be remediable under *Virginia Pharmacy Board*, the remedy of one defrauded is a lawsuit or an agency proceeding based on common-law notions of fraud that are separated by a world of difference from the realm of politics and government. What time, legal decisions, and common sense have so widely severed, I declined to join in *Virginia Pharmacy Board*, and regret now to see the Court reaping the seeds that it there sowed. For in a democracy, the economic is subordinate to the political, a lesson that our ancestors learned long ago, and that our descendants will undoubtedly have to relearn many years hence.

The Court concedes that the state interest in energy conservation is plainly substantial, as is the State's concern that its rates be fair and efficient. It also concedes that there is a direct link between the Commission's ban on promotional advertising and the State's interest in conservation. The Court nonetheless strikes down the ban on promotional advertising because the Commission has failed to demonstrate, under the final part of the Court's four-part test, that its regulation is no more extensive than necessary to serve the State's interest. In reaching this conclusion, the Court conjures up potential advertisements that a utility might make that conceivably would result in net energy savings. The Court does not indicate that the New York Public Service Commission has in fact construed its ban on "promotional" advertising to preclude the dissemination of information that clearly would result in a net energy savings, nor does it even suggest that the Commission has been confronted with and rejected such an advertising proposal. The final part of the Court's test thus leaves room for so many hypothetical "better" ways that any ingenious lawyer will surely seize on one of them to secure the invalidation of what the state agency actually did. . . .

Ordinarily it is the role of the State Public Service Commission to make factual determinations concerning whether a device or service will result in a net energy savings and, if so, whether and to what extent state law permits dissemination of information about the device or service. Otherwise, as here, this Court will have no factual basis for its assertions. And the State will never have an opportunity to consider the issue and thus to construe its law in a manner consistent with the Federal Constitution. . . .

It is, in my view, inappropriate for the Court to invalidate the State's ban on commercial advertising here, based on its speculation that in some cases the advertising may result in a net savings in electrical energy use, and in the cases in which it is clear a net energy savings would result from utility advertising, the Public Service Commission would apply its ban so as to proscribe such advertising. Even assuming that the Court's speculation is correct, I do not think it follows that facial invalidation of the ban is the appropriate course. . . .

For the foregoing reasons, I would affirm the judgment of the New York Court of Appeals.

Sorrell v. IMS Health Inc.
SUPREME COURT OF THE UNITED STATES
131 S. Ct. 2653 (2011)

Justice Anthony KENNEDY delivered the Court's opinion:

. . . Pharmaceutical manufacturers promote their drugs to doctors through a process called "detailing." This often involves a scheduled visit to a doctor's office to persuade the doctor to prescribe a particular pharmaceutical. Detailers bring drug samples as well as medical studies that explain the "details" and potential advantages of various prescription drugs. Interested physicians listen, ask questions, and receive followup data. Salespersons can be more effective when they know the background and purchasing preferences of their clientele, and pharmaceutical salespersons are no exception. Knowledge of a physician's prescription practices—called "prescriber-identifying information"—enables a detailer better to ascertain which doctors are likely to be interested in a particular drug and how best to present a particular sales message. Detailing is an expensive undertaking, so pharmaceutical companies most often use it to promote high-profit brand-name drugs protected by patent. Once a brand-name drug's patent expires, less expensive bioequivalent generic alternatives are manufactured and sold.

Pharmacies, as a matter of business routine and federal law, receive prescriber-identifying information when processing prescriptions. Many pharmacies sell this information to "data miners," firms that analyze prescriber-identifying information and produce reports on prescriber behavior. Data miners lease these reports to pharmaceutical manufacturers subject to nondisclosure agreements. Detailers, who represent the manufacturers, then use the reports to refine their marketing tactics and increase sales.

In 2007, Vermont enacted the Prescription Confidentiality Law. The measure is also referred to as Act 80. It has several components. The central provision of the present case is § 4631(d).

> A health insurer, a self-insured employer, an electronic transmission intermediary, a pharmacy, or other similar entity shall not sell, license, or exchange for value regulated records containing prescriber-identifiable information, nor permit the use of regulated records containing prescriber-identifiable information for marketing or promoting a prescription drug, unless the prescriber consents. . . . Pharmaceutical manufacturers and pharmaceutical marketers shall not

use prescriber-identifiable information for marketing or promoting a prescription drug unless the prescriber consents. . . .

The quoted provision has three component parts. The provision begins by prohibiting pharmacies, health insurers, and similar entities from selling prescriber-identifying information, absent the prescriber's consent. The parties here dispute whether this clause applies to all sales or only to sales for marketing. The provision then goes on to prohibit pharmacies, health insurers, and similar entities from allowing prescriber-identifying information to be used for marketing, unless the prescriber consents. This prohibition in effect bars pharmacies from disclosing the information for marketing purposes. Finally, the provision's second sentence bars pharmaceutical manufacturers and pharmaceutical marketers from using prescriber-identifying information for marketing, again absent the prescriber's consent. The Vermont attorney general may pursue civil remedies against violators.

Separate statutory provisions elaborate the scope of the prohibitions. . . . "Marketing" is defined to include "advertising, promotion, or any activity" that is "used to influence sales or the market share of a prescription drug." § 4631(d) further provides that Vermont's Department of Health must allow "a prescriber to give consent for his or her identifying information to be used for the purposes" identified. . . . Finally, the Act's prohibitions on sale, disclosure, and use are subject to a list of exceptions. For example, prescriber-identifying information may be disseminated or used for "health care research"; to enforce "compliance" with health insurance formularies, or preferred drug lists; for "care management educational communications provided to" patients on such matters as "treatment options"; for law enforcement operations; and for purposes "otherwise provided by law."

Act 80 also authorized funds for an "evidence-based prescription drug education program" designed to provide doctors and others with "information and education on the therapeutic and cost-effective utilization of prescription drugs." An express aim of the program is to advise prescribers "about commonly used brand-name drugs for which the patent has expired" or will soon expire. Similar efforts to promote the use of generic pharmaceuticals are sometimes referred to as "counter-detailing." The counter-detailer's recommended substitute may be an older, less expensive drug and not a bioequivalent of the brand-name drug the physician might otherwise prescribe. Like the pharmaceutical manufacturers whose efforts they hope to resist, counterdetailers in some states use prescriber-identifying information to increase their effectiveness. States themselves may supply the prescriber-identifying information used in these programs. . . .

Act 80 was accompanied by legislative findings. Vermont found, for example, that the "goals of marketing programs are often in conflict with the goals of the state" and that the "marketplace for ideas on medicine safety and effectiveness is frequently one-sided in that brand-name companies invest in expensive pharmaceutical marketing campaigns to doctors." Detailing, in the legislature's view, caused doctors to make decisions based on "incomplete and biased information." Because they "are unable to take the time to research the quickly changing pharmaceutical market," Vermont doctors "rely on information provided by pharmaceutical representatives." The legislature further found that detailing increases the cost of health care and health insurance; encourages hasty and excessive reliance on brand-name drugs, before the profession has observed their effectiveness as compared with older and less expensive generic alternatives; and fosters disruptive and repeated marketing visits tantamount to harassment. . . . Use of prescriber-identifying data also helps detailers shape their messages by "tailoring" their "presentations to individual prescriber styles, preferences, and attitudes."

The present case involves two consolidated suits. One was brought by three Vermont data miners, the other by an association of pharmaceutical manufacturers that produce brand-name drugs. . . . Contending that § 4631(d) violates their First Amendment rights as incorporated by the Fourteenth Amendment, the respondents sought declaratory and injunctive relief. . . .

After a bench trial, the United States District Court for the District of Vermont denied relief. The District Court found that "[p]harmaceutical manufacturers are essentially the only paying customers of the data vendor industry" and that, because detailing unpatented generic drugs is not "cost-effective," pharmaceutical sales representatives "detail only branded drugs." . . . The United States Court of Appeals for the Second Circuit reversed and remanded. It held that § 4631(d) violates the First Amendment by burdening the speech of pharmaceutical marketers and data miners without an adequate justification. . . . The decision of the Second Circuit is in conflict with decisions of the United States Court of Appeals for the First Circuit concerning similar legislation enacted by Maine and New Hampshire. Recognizing a division of authority regarding the constitutionality of state statutes, this Court granted certiorari.

The beginning point is the text of § 4631(d). In the proceedings below, Vermont stated that the first sentence . . . prohibits pharmacies and other regulated entities from selling or disseminating prescriber-identifying information for marketing. The information, in other words, could be sold or given away for purposes other than marketing. . . . At oral argument in this Court, however, the state for the first time advanced an alternative reading . . . namely, that pharmacies, health insurers, and similar entities may not sell prescriber-identifying information for any purpose, subject to the statutory exceptions set out [in the law]. It might be argued that the state's newfound interpretation comes too late in the day. . . . For the state to change its position is particularly troubling in a First Amendment case, where plaintiffs have a special interest in obtaining a prompt adjudication of their rights, despite potential ambiguities of state law.

In any event, § 4631(d) cannot be sustained even under the interpretation the state now adopts. As a consequence this Court can assume that the opening clause . . . prohibits pharmacies, health insurers, and similar entities from selling prescriber-identifying information, subject to the statutory exceptions set out . . . Under that reading, pharmacies may sell the information to private or academic researchers, but not, for example, to pharmaceutical marketers. There

is no dispute as to the remainder of § 4631. It prohibits pharmacies, health insurers, and similar entities from disclosing or otherwise allowing prescriber-identifying information to be used for marketing. And it bars pharmaceutical manufacturers and detailers from using the information for marketing. The questions now are whether § 4631(d) must be tested by heightened judicial scrutiny and, if so, whether the state can justify the law.

On its face, Vermont's law enacts content- and speaker-based restrictions on the sale, disclosure, and use of prescriber-identifying information. The provision first forbids sale subject to exceptions based in large part on the content of a purchaser's speech. For example, those who wish to engage in certain "educational communications" may purchase the information. The measure then bars any disclosure when recipient speakers will use the information for marketing. Finally, the provision's second sentence prohibits pharmaceutical manufacturers from using the information for marketing. The statute thus disfavors marketing, that is, speech with a particular content. More than that, the statute disfavors specific speakers, namely pharmaceutical manufacturers. As a result of these content- and speaker-based rules, detailers cannot obtain prescriber-identifying information, even though the information may be purchased or acquired by other speakers with diverse purposes and viewpoints. Detailers are likewise barred from using the information for marketing, even though the information may be used by a wide range of other speakers. For example, it appears that Vermont could supply academic organizations with prescriber-identifying information to use in countering the messages of brand-name pharmaceutical manufacturers and in promoting the prescription of generic drugs. But § 4631(d) leaves detailers no means of purchasing, acquiring, or using prescriber-identifying information. The law on its face burdens disfavored speech by disfavored speakers.

Any doubt that § 4631(d) imposes an aimed, content-based burden on detailers is dispelled by the record and by formal legislative findings. As the District Court noted, "[p]harmaceutical manufacturers are essentially the only paying customers of the data vendor industry"; and the almost invariable rule is that detailing by pharmaceutical manufacturers is in support of brand-name drugs. Vermont's law thus has the effect of preventing detailers—and only detailers—from communicating with physicians in an effective and informative manner. Formal legislative findings accompanying § 4631(d) confirm that the law's express purpose and practical effect are to diminish the effectiveness of marketing by manufacturers of brand-name drugs. . . . The legislature designed § 4631(d) to target those speakers and their messages for disfavored treatment. "In its practical operation," Vermont's law "goes even beyond mere content discrimination, to actual viewpoint discrimination." Given the legislature's expressed statement of purpose, it is apparent that § 4631(d) imposes burdens that are based on the content of speech and that are aimed at a particular viewpoint.

Act 80 is designed to impose a specific, content-based burden on protected expression. It follows that heightened judicial scrutiny is warranted. The Court has recognized that the "distinction between laws burdening and laws banning speech is but a matter of degree" and that the "Government's content-based burdens must satisfy the same rigorous scrutiny as its content-based bans."

The First Amendment requires heightened scrutiny whenever the government creates "a regulation of speech because of disagreement with the message it conveys." . . . Even if the hypothetical measure on its face appeared neutral as to content and speaker, its purpose to suppress speech and its unjustified burdens on expression would render it unconstitutional. Commercial speech is no exception. A "consumer's concern for the free flow of commercial speech often may be far keener than his concern for urgent political dialogue." That reality has great relevance in the fields of medicine and public health, where information can save lives.

The State argues that heightened judicial scrutiny is unwarranted because its law is a mere commercial regulation. It is true that restrictions on protected expression are distinct from restrictions on economic activity or, more generally, on nonexpressive conduct. It is also true that the First Amendment does not

prevent restrictions directed at commerce or conduct from imposing incidental burdens on speech. . . . But § 4631(d) imposes more than an incidental burden on protected expression. Both on its face and in its practical operation, Vermont's law imposes a burden based on the content of speech and the identity of the speaker. While the burdened speech results from an economic motive, so too does a great deal of vital expression. Vermont's law does not simply have an effect on speech, but is directed at certain content and is aimed at particular speakers. . . .

Vermont further argues that § 4631(d) regulates not speech but simply access to information. Prescriber-identifying information was generated in compliance with a legal mandate, the state argues, and so could be considered a kind of governmental information. . . . An individual's right to speak is implicated when information he or she possesses is subjected to "restraints on the way in which the information might be used" or disseminated. . . . It is true that the respondents here . . . do not themselves possess information whose disclosure has been curtailed. That information, however, is in the hands of pharmacies and other private entities. There is no question that the "threat of prosecution . . . hangs over their heads." . . . [R]estrictions on the disclosure of government-held information can facilitate or burden the expression of potential recipients and so transgress the First Amendment. Vermont's law imposes a content- and speaker-based burden on respondents' own speech. That consideration . . . requires heightened judicial scrutiny.

The state also contends that heightened judicial scrutiny is unwarranted in this case because sales, transfer, and use of prescriber-identifying information are conduct, not speech. Consistent with that submission, the United States Court of Appeals for the First Circuit has characterized prescriber-identifying information as a mere "commodity" with no greater entitlement to First Amendment protection than "beef jerky." In contrast the courts below concluded that a prohibition on the sale of prescriber-identifying information is a content-based rule akin to a ban on the sale of cookbooks, laboratory results, or train schedules.

This Court has held that the creation and dissemination of information are speech within the meaning of the First Amendment. Facts, after all, are the beginning point for much of the speech that is most essential to advance human knowledge and to conduct human affairs. There is thus a strong argument that prescriber-identifying information is speech for First Amendment purposes.

The state asks for an exception to the rule that information is speech, but there is no need to consider that request in this case. The state has imposed content- and speaker-based restrictions on the availability and use of prescriber-identifying information. So long as they do not engage in marketing, many speakers can obtain and use the information. But detailers cannot. Vermont's statute could be compared with a law prohibiting trade magazines from purchasing or using ink. Like that hypothetical law, § 4631(d) imposes a speaker- and content-based burden on protected expression, and that circumstance is sufficient to justify application of heightened scrutiny. As a consequence, this case can be resolved even assuming, as the state argues, that prescriber-identifying information is a mere commodity.

In the ordinary case it is all but dispositive to conclude that a law is content-based and, in practice, viewpoint-discriminatory. The state argues that a different analysis applies here because, assuming § 4631(d) burdens speech at all, it at most burdens only commercial speech. As in previous cases, however, the outcome is the same whether a special commercial speech inquiry or a stricter form of judicial scrutiny is applied. For the same reason there is no need to determine whether all speech hampered by § 4631(d) is commercial, as our cases have used that term.

Under a commercial speech inquiry, it is the state's burden to justify its content-based law as consistent with the First Amendment. To sustain the targeted, content-based burden § 4631(d) imposes on protected expression, the state must show at least that the statute directly advances a substantial governmental interest and that the measure is drawn to achieve that interest. There must be a "fit between the legislature's ends and the means chosen to accomplish those ends." As in other contexts, these standards ensure not only that

the state's interests are proportional to the resulting burdens placed on speech but also that the law does not seek to suppress a disfavored message.

The state's asserted justifications for § 4631(d) come under two general headings. First, the state contends that its law is necessary to protect medical privacy, including physician confidentiality, avoidance of harassment, and the integrity of the doctor-patient relationship. Second, the state argues that § 4631(d) is integral to the achievement of policy objectives—namely, improved public health and reduced health-care costs. Neither justification withstands scrutiny.

Vermont argues that its physicians have a "reasonable expectation" that their prescriber-identifying information "will not be used for purposes other than . . . filling and processing" prescriptions. It may be assumed that, for many reasons, physicians have an interest in keeping their prescription decisions confidential. But § 4631(d) is not drawn to serve that interest. Under Vermont's law, pharmacies may share prescriber-identifying information with anyone for any reason save one: They must not allow the information to be used for marketing. Exceptions further allow pharmacies to sell prescriber-identifying information for certain purposes, including "health care research." § 4631(e). And the measure permits insurers, researchers, journalists, the state itself, and others to use the information. . . .

Perhaps the state could have addressed physician confidentiality through "a more coherent policy." . . . But the state did not enact a statute with that purpose or design. Instead, Vermont made prescriber-identifying information available to an almost limitless audience. The explicit structure of the statute allows the information to be studied and used by all but a narrow class of disfavored speakers. Given the information's widespread availability and many permissible uses, the state's asserted interest in physician confidentiality does not justify the burden that § 4631(d) places on protected expression.

The State points out that it allows doctors to forgo the advantages of § 4631(d) by consenting to the sale, disclosure, and use of their prescriber-identifying information. See § 4631(c)(1). . . . Vermont has given its doctors a contrived choice: Either consent, which will allow your prescriber-identifying information to be disseminated and used without constraint; or, withhold consent, which will allow your information to be used by those speakers whose message the state supports. Section 4631(d) may offer a limited degree of privacy, but only on terms favorable to the speech the state prefers. . . . [T]he state has conditioned privacy on acceptance of a content-based rule that is not drawn to serve the state's asserted interest. To obtain the limited privacy allowed by § 4631(d), Vermont physicians are forced to acquiesce in the state's goal of burdening disfavored speech by disfavored speakers.

. . . Rules that burden protected expression may not be sustained when the options provided by the state are too narrow to advance legitimate interests or too broad to protect speech. As already explained, § 4631(d) permits extensive use of prescriber-identifying information and so does not advance the state's asserted interest in physician confidentiality. The limited range of available privacy options instead reflects the state's impermissible purpose to burden disfavored speech.

The state also contends that § 4631(d) protects doctors from "harassing sales behaviors." "Some doctors in Vermont are experiencing an undesired increase in the aggressiveness of pharmaceutical sales representatives," the Vermont Legislature found, "and a few have reported that they felt coerced and harassed." It is doubtful that concern for "a few" physicians who may have "felt coerced and harassed" by pharmaceutical marketers can sustain a broad content-based rule like § 4631(d). Many are those who must endure speech they do not like, but that is a necessary cost of freedom. In any event the State offers no explanation why remedies other than content-based rules would be inadequate. Physicians can, and often do, simply decline to meet with detailers, including detailers who use prescriber-identifying information. Doctors who wish to forgo detailing altogether are free to give "No Solicitation" or "No Detailing" instructions to their office managers or to receptionists at their places of work. . . .

Vermont argues that detailers' use of prescriber-identifying information undermines the doctor-patient relationship by allowing detailers to influence treatment decisions. According to the state, "unwanted pressure occurs" when doctors learn that their prescription decisions are being "monitored" by detailers. Some physicians accuse detailers of "spying" or of engaging in "underhanded" conduct in order to "subvert" prescription decisions. And Vermont claims that detailing makes people "anxious" about whether doctors have their patients' best interests at heart. But the state does not explain why detailers' use of prescriber-identifying information is more likely to prompt these objections than many other uses permitted by § 4631(d). In any event, this asserted interest is contrary to basic First Amendment principles. Speech remains protected even when it may "stir people to action," "move them to tears," or "inflict great pain." The more benign and, many would say, beneficial speech of pharmaceutical marketing is also entitled to the protection of the First Amendment. If pharmaceutical marketing affects treatment decisions, it does so because doctors find it persuasive. Absent circumstances far from those presented here, the fear that speech might persuade provides no lawful basis for quieting it.

The state contends that § 4631(d) advances important public policy goals by lowering the costs of medical services and promoting public health. If prescriber-identifying information were available for use by detailers, the state contends, then detailing would be effective in promoting brand-name drugs that are more expensive and less safe than generic alternatives. This logic is set out at length in the legislative findings accompanying § 4631(d). Yet at oral argument here, the state declined to acknowledge that § 4631(d)'s objective purpose and practical effect were to inhibit detailing and alter doctors' prescription decisions. The state's reluctance to embrace its own legislature's rationale reflects the vulnerability of its position.

While Vermont's stated policy goals may be proper, § 4631(d) does not advance them in a permissible way. As the Court of Appeals noted, the "state's own explanation of how" § 4631(d) "advances its interests cannot be said to be direct." The state seeks to achieve its policy objectives through the indirect means of restraining certain speech by certain speakers—that is, by diminishing detailers' ability to influence prescription decisions. Those who seek to censor or burden free expression often assert that disfavored speech has adverse effects. But the "fear that people would make bad decisions if given truthful information" cannot justify content-based burdens on speech. These precepts apply with full force when the audience, in this case prescribing physicians, consists of "sophisticated and experienced" consumers.

As Vermont's legislative findings acknowledge, the premise of § 4631(d) is that the force of speech can justify the government's attempts to stifle it. Indeed the state defends the law by insisting that "pharmaceutical marketing has a strong influence on doctors' prescribing practices." This reasoning is incompatible with the First Amendment. In an attempt to reverse a disfavored trend in public opinion, a state could not ban campaigning with slogans, picketing with signs, or marching during the daytime. Likewise the state may not seek to remove a popular but disfavored product from the marketplace by prohibiting truthful, nonmisleading advertisements that contain impressive endorsements or catchy jingles. That the state finds expression too persuasive does not permit it to quiet the speech or to burden its messengers.

The defect in Vermont's law is made clear by the fact that many listeners find detailing instructive. Indeed the record demonstrates that some Vermont doctors view targeted detailing based on prescriber-identifying information as "very helpful" because it allows detailers to shape their messages to each doctor's practice. Even the United States, which appeared here in support of Vermont, took care to dispute the state's "unwarranted view that the dangers of [n]ew drugs outweigh their benefits to patients." There are divergent views regarding detailing and the prescription of brand-name drugs. Under the Constitution, resolution of that debate must result from free and uninhibited speech. . . . The choice "between the dangers of suppressing information, and the dangers of its misuse if it is freely available," is one that "the First Amendment makes for us."

Vermont may be displeased that detailers who use prescriber-identifying information are effective in promoting brand-name drugs. The state can express

that view through its own speech. But a state's failure to persuade does not allow it to hamstring the opposition. The state may not burden the speech of others in order to tilt public debate in a preferred direction. "The commercial marketplace, like other spheres of our social and cultural life, provides a forum where ideas and information flourish. Some of the ideas and information are vital, some of slight worth. But the general rule is that the speaker and the audience, not the government, assess the value of the information presented."

It is true that content-based restrictions on protected expression are sometimes permissible, and that principle applies to commercial speech. Indeed the government's legitimate interest in protecting consumers from "commercial harms" explains "why commercial speech can be subject to greater governmental regulation than noncommercial speech." Here, however, Vermont has not shown that its law has a neutral justification. The state nowhere contends that detailing is false or misleading within the meaning of this Court's First Amendment precedents. Nor does the state argue that the provision challenged here will prevent false or misleading speech. The state's interest in burdening the speech of detailers instead turns on nothing more than a difference of opinion.

• • •

The capacity of technology to find and publish personal information, including records required by the government, presents serious and unresolved issues with respect to personal privacy and the dignity it seeks to secure. In considering how to protect those interests, however, the state cannot engage in content-based discrimination to advance its own side of a debate.

If Vermont's statute provided that prescriber-identifying information could not be sold or disclosed except in narrow circumstances then the state might have a stronger position. Here, however, the state gives possessors of the information broad discretion and wide latitude in disclosing the information, while at the same time restricting the information's use by some speakers and for some purposes, even while the state itself can use the information to counter the speech it seeks to suppress. Privacy is a concept too integral to the person and a right too essential to freedom to allow its manipulation to support just those ideas the government prefers.

When it enacted § 4631(d), the Vermont Legislature found that the "marketplace for ideas on medicine safety and effectiveness is frequently one-sided in that brand name companies invest in expensive pharmaceutical marketing campaigns to doctors." "The goals of marketing programs," the legislature said, "are often in conflict with the goals of the state." The text of § 4631(d), associated legislative findings, and the record developed in the District Court establish that Vermont enacted its law for this end. The state has burdened a form of protected expression that it found too persuasive. At the same time, the state has left unburdened those speakers whose messages are in accord with its own views. This the state cannot do.

The judgment of the Court of Appeals is affirmed. *It is so ordered.*

JUSTICE STEPHEN BREYER, with whom JUSTICE RUTH BADER GINSBURG and JUSTICE ELENA KAGAN join, dissenting.

The Vermont statute before us adversely affects expression in one, and only one, way. It deprives pharmaceutical and data-mining companies of data, collected pursuant to the government's regulatory mandate, that could help pharmaceutical companies create better sales messages. In my view, this effect on expression is inextricably related to a lawful governmental effort to regulate a commercial enterprise. The First Amendment does not require courts to apply a special "heightened" standard of review when reviewing such an effort. And, in any event, the statute meets the First Amendment standard this Court has previously applied when the government seeks to regulate commercial speech. For any or all of these reasons, the Court should uphold the statute as constitutional.

NOTES

Chapter 1

1. 505 U.S. 833, 854 (1992).

2. Alberto Luperon, *Election Law Expert: If Electoral College Abandons Trump, May Go Against Rule of Law*, Law Newz, Nov. 25, 2016, lawnewz.com/high-profile/election-law-expert-if-electoral-college-abandons-trump-may-go-against-rule-of-law.

   Garrett Epps, *The Electoral College Wasn't Meant to Overturn Elections*, Atlantic, Nov. 27, 2016, www.theatlantic.com/politics/archive/2016/11/the-electoral-college-shouldnt-save-us-from-trump/508817.

3. 2 U.S.C. § 441b (McCain–Feingold Act).

4. FEC v. Wisconsin Right to Life Inc., 551 U.S. 449, 534 (2007) (Souter, J., dissenting).

5. Citizens United v. FEC, 530 F. Supp. 2d 274 (D.D.C. 2008).

6. 558 U.S. 310 (2010).

7. *See* Dr. Seuss, The Lorax (1971). (Dr. Seuss is Theodor Seuss Geisel's pseudonym.)

8. Kenneth Grady, *The Election, the Rule of Law, and the Role of Lawyers*, SeytLines, Nov. 17, 2016, www.seytlines.com/2016/11/the-election-the-rule-of-law-and-the-role-of-lawyers.

9. Marbury v. Madison, 5 U.S. (1 Cranch) 137, 163 (1803).

10. *See, e.g.,* John Gardner, *The Supposed Formality of the Rule of Law, in* Law as a Leap of Faith 205 (2012).

11. Moeen H. Chema, *The Politics of the Rule of Law,* 24 Mich. St. J. Int'l L. 449, 492 (2015).

12. *See, e.g.,* Kristina Davis, *El Cajon Protesters Ask Judge for Right to Assemble,* San Diego Union-Trib., Oct. 26, 2016, www.sandiegouniontribune.com/news/courts/sd-me-unlawful-assembly.

13. Cal. Penal Code §§ 407 & 408 (unlawful assembly). *See also* Cal. Penal Code, §§ 409 & 416 (failure to disperse).

14. Kristina Davis, *Arrests of Protesters at Shooting Site in El Cajon Can Continue, Judge Rules,* L.A. Times, Nov. 5, 2016, www.latimes.com/local/lanow/la-me-ln-alfred-olango-ruling.

15. Chief Rabbi Lord Sacks, *Passover Tells Us: Teach Your Children Well,* HuffPost Blog, Apr. 17, 2011, www.huffingtonpost.com/chief-rabbi-lord-sacks/passover-message-for-huff_b_849623.html.

16. Planned Parenthood of Southeastern Pa. v. Casey, 505 U.S. 833, 854 (1992).

17. Kenneth Grady, *The Election, the Rule of Law, and the Role of Lawyers*, SeytLines, Nov. 17, 2016, www.seytlines.com/2016/11/the-election-the-rule-of-law-and-the-role-of-lawyers.

18. Johnson v. Department of Justice, 341 P.3d 1075, 1082 (Cal. 2015).

19. 5 U.S. 137, 177 (1803).

20. *See, e.g.,* David Ardia, *Free Speech Savior or Shield for Scoundrels? An Empirical Study of Intermediary Immunity Under Section 230,* Citizen Media L. Project Blog, June 30, 2010, www.citmedialaw.org/blog.

21. *President Barack Obama's State of the Union Address,* Jan. 28, 2014, whitehouse.gov.

22. Exec. Order No. 13769, *Protecting the Nation From Foreign Terrorist Entry Into the United States,* Jan. 27, 2017, www.whitehouse.gov/the-press-office/2017/01/27/executive-order-protecting-nation-foreign-terrorist-entry-united-states. *See also* Alicia A. Caldwell & Jill Colvin, *A Look at Trump's Executive Order on Refugees, Immigration,* AP, Jan. 30, 2017, www.usnews.com/news/politics/articles/2017-01-27/a-look-at-trumps-executive-order-on-refugees-immigration.

23. Washington v. Trump, No. 17-35105 (9th Cir. Feb. 9, 2017) (per curiam) cdn.ca9.uscourts.gov/datastore/opinions/2017/02/09/17-35105.pdf.

24. Aktepe v. United States, 105 F.3d 1400, 1402 (11th Cir. 1997) (citing Japan Whaling Ass'n v. American Cetacean Soc., 478 U.S. 221, 230 [1986]).

25. Stephanie Condon, *After 148 Years, Mississippi Finally Ratifies 13th Amendment,* CBS News, Feb. 18, 2013, www.cbsnews

.com/8301-250_162-57569880/
after-148-years-mississippi-finally-
ratifies-13th-amendment-which-
banned-slavery/.

26. Wa. St. Const., art. 1, § 7.

27. K.E. Gill, *Visual Guide: The
Balance of Power Between Congress
and the White House
(1901–2017),* WiredPen,
wiredpen.com/resources/political-
commentary-and-analysis/a-
visual-guide-balance-of-power-
congress-presidency.

28. Susan Dente Ross, *Access and New
Media Technology: Teleconferencing,
Telecommuting, and Public Access,*
in Access Denied: Freedom of
Information in the Information
Age 65 (Charles Davis & Sig
Splichal eds., 2000).

29. Reno v. American Civil Liberties
Union, 521 U.S. 844 (1997).

30. 5 U.S. 137 (1803).

31. Dept. of Justice v. Reporters
Comm. for Freedom of the Press,
489 U.S. 749 (1989).

32. *See, e.g.,* Red Lion Broadcasting
Co. v. FCC, 395 U.S. 367
(1969); Miami Herald Pub. Co. v.
Tornillo, 418 U.S. 241 (1974).

33. Agostini v. Felton, 521 U.S. 203
(1997) (rev'g Aguilar v. Felton,
473 U.S. 402 (1985)).

34. *See, e.g.,* Keeton v. Hustler
Magazine Inc., 465 U.S. 770
(1984) (overturning lower court
ruling dismissing libel suit filed
by resident of New York against
Ohio corporation in New
Hampshire court). *See also* New
York Times Co. v. Sullivan, 376
U.S. 254 (1964) (in which trial
and first appeal were heard in
Alabama courts).

35. Daimler AG v. Bauman, 134 S.
Ct. 746 (2014).

36. Rich Samp, *With* Bauman v.
DaimlerChrysler, *High Court
May Have Put Brakes on Forum
Shopping,* Forbes, Feb. 4,
2014, www.forbes.com/sites/
wlf/2014/02/04/with-bauman-
v-daimlerchrysler-high-court-
may-have-put-brakes-on-forum-
shopping.

37. 28 U.S.C. § 1292(a)(1).

38. U.S. Const. art. III, § 1.

39. *Briefing Paper,* SCOTUSBlog, June
28, 2010, www.scotusblog.com/
wp-content/uploads/2010/06/
Kagan-issues_ideology-June-29
.pdf; *see also* Mark Tushnet, In the
Balance: Law and Politics on the
Roberts Court (2013).

40. *Analysis: Justice Kagan—Giving
Liberals a Rhetorical Lift,*
Thompson Reuters News
& Insight, Feb. 23, 2013,
newsandinsight.thomsonreuters
.com/Legal/News/2012/04_-_
April/Analysis__Justice_Kagan—
Giving_liberals_a_rhetorical_lift/.

41. Mark Tushnet, *Opinions: Five
Myths About the Roberts Court,*
Wash. Post, Oct. 11, 2013, www
.washingtonpost.com/opinions/
five-myths-about-the-roberts-
court/2013/10/11/69924370-
30f4-11e3-8627-c5d7de0a046b_
story.html.

42. The Volokh Conspiracy, www
.volokh.com/posts/1212602633
.shtml (posted Aug. 3, 2008).

43. Alicia Parlapiano & Karen
Yourish, *Where Neil Gorsuch
Would Fit on the Supreme Court,*
Feb. 1, 2017, www.nytimes.
com/interactive/2017/01/31/us/
politics/trump-supreme-court-
nominee.html?_r=0.

44. Richard Wolf, *About 2,000
Petitions Await Supreme Court's
Return,* USA Today, Sept. 23,

2013, www.usatoday.com/
story/news/nation/2013/09/23/
supreme-court-petitions-
prisoners-clerks/2843401/.

45. *See, e.g.,* Gregory A. Caldeira &
John R. Wright, *The Discuss List:
Agenda Building in the Supreme
Court,* 24 Law & Society Rev. 807
(1990).

46. Lisa McElroy, Citizens United v.
FEC *in Plain English,* SCOTUS
Blog, Jan. 22, 2010, www
.scotusblog.com/2010/01/
citizens-united-v-fec-in-plain-
english/.

47. Adam Liptak, *Justices, 5–4, Reject
Corporate Spending Limit,* N.Y.
Times, Jan. 21, 2010, www
.nytimes.com/2010/01/22/us/
politics/22scotus.html.

48. Glenn Greenwald, *What the
Supreme Court Got Right,* Salon,
Jan. 22, 2010, www.salon.com/
news/opinion/glenn_greenwald/
2010/01/22/citizens_ united.

49. Samuel D. Warren & Louis D.
Brandeis, *The Right to Privacy,* 4
Harv. L. Rev. 193 (1890).

50. Ofra Bikel, *The Plea: Introduction,*
Frontline, June 17, 2004, www
.pbs.org/wgbh/pages/frontline/
shows/plea/etc/synopsis.html.

51. Nike v. Kasky, 539 U.S. 654 (2003).

52. Nikebiz.com, *The Inside Story
Press Release: Nike Inc. and
Kasky Announce Settlement of*
Kasky v. Nike *First Amendment
Case,* www.nike.com/
nikebiz/news/pressrelease.
jhtml?year=2003&month=09
&letter=f (posted Sept. 2003).

53. *Government Survey Shows 97
Percent of Civil Cases Settled,*
Phoenix Bus. J., May 27,
2004, www.bizjournals.com/
phoenix/stories/2004/05/31/
newscolumn5.html?page=all.

54. Mourning v. Family Publishing Service, 411 U.S. 356, 382 (1973). *See also* Adickes v. Kress & Co., 398 U.S. 144, 157 (1970); United States v. Diebold Inc., 369 U.S. 654, 655 (1962).

55. *See* Anderson v. Liberty Lobby Inc., 477 U.S. 242 (1986).

56. Stephen B. Burbank, *Vanishing Trials and Summary Judgment in Federal Civil Cases: Drifting Toward Bethlehem or Gomorrah?*, 1 J. Empirical Leg. Studies 591 (2004).

57. Washington Post Co. v. Keogh, 365 F.2d 965, 968 (D.C. Cir. 1966).

58. *See* New York Times Co. v. Sullivan, 376 U.S. 254 (1964).

59. *See, e.g.,* 44 Liquormart v. Rhode Island, 517 U.S. 484 (1996).

60. *See* New York Times Co., 376 U.S. 254.

61. *See, e.g.,* Dan Eggen & T. W. Farnam, *More Setbacks for Campaign Finance Rules*, Wash. Post, July 15, 2010, at A17; Green Party of Connecticut v. Garfield, 616 F.3d 189 (2d Cir. 2010); Long Beach Area Chamber of Commerce v. City of Long Beach, 603 F.3d 684 (9th Cir.), *cert. denied*, 562 U.S. 896 (2010); SpeechNow.org v. FEC, 599 F.3d 686 (D.C. Cir.), *cert. denied*, 562 U.S. 1003 (2010); Citizens United v. FEC, 558 U.S. 310 (2010).

62. *Connecticut Campaign Finance Decisions from Second Circuit:* Green Party v. Garfield, Const. L. Prof Blog, July 13, 2010, lawprofessors.typepad.com/ conlaw/2010/07/connecticut-campaign-finance-decisions-from-second-circuit-green-party-v-garfield.html.

63. Michael Cummins, Citizens United and the Roberts Court, Campaign for Liberty, June 30, 2010, www.campaignforliberty .com/article.php?view=978.

64. Damon W. Root, Citizens United, *Stare Decisis,* and the Chicago Gun Case, Reason, Jan. 22, 2010, reason.com/blog/2010/01/22/ citizens-united-stare-decisis.

65. 5 U.S. 137 (1803).

Chapter 2

1. Palko v. Connecticut, 302 U.S. 319 (1937).

2. Gitlow v. New York, 268 U.S. 652 (1925).

3. Note that even Justice Hugo Black, viewed as nearly a First Amendment absolutist, acknowledged that the authors of the First Amendment accepted some restraints on speech.

4. *See* Jonathan Peters, *WikiLeaks, the First Amendment, and the Press,* Harv. L. & Pol'y Rev., Apr. 18, 2011, hlpronline.com; Bland v. Roberts, 857 F. Supp. 2d 599 (E.D. Va. 2012).

5. Potter Stewart, *Or of the Press,* 26 Hastings L.J. 631 (1975); David A. Anderson, *The Origins of the Press Clause,* 30 UCLA L. Rev. 455 (1983); M. Ethan Katsh, *Rights, Camera, Action: Cyberspatial Settings and the First Amendment,* 104 Yale L.J. 1681 (1995).

6. *See* Texas v. Johnson, 491 U.S. 397 (1989) (striking down conviction for flag burning).

7. Adam Liptak, *Study Challenges Supreme Court's Image as Defender of Free Speech*, N.Y. Times, Jan. 8, 2012, at A21 (citing Monica Youn, The Roberts Court's Free Speech Double Standard (2012)).

8. 134 S. Ct. 2369 (2014).

9. United States v. Stevens, 559 U.S. 460 (2010).

10. 315 U.S. 568, 571–72 (1942).

11. 134 S. Ct. 2369, 2378 (2014).

12. *Id.*

13. *Id.* at 2379.

14. United States v. Alvarez, 132 S. Ct. 2537 (2012).

15. 18 U.S.C. § 704(b).

16. United States v. Swisher, 771 F.3d 514 (9th Cir. 2014).

17. John Milton, *Areopagitica* (1st ed. n.p. 1644), in Great Books of the Western World 409 (1952).

18. John Locke, The Second Treatise of Civil Government (1690).

19. Jean-Jacques Rousseau, The Social Contract (1762).

20. 4 William Blackstone, Commentaries 151–52 (London: 1769).

21. *Id.*

22. Frederick S. Siebert, Freedom of the Press in England 1476–1776, at 10 (1952); Leonard Levy, Legacy of Suppression (1960).

23. *See, e.g.,* Leonard Levy, Legacy of Suppression (1960); Leonard Levy, Emergence of a Free Press (1985). *But see* Zechariah Chafee, Free Speech in the United States 2 (1941) (arguing First Amendment was designed to eliminate law of sedition forever).

24. *See* James Morton Smith, Freedom's Fetters (1956).

25. *See* New York Times Co. v. Sullivan, 376 U.S. 254 (1964).

26. *See, e.g.,* John Stuart Mill, On Liberty (1859); Alexander Meiklejohn, Free Speech and Its Relation to Self-Government (1948); Thomas I. Emerson, The System of Free Expression (1970);

Cass Sunstein, Democracy and the Problem of Free Speech (1993).

27. *See, e.g.,* Vincent Blasi, *The Checking Value in First Amendment Theory,* 1977 Am. B. Found. Res. J. 521 (1977).

28. *See, e.g.,* Catharine MacKinnon, Feminism Unmodified, Discourses on Life and Law (1987); Words That Wound: Critical Race Theory, Assaultive Speech, and the First Amendment (Mari J. Matsuda et al. eds., 1993).

29. *See, e.g.,* Lee C. Bollinger, The Tolerant Society: Freedom of Speech and Extremist Speech in America (1986).

30. 376 U.S. 254 (1964).

31. *See, e.g.,* C. Edwin Baker, *Scope of the First Amendment Freedom of Speech,* 25 UCLA L. Rev. 964 (1978).

32. 395 U.S. 367 (1969).

33. *Id.* at 387, 389.

34. 418 U.S. 241, 256 (1974).

35. *Id.*

36. *Id.,* at 258.

37. Ithiel de Sola Pool, Technologies of Freedom (1983).

38. *See* Lovell v. Griffin, 303 U.S. 444, 452 (1938); Burstyn v. Wilson, 343 U.S. 495 (1952).

39. Kovacs v. Cooper, 336 U.S. 77, 97 (1949) (Jackson, J., concurring).

40. Minneapolis Star & Tribune Co. v. Minnesota Comm'r of Revenue, 460 U.S. 575, 585 (1983).

41. *See, e.g.,* Red Lion Broadcasting Co. v. FCC, 395 U.S. 367 (1969).

42. *See, e.g.,* Turner Broadcasting Sys. Inc. v. FCC, 512 U.S. 622 (1994); Turner Broadcasting Sys. Inc. v. FCC, 520 U.S. 180 (1997).

43. Pew Research Center, *Who Owns the News Media,* Jun. 26, 2012, www.journalism.org/2012/06/26/who-owns-news-media-database-summary-findings.

44. Project for Excellence in Journalism of the Columbia University Graduate School of Journalism, *Overview: The State of the News Media 2005, An Annual Report on American Journalism,* www.journalism.org.

45. Project for Excellence in Journalism of the Columbia University Graduate School of Journalism, *Journalist Survey: The State of the News Media 2004, An Annual Report on American Journalism,* www.journalism.org.

46. 283 U.S. 697 (1931).

47. *Id.*

48. 403 U.S. 713 (1971).

49. *Id.* at 714.

50. Nebraska Press Ass'n v. Stuart, 427 U.S. 539, 559 (1976).

51. New York Times Co. v. Jascalevich, 439 U.S. 1317 (1978); Nebraska Press Ass'n v. Stuart, 427 U.S. 539 (1976).

52. Kathryn Foxhall, *When Censorship Becomes a Cultural Norm,* Editor & Publisher, May 16, 2014, www.editorandpublisher.com/feature/when-censorship-becomes-a-cultural-norm2014-05-15t11-11-19.

53. CBS v. Davis, 510 U.S. 1315 (1994) (Blackmun, J., Circuit Justice).

54. Miami Herald Publ'g Co. v. McIntosh, 340 So. 2d 904, 910 (Fla. 1977).

55. Barclays v. TheFlyontheWall.com, 700 F. Supp. 2d 310 (S.D.N.Y. 2010).

56. Barclays v. TheFlyontheWall.com, 650 F.3d 876 (2d Cir. 2011).

57. *Julius Baer Bank and Trust v. WikiLeaks,* Citizen Media Law Project, Feb. 18, 2008, www.citmedialaw.org.

58. CBS, 510 U.S. at 1320.

59. Brown v. Town of Cary, 706 F.3d 294 (4th Cir. 2013).

60. 135 S. Ct. 2218 (2015).

61. *Id.* at 2227.

62. *Id.*

63. *Id.* at 2236 (Breyer, J., concurring).

64. *Id.* at 2239 (Kagan, J., concurring).

65. Norton v. City of Springfield, 806 F.3d 411 (7th Cir., Aug. 7, 2015).

66. Hill v. Colorado, 530 U.S. 703 (2000).

67. Burson v. Freeman, 504 U.S. 191 (1992).

68. U.S. Const. art. I, § 8, (giving Congress authority "to regulate Commerce with foreign nations, and among the several states, and with the Indian Tribes").

69. 502 U.S. 105 (1991).

70. *Id.*

71. United States v. O'Brien, 391 U.S. 367 (1968).

72. *Id.*

73. Ward v. Rock Against Racism, 491 U.S. 781 (1989). *See also* Matthew D. Bunker & Emily Erickson, *The Jurisprudence of Precision: Contrast Space and Narrow Tailoring in First Amendment Doctrine,* 6 Comm. L. & Pol'y 259 (2001).

74. Forsyth County, Ga. v. The Nationalist Movement, 505 U.S. 123 (1992).

75. Ward v. Rock Against Racism, 491 U.S. 781 (1989).

76. 530 U.S. 703 (2000).

77. 134 S. Ct. 2518 (2014).

78. Virginia v. Black, 538 U.S. 343, 365 (2003).

79. Meyer v. Grant, 486 U.S. 414 (1988).

80. *See, e.g.,* Buckley v. Valeo, 424 U.S. 1 (1976).

81. Susan B. Anthony List v. Driehaus, 779 F.3d 628 (6th Cir. 2015).

82. Susan B. Anthony List v. Driehaus, 525 Fed. Appx. 415 (6th Cir. 2013); *rev'd,* 134 S. Ct. 2334 (2014).

83. Susan B. Anthony List v. Driehaus, 814 F.3d 466 (6th Cir. 2016).

84. AP, *U.S. Supreme Court to Consider Ohio Ban on Campaign Lies,* Times-Picayune, Apr. 16, 2014, www.nola.com/politics/index.ssf/2014/04/us_supreme_court_to_consider_o.html.

85. Sarah Kessler, *Reporter Put on Leave After Refusing to Remove Facebook Post,* Mashable Social Media, June 14, 2012, www.mashable.com.

86. Nelson v. McClatchy, 936 P.2d 1123 (Wash. 1997).

87. *See, e.g.,* Perry v. Sindermann, 408 U.S. 593 (1972). For discussion of parallel treatment of public school students, see Chapter 3 and Tinker v. Des Moines Independent Community School Dist., 393 U.S. 503 (1969).

88. *See, e.g.,* Pickering v. Board of Education, 391 U.S. 563 (1968); Snepp v. United States, 444 U.S. 507 (1980); Toni M. Massaro, *Significant Silences: Freedom of Speech in the Public Sector Workplace,* 61 S. Cal. L. Rev. 1 (1987); Sissela Bok, Secrets (1993). *But see* Daniel N. Hoffman, Governmental Secrecy and the Founding Fathers: A Study in Constitutional Controls (1981); Benjamin S. DuVal Jr., *The Occasions of Secrecy,* 47 U. Pitt. L. Rev. 579 (1986); Seth F. Kreimer, *Sunlight Secrets and Scarlet Letters: The Tension Between Privacy and Disclosure in Constitutional Law,* 140 U. Pa. L. Rev. 1 (1991); Kermit L. Hall, *The Virulence of the National Appetite for Bogus Revelation,* 56 Md. L. Rev. 1 (1997); Freedom at Risk: Secrecy, Censorship, and Repression in the 1980s (Richard O. Curry ed., 1998).

89. Heffernan v. City of Paterson, 136 S. Ct. 1412 (2016).

90. 547 U.S. 410 (2006).

91. *Id.* at 422.

92. Borough of Duryea v. Guarnieri, 564 U.S. 379 (2011).

93. *Id.* at 392.

94. *Id.*

95. *Id.*

96. Harris v. Quinn, 134 S. Ct. 2618 (2014).

97. Agency for Int'l Dev. v. Alliance for Open Society Int'l Inc., 133 S. Ct. 2321 (2013).

98. *Id.*

99. *Id.* at 2328.

100. Friedrichs v. California Teachers Assoc., 135 S. Ct. 2993 (2016).

101. 135 S. Ct. 2239, 2249 (2015).

102. Pleasant Grove City v. Summum, 555 U.S. 460 (2009).

103. *Id.*

104. *Id.* at 481.

105. 558 U.S. 310 (2010).

106. *See, e.g.,* American Tradition Partnership v. Bullock, 132 S. Ct. 2490 (2012) (per curiam); Texans for Free Enter. v. Tex. Ethics Comm'n, 732 F.3d 535 (5th Cir. 2013); Wis. Right to Life v. Barland, 751 F.3d 804 (7th Cir. 2014); *c.f.* Bluman v. FEC, 132 S. Ct. 1087 (2012) (summary judgment upholding ban on foreign political contributions); Republican Party v. King, 741 F.3d 1089 (10th Cir. 2013).

107. McCutcheon v. FEC, 134 S. Ct. 1434 (2014).

108. *Id.* at 1450.

109. Nicholas Confessore, *Koch Brothers' Budget of $889 Million for 2016 Is on Par With Both Parties' Spending,* N.Y. Times, Jan. 26, 2015, www.nytimes.com/2015/01/27/us/politics/kochs-plan-to-spend-900-million-on-2016-campaign.html.

110. Kathleen Gray, *Betsy DeVos Appointment Means Less Cash for GOP,* Detroit Free Press, Jan. 31, 2017, www.freep.com/story/news/politics/2017/01/31/betsy-devos-education-secretary-contributions/97161958.

111. Ysursa v. Pocatello Educ. Ass'n, 555 U.S. 353 (2009).

112. McIntyre v. Ohio Election Comm'n, 514 U.S. 334, 357 (1995).

113. *See* Talley v. California, 362 U.S. 60 (1960); Buckley v. Amer. Const. L. F., 525 U.S. 182 (1999); Watchtower v. Stratton, 536 U.S. 150 (2002).

114. Doe v. Reed, 561 U.S. 186 (2010).

115. Doe v. Reed, 823 F. Supp. 2d 1195 (W.D. Wash. 2011).

116. Hague v. Comm. for Industrial Org., 307 U.S. 496, 515 (1939).

117. *See, e.g.,* Susan Dente Ross, *An Apologia to Radical Dissent and a Supreme Court Test to Protect It,* 7 Comm. L. & Pol'y 401 (2002); Ronald J. Krotoszynski

Jr., *Essay: Celebrating Selma: The Importance of Context in Public Forum Analysis,* 104 Yale L.J. 1411 (1995).

118. *See, e.g.,* Skokie v. Nat'l Socialist Party of America, 439 U.S. 916 (1978); Hess v. Indiana, 414 U.S. 105 (1973); Brown v. Louisiana, 383 U.S. 131 (1966); Edwards v. South Carolina, 371 U.S. 229 (1963); NAACP v. Claiborne Hardware Co., 458 U.S. 886 (1982); Gregory v. City of Chicago, 394 U.S. 111 (1969); Grayned v. Rockford, 408 U.S. 104 (1972).

119. 562 U.S. 443 (2011).

120. Grayned v. Rockford, 408 U.S. 104, 116 (1972); Perry Educ. Ass'n v. Perry Local Educators' Ass'n, 460 U.S. 37 (1983).

121. *See, e.g.,* Hague v. Comm. for Industrial Org., 307 U.S. 496 (1939).

122. Coe v. Town of Blooming Grove, 429 F. App'x 55 (2d Cir. 2011).

123. Bell v. Keating, 697 F.3d 445 (7th Cir. 2012).

124. *See, e.g.,* Frisby v. Schultz, 487 U.S. 474 (1988); Madsen v. Women's Health Center Inc., 512 U.S. 753 (1994). *But see* Scheidler v. Nat'l Org. for Women, 537 U.S. 393 (2003) (removing civil injunction on anti-abortion protesters and rejecting claim that their protests constituted illegal extortion and racketeering).

125. Reichle v. Howards, 132 S. Ct. 2088 (2012).

126. *See, e.g.,* Greer v. Spock, 424 U.S. 828 (1976).

127. *See, e.g.,* Smith v. Exec. Dir. of the Indiana War Memorials

Comm'n, 742 F.3d 282 (7th Cir. 2014); Miller v. City of Cincinnati, 622 F.3d 524 (6th Cir. 2010), *cert. denied,* 536 U.S. 974 (2011).

128. *See, e.g.,* United States v. Albertini, 472 U.S. 675 (1985); Los Angeles City Council v. Taxpayers for Vincent, 466 U.S. 789 (1984); United States v. Kokinda, 497 U.S. 720 (1990).

129. *See, e.g.,* Adderley v. Florida, 385 U.S. 39 (1966).

130. *See, e.g.,* Amalgamated Food Employees Union v. Logan Valley Plaza Inc., 391 U.S. 308 (1968); Hudgens v. National Labor Relations Board, 424 U.S. 507 (1976); PruneYard Shopping Center v. Robins, 447 U.S. 74 (1980). *But see* Lloyd Corp., Ltd. v. Tanner, 407 U.S. 551 (1972).

131. PruneYard Shopping Center, 447 U.S. 74.

132. Glickman v. Wileman Bros. & Elliott, 521 U.S. 457, 505 n.2 (1997) (Souter, J., dissenting).

133. *See, e.g.,* David F. Freedman, *Press Passes and Trespasses: Newsgathering on Private Property,* 84 Colum. L. Rev. 1298 (1984).

134. *See, e.g.,* Bd. of Regents of the Univ. of Wis. v. Southworth, 529 U.S. 217 (2000); Rosenberger v. Rector & Visitors of the Univ. of Virginia, 515 U.S. 819 (1995).

135. *See, e.g.,* Grosjean v. Am. Press Co., 297 U.S. 233 (1936); Minneapolis Star & Tribune Co. v. Minnesota Comm'r of Revenue, 460 U.S. 575 (1983); Arkansas Writers' Project v. Ragland, 481 U.S. 221 (1987). *But see* Leathers v. Medlock, 499 U.S. 439 (1991).

136. NEA v. Finley, 524 U.S. 569 (1998).

137. Island Trees Union Free School Dist. Bd. of Ed. v. Pico, 457 U.S. 853 (1982).

138. Wooley v. Maynard, 430 U.S. 705, 714 (1977).

139. *See, e.g.,* Boy Scouts of America v. Dale, 530 U.S. 640 (2000).

140. Hurley v. Irish-American Gay, Lesbian and Bisexual Group of Boston, 515 U.S. 557, 575 (1995).

141. Brian MacQuarrie et al., *Strife Forgotten Amid Inclusive St. Patrick's Day Parade,* Boston Globe, March 18, 2015, www.bostonglobe .com/metro/2015/03/15/ preparations-under-way-for-this-afternoon-patrick-day-parade/ XBloZY1z2vTe9SZnev8qyN/ story.html.

142. Citizens United v. Gessler, 773 F.3d 200 (10th Cir. 2014).

Chapter 3

1. Schenck v. United States, 249 U.S. 47, 52 (1919).

2. Elonis v. United States, 135 S. Ct. 2001 (2015), *conviction aff'd on remand,* 841 F.3d 589 (3d Cir. 2016).

3. Geoffrey R. Stone, *Free Speech and National Security,* 84 Ind. L.J. 939 (2009).

4. Vincent Blasi, *The Pathological Perspective and the First Amendment,* 85 Colum. L. Rev. 449, 450 (1985).

5. Margaret A. Blanchard, Revolutionary Sparks 489 (1992); Margaret A. Blanchard, *"Why Can't We Ever Learn?" Cycles of Stability, Stress and Freedom of Expression in United States History,* 7 Comm. L. & Pol'y 347 (2002); Martin E. Halstuk, *Policy of Secrecy—Pattern of Deception: What Federalist Leaders Thought About a Public Right to Know,*

1794–98, 7 Comm. L. & Pol'y 51 (2002); Susan D. Ross, *An Apologia to Radical Dissent and a Supreme Court Test to Protect It,* 7 Comm. L. & Pol'y 401 (2002).

6. Holder v. Humanitarian Law Project, 561 U.S. 1 (2010).

7. The Uniting and Strengthening America by Providing Appropriate Tools Required to Intercept and Obstruct Terrorism Act of 2001, Pub. L. No. 107–56, 115 Stat. 272; USA PATRIOT Improvement and Reauthorization Act of 2005, 18 U.S.C. § 2709, Pub. L. No. 109–177, 120 Stat. 192 (2006).

8. Office of the Coordinator for Counterterrorism, *Foreign Terrorist Organizations,* U.S. Department of State, Jan. 19, 2010, www.state.gov/s/ct/rls/other/des/123085.htm.

9. *Humanitarian Law Project,* 561 U.S. at 6.

10. *Id.* at 3.

11. *Id.*

12. United States v. Mehanna, 735 F.3d 32 (1st Cir. 2013).

13. 561 U.S. 1 (2010).

14. USA PATRIOT Act, 18 U.S. Code § 2339A.

15. *Decision Today Threatens Writers and Journalists, Academic Researchers, Translators and Even Ordinary Web Surfers,* Dec. 20, 2011, www.aclu.org/news/mehanna-verdict-compromises-first-amendment-undermines-national-security; Nikolas Abel, United States vs. Mehanna, *the First Amendment, and Material Support in the War on Terror,* 54 B.C.L. Rev. 711 (2013), lawdigitalcommons.bc.edu/bclr/vol54/iss2/7.

16. *See, e.g.,* Marguerite Rigoglioso, *Civil Liberties and the Law in the Era of Surveillance,* 49 Stanford L. [Cover Story], No. 91, Nov. 13, 2014; *Top Ten Abuses of Power Since 9/11,* www.aclu.org/other/top-ten-abuses-power-911.

17. William H. Rehnquist, All the Laws but One 224 (1998).

18. Kleindienst v. Mandel, 408 U.S. 753, 773 (1972) (Douglas, J., dissenting).

19. Doe v. Backpage.com, 817 F.3d 12 (1st Cir. 2016), *cert. denied,* 137 S. Ct. 622 (2017).

20. Eric Goldman, *Big Win for Free Speech Online in Backpage Lawsuit,* Forbes, Mar. 17, 2016, http://www.forbes.com/sites/ericgoldman/2016/03/17/big-win-for-free-speech-online-in-backpage-lawsuit/#4898ea3e3a54.

21. 137 S. Ct. 622 (2017).

22. 104 F. Supp. 3d 149 (N.D. Cal. 2016), *aff'd,* 104 F. Supp. 3d 149 (N.D. Cal. 2016), *aff'd,* 817 F.3d 212 (1st Cir. 2016), *cert. denied,* 137 S. Ct. 622 (2017).

23. Chaplinsky v. New Hampshire, 315 U.S. 568, 572 (1942).

24. Schenck v. United States, 249 U.S. 47, 52 (1919).

25. *Id.*

26. *Id.*

27. Frohwerk v. United States, 249 U.S. 204 (1919).

28. *Id.* at 208–09.

29. Debs v. United States, 249 U.S. 211 (1919).

30. Abrams v. United States, 250 U.S. 616 (1919).

31. *Id.* at 628 (Holmes, J., dissenting).

32. *Id.* at 630.

33. Dennis v. United States, 341 U.S. 494 (1951); Scales v. United States, 367 U.S. 203 (1961).

See also Whitney v. California, 274 U.S. 357 (1927); Kent Greenawalt, *Speech and Crime,* 1980 Am. B. Found. Res. J. 645 (1980).

34. Gitlow v. New York, 268 U.S. 652 (1925).

35. *Id.* at 669.

36. *Id.* at 667.

37. *Id.* at 673 (Holmes, J., dissenting).

38. *Id.* at 666.

39. Whitney v. California, 274 U.S. 357 (1927).

40. *Id.* at 377–78 (Brandeis, J., concurring).

41. *Id.* at 379 (emphasis added).

42. Am. Communications Ass'n v. Douds, 339 U.S. 382, 448–49 (1950) (Black, J., dissenting).

43. Dennis v. United States, 341 U.S. 494 (1951); Kunz v. New York, 340 U.S. 290, 300 (1951); Yates v. United States, 354 U.S. 298 (1957).

44. *See* Liezl Irene Pangilinan, Note: *"When a Nation Is at War": A Context-Dependent Theory of Free Speech for the Regulation of Weapon Recipes,* 22 Cardozo Arts & Ent. L.J. 683 (2004).

45. 395 U.S. 444 (1969).

46. *Id.* at 447.

47. *Id.* at 448.

48. 414 U.S. 105 (1973) (per curiam).

49. *Alabama Top Court Denies Industry Motion to Dismiss GTA Killer Suit,* Game Politics, Mar. 29, 2006, gamepolitics.livejournal.com/244744.html.

50. Dana Beyerle, *"Grand Theft Auto" Killer's Sentence Upheld,* Gadsden Times, Feb. 17, 2012, www.gadsdentimes.com/

news/20120217/grand-theft-auto-killers-sentence-upheld.

51. Herceg v. Hustler Magazine, 814 F.2d 1017 (5th Cir. 1987), *cert. denied*, 485 U.S. 959 (1988).

52. Yakubowicz v. Paramount Pictures Corp., 536 N.E.2d 1067 (Mass. 1989).

53. Rice v. Paladin Enterprises Inc., 128 F.3d 233 (4th Cir. 1997), *cert. denied*, 523 U.S. 1074 (1998).

54. *Id.* at 244.

55. Martin Garbus, *State of the Union for the Law of the New Millennium, the Internet, and the First Amendment*, 1999 Ann. Surv. Am. L. 169, 173–74.

56. *See* Dave Itzkoff, *Scholar Finds Flaws in Work by Archenemy of Comics*, N.Y. Times, Feb. 20, 2013, at C1.

57. Am. Acad. of Pediatrics, *Family Life: TV Violence* (2013), www .healthychildren.org/English/ family-life/Media/Pages/TV-Violence.aspx.

58. *Sunday Dialogue: Mayhem on Our Screens,* N.Y. Times, Jan. 27, 2013, at SR2; Tracy Reilly, *The "Spiritual Temperature" of Contemporary Popular Music: An Alternative to the Legal Regulation of Death-Metal and Gangsta-Rap Lyrics*, 11 Vand. J. Ent. & Tech. L. 335 (2009).

59. *See, e.g.*, Ty Burr, *An Uncertain Line Between Fantasy's Lure, Nightmare*, Boston Globe, July 21, 2012, at A1; Nolan Finley, *Missing the Real Lessons From Arizona*, Detroit News, Jan. 20, 2011, at B1; Marc Fisher et al., *Lanza's Isolated Life Stymies Investigators*, Wash. Post, Dec. 23, 2012, at A1.

60. *See generally* John Charles Kunich, *Shock Torts Reloaded*, 6

Appalachian J.L. 1 (2006); John Charles Kunich, *Natural Born Copycat Killers and the Law of Shock Torts*, 78 Wash. U.L.Q. 1157 (2000).

61. Zamora v. Columbia Broadcasting System, 480 F. Supp. 199, 200 (S.D. Fla. 1979).

62. *Id.* at 201, 205.

63. Timothy D. Reeves, *Tort Liability for Manufacturers of Violent Video Games*, Ala. L. Rev. 519 (2009); Jonathan M. Proman, *Liability of Media Companies for the Violent Content of Their Products Marketed to Children*, 78 St. John's L. Rev. 426 (2004).

64. Brown v. Ent. Merchants Ass'n, 564 U.S. 786 (2011).

65. *Id.*

66. *Id.*

67. *Id.* at 794.

68. *Id.* at 790.

69. *Id.* at 806.

70. Olivia N. v. Nat'l Broadcasting Co., 126 Cal. App. 3d 488 (1981).

71. Sanders v. Acclaim Entertainment Inc., 188 F. Supp. 2d 1264 (D. Colo. 2002).

72. James v. Meow Media Inc., 300 F.3d 683 (6th Cir. 2002), *cert. denied*, 537 U.S. 1159 (2003).

73. *Id.* at 693.

74. Eimann v. Soldier of Fortune Magazine Inc., 880 F.2d 830, 832 (5th Cir. 1989), *cert. denied*, 493 U.S. 1024 (1990).

75. Norwood v. Soldier of Fortune Magazine Inc., 651 F. Supp. 1397 (W.D. Ark. 1987).

76. *Id.* at 1403.

77. Braun v. Soldier of Fortune Magazine Inc., 968 F.2d 1110 (11th Cir. 1992), *cert. denied*, 506 U.S. 1071 (1993).

78. Eimann v. Soldier of Fortune Magazine Inc., 880 F.2d 830, 834 (5th Cir. 1989), *cert. denied*, 493 U.S. 1024 (1990).

79. *Id.* at 834.

80. *See* April M. Perry, Comment: *Guilt by Saturation: Media Liability for Third-Party Violence and the Availability Heuristic*, 97 NW. U.L. Rev. 1045, 1055–56 (2003).

81. Watters v. TSR Inc., 904 F.2d 378 (6th Cir. 1990).

82. 403 U.S. 15 (1971).

83. *Id.* at 25.

84. State v. Packingham, 748 S.E. 2d 146 (N.C. 2013); 777 S.E.2d 738 (N.C. 2015), *cert. granted*, 137 S. Ct. 368 (2016)—*rev'd*, 137 S. Ct. 1730 (2017).

85. Packingham, 777 S.E.2d 738 (2015).

86. Packingham, 137 S. Ct. 1730 (2017).

87. Ashcroft v. Free Speech Coalition, 535 U.S. 234 (2002).

88. Abu-Jamal v. Kane, 105 F. Supp. 3d 448 (M.D. Pa. 2015).

89. Revictimization Relief Act, 18 Pa. Cons. Stat. § 11.101 *et seq.* (2014).

90. Abu-Jamal, 105 F. Supp. 3d 448.

91. *Id., citing* Simon & Schuster, Inc. v. Members of N.Y. State Crime Victims Bd., 502 U.S. 105, 118 (1991).

92. *Id.* at 463.

93. Martin H. Redish, *Advocacy of Unlawful Conduct and the First Amendment: In Defense of Clear and Present Danger*, 70 Cal. L. Rev. 1159, 1162 (1982).

94. Gitlow v. New York, 268 U.S. 652, 673 (1925).

95. Chaplinsky v. New Hampshire, 315 U.S. 568 (1942).

96. *Id.* at 571–72.

97. Terminiello v. Chicago, 337 U.S. 1, 3 (1949).

98. *Id.* at 4 (emphasis added).

99. *Id.*

100. *Id.*

101. *See, e.g.,* Gooding v. Wilson, 405 U.S. 518 (1972).

102. R.A.V. v. City of St. Paul, 505 U.S. 377 (1992).

103. 505 U.S. 377, 384–85, 386 (1992).

104. United States v. Stevens, 559 U.S. 460 (2010).

105. *Id.* at 472.

106. Virginia v. Black, 538 U.S. 343 (2003).

107. *Id.* at 394.

108. *See* Watts v. United States, 394 U.S. 705 (1969).

109. Elonis, 135 S. Ct. 2001 (2015).

110. Eugene Volokh, *The Supreme Court Doesn't Decide When Speech Becomes a Constitutionally Unprotected "True Threat,"* Wash. Post., June 1, 2015, www.washingtonpost.com/ news/volokh-conspiracy/ wp/2015/06/01/the-supreme- court-doesnt-decide- when-speech-becomes-a- constitutionally-unprotected- true-threat/.

111. Elonis, 135 S. Ct. 2001 (2015).

112. *Id.* at 2009.

113. *Id.* at 2013.

114. United States v. Elonis, 841 F.3d 589, 596 (3d 2016), *rev'd,* 135 S. Ct. 2001 (2015).

115. United States v. Bagdasarian, 652 F.3d 1113 (9th Cir. 2011).

116. United States v. Jeffries, 692 F.3d 473, 485 (6th Cir. 2012).

117. MK Mallonee and Pamela Brown, *Facebook Threats Case Heard at Supreme Court*, CNN, Dec. 1, 2014, www.cnn.com/2014/12/01/ politics/supreme-court-elonis-vs-u- s-free-speech/.

118. United States v. O'Brien, 391 U.S. 367, 376 (1968).

119. Tinker v. Des Moines Indep. Cmty. Sch. Dist., 393 U.S. 503, 505 (1969).

120. United States v. O'Brien, 391 U.S. 367 (1968).

121. Texas v. Johnson, 491 U.S. 397 (1989). The Supreme Court has said symbolic speech exists and warrants First Amendment protection when (1) speech and action combine, (2) there is an intent to convey a message and (3) witnesses are likely to understand that message.

122. *Id.* at 414.

123. Hess v. Indiana, 414 U.S. 105 (1973).

124. Bd. of Educ., Island Trees Union Free Sch. Dist. v. Pico 457 U.S. 853 (1982).

125. *Id.* at 857.

126. *Id.* at 868.

127. *Id.* at 870.

128. Parents, Families and Friends of Lesbians and Gays v. Camdenton R-111 Sch. Dist., 853 F. Supp. 2d 888 (W.D. Mo. 2012).

129. Michael Winerip, *School District Told to Replace Web Filter Blocking Pro-Gay Sites*, N.Y. Times, March 26, 2012, www .nytimes.com.

130. Wooley v. Maynard, 430 U.S. 705, 714 (1977) (Burger, C.J.).

131. West Virginia State Bd. of Educ. v. Barnette, 319 U.S. 624 (1943).

132. Ambach v. Norwick, 441 U.S. 68 (1979).

133. *See, e.g.,* Epperson v. Arkansas, 393 U.S. 97 (1968); Edwards v. Aguillard, 482 U.S. 578 (1987); Pickering v. Bd. of Educ., 391 U.S. 563 (1968).

134. Barnette, 319 U.S. at 642.

135. Mark C. Rahdert, Point of View: *The Roberts Court and Academic Freedom*, Chronicle Higher Educ., July 27, 2007, chronicle. com/forums/index.

136. Tinker v. Des Moines Indep. Cmty. Sch. Dist., 393 U.S. 503 (1969).

137. Erwin Chemerinsky, *Students Do Leave Their First Amendment Rights at the Schoolhouse Gates: What's Left of* Tinker? 48 Drake L. Rev. 527 (2000).

138. Tinker, 393 U.S. at 508.

139. *Id.*

140. *Id.* at 506.

141. *Id.* at 509.

142. Grayned v. Rockford, 408 U.S. 104 (1972).

143. Morse v. Frederick, 551 U.S. 393 (2007).

144. *Id.* at 410.

145. *Id.* at 445 (Stevens, J. dissenting).

146. Bethel School District v. Fraser, 478 U.S. 675 (1986).

147. *Id.*

148. Hazelwood v. Kuhlmeier, 484 U.S. 260 (1988).

149. *Id.* at 271.

150. *Id.* at 270–71.

151. *Id.* at 270.

152. *Id.* at 273 n.7.

153. A.M. v. Taconic Hills Cent. Sch. Dist., 510 F. App'x 3 (2d Cir. 2013), *cert. denied*, 134 S. Ct. 196 (2013).

154. K.A. *ex. rel.* Ayers v. Pocono Mt. Sch. Dist., 710 F. 3d 99 (3d Cir. 2013).

155. Taylor v. Roswell Ind. Sch. Dist., 713 F.3d 25 (10th Cir. 2013).

156. Hardwick v. Heyward, 711 F.3d 426 (4th Cir.), *cert. denied*, 134 S. Ct. 201 (2013).

157. B.H. *ex rel.* Hawk v. Easton Area Sch. Dist., 725 F.3d 293 (3d Cir. 2013), *cert. denied*, 134 S. Ct. 1515 (2014).

158. Zamecnik v. Indian Prairie Sch. Dist., 636 F.3d 874 (7th Cir. 2011).

159. D.J.M. v. Hannibal Pub. Sch. Dist. #60, 647 F.3d 754 (8th Cir. 2011).

160. *Id.*

161. Kowalski v. Berkeley County Schools, 652 F.3d 565 (4th Cir. 2011), *cert. denied*, 565 U.S. 1173 (2012).

162. Doninger v. Niehoff, 527 F.3d 41 (2d Cir. 2008).

163. Snyder v. Blue Mountain Sch. Dist., 650 F.3d 915 (3d Cir. 2011) (en banc), *cert. denied*, 565 U.S. 1156 (2012); Layshock v. Hermitage Sch. Dist., 593 F.3d 249 (3d Cir. 2010), *cert. denied*, 565 U.S. 1156 (2012).

164. Bd. of Regents of Univ. of Wis. System v. Southworth, 529 U.S. 217, 234 n.7 (2000).

165. Widmar v. Vincent, 454 U.S. 263, 274 (1981).

166. Bethel Sch. Dist. v. Fraser, 478 U.S. 675, 683 (1986). *See also* Edwards v. Aguillard, 482 U.S. 578, 583 (1987).

167. *See, e.g.,* Bd. of Regents, 529 U.S. 217 (2000); Rosenberger v. Rector and Visitors of the Univ. of Va., 515 U.S. 819 (1995).

168. Rosenberger, 515 U.S. at 833.

169. *See, e.g.,* Bd. of Regents, 529 U.S. 217; Rosenberger, 515 U.S. 819.

170. Bd. of Regents, 529 U.S. at 239 (Souter, J., concurring).

171. Papish v. Board of Curators of the University of Missouri, 410 U.S. 667, 670 (1973).

172. *Id.; see also* Bd. of Regents, 529 U.S. at 233.

173. Bd. of Regents, 529 U.S. at 242–43 (Souter, J., dissenting).

174. Note that the Court said this public forum also enhanced the university's curricular goals, but public forum analysis typically protects precisely those types of speech that would not be embraced by the government agency providing the forum.

175. Christian Legal Society v. Martinez, 561 U.S. 661 (2010).

176. *Id.* at 686.

177. Tinker v. Des Moines Indep. Cmty. Sch. Dist., 393 U.S. 503, 506 (1969).

178. Christian Legal Society, 561 U.S. at 706 (Alito, J., dissenting).

179. Greg Lukianoff, *Feigning Free Speech on Campus*, N.Y. Times, Oct. 25, 2012, www.nytimes.com.

180. Hosty v. Carter, 412 F.3d 731 (7th Cir. 2005), *cert. denied*, 546 U.S. 1169 (2006).

181. Kincaid v. Gibson, 236 F.3d 342 (6th Cir. 2001) (en banc).

182. *Id.* at 346.

183. OSU Student Alliance v. Ray, 699 F.3d 1053 (9th Cir. 2012), *cert denied*, 134 S. Ct. 70 (2013).

184. Tatro v. Univ. of Minn., 816 N.W.2d 509 (Minn. 2012).

185. *Id.* at 517.

186. *Id.* at 513.

187. *Id.* at 521.

188. *Id.* at 511–12.

189. *Id.* at 521.

190. Oyama v. Univ. of Hawaii, 813 F.3d 850 (9th Cir. 2015), *cert. denied*, 136 S. Ct. 2520 (2016).

191. Keefe v. Adams, 840 F.3d 523 (8th Cir. 2016), *cert. denied*, 137 S. Ct. 1448 (2017).

192. Hazelwood v. Kuhlmeier, 484 U.S. 260 (1988).

193. *Compare, e.g.,* Keefe, 840 F.3d at 532) (relying on *Hazelwood* to affirm the authority of the university to expel a student for unprofessional off-campus Facebook posts about classmates that were reasonably related to and materially disrupted the graduate nursing program) *with* Oyama, 813 F.3d at 863 (not relying on *Hazelwood* and creating a new test to affirm the authority of the university to deny student teacher placement for a student's inappropriate remarks). *See also,* Ward v. Polite, 667 F.3d 727, 733–34 (6th Cir. 2012) (applying *Hazelwood* to establish authority of the university to impose regulations on speech that are "reasonably related to legitimate pedagogical concerns. . . . Nothing in *Hazelwood* suggests a stop-go distinction between student speech at the high school and university levels, and we decline to create one."); Keeton v. Anderson-Wiley, 664 F.3d 865, 875–76 (11th Cir. 2011) (relying on *Hazelwood* to reject graduate student claim to affirm university authority to control of graduate student speech within a "school-sponsored expressive activity" because graduate program standards constitute a nonpublic forum for government speech); Flint v. Dennison, 488 F.3d 816, 829 n.9 (9th Cir. 2007) (applying *Hazelwood* to college student campaign spending); Hosty v. Carter, 412

F.3d 731, 735 (7th Cir. 2005) (en banc) ("We hold . . . that *Hazelwood*'s framework applies to subsidized student newspapers at colleges as well as elementary and secondary schools"); Axson-Flynn v. Johnson, 356 F.3d 1277, 1285, 1289–93 (10th Cir. 2004) (concluding that a graduate student's speech "constitutes 'school-sponsored speech' and is thus governed by *Hazelwood*"); Student Gov't Ass'n v. Bd. of Trs. of Univ. of Mass., 868 F.2d 473, 480 n.6 (1st Cir. 1989) ("*Hazelwood* . . . is not applicable to college newspapers").

194. Oyama, 813 F.3d at 862.

195. *Id.* at 863.

196. *Id.* at 855, 860.

197. *Id.* at 870 ("the University could look to what Oyama *said* as an indication of what he would *do* once certified") (emphasis in original).

198. Keefe v. Adams, 840 F.3d 523, 532 (8th Cir. 2016), *cert denied*, 137 S. Ct. 1448 (2017).

199. *Id.* at 526.

200. *Id.* at 528.

201. *Id.* at 531.

202. *Id.*

203. Keefe v. Adams, *cert. denied*, 137 S. Ct. 1448 (2017). *See also* Conner Mitchell, *Supreme Court Declines to Hear Free Speech Case*, SPLC on the Blog, Apr. 4, 2017, splc.org.

204. Roxann Elliott, *Court of Appeals Rules in Favor of Community College That Removed Nursing Student Over Facebook Posts*, SPLC, Nov. 3, 2016, www.splc.org/blog/splc/2016/11/keefe-eighth-circuit.

205. Frank LoMonte, *Appeals Court Won't Apply* Hazelwood *to*

Teacher Trainee's Case, Instead Creates New "Professional Standards" Exception, SPLC, Dec. 29, 2015, www.splc.org/blog/splc/2015/12/oyama-hawaii-ninth-circuit-college-hazelwood-ruling.

206. Richard Perez-Pena, *Editors Quit at University of Georgia*, N.Y. Times, Aug. 17, 2012, www.nytimes.com.

207. Alexis Steven, *Editors Rejoin UGA Student Newspaper*, Aug. 20, 2012, www.ajc.com.

208. *Michele Nagar Fired for Diversity's Sake*, July 22, 2004, www.campusreportonline.net/main/articles.php?id=139.

209. *SPJ Members Issue Resolution Condemning Kansas Adviser's Firing*, Oct. 6, 2004, www.splc.org; *SPLC Condemns Kansas State's "Bizarre" Interpretation of the First Amendment*, July 21, 2004, www.splc.org/newsflash.

210. *Johnson Fired From Position of Director, Collegian Adviser*, Kan. St. Collegian, May 11, 2004, at 1.

211. *Newspaper Content Analysis Given in Reasons Not to Reappoint Collegian Adviser*, Kan. St. Collegian, May 18, 2004, www.kstatecollegian.com/article.php?a=2141.

212. *See* Lane v. Simon, 2005 U.S. Dist. LEXIS 11330 (D. Kan. 2005), *vacated and remanded*, 2007 U.S. App. LEXIS 17814 (10th Cir., July 26, 2007).

213. *See, e.g.,* Dinesh D'Souza, Illiberal Education: The Politics of Race and Sex on Campus (1992).

214. *See, e.g.,* The Price We Pay: The Case Against Racist Speech, Hate Propaganda, and Pornography (Laura Lederer & Richard Delgado eds., 1994).

215. *See, e.g.,* Andrew Altman, *Liberalism and Campus Hate Speech,* in Campus Wars: Multiculturalism and the Politics of Difference (John Arthur & Amy Shapiro eds., 1993).

216. *See, e.g.,* Doe v. Univ. of Mich., 721 F. Supp. 852 (E.D. Mich. 1989); UWM Post v. Univ. of Wis. Bd. of Regents, 774 F. Supp. 1163 (E.D. Wis. 1991); Dambrot v. Central Mich. Univ., 839 F. Supp. 477 (E.D. Mich. 1993).

217. Doe v. Univ. of Mich., 721 F. Supp. 852, 864 (E.D. Mich. 1989).

218. Arati R. Korwar, War of Words: Speech Codes at Public Colleges and Universities (1994); Jon B. Gould, *The Precedent That Wasn't: College Hate Speech Codes and the Two Faces of Legal Compliance*, 35 Law & Soc'y Rev. 345 (2001).

219. Greg Lukianoff, *Spotlight on Speech Codes 2013: The State of Free Speech on Our Nation's Campuses*, The Foundation for Individual Rights in Education, www.thefire.org.

220. Wildmon v. Berwick Universal Pictures, 803 F. Supp. 1167 (D. Miss. 1992), *aff'd without opinion*, 979 F.2d 21 (5th Cir. 1992).

221. Savage v. Pacific Gas and Electric Co., 26 Cal. Rptr. 2d 305 (Cal. Ct. App. 1993).

Chapter 4

1. New York Times Co. v. Sullivan, 376 U.S. 254, 270–72 (1964).

2. *See, e.g.,* Diane Leenheer Zimmerman, *Defamation in Fiction: Real People in Fiction:*

Cautionary Words About Troublesome Old Torts Poured Into New Jugs, 51 Brooklyn L. Rev. 355 (1985).

3. Milkovich v. Lorain Journal Co., 497 U.S. 1, 22 (1990) (Rehnquist, C.J.).

4. Rosenblatt v. Baer, 383 U.S. 75, 86 (1966).

5. Dun & Bradstreet Inc. v. Greenmoss Builders Inc., 472 U.S. 749, 757 (1985).

6. *See* Gavin Clark, Famous Libel and Slander Cases of History (1950).

7. M. Lindsay Kaplan, The Culture of Slander in Early Modern England 9 (1997).

8. *See, e.g.,* Norman L. Rosenberg, Protecting the Best Men: An Interpretive History of the Law of Libel (1986).

9. Van Vechten Veeder, *The History and Theory of the Law of Defamation*, 3 Colum. L. Rev. 546, 565 (1903) (quoting De Libellis Famois, 5 Co. Rep. 125 (1606)).

10. *Id.*

11. J.H. Baker, An Introduction to English Legal History 506 (3d ed. 1990).

12. 4 William Blackstone, Commentaries 152 (1979).

13. *Id.*

14. Milkovich v. Lorain Journal Co., 497 U.S. 1, 12 (1990) (Rehnquist, C.J.).

15. Sedition Act of 1798, ch. 74, 1 Stat. 596 (1798).

16. John Marshall, *Report of the Minority on the Virginia Resolutions*, 6 J. House of Delegates (Va.) 93–95 (Jan. 22, 1799), *reprinted in* 5 The Founders' Constitution 136–38 (Philip B. Kurland & Ralph Lerner eds., 1987).

17. *Id.* at 138.

18. James Madison, *The Virginia Report of 1799–1800, Touching the Alien and Sedition Laws, reprinted in* The Founders' Constitution 141–42 (1986).

19. *See, e.g.,* Whitney v. California, 274 U.S. 357, 374–77 (1927) (Brandeis, J., concurring) ("The best answer for bad speech is more speech").

20. Merriam-Webster Dictionary, Jan. 24, 2017, www.merriam-webster.com/dictionary/fact.

21. Merriam-Webster Dictionary, Feb. 2, 2017, www.merriam-webster.com/dictionary/opinion.

22. *New Developments 2012*, MLRC Bulletin, Dec. 2012, at 65; *see, e.g.,* Martin v. Daily News LP, 951 N.Y.S.2d 87 (N.Y. Sup. 2012).

23. Diamond Ranch Academy Inc. v. Filer, 44 Med. L. Rep. 1486 (D. Utah Feb. 17, 2016).

24. *New Developments 2012*, MLRC Bulletin, Dec. 2012, at 65; *see, e.g.,* Martin v. Daily News LP, 951 N.Y.S.2d 87 (N.Y. Sup. 2012).

25. Enigma Software Group USA LLC v. Bleeping Computer LLC, 194 F. Supp. 3d 263 (S.D.N.Y. 2016).

26. Cubby Inc. v. CompuServe Inc., 776 F. Supp. 135 (S.D.N.Y. 1991) (holding that the ISP is not responsible for content posted).

27. Stratton Oakmont v. Prodigy Servs. Co., 1995 N.Y. Misc. LEXIS 229 (N.Y. Sup. Ct., May 24, 1995) (holding that because Prodigy claimed to monitor its content, the ISP is placed in the role of publisher).

28. Zeran v. America Online Inc., 129 F.3d 327, 330 (4th Cir. 1997).

29. *Id.* at 330.

30. *Id.*

31. *Id.* at 331.

32. Universal Communication Systems Inc. v. Lycos Inc., 478 F.3d 413 (1st Cir. 2007).

33. *Id.* at 418–19.

34. Dimeo v. Max, 433 F. Supp. 2d 523 (E.D. Pa. 2006).

35. McIntyre v. Ohio Elections Commission, 514 U.S. 334, 357 (1995).

36. Ashley I. Kissinger, Katharine Larsen & Matthew E. Kelley, *Protections for Anonymous Online Speech*, 2 Comm. L. in the Digital Age 532 (2012). (Good faith is only applied in the state of Virginia.)

37. Dendrite International Inc. v. Doe No. 3, 342 N.J. Super. 134 (July 11, 2001).

38. Doe v. Cahill, 884 A.2d 451, 457 (Del. 2005).

39. Restatement (Second) of Torts § 564A cmt. b (1976).

40. Neiman-Marcus v. Lait, 13 F.R.D. 311, 316 (S.D.N.Y. 1952).

41. Doe v. Hagar, 765 F.3d 855 (2014).

42. *See* Restatement (Second) of Torts § 559 (1997).

43. *See* W. Page Keeton et al., Prosser and Keeton on the Law of Torts § 111, at 773–78 (5th ed. 1984).

44. *See* Restatement (Second) of Torts § 559 cmt. e.

45. *See, e.g.,* Kimmerle v. New York Evening Journal Inc., 262 N.Y. 99 (1933).

46. Yonaty v. Mincolla, N.Y.S. 2d 774 (N.Y. App. 2012).

47. Burke v. Gregg, 55 A.3d 212 (R.I. 2012).

48. *New Developments 2012*, MLRC Bulletin, Dec. 2012, at 51.

49. Kaelin v. Globe Communications, 162 F.3d 1036 (9th Cir. 1998).

50. *Id.* at 1042.

51. Knutt v. Metro Int'l, 938 N.Y.S.2d 134 (N.Y. App. Div. 2012).

52. Cochran v. NYP Holdings Inc., 58 F. Supp. 2d 1113, 1121 (C.D. Cal. 1998).

53. Texas Beef Group v. Oprah Winfrey, 11 F. Supp. 2d 858, 862 (N.D. Tex. 1998). The program had been tape recorded on Apr. 11, 1996.

54. *Id.*

55. *Id.*

56. *Id.* The ruling was also based on the failure of the plaintiffs to prove that cattle are perishable food, a requirement under the Texas False Disparagement of Perishable Food Products Act. The plaintiffs sued for the alleged violation of this provision of the act.

57. Philadelphia Newspapers Inc. v. Hepps, 475 U.S. 767, 776–77 (1986).

58. Masson v. New Yorker Magazine Inc., 501 U.S. 496, 516–17 (1991).

59. Dolcefino and KTRK Television v. Turner, 987 S.W.2d 100, 109 (Tex. Ct. App. 1998).

60. Yeakey v. Hearst Communications Inc., 234 P.3d 332 (Wash. App. 2010).

61. Stevens v. Iowa Newspapers Inc., 728 N.W.2d 823 (Iowa 2007).

62. Cheney v. Daily News LP, 2016 WL 3902639 (3d Cir. July 19, 2016) (unpublished).

63. Manzari v. Assoc. Newspapers Ltd., 830 F.3d 881 (9th Cir. 2016).

64. 376 U.S. 254 (1964).

65. *See, e.g.,* Harry Kalven Jr., *The New York Times Case: A Note on "The Central Meaning of the First Amendment,"* 1964 Sup. Ct. Rev. 191.

66. New York Times Co. v. Sullivan, 376 U.S. 254, 272 (1964).

67. *Id.* at 270.

68. *Id.* at 266.

69. *Id.* at 279.

70. *Id.* at 270.

71. *Id.* at 278.

72. *See, e.g.,* Lawrence Friedman, American Law in the 20th Century 341 (2002).

73. Goldwater v. Ginzburg, 414 F.2d 324 (2d Cir. 1969), *cert. denied,* 396 U.S. 1049 (1970).

74. Masson v. New Yorker Magazine Inc., 501 U.S. 496, 517 (1991).

75. Air Wis. Airlines Corp. v. Hoeper, 134 S. Ct. 852 (2014).

76. *Id.*

77. *Id.* at 864.

78. Curtis Publishing Co. v. Butts, 388 U.S. 130, 158 (1967).

79. Associated Press v. Walker, 388 U.S. 130, 140 (1967).

80. *Id.* at 157–59.

81. St. Amant v. Thompson, 390 U.S. 727, 731 (1968).

82. Herbert v. Lando, 441 U.S. 153 (1979).

83. Harte-Hanks Communications Inc. v. Connaughton, 491 U.S. 657 (1989).

84. Rosenblatt v. Baer, 383 U.S. 75, 85 (1966).

85. *Id.* at 86.

86. *Id.* at 87.

87. 388 U.S. 130, 163 (1967) (Warren, C.J., concurring).

88. *Id.* at 163–64.

89. 418 U.S. 323, 345 (1974).

90. *Id.*

91. *Id.* at 344.

92. *Id.* at 345.

93. Curtis Publishing Co. v. Butts and Associated Press v. Walker, 388 U.S. 130, 163 (1967).

94. Wolston v. Reader's Digest Ass'n, 443 U.S. 157 (1979).

95. Time Inc. v. Firestone, 424 U.S. 448 (1976).

96. Hutchinson v. Proxmire, 443 U.S. 111 (1979).

97. *Id.* at 135.

98. Chuy v. Philadelphia Eagles Football Club, 431 F. Supp. 254, 276 (E.D. Pa. 1977).

99. Renner v. Donsbach, 749 F. Supp. 987 (W.D. Mo. 1990).

100. *See, e.g.,* Williams v. Pasma, 656 P.2d 212 (Mont. 1982).

101. Gertz v. Robert Welch Inc., 418 U.S. 323, 351 (1974).

102. *Id.* at 345.

103. Tillman v. Freedom of Information Commission, 2008 Conn. Super. LEXIS 2120, *25 (Aug. 15, 2008).

104. Dun & Bradstreet Inc. v. Greenmoss Builders Inc., 472 U.S. 749 (1985).

105. *Id.* at 783.

106. *Id.* at 774.

107. Michael K. Cantwell, *Exploring the Issue of "Strict Liability" for Defamation,* MLRC Bulletin, Dec. 2012, at 3.

108. Id.

109. Obsidian Finance Group LLC v. Cox, 812 F. Supp. 2d 1220 (D. Ore. 2011).

110. Obsidian Finance Group LLC v. Cox, 740 F.3d 1284 (9th Cir. 2014).

111. *Id.* at 1290–91.

112. Restatement (Second) of Torts § 46 (1965) cmt. j.

113. *See, e.g.,* Gouin v. Gouin, 249 F. Supp. 2d 62 (D. Mass. 2003).

114. *See* Charles E. Cantu, *An Essay on the Tort of Negligent Infliction of Emotional Distress in Texas: Stop Saying It Does Not Exist*, 33 St. Mary's L.J. 455, 458 (2002).

115. Restatement (Second) of Torts § 46 (1965).

116. *Id.* cmt. d.

117. *Id.*

118. Showler v. Harper's Magazine Foundation, 222 Fed. Appx. 755 (10th Cir.), *cert. denied*, 552 U.S. 825 (2007).

119. Alvarado v. KOB-TV LLC, 493 F.3d 1210, 1222 (10th Cir. 2007).

120. Hatfill v. New York Times, 532 F.3d 312 (4th Cir.), *cert. denied*, 555 U.S. 1085 (2008).

121. *See* Scott Shane & Eric Lichtblau, *New Details on F.B.I.'s False Start in Anthrax Case*, N.Y. Times, Nov. 26, 2008, at A23.

122. Best v. Malec, 2010 U.S. Dist. LEXIS 58996 (N.D. Ill., June 11, 2010).

123. KOVR-TV Inc. v. Superior Court, 37 Cal. Rptr. 2d 431 (Cal. App. 1995).

124. Estate of Duckett v. Cable News Network, 2008 U.S. Dist. LEXIS 88667 (M.D. Fla., July 31, 2008), *quoting* Williams v. City of Minneola, 575 So. 2d 683, 691 (Fla. Ct. App. 1991).

125. Restatement (Second) of Torts § 46(1) (1965).

126. 376 U.S. 254 (1964).

127. Hustler Magazine Inc. v. Falwell, 485 U.S. 46 (1988).

128. *See* Rodney Smolla, Smolla and Nimmer on Freedom of Speech § 24.10 (2012). *See also* Rodney A. Smolla, Jerry Falwell v. Larry Flynt: The First Amendment on Trial (1988).

129. Falwell v. Flynt, 797 F.2d 1270 (4th Cir.), *rehearing en banc denied*, 805 F.2d 484 (4th Cir. 1986).

130. Hustler Magazine Inc. v. Falwell, 485 U.S. 46 (1988).

131. Snyder v. Phelps, 562 U.S. 443, 444 (2011).

132. *Id.* at 448.

133. Snyder v. Phelps, 580 F.3d 206 (4th Cir. Md. 2009).

134. Snyder, 562 U.S. at 452.

135. Honoring America's Veterans and Caring for Camp Lejeune Families Act, 38 U.S.C. § 101.

136. *See, e.g.,* Neilson v. Union Bank of Cal., N.A., 290 F. Supp. 2d 1101, 1142 (C.D. Calif. 2003).

137. *See, e.g.,* Dowty v. Riggs, 385 S.W.3d 117 (Ark. 2010).

138. *See, e.g.,* Nelson v. Harrah's Entertainment Inc., 2008 U.S. Dist. LEXIS 46524 (N.D. Ill., June 13, 2008).

139. *See* Camper v. Minor, 915 S.W.2d 437, 440 (Tenn. 1996).

140. *Id.*

141. Hyde v. City of Columbia, 637 S.W.2d 251 (Mo. Ct. App. 1982).

Chapter 5

1. Gertz v. Robert Welch Inc., 418 U.S. 323, 339–40 (1974).

2. The expression "SLAPP" was initially coined by two University of Denver professors. *See* Penelope Canan & George W. Pring, *Studying Strategic Lawsuits Against Public Participation: Mixing Quantitative and Qualitative Approaches*, 22 Law & Soc'y Rev. 385 (1988).

3. *See, e.g.,* Cal. Code Civ. Proc. § 425.16 (stating, in part, "The Legislature finds and declares that there has been a disturbing increase in lawsuits brought primarily to chill the valid exercise of the constitutional rights of freedom of speech and petition for the redress of grievances. The Legislature finds and declares that it is in the public interest to encourage continued participation in matters of public significance, and that this participation should not be chilled through abuse of the judicial process. . . . A cause of action against a person arising from any act of that person in furtherance of the person's right of petition or free speech under the United States or California Constitution in connection with a public issue shall be subject to a special motion to strike, unless the court determines that the plaintiff has established that there is a probability that the plaintiff will prevail on the claim").

4. Kevin T. Baine, Grey C. Callaham & Nicholas Gamse, *Defamation Law Case Summaries for PLI*, 2 Comm. L. in the Digital Age 32–39 (2014); Royalty Network Inc. v. Harris, 756 F.3d 1351 (11th Cir. July 10, 2014).

5. Abbas v. Foreign Policy Group, LLC, 783 F.3d 1328, 1332 (2015).

6. *Id.* at 1338.

7. Competitive Enterprise Institute v. Michael E. Mann, 2016 D.C. App. Lexis 435 (Dec. 22, 2016).

8. *Id.*

9. *Id.* at *49.

10. Sarver v. Chartier, 813 F.3d 891 (9th Cir., Feb. 17, 2016).

11. Travelers Cas. Ins. Co. v. Hirsh, 831 F.3d 1179 (9th Cir.

Aug. 3, 2016) (Kozinski, J., concurrence).

12. *Defamation and Related Claims*, Comm. L. in the Digital Age 2016 (Nov. 10, 2016).

13. Moreno v. Crookston Times and McDaniel, 2002 Minn. App. LEXIS 12 (Minn. 2002).

14. Hurst v. Capital Cities Media Inc., 754 N.E.2d 429 (Ill. App. 2001).

15. Weimer v. Rankin, 790 P.2d 347 (Ida. 1990).

16. DMC Plumbing and Remodeling v. Fox News Network, No. 12-cv-12867, 2012 U.S. Dist. LEXIS 167318 (E.D. Mich. Nov. 26, 2012); *New Developments 2012*, MLRC Bulletin, Dec. 2012, at 60–61.

17. Milligan v. U.S., 670 F. 3d 686, 698 (6th Cir. 2012).

18. Kevin T. Baine, Grey C. Callaham & Nicholas Gamse, *Defamation Law Case Summaries for PLI*, 2 Comm. L. in the Digital Age 15 (2014); Barhoum v. NYP Holdings Inc., 2014 Mass. Super. LEXIS 52 (Mass. Super. Ct. March 10, 2014).

19. Barhoum v. NYP Holdings Inc. 2014 Mass. Super. LEXIS 52 (Mass. Super. Ct. March 10, 2014).

20. *New Developments 2012*, MLRC Bulletin, Dec. 2012, at 61.

21. *But see, e.g.,* Lee v. Dong-A Ilbo, 849 F.2d 876 (4th Cir. 1988) (ruling that the privilege does not extend to official reports issued by governments other than those in the United States).

22. Cowley v. Pulsifer, 137 Mass. 392, 394 (1884).

23. Liquori v. Republican Co., 396 N.E.2d 726, 728 (Mass. App. 1979).

24. Salzano v. North Jersey Media Group, 201 N.J. 500, 520 (2010).

25. Piscatelli v. Smith, 35 A.3d 1140 (Md. Ct. App. 2012).

26. Allen v. Ray, 87 A.3d 890 (Pa. Super. Ct. 2013) (table).

27. Tacopina v. O'Keeffe, 43 Med. L. Rep. 3180 (S.D.N.Y. Sept. 4, 2015), *aff'd,* 645 F. App'x 7 (2d Cir. 2016).

28. Traylor v. Kopp, 43 Med. L. Rep. 2248 (Conn. Super. Ct. July 2, 2015).

29. McIntosh v. The Detroit News Inc., 2009 Mich. App. LEXIS 128 (Jan. 22, 2009).

30. Gertz v. Robert Welch Inc., 418 U.S. 323, 339–40 (1974).

31. Moldea v. New York Times, 793 F. Supp. 335, 337 (D.D.C. 1992).

32. Moldea v. New York Times, 22 F.3d 310, 315 (D.C. Cir. 1994).

33. L. Fowler V. Harper & Fleming James Jr., Law of Torts § 5.28, at 456 (1956).

34. *See* Restatement of Torts § 606 (1938).

35. Restatement (Second) of Torts § 566 (1977) cmt. a.

36. Milkovich v. Lorain Journal Co., 497 U.S. 1, 14 (1990) (Rehnquist, C.J.).

37. Justin Jouvenal, *Injunction Over Negative Yelp Review Overturned by Virginia Supreme Court*, Wash. Post, Jan. 2, 2013, articles. washingtonpost.com/2013-01-02/ local/36212098_1_yelp-online-reviews-injunction.

38. Aditi Mukherji, *Yelp Defamation Lawsuit Ends in a Draw*, Findlaw .com, Feb. 3, 2014, blogs.findlaw .com/free_enterprise/2014/02/ yelp-defamation-lawsuit-ends-in-a-draw.html.

39. *See* Gertz v. Robert Welch Inc., 418 U.S. 323, 339–40 (1974).

40. Citizen Publishing Co. v. U.S., 394 U.S. 131, 139–40 (1969).

41. Whitney v. California, 274 U.S. 357, 375 (1927) (Brandeis, J., concurring).

42. New York Times Co. v. Sullivan, 376 U.S. 254 (1964).

43. *Id.*

44. Ollman v. Evans, 750 F.2d 970 (D.C. Cir. 1984).

45. *Id.*

46. Janklow v. Newsweek, 788 F.2d 1300, 1305 (8th Cir. 1986).

47. Spelson v. CBS Inc., 581 F. Supp. 1195 (N.D. Ill. 1984); Anderson v. Liberty Lobby Inc., 746 F.2d 1563 (D.C. Cir. 1984), *aff'd on other grounds*, 477 U.S. 242 (1986); Henderson v. Times Mirror Co., 669 F. Supp. 356 (D. Colo. 1987); Dow v. New Haven Indep. Inc., 549 A.2d 683 (Conn. 1987).

48. Gertz v. Robert Welch Inc., 418 U.S. 323, 339 (1974).

49. Milkovich v. Lorain Journal Co., 497 U.S. 1, 4 (1990).

50. *Id.* at 1.

51. *Id.* at 18.

52. *Id.*

53. *Id.* at 21.

54. Couloute v. Ryncarz, 2012 U.S. Dist. LEXIS 20534 (S.D.N.Y. Feb. 15, 2012).

55. Wampler v. Higgins, 752 N.E.2d 962 (Ohio 2001).

56. Madsen v. Buie, 454 So. 2d 727, 729 (Fla. Dist. Ct. App. 1984).

57. Hustler Magazine Inc. v. Falwell, 485 U.S. 46 (1988).

58. Greenbelt Cooperative Publishers Ass'n Inc. v. Bressler, 398 U.S. 6, 7–8 (1970).

59. Seaton d/b/a Grand Resort Hotel & Convention Cntr. v. TripAdvisor, 2012 U.S. Dist. LEXIS 118584 (E.D. Tenn., Aug. 22, 2012)

60. Grand Resort Hotel & Convention Cntr. v. TripAdvisor, 728 F.3d 592, 594 (6th Cir. 2013).

61. *Id.* at 596.

62. *Id.*

63. Silberman v. Georges, 456 N.Y.S.2d 395 (1982).

64. New Times Inc. v. Isaacks, 91 S.W.3d 844, 850 (Tex. 2002).

65. New Times Inc. v. Isaacks, 146 S.W.3d 144 (Tex. 2004), *cert. denied*, 545 U.S. 1105 (2005).

66. 47 U.S.C. §§ 230 (c)(1), (e)(3).

67. RonNell Andersen Jones, *Developments in the Law of Social Media*, Comm. L. in the Digital Age (2016).

68. *Legal Guide for Bloggers, Section 230 Protections*, Electronic Frontier Found., www.eff .org/issues/bloggers/legal/ liability/230.

69. *Id.*

70. Although this was not a libel case (the underlying right of publicity is discussed in Chapter 6), the court's ruling broadly applied to how Section 230 is used by services like Facebook to defend libel and privacy claims.

71. Fraley v. Facebook Inc., 830 F.Supp. 2d 801-02 (N.D. Cal. 2011).

72. Jones v. Dirty World Entm't Recordings, 755 F.3d 398, 401 (6th Cir. 2014).

73. *Id.* at 417.

74. *Id.*

75. Doe No. 14 v. Internet Brands, Inc., 824 F. 3d 846, 850 (9th Cir. 2016).

76. *Id.* at 851.

77. Edwards v. National Audubon Society, 556 F.2d 113 (2d Cir. 1977) (ruling that "when a responsible, prominent organization . . . makes serious charges against a public figure, the First Amendment protects the accurate and disinterested reporting of those charges, regardless of the reporter's private views of their validity. . . . We do not believe that the press may be required under the First Amendment to suppress newsworthy statements merely because it has serious doubts regarding their truth."). *Id.* at 120.

78. Dan Laidman, *When the Slander Is the Story: The Neutral Report Privilege in Theory and Practice*, 17 UCLA Ent. L. Rev. 74, 76 (2010).

79. McKinney v. Avery Journal Inc., 393 S.E.2d 295 (N.C. 1990).

80. Auvil v. CBS, 140 F.R.D. 450 (E.D. Wash. 1991).

81. *See* Firth v. State of New York, 775 N.E.2d 463 (N.Y. 2002), which outlines the principles of applying the single-publication rule to the internet and which is often used as a precedent to support similar cases in other states and in the federal court system.

82. Cardillo v. Doubleday & Co. Inc., 518 F.2d 638 (2d Cir. 1975) (ruling that the passages of a book whose authors wrote that a habitual criminal was involved in various other criminal activities did not constitute actual malice).

83. Liberty Lobby Inc. v. Anderson, 746 F.2d 1563 (D.C. Cir. 1984),

rev'd on other grounds, 477 U.S. 242 (1986).

84. *Id.* at 1568.

85. *Id.*

86. Logan v. District of Columbia, 447 F. Supp. 1328 (D.D.C. 1978).

87. Masson v. New Yorker Magazine Inc., 501 U.S. 496, 523 (1991).

88. Mourning v. Family Publ'ns. Serv., 411 U.S. 356, 382 (1973). *See also* Adickes v. Kress & Co., 398 U.S. 144, 157 (1970); U.S. v. Diebold Inc., 369 U.S. 654, 655 (1962).

89. *See* Anderson v. Liberty Lobby Inc., 477 U.S. 242 (1986).

90. Washington Post Co. v. Keogh, 365 F.2d 965, 968 (D.C. Cir. 1966).

91. Hutchinson v. Proxmire, 443 U.S. 111, 120 n.9 (1979).

92. Anderson v. Liberty Lobby Inc., 477 U.S. 242, 244, 256 (1986).

93. Bell Atlantic Corp. v. Twombly, 550 U.S. 544 (2007).

94. Ashcroft v. Iqbal, 556 U.S. 662 (2009).

95. Suja A. Thomas, *The New Summary Judgment Motion: The Motion to Dismiss Under Iqbal and Twombly*, Ill. Pub. L. and Legal Theory Res. Papers Series (Oct. 27, 2009), www.parker-international.com/public/2009_ Public/SSRN-id1494683.pdf.

96. Schatz v. Republican State Leadership Committee, 669 F.3d 50, 57 (1st Cir. 2012).

97. Mayfield v. NASCAR, 674 F. 3d 369 (4th Cir. 2012).

98. Michel v. NYP Holdings Inc., 816 F. 3d 686 (11th Cir. 2016).

99. *See, e.g.,* Keeton v. Hustler Magazine Inc., 465 U.S. 770 (1984) (overturning a lower court

ruling dismissing a libel suit filed by a resident of New York against an Ohio corporation in a New Hampshire court). *See also* New York Times Co. v. Sullivan, 376 U.S. 254 (1964) (where the trial and first appeal were heard in Alabama courts).

100. Young v. New Haven Advocate, 315 F.3d 256, 261 (4th Cir. 2002), *cert. denied,* 538 U.S. 1035 (2003).

101. *Id.* at 263.

102. *Id.*

103. John C. Martin, *The Role of Retraction in Defamation Suits,* 1993 U. Chi. Legal F. 293, 294 (1993).

104. Two states' retraction statutes apply only to newspapers. *See* Minn. Stat. Ann. 548.06 (1987); S.D. Codified Laws 20–11–7 (1995). Two others include media other than newspapers but exclude radio and television. *See* Wis. Stat. 895.05 (1998); Okla. Stat. tit. 12, § 1446a.

105. Dennis Hale, *The Impact of State Prohibitions of Punitive Damages on Libel Litigation: An Empirical Analysis,* 5 Vand. J. Ent. L. & Prac. 96, 100 (2003).

106. Boswell v. Phoenix Newspapers Inc., 730 P.2d 186 (Ariz. 1986).

107. Ariz. Rev. Stat. §§ 12–653.02 and 12.653.03.

108. Ariz. Const., art. 18, § 6.

109. In its entirety, the column reads as follows:

Yesterday in the Franklin County Common Pleas Court, judge Paul Martin overturned an Ohio High School Athletic Assn. decision to suspend the Maple Heights wrestling team from this year's state tournament.

It's not final yet—the judge granted Maple only a temporary injunction against the ruling—but unless the judge acts much more quickly than he did in this decision (he has been deliberating since a Nov. 8 hearing) the temporary injunction will allow Maple to compete in the tournament and make any further discussion meaningless.

But there is something much more important involved here than whether Maple was denied due process by the OHSAA, the basis of the temporary injunction.

When a person takes on a job in a school, whether it be as a teacher, coach, administrator or even maintenance worker, it is well to remember that his primary job is that of educator. There is scarcely a person concerned with school who doesn't leave his mark in some way on the young people who pass his way—many are the lessons taken away from school by students which weren't learned from a lesson plan or out of a book. They come from personal experiences with and observations of their superiors and peers, from watching actions and reactions.

Such a lesson was learned (or relearned) yesterday by the student body of Maple Heights High School, and by anyone who attended the Maple-Mentor wrestling meet of last Feb. 8.

A lesson which, sadly, in view of the events of the past year, is well they learned early.

It is simply this: If you get in a jam, lie your way out.

If you're successful enough, and powerful enough, and can sound sincere enough, you stand an excellent chance of making the lie stand up, regardless of what really happened.

The teachers responsible were mainly head Maple wrestling coach, Mike Milkovich, and former superintendent of schools H. Donald Scott.

Last winter they were faced with a difficult situation. Milkovich's ranting from the side of the mat and egging the crowd on against the meet official and the opposing team backfired during a meet with Greater Cleveland Conference rival Metor [*sic*], and resulted in first the Maple Heights team, then many of the partisan crowd attacking the Mentor squad in a brawl which sent four Mentor wrestlers to the hospital.

Naturally, when Mentor protested to the governing body of high school sports, the OHSAA, the two men were called on the carpet to account for the incident.

But they declined to walk into the hearing and face up to their responsibilities, as one would hope a coach of Milkovich's accomplishments and reputation would do, and one would certainly expect from a man with the responsible poisition [*sic*] of superintendent of schools.

Instead they chose to come to the hearing and misrepresent the things that happened to the OHSAA Board of Control, attempting not only to convince the board of their own innocence, but, incredibly, shift the blame of the affair to Mentor.

I was among the 2,000-plus witnesses of the meet at which the trouble broke out, and I also attended the hearing before the OHSAA, so I was in a unique position of being the only non-involved party to observe both the meet itself and the Milkovich-Scott version presented to the board.

Any resemblance between the two occurrences [*sic*] is purely coincidental.

To anyone who was at the meet, it need only be said that the Maple coach's wild gestures during the events leading up to the brawl were passed off by the two as "shrugs," and that Milkovich claimed he was "Powerless to control the crowd" before the melee.

Fortunately, it seemed at the time, the Milkovich-Scott version of the incident presented to the board of control had enough contradictions and obvious untruths so that the six board members were able to see through it.

Probably as much in distasteful reaction to the chicanery of the two officials as in displeasure over the actual incident, the board then voted to suspend Maple from this year's tournament and to put Maple Heights, and both Milkovich and his son, Mike Jr. (the Maple Jaycee coach), on two-year probation.

But unfortunately, by the time the hearing before Judge Martin rolled around, Milkovich and Scott apparently had their version of the incident polished and reconstructed, and the judge apparently believed them.

"I can say that some of the stories told to the judge sounded pretty darned unfamiliar," said Dr. Harold Meyer, commissioner of the OHSAA, who attended the hearing. "It certainly sounded different from what they told us."

Nevertheless, the judge bought their story, and ruled in their favor.

Anyone who attended the meet, whether he be from Maple Heights, Mentor, or impartial observer, knows in his heart that Milkovich and Scott lied at the hearing after each having given his solemn oath to tell the truth.

But they got away with it.

Is that the kind of lesson we want our young people learning from their high school administrators and coaches?

I think not.

Chapter 6

1. Riley v. California, 134 S. Ct. 2495 (2014).

2. *Id.*

3. U.S. Const. amend. IV.

4. The "First Amendment has a penumbra where privacy is protected from governmental intrusion." Griswold v. Connecticut, 381 U.S. 479, 482 (1965).

5. *Id.* at 481.

6. U.S. Const. amend. V.

7. Jeffery A. Smith, *Moral Guardians and the Origins of the Right to Privacy*, 10 Journalism & Comm. Monographs 65 (2008).

8. Samuel D. Warren & Louis D. Brandeis, *The Right to Privacy*, 4 Harv. L. Rev. 193 (1890).

9. Warren and Brandeis rested their contention on an English case, Prince Albert v. Strange, 64 Eng. Rep. 293 (V.C. 1848), on appeal, 64 Eng. Rep. 293 (1849). But not until 2001 did English courts explicitly recognize a right to privacy. *See* Douglas v. Hello! Ltd., [2001] W.L.R. 992, 1033, ¶ 110 ("We have reached a point at which it can be said with confidence that the law recognizes and will appropriately protect a right of personal privacy") (per Sedley, L.J.).

10. *See* Don R. Pember, Privacy and the Press (1972).

11. William L. Prosser, *Privacy*, 48 Cal. L. Rev. 383 (1960).

12. Media Law Resource Center, Media Privacy and Related Law 50-State Survey 2016–2017 (2017).

13. Restatement (Second) of Torts § 652I.

14. *See, e.g.,* Restatement (Third) of Unfair Competition § 46 cmt. d (right of publicity limited to "natural persons").

15. Restatement (Second) of Torts § 652E cmt. b, illus. 1.

16. Spahn v. Julian Messner, 233 N.E.2d 840 (N.Y. 1967).

17. Solano v. Playgirl Inc., 292 F.3d 1078, 1082 (9th Cir.), *cert. denied*, 537 U.S. 1029 (2002).

18. See Restatement (Second) of Torts § 652E.

19. *Id.* at § 652I cmt. c.

20. *Id.* at § 652D cmt. a.

21. *See, e.g.,* Solano v. Playgirl Inc., 292 F.3d 1078 (9th Cir.), *cert. denied*, 537 U.S. 1029 (2002).

22. *See, e.g., id.*

23. *See, e.g.,* Eberhardt v. Morgan Stanley Dean Witter Trust FSB, 2001 U.S. Dist. LEXIS 1090 (N.D. Ill. 2001).

24. Howard v. Antilla, 294 F.3d 244 (1st Cir. 2002).

25. Moriarty v. Greene, 732 N.E.2d 730 (Ill. App. Ct. 2000).

26. Kelson v. Spin Publications Inc., 1988 U.S. Dist. LEXIS 4675 (D. Md. 1988).

27. Peoples Bank & Trust Co. v. Globe International, 978 F.2d 1065 (8th Cir. 1992), *on remand*, Mitchell v. Globe International Publ'g Inc., 817 F. Supp. 72 (W.D. Ark.), *cert. denied*, 510 U.S. 931 (1993).

28. Time Inc. v. Hill, 385 U.S. 374 (1967).

29. State courts or federal courts applying state law to follow *Gertz* rather than *Hill* and *Cantrell*, thus not requiring private false light plaintiffs to prove actual malice, include Alabama, Delaware, Kansas, Utah, West Virginia and the District of Columbia. MEDIA LAW RESOURCE CENTER, MEDIA PRIVACY AND RELATED LAW 50-STATE SURVEY 2016–2017 (2017).

30. State courts or federal courts applying state law to follow *Hill* and *Cantrell* rather than *Gertz*, thus requiring private false light plaintiffs to prove actual malice, include Arkansas, California, Connecticut, Florida, Georgia, Illinois, Indiana, Iowa, Kentucky, Maine, Michigan, Mississippi, Montana, Nebraska, Nevada, New Jersey, Oklahoma, Oregon, Pennsylvania, Tennessee and Washington. *Id.*

31. *See* HARVEY L. ZUCKMAN ET AL., MODERN COMMUNICATIONS LAW 357–61 (1999).

32. *See id.* at 360–61 (1999).

33. *E.g.,* Veilleux v. NBC, 206 F.3d 92, 134 (1st Cir. 2000), said opinion could be a false light defense, while Boese v. Paramount Pictures Corp., 952 F. Supp. 550, 558–59 (N.D. Ill. 1996), said opinion is not a false light defense.

34. *See* ZUCKMAN ET AL., *supra* note 80, at 351–52 (1999).

35. Sarver v. Chartier, 813 F.3d 891, 901–902 (9th Cir. 2016).

36. *Id.*

37. Thomas Burke, *Last Year's Key Anti-SLAPP Decisions*, LAW360.COM, Feb. 3, 2017, www.law360.com/articles/888023/last-year-s-key-california-anti-slapp-decisions.

38. Kelli L. Sager, *Address at the 2014 Practising Law Institute's Communication in the Digital Age* (Nov. 13, 2014).

39. *Id.* See also Kelli L. Sager & Karen A. Henry, *Developments in Misappropriation and Right of Publicity Law—2014*, 2 COMM. LAW IN THE DIGITAL AGE 3–18 (2014).

40. MEDIA LAW RESOURCE CENTER, MEDIA PRIVACY AND RELATED LAW 50-STATE SURVEY 2016–2017 (2017).

41. RESTATEMENT (THIRD) OF UNFAIR COMPETITION § 46.

42. N.Y. Civil Rights Law §§ 50–51.

43. Haelan Laboratories Inc. v. Topps Chewing Gum Inc., 202 F.2d 866 (2d Cir. 1953).

44. *See* J. THOMAS MCCARTHY, THE RIGHTS OF PUBLICITY AND PRIVACY §§ 1:27, 4:7 (2013).

45. Some states, such as Georgia, New Jersey and Utah, and the U.S. Court of Appeals for the Second Circuit have decided by common law that the right of publicity survives after death. Statutes in 10 states say the same. Some states, such as Illinois and Ohio, and the U.S. Courts of Appeals for the Sixth and Seventh Circuits say by common law that the right of publicity ends when a person dies. Five states agree by statute: Arizona, Massachusetts, New York, Rhode Island and Wisconsin. *See* J. THOMAS MCCARTHY, THE RIGHTS OF PUBLICITY AND PRIVACY §§ 1:27, 4:7 (2013).

46. By statute: California, Florida, Illinois, Indiana, Kentucky, Nebraska, Nevada, Ohio, Oklahoma, Pennsylvania, Tennessee, Texas, Virginia, Washington. By common law: Connecticut, Georgia, Michigan, New Jersey, Utah. MCCARTHY, supra note 44, §§ 9:20–9:39 (2013).

47. *Id.* § 9:18. For example, Virginia limits the right of publicity to 20 years after a person's death, Indiana and Oklahoma allow the right to last 100 years after a person's death and Nebraska has no stated duration. *Id.*

48. *New Developments 2012*, MLRC BULLETIN, Dec. 2012, 68–71.

49. Milton H. Greene Archives v. Marilyn Monroe LLC, 692 F. 3d 983 (9th Cir. 2012).

50. Hebrew University of Jerusalem v. General Motors LLC, 903 F. Supp. 2d 932 (C.D. Cal 2012).

51. *In re* Estate of Reynolds, 327 P. 3d 213 (Ariz. Ct. App. 2014).

52. Mark Wolski, *Minnesota Lawmaker Pulls Prince Right of Publicity Bill*, BNA.COM, May 20, 2016, www.bna.com/minnesota-lawmaker-pulls-n57982072729/.

53. Bing Crosby v. HLC Properties Ltd., 167 Cal. Rptr. 3d 115 (Cal. Ct. App. 2014).

54. *See, e.g.,* Dalbec v. Gentleman's Companion Inc., 828 F.2d 921 (2d Cir. 1987).

55. Jennifer Rothman, *Harris Faulkner Hamster Case Settles*, RightofPublicityRoadmap .com, Oct. 7, 2016, www .rightofpublicityroadmap. com/news-commentary/harris-faulkner-hamster-case-settles.

56. *See* McCarthy, *supra* note 44, § 3:7.

57. Abdul-Jabbar v. General Motors Corp., 85 F.3d 407 (9th Cir. 1996).

58. Martin v. Wendy's International Inc., 2016 WL 1730648, No. 15 C 6998 (N.D. Ill. May 2, 2016).

59. Jackson v. Odenat, et al. 9 F. Supp. 3d 342 (S.D.N.Y. March 24, 2014).

60. Prudhomme v. The Procter & Gamble Co., 800 F. Supp. 390 (E.D. La. 1992).

61. Midler v. Ford Motor Co., 849 F.2d 460 (9th Cir. 1988). A federal district court denied Midler punitive damages, but the jury awarded $400,000 in compensatory damages. The Ninth Circuit affirmed. Midler v. Young & Rubicam Inc., 944 F.2d 909 (9th Cir. 1991), *cert. denied*, 503 U.S. 951 (1992).

62. White v. Samsung Electronics America Inc., 971 F.2d 1395 (9th Cir. 1992), *cert. denied*, 508 U.S. 951 (1993).

63. Wendt v. Host International Inc., 125 F.3d 806 (9th Cir. 1997), *cert. denied*, 531 U.S. 811 (2000).

64. *Norm and Cliff Cheered by Lawsuit*, Chi. Trib., June 22, 2001, at C2.

65. *See, e.g.*, Cardtoons L.C. v. Major League Baseball Players Assoc., 95 F.3d 959 (10th Cir. 1996).

66. ETW Corp. v. Jireh Publishing Inc., 332 F.3d 915, 924 (6th Cir. 2003).

67. Leviston v. Jackson III, a/k/a 50 Cent, 980 N.Y.S. 2d. 716 (2013).

68. Zacchini v. Scripps-Howard Broadcasting Co., 433 U.S. 562 (1977).

69. C.B.C. Distribution and Marketing Inc. v. Major League Baseball Advanced Media L.P., 505 F.3d 818 (8th Cir. 2007), *cert. denied*, 553 U.S. 1090 (2008).

70. *See* Mark S. Lee, *Agents of Chaos: Judicial Confusion in Defining the Right of Publicity-Free Speech Interface*, 23 Loyola L.A. Ent. L. Rev. 471, 488 (2003).

71. Haelan Laboratories Inc. v. Topps Chewing Gum Inc., 202 F.2d 866, 868 (2d Cir.), *cert. denied*, 346 U.S. 816 (1953).

72. Cardtoons L.C. v. Major League Baseball Players Association, 95 F.3d 959, 962 (10th Cir. 1996).

73. *Id.* at 976.

74. Factors Etc. Inc. v. Pro Arts Inc., 579 F.2d 215 (2d Cir. 1978); Brinkley v. Casablancas, 438 N.Y.S.2d 1004 (App. Div. 1981); Titan Sports Inc. v. Comics World Corp., 870 F.2d 85 (2d Cir. 1989).

75. Paulsen v. Personality Posters Inc., 299 N.Y.S.2d 501 (S. Ct. 1968); Montana v. San Jose Mercury News Inc., 40 Cal. Rptr. 2d 639 (Ct. App. 1995).

76. Eriq Gardner, *Lindsay Lohan Loses Lawsuit Against Pitbull Over Hit Song*, The Hollywood Reporter, Feb. 21, 2013, www .hollywoodreporter.com/thr-esq/ lindsay-lohan-loses-lawsuit-pitbull-423228.

77. Rogers v. Grimaldi, 875 F.2d 994, 999 (2d Cir. 1989).

78. Parks v. LaFace Records, 329 F.3d 437, 442 (6th Cir. 2003), *cert. denied*, 540 U.S. 1074 (2003).

79. *See* Campbell v. Acuff-Rose Music, 510 U.S. 569 (1994);

Pierre N. Leval, *Toward a Fair Use Standard*, 103 Harv. L. Rev. 1105, 1111 (1990).

80. Comedy III Prods. Inc. v. Gary Saderup Inc., 106 Cal. Rptr. 2d 126 (Cal. 2001).

81. For a thorough and critical discussion of the Three Stooges decision, see F. Jay Daugherty, *All the World's Not a Stooge: The "Transformativeness" Test for Analyzing a First Amendment Defense to a Right of Publicity Claim Against Distribution of a Work of Art*, 27 Col. J. L. & Arts 1 (2003).

82. Comedy III Prods. Inc., 106 Cal. Rptr. 2d at 140.

83. Steve Berkowitz, *Payouts for College Athletes From EA Sports Distributed Soon*, USAToday .com, Nov. 7, 2015, www .usatoday.com/story/sports/ college/2015/11/07/ncaa-college-ea-sports-lawsuit-payouts/75367410/.

84. Keller v. EA Inc., 2010 U.S. Dist. LEXIS 10719 (N.D. Calif. Feb. 8, 2010).

85. Hart v. EA Inc., 808 F. Supp. 2d 757 (D.N.J. 2011).

86. *Id.* at 787.

87. Hart v. EA Inc., 2013 U.S. App. LEXIS 10171 (3d Cir., N.J., May 21, 2013).

88. Anne Bucher, *EA, NCAA Video Game Likeness Class Action Settlement*, Top Class Actions, Oct. 24, 2014, topclassactions .com/lawsuit-settlements/open-lawsuit-settlements/42811-ea-ncaa-video-game-likeness-class-action-settlement/.

89. Derek Svendsen, *Former Student-Athletes File Lawsuit to Protect Their Rights of Publicity: Recap of Marshall*

v. ESPN (filed 10/3/14), Sport in Law, Oct. 15, 2014, sportinlaw.com/2014/10/15/former-student-athletes-file-lawsuit-to-protect-their-rights-of-publicity-recap-of-marshall-v-espn-filed-10314/.

90. Javon Marshall et al. v. ESPN et al., 2016 U.S. App. LEXIS 15292 (6th Cir. 2016).

91. Steve Berkowitz, *Judges Who Ruled Against EA Sports Set to Hear NCAA Appeal in O'Bannon*, USA Today, Jan. 23, 2015, www.usatoday.com/story/sports/college/2015/01/23/obannon-class-action-lawsuit-ncaa-appeal-keller-case/22242583/.

92. Moore v. Weinstein Co. LLC, 545 Fed. App'x. 405 (6th Cir. 2013).

93. Winter v. DC Comics, 69 P.3d 473 (Cal. 2003).

94. *Id.* at 478 (*quoting* Comedy III Prods. Inc. v. Gary Saderup Inc., 106 Cal. Rptr. 2d 126, 140 (2001)).

95. Doe v. TCI Cablevision, 110 S.W.3d 363 (Mo. 2003), *on remand*, Doe v. McFarlane, 207 S.W.3d 52 (Mo. Ct. App. 2006).

96. Seale v. Gramercy Pictures, 949 F. Supp. 331 (E.D. Pa. 1996), *aff'd without opinion*, 156 F.3d 1225 (3d Cir. 1998).

97. Rosemont Enterprises Inc. v. Random House Inc., 294 N.Y.S.2d 122 (Sup. 1968), *judgment aff'd*, 301 N.Y.S.2d 948 (App. Div. 1969).

98. *See, e.g.*, Tyne v. Time Warner Entertainment Co., 336 F.3d 1286 (11th Cir. 2003).

99. Booth v. Curtis Publishing Co., 223 N.Y.S.2d 737 (N.Y. Sup. Ct.), *aff'd*, 228 N.Y.S.2d 468 (1962).

100. Cher v. Forum International, 692 F.2d 634 (9th Cir. 1982), *cert. denied*, 462 U.S. 1120 (1983).

101. Jordan v. Jewel Food Stores Inc., 743 F.3d 509 (7th Cir. 2014).

102. Schifano v. Greene County Greyhound Park Inc., 624 So. 2d (Ala. 1993).

103. Netzer v. Continuity Graphic Associates Inc., 963 F. Supp. 1308 (S.D.N.Y. 1997).

104. Restatement (Second) of Torts § 652B.

105. Media Law Resource Center, Media Privacy and Related Law 50-State Survey 2016–2017 (2017).

106. *Current Unmanned Aircraft State Law Landscape*, NCSL.org, Mar. 20, 2017, www.ncsl.org/research/transportation/current-unmanned-aircraft-state-law-landscape.aspx.

107. Webb v. CBS Broadcasting Inc., 2009 U.S. Dist. LEXIS 38597, at *9 (N.D. Ill., May 7, 2009).

108. *See, e.g.,* Broughton v. McClatchy Newspapers Inc., 588 S.E.2d 20 (N.C. App. 2003).

109. Boring v. Google Inc., 362 Fed. Appx. 273 (3d Cir.), *cert. denied*, 562 U.S. 836 (2010).

110. Hill v. Colorado, 530 U.S. 703 (2000).

111. Cal. Civ. Code § 1708.8.

112. Tracy Bloom, *New Laws Set to Take Effect in California for 2014*, KTLA.com, Dec. 31, 2013, ktla.com/2013/12/31/new-laws-set-to-go-into-effect-in-california-for-2014/.

113. Shulman v. Group W Productions Inc., 74 Cal. Rptr. 2d 843, *opinion modified*, 1998 Cal. LEXIS 4846 (Cal. 1998).

114. United States v. Maldonado-Norat, 122 F. Supp. 2d 264 (D.P.R. 2000).

115. Le Mistral Inc. v. Columbia Broadcasting System, 402 N.Y.S.2d 815 (1978).

116. Medical Laboratory Management Consultants v. American Broadcasting Cos. Inc., 306 F.3d 806, 819 (9th Cir. 2002).

117. Belluomo v. KAKE TV & Radio Inc., 596 P.2d 832 (Kan. App. 1979).

118. Machleder v. Diaz, 538 F. Supp. 1364 (S.D.N.Y. 1982).

119. Desnick v. American Broadcasting Cos. Inc., 44 F.3d 1345 (7th Cir. 1995).

120. Carter v. Superior Court of San Diego County, 2002 Cal. App. Unpub. LEXIS 5017 (Ct. App. 2002).

121. Dietemann v. Time Inc., 449 F.2d 245, 249 (9th Cir. 1971).

122. *Id.*

123. *See* John J. Walsh et al., *The Constitutionality of Consequential Damages for Publication of Ill-Gotten Information*, 4 Wm. & Mary Bill Rts. J. 1111, 1137–40 (1996).

124. Medical Laboratory Management Consultants v. American Broadcasting Cos. Inc., 30 F. Supp. 2d 1182 (D. Ariz. 1998), *aff'd on other grounds,* 306 F.3d 806 (9th Cir. 2002).

125. Sanders v. American Broadcasting Cos. Inc., 978 P.2d 67, 74 (Cal. 1999).

126. Brents v. Morgan, 299 S.W. 967 (Ky. Ct. App. 1927).

127. Restatement (Second) of Torts § 652D.

128. Michaels v. Internet Entertainment Group, 5 F. Supp. 2d 823, 842 (C.D. Cal. 1998).

129. MEDIA LAW RESOURCE CENTER, MEDIA PRIVACY AND RELATED LAW 50-STATE SURVEY 2016–2017 (2017). Four states have rejected the tort—Nebraska, New York, North Carolina and Virginia.

130. *See, e.g.,* Jones v. U.S. Child Support Recovery, 961 F. Supp. 1518 (D. Utah 1997). A debt collection agency sent a WANTED poster to the employer of a divorced parent who was behind on child support payments.

131. *See, e.g.,* Y.G. v. Jewish Hospital of St. Louis, 795 S.W.2d 488 (Mo. Ct. App. 1990). A couple, pregnant with triplets after an in vitro fertilization process, were invited to and attended a social gathering for couples who were part of a hospital's in vitro program. The hospital promised there would be no publicity. However, a television station reporting team was at the gathering, photographing and trying to interview the couple. The couple's pictures were part of the station's television report. The couple had not told anyone they were part of the in vitro program.

132. *See, e.g.,* Baugh v. CBS Inc., 828 F. Supp. 745 (N.D. Cal. 1993). Without permission, a television program taped and showed the aftermath of a domestic violence incident.

133. *See, e.g.,* Michaels v. Internet Entertainment Group, 5 F. Supp. 2d 823, 842 (C.D. Cal. 1998). Musician Bret Michaels brought a private facts suit against an internet adult entertainment company for distributing a videotape showing Michaels and actress Pamela Anderson

Lee having sex. Michaels and Lee made the tape, which an unknown person apparently stole and sold to the internet company.

134. See Robert C. Post, *The Social Foundations of Privacy: Community and Self in the Common Law Tort,* 77 CAL. L. REV. 957, 983–984 (1989).

135. RESTATEMENT (SECOND) OF TORTS § 652D cmt. c.

136. *See* M.G. v. Time Warner Inc., 107 Cal. Rptr. 2d 504, 511 (Cal. App. 2001).

137. Sandler v. Calcagni, 565 F. Supp. 2d 184 (D. Me. 2008).

138. *Id.* at 198.

139. RESTATEMENT (SECOND) OF TORTS § 652D cmts. g, h.

140. The Restatement also adopted the test. *Id.* cmt. h.

141. Virgil v. Time Inc., 527 F.2d 1122 (9th Cir. 1975), *cert. denied,* 425 U.S. 998 (1976).

142. Virgil v. Sports Illustrated Inc., 424 F. Supp. 1286 (S.D. Cal. 1976).

143. Michaels v. Internet Entertainment Group Inc., 5 F. Supp. 2d 823 (C.D. Cal. 1998).

144. Gehres Law Group, *Gehres Law Group Reviews the Constitutional Issues in Hulk Hogan v. Gawker,* GEHRESLAW.COM, Mar. 22, 2016, gehreslaw.com/tag/hulk-hogan-civil-case/.

145. Gawker Media LLC v. Bollea, 129 So. 3d 1196 (Fla. Dist. Ct. App. 2014).

146. Sydney Ember, *Gawker and Hulk Hogan Reach $31 Million Settlement,* N.Y. TIMES, Nov. 2, 2016, www.nytimes .com/2016/11/03/business/

media/gawker-hulk-hogan-settlement.html?_r=1.

147. Max Kennerly, *Hulk Hogan v. Gawker Legal FAQ— In Their Lawyers' Words,* LITIGATIONANDTRIAL.COM, May 26, 2016, www.litigationandtrial .com/2016/05/articles/attorney/ hogan-v-gawker-legal-faq/.

148. Diaz v. Oakland Tribune, 188 Cal. Rptr. 762 (1983).

149. Sidis v. F-R Publishing Corp., 113 F.2d 806 (2d Cir.), *cert. denied,* 311 U.S. 711 (1940).

150. RESTATEMENT (SECOND) OF TORTS § 652D, requires the private facts to be disseminated "to the public at large, or to so many persons that the matter must be regarded as substantially certain to become one of public knowledge."

151. *See* Patrick J. McNulty, *The Public Disclosure of Private Facts: There Is Life After* Florida Star, 50 DRAKE L. REV. 93, 100 (2001).

152. See Beaumont v. Brown, 257 N.W.2d 522, 531 (Mich. 1977), *overruled in part on other grounds,* Bradley v. Saranac Board of Education, 565 N.W.2d 650 (1997).

153. Florida Star v. B.J.F., 491 U.S. 524, 541 (1989).

154. *See id.* at 536–37.

155. 491 U.S. 524 (1989).

156. Cox Broadcasting Corp. v. Cohn, 420 U.S. 469 (1975).

157. Oklahoma Publishing Co. v. District Court, 430 U.S. 308 (1977).

158. Smith v. Daily Mail, 443 U.S. 97 (1979).

159. Bartnicki v. Vopper, 532 U.S. 514 (2001).

160. *See, e.g.,* Carafano v. Metrosplash, 207 F. Supp. 2d

1055 (C.D. Cal. 2002), *aff'd on other grounds*, 339 F.3d 1119 (9th Cir. 2003).

161. *See, e.g.,* United States v. Smith, 992 F. Supp. 743 (D.N.J. 1998).

162. *See, e.g.,* Doe v. New York City, 15 F.3d 264 (2d Cir. 1994).

163. *Wyden Offers Bill Calling on President-Elect Trump, Future Presidential Nominees to Release Tax Returns*, SENATE.GOV, Jan. 4, 2017, www.finance .senate.gov/ranking-members-news/wyden-offers-bill-calling-on-president-elect-trump-future-presidential-nominees-to-release-tax-returns.

164. *See* Green v. Chicago Tribune Co., 675 N.E.2d 249 (Ill. App. Ct. 1996), *appeal denied*, 679 N.E.2d 379 (Ill. 1997).

165. *See, e.g., In re* Doubleclick Inc. Privacy Litation, 154 F. Supp. 2d 497 (S.D.N.Y. 2001).

166. Jordan Robertson, *What Your Phone App Doesn't Say: It's Watching*, SAN JOSE MERCURY NEWS, July 30, 2010, advance.lexis.com/Go ToContentView?requestid= 440dbd6c-f591-6e1b-e7be-40c6b5931869&crid=32d 39741-2819-6d42-9176-2577875dfeb0.

167. Associated Press, *Uber's Redesigned App Wants to Mine Personal Information on Your Phone*, L.A. TIMES, Nov. 2, 2016, www.latimes.com/business/technology/la-fi-tn-uber-privacy-20161102-story.html.

168. Cyrus Farivar, *Uber to Encrypt Rider Geo-location Data, Pay $20,000 to Settle NY Privacy Flap*, ARSTECHNICA.COM, Jan. 8, 2016, arstechnica.com/tech-policy/2016/01/uber-to-encrypt-rider-geo-location-data-pay-20000-to-settle-ny-privacy-flap/.

169. Fed. Trade Comm'n, *FTC Issues Final Commission Report on Protecting Consumer Privacy* (March 26, 2012), ftc.gov/opa/2012/03/privacyframework .shtm.

170. Declan McCullagh, *FTC Says Current Privacy Laws Aren't Working*, CNET NEWS, June 22, 2010, news.cnet.com/8301–13578_3–20008422–38.html.

171. Josh Constine, *Facebook Now Has 2 Billion Monthly Users . . . And Responsibility*, TECHCRUNCH .COM, June 27, 2017, techcrunch .com/2017/06/27/facebook-2-billion-users/.

172. Fed. Trade Comm'n, *Data Brokers: A Call for Transparency and Accountability* (May 2014), www.ftc.gov/system/files/documents/reports/data-brokers-call-transparency-accountability-report-federal-trade-commission-may-2014/140527databrokerreport.pdf.

173. *Id.*

174. Jane Kirtley, *Global Privacy and Data Protection—2014*, II COMM. LAW IN THE DIGITAL AGE 405 (2014).

175. Fed. Trade Comm'n, *Internet of Things: Privacy and Security in a Connected World* (Jan. 27, 2015), ftc.gov/system/files/documents/reports/federal-trade-commission-staff-report-november-2013-workshop-entitled-internet-things-privacy/150127iotrpt.pdf.

176. Alex Fitzpatrick, *Google Fined $7 Million in Street View Privacy Settlement*, MASHABLE.COM, March 12, 2013, mashable .com/2013/03/12/google-street-view-settlement/.

177. Emily Field, *Cellphone Cos. Duck Some Claims in Consumer Privacy MDL*, LAW360, Jan. 22, 2015, www.law360.com/articles/613856/cellphone-cos-duck-some-claims-in-consumer-privacy-mdl.

178. Spokeo Inc. v. Robins, 136 S. Ct. 1540 (2016).

179. *Id.*

180. Jane Kirtley, *Private Data Collection: Global Privacy and Data Protection*, COMM. LAW IN THE DIGITAL AGE 2016 (2016).

181. Video Privacy Protection Act, 18 U.S.C.A. § 2710(b).

182. *In re* Hulu Privacy Litigation, 2012 WL 3282960 (N.D. Cal. 2012).

183. Kirtley, *supra* note 238, at 13.

184. City of Ontario v. Quon, 560 U.S. 746 (2010).

185. O'Connor v. Ortega, 480 U.S. 709 (1987).

186. Ray Lewis, Comment: *Employee E-mail Privacy Still Unemployed: What the United States Can Learn From the United Kingdom*, 67 LA. L. REV. 959 (2007); *see also* Smyth v. Pillsbury Co., 914 F. Supp. 97, 101 (E.D. Pa. 1996).

187. 50 U.S.C. §§ 1804(a)(7)(B), 1823(a)(B) (2003).

188. United States v. Jones, 132 S. Ct. 945 (2012).

189. Katz v. United States, 389 U.S. 347 (1967) (Harlan, J. concurring).

190. Daniel T. Pesciotta, *I'm Not Dead Yet: Katz, Jones, and the Fourth Amendment in the 21st Century*, 63 CASE W. RES. 187, 198 (2012).

191. 132 S. Ct. 945.

192. Florida v. Jardines, 133 S. Ct. 1409 (2013).

193. Riley v. California, 134 S. Ct. 2473, 2488-89 (2014).

194. Robert Corn-Revere, *Protecting the Tools of Modern Journalism*, Comm. Law., Sept. 14, 2014, www.americanbar.org/publications/communications_lawyer/2014/september14/protecting.html.

195. Brendan Sasso, *Lawmakers Push Bill to Limit GPS Tracking*, Hill, March 21, 2013, thehill.com/blogs/hillicon-valley/technology/289575-lawmakers-push-bill-to-limit-gps-tracking.

196. Geolocation Privacy and Surveillance Act, S. 237, 114th Cong., 2nd Sess. (2015), www.congress.gov/bill/114th-congress/senate-bill/237; Geolocation Privacy and Surveillance Act, S. 395, 115th Cong., 1st Sess. (2017), www.congress.gov/bill/115th-congress/senate-bill/395/text.

197. Pub. L. No. 99-1508, 100 Stat. 1848 (1986), codified at 18 U.S.C. §§ 2510–2522. Title II of the ECPA is called the Stored Communications Act, codified at 18 U.S.C., ch. 121 §§ 2701–2712.

198. Ellen Nakashima, *Senate Panel Backs E-mail Privacy Bill*, Wash. Post, Nov. 29, 2012, articles.washingtonpost.com/2012-11-29/world/35586082_1_law-enforcement-privacy-law-e-mail-content.

199. Electronic Communications Privacy Act Amendments Act of 2015, S. 356, 114th Cong., 2nd Sess. (2015), www.congress.gov/bill/114th-congress/senate-bill/356; *see also* House

to Consider Narrow Update for Communication Privacy Law, EPIC.org, Feb. 7, 2017, epic.org/privacy/ecpa/.

Chapter 7

1. Branzburg v. Hayes, 408 U.S. 665, 728 (1972).

2. *See, e.g.,* Erwin Chemerinsky, *Protect the Press: A First Amendment Standard for Safeguarding Aggressive Newsgathering*, 33 Univ. Richmond L. Rev. 1143 (2000).

3. Branzburg, 408 U.S. 665.

4. Cindy Gierhart, *New York City Settles for $18 Million Over RNC Arrests*, Meta-News, Jan. 16, 2014, www.rcfp.org/category/tags/newsgathering#sthash.Y1ajjX3o.dpuf.

5. Bell v. Keating, 697 F.3d 445 (7th Cir. 2012).

6. Beacon Journal Publishing Co. Inc. v. Blackwell, 389 F.3d 683 (6th Cir. 2004), *cert. dismissed*, 544 U.S. 915 (2005).

7. PG Publishing Co. v. Aichele, 705 F.3d 91 (3d Cir.), *cert. denied*, 133 S. Ct. 2771 (2013).

8. Richmond Newspapers Inc. v. Virginia, 448 U.S. 555 (1980); Globe Newspaper Co. v. Superior Court for Norfolk County, 457 U.S. 596 (1982); Press-Enterprise Co. v. Superior Court of California for Riverside County, 478 U.S. 1 (1986).

9. Leigh v. Salazar, 677 F.3d 892 (9th Cir. 2012).

10. Leigh v. Salazar, 954 F. Supp. 2d 1090 (D. Nev. 2013).

11. Ketcham v. United States Nat'l Park Serv., 2016 U.S. Dist. LEXIS 178823 (D. Wyo., May 5, 2016).

12. James Dao, *Military Announces New Social Media Policy*, N.Y. Times, Feb. 26, 2010, atwar.blogs.nytimes.com/2010/02/26/military-announces-new-social-media-policy/?_r=0.

13. Gina Lubrano, *Who Paid for the Media in Iraq?*, San Diego Union-Tribune, June 23, 2003, at B-7. *See also* Jack Shafer, *Full Metal Junket: The Myth of the Objective War Correspondent*, Slate (Mar. 5, 2003), slate.msn.com/id/2079703.

14. City of Oak Creek v. Ah King, 436 N.W.2d 285 (Wis. 1989).

15. Letter from James Madison to W. T. Barry (Aug. 4, 1822), in 9 The Writings of James Madison, 1819–1836, at 103 (Galliard Hunt ed. 1910).

16. *See, e.g.*, Shannon E. Martin, Freedom of Information: The News the Media Use (2008).

17. The Government in the Sunshine Act, 5 U.S.C. § 552b (1976).

18. The Freedom of Information Act (FOIA), 5 U.S.C. § 552 (1966).

19. Advisory Committee Act, 5 U.S.C. App. 2 (1972).

20. Seven states provide access to government meetings and records in one law. They are Arkansas, Connecticut, Maine, Missouri, North Dakota, South Carolina and Virginia.

21. Susan Dente Ross, *Break Down or Breakthrough in Participatory Government? How State Open Meetings Laws Apply to Virtual Meetings*, 19 Newspaper Res. J. 31 (1998).

22. The Michigan Open Meetings Act and Freedom of Information Act, 1976 PA 267, MCL 15.261

et seq. (1976), www.legislature
.mi.gov/documents/Publications/
OpenMtgsFreedom.pdf.

23. Acosta v. City of Costa Mesa, 718
F.3d 800 (9th Cir. 2013).

24. The Honest Leadership and Open
Government Act of 2007, Pub.
L. No. 110–81, 121 Stat. 735
(2007).

25. Dep't of the Air Force v. Rose,
425 U.S. 352, 361 (1976).

26. 5 U.S.C. § 552(f)(1).

27. *See* Kissinger v. Reporters Comm.
for Freedom of the Press, 445
U.S. 136, 156 (1980). *But
cf.* United States v. Clarridge,
811 F. Supp. 697 (D.D.C.
1992) (holding that the Tower
Commission was an "agency" for
purposes of 18 U.S.C. § 1001).
Compare Meyer v. Bush, 981
F.2d 1288 (D.C. Cir. 1993)
(holding that FOIA does not
reach President's Task Force on
Regulatory Relief, comprising
vice president and certain cabinet
members), National Security
Archive v. Archivist of the United
States, 909 F.2d 541 (D.C.
Cir. 1990) (holding that FOIA
does not reach Office of Counsel
to President), Rushforth v.
Council of Economic Advisers,
762 F.2d 1038 (D.C. Cir. 1985)
(holding that FOIA does not reach
CEA) and Pacific Legal Found.
v. Council on Envtl. Quality,
636 F.2d 1259 (D.C. Cir. 1980)
(holding that FOIA does not
reach CEQ) with Energy Research
Found. v. Defense Nuclear
Facilities Safety Bd., 917 F.2d 581
(D.C. Cir. 1990) (holding that
Board is agency for purposes of
FOIA and Sunshine Act). The
Sunshine Act incorporates FOIA's
definition of "agency."

28. Goland v. CIA, 607 F.2d 339,
345 (D.C. Cir. 1978). In Forsham
v. Harris, 445 U.S. 169, 178
(1980), the Supreme Court
declared that Congress "did not
provide any definition of 'agency
records.'"

29. Note: *A Control Test for
Determining "Agency Record" Status
Under the Freedom of Information
Act*, 85 Colum. L. Rev. 611, 616
(1985).

30. *See, e.g.,* Note: *The Definition
of "Agency Records" Under the
Freedom of Information Act*,
31 Stan. L. Rev. 1093, 1093
(1979); Note: *What Is a Record?
Two Approaches to the Freedom
of Information Act's Threshold
Requirement*, 1978 B.Y.U. L.
Rev. 408, 408; Nichols v. United
States, 325 F. Supp. 130, 134
(D. Kan. 1971), *aff'd on other
grounds*, 460 F.2d 671 (10th Cir.),
cert. denied, 409 U.S. 966 (1972).

31. Forsham v. Harris, 445 U.S.
at 178.

32. *Id.* at 184.

33. Goland v. CIA, 607 F.2d 339
(D.C. Cir. 1978).

34. *Id.* at 347.

35. *See e.g.,* Mark Carreau, *Another
Shuttle, Another Breach*, Houston
Chron., July 9, 2003, at A1; Lee
Hockstader, *Release of Challenger
Tape Ordered*, Wash. Post, July
30, 1988, at A8; John Schwartz
& Matthew L. Wald, *Earlier
Shuttle Flight Had Gas Enter Wing
on Return*, N.Y. Times, July 9,
2003, at A14; Ralph Vartabedian,
*E-Mail to Columbia Discounted
Danger*, L. A. Times, July 1, 2003,
at A12.

36. David Cuillier & Charles
N. Davis, The Art of Access:
Strategies for Acquiring

Public Records (2010). *See also*
www.theartofaccess.com.

37. David Cuillier, *Honey v. Vinegar:
Testing Compliance-Gaining
Theories in the Context of Freedom
of Information Laws*, 15 Comm. L
& Pol'y 203–29 (2010).

38. Reporters Committee for
Freedom of the Press, *How to Use
the Federal FOIA Act*, www.rcfp
.org/federal open government
guide (last visited July 26, 2017).

39. Reporters Committee for
Freedom of the Press, *FOI Letter
Generator*, www.rcfp.org/foi
(last visited July 26, 2017).

40. Citizens for Responsibility and
Ethics in Washington v. Fed.
Election Comm., 711 F.3d 180
(D.C. Cir. 2013).

41. Amy Harder, *Citizens Group Wins
FOIA Battle With Nuclear Agency*,
Reporters Committee for
Freedom of the Press,
Apr. 4, 2008, http://www.rcfp
.org/browse-media-law-resources/
news/citizens-group-wins-foia-
battle-nuclear-agency.

42. FOIA Improvement Act, Pub. L.
No. 114–185 (2016).

43. ACLU v. CIA, 710 F.3d 422
(D.C. Cir. 2013), *aff'd*, 640 Fed.
App'x 9 (D.C. Cir. 2016).

44. Electronic Freedom of
Information Act Amendments of
1996, Pub. L. No. 104–231, §
1–12, 110 Stat. 3048 (1996).

45. TPS Inc. v. Dep't. Def., 330 F.3d
1191 (9th Cir. 2003).

46. *See, e.g.,* Richard Matthews et al.,
*State-by-State Report on Permanent
Public Access to Electronic Government
Information*, Univ. of Ga. L.
(2003), http://digitalcommons.
law.uga.edu/cgi/viewcontent.
cgi?article=1009&context=law_lib_
artchop.

47. Some studies indicate that FOIA use is very low among journalists. *See, e.g.,* Heritage Foundation, *Media Center Study Finds Little FOIA Use by Journalists*, Dec. 1, 2001, www.heritage.org/Research/Reports/2001/12/Media-Center-Study-Finds-Little-FOIA-Use-by-Journalists (showing that only 5 percent of FOIA requests came from journalists).

48. Freedom of Information Foundation of Texas, *Withholding Information,* Texas Pub. Info. Act, foift.org/resources/texas-public-information-act (last visited July 26, 2017).

49. 5 Ill. Comp. Stat. 140/1–1.

50. Tennessee Public Records Act, T.C.A. § 10–7–301 (6).

51. Lake v. City of Phoenix, 218 P.3d 1004, 1007 (Ariz. 2009).

52. *Id.*

53. O'Neill v. City of Shoreline, 240 P.3d 1149 (Wash. 2010).

54. AP v. Canterbury, 688 S.E.2d 317 (W. Va. 2009); Howell Education Association v. Howell Board of Education, 789 N.W.2d 495 (Mich. App. 2010); Convertino v. U.S. DOJ, 674 F. Supp. 2d 97 (D.D.C. 2009).

55. Nissen v. Pierce County, 357 P.3d 45 (Wash. 2015).

56. *Id.* at 56 (emphasis in original).

57. *Id.* at 57.

58. City of San Jose v. Superior Court, 389 P.3d 848 (Cal. 2017); Assoc. of Calif. Cities--Orange Cty., *California Supreme Court Ruling on Public Agency Disclosure of Private Communications*, www.accoc.org/wp-content/uploads/2017/03/CPRA-Memo.pdf (last visited July 26, 2017).

59. Daxton R. "Chip" Stewart, *Let the Sunshine In, or Else: An Examination of the "Teeth" of State and Federal Open Meetings and Open Records Laws*, 15 Comm. L. & Pol'y 265, 307–08 (2010).

60. Record at 1279, Cohen v. Cowles Media Co. (No. 90–634) (testimony of Bernard Casserly, characterizing the use of confidential sources as "a way of life in the profession of journalism").

61. Record at 694, Cohen v. Cowles Media Co., 501 U.S. 663 (testimony of Arnold Ismach).

62. *See, e.g.,* Brief of Petitioner, Cohen v. Cowles Media Co., 501 U.S. 663 (1990). One of the best known examples of investigative journalism, The Washington Post's uncovering of the Watergate scandal, was driven by a confidential source the reporters dubbed "Deep Throat." *See* Bob Woodward, The Secret Man: The Story of Watergate's Deep Throat (2005).

63. Cohen v. Cowles, 501 U.S. 663 (1991).

64. *Id.*

65. *Id.* at 669.

66. Buehler v. City of Austin, 824 F.3d 548 (5th Cir. 2016), *cert. denied,* Spoor v. Hamoui, 2017 U.S. Dist. LEXIS 2546 (M.D. Fla., Jan. 9, 2017).

67. Gericke v. Begin, 753 F.3d 1 (1st Cir. 2014).

68. Glik v. Cunniffe, 655 F.3d 78 (1st Cir. 2011).

69. *See, e.g.,* Buehler v. City of Austin, A-13-CV-1100 ML (W.D. Tex. July 24, 2014); Ramos v. Flowers, 56 A.3d 869 (N.J. Super. Ct. App. Div. 2012); Copwatch of E. Atlanta v. City of Atlanta, City of Atlanta Res. No. 11-R-0288 (Mar. 1, 2011).

70. Allen Etzler, *U.S. Justice Department Issues Letters Supporting Citizens Recording Police Officers*, Cap. News Serv., Apr. 26, 2013, cnsmaryland.org/2013/04/26/u-s-justice-department-issues-letters-supporting-citizens-recording-police-officers/.

71. *Ex parte* Thompson, 414 S.W.3d 872 (Tex. App 2013), *aff'd* 442 S.W.3d 325 (2014).

72. American Civil Liberties Union of Illinois v. Alvarez, 679 F.3d 583 (7th Cir.), *cert. denied*, 133 S. Ct. 651 (2012).

73. Animal Legal Defense Fund v. Otter, 118 F. Supp. 3d 1195 (D. Id. 2015). *See also* Animal Legal Defense Fund v. Herbert, No. 13-00679 (D. Utah Aug. 8, 2014) (denying the state's motion to dismiss a First Amendment and equal protection challenge to Utah's ag-gag law); People for the Ethical Treatment of Animals Inc. v. Cooper, No. 16-CV-25 (D. N.C. 2016) (pending constitutional challenge to the North Carolina ag-gag law).

74. Idaho Code § 18-7042 (2016).

75. Iowa Code § 717A.3A (2016); Kan. Stat. Ann. § 47-1825 (2016); Mont. Code Ann. § 80-30-101 (2015); Mo. Rev. Stat. § 578.405.1 (2015); N.C. Gen. Stat. § 99A-2 (2016); N.D. Cent. Code § 12.1-21.1-03 (2016); Utah Code Ann. § 76-6-112 (Lexis Nexis 2016). *See also* Marshall Tuttle, *Finally a Solution? How Animal Legal Defense Fund v. Otter Could Affect the Constitutionality of Iowa's Ag-Gag Law*, 21 Drake J. Agric. L. 237 (2016); Matthew Shea, *Punishing Animal Rights Activists for Animal Abuse*, 48 Colum. J.L. & Soc. Probs. 337 (2015).

76. Heff Zalesin, *Paragliding Journalist Arrested After Photographing Kansas Feedlot*, July

15, 2013, www.rcfp.org/category/tags/newsgathering#sthash.YlajjX3o.dpuf.

77. *George Steinmetz Wonders: Was It Worth Getting Arrested for National Geographic Cover Story Photos?*, Photo District News, May 1, 2014, pdnpulse.pdnonline.com/2014/05/george-steinmetz-wonders-worth-getting-arrested-national-geographic-cover-story-photos.html.

78. Animal Enterprise Terrorism Act, 18 U.S.C.A. § 43 (West 2014).

79. Steve Cain, *A Practical Guide to Taping Conversations in the 50 States and D.C.*, Expert Pages, expertpages.com/news/taping_conversations.htm.

80. The 12 states are California, Connecticut, Florida, Illinois, Maryland, Massachusetts, Michigan, Montana, Nevada, New Hampshire, Pennsylvania and Washington. *See* Laws on Recording Conversations in All 50 States, MWL Law, Mar. 3, 2017, www.mwl-law.com/wp-content/uploads/2013/03/LAWS-ON-RECORDING-CONVERSATIONS-CHART.pdf.

81. State v. Geraw, 795 A.2d 1219 (Vt. 2002).

82. Steve Cain, *supra* n. 74. The states are Alabama, Arkansas, California, Delaware, Georgia, Hawaii, Kansas, Maine, Michigan, Minnesota, New Hampshire, South Dakota and Utah.

83. Calif. Penal Code § 632.

84. *Id.* at § 632(a).

85. Vera v. O'Keefe, 2012 U.S. Dist. LEXIS 112406 (S.D. Cal. Aug. 9, 2012).

86. Rick Ungar, *James O'Keefe Pays $100,000 to ACORN Employee He Smeared*, Forbes, Mar. 8, 2013, www.forbes.com/sites/rickungar/2013/03/08/james-okeefe-pays-100000-to-acorn-employee-he-smeared-conservative-media-yawns.

87. Sigma Delta Chi v. Speaker, Maryland House of Delegates, 310 A.2d 156 (Ct. App. Md. 1973).

88. *Id.*

89. *See also* Ronald L. Goldfarb, TV or Not TV: Television, Justice, and the Courts 56–95 (1998).

90. Erin Coyle & Eric Robinson, *Chilling Journalism: Can Newsgathering Be Harassment or Stalking?* 22 Comm. L. & Pol'y 65 (2017).

91. *Id.* n. 422 & 423. The states are Colorado, Delaware, Idaho, Illinois, Louisiana, Maine, New Jersey, Ohio and Vermont.

92. Galella v. Onassis, 353 F. Supp. 196 (S.D.N.Y. 1972).

93. Galella v. Onassis, 487 F.2d 986 (2d Cir. 1973).

94. Wolfson v. Lewis, 924 F. Supp. 1413 (E.D. Pa. 1996).

95. Food Lion Inc. v. Capital Cities Inc./ABC, 964 F. Supp. 956, 959 (M.D. N.C. 1997).

96. *See generally,* Jane Kirtley, *It's the Process, Stupid: Newsgathering Is the New Target*, Colum. Jour. Rev. (Sept./Oct. 2000).

97. *Id.* "The duty of loyalty recognized in this case requires an employee to use her efforts, while working, for the service of her employer. The jury found that each of the producers violated this duty by failing to make a good faith effort toward performing the job requirements of her employer Food Lion as a result of the time and attention she was devoting to her investigation for ABC and by performing specific acts on behalf of ABC which proximately resulted in damage to Food Lion."

98. *Id.*

99. Food Lion Inc. v. Capital Cities Inc./ABC, 964 F. Supp. 956, 959 (M.D. N.C. 1997).

100. Food Lion Inc. v. Capital Cities Inc./ABC, 194 F.3d 505, 526 (4th Cir. 1999) (Niemeyer, J., dissenting).

101. According to one of the attorneys involved, ABC's bill from one of the law firms handling the appeal only was in the "six figures" (personal communication on file with authors).

102. *Hidden Cameras, Hard Choices*, "Primetime Live" (Feb. 12, 1997). After the trial portion of the case, ABC's "Primetime Live" broadcast interviews with members of the jury. One juror said that on a scale of 1 to 10, with 10 being the worst, ABC's wrongdoing was a 10. "Because the—the girls were telling stories to get into a man's personal business, and they even made up stories to get in." This same juror said she wanted the punitive damages levied against ABC to be $1 billion. *Id.*

103. Special Force Ministries v. WCCO Television, 584 N.W. 2d 789 (Minn. 1998).

104. Veilleux v. NBC, 8 F. Supp. 2d 23, 30 (D. Me. 1998).

105. Veilleux v. NBC, 206 F.3d 92, 105 (1st Cir. 2000).

106. Nancy Garland, *Settlement Reached in "Dateline" Suit*, Bangor Daily News, Sept. 1, 2000.

107. *See, e.g.,* Miller v. NBC, 232 Cal. Rptr. 668, 677 (Cal. Ct. App. 1986): "The essence of the cause of action for trespass is an 'unauthorized entry' onto the land of another."

108. Miller v. NBC, 232 Cal. Rptr. 668, 682 (Cal. Ct. App. 1986).

109. *Id.* at 684 (*quoting* Dietemann v. Time Inc., 449 F.2d 245, 249 (1971)).

110. "At trial, Paul Berger was acquitted of federal charges of violating laws protecting eagles and found guilty of misdemeanor use of a pesticide." Nancy L. Trueblood, Comment: *Curbing the Media: Should Reporters Pay When Police Ride-Alongs Violate Privacy?*, 84 Marq. L. Rev. 541, 560 n.131 (2000).

111. Hanlon v. Berger, 526 U.S. 808 (1999).

112. *Obituaries,* St. Petersburg (Fla.) Times, Apr. 20, 2003, at 21A.

113. Wilson v. Layne, 526 U.S. 603, 607 (1999).

114. *Id.* at 611 (1999).

115. *Id.*

116. *Id.* at 613.

117. *Id.* at 614.

118. *See, e.g.,* Shulman v. Group W Productions Inc., 955 P.2d 469 (Cal. 1998) (ruling that outfitting a nurse with a wireless microphone, then videotaping her rescue of two people in an overturned automobile at the bottom of an embankment, then broadcasting the tape, constituted intrusion).

119. Video Voyeurism Prevention Act, 18 U.S.C. § 1801 (2004).

120. National Center for Victims of Crime, *Video Voyeurism Laws,* victimsofcrime.org/docs/Policy/Vid%20Voy%20Aug%202009.pdf?sfvrsn=0 (last visited July 26, 2017).

121. *Ex parte* Thompson, 442 S.W.3d 325 (Tex. Crim. App. 2014).

122. Greg Tsioros, *Photography Laws in Texas: When Taking Pictures Becomes a Crime,* June 1, 2016, www.txcrimdefense.com/photography-laws-in-texas-when-taking-pictures-becomes-a-crime/.

123. The 13 states are Alabama, Arkansas, California, Delaware, Georgia, Hawaii, Kansas, Maine, Michigan, Minnesota, New Hampshire, South Dakota and Utah. More information is available from Reporters Committee for Freedom of the Press at www.rcfp.org/first-amendment-handbook/introduction-recording-state-hidden-camera-statutes#sthash.dUANcVc4.dpuf.

124. *See* Reporters Committee for Freedom of the Press, *A Practical Guide to Taping Phone Calls and In-Person Conversations in the 50 States and D.C.* (2012), www.rcfp.org/taping. This section draws from the Reporters Committee's excellent guide to state and federal recording laws.

125. FAA, Small Unmanned Aircraft Rule, Part 107, June 21, 2016, www.faa.gov/news/fact_sheets/news_story.cfm?newsId=20516.

126. *Aerial Photographers: Drone Laws You Need to Know Before Flying,* SLR Lounge, Mar. 12, 2016, www.slrlounge.com/aerial-photographers-drone-laws-need-know-flying-infographic (citing laws in Arkansas, California, Florida, Mississippi, Tennessee, Texas, Chicago, New York City and Pittsburgh). *See also* Alissa M. Dolan & Richard M. Thompson II, *Integration of Drones Into Airspace: Selected Legal Issues,* Cong. Research Serv., R42940 (2013). *See* Fla. Stat. § 934.50 (2013); 2013 Idaho Sess. Laws 850-60; 725 Ill. Comp. Stat. 167/0 (2014); Tex. Gov't Code Ann. § 423.001.008; Utah Doce Ann. §§ 63G-18-101-05; 2013 Va. Acts 755; Wis. Stat. § 942.10 (2013).

127. *Current Unmanned Aircraft State Law Landscape,* Nat'l Conf. of State Legislatures, Jan. 5, 2017, www.ncsl.org/research/transportation/current-unmanned-aircraft-state-law-landscape.aspx.

128. *California Governor Outlaws Paparazzi Drones, Days After Approving Police UAVs,* RT, Oct. 1, 2014, rt.com/usa/192120-california-bans-paparazzi-drones/.

129. Tex. Gov't Code Ann. § 423.001.008.

130. Bart Jansen, *FAA Seeks $1.9 Million Fine From Drone Company SkyPan,* USA Today, Oct. 6, 2015, www.usatoday.com/story/news/2015/10/06/faa-drone-fine-skypan-19-million/73441850.

131. Bart Jansen, *Drone-Photography Company Fined $200,000 by FAA,* USA Today, Jan. 17, 2017, www.usatoday.com/story/news/2017/01/17/faa-drone-skypan/96671342.

132. 18 U.S.C. § 2510(1).

133. *See, e.g.,* Rafe Needleman & Felisa Yang, *Internet Calling: What It Is,* CNET, May 6, 2005, reviews.cnet.com/4520–9140_7–5131539–1.html; Robert Valdes & Dave Roos, *How VoIP Works,*

HowStuffWorks, May 9, 2001, computer.howstuffworks.com/ip-telephony.htm.

134. Wiretap Act, 18 U.S.C. § 2510 (2002) (defining the "aural transfer" that occurs in wire communication as "a transfer containing the human voice at any point between and including the point of origin and the point of reception").

135. Stored Communications Act, 18 U.S.C. §§ 2701–2711 (2000).

136. Eric Koester, *VoIP Goes the Bad Guy: Understanding the Legal Impact of the Use of Voice Over IP Communications in Cases of NSA Warrantless Eavesdropping*, 24 J. Marshall J. Computer & Info. L. 227, 234 (2006).

137. Vindu Goel & Nicole Perlroth, *Yahoo Says 1 Billion User Accounts Were Hacked*, N.Y. Times, Dec. 14, 2016, www.nytimes.com/2016/12/14/technology/yahoo-hack.html.

138. Electronic Communications Privacy Act, 18 U.S.C. § 2511.

139. Computer Fraud and Abuse Act, Pub. L. No. 99-508, 100 Stat. 1848 (1986) and 18 U.S.C. § 1030.

140. Pam Greenberg, *Computer Crime Statutes*, Nat'l Conf. of State Legislatures, June 27, 2014, www.ncsl.org/research/telecommunications-and-information-technology/computer-hacking-and-unauthorized-access-laws.aspx.

141. *Justice Department Drops News Corp Probe Related to Phone Hacking*, Reuters, Feb. 2, 2015, www.reuters.com/article/2015/02/02/us-newscorp-probe-idUSKBN0L62AX20150202.

142. Jessup-Morgan v. America Online Inc., 20 F. Supp. 2d 1105 (E.D. Mich. 1998).

143. Foreign Intelligence Surveillance Act, 50 U.S.C. § 1802.

144. *Monitoring Journalists' Calls*, Reporters Committee for Freedom of the Press, www.rcfp.org/browse-media-law-resources/digital-journalists-legal-guide/monitoring-journalists-calls (last visited July 26, 2017).

145. See *A Practical Guide to Taping Phone Calls and In-Person Conversations in the 50 States and D.C.*, Reporters Committee for Freedom of the Press, 2012, www.rcfp.org/taping.

146. *Id.*

147. *Id.*

148. 18 U.S.C. § 2511(2)(d).

149. *See* Use of Recording Devices in Connection with Telephone Service, 2 F.C.C.R. 502 (1986).

150. *See id.*

151. 47 C.F.R. § 73.1206.

152. Bartnicki v. Vopper, 532 U.S. 514, 518–19 (2001).

153. 18 U.S.C. § 2511(1)(c).

154. *Id.* at 525.

155. *Id.* at 534, 535.

156. Wiretap Act, 18 U.S.C. §§ 2510(2), 2511(1)(a), (c), (d).

157. Bowens v. Aftermath Entertainment, 254 F. Supp. 2d 629 (E.D. Mich. 2003), *summary judgment granted*, 364 F. Supp. 2d 641 (E.D. Mich. 2005).

158. RonNell Anderson Jones & Lyrissa Barnett Lidsky, *Recent Developments in the Law of Social Media Communications, in* 3 Comm. L. in the Digital Age 2012, at 75, 85 (2012).

159. *See* Memorandum for Heads of All Federal Departments and Agencies (Oct. 12, 2001) from Atty. Gen. John Ashcroft, www.usdoj.gov/foia/011012.htm: "I encourage your agency to carefully consider the protection of all such values and interests when making disclosure determinations under FOIA. Any discretionary decision by your agency to disclose information protected under FOIA should be made only after full and deliberate consideration of the institutional, commercial, and personal privacy interests that could be implicated by disclosure of the information. . . . When you carefully consider FOIA requests and decide to withhold records, in whole or in part, you can be assured that the Department of Justice will defend your decisions unless they lack a sound legal basis or present an unwarranted risk of adverse impact on the ability of other agencies to protect other important records."

160. *New Attorney General FOIA Memorandum Issued*, Fed'n Amer. Scientists, Oct. 15, 2001, www.fas.org/sgp/foia/ashcroft.html.

161. *See, e.g.,* Mark Fitzgerald, *The War of Fog in D.C.*, Editor & Publisher, Apr. 7, 2003, at 16.

162. *See, e.g.,* Brett Strohs, *Protecting the Homeland by Exemption: Why the Critical Infrastructure Information Act of 2002 Will Degrade the Freedom of Information Act*, 2002 Duke L. & Tech. Rev. 18 (2002).

163. *Memorandum for the Heads of Executive Departments and Agencies,* White House, Jan. 23, 2009, www.whitehouse

.gov/the_press_office/
FreedomofInformationAct.

164. *US Agencies Are Still Slow to Open Files*, Boston Globe, Mar. 15, 2010, at 2.

165. Ted Bridis, *Obama Administration Sets New Record for Withholding FOIA Requests*, AP, Mar. 18, 2015, www.pbs .org/newshour/rundown/obama-administration-sets-new-record-withholding-foia-requests/.

166. *See* Exec. Order No. 12958, § 4.2 (b), www.fas.org/sgp/bush/drafteo.html.

167. CIA v. Sims, 471 U.S. 159, 183 (1985).

168. ACLU v. U.S. DOJ, 681 F.3d 61 (2d Cir. 2012).

169. Dep't of the Air Force v. Rose, 425 U.S. 352, 369–70 (1976).

170. Milner v. Dep't of Navy, 562 U.S. 562 (2011).

171. Chrysler v. Brown, 441 U.S. 281, 292 (1979).

172. Russell v. Dep't of the Air Force, 682 F.2d 1045, 1048 (D.C. Cir. 1982).

173. FOIA Improvement Act of 2016, Pub. L. No. 114-185 (2016).

174. DOI and BIA v. Klamath Water Users Protective Association, 532 U.S. 1, 7 (2001) (*quoting* Dep't of Air Force v. Rose, 425 U.S. 352, 361 (1976)).

175. Cochran v. United States, 770 F.2d 949, 956 (11th Cir. 1985).

176. *See* U.S. DOJ v. Reporters Comm. for Freedom of the Press, 489 U.S. 749 (1989).

177. FCC v. AT&T, 562 U.S. 397 (2011).

178. U.S. DOJ v. Reporters Comm. for Freedom of the Press, 489 U.S. 749 (1989).

179. *Id.* at 765.

180. Nat'l Archives and Records Admin. v. Favish, 541 U.S. 157 (2004).

181. *Id.* at 173.

182. Reporters Comm. for Freedom of the Press, 489 U.S. at 773.

183. FCC v. AT&T Inc., 562 U.S. 397 (2011).

184. *Congress Repeals Dodd-Frank Exemption for SEC*, Stroock & Stroock & Lavan LLP, Oct. 13, 2010, www.stroock.com/SiteFiles/Pub996.PDF.

185. Privacy Act, 5 U.S.C. § 552a (1974).

186. Federal Educational Rights and Privacy Act, 20 U.S.C. § 1232g. (The nickname "Buckley Amendment" refers to the U.S. senator who introduced the bill, James Buckley of New York.)

187. *See* 34 C.F.R. § 99.3.

188. Clery Act, 20 U.S.C. § 1092(f) (1990).

189. Red & Black Publishing Co. v. Board of Regents, Univ. of Georgia, 427 S.E.2d 257 (Ga. 1993); Doe v. Red & Black Publishing Co., 437 S.E.2d 474 (Ga. 1993).

190. Red & Black Publishing Co., 427 S.E.2d 257.

191. United States v. Miami University, 294 F.3d 797 (6th Cir. 2002).

192. Health Insurance Portability & Accountability Act, Pub. L. 104–191, 110 Stat. 1936 (1996).

193. Driver's Privacy Protection Act, 18 U.S.C. §§ 2721–2725 (1994).

194. Reno v. Condon, 528 U.S. 141 (2000).

195. Dahlstrom v. Sun-Times Media, LLC, 777 F.3d 937 (7th Cir. 2015), *cert. denied*, 136 S. Ct. 689 (2015).

Chapter 8

1. Sheppard v. Maxwell, 384 U.S. 333, 362 (1966).

2. *See, e.g.*, *CNN Special Report: Married to A Murderer: The Drew Peterson Story*, CNN, June 25, 2015, www.cnn.com/videos/tv/2015/06/25/exp-cnn-creative-marketing-cnn-special-report-married-to-a-murderer.cnn; Jamie Stengle, *Randy Travis DUI: Country Music Star Enters Guilty Drunk Driving Plea*, Huff. Post, Jan. 13, 2013, huffingtonpost .com.

3. Mark Wilson, *Adnan Syed, Subject of "Serial," Asks for Another Appeal*, FindLaw, Jan. 14, 2015, blogs.findlaw.com.

4. See, e.g., Kimberly Gross & Sean Aday, The Scary World in Your Living Room and Neighborhood: Using Local Broadcast News, Neighborhood Crime Rates, and Personal Experience to Test Agenda Setting and Cultivation, 53 J. Comm. 411 (2003); Meredith Diane Lett et al., Examining Effects of Television News Violence on College Students Through Cultivation Theory, 21 Comm. Res. Rep. 39 (2004); Daniel Romer et al., Television News and the Cultivation of Fear of Crime, 53 J. Comm. 88 (2003).

5. Gannett v. DePasquale, 433 U.S. 368 (1979).

6. *Id.* at 378.

7. *Id.* at 383 (1979).

8. *Id.* at 415, 423.

9. Richmond Newspapers Inc. v. Virginia, 448 U.S. 555 (1980).

10. *Id.* at 569.

11. *Id.* at 581.

12. *Id.* at 575.

13. *See, e.g., Tsarnaev Convicted on All Counts*, Here & Now, Apr. 8, 2015, hereandnow.wbur.org/2015/04/08/tsarnaev-trial-verdict.

14. Rapid City Journal v. Delaney, 804 N.W.2d 388 (S.D. 2011).

15. Globe Newspaper Co. v. Superior Court for Norfolk County, 457 U.S. 596 (1982).

16. *Id.* at 606.

17. Press-Enterprise (I) v. Superior Court of Calif., 464 U.S. 501 (1984); Press-Enterprise (II) v. Superior Court of Calif., 478 U.S. 1 (1986).

18. Presley v. Georgia, 558 U.S. 209 (2010).

19. *Id.* at 214.

20. *Id.* at 215.

21. Chandler v. Florida, 449 U.S. 560 (1981).

22. *Judicial Conference Extends Pilot Project to Evaluate Cameras in Federal Courts*, Fed. Evidence Rev., Sept. 26, 2013, federalevidence.com/blog/2013/september/judicial-conference-extends-pilot-project-evaluate-cameras-federal-district-cour.

23. *Judicial Conference Says "No" to Expanding Cameras Pilot Program*, Mar. 15, 2016, fixthecourt.com/2016/03/judicial-conference-says-no-to-expanding-cameras-pilot-program/.

24. Michael Lambert, *Courtroom Camera Pilot Program Grounded*, Reporters Comm. for Freedom of the Press, Spring 2016, www.rcfp.org/browse-media-law-resources/news-media-law/news-media-and-law-spring-2016/courtroom-camera-pilot-prog.

25. *Id.*

26. Hollingsworth v. Perry, 558 U.S. 183 (2010).

27. Lisa Leff, *Court Won't Order California Officials to Appeal Ruling That Struck Down Gay Marriage Ban*, L.A. Times, Sept. 8, 2010, www.latimes.com/sns-ap-us-gay-marriage-trial,0,3059623.story.

28. Kathy Kirby, *Cameras in the Court: A State-by-State Guide*, RTDNA, Summer 2012, https://rtdna.org/article/cameras_in_the_court_a_state_by_state_guide_updated.

29. *See* Rule 2.450, Rules of Judicial Administration, Florida Rules of Court (2008); Florida v. Palm Beach Newspapers, 395 So. 2d 544 (1981).

30. *See Electronic Access to the Courts*, Sup. Ct. Rule 1:19 (Mass. 2012), www.mass.gov/courts/case-legal-res/rules-of-court/sjc/sjc119.html.

31. Sup. Ct. Rule 10–8 & 10–9 (S.D. 2011).

32. Ill. Code of Judicial Conduct, Rule 63 (A) (7).

33. 735 Ill. Code Civil Procedure 5/Art. VII, Part 7, § 8–701, Broadcast or Televised Testimony.

34. C. Danielle Vinson & John S. Ertter, *Entertainment or Education: How Do Media Cover the Courts?* 7 Harv. Int'l J. Press/Politics 80 (2002).

35. Comment: *Social Media's Attack on the Impartial Jury*, Kemp, Ruge & Green LG, 2017, kemprugegreen.com/social-medias-attack-on-the-impartial-jury/.

36. James Podgers, *Social Media Is New Norm, but Courts Still Grappling With Whether to Let Cameras In*, ABA J. (Aug. 8, 2010), www.abajournal.com/news/article/social_media_is_norm_but_courts_still_grappling_with_whether_to_let_cameras/.

37. State v. Smith, No. M2010–01384–SC–R11–CD (2013).

38. *See, e.g., Kan. Reporter Gets OK to Use Twitter to Cover Federal Gang Trial*, Assoc. Press, Mar. 6, 2009, www.firstamendmentcenter.org/news.aspxid=21329&SearchString=media.

39. Dana Liebelson, *Judge Approves Web Coverage of Hearing*, Reporters Comm. for Freedom of the Press News, Jan. 16, 2009, www.rcfp.org/newsitems/index.php?i=9903.

40. *1st Circuit Won't Allow Song-Swapping Hearing to Be Webcast*, Assoc. Press, Apr. 17, 2009, www.firstamendmentcenter.org/news.aspxid=21491&SearchString=media; *RIAA v. Tenenbaum Verdict*, Law & Fin. Mgmt. Channel, Aug. 10, 2009, lawfinancechannel.squarespace.com/law-finance-channel/2009/8/10/riaa-v-tenenbaum-verdict.html.

41. Am. Assoc. for Justice, *Texts and "Tweets" by Jurors, Lawyers Pose Courtroom Conundrums*, 45 Trial News & Trends (Aug. 2009), www.justice.org/cps/rde/xchg/justice/hs.xsl/10049.htm.

42. Laurie Sullivan, *Courtroom Bans on Social Media Spreading Across United States*, Online Media Daily, Mar. 10, 2010, www.firstamendmentcoalition.org/2010/03/courtroom-bans-on-social-media-spreading-across-united-states/.

43. Nixon v. Warner Communications, 435 U.S. 589 (1978).

44. *Id.* at 608–11.

45. United States v. Daoud, 755 F.3d 479 (7th Cir. 2014), *cert. denied*, 135 S. Ct. 1456 (2015); *Justices Won't Give Lawyers Access to Secret Court Records*, Assoc. Press, Feb. 23, 2015, www.foxnews.com/politics/2015/02/23/

46. Pub. L. 95–511, 92 Stat. 1783, 50 U.S.C. ch. 36.

47. United States v. Dimora, 862 F. Supp. 2d 697 (N.D. Ohio 2012).

48. Florida Star v. B.J.F., 491 U.S. 524 (1989).

49. Robert Timothy Reagan et al., *Sealed Settlement Agreements in Federal District Court*, Fed. Judicial C'tr (2009).

50. Ind. Code § 5–15–3–3, § 5–14–3–4.

51. *See* Nast v. Michels, 730 P.2d 54 (Wash. 1986).

52. *State ex rel.* Cincinnati Enquirer v. Winkler, 805 N.E.2d 1094 (Ohio 2004).

53. United States v. Silver, 2016 U.S. Dist. LEXIS 51057 (S.D.N.Y. Feb. 23, 2016).

54. U.S. Courts, *Judicial Privacy Policy Page: Privacy Policy*, Mar. 2008, www.privacy.uscourts.gov/b4amend.htm; Alan Carlson & Martha Wade Steketee, Public Access to Court Records: Implementing the CCJ/COSCA Guidelines Final Project Report (2005), www.ncsconline.org/WC/Publications/Res_PriPub_PubAccCrtRcrds_FinalRpt.pdf; Martha Wade Steketee & Alan Carlson, Developing CCJ/COSCA Guidelines for Public Access to Court Records: A National Project to Assist State Courts, at vi (State Justice Institute) (Oct. 18, 2002), www.courtaccess.org/modelpolicy/18Oct2002FinalReport.pdf.

55. A Quiet Revolution in the Courts: Electronic Access to State Court Records (Aug. 2002), www.cdt.org/publications/020821courtrecords.shtml.

56. Oonagh Doherty & Sara Tonneson, *How to Look Up Court Records on the Internet*, Mass. Justice Project, www.masslegalservices.org/content/how-look-court-records-internet-links-online-access-records-other-states.

57. Anna M. Phillips, *Court Papers Going Online*, Tampa Bay Times, Mar. 14, 2015, tampabay.com.

58. *Access Case Records,* Minn. Judicial Branch, www.mncourts.gov/Access-Case-Records.aspx.

59. Privacy/Public Access to Court Records, State Links, www.ncsc.org/topics/access-and-fairness/privacy-public-access-to-court-records/state-links.aspx.

60. Samuel Warren & Louis D. Brandeis, *The Right to Privacy*, 4 Harv. L. Rev. 193 (1890).

61. Final Report Minn. Sup. Ct Advisory Committee and Order on Rules of Public Access to Records of the Judicial Branch. Minn Court Rules: Record Access Rules Order No. C4–85–1848, Minn. Statutes; *Developing CCJ/COSCA Guidelines for Public Access to Court Records: A National Project to Assist State Courts*, State Justice Institute (Oct. 18, 2002), www.courtaccess.org/modelpolicy/18Oct2002FinalReport.pdf.

62. U.S. DOJ v. Reporters Committee for Freedom of the Press, 489 U.S. 749 (1989).

63. General Rule 31, adopted Oct. 7, 2004, by the Washington

Supreme Court. *See* www.courts.wa.gov/newsinfo/?fa=newsinfo.pressdetail&newsid=484.

64. Estes v. Texas, 381 U.S. 532 (1965).

65. The Pulitzer Prizes, *1963 Winners*, www.pulitzer.org/awards/1963.

66. Patton v. Yount, 467 U.S. 1025 (1984).

67. Sheppard v. Maxwell, 384 U.S. 333 (1966).

68. *Id.* at 340.

69. Interactive Media Lab, *Sheppard v. Maxwell* (1966), College of Journalism and Communications, University of Florida, iml.jou.ufl.edu/projects/Spring01/Woell/Sheppard.html.

70. News Media Barred From Hearing in Slaying of NFL Player, Assoc. Press, Apr. 7, 2011, www.ap.com.

71. Mu'Min v. Virginia, 500 U.S. 415 (1991).

72. Batson v. Kentucky, 476 U.S. 79 (1986); J.E.B. v. Alabama, 511 U.S. 127 (1994).

73. Sluss v. Commonwealth, 381 S.W.3d 215 (Ky. 2012).

74. *Id.* at 222, 223 (emphasis added).

75. Sluss v. Commonwealth, 450 S.W.3d 279 (Ky. 2014).

76. *Id.* at 285.

77. Jess Sullivan, *Judge: Juror's Twitter Messages During Trial Not Prejudicial*, Daily Republic, Apr. 4, 2015, www.dailyrepublic.com/news/crimecourts/.

78. *Id.*

79. Katharine Q. Seelye, *Surveys Show Bias of Potential Jurors in Boston Bombing Trial*, Int'l N.Y. Times, Jan. 23, 2015, www.nytimes.com/2015/01/23/.

80. *Id.*

81. Betterman v. Montana, 136 S. Ct. 1609 (2016).

82. *Id.* at 723.

83. Jeff Mordock, *Anxiety Caused by Trial Delays Is Prejudicial to Defense, Court Rules*, Del. L. Weekly, Jan. 7, 2015, www .delawarelawweekly.com/ id+1202714079771.

84. *Id.*

85. United States v. Velarde, 2015 U.S. App. LEXIS 5470 (10th Cir. 2015) (finding failure to file necessary pretrial motion for dismissal under Speedy Trial Act or to show delay caused prejudice).

86. *See, e.g.,* United States v. Shryock, 342 F.3d 948 (9th Cir. 2003), *cert. denied,* 541 U.S. 965 (2004).

87. Tex. Crim. Proc. Code Ann. § 35.29 (1994).

88. United States v. Wecht, 537 F.3d 222 (3d Cir. 2008); United States v. Blagojevich, 612 F.3d 558 (7th Cir. 2010).

89. United States v. Blagojevich, 614 F.3d 287 (7th Cir. 2010).

90. Mu'Min v. Virginia, 500 U.S. 415 (1991).

91. *Id.*

92. Butterworth v. Smith, 494 U.S. 624 (1990).

93. Chuck Murphy, *Good Intentions, Bad Results in Judge's Gag Order*, Denver Post, Aug. 5, 2012, at 18-A.

94. Jeremy P. Meyer & Kurtis Lee, *Judge Expands Gag Order in Shooting Case to Include University*, Denver Post, July 27, 2012, at 6-A; *Colo. Shooting Suspect Objects to Ending Gag Order*, Bismark Tribune, Feb. 6, 2013.

95. People v. Holmes, Motion Regarding Reconsideration of Pre-trial Publicity Orders,

Feb. 12, 2013, www .courts.state.co.us/userfiles/ file/Court_Probation/18th_ Judicial_District/18th_ Courts/12CR1522/Order.

96. *Court's Gag Order in Michigan Jail Corruption Case Reversed*, Prison Legal News, Apr. 1, 2016, at 58, www .prisonlegalnews.org/news/2016/ apr/1/courts-gag-order-michigan- jail-corruption-case-reversed.

97. People v. Sledge, 2015 Mich. App. LEXIS 1831 (Mich. Ct. App. 2015).

98. Richmond Newspapers Inc. v. Virginia, 448 U.S. 555 (1980).

99. *In re* Wall St. Journal, 601 Fed. Appx. 215 (4th Cir. Mar. 5, 2015).

100. Ruthann Robson, *West Virginia District Judge's Extensive "Gag" and Sealing Order in Blankenship Trial*, Constitutional L. ProfBlog, Jan. 8, 2015, lawprofessors.typepad.com/ conlaw/2015/01.

101. United States v. Blankenship, 79 F. Supp. 3d 613, 618 (S.D. W.Va. 2015).

102. *In re* Wall St. Journal, 601 Fed. Appx. at 218.

103. Sheppard v. Maxwell, 384 U.S. 333, 342 (1966).

104. Caperton v. Massey, 556 U.S. 868, 870 (2009).

105. Republican Party of Minn. v. White, 536 U.S. 765 (2002).

106. *Id.* at 787.

107. United States v. Bryan, 339 U.S. 323, 331 (1950).

108. Branzburg v. Hayes, 408 U.S. 665, 710 (1972) (Powell, J., concurring).

109. *See, e.g., National Security Letters*, Electronic Privacy Info. Ctr., epic.org/privacy/nsl/. *See also*

Daniel J. Malooly, *Searches Under FISA: A Constitutional Analysis,* 35 Am. Crim. L. Rev. 411 (1997–1998).

110. Zurcher v. Stanford Daily, 436 U.S. 547, 563–64 (1978).

111. Report of the Committee of the Judiciary: Free Flow of Info. Act, S. Rep. No. 113-118, at §B (2013).

112. *See Paying the Price: A Recent Census of Reporters Jailed or Fined for Refusing to Testify*, Reporters Comm. for Freedom of the Press, www.rcfp.org/jail.html (last visited July 28, 2016). See also Edmond J. Bartnett, *Columnist Loses in Contempt Case*, N.Y. Times, Oct. 1, 1958, at 30 (explaining the jailing of reporter Marie Torre for refusing to disclose a source of information); Ross E. Milloy, *Writer Who Was Jailed in Notes Dispute Is Freed*, N.Y. Times, Jan. 5, 2002, at A8 (detailing Vanessa Leggett's incarceration and release).

113. *In re* Grand Jury Subpoena (Miller), 397 F.3d 964 (D.C. Cir. 2005).

114. *New York Times Reporter Jailed* (Oct. 28, 2005), www .cnn.com/2005/LAW/07/06/ reporters.contempt.

115. Miller v. United States, 545 U.S. 1150 (2005).

116. Carol D. Leonnig, *N.Y. Times Reporter Jailed*, Wash. Post, July 7, 2005, at A1.

117. Adam Liptak, *Reporter Jailed After Refusing to Name Source*, N.Y. Times, July 7, 2005, at A1.

118. Grand Jury Subpoena (Josh Wolf), 201 F. Appx. 430 (9th Cir. 2006).

119. Jesse McKinley, 8-Month Jail Term Ends as Maker of Video Turns Over a Copy, N.Y. Times, Apr. 4, 2007, at A9.

120. *In re* Grand Jury Subpoenas, No. 01–20745 (5th Cir. Aug. 17, 2001) (unpublished) (per curiam), *cert. denied*, 535 U.S. 1011 (2002).

121. Smith v. Daily Mail, 443 U.S. 97, 107 (1979).

122. Kent v. United States, 383 U.S. 541, 556 (1966).

123. *In re* Gault, 387 U.S. 1, 33, 36–37 (1967).

124. Kristin N. Henning, *Eroding Confidentiality in Delinquency Proceedings: Should Schools and Public Housing Authorities Be Notified?* 79 N.Y.U. L. Rev. 520 (2004). States that presumptively close juvenile proceedings are Alabama, Alaska, Illinois, Kentucky, Massachusetts, Mississippi, New Jersey, New York, Oklahoma, Rhode Island, South Carolina, Tennessee, Vermont, West Virginia, Wisconsin and Wyoming, as well as the District of Columbia; Kristin N. Henning, *Eroding Confidentiality in Delinquency Proceedings: Should Schools and Public Housing Authorities Be Notified?* 79 N.Y.U. L. Rev. 520 (2004). States with presumptively open proceedings are Arizona, Arkansas, Colorado, Florida, Georgia, Iowa, Kansas, Maryland, Michigan, Montana, Nevada, New Mexico, North Carolina, Ohio and Washington. States with open proceedings for children over a certain age or charged with certain offenses are California, Delaware, Hawaii, Idaho, Indiana, Louisiana, Maine, Minnesota, Missouri, North Dakota, Pennsylvania, South Dakota, Texas, Utah and Virginia.

125. *Child Advocates Win Fight to Open Juvenile Courts*, 11Alive, Nov. 14, 2013, www.11alive.com/ story/news/local/investigations/ dfcs/2014/03/06/1953976/; Garrett Therolf, *L.A. Judge Orders Juvenile Courts Opened to Press*, L.A. Times, Feb. 1, 2012, articles. latimes.com/2012/feb/01/local/ la-me-open-courts-20120131; Jack Brammer, *Ky. Senate Approves a Bill to Open Some Juvenile Court Proceedings to the Public*, Lexington Herald Leader, Mar. 10, 2014, Kentucky.com; W.M. Horne, *The Movement to Open Juvenile Courts: Realizing the Significance of Public Discourse in First Amendment Analysis*, 39 Ind. L. J. 659 (2012); Robert E. Shepherd, *Collateral Consequences of Juvenile Proceedings: Part II, Media Exposure*, 15 Crim. J. Mag. (2000), www.abanet.org/crimjust/ juvjus/cjmcollconseq1.html; Barbara White Stack, *The Trend Toward Opening Juvenile Court Is Now Gaining Momentum*, Sept. 23, 2001, old.post-gazette.com.

126. *Id.*

127. Commonwealth v. Barnes, 963 N.E.2d 1156 (Mass. 2012).

128. Kristen Rasmussen, *Access to Juvenile Justice*, Reporters Comm. for Freedom of the Press (2012), www.rcfp .org/rcfp/orders/docs/SJAJJ .pdf.

129. *Id.*, *see* Howard Snyder & Melissa Sickmund, *Juvenile Offenders and Victims: 2006 National Report*, NCJJ & U.S. DOJ, Office of Juv. Just. & Delinquency Prevention (Mar. 2006), www .ojjdp.ncjrs.gov/ojstatbb/nr2006/.

130. Commonwealth v. Chism, 2015 Mass. Super. LEXIS 14 (Mass. Super. Ct., Mar. 3, 2015); 2015 Mass. Super. LEXIS 1 (Mass. Super. Ct., Jan. 23, 2015).

131. Ralph Ellis & Jason Hanna, *Teen Sentenced to at Least 40 Years in Massachusetts Teacher Killing*, CNN, Feb. 26, 2016, www.cnn.com/2016/02/26/us/ massachusetts-teacher-killing-sentence/.

132. Shira Schoenberg, *Massachusetts Lawmakers to Consider Raising Juvenile Court Age*, MassLive, www.masslive.com/ politics/index.ssf/2017/02/ massachusetts_lawmakers_to_ con.html.

133. For a summary of these statutes, see American Prosecutors Research Institute, Rape Shield Laws, www.arte-sana.com/ articles/rape_shield_laws_us.pdf.

134. Nat'l Dist. Att'ys Assoc., *Rape Shield Summary Chart* (Jan. 2010), www.ndaa.org/ pdf/NCPCA%20Rape%20 Shield%202011.pdf.

135. *See, e.g.*, Colo. Rape Shield Law § 18–3–407 (2)(a).

136. Batey v. Haas, 573 F. Appx. 16531 (6th Cir. 2014), *cert. denied*, 135 S. Ct. 2320 (2015).

137. United States v. Reynolds, 345 U.S. 1 (1953).

138. *The State Secrets Privilege*, Electronic Frontier Found., Dec. 4, 2012, www.eff.org/nsa-spying/state-secrets-privilege.

139. Open the Government, 2008 Secrecy Report Card (2008), www.openthegovernment.org/ otg/SecrecyReportCard08.pdf.

140. Glenn Greenwald, *Obama Wins the Right to Invoke "State Secrets" to Protect Bush Crimes*, Salon, Sept. 8, 2010, www .salon.com/news/opinion/glenn_ greenwald/2010/09/08/obama; Charlie Savage, *Court Dismisses a Case Asserting Torture by CIA*,

N.Y. TIMES, Sept. 8, 2010 www
.nytimes.com/2010/09/09/
us/09secrets.html?_r=1&hp.

141. *In re* Sealed Case, 494 F.3d 139
(App. D.C. 2007).

142. Ginnie Graham, *Courts
Keeping Cases Secret*, TULSA
WORLD, Aug. 10, 2008, www
.tulsaworld.com/news/article.
aspx?articleID=20080810_11_
A1_hDistr562350.

143. Press-Enterprise (I) v. Superior
Court, 464 U.S. 501, 510
(1984).

144. *See, e.g., In re* Globe Newspaper
Co., 920 F.2d 88 (1st Cir. 1990).

145. *See, e.g.,* Don J. DeBenedictis,
The National Verdict, A.B.A.
J., Oct. 1994, at 52, 54 (citing
poll finding 86 percent of those
people questioned thought media
had some effect on trial fairness);
Edith Greene, *Media Effects on
Jurors*, 14 LAW & HUMAN BEHAV.
439, 448 (1990).

146. In *re* the Charlotte Observer v.
Bakker, 882 F. 2d. 850 (4th Cir.
1989).

147. Claire S.H. Lim, J.M.
Snyder & David Stromberg,
*Media Influence on Courts:
Evidence From Civil Case
Adjudication* (2010), www
.economics.cornell.edu/csl228/
Media_paper_2010.pdf; JON
BRUSCHKE & WILLIAM LOGES,
FREE PRESS VS. FAIR TRIALS:
EXAMINING PUBLICITY'S ROLE
IN TRIAL OUTCOMES (2004);
Vincent Carroll, *Overreacting
to Pretrial Publicity*, DENV.
POST, Aug. 19, 2012, www
.denverpost.com/ci_
21331048/overreacting-
pretrial-publicity?IADID=.

148. ABC Inc. v. Stewart, 360 F.3d 90
(2d Cir. 2004).

149. AMD v. Intel Antitrust
Litigation, are.berkeley.
edu/~sberto/AMDIntel.pdf (last
visited July 28, 2017).

150. AMD v. Intel Corp., 2006 U.S.
Dist. LEXIS 72722 (D. Del.
Sept. 26, 2006).

151. *In re* Intel Corp. Microprocessor
Antitrust Litigation,
Consolidated Action: Motion
to Intervene for Purpose of
Unsealing Judicial Records and
for Partial Reassignment, C.A.
No. 05–441-JJF (D. Del. Aug.
21, 2008).

152. Intel Corp. v. AMD, 524 U.S.
241 (2004).

153. Greg Sandoval & Declan
McCullagh, *Judge Seals
Courtroom in MPAA DVD-
Copying Case*, CNET NEWS,
Apr. 24, 2009, news.cnet
.com/8301–13578_3–
10227195–38.html. *See also*
RealNetworks Response to
RealDVD Preliminary Injunction
Ruling, Aug. 11, 2009, www
.realnetworks.com/pressroom/
releases/2009/realdvd_initial_
ruling.aspx; Bill Rosenblatt,
*MPAA Wins Settlement in
RealDVD Case*, Mar. 4, 2010,
copyrightandtechnology
.com/2010/03/04/mpaa-
wins-settlement-in-realdvd-
case/.

154. Peña Rodriguez v. Colorado,
OYEZ, www.oyez.org/
cases/2016/15-606 (finding
that juror reliance on racial
animus jeopardizes a fair trial
and overcomes the Rules of
Evidence that preclude admission
of testimony into the deliberative
process of the jury).

155. Nebraska Press Ass'n v. Stuart,
427 U.S. 539 (1976).

156. Federated Pub. Inc. v. Kurtz, 615
P.2d 440 (Wash. 1980).

157. Federated Pub. Inc. v. Swedberg,
633 P.2d 74 (Wash. 1981), *cert.
denied*, 456 U.S. 984 (1982).

158. Nebraska Press Ass'n, 427 U.S.
539 (1976).

159. Butterworth v. Smith, 494 U.S.
624 (1990).

160. Multimedia Holdings Corp. v.
Circuit Court of Fla., 544 U.S.
1301 (2005); Justice Kennedy
Denies Application for Stay in
Prior Restraint Case; First Coast
News v. Circuit Court of Florida,
St. Johns County, MEDIA L.
PROF BLOG, Apr. 25, 2005,
lawprofessors.typepad.com/
media_law_prof_blog/2005/04/
justice_kennedy.html.

161. Multimedia Holdings Corp. v.
Circuit Court of Fla., 544 U.S.
1301, 1304 (2005).

162. Seattle Times v. Rhinehart, 467
U.S. 20 (1984).

163. Alabama Gas Corp. v. Advertiser
Co., CV-2014-000488.00
(Ala. Cir. Ct., Sept. 23,
2014), s3.documentcloud
.org/documents/1303999/
filing.pdf.

164. Maane Khatchatourian, *Mark
Boal Settles Bowe Bergdahl
Lawsuit, Won't Turn Over Tapes*,
VARIETY, Dec. 13, 2016, variety
.com/2016/film/news/mark-
boal-bowe-bergdahl-lawsuit-
settled-1201941202.

165. See, e.g., Nathan Swinton,
Privileging a Privilege: Should
the Reporter's Privilege Enjoy the
Same Respect as the Attorney-
Client Privilege?, 19 GEO. J.
LEGAL ETHICS 979 (2006).

166. See, generally, David
Rudenstine, A Reporter Keeping
Confidences: More Important

Than Ever, 29 Cardozo L. Rev. 1431 (2008).

167. Branzburg v. Hayes, 408 U.S. 665, 710 (1972).

168. *Id.* at 674.

169. *Id.* at 709.

170. *Id.* at 710.

171. *Id.* at 712.

172. *Id.* at 725.

173. *Id.*

174. *Id., quoting* Time Inc. v. Hill, 385 U.S. 374, 389 (1967).

175. *Id.* at 739.

176. *Id.* at 743.

177. *See, e.g.,* United States v. Lloyd, 71 F.3d 1256 (7th Cir. 1995) (finding that a district court did not abuse discretion in quashing a subpoena in a criminal case); LaRouche v. NBC, 780 F.2d 1134 (4th Cir. 1986) (finding that a lower court correctly applied privilege when it quashed subpoenas for journalists in a libel case); United States v. Caporale, 806 F.2d 1487 (11th Cir. 1986) (recognizing qualified privilege in a criminal case); Zerilli v. Smith, 656 F.2d 705 (D.C. Cir. 1981) (recognizing existence of federal privilege in a civil case in which journalists were not parties); Miller v. Transamerican Press Inc., 621 F.2d 721 (5th Cir. 1980) (finding that journalists have a First Amendment privilege, although it is not absolute); United States v. Cuthbertson, 630 F.2d 139 (3d Cir. 1980) (stating that federal privilege exists in both civil and criminal cases); Silkwood v. Kerr-McGee, 563 F.2d 433 (10th Cir. 1977) (recognizing privilege and finding that a documentary filmmaker could assert it); Cervantes v. Time Inc., 464 F.2d 986 (8th Cir. 1972) (determining that a magazine could assert

privilege in a libel case); Bursey v. United States, 466 F.2d 1059 (9th Cir. 1972) (finding that newspaper employees could assert privilege to quash grand jury subpoenas); Baker v. F & F Investment Co., 470 F.2d 778 (2d Cir. 1972) (recognizing privilege in a civil case).

178. Alharbi v. The Blaze, Civil Action No. 14-11550-PBS (D. Mass. Aug. 9, 2016).

179. Eric Holder Says Putting Reporter James Risen Through Hell Is a Good "Example" of DOJ Process for Leak Investigations, Tech Dirt, Feb. 19, 2015, www.techdirt.com/articles/20150218/17531730067/.

180. United States v. Sterling, 724 F.3d 482 (4th Cir. 2013), *cert. denied*, 134 S. Ct. 2696 (2014).

181. Id.; see also Charlie Savage, Court Tells Reporter to Testify in Case of Leaked C.I.A. Data, N.Y. Times, July 19, 2013, at A1.

182. Alan Feuer, *Times Reporter Can't Be Compelled to Testify in Baby Hope Case, Court Rules*, N.Y. Times, Oct. 20, 2016, www .nytimes.com/2016/10/21/nyregion/times-reporter-baby-hope-case.html.

183. Phoenix Newspapers Inc. v. Arizona, No. 1 CA–SA 16–0096 (Ariz. Ct. App., Aug. 11, 2016).

184. State v. Benson, 44 Media L. Rep. 2094 (Del. Super. Ct. 2016).

185. Peck v. City of Boston (*In re* Slack), 768 F. Supp. 2d 189 (D.D.C. 2011).

186. Keefe v. City of Minneapolis v. Star Tribune Media Co., 2012 U.S. Dist. LEXIS 187017, at *12–*13 (D. Minn. May 25, 2012).

187. Amended Memo. Op. and Order Re: Cowles Publishing Motion to Quash Subpoena Duces Tecum, Jacobson v. John Doe, Case No. CV-12-2098 (Idaho Dist. Ct., July 10, 2012).

188. Chevron Corp. v. Berlinger, 629 F.3d 297 (2d Cir. 2011).

189. *In re* McCray, 928 F. Supp. 2d 748 (S.D. N.Y. 2013), *aff'd* 991 F. Supp. 2d 464 (S.D. N.Y. 2013).

190. *In re* McCray, 2013 U.S. Dist. LEXIS 31142, at *10 (S.D. N.Y. Mar. 5, 2013).

191. Branzburg v. Hayes, 408 U.S. 665, 706 (1972).

192. Christine Tatum, *Federal Shield Would Protect Public's Right to Know*, Society of Professional Journalists, www.spj.org/rrr .asp?ref=58&t=foia.

193. Marina Riker, *Media Shield Law 2015: Who's Really a Journalist?*, (Honolulu) Civil Beat, Feb. 20, 2015, www.civilbeat.com.

194. Brett Oppegaard, *Reader Rep: Hawaii Should Reinstate Shield Law Immediately*, (Honolulu) Civil Beat, Nov. 7, 2016, www .civilbeat.org/2016/11/reader-rep-hawaii-should-reinsate-its-shield-law-immediately/.

195. Kyle Schmauch, Press Release: *Governor Signs Bill Protecting Freedom of the Press*, Zolnikov State Legislature, Apr. 9, 2015, danielzolnikov.com/press-release-governor-signs-bill-protecting-freedom-of-the-press/.

196. Cindy Gierhart, Colorado Considers Bill to Bolster Reporter Shield Law, Reporters Comm. for Freedom of the Press, Jan. 16, 2014, rcfp.org; Nate Rabner, Journalists Urge

Expansion of Media Shield Law in Maryland to Protect Against Out-of-State Subpoenas, Capital News Service, Feb. 3, 2015, www.foxnews.com/politics/2015/02/03/journalists-urge-expansion; Marina Riker, Media Shield Law 2015: Who's Really a Journalist?, (Honolulu) Civil Beat, Feb. 20, 2015, www.civilbeat.com.

197. Castellani v. Scranton Times, 956 A.2d 937 (Pa. 2008).

198. Andy Mannix, *Battle Over "First 48" TV Footage Now Embroils Up to 12 Court Cases*, Star Trib., Mar. 18, 2016, www.startribune.com/battle-over-first-48-footage-turning-into-drama-for-prosecutors/372623831.

199. *Television Program's Refusal to Disclose Footage Raises Questions Over Minnesota Shield Law*, Silha Ctr Bulletin, Jun. 20, 2016, silha.umn.edu/news/SILHACENTERTVprogramand MinnShieldLaw UniversityofMinnesota.html.

200. Minn. Stat. Ann. § 595.023.

201. Mike Masnick, *Pennsylvania Court Says Bloggers Protected by Journalist Shield Law*, Techdirt, Mar. 30, 2017, www.techdirt.com/articles/20170328/00200337021/pennsylvania-court-says-bloggers-protected-journalist-shield-law-dont-have-to-reveal-commenter-ip-addresses.shtml.

202. Javens v. Does, No. 10550-2016 (Beaver Cty. Ct. C.P., Penn., Mar. 7, 2017).

203. Matera v. Superior Court, 825 P.2d 971 (Ariz. Ct. App. 1992).

204. Too Much Media v. Hale, 993 A.2d 845 (N.J. App. Div. 2010).

205. Too Much Media v. Hale, 20 A.3d 364, 382 (N.J. 2011).

206. Johns-Byrne Co. v. TechnoBuffalo, No. 2011-L-009161 (Ill. Cir. Ct. Jan. 13, 2012); *see* James C. Goodale et al., *Reporter's Privilege—Recent Developments 2011–2012, in* 2 Comm. L. in the Digital Age 2012, at 25–26 (2012).

207. Ashley I. Kissinger, Katharine Larsen & Matthew E. Kelley, *Protections for Anonymous Online Speech, in* 2 Comm. L. in the Digital Age 2012, at 534 (2012).

208. Kevin Ellis, *Judge Gives Online Commenters First Amendment Protection*, Gaston Gazette, July 28, 2010, www.gastongazette.com/waptest/news/judge-49409-online-amendment.html. *See, also,* Samantha Fredrickson, *Anonymous Bloggers Protected by Shield Law, Judge Find*, Reporters Comm. for Freedom of the Press, Sept. 4, 2008, https://www.rcfp.org/browse-media-law-resources/news/anonymous-bloggers-protected-shield-law-judge-finds.

209. The states are Delaware, Minnesota and New York.

210. Republic of Kazakhstan v. Does 1-100, No. 73391-5-1 (Wn. App., Feb. 22, 2016).

211. People v. McKee, 24 N.E. 3d 75 (Ill. 2014); Ken Schmetterer & Joe Roselius, *Reporter's Privilege*, Editor & Publisher, Mar. 16, 2015, www.editorandpublisher.com/Features/Article/Reporter-s-Privilege.

212. Brokers' Choice of America v. NBC Universal, 757 F.3d 1125 (10th Cir. 2014).

213. Obsidian Financial Group v. Cox, 2011 U.S. Dist. LEXIS 137548 (D. Ore. Nov. 30, 2011).

214. *Id.* at *13.

215. Obsidian Financial Group v. Cox, 2012 U.S. Dist. LEXIS 43125, at *20 (D. Ore. Mar. 27, 2012).

216. Lipsky v. Durant, No. 11–0798 (Tex. Dist. Ct. May 15, 2012).

217. *New Jersey Shield Law Does Not Extend to Blogger*, 16:3 Silha Ctr. Bulletin (Sum. 2011), http://silha.umn.edu/news/Summer2011/StateShieldLaws.html.

218. United States v. Nixon, 418 U.S. 683 (1974).

219. 42 U.S.C. § 2000aa.

220. Charlie Savage, *Holder Tightens Rules on Getting Reporters' Data*, N.Y. Times, July 12, 2013, www.nytimes.com/2013/07/13/us/holder-to-tighten-rules-for-obtaining-reporters-data.html?_r=1&.

221. *Id.*

222. *N.J. Newspaper Cries Foul After Police Seize Stolen Water Meter*, NBC New York, Dec. 21, 2016, www.nbcnewyork.com/news/local/Newspaper-Water-Meter-Seized-NJ-New-Jersey-New-Brunswick-407766655.html.

223. United States v. Cotterman, 709 F.3d 952 (9th Cir. 2013), *cert. denied*, 134 S. Ct. 899 (2014).

224. *Government Obtains Wide AP Phone Records in Probe*, Assoc. Press, May 13, 2013, www.ap.org/ap-in-the-news/2013/govt-obtains-wide-ap-phone-records-in-probe; Charlie Savage

& Leslie Kaufman, *Phone Records of Journalists Seized by U.S.*, N.Y. Times, May 13, 2013, www .nytimes.com/2013/05/14/us/ phone-records-of-journalists-of-the- associated-press-seized-by-us.html.

225. *Audrey Hudson Wins Settlement in Reporter Privacy Rights Case*, Harris, Wiltshire & Grannis LLP, Sept. 30, 2014, www .hwglaw.com/audrey-hudson- wins-settlement-in-reporter- privacy-rights-case.

Chapter 9

1. Protecting and Promoting the Open Internet, 2015 FCC LEXIS 1008 (Mar. 12, 2015) (Wheeler, Chair, concurring).

2. Joseph Turow, Media Today: Mass Communication in a Converging World (6th ed.) (2017).

3. *Id.*

4. Wireless Ship Act of 1910, Pub. L. 262, 36 Stat. 629.

5. *See* Thomas G. Krattenmaker, Telecommunications Law and Policy 3–4 (1994).

6. Radio Act of 1912, Pub. L. 264, 37 Stat. 302.

7. United States v. Zenith Radio Corp., 12 F.2d 614 (N.D. Ill. 1926).

8. Radio Act of 1927, Pub. L. 69–632, ch. 169, 44 Stat. 1162.

9. FRC v. Nelson Bros., 289 U.S. 266 (1933).

10. Communications Act of 1934, Ch. 652, 48 Stat. 1064.

11. FCC, What We Do (Apr. 4, 2017), www.fcc.gov/about-fcc/ what-we-do.

12. Mike M. Ahlers, *RIP Excessively Loud TV Commercials*, CNN, Dec. 13, 2012, www.cnn .com/2012/12/13/showbiz/tv-ad- volume.

13. 47 U.S.C. § 153(6).

14. 47 U.S.C. § 605.

15. 47 U.S.C. § 309(j); 47 C.F.R. §§ 73.5000–73.5009; Competitive Bidding Order, 13 F.C.C.R. 15920 (1998).

16. 47 U.S.C. §§ 308(b), 319(a).

17. 47 U.S.C. § 310(b).

18. 47 C.F.R. § 73.3555(a).

19. 47 C.F.R. § 73.3555(e); Consolidated Appropriations Act of 2004, Pub. L. No. 108–199, § 629, 118 Stat. 3, 99.

20. 47 C.F.R. § 73.3555(b); Review of the Commission's Regulations Governing Television Broadcasting, 14 F.C.C.R. 12903, 12907–8 (1999).

21. 47 C.F.R. § 73.3555(c).

22. Consolidated Appropriations Act of 2004, Pub. L. 108–199, § 629, 118 Stat. 3, 86ff.

23. 2006 Quadrennial Review, 23 F.C.C.R. 2010 (2008).

24. FCC, FCC's Review of the Broadcast Ownership Rules, www.fcc.gov/guides/review- broadcast-ownership-rules (last visited May 19, 2015).

25. Gautham Nagesh, *FCC Bans Ad Sales Pacts Between Same-Market TV Stations*, Wall St. J., Mar. 31, 2014, www.wsj.com/articles/SB10 0014240527023041572045794 73492565989378.

26. Prometheus Radio Project v. FCC, 824 F.3d 33 (3d Cir. 2016).

27. Kathleen Kirby, *Communication Law 2016*, Comm. Law in Digital Age 2016 (2016).

28. David Shepardson, *Update: 2-U.S. FCC to Reverse Rules on TV Station Purchases*, CNBC, Mar. 30, 2017, www.cnbc.com/2017/03/30/ reuters-america-update-2-us-fcc-

to-reverse-rules-on-tv-station- purchases.html.

29. Joseph Burstyn Inc. v. Wilson, 343 U.S. 495, 503 (1952).

30. National Broadcasting Co. v. United States, 319 U.S. 190 (1943).

31. *Id.* at 213.

32. Red Lion Broadcasting Co. Inc. v. FCC, 395 U.S. 367 (1969).

33. Miami Herald Pub. Co. v. Tornillo, 418 U.S. 241 (1974).

34. FCC v. League of Women Voters of California, 468 U.S. 364, 376 n.11 (1984).

35. FCC v. Pacifica Found., 438 U.S. 726 (1978).

36. *See* Robinson v. American Broadcasting Co., 441 F.2d 1396, 1399 (6th Cir. 1971).

37. *See, e.g.,* 47 U.S.C. §§ 302(a), 307(d), 309(a) and 316(a).

38. Peter J. Boyer, *Under Fowler FCC Treated TV as Commerce*, N.Y. Times, Jan. 19, 1987, www .nytimes.com/1987/01/19/arts/ under-fowler-fcc-treated-tv-as- commerce.html.

39. Roger Cheng, *The US Government's Wireless-Spectrum Auction: Why It Matters*, CNET, Oct. 19, 2014, *available at* www.cnet.com/news/the-us- government-is-auctioning-off- wireless-spectrum-why-you- should-care-faq/.

40. FirstNet, *Guiding Principles*, www.firstnet.gov/about/guiding- principles (last visited May 19, 2015).

41. *Id.*

42. Amanda Vicinanzo, Emergency Management/Disaster Preparedness Interoperable Communications Show Dramatic Improvement Since 9/11, but

Problems Remain, HOMELAND SEC. TODAY, Nov. 20, 2014, www.hstoday.us/focused-topics/emergency-managementdisaster-preparedness/single-article-page/interoperable-communications-show-dramatic-improvement-since-911-but-problems-remain/07977cadc92ca4f7fd04fbfa33f15341.html.

43. *FirstNet Commends FCC on Taking Critical Steps in Planning for the Nationwide Public Safety Broadband Network*, FIRSTNET, Aug. 26, 2016, www.firstnet.gov/news/firstnet-commends-fcc-taking-critical-steps-planning-nationwide-public-safety-broadband-network.

44. Great Lakes Broadcasting, 3 F.R.C. Ann. Rep. 34 (1929).

45. Editorializing by Broadcast Licensees, 13 F.C.C. 1246 (1949).

46. *Id.* at 1257–58.

47. Red Lion Broadcasting Co. Inc. v. FCC, 395 U.S. 367, 391 (1969).

48. Syracuse Peace Council, 2 F.C.C.R. 5043 (1987).

49. Syracuse Peace Council v. FCC, 867 F.2d 654 (D.C. Cir. 1989), *cert. denied*, 493 U.S. 1019 (1990).

50. Radio-Television News Directors Ass'n v. FCC, 229 F.3d 269 (D.C. Cir. 2000).

51. 47 U.S.C. § 399; FCC v. League of Women Voters of California, 468 U.S. 364 (1984).

52. Dylan Matthews, *Everything You Need to Know About the Fairness Doctrine in One Post*, WASH. POST, Aug. 23, 2011, https://www.washingtonpost.com/blogs/ezra-klein/post/everything-you-need-to-know-about-the-fairness-doctrine-in-one-post/2011/08/23/gIQAN8CXZJ_blog.html.

53. 47 U.S.C. § 326.

54. *See, e.g.,* 47 C.F.R. 73.1940.

55. Paramount Pictures Corp., 3 F.C.C.R. 245, 246 (Mass Media Bureau 1988).

56. *Id.*

57. Time-Telepictures Television, 17 F.C.C.R. 16273 (2002).

58. Multimedia Entm't Inc., 9 F.C.C.R. 2811 (Political Programming Branch 1994).

59. Infinity Broadcasting, 18 F.C.C.R. 18603 (Media Bureau 2003).

60. Arkansas Educ. Television Comm'n v. Forbes, 523 U.S. 666 (1998).

61. 47 U.S.C. § 315(b).

62. 47 U.S.C. §§ 317, 507.

63. Farmers Educ. and Cooperative Union v. WDAY Inc., 360 U.S. 525 (1959).

64. 47 U.S.C. § 312(a)(7).

65. CBS v. FCC, 453 U.S. 367 (1981).

66. *Id.*

67. *Id.* at 387.

68. *Id.* at 387–88.

69. 26 U.S.C. § 527.

70. *Top Individual Contributors to Federally Focused 527 Organizations, 2012 Election Cycle*, OPEN SECRETS, www.opensecrets.org/527s/527indivs.php (last visited July 31, 2017).

71. Kate Phillips, Settlements Including Fines Are Reached in Election Finance Cases of Three Groups, N.Y. TIMES, Dec. 14, 2006, at A38.

72. Children's Television Act of 1990, Pub. L. 101–437, 104 Stat. 996.

73. 47 C.F.R. § 73.520, 73.671.

74. Children's Television Programming, 6 F.C.C.R. 7199 (1990).

75. Children's Television Report and Policy Statement, 50 F.C.C.2d 1, 13–14 (1974).

76. Children's Television Programming, 6 F.C.C.R. 2111 (1991); Children's Television Programming, 6 F.C.C.R. 5093 (1991).

77. Children's Television Programming; Revision of Programming Policies for Television Broadcast Stations, 11 F.C.C.R. 10660 (1996).

78. *Id.* at 10730.

79. FCC, PROTECTING CHILDREN FROM OBJECTIONABLE CONTENT ON WIRELESS DEVICES (Apr. 4, 2017), www.fcc.gov/guides/protecting-children-objectionable-content-wireless-devices.

80. 47 C.F.R. § 73.1217.

81. Ch. 287, 37 Stat. 302, 308.

82. Ch. 169, 44 Stat. 1162, 1172.

83. 47 U.S.C. § 325(a).

84. *See* Justin Levine, *A History and Analysis of the Federal Communications Commission's Response to Radio Broadcast Hoaxes*, 52 FED. COMM. L.J. 273, 277–79 (2000); HADLEY CANTRIL, THE INVASION FROM MARS (1940).

85. *See, e.g.,* Tim Crook, *The Psychological Power of Radio*, www.irdp.co.uk/hoax.htm (last visited Aug. 1, 2017).

86. *See* Levine, *supra* note 84, at 280–87.

87. 47 C.F.R. § 73.1217.

88. 47 U.S.C. § 399B.

89. 47 U.S.C. § 399b(A).

90. Minority TV Project Inc. v. FCC, 649 F. Supp. 2d 1025 (N.D. Cal. 2009), *aff'd*, 736 F. 3d 1192 (9th Cir. 2013), *cert. denied*, 134 S. Ct. 2874 (2014).

91. 47 U.S.C. § 396(g)(1)(A).

92. FCC v. League of Women Voters of California, 468 U.S. 364 (1984).

93. *Id.* at 402.

94. Alana Abramson, *The Organization Behind PBS and NPR Calls Trump's Proposed Cuts "Devastating,"* TIME, Mar. 16, 2017, http://time.com/4703652/ trump-budget-corporation-for-public-broadcasting/.

95. *See* James C. Goodale & Rob Frieden, All About Cable and Broadband § 1.02 (2015).

96. Frontier Broadcasting Co., 24 F.C.C. 251 (1959).

97. Carter Mountain Transmission Corp., 32 F.C.C. 459 (1962), *aff'd,* 321 F.2d 359 (D.C. Cir. 1963), *cert. denied,* 375 U.S. 951 (1963).

98. United States v. Southwestern Cable Co., 392 U.S. 157 (1968).

99. Cable Communications Policy Act of 1984, Pub. L. No. 98–549, 98 Stat. 2779.

100. Cable Television Consumer Protection and Competition Act of 1992, Pub. L. No. 102–385, 106 Stat. 1460.

101. Telecommunications Act of 1996, Pub. L. No. 104–104, 110 Stat. 56.

102. Turner Broadcasting System Inc. v. FCC, 512 U.S. 622 (1994).

103. Denver Area Educ. Telecomm. Consortium Inc. v. FCC, 518 U.S. 727 (1996) (plurality opinion).

104. *See* United States v. Playboy Entm't Group Inc., 529 U.S. 803 (2000).

105. 512 U.S. 622 (1994).

106. 518 U.S. 727 (1996) (plurality opinion).

107. *Id.* at 743.

108. *Supra* note 104.

109. *Id.*

110. Elliot Harmon, *What Happened to Unlocking the Box? 2016 In Review,* EFF.org, Dec. 26, 2016, www.eff.org/deeplinks/2016/12/ what-happened-unlocking-box-2016-review.

111. *Major Pay-TV Providers Lost About 125,000 Subscribers in 2014,* LEICHTMAN RESEARCH GROUP, May 20, 2015, www .leichtmanresearch.com/ press/030315release.html.

112. Nat'l Ass'n of Broadcasters v. FCC, 740 F.2d 1190 (D.C. Cir. 1984).

113. Satellite Home Viewer Improvement Act of 1999, Pub. L. No. 106–113, § 1001–1012, 113 Stat. 1501. The act was upheld in Satellite Broadcasting and Comm'n Ass'n v. FCC, 275 F.3d 337 (4th Cir. 2001), *cert. denied,* 536 U.S. 922 (2002).

114. Direct Broadcast Satellite Public Interest Obligations, 13 F.C.C.R. 23254 (1998); 47 C.F.R. § 100.5.

115. Direct Broadcast Satellite Public Interest Obligations, 19 F.C.C.R. 5647 (2004).

116. *Id.*

117. FCC, ANNUAL ASSESSMENT OF THE STATUS OF COMPETITION IN THE MARKET FOR THE DELIVERY OF VIDEO PROGRAMMING (May 6, 2016), transition.fcc .gov/Daily_Releases/Daily_ Business/2016/db0506/DA-16-510A1.pdf.

118. 47 U.S.C. §§ 534 (commercial stations), 535 (noncommercial stations).

119. Turner Broadcasting System Inc. v. FCC, 520 U.S. 180 (1997).

120. United States v. O'Brien, 391 U.S. 367 (1968).

121. Cablevision Sys. Corp. v. FCC, 570 F.3d 83 (2d Cir. 2009), *cert. denied,* 560 U.S. 918 (2010).

122. In the Matter of Implementation of Section 103 of the STELA Reauthorization Act of 2014, Totality of the Circumstances Test, Notice of Proposed Rulemaking, MB Docket No. 15-216 (rel. Sep. 2, 2015).

123. *Id.*

124. *Id.*

125. 47 U.S.C. § 531.

126. *See, e.g.,* Denver Area Educ. Telecomm. Consortium Inc. v. FCC, 518 U.S. 727, 761–62 (1996).

127. 47 U.S.C. §§ 531(e) (public access), 532(c)(2) (leased access).

128. Cable Television Consumer Protection and Competition Act of 1992, Pub. L. No. 102–385, § 25, 106 Stat. 1460.

129. Daniels Cablevision Inc. v. United States, 835 F. Supp. 1 (D.D.C. 1993).

130. Appropriate Framework for Broadband Access to the Internet Over Wireline Facilities, 20 F.C.C.R. 148653 (2005).

131. United States v. Southwestern Cable Co., 392 U.S. 157 (1968); United States v. Midwest Video Corp., 406 U.S. 649 (1972) (*Midwest I*); United States v. Midwest Video Corp., 440 U.S. 689 (1979) (*Midwest II*).

132. NCTA v. Brand X Internet Services, 545 U.S. 967 (2005).

133. Telecommunications Act of 1996, 47 U.S.C. §§ 201–209, 251(a)(1).

134. High-Speed Access to the Internet Over Cable and Other

Facilities, 17 F.C.C.R. 4798 (2002).

135. FCC, FCC Proposes to Modernize MVPD Definition (Dec. 19, 2014), www.fcc .gov/document/fcc-proposes-modernize-mvpd-definition.

136. FCC, Annual Assessment of the Status of Competition in the Market for the Delivery of Video Programming (May 6, 2016), transition.fcc .gov/Daily_Releases/Daily_ Business/2016/db0506/DA-16-510A1.pdf. *See also* Applications of Comcast Corp., General Electric Co., and NBC Universal Inc. for Consent to Assign Licenses and Transfer Control of Licenses, MB Docket No. 10-56, Memorandum Opinion and Order, 26 FCC Rcd 4238, 4357, App. A (2011).

137. *Id.*

138. FCC, *supra* note 136.

139. FCC, *Protecting and Promoting the Open Internet*, GN Docket No. 14-28, Report and Order on Remand, Declaratory Ruling and Order, 30 FCC Rcd 5601 (2015).

140. FCC, *Independent Programming NOI* (Feb. 18, 2016), www.fcc .gov/document/independent-programming-noi.

141. *Id.*

142. Lee Drutman & Zander Furnas, *Who's Putting the Most Money Against Net Neutrality?* DailyDot, Sept. 5, 2014, available at www.dailydot.com/ politics/lobbyists-net-neutrality-fcc/.

143. Broadband Industry Practices, 223 F.C.C.R. 13028 (2008).

144. Comcast Corp. v. FCC, 600 F.3d 642, 644 (D.C. Cir. 2010).

145. *In re* Preserving the Open Internet, 25 F.C.C.R 17905 (2010).

146. Verizon v. FCC, 740 F. 3d 623, 628 (D.C. Cir., 2014).

147. Recent Case: Telecommunications Law, Internet Regulation: D.C. Circuit Holds That Federal Communication Commission Violated Communications Act in Adopting Open Internet Rules, 127 Harv. L. Rev. 2565, 2574 (2014).

148. 47 C.F.R. Title II, §20.15.

149. Protecting and Promoting the Open Internet, 80 Fed. Reg. 19737 (Apr. 13, 2015).

150. Protecting and Promoting the Open Internet, 2015 FCC LEXIS 1008 (Mar. 12, 2015) (Wheeler, Chair, concurring).

151. *Id.* (Pai, dissenting).

152. FCC, *List of Pending Appellate Cases* (Feb. 24, 2016), transition. fcc.gov/Daily_Releases/Daily_ Business/2016/db0224/DOC-337898A1.pdf.

153. United States Telecom Association v. FCC, No. 15-1063, 2016 WL 3251234 (rel. June 14, 2016).

154. Alina Selyukh and David Greene, *Tackling Net Neutrality Violations "After the Fact,"* NPR, May 5, 2017, www.npr.org/ sections/alltechconsidered/ 2017/05/05/526916610/ fcc-chief-net-neutrality-rules-treating-internet-as-utility-stifle-growth.

155. Reno v. ACLU, 521 U.S. 844 (1997).

156. Telecommunications Act of 1996, Pub. L. No. 104–104, Title V, §§ 501–561, 110 Stat. 56, 133–43 (codified at 18

U.S.C. §§ 1462, 1465, 2422 and at scattered sections of 47 U.S.C.).

157. Reno v. ACLU, 521 U.S. at 869.

158. *Id.* at 853.

159. Miller v. California, 413 U.S. 15 (1973).

Chapter 10

1. Jacobellis v. Ohio, 378 U.S. 184, 197 (1964) (Stewart, J., concurring).

2. Martin Cogan, *In the Beginning, There Was a Nipple*, ESPN, Jan. 28, 2014, espn.go.com/espn/ feature/story/_/id/10333439/ wardrobe-malfunction-beginning-there-was-nipple.

3. *Obscene*, Merriam-Webster, www.merriam-webster.com/ dictionary/obscene (last visited May 6, 2015).

4. *See* Margaret A. Blanchard, Revolutionary Sparks: Freedom of Expression in Modern America (1992).

5. Heywood Broun & Margaret Leech, Anthony Comstock 265 (1927).

6. Robert Corn-Revere, *New Age Comstockery*, 4 CommLaw Conspectus 173, 173 (1996).

7. An Act for the Suppression of Trade in, and Circulation of, Obscene Literature and Articles of Immoral Use, ch. 258, § 2, 17 Stat. 598, 599 (1873).

8. Amendment to the Comstock Act, ch. 186, § 1, 19 Stat. 90.

9. Margaret A. Blanchard, *The American Urge to Censor*, 33 Wm. & Mary L. Rev. 741, 749 (1992).

10. L.R. 3 Q.B. 360, 371 (1868).

11. United States v. One Book Called "Ulysses," 5 F. Supp. 182, 184, 185 (S.D.N.Y. 1933), *aff'd sub nom.* United States v. One Book Entitled Ulysses, 72 F.2d 705 (2d Cir. 1934).

12. 18 U.S.C. §§ 1460–1470.

13. 18 U.S.C. §§ 1470, 2252B; 47 U.S.C. §§ 223(d), 231.

14. Roth v. United States, 354 U.S. 476, 489 (1957).

15. Miller v. California, 413 U.S. 15 (1973).

16. *Id.* at 18.

17. *Id.* at 22.

18. *Roth*, 354 U.S. at 487 n.20.

19. Smith v. United States, 431 U.S. 291, 305 (1977); Hamling v. United States, 418 U.S. 87, 104–5 (1974).

20. Ward v. Illinois, 431 U.S. 767 (1977).

21. Mishkin v. New York, 383 U.S. 502, 508–09 (1966).

22. United States v. Thomas, 74 F.3d 701 (6th Cir.), *cert. denied*, 519 U.S. 820 (1996).

23. Ashcroft v. ACLU, 535 U.S. 564, 597 (2002) (Kennedy, J., concurring in the judgment).

24. *Id.* at 590 (Breyer, J., concurring in part and concurring in the judgment).

25. *Id.* at 586–89 (O'Connor, J., concurring in part and concurring in the judgment).

26. United States v. Kilbride, 584 F.3d 1240 (9th Cir. 2009).

27. United States v. Little, 365 F. App'x 159 (11th Cir. 2010).

28. Miller v. California, 413 U.S. 15, 25 (1973).

29. Jenkins v. Georgia, 418 U.S. 153 (1974).

30. Ward v. Illinois, 431 U.S. 767 (1977).

31. *Jenkins*, 418 U.S. at 160.

32. Pope v. Illinois, 481 U.S. 497 (1987).

33. Luke Records Inc. v. Navarro, 960 F.2d 134 (11th Cir.), *cert. denied*, 506 U.S. 1022 (1992).

34. Butler v. Michigan, 352 U.S. 380, 383 (1957).

35. *Id.*

36. Ginsberg v. New York, 390 U.S. 629 (1968).

37. 18 U.S.C. § 2256(8).

38. New York v. Ferber, 458 U.S. 747 (1982).

39. *Id.* at 758.

40. 18 U.S.C. §§ 2251(a), 2252(b) (4), 2256(8).

41. 18 U.S.C. § 2256(2)(A).

42. John A. Humbach, *"Sexting" and the First Amendment*, 37 Hastings Const. L.Q. 433, 446 (2010).

43. United States v. Knox, 32 F.3d 733, 737 (3d Cir. 1994), *cert. denied*, 513 U.S. 1109 (1995).

44. *Id.*

45. Erica Goode, *Life Sentence for Possession of Child Pornography Spurs Debate Over Severity*, N.Y. Times, Nov. 5, 2011, at A9.

46. Ashcroft v. Free Speech Coalition, 535 U.S. 234 (2002).

47. United States v. Williams, 553 U.S. 285 (2008).

48. *Id.* at 307.

49. United States v. Anderson, 759 F. 3d 891 (8th Cir. 2014).

50. *Id.* at 896.

51. 18 U.S.C. § 2259.

52. *See* Emily Bazelon, *Money Is No Cure*, N.Y. Times, Jan. 27, 2013, § 8 (Magazine), at 22.

53. United States v. Monzel, 641 F.3d 528 (D.C. Cir.), *cert. denied*, 565 U.S. 1072 (2011); United States v. Kearney, 672 F.3d 81 (1st Cir. 2012), *cert. dismissed*, 133 S. Ct. 1521 (2013); United States v. Aumais, 656 F.3d 147 (2d Cir. 2011); United States v. Crandon, 173 F.3d 122 (3d Cir.), *cert. denied*, 528 U.S. 855 (1999); United States v. Burgess, 684 F.3d 445 (4th Cir.), *cert. denied*, 133 S. Ct. 490 (2012); United States v. Evers, 669 F.3d 645 (6th Cir. 2012); United States v. Laraneta, 700 F.3d 983 (7th Cir. 2012), *cert. denied*, 134 S. Ct. 235 (2013); United States v. Fast, 709 F.3d 712 (8th Cir. 2013); United States v. Kennedy, 643 F.3d 1251 (9th Cir. 2011); United States v. McGarity, 669 F.3d 1218 (11th Cir.), *cert. denied*, 133 S. Ct. 378 (2012).

54. *In re* Amy Unknown, 701 F.3d 749 (5th Cir. 2012) (*en banc*), *cert. granted sub nom*, Paroline v. United States, 2013 U.S. LEXIS 4943 (June 27, 2013).

55. Paroline v. United States, 134 S. Ct. 1710 (2014).

56. *In re* Amy Unknown, 754 F.3d 296 (2014).

57. *Paroline*, 134 S. Ct. at 1730 (Roberts, C.J., dissenting).

58. *Id.* at 1737 (Sotomayor, J., dissenting).

59. Mary Margaret Giannini, *Continuous Contamination: How Traditional Criminal Restitution Principles and §2259 Undermine Cleaning Up the Toxic Waste of Child Pornography Possession*, 40 New. Eng. J. on Crim. & Civ. Confinement 21, 25–26 (2014).

60. *Sexting*, Merriam-Webster, www.merriam-webster.com/dictionary/sexting (last visited Mar. 5, 2017).

61. *See, e.g.,* A.H. v. State, 949 So. 2d 234 (Fla. Dist. Ct. App. 2007).

62. States with sexting laws include Arizona, Arkansas, Connecticut, Florida, Georgia, Hawaii, Illinois, Louisiana, Nebraska, Nevada, New Jersey, New York, North Dakota, Pennsylvania, Rhode Island, South Dakota, Texas, Utah, Vermont and West Virginia. Sameer Hinduja & Justin Patchin, *State Sexting Laws: A Brief Review of State Sexting Laws and Politics,* Cyberbullying Res. Center, Jan. 2017, cyberbullying.us/state-sexting-laws.pdf.

63. Nathan Koppel & Ashby Jones, *Are "Sext" Messages a Teenage Felony or Folly?* Wall St. J., Aug. 25, 2010, at D1.

64. Ronak Patel, *Taking It Easy on Teen Pornographers: States Respond to Minors' Sexting,* 13 J. High Tech L. 574 (2013).

65. National Campaign to Prevent Teen and Unplanned Pregnancy, *Teenage Sexting Statistics,* DoSomething.org, Apr. 2014, www.dosomething.org/facts/11-facts-about-sexting.

66. Stanley v. Georgia, 394 U.S. 557 (1969).

67. *Id.* at 568.

68. 18 U.S.C. § 2252A; Osborne v. Ohio, 495 U.S. 103 (1990).

69. *Osborne,* 495 U.S. 103.

70. Joseph Burstyn Inc., v. Wilson, 343 U.S. 495 (1952).

71. Times Film Corp. v. City of Chicago, 365 U.S. 43 (1961).

72. Freedman v. Maryland, 380 U.S. 51 (1965).

73. Pub. L. No. 91-452, 84 Stat. 922 (1970), codified at 18 U.S.C. §§ 1961–1968 (as amended by USA PATRIOT Act of 2001, Pub. L. No. 107–56, § 813, 115 Stat. 272, 382).

74. *See* Teresa Bryan et al., *Racketeer Influenced and Corrupt Organizations,* 40 Am. Crim. L. Rev. 987 (2003).

75. Alexander v. United States, 509 U.S. 544 (1993).

76. 18 U.S.C. § 1464; 47 C.F.R. § 73.3999.

77. 18 U.S.C. § 1464.

78. FCC v. Pacifica Found., 438 U.S. 726, 739 (1978).

79. *Id.* at 740.

80. Miller v. California, 413 U.S. 15 (1973).

81. *Id.* at 727.

82. Enforcement of Prohibitions Against Broad. Indecency, 8 F.C.C.R. 704, 705 n.10 (1993).

83. Pub. L. 69-632, ch. 169, § 29, 44 Stat. 1162 (1927); ch. 652, § 326, 48 Stat. 1064 (1934).

84. 18 U.S.C. § 1464.

85. 47 U.S.C. § 503(b)(1)(D).

86. *See, e.g.,* Sable Communications of California Inc. v. FCC, 492 U.S. 115, 126 (1989).

87. 47 U.S.C. § 326.

88. *See, e.g.,* Application of The Jack Straw Memorial Foundation for Renewal of the License of Station KRAB-FM, Seattle, Wash., 21 Rad. Reg. 2d (P&F) 505 (1971).

89. Sonderling Broad. Corp., 41 F.C.C.2d 777, 782 (1973), *aff'd,* Illinois Citizens Comm. for Broad. v. FCC, 515 F.2d 397 (D.C. Cir. 1974).

90. George Carlin, FCC Transcript: *Filthy Words,* law2.umkc.edu/faculty/projects/ftrials/conlaw/filthywords.html (last visited Aug. 2, 2017).

91. Pacifica Found. 56 F.C.C.2d 94 (1975) (the words, as listed in the FCC's decision, are "shit, piss, fuck, cunt, cocksucker, motherfucker, and tits").

92. Citizen's Complaint Against Pacifica Found. Station WBAI (FM), N.Y, N.Y, 56 F.C.C.2d 94 (1975).

93. FCC v. Pacifica Found., 438 U.S. 726, 750 (1978).

94. *Id.*

95. *Id.*

96. Pacifica Found., 2 F.C.C.R. 2698, 2699 (1987).

97. *In re* Infinity Broad. Corp. of Penna., 2 F.C.C.R. 2705 (1987); *In re* Pacifica Found., 2 F.C.C.R. 2698 (1987); *In re* Regents of the Univ. of Cal., 2 F.C.C.R. 2703 (1987); New Indecency Enforcement Standards to Be Applied to All Broad. & Amateur Radio Licensees, 2 F.C.C.R. 2726 (1987).

98. 2 F.C.C.R. 2726 (1987). The D.C. Circuit upheld the FCC's more expansive indecency definition. Action for Children's Television v. FCC, 852 F.2d 1332 (D.C. Cir. 1988) (ACT I).

99. 438 U.S. at 772.

100. *In re* Indus. Guidance on the Comm'n's Case Law Interpreting 18 U.S.C. § 1464 & Enforcement Policies Regarding Broad. Indecency, 16 F.C.C.R. 7999, 8002–3 (2001).

101. *In re* Complaints Against Various Broad. Licensees Regarding Their Airing of the "Golden Globe Awards" Program, 19 F.C.C.R. 4975 (2004).

102. *In re* Complaints Regarding Various Television Broad. Between Feb. 2, 2002 & Mar. 8, 2005, 21 F.C.C.R. 2664 (2006).

103. *See* Fox Television Stations Inc. v. FCC, 613 F.3d 317, 324 (2d Cir. 2010), *vacated by, remanded by* FCC v. Fox Television Stations Inc., 567 U.S. 239 (2012).

104. FCC v. Fox Television Stations Inc., 556 U.S. 502 (2009).

105. *In re* Complaints Against Various Television Licensees Regarding Their Broadcast on Nov. 11, 2004, of the ABC Television Network's Presentation of the Film "Saving Private Ryan," 20 F.C.C.R. 4507 (2005).

106. *Fox Television Stations*, 556 U.S. 239.

107. Fox Television Stations Inc. v. FCC, 613 F.3d 317, 322 (2d Cir. 2010), *vacated by, remanded by* 556 U.S.239 (2012).

108. Complaints Against Various Television Licensees Concerning Their Feb. 1, 2004, Broad. of the Super Bowl XXXVIII, 19 F.C.C.R. 19230 (2004).

109. CBS Corp. v. FCC, 535 F.3d 167, 174 (3d Cir. 2008), *vacated and remanded*, 556 U.S. 1218 (2009).

110. 556 U.S. 1218 (2009).

111. CBS Corp. v. FCC, 663 F.3d 122 (3d Cir. 2011), *cert. denied*, 567 U.S. 953 (2012).

112. FCC v. Fox Television Stations Inc., 567 U.S. 239, 258 (2012).

113. FCC, FCC Reduces Backlog of Broadcast Indecency Complaints by 70% (More Than One Million Complaints); Seeks Comment on Adopting Egregious Cases Policy (Apr. 1, 2013), www.fcc.gov/document/fcc-cuts-indecency-complaints-1-million-seeks-comment-policy.

114. 47 C.F.R. § 73.3999.

115. Action for Children's Television v. FCC, 58 F.3d 654 (D.C. Cir. 1995) (*en banc*), *cert. denied*, 516 U.S. 1043 (1996) (*ACT III*).

116. FCC, FCC V-Chip Task Force Releases Updated Survey on the Encoding of Video Programming, 2000 FCC LEXIS 143 (2000).

117. Implementation of Section 551 of the Telecommunications Act of 1996; Video Programming Ratings, 13 F.C.C.R. 8232, 8237 (1998).

118. *See* MPAA, *Classification and Rating Administration, Questions & Answers: Everything You Always Wanted to Know About the Movie Rating System*, www.mpaa.org/film-ratings/ (last visited Mar. 4, 2017).

119. Cruz v. Ferre, 755 F.2d 1415 (11th Cir. 1985), citing FCC v. Pacifica Found., 438 U.S. 726 (1978).

120. *See, e.g.,* Community Television of Utah Inc. v. Roy City, 555 F. Supp. 1164 (D. Utah 1982); Home Box Office Inc. v. Wilkinson, 531 F. Supp. 987 (D. Utah 1982).

121. 47 U.S.C. § 532(h) (franchising authorities may prohibit leased access programming that is "obscene or is in conflict with community standards in that it is lewd, lascivious, filthy or indecent, or is otherwise unprotected by the Constitution of the United States"); 47 U.S.C. § 544(d)(i) (franchising authorities may require a franchise to prohibit obscene or "otherwise unprotected" programming); 47 U.S.C. § 558 (franchising authorities may enforce state or local laws forbidding obscenity and "other similar laws").

122. 47 U.S.C. § 544(d)(2).

123. Various Complaints Against the Cable/Satellite Television Program "Nip/Tuck," 20 F.C.C.R. 4255, 4255 (2005), *quoting* Violent Television Programming and Its Impact on Children, Notice of Inquiry, 19 F.C.C.R. 14394, 14403 (2004).

124. Denver Area Educ. Telecomm. Consortium Inc. v. FCC, 518 U.S. 727 (1996) (ruling on Pub. L. No. 102-385, § 10, 106 Stat. 1486).

125. *Id.*

126. 47 U.S.C. § 531(e).

127. Telecommunications Act of 1996, Pub. L. 104–104, §§ 504, 505, 110 Stat. 136.

128. Implementation of Section 505 of the Telecommunications Act of 1996, 12 F.C.C.R. 5212 (1997).

129. United States v. Playboy Entm't Group Inc., 529 U.S. 803 (2000).

130. Michael Castleman, *Dueling Statistics: How Much of the Internet Is Porn?* Psychology Today, Nov. 3, 2016, www.psychologytoday.com/blog/all-about-sex/201611/dueling-statistics-how-much-the-internet-is-porn.

131. *See, generally,* Amitai Etzioni, *Do Children Have the Same First Amendment Rights as Adults? On Protecting Children From Speech*, 79 Chi.-Kent L. Rev. 3 (2004).

132. Pub. L. No. 104–104, § 502, 110 Stat. 56 (1996) (codified at 47 U.S.C. §§ 223(a)(1)(B)(ii), 223(d)).

133. Reno v. ACLU, 521 U.S. 844 (1997).

134. *Id.* at 877.

135. Pub. L. No. 105–277, §§ 1401–1406, 112 Stat. 1681 (codified at 47 U.S.C. § 231).

136. ACLU v. Reno, 31 F. Supp. 2d 473 (E.D. Pa. 1999).

137. ACLU v. Reno, 217 F.3d 162 (3d Cir. 2000).

138. Ashcroft v. ACLU, 535 U.S. 564 (2002).

139. ACLU v. Ashcroft, 322 F.3d 240 (3d Cir. 2003).

140. Ashcroft v. ACLU, 542 U.S. 656 (2004).

141. ACLU v. Gonzales, 478 F. Supp. 2d 775 (E.D. Pa. 2007).

142. ACLU v. Mukasey, 534 F.3d 181 (3d Cir. 2008), *cert. denied,* 555 U.S. 1137 (2009).

143. ACLU v. Ashcroft, 322 F.3d 240, 268 (3d Cir. 2003).

144. Mukasey v. ACLU, 555 U.S. 1137 (2009).

145. Pub. L. 104–208, 110 Stat. 3009.

146. 18 U.S.C. § 2256(8)(B), (D).

147. Ashcroft v. Free Speech Coalition, 535 U.S. 234 (2002).

148. Pub. L. 108–21, §§ 102–601, 117 Stat. 650.

149. United States v. Williams, 553 U.S. 285 (2008).

150. Pub. L. No. 106–554, 114 Stat. 2763A-335 (2000).

151. United States v. American Library Ass'n, 539 U.S. 194 (2003).

Chapter 11

1. Barack Obama, *Remarks by the President at the Export-Import Bank's Annual Conference*, WHITE HOUSE, Mar. 11, 2010, www .whitehouse.gov/the-press-office/ remarks-president-export- import-banks-annual-conference.

2. 17 U.S.C. § 102(a).

3. U.S. CONST. art. I, § 8, cl. 8.

4. *Id.*

5. 8 Anne, C. 19 (1710).

6. U.S. CONST. art. I, § 8, cl. 8.

7. Act of May 31, 1790, ch. 15, 1 Stat. 124.

8. Wheaton v. Peters, 33 U.S. 591 (1834).

9. Act of Feb. 3, 1831, 4 Stat. 436 (musical compositions); Copyright Act of 1865, 13 Stat. 540 (photographs); Act of July 8, 1870, 16 Stat. 212 (paintings).

10. Pub. L. No. 60–349, 35 Stat. 1075.

11. Berne Convention Implementation Act of 1988, Pub. L. 100–568, 102 Stat. 2853.

12. Digital Millennium Copyright Act of 1998, Pub. L. 105–304, 112 Stat. 2860.

13. 17 U.S.C. § 1201.

14. *See, e.g.,* 321 Studios v. MGM Studios Inc., 307 F. Supp. 2d 1085 (N.D. Cal. 2004).

15. 17 U.S.C. § 1202.

16. 18 U.S.C. § 102(a).

17. *See* Burrow-Giles Lithographic Co. v. Sarony, 111 U.S. 53 (1884).

18. Boisson v. Banian Ltd., 273 F.3d 262, 268 (2d Cir. 2001).

19. *See, e.g., id.*; Amer. Dental Ass'n v. Delta Dental Plans Ass'n, 126 F.3d 977 (7th Cir. 1997).

20. 17 U.S.C. § 103.

21. 17 U.S.C. § 102(a).

22. *Id.*

23. Star Athletica LLC v. Varsity Brands Inc., 137 S. Ct. 1002 (2017).

24. U.S. Copyright Office, *Useful Articles*, www.copyright.gov/ register/va-useful.html (last visited May 12, 2017).

25. Gene Quinn and Steve Brachmann, *Copyrights at the Supreme Court: Star Athletica v. Varsity Brands*, IPWATCHDOG, Mar. 22, 2017, www.ipwatchdog .com/2017/03/22/copyrights- supreme-court-star-athletica-v- varsity-brands/id=79767/.

26. *Star Athletica LLC,* 137 S. Ct. at 1007.

27. Bruce Keller, Communications Law in the Digital Age: Intellectual Property, COMM. L. IN THE DIGITAL AGE (2016).

28. 17 U.S.C. § 301.

29. *See* Wheaton v. Peters, 33 U.S. 591 (1834).

30. Feist Pubs. Inc. v. Rural Tel. Serv. Co. Inc., 499 U.S. 340, 340 (1991).

31. *See* 17 U.S.C. § 102(b).

32. Feist Pubs. Inc., 499 U.S. 340.

33. Phantom Alert, Inc. v. Google, Inc., No. 15-cv-03986-JCS (N.D. Cal., Mar. 8, 2016).

34. Media.net Advert. FZ-LLC v. NetSeer Inc., 156 F. Supp. 3d 1052 (N.D. Cal. 2016).

35. 17 U.S.C. § 105.

36. John F. Harris & Jim VandeHei, *Editors' Note*, POLITICO, Oct. 13, 2013, www.politico.com/news/ stories/1011/65940.html.

37. Christine Haughney, *Time and CNN Reinstate Journalist After Review*, N.Y. TIMES, Aug. 17, 2012, at B2.

38. JAYSON BLAIR, BURNING DOWN MY MASTER'S HOUSE: MY LIFE AT THE NEW YORK TIMES (2004).

39. Margaret Sullivan, *Repairing the Credibility Cracks*, N.Y. TIMES, May 5, 2013, at SR12.

40. 17 U.S.C. § 201(a).

41. 17 U.S.C. § 201(b).

42. 17 U.S.C. §§ 101, 201.

43. Community for Creative Non-Violence v. Reid, 490 U.S. 730 (1989).

44. 17 U.S.C. § 101.

45. *Community for Creative Non-Violence*, 490 U.S. at 730.

46. 17 U.S.C. § 201 (c).

47. New York Times Co. Inc. v. Tasini, 533 U.S. 483 (2001).

48. 17 U.S.C. § 106.

49. Sony Corp. of America v. Universal City Studios Inc., 464 U.S. 417 (1984).

50. Audio Home Recording Act of 1992, Pub. L. No. 102–563, 106 Stat. 4244 (codified at 17 U.S.C. §§ 1001–1010).

51. Peter Mayer Publishers Inc. v. Shilovskaya, 11 F. Supp. 3d 421 (S.D.N.Y. 2014).

52. Agence France Presse v. Morel, 934 F. Supp. 2d 547 (S.D.N.Y. 2013).

53. *Id.*

54. Joseph Ax, *Photographer Wins $1.2 Million From Companies That Took Pictures Off Twitter*, Reuters, Nov. 22, 2013, www .reuters.com/article/2013/11/22/ us-media-copyright-twitter-idUSBRE9AL16F20131122.

55. 17 U.S.C. § 106(4).

56. WNET, Thirteen v. Aereo Inc., 712 F. 3d 676, 685 (2d Cir. 2013), *rev'd and remanded sub nom.* ABC Inc. v. Aereo Inc., 134 S. Ct. 2498 (2014).

57. Teleprompter Corp. v. Columbia Broad. Sys., 415 U.S. 394 (1974); Fortnightly Corp. v. United Artists Television Inc., 392 U.S. 390 (1968).

58. 17 U.S.C. § 111.

59. 17 U.S.C. § 119; Satellite Home Viewer Improvement Act of 1999, Pub. L. No. 106–113, §§ 1001–1012, 113 Stat. 1501.

60. American Broadcasting Companies Inc. v. Aereo Inc., 134 S. Ct. 2498 (2014).

61. *Id.*

62. Corinee Lestch, *Aereo Suspends Video Streaming After Supreme Court Decision*, N.Y. Daily News, June 29, 2014, www .nydailynews.com/news/national/ aereo-suspends-streaming-service-supreme-court-decision-article-1.1847702.

63. Matthew Syrkin, *U.S. Television on the Internet and the New "MVPDS,"* Hughes, Hubbard & Reed, Mar. 18, 2015, www .hugheshubbard.com/news/u-s-television-on-the-internet-and-the-new-mvpds-updated.

64. FilmOn X LLC v. Window to the World Commc'ns, Inc. 13 C 8451 (N.D. Ill., Mar. 23, 2016); *see also* Jeffrey P. Cunard, Jared I. Kagan & Holly S. Norgard, *Intellectual Property 2016: Select Developments*, Comm. Law in the Digital Age, Nov. 10, 2016.

65. 17 U.S.C. § 106.

66. Digital Performance Right in Sound Recordings Act, Pub. L. No. 104–39, 109 Stat. 336, *as amended by* DMCA, Pub. L. 105–304, 112 Stat. 2860.

67. 17 U.S.C. § 108.

68. 17 U.S.C. § 109(a).

69. The Supreme Court provides a brief history and interpretation of the first-sale doctrine in Quality King Distributors Inc. v. L'Anza Research Int'l Inc., 523 U.S. 135 (1998).

70. Kirtsaeng v. John Wiley & Sons Inc., 568 U.S. 519 (2013).

71. 17 U.S.C. § 109(b)(1)(A); Computer Software Rental Amendments, Pub. L. No. 101–650, tit. viii, 104 Stat. 5089, 5134–35; Record Rental Amendment of 1984, Pub. L. No. 98–450, 98 Stat. 1727.

72. Capitol Records LLC v. ReDigi Inc., 934 F. Supp. 2d 640 (S.D.N.Y. 2013).

73. 17 U.S.C. §§ 203(a), 304(c).

74. U.S. Const. art I, § 8, cl. 8.

75. 17 U.S.C. § 302(a).

76. 17 U.S.C. § 302(c).

77. *Eldred v. Ashcroft*, 537 U.S. 186 (2003).

78. *Id.*

79. This was "due to (i) failure to comply with copyright formalities, (ii) lack of subject matter protection, or (iii) lack of national eligibility due to the absence of copyright relations with the" United States. Dan Laidman, *Golan v. Holder and the Controversial New Efforts to Update IP Law for the Internet Age*, Davis Wright Tremaine, March 12, 2012, www.lexology.com/ library/detail.aspx?g=2d5e85f7-9b48-4c6a-beff-c63c25335859.

80. 17 U.S.C. § 104A.

81. Laidman, *supra* note 80.

82. Golan v. Holder, 565 U.S. 302 (2012).

83. *Id.* at 311.

84. 17 U.S.C. § 401(c).

85. Arnstein v. Porter, 154 F.2d 464 (2d Cir. 1946).

86. Shyamkrishna Balganesh, *The Questionable Origins of the Copyright Infringement Analysis*, 68 Stan. L. Rev. 791 (April 2016).

87. Sid & Marty Krofft Television Prods. Inc. v. McDonald's Corp., 562 F.2d 1157 (9th Cir. 1977).

88. Nicole Lieberman, Un-Blurring Substantial Similarity: Aesthetic Judgments and Romantic Authorship in Music Copyright Law, 6 N.Y.U. J. Intell. Prop. & Ent. Law 92 (2016).

89. *Id.* at 137. *See also* Computer Assocs. Int'l v. Altai Inc. 982 F. 2d 693, 713 (2d Cir. 1992).

90. Feist Pubs. Inc. v. Rural Tel. Serv. Co. Inc., 499 U.S. 340 (1991).

91. 17 U.S.C. § 504(c).

92. *See, e.g.,* Kalem Co. v. Harper Bros., 222 U.S. 55 (1911) (producer of infringing film violated copyright law although movie theaters, not producer, showed film to public); 17 U.S.C. §§ 106, 501(a).

93. Sony Corp. of America v. Universal City Studios Inc., 464 U.S. 417 (1984).

94. *Id.*

95. Cartoon Network LP v. CSC Holdings Inc., 536 F.3d 121 (2d Cir. 2008), *cert. denied*, 557 U.S. 946 (2009).

96. MGM Studios Inc. v. Grokster Ltd., 545 U.S. 913 (2005).

97. Columbia Pictures Indus. Inc. v. Fung, 710 F.3d 1020 (9th Cir.), *cert. dismissed*, 134 S. Ct. 624 (2013).

98. Flava Works Inc. v. Gunter, 689 F.3d 754 (7th Cir. 2012).

99. 17 U.S.C. § 507.

100. *See, e.g.,* Dam Things From Denmark v. Russ Barrie & Co., 290 F.3d 548, 560 (3d Cir. 2002).

101. *See* Pierre N. Leval, *Toward a Fair Use Standard*, 103 Harv. L. Rev. 1105, 1105 (1990).

102. 17 U.S.C. § 107.

103. Leval, *supra* note 102, at 1110.

104. Campbell v. Acuff-Rose Music Inc., 510 U.S. 569, 578 (1994).

105. Harper & Row Publishers Inc. v. Nation Enter., 471 U.S. 539 (1985).

106. *See* 4 Melville Nimmer & David Nimmer, Nimmer on Copyright § 13.05[A][1] (2013).

107. *Campbell*, 510 U.S. at 579.

108. *Id.* at 569.

109. See Nimmer & Nimmer, *supra* note 107, at § 13.05[C][1].

110. Brownmark Films LLC v. Comedy Partners, 682 F.3d 687 (7th Cir. 2012).

111. Keeling v. Hars, 809 F. 3d 43 (2d Cir. 2015), *cert. denied*, 136 S. Ct. 2519 (2016).

112. Fox News Network LLC v. TVEyes Inc. 43 F. Supp. 3d 379 (S.D.N.Y. 2014).

113. White v. West Publ'g Corp., 29 F. Supp. 3d 396 (S.D.N.Y. 2014).

114. Authors Guild v. Google Inc., 804 F.3d 202 (2d Cir. 2015), *cert. denied*, 136 S. Ct. 1658 (2016).

115. Authors Guild v. HathiTrust, 902 F. Supp. 445 (S.D.N.Y. 2012).

116. *Authors Guild*, 804 F.3d 202.

117. Bouchat v. Baltimore Ravens Ltd. P'ship, 737 F. 3d 932 (4th Cir.), *cert. denied*, 134 S. Ct. 2319 (2014).

118. TCA Television Corp. v. McCollum, 839 F. 3d 168 (2d Cir., Oct. 11, 2016).

119. *See* Nimmer & Nimmer, *supra* note 107, at § 13.05[A][2].

120. Salinger v. Random House Inc., 811 F.2d 90 (2d Cir. 1987), *cert. denied*, 484 U.S. 890 (1988).

121. 17 U.S.C. § 107; Pub. L. No. 102–492, 106 Stat. 3145.

122. A.V. v. iParadigms LLC, 562 F.3d 630 (4th Cir. 2009).

123. *Id.* at 642.

124. *See* Fox News Network LLC v. TVEyes Inc. 43 F. Supp. 3d 379 (S.D.N.Y. 2014); White v. West Publ'g Corp., 29 F. Supp. 3d 396 (S.D.N.Y. 2014).

125. Bill Graham Archives v. Dorling Kindersley Ltd., 448 F.3d 605 (2d Cir. 2006).

126. Benny Evangelista, *Consumers Can Now Pass Go, Collect Any App*, S.F. Chron., July 27, 2010, at D1.

127. Basic Books Inc. v. Kinko's Graphics Corp., 758 F. Supp. 1522, 1534 (S.D.N.Y. 1991).

128. Campbell v. Acuff-Rose Music Inc., 510 U.S. 569, 587 (1994).

129. *See, e.g.,* Authors Guild Inc. v. Google Inc. 954 F. Supp. 2d 282 (S.D.N.Y. 2013), *aff'd*, 804 F.3d 202 (2d Cir. 2015), *cert. denied*, 136 S. Ct. 1658 (2016); Authors Guild Inc. v. HathiTrust, 755 F. 3d 87 (2d Cir. 2014).

130. *See, e.g.,* Playboy Enter. Inc. v. Russ Hardenburgh Inc., 982 F. Supp. 503 (N.D. Ohio 1997).

131. Pub. L. 105–304, 112 Stat. 2860.

132. 17 U.S.C. § 512(c).

133. Perfect 10 Inc. v. Google Inc., 2010 U.S. Dist. LEXIS 75071 (C.D. Cal., July 26, 2010), *aff'd*, 653 F.3d 976 (9th Cir. 2011), *cert. denied*, 565 U.S. 1245 (2012).

134. UMG Recordings Inc. v. Veoh Networks Inc., 718 F.3d 1006 (9th Cir. 2013); *see also* Io Group Inc. v. Veoh Networks Inc., 586 F. Supp. 2d 1132 (N.D. Cal. 2008).

135. Viacom Int'l Inc. v. YouTube Inc., 940 F. Supp. 2d 110

(S.D.N.Y. 2013), *on remand from* Viacom Int'l Inc. v. YouTube Inc., 676 F.3d 19 (2d Cir. 2012); *see* Meg James, *YouTube Prevails in Viacom Copyright Suit*, L.A. Times, Apr. 19, 2013, at B3.

136. Capitol Records LLC v. Vimeo LLC, 972 F. Supp. 2d 537 (S.D.N.Y. 2014), *aff'd in part, vacated in part*, 826 F.3d (2d Cir. 2016), *cert. denied*, 137 S. Ct. 1374 (2017).

137. Evan Sheres, *Disabling the "Red Flag" Doctrine: Missed Opportunity to Establish Reasonable Precedent in* Capitol Records v. Vimeo, Copyright Alliance, Sept. 25, 2013, copyrightalliance.org/2013/09/ disabling_red_flag_doctrine_ missed_opportunity_establish_ reasonable_precedent_capitol# .VVfrRuu25kg.

138. *Capitol Records LLC*, 972 F. Supp. 2d 537.

139. Wolk v. Photobucket.com Inc., 569 Fed. Appx. 51 (2d Cir. 2014).

140. BWP Media USA Inc. v. Clarity Digital Group LLC 820 F. 3d 1175 (10th Cir. 2016).

141. Perfect 10 Inc. v. Amazon.com, 508 F.3d 1146, 1160–61 (9th Cir. 2007).

142. Amanda Lenhart & Mary Madden, *Music Downloading, File-Sharing and Copyright*, Pew Research Center, July 31, 2003, www.pewinternet .org/2003/07/31/music- downloading-file-sharing-and- copyright/.

143. A&M Records Inc. v. Napster Inc. 239 F.3d 1004 (9th Cir. 2001).

144. Capitol Records Inc. v. Thomas- Rasset, 692 F.3d 899 (8th Cir.

2012), *cert. denied*, 133 S. Ct. 1584 (2013).

145. Sony BMG Music Ent. v. Tenenbaum, 660 F.3d 487 (1st Cir. 2011), *cert. denied*, 132 S. Ct. 2431 (2012).

146. MGM Studios Inc. v. Grokster Ltd., 545 U.S. 913 (2005).

147. *Id.* at 922, 940.

148. Sony Corp. of America v. Universal City Studios Inc. 464 U.S. 417 (1984).

149. *CCI Provides First Copyright Alert System Progress Report Highlighting Initial Accomplishments*, CCI, May 28, 2014, www .copyrightinformation.org/ press-release/cci-provides- first-copyright-alert-system- progress-report-highlighting- initial-accomplishments/.

150. 15 U.S.C. § 1127.

151. Qualitex Co. v. Jacobson Products Co. Inc., 514 U.S. 159 (1995).

152. Ride the Ducks LLC v. Duck Boat Tours Inc., 2005 U.S. Dist. LEXIS 4422 (E.D. Pa. Mar. 21, 2005), *aff'd*, 138 Fed. Appx. 431 (3d Cir. Pa. 2005).

153. *See* Anne Gilson LaLonde, Gilson on Trademarks § 10A.09[5] (2013).

154. 15 U.S.C. § 1051 *et seq.*

155. 15 U.S.C. § 1125(a).

156. 15 U.S.C. § 1052.

157. PACCAR Inc. v. TeleScanTechnologies LLC, 319 F.3d 243 (6th Cir. 2003).

158. Bebe Stores Inc. v. May Dep't Stores Int'l, 313 F.3d 1056 (8th Cir. 2002) (per curiam).

159. Standard Brands Inc. v. Smidler, 151 F.2d 34 (2d Cir. 1945).

160. *See* Anne Gilson LaLonde, Gilson on Trademarks § 2.04[1] (2013).

161. Sara Lee Corp. v. Kayser- Roth Corp., 81 F.3d 455, 464 (4th Cir. 1996).

162. Circuit City Stores Inc. v. CarMax Inc., 165 F.3d 1047 (6th Cir. 1999).

163. Japan Telecom Inc. v. Japan Telecom of America Inc., 287 F.3d 866, 873 (9th Cir. 2002).

164. Boston Beer Co. LP v. Slesar Bros. Brewing Co. Inc., 9 F.3d 175 (1st Cir. 1993).

165. Hamilton-Brown Shoe Co. v. Wolf Bros. & Co., 240 U.S. 251 (1918).

166. M. Fabrikant & Sons Ltd. v. Fabrikant Fine Diamonds Inc., 17 F. Supp. 2d 249 (S.D.N.Y. 1998).

167. Anne Gilson LaLonde, Gilson on Trademarks § 2.08[1] (2013).

168. Harley-Davidson Inc. v. Grottanelli, 164 F.3d 806 (2d Cir. 1999).

169. Small Bus. Assistance Corp. v. Clear Channel Broad. Inc., 210 F.3d 278 (5th Cir. 2000).

170. *See* Sung In, Note: *Death of a Trademark: Genericide in the Digital Age*, 21 Rev. Litig. 159 (2002).

171. *See, e.g.,* George K. Chamberlin, Annotation: *When Does Product Mark Become Generic Term or "Common Descriptive Name" So as to Warrant Cancellation of Registration of Mark*, 55 A.L.R. Fed. 241 (2004).

172. *See* Anne Gilson LaLonde, Gilson on Trademarks § 2.02[6] (2013).

173. 15 U.S.C. § 1051.

174. 15 U.S.C. § 1052(a).

175. 15 U.S.C. § 1052 (b), (c), (d), (e).

176. 15 U.S.C. § 1091.

177. *In re* Tam, 808 F.3d 1321 (D.C. Cir. 2015), *cert granted*, 137 S. Ct. 30 (2016).

178. *Id.*

179. *Id.* at 1327–1328.

180. Matal v. Tam, 137 S. Ct. 1744, 1748 (2017).

181. Susan Neuberger Weller, *U.S. Supreme Court Denies Redskins' Petition to Join SLANTS Case*, Copyright & Trademark Matters, Oct. 3, 2016, www .copyrighttrademarkmatters. com/trademark/disparaging-marks-trademark/.

182. Robert Barnes, *Can Disparaging Trademarks Be Denied? The Supreme Court Is Skeptical*, Wash. Post, Jan.18, 2016, www.washingtonpost.com/ politics/courts_law/supreme-court-skeptical-of-governments-withholding-disparaging-trademarks/2017/01/18/ b97b6752-dd05-11e6-918c-99ede3c8cafa_story.html?utm_ term=.f3779d109e82.

183. 15 U.S.C. §§ 1052, 1072, 1115.

184. 15 U.S.C. § 1115(a), (b).

185. 15 U.S.C. § 1058.

186. 15 U.S.C. § 1059.

187. Pub. L. 106–113, 113 Stat. 1536.

188. E. & J. Gallo Winery v. Spider Webs Ltd., 286 F.3d 270 (5th Cir. 2002).

189. Brookfield Communications Inc. v. West Coast Ent. Corp., 174 F.3d 1036 (9th Cir. 1999).

190. Ty Inc. v. Perryman, 306 F.3d 509, 513 (7th Cir. 2002), *cert. denied*, 538 U.S. 971 (2003).

191. 15 U.S.C. § 1125(a)(1) (Lanham Act—U.S. trademark law).

192. *See, e.g.,* Triangle Publ'ns v. Knight-Ridder Newspaper Inc., 626 F.2d 1171 (5th Cir. 1978).

193. Deere & Co. v. MTD Products Inc., 41 F.3d 39 (2d Cir. 1994).

194. Infostream Group Inc. v. Avid Life Media Inc., 2013 U.S. Dist. LEXIS 161940 (C.D. Cal., 2013).

195. Facebook Inc. v. Teachbook.com LLC, 819 F. Supp. 2d 764, 781 (N.D. Ill. 2011).

196. *Tacking*, MarkLaw, www .marklaw.com/index.php?option= com_content&view=article&id= 292:tacking&catid=41:t&Item id=19 (last visited May 17, 2015).

197. *Pepsi Logo Timeline: The Evolution of the Company's Brand*, Huff. Post, July 30, 2015, www.huffingtonpost .com/2012/12/28/pepsi-logo-timeline_n_2279676.html.

198. *Id.*

199. Hana Financial Inc. v. Hana Bank, 135 S. Ct. 907 (2015).

200. Mark Wilson, *What Is Trademark Tacking*, FindLaw, Jan. 21, 2015, blogs.findlaw.com/ free_enterprise/2015/01/what-is-trademark-tacking.html.

201. *See* Applicant of E. I. DuPont de Nemours & Co., 476 F.2d 1357, 1361 (C.C.P.A. 1973).

202. 15 U.S.C. §§ 1125(c), 1127.

203. Anne Gilson LaLonde, Gilson on Trademarks § 5A.01[5], [6] (2013).

204. Moseley v. V Secret Catalogue Inc., 537 U.S. 418 (2003).

205. *Id.* at 434.

206. 15 U.S.C. § 1115(b).

207. 15 U.S.C. § 115(b)(4).

208. Overstock.com v. NoMoreRack. com, 2014 U.S. Dist. LEXIS 89620 (2014).

209. Webceleb Inc. v. Procter & Gamble Co. 554 Fed. Appx. 606 (9th Cir. 2014).

210. New Kids on the Block v. News America Publ'g Inc., 971 F.2d 302 (9th Cir. 1992).

211. 15 U.S.C. § 1125(c)(3).

Chapter 12

1. Va. State Bd. of Pharmacy v. Va. Citizens Consumer Council, 425 U.S. 748, 762, 763, 764 (1976).

2. Sorrell v. IMS Health Inc., 564 U.S. 552 (2011).

3. *See, e.g.,* Alexander Meiklejohn, Free Speech and Its Relation to Self-Government (1948).

4. Valentine v. Chrestensen, 316 U.S. 52, 54 (1942).

5. *Id.*

6. New York Times Co. v. Sullivan, 376 U.S. 254 (1964).

7. *Id.*

8. *Id.* at 266.

9. Test Masters Educ. Servs. Inc. v. Robin Singh Educ. Servs. Inc., 799 F.3d 437, 453 (5th Cir. 2015), *cert. denied*, 137 S. Ct. 499 (2016).

10. 16 C.F.R. § 255.5.

11. Sarver v. Chartier, 813 F.3d 891 (9th Cir. 2016).

12. Enigma Software Group USA LLC v. Bleeping Computer LLC, 194 F. Supp. 3d 25 (S.D.N.Y. 2016).

13. Pittsburgh Press Co. v. Pittsburgh Comm'n on Human Relations, 413 U.S. 376, 389 (1973).

14. Bigelow v. Virginia, 421 U.S. 809 (1975).

15. Roe v. Wade, 410 U.S. 113 (1973).

16. *Bigelow*, 421 U.S. at 809, 822.

17. *Id.* at 817.

18. *Id.* at 820.

19. Va. State Bd. of Pharmacy v. Va. Citizens Consumer Council, 425 U.S. 748, 762 (1976).

20. *Id.* at 762.

21. Central Hudson Gas & Electric Corp. v. Public Service Commission of New York, 447 U.S. 557 (1980).

22. *Id.* at 561 (emphasis added).

23. Board of Trustees of the State University of New York v. Fox, 492 U.S. 469 (1989).

24. *Id.* at 480.

25. 44 Liquormart Inc. v. Rhode Island, 517 U.S. 484, 507 (1996).

26. *Id.* at 503.

27. *Id.* at 500.

28. *Id.* at 518.

29. Sorrell v. IMS Health Inc., 564 U.S. 552 (2011).

30. Retail Digital Network LLC v. Appelsmith, 810 F.3d 638 (9th Cir. 2016), *and aff'd at* 861 F.3d 839 (9th Cir. 2017).

31. Crazy Ely W. Vill. LLC v. City of Las Vegas, 618 F. App'x 904 (9th Cir. 2015).

32. American Meat Inst. v. USDA, 760 F.3d 18, 26 (D.C. Cir. 2014).

33. *Id.*

34. 15 U.S.C. § 1125.

35. FTC v. DirecTV, Case3:15-cv-01129 (N.D. CA. Mar. 11, 2015), www.ftc.gov; Linda Wagar, *FTC Takes DirecTV to Court for Alleged Deceptive Advertising Practices*, WDAF-TV, Mar. 23, 2015, fox4kc.com/2015/03/23/ftc-takes-directv-to-court-for-alleged-deceptive-advertising-practices.

36. 15 U.S.C. § 1125.

37. Roscoe B. Starek III, *Myths and Half-Truths About Deceptive Advertising*, ADDRESS TO THE NATIONAL INFOMERCIAL MARKETING ASSOCIATION (Oct. 15, 1996), www.ftc.gov/speeches/starek/nima96d4.htm.

38. FTC POLICY STATEMENT BY CHAIRMAN JAMES C. MILLER III (Oct. 14, 1983), www.ftc.gov/public-statements/1983/10/ftc-policy-statement-deception.

39. Grubbs v. Sheakley Group Inc., 807 F.3d 785, 800 (6th Cir. 2015).

40. *Id.* at 803.

41. Radiance Found. Inc. v. NAACP, 786 F.3d 316, 320 (4th Cir. 2015).

42. L.A. Taxi Coop. Inc. v. Uber Technologies Inc., 114 F. Supp. 3d 852, 858 (N.D. Cali. 2015).

43. Zauderer v. Office of Disciplinary Counsel of Supreme Court of Ohio, 471 U.S. 626, 651 (1985).

44. Fed. Trade Comm'n, *.Com Disclosures: Information About Online Advertising* (May 2000), www.ftc.gov/os/2000/05/0005dotcomstaffreport.pdf; Fed. Trade Comm'n, *.Com Disclosures: How to Make Effective Disclosures in Digital Advertising* (Mar. 2013), ftc.gov/os/2013/03/130312dotcomdisclosures.pdf.

45. Fed. Trade Comm'n, *Enforcement Policy Statement on Deceptively Formatted Advertisements* (2015), www.ftc.gov/system/files/documents/public_statements/896923/151222deceptiveenforcement.pdf; Fed. Trade Comm'n, *Native Advertising: A Guide for Business* (Dec. 2015), www.ftc.gov/tips-advice/business-center/guidance/native-advertising-guidebusinesses.

46. Fed. Trade Comm'n, *Lord & Taylor Settles FTC Charges It Deceived Consumers Through Paid Article in an Online Fashion Magazine and Paid Instagram Posts by 50 "Fashion Influencers"* (Mar. 15, 2016), www.ftc.gov/news-events/press-releases/2016/03/lordtaylor-settles-ftc-charges-it-deceived-consumers-through.

47. Fed. Trade Comm'n, *Complaint, In the Matter of Lord & Taylor, LLC* (Docket No. C-4576) (March 15, 2016), www.ftc.gov/system/files/documents/cases/160523lordtaylorcmpt.pdf.

48. Fed. Trade Comm'n, *FTC Approves Final Lord & Taylor Order Prohibiting Deceptive Advertising Techniques* (May 23, 2016), www.ftc.gov/newsevents/press-releases/2016/05/ftc-approves-final-lord-taylor-orderprohibiting-deceptive.

49. Patrick Coffee, *FTC Slams Lord & Taylor for Not Disclosing Paid Social Posts and Native Ads*, ADWEEK, March 15, 2016, www.adweek.com/news/advertising-branding/ftc-slamslord-taylor-deceiving-customers-not-disclosing-its-native-ads-170229.

50. Fed. Trade Comm'n, *Agreement Containing Consent Order, In re Machinima, Inc.*, File No. 1423090 (Mar. 17, 2016).

51. *See* Fed. Trade Comm'n, *Closing Letter, Microsoft/Starcom*, File No. 142-3090 (Aug. 26, 2015), www.ftc.gov/system/files/documents/closing_letters/nid/150902machinima_letter.pdf.

52. Aaron Burstein, *FTC Puts "Influencers" on Notice: Disclose Marketing Relationships in Social Media Post*, BROADCAST L. BLOG, Apr. 26, 2017, http://www.broadcastlawblog.com/2017/04/articles/ftc-puts-influencers-on-notice-disclose-marketing-relationships-in-social-media-posts/?utm_

source=David+Oxenford%2C+
Esq+-+Broadcast+Law+
Blog&utm_campaign=84656aaedb
-RSS_EMAIL_CAMPAIGN.

53. *See, e.g.,* Fed. Trade Comm'n,
*Closing Letter, AnnTaylor Stores
Corp.,* File No. 102-3147 (Apr.
20, 2010), www.ftc.gov/os/closin
gs/100420anntaylorclosingletter
.pdf; Fed. Trade Comm'n, *Closing
Letter, Cole Haan,* File
No. 142-3041 (Mar. 20, 2014),
www.ftc.gov/system/files/
documents/closing_letters/
cole-haan-inc./140320
colehaanclosingletter.pdf.

54. *Guides Concerning the Use of
Endorsements and Testimonials in
Advertising,* 16 C.F.R. pt. 255
(2014), ftc.gov/os/2009/10/0910
05revisedendorsementguides.pdf;
Fed. Trade Comm'n, *The FTC's
Endorsement Guides: What People
Are Asking* (May 2015), www.ftc
.gov/system/files/documents/
plain-language/pdf-0205-
endorsement-guides-faqs_0.pdf.

55. 15 U.S.C. § 7701.

56. 15 U.S.C. § 7704(a)(1).

57. 16 C.F.R. § 255.5.

58. Van Hollen v. FEC, 74 F. Supp.
3d 407 (D.D.C. 2014), *reversed by*
811 F.3d 486 (D.C. Cir. 2016).

59. *Id.* (emphasis added).

60. Rubin v. Coors Brewing Co., 514
U.S. 476, 490 (1995).

61. Educ. Media Co. at Va. Tech. Inc.
v. Insley, 731 F.3d 291 (4th Cir.
2013).

62. Educ. Media Co. at Va. Tech. v.
Swecker, 2008 U.S. Dist. LEXIS
124685 (E.D. Va., June 19,
2008), *vacated,* 602 F.3d 583
(4th Cir. 2010).

63. 44 Liquormart Inc. v. Rhode
Island, 517 U.S. 484, 507 (1996).

64. Capital Broad. Co. v. Mitchell,
333 F. Supp. 582 (D.D.C. 1971).

65. Lorillard Tobacco Co. v. Reilly,
533 U.S. 525, 569 (2001).

66. *Id.* at 558.

67. Coyne Beahm Inc. v. FDA, 966 F.
Supp. 1374 (M.D.N.C. 1997).

68. *The Facts on the FDA's New
Tobacco Rule,* U.S. Food &
Drug Admin., Apr. 8, 2017,
www.fda.gov/ForConsumers/
ConsumerUpdates/ucm506676
.htm

69. Family Smoking Prevention and
Tobacco Control Act (FSPTCA),
Pub. L. No. 111–31, 123 Stat.
1776 (2009).

70. Steven Reinberg, *U.S. Abandons
Effort to Place Graphic Labeling on
Cigarettes,* HealthDay, Mar. 20,
2013, health.usnews.com.

71. Discount Tobacco City & Lottery
Co. v. United States, 674 F.3d
509 (6th Cir. 2012), *cert. denied,*
133 S. Ct. 1996 (2013); R.J.
Reynolds Tobacco Co. v. FDA,
696 F.3d 1205 (D.C. Cir. 2012),
cert. denied, 133 S. Ct. 1996
(2013).

72. *R.J. Reynolds Tobacco Co.,* 696
F.3d 1205.

73. *See, e.g., Discount Tobacco City,*
674 F.3d at 524–25.

74. Discount Tobacco City & Lottery
Co. v. United States, *cert. denied,*
133 S. Ct. 1996 (2013); R.J.
Reynolds Tobacco Co. v. FDA,
cert. denied, 133 S. Ct. 1996
(2013).

75. Stephanie Strom, *U.S. Judge
Rejects Gruesome Cigarette Labels,*
N.Y. Times, Feb. 29, 2012,
www.nytimes.com.

76. Mark Bittman, *The Right to Sell
Kids Junk,* Opinionator, Mar.
27, 2012, opinionator.blogs

.nytimes.com/2012/03/27/the-
right-to-sell-kids-junk/.

77. United States v. Edge Broad., 509
U.S. 418 (1993).

78. *Id.* at 428.

79. Greater New Orleans Broad.
Ass'n. Inc. v. United States, 527
U.S. 173 (1999).

80. *Id.*

81. Sorrell v. IMS Health Inc., 564
U.S. 552 (2011).

82. Vt. Stat. Ann., Tit. 18, § 4631
(Supp. 2010).

83. *Sorrell,* 564 U.S. at 580.

84. *Id.* at 602.

85. *One Year Later: The Consequences
of Sorrell v. IMS Health Inc.,*
Justice Watch, July 2, 2012,
afjjusticewatch.blogspot
.com//2012/07/one-year-later-
consequences-of-sorrell.html.

86. *Id.*

87. Tracy Rifle & Pistol LLC v.
Harris, 118 F. Supp. 3d 1182
(E.D. Cal. 2015), *aff'd,* 637 F.
App'x 401 (9th Cir. 2016).

88. Seattle Mideast Awareness
Campaign v. King County, 781
F.3d 489 (9th Cir. 2015).

89. AFDI v. Mass. Bay Transportation
Authority, 781 F.3d 571 (1st Cir. 2015),
cert. denied, 136 S. Ct. 793 (2016).

90. AFDI v. Southeastern Pa.
Transportation Authority, 2015
U.S. Dist. LEXIS 29571 (E.D.
Pa., Mar. 11, 2015).

91. *Id.*

92. First Nat'l Bank of Boston v.
Bellotti, 435 U.S. 765 (1978).

93. *See, e.g.,* FEC v. Nat'l Right to Work
Comm., 459 U.S. 197 (1982); FEC
v. Nat'l Conservative Political Action
Comm., 470 U.S. 480 (1985);
FEC v. Massachusetts Citizens for
Life Inc., 479 U.S. 238 (1986); and
Austin v. Mich. State Chamber of
Commerce, 494 U.S. 652 (1990).

94. Citizens United v. FEC, 558 U.S. 310 (2010).

95. Nike Inc. v. Kasky, 539 U.S. 654 (2003).

96. Kasky v. Nike Inc., 45 P.3d 243, 258 (Cal. 2002).

97. *Id.* at 263.

98. *See, e.g.,* Bates v. State Bar of Ariz., 433 U.S. 350 (1977).

99. *Id.*

100. Kiser v. Kamdar, 831 F.3d 784 (6th Cir. 2016).

101. 15 U.S.C. § 6501 *et seq.*

102. Fed. Trade Comm'n, *Two App Developers Settle FTC Charges They Violated Children's Online Privacy Protection Act* (Dec. 17, 2016), www.ftc.gov/newsevents/press-releases/2015/12/two-app-developers-settle-ftccharges-they-violated-childrens.

103. 16 C.F.R. § 312 *et seq.*; *see also* Seena Gressin, COPPA: *When Persistence Doesn't Pay,* BUSINESS BLOG, Dec. 17, 2015, www.ftc.gov/news-events/blogs/businessblog/2015/12/coppa-when-persistence-doesnt-pay.

104. FTC v. Corzine, No. Civ.-S-94–1446 (E.D. Ca. 1994).

105. Jessica Guynn, *FTC Calls on Online Ad Industry to Agree on Do-Not-Track Standard,* L.A. TIMES, Apr. 17, 2013, www.latimes.com/business/technology/la-fi-tn-ftc-online-ad-industry-do-not-track-20130417,0,5397711.story.

106. Fed. Trade Comm'n, *FTC Testifies on Do Not Track Legislation* (Dec. 2, 2010), www.ftc.gov/opa/2010/12/dnttestimony.shtm.

107. Laura Sydell, *Microsoft Adds "Do Not Track" Option to Internet Explorer 9,* ALL TECH CONSIDERED, Dec. 8, 2010, www.npr.org/blogs/alltechconsidered/2010/12/09/131914019/microsoft-ads-do-not-track-option-to-internet-explorer-9.

108. 15 U.S.C. §§ 7701–7713 (2004).

109. Fed. Trade Comm'n, *FTC Approves New Rule Provision Under the CAN-SPAM Act* (May 12, 2008), www.ftc.govopa/2008/05/canspam.shtm.

110. These states are Alaska, Arizona, Arkansas, California, Colorado, Connecticut, Delaware, Florida, Georgia, Idaho, Illinois, Indiana, Iowa, Kansas, Louisiana, Maine, Maryland, Michigan, Minnesota, Missouri, Nevada, New Mexico, North Carolina, North Dakota, Ohio, Oklahoma, Pennsylvania, Rhode Island, South Dakota, Tennessee, Texas, Utah, Virginia, Washington, West Virginia, Wisconsin and Wyoming.

111. Va. Code Ann. § 18.2–152.3:1.

112. *See Virginia: Spam Law Struck Down on Grounds of Free Speech,* N.Y. TIMES, Sept. 13, 2008, at A17.

113. Jaynes v. Virginia, 666 S.E.2d 303, 314 (Va. 2008), *cert. denied,* 556 U.S. 1152 (2009).

114. 47 U.S.C. § 227(b)(1)(A) (1991).

115. Nack v. Walburg, No. 11–1460 (8th Cir. May 21, 2013), law.justia.com/cases/federal/appellate-courts/ca8/11-1460/11-1460-2013-05-21.html.

116. 15 U.S.C. 1125, § 43 (a)(1)(A)(B).

117. Aaron Taube, *Coca-Cola Loses Huge False-Advertising Case in Supreme Court,* BUSINESS INSIDER, Jun. 12, 2014, www.businessinsider.com/scotus-revives-false-ad-claims-against-coke-2014-6.

118. POM Wonderful LLC v. Coca-Cola Co., 134 S. Ct. 2228, 2241 (2014).

119. Lexmark v. Static Control, 134 S. Ct. 1377 (2014).

120. *Id.* at 1390, 1391.

121. Eric Goldman, *Supreme Court Changes False Advertising Law Across the Country,* FORBES, Mar. 26, 2014, www.forbes.com/sites/ericgoldman/2014/o3/26/supreme-court-changes-false-advertising-law-across-the-country.

122. Fed. Trade Comm'n, *Three Home Loan Advertisers Settle FTC Charges; Failed to Disclose Key Loan Terms in Ads* (Jan. 8, 2009), www.ftc.gov/opa/2009/01/anm.shtm.

123. POM Wonderful v. FTC, 777 F.3d 478 (D.C. Cir. 2015), *cert. denied,* 136 S. Ct. 1839 (2016).

124. *Id.*

125. Fed. Trade Comm'n, *Decision and Order: American Nationwide Mortgage Co.,* Docket No. C-2429 (Feb. 17, 2009), www.ftc.gov/sites/default/files/documents/cases/2009/01/090108americancmpt.pdf.

126. Fed. Trade Comm'n, *Rite Aid Settles FTC Charges That It Failed to Protect Medical and Financial Privacy of Customers and Employees* (July 27, 2010), www.ftc.gov/opa/2010/07/riteaid.shtm.

127. Fed. Trade Comm'n, *Three CortiSlim Defendants to Give Up $4.5 Million in Cash and Other Assets* (Sept. 21, 2005), www.ftc.gov/opa/2005/09/windowrock.shtm.

128. Lesley Fair, *Substantiation: The Science of Compliance, Fed. Trade Comm'n*, Dec. 15, 2011, www.ftc.gov/news-events/blogs/business-blog/2011/12/science-reliance-compliance.

129. In the Matter of Tropicana Products Inc., FTC Complaint, Docket No. C-4145 (2005), www.ftc.gov/os/caselist/0423154/050825comp0423154.pdf.

130. Warner-Lambert Co. v. FTC, 562 F.2d 749 (1977), *cert. denied*, 435 U.S. 950 (1978).

131. *Id.* at 762, 764.

132. Michael B. Mazis, *FTC v. Novartis: The Return of Corrective Advertising?*, 20 J. Pub. Pol'y & Market'g 114 (2001).

133. *Id.*

134. Fed. Trade Comm'n, *FTC Charges Marketers With Making Unsubstantiated Claims That They Could Eliminate Consumers' Debt* (Dec. 2, 2010), www.ftc.gov/opa/2010/12/ffdc.shtm.

135. Minority TV Project v. FCC, 134 S. Ct. 2874 (2014).

136. Minority TV Project v. FCC, 736 F.3d 1192 (9th Cir. 2013).

GLOSSARY

A

absolute privilege A complete exemption from liability for the speaking or publishing of defamatory words of and concerning another because the statement was made within the performance of duty such as in judicial or political contexts.

actual malice In libel law, a statement made knowing it is false or with reckless disregard for its truth.

ad hoc balancing Making decisions according to the specific facts of the case under review rather than more general principles.

administrative law The orders, rules and regulations promulgated by executive branch administrative agencies to carry out their delegated duties.

admonitions Judges' instructions to jurors warning them to avoid potentially prejudicial communications.

advisory opinion A Federal Trade Commission measure that offers formal guidance on whether a specific advertisement may be false or misleading and how to correct it.

affirm To ratify, uphold or approve a lower court ruling.

all-purpose public figure In libel law, a person who occupies a position of such persuasive power and influence as to be deemed a public figure for all purposes. Public figure libel plaintiffs are required to prove actual malice.

amicus brief A submission to the court from amicus curiae, or "friends of the court," which are interested individuals or organizations that are parties in the case.

appellant The party making the appeal; also called the petitioner.

appellee The party against whom an appeal is made.

appropriation Using a person's name, picture, likeness, voice or identity for commercial or trade purposes without permission.

artistic relevance test A test to determine whether the use of a celebrity's name, picture, likeness, voice or identity is relevant to a disputed work's artistic purpose. It is used in cases regarding the infringement of a celebrity's right of publicity.

as applied A legal phrase referring to interpretation of a statute on the basis of actual effects on the parties in the present case.

B

Berne Convention The primary international copyright treaty adopted by many countries in 1886 and by the United States in 1988.

black-letter law Formally enacted, written law that is available in legal reporters or other documents.

bootstrapping In libel law, the forbidden practice of a defendant claiming that the plaintiff is a public figure solely on the basis of the statement that is the reason for the lawsuit.

broadband A high-capacity transmission technique that uses a wide range of frequencies, which enables a large number of messages to be communicated simultaneously.

broadcasting Defined by the Communications Act of 1934 as use of the electromagnetic spectrum to send signals to many listeners and viewers simultaneously.

burden of proof The requirement for a party to a case to demonstrate one or more claims by the presentation of evidence. In libel law, for example, the plaintiff has the burden of proof.

C

categorical balancing The practice of deciding cases by weighing different broad categories, such as political speech, against other categories of interests, such as privacy, to create general rules that may be applied in later cases with similar facts.

cease and desist order An administrative agency order prohibiting a person or business from continuing a particular course of conduct.

child pornography   Any image showing children in sexual or sexually explicit situations.

chilling effect   The discouragement of a constitutional right, especially free speech, by any government practice that creates uncertainty about the proper exercise of that right.

clear and present danger   Doctrine establishing that restrictions on First Amendment rights will be upheld if they are necessary to prevent an extremely serious and imminent harm.

commercialization   The appropriation tort used to protect people who want privacy; prohibits using another person's name or likeness for commercial purposes without permission.

common law   Judge-made law comprised of the principles and traditions established through court rulings; precedent-based law.

Communications Decency Act   The part of the 1996 Telecommunications Act that largely attempted to regulate internet content. The Communications Decency Act was successfully challenged in *Reno v. American Civil Liberties Union* (1997).

compelling interest   A government interest of the highest order, an interest the government is required to protect.

concurring opinion   A separate opinion of a minority of the court or a single judge or justice agreeing with the majority opinion but applying different reasoning or legal principles.

conditional (or qualified) privilege   An exemption from liability for repeating defamatory words of and concerning another because the original statement was made within the performance of duty such as in judicial or political contexts; usually claimed by journalists who report statements made in absolutely privileged situations; this privilege is conditional (or qualified) on the premise that the reporting is fair and accurate.

consent order   An agreement between the Federal Trade Commission and an advertiser stipulating the terms that must be followed to address problematic advertising; also called a consent agreement.

constitutional law   The set of laws that establish the nature, functions and limits of government.

content-based laws   Laws enacted because of the message, the subject matter or the ideas expressed in the regulated speech.

content-neutral laws   Laws that incidentally and unintentionally affect speech as they advance other important government interests.

continuance   Postponement of a trial to a later time.

contributory infringement   The participation in, or contribution to, the infringing acts of another person.

copyright   An exclusive legal right used to protect intellectual creations from unauthorized use.

corrective advertising   The Federal Trade Commission power to require an advertiser to advertise or otherwise distribute information to correct false or misleading advertisement claims.

D

damages   Monetary compensation that may be recovered in court by any person who has suffered loss or injury. Damages may be compensatory for actual loss or punitive as punishment for outrageous conduct.

data broker   An entity that collects and stores personal information about consumers, then sells that information to other organizations.

de novo   Literally, "new" or "over again." On appeal, the court may review the facts de novo rather than simply reviewing the legal posture and process of the case.

defamation   A false communication that harms another's reputation and subjects him or her to ridicule and scorn; incorporates both libel and slander.

defendant   The party accused of violating a law, or the party being sued in a civil lawsuit.

deference   The judicial practice of interpreting statues and rules by relying heavily on the judgments and intentions of the administrative experts and legislative agencies that enacted the laws.

demurrer   A request that a court dismiss a case on the grounds that although the claims are true they are insufficient to warrant a judgment against the defendant.

deposition   Testimony by a witness conducted outside a courtroom and intended to be used in preparation for trial.

designated public forum   Government spaces or buildings that are available for public use (within limits).

discovery   The pretrial process of gathering evidence and facts. The word also may refer to the specific items of evidence that are uncovered.

discretion   The authority to determine the proper outcome.

disparaging mark   A trademark that consists of or comprises immoral, deceptive or scandalous matters; or matters that may disparage or falsely suggest a connection with people and/or symbols that may bring them into contempt or disrepute. Section 2(a) of the Lanham Act prevents the Patent and Trademark Office from registering these trademarks.

dissenting opinion   A separate opinion of a minority of the court or a single judge or justice disagreeing with the result reached by the majority and challenging the majority's reasoning or the legal basis of the decision.

distinguish from precedent   To justify an outcome in a case by asserting that differences between that case and preceding cases outweigh any similarities.

distortion   Occurs when facts are omitted or the context in which material is published makes an otherwise accurate story appear false.

doctrines   Principles or theories of law that shape judicial decision making (e.g., the doctrine of content neutrality).

Driver's Privacy Protection Act   Federal legislation that prohibits states from disclosing personal information that drivers submit in order to obtain a driver's license.

due process   Fair legal proceedings. Due process is guaranteed by the Fifth and 14th Amendments to the U.S. Constitution.

E

electromagnetic spectrum The range of wavelengths or frequencies over which electromagnetic radiation extends.

Electronic Freedom of Information Act   A 1996 amendment to the Freedom of Information Act that applies the act to electronically stored information.

electronic media   Broadcast and newer forms of media that utilize electronic technology or the digital encoding of information to distribute news and entertainment. Does not include media, like newspapers, historically distributed in printed form.

embellishment   Occurs when false material is added to otherwise true facts.

emotional distress   Serious mental anguish.

en banc   Literally, "on the bench" but now meaning "in full court." The judges of a circuit court of appeals will sit en banc to decide important or controversial cases.

equity law   Law created by judges to decide cases based on fairness and ethics and also to determine the proper remedy.

executive orders   Orders from a government executive, such as the president, a governor or a mayor, that have the force of law.

experience and logic test   A doctrine that evaluates both the history of openness and the role it plays in ensuring the credibility of a process to determine whether it is presumptively open.

F

facial challenge   A legal argument that the challenged law or policy is unconstitutional in every application; there are no situations in which the law can be interpreted to be constitutional.

facial meaning   The plain and straightforward meaning.

fact finder   In a trial, a judge or the jury determining which facts presented in evidence are accurate.

fair comment and criticism   A common law privilege that protects critics from lawsuits brought by individuals in the public eye.

fair report privilege   A privilege claimed by journalists who report events on the basis of official records. The report must fairly and accurately reflect the content of the records; this is the condition that sometimes leads to this privilege being called "conditional privilege."

fair use   A test courts use to determine whether using another's copyrighted material without permission is legal or an infringement. Also used in trademark infringement cases.

fairness doctrine   The Federal Communications Commission rule requiring broadcast stations to air programs discussing public issues and include a variety of views about controversial issues of public importance.

false light   A privacy tort that involves making a person seem in the public eye to be someone he or she is not. Several states do not allow false light suits.

Family Educational Rights and Privacy Act   A federal law that protects the privacy of student education records. Also known as the Buckley Amendment.

Federal Communications Commission   An independent U.S. government agency, directly responsible to Congress, charged with regulating interstate and international communications by radio, television, wire, satellite, cable and broadband. The Communications Act of 1934 established the Federal Communications Commission; its jurisdiction covers the 50 states, the District of Columbia and U.S. possessions.

Federal Radio Commission A federal agency established by the Radio Act of 1927 to oversee radio broadcasting. The Federal Communications Commission succeeded the Federal Radio Commission in 1934.

Federal Trade Commission A federal agency created in 1914. Its purpose is to promote free and fair competition in interstate commerce; this includes preventing false and misleading advertising.

federalism A principle according to which the states are related to yet independent of each other and are related to yet independent of the federal government.

fictionalization Occurs when some truth, such as a person's name or identifying characteristics, is part of a largely fictional piece.

fighting words Words not protected by the First Amendment because they cause immediate harm or illegal acts.

first-sale doctrine Once a copyright owner sells a copy of a work, the new owner may possess, transfer or otherwise dispose of that copy without the copyright owner's permission.

for-cause challenge In the context of jury selection, the ability of attorneys to remove a potential juror for a reason the law finds sufficient, as opposed to a peremptory challenge.

forum shopping A practice whereby the plaintiff chooses a court in which to sue because he or she believes the court will rule in the plaintiff's favor.

Freedom of Information Act The federal law that requires records held by federal government agencies to be made available to the public, provided that the information sought does not fall within one of nine exempted categories.

G

gag orders A nonlegal term used to describe court orders that prohibit publication or discussion of specific materials.

generally applicable law A law that is enforced evenly, across the board. Within First Amendment contexts, it is the idea that the freedom of the press clause does not exempt news organizations from obeying general laws.

Government in the Sunshine Act Sometimes referred to as the Federal Open Meetings Law, an act passed in 1976 that mandates that meetings of federal government agencies be open to the public unless all or some part of a meeting is exempted according to exceptions outlined in the law.

grand jury A group summoned to hear the state's evidence in criminal cases and decide whether a crime was committed and whether charges should be filed; grand juries do not determine guilt.

H

hate speech A category of speech that includes name-calling and pointed criticism that demeans others on the basis of race, color, gender, ethnicity, religion, national origin, disability, intellect or the like.

Health Insurance Portability and Accountability Act A federal law protecting against health professionals and institutions revealing individuals' private medical records.

Hicklin rule Taken from a mid-19th-century English case and used in the United States until the mid-20th century, a rule that defines material as obscene if it tends to corrupt children.

holding The decision or ruling of a court.

I

impanel To select and seat a jury.

important government interest An interest of the government that is substantial or significant (i.e., more than merely convenient or reasonable) but not compelling.

incorporation doctrine The 14th Amendment concept that most of the Bill of Rights applies equally to the states.

indecency A narrow legal term referring to sexual expression and expletives inappropriate for children on broadcast radio and television.

industry guides In advertising, a Federal Trade Commission measure that outlines the FTC's policies concerning a particular category of product or service.

infringement The unauthorized manufacture, sale or distribution of an item protected by copyright, patent or trademark law.

injunction A court order prohibiting a person or organization from doing some specified act.

intellectual property law   The legal category including copyright, trademark and patent law.

intentional infliction of emotional distress   Extreme and outrageous intentional or reckless conduct causing plaintiffs severe emotional harm; public official and public figure plaintiff must show actual malice on defendant's part.

intermediate scrutiny   A standard applied by the courts to review laws that implicate core constitutional values; also called heightened review.

intrusion upon seclusion   Physically or technologically disturbing another's reasonable expectation of privacy.

involuntary public figure   In libel law, a person who does not necessarily thrust himself or herself into public controversies voluntarily but is drawn into a given issue.

J

judicial review   The power of the courts to determine the meaning of the Constitution and decide whether laws violate the Constitution.

jurisdiction   The geographic or topical area of responsibility and authority of a court.

L

Lanham Act   A federal law that regulates the trademark registration process but also contains a section permitting business competitors to sue one another for false advertising.

laws of general application   Laws such as tax and equal employment laws that fall within the express power of government. Laws of general application are generally reviewed under minimum scrutiny.

legislative history   Congressional reports and records containing discussions about proposed legislation.

libel per quod   A statement whose injurious nature requires proof.

libel per se   A statement whose injurious nature is apparent and requires no further proof.

libel-proof plaintiff   A plaintiff whose reputation is deemed to be so damaged already that additional false statements of and concerning him or her cannot cause further harm.

limited-purpose public figure   In libel law, those plaintiffs who have attained public figure status within a narrow set of circumstances by thrusting themselves to the forefront of particular public controversies in order to influence the resolution of the issues involved; this kind of public figure is more common than the all-purpose public figure.

litigated order   A Federal Trade Commission order filed in administrative court and enforceable by the courts whose violation can result in penalties, including fines of up to $10,000 per day.

lowest unit rate   Generally a station's minimum advertising rate and the maximum rate a broadcaster or cable system may charge a politician for advertising time during the 45 days before primary elections and the 60 days before general elections.

M

memorandum order   An order announcing the vote of the Supreme Court without providing an opinion.

metadata   A set of data that describes and gives information about other data.

modify precedent   To change rather than follow or reject precedent.

moot   Term used to describe a case in which the issues presented are no longer "live" or in which the matter in dispute has already been resolved; a case is not moot if it is susceptible to repetition but evades review.

motion to dismiss   A request to a court to reject a complaint because it does not state a claim that can be remedied by law or is legally lacking in some other way.

multichannel video programming distributors   An entity, including cable or direct broadcast satellite services, that makes multiple channels of video programming available for purchase.

must-carry rule   Regulations enacted under the federal cable law that require multichannel video programming distributors to transmit local broadcast television stations.

N

native advertising   Ads designed to resemble the editorial content of the medium where they appear. The Federal Trade Commission has said this may be deceptive if it makes it difficult for consumers to distinguish advertising from editorial content.

negligence   Generally, the failure to exercise reasonable or ordinary care.

negligent infliction of emotional distress   Careless breach of a duty that causes the plaintiff severe emotional harm.

net neutrality   The principle that holds that internet service providers cannot charge content providers to speed up the delivery of their goods—all internet traffic is treated equally.

neutral reportage   In libel law, a defense accepted in some jurisdictions that says that when an accusation is made by a responsible and prominent organization, reporting that accusation is protected by the First Amendment even when it turns out the accusation was false and libelous.

nonpublic forum   Government-held property that is not available for public speech and assembly purposes.

notice of proposed rulemaking   A notice issued by the Federal Communications Commission announcing that the commission is considering changing certain of its regulations or adopting new rules.

O

O'Brien **test**   A three-part test used to determine whether a content-neutral law is constitutional.

obscenity   The dictionary defines it as relating to sex in an indecent, very offensive or shocking way. The legal definition of obscenity comes from *Miller v. California*—material is determined to be obscene if it passes the *Miller* test.

online video distributor   An entity that provides video programming using the internet or internet protocol–based transmission paths.

opinion letter   An informal Federal Trade Commission communication providing general advice about advertising techniques.

original intent   The perceived intent of the framers of the First Amendment that guides some contemporary First Amendment application and interpretation.

original jurisdiction   The authority to consider a case at its inception, as contrasted with appellate jurisdiction.

originalists   Supreme Court justices who interpret the Constitution according to the perceived intent of its framers.

overbroad law   A principle that directs courts to find laws unconstitutional if they restrict more legal activity than necessary.

overrule   To reverse the ruling of a lower court.

overturn precedent   To reject the fundamental premise of a precedent.

P

patently offensive   Term describing material with hard-core sexual conduct.

PEG access channels   Channels that cable systems set aside for public, educational and government use.

per curiam opinion   An unsigned opinion by the court as a whole.

peremptory challenge   During jury selection, a challenge in which an attorney rejects a juror without showing a reason. Attorneys have the right to eliminate a limited number of jurors through peremptory challenges.

plagiarism   Using another's work or ideas without attribution.

plaintiff   The party who files a complaint; the one who sues.

political questions   Questions not subject to judicial review because they fall into areas properly handled by another branch of government.

pornography   A vague—not legally precise—term for sexually oriented material.

precedent   The outcome of a previous case that establishes a rule of law that courts within the same jurisdiction rely on to determine cases with similar issues.

predominant use test   In a right of publicity lawsuit, a test to determine whether the defendant used the plaintiff's name or picture more for commercial purposes or protected expression.

prior restraint   Action taken by the government to prohibit publication of a specific document or text before it is distributed to the public; a policy that requires government approval before publication.

private facts   The tort under which individuals or media are sued for publishing highly embarrassing private information that is not newsworthy or lawfully obtained from a public record.

private figure   In libel law, a plaintiff who cannot be categorized as either a public figure or a public official. Generally, in order to recover damages, a private figure is required to prove not actual malice but merely negligence on the part of the defendant.

probable cause   The standard of evidence needed for an arrest or to issue a search warrant. More than mere suspicion, it is a showing through reasonably trustworthy information that a crime has been or is being committed.

promissory estoppel   A legal doctrine requiring liability when a clear promise is made and relied on and injury results from the broken promise.

proximate cause   The legal determination of whether it is reasonable to conclude the defendant's actions led to the plaintiff's injury.

prurient interest   Lustful thoughts or sexual desires.

public domain   The sphere that includes material not protected by copyright law and therefore available for use without the creator's permission.

public figure   In libel law, a plaintiff who is in the public spotlight, usually voluntarily, and must prove the defendant acted with actual malice in order to win damages.

public forum   Government property held for use by the public, usually for purposes of exercising rights of speech and assembly.

public record   A government record, particularly one that is publicly available.

puffery   Advertising that exaggerates the merits of products or services in such a way that no reasonable person would take the ad seriously. Usually, puffery is not illegal given that a reasonable person understands the claim is not to be taken literally.

Q

quash   To nullify or annul, as in quashing a subpoena.

R

radio frequency   Any one of the electromagnetic wave frequencies that lie in the range extending from around 3 kHz to 300 GHz, which includes those frequencies used for communications or radio signals.

rational review   A standard of judicial review that assumes the constitutionality of reasonable legislative or administrative enactments and applies minimum scrutiny to their review.

reasonable person   The law's version of an average person.

reckless   Word used to describe actions taken with no consideration of the legal harms that might result.

red flag knowledge   When an internet service provider or website is aware of facts that would make infringement obvious to a reasonable person.

remand   To send back to the lower court for further action.

reporter's privilege   The concept that reporters may keep information such as source identity confidential. The rationale is that the reporter–source relationship is similar to doctor–patient and lawyer–client relationships.

restraining order   A court order forbidding an individual or group of individuals from doing a specified act until a hearing can be conducted.

retraction statutes   In libel law, state laws that limit the damages a plaintiff may receive if the defendant had issued a retraction of the material at issue. Retraction statutes are meant to discourage the punishment of any good-faith effort of admitting a mistake.

retransmission consent   Part of the federal cable television law allowing broadcast television stations to negotiate.

ride-along   A term given to the practice of journalists and other private citizens accompanying government officials—usually those in law enforcement or other emergency response personnel—as they carry out their duties.

right of publicity   The appropriation tort protecting a celebrity's right to have his or her name, picture, likeness, voice and identity used for commercial or trade purposes only with permission.

rule of law   The standards of a society that guide the proper and consistent creation and application of the law.

S

safe harbor   The takedown notification provision of the Digital Millennium Copyright Act that protects internet service providers and video-sharing websites from claims of infringement when they do not know about the infringement, do not earn money from the infringement and promptly comply with a takedown notice.

safe harbor policy   A Federal Communications Commission policy designating 10 p.m. to 6 a.m. as a time when broadcast radio and television stations may air indecent material without violating federal law or FCC regulations.

satellite market modification rule   Part of the Satellite Television Extension and Localism Act Reauthorization Act of 2014 that allows a television station, satellite operator or county government to request the addition or deletion of communities from a broadcast station's local television market.

search warrant   A written order issued by a judge, directed to a law enforcement officer, authorizing the search and seizure of any property for which there is reason to believe it will serve as evidence in a criminal investigation.

Sedition Act of 1798   Federal legislation under which anyone "opposing or resisting any law of the United States, or any act of the President of the United States," could be imprisoned for up to two years. The act also made it illegal to "write, print, utter, or publish" anything that criticized the president or Congress. The act expired in 1801 and ultimately was seen as a direct violation of the First Amendment.

seditious libel   Communication meant to incite people to change the government; criticism of the government.

sequestration   The isolation of jurors to avoid prejudice from publicity in a sensational trial.

serious social value   Material cannot be found obscene if it has serious literary, artistic, political or scientific value determined using national, not local/community, standards.

shield laws   State laws that protect journalists from being found in contempt of court for refusing to reveal sources.

single-publication rule   A rule that limits libel victims to only one cause of action even with multiple publications of the libel, common in the mass media and on websites.

SLAPP (strategic lawsuit against public participation)   A lawsuit whose purpose is to harass critics into silence, often to suppress those critics' First Amendment rights.

sound-alike   Someone whose voice sounds like another person's voice. Sound-alikes may not be used for commercial or trade purposes without permission or a disclaimer.

spectrum scarcity   The limitation to the number of segments of the broadcast spectrum that may be used for radio or television in a specific geographical area without causing interference. Spectrum scarcity is the primary reason courts permit greater regulation of broadcasters than print media.

standing   The position of a plaintiff who has been injured or has been threatened with injury. No person is entitled to challenge the constitutionality of an ordinance or statute unless he or she has the required standing—that is, unless he or she has been affected by the ordinance or statute.

stare decisis   The doctrine that courts follow precedent; the basis of common law, it literally means to stand by the previous decision.

Statute of Anne   The first copyright law, adopted in England in 1710, protected authors' works if they registered them with the government.

statutory construction   The process by which courts determine the proper meaning and application of statutes.

statutory damages   Damages specified in certain laws. Under these laws, copyright being an example, a judge may award statutory damages even if a plaintiff is unable to prove actual damages.

statutory law   Written law formally enacted by city, county, state and federal legislative bodies.

strict construction   Courts' narrow interpretation and application of a law based on the literal meaning of its language. Especially applied in interpreting the Constitution.

strict liability   Liability without fault; liability for any and all harms, foreseeable or unforeseen, which result from a product or an action.

strict scrutiny   A court test for determining the constitutionality of laws aimed at speech content, under which the government must show it is using the least restrictive means available to directly advance its compelling interest.

subpoena   A command for someone to appear or testify in court or to turn over evidence, such as notes or recordings with penalties for noncompliance.

substantiation   The authority of the Federal Trade Commission to demand that an advertiser prove its advertised claims.

summary judgment   The resolution of a legal dispute without a full trial when a judge determines that undisputed evidence is legally sufficient to render judgment.

summons   A notice asking an individual to appear at a court. Potential jurors receive such a summons.

supremacy Article 4, Part 2 of the U.S. Constitution (commonly called the Supremacy Clause) establishes that federal law takes precedence over, or supersedes, state laws.

symbolic expression Action that warrants some First Amendment protection because its primary purpose is to express ideas.

T

tacking Allows a trademark owner to slightly alter a trademark without abandoning ownership of the original mark.

textualists Judges—in particular, Supreme Court justices—who rely exclusively on a careful reading of legal texts to determine the meaning of the law.

time/place/manner laws A First Amendment concept that laws regulating the conditions of speech are more acceptable than those regulating content; also, the laws that regulate these conditions.

tort A private or civil wrong for which a court can provide remedy in the form of damages.

tortious newsgathering The use of reporting techniques that are wrongful and unlawful and for which the victim may obtain damages in court.

trade regulation rule A broadly worded statement by the Federal Trade Commission that outlines advertising requirements for a particular trade.

trademark A word, name, symbol or design used to identify a company's goods and distinguish them from similar products other companies make.

traditional public forum Lands designed for public use and historically used for public gathering, discussion and association (e.g., public streets, sidewalks and parks). Free speech is protected in these areas.

transformative use test A test to determine whether a creator has transformed a person's name, picture, likeness, voice or identity for artistic purposes. If so, the person cannot win a right of publicity suit against the creator.

Transmit Clause Part of the 1976 Copyright Act that says a broadcast network is performing when it transmits content; a local broadcaster is performing when it transmits the network broadcast; and a cable television system performs when it retransmits a broadcast to its subscribers.

true threat Speech directed toward one or more specific individuals with the intent of causing listeners to fear for their safety.

U

underinclusive A First Amendment doctrine that disfavors narrow laws that target a subset of a recognized category for discriminatory treatment.

USA PATRIOT Act The Uniting and Strengthening America by Providing Appropriate Tools Required to Intercept and Obstruct Terrorism Act of 2001. The act gave law enforcement agencies greater authority to combat terrorism.

V

vague laws Laws that either fail to define their terms or use such general language that neither citizens nor judges know with certainty what the laws permit or punish.

variable obscenity The concept that sexually oriented material not obscene for adults may be obscene if distributed to minors.

venire Literally, "to come" or "to appear"; the term used for the location from which a court draws its pool of potential jurors, who must then appear in court for voir dire; a change of venire means a change of the location from which potential jurors are drawn.

venue The locality of a lawsuit and of the court hearing the suit. Thus, a change of venue means a relocation of a trial.

vice products Products related to activities generally considered unhealthy or immoral or whose use is restricted by age or other condition. The category includes alcohol, tobacco, firearms, sexually explicit materials and drugs.

viewpoint-based discrimination Government censorship or punishment of expression based on the ideas or attitudes expressed. Courts will apply a strict scrutiny test to determine whether the government acted constitutionally.

voir dire Literally, "to speak the truth"; the questioning of prospective jurors to assess their suitability.

voluntary compliance The general Federal Trade Commission practice to allow advertisers to follow FTC rules and correct violations before the commission takes action.

W

Wiretap Act   A federal law to protect the privacy of phone calls and other oral communications that makes it illegal to intercept, record, disseminate or use a private communication without a participant's permission. The law allows the government to bring criminal charges and those whose privacy was violated to sue for civil damages.

work made for hire   Work created when working for another person or company. The copyright in a work made for hire belongs to the employer, not the creator.

writ of certiorari   A petition for review by the Supreme Court of the United States; *certiorari* means "to be informed of."

Z

Zapple rule   A political broadcasting rule that allows a candidate's supporters equal opportunity to use broadcast stations if the candidate's opponents' supporters use the stations.

CASE INDEX

SUBJECT INDEX